SECOND A

THE ANTIQUE TRADER

ANTIQUES & COLLECTIBLES PRICE GUIDE

Edited by Catherine Murphy

A comprehensive price guide to the entire field of antiques and collectibles for 1986 market.

Illustrated

The Babka Publishing Co.

P.O. Box 1050

Dubuque, Iowa 52001

ISBN: 0-930625-01-3

Library of Congress Catalog Card No. 85-071173

Additional copies of this book may be ordered from:

THE BABKA PUBLISHING CO.
P.O. Box 1050
Dubuque, Iowa 52001

$11.95 plus $1.00 postage and handling.

A WORD
TO THE READER

The Antique Trader has been publishing a Price Guide for fifteen years. *The Antique Trader Price Guide to Antiques and Collectors' Items* has been available by subscription and on newsstands across the country, first as a semi-annual and then as a quarterly publication, and since 1984 it has been published on a bi-monthly basis. This periodical will continue to be published bi-monthly, in magazine format, for subscription and newsstand distribution.

In 1985, in response to numerous requests to combine the material of the bi-monthly issues and provide a large, complete price guide, the first edition of *The Antique Trader Antiques & Collectibles Price Guide* was issued and it met with a cordial reception from collectors across the country. At that time, we promised to issue a comprehensive guide each year and the book you now hold in your hands is the 1986 guide to the entire field of antiques and collectibles.

This book is the most current price listing available. We think it is also the most reliable book for dealers and collectors to turn to for realistic values of antiques and collectibles. Prices listed in this guide have not been unrealistically set at the whim of an editor who has no material at hand to substantiate the listed values. The Antique Trader Price Guide staff has always used a very methodical compilation system that is supported by experts from across the country as we select listings for the various categories. Prices are derived from antique shops, advertisements, auctions, and antique shows, and on-going records are maintained. Items are fully described and listings are carefully examined by experts who discard unreasonable exceptions to bring you the most reliable, well-illustrated and authoritative Price Guide available.

Our format enables us to maintain a wide range of both antique and collectible items in a running tabulation to which we are continually adding information and prices. Items are diligently researched and clearly described. As new avenues of collecting interest are aroused, new categories are added and if this interest continues and a definite market is established, this material becomes a part of the Price Guide. If collector interest wanes in a given area, material relating to this segment of collecting is withdrawn for a specific period of time.

This year Billiken Collectibles, Franklin Maxim Wares and Maud Humphrey Illustrations have been included in the general listing for the first time and Goldscheider Wares, Hutschenreuther porcelain, Bernard Moore, Pisgah Forest and Rosemeade potteries have been added under the heading of Ceramics.

Six *"Special Focus"* segments on popular areas of collecting are highlighted in this issue. Advertising Postcards, China Head Dolls, Red Wing Stoneware Pottery, Soft Drink Bottles, Sugar Bowls and Wicker Furniture are each treated in a section that provides fine background material, tips on collecting and profuse illustrations of priced items.

This book should be used only as a *guide* to prices and is not intended to set prices. Prices do vary from one section of the country to another and auction prices, which are incorporated into this guide, often have an even wider variation. Though prices have been double-checked and every effort has been made to assure accuracy, neither the compilers, editor or publisher can assume responsibility for any losses that might be incurred as a result of consulting this guide, or of errors, typographical or otherwise.

This guide follows an alphabetical format. All categories are listed in alphabetical order. Under the category of Ceramics, you will find all types of pottery, porcelain, earthenware china, parian and stoneware listed in alphabetical order. All types of glass, including Art, Carnival, Custard, Depression, Pattern and so on, will be found listed alphabetically under the category of

Glass. A complete Index and cross-references in the text have also been provided.

We wish to express sincere appreciation to the following authorities who help in selecting material to be used in this guide: Robert T. Matthews, West Friendship, Maryland; Connie Morningstar, Salt Lake City, Utah; Cecil Munsey, Poway, California; J. Michael and Dorothy T. Pearson, Miami Beach, Florida; Bob Rau, Portland, Oregon; Jane Rosenow, Dickeyville, Wisconsin; Ruth Schinestuhl, Absecon, New Jersey and Vera Tiger, Colorado Springs, Colorado.

We wish to pay tribute to the authors of our *"Special Focus"* segments: "Advertising Postcards" by Sally S. Carver, Chestnut Hill, Massachusetts; "China Head Dolls" by Sybill M. McFadden, Lakewood, New York; "Red Wing Stoneware Pottery" by Gail DePasquale, Leavenworth, Kansas; "Soft Drink Bottles" by Cecil Munsey, Poway, California; "Sugar Bowls" by Kyle Husfloen, Galena, Illinois and "Wicker Furniture" by Connie Morningstar, Salt Lake City, Utah. Each has made an outstanding contribution to this issue of The Antique Trader Antiques & Collectibles Price Guide for 1986 and we are indebted to them for their diligence in helping us bring reliable reference material to our readers.

Photographers who have contributed to this issue include: E.A. Babka, Dubuque, Iowa; Stanley L. Baker, Minneapolis, Minnesota; Dorothy Beckwith, Platteville, Wisconsin; Donna Bruun, Galena, Illinois; Marie Bush, Amsterdam, New York; David and Herman C. Carter, Tulsa, Oklahoma; J.D. Dalessandro, Cincinnati, Ohio; Gail DePasquale, Leavenworth, Kansas; Bill Freeman, Birmingham, Alabama; Vicki Gross, Hillsboro, Oregon; Jeff Grunewald, Chicago, Illinois; William Heacock, Marietta, Ohio; Kyle Husfloen, Galena, Illinois; Joan C. LeVine, New York, New York; Mariann Marks, Honesdale, Pennsylvania; Jim Martin, Monmouth, Illinois; James Matthews, Fort Worth, Texas; Sybill M. McFadden, Lakewood, New York; James Measell, Berkley, Michigan; Donald Moore, Alameda, California; Cecil Munsey, Poway, California and Ruth Schinestuhl, Absecon, New Jersey.

For other photographs, artwork, data or permission to photograph in their shops, we express sincere appreciation to the following auctioneers, galleries, shops and individuals: The American Graniteware Association, Downers Grove, Illinois; David and Linda Arman, Woodstock, Connecticut; Susan and Al Bagdade, Northbrook, Illinois; Bell Tower Antique Mall, Covington, Kentucky; Paul Bussan, Sterling, Illinois; Arthur Cass, Dubuque, Iowa; Norman and Dianna Charles, Hagerstown, Indiana; Christie's, New York, New York; Mrs. J. Ciparchia, Norwood, New Jersey; Court Antiques, Pekin, Illinois; D. & L. Antiques, North Berwick, Maine; Edith Dragowick, Epworth, Iowa; T. Emert, Cincinnati, Ohio; Frasher's Doll Auction Service, Oak Grove, Missouri; Garth's Auctions, Inc., Delaware, Ohio; Glick's Antiques, Galena, Illinois; Vicki Gross, Hillsboro, Oregon; Grunewald Antiques, Hillsborough, North Carolina; Gene Harris Auction Center, Marshalltown, Iowa and Hidden Treasures Auctions & Appraisals, Milwaukee, Wisconsin.

Also to Jane's Antiques, Dickeyville, Wisconsin; Jeanne & Keith Antiques, Cassville, Wisconsin; Tom Junk, South Charlestown, Ohio; Mrs. Robert Kubesheski, Dubuque, Iowa; Marie's Antiques, Amsterdam, New York; Virginia Marshall, St. Louis, Missouri; J. Martin, Mount Orab, Ohio; Rosemary Meyer, Dubuque, Iowa; Virginia Miller, East Dubuque, Illinois; The Nippon Room, Rexford, New York; Phillips, New York, New York; Tammy Roth, East Dubuque, Illinois; John Schleicher Antiques, Dickeyville, Wisconsin; Shirley's Glasstiques, Brunswick, Ohio; Mr. and Mrs. John Shuman III, Pottstown, Pennsylvania; Robert W. Skinner, Inc., Bolton, Massachusetts; Sotheby's, New York, New York; Doris Spahn, East Dubuque, Illinois; Stratford Auction Center, Delaware, Ohio; Sybill's Museum of Antique Dolls and Toys, Lakewood, New York; Robert W. Taylor, Richmond, Virginia; Time Was Museum, Mendota, Illinois; Doris Virtue, Galena, Illinois; Marguerite Wade, Andrew, Iowa; Williams Auctions, Harrisonville, Missouri and Woody Auction Service, Douglass, Kansas.

The staff of The Antique Trader Antiques & Collectibles Price Guide welcomes all letters from readers, especially those of constructive critique, and we make every effort to personally respond to correspondence addressed to us in care of Babka Publishing Company.

Catherine Murphy, Editor

ABC PLATES

These children's plates were popular in the late 19th and early 20th centuries. An alphabet border was incorporated with nursery rhymes, maxims, scenes or figures in an apparent attempt to "spoon feed" a bit of knowledge at meal time. They were made of ceramics, glass and metal. A recent boon to collectors is the fine book, "A Collector's Guide to ABC Plates, Mugs and Things" by Mildred L. and Joseph P. Chalala. Also see GRANITEWARE.

CERAMIC

Franklin Maxim Plate

4½" d., shepherd scene black transfer center highlighted in polychrome enameling, embossed alphabet border (hairlines & minor stains) $45.00

5" d., boy goat herder w/horn, dog & goat transfer center, embossed alphabet border 75.00

5¼" d., "Harry Baiting His Line - For To Fish He Doth Incline," polychrome transfer of boy fishing beneath tree center, embossed alphabet border, Elsmore & Son, 1872-87 . . . . .60.00

5¼" d., "Shuttlecock," black transfer scene of youths playing center, highlighted in red, green & yellow enameling, embossed alphabet border, J. & G. Meakin 65.00

5 3/8" d., Franklin Maxim, "Keep Thy Shop And Thy Shop Will Keep Thee," J. & G. Meakin, 1851-90 (ILLUS.) 70.00

5½" d., "Behold Him Rising From the Grave, etc.," religious scene transfer center, embossed alphabet border, J. & G. Meakin, 1851-90 . . . . .60.00 to 75.00

5½" d., "Harry Baiting His Line - For a Fish He Doth Incline," polychrome transfer scene center, embossed alphabet border, Elsmore 60.00

5½" d., "Harvest Home," color transfer scene center of bringing home hay wagon, embossed alphabet border, J. & G. Meakin, 1851-90 . . . . . .55.00

Alphabet Plate

6" d., child musicians, mulberry transfer scene center, printed alphabet border (ILLUS.) 40.00

6" d., children (2) rolling hoops transfer scene center, embossed alphabet border, Staffordshire, 1840s 35.00

6¼" d., "Thoroughbreds," brown transfer of sheep grazing in pasture center, gilt alphabet border 39.00

6½" d., Deaf & Dumb sign language plate, pr. elegantly dressed cats pink transfer center w/inner rim pink transfer of hands forming sign language representing embossed letters on outer rim alphabet, H. Aynsley & Co., Longton, England, ca. 1904 . . . . .150.00

6½" d., "Old Mother Hubbard," color transfer of woman & dog center, printed alphabet border (small rim flake) 58.00

6¾" d., Franklin Maxim, "For Age and Want Save While You May - No Morning Sun Lasts All Day," black transfer scene center, embossed alphabet border . . . . .60.00 to 68.00

6¾" d., Franklin Maxim, "For Age and Want Save While You May - No Morning Sun Lasts All Day," pink transfer scene center, embossed alphabet border 80.00

6¾" d., Franklin Maxim, "He That Hath a Trade Hath An Estate - Industry Pays Debts While Despair Increaseth Them," transfer scene of blacksmith center, embossed alphabet border (faint crow's foot on back) 45.00

7" d., "Mother and Daughter," multi-colored transfer center, embossed alphabet border 59.00

7" d., "Old Woman - Old Woman," deep feeding dish-type, color transfer center, alphabet border, E. McNichol, East Liverpool, Ohio, 1890-1920 . . . . . 37.50

7" d., "The Drive," color transfer scene of couple riding in cart center, embossed alphabet border, Staffordshire 40.00

7 3/16" d., Aesop's Fables, "The Fox and The Grapes," color transfer scene center, printed alphabet border, Brownhills Pottery Co., Tunstall, ca. 1875 . . . . 55.00

7¼" d., Robinson Crusoe, "Crusoe at Work," color transfer of Crusoe center, printed alphabet border, Brownhills Pottery Co., ca. 1887 . . . . . . 77.50

7¼" d., Robinson Crusoe, "Crusoe Viewing the Island," brown & color scene of Crusoe w/binoculars in boat center, printed alphabet border, Brownhills Pottery Co., ca. 1877 . . . . 60.00 to 80.00

7 3/8" d., famous "Oriental Hotel," brown transfer scene of hotel center, embossed alphabet border, Brownhills Pottery Co., Tunstall, 1872-96 . . . . 80.00
1872-96 . . . . 80.00

7½" d., humorous scene, color transfer of man sliding down hill center, embossed alphabet border, Staffordshire, unmarked 65.00

8" d., zebra hunt center, embossed alphabet border, Staffordshire 65.00

8 1/8" d., Deaf & Dumb sign language plate, owls at school green transfer center w/inner rim transfer of hands forming sign language representing embossed letters of outer rim alphabet, highlighted w/polychrome enameling, H. Aynsley & Co., Longton, England, ca. 1904 . . . . 90.00

8¼" d., "A Sioux Indian Chief," brown transfer scene of Indian astride horse center, embossed alphabet border, Charles Allerton & Sons, England, ca. 1890 . . . . 60.00

8¼" d., "F is for the Fowls and the Farm where they Feed - G is for the Girlie who feeds them so well," pink transfer scene of girl feeding barnyard fowl, embossed alphabet border, Staffordshire 85.00

8¼" d., hunting scene color transfer of 2 Scottish highlanders w/dogs & guns, one viewing stags in the distance through binoculars, embossed alphabet border, Staffordshire . . . 65.00

"American Sports - Base Ball Striker & Catcher," brown transfer center, embossed alphabet border 100.00

Baby Bunting & Little Dog Bunch 55.00

Boy crossing over stile transfer scene center, embossed alphabet border, Staffordshire 80.00

GLASS

Clock Face ABC Plate

6" d., clock face center w/Roman & Arabic numerals, alphabet border, clear (ILLUS.) 40.00

6" d., ducks w/ducklings center, alphabet border, clear 45.00

6" d., elephant w/howdah on back & 3 tiny figures in howdah waving flag, alphabet border, clear, signed "R. & C." (Ripley & Co.) on howdah . . . . 120.00 to 150.00

6" d., hen & chicks center, alphabet border, clear 40.00

Garfield ABC Plate

6" d., President Garfield bust center, alphabet border, clear, ca. 1885 (ILLUS.) 55.00

6" d., Sancho Panza & Dapple center, alphabet border, frosted & clear 48.00

6" d., star medallion center, alphabet border, clear 40.00

6¼" d., "Christmas Morn," center scene of children w/toys, fireplace w/stockings, Christmas tree, & mother & father peeking from behind door, alphabet border, frosted & clear 165.00

6¼" d., rayed center, alphabet border,
scalloped & beaded edge, clear 18.00
7½" d., stork center, alphabet border,
marigold Carnival glass 55.00
Emma (girl's bust) center, alphabet
border, frosted & clear, Bryce Higbee
Glass Co., Pittsburgh, Pa. 45.00
Rover (bulldog) center, alphabet bor-
der, amber . . . . 37.00 to 50.00
Stork center, alphabet border, frosted
& clear, Iowa City Glass Co. . . 70.00 to 95.00

TIN

Tin Plate with Alphabet & Numbers

3" d., girl & boy rolling hoop color-
printed center scene, alphabet
border, miniature 85.00
3½" d., girl on swing color-printed
center scene, alphabet
border . . . . 30.00 to 37.50
4" d., kittens (2) color-printed center
scene, alphabet border, "Ohio Art
Co." 28.00
5 5/8" d., George Washington bust &
13 stars embossed center, alphabet
border 75.00
6" d., alphabet & numbers embossed
center (ILLUS.) 30.00
6" d., "Jumbo" elephant embossed
center, alphabet border 75.00
8" d., Hi Diddle Diddle embossed
center scene w/cat & fiddle & cow
jumping over moon, alphabet
border 55.00
8" d., "Mary Had a Little Lamb"
embossed center scene & verse,
alphabet border 75.00
8" d., "Who Killed Cock Robin"
embossed center scene & verse,
alphabet border 60.00
"Bunny Teacher," color-printed scene
of bunny teacher & pupils center,
alphabet w/animal figures over
clouds border 65.00
"Jack and Jill" color-printed scene &
verse center, alphabet border
(ILLUS.) 45.00

"Jack & Jill" Printed Tin Plate

"Mary Had A Little Lamb" color-printed
center scene, alphabet border 65.00

ADVERTISING CARDS

"Black Cat Hosiery"

*The Victorian trade card evolved from in-
formal calling cards and hand decorated
notes. From the 1850s through the 1890s,
the American home was saturated with
these black-and-white and choromolitho-
graphed advertising cards given away with
various products. Also see SCRAPBOOKS
& ALBUMS.*

Assorted chromolithographs, 1880s,
set of 24 . . . . $20.00
Assorted chromolithographs, 19th c.,
set of 165 . . . . 132.00
Bitters, "Burdock Blood Bitters,"
colorful scene of children 8.00

Cigarettes, "Helmar Turkish Trophies,"
ladies by the artist Hamilton King,
large size, set of 6 ....50.00

Cigarettes, "Helmar Turkish," coat-of-
arms of various countries, set of 54 ..150.00

Cigarettes, "Old Judge," folding-type
entitled "Stolen Sweets," front
w/mother approaching smoking
barrel opening to reveal 3 mis-
chievious boys smoking cigarettes,
4 x 4½", opening to 4 x 9" 75.00

Cigars, "Hustler Little Cigars," flags of
different countries, set of 32........20.00

Cocoa, "Van Houten's," chromolithograph w/child 5.00

Coffee, "C.D. Kenny," chromolithograph
of baby on pillow, large............12.00

Coffee, "McLaughlin's," Inauguration
of President Lincoln 15.00

Coffee, "McLaughlin's," Romeo & Juliet
scene 15.00

Coffee, "Panama Coffee," die-cut,
Raphael Tuck type, fairy tales,
etc., assorted set of 14.............30.00

Cologne, "Hoyt's German Cologne,"
chromolithograph of children w/doll ..4.00

Fertilizer, "Frank Coe," reproduction
of Rosa Bonheur's "Horse Fair"
painting, 1912 ....15.00

Food product, "Heinz," aviation series,
set of 20 ....39.00

Hosiery, "Black Cat Brand," die-cut
black cat wearing yellow ribbon,
"Chicago-Kenosha Hosiery Co.,
Kenosha, Wisconsin," 6" h. (ILLUS.)...24.00

"Clipper Mower"

Lawn mower, "Clipper," chromolithograph
of girl pushing lawn mower while
adults play croquet in background,
6 x 3½" (ILLUS.) 4.50

Metamorphic, "Packard" automobiles,
car moves along mountainous highway, 11 x 6"......................35.00

Patent medicine, assorted set of 10.....15.00

Patent medicine, "Ayer's Cherry
Pectoral," chromolithograph of
toddlers standing beside huge bottle ..3.00

Patent medicine, "Dr. White's,"
w/children........................6.00

Pickles, "Heinz," die-cut girl in
cucumber.........................8.00

Sad irons, "Mrs. Potts Irons," black &
white 4.00

Sewing machines, "Singer," Costumes of
All Nations series, Columbian Exposition, 1893, set of 14..............50.00

Soap, "R.W. Bell & Co.," w/elephant.....7.00

Soap, "Sweet Home," chromolithograph of little girls, large 6.50

"Tulip Soap" Advertising Card

Soap, "Tulip," chromolithograph of 2 little girls, one holding
a doll (ILLUS.) 2.00

Stoves, "Acorn Range," chromolithograph of Victorian woman at stove 3.75

Stoves, "Garland Stoves," chromolithograph of little girls seated on
bench peeling apples w/stove in
background 3.00

Stoves, "Quick Meal," cast iron cook
stove, 1908.......................4.00

Thread, "J.P. Coats," black boy seated
on spool, crows in foreground & sun
overhead, "We Never Fade".........12.00

Thread, "Corticelli," chromolithograph
of little girl in fur-trimmed hat &
coat carrying a muff (ILLUS.).........2.00

"Corticelli" Knitting Silk, Spool Silk and Wash Silks are Superb.

"Corticelli" Thread Card

Tobacco, "Duke's Honest Long Cut,"
   actors, actresses, & boxer John L.
   Sullivan, set of 34 . . . . .18.50
Tobacco, "Players," Castles & Coat of
   Arms series, set of 27 . . . . .5.50
Tobacco, "Players," Struggle for
   Existence series, set of 25 . . . . .6.00
Tobacco, "Players," World War I Army
   Corps division symbols, 1914-18,
   set of 50 . . . . .18.00
Toys, "McLoughlin," chromolithograph
   of Victorian baby & dog, "Jingle
   Jingle" & "Bow-Wow-Wow,"
   6¾ x 5½" 10.00

ADVERTISING ITEMS

Thousands of objects made in various materials, some intended as gifts with purchases, others used for display or given away for publicity, are now being collected. They range from ash and drink trays to razors. Also see ADVERTISING CARDS, ALMANACS, AUTOMOBILE LITERATURE, AVIATION COLLECTIBLES, BANKS, BASEBALL MEMORABILIA, BIG LITTLE BOOKS, BILLIKEN COLLECTIBLES, BOOKMARKS, BOTTLE OPENERS, BOTTLES & FLASKS, BREWERIANA, BROWNIE COLLECTIBLES, BUTTON HOOKS, CALENDAR PLATES, CAMPBELL KID COLLECTIBLES, CANS & CONTAINERS, CARNIVAL GLASS, CHARACTER COLLETIBLES, CIGAR & CIGARETTE CASES, HOLDERS & LIGHTERS, CIGAR & TOBACCO CUTTERS, COCA-COLA ITEMS, COFFEE GRINDERS, COOKBOOKS, CORKSCREWS, FIRE FIGHTING COLLECTIBLES, FOOT & BOOT SCRAPERS, GRANITEWARE, JEWEL TEA AUTUMN LEAF WARE, KEWPIE COLLECTIBLES, KITCHENWARES, KNIVES, MAGAZINES, MATCH SAFES & CONTAINERS, METALS, OLD SLEEPY EYE POTTERY, PAPER DOLLS, PARRISH ARTWORK, POSTCARDS, POSTERS, RAILROADIANA, SIGNS & SIGNBOARDS, SPOOL, DYE & ALLIED CABINETS, TOKENS, TRAYS, VIENNA ART TIN PLATES, WATCH FOBS, WORLD FAIR COLLECTIBLES, WRITING ACCESSORIES and ZEPPELIN COLLECTIBLES.

Angel food cake pan, "Swans Down,"
   tin, 1923 patent . . . .$10.00 to 18.50
Ash tray, "Camel Cigarettes," tin 20.00
Ash tray, "Chrysler Transmissions -
   May 1955," Roseville Pottery, Hyde
   Park patt., green & brown 18.00
Ash tray, "Du Bonnet," metal, man
   in chair pouring drink from wine
   bottle . . . . .15.00 to 20.00
Ash tray, "Ford Motor Co.," brass,
   upright back cast w/embossed
   "XM-151" jeep 38.00
Ash tray, "Jewel Stoves & Ranges,"
   cast iron, horseshoe shape 15.00
Ash tray, "Kelly Tires," rubber tire
   shape w/green glass insert "Every-
   body Knows Us" . . . . .12.00 to 17.00
Ash tray, "Michelin Tires," rubber tire
   shape w/clear glass insert 15.00
Ash tray, "Mountain States Tele-
   phone," porcelain 47.00

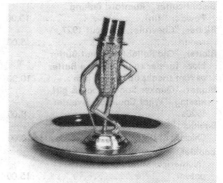

Planters Peanuts Ash Tray

Ash tray, "Planters Peanuts," gold
   finish metal w/figure of Mr. Peanut
   center (ILLUS.) .18.00
Ash tray, "Planters Peanuts," silver
   finish metal w/figure of Mr. Peanut
   center, "Planters Peanuts 1909-
   1956" .42.50 to 50.00

Ash tray, "Thor" (washing machine), graniteware, fluted rim, apple green w/white speckles, understamped "Lusterlite - 123," 6" d..............25.00

Ash tray w/matchbox holder center, "Philip Morris Cigarettes," ceramic, "Johnny" pictured, marked Germany........................95.00

Bank, "Electrolux," model of a refrigerator, pot metal, 4" h.....................20.00 to 35.00

Bank, "Red Goose Shoes," chalkware, 5"................................30.00

Banner, "DeLaval Cream Separator," canvas, lady pouring milk & boy carrying milk can, cows, cream separator & automatic milker in operation, "Sooner or Later You Will Use a DeLaval Cream Separator & Milker," colorful, 120 x 34"........525.00

Banner, "San Felice Cigars," cloth, 141 x 26½".........................65.00

Baseball scorekeeper, "Sen-Sen Gum"...9.00

Beater jar, "Christmas Greetings, Peter's Store, Alexander, Iowa," utilitarian crockery w/blue band.....75.00

Beater jar, "Wesson for Good Things to Eat," utilitarian crockery, blue & white..............................60.00

Bill clip, "Mars Bars," replica of candy bar................................8.00

Bill hook, "Ceresota Flour," metal w/chromolithographed cardboard insert of boy......................35.00

Bill hook, "Red Goose Shoes," w/goose..........................12.50

Biscuit cutter, "Cottolene Shortening," tin................................6.00

Biscuit cutter, "Horsfords," tin..........7.00

Biscuit cutter, "Rumford Baking Powder," tin.....................10.00

Blotter, "Chevrolet," die-cut 1927 sedan............................5.00

Blotter, "Old Reliable Peanut Butter," black farmer saying "Some Butter" as ram sneaks up behind him........10.00

Blotter, "Quaker Sugar," boy & girl kissing, "What Could Be Sweeter," 1920s.............................8.00

Booklet, "Bon Ami," entitled "The Chick That Never Grew Up"...5.00 to 10.00

Booklet, "Ceresota Flour," entitled "Numerical Mind Reader," 1904 patent...........................15.00

Booklet, "Colgate-Palmolive," entitled "Jungle Pow Wow," 1911...........12.00

Booklet, "Diamond Salt Co.," entitled "101 Uses of Salt," 1914.............12.00

Booklet, "Honest Scrap Tobacco," 1910, black cat & dog on cover...........28.00

Booklet, "Jello," entitled "The Jello Girl Gives a Party," w/illustrations by Rose O'Neill......................19.00

Booklet, "Wheeler-Wilson Sewing Machines," 1889, 4 pp..............10.00

Booklet, "Wrigleys Gum," entitled, "Mother Goose," 1915.............10.00

Bookmark, "Cracker Jack," tin, die-cut & color-printed Bulldog, 3".........11.50

Bookmark, "Cracker Jack," tin, die-cut & color-printed Spaniel dog.........20.00

Bookmark, "Planters Peanuts," die-cut Mr. Peanut w/top hat & cane, "Greetings from the World's Fair 1939"............................25.00

Bowl, cereal, "Quaker Oats," Quaker man & oats decor.................50.00

Box opener & nail puller, "Webster's Candy," cast iron...............27.00

Broom rack, "Kentucky Cardinal Cigar," holds 5 brooms, cast iron w/embossed tin sign w/red bird either side......................250.00

Calendar, 1882, "Youth's Companion Magazine," folding-type, 6 bright floral panels, reverse lists coming articles..........................35.00

Calendar, 1887, "Hood's Sarsaparilla," chromolithograph of little girl in bonnet at top, printed by Major, Knapp & Co., New York............95.00

Calendar, 1889, "Hood's Sarsaparilla," die-cut chromolithograph bust portrait of little girl in bonnet, w/pad..........................25.00

Calendar, 1890, "Hillman Telegraph," 3 shoeshine boys................85.00

Calendar, 1890, "Hood's Sarsaparilla," bust profile portrait of little girl, w/pad..........................25.00

Calendar, 1892, "Hood's Sarsaparilla," circle of children's faces, w/pad.....30.00

Calendar, 1895, "Arm & Hammer Soda," pocket-type.................10.00

Calendar, 1895, "Hood's Sarsaparilla," heart-shaped, small girls wearing summer & winter bonnets at top, illustrated by Maude Humphrey................98.00 to 110.00

Calendar, 1895, "Phoenix Mutual Life Insurance," Victorian children, 4 pp., 7 x 5"............................32.00

Calendar, 1898, "Hood's Sarsaparilla," bust portrait of little blonde girl reserved in round medallion surrounded by florals, w/pad, overall 8½" w., 10½" h...................41.00

Calendar, 1898, "Winchester Ammunition," hunter & elk at top, duck hunter below...................600.00

Calendar, 1899, "Hood's Sarsaparilla," bust portrait of beautiful brunette woman, w/pad............35.00 to 40.00

Calendar, 1900, "Dupont Powder Co.," ram jumping ravine at top half; hunters & dogs in heavy brush bottom half, 14 x 28".............250.00

Calendar, 1903, "Fairbank's Fairy
Soap" 125.00
Calendar, 1903, "Prudential Insur-
ance," beautiful girl, Forbes litho-
graph 10.00
Calendar, 1906, "Fleischmann's Yeast,"
horse-drawn wagon & street scene,
10 x 14".........................45.00
Calendar, 1907, "World's Star Knitting
Co., Michigan," 3-dimensional Dutch
comic 65.00
Calendar, 1909, "Peters Shot Gun
Shells," hunters, dog on point
w/puppies, 14 x 27" 250.00
Calendar, 1909, "The Prudential Life
Ins. Co.," Victorian lady in color 15.00
Calendar, 1910, "Hood's Sarsaparilla,"
bust portrait of little girl wearing
large bow in her long curly hair,
w/pad...........................50.00
Calendar, 1911, "Ceresota Flour,"
Ceresota boy 95.00
Calendar, 1917, "Chero Cola," brunette
holding bottle, wooden frame,
36 x 20".........................295.00
Calendar, 1920, "Atlantic Tea,"
embossed die-cut girl in red outfit
w/rifle over shoulder & 2 hunting
dogs, 17" 35.00
Calendar, 1929, "Kennel Shop, Concord,
Mass.," dogs (6) playing cards,
colored.........................22.00
Calendar, 1935-37, "DeLaval Cream
Separators," various historical
scenes & DeLaval factory at Pough-
keepsie, New York on Hudson River,
17 x 9"..........................25.00
Calendar, 1944, "Merita Bread," Lone
Ranger pictured 50.00
Candy scale, "Wrigley's Gum," brass ..200.00
Cap, "Checker Cab," front emblem
w/taxi cab & 1951 brass cab license
on side 25.00
Change receiver, "Baby Ruth Candy,"
glass & tin 85.00
Change receiver, "Cutacura," clear
glass 25.00
Charm bracelet, "Planters Peanuts,"
brass chain w/four Mr. Peanuts & 2
nuts............................15.00
Cigar box opener, "Laurel Stoves," cast
iron hatchet embossed "Axe of All
Nations" & Carrie Nation on back,
1901, 4" l.......................47.50
Cigar box opener, "Zorns, Philadelphia," nickel-plated iron, cast
w/ship's figurehead of woman 45.00
Cigar lighter-lamp combination, "Lillian
Russell 5-cent Cigar," counter model,
ornate oil font, 4 panel pierced
copper-plated tin shade w/adver-
tising, 1880s....................950.00
Cigarette flannels, Flag series, set of
12 ....15.00

Cigarette lighter, "Chesterfield
Cigarettes" 12.00
Clock, "Calumet Baking Powder," wall
regulator, Sessions Clock Co........750.00
Clock, "La Reforma 5 cent Cigar,"
wall regulator, Gilbert Clock Co.,
oak case........................850.00
Cologne bottle, "Rich Secker Sweet
Cologne, New York" etched on
spatter glass, applied clear handles,
8½" h. 60.00
Condensed milk can opener, "Pet
Milk," embossed w/can of "Pet"
milk & hand using opener 11.00
Cookbook, "Sleepy Eye Flour Mills,"
square, colorful portrait of Old
Sleepy Eye.............225.00 to 290.00
Corkscrew, "Listerine" 4.00
Counter display, "Antique Bourbon,"
composition figure of 19th c. baseball
player w/bat in hand, mid-20th c.,
44½" h. 99.00
Counter display, "Grand Union Tea
Co.," cardboard, die-cut figure of
child in swing, 1936, 36" h. 45.00
Counter display, "Green River
Whiskey," composition figure group
of black man & horse w/rat on
saddle, 13" l., 10½" h. ....195.00 to 225.00
Counter display, "Hickory Children's
Garters," die-cut wood, children
under umbrella, colorful 95.00
Counter display, "Hire's Root Beer,"
cardboard, easel-type, die-cut Hire's
Kid w/package, ca. 1900 ....175.00
Counter display, "Mother Goose
Shoes," papier mache full figure
Mother Goose 110.00
Counter display, "Moxie," die-cut card-
board of Frank Archer over box......95.00

"Munsingwear" Counter Display

Counter display, "Munsingwear," hard
vinyl model of a penguin, 7" h.
(ILLUS.)..........................7.50

Counter display, "Sheaffer Pen Co.,"
cardboard, colorful winter snow
scene of village w/steepled churches
& children bearing gifts, dated 1925,
36 x 26"............................49.00
Counter display, "White Horse
Whiskey," chalkware model of a
horse ....70.00 to 100.00
Counter display, "Whitman's
Chocolates," cardboard, easel-type
die-cut Santa w/sleigh & reindeer,
large...............................35.00
Counter display box, "Jap Rose Soap,"
wooden, geisha girl decor, holds 50
bars................................95.00
Counter display case, "Newport
Garters - 25 cents," wooden w/lift-
top.................................55.00
Counter display case, "Zeno Gum," oak
w/marquee & glass slant front,
18½ x 10 x 8" ....295.00 to 395.00
Counter display jar, "Curtis Chicos
Spanish Peanuts - 5 Cents," clear
glass, "by the makers of Baby Ruth
Candy Bars," tin lid, 11½" h. 105.00
Counter display jar, "Planters Pea-
nuts," clear glass barrel-shaped jar,
original glass lid w/peanut
finial..................165.00 to 195.00
Counter display jar, "Planters Peanuts," clear glass "clipper" jar, metal
lid 57.00
Counter display jar, "Planters Pea-
nuts," clear glass rectangular jar
w/red, white & blue decal, w/lid.....75.00
Counter display jar, cov., "Tom's
Roasted Peanuts," clear glass 35.00
Counter display penny sucker holder,
"Chief Watta Pop," bust of Indian
Chief w/suckers forming feathers in
headdress ....110.00 to 125.00

"H.J. Heinz Co." Crock

Crock, "H.J. Heinz Co., Pittsburgh,
U.S.A.," stoneware w/die-stamped
borders & emblem "Keystone

Pickling & Preserving Works," 6" d.,
6" h. (ILLUS.) 100.00
Cuff links, "Lucky Strike," miniature
cigarette packs, 1930s, pr. 135.00
Door push plate, "Chesterfield
Cigarettes," metal 15.00
Door push plate, "Pepsi Cola," heavy
metal 20.00
Door push plate, "Polar Bear Tobacco,"
bear pictured, 7 x 3½"..............47.50
Fan, folding-type, "Hamburg-Amerika
Lines," 11-stick 45.00
Fan, folding-type, "Moxie," celluloid ...50.00
Fan, "Hoffman Willis Ice Cream Co.,"
cardboard, photograph of little girls
eating ice cream, early 20th c. 15.00
Fan, "Maxwell-Chrysler," cardboard,
colorful scene of woman driving 20.00
Fan, "Moxie," cardboard, color portrait
of Muriel Ostriche, 1916 ....30.00
Fan, "Putnam Dyes," cardboard,
colorful scene of General Putnam
escaping British dragoons..........12.50

"Old Sleepy Eye" Fan

Fan, "Sleepy Eye Mills," cardboard,
portrait of Victorian lady front,
advertising for "Cream" & "Hummer"
flour reverse (ILLUS.) 90.00
Flour sack, "Cake Walk," cloth,
strutting black couple pictured.......35.00
Flour sack, "Ethan Allen Flour," cloth 5.00
Fork, "Planters Peanuts," silverplate,
figural Mr. Peanut handle 30.00
Game, "Will's Woodbine Tobacco,"
Dominoes, tin black & white game
pieces in green box w/white
lettering, complete, 7½ x 2 1/8 x
1¼"...............................45.00
Gasoline pump top globe, "Atlantic
White Flash," milk white glass 185.00

Gasoline Pump Globes

Gasoline pump top globe, "Mobilgas,"
  milk white glass w/red Pegasus
  (ILLUS. left) 160.00
Gasoline pump top globe, "Standard,"
  milk white glass crown w/red paint,
  16" d., 17" h. 230.00
Gasoline pump top globe, "Standard,"
  milk white glass crown w/gold
  paint....................195.00 to 250.00
Gasoline pump top globe, "Texaco,"
  milk white glass flattened globe
  w/Texaco star (ILLUS.
  right) ....200.00 to 350.00
Gum stand, "Clark's Teaberry," amber
  pressed glass 38.00
Gum stand, "Clark's Teaberry," clear
  pressed glass ....25.00 to 35.00
Gum stand, "Clark's Teaberry," green
  pressed glass 37.50
Gum stand, "Clark's Teaberry," vaseline pressed glass ....35.00 to 55.00
Hobby horse, "Simples Flexi Shoes for
  Children," spring-type..............90.00
Jigsaw puzzle, "McKesson Drugs,"
  entitled "Our Gang," 1932,
  mounted.........................60.00
Juice reamer, "Sunkist," green opaque
  glass 22.50
Juice reamer, "Sunkist," milk white
  glass 12.50

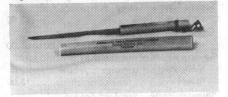

Letter Opener & Case

Letter opener, "Associated Rug & Furniture Cleaners," bamboo handle &
  case, sword-shaped blade, 8½" l.
  (ILLUS.) 8.00
Loaf pan, "Deckers," tin 12.50
Marble box, "Akro Agate," tin, boys &
  girls playing marbles pictured,
  1920-30..........................75.00
Match holder, table model, "Richmond
  Stove Co.," cast iron, model of a
  turtle w/shell-lift lid...............85.00

Wall Match Box with Advertising

Match holder, wall-type, "Blue Ribbon
  Store," color-printed tin, red & white,
  4" w., 7" h. (ILLUS.)................12.50
Match holder, wall-type, "Dr. Pepper,"
  tin, green 20.00
Match safe, pocket-type, "Arm &
  Hammer Baking Soda," gutta
  percha ....35.00 to 42.00
Match safe, pocket-type, "Wylie Coal,"
  brass, dated 1890 ....20.00
Measuring cup, "Kellogg's," pink
  transparent glass, w/three
  spouts ....15.00 to 25.00
Mechanical pencil, "Planters Peanuts,"
  Mr. Peanut at top 10.00
Mirror, hand-type, "Princess Cox
  Stoves," Art Nouveau style.........28.00
Mirror, pocket-type, "Chevrolet,"
  2 x 3"............................17.50
Mirror, pocket-type, "Continental
  Cubes Tobacco," beautiful woman ..125.00
Mirror, pocket-type, "Pacific Shoes,"
  high button shoe pictured..........25.00
Mirror, pocket-type, "Skeezix Shoes,"
  Skeezix & various birthstones 65.00

"Ceresota Flour" Pocket Mirror

Mirrors, pocket-type, "Ceresota Flour,"
"Victor" & "Horlick's Malted Milk,"
1st quarter 20th c., set of 3 (ILLUS.
of one) 198.00

Mirror, wall-type, "We Sell Arrow
Brand Collars & Cuffs," ornate
frame, 11 x 15" 75.00

Monkey wrench, "Indian Motorcycles,"
cast iron 19.00

Mug, "Armour's Vigoral," china, pink
carnation decor ....15.00 to 20.00

Mug, "Baker's Chocolate," china,
La Belle Chocolatiere in red on side,
"Made expressly for Walter Baker &
Co.".............................60.00

Mug, "Borden's Dairy," ceramic,
w/Elmer 12.00

Mug, "Doe-Wah-Jack (Dowagiac,
Michigan) Round Oak Stoves," milk
white glass, stoves, ranges &
furnaces pictured, "Compliments of
Estate of Beckwith 1907" on base....150.00

Napkin ring, "Universal Theatres," tin ...9.00

Paint book, "Planters Peanuts,"
entitled "Presidents of the U.S.,"
1932 ....10.00 to 20.00

Pancake turner, "Log Cabin Syrup,"
lithographed log cabin..............17.50

Paper clip, "Manhattan Fire & Marine
Insurance Co.," Indian pictured 45.00

Paperweight, "Adlay Trucking - Always
on Time," bronze sun dial replica,
4¾" d. 20.00

Paperweight, "Thatcher Boilers,
Ranges & Furnaces," cast iron
model of a boiler 30.00

Pencil box, "Red Goose
Shoes" ....50.00 to 75.00

Perfume flask, "Lydia Pinkham's Pills
for Constipation," purse-type, silverplate, 2½" 37.50

Pinback button, "Case Threshing
Machine," w/eagle 16.00

Pinback button, "High Admiral
Cigarettes," w/yellow kid & "Wot Do
Ye Tink Of Me Suit," No. 53, 1896 ....55.00

Pinback button, "Lion Coffee" 16.00

Pinback button, "Lionel Toy Trains,"
Lionel Engineers Club 12.00

Pinback button, "Philip Morris," celluloid, "Johnny" pictured 12.00

Pinback button, "Sharples Separator,"
lady using separator 15.50

Pitcher, "Fern Brand Coffee - Little
Falls, Minn.," utilitarian crockery,
Cherry Band patt., blue & white 210.00

Plate, "Urban's Liberty Flour, Buffalo,
N.Y.," pink translucent glass, 8" d. ...20.00

Plate, "Compliments of Wirtz & Haber-
garten, Waconia, Minn.," china,
multicolor transfer of harness racing
scene on white, D.E. McNicol, East
Liverpool, Ohio, 9½" d. (ILLUS.) 55.00

Complimentary Plate

Platter, "Buick Automobiles," china,
Buick logo & Orange Lodge emblem,
"Scammell's, Trenton" backstamp,
oval 45.00

Playing cards, "Lion Coffee," Mother
Goose decor 18.00

Print, "Cream of Wheat," entitled
"Case of Desertion," little black boy,
1909, framed 15.00

Radio, "Pepsi-Cola," bottle-shaped,
ca. 1930s, 24" h. 425.00

Radio, "Pepsi-Cola," model of a cooler,
R.C.A............................225.00

Radio, "Sinclair Oil Co.," Dinny
dinosaur on front, original box 35.00

Rat trap, "Anchor Brand Clothes
Wringers - Sure Catch" 12.00

Ruler, "Zeno Gum"...................20.00

Scale, "Planters Peanuts," w/large
figure of Mr. Peanut standing behind
platform, drop penny into Mr.
Peanut's hat to read your weight ..5,200.00

Scoop, "James Lutted, Buffalo, N.Y.,"
embossed glass 75.00

Scoop, "Planters Peanuts,"
tin ....45.00 to 65.00

Sewing kit, "Calvert Whiskey,"
embossed tin container, yellow
tassel 15.00

Shipping crate, "Rumford Baking
Powder," wooden, die-stamped
sides, holds dozen 1-lb. cans 20.00

Shipping crate, "Stickney & Poors
Mustard," wooden, die-stamped
fireside scene, 16 x 8" 50.00

Shipping crate, "Van Houten Cocoa,"
wooden 27.00

Shoe horn - button hook combination,
"Physical Culture Shoes, Passaic,
N.J." 8.00

Soap dish, hanging-type, "Arbee Flour,
Hubbard Milling, Mankato," tin 16.00

"Cherry Chic" Soda Fountain Dispenser

Soda fountain syrup dispenser, "Cherry Chic," ceramic globe-shaped dispenser molded w/red cherries & green leaves in relief on blue ground, manufactured by J. Hungerford Smith Co., Rochester, New York, ca. 1925, 9" d., 11½" h. (ILLUS.) . . . 1,595.00

"Ward's Lime Crush" Dispenser

Soda fountain syrup dispenser, "Ward's Lime Crush," ceramic, floral base (ILLUS.) 575.00
Soda fountain syrup dispenser, "Ward's Orange Crush," ceramic, black base 335.00
Soda fountain syrup dispenser, "Welch-Ade," milk white glass, dated 1917 . . . . .110.00
Song book, "Alka Seltzer," 1937 . . . . .5.00
Statue, "Planters Peanuts," cast iron figure of Mr. Peanut, 38" h. 2,450.00
Stickpin, "C.D. Kenny Co.," portrait decor, oval. 40.00
Stickpin, "Moline Plow Co." 35.00

Stickpin, "Swift's Silver Lard," maple leaf shape 18.00

"Baker's Chocolate" Tin Table

Table, "Baker's Chocolate," tin, urn-shaped pedestal on platform w/full-length portrait of La Belle Chocolatiere, tray top (ILLUS.) 1,350.00
Tape measure, "Cawston Ostrich Farm, South Pasadena, Calif.," ostrich & child each side .18.50
Tape measure, "General Electric Refrigerators," celluloid 16.00
Teapot, "Lipton Tea," maroon-glazed ceramic 18.00
Teaspoon, demitasse, "Towle's Log Cabin Syrup," silverplate . . . .10.00 to 18.00
Teaspoon, "Towle's Log Cabin Syrup," silverplate 16.50
Thermometer, "Carter's Ink," granite-ware, black & white w/red lettering, 7 x 27" . . . . .75.00 to 100.00
Thermometer, "Moxie," graniteware, picture of man pointing finger, 16 x 10" . . . . .135.00 to 175.00
Thermometer, "Ramon's Pills," wooden back, 8½ x 21" 65.00
Thermometer, "Red Seal Batteries," graniteware 60.00

"Clark's O.N.T. Thread" Box

Thread box, "Clark's O.N.T. Spool
Cotton," blue velvet exterior
(ILLUS.) 15.00
Toy clicker, "Marbis Soda Cracker,"
tin, model of a shoe 25.00
Toy doll, "Arbuckle Coffee," uncut
cloth Jill (of Jack & Jill), 1931 ....55.00
Toy doll, "Planters Peanuts," wood-
jointed Mr. Peanut 135.00

"Cracker Jack" Whistle

Toy whistle, "Cracker Jack," tin, owl
replica (ILLUS.) 6.50
Toy whistle, "Peter's Weatherbird
Shoes," tin, rooster weathervane
pictured 10.00
Toy whistle, "Red Goose Shoes,"
tin......................7.50 to 15.00
Whiskey shot glass, "Hayner Distilling,
St. Louis, Dayton," etched clear
glass 15.00

ALMANACS

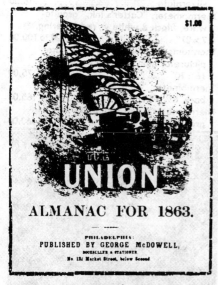

$1.00

PHILADELPHIA:
PUBLISHED BY GEORGE McDOWELL,
BOOKSELLER & STATIONER
No. 12½ Market Street, below Second

ALMANAC FOR 1863.

The Union Almanac

*Almanacs have been published for de-
cades. Commonplace ones are available at*

*$4 to $12; those representing early printings
or scarce ones are higher.*

American Telephone & Telegraph
Almanac, 1935 ....$10.00
Ayer's American Almanac,
1885 ....3.00 to 5.50
Bucklen's Almanac, 1914...............5.00
Der Lutherische Kalender fur das jahr
1860, Allentown, Pa. 7.50
Dr. S.S. Fitch's Almanac, 1868 ....12.00
Dr. Jayne's Medical Almanac, 1912,
32 pp. 5.00
Dr. Kilmer's Swamp Root Almanac,
1918 ....3.00
Dr. Kilmer's Swamp Root Almanac,
1926 ....9.00
Dr. Kilmer's Swamp Root Almanac,
1933 ....7.50
Dr. Miles Almanac, 1920 or 1929, each ...1.25
Dr. Pierce's Happiness in the Home
Almanac, 1928, 32 pp. 3.00
Dr. Thatcher's Almanac, 1923.........5.00
Family Christian Almanac, 1862.........7.00
The Family Health Almanac, 1876,
published at the Office of the
Health Reformer, Battle Creek,
Michigan, 46 pp. 8.50
Farmer's Almanack, 1829, Robert B.
Thomas, 28 pp. 10.00
Farmer's and Mechanic's Almanac,
1853 ....8.50
Father Abraham's Almanac, 1808,
Philadelphia 20.00
Fleming Bros. Almanac, 1923 ....5.00
Foley's Family Almanac, 1914..........2.50
Hazeltine's Pocket Almanac, 1886,
1889, 1892 or 1896, each 5.00
Herbalist Almanac, 1931, Indian pictured
on cover 1.50
Hoofland's Almanac and Family Receipt
Book for Everybody's Use, 1878,
Philadelphia 7.50
Hostetter's Illustrated United States
Almanac, 1862, for the use of
merchants, mechanics, farmers &
planters & all families, Pittsburgh,
32 pp. 10.00
Hostetter's Illustrated United States
Almanac, 1870 ....12.00
Low's Almanac, 1809 ....15.00
Lum & Abner's Almanac, 1936 ....18.00
Moffat's Medical and Agricultural
Almanack, 1846, w/advertising for
Phoenix Bitters & details of 40 cures,
48 pp. 4½ x 7½'' 20.00
National Temperance Almanac &
Teetotaler Yearbook, 1899 ....5.00
New Appeal, 1918, 352 pp. 4.00
New England Farmer's Almanac, 1848,
1849 or 1854, each 3.00
The North American Almanac, 1847,
18 pp. 10.00

The Old Farmer's Almanack, 1834,
Robert B. Thomas, 36 pp. 10.00
The Old Farmer's Almanack, 1857,
Robert B. Thomas, 30 pp. 7.50
Phelps Almanac, 1881 . . . . .3.00
Piso Pocket Almanac, 1897 or 1898,
each 5.00
Rawleigh's Almanac, 1918 . . . . .5.00
Rawleigh's Almanac, 1927, 64 pp. 4.00
Seven Barks Almanac, 1889, w/por-
trait "Gallery of Our Governors" 8.00
Shaker Almanac, 1882 . . . . .18.50
Shaker Almanac, 1883 . . . . .15.00
Shaker Almanac, 1886, 32 pp. 50.00
Simmons' Liver Regulator Almanac,
1903 . . . . .16.00
Standard Almanac, 1889 . . . . .3.00
Tribune Almanac and Political Register,
1878, New York 7.50
The Union Almanac, 1863,
Philadelphia (ILLUS.) 10.00
Universal Almanac & Catalogue of
Seeds, 1893, D.M. Ferry & Co.,
48 pp. 15.00
Vinegar Bitters Almanac, 1872 . . . . .15.00
Watkins Almanac, 1916 . . . . .2.00
World Almanac & Book of Facts, 1930,
936 pp. 6.00

ART DECO

Art Deco Bangle Bracelets

Interest in Art Deco, a name given an art movement stemming from the Paris International Exhibition of 1925, is at an all-time high and continues to grow. This style flowered in the 1930s and actually continued into the 1940s. A mood of flippancy is found in its varied character-istics--zigzag lines resembling the lightning bolt, sometimes steppes, often the use of sharply contrasting colors such as black and white and others. Look for Art Deco prices to continue to rise.

Ash tray, bronze figural lady on
green onyx base, 8 x 6" base,
5¼" h. figure $125.00
Ash tray, chrome figural nude lady on
black-glazed pottery base 45.00

Bookends, bronze finish metal, figural
race horse & jockey, pr. 65.00
Bookends, chrome, 3-dimensional
wolf heads, pr. 45.00
Bracelets, bangle-type, celluloid, black
elongated diamond forms in white,
1920s, set of 3 (ILLUS.) 30.00
Bracelet, bangle-type, 14k green gold,
w/finely detailed coiled snake in
black & white enamel, 2 3/8" l.
snake, 3/8" w. bracelet 350.00
Bracelet, bangle-type, gold-filled,
engraved Deco hearts, florals, etc. 49.00
Bracelet, rhinestone, hand-set flexible-
type w/three rows of rhinestones,
early 1940s 45.00
Bracelet, sterling silver, flowered links,
Georg Jensen .65.00
Bust of an Art Deco lady, green
onyx, 4½" h., on 2 x 1½" base 35.00
Candlesticks, silverplate, tubular form
on square foot, stylized floral
candle nozzle, 11¼" h., pr. 35.00
Carpet, knotted wool & silk, camel
ground w/thin brown double borders, field w/overlapping rectangles
in shades of brown & rose, fringed
border, French, ca. 1930, 12' 10" x
9' 4" 1,870.00

Art Deco Cameo Glass

Centerpiece bowl, cameo-carved brown
glass w/polished squared motifs
on deeply etched ground, signed
"Daum Nancy," ca. 1930, 14" d.
(ILLUS.) 2,970.00

Tiffany Bronze Cigarette Box

Cigarette box w/hinged lid, bronze
w/applied 18k gold trim, oblong
form w/sloping sides & splayed
bracket feet, applied 18k gold panel
on lid engraved w/hieroglyphs & 18k
gold pyramid on front, engraved "M.

Friedsam/one of those who helped to build the pyramid" inside cover, lined cedarwood base, Tiffany & Co., New York, 1907-47, 8" l. (ILLUS.) 385.00

Cigarette holder, black Bakelite & silver, 3" l. 15.00

Cigarette lighter, table model, marbleized glass baseball shape. 65.00

Clock, table model, Elgin 7-jewel movement, brushed brass triangular case w/pr. enameled swinging doors studded w/brass stars opening to white dial w/brass numerals on black ground, 4" w., 4" h. 60.00

Cocktail set: cocktail pitcher, 6 goblets & tray; vari-colored glass goblet bowls on chrome stems & chrome tray, signed Farber Bros., 8 pcs. 125.00

Cocktail set: pitcher & 8 glasses; clear glass w/applied black reeding, signed Steuben, 9 pcs. 595.00

Cocktail shaker, black amethyst glass & chrome 15.00

Danish Silver Coffee Set

Coffee service: cov. coffee pot, creamer & waste bowl; silver, hammered sides, stained wood handles set at right angles, Georg Jensen, Copenhagen, ca. 1925, 3 pcs. (ILLUS.) 880.00

Coffee service: cov. coffee pot, creamer & sugar bowl; silverplate, oval faceted shape tapering to molded spreading foot, applied on two sides w/tapering ridged bands & oblong cartouches enclosing geometric designs, American, ca. 1930, 3 pcs. 137.00

Cuff links, 14k green gold, 4 identical sides w/raised carved platinum trim, ¾ x 7/17" oblong, pr. 76.00

Desk set: 4½" sq. pyramid form inkwell w/hinged lid & milk white glass insert, pen tray, rocker blotter & sponge-holder; brass w/silverplate trim, marked Bradley & Hubbard, 4 pcs. 125.00

Dresser set: pr. cologne bottles & cov. jar; cut & polished crystal w/enameled floral decor, 3 pcs. 150.00

Dresser set: cov. puff jar & 2 perfume bottles; porcelain, figural ballerinas in pink, marked "Bavaria," 3 pcs. 195.00

Dresser tray, blue mirrored glass 20.00

Figure of a dancing girl, pewter, on amber onyx base, 8" h. 150.00

Figure of a dancing girl, porcelain, white, marked Japan, 8" h. 18.00

Figure of Harlequin holding a dagger above head, porcelain, Bing & Grondahl, 8" h. 275.00

Figure of a Court Jester dancing, gilt bronze w/ivory face & hands, marked "Germany," 11" h. 1,250.00

Fish bowl in brass holder cast w/Art Deco lady & dog in crescent moon 125.00

Flower frog, pottery, figural Art Deco nude dancing w/scarf, white glaze, 8" h. 18.00

Handkerchief box, cov., Lucite (transparent plastic), w/Art Deco nude on cover. 25.00

Incense burner, pot metal, figural Art Deco lady kneeling on pillow, marked "Aronson," 1923 . . . . .95.00

Art Deco Jewelry Box

Jewelry box w/hinged lid, silverplate, stylized nude figure on lid, marked "W.B. Mfg. Co.," 5 x 5" base, 6" h. (ILLUS.) 55.00

Art Deco Lamp

Lamp, pot metal base w/musicians
flanking amber glass globe, gilt
finish, 12 x 4" base, overall 9" h.
(ILLUS.)..........................75.00
Lamp, bronze finish metal, figural nude
ladies (2) supporting gilt finish
oblong shade, 13" h. 285.00
Lamp, copper finish metal base cast
w/three figural Art Deco nudes in a
circle supporting an amber "crackle"
glass ball-shaped 5½" d. globe,
14" h. 165.00
Lamp, model of a ship, blue satin
glass base w/nickel-plated deck
& sails............................52.00
Lamps, blue satin glass, figural nude
playing harp, 12 x 6", pr...........300.00

Art Deco Chrome Lamps

Lamps, chrome, domical shade, cylindrical standard, circular base,
French, ca. 1925, 19" h., pr.
(ILLUS.) 1,875.00
Letter rack, folding-type, brass, 3-com-
partment w/hinged 3-section stamp
box at base, stylized cut-out floral
design, marked E.S. Gesch., 6" l.,
5" h. 52.00
Mechanical pencil for watch chain,
sterling silver 12.00
Mirror, hand-type, gutta percha, basket of fruit & leaf scroll decor 25.00
Necklace, black & amber glass beads,
Bohemian, 54" l. 55.00
Necklace, choker-type, black glass
beads w/velvet ribbon tie 35.00
Necklace, rhinestone, intricate Art
Deco design, marked Weiss 42.00
Pen stand, gilt spelter 5" h. figure of
an Art Deco lady w/ivorene face
wearing male medieval costume &
holding a sword, on beige marble
5 x 2½" base 75.00
Pin tray, china, h.p. profile portrait of
beautiful girl, 1920s, Japan, 5"......20.00
Pitcher, water, frosted glass w/black
trim, 10" h........................35.00
Powder box, frosted glass base,

chrome top w/black enameled
designs...........................8.00
Powder box, onyx base, metal cover
w/Deco lady finial 36.00
Powder box & cover w/figural Deco
lady & dogs finial, pink frosted
glass 38.00
Ring, lady's, 14k gold w/emerald-cut
synthetic aquamarine set flanked by
small snythetic rubies 77.00
Ring, lady's, 14k gold w/emerald-cut
deep purple amethyst set flanked by
white gold butterfly each side 275.00
Tea set: teapot, creamer & open
sugar bowl; chrome, tall forms,
marked Krome Kraft, 3 pcs. 36.00
Tea set: ball-shaped teapot w/upright
spout, creamer, cov. sugar bowl &
round tray; chased chrome w/French
ivory (celluloid) handles, 4 pcs. 125.00
Tea set: teapot w/reed-covered swing
handle, tea caddy, condensed milk
can holder, cov. sugar bowl & tray;
silverplate, straight-sided forms
w/horizontal grooves, circle finials &
handles, 5 pcs. 125.00

Traveling Accessories

Traveling toilet accessories: dental
cream, cold cream, talcum powder &
toilet soap; in original box w/Art Deco
lady lettered "Colgate's Week-End
Package," ca. 1927, 5 x 3" box
(ILLUS.) 10.00
Tray, serving, chrome, w/four cobalt
blue glass inserts, 15" l............65.00
Vase, art pottery, bulbous, incised
swirl designs, tan, white & green
semi-matte glaze w/glossy green
drip, Belgium, 3½" h. 12.00
Vase, art pottery, 2-handled, burgundy
& grey glaze, marked Belgium
Faience Rib Thulin, 8" h. 185.00
Vase, silverplate, pear-shaped body
w/bulbous ribs supported by three
2 1/8" h. full figure draped nude
ladies, marked Silvercraft, 9" h. 48.00
Vase, pottery, matte grey ground
w/shadow flowers, glossy cobalt blue
top band & trim & large glossy
blue, rose, white & gold stylized
florals around center w/small band of

same at base, marked "Amphora,"
6 3/8" widest d., 9 1/8" h. 175.00
Vase, blue glass w/silver deposit
trim, 10½" h. 75.00
Vase, art pottery, molded w/pr. nude
females in relief, ivory w/blue
interior, 11½" h. 85.00
Whisk broom, pink bristles on sterling
silver handle 24.00

ART NOUVEAU

*Art Nouveau's primary thrust was be-
tween 1890 and 1905 but commercial Art
Nouveau productions continued until about
World War I. This style was a rebellion
against historic tradition in art. Using
natural forms as inspiration, it is primarily
characterized by undulating or wave-like
lines. Many objects were made in materials
ranging from glass to metals. While interest
in Art Nouveau still remains high,
especially for jewelry in the Nouveau taste,
prices appear to be leveling off. Also see
CANDLESTICKS & CANDLE HOLDERS
and METALS.*

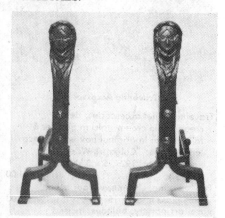

Art Nouveau Andirons

Andirons, bronze & patinated metal,
terminals cast w/head of Art Nouveau woman w/flowers in her hair,
probably French, ca. 1900, 27" h.,
pr. (ILLUS.) $1,980.00
Bookends, cast iron, figural dancing
nudes, pr. 37.50
Bookmark, sterling silver 25.00
Bowl, pewter w/Moorcroft pottery insert
w/enameled blue plums, "Liberty &
Co. Tudric Pewter," 11 x 8"
(ILLUS.) 285.00

Liberty & Co. Tudric Pewter

Bowl, pewter, fluted rim w/tulips &
leaves in relief, "Kayserzinn,"
11 x 11" 68.00
Bowl, sterling silver, undulating lines,
footed, 12½" d. 750.00
Brooch, gold & plique-a-jour enamel,
pr. central plique-a-jour enamel fan-
shaped panels set w/three rose-cut
diamonds topped by single European
cut diamond within gold mount,
ca. 1900 . . . . .715.00
Bust of Art Nouveau maiden, chalk-
ware w/bronze finish 90.00
Button hook, sterling silver hollow
handle . . . . .15.00 to 25.00
Candle sconce, wall-type, bronze &
stained glass w/heart-shaped
cut-outs, 12" h. 125.00
Centerpiece bowl, sterling silver, in the
"Martele" style, shaped oval
w/broad everted rim, embossed &
chased w/irises & primrose, hollow
slipper feet, gilt interior, The
Gorham Co., Providence, R.I., ca.
1905, 18½" l. 5,500.00

French Silver Chocolate Pot

Chocolate pot, cov., silver, tapering
cylinder chased & embossed w/undu-
lating tulips & stems & engraved
w/monogram, carved ivory handle,
hinged lid w/swirling ivory bud

finial, Cardeilhac, Paris, ca. 1900,
9 5/8" h. (ILLUS.) 3,850.00
Clothes brush, sterling silver, volup-
tuous Art Nouveau female in relief,
6" l. 57.50
Cologne bottle w/matching stopper, clear
glass w/overall ornate sterling
silver overlay, 5½ x 5" 135.00
Dish, pewter, leaf-shaped w/stem
handle & fluted irregular edge
molded w/florals, marked "Silberzinn,"
11 x 9" 90.00
Dish, sterling silver, "repousse"
swirling waves w/swimming mermaid, Simpson, Hall & Miller,
1895-98, 6½" w. 195.00

Bronze Ewer

Ewer, bronze, cast w/Nouveau maiden
handle & swan in relief on vase,
6" h. (ILLUS.) 65.00
Eyeglass case, sterling silver, engraved
Art Nouveau iris decor, Blackinton
Co., 5 x 2" 95.00

Silvered Bronze Art Nouveau Figure

Figure of an Art Nouveau woman
within a floriform wrap, silvered
bronze w/turquoise "jewels" set in
iris-like petals, Austrian, foundry
mark of Franz Bergmann, ca. 1900,
11½" h. (ILLUS.). 1,650.00
Fish platter, pewter, fish, pond lilies
& dragonfly decor, "Kayserzinn,"
24 x 11". 250.00
Flask, silverplate, w/screw-on cup
cap, engraved Nouveau maiden &
initial, 6" l. 45.00
Flask, sterling silver, "repousse"
florals 275.00

French Gilt-Bronze Garniture Set

Garniture set: clock & 3-light candle
holders; gilt-bronze, cast from
models by Charles Jonchery, France,
early 20th c., 15" h. clock & approximately 11" h. candlesticks, 3 pcs.
(ILLUS. of part) 4,180.00

Goldfish Bowl

Goldfish bowl, on bronze base w/three
figural mermaids, "Verona Art
Works," 12" across stand, 4½" h.
bowl (ILLUS.) 95.00
Hair brush & hand mirror, sterling
silver handles & backs, typical
Nouveau lines, pr. 52.50
Inkwell-lamp, bronze, base in the form
of lily pads supporting a blossom
form inkwell w/detachable cover,
surmounted by a young woman
leaning forward & supporting a
heavy open poppy blossom enclosing

a light, woman wearing a flower-
form hat to match cover of inkwell,
brown patina, inscribed Leo Laporte
Blairsy, early 20th c., 16¼" h......5,500.00
Jewelry box w/hinged lid, silverplate,
footed, Art Nouveau female masks &
florals within panels, original lining,
6" sq. 65.00

"Loie Fuller" Lamp

Lamp, gilt bronze, figure of Loie
Fuller, her arms extended into her
billowing draperies concealing 2 light
sockets, after Francois-Raoul Larche,
early 20th c., 18" h. (ILLUS.)......19,250.00
Match safe, pocket-type, sterling
silver, bust of Art Nouveau woman
w/flowing hair in relief 55.00

Art Nouveau Mirror

Mirror, wall-type, beveled mirror plate
within patinated bronze frame w/floral

crest & undulating sides above Art
Nouveau woman's face at base,
ca. 1910, 11¾" h. (ILLUS.) 200.00
Mirror, dresser-type w/easel back,
patinated metal frame w/stylized
iris enclosing beveled oval mirror
plate, 16" h......................75.00
Mirror, hand-type, silverplate, Art
Nouveau woman's head w/flowing
hair & embossed florals overall,
beveled mirror, 9½ x 4½" 75.00
Mirror, hand-type, sterling silver, Art
Nouveau lady's head w/flowing
hair & florals in relief 125.00
Mirror, hand-type, sterling silver,
lilies or tulips in high relief, small
size ....50.00 to 95.00
Mustache comb, folding-type, tortoise
shell comb in sterling silver,
1 5/8 x 3/8", 3" l. opened 45.00
Nail file, sterling silver handle w/busts
of cherubs & scrollwork 30.00
Nut dishes, sterling silver, florals in
relief & monogram, set of 6 ....100.00
Paper clip, brass floriform w/yellow
slag glass insets, 4¼" 50.00
Paper clip, brass, figural swan........65.00
Paperweight, sterling silver semi-nude
female figure on brass base, 6" h.....95.00
Pendant necklace, 14k gold, detailed
profile of woman w/long flowing hair
hair & flowers, tiny diamond nestled
within her hair, 18" chain 210.00
Perfume bottle, crystal encased in
metal spider web cast w/spiders,
dragonflies, flowers & tiny raised
beading, 6½" h. 85.00
Picture, woven silk, seven dancing
girls, framed, small 45.00
Pin, sterling silver, nude Art Nouveau
maiden w/butterfly wings, 2" 45.00
Pin tray, brass, Art Nouveau maiden
w/flaring skirt, 6 x 7".............62.00
Pitcher, lemonade, mold-blown clear
glass w/interior ribbing & applied
handle, enameled white florals,
flowing tendrils & buds w/green
leaves, gold trim, 10¼" h. 55.00
Salad fork, sterling silver, semi-nude
Art Nouveau maiden handle, Tiffany
& Co.............................140.00
Serving dish, pewter, 3-compartment
w/center handle, iris decor, "Orivit,"
large...........................150.00
Serving spoon, sterling silver, Art
Nouveau nude lady handle..........95.00
Stein, pewter, eagle's beak spout &
wings at base, "Kayserzinn,"
13½" h. 495.00
Tea & coffee service: cov. tea & coffee
pots, hot water jug, creamer, cov.
sugar bowl & 2-handled tray; silverplate, swirling panel forms on

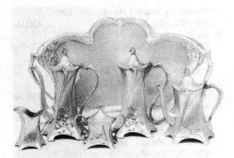

Tea & Coffee Service

bracket feet embossed & chased
w/berried leaves & covers w/open-
work stem finials, marked Wurttem-
bergische Metallwarenfabrik,
Geislingen, Germany, ca. 1900,
25½" w. tray, 6 pcs. (ILLUS.) 2,860.00
Tea infuser, sterling silver, hinged
ball w/"repousse" florals overall,
w/chain & ring, 2¼" d. 165.00
Teaspoon, sterling silver, figural Art
Nouveau nude lady handle 75.00
Thermometer, desk-type, bronze Art
Nouveau maiden leaning against
pedestal supporting thermometer,
marble base 75.00
Tray, pewter, 4-leaf clover shape
cast w/bumblebees, "Kayserzinn,"
6" w.....................60.00 to 75.00
Vase, art pottery, pierced handles,
enameled stork decor on earth-tone
ground w/enameled cobalt blue top
& base, signed "Amphora," 5" h. 80.00
Vase, porcelain, relief-molded &
pierced decor, "Rorstrand," Sweden,
9" h. 250.00
Vases, pewter, trumpet-shaped, cast
w/leafage, 3 pierced antler form
handles continuing to steer's skull
in the flaring round base, "Kayserzinn," ca. 1900, 14¼" h., pr. 770.00
Vase, sterling silver, in the "Martele"
style, elongated lobed pear form
w/everted wavy rim & 4 slipper feet,
embossed & chased grape bunches,
leaves & florals, The Gorham Co.,
Providence, R.I., 1898, 19¼" h. ...8,250.00
Vase, art pottery, shouldered ovoid
flanked by whiplash handles, deep
brown drip glaze over pale celadon
green, w/gilt metal mounts, France,
ca. 1900, 21½" h. 275.00
Whisk broom, sterling silver handle,
small..........................48.00
Wine cooler, pewter, 6 molded scallop
shells around upper part & relief-
molded fronds, "Orivit," 1881-1901,
8" h. 225.00
Yarn box & scissors holder, brass,
embossed w/Art Nouveau lady

w/flowing hair, butterfly, fan &
chrysanthemums, ca. 1900, 4" w.,
3" h. 69.00

AUDUBON PRINTS

Barred Owl

*John James Audubon, American orni-
thologist and artist, is considered the finest
nature artist in history. About 1820 he
conceived the idea of having a full color
book published portraying every known
species of American bird in its natural
habitat. He spent years in the wilderness
capturing the beauty in vivid color only to
have great difficulty finding a publisher. In
1826 he visited England, received immediate acclaim, and selected Robert Havell as
his engraver. "Birds of America," when
completed, consisted of four volumes of 435
individual plates, double-elephant folio size,
which are a combination of aquatint,
etching and line engraving. W. H. Lizars of
Edinburgh engraved the first ten plates of
this four volume series. These were later
retouched by Havell who produced the
complete set between 1827 and early 1839.
In the early 1840s, another definitive work,
"Viviparous Quadrupeds of North America," containing 150 plates, was published
in America. Prices for Audubon's original
double-elephant folio size prints are very
high and beyond the means of the average
collector. Subsequent editions of "Birds of
America," especially the chromolithographs
done by Julius Bien in New York (1859-60)*

and the smaller octavo (7 x 10½") edition of prints done by J.T. Bowen of Philadelphia in the 1840s are those that are most frequently offered for sale.

American Redstart - Plate XL (40), hand-colored engraving & aquatint plate from "The Birds of America," printed by Robert Havell, Jr., London, 1827-39, 19 3/8 x 12 1/8" $1,650.00

Arkansas Flycatcher, Swallow-Tailed Flycatcher or Says Fly-Catcher - Plate CCCLIX (359), hand-colored engraving & aquatint plate from "The Birds of America," printed by Robert Havell, Jr., London, 1827-39, 21¾ x 14" 1,430.00

Barred Owl - Plate XLVI (46), hand-colored engraving & aquatint plate from "The Birds of America," printed by Robert Havell, Jr., London, 1827-39, 38¼ x 25 5/8" (ILLUS.) 5,500.00

Bay-Breasted Warbler - Plate LXIX (69), hand-colored engraving & aquatint plate from "The Birds of America," printed by Robert Havell, Jr., London, 1827-39, 19½ x 12¼" 1,430.00

Bird of Washington

Bird of Washington or Great American Sea Eagle - Plate XI (11), hand-colored engraving & aquatint plate from "The Birds of America," printed by Robert Havell, Jr., London, 1827-39, 38¼ x 25 5/8" (ILLUS.) . . . . 3,300.00 to 5,225.00

Black or Surf Duck - Plate CCCXVII (317), hand-colored engraving & aquatint plate from "The Birds of America," printed by Robert Havell, Jr., London, 1827-39, 21¼ x 30¼" 2,090.00

Black Backed Gull - Plate CCXLI (241), hand-colored engraving & aquatint plate from "The Birds of America,"

printed by Robert Havell, Jr., London, 1827-39, 38 1/8 x 25½" 2,420.00

Black-Winged Hawk - Plate CCCLII (352), hand-colored engraving & aquatint plate from "The Birds of America," printed by Robert Havell, Jr., London, 1827-39, 30 3/8 x 21¼" 2,310.00

Blue-Bird - Plate CXIII (113), hand-colored engraving & aquatint plate from "The Birds of America," printed by Robert Havell, Jr., London, 1827-39, 19½ x 12 3/8" . . . . 2,420.00 to 2,970.00

Blue-Green Warbler - Plate XLIX (49), hand-colored engraving & aquatint plate from "The Birds of America," printed by Robert Havell, Jr., London, 1827-39, 19 5/8 x 12¼" 1,045.00

Blue-Grey Fly-Catcher - Plate LXXXIV (84), hand-colored engraving & aquatint plate from "The Birds of America," printed by Robert Havell, Jr., London, 1827-39, 19½ x 12¼" 1,320.00

Canvas Backed Duck - Plate CCCI (301), Amsterdam Edition (exact facsimile of the Havell Edition, printed in 1971 on rag paper & limited to 250), 25½ x 38 1/8" 1,400.00

Carolina Turtle Dove (Mourning Dove) - Plate XVII (17), hand-colored engraving & aquatint plate from "The Birds of America," printed by Robert Havell, Jr., London, 1827-39, 26¾ x 20¾" 13,200.00

Carolina Turtle Dove (Mourning Dove) - Plate XVII (17), Amsterdam Edition, 1971, 26¾ x 20¾" 750.00

Florida Jay - Plate LXXXVII (87), hand-colored engraving & aquatint plate from "The Birds of America," printed by Robert Havell, Jr., London, 1827-39, 25¾ x 20½" 4,125.00

Great Blue Heron - Plate CCXI (211), Amsterdam Edition, 1971, 38 1/8 x 25½" 1,500.00

Great Carolina Wren - Plate LXXVIII (78), hand-colored engraving & aquatint plate from "The Birds of America," printed by Robert Havell, Jr., London, 1827-39, 19 3/8 x 12 1/8" . . . . 1,540.00 to 2,750.00

Great-Footed Hawk - Plate XVI (16), hand-colored engraving & aquatint plate from "The Birds of America," printed by Robert Havell, Jr., London, 1827-39, 25 5/8 x 38¼" . . . . 2,530.00 to 3,080.00

Great White Heron - Plate CCLXXXI (281), hand-colored engraving & aquatint plate from "The Birds of America," printed by Robert Havell, Jr., London, 1827-39, 25½ x 38 1/8" . . 18,700.00

Hermit Thrush - Plate LVIII (58), hand-
colored engraving & aquatint plate
from "The Birds of America," printed
by Robert Havell, Jr., London,
1827-39, 19 3/8 x 12 1/8" 1,430.00
House Wren - Plate LXXXIII (83), hand-
colored engraving & aquatint plate
from "The Birds of America," printed
by Robert Havell, Jr., London,
1827-39, 19½ x 12¼" 3,960.00
Indigo Bird - Plate LXXIV (74), hand-
colored engraving & aquatint plate
from "The Birds of America," printed
by Robert Havell, Jr., London,
1827-39, 19 5/8 x 12¼"..........1,760.00
Ivory-Billed Woodpecker - Plate LXVI
(66), hand-colored engraving & aquatint plate from "The Birds of America," printed by Robert Havell, Jr.,
London, 1827-39, 38¼ x 25 5/8" ..17,600.00
Kentucky Warbler - Plate XXXVIII (38),
hand-colored engraving & aquatint
plate from "The Birds of America,"
printed by Robert Havell, Jr.,
London, 1827-39, 19½ x 12¼".....1,210.00
Lazuli Finch, Clay-Coloured Finch or
Oregon Snow Finch - Plate CCCXCVIII
(398), hand-colored engraving &
aquatint plate from "The Birds of
America," printed by Robert Havell,
Jr., London, 1827-39, 19½ x
12¼" 1,100.00

Puffin

Puffin - Plate CCXIII (213), hand-colored
engraving & aquatint plate from "The
Birds of America," printed by Robert
Havell, Jr., London, 1827-39,
12¼ x 19½" (ILLUS.) 5,720.00
Purple Martin - Plate XXII (22), hand-
colored engraving & aquatint plate
from "The Birds of America," printed
by Robert Havell, Jr., London,
1827-39, 25½ x 20½" 2,860.00
Red Shouldered Hawk, male & female,
hand-colored engraving & aquatint
plate from "Birds of America,"
engraved by R. Havell 250.00
Snowy Heron or White Egret (Snowy
Egret) - Plate CCXLII (242), Amsterdam Edition, 1971, 25¾ x 20½" ...1,400.00
Snowy Owl - Plate CXXI (121),
Amsterdam Edition, 1971, 38¼ x
25 5/8" (ILLUS.) 1,100.00

Snowy Owl

Towhe Bunting - Plate XXIX (29), hand-
colored engraving & aquatint plate
from "The Birds of America," printed
by Robert Havell, Jr., London,
1827-39, 19 5/8 x 12 3/8" 2,420.00

Velvet Duck

Velvet Duck - Plate CCXLVII (247),
hand-colored engraving & aquatint
plate from "The Birds of America,"
printed by Robert Havell, Jr.,
London, 1827-39, 20 5/8 x 29 7/8"
(ILLUS.) 2,090.00
Virginian Patridge - Plate LXXVI (76),
hand-colored engraving & aquatint
plate from "The Birds of America,"
printed by Robert Havell, Jr.,
London, 1827-39, 25 5/8 x 38¼" ..19,250.00
Whooping Crane - Plate CCXXVI (226),
Amsterdam Edition, 1971, 38 1/8 x
25½" 1,100.00
Wild Turkey...Male - Plate I (1), hand-
colored engraving & aquatint plate
from "The Birds of America," printed
by Robert Havell, Jr., London,
1827-39, 38 1/8 x 25½"..........24,200.00
Yellow-Crowned Heron - Plate
CCCXXXVI (336), hand-colored
engraving & aquatint plate from

"The Birds of America," printed by
Robert Havell, Jr., London, 1827-39,
38¼ x 25 5/8" 11,550.00

AUTOGRAPHS

*Values of autographs and autograph let-
ters depend on such factors as content,
scarcity and the fame of the writer. Values
of good autograph material continue to rise.
A.L.S. stands for "autographed letter
signed;" L.S. for "letter signed."*

Benton, Thomas H., (1889-1975) American
  artist, pencil A.Ms. S., his recipe for
  egg nog, at lower left appears a
  small pencil caricature of a man
  imbibing the drink, 1 p. $150.00
Burns, George & Allen, Gracie,
  comedians, photograph signed,
  8 x 10" 35.00
George V, (1865-1936) King of
  England, photograph signed, 1909 ..150.00
Gershwin, George, (1898-1937) American
  composer, L.S., New York, Jan. 20,
  1936, to Keane Waters of the
  Lyceum Theatre, ½ p. 350.00
Grant, Ulysses S., (1822-1885) Commander of Union Armies at the close
  of the Civil War & 18th President
  of the United States, Lieutenant's
  Commission in United States Navy on
  parchment signed, March 21, 1870 ..175.00
Grant, Ulysses S., (1822-1885) Commander of Union Armies at the close
  of the Civil War & 18th President
  of the United States, partly-printed
  document signed, Washington, March
  26, 1869, appointment of a deputy
  postmaster at Troy, Pa., countersigned by Hamilton Fish, Secretary of
  State, 1 p. 425.00
Grant, Ulysses S., (1822-1885) Commander of Union Armies at the close
  of the Civil War & 18th President
  of the United States, printed whaleship document signed, July 17, 1871,
  ship's passport in 4 languages
  issued to shipmaster Edwin A.
  Potter, countersigned by Secretary of
  State Hamilton Fish 880.00
Harrison, Benjamin, (1833-1901) 23rd
  President of the United States, A.L.S.,
  Washington, Dec. 29, 1889, to
  Commodore A.E. Bateman, 1 p.,
  w/partly-engraved invitation to a
  reception by President & Mrs.
  Harrison, 1891, 2 pcs...............600.00
Jefferson, Thomas, (1743-1826) 3rd
  President of the United States,

A.L.S., Washington, March 12, 1805,
  to Mrs. Ann Welsh, 1 p. French-
  matted w/bust engraving of Jefferson
  & contained under glass in brown
  wooden frame, overall 15 x 18"
  oblong............................3,900.00
Marshall, John, (1776-1835) Chief
  Justice, A.L.S., Department of State,
  Washington, June 25, 1800, to Israel
  Whelan, 2 pp....................2,100.00
Monroe, Marilyn, (1926-1962) American
  movie star, A.L.S., West L.A., Calif,
  no date but w/original envelope
  postmarked April 13, 1944, to Mrs.
  Janiece Wright in Sandy, Utah,
  3 pp., 2 pcs. 3,500.00
Pierce, Franklin, (1804-1869) 14th
  President of the United States,
  printed whaleship document signed,
  October 10, 1853, ship's passport in
  4 languages issued to shipmaster
  William Jernegan II & signed by
  President Pierce & countersigned by
  Secretary of State W.L. Marcy 990.00
Pound, Ezra, (1885-1972) American
  poet, essayist & critic, A.L.S., Hotel
  Eden, Sirmione, Lago di Garda, no
  date (but early 1910), to the
  publisher Elkin Mathews, concerning
  the publication of "Canzoni," 4 pp. ..660.00
Revere, Paul, (1735-1818) American
  patriot, A.L.S., Boston, March 25,
  1810, to his son Joseph Warren,
  1 p............................5,000.00
Roosevelt, Theodore, (1858-1919) 26th
  President of the United States, L.S.,
  N.Y.C., Sept. 14, 1916, to Hamilton
  Fish, 1 p........................900.00
Rosetti, Dante Gabriel, (1828-1882)
  English painter & poet, A.L.S., Aldrich
  Lodge near Bogner, November 30,
  1875, to "my dear Philip," 4 pp. 247.00
Ruby, Jack (Kennedy assassination),
  murderer of Lee Harvey Oswald,
  A.L.S., County Jail, Dec. 6, 1963, to
  Harold Bush, w/original holograph
  envelope, 1 p......................275.00
Stanford, Leland, (1824-1893) American
  railroad magnate, A.L.S. as president
  of the Central Pacific Railroad Co.,
  Salt Lake City, Dec. 3, 1868, to John
  W. Campbell, 1 p.................475.00
Tucker, Sophie, photograph signed,
  5 x 7"............................40.00
Wolfe, Thomas, (1900-1938) American
  novelist, autograph manuscript of his
  article entitled "What a Writer
  Reads," written for Charles Scrib-
  ner's & Sons "The Bookbuyer," in
  pencil, 30 pp. in cloth folder &
  morocco-backed slipcase........4,675.00

AUTOMOBILE ACCESSORIES

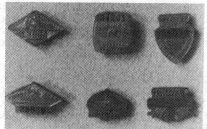

Chauffeur's Badges

Bumper & grill, "Chrysler Airflow," cast
iron, 1936, 70% original paint $75.00
Chauffeur's badge, California,
1935-36 ....15.00
Chauffeur's badge, Illinois, 1918 ....35.00
Chauffeur's badge, Illinois, 1948 ....13.50
Chauffeur's badge, Indiana, 1935 ....5.00
Chauffeur's badge, Iowa, 1940 ..5.00 to 12.00
Chauffeur's badge, Michigan, 1931 .....10.00
Chauffeur's badge, Michigan, 1938 .....7.50
Chauffeur's badge, Minnesota, 1928 .....5.00
Clock, "Hudson Super 6," Waltham 120.00
Coil case, "Ford Model T," wooden,
w/coils 35.00
Duster, yellow cotton.................45.00
Fender skirts, "Ford Thunderbird,"
1963, pr..........................100.00

Early Gear Shift Knobs

Gear shift knob, "Buick," marble
glass 25.00
Gear shift knob, marbleized green &
white glass ....20.00 to 35.00
Gear shift knob, model of a skull,
amber w/red eyes 15.00
Goggles, folding-type w/dust shields,
tinted, metal case, "Willson
Goggles" 15.00
Head lamp, "Maxwell," brass 45.00
Head lamps, "Powell & Hammer Ltd.,
England," brass, ca. 1905, pr.......450.00
Hood ornament, "Armstrong-Siddeley,"
sphinx, on wooden base, 1930s 75.00
Hood ornament, "Chevrolet," 1950s 20.00
Hood ornament, "Chrysler," 1950s 20.00
Hood ornament, "Dodge," ram
w/horns 10.00

Hood ornament, "Lincoln," leaping
Greyhound, on wooden base, 1930s ..85.00
Hood ornament, "Mack" Bulldog,
chrome 25.00
Hood ornament, "Oldsmobile," 1950s...30.00
Hood ornament, "Packard," Goddess of
Speed, on wooden base, 1920s 47.50
Hood ornament, "Pontiac," Indian
head, 1950s 42.50
Hood ornament, "Spirit of Triumph,"
winged male w/wheel, on wooden
base, 1930s 75.00
Hood ornament, nude lady w/long
flowing hair 42.50
Horn, brass bulb-type, 3-coil, for right
hand mount 40.00
Horn, "Klaxon," Stewart 14-A 40.00
Horn, "Ooga," hand-operated No. 2
model, red over steel, E.A. Labora-
tories 28.00
Hub caps, 1963 Ford Thunderbird,
spinner-type, set of 4 ....300.00
Jack, "Cadillac" in script 17.50
Jack, "Ford" in script ....17.50 to 25.00
License plate, 1916, New Hampshire,
graniteware 18.00
License plate, 1917, New Hampshire,
graniteware 27.50
License plate, 1919, California, granite-
ware 27.50
License plate, 1920, New Hampshire ...15.00
License plate, 1922, Nebraska 14.00
License plate, 1924, California 15.50
License plate, 1924, Minnesota 12.50
License plates, 1928, California, pr. 30.00
License plates, 1928, Oklahoma, pr. ...12.50
License plates, 1929, Michigan, pr. 10.00
License plates, 1931, Michigan, pr. 30.00
License plates, 1933, Maine, pr.........15.00
License plates, 1933, North Dakota,
graniteware, w/original wrappers,
pr................................15.00
License plates, 1937, New Mexico, pr. ..18.00
License plates, 1939, Michigan, granite-
ware, w/original wrappers, pr.......15.00
License plates, 1940, Texas, pr. 10.00
License plates, 1944, Nevada, pr. 20.00
License plate, 1948, Maine, brass 18.00
License plates, 1948, New Mexico, pr. ..15.00
Luggage rack, running board type,
wrought iron, black ....18.00 to 30.00
Monkey wrench, "Ford" in script 5.50
Motometer, "Boyce," for Willys Six,
1913-14 patent....................50.00
Motometer, "Chandler"...............65.00
Motometer, "Nash 6," w/wings 95.00
Oil can, "Ford" in script 13.50
Pliers, "Ford" in script 12.50
Radiator cap w/winged hood orna-
ment, "Chrysler," brass, 1927........45.00
Radiator cap, "Stutz," silvered bronze,
Art Deco style, sun god 150.00
Radiator cap, metal, devil thumbing his
nose, 5" 40.00

"Chevrolet" Radiator Emblem

Radiator emblem, "Chevrolet," blue &
  white porcelain, 4 x 1½" (ILLUS.).....22.00
Radiator emblem plates, "Dodge," blue
  & white enameled metal, round,
  1918, "Dodge," brushed metal, round
  & "Chevrolet," logo-type, set of 3 ....50.00
Radiator emblem plate, "Essex" 12.00
Radiator emblem plate, "Kaiser".......17.00
Radiator emblem plate, "De Soto,"
  1930s.....................................8.00
Screwdriver, "Ford" in script 8.00
Side light, "Gray & Davis, Amesbury,
  Mass.," brass, 6¼" d. 40.00
Spare tire cover, "Pontiac," early
  1930s, 2-piece 160.00
Spark plug wrench, "Ford Model T" in
  script..................................2.50
Spark plug wrench, "Maxwell" 4.00
Speedometer, "Ford," w/July 1909
  patent................................55.00
Speedometer, "Stewart" 45.00
Tire pressure gauge, "Schrader,"
  brass, 1923 ....8.00 to 12.00
Tire pump, brass w/wood handle 50.00
Tire pump, "Ford" in script, cast iron....16.00
Vase, clear glass hexagon w/etched
  floral designs, in Art Deco style
  metal holder 95.00
Vase, cobalt blue pressed glass,
  w/original bracket, 7½" h..........175.00
Vases, vaseline Satin glass, pr. 55.00
Wheel w/wooden spokes, "Ford" on
  hub 95.00
Wrench, crescent-type, "Ford" in script,
  1918 ....12.50
Wrench, "Maxwell 2"...................20.00

AUTOMOBILE LITERATURE

Auburn owner's manual, 1933 ....$10.00
Auto Blue Book, 1910, Vol. 1 ....20.00
Auto Blue Book, 1913, Vol. 4, 1088 pp. ..55.00
Auto Trade Catalog, "Radco," 1930,
  labor price book for auto repairs,
  lists all 1930 car models.............17.50
Auto Trade Journal, Jan. 1917, New
  York Show No. 522, new cars
  illustrated 25.00
Buick catalog, 1955, all models pictured
  in color...............................25.00
Buick owner's manual, 1940 ....25.00

Cadillac instruction manual, 1913,
  4th edition, 30 pp...................65.00
Cadillac showroom brochure, 1928 .....50.00
Chevrolet sales brochure, 1936 ....20.00
DeSoto sales booklet, 1940............20.00
Dodge Brothers 1½-ton truck instruction
  book, 1931 ....16.00
Dodge manual & lubrication chart, 1921,
  44 pp. 25.00
Dodge Six owner's manual, 1935 ....15.00
Edsel maintenance manual, 1960.......30.00
Essex Super-6 brochure, 1920s, 5 color
  illustrations, 6 pp. 25.00
Ford auto & truck shop manual, 1948
  or 1949, each.........................18.00
Ford Model T owner's manual, 1922 or
  1925, each 20.00
Reo Flying Cloud sales brochure, 1935 ..20.00
Studebaker booklet, "A Century of
  Wheels, 1852-1952," Longstreet......15.00
Terraplane owner's manual, 1932 .....25.00
Whippet sales booklet, 1929..........20.00
Willys Knight sales brochure, Model
  84 ....25.00

AUTOMOBILES

Plymouth 1931 Convertible

Buick, 1937 coupe, Model 46 ....$7,500.00
Buick, 1963 convertible, special
  edition (needs new top & paint) ...1,975.00
Buick, 1963 Wildcat, 4-door, air con-
  ditioning, power brakes, power
  steering, power windows & seat
  (needs paint & headliner) 1,475.00
Cadillac, 1933 V-12 limousine 35,000.00
Cadillac, 1941 Fleetwood sedan 7,500.00
Cadillac, 1958 4-door hardtop
  sedan 4,000.00
Cadillac, 1966 Fleetwood El Dorado
  convertible, light blue w/white
  interior, automatic & power 4,750.00
Chevrolet, 1936 2-door sedan 2,000.00
Chevrolet, 1946 Fleetline 4-door
  sedan 1,800.00
Chevrolet, 1967 Impala convertible,
  red & white....................6,500.00

Chrysler, 1947 Windsor sedan, all
original 1,400.00
Chrysler, 1967 Crown Imperial 4-door
sedan, power steering, windows &
seats 5,000.00
Dodge, 1947 4-door sedan 1,500.00
Edsel, 1958 Pacer, 2-door, hardtop,
400 V-8, push-button automatic
transmission, power steering 3,000.00
Ford, 1914 Model T, w/brass radiator,
head lamps & horn 22,500.00
Ford, 1930 Model A (needs work) 2,500.00
Ford, 1955 Thunderbird, red,
restored 18,000.00
Ford, 1962 Falcon, stick shift, new
paint 1,500.00
Ford, 1963 Falcon Sprint convertible,
red interior, white exterior 2,500.00
Ford, 1965 Thunderbird convertible,
white & blue, restored 9,500.00
Kaiser, 1948 4-door sedan, all
original 2,800.00
Lincoln, 1956 Premiere 4-door sedan,
baby blue & white, 53,000 actual
miles 5,500.00
Mercedes, 1967 280 SE, rosewood
interior 5,000.00
Mercury, 1971 Cougar convertible,
white & green 8,000.00
Oldsmobile, 1930 sport coupe, dual
fender mount spare tires, wood
spoke wheels, trunk rack, rebuilt
engine & transmission 8,000.00
Overland, 1916 Model 75B 4-door
touring car, restored, new leather
top & side curtains 12,000.00
Plymouth, 1931 convertible, restored
(ILLUS.) . . . . .12,000.00 to 15,000.00
Plymouth, 1949 Club coupe, rebuilt
motor, new paint 1,800.00
Plymouth, 1966 Fury convertible,
black & gold 6,500.00
Pontiac, 1934 2-door coupe, 6,700
actual miles 5,600.00
Porsche, 1963 356-B Super coupe,
total body & engine restoration . .12,750.00
Rolls Royce, 1958 Silver Cloud sedan,
restored 33,000.00
Star, 1923 touring car 3,500.00
Studebaker, 1950 Champion Six 2-door
sedan, overdrive, 35,130 actual
miles 3,500.00

AVIATION COLLECTIBLES

Recently much interest has been shown in collecting items associated with the early days of the "flying machine." In addition to relics, flying adjuncts and literature relating to the early days of flight, collectors also seek out items that picture the more renowned early pilots, some of whom became folk-heroes in their own lifetimes, as well as the early planes themselves.

"Lucky Lindy Perfume"

Bank, bust of Charles Lindbergh,
aluminum, dated $65.00
Bank, bust of Charles Lindbergh,
"Lindy," dated 1928, heavy metal or
lead 120.00
Book, "Flying with Lindbergh," Keyhoe,
published New York, 1929 . . . . .7.50
Book, "Golden Book of Airplanes," 1950,
88 pp. 5.00
Book, "The Lindberghs," P.J. O'Brien,
illustrated, 1935 . . . . .20.00
Book, "Search for Amelia Earhart,"
Goerner, first edition, 1966,
w/dust jacket 6.00
Booklet, "How To Fly A Piper Cub,"
1945, 30 pp. 15.00
Box, Charles Lindbergh & "Spirit of St.
Louis" pictured on lid, mirror inside . .60.00
Box, cover w/figural woman aviator
standing before biplane propeller,
brass, 1½" d. .45.00
Bust of Charles Lindbergh, plaster,
signed 60.00
Catalog, "The American Eagle,"
A.E. Aircraft Corp., Kansas City,
Kansas, Lindbergh-type airplanes
pictured, 1928, 24 pp. 30.00
Catalog, "Madison Square Garden Expo,"
March 1919, w/photographs 28.00
Collar box, cov., bentwood round,
Orville & Wilbur Wright pictured on
cover w/inscription "The First Aeroplane
Flight, Dec. 17, 1903, Kitty Hawk"
& "Kill Devil Hill, Dare County,
N.C.," 5½" d., 2¾" h. 85.00
Game, "Lucky Lindy," 1927, original box
w/instructions .32.50
Medallion, bronze, bust of Charles
Lindbergh in relief, 1927, 3" d. 45.00
Newspaper, "New York Times,"

pictorial souvenir Lindbergh edition,
June 23, 1927, 32 pp. 35.00
Pencil box, tin w/blue decals of
airplane & Lindbergh 37.50
Pencil sharpener, metal, model of
airplane w/removable propeller-
nose 30.00
Perfume bottle, clear glass, "Lucky
Lindy Perfume" label, each vial
(ILLUS. of counter display w/num-
erous bottles) .10.00

Charles Lindbergh Pictures

Photographs of Charles Lindbergh,
small close-up bust portrait & Lindbergh beside his plane, in blue-
painted tin frame w/enameled red
flower at crest, 2¾" w. (ILLUS.) 12.50
Pin, brass, "The Spirit of St. Louis"
airplane, original card 35.00
Pinback button, "Two Great Flyers,"
pictures Lindbergh & sled, advertising premium for "Flexible Flyer"
sleds 24.50
Plate, commemorative, 1927 Lindbergh
New York to Paris flight, Limoges
china, 8½" d. . . . . .35.00 to 45.00
Postcard, "Lincoln Beachey, World's
Most Daring Aviator" 35.00
Print, World War I fighter planes
after A.B. Dineen, red velvet matt,
original gold & blue frame, 29 x 25" . .35.00
Program, 1927 Lindbergh reception 17.00
Propeller, wooden, 8' l. 395.00
Sheet music, "Eagle of the U.S.A." 15.00
Sheet music, "Like an Angel You Flew
Into Everyone's Heart," dedicated to
Charles Lindbergh 12.50
Sheet music, "Lindy Did It" 10.00
Sign, "Bulova Watch," metal, bust
portrait of Charles Lindbergh,
10¾ x 7½" 34.00
Tapestry, woven w/Lindbergh portrait
& "Spirit of St. Louis" airplane center
& scenes of New York & Paris
each end, 55 x 20 . . . . .125.00
Tray, brass, etched biplane in flight,
8" oval 45.00
Watch fob, Spirit of St. Louis, w/tiny
compass 50.00
Year book, Aircraft, 1929 . . . . .50.00

BABY MEMENTOES

McNicol Pottery Baby's Bowl

*Everyone dotes on the new baby and
through many generations some exquisite
and unique gifts have been carefully
selected with a special infant in mind.
Collectors now seek items from a varied
assortment of baby mementoes, once tokens
of affection to the newborn babe. Also see
ABC PLATES, BUSTER BROWN COL-
LECTIBLES, CAMPBELL KID COL-
LECTIBLES, CHILDREN'S MUGS,
CRADLES, FRANKLIN MAXIM
WARES and TEXTILES.*

Baby's record book, "Baby's Biography,"
illustrated by Frances Brundage,
1891 . . . .$45.00
Baby's record book, illustrated by
Frances Brundage, published by
Raphael Tuck, 1910 . . . . .65.00
Baby's record book, 12 color & 30
black & white illustrations by Maud
Humphrey, 1898, 11 x 9" . . .100.00 to 150.00
Bonnet, crocheted cotton, lined,
white 15.00
Bonnet, crocheted cotton, Irish-type
crochet w/rosettes, off-white 22.00
Bonnet, embroidered white cotton
w/lace & ribbon trim 10.00
Bonnet, fine white cotton, Amish,
1930s 50.00
Bowl, white earthenware china, boy on
rocking horse & dog center decor,
gilt design rim, D. E. McNicol Pottery,
East Liverpool, Ohio, 1892-1920, 7" d.
(ILLUS.) 18.00
Christening gown, white cotton
w/tucks & panel of lace at front,
Victorian, 34" l. . . . . .25.00 to 40.00
Christening gown, white cotton eyelet,
ca. 1900, 38" l. 75.00
Christening gown, white cotton, w/tiny
tucks & embroidery, ca. 1820, 40" l. . .65.00
Christening gown, white cotton w/lace
inserts & tucks at bodice, sleeves &
hem, 40" l. 45.00
Christening gown, white cotton w/full-

length panel of smocking & lace,
41" l. 47.50

Christening gown, white cotton
w/numerous rows of tucks, white
eyelet lace inserts & eyelet lace trim,
Victorian, 41" l. . . . . 65.00 to 85.00

Comb, celluloid & sterling silver 29.00

Comb & brush, celluloid, creamy ivory
w/pink roses decor, original box,
2 pcs. 20.00

Cup, china, "Mother Hubbard" &
"Farmer's Wife" decor, Hanley,
England, 1890s 25.00

Cup, silverplate, "ABC" border,
Oneida 85.00

Feeding dish, china, skating scenes
decor, Royal Doulton, 1920s 100.00

Feeding dish, heavy earthenware
pottery, "Baby's Plate," w/large
teddy bear & toys decor 45.00

Feeding dish, heavy earthenware china,
Campbell Kids decor after Grace
Drayton, Buffalo Pottery . . . . 50.00 to 75.00

Feeding dish, heavy earthenware china,
children playing decor, marked
Germany, ca. 1900 . . . . 50.00

Feeding dish w/hot water compartment,
heavy earthenware pottery w/tin base
& spout, Little Boy Blue nursery
rhyme decor, Staffordshire 65.00

Feeding spoon, silverplate, "Little Bo
Peep" patt., Wm. Rogers & Son 18.00

Feeding spoon, sterling silver, figural
stork w/baby handle, engraved
"December" & holly in bowl,
Wallace 45.00

Feeding spoon, sterling silver, Grande
Baroque patt. 30.00

Feeding spoon w/curved handle, ster-
ling silver, figural kitten handle 22.00

Feeding spoon w/curved handle, sterling silver, monogrammed, Watrous
Mfg. Co., International Silver, ca.
1898 . . . . 20.00 to 35.00

Flatware: youth size knife, fork &
spoon; sterling silver, Wave Edge
patt., Tiffany & Co., New York,
3 pcs. 95.00

Food pusher, sterling silver, curved
handle w/embossed cupid, dated
1894 . . . . 48.00

Food pusher, sterling silver, Fleur-de-
lis patt., Alvin Silver Co. . . . . 38.00 to 45.00

Food pusher, sterling silver, Renaissance patt., Tiffany & Co., New
York 125.00

Food pusher, sterling silver, long
"rococo" handle, Dominick &
Haff . . . . 42.00 to 50.00

Food pusher, sterling silver, figural
cupid loop handle, Reed & Barton 58.00

Fork & spoon, sterling silver, Wild
Rose patt., pr. 39.00

Hair brush, sterling silver, Art Nouveau
style, engraved name 25.00

Mug, sterling silver, plain 45.00

Plate, pressed clear glass, "Hey Diddle
Diddle" scene center, dancing
bears border 80.00

Plate, pressed clear glass, "Little Bo
Peep" scene center, dancing bears
border 80.00

Plate, pressed clear glass, "This Little
Pig Went to Market" scene center
w/pig drawing cart, dancing Dutch
boys & girls border 80.00

Plate, printed tin, clown riding pig
decor, 1910 . . . . 40.00

Rattle, celluloid, figural beaked bird
wearing top hat 50.00

Rattle, celluloid, figural chick in high-
buttoned shoe 13.00

Rattle, celluloid, figural peacock,
ca. 1900 . . . . 15.00

Rattle, celluloid, figural rhinoceros
& bear 10.00

Rattle, celluloid & wood, happy & sad
dog faces 12.00

Rattle, pine carved block w/key end,
18th cent., 8" l. 57.00

Rattle, silverplate, figural English
Bobby on ring, 2" 65.00

Sterling Silver Dumbbell Rattle

Rattle, sterling silver, ca. 1890 (ILLUS.) . . 95.00

Rattle, sterling silver, flat disc
embossed w/"Cat and The Fiddle"
scene on mother-of-pearl teething
ring, 1¼" d. disc 48.00

Rattle, sterling silver, "Ride a Cock
Horse," child riding broomstick horse
in relief each side, mother-of-pearl
teething ring at top, 2 bells at
sides, 3¾" 125.00

Rattle-Whistle

Rattle, sterling silver w/coral teether-
handle, whistle over cast form hung
w/bells (missing one), England,
18th c., 5½" l. (ILLUS.) 550.00

Rattle, sterling silver w/coral handle,

whistle over ornately tiered form
incorporating 2 rows of bells,
Europe, 19th c., 6½" l. 165.00
Rattle, sterling silver w/mother-of-pearl
handle, w/attached bells, 19th c.
(teether missing) 275.00
Ring, wide 14k gold band 25.00
Saucer, printed tin, Peter Rabbit scene
by Harrison Cady, w/Buster Bear,
Tommy Turtle, etc. 110.00
Shoes, hightop style w/buttons at
sides, white leather, pr. 25.00
Teething ring, mother-of-pearl ring
w/sterling silver bell chased w/Peter
Rabbit 65.00

BANKS

*Original early mechanical and still banks
are in great demand with collectors. There
are many reproductions of both mechanical
and early cast iron still banks and the
novice collector is urged to exercise caution.
Prices for early bank toys continue to climb
and recent toy and bank auctions have
contributed significantly to this price rise.
In fact, the rarer mechanical banks are
seldom offered for sale but usually traded
with fellow collectors attempting to upgrade
existing collections. Some of the very rare
mechanical and still banks may come to the
market only once during a period of several
years. Numbers before mechanical banks
refer to those in John Meyer's "Handbook
of Old Mechanical Banks." Numbers before
still banks refer to those in Hubert B.
Whiting's book, "Old Iron Still Banks."
Prices are for banks in good original
condition with good paint and no repairs,
unless otherwise noted. Also see ADVER-
TISING ITEMS, AVIATION COL-
LECTIBLES, BILLIKEN COLLECT-
IBLES, CHALKWARE, CHARACTER
COLLECTIBLES and DISNEY COL-
LECTIBLES.*

MECHANICAL

Bad Accident Mechanical Bank

Meyer No.
4 　Always Did 'Spise a Mule (on
　　bench) . . . .$440.00 to 550.00
5 　Always Did 'Spise a Mule (riding
　　mule) . . . . .400.00 to 600.00
9 　Bad Accident (ILLUS.) 2,090.00

Boy Robbing Bird's Nest Bank

20 　Boy Robbing Bird's Nest
　　(ILLUS.) .3,300.00

Boy Scout Mechanical Bank

21 　Boy Scout (ILLUS.) . .3,575.00 to 4,400.00
26 　Buffalo - Bucking 2,200.00
33 　Cabin . . . . .275.00 to 450.00
39 　Cat & Mouse 2,200.00
45 　Chinaman - reclining 1,750.00
49 　Clown on Globe . . . . . . .600.00 to 800.00
53 　Creedmore - Soldier aims rifle at
　　target in tree trunk 350.00
54 　Creedmore - New (Tyrolese
　　Bank) 375.00
56 　Darktown Battery 800.00
57 　Dentist . . . . .1,450.00 to 2,500.00
58 　Dinah . . . . .165.00 to 350.00
63 　Dog on Oblong Base. 550.00
69 　Dog Speaking 500.00
71 　Dog - Trick 250.00
75 　Eagle & Eaglets 350.00
82 　Elephant with Man in Howdah . . .300.00
85 　Elephant - Jumbo, tiny, 2½" h. . . .495.00
88 　Elephant & Three Clowns on
　　Tub 835.00

99	Frogs - Two	500.00
102	Frog on Round Lattice Base	350.00
110	Globe on Stand	215.00
111	Globe on Arc	150.00
118	Hall's Excelsior	245.00 to 300.00
123	Hold the Fort (flag missing from staff)	1,300.00
124	Home Bank - Door w/three-paneled window on each side & 3 steps leading to door, man in doorway, 4¼ x 4½ x 5½" h.	725.00
	Hoopla (replaced hoop)	200.00
127	Humpty Dumpty	345.00
128	Independence Hall Tower	310.00
129	Indian Shooting Bear	1,300.00

Musical Savings Mechanical Bank

Joe Socko Tin Mechanical Bank

	Joe Socko, tin, 1930s (ILLUS.)	225.00
132	Jolly Nigger - Shephard Hardware Co., Buffalo, N.Y., March 14, 1882	285.00 to 300.00
133	Jolly Nigger, red coat, white collar, blue tie (aluminum)	125.00
135	Jolly Nigger with High Hat	365.00
136	Jolly Nigger with Straw Hat	125.00
137	Jolly Nigger - Starkie Patent, red coat, white collar, blue tie (aluminum)	70.00 to 135.00
138	Jonah and the Whale	650.00 to 825.00
143	Leap Frog	1,250.00 to 1,700.00
147	Lion and Monkeys	365.00 to 425.00
148	Lion Hunter	1,200.00 to 1,750.00
150	Little Joe	385.00
153	Magic	1,870.00
154	Magician	1,760.00
156	Mason & Hod Carrier	1,650.00
165	Monkey & Parrot	175.00 to 385.00
169	Mule Entering Barn	535.00 to 625.00
171	Multiplying Bank	220.00
172	Musical Savings - Regina, wood & metal, w/six 8" discs (ILLUS.)	5,800.00
174	New Bank - Building & Guard	500.00
175	North Pole	1,600.00
176	Novelty	350.00

178	Organ Bank - with Monkey, Boy & Girl	275.00 to 380.00
182	Owl - Turns Head	195.00 to 325.00
186	Panorama Bank	4,675.00
189	Pelican	1,150.00 to 1,870.00
194	Pig in High Chair	300.00
196	Pony - Trick	350.00 to 425.00
203	Punch & Judy	550.00 to 695.00
212	Rooster	195.00 to 400.00
214	Santa Claus at Chimney	450.00 to 895.00
216	Scotchman - tin	775.00
219	Squirrel - Saving, lead	275.00
220	Squirrel & Tree Stump	450.00 to 700.00
222	Stump Speaker	765.00
224	Tammany	175.00
226	Teddy & the Bear in Tree	425.00 to 550.00
231	Uncle Sam with Umbrella	535.00
235	Uncle Tom	190.00
237	William Tell	375.00 to 550.00
244	World's Fair Bank - with Columbus & Indian	685.00
245	Zoo	610.00 to 825.00

STILL
Whiting No.

	Amish Boy with Pig - seated on bale of straw, painted pot metal, key-lock trap	65.00
299	Apple on Twig & Leaf - with bumblebee on face of apple, 3½" h.	550.00 to 850.00
	Automobile - 1910 Stanley, bronze finish pot metal, Banthrico	35.00
	Automobile - 1915 Chevrolet coupe, bronze finish pot metal, Banthrico (after 1964)	35.00
	Automobile - 1926 Pontiac Coupe, bronze finish pot metal, Banthrico	35.00
	Automobile - 1927 Ford Sedan, bronze finish pot metal, Banthrico	35.00

159 Automobile - early model
w/large wheels, 5½" l.,
3½" h. 500.00

157 Automobile - Tudor sedan
w/large wheels & passengers,
5½" l. ....365.00 to 450.00

307 Bank Building - small - "Bank"
over door, 2½" w., 3¼" h. 30.00

380 Bank Building - "City Bank," slot
in roof, 3" w., 4" h. 50.00

306 Bank Building - "Bank" over door,
cupola on roof, 3½ x 2¾",
4¼" h. 42.50

413 Bank Building - multi-windowed
skyscraper w/four turrets,
2¼" sq., 4½" h. 30.00

421 Bank Building - "Bank" at top on
front, 4" w., 4¾" h. 37.50

412 Bank Building - multi-windowed
skyscraper w/four turrets,
large, 2½" sq., 5½" h. 50.00

283 Barrel, 2¼" d., 2¾" h. 60.00

10 Baseball Player, 5¾" h. 90.00

142 Battleship Maine - small, 4½" w.,
4½" h. 225.00

146 Battleship Oregon - large, 6" l.,
5" h. 237.50

331 Bear - "Teddy" on side, 4" l.,
2½" h. 85.00

330 Bear - standing & begging,
5½" h. 50.00

329 Bear - standing w/paws clasped
at waist, 5½" h. 80.00

169 Beehive - small bear robbing
hive, 7" h. 210.00

Billiken Bank

50 Billiken - marked on base,
2¼" w., 4¼" h. (ILLUS.).........72.50

48 Billiken - "Good Luck" - on
throne, 6¼" h. 85.00

107 Bird Dog, 5½" l., 3½" h. 39.00

209 Bird on Stump, 4¾" h. 190.00

174 Bismark Pig, 7½" l., 3½" h. 152.50

14 Boy Scout, 6" h. 87.50

208 Buffalo, 4½" l., 3" h. 75.00

2 Buster Brown & Tige, 5" h. 130.00

398 Buster Brown & Tige Cashier,
4½" w., 5" h. 450.00

202 Camel - small, 4¾" h. 65.00

45 Campbell Kids, 3¼" h. 165.00

38 Captain Kidd - with shovel beside
tree, 5½" h. 225.00

Carpenter Safe - with carpenter
holding saw in front of house,
J.M. Harper, 1907 ....1,100.00

241 Cash Register, 4" h. 110.00

248 Cat - seated, 4" h. 80.00

244 Cat with Bow Tie, 4½" h. 75.00

Charles Lindbergh Bust -
aluminum, 6¼" h. 110.00

393 Charlie Chaplin beside Barrel -
candy container conversion,
3" w., 3¾" h. 120.00

Charlie McCarthy - standing,
composition, 1930s, 9" h. 65.00

303 Chest - pirate-type w/domed
lid, 2 x 2¾", 2" h. 45.00

Circus Elephant - seated &
wearing child's straw sailor hat
w/ribbon, 4" h. 125.00

29 Clown, 6¼"h 75.00

Combination Safe - "Security Safe
Deposit," 2 dials, "Pat'd Feby 15,
'81 & Mar 1, '87" on base, 75%
original black paint w/traces of
gilt trim, 2 7/8 x 2 5/8",
3 7/8" h. 95.00

Combination Safe - "Ideal Safe
Deposit," brass handle, 3 x 2¼",
4 1/8" h. 48.00

Combination Safe - "Burglar Proof
House Safe," elaborate floral
panels, "J. & E. Stevens Co.,
Cromwell, Conn., pat'd Aug.
17, 1897," 6" h. 90.00

439 Combination Safe - "Globe
Savings Fund 1888," w/drawer
at top, 5½ x 4¼", 7" h. 285.00

188 Cow - small, 4½" l., 2½" h. 120.00

200 Cow, 5½" l., 3¼" h. 95.00

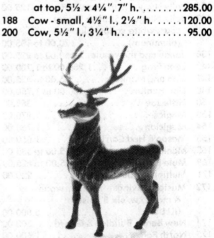

Large Deer

31 BANKS - STILL

196 Deer - large, 9" h.
(ILLUS.) .... 95.00 to 165.00
260 Derby Hat - "Pass Around the
Hat," 3" d., 1¾" h. 100.00
261 Dog - Basset Hound, 4¼" l.,
3" h. 750.00
105 Dog - Bulldog - seated, 4¼" h. 55.00
114 Dog - Boston Bulldog, seated,
5" l., 4½" h. 125.00
112 Dog - Boston Bulldog - standing,
5¼" h., 5" l. 75.00

English Bulldog

102 Dog - English Bulldog, seated,
3¾" h. (ILLUS.) .... 60.00 to 85.00
109 Dog - Spaniel, 6" l., 3¾" h. 130.00
54 Dog on Tub, 4" h. 56.50
106 Dog with Pack - small, 5½" l. 50.00
113 Dog with Pack - large, 8" l. 75.00
198 Donkey - with saddle - small,
4½" l., 4½" h. 45.00
325 Duck - original red & blue paint,
5" w., 4" h. 195.00
323 Duck on Tub - "Save for a Rainy
Day," 5¼" h. 115.00
Eiffel Tower - England, 1908,
8¾" h. 450.00
69 Elephant - small, 3¼" l., 2½" h. .. 60.00
65 Elephant, 4¾" l., 3½" h. 195.00
62 Elephant - large, 7¾" l., 4¾" h. ... 70.00
72 Elephant - "G.O.P.," 5½" l.,
4" h. .... 110.00 to 150.00
74 Elephant drawing Chariot, 8" l.,
3½" h. .... 195.00 to 450.00
55 Elephant on Bench on Tub,
4" h. 165.00
75 Elephant on Wheels, 4" l., 4" h. .. 200.00
149 Ferry Boat - one stack, 7¾" l. 155.00
9 Fireman, 5½" h. 165.00
409 Flat Iron Building - 3-sided
building, 3 x 3½" base, 5½" h. .. 76.50
23 Foxey Grandpa, 4¾" h. 170.00
Franklin D. Roosevelt Bust - "New
Deal" on base, Kenton 1933-36,
5" h. 175.00
129 Furnace - "Mellow" on door,
3" d., 3½" h. 65.00
294 General Butler - "Bonds & Yachts
for Me - For the Masses This
is $1,000,000," w/patent of
1878, 6½" h. (ILLUS) 1,760.00

General Butler

312 General Pershing, 8" h. 100.00
88 General Sheridan - astride
cavalry horse, 5½" h. 450.00
311 George Washington Bust - on gilt
pedestal base w/slot,
8" h. .... 175.00 to 435.00
237 G.E. Refrigerator - white,
4½" h. 65.00
19 "Give Me Penny," 5½" h. 185.00
214 Goose, 3¾" h. .... 85.00 to 105.00
215 Goose - "Red Goose Shoes" -
small, 3¾" h. .... 110.00 to 150.00
212 Goose - "Red Goose Shoes" -
large," 4½" h. 145.00
86 Horse - small, 3¼" l.,
2¾" h. .... 125.00 to 170.00
82 Horse - "Beauty," 5" l., 4" h. 62.50
84 Horse - "Good Luck" on side,
5" l., 4" h. 110.00
56 Horse on Tub, 5¼" h. 160.00
87 Horse on Wheels, 4½" l., 5" h. ... 170.00
77 Horse Prancing, 4" h. 40.00
78 Horse Prancing on Oblong Base,
7½" h. 65.00
79 Horse with Saddle, 5½" l.,
4¼" h. 260.00
83 Horseshoe with Buster Brown &
Tige, 4" h. 110.00

Small House with Porch

404 House with Porch - small, 3" h.
     (ILLUS.) 47.50
377 House with Porch - cottage-type
     house w/people on porch,
     3" w., 3¾" h. 135.00
156 Ice Cream Freezer - "Save Your
     Money and Freeze It," 2½" d.,
     4" h. 250.00
451 Independence Hall - main central
     portion, 6½" w., 9" h. 265.00
447 Independence Hall - large, 8" w.,
     3½" deep, 10¼" h. 475.00
39   Indian, 6" h. . . . . .175.00 to 235.00
     Indian Chief Bust - pot metal,
     3½" h. 45.00
     Keylock safe - "Inland Security
     Co., Kansas City, Mo.," w/key . . .25.00

Kitten with Ribbon at Neck

335 Kitten with Ribbon at Neck,
     4¾" h. (ILLUS.) 60.00
192 Lamb - small, 4" l., 3" h. 100.00
281 Liberty Bell - "Sesqui 1926 Cen-
     tennial," 3¾" h. 30.00
273 Liberty Bell - "Proclaim Liberty
     Throughout All the Land Unto
     All the Inhabitants There Of,"
     J.M. Harper, 1905, 4" h. 375.00
259 Lincoln High Hat - "Pass Around
     the Hat," 2¼" h. 85.00
91   Lion - medium, 4½" l., 3½" h. 25.00
90   Lion - medium, 5" l., 4" h. 37.50
93   Lion - standing, 5¼" l., 3¾" h. 48.00

Large Lion Still Bank

89   Lion - large, 6¼" l., 5¼" h.
     (ILLUS.) . . . . .65.00 to 100.00
58   Lion on Tub, 5¼" h. 75.00
95   Lion on Wheels, 4½" l., 5" h. 160.00
126 Mail Box, 1¾' x 1½" base,
     3¾" h. . . . . .35.00 to 45.00
117 Mail Box - "U.S. Mail,"
     w/movable slot, 4" h. 26.50
382 Mail Box - wall-type, 2¼" w.,
     5" h. 65.00
116 Mail Box - American Eagle on
     front, 3¼" w., 5" h. 90.00
20   Mammy - with polka dot
     scarf . . . . .60.00 to 75.00
17   Mammy with Spoon, 5¾" h. 90.00
154 Marrietta Silo - "Saves You
     Money," 5¾" h. 415.00
1   Mary & Little Lamb, 4½" h. 355.00
435 Metropolitan Safe - with brass
     figure of guard on side, 4" sq.,
     5¾" h. 150.00
26   Middy Bank - English Admiralty
     character, 5¼" h. 135.00
266 Moody & Sankey - "Hold the Fort,"
     4¼ x 3½", 4½" h. 800.00

Mosque Bank

415 Mosque - small, 3" h. (ILLUS.) 30.00
8   Mulligan the Cop, 5½" h. 135.00
13   Mutt & Jeff - colorful old paint . . .115.00
     "Our Empire Bank" - bust of King
     George V & Queen Mary in
     relief, English, 6½" h. 105.00
204 Owl on Stump - "Be Wise, Save
     Money," 4¼" h. 85.00
203 Owl, 2½" sq. base, 5" h. 162.50

Seated Pig Bank

179 Pig - seated, 3" h. (ILLUS.) ....30.00 to 38.00
178 Pig - seated, w/bow at neck, 5" l., 3" h. 120.00
173 Pig - small, 2¼" h. 150.00
182 Pig - "Decker's Iowana," 4¼" l., 2¼" h. 85.00
177 Pig - "I made Chicago Famous" embossed on side, 4" l., 2¼" h. ...95.00
176 Pig, 7" l., 3¼" h. 70.00
Pirate with Guns - seated on chest, pot metal, 5¾" h. 30.00
292 Plymouth Rock, 4" l., 1¾" h. 800.00
427 Presto Still - small, 2¼" w., 3¼" h. 22.50

Medium Presto Still Bank

426 Presto Still - medium, 2¾" w., 3½" h. (ILLUS.) 26.50
425 Presto Still - large, 3½" w., 4" h. 45.00
337 Puppy Dog - "Fido" on collar, 5" h. 145.00
338 Puppy Dog with Bee, 5" l. 90.00
141 Radio - "Crosley No. 70," 4" w., 4¼" h. 110.00
Radio - "Majestic," cabinet-style ..57.50
Refrigerator - "Mayflower Electric," 5" h. 85.00
Refrigerator - "Servel Electrolux" .38.00
Reid Library, Lake Forest College - porcelain-coated cast iron replica of building, 1930s, 5¼ x 3½ x 2 1/8" 192.50
252 Rhino, 5" l., 2½" h. 315.00
187 Rooster - silver w/red comb & wattles, 4¾" h. 68.00
347 Safe - keylock-type, embossed & colored florals on sides, 4½" sq., 4½" h. 82.50
16 Sailor, 5¾" h. 95.00
31 Santa - large, 7" h. 325.00
Santa Claus - sleeping in large chair, pot metal, original paint, 1950s, Banthrico, 6½ x 6" 52.50
Satchel (or carpetbag) - bronze finish heavy steel, 5¾" w., 3¼" h. 160.00
110 Scotty Dog - seated, 5" h. 75.00
108 Scotty Dog - standing, 4¾" l., 3¼" h. 168.00
199 Seal on Rock, 4¼" l., 3½" h. 250.00
385 Shell - World War I de-activated shell, 1½" d., 8" h. 42.50
357 Small House - single story, 2¼" w., 3" h. 45.00
250 Squirrel with Nut, 3" w., 4" h. 425.00
442 State Bank - smallest size, 2" w., 3" h. 60.00
445 State Bank - medium, 4½ x 3½", 6" h. 80.00
269 Statue of Liberty - small, 6" h. 60.00
268 Statue of Liberty - large, 9½" h. 175.00
164 Streetcar - "Main Street," w/passengers, 1¾ x 6½", 3" h. (no wheels) 295.00
163 Tank - World War I, "U.S. Tank Bank" on side, 4" l, 1¾" h. 42.00
162 Tank - World War I, 4½" l., 2½" h. 72.50
309 Teddy Roosevelt, 5" h. 175.00
236 Three Monkeys - "See, Hear & Speak No Evil" on base, 3¼" w., 3¼" h. 225.00
175 Thrifty Pig - "The Wise Pig - Save A Penny Yesterday, etc.," 6½" h. 62.50
172 Time Around the World - printed cards inside visible through windows to indicate times at 24 world capitols when noon in Washington, D.C., 4" h. 250.00

Tower Bank

437 Tower Bank - door opens by combination, 7" h. 360.00
265 Trolley Car - small, 4½" l., 2½" h. 250.00
193 Turkey - small, 3½" h. 70.00
41 Two-Faced Devil, 4¼" h. 390.00
44 Two-Faced Woman - small ....60.00 to 85.00
Uncle Sam 3-Coin Register, rolled steel, ca. 1912, 6¼ x 4½ x 5¼" 25.00

387 Woolworth Building - small,
     5¾" h. 25.00
167 World War I Hat, 3¾" widest d. 90.00
40   World War I Soldier, 7" h. 300.00
171 Zeppelin Airship - "Graf Zeppe-
     lin" on side, 6¾" l.....100.00 to 115.00

GLASS

Advertising "Pittsburgh Paints"

Baseball, clear glass w/white-painted
  interior & Mobil Oil "flying red
  horse" Pegasus, w/tin screw-on
  closure, Heffelfinger Publications,
  N.Y., 3" d., 3½" h. 25.00
Charlie Chaplin beside barrel, painted
  clear glass...............90.00 to 120.00
Duck, clear glass 10.00
Happy Fats standing on drum, clear
  glass, 4½" h......................160.00
House, advertising "Pittsburgh Paints,"
  clear glass, 2¼ x 3¼ x 2½" h.
  (ILLUS.) 25.00
Independence Hall, clear glass,
  4¼" h. 45.00
Log cabin, clear glass................25.00
Log cabin, milk white glass w/brown
  paint, opening in chimney for coins...75.00
"Lucky Joe," Nash's Mustard container,
  clear glass.................9.50 to 14.00
Monkey, clear glass 32.00
Owl, clear glass 15.00
Owl, ruby red glass, 7" h. 97.50
"Snoopy" dog, clear glass 10.00

POTTERY

Acorn, white clay pottery w/mottled
  brown Rockingham glaze, 3½" h. 35.00
Apple, earthenware pottery, layered
  old dark red paint, 3 1/8" h. 60.00
Barrel, earthenware pottery, old red
  paint w/gold striping, 3½" h........30.00
Bird on round base, white clay
  pottery, embossed feather detail,
  brownish amber glaze, 5" h.........75.00
Cabin, earthenware pottery, green &
  white glaze w/blue window, 5½" l. ..55.00
Child's head, sewer tile pottery,
  tooled hair & eyebrows, inset

white eyes & teeth, incised "June,"
  5" h. 200.00
Crown, Rockingham glaze pottery,
  "Bank of England - E.R. II" 35.00
Dog's head, Roseville Pottery, mottled
  brown glaze, ca. 1900, 4" h. 60.00
Eagle w/shield, Staffordshire pottery,
  green, yellow & blue highlights,
  ca. 1840 ....250.00
Frog, Roseville Pottery, mottled green &
  black glaze 63.00
Gypsy fortune teller bust, majolica,
  3½" h. 40.00
Keg, earthenware pottery, worn
  original red paint, gold striping,
  3¼" h. 20.00
Man seated & holding pitcher
  impressed "Money Taken In Here,"
  mottled brown Rockingham glaze
  pottery (minor small flakes) 60.00
Pear, white clay pottery, yellow
  glazed body, green stem, 4" h.
  (chips on stem & coin slot)..........75.00
Pig in recumbent position, white clay
  pottery, green glaze, 5 3/8" l.
  (minor chips on snout) 35.00
Pig seated, Roseville Pottery, brown &
  yellow spots, early 1900s, 5½ x 4" ...45.00
Pig standing, white clay pottery, blue
  & brown sponge-spatter decor,
  3¾" l....................100.00 to 125.00
Pig standing, earthenware pottery,
  marbleized glaze, marked "Austria,"
  4½" l.............................40.00

Pig Bank

Pig standing, earthenware pottery,
  streaked rust & blue top &
  cream-glazed bottom, impressed
  numbers on base, 5" l. (ILLUS.).......45.00
Pig standing, white clay pottery, amber
  glaze w/yellow spots, 5¾" l. (minor
  glaze wear) 25.00
Pig standing, white clay pottery, amber
  glaze & large yellow spots, 7½" l.
  (glaze wear on one ear) 35.00
Pig standing, earthenware pottery,
  mottled brown, yellow & blue glaze ..30.00
Pig standing, mottled brown Rockingham
  glaze, ca. 1845 ....50.00 to 75.00
Pig standing, Roseville Pottery, brown
  sponge-daubed spots, early
  1900s ....55.00 to 92.00

Urn, cov., stoneware pottery, cobalt
  blue glaze, 6¼" h. 125.00

TIN

"Home Bank"

Advertising, "Amalie Motor Oil," oil
  can shape 20.00
Advertising, "Atlas Battery," replica
  of battery 12.50
Advertising, "Bokar Coffee" (A & P),
  black . . . . .7.00 to 10.00
Advertising, "Diamond 760 Motor Oil,"
  3½" h. 12.00
Advertising, "Eight O'clock Coffee"
  (A & P), red . . . . .7.00 to 10.00
Advertising, "High Lindens Coffee,"
  3" h. 27.00
Advertising, "Parsley Brand Salmon,"
  3¼" h. 45.00
Advertising, "Pennzoil" 15.00
Advertising, "Phillips 66 Trop-Artic
  Oil" . . . . .8.00 to 15.00
Advertising, "Red Circle Coffee"
  (A & P), red . . . . .8.50 to 12.00
Advertising, "Sun Oil Co.," blue
  triangle design 10.00
Advertising, "Towles' Log Cabin
  Syrup," log cabin replica . . . . .18.00 to 40.00
Advertising, "Triton Motor Oil" 20.00
Advertising, "Wolf's Head Motor Oil,"
  3½" h. 9.00
Barrel, "Happy Days," Chein . . .15.00 to 20.00
Baseball on stand, "Official League
  Ball," Ohio Art Co. 20.00
Ben Franklin register bank 45.00
Brick house, 3¼" h. 80.00
Cash register, "U Save a Penny" 30.00
Cash register, "Uncle Sam's Register
  Bank," original black w/brass trim,
  6" h. 30.00
Church, "Day by Day - a Penny a
  Meal," Chein, 6½" l. 35.00
Clown's head, semi-mechanical,
  Chein 40.00
Combination safe, "Mascot," J. Chein &
  Co., 4" h. 45.00
Cylinder w/pierced sides, dome-top
  lid w/slot, 2½" h. 40.00

Drum, color printed piggy banks &
  Spanish boy walking around sides,
  3" 15.00
Football, 2¼" w. 17.00
"Home Bank" w/clock above door,
  Chein (ILLUS.) 30.00
House, "Save for a Home - American
  Exchange Nat. Bank of St. Louis,"
  3 5/8" l. 185.00
House, "Bank" stenciled over door,
  red & blue, 3 7/8" h. 40.00
Log cabin, Chein, 3" h. 35.00

Monkey Bank by J. Chein & Co.

Monkey on base, semi-mechanical,
  tips hat, Chein, ca. 1900 (ILLUS.) 225.00
Oval, color printed squirrel & owl on
  sides, 3" h. .55.00
"Post Office Savings Post," old "Salt"
  pointing to slot w/thumb, 4½" 15.00
Trunk, patented 1888 . . . . .18.00
Water heater, "Welsbach" decal,
  7½" h. 100.00
World globe, Chein . . . . .10.00 to 15.00
World globe, Ohio Art Co., 3½" d. 12.50

_____

BAROMETERS

Stick-type, curly walnut, brass-
  plated white metal, face engraved
  "Charles Wilder, Peterboro, N.H.,"
  37¼" h. $665.00
Stick-type, black walnut, long oblong
  case w/rounded top fitted
  w/barometer in top section, thermometer in middle & date slot at
  base, Timby's patent, "Manufactured
  and Sold by A.D. More, Boston,"
  ca. 1857, 41" h. 440.00
Stick-type, inlaid mahogany, broken
  pediment cresting above quarter-
  veneered & glazed hinged door &
  molded quarter-veneered body

w/triple string borders, fitted
w/engraved brass barometer &
thermometer dials, A. Pozzoly,
London, 1st quarter 19th c.,
37½" h. 660.00

Stick-type Mahogany Barometer

Stick-type, mahogany, molded cornice
above hinged & glazed door opening
to a metal dial engraved w/weather
conditions & inscription "L. C. Francis,
Philada." above shaped pendant,
ca. 1790, 38" h. (ILLUS.) 2,310.00
Stick-type, oak, fitted w/barometer,
thermometer & altitude indicator,
polychrome lithographed paper back,
marked "Barometer by the late
Admiral Fitzroy," late 19th c.,
39" h. 550.00
Wheel-type, giltwood & gilt-gesso,
circular silvered dial centered by an
engraved composite patera w/a
molded giltwood frame w/sanded
inner rim & surmounted by an urn
issuing fronds & flowers &
w/elaborate pierced floral scrolls
flanking the case w/twin mirrored
panels below hung w/bellflower
swags, George III period, last
quarter 18th c......................825.00
Wheel-type, mahogany, broken arch
pediment w/line inlay above
barometer, hygrometer & thermometer dials w/level below, A.
Molinari Halesworth, 19th c.,
39" h. 275.00
Wheel-type, inlaid mahogany, fitted
w/barometer & thermometer flanked
flanked by inlaid shell designs &
paterae, signed "Holbn, London,"
late George III period, 1st quarter
19th c., 39" h. 770.00

Wheel-type, rosewood, banjo form
case fitted w/hygrometer dial,
arched thermometer, small mirror &
circular barometer dial, England,
19th c., 37" h. 275.00

BASEBALL MEMORABILIA

Gil Hodges Baseball Card

   *Baseball was named by Abner Doubleday
as he laid out a diamond-shaped field with
four bases at Cooperstown, New York, in
1839. A popular game from its inception, by
1869 it was able to support its first all-
professional team, the Cincinnati Red
Stockings. The National League was
organized in 1876 and though the American
League was first formed in 1900, it was not
officially recognized until 1903. Today, the
"national pastime" has millions of fans and
collecting baseball memorabilia has become
a major hobby with enthusiastic collectors
seeking out items associated with players
such as Babe Ruth, Lou Gehrig, and others,
who became legends in their own lifetimes.
Though baseball cards, issued as advertising premiums for bubble gum and other
products, seem to dominate the field there
are numerous other items available. Also
see BANKS.*

Almanac, "Mutual Baseball Almanac,"
1954, hard cover $6.00
Baseball, autographed by Don Sutton...20.00
Baseball, autographed by 1938
Athletics, including Connie Mack,
Hal Wagner, Wally Moses & Nick
Etten 300.00
Baseball, autographed by 1939 Yankees,
including Lou Gehrig, Charlie Keller,
Lefty Gomez & Joe DiMaggio 350.00
Baseball card, 1950, Bowman Gum, Yogi
Berra (No. 46) 27.50
Baseball card, 1950, Bowman Gum, Lou
Boudreau (No. 94) 7.50
Baseball card, 1950, Bowman Gum,
Roy Campanella (No. 75)............31.00
Baseball card, 1950, Bowman Gum,
Phil Rizzuto (No. 11) 14.50

Baseball card, 1951, Bowman Gum,
Mickey Mantle 275.00
Baseball card, 1950, Bowman Gum,
Enos Slaughter (No. 35) 7.25
Baseball card, 1950, Bowman Gum,
Duke Snider (No. 77) 20.00
Baseball card, 1951, Bowman Gum,
Whitey Ford (No. 1) 54.00
Baseball card, 1953, Bowman Gum,
Mickey Mantle (No. 59) 150.00
Baseball card, 1933, Goudey Gum,
Babe Ruth (No. 149) 350.00
Baseball card, 1952, Topps Gum, Bill
Dickey (No. 400) 170.00
Baseball card, 1952, Topps Gum, Willie
Mays (No. 261) 250.00
Baseball card, 1953, Topps Gum,
Mickey Mantle (No. 82) 215.00
Baseball card, 1953, Topps Gum,
Jackie Robinson (No. 1) 39.50
Baseball card, 1954, Topps Gum, Billy
Martin (No. 13) 16.50
Baseball card, 1954, Topps Gum,
Whitey Ford 10.00
Baseball card, 1955, Topps Gum, Hank
Aaron (No. 47) . . . . .13.50 to 23.00
Baseball card, 1960, Topps Gum, Gil
Hodges, No. 295 (ILLUS.) 1.50
Baseball card, 1963, Topps Gum,
Frank Robinson 7.00
Baseball card, 1967, Topps Gum,
Hank Aaron 9.00
Baseball card, 1969, Topps Gum, Pete
Rose 15.00
Baseball card, 1970, Topps Gum,
Johnny Bench 35.00
Bat, miniature, "Louisville Slugger -
Lefty Grimm". 20.00
Bat miniature, 1932 World Series - New
York Yankees & Chicago Cubs,
18" l. 100.00
Book, "America's National Game,"
written by Albert G. Spalding,
w/pull-out picture of New Polo
Grounds New York City, 1911 . . . . .95.00
Book, "Little Red Book of Baseball,"
1966 . . . . .10.00
Book, "Lucky Strike Baseball Guide,"
1956 . . . . .6.50
Book, "Official Baseball Rules," 1942 . . . .7.50
Book, "Spalding's How to Umpire," by
Billy Evans, 1920, 90 pp. 8.50
Book, "Spalding's Score Book," 1934 . . . . .7.00
Book, "Who's Who in Major League
Baseball," 1946 . . . . .6.00
Cigarette flannels, various baseball
players pictured, set of 20 . . . . .150.00
Doll, "Jackie Robinson," composition,
molded & painted hair & features
w/side-glancing eyes, 5-piece body,
dressed in Dodgers uniform, w/paper
label "Mf'd. by Allied Grand Doll
Mfg. Co., Inc., Brooklyn, N.Y.,"
12½" h. (ILLUS.) 357.00

Jackie Robinson Doll

Figure of Babe Ruth w/bat, Hartland . . .75.00
Magazine, "Life," May 28, 1941,
"DiMaggio Ends Hitting Streak" 7.50
Nodding figure, Roger Maris,
composition .20.00
Pencil, Stan Musial 12.00
Pencil clip, Satchel Paige, St. Louis
Browns 14.00
Photograph, 1887 Detroit club 45.00
Photograph, Babe Ruth, black & white . . .60.00
Photographs, 1941 Boston Red Sox,
24 black & white photographs in
envelope 25.00
Pinback button, Mickey Mantle, 1950s,
3" d. 7.50
Pinback button, Ted Williams, Boston
Red Sox, 1940s, 1¼" 5.00
Print, "The Immortal Babe," full figure
image w/seven smaller vignettes at
bottom, by R. H. Palenske 65.00
Program, Boston Braves, 75th Anni-
versary, 1876-1951 . . . . .20.00
Record Book for 1954 World Series,
Gillette advertising 10.00
Scorecard, 1928 World Series, St. Louis
players pictured 20.00
Scorecard, in the form of a catcher's
mitt, advertising "Rose Distillers,"
1905 . . . . .45.00
Watch fob - scorekeeper, Babe Ruth
pictured front, scorer reverse 100.00
Wrist watch, Babe Ruth,
1930s . . . . .125.00 to 250.00
Yearbook, 1965 New York Yankees . . .100.00
Yearbook, 1967 New York Yankees 20.00

BASKETS

Chilcotin Indian Basket

The American Indians were the first basket weavers on this continent, and, of necessity, the early Colonial settlers and their descendents pursued this artistic handicraft to provide essential containers for berries, eggs and endless other items to be carried or stored. Rye straw, split willow and reeds are but a few of the wide variety of materials used. The Nantucket baskets, plainly and sturdily constructed, along with the baskets woven by American Indians and at the Shaker settlements, would seem to draw the greatest attention in an area of collecting where interest remains high.

American Indian cov. basket, Mescalaro
  Apache, reddish brown & natural
  design, 14½ x 10½", 7" h. $70.00
American Indian basket, Klamath,
  coilwork construction, woven geometric designs, ca. 1920, 3½" d. 98.50
American Indian basket, Popago, coilwork construction, woven in natural
  & dark brown, plain center w/seven
  standing figures around shallow rim,
  9¼" d., 2¼" h. 145.00
American Indian basket, Upper Wisconsin tribe, woven split wood
  w/swing handle, ca. 1930, 11" d.,
  8½" h. 60.00
American Indian basket, Popago,
  woven Yucca coilwork construction, dark brown & natural
  design, 13¾" d., 1½" h. 75.00
American Indian basket, woven w/five
  serrated columns radiating from the
  tondo, 5 human figures below the
  rim, 17 5/16" d....................605.00
American Indian basket, White Mountain
  Apache, woven w/figures of men &
  animals w/geometric designs &
  star center, dark brown & natural,
  18" d., 3¼" h. 1,150.00
American Indian basket, Wisconsin
  tribes, woven faded & natural
  splint w/curlique banding, w/swing-
  ing bentwood handle, 1940s, 18 x
  12½", 9½" h. 75.00
American Indian burden basket,
  Chilcotin, flaring rectangular form,

woven from cedar root & imbricated
  in rush & cherry bark w/three
  rows of birds around sides, a row
  of geometric devices at the rim,
  metal wire binding w/four hide
  loops attached for suspension,
  14 3/8" l. (ILLUS.) 2,090.00
American Indian burden basket, Pima,
  giho or kiaha, composed of a
  saguaro stick frame & woven in
  agave fiber in a lace coiling technique, horsehair ropes, remains of
  red & blue pigment, 17" l. 550.00
American Indian utility basket, Hupa,
  twined, decorated in overlay technique
  w/pattern of broad vertical serrated
  zig-zags alternating w/parallel
  zig-zag lines, a row of right
  triangles below the openwork section
  at the rim, steel hoop on interior
  for support, 23½" h. 880.00
Berry basket, woven splint, bentwood
  handle, 7 x 7" 50.00
"Buttocks" basket, 18-rib construction,
  woven splint, 16½ x 12" oblong,
  8" h. plus bentwood handle (minor
  wear) 65.00
"Buttocks" basket, 20-rib construction,
  woven oak splint, early 20th c.,
  13½ x 12½", 6" h. plus bentwood
  handle 85.00
"Buttocks" basket, 22-rib construction,
  woven natural & colored splint,
  14 x 12" oblong, 6½" h. plus
  bentwood handle 155.00
"Buttocks" basket, 22-rib construction,
  woven oak splint, 17" d., 9½" h.
  plus bentwood handle (minor wear) .150.00
"Buttocks" basket, 24-rib construction,
  woven natural & brown oak splint,
  14 x 13½", 7" h. plus bentwood
  handle 175.00

"Buttocks" Basket

"Buttocks" basket, 24-rib construction,
  woven hickory splint, 14½ x 12½"
  oblong, 7" h. plus bentwood handle
  (ILLUS.) 95.00
Cheese basket, woven oak splint, 9" d.,
  5½" h. (ILLUS. right).............300.00
Cheese basket, woven oak splint,
  19th c., 15" d., 8" h. 495.00

Cheese Baskets

Cheese basket, woven oak splint,
w/side handles, 22" d. (ILLUS. left) ..330.00
Egg gathering basket, tightly woven
hickory splint, melon-ribbed, arched
bentwood handle, nut brown patina,
ca. 1880, 9" d., 5" h. 150.00
Field (or gathering) basket, woven
splint, 13" d. top, square base
w/three hand-hewn braces, w/swing-
ing bentwood handle, 9½" h........195.00
Field (or gathering) basket, woven
splint w/bentwood rim & handles,
20½ x 19½", 12¾" h. 135.00
Market (or utility) basket, woven
splint w/faded red on wrapped edge,
9 x 8¼", 7" h. plus bentwood
handle 100.00
Market (or utility) basket, woven red,
green & yellow splint, 11" d., 5" h.
plus bentwood handle 70.00
Market (or utility) basket, woven
narrow splint, swivel handle
w/bentwood fasteners, 11" d.,
7½" h. plus bentwood handle 135.00
Market (or utility) basket, cov., woven
splint w/red & blue watercolor
designs, 11" d., 9½" h. plus bentwood handle 150.00
Market (or utility) basket, woven
splint, worn dark green paint, 12" d.,
6½" h. plus bentwood handle 185.00
Market (or utility) basket, woven
hickory splint, 12¾" d., 7½" h.
plus bentwood handle 70.00
Market (or utility) basket, woven
splint, worn old blue paint, 13 x 12"
square, 7" h. plus bentwood
handle 135.00
Market (or utility) basket, woven oak
splint, 13" d., 12" h., plus bentwood
handle 55.00
Market (or utility) basket, woven
natural & faded red & black splint,
13½ x 12½" oval, 6¾" h. plus
bentwood handle 130.00

Market (or utility) basket, woven
splint, 15" d., 10" h. plus bentwood
handle 85.00
Market (or utility) basket, woven oak
splint, 15" oblong, 11½" h. to top of
wide bentwood handle 110.00
Market (or utility) basket, woven split
wood, w/two wooden strengthening
battens in bottom, 16¼ x 11¾"
oblong, 6¾" h. plus sturdy bentwood
handle 125.00
Market (or utility) basket, woven
splint, 19¼ x 14½", 8" h. plus wide
bentwood handle 165.00

Melon Basket

Melon basket, 18-rib construction,
woven hickory splint, 7 x 6½"
rounded oval, 4½" h. plus bentwood handle (ILLUS.) 105.00
Melon basket, 18-rib construction,
woven oak splint w/diamond design
at base of bentwood handle, 12 x
11½", 5½" h. plus handle..........95.00
Melon basket, 22-rib construction,
woven oak splint, 16" d., 10" h. plus
well-shaped wooden handle 105.00
Nantucket lightship basket, wooden
base, tightly woven rattan sides,
bentwood swing handle secured by
copper rivets, 8" d., 5½" h. (minor
damage to rim) 425.00
Nantucket lightship basket, wooden
base, tightly woven rattan sides,
stationary bentwood handle, 9 1/8 x
6½" oval, 4" h. plus handle 450.00

Picnic Hamper

Picnic (or storage) hamper w/double-
hinged cover, woven willow,
suitcase-type, 18½ x 13¼" oblong,
10" h. (ILLUS.) 30.00
Rye straw (bread) basket, coilwork construction, chip-carved bentwood rim
handles, 5½" d., 3¼" h. 275.00
Rye straw (bread) basket, coilwork
construction, rim handles, 15" d.,
7½" h. 145.00
Satchel-type basket, woven narrow
splint, bleached finish, 11" l., 5" w.,
8" h. plus carrying handles 90.00
Sewing basket, cov., woven sweet-
grass, 3¼" d., 1¼" h. 12.00
Sewing basket, cov., woven sweet-
grass, w/sewing novelties, 9" d. 30.00
Sewing basket, cov., woven reed,
w/Chinese coins & Peking glass
beads on lid, 5¾" d. 12.50
Sewing basket, cov., woven reed,
w/Chinese coins, Peking glass rings
& tassels on lid, 9" d. 19.50
Shaker bushel basket, woven splint
wood, double-wrapped rim, stamped
"L.T. Colby" on handle, Enfield, New
Hampshire, 18½" d., 17½" h. 165.00
Shaker field (or gathering) basket,
tightly woven ash splint, single-
wrapped rim & wooden side handles,
old brown patina, Sabbathday Lake,
18" d., 7¼" h. 825.00
Shaker field (or gathering) basket,
woven ash splint, footed base, hoop
handles at sides, 18¼" d., 10" h. 165.00
Shaker field (or gathering) basket,
woven ash splint, double-wrapped
handles, "Sisters Basket" written on
side, 38 x 26", overall 18½" h. 495.00
Shaker basket w/attached sliding lid,
woven narrow splint w/bentwood
handle, 6" top d., overall 8" h. 181.50
Storage basket, open, woven splint
w/delicate potato print floral
designs in faded red & blue, square
base w/rounded top, 11¾" d.,
5 3/8" h. (rim lacing incomplete) 85.00
Storage basket, open, woven narrow
hickory splint, w/carved wooden rim
handles, 12½" d., 5½" h. 95.00
Storage basket, open, woven oak
splint, w/carved wooden rim
handles, old white paint, 11" d.,
5" h. 60.00
Storage basket, open, woven oak
splint, square base, round top,
12¾" top d., 5¾" h. 45.00
Storage basket, cov., woven splint,
attached lid slides on uprights of
bentwood handle, 12" d., 10" h. plus
handle 85.00

BEADED & MESH BAGS

Multicolored Beaded Bag

Beaded and mesh bags, popular earlier in this century, are now in great demand. Ladies have found them to be the perfect accessory to the casual long gowns now so fashionable. Sterling silver bags and those set with precious stones bring high prices, but the average glass beaded bag is much lower.

Beaded, black beading, envelope clutch-
type, made in France, 5 x 8" $45.00
Beaded, black beading forming house
design, metal clasp & chain handle . . .75.00
Beaded, black beading on burgundy,
drawstring-type w/beaded fringe 35.00
Beaded, blue-black beading, drawstring-
type, 4½" w., 13" l. 35.00
Beaded, blue beading in vertical stripes,
drawstring-type, large 25.00
Beaded, blue & cream beading, ornate
frame w/embossed bird design,
4 x 7" 55.00
Beaded, blue & silver beading, lattice
design & florals w/heavy fringe,
drawstring-type w/ornate silver finish
metal pear-shaped dangles on cord,
silk lining 40.00
Beaded, blue Carnival glass beading,
metal frame w/embossed floral
design 68.00
Beaded, marigold Carnival glass
beading on red ground,
expandable metal closure 55.00
Beaded, marcasite beading forming
diamond pattern on pink fabric,
w/beaded fringe, silverplate frame,
9½ x 5½" 48.00
Beaded, multicolored beading in checker-
board pattern, w/black beaded fringe,
jewel-set gilt metal frame, w/chain
handle, 7" w., 11" l. (ILLUS.) 75.00
Beaded, multicolored beading on
white, w/fringe, metal frame
w/pierced design, chain handle 45.00
Beaded, multicolored beading forming
peacock design on white velvet
fabric 45.00

Multicolored Beaded Bag

Beaded, multicolored beading forming
a floral design on blue beaded
ground, w/beaded fringe, celluloid
link handle, 7" w., 11" l. (ILLUS.) 38.00
Beaded, silver bugle beads, kid
leather lining, German silver frame,
ca. 1910 . . . . .45.00
Brass mesh, reticulated frame set
w/multicolored jewels, w/chain
handle, 5¼" w., 6" l. 35.00
Enameled mesh, apricot & blue design
on gold ground 45.00
Enameled mesh, black & white Art
Deco design, Whiting-Davis 37.50
Enameled mesh, blue & white design,
silver finish metal compact top
w/blue jeweled clasp 60.00
Enameled mesh, green, white & pink
design, Whiting-Davis 45.00
Enameled mesh, turquoise blue & black
Art Deco geometric design, Whiting-
Davis. 45.00
German silver mesh, Art Nouveau
style . . . . .45.00 to 85.00
Gold finish mesh, Whiting-Davis 25.00
Gold finish mesh w/iridescent tones,
Whiting-Davis .45.00
Silver finish mesh, chain handle,
early 1900s. 40.00
Silver finish mesh, Art Deco style,
Whiting-Davis .35.00
Sterling silver mesh, frame chased
w/scrolling florals, base w/tassels . .115.00

BELLS

Altar sanctuary bell, brass, embossed
animals & "Qui Me Tangit: Vocem
Meam Audit" (Who rings me: Hears
My Voice), 4½" d., 7" h. $100.00

Altar sanctuary "Sanctus" bell, brass,
large 135.00
Animal bell, cow, brass w/iron clapper,
7" h. 38.00
Animal bell, cow, brass w/lead
clapper, "Chiantell Fondeur, 1878,
Saignegier," 4½" d., 4½" h. 128.00
Animal bell, sheep, brass, 3 x 4" 30.00

Sheep Bell

Animal bell, sheep, sheet iron,
w/original label "Holstein Sheep
Bell No. 6," 3½" h. (ILLUS.) 12.00
China bell, Nippon, h.p. continuous
scene w/cobalt blue top & bottom
borders, w/wooden clapper,
3½" h. 150.00
Church steeple bell, bronze, w/wrought
iron yoke, cast by Fulton,
ca. 1838 . . . . .1,500.00
Church steeple bell, cast iron,
Hollsboro, Ohio, 1886, No. 2 yoke . . .225.00
Commemorative bell, World War II
"Victory" bell, cast from metal of
German aircraft shot down over
Britain, "V" on handle & embossed
bust portraits of Churchill, Stalin &
Roosevelt on sides, 5½" h. 60.00
Dinner chimes, brass, 4 graduated
bells hung from stand, marked
"China," w/striker 85.00
Dinner gong, brass, bell suspended
from framework cast w/grape
clusters & leaves, 11¼" d. gong,
14½" h. stand, w/striker 115.00
Figural bell, brass, Victorian lady in
hooped skirt carrying umbrella, her
legs & feet forming clapper, 3¾" h. . .40.00
Figural bell, brass, owl w/well-defined
features & feathers, 4" h. (ILLUS.) 35.00
Figural bell, brass, lady in
Elizabethan dress, 2¼" d., 4" h. 44.00
Figural bell, brass, pomade seller
w/nodding head, 2½" d., 4" h. 195.00
Figural bell, brass, Colonial maiden
w/tiered skirt, wearing cross &
cap, 3½" d., 4¾" h. 65.00
Figural bell, brass, old woman carrying
pot, her feet form the clapper,
2½" d., 5" h. .75.00

Brass "Owl" Bell

Figural bell, brass, lady in 18th century
attire w/powdered wig & hooped
skirt, 3½" d., 5" h. 70.00
Figural bell, brass, Southern Belle
carrying basket of flowers,
2½ x 4¼", 5½" h. 69.00
Figural bell, brass, lady wearing hat
& full layered skirt embossed
w/flowers, carrying basket, 6" h. 65.00
Figural bell, brass, Colonial lady
w/tiered skirt & shawl, 3¼" d.,
6½" h. 110.00
Figural bell, sterling silver w/vermeil
(silver-gilt) work, Colonial lady,
3¼" h. 285.00

Cut Glass Bell

Glass bell, clear cut glass, Brilliant
Period, Libbey's Puritana patt.,
4½" h. (ILLUS.) 375.00
Glass bell, clear cut glass, Brilliant
Period cutting w/pinwheels, etc.,
notched handle, 5¾" h. 295.00
Glass bell, cranberry w/cream opaque
handle, Diamond Quilted patt.,
10" h. 225.00
Glass bell, cranberry w/applied white

rim & clear handle threaded w/cobalt
blue & white latticinio, w/clear berry
clapper, 11" h. 250.00
Glass bell, cranberry w/applied clear
handle & green clapper, 12" h. 185.00
Glass bell, Custard, souvenir-type
inscribed "Alamo - Built 1718, San
Antonio, Texas" & gilt band 95.00
Glass bell, Nailsea-type, clear
w/opaque white & vaseline loopings,
19th c., 11½" h. 400.00
Glass bell, Nailsea-type, amethyst
w/opaque white loopings, colorful
handle, ca. 1860, 12" h. 395.00
Glass bell, Nailsea-type, opaque white
w/green loopings, ca. 1860 . . . . .400.00
Hand bell, brass, tutonic bust portraits in relief each side, 3" d., 4" h. . .75.00
Hand bell, brass, cast w/swan in
relief each side, 3 3/8" d., 4½" h. 75.00
Hand bell, brass, embossed design on
bell, openwork handle, 3¼" d.,
5¼" h. 55.00
Hand bell, brass, figural French
peasant woman w/jug handle,
5¾" h. 79.00
Hand bell, brass, figural Indian
head handle, 3¼" d., 7¼" h. 95.00
Hemony bell, brass, spuriously cast
w/"F. Hemony Me Fecit Anno 1569,"
w/figural bear & shield handle,
4¾" d., 7 7/8" h. 175.00
Hemony bell, bell metal, spuriously cast
w/"F. Hemony Me Fecit Anno 1569"
& "Jacob Serke etc." 235.00
Locomotive bell, bronze, embossed
"C. & N.W. R.R." (Chicago & North-
western), w/yoke & cradle, 13" d. . . .850.00
Locomotive bell, bronze, w/yoke &
cradle, 15" d. .875.00

School Teacher's Hand Bells

School teacher's hand bell, bell metal
w/turned wood handle,
6 3/8" h. . . . . .30.00 to 48.00
School teacher's hand bell, brass
w/turned wood handle,
8½" h. .40.00 to 55.00

School teacher's hand bell, brass
　w/turned wood handle,
　10" h. .55.00 to 85.00
Ship's bell, brass, 18" h. 247.00
Shop entrance bell, brass, w/coiled
　spring & wrought iron
　mounting. . . . . .75.00 to 85.00
Sleigh cutter bells, 4 brass open end
　chimes on metal strap 75.00
Sleigh bells, 13 graduated brass crotal-
　type bells on 57" leather strap 145.00
Sleigh bells, 26 graduated brass crotal-
　type bells on leather strap 245.00
Sleigh bells, 32 small brass crotal-
　type bells on leather strap w/cotter
　keys . . . . .175.00 to 195.00
Tap bell, nickel-plated brass on brass
　base, 1870s, large 75.00
Town crier's bell, brass w/turned
　wood handle, early 19th c., 7" d.,
　13½" h. 210.00
Trolley car bell, brass, "St. Louis
　Car Co.," complete . . . . .75.00 to 90.00

BIG LITTLE BOOKS

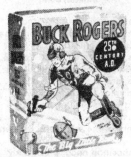

Buck Rogers 25th Century A.D.

The original "Big Little Books" series of small format was originated in the mid-30s by Whitman Publishing Co., Racine, Wis., and covered a variety of subjects from adventure stories to tales based on comic strip characters and movie and radio stars. The publisher originally assigned each book a serial number. Most prices are now in the $8.00-$20.00 range with scarce ones bringing more.

Alice in Wonderland, 1934 . . . .$25.00
Alley Oop & Dinny, 1935 . . . . .6.00
Betty Boop - Snow White 45.00
The Border Eagle, 1938 . . . . .10.00
Bringing Up Father, 1936 . . . . .19.50
Buck Rogers 25th Century A.D. (ILLUS.) . .8.00
Buck Rogers - Depth Men of Jupiter. 25.00
Bugs Bunny & His Pals, 1945 . . . . .18.50
Captain Frank Hawks Air Ace & the
　League of Twelve 10.00

Capt. Marvel - Return of Scorpion 40.00
Chester Gump at Silver Creek Ranch,
　1933 . . . . .7.00
Chuck Malloy Railroad Detective
　on Streamliner, 1938 . . . . .9.00
Cinderella & the Magic Wand, Walt
　Disney, 1950 . . . . .9.00
Dan Dunn & the Crime Master, 1937 . . . .12.00
David Copperfield, 1934 . . . . .15.00
Desert Eagle Rides Again, Zane Grey 7.50
Dick Tracy & the Boris Arson Gang,
　1935 . . . . .7.00
Dick Tracy & the Racketeer Gang. 12.00
Donald Duck & the Ghost of
　Morgan's Treasure, 1946 . . . . .20.00
Flash Gordon & the Monsters of Mongo,
　ca. 1935 . . . . .75.00
Flash Gordon & the Witch Queen of
　Mongo 56.00
Frank Buck Presents Ted Towers,
　Animal Master, 1935 . . . . .11.00
Gene Autry - Gunsmoke Reckoning 25.00
Guns in the Roaring West, 1937 . . . . .9.00
Hall of Fame of the Air, 1936 . . . . .20.00
Houdini's Book of Magic, 1927, Amoco
　premium 35.00
Invisible Scarlet O'Neil Versus King of
　the Slums, 1946. . . . . .9.00
Jim Craig State Trooper & the Kid-
　napped Governor, 1938. . . . . .7.00
Jim Starr of the Border Patrol, 1937 . . . . .9.50
Jungle Jim & the Vampire Woman. 6.00
Just Kids, 1932, No. 283 . . . . .6.00
Ken Maynard - Western Justice 10.00
Li'l Abner - Among the Millionaires,
　1939 . . . . .18.00
Little Men. 11.50
Little Orphan Annie & Chizzler 25.00
Little Orphan Annie & the Mysterious
　Shoemaker 20.00
Lone Ranger - Secret Killer 10.00
Lone Star Martin's Texas Rangers 18.00
Mickey Mouse the Detective, 1934 . . . . .31.00
Mickey Mouse & the Stolen Jewels,
　1949 . . . . .30.00
Mr. District Attorney, 1941, "movie
　flip" page corners. 20.00
Mr. District Attorney on the Job,
　"movie-flip" page corners, 1941. . . . . .15.00
Og, Son of Fire, 1936 . . . . .14.00
Once Upon a Time, 1933 . . . . .12.00
Peggy Brown in the Big Haunted
　House, 1940. . . . . .13.50
The Phantom, 1936 . . . . .28.50
Popeye & the Deep Sea Mystery, 1939 . .25.00
Popeye the Super Fighter, 1942 . . . . .15.00
Radio Patrol Outwitting the Gang
　Chief, 1939 . . . . .8.00
Red Barry, Hero of the Hour, 1935 . . . . . .8.00
The Return of Tarzan, 1936 . . . . .20.00
Riders of Lone Trails, 1937. . . . . .8.00
Robinson Crusoe, 1933. . . . . .19.00
Shirley Temple - "The Little Colonel,"
　1935 . . . . .25.00

Sir Lancelot, 1958 ....12.50
Skeezix in Africa, 1934 ....15.00
Skyroads with Clipper Williams of the
    Flying Legion, 1938..................12.00
Smilin' Jack Flying High With Down-
    wind, "movie-flip" page corners,
    1942 ....20.00
Smitty, Golden Gloves Tournament,
    1934 ....12.00
Son of Tarzan, 1939 ....17.00
Story of Clara Belle Cow, Walt Disney
    1066 Series, 1938 ....23.00
Story of Donald Duck, Walt Disney
    1066 Series, 1938 ....28.00
Tailspin Tommy, The Dirigible Flight to
    the North Pole, 1934...............20.00
Tarzan's Revenge, 1938 ....20.00
Tarzan the Untamed, 1941 ....12.00
Terry & The Pirates, 1935.............18.00
Terry & War in the Jungle, 1946 ....15.00
The Texas Kid, 1937 ....10.00
The Three Musketeers, 1935............8.50
Tim McCoy in The Prescott Kid, 1935 ....15.00
Tim McCoy in The Westerner, 1936 .....15.00
Tim Tyler's Luck, 1937 ....18.00
Tom Beatty, Ace of the Service, 1934 ...11.50
Tom Beatty Scores Again, 1937 ....11.00
Tom Mix & the Hoard of Montezuma,
    1937 ....18.50
Tom Mix in The Fighting Cowboy, 1935 ..22.00

Tom Mix in The Range War

Tom Mix in The Range War, 1937
    (ILLUS.) 15.00
Uncle Sam's Sky Defenders, "movie-
    flip" page corners, 1941.............10.00
Uncle Wiggily's Adventures, 1946 ....8.00
Wells Fargo, 1938 ....9.50
Zip Saunders, King of Speedway, 1939 ..10.00

BILLIKEN COLLECTIBLES

*The Billiken craze swept this country in
the early years of this century. A symbolic
good luck figure was created in the form of
an Oriental-type pixie with slanting*

*eyebrows and a pointed head. A doll, copy-
righted in 1909 by the Billiken Company
and produced by Horsman Company of New
York, was an immediate success and soon
stamp boxes, tape measures, bridge pads,
blotters, picture frames and other items
with Billiken decoration began to appear on
merchant's shelves. Today these celluloid,
leather, china and paper items are
attracting collectors.*

Billiken Bank

Bank, cast iron, figure of seated
    Billiken, marked "Billiken" on base,
    2¼" w., 4¼" h. (ILLUS.)...........$72.50
Bookends, chalkware, "Billie Can" &
    "Billie Can't," copyright by Russel
    Roberts, pr. 35.00
Counter display figure, chalkware, "The
    Billy Kid wears Billiken Shoes,"
    16" h. 95.00
Cup, silverplate, 4 embossed Billiken
    figures 55.00
Doll, composition head, plush body,
    Horsman label, 1909, 12" ..195.00 to 295.00
Door stop, cast iron, jewel inset head,
    name on base, 7" h.................25.00
Figure, bisque 45.00
Figure, chalkware, "God of Good
    Luck," painted brown, 6" h. 20.00
Figure on stand, metal, w/label "Billiken
    Co."..............................125.00
Figure group, bisque, Billiken astride
    dolphin, 3" l. 45.00
Hatpin holder, brass, figural Billiken,
    w/velvet cover 125.00
Incense burner, white pot metal,
    figural Billiken, original box w/color-
    printed Billiken on lid, marked
    "Nippon" 45.00
Knife, fork & spoon, silverplate, "Good
    Luck" & Billiken handles, set.........55.00
Match safe, brass, figural Billiken 200.00
Postcard, 1908, Billiken Co., Chicago 6.50
Salt shaker, clear glass w/pewter lid ...42.50
Salt & pepper shakers, china, pr........25.00

Salt & pepper shakers, milk white
glass, pr. 150.00
Stickpin, sterling silver 14.50
Token, "Good Luck - The God of Things
as They Ought To Be," 1908......... 15.00

BOOKENDS

Pressed Glass Horse Bookends

Also see ART DECO, ART NOUVEAU, BILLIKEN COLLECTIBLES and ROY-CROFT ITEMS.

Art pottery, figure of cherub, American Encaustic Tiling Co., Zanesville, Ohio, pr..................... $75.00
Art pottery, model of Polar bear,
impressed Cowan Pottery mark,
pr............................... 175.00
Bronze, figure of Buddha, "dore"
finish, signed Tiffany Studios &
numbered, pr..................... 195.00
Bronze, male figures (2) after Isidore
Konti, signed Roman Bronze Works,
New York, ca. 1862, 6 5/8" h., pr. ... 198.00
Bronze, model of owl, standing on
open book, signed Krupka, 9" h.,
pr............................... 160.00
Bronze, model of Scottie dog, tiered
multicolored onyx base, pr. 85.00
Bronze, Zodiac patt., signed
Tiffany Studios, pr................ 175.00
Bronze-finish pot metal, model of
reclining Whippet dog, pr. 38.00
Cast iron, cluster of acorns & oak
leaves, 7" h., pr.................. 50.00
Cast iron, Dickens' characters in
relief, marked Bradley & Hubbard,
6" h., pr......................... 40.00
Cast iron, "End of Trail," weary
Indian astride horse, original
paint, pr. 30.00
Cast iron, model of Irish setter dog,
ca. 1920, pr..................... 35.00

Pressed glass, figure of woman astride
horse, clear, 6" h., pr. 55.00
Pressed glass, model of owl, pink
frosted, pr. 90.00
Pressed glass, model of rearing horse,
clear, L.E. Smith, 1940s, 8" h.,
pr. (ILLUS. of one) 35.00
Wooden, semi-circle mounted w/cast
iron snow bird, 9½" w., pr. 45.00

BOOKMARKS

Paper Bookmark with Advertising

Also see ADVERTISING ITEMS, ART NOUVEAU and TEXTILE COLLECT-IBLES - Stevengraphs.

Advertising, "Antiphlogistine," silver-
plate, embossed old-fashioned
nurse $28.00
Advertising, "Cracker Jack," tin,
w/dog........................... 15.00
Advertising, motion picture "Jane
Eyre," Katharine Hepburn pictured ... 15.00
Advertising, "W. H. Foote & Co.,"
Clothing, Westfield, Mass.," paper
(ILLUS.) 2.00
Advertising, "Yale Coffee" 5.00
Advertising, "Zeno Chewing Gum," 2
lovebirds & countryside decor 10.00
Celluloid, "Greetings," floral decor 2.50
Ivory, carved monkey, macrame page
marker w/jade attachments......... 39.00
Sterling silver, embossed elk's head.... 18.00
Woven silk, Admiral Dewey portrait..... 9.00
Woven silk, Mrs. Grover Cleveland
pictured at World's Fair, 1898 .... 25.00
Woven silk, Statue of Liberty, Paris,
1878 .... 65.00

BOOTJACKS

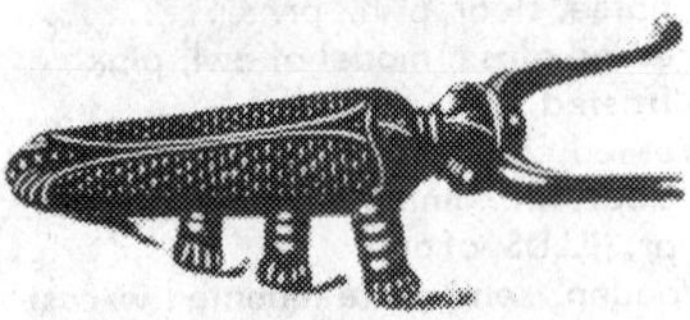

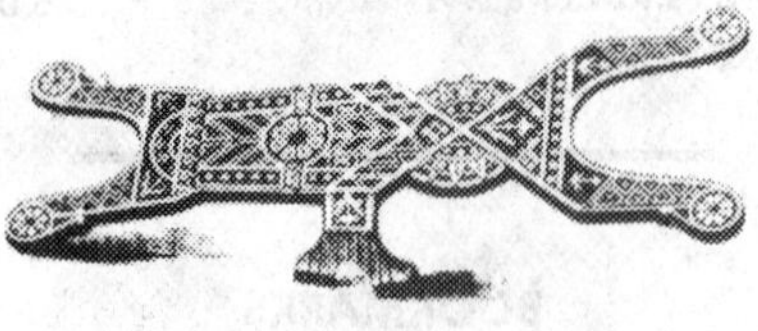

Cast Iron Bootjacks

Cast iron, cricket or beetle form, 9¼" l. (ILLUS. top) $35.00
Cast iron, cricket or beetle form, embossed lacy design, 11¾" l. (ILLUS. bottom) 25.00
Cast iron, figural "Naughty Nellie," traces of original paint ...... 65.00 to 70.00
Cast iron, figural "Naughy Nellie," worn black paint, 9½" l. 45.00
Cast iron, openwork lacy design w/"Try Me" 57.00
Cast iron, openwork design incorporating 2 hearts 35.00
Cast iron, wishbone-shaped w/curling ends on arched feet 130.00

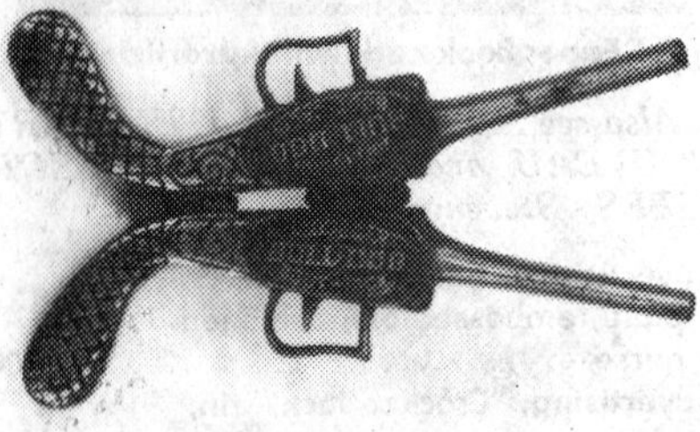

"American Bulldog Bootjack"

Cast iron, folding-type, cast in the form of a revolver, "The American Bull Dog Boot Jack," 8¼" l. (ILLUS.) 75.00
Wooden (maple, birch or walnut), plain, refinished .... 20.00 to 30.00
Wooden (maple, birch or walnut), plain, refinished .... 20.00 to 30.00
Wooden, traveling model, folding-type w/hinges 30.00

BOTTLE OPENERS

Corkscrews were actually the first bottle openers and these may date back to the mid-18th century, but bottle openers, as we know them today, are strictly a 20th century item and come into use only after Michael J. Owens invented the automatic bottle machine in 1903. Avid collectors have spurred this relatively new area of collector interest that requires only a modest investment. Our listing, by type of metal, encompasses the four basic types sought by collectors: advertising openers; full figure openers which stand alone or hang on the wall; flat figural openers such as the lady's leg shape; and openers with embossed, engraved or chased handles. Also see BREWERIANA and CORKSCREWS.

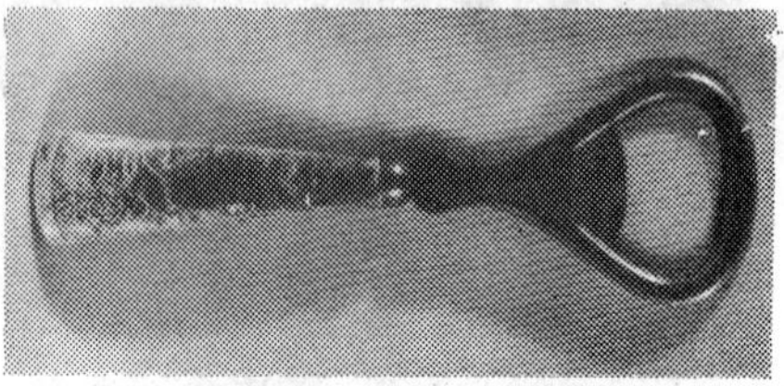

Opener with Sterling Silver Handle

Advertising "Arrow Beer," metal, bottle-shaped $8.00
Advertising, "Drink California Grapine - 5 cents" 15.00
Advertising, "Emerson's Ginger Mint Julep," bottle-shaped, ca. 1900 ...... 20.00
Advertising, "Haworth's Havannas," model of a hatchet 15.00
Advertising, "Heinz 57" 6.00
Advertising, "Tavern Pale Beer," metal, bottle-shaped 5.00
Advertising, "White Rock Water & Gingerale," chrome, engraved nymph 12.00
Brass, flat figural corn stalk 5.00
Brass, full figure Dachshund dog w/smooth collar 30.00
Brass, full figure dolphin jumping 60.00
Brass, full figure nude lady .... 30.00 to 45.00
Brass, full figure parrot, large, Wilton Products .... 12.00 to 20.00
Brass, full figure rooster w/opener in tail 20.00
Bronze, full figure nude lady holding wreath-opener above her head 30.00
Bronze, full figure nude lady, ca. 1920, heavy 90.00
Cast iron, full figure Art Deco parrot.... 32.50
Cast iron, full figure "Dinky Dan" schoolboy, original paint (made for Gadzik) 50.00
Cast iron, full figure donkey seated & braying 20.00
Cast iron, full figure donkey seated & braying w/lips curled back to show teeth .... 25.00 to 30.00
Cast iron, full figure drunk at sign post, "St. Petersburg, Florida" .... 12.00 to 19.00

Cast iron, full figure drunk in straw
  hat at sign post, original
  paint......................50.00 to 60.00
Cast iron, full figure Mademoiselle by
  lamp post on ash tray base..........21.50
Cast iron, full figure pelican, hollow
  mold, original paint................30.00
Cast iron, full figure rooster, original
  paint...............................32.50
Cast iron, wall-type, false teeth,
  original paint......................75.00
Cast iron, wall-type, four-eyed bald
  headed man 35.00
Cast iron, wall-type, four-eyed country
  boy w/red hair 70.00
Cast iron, wall-type, four-eyed man
  w/mustache & 3 front teeth 75.00
Silverplate key shape w/corkscrew,
  marked "Napier" 22.00
Stag's horn handle w/brass ferrule &
  opener end, 3" 12.00
Stag's horn handle w/sterling silver
  mounts, 1864 patent, 7" l...........28.00

BOTTLES

Glass bottles and flasks have been made since ancient times and the first attempt to manufacture glass in the new world took place at the Jamestown, Virginia settlement, probably between 1609 and 1617. Over one-hundred years passed before another glass factory could survive more than a decade. Caspar Wistar and subsequently his son, operated a glasshouse, from 1739 to 1779, in New Jersey where bottles and other utilitarian wares were produced from ordinary window glass and green, or bottle, glass. Henry William Stiegel, whose glass factory opened in Manheim, Pennsylvania in 1763, produced a fine quality glass in the European tradition by employing German, Venetian and English glass blowers. The quality of Stiegel's glass was so fine that today it is difficult to distinguish from the Continental glasswares produced during the same time span. Today, almost all early glass made in colonial America is categorized as being either Jersey-type or Stiegel-type though few pieces can be positively identified.

Bottles and flasks were either free-blown or pattern-molded and expanded. Stiegel bottles are typically pattern-molded. The Pitkin glasshouse, near Hartford, Connecticut produced bottles of all kinds, but "pitkin" has become a generic term for a flask that is fine-ribbed vertically or spirally, or possibly in a combination of

both. A "chestnut" bottle is a globular or ovoid bottle with a tapered neck, somewhat resembling the American chestnut and can be free-blown or pattern-molded and expanded.

"Ludlow," a term often applied to chestnut bottles, is derived from the fact that early bottle collectors assumed all chestnut-form bottles were made at a glassworks that operated at Ludlow, Massachusetts about 1815. Carboys are large bottles that usually held corrosive liquids and often were encased in wooden crates, while demijohns are usually large narrow-necked wine bottles often originally encased in wicker.

"Bitters" were merely a means of evading a tax on gin imposed by George II of England. Gin merchants added herbs to the gin and sold it for medicinal purposes, evading the tax levy and retaining their margin of profit. For the same reason, Bitters became popular in colonial America. Case bottles are square-bodied bottles that are sometimes tapered. Case gin bottles and other early bottles before the mid-19th century will have pontil scars and applied lips. Sometimes gin and wine bottles have an applied "seal," a glob of molten glass applied to the shoulder or body that is subsequently stamped with a seal. These are referred to as "seal" bottles.

Historical flasks have national themes with portraits of national heroes, prominent people and presidents or patriotic themes. Historical and pictorial flasks constitute a well-researched area of bottle collecting. Figural, ink and nursing bottles represent still other aspects of the overall bottle collecting hobby.

J. Michael Owens patented his automatic bottle making machine in 1891 and, by the very early 1900s, hand blowing of bottles gave way to this automated procedure. Bottles do not have to be hand-blown to be collectible and many of the beer, soda and whiskey bottles that are avidly collected today are those made by machine. A good reference for the beginning bottle collector is Cecil Munsey's "The Illustrated Guide to Collectible Bottles." Collectors of historical flasks will find invaluable material in George and Helen McKearin's comprehensive work, "American Glass."

BARBER
Amethyst, Daisy & Dot patt., original
  stopper..........................$90.00
Amethyst, enameled decor (no
  stopper) 65.00
Blue opaque, bulbous, pedestal base,
  enameled gold decor, original
  stopper...........................85.00

Blue translucent, melon-ribbed, enameled
decor, 8½" h. (no stopper) 65.00

Clambroth Barber Bottle

Clambroth, octagonal neck, original
pewter stopper, 7" h. (ILLUS.). 60.00
Clambroth, lettered "Water" in red
(no stopper). 25.00
Cranberry, ring neck, Inverted Thumb-
print patt., original stopper 120.00
Cranberry opalescent, Hobnail patt.
(no stopper) . . . . .110.00 to 125.00
Cranberry opalescent, Stripe patt. (no
stopper) 95.00
Electric blue, Hobnail patt., original
stopper, 7¾" h. 105.00
Mary Gregory type, green, white
enameled girl w/butterfly net (no
stopper) 190.00
Milk white, lettered "Bay Rum," wild
flowers decor, original stopper 55.00
Milk white, lettered "Witch Hazel," red
floral decor, open pontil, original
stopper. 60.00
Purple translucent, melon-ribbed,
enameled decor, original stopper,
8½" h. 65.00
Sapphire blue, Inverted Thumbprint
patt. (no stopper) 50.00

BITTERS

Abbott Aromatic Bitters, amber. 30.00
Abbott's Bitters, w/C.W. Abbott & Co.,
Baltimore on shoulder & Abbott &
Co., Baltimore, Md. on base, round,
amber, w/90% of label, 8¼" h. 55.00
Atwood's Jannaice Bitters, Formerly
Made by Moses Atwood, George-
town, Mass., 12-sided, aqua,
6 1/8" h. 30.00
Atwood's Quinine Tonic, rectangular,
aqua, 8 7/16". .72.50
Augauer, green, w/partial label 50.00

Ayer (Dr. M.C.) Restorative Bitters,
Boston, Mass., rectangular, aqua,
8 7/8" h. 170.00
Baker's Orange Grove, square
w/roped corners, orange-amber,
¾ qt. 150.00
Baker's Orange Grove, square
w/roped corners, puce, ¾ qt. 255.00
Baxter's (Dr.) Mandrake, Lord Bro's
Proprietors, Burlington, Vt.,
12-sided, smooth base, aqua,
6½" h. 18.50
Bell's (Dr.) Blood Purifying Bitters - The
Great English Remedy, rectangular,
amber, 9¾" h. . . . . .175.00 to 250.00
Big Bill's Best, square, orange-amber . . .98.50
Blake's (Dr.) Aromatic, New York,
rectangular, pontil, aqua, pt. 140.00
Boerhaves Holland Bitters, B. Page Jr.
& Co., Pittsburgh, Pa., rectangular,
aqua, 8" h. 125.00
Boker's Stomach, lady's leg shape,
amber, w/label . . . . .25.00 to 55.00
Bourbon Whiskey, barrel-shaped,
puce 225.00
Bowe's Cascara Bitters Has No Equal,
P. F. Bowe, Waterbury, Connecticut,
square, clear, 9 5/8" h. 135.00
Boyce's (Dr.) Tonic, 12-sided, aqua,
7¾" h. . . . . .55.00 to 75.00
Brown's Celebrated Indian Herb, fig-
ural Indian Queen, amber. 320.00
Brown's Celebrated Indian Herb,
Patented Feb. 11, 1868, figural Indian
Queen, amber, 12¼" h. 495.00
Brown's Celebrated Indian Herb,
Patented Feb. 11, 1868, figural Indian
Queen, yellow-amber, 12¼" h. 370.00
Brown's Celebrated Indian Herb,
Patented 1868, figural Indian Queen,
honey amber, 13½" h. . . .595.00 to 1,975.00
Brown's Iron, square, applied top,
amber, pt. 18.50
Brown's Iron, square, applied top,
citron yellow, pt. 35.00
Brown (F.) Sarsaparilla & Tomato,
oval, pontil, aqua, 9½" h. 225.00
Bull's (Dr. John) Compound Cedron
Bitters, Louisville, Ky., square,
amber, 10" h. 225.00
Burdock Blood, Buffalo, N.Y.,
amethyst 25.00
Burdock Blood, rectangular, clear 35.00
Byrne's (Prof. Geo. J.) Great Universal
Compound Stomach, cabin-shaped,
amber. 850.00
Caldwell's (The Great Dr.) Herb Tonic,
triangular, amber. 140.00
California Fig, California Extract of Fig
Co., San Francisco, Cal., square,
amber, 10" h. .90.00
California Fig & Herb, square,
amber . . . . .35.00 to 42.00

Campbell's (Dr.) Scotch Bitters, strap-
 sided flask, amber, ¼ pt. (dug) 100.00
Caroni, cylindrical, green, 8¼" h. 135.00
Caroni, cylindrical, olive green, ½ pt. . . 18.00
Carpathian Herb, square, amber,
 ¾ qt. 25.00
Carson's (Dr.) Stomach, aqua 90.00
Clarke's (Dr.) Vegetable Sherry Wine,
 Sharon, Mass., aqua, gal. 175.00
Cole Brothers Vegetable, aqua 45.00
Cole Bros. Vegetable, Binghamton,
 N.Y., rectangular, aqua, w/label,
 7 7/8" h. 185.00
Colton's (J.W.) Nervine Strengthening,
 square, smooth base, amber, pt.,
 8 3/8" h. 145.00
Columbo Peptic, amber 32.00
Curtis & Perkins Wild Cherry, pontil,
 aqua, original label . . . . 82.50 to 95.00
Damaiana, round, aqua, 11¾" h. 52.50
Dandelion (XXX), rectangular strap
 flask, clear, 7¼" h. 70.00
D'Artagnan To-Ni-Ta, amber 25.00
Devil-Cert Stomach, round, clear 40.00
DeWitt's Stomach, strap-sided oval,
 amber, 7½" h. 40.00
Doyle's Hop, 1872, square, amber 25.00
Drake's Plantation, cabin-shaped,
 4-log, amber 70.00
Drake's Plantation, cabin-shaped,
 4-log, yellow . . . . 85.00 to 125.00
Drake's Plantation, cabin-shaped,
 5-log, honey amber, ¾ qt. 170.00
Drake's Plantation, cabin-shaped,
 5-log, light golden yellow 200.00
Drake's Plantation, cabin-shaped,
 6-log, amber 62.50
Drake's Plantation, cabin-shaped,
 6-log, lemon amber 75.00
Drake's Plantation, cabin-shaped,
 6-log, puce 120.00
Drake's Plantation, cabin-shaped,
 6-log, salmon pink (apricot) 165.00
Drake's Plantation, cabin-shaped,
 6-log, yellow-green 450.00

Electric Brand Bitters

Electric Brand, H.E. Bucklen & Co.,
 square, amber (ILLUS.) 30.00
Fenner's (Dr. M.M.) Capitol, rectangu-
 lar, aqua, 9 1/8" h. 37.50
Fisch's (Dr.), figural fish,
 amber . . . . 110.00 to 195.00
Fish (The), W.H. Ware Patented 1886,
 figural fish, amber, 11½" h. 150.00
Forrest's (Dr.) Shamrock, blown, clear,
 w/label only 55.00
Gentiana Root & Herb, Seth E. Clapp &
 Co. Sole Proprietors, Boston, Mass.,
 square case gin shape, aqua,
 9 7/8" h. 225.00
Genuine Black Walnut Bitters, A. Graf
 & Co., St. Louis, Mo. Sole Proprietors,
 square, clear, 7¾" h. 160.00
German Hop, square w/roofed
 shoulders, amber, ¾ qt. 85.00
Globe (The) Tonic, amber, w/labels 65.00
Gotthard (St.), amber 50.00
Graves & Son Tonic Bitters, Louisville,
 Ky., square, aqua, 10" h. 250.00

Greeley's Bourbon Bitters

Greeley's Bourbon, barrel-shaped
 w/ten hoops above & below center
 band, tangerine-puce
 (ILLUS.) . . . . 225.00 to 265.00
Greeley's Bourbon, barrel-shaped
 w/ten rings above & below center
 band, purple . . . . 225.00 to 395.00
Greer's Eclipse, amber 75.00
Hall's (E.E.), New Haven, established
 1842, barrel-shaped,
 amber . . . . 95.00 to 115.00
Hardy's (Dr. Manly) Genuine Jaundice,
 rectangular, aqua . . . . 55.00 to 90.00
Harter's (Dr.) Wild Cherry, rectangular,
 amber 24.00
Harter's (Dr.) Wild Cherry,
 aqua . . . . 20.00 to 27.50
Hartwig Kantorowicz, Posen Hamburg,
 Germany, clear 65.00

Hepatic Bitters

Hepatic, New York, dark amber
(ILLUS.)............................225.00
Herb (H.P.) Wild Cherry, cabin-shaped,
amber...........................245.00

Holtzermann's & Pineapple Bitters

Holtzerman's Patent Stomach, cabin-
shaped, amber (ILLUS. left).........165.00
Home, square, amber 78.50
Hoofland's (Dr.) German, aqua, pt......45.00
Hop & Iron, Utica, N.Y., square, amber,
original label, pt. 42.00
Hopkin's (Dr. A.S.) Union Stomach,
square, amber, ¾ qt. 190.00
Hostetter's (Dr.) Stomach, amber 12.50
Hostetter's (Dr.) Stomach, square,
olive green, ¾ qt. ....60.00 to 80.00
Hutchings Dyspepsia, pontil, aqua
(dug).............................125.00
Johnson's Calisaya, square, collared
mouth w/ring, amber, 10" h. 125.00
Kaiser Wilhelm Bitters Co., Sandusky,
Ohio, round, amber, 10 1/8" h. 95.00
Kaiser Wilhelm Bitters Co., Sandusky,
Ohio, round, clear,
10 1/8" h.................40.00 to 50.00

Kelly's Old Cabin, cabin-shaped,
amber.............................500.00
Keystone, barrel-shaped, amber,
¾ qt. ....295.00 to 375.00
Kimball's Jaundice, golden amber.....250.00
Kimball's Jaundice, Troy, N.H., rec-
tangular, greenish olive, 7" h. 295.00
Kimball's Jaundice, olive amber 250.00
King Solomon's, amber 125.00
King's 25 Cent Bitters, King Bitter Co.,
Rochester, New York, oval, aqua,
6¾" h. 155.00
Koehler & Hinrichs Red Star Stomach ..140.00
Lacour's, golden amber.............495.00
Langenbach's Dysentery Cure, bimal ...30.00
Langley's (Dr.) Root & Herb, square,
collared mouth, original label,
amber, ½ pt......................42.50
Langley's (Dr.) Root & Herb, J.O.
Langley, proprietor, round, amber,
6" h. 75.00
Langley's (Dr.) Root & Herb, J.O.
Langley, proprietor, round, aqua,
6" h. 75.00
Langley's (Dr.) Root & Herb, 76 Union
St., Boston, round, aqua 40.00
Langley's (Dr.) Root & Herb, 99 Union
St., Boston, pontil, aqua, ¾ qt. 30.00
Lash's Bitters Co., New York - Chicago,
San Francisco, round back-bar type
w/fluted shoulders, amber, 11" h. ..145.00
Lash's Bitters Co., N.Y. - Chicago, S.F.,
round, amber 55.00
Lash's Bitters Co., New York - Chicago,
San Francisco, round, clear.........65.00

Lash's Bitters

Lash's Kidney & Liver, square, amber,
w/label, 9½" h. (ILLUS.) 30.00
Lash's Liver, Nature's Tonic Laxative,
square, amber, 9 3/8" h............85.00
Lash's Natural Tonic, amber, label
only..............................12.50

Leonard's (Mrs.) Dock & Dandelion,
L.C. Sargent Propr., Lynn, Mass.,
rectangular, clear, 8 1/8" h. 100.00
Litthauer Stomach, square case gin
shape, milk white, 9½" h. 150.00
Loew's (Dr.) Celebrated Stomach,
green, large 125.00
Lyman's Dandelion, C. Sweet & Bro.,
Gangor, Me., rectangular, aqua,
¾ qt., 10½" h. (hazy) 245.00
Malt Company, Boston, U.S.A., round,
smooth base, green, pt.,
9" h. . . . . 22.50 to 30.00
Marshall's, "The Best Laxative and
Blood Purifier," square, amber,
8 5/8" h. 37.50
McConnon's Stomach Bitters,
McConnon & Company, Winona,
Minn., square, amber, 8¾" h. 195.00
McKeever's Army, drum-shaped,
shoulders covered w/cannonballs,
amber, ¾ qt. 1,750.00
Mishler's Herb, square, golden amber,
9" h. 42.50
Mist of the Morning, barrel-shaped,
amber. 200.00
Morning Star, triangular,
amber . . . . 130.00 to 175.00
Moulton's Oloroso, embossed pineapple
& vertical ribs, aqua . . . . . 265.00 to 300.00
National, figural ear of corn, amber,
¾ qt. 200.00
National, figural ear of corn, light
yellow w/green tint 285.00
National, figural ear of corn, puce,
¾ qt. 600.00
National, Patent 1867, figural ear of
corn, amber, 12 5/8" h. 245.00
New York Hop Bitters Co., embossed
flag. 120.00 to 155.00
Niagara Star (John W. Steele's), square
w/roofed shoulders, 3 stars on roof
& 1864, collared mouth w/ring,
amber, 10" h. 295.00

O-Jib-Wa, clear, original paper labels
front & back dated 1949, threaded top
for cap, 7½" h. (ILLUS.) 6.00
Old Continental, rectangular w/roofed
shoulders, amber, 9 7/8" h. 295.00
Old Homestead Wild Cherry, cabin-
shaped, amber, 9 7/8" h. . . 140.00 to 195.00
Old Sachem Bitters & Wigwam Tonic,
barrel-shaped, amber 180.00
Old Sachem Bitters & Wigwam Tonic,
barrel-shaped, amethyst. 485.00
Old Sachem Bitters & Wigwam Tonic,
barrel-shaped, puce. 225.00
O'Leary's 20th Century, square, amber,
8½" h. 265.00
Oswego, oval, amber, 7" h. 90.00
Oxygenated for Dyspepsia, Asthma &
General Debility, rectangular, aqua,
½ pt., 7 5/8" h. 65.00
Parmelee's Mandrake & Dandelion
Jaundice Anti Bilious & Liver,
12-sided, aqua, 6¼" h. 60.00
Pendleton's Pineapple Bitters, Nash-
ville, T., 3 sunken panels, amber,
9" h. 450.00
Pepsin Calisaya, Dr. Russell Med. Co.,
rectangular, green, pt., 7 7/8" h. 100.00
Peruvian, square, smooth base,
amber. 50.00
Peychaud's American Aromatic Bitter
Cordial, L.E. Jung sole proprietor,
New Orleans, round, amber, 6" h. . . . 50.00
Peychaud's Bitter Cordial, cylindrical,
amber. 17.50
Phoenix, John Moffat, New York, rec-
tangular w/wide beveled corners,
aqua, ½ pt. 55.00
Pierce's (Dr.) Indian Restorative, rec-
tangular, pontil, aqua 37.50
Pineapple, J.C. & Co., pineapple-
shaped, amber, ¾ qt. 165.00
Pineapple, W. & Co., medium amber
(ILLUS. right) 350.00

Pond's Genuine Laxative Bitters

O-Jib-Wa Bitters

Pond's Genuine Laxative, amber,
paper label (ILLUS.) 30.00

Pond's Kidney & Liver, square, amber,
    9½" h. 42.50
Poor Man's Family, rectangular, aqua,
    ½ pt. 30.00
Porter (Mr. Zadoc) Medicated Stomach,
    rectangular, aqua, w/label 165.00
Prickley Ash, square, amber, ¾ qt. 28.50
Prickley Ash, square, olive yellow,
    ¾ qt. 95.00
Prune Stomach & Liver, square,
    amber 80.00
Red Jacket, Monheimer & Co., square,
    amber, ¾ qt. 50.00
Rex Kidney & Liver, amber 22.50
Rex Kidney and Liver, The Best
    Laxative and Blood Purifier, square,
    amber, w/50% of label, 9 5/8" h. 85.00
Richardson's (S.O.), rectangular
    w/wide beveled corners, aqua, pt. ...55.00
Richardson's (S.O.), rectangular
    w/wide beveled corners, green, pt. ..35.00
Rising Sun, John C. Hurst, Philada.,
    square, amber, 9 3/8" h. 120.00
Roback's (Dr. C.W.) Stomach, barrel-
    shaped, golden amber, ¾ qt. 110.00
Root's (John), rectangular w/roofed
    shoulders, aqua, ¾ qt. 115.00
Royal Pepsin Stomach, amber,
    7 3/8" h. 285.00
Royal Pepsin Stomach, amber,
    8¾" h. 165.00
Rush's, amber 37.50
Ryder's (Dr.) Clover, rectangular,
    amber, 7¼" h. 145.00
S & S, Der Doktor, square, clear,
    9½" h. 65.00
Saint Jacobs, dark blackish amber 65.00
Sanborn's Kidney & Liver, amber,
    10" h. 100.00
Sarasina Stomach, square, amber,
    9 1/8" h. 95.00
Schroeder's, lady's leg shape, amber,
    12½" h. 440.00
Severa (W.F.) Stomach, square,
    amber 125.00
Simon's Centennial, bust of Washing-
    ton, aqua, ¾ qt., 9¾" h. 295.00
Solomon's Strengthening & Invigor-
    ating, cobalt blue 575.00
Stewart's (Dr.) Tonic, rectangular,
    amber 125.00
Suffolk, figural pig, pontil, canary
    yellow 500.00
Suffolk, figural pig, yellow amber 500.00
Sun Kidney and Liver, Vegetable
    Laxative, Bowel Regulator & Blood
    Purifier, square, amber, 9½" h. 145.00
Sweet's (Dr. J.) Strengthening, square,
    aqua, 8¼" h. 150.00
Tippecanoe, H.H. Warner Co., tree
    bark design w/canoe, golden
    amber, ¾ qt. 68.00
Tonola, Trade Mark, Philadelphia,
    w/eagle, square, aqua, 8¼" h. 155.00

Van Dyke's (Dr.) Holland, rectangular,
    clear, 9½" h. 30.00
Von Hopf's (Dr.) Curacoa, Chamber-
    lain & Co., Des Moines, Iowa,
    rectangular, amber, 70% label,
    ½ pt., 7½" h. 85.00
Von Koster Stomach, Fairfield, Conn.,
    square, amber, 9" h. 225.00
Wahoo (Dr. E. Dexter Loveridge),
    cabin-shaped, yellow olive green ...225.00
Wait's Kidney & Liver, square, amber,
    8¾" h. 67.50
Wakefield's Strengthening, rectangular
    w/beveled corners, aqua 45.00
Warner's Safe, Rochester, N.Y., oval,
    amber, 9½" h. 750.00
West India Stomach, square, amber,
    8½" h. 48.50
West India Stomach, square, yellow,
    8½" h. 55.00
Whitcomb's (Faith) Nerve, rectangular,
    aqua, pt. 35.00
Whitwell's Temperance, pontil, light
    green (base flake) 100.00
Wilder's (Edw.) Stomach, building
    shape, clear 150.00
Wilson's (Dr.) Herbine, aqua 22.00
Woodcock Pepsin, Schroder's Med. Co.,
    amber 90.00
Wood's (Dr.) Sarsaparilla & Wild
    Cherry, pontil, aqua 145.00
Yamara Cordial, Yamara Medicine Co.,
    Chicago, Ill., U.S.A., rectangular,
    clear, 9¼" h. 895.00
Yerba Buena, flask-shaped, amber,
    8½" h. 45.00
Yerba Buena, rectangular strap-sided
    flask, amber, 9½" h. 165.00
Yochim Bros. Celebrated Stomach,
    square, amber 55.00
Young's (Dr.) Wild Cherry, rectangular,
    amber, 8½" h. 245.00
Zingari, amber 180.00

DRUG STORE BOTTLES & JARS

Drug Store Jars

Aqua mold-blown glass bottle,
    embossed "J. Tucker Druggist -
    Mobile," open pontil, 7½" h. 75.00

Blue-green mold-blown glass bottle, embossed "C.W. Merchant Chemist, Lockport, N.Y.," iron pontil 65.00

Clear apothecary jar, mold-blown glass globe on pedestal base w/pressed design around straight-sided collared neck, 13" h. (clear glass lid w/damage) 90.00

Clear apothecary jars, glass cylinders w/ground glass lids, various sizes, each (ILLUS.) . . . . .10.00 to 35.00

Clear mold-blown glass bottle, embossed "McIntosh & Kubon Prescription Druggists, Fairbanks, Alaska" 50.00

Clear mold-blown glass bottle, w/label, ½ gal. 25.00

Clear pressed glass bottle, embossed "G.A. Grimm Red Cross Drug Store, Dubuque, Iowa" 4.50

Clear pressed glass bottle, w/paper label "Shaker Witch Hazel," cork stopper, 7¼" h. 20.00

Clear pressed glass bottle, embossed "Trunk Bro's, Denver, Colo." & trunk, 5" h. 18.00

Cobalt blue apothecary jar, mold-blown glass cylinder, whittled mold marks, 4¾" d., 12¼" h. 90.00

Emerald green mold-blown glass bottle, embossed "Owl Drug Co.," applied blob top, 9¾" h. 75.00

Milk white mold-blown glass bottle, embossed "M.K. Paine Druggist & Apothecary, Windsor, Vt." 145.00

Milk white pressed glass bottle, embossed monogram of "Jno. Sullivan, Pharmacist, Boston" . . . . .10.00 to 16.00

FIGURAL

Cod Liver Oil Bottle

Bear, Kummel-type, black-amber glass 40.00

Bear, Kummel-type, black-amethyst glass 85.00

Bear, Kummel-type, milk white glass . .135.00

Bear, Kummel-type, purple glass, w/some label .40.00

Book, white clay pottery, mottled brown-black glaze, 6¼" h. 45.00

Bust of Grover Cleveland, frosted & clear glass, 10" h. 135.00

Bust of Kate Klaxton, clear glass 175.00

Carrie Nation, clear glass 62.50

Children climbing tree, clear glass w/frosted children, pontil, 11¾" h. . .15.00

Cigar, amber glass, 7 3/8" l. 32.50

Coachman, "Van Dunck's Genever," puce glass 120.00

Cucumber, green-glazed pottery 28.00

Ear of corn, green carnival glass, 5" h. 225.00

Ear of corn, marigold carnival glass, 5" h. 200.00

Eiffel Tower, clear glass 30.00

Fish, Eli Lily Co. Cod Liver Oil, amber glass, 6¼" h. (ILLUS.) 25.00

Fish, clear pressed glass w/applied green glass eyes, "Dobson's Shad-Ro-Branco Wine," Portugal, 1969 . . . . .15.00

Grant's Tomb, milk white glass 192.50

Grape cluster, clear glass 17.50

Lady's leg, amber glass, embossed "Nuyens" at shoulder 20.00

Lady's Leg Bottle

Lady's leg in high button shoe on base, frosted & clear glass w/painted details (ILLUS.) 125.00

Matador, milk white glass 120.00

Pig, mottled brown Rockingham-glazed pottery, good details 650.00

Pineapple, amber glass, 9 1/8" h. 200.00

Saddle, black glass, applied rings at neck, 9" l. 72.00

Snowman, milk white glass 135.00

Statue of Liberty base, milk white glass, w/metal figural Statue of Liberty on cover, 1880-90, 15¼" h. . . .200.00

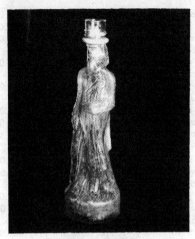

Uncle Sam Bottle

Uncle Sam, clear glass (ILLUS.) 45.00
Violin, amethyst (deep) glass, pontil . . .25.00
Violin, cobalt blue glass 13.00

FLASKS

*(Numbers used below refer to those used
in the McKearins' "American Glass.")*

"Corn for the World" Flask

"Albany Glass Works" in semi-circle
    around bust of Washington, "Albany,
    N.Y." below - Full-rigged Ship
    Sailing, plain lip, vertically ribbed
    edges, pontil, amber, pt. (GI-28) 870.00
American Eagle - Bunch of Grapes,
    plain lip, vertical ribbing, pontil,
    aqua, ½ pt. (GII-56) . . . . . . .175.00 to 200.00
American Eagle - Bunch of Grapes,
    plain lip, vertical ribbing, pontil,
    light aqua, qt. (GII-55) 100.00
American Eagle on shield & flag
    w/"Continental" below - Indian &

dog w/"Cunninghams & Co.,
    Pittsburgh, Pa." below, smooth
    edges, aqua, qt. (GII-142) 150.00
American Eagle on oval - U.S. Flag
    w/"Coffin & Hay." above &
    "Hammonton" below, plain lip,
    vertically ribbed edges, pontil,
    aqua, qt. (GII-48) . . . . .150.00 to 175.00
American Eagle standing on wreath of
    laurel branches & "Liberty" above -
    "Willington Glass Co., West
    Willington, Conn.," plain lip, round-
    ed collar, smooth edges, olive
    green, qt. (GII-61) . . . . .140.00 to 175.00
"Baltimore" Monument - "Corn For The
    World" above ear of corn, plain lip,
    smooth edges, pontil, clear green,
    ½ pt., GVI-7 (ILLUS.) 750.00
"Benjamin Franklin" above bust - "T.W.
    Dyott, M.D." above bust, plain lip,
    "Where Liberty Dwells There Is My
    Country" & "Kensington Glass Works
    Philadelphia" on edges, pontil, aqua,
    pt. (GI-94) .155.00
"Benjamin Franklin" above bust - "T.W.
    Dyott, M.D." above bust, w/"Eripuit
    Coelo Fulmen. Sceptrumque
    Tyrannis" & "Kensington Glass
    Works, Philadelphia" plain lip,
    vertically ribbed edges, pontil,
    aqua, qt. (GI-96) 400.00
Chestnut, 24 vertical ribs, smoky
    amber, Midwestern, ½ pt. 275.00
Chestnut, 24 vertical ribs, yellow-
    green, ½ pt. .550.00
Chestnut, 24 vertical ribs, golden
    amber, 8½" h. 900.00
Chestnut, 24 ribs swirled to left,
    greenish aqua, qt. 85.00
Chestnut, 24 swirled ribs, square
    flanged lip, amber, 9" h. 170.00
Chestnut, brilliant yellow, 9" 150.00
Cornucopia - Urn with Produce, plain
    lip, vertically ribbed edges, pontil,
    olive amber, pt. (GIII-4) . . . . .50.00 to 80.00
Cornucopia - Urn with Produce, plain
    lip, vertically ribbed edges, pontil,
    olive green, pt. (GIII-4) 60.00
Double American Eagle, plain lip,
    horizontally corrugated edges,
    pontil, aqua, pt. (GII-24) . . .120.00 to 165.00
Double American Eagle, plain lip,
    horizontally corrugated edges,
    pontil, yellow-green, pt. (GII-24) 500.00
Double American Eagle on oval frame
    & surrounded by 23 rays, plain lip,
    vertically ribbed edges, pontil,
    greenish aqua, pt. (GII-40) . .95.00 to 105.00
Double American Eagle holding arrows
    in talons w/oval frame below,
    smooth edges, aqua, qt. (GII-91) 100.00
Double Scroll, plain lip, vertical
    medial rib, pontil, aqua, ½ pt.,
    GIX-37 (ILLUS.) 200.00

Double Scroll Flask

Double Scroll, plain lip, heavy vertical medial rib, pontil, bluish aqua,
½ pt. (GIX-31) . . . . .78.00 to 125.00
Double Scroll, plain lip, heavy vertical
medial rib, pontil, golden amber,
½ pt. (GIX-34) 440.00
Double Scroll, plain lip, heavy vertical
medial rib, pontil, aqua, pt.
(GIX-11) . . . . .55.00 to 65.00
Double Scroll, plain lip, heavy vertical
medial rib, pontil, sea green, pt.
(GIX-14) 350.00
Double Scroll, plain lip, heavy vertical
medial rib, pontil, aqua, qt.
(GIX-51) .1,800.00
Double Scroll, plain lip, vertical medial
rib, aqua, gal. (GIX-30) 75.00
Double "Success To The Railroad,"
plain lip, vertically ribbed edges,
pontil, olive amber, pt. (GV-3) 150.00
Double "Success To The Railroad,"
plain lip, vertically ribbed edges,
pontil, olive amber, pt. (GV-5) 157.00
Double Sunburst w/"KEEN" in oval,
plain lip, horizontal corrugations,
pontil, golden amber, ½ pt.
(GVIII-9) 100.00
Double Sunburst w/twenty-four rays,
plain lip, horizontally corrugated
edges, pontil, olive green, ½ pt.
(GVIII-18) 325.00
Double (elongated) Sunburst w/twelve
rays in small sunken oval panel,
plain lip, entirely vertical ribbed,
pontil, blue-green, ¾ pt.
(GVIII-29) . . . . .150.00 to 260.00
Double Sunburst, plain lip, horizon-
tally corrugated edges, pontil,
light greenish blue, pt. (GVIII-2) 350.00
Double Sunburst, plain lip, horizontally
corrugated edges, pontil, brilliant
green, pt. (GVIII-1) 560.00
Double Sunburst, plain lip, horizontally
corrugated edges, pontil, clear, pt.
(GVIII-1) 350.00
"Genl. Taylor" above bust - Baltimore

Monument w/"Fells Point" above &
"Balt." below, plain lip, vertically
ribbed edges, pontil, deep olive
yellow, pt. (GI-73) . . . . . . .575.00 to 650.00
"General Washington" above bust -
American Eagle on oval, plain lip,
horizontal beading w/vertical
medial rib, pontil, light green, pt.
(GI-2) . . . . .300.00 to 395.00
"G. Washington" above bust -
American Eagle on oval w/eleven
stars above & 1 at left, plain lip,
horizontal beading w/vertical
medial rib, pontil, light green, pt.
(GI-10) 450.00
Grant profile bust in laurel wreath -
American Eagle on shield & "Union"
in oval frame below, plain lip,
smooth edges, aqua, pt. (GI-79) 200.00
"Jeny Lind" calabash w/portrait bust -
View of Glasshouse w/"Glass
Factory" above, broad sloping collar,
heavy vertical ribbing, pontil, aqua,
qt. (GI-102) 65.00
"Jeny Lind" calabash w/three-quarter
figure wearing broad decorated
bertha - View of Glass House, broad
sloping collar, heavy vertical ribbing,
pontil, aqua, qt. (GI-103) 79.00
"La Fayette" above bust, "T.S." below -
"De Witt (backwards D) Clinton"
above bust, "Coventry C-T" below,
plain lip, horizontally corrugated
edges, pontil, light olive amber, pt.
(GI-80) 585.00
"Liberty" above American Eagle -
"Willington Glass Co., West
Willington, Conn.," plain lip, smooth
edges, pontil, green, pt. (GII-64) 145.00
Masonic Emblems - American Eagle &
oval frame w/"J.K.B.," tooled neck,
vertically ribbed edges, pontil,
yellow-green, pt. (GIV-4) 845.00
Masonic Emblems - American Eagle &
plain oval frame, plain lip, smooth
edges w/vertical medial rib, olive
green, ½ pt. (GIV-24) 175.00
Masonic Emblems - American Eagle,
"Janesville, Ohio" & "J. Shepard
(backwards S) & Co.," plain lip,
vertically ribbed edges, pontil,
honey amber, pt. (GIV-32) 475.00
Masonic Emblems w/Clasped Hands &
"Union" - American Eagle on shield
& "A.R.S.," broad sloping collar,
fluted edges, pontil, aqua, qt.
(GIV-42) 65.00
Pitkin, 36 swirled ribs, blown, olive
amber, 5¼" h. 140.00
Pitkin, 36 ribs swirled to right,
sheared mouth, pontil, forest
green 198.00
"Success To The Railroad" - American
Eagle, plain lip, vertically ribbed

edges, pontil, dark olive amber, pt.
(GV-8) . . . . .95.00 to 165.00
Summer Tree - Winter Tree, plain lip,
smooth edges, pontil, black, qt.
(GX-19). 485.00
Taylor above "Rough and Ready" -
"Major Ringgold" w/bust, plain lip,
vertical ribbing, pontil, aqua, pt.
(GI-71) 155.00
Taylor, "Zachary Taylor" & "Rough &
Ready" - "Corn For The World"
above tall corn stalk, plain lip,
smooth edges, pontil, aqua, pt.
(GI-75) 325.00
Washington bust w/"Fells" above &
"Point" below - Baltimore Monu-
ment w/"Balto" below, plain lip,
horizontal beading w/vertical med-
ial rib, pontil, aqua, pt. (GI-20) 105.00
Washington, "The Father Of His
Country" - Taylor, "Gen. Taylor
Never Surrenders" & "Dyottville
Glass Works, Philad.a," plain lip,
smooth edges, aqua, qt. (GI-37) 80.00
Washington, "The Father of His
Country" - Taylor, plain lip, smooth
edges, pontil, aqua, qt. (GI-45) 125.00

INKS

Carter's Cathedral Ink

Barrel-shaped, mold-blown light green
glass, pontil. 70.00
Boat-shaped, pressed clambroth glass,
embossed "Pat'd Aug. 9, 1870,"
w/hinged metal cap, attributed to
the New England Glass Co., 5½" l. . .125.00
Cone-shaped, aqua mold-blown glass,
embossed "H. & T. Red Ink," open
pontil (dug) 120.00
Cone-shaped, aqua mold-blown glass,
embossed "Wood's Black Ink
Portland," open pontil, 2¼" d.,
2½" h. 120.00
Cone-shaped, emerald green mold-
blown glass, applied lip, embossed
"Carter's 1897" on base 15.00

Cone-shaped, medium green mold-
blown glass, 2" h. 16.00
Cone-shaped, olive-amber mold-
blown glass w/greenish tint,
pontil 100.00
Cylindrical, amber mold-blown glass,
pontil, 4 oz. .85.00
Cylindrical, amber glass, embossed
"Sanford" 16.00
Cylindrical, aqua glass, 2" d., 3" h. 2.00
Cylindrical, cobalt blue mold-blown
glass, pontil, 3" h. 70.00
Domed cylinder, light olive yellow
mold-blown glass, sheared lip,
embossed "Bertinguiot" on side,
2½" d., 2¼" h. 150.00
Domed w/offset neck, amber mold-
blown glass, embossed "J. & IEM"
in rounded end opposite 6 panels,
polished pontil, 1 5/8" h. 66.00
Figural "Ma" & "Pa" Carter, porcelain,
marked "Carter's Inx" on base, pr. . .125.00
Hexagonal, cobalt blue mold-blown
glass, pontil .55.00
Master size, aqua mold-blown glass,
12-sided, embossed vertically
"Harrison's Columbian Ink,"
6" h. .40.00 to 75.00
Master size, cobalt blue glass, "Carter's
Cathedral," w/Gothic arch
"windows," ½ pt. . . . . .55.00 to 70.00
Master size, cobalt blue glass, "Carter's
Cathedral," w/Gothic arch "win-
dows," qt. (ILLUS.) 55.00
Master size, cobalt blue glass cylinder,
embossed "Carter's" on base & "32
Fluid Oz." on shoulder, 9½" h. 15.00
Master size, cobalt blue glass cylinder
w/red & white label "Raiguel's
Recording Writing Ink, Philadel-
phia". 27.00
Master size, cobalt blue pressed glass
cylinder embossed "S. Stafford,
Inc., Made in U.S.A." on base, 6" h. . .22.50
Octagonal, aqua mold-blown glass,
embossed "Harrison's Columbian
Ink," 4" h. 45.00
Octagonal, fiery opalescent mold-
blown glass, straight-sided octagon
w/original stopper, embossed "Penn
Mfg. Works, P. Garrett & Co.,
Philada." on base, 3" d., 3" h. 175.00
Octagonal, golden amber mold-
blown glass, sheared lip, pontil,
1 7/8" h. 308.00
Octagonal, green mold-blown bottle
attributed to Stoddard 75.00
Square w/pinched in sides, clear glass,
embossed "Diamond Ink Co.,
Milwaukee". .10.00
Square, aqua glass, "Caw's Black Ink,"
original paper label w/black crow
trademark (ILLUS.). . . . . .10.00 to 15.00

mmm mm mmmmm mmmmmmmmmmmmmmmmmmmmmmmmmmmmmmmmmmmmmmmmm

Caw's Ink Bottle

Stoneware pottery bottle, small size....10.00
Teakettle-type fountain inkwell, sapphire blue mold-blown glass..................265.00 to 295.00
Triangular w/offset neck, green mold-blown glass, embossed "Allings Patd Apl 25 1871," 2½ x 2½", 1 7/8" h..........................50.00
Twelve-sided, yellow-green mold-blown glass, embossed "Butler's Ink, Cincinnati," pontil, 2" d., 2" h. ...190.00
Umbrella-type (paneled cone-shape), aqua mold-blown glass, 8-sided, embossed "Stick Well & Co.," 3" h. (dug)..........................35.00
Umbrella-type (paneled cone shape), deep amber mold-blown glass, 8-sided, sheared lip, 2¼" d., 2½" h...........................95.00
Umbrella-type (paneled cone shape), olive yellow glass, 8-sided, rolled mouth, pontil, 2¼" h..............77.00
Umbrella-type (paneled cone shape), teal blue mold-blown glass, 8-sided, tooled mouth, pontil, 2½" h. 275.00

MEDICINES

Adams' (Dr. A.L.) Liver Balsam, deep aqua...........................105.00
Allen's (Mrs.) World Hair Restorer, dark red violet...................90.00
Allen's (Mrs.) World Hair Restorer, light golden amber.....................10.00
Allen's (Mrs.) World Hair Restorer, yellow w/green cast...............85.00
Ayer's (Dr. J.C.) Ague Cure, rectangular, aqua, 7" h.....................10.00
Ayer's Hair Vigor, cobalt blue, 6½" h. ...18.50
Baker's (Dr.) Pain Panacea, rectangular, pontil, aqua, 5" h.......30.00
Baker's (Dr.) Tonic Laxative, Keokuk, Iowa, indented panels, golden amber..........................18.00

Barry's Tricopherous for the Skin and Hair, aqua.......................20.00
Bromo-Seltzer, round, cobalt blue, 4" h...............................1.50
Browder's (Dr.) Compound Syrup of Indian Turnip, rectangular, aqua, 7" h. 76.00
Buckhout's (E.A.) Dutch Liniment, Prepared at Mechanicville Saratoga Co., N.Y., rectangular, embossed Dutchman, aqua, 4 5/8" h. 295.00
Burdsall's (J.R.) Arnica Liniment, rectangular, grey, flint, 5½" h. 60.00
Cann's Kidney Cure, 1876, clear, 8½" h. 22.50
Chamberlain's Cough Remedy, Des Moines, Iowa, U.S.A., rectangular, aqua to blue-green at corker top, 5¾" h. 9.25

Clemen's Indian Tonic Bottle

Clemen's Indian Tonic prepared by Geo. W. House, oval, w/embossed Indian, pontil, aqua, w/95% label, 5½" h. (ILLUS.) 295.00
Cole Bros. Restorative Balsam, rectangular, aqua, 6 1/8" h............22.50
Corbin's German Drops, pontil, aqua ..125.00
Covert's Balm of Life, rectangular w/beveled corners, pontil, olive green (extra long neck)............825.00
Crook's (Dr.) Wine of Tar, square, green, 8¾" h. 38.00
Curtis' Hygeana or Inhaling Hygean Vapor and Cherry Syrup, rectangular, clear 75.00
Daniel's (Dr.) Colic Cure No. 2, clear, 3½" h. 5.00
Davis' (Perry) Pain Killer, rectangular, pontil, aqua, 4 5/8" h. 19.00
Davis' (Perry) Pain Killer, rectangular, pontil, aqua, 6" h.................2.50
Dickenson (Geo.) Alterative Balsam, Hartford, Conn., rectangular, aqua...12.50

Dodge's Rheumatic Liniment, rectangular, open pontil, black 1,100.00
Donnaud's Gout Remedy, round, aqua,
6" h. 350.00
Dyer's Healing Embrocation, Provi-
dence, R.I., pontil, aqua,
6¼" h. ....37.00 to 59.00
Fenner's (Dr. M.M.) Kidney & Backache
Cure, oval, amber, w/95% label,
10" h. ....18.00 to 25.00
Fitch (Dr. S.S.), 714 Broadway, N.Y.,
oval, aqua, 6 3/8" h. (dug) 10.00
Foley's Kidney & Bladder Cure,
Chicago, U.S.A., rectangular, amber,
4¼" h. 7.50
Foley's Kidney & Bladder Cure,
Chicago, U.S.A., rectangular, amber,
7½" h. 17.50
Franklin's Eagle Hair Restorer,
Columbus, Ohio, orange-amber 65.00
Fruiticura Womans Tonic, clear 25.50
Gibb's Bone Liniment, 8-sided, open
pontil, olive green, 6½" h. 650.00
Glover's Imperial Distemper Cure, H.
Clay Glover, New York, amber,
5 1/8" h. 9.75
Glover's Imperial Mange Cure, amber ...7.50
Graydon (Dr. T.W.), Cincinnati, O.,
Diseases of the Lungs, square,
amber, 7¼" h. 20.00
Gray's Balsam, Best Cough Cure,
rectangular, aqua, 6½" h. 18.50
Grove's Tasteless Chill Tonic, aqua,
6" h. 10.00
Haynes (Dr.) Arabian Balsam, E.
Morgan & Sons, Providence, R.I.,
12-sided, aqua, 4 1/8" h. 5.00
Henry's Calcined Magnesia 15.00
Hick's Capudine for all Headaches,
Colds & Gripp, etc., rectangular,
amber, 2¾" h. 6.00
Hoofland's Balsamic Cordial, aqua,
6¾" h. 115.00
Hunter's Pulmonary Balsam or Cough
Syrup, J. Curtis Prop., Bangor, Me.,
rectangular, aqua, 6" h. .....65.00 to 75.00
Hurds Cough Balsam, partial label,
open pontil, aqua 49.00
Indian Vegetable Balsam 73.00
Jayne's (Dr. D.) Alterative, rectangu-
lar, aqua, 7" h. ....17.00 to 24.00
Jayne's (Dr. D.) Liniment or Counter
Irritant, rectangular, aqua,
5 1/8" h. 35.00
Jayne's (Dr. D.) Tonic Vermifuge,
Philada., square, aqua, 4 7/8" h. 25.00
Jewitt's (Dr.) Pulmonary Elixir, open
pontil, aqua, w/label 75.00
Keeley's (Dr. L.E.) Gold Cure For
Drunkenness, flat-paneled oval,
clear, 5½" h. ....32.00 to 50.00
Kendall's (Dr. B.J.) Spavin Cure,
12-sided, amber, 5½" h. 7.50
Kennedy's (Dr.) Medical Discovery,

Roxbury, Mass., rectangular, light
emerald green 43.50
Kidder's (Mrs. E.) Cordial, Boston,
aqua 48.00
Kilmer's (Dr.) Herbal Extract,
rectangular, aqua, 4½" h. 20.00
Kilmer's (Dr.) Swamp-Root Kidney, Liver
& Bladder Cure, Binghamton, N.Y.,
rectangular, aqua, small sample
size, 3¼" h. ....3.00 to 6.50
Kodol Dyspepsia Cure, rectangular,
aqua, 6¾" h. 10.00

H. Lake's Indian Specific

Lake's Indian Specific, rectangular
w/deeply beveled corners & raised
frame around embossing, aqua-
green, 8¼" h. (ILLUS.) 325.00
Leonardi Blood Elixir, Tampa, Fla.,
rectangular, amber 18.00
Leon's (Dr.) Electric Hair Renewer,
Ziegler & Smith, Philada., indented
panels, black amethyst 195.00
Lindsay's Blood Searcher, aqua 35.00
Lindsay's Blood Searcher, clear 18.00
McLean's (Dr. J.H.) Strengthening
Cordial & Blood Purifier, aqua 18.00
Merchant's (G.W.) Gargling Oil, rec-
tangular, open pontil, green,
7 1/8" h. 55.00
Mexican Mustang Liniment, round,
pontil, aqua, 4" h. 12.00
Miles (Dr.) New Heart Cure, rectagu-
lar, aqua, 8 3/8" h. 14.00
Miles' (Dr.) Restorative Nervine, aqua,
8½" h. 6.00
Miller's (Dr. J.R.) Magnetic Balm, rec-
tangular, aqua, 4¾" h. 22.50
Moxie Nerve Food, round, aqua,
9¾" h. ....7.00 to 15.00
Osgood's India Cholagogue, New York,
rectangular, pontil, aqua, 5 3/8" h. 24.50

Paine's Celery Compound, square,
amber, 9¾" h. . . . . .8.00 to 12.50

Parker's Hair Balsam Bottle

Parker's Hair Balsam, New York,
amber, 7" h. (ILLUS.) 3.00
Parker's Hair Balsam, pale yellow-
green 18.00
Pinkham's (Lydia) Vegetable Com-
pound, oval, aqua, 8½" h. 10.00
Pond's Extract, oval, aqua, 5½" h. 25.00
Porter's (Madame Zadoc) Curative
Balsam 35.00
Pratt's Distemper & Pink Eye Cure,
amber, 6¾" h. 18.50
Ridgway's Acme Liniment, rectangular
w/rounded sides, amber, 7 7/8" h. . . .12.50
Roberson's (Prof. Wm.) Hair Renewer,
indented panels, dark amethyst
(professionally cleaned) 155.00
Roberts's (M.B.) Vegetable Embro-
cation, round, pontil, light lime
green, 5" h. 80.00
Roger's (Dr. A.) Liverwort, Tar and
Canchalagua, rectangular, aqua,
7½" h. 45.00
Sanford's (Dr.) Invigorator, Sanford &
Co. Proprietors, N.Y., rectangular,
aqua, 6 1/8" h. . . . . .58.00 to 96.00

Sanford's Liver Invigorator

Sanford's (Dr.) Liver Invigorator, rectangular, aqua, 7¼" h. (ILLUS.) 65.00
Sanford's Radical Cure, rectangular,
cobalt blue, 7 5/8" h. 20.00
Sawens' (Dr.) Cough Balsam, rec-
tangular, aqua, 6" h. 32.00
Schenck's (J.H.) Sea Weed Tonic,
square, iron pontil, aqua, 8 3/8" h. . . .125.00
Scott's Emulsion of Cod Liver Oil, rectangular, aqua, 9¼" h. 10.00
Scovell Blood & Liver Syrup, Cincinnati,
aqua 12.00
Shaker Anodyne, Nth Enfield, N.H.,
w/partial paper label, aqua,
3¾" h. 30.00
Sparks' Kidney & Liver Cure, oval
w/flat front, aqua. 9.00
Swaim's Panacea, rectangular, pontil,
light forest green 135.00
Tebbetts (Dr.) Hair Regenerator,
puce 150.00
Thatcher's (Dr.) Liver & Blood Syrup,
Chattanooga, Tenn., amber,
8 3/8" h. 6.00
Thomson's Compound Syrup of Tar and
Wood Naphtha, rectangular, aqua,
5¾" h. 62.50
Tobias' Venetian Liniment, aqua,
5¾" h. 27.50
Tom's Russian Liniment, square, aqua,
4½" h. 85.00
Townsend's (Dr.) Sarsaparilla, olive
green 100.00
University of Free Medicines, Philada.,
6-sided, aqua .95.00
Velvetina Skin Beautifier, Omaha,
U.S.A., rectangular, milk white,
5½" h. 35.00
Veno's Lightning Cough Cure, aqua,
5 3/8" h. . . . . .5.00 to 10.00
Warner's Safe Cure Co., round, amber,
4¼" h. 22.50
Warner's Safe Cure, Melbourne,
amber, pt. 37.50
Warner's Safe Diabetes Cure, oval,
amber, 9¾" h. 50.00
Warner's Safe Kidney & Liver Cure,
oval, amber, 9¾" h. 20.00
Warner's Safe Nervine, H.H. Warner
& Company, Rochester, New York,
amber, ½ pt. .35.00
Warner's Safe Rheumatic Cure,
Rochester, N.Y., U.S.A., amber,
w/original paper label, 9¼" h. 38.00
Weaver's (Dr. S.A.) Canker & Salt
Rheum Syrup & Cerate, oval, aqua,
9" h. 65.00
Williams' (Dr. James) Anti-Dyspeptic
Elixir, aqua, 6½" h. 70.00
Winans Brothers' Indian Cure,
embossed & full label, 9¼" h. 145.00
Wishart's (Dr. L.Q.C.) Pine Tree Tar
Cordial, square, emerald green,
9½" h. 42.50

Wistar's Balsam of Wild Cherry,
   Cincinnati, O., 8-sided, deep aqua . . .30.00
Woods (Professor) Hair Restorative,
   aqua 20.00

MILK

Half Pint & Quart Milk Bottles

Amber, embossed "Fenn's Guernsey
   Dairy," qt. 8.00
Amber, embossed "Mayer, Rochester,
   N.Y.," qt. 50.00
Amber, embossed "San Rafael, Cali-
   fornia," qt. 5.00
Amber, white pyroglaze cow, bottle
   & shield, qt. 5.50
Clear, "baby face" top, ½ pt. 30.00
Clear, "baby face" top, pt. 26.00
Clear, "baby face" top, embossed
   "Royal Dunloggin Farms," pt. 15.00
Clear, double "baby face" top,
   qt. . . . . .22.00 to 30.00
Clear, "cop face" top w/molded hair
   on back of head, embossed "Cop-the-
   Cream," 2 children, cow & milkman,
   qt. . . . . .18.00 to 25.00
Clear, cream-top, embossed doctor 1
   side & steer's head other, dated
   1925, pt. 14.00
Clear, cream-top, embossed "Bordens,"
   qt. 9.50
Clear, cream-top, embossed "Meadow
   Gold," qt. 24.50
Clear, cream-top, embossed "Otto
   Milk, Pittsburg, Pa. - Pat. Mar.
   3-25," w/spoon, qt. 30.00
Clear, embossed "Quality," miniature,
   ¾ oz. 6.00
Clear, embossed "Tastemark," miniature,
   ¾ oz. 6.00
Clear, embossed "Erickson," ½ pt. 3.50
Clear, embossed "Half Pint Liquid,
   Hills Bros., Canton, N.Y.," ½ pt. 5.00
Clear, embossed "Milky Way," ½ pt. 3.50
Clear, embossed "Pin Ball, Maine
   Creamery," ½ pt. 10.00

Clear, embossed "Roberts," ½ pt. 3.50
Clear, embossed "Thurston Dairy,
   Taylorsville, N.C.," ½ pt. 3.00
Clear, embossed baby w/foot in mouth
   on side, ½ pt. .10.00
Clear, embossed "E.M. Bleacher,
   Lancaster, Pa." & anchor, pt. 25.00
Clear, embossed "Lincoln Nebraska
   Dairy," pt. 3.00
Clear, embossed "Poudre Valley Colorado
   Creamery," pt. .3.50
Clear, embossed "Iowa Guernsey Dairy,
   Ames, Iowa," qt. 5.00
Clear, embossed "Koontz Creamery" &
   mother pushing baby in carriage &
   "The Carriage Trade," qt. . . . .10.00 to 15.00
Clear, embossed "Larrimore Dairy,
   Seaford, Delaware" & boy & girl
   walking arm in arm, qt. 15.00
Clear, embossed "Mills Pure Pasteurized
   Milk" & Dutch windmill, qt. 15.00
Clear, embossed "Pin Ball - Empire
   Patent," qt. 10.00
Clear, embossed "Robert's Dairy -
   Omaha," round, qt. 10.00
Clear, embossed "Victory Comes a
   Little Closer Every Time You Buy a
   War Bond," Pennsylvania dairy, qt. . . .22.00
Green, embossed man milking cow,
   w/porcelain stopper, 1884 . . . . .45.00
Purple, embossed "Hampden" & steer's
   head, ½ pt. 10.00

MINERAL WATERS

Congress Spring Co. "C" Bottle

Ballston Spa, A & S monogram each
   side, Artesian Spring, Ballston, N.Y.,
   large bubbles, green, pt. 75.00

Ballston Spa Mineral Water, emerald
green, pt. 30.00
Ballston Spa Mineral Water, yellow
olive, pt. 45.00
Boardman (J.), N.Y. Mineral Water,
8-sided, iron pontil, cobalt blue 75.00
Boyd & Beard Mineral Water, iron
pontil, emerald green 68.00
Buffalo Lithia Mineral Water, aqua,
½ gal. 18.00
Champion Spouting Spring, Saratoga
Mineral Spring, C.S. Co. S. Limited,
Saratoga, N.Y., blue-aqua, pt. (chip
on base) 20.00
Clarke & White, N.Y., olive green, pt. . .25.00
Congress & Empire Spring, Hotchkiss'
Sons, C. & W. monogram, Saratoga,
New York, light yellowish olive
green, ½ pt. 150.00
Congress & Empire Spring Co.,
Hotchkiss Sons, Saratoga, green 30.00
Congress Spring Co., Saratoga, N.Y.,
green, pt. 22.50
Congress Springs Co., Saratoga, N.Y.,
dark green, qt. 35.00
Congress Spring Co., "C" monogram,
Saratoga, N.Y., green, pt. (ILLUS.) . . .80.00
Darlen Mineral Springs, Tifft & Perry
Darlen, Centre, N.Y., green, pt. 150.00
Geyser Springs, Avery N. Lord, 66
Broad Street, Utica, N.Y., aqua, qt. . . .45.00

Hathorn Spring Bottle

Hathorn Spring, Saratoga, N.Y.,
amber, pt. (ILLUS.) 22.00
Hathorn Spring, Saratoga, N.Y.,
black, pt. 24.00
Hathorn Spring, Saratoga, N.Y.,
amber, qt. 20.00
Hotchkiss' Sons Congress, emerald
green, pt. 39.00

John Ogden's Mineral Water, Pittsburgh, blob top, iron pontil, blue-
aqua 55.00
John Ogden's Mineral Water, Pitts-
burgh, blob top, pontil, green-
aqua 40.00
John Ryan, Excelsior Mineral Water
1859, Savannah, Ga., cobalt blue 57.50
Kennedy (J.) Mineral Water, Pittsburgh, Pa., iron pontil, green-aqua. . .40.00
New Almaden (A.P.) Vichy Water,
California, whittled, grass green,
applied ring top . . . . .275.00 to 350.00
Nicholson (A.) Mineral Water, Pitts-
burgh, tapered top, pontil, green-
aqua 50.00
Pablo Mineral Water, blob top 25.00
Pine Hill Crystal Water, New York,
5-pt. 60.00
Poland Mineral Spring, aqua, label 25.00

Saratoga Red Spring Bottle

Saratoga Red Spring, emerald green,
pt. (ILLUS.) 85.00
Tonbridge Mineral Water Co. B, blob
top, pt. 40.00

NURSING
Clear, double-ended oval, mold-blown
w/dimples 16.00
Clear, double-ended oval, embossed
"Albert" 16.00
Clear, double-ended oval, embossed
"Griptite" 16.00
Clear, turtle-shaped, mold-blown 95.00
Clear, turtle-shaped, embossed "Acme
Nursing Bottle" & monogram within
8-point star, oval, 6" l. 28.00
Clear, turtle-shaped, embossed
"Columbia" 30.00

Clear, pressed glass, embossed "The
Best"............................38.00
Clear, pressed glass, embossed cats ...20.00

"Happy Baby" Nursing Bottle

Clear, pressed glass, embossed "Happy
Baby" & baby each side, 8 oz.
(ILLUS.) ....12.50 to 15.00
Clear, pressed glass, embossed
"Humpty Dumpty," 8 oz. ......8.00 to 12.00
Clear, pressed glass, embossed "Royal
Nurser" & monogram...............16.00
Clear, pressed glass, embossed Scottie
dogs, 8 oz. 10.00
Clear, pressed glass, embossed "Sonny
Boy" & crawling baby..............18.00
Clear, shoe-shaped w/extended neck,
embossed "N. Wood & Sons" 40.00
Pale blue, embossed "The Peerless
Nurser" 45.00

PEPPERSAUCES

"E.R. Durkee" Peppersauce Bottle

Beehive, aqua.......................16.00
Cathedral arches, 4-sided, open pontil,
aqua, 8½" h. (dug)................28.00
Cathedral arches, 6-sided, open pontil,
aqua 40.00
Indented panels, 8-sided, "Yankee
Sauce Hodges & Cross," aqua........65.00
Ridge-sided tapering square,
embossed "E.R. Durkee & Co., N.Y."
& "Pat'd Feb. 17, 1874" on base,
emerald green, 7¾" h. (ILLUS.) 30.00
Ridge-sided tapering square,
unmarked, green 22.00
Six-sided, open pontil, aqua (dug)......40.00

PICKLE BOTTLES

Cathedral Pickle Bottles

Aqua, cathedral-type w/gothic arch
windows, "SJG" monogram, pt.......48.00
Aqua, 4 panels, petal pattern top
shoulders, open pontil, 7 5/8" h. 50.00
Aqua, cathedral-type w/gothic arch
windows, 11½" h. 60.00
Aqua, cathedral-type w/gothic arch
windows, large (ILLUS. right) 120.00
Cornflower blue, cathedral-type
w/gothic arch windows, very large
(ILLUS. left) 300.00
Green-aqua, cathedral-type w/gothic
arch windows, ½-gal. 130.00
Light green, cathedral-type w/gothic
arch windows & cross-hatched
panels, 7½" h. 125.00
Deep emerald green, cathedral-type
w/gothic arch windows, 4-sided,
large (minor lip chip) 200.00
Medium emerald green, cathedral-type
w/gothic arch windows, very large
(ILLUS. center)...................700.00
Sage green, cathedral-type w/gothic
arch windows, pt. (cracked) 50.00
Yellow-amber, embossed "Sanborn
Parker & Co., Boston, Pickles,"
sheared & ground lip, 7¼" h. 125.00

SOFT DRINK BOTTLES

(A Chronological History)

by Cecil Munsey

The history of soft drinks began with man's discovery of natural mineral waters. The exact date is unkown but in 400 B.C. the Greek physician Hippocrates wrote a book entitled *Airs, Waters, and Places.* Physicians and scientists throughout the ages have studied mineral waters.

It was Bewley (England), in 1767, who was first to prepare a mixture of bicarbonate with carbonated water. His mixture later became known as "soda water," a term which has become generic for soft drinks.

In 1789 Paul, Schweppe, and Gosse (Switzerland) started an artificial mineral water business in Geneva. In 1794 Schweppe left Geneva and opened his own business in Bristol, England. Products bearing the Schweppe name are still being produced and sold today.

In the United States, in 1809, the first patent for preparing artificial mineral water was issued to Joseph Hawkins. Seventeen years later, in 1826, John Clarke (New York City) operated a shop for bottling the effervescent waters of Saratoga Springs. He was able to produce 1,200 bottles a day. Bottles from the Saratoga area have long been prized by collectors for their historical value and their beautiful colors -- greens, blues, ambers.

As early as 1824 the U.S. Dispensatory (Philadelphia) published recipes for soda water flavoring syrups -- sarsaparilla, lemon, strawberry, raspberry, and ginger. By 1837 flavoring syrups for soda water, made from fruit juices, were being used at apothecary shops. A few years later, in 1843, several bottling shops for making soda water opened in New York City. The 1850 census reported 64 plants for making bottled soda water in the United States.

The closures for early soft drink bottles were cork. In 1857 Henry W. Putnam (Cleveland) invented a wire clamp retainer for bottle corks. For the next three decades a wide variety of bottle closures were invented and marketed (Figure A). Collecting examples from this period has long been a common pursuit of some bottle collectors.

Figure A: *Early soft drink bottle closures.*

The 1860 census reported 123 plants for bottling soda water operating in the United States. A year later, in 1861, Dows (Boston) made the first marble soda fountain *and* became the first to bottle ginger ale in the United States.

John Matthews, Jr. (New York) invented and patented the gravitating stopper for soft drink bottles. This was a popular bottle closure for many years.

In 1866 Cantrell & Cochrane (Ireland) entered the American trade with ginger ale bottled in Ireland. The origin of ginger ale is generally credited to Dr. Cantrell who began its manufacture in the early 1850's.

The census for 1870 reported 387 soda water bottling plants operating in the United States. The census also showed 13 firms engaged in the manufacture of soda water apparatus for soda fountains.

In 1873 the internal ball-stoppered bottle closure was patented in the United States by Hiram Codd (England) who had a prior British patent. Breaking the bottles to obtain the marbles in the neck has, as collectors have sadly discovered, reduced the numbers of these historic bottles. A year later, in 1874, Charles de Quillfeldt (New York) patented the "Lightning Stopper." This adaptable closure (used also on fruit jars) was first used in 1875.

In 1876 Charles E. Hires (Philadelphia) began the manufacture of his now famous Hires Root Beer extract. The product was successfully presented at the Centennial Exhibition. Hires products are still on the market today.

Charles G. Hutchinson (Chicago), in 1879, patented a spring-type internal bottle closure which became widely known as the "Hutchinson" stopper. A year later the census reported 512 plants for making bottled soda water in operation in the United States. In the same year James Vernor (Detroit) began making Vernor's Ginger Ale -- a product still on the market today.

In 1881 the Clicquot Club Company (Millis, Massachusetts) began the manufacture of ginger ale and other beverages. Two years later, in 1883, White Rock mineral waters (Waukesha, Wisconsin) were first produced. Both companies still exist today.

In 1885 William Painter (Baltimore) invented a single-use bottle seal which later became known as the "Baltimore Loop Seal." In the same year the Moxie Nerve Food Company (Boston) began the manufacture of its famous soft drink --Moxie. Also created in 1885 was Dr. Pepper (Waco, Texas). This soft drink was perfected by R. S. Lazenby. Dr. Pepper was not bottled, however, until 1888.

Coca-Cola was invented in 1886 by John S. Pemberton (Atlanta). It was first bottled in 1894 by Joseph A. Biedenharn (Vicksburg, Mississippi).

The census of 1890 reported 1,377 plants for making bottled soda water in operation in the United States -- 15 bottling plants in San Francisco and 3 in Los Angeles.

In 1892 William Painter (Baltimore) was granted a patent for the "Crown" cap closure, the one that became standard in the industry. He actually invented it in 1889 while his previous invention, the "Baltimore Loop Seal," was enjoying great popularity.

In 1893 Hires Root Beer (Philadelphia) was first bottled by Crystal Bottling Company. Others were soon bottling the famous root beer.

Three years later, in 1896, Caleb D. Bradham (New Bern, North Carolina) developed "Brad's Drink" which, in 1901, became the now famous Pepsi-Cola. Three years closer to the turn of the century, in 1889, Benjamin F. Thomas and Joseph B. Whitehead were granted the bottling rights to Coca-Cola in most of the continental United States.

The 1900 census reported 2,763 bottling plants operating in the United States.

In 1903 Michael J. Owens (Toledo) invented the first automatic machine for blowing glass bottles. Collectors use this invention to separate hand-blown and semi-automatically blown bottles from automatically blown bottles. Bottle seams go all the way to the top of the bottle on automatically blown bottles. Automatically blown bottles were first placed on the market in 1907.

The 1910 census reported 4,916 bottling plants operating in the United States.

Five years later, in 1915, Alexander Samuelson designed the traditional Coca-Cola "hobble-skirt" bottle. (In 1960 this became the first bottle ever registered as a trademark.) A year later, in 1916, Orange Crush was introduced as a franchised bottled drink by J.M. Thompson (Chicago).

The 1920 census reported 5,194 bottling plants operating in the United States.

Figure B: *Some special Crown cap bottle designs of the 1920's and 1930's. These kinds of soda water bottles are only recently being sought by serious collectors. As the supply dwindles the prices will increase. The average price for such bottles is now $10.*

Between 1920 and 1930, following the lead of The Coca-Cola Company, numerous bottling companies developed and used designed bottles (Figure B). Bottle collectors are only now beginning to take a real interest in specimens from this period.

In 1928 Seven-Up was introduced by C. G. Grigg of the Howdy Company (St. Louis, Missouri). Two years later, in 1930, the soft drink industry reported 7,648 bottling plants were operating in the United States. Bireley's Orange drink was introduced in 1930. Mission Orange, in a black glass bottle, was introduced in 1933.

The year 1934 was a significant one for soft drinks in that Pepsi-Cola introduced the first successful 12-oz. bottle. Also, 1934 was the year that the industry first made use of the "applied color label" which eventually made paper labels as well as bottle/product identification by embossing obsolete. Applied color labels give the appearance of lettering and designs, having been baked on the bottle; the process is still very much in use today.

In 1935 Royal Crown Cola was introduced by the Nehi Corporation. Dad's Old Fashioned Root Beer was introduced two years later in 1937. Squirt was introduced the next year, in 1938.

In 1940 Grapette entered the soft drink field and the industry reported a drop in bottling plants from 7,648 in 1930 to 6,118 in the United States. The number of plants increased to 6,662 by 1950.

Soft drink bottles of the 1800's and early 1900's have long been of collecting interest. Only recently have collectors been seeking bottles of the 1920's, 1930's, and the 1940's. They are unusual in many ways and certainly of historic interest. As these bottles become harder to find collectors will express increasing interest in even more current bottles. It is never too early to collect for eventual historic and monetary value.

(Editor's Note: *Cecil Munsey is a bottle enthusiast who follows the bottle collecting hobby closely. An educator with a Ph. D., he serves as the Coordinator for Planning, Research and Evaluation of the San Diego County Office of Education, San Diego, California. Through the years. Dr. Munsey has researched and written several books for collectors, including:* The Illustrated Guide to the Collectibles of Coca-Cola *(1972);* Disneyana - Walt Disney Collectibles *(1974); and* The Illustrated Guide to Collecting Bottles *(1970), all published by Hawthorn Books, Inc., New York City. He has authored books related to the education field and contributed numerous articles to a wide variety of magazines and journals. The* Illustrated Guide to Collecting Bottles, *a widely used reference for the beginning bottle collector, has been kept in print by E.P. Dutton, Inc. (2 Park Ave., New York), and may be ordered through any book store.)*

*   *   *   *   *

SODAS & SARSAPARILLAS

Anthony, soda, stubby, iron pontil,
  teal green . . . . .75.00 to 100.00
Beard's Mineral Water, F. & B. Boston,
  soda, bulbous lip, emerald green,
  7" h. 15.00
Bertram, Philadelphia, soda, squat,
  dark aqua 20.00
Brownell, New Bedford, soda, iron
  pontil, cobalt blue 125.00
Buffum Sarsaparilla & Lemon, iron
  pontil, blue 350.00
California Soda Works, H. Ficken,
  San Francisco, eagle, blob top,
  aqua .20.00 to 30.00

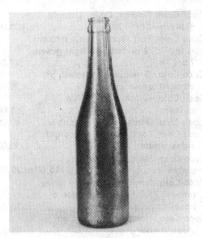

Canada Dry Ginger Ale

Canada Dry, marigold Carnival
  glass . . . . .20.00 to 24.00
Caspar (J. & H.) Cream Soda, applied
  top, aqua, 5½" h. 38.00
Chadsey & Bro., New York, soda,
  bulbous lip, sapphire blue, 6¼" h. . . .40.00
Charles Clark, Charleston, S.C., soda,
  graphite pontil, dark green (dug) 75.00
Coca-Cola, Ada, Okla., Pat'd Dec. 25,
  1923, green 75.00
Coca-Cola, Ardmore, Okla., straight
  sides, clear w/pale greenish tint,
  7½" h. 65.00

Amber Coca-Cola Bottle

Coca-Cola, Baltimore, Maryland,
  straight sides, amber 50.00
Coca-Cola, Biedenharn Candy Co.,
  Vicksburg, Miss. (dug) 125.00
Coca-Cola, Cleveland, Ohio, plain,
  amber 25.00
Coca-Cola, Columbus, Ohio, 6½ oz. 3.25
Coca-Cola, Dayton, Ohio, amber,
  dated 1917 . . . . .75.00
Coca-Cola, Dayton, Tennessee, straight
  sides, amber .225.00

Coca-Cola, Findlay, Ohio, straight
sides, amber 100.00
Coca-Cola, Fort Worth, Tex., straight
sides, 1572 on bottom, light green,
7 5/8" h. 47.50
Coca-Cola, Greenville, Mississippi,
straight arrow, amber 75.00
Coca-Cola, Huntington, W. Va.,
amber 65.00
Coca-Cola, Huntsville, Ala., amber 40.00
Coca-Cola, Louisville, Ky., straight
sides, amber, 7½" h. 55.00
Coca-Cola, Memphis, Tenn.,
amber .... 15.00 to 20.00
Coca-Cola, Nashville, straight sides,
amber, 7½" h. (minor bruise at
base)............................ 25.00
Coca-Cola, Norfolk, Va., straight
sides, amber 35.00
Coca-Cola, Pittsburgh, amber 28.00
Coca-Cola, Portland, Oregon, straight
sides, amber 115.00
Coca-Cola, Portsmouth, Ohio, straight
sides, amber 125.00
Coca-Cola, Salisbury, Maryland, straight
sides, amber 100.00
Coca-Cola, Shelbyville, Tennessee,
straight sides, amber............. 100.00
Coca-Cola, Tullahoma, Tennessee,
straight sides, amber.............. 75.00
Coca-Cola, Verner Springs Water Co.,
Greenville, S.C. 25.00
Coca-Cola, Williamsport, Pa., amber .. 115.00

Cochran & Company's Belfast Ginger Ale
Cochran & Company Belfast Ginger Ale,
embossed & paper label, imported by
Goldberg, Bowen & Company of San
Francisco & Oakland, California -
Sole Agents for Pacific Coast, cork
closure, light green, ca. 1890
(ILLUS.)............................ 65.00

Crawford (M.T.), Hartford, Conn.,
soda, iron pontil, cobalt blue 150.00
Crawford (M.T.), Springfield on front,
Union Glass Works, Phila. on back,
soda, squat, 10-paneled mug base,
iron pontil, cobalt blue 125.00
Cripple Creek Bottling Works, Colo.,
soda, Hutchinson stopper 25.00
Crystal Soda Water Co., Patented Nov.
12, 1872, footed base, blob top,
cobalt blue (small ding on inside lip) .. 60.00

Sun-Colored Purple Soft Drink Bottle
Dan McPolin, Park City, Utah, soda,
Hutchinson stopper, sun-colored purple
(from clear) because of high
manganese content of glass, ca. 1915
(ILLUS.)......................... 250.00
Deegan (J.), Pottsville, Pa., soda,
amber........................... 75.00
Di Filippo & Co., Camden, N.J., soda,
10-sided, blob top, aqua, 9" h. 10.00
Dr. Pepper seltzer bottle, Memphis,
Tn., amber 135.00
Eastern Cider Co., soda, amber 25.00
Eclipse Carbonating Co., St. Louis,
soda, Hutchinson stopper, amber ... 225.00
Einwechter & Fulton, Philada., soda,
wire & cork stopper, green 80.00
Elephant Steam Bottling Works, Bingham,
Ala., soda, embossed elephant,
Hutchinson stopper 17.50
Elliott (H.A.), Idaho Springs, Colo.,
soda, Hutchinson stopper 55.00
Empire Soda Works, Vallejo, Calif,
Hutchinson stopper, aqua 20.00
Engall's Bros., Portland, Me., soda,
squat, aqua 20.00
Fairbanks & Beard, Howard St., Boston,
soda, blue-green 35.00

Ghirardell's Branch Oakland, soda,
   blob top, whittled, cobalt blue 75.00
Grone (S.) & Co., St. Louis, Mo., soda,
   long neck, blob top, aqua 5.00
Gypsum City Bottling Works, Ft.
   Dodge, soda, blob top 8.50
H.L. & J.W. Brown, Hartford, Ct.,
   soda, pontil, dark black olive 75.00
Hamacua Soda Works, Hutchinson
   stopper, aqua-blue. 50.00

Henry Kuck Soda Bottle

Henry Kuck, Savannah, Ga., soda,
   cork closure, blue, ca. 1890 (ILLUS.) .175.00
Henry Woertz, Elgin, Illinois, soda,
   Hutchinson stopper, aqua 6.00

1915 Hires Root Beer Bottle

Hires Root Beer, Philadelphia, Pennsylvania, Crown cap, light green,
   ca. 1915 (ILLUS.) 35.00

1920 Hires Root Beer

Hires Root Beer, Philadelphia, Penn-
   sylvania, embossed, Crown cap,
   deep amber, ca. 1920 (ILLUS.) 30.00
Huberty (J.) & Co., Canton, O.,
   soda, squat, aqua, 7½" h. 75.00
Hygeia Soda Works, Kahului, soda,
   Hutchinson stopper, aqua . . .45.00 to 65.00
Jacksons Napa Soda, aqua, 7½" h. 12.00
John Ryan Excelsior Ginger Ale,
   amber, 1870s .40.00
John Ryan Excelsior Sodaworks, 1866,
   Savannah, Georgia, blob top, cobalt
   blue. 25.00
John Ryder, Mt. Holly, N.J., soda,
   blob top 45.00
Johnston & Co., Philadelphia, soda,
   squat, dark aqua 20.00
Jones's Sarsaparilla, Williamsport, Pa.,
   aqua 125.00
Kayo, soda, pictures Kayo holding
   bottle on clear. 20.00
Kimball & Co., soda, blob top, blue 60.00
Knickerbocker (W.P.) Soda Water, 164
   18th St., N.Y., 10-sided, iron pontil,
   cobalt blue 135.00
Kroger Bros., Butte, Mt. in oval slug
   plate, soda, Hutchinson stopper,
   aqua, 6½" h. 550.00
McLanglin (A.), Philada., soda, green . .65.00
Mellor & Sons, Manchester, soda,
   w/Codd's marble-stoppered closure,
   clear, ca. 1890 . . . . .25.00
Morimoto Soda Works, Fresno, Calif.,
   vertically embossed Japanese characters center, Hutchinson stopper,
   1890s. 75.00
Morton (W.), Trenton, N.J., soda,
   monogram on reverse, saratoga
   green 45.00

Moxie Bottle

Moxie, embossed & paper label, Boston,
Massachusetts, Crown cap, light
green, ca. 1910 (ILLUS.) 20.00

Orange Crush Bottle

Orange Crush, Chicago, Illinois, soda,
ribbed, Crown cap, clear, ca. 1920
(ILLUS.) 20.00
Orange Crush, soda, ribbed, Crown
cap, emerald green, Pat. July 20,
1920, 7 oz. 15.00
Ormsbyd (L.), soda, blob top, blue 60.00
Pablo (S.), Elysian Fields St. N.O., soda,
squat, embossed eagle, iron pontil,
blue-aqua 45.00
Pacific & Puget Sound Soda Works,
Seattle, Hutchinson stopper 150.00
Pacific Soda Works, Classen & Co.,
San Francisco, blob top, aqua-green . .45.00

Pepsi Cola, P.C. in script center, green,
12 oz. 12.00
Pepsi Cola, Boston, Mass., amber 40.00

1890s Bottle with Codd Stopper

Roberts (J.), Castleford, England,
embossed castle turret w/flag,
w/Codd's marble-stoppered closure,
light green, ca. 1890 (ILLUS.) 35.00
Ross & Co. Trademark, Weston Super-
mare, soda, w/Codd's marble-stoppered
closure, clear, ca. 1890 . . . . .25.00
Salida Bottling Works, Salida, Colo.,
soda, Hutchinson stopper 35.00
Samuel C. Palmer, Belfast Ginger Ale,
Washington, D.C. 10.00

San Francisco Glass Works Bottle

San Francisco Glass Works, soda, cork
closure, light green, ca. 1890
(ILLUS.) 200.00

Schwertfecer (F.L.), Muscatine, Iowa,
soda, blob top, pale green, 6" h. 35.00
Seedorf (H.C.), Charleston, soda,
graphite pontil, square slug plate,
blue. 145.00
Seitz & Bro., Easton, Pa., soda, squat,
pontil, cobalt blue 75.00
Seitz & Bro., Easton, Pa., soda, squat,
pontil, cornflower blue 50.00

"7-Up Settles the Stomach"

Seven-Up Lithiated Lemon Soda, Salt
Lake City, Utah, embossed & paper
label ("Seven-Up Settles the Stomach -
For Hospital or Home Use - 7-Up
is more than a mixer. It blends out
the harsh features. Dispels Hang-
over...takes the 'ouch' out of
grouch"), Crown cap, clear, ca. 1930
(ILLUS.) 50.00

Shaw's Wakefield Soda

Shaw's (E.P.) Wakefield, soda, emerald
green, threaded lip, 9¼" h. (ILLUS.) . .90.00
Skodas Sarsaparilla, amber . . . .20.00 to 35.00
Smith (A.P.), Charleston, S.C., soda,
graphite pontil, deep blue (small
lip chip - dug). 125.00
Smith (L.C.), soda, cobalt blue 50.00
South Range Bottling Works, South
Range, Mich., soda, Hutchinson
stopper, aqua .7.00
Sullivan Bros. (fancy monogram),
Providence, R.I., soda, Lightning
stopper w/clamp, clear, 9¼" h. 2.50
Taylor & Co. Soda Waters, San
Francisco, Eureka, pontil, cobalt
blue (dug) 65.00
Twitchell T Philada., soda, smooth
bottom, green .80.00
Union Glass Works, soda, slug plate,
blob top, green 30.00

Unmarked 12-Sided Bottle

Unmarked 12-sided soda, Hutchinson
stopper, amber, ca. 1905 (ILLUS.) . . .150.00
W. Morton, Trenton, N.J., soda, mono-
gram on reverse, Saratoga green 45.00
W.W. Lake, Jackson, Miss., soda,
Hutchinson stopper, aqua, 7" h. 12.50
Western Soda Works, embossed deer's
head w/large antlers, Hutchinson
stopper, blue-aqua. 28.00
Wilson & Bates, King St., Glossop,
Kindly Return Bottle, soda,
embossed dragon, internal screw
threads, aqua, 8½" h. 17.50
Yagers Sarsaparilla, yellow amber
(small lip chips) 30.00
Ziegler's Soda Works, Tuscon, Ariz.,
10-sided mug base, Hutchinson
stopper, aqua .138.00

(End of Special Focus)

WHISKEY & OTHER SPIRITS

Sheboygan, Wisconsin Beer Bottle

Ale, stoneware pottery, grey w/cobalt
blue swash over incised lettering on
sides & at round "doughnut" top
opening 40.00

Beer, "Eldorado Brewing Company,
Stockton, California," honey amber,
qt. 55.00

Beer, "Elgin Eagle," amber 10.00

Beer, "Foxhead 400," enameled label,
amber, 8 oz. 12.00

Beer, "Groesch," embossed label,
amber, porcelain stopper 5.00

Beer, "Gutsch Brewing Co., Sheboygan, Wis. USA," embossed, paneled
base, round sides, amber, 8¾" h.
(ILLUS.) 17.50

Beer, "Honolulu Brewing Co., Honolulu, T.H.," blob top, aqua, qt. 35.00

Beer, "Indianapolis Brewing Co.,"
embossed, amber, twenty-four 6 oz.
bottles in original wooden crate 57.50

Beer, "John Rapp & Son," amber, pt. 20.00

Beer, "Kings," embossed & original
paper labels, amber, picnic, 20" h. ... 90.00

Beer, "Lucky," enameled label, amber,
8 oz. 9.00

Beer, "North Star," enameled label,
amber, 8 oz. 12.00

Beer, "Old Timers," enameled label,
amber, 8 oz. 12.00

Beer, "Rolling Rock," enameled label,
amber, 8 oz. 9.00

Beer, "Schlitz," amber, 1954, 16 oz. 22.00

Beer, "Schlitz Brewing Co.," embossed
"Not To Be Sold," amber 60.00

Beer, "Schlitz," royal ruby, qt. 30.00

Beer, "Walters," enameled label,
8 oz. 12.00

Beer, stoneware pottery, various
impressed marks, qt., each 40.00

Case gin, "Blankenheym & Nolet,"
sloping collar, olive green, qt. 26.50

Case gin, "C.W. Herwig," embossed
king's crown, forest green, 9¾" h. ... 26.00

Case gin, "Vanderveer Medicated Gin
or Real Schnapps," embossed on 3
sides, smooth base, ca. 1860, half-
pint 65.00

Gin, "Charles London Cordial," teal
green, pt. 35.00

Gin, "Gordon's," olive green, pt. 22.00

Gin, "London Jockey Clubhouse,"
embossed horse & jockey, iron
pontil, citron 335.00

Gin, "Peters," embossed dog, green ... 45.00

Gin, "Van Den Herch & Co.," applied
seal w/bell, olive green, 10½" h. 45.00

Schnapps, "Udolpho Wolfe's," pontil,
olive green 75.00

Sloe gin, "Baird's Special," lady's leg
shape, amber, qt. 30.00

Whiskey, "A.M. Bininger & Co., 38
Broadway, N.Y., Old Kentucky
Bourbon," barrel-shaped w/rings
above marked center band, golden
amber, 8" h. 175.00

Whiskey, "A.M. Bininger," cannon-
shaped, honey amber 308.00

Whiskey, "Cuckoo Whiskey,"
embossed bird, clear, qt. (some
stain) 12.50

Early Whiskey Bottles

Whiskey, "Chapin & Gore Sour Mash,
1867," barrel-shaped, amber (ILLUS.
left) 75.00

Whiskey, flask w/embossed 5-point
star within lozenge-shaped panel,
amber (ILLUS. right) 30.00

Whiskey, "Chapin & Gore," embossed
"Hawley Glass Co." on base, inside-
threaded top, amber, 4/5 qt. 75.00

Whiskey, "Chestnut Grove," ewer form
w/applied handle,
amber ....110.00 to 150.00
Whiskey, "The F. Chevalier Castle
Whiskey, San Francisco, Cal.,"
amber, 4/5 qt......................40.00
Whiskey, "Cordova Rye Whiskey -
Wood, Polard & Co., Boston,"
etched label on clear, square........22.00
Whiskey, "J.H. Cutter," bar bottle,
fluted neck, clear 25.00
Whiskey, "R.B. Cutter's Pure Bourbon,"
handled jug, pontil, amber.........175.00

"Deer Lick" Whiskey Flask

Whiskey, "Deer Lick," clear flask
w/paper label, pt. (ILLUS.) 10.00
Whiskey, "Duffy Crescent (moon)
Saloon," pig bottle, sheared mouth,
golden amber 660.00
Whiskey, "Duffy Malt," golden amber,
pt...............................15.00
Whiskey, "Duffy Malt - Rochester,"
amber, qt.........................8.00
Whiskey, "Fulton Kentucky," jug,
earthenware pottery, 3-gal.........195.00
Whiskey, "Golden Gate All Rye,"
square, embossed girl on moon,
yellow-amber, qt..................45.00
Whiskey, "Golden Wedding," marigold
Carnival glass, pt. 10.00
Whiskey, "Green Mountain," qt.......18.00
Whiskey, "The Hayner Distilling Co.,
Dayton, St. Louis, Atlanta, St. Paul
Distillers," amber, qt. 21.50
Whiskey, "The Hayner Distilling Co.,
Dayton, St. Louis, Atlanta, St. Paul
Distillers," clear, qt................10.00
Whiskey, "Jessie Moore," blob top,
yellow-amber 60.00
Whiskey, "Little Brown Jug, Old 1869
Rye Whiskey, Distilled by S.T. Suit
Distilling Co., Suitland, Md.," brown-
amber, qt. 75.00
Whiskey, "Medford," amber label
under glass, blob top 40.00

Whiskey, "Mohawk," Indian warrior,
rolled lip, yellow-amber, 12¼" h. ...522.50
Whiskey, "Old Continental," acorn-
shaped jug, yellow-amber, 3½" h. ...950.00
Whiskey, "Old Joe Gideon Whiskey,
Gideon Bro. Mono.," slug plate,
amber, fifth 15.00
Whiskey, "Old Joel - Oldest Distillery
in Anderson Co, Founded 1818,
McBrayer, Ky.," ½ gal..............75.00
Whiskey, "Old Quaker," flask 10.00
Whiskey, "H. Pharazyn," figural Indian
warrior, rolled lip, yellow-amber ...687.50
Whiskey, "Roehling & Schutz," cabin-
shaped, tooled mouth, smooth base,
amber, 9¾" h. 88.00
Whiskey, "H.A. Schunk Pure Family
Liquors, Dubuque, Iowa," ½ gal......55.00
Whiskey, "Schwartz, Klein Co.
Distillers, Wholesalers, 401 E.
Federal Cor. Basin, Youngstown,
Ohio," gal........................42.00
Whiskey, "Star," vertical ribbed jug
w/applied handle, light amber 400.00
Whiskey, "Willington Glass Works,"
cylinder, dark amber 55.00
Wine, "PC Brooks Wine 1820," deep
olive amber, pontil, 10¼" h. 176.00
Wine, "Klein & Pauntz - Wholesale,
Retail Wine & Liquors - Minneapolis,
Minn." ½ pt. 50.00
Wine, mallet-shaped w/high kick-up,
applied lip, olive amber, slightly
misshapen, mid-18th c. 195.00
Wine, olive green glass, applied smug
top, kick-up bottom, rough pontil,
Revolutionary War period, 10" h......75.00

Wine Demijohn

Wine demijohn, open pontil, olive
green, 17½" h. (ILLUS.) 105.00
Wine, demijohn, free-blown, olive
green, in wicker cover, ca. 1820,
19½" h. 150.00

(End of Bottle Section)

BOY SCOUT ITEMS

Boy Scout Poster

Boy Scout rules and regulations, hand-books and accouterments have changed with the times. Early items associated with this movement are now being collected. A sampling follows.

Beadwork loom for Indian beadwork
   project, original box, 1930s $25.00
Book, "How Book of Scouting," 1929 .....9.00
Booklet, "Merit Badge Life Saving,"
   1944 ....5.00
Bookmark & letter opener, "Cub Scout"
   insignia, original package 5.00
Bugle, brass ....17.50 to 49.00
Calendar, 1931, "Scout Memories,"
   Norman Rockwell, 16" w., 34" h. 95.00
Calendar, 1967, Norman Rockwell
   illustration 2.50
Camp set, knife, fork & spoon in case
   w/emblem, ca. 1940, set 15.00
Cup, tin, folding-type, eagle at top 15.00
Diary for 1928 (unused) 20.00
First Aid kit, 1933 ....12.00 to 22.00
First Aid kit, tin box w/contents,
   1942 ....10.00
Flannel square, "Honor Unit - 1857-
   1957," purple & yellow, bear center,
   9 x 7".........................50.00
Flashlight, brass 12.50
Game of Scouting, 1928 ....50.00
Handbook, 1937, Norman Rockwell
   cover.........................15.00
Handbook, 1948, Norman Rockwell
   cover..........................6.00
Hatchet...........................19.00
Jacket patch, "1964 Jamboree" 15.00
Knickers, cotton, khaki, 1940 ....20.00

Knife, pocket-type, Cub Scout emblem,
   Camillus Cutlery 10.00
Knife, pocket-type, "Imperial," in original
   box, 1927 ....25.00
Knife, sheath-type w/scabbard, 7½" l. ..20.00
Knife, sheath-type, Remington No.
   RH51 ....60.00
Magazine, "Scouting," 1924 or 1927, bound
   volume, each....................12.00
Manual, 1931, First Class Helps 20.00
Membership card, 1911, tri-fold........25.00
Neckerchief, "1969 Jamboree" 6.00
Neckerchief slide, brass, embossed
   Statue of Liberty 16.00
Pamphlet, Merit Badge series, "Pigeon
   Raising," 1934 ....8.50
Poster, "Come on Everybody," Norman
   Rockwell, 10½ x 17" 35.00
Poster, "U.S.A. Bonds - Weapons for
   Liberty," J.C. Leyendecker, 1918,
   29¾ x 19 5/8" (ILLUS.) .....160.00 to 200.00
Ring, sterling silver, "Cub Scout,"
   1920s..........................10.00
Uniform buttons, celluloid, 2 different
   styles, pr.........................10.00
Uniform shirt, size 10-12, 1920-30 .....20.00
Watch fob, early 1900s...............20.00
Yearbook for 1915, 243 pp......18.00 to 25.00
Yearbook for 1928 ....10.00
Yearbook for 1930 ....6.00

BREWERIANA

Cone-Top Beer Cans

Beer is still popular in this country but the number of breweries has greatly diminished. More than 1,900 breweries were in operation in the 1870s but we find fewer than 40 supplying the demands of the country a century later. The small local brewery has either been absorbed by a larger company or forced to close, unable to meet the competition. Advertising items used to promote the various breweries, especially those issued prior to prohibition, now attract an ever growing number of collectors. The breweriana items listed are a sampling of the many items available. Also see BOT-TLES, CORKSCREWS, SIGNS & SIGN-BOARDS and TRAYS.

Ale set: tankard pitcher & 4 mugs;
  pottery, "Leisey Brewing Co." in gilt
  on green glazed ground, 1880,
  5 pcs. $240.00
Bank, "Metz Beer," barrel-shaped 15.00
Bank, "Pabst Blue Ribbon," tin, round 8.50
Beer case, "Goetz Co., St. Joseph,
  Mo.," wood & tin, 20¼ x 12½",
  10¾" h. 45.00
Beer glass, "American Brew. Co.,
  Rochester, New York," clear glass
  w/eagle on shield pictured 45.00
Beer glass, "Bartholomay," clear glass
  w/winged wheel logo 18.00
Beer glass, "W.F. Lemp," clear glass,
  stemmed 24.00
Beer glass, "G. Piel Bros., Real Ger-
  man Lager Beer," clear glass
  w/frosted lettering 37.50
Beer glass, "West End Brewery," clear
  glass, Miss Liberty draped in flag
  pictured 45.00
Beer growler (pail used for carry-outs),
  tin, w/lid & wire bail handle, 3¾" d.,
  3" h. 10.00
Bottle opener, "East India Ale," white
  label, scimitar-shaped 25.00
Bottle opener, "Esslinger's Beer" 12.50
Bottle opener, "Fehr's," wooden bottle-
  shaped handle 12.00
Bottle opener, "Globe Brewing," metal,
  flat figure girl wading in water 25.00
Bottle opener, "Metz Beer," metal,
  key-shaped 25.00
Bottle opener, "Molson's Ale," celluloid
  handle 15.00
Bottle opener, "St. Pauli Beer, A Great
  German Beer," metal, embossed St.
  Pauli girl holding beer mug, 4 1/8" . . . 25.00
Bottle opener, "Schlitz Beer," wooden
  bottle-shaped handle, 3½" l. 16.00
Bottle opener, "Stegmaier's Gold
  Medal Beer," 1933 . . . . 9.00
Bottle opener w/corkscrew, "Eldredge
  Brew. Co., Portsmouth, N.H.," brass,
  bottle-shaped 35.00
Calendar, 1897, "Iroquois Brewing
  Co.," 12 x 17" 250.00
Calendar, 1916, "Pabst Malt Extract,"
  beautiful lady pictured 65.00
Calendar, 1972, "Schlitz Brewing Co.,"
  circus parade pictured 10.00
Can, cone-top, "Leinenkugels,"
  12 oz. 15.00
Can, cone-top, "Neuweilers," 12 oz. . . . 64.00
Can, cone-top, "Oertels 92," 12 oz. 20.00
Can, cone-top, "Kuebler Cream Ale,"
  32 oz. 500.00
Can, flat-top, "Kruegers Cream Ale,"
  12 oz. 65.00

Can, flat-top, "Scotch Thistle Brand
  Ale," New York 130.00

Boston Beer Co. Clock

Clock, wall-type, "Boston Beer Co.,"
  gilt & polychrome reverse painting
  on glass depicting a keg lid w/bar-
  ley & hops wreath, 8-day lever move-
  ment, spring driven, New Haven
  Clock Co., ca. 1900, 14" d. (ILLUS.) . . . 605.00
Clock, "Potosi Brewing Co., Holiday
  Beer," glass & metal 65.00
Coaster, "Fehr's," cardboard, King &
  Queen pictured 40.00
Coaster, "King's Beer" 35.00
Corkscrew, "Anheuser-Busch," chrome-
  plated brass, bottle-shaped, dated
  1897 . . . . 35.00
Corkscrew, "Drink Lemp, St. Louis,"
  brass, bullet-shaped 27.50
Corkscrew, "C. Birkhofer Brew. Co.,
  Minneapolis, Minnesota," wooden
  handle 38.00
Counter display, "Pabst Blue Ribbon
  Beer," metal, bartender holding 4
  glasses of beer . . . . 65.00 to 80.00
Counter display figure, "Mr. Pickwick -
  Ale That Is Ale," papier mache 35.00
Counter display jar, "Piel Bros.,"
  metal, keg-shaped beer foam
  scraper holder, elves decor 40.00
Door push plate, "Pabst," tin 25.00
Fan, "Stroh's Beer," cardboard, tavern
  scene 70.00
Fishing manual, "Grain Belt Beer,"
  1940s 7.50

Early Foam Scrapers

Foam scrapers, "Budweiser" &
"Anheuser-Busch," celluloid, 1890s,
each (ILLUS.) . . . . .25.00 to 30.00
Foam scraper, "Berghoff Beer,"
celluloid 18.00
Foam scraper, "Dobler," celluloid 25.00
Foam scraper, "Engesser Beer," plastic . .9.00
Foam scraper, "Hedrick," plastic 6.00
Foam scraper, "Narragansett Beer,"
celluloid 18.00
Foam scraper, "Pabst Blue Ribbon,"
celluloid . . . . .18.00 to 25.00
Foam scraper, "Quandt Brew. Co.,
Troy, N.Y.," celluloid, red lettering
on cream 35.00
Foam scraper, "Ruppert Mellow Light
Beer-Ale," plastic 12.00
Key chain w/fob, "Schlitz," brass,
barrel-shaped .10.00
Letter opener, "Budweiser," brass,
Anheuser-Busch eagle on end 45.00
Salt & pepper shakers, "Blatz Pilsner
Beer," small amber glass bottles
w/labels, pr. 10.00
Sign, "Carling's Ale," tin, "Nine Pints
of the Law," w/nine Keystone cops
imbibing 75.00
Sign, "Coors Beer," tin, riverboat
scene 446.00
Sign, "Gulf Brewing Co., Sparkling
Ale, Utica, N.Y.," reverse painting
on glass, oak frame, 32 x 26" 395.00
Sign, "Hamm's," revolving, waterfalls,
canoe & camp site 650.00
Sign, "Harvard Beer," lithographed tin,
young woman seated at a table in
a Turkish interior, pouring glass of
beer, original wooden frame, ca.
1910, 35¾ x 26¾" 605.00
Sign, "Hudepohl Beer," self-framed
tin, old man smoking corn cob pipe
w/bottle on table 185.00
Sign, "Kato Beer," convex glass, eagle
pictured, 15" d. 125.00
Sign, "Old Towne Ale," reverse
painting on glass, 1930s 70.00
Sign, "Patrick Henry Fine Beer," self-
framed tin, Patrick Henry before
Virginia Assembly, artist-signed,
17 x 13" 195.00
Sign, "Progress Beer," cardboard,
black men playing cards, 25 x 19" 97.50
Sign, "White Rock Beer," tin, girl
leaning on tiger, pre-prohibition 245.00
Stein, "Bartholomay," Mettlach 265.00
Stein, "Wiedemann Brewing Co.,"
Rookwood 125.00
Tape measure, "Phoenix Beer,"
"Buffalo's Famous Brew" 8.50
Tap knob, "Gettleman Rathskellar" 32.00
Thermometer, "Rochester Brewing,"
12" d. 49.00
Thimble, "Old Union Pale Beer,"
aluminum. 8.00

Tray, "Bartholomay Beer, Rochester,"
brass, 12" d. .95.00
Vienna Art tin plate, "Anheuser-
Busch," portrait of girl,
1905 .40.00 to 60.00
Watch fob, "Blatz Beer," barrel-
shaped 67.50

BRONZES

Lion & Serpent

*Small bronzes, used as decorative
adjuncts in today's homes, continue to
attract interest. Particularly appealing to
collectors today are "les animaliers" of the
19th century French school of sculptors who
turned to animals for their subject-matter.
These, together with figures in the Art Deco
and Art Nouveau taste, are very popular
with collectors and available in a wide price
range. Also see ART DECO and ART
NOUVEAU.*

Barrias, Louis-Ernest, figure of Nature
unveiling herself before Science,
raising a silvered cloak from her
head & shoulders, scarab holding
her gilt robes below her breast,
ca. 1900, 23" h. . . . . . .$4,125.00 to 4,950.00
Barye, Antoine-Louis, group of lion
crushing a coiling serpent w/his right
paw, brown patina, late 19th c.,
14" l. (ILLUS.) .605.00
Barye, Antoine-Louis, model of a tiger
walking, greenish black patina, late
19th c., 15" l. .880.00
Boucher, Jean, figure of a Chinese
"Sorceress," clothed in elaborate
headdress & flowing brocade robe,
opening a vaporous incense burner,
standing upon a coiling serpent,
black patina, ca. 1913, 26½" h. . . .2,640.00
Cain, Auguste-Nicholas, group of a
partridge feeding her 8 young
clustered about a rocky outcrop &
w/some attacking a snail, brown
patina, late 19th c., 18¼" h. 990.00

Carrier-Belleuse, Albert-Ernest, figure of a maiden stepping through rushes, an overturned water jug at her feet, parcel gilt-bronze, late 19th c., 18" h. 880.00

Carrier-Belleuse, Albert-Ernest, figure of a female w/upswept hair dancing w/her left leg raised, wearing clinging robes w/lengths of drapery falling from her upheld arms, golden brown patina, early 20th c., 27" h.........................1,980.00

Carrier-Belleuse, Albert-Ernest, figure of a woman chained to a stump w/shield & quiver at her side & foot resting on her helmet, brown to golden bronze patina, late 19th c., 29½" h.......................1,870.00

"Indiscreet" after Chiparus

Chiparus, Demetre, entitled "Indiscreet," figure of a woman wearing a floppy hat & full skirt, admonishing a bird perched on her outstretched arm, gilt-bronze & ivory, brown onyx socle, ca. 1925, restorations, 17½" h. (ILLUS.)...............2,530.00

Chiparus, Demetre, figure of a Cabaret dancer, cold-painted bronze & ivory, grey marble base, overall 23½" h.......................13,200.00

Chiparus, Demetre, figure of an Egyptian dancer, standing w/arms raised, silvered-bronze, truncated ochre & verde antico marble plinth, ca. 1925, overall 27¼" h.........2,860.00

Chiparus, Demetre, figure group, "Persian Dance," male & female dancer, silvered & gilt bronze & ivory, elaborate brown & green marble base, overall 20¾" h......8,800.00

Colin, George, figure of Icarus w/arms outstretched, strapped to large

feathered wings, leaning forward in position for flight, rocky base, golden brown & reddish patina, ca. 1900, 28" h. 1,980.00

Dalou, Aime-Jules, figure of a mermaid rising from a wavecrest, holding a lyre as she throws back her tresses, rich brown patina, late 19th c., 13¾" h. 3,410.00

Delabrierre, Paul-Edouard, group of a Retriever dog & 2 pheasants, dog on rocky outcrop, his prey hidden below, brown & golden brown patina, late 19th c., 18" l..........1,045.00

Dumaige, Etienne-Henri, figure of a classically garbed young woman holding an oil lamp, late 19th c., 27" h........................1,540.00

Duret, Francisque-Joseph, figure of a young Neapolitan boy, wearing gathered breeches, dancing the tarantella on a ground scattered w/crustaceans, brown patina, late 19th c., 38" h................3,300.00

Fratin, Christophe, group of 3 wolves attacking a cow, black-brown patina, shaped black wood plinth, late 19th c., 12¼" l. bronze........550.00

Fremiet, Emmanuel, equestrian figure, Louis D'Orleans on horse, rectangular leaf-molded base, coppery brown patina, late 19th c., 20" h. 935.00

Frolich, Finn-Haekon, bust of a woman, her long tresses knotted loosely at the back of her neck, on a socle cast w/blossoms & the title, brown patina, ca. 1899, 24¾" h.........1,100.00

Gaudex, Adrien-Etienne, figure of Marguerite, wearing Renaissance clothing & holding daisy in one hand, golden-brown patina, circular base w/attached plaque, late 19th c., 24½" h......................1,650.00

Bust of Voltaire after Houdon

Houdon, Jean-Antoine, bust of Voltaire
smiling, turned socle, brown patina,
late 19th c., overall 18" h. (ILLUS.) 715.00
Kauba, Carl, figure of an Indian,
6" h. 350.00
Mene, Pierre-Jules, model of a bull,
4 x 2½". 350.00
Mene, Pierre-Jules, model of a Cari-
bou deer standing, rectangular
base w/detailed terrain, 7½" l.,
5" h. 345.00
Mene, Pierre-Jules, model of a stal-
lion standing, dark brown patina,
rectangular base w/detailed terrain,
9½" l., 7½" h. 595.00
Moreau, Mathurin, figure of Psyche
w/a length of drapery about her
waist, seated on a rocky base cast
w/leafage, brown patina, late
19th c., 21" h. 1,100.00
Moreau, Mathurin, figure of a barefoot
woman in mobcap harvesting grapes
on rocky base, hoisting a heavy
basket of grapes, brown patina,
late 19th c., 27½" h. 2,310.00

Nymph Figure after Moreau

Moreau, Mathurin, figure of a partly
clad nymph, standing before a
grotto-like formation, brown patina,
shaped onyx base, late 19th c.,
31" h. (ILLUS.). 2,530.00
Picault, Emile Louis, figure of a nude
female, "A L'ideal," standing before
a garden wall cast w/flowering leafage & a lyre, golden brown patina,
late 19th c., 41" h. 3,190.00
Villanis, Emanuelle, figure of Melodie
in classical dress seated on rocky
base, holding lyre & looking off
w/dreamy gaze, golden green &
brown patina, ca. 1900, 24¾" h. 1,210.00

BROWNIE COLLECTIBLES

Brownie Figural Picture Frame

*The Brownies were creatures of fantasy
created by Palmer Cox, artist-author, in
1887. Early in this century, numerous
articles with depictions of or in the shape of
Brownies appeared. Also see BANKS.*

Ash tray, china, "Cox Brownies," R.S.
Germany, 1913 . . . .$45.00
Book, "The Brownie Year Book," by
Palmer Cox, 1895 . . . . .75.00
Book, "Brownies & Prince Florimel,"
by Palmer Cox, 1918, first edition 45.00
Book, "The Monk's Victory," by Palmer
Cox, Brownies decor cover, 1901 . . . . .25.00
Creamer, china, Brownies decor,
4½" h. 65.00
Demitasse spoon, silverplate, enam-
eled Brownie handle 29.00
Figure, Brownie Canadian, Chinaman
or Soldier, chromolithographed
paper on wood, stands in wooden
base, verse on back, 1892, 12" h.,
each 35.00
Fork, child's, silverplate, w/Brownie
on handle. 15.00
Game, "Horseshoes," two 11½" d. tin
pads w/Brownies pitching horseshoes decor & 4 rubber horseshoes
marked "Brownies" . . . . .40.00 to 65.00
Paint book, Whitman No. 669-10 . . . . . .25.00
Patent medicine bottle, "Little
Brownies Laxative - works while you
sleep," original box 20.00
Picture frame, bronze-finish pot metal,
cast w/full figure Dude, Canadian,
Highlander & Irishman Brownies
perched on sides & top, free-standing
frame on rococo base, 5¾" h.,
together w/lithographed scene of
the Brownie in two string hammock,
11 7/8 x 9 3/8", 2 pcs. (ILLUS. of
picture frame) 302.50

Plate, china, scalloped rim w/Brownies
(16) decor border, 2 Brownies center,
colorful, Limoges, 8½" d. 85.00
Ruler, Brownies decor on front, advertisement for "Mrs. Winslow's Sooth-
ing Syrup" reverse 20.00
Salt & pepper shakers w/original tops,
white opaline glass, Brownies decor,
Mt. Washington, 2½" h., pr........475.00
Salt & pepper shakers w/original tops,
white opaline glass, w/Brownies
swimming & running on the beach,
Mt. Washington, 4" h., pr..........290.00
Sheet music, "Dance of the Brownies,"
1895 ....30.00
Sheet music, "Frolic of the Brownies,"
1896 ....30.00
Soda bottle, embossed Brownies
decor 45.00
Stickpin, Brownie Uncle Sam 18.00
Thimble holder, silverplate, Brownie
on rectangular base 45.00
Toy, "Movie," tin, 3-hole w/cardboard
pictures of Brownies 45.00

surrounded by enameled florals,
4½ x 2½"...........................75.00
Belt buckle, lady's, pink-tinged
mother-of-pearl shell, each section
1½" l. (ILLUS.).....................12.50
Belt buckle, lady's, white jade, carved
standing dragon facing Foo dog head,
China, late 19th c., 3½" l. 100.00
Belt buckles, man's, bronze, 2-part,
in the form of coins w/bats, dragon
head hooks, China, late 19th c.,
4¼" l., set of 3 ....50.00
Belt buckle, man's, silver, 2-part
w/dagger closure, Russian, ca. 1890,
2¾ x 2"..........................165.00
Shoe buckles, paste diamond brilliants
closely set in two circles, pr..........52.00
Shoe buckles, rhinestone-studded, pr...12.00
Shoe buckles, silvered metal, Art
Nouveau style set w/center cameo,
pr................................52.00

BUCKLES

Lady's Belt Buckle

*When it was the height of popularity
between 1650 and 1800, the lowly buckle
was considered a fashionable status symbol
denoting the wearer's wealth by the
material from which it was made. Gold,
silver, pewter, iron and tin buckles were
made in a variety of forms. Though buckle
collectors strive to acquire at least a few
18th century examples, they also seek out
later buckles in desirable forms that are
more affordable. Listed by type as well as
material, the following buckles sold within
recent months.*

Belt buckle, Civil War uniform, Con-
federate States Army.............$65.00
Belt buckle, lady's, cloisonne, vase,
florals & incense burner decor,
China, 3" oval 235.00
Belt buckle, lady's, cloisonne, lotus
blossoms, etc., on black, 2¾ x
1 5/8" 50.00
Belt buckle, lady's, gold-washed brass,
Art Nouveau lady w/flowing hair

BUSTER BROWN COLLECTIBLES

Buster Brown Shoe Trees

*Buster Brown was a comic strip created
by Richard Outcault in the New York
Herald in 1902. It was subsequently
syndicated and numerous objects depicting
Buster (and often his dog, Tige) were
produced. Also see BANKS.*

Baby's rattle, sterling silver, Buster in
relief on side, Tige reverse, small ...$45.00
Blackboard portfolio, folding-type, red
leather-like cover, Buster & Tige
decor 75.00
Bone dishes, china, oblong, Buster
Brown & Tige decor, set of 6 ....40.00
Book, "Buster Brown Abroad," by
Richard F. Outcault, 53 black & white
illustrations by author, 1904 copyright,
8½ x 10¼" ....45.00 to 65.00
Book, "Buster Brown Dictionary," 1927,
324 pp. 32.50
Book, "Buster Brown on His Travels,"
by Richard Outcault, 1909, full color,
large size 40.00

Camera, box-type, ca. 1916 . . . . .21.50
Card game, "Buster Brown at the
   Circus w/the Yellow Kid" 225.00
Coloring book 30.00
Creamer, china, Buster Brown & Tige
   decor, large 30.00
Drawing book, advertising "Sterling
   Player Pianos," 1906 (unused) 25.00
Figurine, bisque, 2" h. 30.00
Hatchet (or camping ax) . . . . . . .60.00 to 80.00
Knife, fork & spoon, silverplate, set 65.00
Laundry bag, cloth, 1920s 58.00
Magazine sheet, "Saturday Evening
   Post," 1920, color advertisement
   w/Buster Brown 7.00
Mirror, hand-type, silverplate, small . . .25.00
Mirror, pocket-type, advertising
   "Buster Brown Bread" 40.00
Mustard can, "Buster Brown Mustard,"
   w/lithographed paper label of Buster
   & Tige, 2½" h. .50.00
Paper dolls, Buster Brown w/four
   outfits, Tige w/single clown hat,
   original envelope 350.00
Pinback button, advertising "Buster
   Brown Hose Supports," 1" d. 20.00
Pinback button, advertising "Buster
   Brown Bread," w/Buster &
   Tige .15.00 to 20.00
Plate, china, Buster Brown decor,
   marked "Germany," 7" d. 39.50
Pocket knife, lady's leg shape 55.00
Postcard calendars, 1910, September &
   October, pr. 25.00
Shoes, miniature, original box, pr. 15.00
Shoe trees, celluloid, w/Buster
   Brown & Tige, 9½" l., pr. (ILLUS.) 26.00
Stockings, black cotton, w/original
   Buster Brown & Tige label, size 7,
   pr. 10.00

Buster Brown Tea Set

Tea set: cov. teapot, creamer, cov.
   sugar bowl & 4 c/s; china, Buster
   Brown, Tige & Mary Jane at tea decor,
   11 pcs. (ILLUS. of part) 400.00
Toy clicker, tin 10.00
Toy whistle, tin, advertising "Buster
   Brown Shoes," cylindrical, w/picture
   of Buster & Tige. 15.50
Toy whistle, wooden 7.00

BUTTER MOLDS & STAMPS

Cow Butter Stamp

*While they are sometimes found made of
other materials, it is primarily the two-
piece wooden butter mold and one-piece
butter stamp that attracts collectors. The
molds are found in two basic styles, rounded
cup form and rectangular box form. Butter
stamps are usually round with a protruding
knob handle on the back. Many are factory
made items with the print design made by
forcing a metal die into the wood under
great pressure, while others have the design
chiseled out by hand.*

Acorn mold, wooden, die-stamped
   double design $53.00
Acorn & oak leaves stamp, wooden,
   hand-carved, 4½" d. 95.00
Acorns on branches mold, wooden,
   chip-carved, 2-pc. 50.00
Bird on branch stamp, wooden, hand-
   carved, 3 5/8" d. 90.00
Compass star "lollypop" stamp,
   wooden, hand-carved w/chip-
   carved edge, 8" l. 300.00
Cow mold, wooden, hand-carved,
   hinged case, 6¾ x 5" 125.00
Cow mold, wooden, hand-carved,
   9½ x 6" 295.00
Cow stamp, wooden, hand-carved,
   1-piece w/turned wood handle,
   4¼" d. (ILLUS.) 225.00
Duck flying mold, wooden, hand-
   carved, round, ½ lb. 135.00
Eagle stamp, wooden, hand-carved
   w/rope-carved edge, turned wood
   handle, 4½" d. 625.00
Flower stamp, wooden, hand-carved,
   4¾ x 2¼" 55.00
Flower & leaves mold, wooden, hand-
   carved, w/round case plunger,
   19th c., 3½ x 3½" 95.00
Flower & stylized leaves stamp,
   wooden, hand-carved, 3½" d. 55.00
Geometric star mold, wooden, hand-
   carved 65.00

Heart stamp, wooden, deeply hand-
carved intertwined double heart
design, 1-piece w/knob handle,
18th c., 3½" d. 150.00
House mold, wooden, hand-carved,
9-piece 105.00
Lamb mold, wooden, hand-carved,
miniature 220.00
Leaf molds, wooden, hand-carved,
6¾" l., 2½" h., pr. 176.00
Pineapple mold, wooden, die-stamped
design ....60.00 to 85.00
Pineapple stamp, wooden, hand-
carved, 1-piece w/turned wood
handle, 4 1/8" d....................45.00
Pinwheel stamp, wooden, die-stamped
design, 4½" d. 30.00
Rose stamp, wooden, hand-carved,
long knob handle, 5" d. 245.00
Sheaf of wheat mold, maple, hand-
carved, 19th c.....................55.00
Sheaf of wheat mold, wooden, die-
stamped design 45.00
Sheaf of wheat stamp, maple, hand-
carved, 1-piece, ca. 1870, 4¼" d. 80.00
Songbird stamp, wooden, hand-
carved, 1-piece w/knob handle 280.00
Starflower mold, wooden, die-
stamped design, 4" d. 40.00
Starflower "lollypop" stamp, wooden,
hand-carved, 18th c. 130.00
Strawberry mold, wooden, hand-
carved, barrel-shaped, 3-piece 95.00

Swan Butter Mold

Swan mold, wooden, hand-carved
(ILLUS.) ....120.00 to 135.00
Tulip stamp, wooden, hand-carved,
1-piece w/knob handle, 18th c.,
4" d. 250.00

BUTTON HOOKS

*From the 1860s through the early years of
the 20th century, people buttoned up their*
*shoes, along with many layers of garments
and gloves and the button hook was an in-
dispensable part of everyday life. Produced
in a variety of forms and materials, this
once useful gadget is now a popular collectors' item. Also see ART NOUVEAU.*

Button Hooks

Advertising, "Beck Hazzard Shoes,"
metal $5.00
Advertising, "Bond Street Spats," metal. .8.00
Celluloid handle, plain (ILLUS. top) 7.50
Clear glass, whimsey, 9½" l. 35.00
Gold handle, 9k, Art Nouveau style,
2¾" l. 90.00
Sterling silver handle, Art Nouveau
style ....17.00 to 28.00
Sterling silver handle, Le Secrete de
Fleurs patt., Unger Brothers 77.00
Sterling silver handle, Medallion patt.,
George W. Shiebler & Co., large 195.00
Sterling silver handle, ornate (ILLUS.
bottom) 25.00

BUTTONS

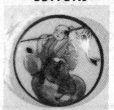

Satsuma Samurai Warrior Button

Brass, ball-shaped, w/stick-like
stamped design, ½" d. $1.00
Brass, filigree stamped border w/floral
center, small 45
Brass, Kate Greenaway type, 2 children
seated on fence, large..............22.00
Brass, w/marcasite center, backmarked "A.P. & CIE* Paris," 1930s,
½" d., set of 8 ....65.00
Brass, marcasite florals on textured
ground, 1930s, ½" d., set of 10 .....125.00
Brass, Maude Adams as Peter Pan,
1906, 1½" d. 22.50
Brass, stamped & die-cut warrior in full
suit of armor on velvet background,
beaded brass rim 15.00
Brass, trumpet flower design, 1 1/8" d. ..8.50
Celluloid, flat disc w/applied brass dog
center, 1 1/8" d. 5.00

China, calico print, set of 6 . . . . .5.00
China, Satsuma, pink iris w/green
 leaves on royal blue ground, ¾ " d. . . .40.00
China, Satsuma, children playing,
 1¼" d. 50.00
China, Satsuma, floral decor w/heavy
 gold trim, 1¼" d. 18.50
China, Satsuma, Geisha girl decor,
 1¼" d. 20.00
China, Satsuma, bamboo decor, small,
 set of 4 . . . . .48.00
China, Satsuma, Samurai warrior,
 1¼" d., set of 6 (ILLUS. of one) 250.00
China, Satsuma, 7 gods of fortune,
 small, set of 7 . . . . .35.00
China, Satsuma, 7 gods of fortune,
 large, set of 7 . . . . .75.00
Cut steel, snowflake design, 2½" d. 12.00
Gilt metal, flat disc, Victorian, late
 18th-early 19th c., card of 24 . . . . .60.00
Jasper ware, classical figures,
 ca. 1850 . . . . .20.00
Silver, angel busts (4) embossed in high
 relief, rope border, Birmingham hall-
 mark for 1904, 1 1/8" d. 28.00
Silver, 6-petal flower w/large bead
 center, concentric ring border,
 marked "980," ¾" d., set of 6 . . . . . . .48.00
Silver & enamel, round w/foliate
 reserve enameled in green & turquoise blue, backmarked "CYMRIC,"
 set of 5, together w/belt buckle
 resembling spreading butterfly
 wings enameled in green & blue
 between chased ridges, in fitted
 case, Liberty & Co., Birmingham,
 possibly designed by Archibald
 Knox, 1902, 7 pcs. 660.00
Sterling silver, embossed florals,
 berries & foliage, marked "Briston,"
 ca. 1900, 1" d. 20.00

CALENDAR PLATES

Calendar plates have been produced in this country since the turn of the century, primarily of porcelain and earthenwares but also of glass and tin. They were made earlier in England. The majority were issued after 1909, largely intended as advertising items.

1906, holly & roses center, w/adver-
 tising, 9" d. $37.50
1908, 2 monks drinking wine, Ohio
 advertising, 9½" d. 68.00
1908, roses center, calendar months
 border 20.00
1909, bird center, 4 seasons calendar
 month border, Maine advertising,
 8¼" d. 16.00

1909, New York State Capitol center,
 green transfer on white, red
 border, 9½" d. 27.50
1909, beautiful woman center, Ansonia,
 Connecticut advertising 45.00
1909, Gibson Girl portrait center,
 calendar months border . . . . .27.00 to 38.00

1910 Advertising Calendar Plate

1910, raspberries & gooseberries
 center, calendar months within holly
 border, 7½" d. (ILLUS.) 22.00
1910, cherubs (2) ringing in New Year
 center, w/advertising 35.00
1910, Mount Vernon center, calendar
 months circled w/pink roses 18.00
1910, lady w/horse center 23.00
1910, ships & windmills center 20.00
1911, floral bouquet center, calendar
 months border, 7" d. 20.00
1911, moonlit water scene center,
 8" d. 35.00
1911, duck in flight center, Texas
 advertising 35.00
1911, Gibson Girl portrait center 35.00
1912, cherubs & fruit center,
 w/advertising 25.00

1912 Advertising Calendar Plate

1912, fruit center, w/advertising
 (ILLUS.) 22.00

1913, early bi-plane in flight center,
7½" d. 42.00
1914, grouse center, signed Beck 40.00
1916, Indian in canoe center 30.00
1919, U.S. & World War I Allies flags
center 30.00
1920, "The Great War," Missouri
advertising 25.00
1921, apple & nuts decor 30.00
1922, roses center, Minnesota
advertising 14.00
1924, dog & game birds center,
Minnesota advertising 32.00

CAMPBELL KID COLLECTIBLES

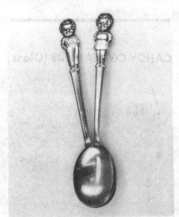

Campbell Kids Soup Spoons

The Campbell Kids were created by Grace Weiderseim (Drayton) at the turn of this century and their first use is said to have been on street car cards. They have been used for years by the Campbell Soup Company in its advertisements and various objects were produced graced with illustrations of them. Also see DOLLS.

Bank, cast iron, figural Campbell
Kids $165.00
Booklet, "Help for the Hostess," 1930s . . 28.00
Bowl, silverplate, Campbell Kid center
decor, Rogers Bros. 45.00
Candy container, papier mache, fig-
ural Campbell Kid 125.00
Cookbook, "Campbell Kids Junior
Cookbook," 1954 . . . . 4.00
Dish, silverplate, Rogers 22.00
Doll, composition, jointed 225.00
Feeding dish, pottery, Campbell Kids
decor, signed Drayton, Buffalo
Pottery . . . . 45.00 to 55.00
Knife, fork & spoon, silverplate, 3 pcs. . . 50.00
Potholder plaques, 1950s, pr. 23.00

Salt & pepper shakers, plastic, red &
white uniforms, yellow hair, made
by "F. & F. Mold & Die Works,
Dayton, Ohio," 4½" h., pr. . . . 22.00 to 28.00
Soup spoons, silverplate, figural
Campbell Kid handles, International
Silver Co., 6" l., pr. (ILLUS.) 22.50
Teaspoon, silverplate, figural Campbell
boy or girl handle, each . . . . . 10.00 to 18.00

CANDLESTICKS & CANDLE HOLDERS

Figural Candlestick

Also see LIGHTING DEVICES.

Candelabrum, bell metal, 4-light,
stepped circular foot, columnar stem
w/elaborately turned finial supporting 4 scrolled adjustable arms
w/vase-shaped candle nozzles &
circular drip pans, 15" h. $220.00
Candle holders, brass, chamberstick-
type, shallow saucer base w/ring
handle, cylindrical stem w/pushup,
4¼" h., pr. 300.00
Candle holder, silver, chamberstick-
type, circular saucer base w/molded
rim & domed center, cylindrical stem
pierced w/a trefoil, shaped flat handle w/pierced decoration & applied
w/a beaded rat-tail, maker's mark
"B.B.," London, James II period,
1686, 5½" d. pan 6,600.00
Candle holder, tin, chamberstick-
type, deep saucer base w/canted
sides & ring handle, cylindrical stem
w/pushup, 8" d., 4¼" h. 95.00
Candle holder, tin, chamberstick-
type, saucer base w/flared rim &
curved handle, cylindrical stem

w/telescoping pushup, worn brown
japanning, embossed "F.A. Rock-
wells Pat. Feb. 27th 1855," 5" h......125.00
Candle holder, wrought iron, miner's
"Sticking Tommy," 7¼" l.....70.00 to 80.00
Candle-holder, wrought iron, miner's
"Sticking Tommy," w/twisted shaft,
12½" l.........................190.00
Candlestick, brass, circular base,
slender tubular spring-loaded stem,
impressed "Cornelius & Baker, Philadelphia," polished, 13" h. (single) ...100.00
Candlestick, bronze, figural Art
Nouveau type woman wearing
turban & half-draped in pleated
skirt, holding candle socket in each
arm, inscribed "Gurschner Depose,"
16¾" h. (ILLUS.)................3,575.00
Candlestick, bronze & glass, disc-form
bronze base & tall slender stem
w/green glass blown through
pierced bronze candle socket,
Tiffany Studios, New York,
ca. 1920, 17" to 20" h.,
each..................275.00 to 550.00
Candlestick, pewter, domed base,
baluster stem, removable bobeche,
7 3/8" h. (single)..................95.00
Candlestick, tin, "hogscraper" w/push-
up marked "Patented 1853" & hanging lip, 5" h. (single)..............125.00
Candlestick, wrought iron spiral
w/pushup & hanging lip on wooden
base, 8½" h. (single).............115.00
Candlesticks, brass, neo-classical
style, polished, 4¾" h., pr.........130.00

"Capstan" Candlesticks

Candlesticks, brass, "capstan," flaring
base, incised mid-drip pan, molded
candle nozzle, probably Spanish,
16th c., 5" h., pr. (ILLUS.) 1,210.00
Candlesticks, brass, stepped base,
beehive stem, plain candle nozzle,
w/pushup, English Registry mark,
8" h., pr.........................125.00
Candlesticks, brass, domed & stepped
base, baluster-turned & blocked
stem, square candle socket, w/push-
up, Victorian, 10 7/8" h., pr........150.00
Candlesticks, brass, domed & stepped
base, ring-turned stem w/wide mid-
stem drip pans, elongated candle

socket, post sections screw together,
polished, 20¼" h., pr.............850.00
Candlesticks, pewter, domed bead-
molded foot, baluster stem, vasiform
candle nozzle w/flaring bead-
molded bobeche, w/pushup, 19th c,
10¼" h., pr......................220.00
Candlesticks, silver, circular base,
short tri-level circular candle nozzle,
designed by Harold Nielsen,
executed by Georg Jensen, 1¼" h.,
pr..............................605.00
Candlesticks, silverplate, square base
accented w/cast floral collar,
tapering stem, baluster-shaped
candle socket, Gorham Mfg. Co.,
Providence, Rhode Island, ca. 1890,
10" h., set of 4 ....192.50

CANDY CONTAINERS (Glass)

Airplane Candy Container

*Along with other early toys, interest in
glass candy containers has escalated in the
past five years and scarce, early versions of
certain containers bring very high prices.
*Indicates the container might not have
held candy originally. +Indicates this
container might also be found as a
reproduction. ‡Indicates this container was
also made as a bank. All containers are
glass unless otherwise indicated.*

Airplane - marked "Spirit of Saint
Louis" on metal wings, w/clamp-on
nose cap & tin propeller, tin wheels,
all original, ca. 1927, 4½" l. $285.00
Airplane - w/left side rear door, metal
screw cap & tin propeller, painted
wing & wheels, probably 1930s,
4 5/8" l. (ILLUS.) 140.00
Airplane - w/tin wing, marked "Patent
113053" on glass body, w/front cork
closure & tin propeller, T.H. Stough
Co., 1939, 4 5/8" l. 87.50
Airplane - "P-38" Lightning, all glass,
5½" l., 7 1/8" wing span 145.00

Amos & Andy in Open Air Taxi -
painted figures, marked "Victory
Glass Co., etc.," w/tin closure,
1928-30, 4½" l. 345.00
Automobile - little sedan w/stippled
wheels & top, 3" l. 25.00
+Automobile - electric runabout, w/tin
closure at top, ca. 1914, 3½" l.......75.00

Old Style Limousine

Automobile - old style limousine
marked "Pat. Ap'ld. For" on bottom,
tin slide on top, 3 7/8" l. (ILLUS.) 80.00
Automobile - streamlined touring car,
3 7/8" l. 25.00
Automobile - "Westmoreland Specialty
Co. Limousine," w/tin wheels,
4" l. 125.00
Automobile - sedan w/twelve vents,
w/closure, 4 5/16" l. ....70.00 to 85.00
Automobile - hearse-type, 4 windows
each side w/tassels, spare tire at
rear, w/tin closure on top,
Cambridge Glass Co., ca. 1916,
4 3/8" l. 90.00
+Automobile - streamlined miniature,
partly painted, 4 9/16" l. 32.50
Automobile - limousine w/rear trunk &
tire, marked "V.G. Co., etc.,"
original paint, w/tin closure on top,
ca. 1930, 4 13/16" l. 140.00
*Automobile - phaeton, milk white
glass, marked "Portieux" on base,
4½" l. 75.00
Automobile - V.G. Co. sedan, 4-door,
marked "Avor ¾ oz" & "V.G. Co."
under doors, w/original tin wheels,
5" l. 97.00
Automobile - modern, w/pebbled top,
marked "Victory Glass, etc." on cardboard closure, ca. 1942, 5" l. 30.00
Automobile - electric coupe w/patent
of Feb. 18, 1913, w/closure 75.00
Baby Chick - standing, painted yellow,
w/tin closure, no markings, ca. 1930,
3 3/8" h. 60.00
Barney Google & Ball - painted,
3¾" h. 198.00
Bear on Circus Tub - w/tin spinning
disc & closure, 4¼" h. 250.00
Bell - Liberty Bell w/hanger, green,
w/old closure, 3 3/8" h..............65.00
‡*Bell - "1776 Liberty," amber, 4"
base d., 4 1/8" h. 40.00

Boat - model cruiser, w/cardboard
closure, 4½" l. 25.00
Boat - w/tin portholes in glass hull &
mast sticks attached to tin deck
closure, T.G. Stough patent 1914,
6 3/8" l. ....285.00 to 300.00
Bus - "Victory Lines Special," painted,
w/closure, 4 7/8" l. 70.00
+Camera on Tripod - w/wire legs,
cord & wooden bulb hanging from
lens w/tin closure on back of glass
camera, ca. 1915, 5½" h. 185.00
Cannon on 2-wheel tin carriage mount -
w/tin wheels, 3¾" l. 175.00
Cannon on 2-wheel tin carriage -
w/tin wheels, aluminum cap on glass
cannon, ca. 1908, 4¾" l. 200.00
Cannon - Rapid Fire, metal carriage &
wheels, "West Bros. Co.," sliding tin
closure at top, all original, ca. 1916,
7¾" l. 300.00
Cash Register - clear glass, w/tin
closure, ca. 1913, 3" w., 2 5/8" h. ...160.00
*Chamberstick - w/ring handle & open
base, 2¾" d. 14.50
Charlie Chaplin beside Barrel - figure
beside barrel marked "Geo.
Borgfeldt & Co." on base & w/tin
closure on barrel slotted for use as
bank, ca. 1915, 3 7/8" h. figure
w/some paint 120.00
Chicken on Nest - "Manufactured by
J.H. Millstein Co." on rim of base,
4 5/8" h. 25.00
Chicken - crowing rooster, original
paint, 2 1/8" d., 5" h. 145.00
Clock - alarm-type, rope-beaded
edges, 2 3/8" d. face, 3 5/16" h......140.00
Dirigible - marked "Los Angeles" on
side, painted silver, marked "V.G.
Co., etc.," aluminum screw-on cap
closure, ca. 1929, 5¾" l. 125.00
Dog - Bulldog on oblong base, 3¾" h. ...25.00
Dog - Bulldog, w/gilt collar, on round
base, painted, marked "U.S.A.,"
w/metal screw closure,
4¼" h. ....50.00 to 85.00
Dog - Bulldog on round base, no paint,
w/closure, 4¼" h. ....45.00 to 60.00
*Dog - Hound Pup w/wide screw-on
top, cobalt blue, 3½" h. 15.00
Dog - Hound Pup, w/paper & metal
hat, 3 5/8" h. 12.00
Dog - Hound Pup, w/closure 10.00
Duck on rope top basket - marked
"V.G. Co.," w/tin closure, 1920s,
3 1/8" h. 62.00
Duck - with large head & bill, painted, w/tin closure, 1900s, 3¼" h. 135.00
Elephant - marked "G.O.P." on side,
painted grey, marked "V.G. Co.,"
w/tin closure, ca. 1925, 2 7/8" l.,
2¾" h. (ILLUS.) 115.00

Gray

G.O.P.

U.S.A.

RTM

"G.O.P." Elephant

+Fat Boy on Drum - painted, w/tin
closure on base slotted for use as
bank, ca. 1915, 4 3/8" h. 170.00

Flat Iron - stippled, contoured tin
closure w/three tabs, 1908-13,
3½" l., 2" h. 250.00

Gun - marked "Kolt" on grip & "V.G."
on barrel, w/round tin closure on
handle grip, ca. 1925, 4¼" l. 68.00

Gun - revolver w/square butt,
7 1/8" l. 22.00

Horn - with three valves, some painted
decoration, tin whistle & tin screw
cap closure on belled end, 1920s,
5" l. 125.00

Horn - trumpet shape but no valves,
milk white glass w/painted
decoration, tin screw-on cap closure
on belled end, ca. 1908, 5½" l. 83.00

Hot Doggie - painted, w/closure,
ca. 1925, 5 5/8" l. 275.00

House - bungalow, 1-story w/dormer
in roof, painted, w/tin closure, early
1900s, 2¾ x 2 1/8" base,
2 3/8" h. . . . . .125.00 to 150.00

Iron - electric-type w/string cord,
4½" l. (no closure) 28.50

+Kewpie by Barrel - painted figure,
marked "Geo. Borgfeldt & Co., etc."
under barrel, w/tin closure slotted
for use as bank, ca. 1915 . . . . .87.50

Lamp - miniature w/hurricane-type
shade, 3 1/8" l., 1¾" h. base &
3¼" h. glass chimney 36.50

Lantern - tiny, plain, "J.C. Crosetti Co."
in circle on base, 2¼" h. . . . . .8.50 to 12.00

Lantern - oval globe w/six ribs,
greenish cast, 3 1/8" h. 25.00

Lantern - six vertical ribs, "Pat. Dec.
20, '04" on base, 3¼" h. 20.00

Lantern - all glass w/six vertical ribs,
marked "Pat. Dec. 20, '04, etc.,"
w/metal shaker top closure & wire
bail, 3¼" h. 26.00

Lantern - Beaded No. 1 globe, w/metal

screw-on cap & long bail handle,
original paint, 3½" h. 50.00

Lantern - all glass, marked "Victory
Glass Inc., Jeannette, Pa." around
bottom, 3½" h. 20.00

Lantern - "V.G. Co. No. 2," w/metal
screw-on cap, 3 5/8" h. 25.00

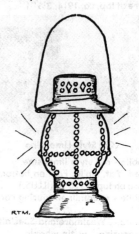

RTM.

Lantern

Lantern - clear glass, pear-shaped
globe w/aluminum top & bottom,
raised beads on ribs, 1920s, 3¾" h.
(ILLUS.). 85.00

Lantern - barn-type No. 2, ruby-flashed,
West Bro's. Co., Grapeville, Pa.,
original closure, ca. 1913, 4¼" h. 75.00

Lantern - large railroad-type, "Stough's
No. 81," w/red-enameled screw-on
cap, 4 3/8" h. .27.50

Lantern - barn-type enclosed in a glass
frame, painted globe & frame,
w/metal screw-on closure at base,
West Bros. Co., ca. 1913, 4½" h. 72.00

*Lantern - "Bond Mono Cell," w/bat-
tery in hanger & light bulb that
switches on when handle is raised,
4½" h. 29.50

Locomotive - "Stough's No. 8," opens
at cab end, 3¾" l. 17.00

Locomotive - American-type w/litho-
graphed tin closure, ca. 1924,
4 3/16" l. 70.00

Locomotive - marked "999" under cab,
w/man in cab window, w/cap
closure in back of cab, Cambridge
Glass Co., ca. 1916, 4 7/16" l. 145.00

Mail Box - painted aluminum, souo
venir, w/closure, 3¼" h. 95.00

Milk bottle - "Dolly's Milk," 3" h. 30.00

Monkey Lamp - glass monkey marked
"See, speak or hear no evil," red
plastic shade covers cap closure on
monkey's head, paper label of "T.H.
Stough Co.," 1950s, 4" h. 100.00

Mug - "Kiddies Drinking Mug," w/card-
board closure, 3 7/16" h. 23.00

+ Mule Pulling 2-Wheeled Barrel with
Driver - painted, some examples
marked "Victory Glass Co.," w/tin
cap closure on barrel, 1930s,
4½" l. .60.00 to 85.00

Nursing Bottle - "Lynne Doll Nurser,"
w/rubber nipple, 2¾" h. . . . .12.00 to 20.00

Owl - painted, unmarked, w/tin cap
closure, 1920s .80.00

Pencil - marked "Baby Jumbo," 5½" l. . .41.00

Rabbit on Base - crouching, some
paint, w/closure, 3¾" l. 80.00

Rabbit - pushing chick in shell cart,
original paint & closure, 4" l.,
3 7/8" h. 225.00

Rabbit - running on log, some paint,
4¼" l. 150.00

Rabbit on Base - sitting w/laid-back
ears, heavy glass, w/tin closure,
early 1900s, 4½" h. 80.00

Rabbit Family on Base - painted
rabbits, clear base, marked "V.G.
Co., etc.," w/tin closure, 1920s,
4¾" h. . . . . .440.00 to 475.00

Rabbit in Egg Shell - gilt-painted rabbit,
marked "V.G., etc.," w/metal
screw-on cap closure, 1920s,
5 1/8" h. . . . . .50.00 to 75.00

Rabbit - feet together, round base,
5¼" h. 45.00

Radio - old-time model w/speaker horn
on top of cabinet, marked "Tune In"
on cabinet & marked "V.G., etc.,"
w/tin closure, ca. 1925 . . . . .98.00

Rocking Horse with Clown Rider - some
parts painted, w/tin closure, 1920s,
4¼" l. 250.00

Santa with Plastic Head

Santa Claus with Plastic Head Closure -
marked "J.H. Millstein Co., etc."
inside plastic head, parts of Santa
airbrush-painted, 1940s, 5 5/8" h.
(ILLUS.) . . . . .55.00 to 75.00

Sign - marked "Don't Park Here,"
w/tin closure, ca. 1925, 4½" h. 128.00

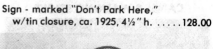

Suitcase Candy Container

Suitcase - clear glass, w/tin closure,
3 5/8" l., 2½" h. (ILLUS.) 37.50

Tank (miniature) - marked "U.S.
Army," T.H. Stough Co., 3 1/8" l. 26.50

Tank - w/man in turret, 1942, 4¼" l. 28.00

Tank with Two Cannons - some parts
painted, marked "Victory Glass Inc."
on cardbaord closure, 1940s, 4¼" l. . . .36.50

Tank - World War I, some paint,
w/closure, 4 5/16" l. 100.00

Telephone - Millstein's "Tot," desk-
type, 2 3/8" h. .22.00

Telephone - candlestick-type, tall
musical toy, w/wooden receiver,
4¼" h. 25.00

Telephone - "West Bro's. Co., 1907,"
pewter mouthpiece & wooden
receiver, 4¼" h. 75.00

Telephone - Lynn-type w/raised dial,
4¾" h. 30.00

Telphone - "Victory Glass Co., Dial
type," wire hanger & wooden
receiver, 4 7/8" h. 30.50

Telephone - dial-type, "VG Co.,"
4 7/8" h. (no wooden receiver) 16.50

Toonerville Depot Line - replica of
Toonerville Trolley, no paint, some
chips, 2 7/8" l., 3½" h. 400.00

Top - spinning-type w/winding disc,
overall 3¾" h. .90.00

Trunk - w/dome top, clear, 3" l.,
2½" h. (no closure) 102.00

Turkey - gobbler, 3½" h. 78.00

Well Bucket - "Ye Olde Oaken Bucket,"
w/tin lid & wire bail handle, overall
4¼" l. . . . . .22.00 to 45.00

Wheelbarrow - w/tin closure over top,
6" l. 75.00

Yellow Taxi - w/radiator cap, 4 3/8" l.,
2¼" h. 150.00

CANES & WALKING STICKS

Whalebone Cane

Canes have been used for thousands of years and probably collected for hundreds of years. Seventeenth and eighteenth century court "dandies" often owned numerous canes, coordinating their use to various costumes and occasions. Today's collector looks for canes made of unique materials or in a unique form. Gadget canes, such as those that convert into a weapon or conceal a whiskey flask in the handle, are probably the most elusive type for the collector to acquire.

Bamboo-carved cane, dog's head
   handle w/glass eyes, labeled "Cross,
   London," 34" l. $35.00
Bone-handled walking stick, carved
   as a lady's leg w/buttoned
   pantaloons & wooden boot end,
   on tapering cylindrical wooden shaft,
   19th c., 34½" l. 165.00
Civil War cane, wooden, camp-carved
   "1st Massachusetts Infantry - Emmits-
   burg Rd. - Meade's Headquarters" . . .95.00
Glass cane, aqua 55.00
Glass cane, light green w/thin black
   stripes in twisted crook handle,
   34" l. 150.00
Glass walking stick, clear, bulbous head,
   swirled tapering shaft, 48½" l. 85.00
Glass walking stick, clear w/interior
   red, yellow & blue spirals, 36" l. 200.00
Gold-handled cane, "repousse" handle,
   ca. 1870 . . . . .300.00
Gold-handled "Presentation" walking stick,
   engraved "Professor McKarg - Class of
   1865" (wide crack in handle) 95.00
Ivory-handled cane, carved w/eagle &
   shield, tooled silver-gilt ferrule
   w/inscription, 35½" l. 230.00
Leather-covered steel core cane,
   w/cast metal lady's leg handle,
   34" l. 70.00
Rattan-wrapped wooden walking stick . 12.50
Sapling walking stick, root handle,
   38" l. 12.50
Whalebone & whale ivory cane,
   angular whale ivory handle carved

as lady's hand w/fold-over cuff,
   faceted whalebone shaft w/metal
   tip, ca. 1860, 31½" l. (ILLUS.) 1,265.00
Wooden "Presentation" cane, curved
   handle w/sterling silver inlay &
   inscription dated "January 1, 1914,"
   w/original cloth sleeve, 36" l. 90.00
Wooden cane, carved entwining snake
   & date "1889" 60.00
Wooden cane, carved American eagle
   & entwined snake 85.00
Wooden walking stick, carved man's
   head handle, vine-twisted shaft,
   painted black, 35" l. 25.00
Wooden walking stick, carved head of man
   wearing fez knob handle, 37" l. 50.00
Wooden walking stick, carved overall
   leaves 45.00
Wooden walking stick, rosewood
   w/sterling silver knob, 35" l. 35.00
Wooden walking stick, nubby shaft
   w/sterling silver knob 75.00

CANS & CONTAINERS

"Superior" Axle Grease

The collecting of tin containers has become quite popular within the past several years. Air-tight tins were at first produced by hand to keep foods fresh, and after the invention of the tin-printing machine in the 1870s, containers were manufactured in a wide variety of shapes and sizes with colorful designs.

Axle grease, Galena Mfg. Co.
   "Superior" Axle Grease can, yellow
   w/green lid (ILLUS.) $7.50
Axle grease, Mica miniature pail,
   2" h. 45.00
Axle grease, Monarch pail, eagles
   pictured 25.00
Baking powder, Calumet 6-oz. can,
   Indian pictured 12.00
Baking powder, Dairy Maid can 9.00
Baking powder, Davis, 1-lb. 8-oz. can. . .10.00
Baking powder, K.C., "25 oz. for 25
   cents" 12.50

Baking powder, Rough Rider can,
Teddy Roosevelt astride horse 15.00
Baking powder, Rumford 1-lb. 8-oz.
can 15.00
Baking powder, Watkins, lady
w/platter of biscuits 12.00
Biscuit, Carr & Co., 2 kittens on lid 20.00
Biscuit, Huntley & Palmers books,
"History of Reading" 138.00
Biscuit, Huntley & Palmers books,
"Waverly Novels" 165.00
Biscuit, Huntley & Palmers, globe,
1907 . . . . .100.00
Biscuit, Huntley & Palmers, ink stand . .125.00
Biscuit, Huntley & Palmers, tavern
scene on sides .65.00

Loose-Wiles Biscuit Box

Biscuit, Loose-Wiles, Hiawatha & bride
on cover, scenes & verse on sides
(ILLUS.) 35.00
Biscuit, Loose-Wiles, Robin Hood
series 35.00
Biscuit, Mutual store bin w/hinged lid,
10½" sq., 11" h. 50.00
Candy, Beach Pops pail, children at
seashore 15.00
Candy, Blue Bird Chocolate Toffee con-
tainer w/hinged lid, 8½ x 8½" 20.00
Candy, Clarks Peanut Brittle can 20.00
Candy, Colgan's Taffy Tulu, cupids 395.00
Candy, Harvino Toffee box, Santa &
children, 4½ x 2" 25.00
Candy, Louis Sherry "Violets" 15.00
Candy, Mello-Mints oval box 7.50
Candy, Old Benson box, Queen Mary,
5 x 8" 9.00
Candy, Riley's Toffee, pr. pheasants on
lid, 4½" d. 6.00
Candy, Riley's Toffee oval can, seated
bear painting & standing bear
w/umbrella, 6½" oval 25.00
Candy, See's pail, sea waves scene 10.00
Candy, Whitman "Salamagundi" 1-lb.
box 20.00
Chalk, An-Du-Septic Dustless Crayon
box (ILLUS.) 14.00
Chocolate, Bowey's Hot Chocolate
Powder canister, black man serving,
orange & gold (no lid) 28.00

An-Du-Septic Chalk Box

Chocolate, Walter Baker's box, 2 x 3" . . .18.00
Cigarettes, Axton-Fisher's Imperial
Doublets flat box 10.00
Cigarettes, Cavalier one hundreds,
oval . . . . .6.00 to 10.00
Cigarettes, Chesterfield flat
fifties . . . . .7.00 to 12.00
Cigarettes, Egyptienne Luxury box 15.00
Cigarettes, Lucky Strike flat fifties,
green, red & gold 9.00
Cigarettes, Melachrino flat fifties 9.00
Cigarettes, Target box 12.00
Cigars, Banquet Hall Little Cigars 20.00
Cigars, Ben Key box 35.00
Cigars, Cinco-Nettes 9.00
Cigars, Club House canister 15.00
Cigars, Custom House canister 90.00
Cigars, Dixie Maid 40.00
Cigars, El Verso box, shepherdess &
sheep, 5 x 3½ x 1" 25.00
Cigars, Good Cheer 85.00
Cigars, Kipps Hand Made box 24.00
Cigars, LaFendrich canister 20.00
Cigars, La Resta container . . . . .25.00 to 40.00
Cigars, MaPaCuba container 42.50
Cigars, Mill-Town Stogies container 75.00
Cigars, Optimo canister 55.00
Cigars, Postmaster canister 25.00
Cigars, Rice's Agent 45.00
Cigars, Richman's 5-cent box 25.00
Cigars, Tom Moore container 18.00
Cigars, Train Master 45.00
Cigars, Two Orphans canister,
Victorian girls, 1909 . . . . .85.00

White Owl Cigars

Cigars, White Owl box (ILLUS.) 15.00

Cocoa, Droste's sample size can 20.00
Cocoa, Droste's square 16 oz. con-
     tainer, Dutch girl & boy 10.00
Cocoa, Monarch sample size, lions 29.00
Cocoa, Watkins square container 20.00
Coconut, Schepp's "cake box,"
     1-shelf 125.00
Coconut, Schepp's "cake box,"
     2-shelf 80.00
Coconut, Schepp's pail, 4¼" d.,
     4½" h. 55.00
Coconut, Schepp's pail, children
     playing, black & green 200.00
Coffee, A & P 8 O'Clock 1-lb. canister 4.00
Coffee, Astor House 1-lb. can 70.00
Coffee, Blue Bird pail 75.00
Coffee, Bokar 1-lb. container w/screw-
     on cap 10.00
Coffee, Campbell 4-lb. container,
     camel, yellow & red 50.00
Coffee, Campbell & Woods bin, red,
     gold & black, pre-1910,
     14 x 18 x 17½" 385.00
Coffee, Fairy Dell 4-lb. pail 43.50
Coffee, Folger's 5-lb. container, ship ... 45.00
Coffee, Forbes trial size 10.00
Coffee, Glendora, sample size 18.00
Coffee, Luzianne 1-lb. container 35.00
Coffee, Mammy's Favorite Brand 4-lb.
     container, black mammy on
     orange 135.00
Coffee, Mothers Joy 1-lb. container 8.00
Coffee, Nash's trial size 15.00
Coffee, Red Wolf 1-lb. can 28.00
Coffee, St. James 5-lb. pail, Philadel-
     phia store pictured 185.00
Coffee, Stock Norton Bros. 100-lb.
     roll-top bin, lady pictured 225.00
Coffee, Strong Heart 1-lb. can 70.00

Wampum Coffee Pail

Coffee, Wampum 5-lb. pail (ILLUS.) 175.00
Coffee, White House half-lb. can 15.00
Coffee, White House 1-lb. can 18.00
Coffee, Wishbone 5-lb. pail, green 43.50
Cold cream, Marcelle 18.00
Cold cream, Rexall Theatrical, 1-lb. 13.50

Crackers, Crescent Tom Thumb box 20.00
Crackers, Dr. Johnson Educator,
     5½ x 5½" 35.00
Crackers, Dr. Johnson Educator box
     w/oak handles, 12 x 7½" 32.50
Flour, Ceresota 25-lb. bin, Ceresota
     boy pictured 675.00
Gum, Adams Spearmint box w/hinged
     lid 105.00
Gum, Clark's Teaberry Pepsin Chewing
     box, 7 x 5 x 3" 70.00
Gum, Yucatan box, 6 x 6" 105.00
Gun powder, DuPont drum, w/eagle ... 60.00
Gun powder, Laflin & Rand Infallible
     drum, blue & gold 28.00
Hair restorer, Clement's, lady w/long
     hair, 4 x 2½" 18.00
Lard, Armour's 4-lb. pail 12.00
Lard, Blue Bell 4-lb. pail 15.00
Lard, Carsten's pail 12.00
Lard, Luters 4-lb. pail, Mammy
     w/spatula & frying pan 45.00
Lard, Morrell's Snow Cap 8-lb. pail 15.00
Lard, R.B. Rice Co., Lee Summit, Mo.
     4-lb. pail 15.00
Lard, Swift's Silver Leaf 2-lb. pail 13.50
Malted milk, Carnation soda fountain
     canister, red & white flower design ... 45.00
Marshmallows, Brock's 5-lb. box 45.00
Marshmallows, Bunte 25-lb. store bin,
     w/child 95.00
Marshmallows, Campbell 1-lb.
     container 10.00
Marshmallows, Campfire 12-oz.
     container 39.50
Marshmallows, Campfire 5-lb.
     container 22.50
Marshmallows, Lyon's Swansdown 4-oz.
     box 55.00
Metal polish, Whiz, elves & auto
     pictured 25.00
Oysters, Jack's 1-lb. pail 28.00
Oysters, Maryland Raw Beauty pail 18.50
Oysters, Pride of the Chesapeake
     1-gal. pail 20.00
Oysters, Wentworth 1-gal. pail 12.50
Patent medicine, Dr. Chase Ointment ... 8.00
Patent medicine, Dr. Legears Nicotine
     Pills, Dr. holding chicken 15.00

Mentholatum Container

Patent medicine, Metholatum purse-
size container, w/little girl
(ILLUS.) .... 6.00 to 7.50
Patent medicine, Rawleigh's Salve 10.00
Patent medicine, Watkins Ointment,
trial size 10.00
Peanut butter, Armour's Veribest 1-lb.
pail, Mother Goose scenes 80.00
Peanut butter, Buffalo 1-lb. pail 60.00
Peanut butter, Canadian Squirrel Brand
pail 300.00
Peanut butter, Credo 1-lb.
pail .... 15.00 to 28.00
Peanut butter, Fi-Na-St (First National)
pail, man in white uniform 35.00
Peanut butter, Flower Brand 1-lb. pail .. 30.00
Peanut butter, Gold Bond 1-lb. pail 40.00
Peanut butter, Jackie Coogan pail.... 150.00
Peanut butter, Lighthouse pail 60.00
Peanut butter, Meadow Sweet pail 100.00
Peanut butter, Monarch 1-lb. pail,
lion's head 28.00
Peanut butter, Monarch "Teenie
Weenie" 2-lb. pail 98.00
Peanut butter, Monarch "Teenie
Weenie" 4-lb. pail................ 125.00
Peanut butter, Old Frontenac pail 75.00
Peanut butter, Old Reliable 1-lb. pail ... 22.00
Peanut butter, Squirrel 1-lb.
pail .... 65.00 to 80.00
Peanut butter, Staple Brand 55-lb.
store bin........................ 25.00
Peanut butter, Swift's Wizard of Oz
5-lb. pail........................ 55.00
Peanuts, Buffalo 25-lb. pail 65.00
Peanuts, Bunnies Salted 10-lb.
container 165.00
Peanuts, Planters Red Pennant 10-lb.
container 110.00
Phonograph needles, RCA Victor,
dog & phonograph 21.00
Sardine, Herald's book-shaped
container 66.50
Spice, "Mexene" chili powder canister,
devil, brewing kettle, 7" 75.00
Spice, Watkins Ginger box, light
green 14.00
Spice, Wigwam Curry Powder box....... 7.50
Syrup, Towle's Log Cabin, plain,
4½" h. 30.00
Syrup, Towle's Log Cabin - Express
Office container 66.50
Syrup, Towle's Log Cabin, cabin-
shaped, cartoon-style w/mother
flapping pancakes & bear at door 70.00
Syrup, Towle's Log Cabin, Stockade
School........................... 70.00
Talcum powder, Apple Blossom .. 3.50 to 5.00
Talcum powder, Cuticura, lady & baby .. 20.00
Talcum powder, Dream Girl can, Art
Nouveau lady 25.00
Talcum powder, Sweetheart can, lady
in evening gown standing between
columns 25.00

Richard Hudnut Yanky Clover Box

Talcum powder, Richard Hudnut Yanky
Clover round box, yellow & green,
5" d. (ILLUS.) 18.00
Tea, Mayfair triangular box 18.50
Tea, McCormick box, black on orange,
1938 .... 11.50

Monarch Tea Box

Tea, Monarch box w/hinged lid
(ILLUS.) 8.00
Tea, Old Fire Side box 25.00
Tea, Swee-Touch Nee trunk-shaped
container, red & gold decor 22.50
Tea, Tetley's box, sunflowers ... 5.00 to 12.00
Tobacco, Blue Label pocket tin 75.00
Tobacco, Brotherhood lunch
box .... 150.00 to 185.00
Tobacco, Buckhorn pocket tin ... 8.50 to 12.00
Tobacco, Charm of the West pocket
tin 85.00
Tobacco, City Club pocket tin 88.00
Tobacco, Edgeworth square container
w/concave sides.................. 30.00
Tobacco, Epicure pocket tin 63.00
Tobacco, Game Fine Cut store bin 288.00
Tobacco, Half & Half pocket tin,
telescopic-type 13.00
Tobacco, Hi-Plane pocket tin, single-
engine plane 34.50
Tobacco, Sweet Cuba Fine Cut slant top
canister, woman's portrait 90.00

Tooth powder, Dr. Wernet's Powder for
False Teeth, hand pours powder on
false teeth, 5½" h. 18.00
Typewriter ribbon, Columbia round
box, twins pictured 10.00

Panama Typewriter Ribbon Box

Typewriter ribbon, Panama round box,
plane flying over canal zone, 2½" d.
(ILLUS.)...........................10.00
Typewriter ribbon, Rainbow round box ..4.00
Veterinary medicine, Bleecker's Carbo-
Pet Cow Salve can 20.00
Wax, Johnson's Wax for Dancing Floors
can, 1920's couple dancing 15.00

CARD CASES

Sterling Silver Card Case

*In a more leisurely and sociable era, ladies
made a ritual of "calling" on new neighbors
and friends. Calling card cases held the
small cards engraved or lettered with the
owner's name and sometimes additionally
decorated. The cases were turned out in a
wide variety of styles and materials which
included gold, silver, ivory, tortoise shell
and leather. A sampling of collectible calling
card cases is listed below. Also see IVORY.*

Coin silver, engraved bird, A. Cole,
New York, 1840, w/original hinged
box $95.00
Ivory, carved scene of figures in a
palace garden, China, 19th c.,
4 3/16 x 2 5/8"...................120.00

Ivory & leather, 2-compartment 65.00
Ivory inlaid w/silver & malachite,
geometric quilted design, 3¼ x 2" ...55.00
Lacquer, oblong w/rounded ends,
black w/yellow striping, central
engraved & hand-colored decoupage
scene of "The Battle of Buena
Vista," 5 7/16 x 2 13/16" 700.00
Mother-of-pearl shell, gentleman's,
4 x 2¾" ....28.00 to 35.00
Ostrich skin 8.00
Sterling silver, gold-washed, engraved
birds, w/chain, marked Gorham 125.00
Sterling silver, engraved bamboo &
floral decor, 3½ x 2½" 85.00
Sterling silver, engraved monogram,
3½ x 3½" (ILLUS.) 65.00
Tortoise shell, Victorian 65.00

CASH REGISTERS

Early "National" Cash Register

*James Ritty of Dayton, Ohio, is credited
with inventing the first cash register. In
1882, he sold the business to a Cincinnati
salesman, Jacob H. Eckert, who subsequently invited others into the business by
selling stock. One of the purchasers of an
early cash register, John J. Patterson, was
so impressed with the savings his model
brought to his company, he bought 25
shares of stock and became a director of the
company in 1884, eventually buying a
controlling interest in the National Manufacturing Company. Patterson thoroughly
organized the company, conducted sales
classes, prepared sales manuals and established salesman's territories. The success of*

the National Cash Register Company is due as much to these well organized origins as to the efficiency of its machines. Early "National" cash registers, as well as other models, are deemed highly collectible today.

Brass, "National," Model 5, fleur-de-lis scrolling designs $800.00

Brass, "National," Model 5, floor model, on oak 5-drawer base 1,400.00

Brass, "National," Model 7, 1889 patent, ca. 1904 ....700.00

Brass, "National," Model 50, w/clock........................1,200.00

Brass, "National," Model 215 ....750.00

Brass, "National," Model 216, original "Amount Purchased" marquee 950.00

Brass, "National," Model 238, ornate scrolled corner brackets, milk white glass shelf 395.00

Brass, "National," Model 247, registers to $7.00........................750.00

Brass, "National," Model 310, candy store model, registers to 50 cents ...875.00

Brass, "National," Model 312, original "Amount Purchased" marquee, burnished....................1,150.00

Brass, "National," Model 313, candy store model, registers from 5 cents to $1.00........................550.00

Brass, "National," Model 317, burnished....................975.00

Brass, "National," Model 333, restored & burnished 795.00

Brass, "National," Model 349, dated 1912 ....375.00 to 550.00

Brass, "National," Model 356, registers from 1 cent to $20.00 ....250.00

Brass, "National," Model 514, candy store model, registers from 1 cent to 59 cents, 10" w.................550.00

Brass, "National," Model 842, w/crank & tape print-out device, white marble slab shelf, registers to $9.99, ca. 1904 ....450.00

Bronze, "National," Model 92, floor model on oak 8-drawer base......1,850.00

Cast iron, "Premier," Model 1 ....450.00

Copper, "St. Louis," 9" w. 450.00

Nickel-plated brass, "National," Model 441, crank-style on oak 5-drawer base, ca. 1913 ....2,000.00

CASTORS & CASTOR SETS

Castor bottles were made to hold condiments for table use. Some were produced in sets of several bottles housed in silverplated frames. The word also is sometimes spelled "Caster."

English Silver Castor Set

Castor set, 3-bottle, cranberry glass bottles, crescent moon shaped silverplate holder, w/spoon...........$160.00

Castor set, 4-bottle, ruby glass Thumbprint patt. bottles, silverplate stand........................300.00

Castor set, 5-bottle, clear glass bottles w/copper wheel engraved decor, revolving silverplate stand 110.00

Castor set, 5-bottle, clear glass Gothic Arch patt. bottles, pewter frame, dated 1858....................135.00

Castor set, 5-bottle, clear glass Honeycomb patt. bottles, silverplate stand, marked Meriden..................165.00

Castor set, 6-bottle, vaseline glass Daisy & Button patt. bottles, revolving silverplate stand w/engraved skirt & ornate bail handle, 18" h.....450.00

Castor set, 7-bottle, silver-mounted clear glass cruets, shakers, bottles & mustard pot, footed silver tray w/strap handle, London hallmark for 1799 (ILLUS.) 560.00

Pickle castor, amber glass Diamond Point patt. insert & lid, ornate footed silverplate frame 160.00

Pickle castor, Amberina glass insert w/enameled decor, silverplate frame 230.00

Pickle castor, amethyst cut to clear glass insert, silverplate frame w/pedestal base, marked James Tufts 225.00

Pickle castor, blue glass Diamond patt. insert, silverplate frame 95.00

Pickle castor, clear glass Block patt. insert, silverplate frame, cover & fork, marked Reed & Barton 75.00

Pickle castor, clear glass Manhattan patt. insert, silverplate frame & fork 80.00

Pickle castor, cranberry glass Diamond Quilted patt. insert w/enam-

eled florals, ornate silverplate
frame, cover & tongs, marked
Pairpoint 265.00
Pickle castor, cranberry glass Optic
patt. insert w/enameled daffodil
blossoms & leaves, silverplate frame
w/side handle & tongs, marked
Tufts 250.00
Pickle castor, cranberry glass Thumb-
print patt. insert w/deep blue
enameled florals, footed silverplate
frame, marked Simpson Hall
Miller 250.00
Pickle castor, green glass insert, silver-
plate frame, 11" h. 110.00
Pickle castor, milk white glass Grape &
Vine patt. insert, footed silverplate
frame w/embossed berries & leaves,
marked Pairpoint 185.00
Pickle castor, sapphire blue glass
insert w/enameled florals & gold
trim, footed silverplate frame &
tongs. 295.00
Pickle castor, double, clear glass
Diamond patt. inserts, ornate ball-
shaped silverplate base supporting
footed frame embossed w/florals &
foliage, embossed covers, tongs &
fork, marked Meriden, ca. 1896 . . . . .225.00
Pickle castor, double, clear glass Fine
Cut patt. inserts, silverplate frame,
covers & tongs, marked Wilcox 155.00
Pickle castor, double, clear glass Twin
patt. inserts, engraved silverplate
frame w/center handle, covers &
tongs. 125.00

Double Pickle Castor

Pickle castor, double, cranberry glass
inserts, silverplate footed frame
w/center handle & covers (ILLUS.) . . .325.00

CAT COLLECTIBLES

Hooked Rug with Striped Cat

*Cats--love them or hate them--you have to
respect the fact that today cats are pets in
almost one-fourth of all households in the
United States. Proud, aloof and indifferent,
their haughty poses have been recaptured in
artwork in a variety of materials through
the years. Other representations catch the
inquisitive, cuddly and playful mood of the
domestic cat. Both have brought a delight-
ful area of collecting to cat lovers across the
country.*

Corkscrew, cast iron, figural Cheshire
cat handle, ca. 1870, 5" $110.00
Hooked rug, striped cat on striped
block background w/dark border, in
shades of beige, brown, blue, red &
magenta, early 20th c., 50 x 33"
(ILLUS.) 1,100.00
Hot water bottle, child's, rubber,
model of a cat .12.00
Lamp, papier mache, model of a black
cat, w/silk shade, 1930s 65.00
Model of a cat in seated position,
brass, on round Akro Agate glass
base, 2½" h. 65.00
Model of a cat standing w/back
arched, cast iron, 4 x 3½" 45.00

Delft Cats

Models of cats in recumbent position,
Delft faience pottery, blue & white,
on oval grassy bases, enriched in
green, ca. 1755, minor repairs to
rims of bases & ears, 4½" l., pr.
(ILLUS.) 2,860.00
Model of a cat in seated position,
stoneware pottery, black, blue &
green on clear glaze, 6¾" h. (minor
ear flake) 250.00

Model of a comical cat w/ribbon tied
around head, pottery, yellow w/dark
brown trim, 4" d., 7 3/8" h. 88.00
Model of a cat in seated position,
Rockingham-glazed pottery,
9½" h. 295.00
Model of a cat kneeling w/hands
clasped in prayer, bronze, Vienna. . . .30.00
Models of kittens playing musical
instruments, porcelain, Japan,
ca. 1920, 1½" h., 4 pcs. 15.00
Pitcher w/cat handle, china, lustre
decor, Czechoslovakia, 4½" h. 10.00
Plate, decal portrait of cat center,
Falcan Ware, England, 9" d. 15.00
Print, entitled "Brother & Sister,"
signed, framed 32.00
String holder, chalkware, model of
a cat 22.00
Thimble holder, silverplate, cat seated
on 3" oval base w/thimble & thread
spindles 55.00
Toy doll cat, bisque head w/molded
leering expression, cloth body,
dressed, marked "Heubach,"
6½" 1,250.00
Tray, bronze, embossed head of a cat
peering at a snail, 6½ x 3½" 75.00

CELLULOID

Powder Box & Hair Receiver

Celluloid was our first commercial plastic and early examples are now "antique" in their own right, having been produced as early as 1868 after the perfection of celluloid by John Wesley Hyatt. Also see ART DECO, BABY MEMENTOES, BREWERIANA, BUTTONS and FANS.

Calendar frame, creamy ivory, w/1924
calendar. $3.00
Cane handle, curved, dog's head
w/inset glass eyes 28.00
Collar & cuff box, cov., creamy ivory,
holly & berries decor 37.50
Collar & cuff box, cov., creamy
ivory, embossed woman decor,
ca. 1890, w/original collars & cuffs . . .60.00
Dresser set: cov. powder box, cov.

hair receiver & hand mirror; creamy
ivory, 3 pcs. .12.00
Dresser set: cov. powder box, cov. hair
receiver & hand mirror; green w/purple
orchid decor, 3 pcs. 18.00
Dresser set: cov. powder box, cov. hair
receiver, hand mirror & dresser tray;
green w/leaping deer decor, 4 pcs. . .28.00
Dresser set: cov. powder box, cov. hair
receiver, pin box w/lift-off cushion,
ring box, hand mirror & tray; creamy
ivory, 6 pcs. .28.00
Dresser set: tray, hand mirror, cov.
powder box, cov. hair receiver, cov.
jewelry box, nail tools & matching
clock; creamy ivory, 12 pcs. 90.00
Glove box, cov., creamy ivory, scenic
decor on lid, ca. 1910 . . . . .35.00
Hair receiver, cov., pearlized green 6.00
Hair receiver & cov. powder box,
creamy ivory, pr. (ILLUS.) 12.00
Handkerchief box, cov., creamy ivory,
scenic decor on lid . . . . .15.00 to 20.00
Manicure box, creamy ivory, complete
w/tools. 45.00
Mustache comb, lady's leg shape,
creamy ivory .15.00
Necktie box, cov., creamy ivory,
embossed florals overall & "Neckties,"
12½" l. 38.00
Picture frame, easel-type, creamy ivory,
9" w., 11" h. .12.00

Celluloid Pin Cushion

Pin cushion w/lift-off plush-covered
top, creamy ivory, 4" d. (ILLUS.) 10.00
Pinback button, "Confederate Reunion,
Petersburg, Va.," flag background,
1905, 1" d. 22.50
Powder box & cover w/cupid finial,
creamy ivory, marked "Germany" . . .15.00
Shoe horn w/high button shoe in relief
on handle, creamy ivory w/painted
highlights. 22.00
Tatting shuttle. .6.00
Toothbrush holder, creamy ivory 5.00
Wedding cake figures of bride & groom,
fully dressed & bride w/veil & flowers,
1940s, 3" h., pr. 20.00

CERAMICS

ADAMS

Adams Columbia Pattern Coffee Pot

The Adams family has been potters in England since 1650. Three William Adamses made pottery, all of it collectible. Most Adams pottery easily accessible today was made in the 19th century and is impressed or marked variously ADAMS, W. ADAMS, ADAMS TUNSTALL, W. ADAMS & SONS, and W. ADAMS & CO. with the word "England" or the phrase "made in England" added after 1891. Wm. Adams & Son, Ltd. continues in operation today. Also see FLOW BLUE, HISTORICAL & COMMEMORATIVE and JASPER WARE.

Bowl, 10" d., footed, Cattle Scenery
   patt., dark blue transfer $195.00
Coffee pot, cov., octagonal, Columbia
   patt., blue transfer, W. Adams,
   ca. 1848 (ILLUS.) 225.00
Cookie jar, cov., enameled medallions
   on cream ground, matte finish 65.00
Creamer, Jeddo patt., mulberry
   transfer 110.00
Cup & saucer, handleless, Beehive
   patt., purple transfer 45.00
Hot water pitcher, Columbia patt.,
   flow blue transfer 125.00
Plate, 7¾" d., soft paste, embossed
   rim & feathered edge highlighted in
   cobalt blue, impressed "Adams"
   mark 45.00
Plate, 9½" d., Spanish Convent patt.,
   light blue transfer 195.00
Plate, 10" d., souvenir, "Governor's
   Palace - Williamsburg, Virginia,"
   flow blue transfer 75.00
Platter, 1890s copy of early Wm.
   Adams patt., blue transfer, large
   (ILLUS.) 85.00

1890's Copy of Early Pattern

Soup plate w/flange rim, Caledonia
   patt., black transfer, 9½" d 36.00
Soup plate w/flange rim, Palestine
   patt., purple transfer, 10¾" d 35.00
Vegetable dish, cov., English country
   scene, dark blue transfer, late
   19th c., 11" oval 55.00
Vegetable tureen, cov., Athens patt.,
   mulberry transfer, ca. 1849, 10" d. . .200.00

AUSTRIAN - MISCELLANEOUS

Hand-painted Austrian Plate

Numerous potteries in Austria produced good-quality ceramic wares over many years. Some factories were established by American entrepreneurs, particularly in the Carlsbad area, and other factories made china under special brand names for American importers. Marks on various pieces are indicated in many listings. Also see KAUFFMANN (Angelique), OYSTER PLATES, ROYAL VIENNA and RING TREES.

Bowl, 9½" d., 2½" h., purple flowers
   center on blue-green shaded to

yellow ground, ruffled rim, gold
trim (Carlsbad) $23.00
Butter pats, blue floral decor, set of 4 ...12.00
Cake plate, pierced handles, scenic
decal center, floral border
(Carlsbad) 30.00
Celery tray, scalloped border, pink
roses & green leaves decor, gold
trim, 12" l. 43.00
Chocolate pot, cov., h.p. pink roses
& emerald green vining decor, gold
trim, 12" h. (Imperial) 100.00
Chocolate set: cov. chocolate pot & 4
c/s; roses decor on green ground,
9 pcs. (Victoria) 110.00
Cookie jar, cov., decal portrait of
classical lady (pseudo beehive
mark) 78.00
Creamer, figural moose head, 4½" h. ..35.00
Cup & saucer, Bluebird patt. (Victoria) ..18.00
Dresser set: tray, hatpin holder,
chamberstick & hair receiver; h.p.
pansies decor, 4 pcs. 150.00
Egg set: egg caddy w/colorful full
figure rooster center & fitted
w/twelve egg cups; pink roses
decor, 13 pcs. (Victoria) 58.00
Ewer, pansy decor on pale green
ground, gold trim, 14" h. (Carlsbad,
Victoria) 70.00
Fish set: 16½ x 11½" oval tray,
9 x 5½" gravy boat w/scrolled
handle & attached underplate &
eight 8¾" d. plates w/scalloped
rims; multicolored fish & seaweed
decor on blue ground, after 1918,
10 pcs. 150.00
Fish set: 20" l. platter, eight 12" d.
plates & sauceboat; underwater scene
w/various species of fish decor,
10 pcs. (Carlsbad) 250.00
Hair receiver, pink roses decor on
shaded pastel green, pink & white
ground, gold trim (M.Z.) 30.00
Pitcher, 6¾" h., molded bamboo
handle w/figural bee, gold decor on
white ground (Stellmacher) 75.00
Pitcher, 8 3/8" h., 4¾" d., Alhambra
patt., maroon, green, creamy white
& grey design w/gold trim 135.00
Pitcher, tankard, 12½" h., 3¾" d., h.p.
pink & white roses w/green leaves
on green shaded to pink ground,
gold rim 170.00
Plaque, pierced to hang, center
portrait of robed ladies playing
harps, dark green & gold border
w/small florals, 11½" d. (Carlsbad,
Victoria) 75.00
Plate, 8½" d., realistic grapes on
shaded pastel yellow to peach
ground, artist-signed (ILLUS.) 45.00
Plate, 8½" d., pansy decal, gold
trim (Carlsbad) 12.50

Plate, 8½" d., bust portrait of
beautiful woman decor, h.p. lilacs
in background, scalloped rim w/gold
tracery (pseudo beehive mark) 65.00

Hand-Painted Austrian China Plate

Plate, 8½" d., dark blue plums on
shaded blue to purple ground, gold
rim, artist-signed (ILLUS.) 45.00
Plate, 9½" d., portrait of "Mdm. Van
Der Geeste" in late 16th c.
costume, burgundy lustre border
w/raised gilt band & elaborate
enameled beading, late 19th c. 260.00
Plate, 9½" d., portrait of "Miss
Hallett," wearing large feathered
maroon hat on high powdered curls
& gauze fichu, elaborate gilt &
cobalt blue rim, late 19th c. 200.00
Plate, 9¾" d., scenic center, green
& gold border, artist-signed 250.00
Plates, 10" d., center portraits of
beautiful blonde & brunette, artist-
signed, pr. 110.00
Platter, 16½" l., shaded pink roses
w/green leaves decor 40.00
Ramekin & underplate, fluted design,
all white 27.50

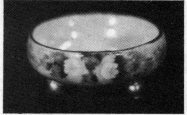

Austrian Salt Dip

Salt dip, h.p. pink roses & green leaves
decor, ca. 1900, 1" h., M.Z. (ILLUS.) ...18.00
Stamp box w/lift-off lid, footed, 2-com-
partment, h.p. roses decor, gold
trim, 4¼ x 3 1/8" 34.00
Stein, tapering cylinder, portrait of
monks sampling ale reserved on
cobalt blue ground, gilt trim,
6 1/8" h. 550.00

Teapot, cov., oval form, gilt finial,
handle & spout, shaded greens
through reds w/heavy gilt scrolling
decor, 8¼" across handle, 4½" h.....58.00
Vase, 5" h., bulbous, decal portrait of
girl w/flowing hair on shaded rust
ground 25.00
Vase, 8¾" h., 5" d., handled, portrait
of beautiful lady, artist-signed
(Victoria) 85.00
Vase, 9" h., 6" d., gold handles, pink &
yellow roses decor on pale green
ground 45.00
Vase, 9½" h., handled, fall flowers
decor on tan & cream ground (blue
Crown mark) 32.00
Vases, 11" h., h.p. portraits of Louis
XIV & Louis XVI, pr. (Carlsbad,
Victoria).......................425.00
Vases, 14" h., elongated teardrop form
w/open handles at sides, h.p.
pastoral scene w/grazing cattle, pr.
(Victoria) 150.00

BAVARIAN - MISCELLANEOUS

Bavarian China Plate

*Ceramics have been produced by various
potteries in Bavaria for many years. Those
appearing for sale in greatest frequency
today having been produced in the 19th and
early 20th centuries. Also see HUTSCHEN-
REUTHER, KOCH, NYMPHENBURG,
PICTORIAL SOUVENIRS, ROSEN-
THAL, ROYAL BAYREUTH and RING
TREES.*

Bowl, 7½" octagon, center decal of 2
parrots, reticulated lavender rim ...$35.00
Bowl, 10¼ x 6½" oval, 2" h., 2-han-
dled, pierced edge, multicolored
floral decor, gold trim (Schumann) ...70.00
Cake plate, pierced handles, iris &

pansies in relief w/fern fronds,
gold trim, 11" d. (R.C.) 50.00
Candle holders, gold reticulated han-
dles midsection to base, teal blue
iridescent, 8½" h., pr...............25.00
Candy dish, scenic decor w/houses &
women, oval 60.00
Canisters, cov., variously lettered
"Sugar," "Prunes," & "Flour" in blue
& blue floral decor, 7" h., set of 3....150.00
Celery dish, Orleans patt., pink roses
decal, Z.S. & Co. (Zeh, Scherzer &
Co.).............................30.00
Child's feeding plate, h.p. scene
w/Dutch children at border, dated
Christmas, 1916 ....38.00
Chocolate set: cov. chocolate pot &
5 c/s; large pink roses decor, gold
trim, 11 pcs. (Royal Crown).........150.00
Chocolate set: cov. chocolate pot & 6
c/s; pink, red & white roses on
smoky blue shaded to off-white
ground, large white leaves border,
13 pcs. (Crown mark)..............235.00
Coffee pot, cov., child's, dolls & bears
decor 75.00
Coffee set, demitasse, lovers in silhouette decor, 23 pcs. (Z.S. & Co.) 150.00
Cookie jar, cov., squatty, large pink
roses w/green foliage & gold trim on
white ground, 8½" d., 5" h. (Z.S. &
Co.).............................32.00
Cup & saucer, large pink roses decor
on pink lustre ground..............35.00
Dish, 2-handled, reticulated rim, overall
h.p. floral decor, 6½ x 4¼" oval 25.00
Dresser bowl w/domed lid centered
w/scene of boy & girl picking grapes
w/gold accents, rococo-molded cobalt
blue base w/gold accents, 8 x 5"
oval, 4½" h. (Schumann)...........68.00
Feeding dish, "The Wing, I felt you
push, I heard you call," artist-
signed...........................67.50
Game plate, center decal of deer,
9" d. (Z.S. & Co.) 45.00
Marmalade (or jam) jar, cov.,
2-handled, grape cluster border,
artist-signed & dated 1915..........65.00
Moustache cup, pink & yellow chrysanthemums decal on white shaded to
pink ground......................32.00
Pitcher, 9" h., bulbous, burnished
gold lizard handle, blackberry
decor on shaded ground, artist-
signed..........................110.00
Plate, 6½" d., scalloped rim, portrait
of beautiful woman wearing purple
hat & holding a purple fan (Wreath
& Crown mark) 72.50
Plate, 8¼" d., fruit cluster decal
w/shaded mauve through pink grape
clusters & realistic pear & apple,
green border (ILLUS.)...............15.00

Hand-Painted Bavarian China Plate

Plate, 9" d., scalloped & embossed rim
w/gold edge, blackberries & blossoms on pastel turquoise ground,
artist-signed (ILLUS.) 45.00
Plate, 13" d., yellow & red roses
decal on shaded ground 55.00
Powder jar, cov., overall roses decor on
pale green ground 25.00

Bavarian Relish Tray

Relish, pierced handles, tulips on
shaded ground, artist-signed
(ILLUS.) 35.00
Teapot, cov., h.p. & w/heavy silver
overlay 125.00
Vase, 5¾" h., h.p. bird & floral
decor, dated 1912 .... 25.00
Vase, 8" h., flattened oval, 2-handled,
green & purple grapes & foliage on
shaded green ground, gold trim 80.00

BECK, R.K.

*Items that are signed R.K. Beck are
sought by a group of specialized collectors.
Beck was a noteworthy wildlife painter and
his original art works have been reproduced
in decal form and applied to plates, platters
and the like, under the glaze. Though these
items are signed R.K. Beck, it should not be
construed that these pieces were hand-*
*painted by Beck since they are merely
derived from his original art work. Also see
BUFFALO POTTERY.*

Fish set: platter & 6 plates; various
game fish depicted, Buffalo Pottery,
7 pcs. $250.00
Game plate, blue scalloped rim,
Mallards swimming, 8¼" d. 24.00
Game plate, Prairie Chicken in flight,
9¼" d. 62.50
Game plate, Elk in forest scene, green
ground, 10" d. 85.00
Game plate, Buck & Doe decor,
12½" d. 65.00
Game plate, (2) Moose at Lake w/for-
est background, w/bronze stand 70.00
Game platter, Buck & Doe in autumn
forest scene 125.00
Game set: platter & 4 plates; platter
w/scene of Buck & Doe in forest glen
& plates w/various deer scenes on
shaded yellow, red & orange ground,
5 pcs. 395.00
Plate, 12" d., Ram & 2 Ewes in glade
at water w/sky in background 110.00

BELLEEK

*Belleek china has been made in Ireland's
County Fermanagh for many years. It is
exceedingly thin porcelain. Several marks
were used, including a hound and harp
(1865-1880), and a hound, harp and castle
(1863-1891). A printed hound, harp and
castle with the words "Co. Fermanagh
Ireland" constitutes the mark from 1891.
Belleek-type china was also made in the
United States last century by several firms,
including Ceramic Art China Works,
Columbian Art Pottery, Lenox Inc., Ott &
Brewer and Willets Manufacturing Co. Also
see COMMEMORATIVE PLATES and
LOTUS WARE.*

AMERICAN

Willets Belleek Mark

Bouillon cup & saucer, 2-handled,
ruffled & gilt rim, h.p. lavender
florals w/ornate gold stems &
leaves (Willets) $135.00
Bowl, 8" d., 1½" h., 2-handled, ruffled

rim w/gold trim, floral decor, artist-
signed (Willets) 145.00
Bowl, 8" d., 5¼" h., footed, Art
Nouveau wild roses decor (Lenox
1897-98 mark) 90.00
Bowl, 9" d., 4" h., shaped rim, h.p.
bust portrait reserved in gilt
latticework hung w/pendant
blossoms (Willets) 325.00
Busts of lady & gentleman, 9¼" h.,
pr. (Lenox) 340.00

Lenox Belleek Coffee Set

Coffee set: cov. coffee pot, creamer,
cov. sugar bowl & pr. c/s; ivory
w/multicolored florals on gold-
ground band, set, Lenox (ILLUS.) 425.00
Cookie jar & cover w/finial, embossed
shoulder outlined w/silver overlay
on cobalt blue (Lenox 1897-98
mark) 115.00
Creamer, lavender shaded to white,
gold trim (Ott & Brewer) 65.00
Cup & saucer, demitasse (Ott &
Brewer) 80.00
Cup & saucer, pink (Ott & Brewer) 150.00
Ewer, pink w/white handle, 8½" h.
(Lenox 1897-98 mark)...............49.00
Fish plate, gold medallions on double
border, colorful red snapper in blue
water center, 9" d. (Willets) 65.00
Hatpin holder, silver overlay decor,
5" h. (Willets) 75.00
Jar, cov., gold paste floral decor,
4¾" h. (Ott & Brewer) 300.00
Marmalade jar, cov., wheat design
on blue ground (Ceramic Art
Company) 95.00
Mug, h.p. berries & leaves on coral
pink to cream ground, 4½" h.
(Willets) 85.00
Mug, h.p. trailing vines & leaves
decor, 5¼" h. (Willets) 125.00
Mugs, berries & ferns decor, artist-
signed, 5½" h., pr. (Willets) 140.00
Mug, 3-handled, "Board of Trade
Meeting-Waldorf Astoria, 1896,"
enameled blue dot & gold floral
decor, miniature (Lenox)...........185.00

Mug, tankard, h.p. Indian in full
headdress (Lenox) 175.00
Perfume jar w/metal cylinder insert,
lily-of-the-valley decor, matte finish
(Ceramic Art Company)............225.00
Pitcher, cider, purple, magenta &
lemon-colored fruit on shaded
ground, gold trim, artist-signed
(Ceramic Art Company)............90.00
Pitcher, tankard, 14" h., h.p. grape
clusters decor (Willets) 130.00
Pitcher, tankard, 16" h., figural dragon
handle, h.p. portrait of the artist
Houghton's dog (Willets) 695.00
Plate, 5½" d., gold-brushed embossed
& scalloped rim, h.p. gold sprays
center (Willets) 45.00
Plate, 8" d., h.p. tiny roses & gold
overall decor (Willets) 95.00
Plate, 9½" d., Tridacna patt., brushed
gold & ornate gold decor on eggshell ground (Ott & Brewer) 275.00
Plate, h.p. tiny Worcester-type red
roses decor (Willets) 120.00
Salt dip, ruffled rim, pink roses
decor (Lenox) 20.00

Lenox Swan Salt Dips

Salt dips, model of swan, Lenox, pr.
(ILLUS.)..........................70.00
Sugar bowl, cov., silver overlay decor
(Lenox) 30.00
Teapot, cov., Cactus patt. w/gold
cactus form handle & gold twig
decor (Ott & Brewer) 395.00
Tea set: cov. teapot, creamer & sugar
bowl; silver overlay decor, 3 pcs.
(Lenox) 125.00
Tea strainer w/underplate, h.p. floral
& gold decor, 2 pcs. (Ceramic Art
Co. - Lenox) 200.00
Tobacco jar, cov., flying geese decor,
artist-signed 295.00
Vase, 4" h., 2 curved gold handles,
bulbous, gold paste decor on cobalt
blue & gold ground (Ott & Brewer)...300.00
Vase, 8 1/8" h., flared top, yellow
glaze (Lenox).....................95.00
Vase, 12" h., bulbous, h.p. red
cabbage roses on dark green
ground (Willets) 420.00
Vase, 14" h., bulbous bottom, slender
flaring neck, waterlilies on aqua-

marine to green ground,
artist-signed 300.00

Vase, 16" h., scalloped gold rim &
gold rococo-molded design at base,
h.p. red & cream roses on green
ground 195.00

Vase, portrait of lion on pale
chocolate ground, attributed to the
artist Houghton (Willets) 395.00

IRISH

Lily Pattern Basket Ware

Basket, Basket Ware, 3-strand,
shamrock shape w/three applied
florals w/leaves & tiny shells at rim,
5½" w. 550.00

Basket, Basket Ware, Lily patt.,
3-strand w/applied lily-of-the-valley
at rim, early impressed mark on
pad, 10½" l. (ILLUS.) 2,000.00

Basket, Basket Ware, handled,
4-strand, applied florals, impressed
Belleek Co. Fermanagh, Ireland on
ribbon pad, 12" l. 1,100.00

Bowl, 6 x 5", shell-shaped, shaded
pink to cream, 1st black mark 135.00

Bread plate, Echinus patt., pink & gilt
trim, 9" d., 1st black mark 145.00

Bread plate, Grasses patt., 1st black
mark 250.00

Bread plate, Limpet patt., 11" d.,
2nd green mark 60.00

Bread plate, Neptune patt., pink trim,
2nd black mark . . . . .120.00 to 150.00

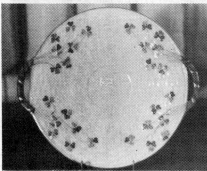

Shamrock-Basketweave Bread Plate

Bread plate, Shamrock-Basketweave
patt., 10½" d., 3rd black mark
(ILLUS.) 55.00

Bust of Charles Stewart Parnell,
11" h., 1st black mark 2,800.00

Bust of Clytie

Bust of Clytie, 2nd black mark
(ILLUS.) 1,000.00

Butter plate, heart-shaped, 2nd black
mark 50.00

Butter plate, Shamrock-Basketweave
patt. w/twig handle, 3rd black
mark 40.00

Cake plate, Neptune patt., green
trim, 2nd black mark 115.00

Candlestick, Thorn patt., 7" h.,
2nd black mark (single) 195.00

Limpet Pattern Coffee Pot

Coffee pot, Limpet patt., 3rd black
mark (ILLUS.) 250.00

Coffee set: cov. coffee pot, creamer,
sugar bowl & 6 demitasse cups &
saucers; Mask patt., 15 pcs. (brown
Castle mark) .475.00

Cookie jar, cov., Shell patt., green
trim, 8" h., 2nd black mark 1,190.00

Creamer, Cleary patt., pink trim, 2nd
  black mark 45.00
Creamer, Echinus patt., 1st black
  mark, large 75.00
Creamer, Harp-Shamrock patt., 1st
  black mark 75.00
Creamer, Hexagon patt., pink trim,
  2nd black mark 125.00
Creamer, Irish Pot patt., 2nd black
  mark 45.00
Creamer, Ivy patt., 1st black mark 75.00
Creamer, Lotus patt., 1st black mark 75.00
Creamer, Mask patt., 1st black mark . .290.00
Creamer & open sugar bowl, Lily patt.,
  green trim, 2nd black mark, pr. 150.00
Creamer & open sugar bowl, Lotus
  patt., 3rd black mark, pr. . . .85.00 to 110.00
Creamer & open sugar bowl, Tridacna
  patt., 1st black mark, pr. . . .95.00 to 110.00
Creamer & open sugar bowl, Toy Shell
  patt., 2nd black mark, pr. 110.00
Cup & saucer, Artichoke patt., white,
  1st black mark 145.00
Cup & saucer, Echinus patt., 1st black
  mark 120.00
Cup & saucer, Harp Shamrock patt.,
  3rd black mark . . . . .85.00 to 98.00
Cup & saucer, Institute patt., pink &
  gilt trim, large size, 1st black mark . .325.00
Cup & saucer, Limpet patt., gold trim,
  3rd black mark . . . . .75.00 to 95.00
Cup & saucer, Neptune patt., green
  trim, 2nd black mark 80.00
Cup & saucer, Neptune patt., pink
  trim, 2nd black mark 125.00
Cup & saucer, Shamrock-Basketweave
  patt., 2nd black mark 55.00
Cup & saucer, Shamrock-Basketweave
  patt., 3rd black mark 48.00
Egg cup, Primrose patt., 1st
  black mark 95.00

Aberdeen Ewer-Vase

Ewer-vase, Aberdeen patt., 6" h.,
  2nd black mark (ILLUS.) . . .425.00 to 575.00
Figurine, "Affection," Grecian-type
  nude w/draped gown, 15" h., 1st
  black mark 1,400.00

Figurine, "Affection," Grecian-type
  nude w/draped gown, 15" h., 2nd
  green mark 375.00
Figurine, "Meditation," 15" h., 2nd
  green mark 525.00
Flower pot, melon-ribbed, applied
  flowers, 5" d., 4¼" h., 2nd black
  mark 198.00
Holy water font, bust of angel, 11",
  2nd black mark 1,150.00
Honey pot w/cover & stand, Grasses
  patt., tan trim, 7" h., 1st black
  mark 725.00
Jardiniere, 3 dolphin feet, swirl-
  molded, applied florals at waisted
  neck, 10½" d., 2nd black mark 1,750.00
Mug, Shamrock-Basketweave patt.,
  2¾" d., 2¾" h., 2nd black mark 67.50
Mug, Thorn patt., 1st black mark 110.00
Mustache cup & saucer, ring handle,
  gilt trim, 1st black mark cup; 2nd
  black mark saucer 195.00
Plate, 6" d., Blarney patt., pink &
  gold trim, 2nd black mark 90.00
Plate., 8" d., Shamrock-Basketweave
  patt., 3rd black mark 35.00
Plate, 8" d., Tridacna patt., 2nd black
  mark 36.00
Plate, 9¼" d., Thorn patt., pink &
  gold trim, 2nd black mark 475.00
Plate, 10" d., Neptune patt., blue trim,
  3rd black mark 85.00
Powder bowl, cov., Mask patt., luster
  highlights, 2nd black mark 195.00
Salt dip, Limpet patt. w/coral legs, 2nd
  black mark 90.00
Salt dip, Shamrock-Basketweave
  patt., 2nd black mark 25.00
Salt dip, seahorse & shell, turquoise
  blue horse & pink shell w/gold trim,
  3 x 5", 4" h. .550.00
Spillholder, cornucopia on rock, 7¾" h.,
  3rd black mark 110.00
Tazza, shell on dolphin base, 9¾" l.,
  3½" h., 1st black mark 275.00
Tea kettle, cov., w/overhead handle,
  Shamrock-Basketweave patt., 6" d.,
  5½" h., 2nd black mark 225.00
Teapot, cov., Harp Shamrock patt.,
  2nd black mark . . . . .200.00 to 235.00

Hexagon Pattern Teapot

Teapot, cov., Hexagon patt., green
trim, 2nd black mark (ILLUS.) 225.00
Teapot, cov., Neptune patt., pink trim,
3rd black mark 225.00
Teapot, cov., Shamrock-Basketweave
patt., 4¼" d., 3½" h., 2nd black
mark. 150.00
Teapot, cover & underplate, Tridacna
patt., individual size, 1st black
mark. 225.00
Tea set: cov. teapot, open sugar bowl,
creamer, 2 c/s & tray; Tridacna
patt., pink trim, 2nd black mark,
8 pcs.. . . . . .1,650.00
Tray, Grasses patt., 15 x 12", 1st
black mark. 595.00
Tray, Neptune patt., green trim, 17 x
14½", 2nd black mark 495.00
Tumbler, Tridacna patt., 2nd black
mark. 112.00
Vase, 6½" h., 3" d., ear of corn, 1st
black mark. 195.00
Vase, 6½" h., tree trunk form, Ivy
patt., 1st black mark 160.00
Vase, 6½" h., tree trunk form, Ivy
patt., 2nd black mark . . . . . . .60.00 to 85.00
Vase, 7"h., Aberdeen patt., 2nd green
mark. 135.00

BENNINGTON

Coachman Bottle

*Bennington wares, which ranged from
stonewares to parian and porcelain, were
made in Bennington, Vt., primarily in two
potteries, one in which Captain John Norton
and his descendants were principals, and
the other in which Christopher Webber
Fenton (also once associated with the
Nortons) was a principal. Various marks are*
*found on the wares made in the two major
potteries, including J. & E. Norton, E. & L.
P. Norton, L. Norton & Co., Norton &
Fenton, Edward Norton, Lyman Fenton &
Co., Fenton's Works, United States Pottery
Co., U.S.P. and others.*

Baker, mottled brown Rockingham
glaze, 10½" oval $135.00
Bed pan, mottled brown Rockingham
glaze. 85.00
Book flask, "Departed Spirits," mottled
brown Rockingham glaze . .275.00 to 500.00
Book flask, Flint Enamel glaze,
5½" h. (in the making flaw at one
corner) 300.00
Bowl, 3¼" d., 2" h., mottled brown
Rockingham glaze 65.00
Bowl, 5½" d., 1½" h., canted sides. 85.00
Coachman (or Toby) bottle, mottled
brown Rockingham glaze, 9¾" h.
(ILLUS.). 385.00
Coachman (or Toby) bottle, mottled
brown Rockingham glaze, 1849
mark, 10½" h.. . . . . .850.00
Creamer, model of a cow, Flint
Enamel glaze, 1849-58, 7" l. (no lid
& some chips) 225.00
Crock, straight-sided cylinder
w/earred handles, stoneware,
cobalt blue slip-quilled lion seated
before a house on grey, impressed
"J. & E. Norton, Bennington, Vt.,"
1850-59, 2-gal. (some discol-
oration). 1,200.00
Crock, slightly ovoid w/earred
handles, stoneware, cobalt blue slip-
quilled bird & branch on grey,
impressed "J. & E. Norton, Benning-
ton, Vt.," 1859-61, 2-gal. 270.00

Stoneware Crock

Crock, straight-sided cylinder
w/earred handles, stoneware,
cobalt blue slip-quilled floral spray
on grey, impressed "E. & L.P. Norton,
Bennington, Vt.," 1861-81, 12½" d.,
12½" h. (ILLUS.) 150.00

Shell Pattern Cuspidor

Cuspidor, Shell patt., mottled brown
  Rockingham glaze (ILLUS.) 145.00
Figure of a baby in a hooded cradle,
  parian, tinted hair & features, 6" l.,
  4" h. 195.00
Jug, ovoid w/strap handle, stoneware,
  brushed brown floral & leaves on
  grey, impressed "L. Norton, Bennington, Vt.," 1828-33, 11¼" h. 425.00
Jug, ovoid w/strap handle, stoneware,
  brushed cobalt blue butterfly on
  grey, impressed "L. Norton & Son,
  Bennington, Vermont," 1833-40,
  13½" h. 247.00
Jug, straight sides, strap handle,
  stoneware, cobalt blue slip-quilled
  squiggly leaf design on grey,
  impressed "J. & E. Norton, Bennington, Vt." label also brushed over in
  cobalt blue, 1850-59,
  14" h. . . . . .185.00 to 215.00
Jug, stoneware, brushed cobalt blue
  3-flower spray on grey, impressed
  "Norton & Fenton, East Bennington,
  Vt.," 1845-57, 3-gal., 14¾" h. 285.00
Jug, stoneware, cobalt blue slip-
  quilled floral spray on grey,
  impressed "J. & E. Norton, Ben-
  nington, Vt.," 1850-59, 4-gal. 525.00
Mixing bowl, mottled brown Rocking-
  ham glaze, 8" d. 65.00
Paperweight, model of a Spaniel dog,
  Flint Enamel glaze, 1849 mark,
  4½" l. 550.00
Pie plate, mottled brown Rockingham
  glaze, 9" d. . . . . .95.00 to 110.00
Pie plate, mottled brown Rockingham
  glaze, 10½" d. . . . . .125.00 to 145.00
Pitcher, 9¾" h., parian, Pond Lily
  patt. 240.00
Pitcher, 10" h., parian, Wild Rose
  patt. 250.00
Soap dish, pierced top, drain hole in
  side, mottled brown Rockingham
  glaze, 4½ x 3" rounded oval, 3" h. . .110.00
Soap dish, pierced top, drain hole in
  side, feather-molded rim, mottled
  brown Rockingham glaze 225.00

Syrup pitcher, parian, Palm Tree patt.
  (no pewter top) 135.00
Syrup pitcher w/original pewter top,
  parian, Climbing Ivy patt., 7" h. 170.00
Toby "barrel" bottle, figural Toby
  seated atop barrel labeled "Old
  Tom," mottled brown Rockingham
  glaze, 8" h. (minor hairline at seam
  on hat) 650.00
Trinket box, cov., parian, figural
  cherub asleep on lid, white w/gilt
  nubs on cherub 60.00
Tulip vase, Flint Enamel glaze in dark
  brown w/touches of yellow & dark
  green, 1849-58, 9" h. . . . . . .250.00 to 400.00
Vases, 8" h., parian, ovoid w/slightly
  flaring rim, applied grape clusters
  at shoulders, blue & white, pr. 150.00
Vase, 8½" h., parian, ovoid w/tall
  neck & shaped rim, applied grapes
  at shoulders, white w/blue-green
  leaves & pink & yellow buds 70.00
Vase, parian, reserved w/profile bust
  portrait of gentleman 230.00

BERLIN (KPM)

Model of a Bird

*The mark, KPM, was used at Meissen
from 1723 to 1725, and was later adopted by
the Royal Factory, Konigliche Porzellan
Manufaktur, in Berlin. At various periods it
has been incorporated with the Branden-
burg sceptre, the Prussian eagle or the
crowned globe. The same letters were also
adopted by other factories in Germany in
the late 19th and 20th centuries. With the
end of the German monarchy in 1918, the
name of the firm was changed to Staatliche
Porzellan Manufaktur and though production was halted during World War II, the
factory was rebuilt and is still in business.*

The exquisite paintings on porcelain produced at the close of the 19th century are eagerly sought by collectors today.

Cream jug, h.p. frolicking cherubs
decor, 4½" h. $290.00

Figure of Cupid in a strident stance, naked but for a pale apricot drapery & offering a rose in one extended hand, base littered w/his bow & several arrows, late 19th c.,
14 5/8" h. 605.00

Figures, Ceres, the goddess of fertility, holding a large cornucopia overflowing w/fruits & flowers, a young putto w/a spade & other farming implements resting at her feet & a young warrior wearing a helmet surmounted by an eagle & carrying a shield molded as a face, 10½" & 5¼" h., respectively, pr. (Ceres w/minor losses) 275.00

Figure group, Venus seated on a shellwork support holding an apple, surrounded by 2 putti w/quiver & arrows, a cupid holding a flaming torch & hunter (possibly Adonis) w/his dog, scroll-molded mound base heightened in gilding, late 19th c., 8½" h. (restoration to hunter's leg) 522.00

Garniture set: pr. 8-light candelabra, large centerpiece bowl & pr. pierced scroll-molded dishes; molded candelabra base supporting a cornucopia issuing 8 gilt-bronze branches terminating in a porcelain socket & bobeche, each painted w/floral sprays & heightened in gilding, late 19th c., 5 pcs. 6,050.00

Model of a bird, naturalistically modeled w/incised feather markings enriched in brown tones, standing on a circular grassy base enriched w/water reeds in shades of green & turquoise, ca. 1870, repair to beak & small base chip, 8" h. (ILLUS.) . . .1,430.00

Painting on porcelain, Romeo & Juliet, 5¾ x 4½". 145.00

Painting on porcelain, bust of young girl w/red hair, ornate frame,
7 x 5". 1,500.00

Painting on porcelain, Gypsy maiden wearing a shawl, w/gold coins dangling about her forehead & leaning against a crimson-colored cushion w/her hands clasped, artist-signed, late 19th c., 9 3/8 x 6¼" 825.00

Painting on porcelain, infant Jesus standing on the Virgin's lap, Saint John & Elizabeth at their side, artist-signed, late 19th c., 9 3/8 x 6¼". 770.00

Painting on porcelain, semi-nude

Lorelei maiden clinging to a rocky outcrop, her blonde tresses blowing about her & w/musical instrument nearby, signed Wagner, late 19th c., 9 3/8 x 6¼" 2,200.00

Painting on porcelain, Ruth in field w/sheaf of wheat under her left arm, artist-signed, late 19th c., framed, 9 3/8 x 6 3/8" 1,100.00

Painting on porcelain, group of Neopolitan urchin boys playing a game of dice, late 19th c.,
10 3/8 x 7 5/8" 2,200.00

Painting on porcelain, tavern scene w/rustic maiden dancing a jig w/an elderly partner while numerous guests congenially look on, 3rd quarter 19th c., 12¼ x 10" 1,870.00

Painting Of Psyche

Painting on porcelain, Psyche, w/scant drapery around her waist, seated on grassy mound at the banks of a stream, 3rd quarter 19th c.,
12 3/8 x 10 1/8" (ILLUS.) 4,400.00

Painting on porcelain, "Temptation of St. Anthony," young woman offering wine to kneeling monk, artist-signed, framed, 14 x 12" 1,870.00

Painting on porcelain, "The Monkey's Feast," interior of a rustic kitchen w/groups of monkeys seated at a heavily laden banquet table w/others seated on floor & carving a bird, grilling oysters or tending to numerous kettles in an open hearth, late 19th c., 15 x 12 1/8" 2,310.00

Painting on porcelain, Hagar & Ishmael leaving the house of Abraham & wandering forlornly into a darkened landscape, 3rd quarter 19th c., 23¼ x 18 5/8" 9,350.00

Plate, 8¼" d., butterfly, bird & dragon-

fly amidst meadow scene center, sky
blue border w/scalloped gilt rim 95.00
Plate, 8½" w., leaf-shaped w/single
handle, h.p. realistic fruit decor,
gold trim, ca. 1870 . . . . 185.00

Berlin Hand-painted Plates

Plates, 8 5/8" d., each w/cluster of
ripening fruit amongst foliage
center, molded lappet border
heightened in gilding, set of 8
(ILLUS. of part) 1,100.00
Plates, 9" d., cupids at various pursuits
reserved on bright blue ground
center, each within gilt band on
cavetto & gilt-edged rim, late 19th
c., set of 6 . . . . 990.00
Platter, 13" l., pierced handles, pink
decor on white ground, gold trim 75.00
"Solitaire" set: cov. teapot, cov. sugar
bowl, cov. milk jug, c/s & tray;
each w/different panel of exotic &
domestic birds in landscapes within
lightly molded basketwork borders,
gilt lappet borders, late 19th c.,
6 pcs. 880.00
Vases, cov., 17" h., each side
w/medallion of lovers relaxing
beneath a tree reserved on wide
cobalt blue band between pale beige
& white borders enriched w/gilding,
late 19th c., pr. 1,540.00

BILOXI (George Ohr) POTTERY

George Ohr Vases

George Ohr, the eccentric potter of Biloxi,
Mississippi, worked from about 1883 to
1906. Some think him to be one of the most
expert throwers the craft will ever see. The
majority of his works were hand thrown,
exceedingly thin-walled items, some of
which have a crushed or folded appearance.
He considered himself the foremost potter

in the world and declined to sell much of his
production, instead accumulated a great
horde to leave as a legacy to his children. In
1972, this collection was purchased for
resale by an antique dealer.

Bank, minaret-shaped on base, brown
glaze, must break to open,
signed $125.00
Bank, pear-shaped, light tan,
unglazed, must break to open,
signed 125.00
Jug, mottled light green glaze, 9 x 7" . . 295.00
Mug, crumpled angular handle, red &
green matte finish, ca. 1900, signed,
4¼" h. 605.00
Pitcher, 10½" h., relief-molded decor,
dated 1892 (handle repair) 275.00
Puzzle mug, gun metal grey glaze 325.00
Vase, 3" h., speckled brown glaze 125.00
Vases, 3¼" & 2¾" h. respectively, one
w/punched & pinched sides, neck
pressed to form 2 opposing spouts,
streaked ochre & burgundy glaze;
the second of pinched & folded form,
orange-mustard glaze spotted
w/green, pr. (ILLUS.) 550.00
Vase, 4¼" h., crimped, overall crystal
globs on deep green, signed 295.00
Vase, 4½" h., bulging body
w/crumpled lip, blue over mottled
pink exterior glaze, mottled brown
interior, ca. 1900, signed 385.00

BISQUE

Bisque Child

Bisque is biscuit china, fired a single time
but not glazed. Some bisque is decorated
with colors. Most abundant from the
Victorian era are figurines and groups, but
other pieces from busts to vases were made
by numerous potteries in the U.S. and
abroad. Also see FAIRY LAMPS.

Animal covered dish, dog w/bone on
basketweave base, white & brown

dog on green blanket atop white
& gilt basket-base, marked "France,"
9 x 6½", 5½" h. $595.00

Busts of boy & girl w/hands to cheeks,
wearing pink & aqua-trimmed white
gowns, 4½" h., pr................325.00

Busts of lady wearing bonnet & gentleman w/hair in long curls, France,
10" h., pr......................425.00

Figure of a child, seated & pulling
at tassel of night cap, 2¼" l.,
2¼" h. (ILLUS.) 65.00

Figure of a black banjo player,
Heubach sunburst mark, 5¾" h. 400.00

Figure of a girl holding up a blue
slipper w/mouse peeking out
of mesh stocking, wearing a
lovely dress, apron & bonnet,
7¾" h. 125.00

Figure of a Dutch girl carrying a
bucket, lavender, peach & green
garments, Heubach, 9½" h. 175.00

Figure of a lady, her shoes in one
hand & holding up her skirts, gold
anchor on her blouse & ruffled
bonnet, Heubach, 11½" h. 165.00

Figure of a girl w/tambourine,
Heubach, 14½" h. 265.00

Figure of a little boy dressed as
Teddy Roosevelt in hunting attire,
Heubach, 16" h. 325.00

Figure of a girl dancing & holding
out her decorated pleated skirt,
on floral base w/tambourine at
her feet, Heubach, 16½" h. 550.00

Figures, boy & girl bubble blowers,
pastel garments, 13" h., pr. 495.00

Figures, boy & girl dressed in Victorian garments & holding brown
seashells, Germany, pr...........375.00

Figure group, boy, girl & dog, girl
in blue riding brown & white dog
& boy wearing tan cap & blue &
white suit holding girl in position,
7¼ x 3¾", 8¾" h. 165.00

Bisque Figure Group

Figure group, 3 boys wearing blue fur-
trimmed caps & coats w/gold
buttons, Germany, late 19th c.,
9½" h. (ILLUS.) 180.00

Figure group, man, woman & child in
boat, pastel colors w/enameled gold
dots in relief, Germany, 13 x 6",
12" h. 390.00

Flower holder vase, figure of Dutch boy
wearing tan breeches & hat & blue
shirt standing beside square vase,
Heubach, 3 3/8" d., 6 3/8" h. 110.00

Bisque Flower Holder

Flower holder vase, boy & girl
supporting lustred cornucopia vase,
pastel pink, blue & orchid garments,
ca. 1890, numered on base, 7¾" h.
(ILLUS.)........................130.00

Flower holder vase, 2 large cupids
supporting flower-form vase
w/pierced top, gold trim, 5¼" w.,
8¾" h. 185.00

Model of a dog, tan & white coat
w/black markings on face, wearing
black collar, 7" l., 4" h. 70.00

Model of a dog, brown & white King
Charles Spaniel w/pink ribbon
around neck, seated on blue pillow
base, 3¾" d., 4 3/8" h. 69.00

Model of a wild boar in standing
position, Germany, 7½" w. base,
4½" h. 130.00

Model of a white dog w/pink & brown
intaglio eyes, wearing rust collar,
Heubach, 5 x 3¾", 9" h. 150.00

Model of a dog dressed as a drummer,
wearing ornate hat w/plume, red,
white & blue jacket & blue & white
striped trousers, marked "Bibi Tapin"
& numbered on base, 3½ x 4½",
10¼" h. 195.00

Nodding figure, seated poodle & bulldog on oval base, 4¾" h. 135.00

Nodding figure, man seated beneath
tree by fence w/hat hanging from

branch, grey & white clothing & tan
tree, 3¼ x 2½", 5½" h.............125.00
Nodding figure, Oriental man pulling
cart, dressed in pink, yellow & blue
w/enameled gold dots in relief,
France, 5 x 3", 7¼" h. 145.00
Nodding figures, Sultan & Sultaness,
soft green w/pink robes & rust hats,
gold trim, 2½" d., 3¾" h., pr. 180.00
Nodding figures, black African man &
woman, pr. 575.00
Piano baby, lying on back & playing
w/toes, Heubach, 4" l. 95.00
Piano baby, seated w/arms extended
& head cocked, intaglio eyes,
Heubach, 4¾" h. 145.00
Piano baby, black, seated, wearing
white pants w/blue trim, blue bands
around neck, Heubach, 5" l........300.00
Piano baby, seated w/legs crossed &
arms extended upward, wearing
pink-trimmed nightgown, 10" h. 400.00
Toothpick holder, crawling baby
w/"cracked" egg on back,
Heubach.......................95.00
Vases, 18 1/8" h., ovoid, white classical maiden's head handles, 4 flaring
feet, classical profiles reserved
within gilt roundel on matt blue
ground, supported on a knop
modeled as a classical male head,
ca. 1880, pr. (repairs & now mounted
as table lamps) 770.00
Whimsey, 2 frogs seated before 2 eggs,
3¼ x 2¾"......................75.00

BLUE WILLOW

Blue Willow Plate

This pseudo-Chinese pattern has been
used by numerous firms throughout the
years. The original design is attributed to
Thomas Minton about 1780 and Thomas
Turner is believed to have first produced the
ware during his tenure at the Caughley
works. The blue underglaze transfer print

pattern has never been out of production
since that time. An oriental landscape
incorporating a bridge, pagoda, trees,
figures and birds, supposedly tells the story
of lovers fleeing a cruel father who wished to
prevent their marriage. The gods, having
pity on them, changed them into birds
enabling them to fly away and seek their
happiness together. Also see BUFFALO
POTTERY.

Ale tankard, angular handle, England,
30 oz. $45.00
Bone dish, Buffalo Pottery, 1914 ....18.00
Bone dish, Ridgway, early 20th c. 10.00
Bouillon cup, 2-handled, Ridgway,
6½" d. 25.00
Bowl, 3½" d., footed, Maastricht 25.00
Bowl, 5" d., Homer Laughlin, U.S.A.,
20th c. 4.00
Bowl, 7¼" d., John Steventon & Sons,
1923-36.........................9.00
Bowl, 8" d., Swinnerton's Ltd.,
early 20th c......................45.00
Butter pat, Allertons ....15.00 to 18.00
Cake stand, England 135.00
Chocolate pot, cov..................65.00
Creamer, child's 7.50
Creamer, Copeland, after 1891 ....22.00
Creamer & cov. sugar bowl, made in
Japan, pr. ....12.00 to 15.00
Cup & saucer, scalloped rim,
Allertons 22.50
Cup & saucer, gold trim, Booths,
20th c...........................18.00
Cup & saucer, Homer Laughlin....5.00 to 7.00
Cup & saucer, Occupied Japan 12.00
Cup & saucer, Petrus Regout
Maastricht 12.00
Cup & saucer, Ridgway, England,
late 19th c. 16.00
Cup & saucer, early 19th c. 60.00
Cup & saucer, ca. 1900, large size 30.00
Dinner set, child's, cov. teapot,
creamer, sugar bowl, four 5" d.
plates, 4 c/s, platter & vegetable
bowl, 17 pcs. 215.00
Egg coddler, Royal Worcester, 2½".....28.00
Egg cup, double, Allertons, 4¼" h......22.50
Egg cup, Japan, 3¾" h. 10.00
Mug, Wood & Sons, 1917-54 ....20.00
Mustard pot, cov., unmarked 95.00
Pancake dish & dome cover, handled,
Japan, 10½" d....................90.00
Pitcher, 5½" h., jug-type, ironstone,
Mason's 95.00
Pitcher, 6" h., Allertons.............110.00
Pitcher, milk, 8½" h., Japan..........35.00
Plate, 6" d., Allertons (ILLUS.) 7.50
Plate, 6" d., Ridgway 5.00
Plate, 6" d., J. Steventon & Sons 5.00
Plate, 6½" d., Petrus Regout
Maastricht 7.00
Plate, 8" d., Allertons 10.00

Plate, 8¾" d., Meakin 7.00
Plate, 9" d., W. Adams 8.00
Plate, 9" d., Japan 4.50
Plate, 9" d., Ridgway 9.00
Plate, 9" d., Wedgwood. 24.00
Plate, 10" d., Brown & Steventon, early
   20th c. 11.00
Plate, 10" d., Dudson Wilcox & Till,
   1902-26 . . . . .12.00
Plate, 10" d., England, 1891-
   1912 .12.00 to 15.00
Plate, 10" d., Homer Laughlin. 7.00
Plate, 10" d., Japan 6.00
Plate, 11" d., Royal Worcester, 1880 . . . .29.00
Plate, 12" d., Homer Laughlin. 10.00
Platter, 10" l., Allertons 25.00
Platter, 12" oval, Ridgway. 33.00
Platter, 13¼ x 10½", Staffordshire,
   late 19th c. 38.00
Platter, 13½" l., Homer Laughlin. 14.00
Platter, 15½" l., Allertons 60.00
Platter, 16¾" l., A. Stevenson,
   1816-30 . . . . .175.00
Salt & pepper shakers, Homer
   Laughlin, pr. 30.00
Sauce dish, Maastricht, 5½" d. . . .5.00 to 7.00
Soup plate w/flange rim, Allertons,
   8" d. 10.00
Soup plate w/flange rim, Maastricht,
   8" d. 30.00
Soup plate w/flange rim, Booth,
   10" d. 15.00
Soup tureen w/cover, ladle & under-
   plate, Burleigh, 3 pcs. 295.00
"Stilton" cheese dish, slant-top lid &
   underplate, 2 pcs. 85.00
Teapot, cov., Allertons 75.00
Teapot, cov., Sadler, 7" h. 30.00
Teapot, cover & underplate 55.00

Child's Tea Set

Tea set, child's: cov. teapot, creamer,
   cov. sugar bowl, 4 c/s & 4 plates;
   original box, Japan, 15 pcs. (ILLUS.
   of part) 110.00
Tea set: cov. teapot, creamer & cov.
   sugar bowl; Japan, 3 pcs. 165.00
Vegetable dish, cov., Thomas
   Dimmock, 10" sq. 150.00
Vegetable dish, cov., square,
   Steventon. 80.00
Vegetable dish, open, Ridgway, 7½ x
   6" oval 38.00
Vegetable dish, open, Allertons, 8 x 6"
   oblong 38.00

BOCH FRERES

Boch Freres Vase

This Belgium firm, founded in 1841 and still in production, first produced stoneware art pottery of mediocre quality, attempting to upgrade their wares through the years. In 1907, Charles Catteau became the art director of the pottery and slowly the influence of his work was absorbed by the artisans surrounding him. All through the 1920s, wares were decorated in a distinctive Art Deco motif that is now eagerly sought along with the hand-thrown gourd form vessels coated with earth-tone glazes that were produced during the same time. Almost all Boch Freres pottery is marked, but the finest wares also carry the signature of Charles Catteau in addition to the pottery mark. Also see TILES.

Bowl, 11" d., 2¼" h., Art Deco style,
   enameled golden yellow & green
   leaves & circles on sandy rough dark
   brown ground, enameled green
   banding interior & exterior $115.00
Vase, 9" h., Art Deco style, stylized
   gulls flying over waves on creamy
   glazed ground 190.00
Vase, 11½" h., baluster-shaped 6
   black roundels w/yellow, fuchsia
   & lavender stylized florals on
   white ground. 110.00
Vase, 11¾" h., ovoid, 3 black panels
   w/h.p. stylized yellow, fuchsia &
   yellow florals .99.00
Vases, 12" h., blue streaked glaze,
   ormolu mounting, pr. 125.00
Vase, 15" h., beige relief florals on
   chocolate-grey ground (ILLUS.) 400.00
Vase, Art Deco style, enameled
   roosters decor. 200.00

BOEHM PORCELAINS

Boehm Bengal Tiger

Although not antique, Boehm porcelain sculptures have attracted much interest, Edward Marshall Boehm excelled in hard porcelain sculptures. His finest creations, inspired by the beauties of nature, are in the forms of birds and flowers. Since his death in 1969, his work has been carried on by his wife at the Boehm Studios in Trenton, New Jersey. In 1971, an additional studio was opened in Malvern, England, where bone porcelain sculptures are produced. We list both limited and non-limited editions of the Boehm Studios.

Arabian Stallion $700.00
Bengal Tiger (ILLUS.) 2,200.00
Blue Jay w/wild raspberries, 1981-82,
    14½" w., 8" d., 17" h. 1,950.00
Bunnies, male & female, pr. 325.00
Cat w/kittens 595.00
Chickadees 1,025.00
Cocker Spaniel 450.00
Cygnet 350.00
Dachshund 400.00
Fledgling Blackburnian Warbler,
    1964 . . . . 275.00
Fledgling Bluejay 225.00
Fledgling Kingfisher 235.00
Fledgling Red Poll 250.00
Lesser Prairie Chickens, 1962, pr. 975.00
Meadowlark, 1957, 8½" h. 925.00
Non pareil Buntings, 1958, 8½" h. 850.00
Robin w/Daffodil, 1964, overall
    13" h. 3,500.00
Swallows 2,100.00
Tree Sparrow, 1963 . . . . 380.00
Tufted Titmice 900.00
Tutankhamen - Shawabty 550.00
Tutankhamen - Votive Shield bas-
    relief 1,500.00
Wood Ducks, 1981-82, 18" w., 11" d.,
    16" h. 3,400.00
Yellow Rhododendron, 1981-82,
    9¾" w., 6" d., 6¼" h. 825.00
Yellow-Throated Warbler 325.00

BUFFALO POTTERY

Buffalo Pottery was established in 1902 in Buffalo, N.Y., to supply pottery for the Larkin Company. Most desirable today is Deldare Ware, introduced in 1908 in two patterns, "The Fallowfield Hunt" and "Ye Olden Times," which featured central English scenes and a continuous border. Emerald Deldare, introduced in 1911, was banded with stylized flowers & geometric designs and had varied central scenes, the most popular being from "The Tours of Dr. Syntax." Reorganized in 1940, the company now specializes in hotel china.

DELDARE

"The Great Controversy" Tankard Pitcher

Bowl, 9" d., The Fallowfield Hunt -
    Breaking Cover $450.00
Bowl, fruit, 9" d., Ye Village
    Tavern . . . . 385.00 to 400.00
Candlestick, shield-back, Village
    Scenes 575.00
Card tray, The Fallowfield Hunt - The
    Return, 7¾" d. 315.00
Card tray, Ye Lion Inn, 7¾" d. 300.00
Creamer, Scenes of Village Life in Ye
    Olden Days 185.00
Creamer & cov. sugar bowl, octagonal,
    Scenes of Village Life in Ye Olden
    Days, pr. 365.00
Cup & saucer, Ye Olden Days 175.00
Dresser tray, Dancing Ye Minuet,
    12 x 9" 525.00
Humidor, cov., bulbous, There was an
    Old Sailor, etc., 8" h. . . . . . . 700.00 to 795.00
Humidor, cov., octagonal, Ye Lion Inn,
    7" h. 475.00
Matchbox holder & ash tray combin-
    ation, Ye Lion Inn, ca. 1925, artist-
    signed, 6½" l., 3¼" h. 200.00

Mug, The Fallowfield Hunt, 2½" h. 400.00
Mug, The Fallowfield Hunt - Breaking
  Cover, 3½" h. 180.00
Mug, Ye Lion Inn, 3½" h.............245.00
Mug, Ye Lion Inn, 4¼" h.............250.00
Mug, Breakfast at the Three Pigeons,
  4½" h. 225.00
Pin tray, Ye Olden Days, artist-signed,
  6¼ x 3½"..........................290.00
Pitcher, 6" h., octagonal, The Fallow-
  field Hunt, artist-signed 360.00
Pitcher, 6" h., octagonal, Their Manner
  of Telling Stories - Which he Returned
  with a Curtsy, artist-
  signed ....265.00 to 325.00
Pitcher, 7" h., The Fallowfield Hunt -
  Breaking Cover 400.00
Pitcher, 7" h., octagonal, "To Spare an
  Old, Broken Soldier" one side, "To
  Advise Me in a Whisper" reverse,
  dated 1923 ....500.00
Pitcher, 8" h., octagonal, The Fallow-
  field Hunt - The Return 500.00
Pitcher, 8" h., octagonal, To Demand
  My Annual Rent - Welcome Me,
  1908 ....450.00
Pitcher, 9" h., octagonal, With a Cane
  Superior Air - This Amazed Me......575.00
Pitcher, 10" h., octagonal, Ye Old
  English Village 550.00
Pitcher, tankard, 12½" h., All You
  Have To Do Is Teach the Dutchman
  English 890.00
Pitcher, tankard, 12½" h., The Hunt
  Supper 550.00
Pitcher, tankard, 12¾" h., The Great
  Controversy, 1908
  (ILLUS.) ....650.00 to 885.00
Plaque, The Fallowfield Hunt - Break-
  fast at the Three Pigeons, pierced to
  hang, 12" d. 475.00

Deldare Plaque & Plate

Plaque, Ye Lion Inn, 1909, 12" d. (ILLUS.
  left)..............................375.00
Plate, 6¼" d., At Ye Lion Inn 145.00
Plate, 7¼" d., Ye Village Street,
  1908 ....118.00
Plate, 7½" d., The Fallowfield Hunt -
  The Start..........................180.00
Plate, 8¼" d., Ye Town Crier 225.00
Plate, 8½" d., The Fallowfield Hunt -
  The Death, 1909 (ILLUS. right).......250.00

Plate, 8½" d., Ye Town Crier 135.00
Plate, 9" d., The Fallowfield Hunt -
  The Start..........................135.00
Plate, 9¼" d., Ye Olden
  Times ....165.00 to 250.00
Plate, 9½" d., The Fallowfield Hunt -
  The Start, artist-signed 180.00
Plate, 9½" d., Ye Olden Times........140.00
Plate, 10" d., The Fallowfield Hunt -
  Breaking Cover, artist-signed 190.00
Plate, chop, 12" d., Ye Lion Inn........550.00
Plate, chop, 14" d., An Evening at Ye
  Lion Inn, pierced to hang, artist-
  signed.............................485.00

Fallowfield Hunt Chop Plate

Plate, chop, 14" d., The Fallowfield
  Hunt - The Start (ILLUS.)...........535.00
Punch bowl, The Fallowfield Hunt,
  14½" d...........................6,500.00
Relish tray, Ye Olden Times, 12 x
  6½".............................350.00
Sugar bowl, cov., Scenes of Village
  Life in Ye Olden Days..............200.00
Teapot, cov., Scenes of Village Life in
  Ye Olden Days, 3¾" h. 355.00
Teapot, cov., Scenes of Village Life in
  Ye Olden Days, 5¾" h. 260.00
Tea tile, Traveling in Ye Olden Days,
  6" d. 265.00
Tea tray, Heirlooms, 13¾ x 10¼" 695.00

EMERALD DELDARE
Card tray, handled, Dr. Syntax Robbed
  of his Property, 7" d. 315.00
Cup & saucer, Dr. Syntax of Liverpool ..375.00
Humidor, cov., Sailor, 8" h.............700.00
Pin tray, Dr. Syntax Received by the
  Maid 725.00
Pitcher, 6" h., Dr. Syntax Stopt by
  Highwaymen......................475.00
Plaque, Lost Sheep, 13½" d. 1,400.00
Plate, 7¼" d., Dr. Syntax Soliloquis-
  ing................................450.00
Plate, 8¼" d., Art Nouveau florals &
  geometric 250.00

Plate, 8½" d., Misfortune at Tulip
Hall 450.00
Plate, 9¼" d., Dr. Syntax - The Gar-
den Trio 325.00
Plate, 9¼" d., Dr. Syntax Losing His
Way...........................295.00
Salt shaker, 3" h. (single) 250.00
Salt & pepper shakers, Art Nouveau
geometric & florals, 3" h., pr.......440.00
Vase, 13½" h., cylindrical, American
Beauty, typical borders w/frieze of
butterflies above flowering plants ..600.00

MISCELLANEOUS

Cinderella Jug

Bowl, cream soup, Blue Willow patt......8.50
Butter pat, multicolored Art Deco
border, dated 1927 ....10.00
Butter tub, 2-handled, w/insert, pink
Apple Blossom decor, 1915 ....21.00
Christmas plate, 1952 ....43.50
Christmas plate, 1954 ....45.00
Christmas plate, 1957 ....43.50
Creamer & cov. sugar bowl, Blue
Willow patt., pr. 70.00
Cup & saucer, Blue Willow patt., 1905 ...31.50
Cup & saucer, Blue Willow patt.,
farmer's size 60.00
Feeding dish, Campbell Kids decor,
7¾" d. ....50.00 to 75.00
Game plate, Fallow Deer, signed R.K.
Beck, 9" d. 48.00
Game plate, Mallard Ducks, green
ground, 9" d. 55.00
Game plate, Wild Ducks, green ground,
9" d. ....38.00 to 60.00
Game platter, Buffalo Hunt, scalloped
edge, 14 x 11" 194.00
Game platter, Deer at Pond, 15 x 11"
oval 65.00
Game set: 15" l. platter & six 9¼" d.

plates; each w/different deer scene,
signed R.K. Beck, 7 pcs............240.00
Gravy boat w/undertray, Blue Willow
patt............................65.00
Jug, Cinderella, 6" h. (ILLUS.) 400.00
Jug, Landing of Roger Williams,
6" h...................350.00 to 385.00
Jug, Whaling City, souvenir of New
Bedford, Massachusetts, 1907,
6" h..........................1,100.00
Jug, Dutch, h.p. windmill scene,
6½" h..........................265.00
Jug, George Washington, blue decor,
gold trim, 7½" h. ....350.00 to 420.00
Jug, Robin Hood, 8¼" h. 375.00
Mug, advertising, "Bing & Nathan,"
monk reverse 70.00
Pitcher, 5" h., bulbous, Blue Willow
patt., 1907 ....75.00
Pitcher, 9" h., Pilgrim .....425.00 to 500.00
Pitcher, 9¼" h., Gloriana 275.00
Pitcher, 9¼" h., John Paul Jones,
1907 ....435.00
Pitcher, 9¼" h., Sailor 550.00
Plate, 4 3/8" d., commemorative,
"Wanamaker Store, 1861-1911
Jubilee" 65.00
Plate, 6" d., Blue Willow patt. 12.00
Plate, 7½" d., commemorative,
Washington's Home at Mt. Vernon,
multicolored 29.00
Plate, 7½" d., historical series,
McKinley Monument 25.00
Plate, 7½" d., historical series,
Niagara Falls, blue-green decor 75.00
Plate, 9" d., Blue Willow patt. 11.00
Plate, 10" d., Bangor patt............38.00
Plate, 10" d., historical series, The
White House, Washington, blue-
green on white 32.00
Plate, dinner, New England Steamship
Co. logo on face, New York, New
Haven & Hartford R.R. 20.00
Platter, 9¼" l., Blue Willow patt.......35.00
Platter, 10½ x 8½" oblong, Blue
Willow patt., 1909.................50.00
Platter, 14 x 11", Blue Willow patt.,
1909 ....70.00
Platter, 15 x 11", pink transfer on
white 22.50
Sugar bowl, cov., Blue Willow patt.,
1907 ....32.50
Toy tea set: cov. teapot, creamer, cov.
sugar bowl & 2 cups; House That
Jack Built decor, 5 pcs. 100.00
Wash basin, Blue Willow patt., 1911 ...175.00

CALIFORNIA FAIENCE

Chauncey R. Thomas and William V. Bragdon organized what was to become the

California Faience pottery in 1916, in Berkeley, California. Originally named after its owners, it later became The Tile Shop, finally adopting the California Faience name about 1924. Always a small operation whose output was a simple style of art pottery, most of which has a matte glaze that was designed for the florist shop trade, it also made colorfully decorated tiles. During the mid-1920s, California Porcelain was produced by this firm for the West Coast Porcelain Manufacturers of Millbrae, California. The great Depression halted art pottery production and none was produced after 1930 although some tiles were made for the Chicago World's Fair about 1932. Collectors now seek out these somewhat scarce pieces that always bear the incised mark of California Faience.

California Faience Mark

Basket, ribbon molded handle, glossy
    pink glaze, overall 10" h. $45.00
Bowl, 12" d., oriental decor, 3-color
    glaze 265.00
Candlesticks, blue to turquoise high
    glaze, 7" h., pr. 235.00
Condiment bottle, Delft-type, figural
    boy 150.00
Console bowl w/flower frog in the
    form of 2 ducks . . . . .375.00 to 450.00
Console bowl w/flower frog, tur-
    quoise interior, black matte finish
    exterior 150.00
Tile, multicolored basket of flowers . . .165.00
Vase, 4" h., glossy blue glaze 75.00
Vase, 4" h., 2" d., cylindrical, yellow
    matte finish .135.00
Vase, 7" h., glossy pink glaze 105.00
Vase, 11" h., 10" d., gourd-shaped,
    mottled glaze w/crystalline high-
    lights. 300.00

CANTON

    This ware has been produced for nearly two centuries in potteries near Canton, China. Intended for export sale, much of it was originally inexpensive blue-and-white hand decorated ware. Late 18th and early 19th century pieces are superior to later ones and fetch higher prices.

Bowl, 4" d., 2" h., Willow patt. variant,
    blue-and-white $55.00
Cup & saucer, Rice patt., blue-and-
    white 75.00

Canton Dessert Dish

Dessert dishes: pr. scalloped oval
    dishes & 3 sq. dishes (major
    damage on 2); enameled "famille-
    rose" decor w/insects in flight,
    pheasants & flowering branches on
    celadon ground, gilt-edged rim,
    mid-19th c., set of 5 (ILLUS. of
    one) 880.00
Dish, leaf-shaped, blue-and-white,
    7 x 5". 80.00
Ginger jar, cov., blue-and-white
    decor, 8" d., 10" h. 410.00
Plate, 8½" d., Willow patt. variant,
    blue-and-white 75.00
Plate, 10" d., blue-and-white, 19th c. . . .95.00
Platter, 10 x 8½" oval, Willow patt.,
    blue-and-white 100.00
Platter, 12¾ x 10½" oval, deep, blue-
    and-white, 19th c. 275.00

Canton Platter

Platter, 15" l., Willow patt. variant
    cavetto & trellis diaper border at
    rim, blue-and-white, 19th c.
    (ILLUS.) 50.00
Platter insert w/drain holes, blue-
    and-white, eggshell glaze, 14 x 11". . .100.00
Serving dish, scalloped rim, Willow

patt. variant, blue-and-white, egg-
shell glaze, 9½" d. 280.00
Serving dish, oval, Willow patt. variant,
blue-and-white, lemon peel glaze,
10¼" l. 150.00
Soup plates, "famille-rose" decor,
Chinese pheasant perched on a
branch of pomegranates amidst
butterflies, sprigs & clusters of
flowers & fruit on celadon ground,
gilt-edged rim, late 19th c.,
9 7/8" d., set of 14 (2 w/minor
cracks) 1,045.00
Sugar bowl, cov., globular w/applied
loop handles at sides, typical
Oriental landscape, blue-and-
white 260.00
Vases, 34¾" h., baluster-shaped
w/bat-form handles at neck, concentric rows of "shou" characters in
various scripts between borders of
floral sprays, precious emblems,
dragons & squirrels amidst flowering
vines, all in slip & "famille rose"
enamels on a pale celadon ground,
19th c., pr. .2,863.00
Vegetable dish, octagonal, Willow
patt. variant, blue-and-white, egg-
shell glaze, 11¾" l. 175.00

CAPO DI MONTE

Capo-di-Monte Covered Box

*Production of porcelain and faience began
in 1736 at the Capo-di-Monte factory in
Naples. In 1743 King Charles of Naples
established a factory there that made wares
with relief decoration. In 1759 the factory
was moved to Buen Retiro near Madrid,
operating until 1808. Another Naples
pottery was opened in 1771 and operated
until 1806 when its molds were acquired by
the Doccia factory of Florence, which has
since made reproductions of original
Capo-di-Monte pieces with the "N" mark*

*beneath a crown. Some very early pieces are
valued in the thousands of dollars but the
subsequent productions are considerably
lower.*

Box, cov., enameled relief-molded
allegorical scenes, brass fittings,
6 13/16 x 6" oval, 5½" h. (ILLUS.). . .$264.00
Cup & saucer, demitasse, branch
handle, maidens & dogs frolicking
in a landscape scene w/trees &
mountainous background 65.00
Cup & saucer, demitasse: cup w/scene
of figures frolicking in a field, gold
interior; saucer w/floral sprays &
cherubs bearing garlands 45.00
Cup & saucer, demitasse, footed, scene
of ducks & heron in marshland
habitat 68.00
Cup & saucer, cherubs in relief, large . . .60.00
Cup & saucer, cherubs & floral garlands
decor, gold trim 55.00
Cup & saucer, Phaeton patt., 1860 . . . . . .75.00
Dresser box w/hinged lid, rectangular
w/cut corners, relief-molded classical figures on lid, side panels
w/cherubs in various pursuits, early
19th c., 3¾ x 3", 2½" h. 210.00
Equestrian figure, soldier on horse-
back, dated 1840, 9 x 8" 350.00
Ewer, semi-nude maidens in relief,
14" h. 110.00
Figure of a fat man playing a tuba,
6" h. 125.00
Figure of a flower girl, ca. 1880, 9" h. . . .325.00
Figure of an elephant lady wearing a
long flowing gown & large hat,
20" h. 575.00
Figure group, hunchback dwarf
musicians (6) & conductor, ca. 1860,
3½" h. 270.00
Perfume bottle, cherubs in a garden in
relief, 3" h. 95.00

CELADON

Chinese Celadon Dish

Celadon is the name given a highly-fired Oriental porcelain featuring a glaze that ranges from olive through tones of green, blue-green and greys. These wares have been made for centuries in China, Korea and Japan. Fine early Celadon wares are costly, later pieces are far less expensive.

Bowl, 5 7/8" d., shallow, flared rim, interior molded w/foliage decor below a plain band encircling the everted rim, plain underside w/single carved line, raised on knife-cut footrim, grey-green glaze, Song Dynasty. $330.00

Censor, 3-footed, on wooden ring base, 1890s, 8" h. 85.00

Dish, shallow w/rounded sides rising to flange rim, impressed central peony medallion within border of carved floral sprays w/combed details, olive green glaze, Ming Dynasty, 13¼" d. (ILLUS.) 990.00

Plate, 8" d., enameled floral decor, early 20th c. 110.00

Plate, 8¾" d., green border, blue & white center scene of Oriental man at table 130.00

Shrimp dish, shell-shaped, polychrome bird & butterfly pattern on celadon green, 1790-1820, 10¾ x 9" 275.00

Teapot, cov., 20th c., 6-cup 60.00

Umbrella stand, cylindrical, bas relief blossoming wisteria on pale green ground, raised stylized floral band on royal blue rim, Japan, late 19th c., 24 5/8" h. 275.00

Vase, 11½" h., sides carved w/large chrystanthemum blossoms on scrolling, leafy stems rising from the base, cylindrical neck carved w/simple lappets, green glaze, unglazed footrim burnt orange in the firing, Ming Dynasty (small glaze chip) 550.00

Vase, 23¼" h., baluster-shaped, applied handles, blue Foo dog decor on pale green, early 20th c. 231.00

Wall pocket, early 20th c., 12" h. 65.00

Korean Celadon Wine Pot

Wine pot & cover w/coiling stem knop, melon-ribbed, C-scroll handle & curving spout, slightly crackled sea green glaze, Koryo Dynasty, Korea (ILLUS.). 11,000.00

CHANTILLY

Chantilly Jardiniere

Chantilly porcelain was made in Oise, France, from 1725. Soft paste porcelain was made until 1800. Subsequently, hard paste wares were made at other factories there. Early decoration, until 1740, was primarily influenced by early Chinese and Japanese porcelains. Later decoration included naturalistic flowers painted or molded in relief.

Butter tub & cover on attached stand, circular, painted in underglaze-blue & enameled w/central carnation sprig surrounded by smaller floral sprigs & insects within a blue-edged rim molded w/basketwork, ca. 1770, 8 1/8" d. $165.00

Cup & saucer, fluted bucket shape cup w/scroll handle, h.p. bouquets & floral sprays, chocolate brown rims, ca. 1745 . . . . .550.00

Cup & saucer, h.p. floral sprays within gilt scroll & foliate surrounds reserved on a blue trellis pattern ground enriched w/gilt dots, gilt rims, ca. 1760 .770.00

Drug jar & cover w/knob finial, Kakiemon-style decor w/a red & green berried foliage cartouche enclosing the name "Baume d'Arceus," reverse & cover decorated w/flower sprays, ca. 1735, 6" h. 2,640.00

Jardiniere, painted Kakiemon palette w/chinoiserie figure one side & tied floral bouquet & insects reverse, dragon handles (w/minor repair) enriched in turquoise & black, red hunting horn mark, ca. 1730, 5¼" h. (ILLUS.) .3,080.00

Jug, cov., pear-shaped, Kakiemon-
style decor in iron-red, yellow,
green, blue & black w/flowering
plants issuing from rockwork & insects, phoenix decor on cover,
scrolling silver mounts w/shell
thumbrest, ca. 1735, 7½" h. 7,150.00
Sauceboats, side handles, double
spouts, blue florals & trim on white,
blue hunting horn mark, 18th c.,
9" l., pr. 390.00

CHELSEA

Chelsea Dish

*This ware was made in London from 1754
to 1770 in England's second porcelain
factory. From 1770 to 1783 it was operated
as a branch of the Derby Factory. Its
equipment was then moved to Derby. It has
been reproduced and ceramics made
elsewhere are often erroneously called
Chelsea.*

Bonbonniere, modeled as a young boy
shearing the mane of a grey boar &
wearing a green hat, puce jacket
& turquoise breeches & with satchel
slung over his shoulder on strap
inscribed "Plus de bruit que de
profit," on a green mound molded
w/leaves & w/applied colorful
florettes; the interior painted
w/yellow, iron-red & purple floral
sprigs within a shaded green leaf
border, w/gold mounts & enameled
cover painted on each side w/floral
sprigs, late red-early gold anchor
period, 1756-60, 2 1/8" h........$1,760.00
Dish, hollyhock leaf shape, center
w/yellow, iron-red, rose, green &
purple pear, strawberries & gooseberries surrounded by 6 jade green
leaves w/puce veins & stems

forming the pierced rim, edge
between leaves heightened in
gilding, late red-early gold anchor
period, ca. 1758, 8¼" d..........2,640.00
Dishes, cabbage leaf shape, center
w/rose, iron-red, blue, yellow &
green floral spray on rose-height-
ened molded veining extending as a
midrib to the curled stalk handle,
crimped edges shaded from deep
green to yellow, red anchor period,
ca. 1755, 9½" l., pr. 3,740.00
Dishes, cabbage leaf shape, painted in
center w/sprig of yellow peaches &
green leaves on rose-veined ground,
crimped rim edged in green shading
to pale yellow, gold anchor period,
ca. 1759, 11" & 11¼" l., pr. 1,760.00
Dish, scalloped edge, h.p. puce, yellow, blue, green & brown floral
bouquet & sprigs & pr. shaded brown
& iron-red moths, red anchor period,
ca. 1755, 12¼" d. (ILLUS.) 880.00
Figure of boy w/rabbit, gold anchor
period, 1758-70, 5½" h..............95.00
Figure of Neptune w/dolphin, 12" h....300.00
Figures of Colonial man & woman, gold
anchor period, 1758-70, 7½" h.,
pr.................................215.00
Figures of man & woman standing
against tree stumps, lamb at feet,
lady holding tambourine, applied
flowers, green, yellow, pink,
lavender, blue & burgundy costumes, 11" h., pr. 710.00
Plate, 8½" d., painted green, red,
purple, yellow & puce sprigs of fruit
& 2 yellow, iron-red, purple &
turquoise butterflies, petal-shaped
rim edged in turquoise, late red
anchor period, ca. 1758 ....770.00
Sauceboat, leaf-shaped body molded at
base w/strawberry vine forming 4
feet, yellow & brown branch handle
entwined w/puce vine bearing iron-
red, yellow & green strawberries,
blossoms & leaves, interior &
exterior w/floral sprays & insects,
barbed rim edged in brown, red
anchor period, ca. 1755, 7½" l. 770.00
Scent bottle w/double stoppers,
modeled as cupid holding pr. of
billing doves & his bow & seated on a
gilt-edged high-domed base painted
on the exterior & interior w/floral
sprays, his head & feather tipped
arrows in quiver forming the
stoppers, bottle & stopper necks
w/gold & gilt-metal mounts, red
anchor period, ca. 1756, 2¾" h......990.00
Soup plate w/flange rim, rose, yellow,
iron-red, green & blue floral spray &
sprigs within a brown-edged rim, red
anchor period, ca. 1755, 9" d.......275.00

CHELSEA LUSTRE WARE

Chelsea Grape Lustre Pattern

The name for this ware is misleading since the design is thought to have originated at the Coalport, Shropshire, England porcelain factory during the 1800s, long after the closing of the Chelsea factory. In this attractive pattern, small grape clusters or sprigs are raised in relief and colored in blue or purple lustre on a white ground, It was a popular pattern from the earliest Victorian years and is often referred to as "Grandmother's Ware."

Bowl, 6½" d., 3½" h. $20.00
Cake plate, 10" d. 39.00
Cup 6.00
Cup plate 20.00
Pitcher, ca. 1840 . . . . .47.50
Plate, 9" d., handled 25.00
Plate, 10" d. 28.00
Ramekin w/underplate, blue lustre
　sprigs 12.00
Tea set: cov. teapot, creamer & cov.
　sugar bowl; purple lustre, 3 pcs.
　(ILLUS. of part) 200.00
Vegetable bowl, oval 22.00

CHINESE EXPORT

Fitzhugh Pattern Bottle & Plate

Large quantities of porcelain have been made in China for export to America from the 1780s, much of it shipped from the ports of Canton and Nanking. A major source of this porcelain was Ching-te-Chen in the Kiangsi province but the wares were also made elsewhere. The largest quantities were blue and white. Prices fluctuate considerably depending on age, condition, decoration, etc. Also see CANTON.

Bottle, blue Fitzhugh patt., small hair
　crack, 19th c. (ILLUS. left) $660.00

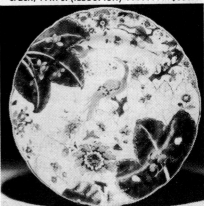

Chinese Export Charger

Charger, Tobacco Leaf patt., under-
　glaze-blue, yellow, rose, iron-red,
　green, turquoise & gilt w/pr.
　pheasants & tree squirrel amidst
　profusion of florals, fruiting branches
　& large overlapping leaves, gilt-
　edged rim, 1760-80, 13¼" d.
　(ILLUS.) 1,870.00
Creamer, helmet-shaped, enameled
　rust-red florals, 5¼" h. 85.00
Dishes, fluted, painted in iron-red,
　turquoise, yellow, purple & gold
　w/peonies & other flowers growing
　behind a fence within a stylized
　spearhead border on the cavetto,
　rim molded w/two rows of petals &
　painted w/four clusters of flowering
　plants, early 18th c., 8½" d., pr. 715.00

Chinese Export Leaf-Shaped Dish

Dishes, leaf-shaped, each modeled as
a "cos" lettuce leaf, rose & white
veining continuing from stem
handle (w/restored tip) & gilt-edged
fluted rim, ca. 1770, 14" l., pr.
(ILLUS. of one) 4,640.00
Hot water dish, orange Fitzhugh
patt., ca. 1810, 13¼" oval 1,980.00
Ink stand, underglaze-blue floral
decor, 10" l. .140.00
Mug, cylindrical body, woven strap
handle, underglaze blue florals
overall, late 18th c., 4 3/8" h. 165.00
Mug, cylindrical, painted on front in
shades of rose, iron-red, green,
"grisaille" & gold w/peonies growing
behind stylized rockwork & a fence,
rim w/iron-red diaper & floral panel
border, ca. 1740, 5½" h. (some
chips) 137.00
Pitcher, 10 7/8" h., jug-type,
Valentine patt., painted in pastel
enamels & gilding w/flaming altar,
pr. of doves on quiver, dogs &
shepherd's crook beneath a tree
in hilly landscape, ca. 1750 . . . . .935.00
Plate, 5½" d., underglaze-blue scene
w/four sages beneath tree, ca. 1750. .65.00
Plates, 6" to 8¾" d., green Fitzhugh
patt., 19th c., some w/minor repair,
set of 5 (ILLUS. of one w/bottle) 715.00
Plate, 7½" d., underglaze-blue decor
w/overglaze enamels in 4 colors,
ca. 1850 . . . . .120.00
Plate, 9" d., "Judgment of Paris,"
painted w/Paris wearing rose
drapery & seated on an iron-red
bench beneath a green & yellow
tree & w/brown & white dog at
his feet, offering a golden apple
to Venus in iron-red drapery while
Juno, Athena & Cupid wearing
green & iron-red drapery look on,
w/iron-red & gilt scroll & shell
border, ca. 1755 . . . . .440.00
Platter, 11 x 8 1/8" oblong w/cut
corners, dramatic genre scene center,
swag border w/lavender diapered
design, late 18th c. 412.50
Platter w/well & tree center, 18½ x
14½" oval, enameled multicolor
decor including vase of flowers,
deer, butterflies, fruit & bats
w/small armorial crest 600.00
Platter, 20¼" oval, blue Fitzhugh patt.,
ca. 1820 . . . . .935.00
Tea bowl, late 18th c., 2 x 3½" 125.00
Vase, 12" h., "famille-noire" decor
w/brown-black enameling, ca.
1900 . . . . .90.00
Vase, 15" h., "famille-rose" decor,
exotic birds, ca. 1890 . . . . .115.00
Waste bowl, enameled rust-red floral
decor, 5¼" d., 2½" h. 90.00

Wine cooler, cylindrical, painted
underglaze-blue, iron-red, gold &
white arms of France above the
Order of Saint Esprit flanked by
clusters of pomegranates, gourds,
chrysanthemums & prunus branches
painted in iron-red, "grisaille,"
white, blue enamel & gold, sides
w/grotesque mask handles beneath
a floral scroll border on the rim,
interior rim w/iron-red & gold diaper
band, ca. 1725, 4 5/8" h. (repaired
rim chip) 2,530.00

CLARICE CLIFF DESIGNS

Bone Dish

*Clarice Cliff was a designer for A.J.
Wilkinson, Ltd., Royal Staffordshire
Pottery, Burslem, England when they
acquired the adjoining Newport Pottery
Company whose warehouses were filled with
undecorated bowls and vases. About 1925,
her flair with the Art Deco style was
incorporated into designs appropriately
named "Bizarre" and "Fantasque" and the
warehouse stockpile was decorated in vivid
colors. These handpainted earthenwares, all
bearing the signature of designer Clarice
Cliff, were produced until World War II and
are now finding enormous favor with
collectors.*

Bone dish, Tonquin patt. (ILLUS.) $12.00
Bowl, 8" d., "Bizarre," cottage & hills
decor 140.00
Bowl, 8" d., "Bizarre," Secret patt. 100.00
Bowl, 9" d., "Fantasque," canterbury
bells decor 125.00
Bowl, 9" octagon, colorful florals on
wavy stems decor 65.00
Bowl, blue parrots decor 95.00
Coffee pot, cov., "Bizarre," green Art
Deco florals & orange leaves on
shaded green to cream ground,
brown base, 4" d., 7" h. 145.00
Cookie jar, cov., Crocus patt.,
w/wicker handle 125.00
Cup & saucer, demitasse, overall blue,

pink, green & lavender Art Deco
decor 45.00
Marmalade jar, "Bizarre," blue, pink,
aqua & yellow Art Deco florals on
green & gold ground, silverplate
rim, cover & handle, 3¾" d.,
4½" h. 118.00
Pitcher, 4" h., jug-type, stylized Art
Deco florals on vivid orange, blue,
lavender, green & tan overall design
ground 145.00
Pitcher, 5¾" h., jug-type, "Bizarre,"
black Art Deco decor on vivid
orange, blue, green & cream
ground 175.00
Pitcher, 6" h., "Bizarre," chicken
decor 75.00
Pitcher, 6¾" h., ring-embossed body,
blue Art Deco trees & tan shrubs
on light grey ground...............110.00
Pitcher, 7" h., octagonal jug-type,
"Fantasque," multicolored decor....175.00
Pitcher, 8" h., octagonal jug-type,
"Bizarre," trees & hillls decor 135.00
Pitcher, 8¼" h., jug-type, orange
Art Decor nasturtium-like florals
& green leaves w/multicolored
mottled dripping on cream ground ..265.00
Plate, "Bizarre," floral decor 29.00
Sugar shaker, My Garden patt., multi-
colored Art Deco florals in relief
at base, mottled tan & gold
ground, 5½" h. 82.50
Toast rack, Crocus patt., Art Deco
orange, blue & purple crocus
w/green & yellow trim, 6¾" l. 95.00
Tray, geometric sunburst decor,
11" l. 175.00
Vase, 4" h., octagonal, "Bizarre,"
Gay Day patt. 45.00
Vase, 8" h., ribbed squat form,
"Bizarre," florals & willow
trees decor 95.00

CLEWELL WARES

Clewell Mark

Though Charles W. Clewell of Canton, Ohio, didn't operate a pottery, he is responsible for a category of fine art pottery through his development of a unique metal coating period on pottery blanks obtained from Owens, Weller and others. By encasing

objects in a thin metal shell, he produced copper and bronze finish ceramics. Later experiments led him to chemically treat the metal coating to attain the blue-green patinated effect associated with copper and bronze. Although he produced metal-coated pottery from 1902 until the mid-1950s, Clewell production was quite limited for he felt no one else could competently re-create his artwork and, therefore, operated a small shop with little help.

Bowl, 4½" d., 1½" h., copper-covered
w/patinated finish, riveted seams,
signed...........................$195.00
Bowl, copper-covered w/green
patinated finish....................320.00
Ewer, paneled, bronze-covered
w/patinated finish, 5¾" h...........95.00
Mug, advertising, copper-covered
w/patinated finish & riveted seams,
porcelain interior, dated 1914 ......175.00
Pitcher, 5¾" h., copper-covered Owens
blank w/green patinated finish 150.00
Vase, bud, 6½" h., copper-covered
w/patinated finish 80.00
Vase, 6½" h., bulbous, copper-covered
w/green patinated finish 350.00

CLIFTON ART POTTERY

Clifton Art Pottery Marks

William A. Long, an organizer of the Lonhuda Pottery, and Fred Tschirner, a chemist, established the Clifton Art Pottery in Newark, New Jersey, in 1905. The first art pottery produced was designated the Crystal Patina line and was decorated with a subdued pale green crystalline glaze which was later also made in shades of yellow and tan. Indian Ware, introduced in 1906, was patterned after the pottery made by the American Indians. These two lines are the most notable in the pottery's production though Tirrube and Robin's-egg Blue lines were also produced. After 1911, production shifted to floor and wall tiles and by 1914 the pottery's name was changed to Clifton Porcelain Tile Company to better reflect this production.

Bowl, 8" d., Indian Ware $85.00
Coffee pot, cov., Indian Ware.........50.00

Flower pot, Indian Ware, dark red clay
w/black & cream geometric designs,
3½" h. 50.00
Humidor, cov., Indian Ware, 6 x 6" 60.00
Teapot, cov., Indian Ware, 7" h. 55.00
Vase, 3½" h., 5½" widest d., Indian
Ware..........................40.00
Vase, 4½" h., green drip glaze, dated
1903 ....55.00
Vase, 5½" h., Indian Ware 50.00
Vase, 6" h., Indian Ware 38.00
Vase, 6" h., handled, Crystal Patina
line, green crystalline glaze, 1906 ...275.00

COALPORT

Coalport Garniture Set

Coalport Porcelain Works operated at
Coalport, Shropshire, England, from about
1795 to 1926 and has operated at Stoke-on-
Trent as Coalport China, Ltd., making bone
china since then.

Cup & saucer, demitasse, pink
w/enameled gold decor & gold cup
interior, ca. 1891.................$135.00
Cup & saucer, swirl-molded, rose-red
dainty floral borders, 1883 English
registry mark 39.00
Figurine, "Judith Anne," plum-colored
dress, hat, muff & shawl, blue necklace, 1920-45 mark, 7" h. 75.00
Garniture set: 3 spill vases; each
painted w/colorful continuous band
of flowers on pink ground within
gilt bandings, ca. 1830, set of 3
(ILLUS.) 825.00
Plate, 8" d., fluted rim, cobalt blue
florals & ornate gold decor on white
ground 65.00
Plate, 9" d., h.p. pink roses & green
garlands, ornate gold trim, made for
Davis Callamore & Co., New York 85.00
Plates, 9" d., white w/gold-trimmed
wavy edges, ca. 1880, set of 4 ....95.00
Plate, castle scene center, ornate blue
& gold rim, artist-signed 200.00
Tea set: cov. teapot & 6 c/s;
cobalt blue florals & vignettes decor
on orange & gold ground, 1870s,
13 pcs. 295.00

Urn, cov., reserved w/scene of "Loch
Achray," w/river, hills, & Roman
ruins on cobalt blue & ivory ground
w/fine gold tracery, attributed to
the artist Percy Simpson, 11" h. 285.00

COPELAND & SPODE

Copeland's Ruins Pattern

W.T. Copeland & Sons, Ltd., have
operated the Spode Works at Stoke,
England, from 1847 to the present. The
name Spode was used on some of its
productions. Its predecessor, Spode, was
founded by Josiah Spode about 1784 and
became Copeland & Garrett in 1843, continuing under that name until 1847.
Listings dated prior to 1843 should be
attributed to Spode. Also see COM-
MEMORATIVE PLATES and TOBY
MUGS & JUGS.

Bowl, 9" d., Spode's Queen Charlotte
patt., painted in iron-red, rose,
underglaze-blue & gilding w/spiral-
ling bands of stylized flowers &
foliage within an iron-red floral vine
border & gilt rim, 1805-10 ....$385.00
Bowl, 10" d., Copeland's Ruins patt.,
flow blue (ILLUS.) 45.00
Bust of Ophelia, 11" h. 375.00
Cheese dish & cover w/acorn finial,
base w/white angels, trees & puppy
in relief on deep green ground......142.50
Creamer, Spode's Tower patt., blue
transfer, 4" h. 48.00
Cup & saucer, Chelsea Garden patt. 42.50
Cup & saucer, Imari patt., cobalt blue,
iron-red & gilt, 1804 ....235.00
Cup & saucer, octagonal, tree decor,
gold Greek Key border, 1890s 40.00
Figurine, Cries of London series -
"Strawberries" 375.00
Fish set: oval platter, sauceboat

w/stand & 12 plates; each w/different identified fish amidst aquatic weeds, in a marine palette of soft green, blue, brown, lavender & grey heightened w/gilding, ca. 1910, 15 pcs. 550.00

Gravy boat, Spode's Camellia patt., blue..............................75.00

Marmalade jar, w/cover & underplate, Spode's Tower patt., blue transfer, 2 pcs. 52.00

Pancake dish & pierced cover, black transfer-printed florals on white ground 75.00

Pitcher, 6¾" h., Winston Churchill commemorative 150.00

Pitcher, 8" h., parian, Chicago fire scene around top & three medallions at center featuring Indians, Capitol w/lady & American Eagle & Settlers, 8 small cameo relief medallions of Mrs. O'Leary's cow, fort, etc., blue & white, designed by Frank E. Burley for limited edition....................350.00

Pitcher, 9" h., salt-glazed grey stoneware, fluted rim, cherubs & goat in relief, 1833-47 mark.............145.00

Plate, 6½" d., Spode's Tower patt., pink transfer 10.00

Plate, 8½" d., Spode's Tower patt., blue transfer 12.00

Plate, 9" d., h.p. flowers, ca. 1940......16.00

Spode's Tower Pattern

Plate, 10½" d., Spode's Tower patt., blue transfer, 1897 (ILLUS.)...........35.00

Plate, dinner, bird decor on magenta ground, ornate gold border 40.00

Plates, dinner, Buttercup patt., set of 8 ....96.00

Platter, 11 x 8½", scalloped shell border, overall cobalt blue fuchsia blossoms & vines w/gold highlights & trim, dated 1887 ....35.00

Platter, 13" l., blue transfer "City of Corinth" 110.00

Platter, 14½" l., Spode's Tower patt., blue transfer 125.00

Platters, 15 7/8" oval, Spode's 967 patt., painted in shades of iron-red, green, underglaze-blue & gilding w/oriental fenced garden within elaborate floral & scroll paneled border, ca. 1810, pr..............1,760.00

Platters, 17" l., Imari-type decor, underglaze-blue, iron-red & gold central basket of flowers within a wide border of floral panels & fans amidst lotus vines, rims edged in brown, Spode "Stone-China" mark, ca. 1814, pr.....................880.00

Punch bowl, Spode's Tower patt., blue transfer, 15½" d. 140.00

Teapot, cov., 6-sided, Spode's Tower patt. 290.00

Teapot, cov. & tea tile, teapot w/frieze of classical ladies dancing w/garlands of flowers on deep blue, 5" d., 5½" h.; tea tile w/floral garlands decor, 5 7/8" d., 2 pcs..............135.00

Tea tile, Spode's Tower patt. 55.00

Toothbrush holder, Spode's Tower patt., blue transfer.................55.00

Urn, Spode's Tower patt., blue transfer, 13" d., 17" h. 695.00

Vase, 5" h., Spode's Tower patt., blue transfer 42.00

Vases, 6¼" h., beaker-shaped, Spode's 967 patt., painted in shades of iron-red, green, peach, underglaze-blue & gilding w/oriental garden within elaborate foliate & scroll border, gilt rim w/molded beading & white enameling, ca. 1810, pr.........................990.00

Vase, 8" h., stick-type w/flaring rim, white floral sprays in relief on blue ground 60.00

Vegetable dish, Chelsea Garden patt. ...55.00

CORDEY

Founded by Boleslaw Cybis in Trenton, New Jersey, the Cordey China Company was the forerunner of the Cybis Studio, renowned for its fine porcelain sculptures. A native of Poland, Boleslaw Cybis was commissioned by his government to paint "el fresco" murals for the 1939 New York World's Fair. Already a renowned sculptor and painter, he elected to remain and become a citizen of this country. In 1942, under his guidance, Cordey China Company began producing appealing busts and figurines, some decorated by applying real lace dipped in liquid clay prior to firing in the kiln. Cordey figures were assigned numbers that were printed or pressed on the base. The Cordey line was eventually phased out of production during the 1950s as the porcelain sculptures of the Cybis Studios became widely acclaimed.

Box, w/figural bluebird & pink floral
on cover, 9" d. $125.00
Box, cov., lady in flowing robes in
relief, blue & oatmeal 35.00
Bust of lady wearing blue lace blouse,
6½" h. 75.00
Bust of girl w/veil, No. 5026, 7" h. 55.00
Busts of Colonial man & Colonial lady
wearing hat, each w/ornate lace,
16" h., pr. 325.00
Cornucopia-vase, roses decor,
No. 7008, 7" h. 25.00
Figure of a beautiful lady, No. 3004,
6¾" h. 80.00
Figure of an Oriental lady, 10½" h. 85.00
Figure of a ballerina dancing, roses,
other florals & lace-trimmed
costume, No. 4101, 10¾" h. 225.00
Figure of a girl, w/rosettes on
costume, 12" h. 115.00
Figure of a lady, wearing plum-colored
dress, long coat & tall hat, all
w/lace & roses, No. 5066, 14" h. 165.00
Figure of a lady grape harvestor
w/basket of grapes, No. 304,
16" h. 120.00
Figure group, Colonial "dandy" & his
lady, lace-trimmed garments,
10½" h. 150.00

Cordey Lamp Base

Lamp, bust of Colonial gentleman
w/lace collar, on gilt base, overall
21" h. (ILLUS.) .150.00
Model of a black & yellow bird on
stump, scroll & floral embellished
base, No. 6023 . . . . .90.00
Model of a bluebird on stump, scroll
& floral embellished base, No. 6004 . .90.00

Model of a lamb, No. 6025 . . . . .117.00
Vase, 8¾" h., ovoid, lady in relief,
blue & oatmeal 90.00

COWAN

Cowan "Jazz" Bowl

R. Guy Cowan first opened a studio pottery in 1913 in Cleveland, Ohio. The pottery continued to operate almost continuously, at various locations in the Cleveland area, until it was forced to close in 1931, due to financial problems. This fine art pottery, which was gradually expanded into a full line of commercial productions, is now sought out by collectors.

Bookends, model of elephant, black
glaze, pr. $375.00
Bowl, 14" d., flared, low circular foot,
glazed in black over vivid turquoise
& sgraffito w/abstract motifs &
symbols of the Jazz Age, ca. 1931,
designed by Viktor Schreckengost,
signed, restored (ILLUS.) 3,520.00
Bowl, octagonal, blue glaze 35.00
Bowl, Chinese red glaze 75.00
Candle holders, model of a frog,
lime green glaze, 3 x 3", pr. 28.00
Candle holders, floral form, ivory
glaze, 4¼" h., pr. 29.00
Candlesticks, bulb-shaped, 2¼" h.,
pr. 15.00
Candy dish, green & ivory glaze,
2½" h. 20.00
Chamberstick, saucer base w/ring
handle, blue lustre finish 24.00
Compote, figural seahorse base,
green & ivory glaze, 3½" h. 20.00
Console bowl, seahorse decor, purple
lustre finish, 16½" d., 6" h. 32.00
Console bowl w/figural kneeling nude
lady flower frog, blue glaze 245.00
Console set: bowl & pr. candle holders;
seahorse decor, ivory glaze, 3 pcs. . . .45.00
Console set: octagonal bowl & pr.
candle holders; blue glaze, 3 pcs. 50.00
Figure of a nude lady, 8½" h. 125.00
Flower bowl w/center divider, pink
glaze, 6" d. 45.00

Flower frog, figural nude lady,
6½" h. 135.00
Flower frog, figural dancing nude lady,
7½" h. . . . . .120.00 to 150.00
Garniture set: vase & pr. candle
holders; figural seahorse bases,
orange lustre finish, 3 pcs. 45.00
Match holder, seahorse base, blue
glaze, 3½" h. 35.00
Strawberry jar, cov., mint green
glaze, large 150.00
Vase, 5" h., orange lustre finish 20.00
Vase, 5" h., bulbous, matte green
shaded to rose finish 50.00
Vase, 6¼" h., blue lustre finish 45.00
Vase, 8½" h., blue lustre finish 30.00
Vase, 9" h., Chinese red glaze 85.00

CUP PLATES (Staffordshire)

Historical Staffordshire Cup Plates

Like their glass counterparts, these small plates were designed to hold a cup while the tea or coffee was allowed to cool in a saucer before it was sipped from the saucer, a practice that would now be considered in poor taste. The forerunner of the glass cup plates, those listed below were produced in various Staffordshire potteries in England. Their popularity waned after the introduction of the glass cup plate in the 1820s. Also see HISTORICAL & COMMEMORATIVE china and CUP PLATES under glass.

Adams (W.) & Sons, Lorraine patt.,
flow blue scenic transfer, ca. 1850. . .$50.00
Adderly (W.), Rhone patt., red trans-
fer, 1876-1905, 4½" d. 20.00
Challinor, Priory patt., light blue
transfer, ca. 1855 . . . . .30.00
Davenport, Cyprus patt., mulberry
transfer 35.00
Malkin, white ironstone, 3¾" d. 40.00
Mayer, Canova patt., green transfer,
ca. 1830 . . . . .30.00
Morley (Francis), Vista patt., medium
blue transfer 30.00
Phillips, Corinth patt., blue blue
transfer 35.00

Ridgway, embossed rim, all white,
3 7/8" d. 25.00
Tams (J.), Castle patt., flowing blue
transfer, ca. 1875 . . . . .38.00
Unmarked Staffordshire, California
scene, historical series, mulberry
transfer 30.00
Unmarked Staffordshire, Floral patt.,
medium blue transfer, ca. 1840 . . . . . .22.00
Unmarked Staffordshire, Georgetown
(lake) scene, light blue transfer. 75.00
Unmarked Staffordshire, Residence of
the Late R. Jordan, historical series,
light blue transfer. 285.00
Wood, pr. w/bust-length oval portraits
of Lafayette & Washington suspended from beak of American eagle &
third plate w/bust-length portrait of
General Andrew Jackson, iron-red
transfer & rim, set of 3 cup plates &
single child's mug, transfer-printed
in black on canary-yellow ground
w/conforming portraits of Lafayette
& Washington, ca. 1824-28, 4 pcs.
(ILLUS. of part) 1,210.00

CYBIS

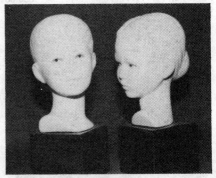

Boy & Girl by Cybis

Though not antique, fine Cybis porcelain figures are included here because of the great collector interest. They are produced in both limited edition and non-numbered series and thus there can be a wide price range available to the collector.

American Wild Turkey,
12 x 13" . . . .$1,800.00 to 1,950.00
Ballerina on Cue, white . . . . .375.00 to 450.00
Ballerina "Red Shoes," 10½" 795.00
Blackfoot Medicine Man w/stand. . . .2,295.00
Boy & Girl Heads on stands, pr.
(ILLUS.). 650.00
Bunny "Mr. Snowball" 38.00
Burro "Fitzgerald" 92.50
Carousel Giraffe. 700.00
Carousel Horse 760.00

Carousel Lion or Tiger, each 600.00
Child Clown Head "Funny Face,"
   10½" 425.00
Cybele 485.00
Deer Mouse in Clover 130.00
Desdemona, No. 90 . . . . .1,650.00
Duckling "Baby Brother," 4½" 75.00
Elephant "Alexander" 225.00
Elizabeth Anne, 5" 200.00
Eros (Cupid) Head, 10" . . . . . .165.00 to 210.00
Eskimo Child Head, 10½" 365.00
First Flight, 4½" 175.00
Goldilocks & Panda Bear 265.00
Gretel, 7" h. 230.00
Indian Girl Head, 10" 450.00
Jeanie w/Light Brown Hair, 9½" h. 400.00
Juliet, 12" 1,600.00
Karina 320.00
King Arthur 1,100.00
Kitten "Chantilly" 135.00
Lady Bug. 95.00
Little Princess .450.00
Madonna with Bird, 11" 325.00
Madonna with Lace Veil, 4½" 260.00
Melissa, 10" 395.00
Mother of Love 185.00
Nefertiti, 12¼" . . . . .1,900.00 to 2,100.00
Onondaga Hiawatha on stand 1,500.00
Pandora, 5" 195.00
Peter Pan 350.00
Pinto Colt 150.00

Pollyanna

Pollyanna (ILLUS.). 300.00
Poppy the Pony 500.00
Priscilla, 14" 975.00
Psyche 200.00
Raffles the Raccoon 295.00
Rapunzel, 8" 500.00
Red Riding Hood 375.00

St. Francis, white w/pink rose at
   feet, 11" h. .350.00
Springtine, 5" .450.00
Suzanne 245.00
Tinkerbell, 7½" 750.00
Turtle "Baron" w/frog on back 95.00
Unicorn, 10 x 13" . . . . .1,400.00 to 1,500.00
Wendy w/doll, 6½" 175.00
Windflower 225.00

DEDHAM

Dedham Paperweight

This pottery was organized in 1866 by Alexander Robertson in Chelsea, Mass., and became A.W. & H. Robertson in 1877. In 1872, the name was changed to Kelsea Keramic Art Works and in 1891 to Chelsea Pottery, U.S.A. About 1894 the pottery was moved to Dedham, Mass., and was renamed Dedham Pottery. Production ceased in 1943. High-fired colored wares & crackle ware were specialties. The rabbit is said to have been the most popular decoration on crackle ware in blue.

Bird house $125.00
Creamer, Rabbit 150.00
Marmalade jar, Rabbit 893.00
Mayonnaise bowl, Elephant 800.00
Mug, Rabbit 110.00
Paperweight, model of a rabbit,
   2¾" l. (ILLUS.) . . . . .250.00 to 285.00
Plate, 6" d., Grape 95.00
Plate, 6" d., Iris .65.00
Plate, 6" d., Peacock. 1,250.00
Plate, 6" d., Pond Lily 95.00
Plate, 6" d., Rabbit . . . . .65.00 to 85.00
Plate, 8" d., Iris .70.00
Plate, 8½" d., Duck 110.00
Plate, 8½" d., Horse Chestnut 125.00
Plate, 8½" d., Rabbit 95.00
Plates, 8½" d., one-earred Rabbit &
   Artichoke, set of 6. . . . . .1,800.00
Plate, 8½" d., Snow Tree 165.00
Plate, 9½" d., Rabbit. . . . . .95.00 to 110.00
Plate, 10" d., Dolphin & Mask 1,500.00
Plate, 10" d., Duck 195.00
Plate, 10" d., Lion, "tapestry" 950.00
Plate, 10" d., Pond Lily (ILLUS.) 85.00

Pond Lily Plate

Plate, "Golden Gate S.F.," pre-bridge landscape w/rising sun center & blue floral border 3,300.00
Salt dishes, model of a walnut on leaf, pr. 1,650.00
Saucer, Rabbit in reverse..........1,102.00
Vase, 5¾" h., green "volcanic" glaze w/highlights, signed "H.R." 275.00
Vase, 8" h., red, orange & black "volcanic" glaze................1,100.00

DELFT

18th Century Dutch Delft

Delft, a tin-glazed pottery, is of a type that originated in Belgium and Italy centuries ago. Because Dutch traders made the city of Delft the center of their world-wide trade on these items, the term "delft" became synonymous with "tin-glazed-pottery." The use of delft to indicate only blue and white is in error since all potters worked in polychrome as well. Delft, faience, and majolica are all tin-glazed pottery. Also see CAT COLLECTIBLES and TILES.

Barber's bowl, deep well painted w/large ship, wide rim w/foliate, scallop & dot borders interrupted by the circular soap well & semicircular

neck notch, blue & white, London, 1760-70, 10" w. $2,750.00
Bowl, 9 1/8" d., Fazackerly patt., polychrome blue, yellow, iron-red, mixed green & manganese floral sprays on fences front, reverse & interior w/floral sprig, Liverpool, ca. 1760 ....440.00
Fuddling cup (English drinking vessel), formed as 3 conjoined baluster-shaped vessels w/entwined rope-twist handles heightened w/blue dashes, front of each w/h.p. blue floral sprig, London, mid-17th c., 3 1/8" h. (minor imperfections)....1,870.00
Models of a dog w/iron-red eyes & a cat w/yellow eyes, each w/manganese markings, iron-red & yellow collar, seated on blue-dotted green base w/yellow-banded edges patterned w/iron-red & green foliate scrollwork, Dutch, mid-18th c., 7¼" h., pr. 2,530.00
Models of a cow standing on oblong base, bodies & bases enriched w/blue flowerheads, foliage & dots, Dutch, ca. 1760, 7¾" l., facing pr. (ILLUS. of one) 2,200.00
Mug, globular w/straight neck & scroll handle, "Bleu Persan," deep blue glaze, splashed on exterior w/spots of opaque white, London, 1680-90, 3 5/8" h. 6,050.00
Pilgrim bottle, blue & white, Dutch, 9" h. 450.00

Delft Pill Slab

Pill slab (for rolling pills), h.p. rhinocerous crest & arms of the Worshipful Society of Apothecaries within scroll-edged scalework crest above shell & pendant ribbon inscribed w/motto "Opiferque Per" in manganese, now mounted on a painted grey board, Bristol, England, 1740-50, 11 x 9 5/8" (ILLUS.) 4,070.00

Pitcher, 6½" h., painted blue-green
decor on white ground, Thoovt &
LaBouchere, 1895 ....85.00
Plaque, pierced to hang, farm scene
decor center, floral & scroll border,
blue & white, 15¼" d. 68.00
Plaque, blue & white, Dutch, mid-19th
c., 22½" oval....................950.00
Plate, 9" d., h.p. w/Justice trampling
on Evil, who holds in his right hand a
scroll inscribed "Place Men," above
them 2 trumpeting cherubs flanking
a garlanded arch inscribed "Libertas
Populi," rim w/sponged manganese
reserved w/blue & white floral & leaf
scroll border, Bristol, 1735-45 .....3,410.00
Plate, 9 1/8" d., scalloped edge, polychrome, bird decor................155.00
Plate, 12 5/8" d., painted in blue
w/central floral spray within a
"woolsack" panel reserved on pale
lavender ground, rim reserved
w/four leaf-shaped panels also
painted w/blue floral sprigs, reverse
w/letter Q & 3 leafy branches in
blue, Bristol, ca. 1750.............605.00
Wet drug jar, globular w/short,
knopped spout, conical foot &
grooved loop handle, painted on
front w/label inscribed "S:PAEONAE"
below a basket of flowers & pr. of
birds amidst branches, beneath the
label an angel's head suspending a
tassel & floral swags, blue & white,
London, 1710-25, 7 5/8" h..........660.00

DERBY & ROYAL CROWN DERBY

Derby King's Pattern

William Duesbury, in partnership with
John and Christopher Heath, established
the Derby Porcelain Works in Derby,
England, about 1750. Duesbury soon
bought out his partners and in 1770
purchased the Chelsea factory and six years
later, the Bow works. Duesbury was
succeeded by his son and grandson. Robert
Bloor purchased the business about 1814
and managed successfully until illness in
1828 left him unable to exercise control. The
"Bloor" Period, however, extends from 1814
until 1848, when the factory closed. Former
Derby workmen then resumed porcelain
manufacture in another factory and this
nucleus eventually united with a new and
distinct venture, Derby Crown Porcelain,
Ltd., 1890.

Butter tub & cover w/iron-red, yellow
& green strawberry sprig knop, front
& reverse w/purple, iron-red, yellow,
green & brown exotic birds, ends &
cover w/butterflies & smaller
insects, rims edged in russet,
ca. 1760, 5" chamfered
rectangle $1,980.00
Coffee pot, cov., Imari patt., qt. 395.00
Cup & saucer, Imari patt., early
20th c. ....69.00 to 80.00
Cup & saucer, Japan patt., 1800-25 .....75.00
Ewer, bulbous, gilded twisted bracket
handle, painted variegated cobalt &
light blue iris accented w/gold &
w/other gold florals & dusting on
cream ground, made for A. Stowell
& Co., Boston, 6½" d., 8½" h. 175.00
Figure of Britannia, wearing white-
plumed lavender helmet, green
mantle & gilt scalework breastplate
over a yellow-lined purple robe
patterned w/gilt-centered iron-red
sprigs, standing before a crouching
russet lion, rose pennant, globe,
cannon & other trophies of war on a
scroll-molded base heightened in
gilding, 1765-70, 10¾" h. (restoration to neck, tip of pennant & some
costume edges)...................770.00
Pitcher, 6½" h., painted multicolored
florals outlined w/gold on cobalt
blue ground, 1881 ....125.00
Plate, 6" d., Imari patt. 39.00
Plates, 8 5/8" d., King's patt., underglaze-blue, iron-red & gold peonies
& other florals beneath prunus tree
within elaborate border, ca. 1825,
set of 12 (ILLUS. of pr.) 1,540.00
Plate, 8¾" d., view of Tissington Spires
Dovedale center, scalloped turquoise
blue border w/encrusted gold &
jeweling, artist-signed 200.00
Plate, Persian type decor, pink
w/elaborate encrusted gold
design.........................250.00
Punch bowl, Japan patt., interior decor
of underglaze-blue, iron-red, salmon,
green, rose, puce & gold peony plant
in a fenced garden surrounded by a
wide border of floral panels
repeated on the exterior, ca. 1820,
11 7/8" d. 1,430.00
Sauceboats, each molded on exterior
w/overlapping leaves edged in pale

green shading to yellow, issuing from a curling stem handle terminating in a rose florette & rose & green bud, painted on exterior & interior in shades of rose, iron-red, yellow, blue & green w/floral sprays & sprigs, 1758-62, 7¼" l., pr. 1,210.00

Teapot, cov., puce, purple, iron-red, yellow & green floral sprays & sprigs, spout & cover rim edged in brown, ca. 1765, 6 1/8" h. (2 small hair cracks) 247.00

Vase, cov., decorated in the Japanese palette w/blue & orange stylized florals on cream ground, heavy gold trim, cobalt blue neck w/heavy gold, made for Geo. G. Shreve & Co., 1884 . . . . .279.00

Japan Pattern Sauce Tureen & Stand

Vegetable dish & pr. oval sauce tureens w/covers & stands, Japan patt., underglaze-blue, iron-red & gilding, ca. 1825, imperfections & minor repairs, 6 5/8" & 8 5/8" tureens & 10½" l. dish, 3 pcs. (ILLUS. of part) . .412.00

DOULTON & ROYAL DOULTON

Doulton & Co., Ltd., was founded in Lambeth, London, about 1858. It was operated there till 1956 and often incorporated the words "Doulton" and "Lambeth" in its marks. Pinder Bourne & Co., Burslem, was purchased by the Doultons in 1878 and in 1882 became Doulton & Co., Ltd. It added porcelain to its earthenware production in 1884. The "Royal Doulton" mark has been used by this factory, which is still in production. Character jugs and figurines are commanding great attention from collectors at the present time. Also see COMMEMORATIVE PLATES, FLOW BLUE, GIBSON GIRL PLATES and TOBY MUGS & JUGS.

DICKENSWARE

Ash pot, Old Charley $100.00
Ash tray, Fagin, 4¼" d. 45.00

Ash tray, Parson Brown 120.00
Bowl, 8¾" sq., 2" h., Mr. Pickwick 87.50
Bowl, 9" octagon, Sam Weller in low relief 85.00
Bust of Mr. Micawber 65.00
Bust of Sam Weller, brown hat, yellow vest, cream shirt & brown tie, 2½" h. 65.00
Candlesticks, Fagin & Sam Weller figures, 6¾" h., pr. 350.00
Cup, Dickens characters in relief, signed Noke .25.00
Cup & saucer, demitasse, Sam Weller on cup, Fagin on saucer 52.50
Cup & saucer, Bill Sykes or Fagin, each 69.00
Cup & saucer, Sam Weller 50.00
Dresser set: 11½ x 7" tray & 3 cov. boxes; Bill Sykes & Fat Boy, 4 pcs. . . .395.00

Dickensware Match Holder

Match holder w/striker, Sam Weller & Mr. Micawber (ILLUS.) 150.00
Mug, 2-handled, Cap'n Cuttle, 4¼" h. . .135.00
Pitcher, 6" h., Tony Weller 175.00
Pitcher, 7" h., square, "Oliver Asks For More" in relief . . . . .170.00 to 225.00
Pitcher, 8" h., Old Peggoty 250.00
Pitcher, 9" h., Mr. Pickwick 175.00
Plate, 4" d., The Artful Dodger & Mr. Micawber, signed Noke 27.50
Plate, 9½" d., The Artful Dodger 55.00
Plate, 10" d., Little Nell 75.00
Teapot, cov., Bill Sykes, 6" h. 225.00
Teapot, cov., Sam Weller 135.00
Vase, 2¾" h., 2 1/8" d., Fagin 88.00
Vase, 3 1/8" h., 2¼" d., Sam Weller 70.00
Vase, 4¾" h., 2" d., Barnaby Rudge 75.00
Vase, 6½" h., The Artful Dodger 115.00
Vase, 9½" h., 3 1/8" d., 2-handled, straight-sided cylinder, Sergeant Buz Fuz 158.00
Whiskey jug, Pickwick Papers 57.00

MISCELLANEOUS

Ash tray, Old Charley, "A" mark, dated 1937 . . . . .125.00

Ash tray, stoneware, large lavender, green & blue bird w/large beak perched on blue rock center, blue & brown ground, 4¼" d., 4 1/8" h. 225.00

Ash tray w/match holder & striker, orange & black playing cards decor on cream ground, 3¼ x 3 5/8", 2 5/8" h. 55.00

Baby's feeding dish, Shakespeare series, "Shylock," 8¼" d., 1¼" h. 110.00

Beaker, brown & blue over tan ground, artist-signed, Doulton-Lambeth, 4½" h. 65.00

Bowl, 3½" d., pedestal base, Titanian Ware, gold bird & leaf decor on blue ground, original paper label.........75.00

Bowl, 4" d., stoneware, incised donkey border, silver rim, signed Hannah Barlow 140.00

Bowl, 7½" d., 3¾" h., collared base, Robin Hood series...............135.00

Bowl, 11" d., floral band interior, mottled purple, red & blue exterior, Sung glaze 450.00

Cake plate, 2-handled, Robin Hood series, "Under the Greenwood Tree".............................110.00

Chamber pot, Night Watchman series, large............................285.00

Character jug, Aramis, small, 3½" h....40.00

Character jug, Aramis, large 65.00

Character jug, 'Ard of 'Earing, miniature, 2¼" h. ....925.00 to 950.00

Character jug, 'Ard of 'Earing, small, 3½" h. ....580.00 to 650.00

Character jug, 'Ard of 'Earing, large, 6" h. 985.00

Character jug, 'Arriet, tiny, 1¼" h. 195.00

Character jug, 'Arriet, miniature, 2¼" h. 68.00

Character jug, 'Arriet, "A" mark, miniature, 2¼" h. 80.00

Character jug, 'Arriet, small, 3½" h. ...80.00

Character jug, 'Arriet, large 170.00

Character jug, 'Arry, tiny, 1¼" h. 190.00

Character jug, 'Arry, miniature, 2¼" h. 65.00

Character jug, 'Arry, "A" mark, miniature, 2¼" h. 72.50

Character jug, 'Arry, small, 3½" h. ....75.00 to 90.00

Cardinal & 'Arry Character Jugs

Character jug, 'Arry, large, 6¾" h. (ILLUS. right) 165.00

Character jug, Auld Mac, tiny, 1¼" h. 210.00

Character jug, Auld Mac, miniature, 2¼" h. 30.00

Character jug, Auld Mac, "A" mark, miniature, 2¼" h.................55.00

Character jug, Auld Mac, "A" mark, small, 3½" h. 45.00

Character jug, Auld Mac, "A" mark, large, 6¾" h....................60.00

Character jug, Beefeater, miniature, 2¼" h. 52.50

Character jug, Beefeater, "A" mark, small, 3½" h. 55.00

Character jug, Beefeater, large 100.00

Character jug, Cap'n Cuttle, miniature, 2¼" h. 85.00

Character jug, Cap'n Cuttle, small, 3½" h. 90.00

Character jug, Cap'n Cuttle, "A" mark, small, 3½" h. 85.00

Character jug, Cap'n Cuttle, large, 6" h. 150.00

Character jug, Captain Hook, small, 3½" h. 275.00

Character jug, Captain Hook, large, 6" h. 345.00

Character jug, Cardinal, tiny, 1¼" h. ..230.00

Character jug, Cardinal, miniature, 2¼" h. 55.00

Character jug, Cardinal, "A" mark, miniature, 2¼" h..................55.00

Character jug, Cardinal, small, 3½" h. 70.00

Character jug, Cardinal, "A" mark, small, 3½" h. 78.00

Character jug, Cardinal, large, 6½" h. (ILLUS. left) 130.00

Character jug, Cavalier, gun handle, "A" mark, miniature, 2¼" h.......55.00

Character jug, Cavalier, small, 3½" h. ...60.00

Character jug, Cavalier, "A" mark, small, 3½" h. 70.00

Character jug, Cavalier, large 125.00

Character jug, Cavalier, "A" mark, large.............................135.00

Character jug, Cliff Cornell, small, 2½" h. ....295.00 to 325.00

Character jug, Cliff Cornell, large, 6¾" h. ....225.00 to 425.00

Character jug, Clown w/red hair, large ....3,500.00 to 3,650.00

Character jug, Clown w/white hair, large ....995.00 to 1,150.00

Character jug, Dick Turpin, "A" mark, miniature, 2¼" h. ....50.00 to 60.00

Character jug, Dick Turpin, gun handle, small, 3½" h. 62.50

Character jug, Dick Turpin, gun handle, mask up, large 110.00

Character jug, Dick Whittington, large, 6" h. ....350.00 to 400.00

Charger, Coaching Days series,
13" d. 170.00
Cookie jar, melon-ribbed, panels of
birds & animals on wide blue
center band, cream ground w/gold
trim, Doulton-Burslem, silverplate
rim, cover & handle, 5¾" d.,
7½" h. 145.00
Cup & saucer, demitasse, King's Ware -
Pied Piper, green & gold on brown
ground 75.00
Cup & saucer, Robin Hood series 65.00
Figurine, "A 'Courting," HN 2004 . . . . . . .435.00
Figurine, "A Gentlewoman," HN 1632,
lavender dress 475.00
Figurine, "A Jester," HN 1702, brown,
purple & red costume 330.00
Figurine, "A Yeoman of the Guard,"
HN 2122 . . . . .610.00
Figurine, "Adrienne," HN 2152, rose-
red dress 135.00
Figurine, "Alice," HN 2158 . . . . .115.00
Figurine, "Angelina," HN 2013, red
dress. 595.00
Figurine, "Babie," HN 1679. . . . .30.00 to 50.00
Figurine, "Baby Bunting," HN 2108 . . . .280.00
Figurine, "Ballerina," HN 2116 . . . . .230.00
Figurine, "Balloon Seller" (The),
HN 583, green shawl, cream dress . .360.00
Figurine, "Bather" (The), HN 687,
purple & blue robe 540.00
Figurine, "Bather" (The), HN 1238, red
& black robe 700.00
Figurine, "Beachcomber," HN 2487 . . . .145.00
Figurine, "Bedtime," HN 1978 . .25.00 to 65.00
Figurine, "Beggar" (The), HN 526, blue
trousers, red sash. 510.00
Figurine, "Beggar" (The), HN 2175,
black coat, orange sash. 535.00
Figurine, "Biddy," HN 1513, red dress,
blue shawl, Potted by Doulton,
1932-51 . . . . .155.00
Figurine, "Blossom," HN 1667, orange
multicolored shawl. 595.00
Figurine, "Boatman" (The), HN 2417 . . . .90.00
Figurine, "Bride" (The), HN 1588, white
flowers 425.00
Figurine, "Bride" (The), HN 1600,
yellow roses .460.00
Figurine, "Bridesmaid," M 11, pink
ruffled dress .275.00
Figurine, "Bridget," HN 2070 . . . . .235.00
Figurine, "Buttercup," HN 2309, pale
yellow dress, green bodice .75.00 to 100.00
Figurine, "Camilla," HN 1710, pink
dress 450.00
Figurine, "Camille," HN 1586, red
bodice & overskirt 400.00
Figurine, "Carolyn," HN 2112 . . . . .255.00
Figurine, "Carrie," HN 2800 . . . . .75.00
Figurine, "Charmian," HN 1569, light
green-blue skirt 675.00
Figurine, "Chloe," M 10, blue ruffled
dress 205.00

Figurine, "Chloe," M 29, red & cream
ruffled gown .245.00
Figurine, "Choir Boy," HN 2141 . . . . .80.00
Figurine, "Christine," HN 1840, pink
dress, blue shawl 560.00
Figurine, "Christmas Parcels,"
HN 2851 . . . . .150.00
Figurine, "Cissie," HN 1809, red
dress .60.00 to 95.00
Figurine, "Clarissa," HN 2345 . . . . .150.00
Figurine, "Clockmaker" (The),
HN 2279 . . . . .220.00
Figurine, "Clothilde," HN 1598, cream
dress, red cape 470.00
Figurine, "Clothilde," HN 1599, flower-
ed dress, red & blue cape 540.00
Figurine, "Columbine," HN 1297, white
line border on dress 575.00
Figurine, "Cookie," HN 2218. . . . . .115.00
Figurine, "Craftsman" (The),
HN 2284 . . . . .430.00
Figurine, "Crouching Nude," HN 457. . .475.00
Figurine, "Cup of Tea,"
HN 2322 . . . . .75.00 to 100.00
Figurine, "Curly Knob," HN 1627 . . . . . .350.00
Figurine, "Cymbals," HN 2699 . . . . .630.00
Figurine, "Dainty May," M 67, pink
skirt, blue overdress 225.00
Figurine, "Darling," HN 1319, black
base 120.00
Figurine, "Darling," HN 1985, white
nightgown. . . . . .25.00 to 45.00

"Daydreams"

Figurine, "Daydreams," HN 1731, pink
bodice, light skirt (ILLUS.) 75.00
Figurine, "Delight," HN 1772, red
dress. 160.00
Figurine, "Denise," M 34, green dress,
blue bodice, red overskirt 300.00
Figurine, "Diana," HN 1986, red dress,
purple hat ties. 100.00
Figurine, "Dinky Doo," HN 1678, blue
bodice, light skirt 55.00

Figurine, "Dorcas," HN 1558, red
dress...........................210.00
Figurine, "Dreamweaver,"
HN 2283 ....185.00 to 215.00
Figurine, "Drummer Boy,"
HN 2679 ....265.00 to 295.00
Figurine, "Easter Day," HN 2039, multi-
colored dress, green hat 265.00
Figurine, "Elfreda,"
HN 2078 ....510.00 to 550.00
Figurine, "Eliza," HN 2543 ....160.00
Figurine, "Elsie Maynard,"
HN 639 ....475.00 to 600.00
Figurine, "Emir," HN 1604, orange &
green scarf 525.00
Figurine, "Ermine Coat" (The),"
HN 1981 ....215.00
Figurine, "Eugene," HN 1520, green &
pink dress 525.00
Figurine, "Evelyn," HN 1622, red
bodice & hat.....................425.00
Figurine, "Fairy," HN 1393, yellow
flowers..........................320.00
Figurine, "Faraway," HN 2133 ....280.00
Figurine, "Fat Boy" (The), HN 555,
blue jacket, white scarf 285.00
Figurine, "Fiona," HN 1924, pink
skirt...........................1,000.00
Figurine, "First Steps," HN 2242 ......600.00
Figurine, "Fleurette,"
HN 1587 ....400.00 to 450.00
Figurine, "Flute," HN 2483 ....950.00
Figurine, "Fortune Teller," HN 2159 ...400.00
Figurine, "French Horn,"
HN 2795 ....650.00 to 750.00
Figurine, "Friar Tuck,"
HN 2143 ....350.00 to 450.00
Figurine, "Gaffer" (The),
HN 2053 ....275.00 to 350.00
Figurine, "Gay Morning," HN 2135,
1954-67 ....195.00 to 235.00

"Genevieve"

Figurine, "Genevieve," HN 1962,
1941-75 (ILLUS.) 190.00
Figurine, "Geraldine," HN 2348 ....135.00
Figurine, "Golden Days," HN 2274.....145.00
Figurine, "Gollywog," HN 2040, blue
overalls, green hat 240.00
Figurine, "Good King Wenceslas,"
HN 2118 ....260.00 to 315.00
Figurine, "Good Morning," HN 2671 ...140.00
Figurine, "Grandma,"
HN 2052 ....270.00 to 350.00
Figurine, "Grand Manner," HN 2723 ...185.00
Figurine, "Granny's Shawl," HN 1647,
red cape ....300.00 to 325.00
Figurine, "Griselda," HN 1993 ....445.00
Figurine, "Harlequinade," HN 585,
purple & green costume 800.00
Figurine, "Hazel," HN 1797, orange &
green dress 350.00
Figurine, "Heart to Heart,"
HN 2276 ....250.00 to 325.00
Figurine, "He Loves Me," HN 2046.....135.00
Figurine, "Henrietta Maria,"
HN 2005 ....375.00 to 425.00
Figurine, "Here A Little Child I Stand,"
HN 1546 ....250.00
Figurine, "Her Ladyship," HN 1977,
1945-59 ....245.00 to 280.00
Figurine, "Hilary," HN2335...110.00 to 135.00
Figurine, "Hinged Parasol" (The),
HN 1578, blue-dotted skirt 525.00
Figurine, "Honey," HN 1909, pink
dress...........................300.00
Figurine, "Honey," HN 1963, red dress,
blue hat & shawl 375.00
Figurine, "Invitation," HN 2170 ....135.00
Figurine, "Irene," HN 1952, red-blue
dress...........................375.00
Figurine, "Ivy," HN 1768, pink hat,
lavender dress ....65.00 to 85.00
Figurines, "Jack" & "Jill," HN 2060 &
HN 2061, pr......................235.00
Figurine, "Janet," HN 1538, blue-red
dress...........................210.00
Figurine, "Janice," HN 2165, dark
overdress........................465.00
Figurine, "Jean," HN 1877, pink dress,
blue shawl 260.00
Figurine, "Jennifer," HN 1484........400.00
Figurine, "Jersey Milkmaid" (The),
HN 2057 ....225.00 to 300.00
Figurine, "Joan," HN 1422, blue dress,
1930-49 ....245.00 to 275.00
Figurine, "Jolly Sailor," HN 2172 ......525.00
Figurine, "Jovial Monk" (The),
HN 2144 ....175.00
Figurine, "June," HN 1690, green
dress...........................320.00
Figurine, "June," HN 1691, pink shoes,
light floral dress 300.00
Figurine, "Kate Hardcastle," HN 1919,
green dress, black base, red
overskirt 550.00

Figurine, "Kathleen," HN1252, pale
pink skirt . . . . 475.00 to 550.00
Figurine, "Katrina," HN 2327 . . . . .215.00
Figurine, "Ko-Ko," HN 1266, black &
white costume . . . . .425.00 to 500.00

"Lady April"

Figurine, "Lady April," HN 1958, red
dress, 1940-59 (ILLUS.) 285.00
Figurine, "Lady April," HN 1965, green
dress 375.00
Figurine, "Lady Betty," HN 1967 . . . . . .210.00
Figurine, "Lady Charmian," HN 1948,
green dress, red shawl . . . .200.00 to 225.00
Figurine, "Lady Charmian," HN 1949,
red dress, green shawl 185.00
Figurine, "Lady Clare," HN 1465 . . . . . . .525.00
Figurine, "Lady Pamela," HN 2718 . . . . .145.00
Figurine, "Lambing Time," HN 1890 . . . .120.00
Figurine, "Laurianne," HN 2719 . . . . . . .130.00
Figurine, "Leading Lady," HN 2269 . . . .135.00
Figurine, "Lido Lady," HN 1220,
flowered blue costume 605.00
Figurine, "Lights Out," HN 2262 . . . . . . .165.00

"Lilac Time"

Figurine, "Lilac Time," HN 2137,
1954-69 (ILLUS.) 250.00
Figurine, "Lily," HN 1798, white shawl,
pink dress 110.00
Figurine, "Linda," HN 2106 . . . . .120.00
Figurine, "Lisa," HN 2310, violet &
white dress 110.00
Figurine, "Little Bridesmaid" (The),
HN 1433, pale yellow dress 115.00
Figurine, "Little Mistress" (The),
HN 1449 . . . . .190.00 to 225.00
Figurine, "Long John Silver," HN 2204,
1957-65 . . . . .445.00
Figurine, "Loretta," HN 2337 . . . . .95.00
Figurine, "Lunchtime," HN 2485 . . . . . . .145.00
Figurine, "Lute," HN 2431 . . . . .950.00
Figurine, "Madonna of the Square,"
HN 2034, light green-blue
costume . . . . .450.00 to 600.00
Figurine, "Maisie," HN 1619, pink
dress 335.00
Figurine, "Mantilla," HN 2712 . . . . .270.00
Figurine, "Margaret," HN 1989 . . . . .250.00
Figurine, "Margaret of Anjou,"
HN 2012 . . . . .445.00
Figurine, "Margery," HN 1413 . . . . . . .325.00
Figurine, "Margot," HN 1628, blue
bodice 565.00
Figurine, "Marguerite," HN 1928, pink
dress 335.00
Figurine, "Marietta," HN 1341, black
costume, red cape 650.00
Figurine, "Marietta," HN 1699, green
dress, red cape 525.00

"Market Day"

Figurine, "Market Day," HN 1991
(ILLUS.) . . . . .295.00 to 325.00
Figurine, "Mary Jane," HN 1990 . . . . . . .285.00
Figurine, "Mary Mary," HN 2044 . . . . . .130.00
Figurine, "Masquerade," HN 599, man,
red jacket 360.00

Figurine, "Masquerade," HN 2251, blue-
green overskirt 350.00
Figurine, "Matilda," HN 2011 . . . . .600.00

"Maureen"

Figurine, "Maureen," HN 1770, red
dress (ILLUS.) .245.00
Figurine, "Mayor" (The), HN 2280 . . . . .345.00
Figurine, "Melanie," HN 2271 . . . . .115.00
Figurine, "Melody," HN 2202 . . . . .235.00
Figurine, "Memories," HN 2030, green
& red dress 310.00
Figurine, "Mendicant" (The),
HN 1365 . . . . .220.00
Figurine, "Mermaid" (The), HN 97,
green seaweed in hair, beige base . .550.00
Figurine, "Midinette," HN 2090, blue
dress 250.00
Figurine, "Midsummer Noon," HN 1899,
red dress, 1939-49 . . . . .400.00
Figurine, "Millicent," HN 1714, pink
shawl 795.00

"Minuet"

Figurine, "Minuet," HN 2019, white
dress, floral print, 1949-71 (ILLUS.) . .220.00
Figurine, "Miss Demure," HN 1440,
pale blue dress 275.00
Figurine, "Miss Muffet," HN 1936, red
coat 150.00
Figurine, "Monica," HN 1458, white
flower-printed dress 165.00
Figurine, "Mother's Helper," HN 2151 . .132.50
Figurine, "Mr. Pickwick," HN 1894,
1938-52 . . . . .275.00
Figurine, "My Pet," HN 2238 . . . . .145.00
Figurine, "Negligee," HN 1219, dark
blue hairband 850.00
Figurine, "Nell Gwynne," HN 1882,
blue skirt 475.00
Figurine, "Nell Gwynne," HN 1887,
orange skirt, green bodice 550.00
Figurine, "New Bonnet" (The), HN 1728,
pink dress, green hat 550.00
Figurine, "Nina," HN 2347 . . . . .140.00
Figurine, "Noelle," HN 2179 . . . . .335.00
Figurine, "Olivia," HN 1995 . . . . .300.00
Fish plates, each w/different fish
species front & identified reverse,
artist-signed, 9½" d., set of 12 . . . .1,500.00
Flask, "Lord Brougham Reform,"
Doulton-Watts, 1830 . . . . .275.00
Flower pot, stoneware, crimped rim,
blueberries & green leaves decor,
brown glaze, 3½ x 3" 35.00
Hot plate, footed, flow blue decor,
gold trim, Doulton-Burslem, 1891 . . .150.00
Humidor, cov., Silicon Ware, applied
fish & floral insets, Doulton-Lambeth,
5½" h. 135.00

"Gallant Fishers" Jardiniere

Jardiniere, Gallant Fishers series
w/motto, 1913-36, 8½" d., 7" h.
(ILLUS.) 175.00
Jardiniere, Falstaff series, ca. 1920,
8" d. 165.00
Jardiniere, flow blue Babes in Woods
series, children playing hide & seek,
9¾" d., 9¼" h. 495.00
Match holder w/striker & 4 ash trays,
double-sided holder w/King of Hearts
decor & 4 trays w/diamonds, hearts,
spades & clubs decor, 1920, 5 pcs. 60.00

Model of lizard, signed George
Tinworth, 5" l. 150.00
Mug, Dutch series, 2 Dutch children
on front in natural colors, 1½" d.,
1¾" h. 55.00
Mug, Leather Ware, simulated black
leather w/silver rim, 6" h. 55.00
Mug, "Ye Olde Cheshire Cheese"
scene, brown glaze 45.00
Pin tray, Dutch series, Dutch figures on
cream, tan & grey ground, Haarlem,
5 x 3¼". 28.00
Pitcher, 2½" h., jug-type, Shakespeare
series, silver rim hallmarked "London
1908". 115.00
Pitcher, 2¾" h., 2" d., Dutch (or
Holland) series w/Dutch families
& children, green handle. 55.00
Pitcher, 4" h., octagonal jug-type,
Gaudy Welsh-type decor, applied
serpent handle 45.00
Pitcher, 6" h., jug-type, Coaching Days
series, 1910-25 . . . . 125.00
Pitcher, 6½" h., 5½" d., embossed
drinking scene, Doulton-Lambeth,
1870-71 mark. 115.00
Pitcher, 6¾" h., Coaching Days
series 130.00
Pitcher, 7½" h., w/pewter lid, h.p.
floral decor, cobalt blue border,
Doulton & Slaters Patent, 1882-1902 .145.00
Pitcher, 8" h., jug-type, Queen
Victoria Commemorative, 1897,
w/silver lip 320.00
Pitcher, 9" h., Foliage Ware, Doulton-
Lambeth . . . . 80.00 to 115.00
Pitcher, 9" h., jug-type, Leather Ware,
simulated brown leather w/stitching,
1885 . . . . 80.00

Elizabethan Men Bowling

Pitcher, 9¼" h., jug-type, relief-
molded scene of Elizabethan men
playing "bowls" on brown shaded to
tan ground (ILLUS.). 185.00
Pitcher, 9¼" h., 5" d., stoneware,
incised white cows grazing on tan,
brown & green ground, glossy
borders, signed Hannah Barlow. 695.00

Pitcher, tankard, stoneware, bear
handle, incised & enameled bear &
flying geese decor, signed Hannah
Barlow & dated 1878. . . . . .960.00
Pitcher, water, "Jack's The Lad for
Work," signed Noke. 125.00
Plates, 7" d., Coaching Days series,
set of 12 . . . . 175.00
Plate, 8½" d., Golf series, "All Fools
Are Not Knaves, But All Knaves
Are Fools" 160.00
Plate, 9½" d., Jackdaw of Rheims
series, "And Off that Terrible Curse
He Took," Cardinal & monks decor . . .48.00
Plate, 10" d., Automobile series, "A
Nerve Tonic" 200.00
Plate, 10" d., Shakespeare series,
Portia, w/character border. 65.00
Plates, 10" d., each w/different orchid,
artist-signed, set of 12 . . . . 2,500.00
Plate, 10¼" d., Coaching Days series . . .60.00
Plate, 10¼" d., h.p. Ludlow castle
scene in realistic colors 165.00
Plate, 10 3/8" d., Arabian Nights
series, "The Arrival of the Unknown
Princess" 95.00
Plate, 10 3/8" d., Automobile series,
"Itch Yer On Guvenor," old auto
broken down on road. 160.00
Plates, 10 3/8" d., French & North
Wales views, artist-signed, pr. 400.00
Plate, 10 3/8" d., Jackdaw of
Rheims series, "And they saved the
Lord Primate on bended knee,"
dated 1906 . . . . 65.00
Plate, 10½" d., flow blue hunting
scene decor, dated 1934 . . . . 79.50
Plate, 10½" d., rack-type, portrait,
"The Falconer" . . . . 55.00 to 75.00
Plate, 10½" d., rack-type, portrait,
"The Jester". 65.00
Plate, 10½" d., Shakespeare series,
Wolsey 65.00
Plate, 10½" d., "Rochester Castle" 60.00
Plate, chop, 13" d., African series,
lions center & animal border 75.00
Plate, chop, 13" d., Treasure Island
series 90.00
Plate, chop, 13 3/8" d., Robin Hood
series, "Under the Greenwood
Tree," realistic colors on cream
ground 158.00
Plate, Old English Inns series, "The
King's Head, Chigwell" 45.00
Salt bowl, stoneware, cupids decor,
signed George Tinworth, 5" d. 275.00
Soap dish, stoneware, dragonfly
decor 75.00
Teapot, cov., stoneware, beige &
brown tapestry ground w/aqua &
white florals, gold trim, Doulton &
Slater's Patent, 1888-1902, 4½" d.,
5¼" h. 175.00

Teapot, cov., Robin Hood series, Robin
  Hood & Friar Tuck decor, 1910-25,
  5½" h. 150.00
Teapot, cov., Glamis Thistle patt. 75.00
Teapot stand, Shakespeare series,
  "Shylock" 65.00
Toothpick holder, cuspidor form,
  stoneware, red & black relief
  card suits at sides on brown
  ground, 2¾" d., 2" h. 48.00
Tureen, cov., "This Is The House That
  Jack Built," 10" d. 90.00
Tyg (3-handled drinking mug), stone-
  ware, incised stags & hounds, signed
  Hannah Barlow, 8" h. 300.00
Vase, 4" h., flow blue Babes in Woods
  series, young girl w/doll & frog 250.00
Vase, 4½" h., Egyptian desert scene
  on green ground 150.00
Vase, 4¾" h., barrel-shaped, Dutch
  (or Holland) series w/Dutch families
  & children 75.00
Vase, 5" h. Sung veined "flambe"
  glaze, brass rim & base 125.00
Vase, 5¼" h., colorful florals & gold
  birds decor, Doulton-Lambeth,
  ca. 1880 . . . . .150.00
Vase, 5¾" h., "Harlech Castle" scene,
  artist-signed 395.00
Vase, 6½" h., Coaching Days series . . .115.00
Vase, 7" h., Zunday Zmocks series,
  signed Noke 100.00
Vase, 8" h., bulbous, flow blue Babes
  in Woods series, girl wearing coat &
  hat & carrying basket 285.00
Vase, 8" h., square, Robin Hood
  series 185.00
Vase, 8" h., stoneware, Art Nouveau
  design on cobalt blue, signed
  Eliza Simmance 140.00
Vase, 8½" h., 3½" d., flow blue
  Babes in Woods series, boys & girls
  playing blindman's buff 275.00

Shakespeare Series Vases

Vases, 9" h., Shakespeare series,
  "Hamlet" & "Ophelia," dated 1911,
  pr. (ILLUS.) .300.00
Vase, 11" h., stoneware, scrolling
  plants decor, signed Frank A.
  Butler 120.00
Vase, 11½" h., 5" d., large gold
  chrysanthemum decor on tan shaded
  to brown ground, artist-signed,
  marked "Faience," ca. 1872 . . . . .195.00

Stoneware Vase by Hannah Barlow

Vase, 12" h., cylindrical, grey stoneware, incised lions, blue foliate
  borders, signed Hannah Barlow &
  dated 1871 (ILLUS.) 650.00
Vases, 19" h., stoneware, baluster-
  shaped, irises & strapwork in relief,
  mottled grey-blue, brown & olive
  glaze, 1902-22, pr. 770.00

Doulton "Whiskey" Jug

"Whiskey" jug, relief-molded blue-
  purple grapes & green leaves,
  butterscotch to deep brown high
  glaze, 6¼" h. (ILLUS.) 275.00
Whiskey jug, Night Watchman's series,
  figural head spout, silver
  stopper & chain, 1903, 11" 225.00

DRESDEN

Dresden Ballerina at Rest

Dresden porcelain has been produced since the type now termed Dresden was made at the nearby Meissen Porcelain Works early in the 18th century. "Dresden" and "Meissen" are often used interchangeably for later wares. "Dresden" has become a generic name for the kind of porcelains produced in Dresden and certain other areas of Germany but perhaps should be confined to the wares made in the city of Dresden. Also see MEISSEN.

Console bowl, open latticework sides
  w/applied multicolored florettes,
  pedestal base w/three 5" h.
  figures w/conforming latticework &
  florettes, 14" w., overall
  18½" h. $1,000.00
Cup & saucer, h.p. scenes of 18th c.
  courtesans, 1¼" miniature 95.00
Cup & saucer, demitasse, 6-footed,
  white w/applied clusters of multicolored florals & h.p. florals
  & leaves 125.00
Cup & saucer, demitasse, swirl-molded,
  blue & gold floral decor on
  yellow ground 42.00
Figure of a boy pushing a wheelbarrow w/moveable front wheel,
  h.p. lavender & green floral decor,
  pseudo Meissen mark, 8½" l., 6" h. .260.00
Figure of a ballerina seated &
  admiring small bouquet, pink &
  white "lace" costume, overall 5½" h.
  (ILLUS.) 125.00
Figure of a lady dancing, pink & white
  "lace" dress, applied florettes,
  7¼" h. 175.00
Figure group, boy seated on sled &
  girl standing, blue, orange, lavender,
  grey, white & green costumes,
  gold trim, marked "Late Dresden,"
  3 1/8 x 4" base, 5" h. 145.00
Figure group, 4 musicians on
  platform on base, 20th c., pseudo
  "crossed swords" mark, 10 x 5½" ...600.00

Figure group, huntsman wearing
  flowered jacket & standing before a
  tree stump, 2 hounds at his feet,
  late 19th c., 15" h. 715.00
Ice cream set: oblong tray & 12
  serving plates; gilt design dividing
  surface into 4 alternating floral
  & figure panels on yellow ground,
  late 19th c., 13 pcs. 275.00
Jar w/domed cover, bulbous, alternating polychrome figure & floral
  reserves on turquoise ground,
  late 19th c., 14¾" h. 95.00
Monkey band figures, ca. 1890, 5" h.,
  8-pc. band 1,100.00
Plate, 9" d., floral decor & embossed
  scrollwork highlighted w/gilt 30.00
Plate, 9½" d., portrait of Marie
  Antoinette, wearing a green turban
  on her powdered curls & ruffle-
  edged gold satin dress, elaborate
  gilt, cobalt blue & white border,
  artist-signed, early 20th c. 225.00
Vase, cover & stand, 39" h. overall,
  bulbous, reserve scene of 18th c.
  lovers in pastoral landscape within
  elaborately molded & gilt floral
  border, applied w/figure of cupid at
  side & base, ca. 1900 ....2,475.00

FAIRINGS, GOSS & CREST

Goss Vase with Swansea Crest

Fairings are brightly-colored small porcelain objects, largely groups and boxes, that were made in molds in Germany and Bohemia and painted in the late 19th and early 20th centuries. Most related to court- ship and marriage, family life, children, animals and the like and bore captions. They were originally sold at fairs and bazaars and as souvenir pieces. In much the same category were the Goss and Crest miniature pieces, made by W.H. Goss at Stoke-on-Trent, England, and other factories, and many bearing crests. All are now widely sought.

Bust of Charles Dickens, Goss, 8" h. . . .$67.50
Bust of Greek lady, Goss, 8" h. 75.00
Bust of Lord Byron, Goss,
   8" h. . . . . .45.00 to 55.00
Bust of Sir Walter Scott, Goss, 5" h. 40.00
Figure, "Daisy," Goss 80.00
Figure, "Peggy," Goss, miniature 87.50
Model of an anvil at Gretna Green
   (crest) 15.00
Model of Robert Burns Cottage, Goss
   (crest) 75.00
Model of a skull, "Alas Poor Yorick,"
   Goss (crest) 95.00
"Returning At One O'Clock in the
   Morning" (fairing) 60.00
"Shall We Sleep First" (fairing) 65.00
Vase, w/crest of Swansea, Goss, crest
   (ILLUS.) 14.00
"When a Man is Married His Troubles
   Begin" (fairing) 82.50

FIESTA WARE

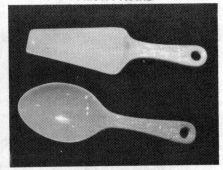

Fiesta Ware Serving Pieces

Fiesta dinnerware was made by the Homer Laughlin China Company of Newell, West Virginia, from the 1930s until the early 1970s. The brilliant colors of this inexpensive pottery have attracted numerous collectors and though it is not even out of production for a decade, it merits inclusion in our price guide.

Ash tray, cobalt blue, ivory, turquoise
   or yellow, each . . . .$20.00 to 35.00
Ash tray, red 40.00
Bowl, fruit, 4¾" to 5½" d., char-
   treuse, forest green, grey, medium
   green, red or rose, each . . . . .10.00 to 15.00
Bowl, 6" d., grey, ivory, medium green,
   red, turquoise or yellow,
   each .10.00 to 20.00
Bowl, individual salad, 7½" d.,
   turquoise 30.00
Bowl, nappy, 8½" d., ivory, light
   green, red or turquoise, each 16.00
Bowl, nappy, 9½" d., yellow 29.50
Bowl, salad, 9½" d., red 125.00

Bowl, fruit, 11¾" d., cobalt blue 48.00
Bowl, cream soup, cobalt blue, forest
   green, ivory or yellow, each 15.00
Cake server, yellow (ILLUS. top) 50.00
Candle holders, bulb-type, green or
   ivory, each pr. .32.00
Candle holders, bulb-type, turquoise,
   pr. 26.00
Candle holders, tripod-type, red, pr. . .105.00
Carafe, cov., forest green or medium
   green, each 65.00
Carafe, cov., turquoise or yellow,
   each 75.00
Casserole, cov., grey 95.00
Casserole, cov., red 50.00
Casserole, cov., yellow 40.00

Fiesta Ware Coffee Pot

Coffee pot, cov., demitasse, stick
   handle, ivory (ILLUS.) 85.00
Coffee pot, cov., red 75.00
Coffee pot, cov., yellow 55.00
Creamer, cobalt blue, grey, medium
   green, red, rose or turquoise,
   each .10.00 to 17.00
Cup & saucer, demitasse, stick handle,
   chartreuse or forest green, each 85.00
Cup & saucer, demitasse, stick handle,
   medium green, red or turquoise,
   each .20.00 to 30.00
Cup & saucer, ring handle, cobalt blue,
   forest green, ivory, light green,
   turquoise or yellow, each 16.50
Cup & saucer, ring handle, chartreuse,
   red or rose, each 19.00
Egg cup, turquoise 30.00
Egg cup, yellow .18.00
Gravy boat, cobalt blue 23.00
Gravy boat, ivory or yellow, each 20.00
Marmalade jar, cov., ivory 80.00
Marmalade jar, cov., yellow 50.00
Mixing bowl, nest-type, red, size
   No. 1 . . . . .55.00
Mixing bowl, nest-type, cobalt blue,
   size No. 2 . . . . .37.00

Mixing bowl, nest-type, yellow, size
No. 3 . . . . .20.00
Mixing bowl, nest-type, turquoise, size
No. 4 . . . . .27.50
Mixing bowl, nest-type, medium
green, size No. 5 . . . . .35.00
Mixing bowl, nest-type, light green,
size No. 6 . . . . .38.00
Mixing bowl, nest-type, red, size
No. 7 . . . . .105.00
Mug, cobalt blue or yellow,
each . . . . .22.00 to 26.00
Mug, forest green, medium green, red
or rose, each . . . . .37.00 to 42.00
Mustard jar, cov., cobalt blue 65.00
Mustard jar, cov., medium green or
yellow, each . . . . .35.00 to 40.00
Onion soup bowl, cov., ivory 140.00
Onion soup bowl, cov., yellow 35.00
Pitcher, juice, disc-type, cobalt blue or
grey, 30 oz., each 50.00
Pitcher, juice, disc-type, forest green
or ivory, 30 oz., each . . . . .28.00 to 33.00
Pitcher, juice, disc-type, yellow,
30 oz. 14.00
Pitcher w/ice lip, globular, ivory or
medium green, 2-qt., each . . .18.00 to 25.00

Fiesta Ware Pitcher

Pitcher w/ice lip, globular, yellow,
2-qt. (ILLUS.) 38.00
Pitcher, water, disc-type, chartreuse or
forest green, each . . . . .65.00 to 70.00
Pitcher, water, disc-type, cobalt blue,
ivory, medium green, turquoise or
yellow, each . . . . .25.00 to 35.00
Plate, 6" d., chartreuse, grey, red,
rose or yellow, each . . . . .4.00 to 5.00
Plate, 7" d., forest green, red, rose
or turquoise, each . . . . .6.00 to 7.00
Plate, 9" d., chartreuse, grey, ivory
or rose . . . . .9.00 to 10.00
Plate, 10" d., chartreuse, grey, red or
rose, each . . . . .18.00 to 20.00
Plate, grill, 10½" d., ivory, light
green or yellow, each 9.00
Plate, grill, 10½" d., cobalt blue, red
or turquoise, each 12.00
Plate, chop, 13" d., cobalt blue,
medium green or red, each . .18.00 to 22.00

Plate, chop, 15" d., green, grey, red,
turquoise or yellow, each . . . .20.00 to 25.00
Platter, 12" oval, medium green,
turquoise or yellow, each 11.00
Platter, 13" oval, cobalt blue, ivory,
red or yellow, each . . . . .12.00 to 14.00
Relish tray, w/five inserts, ivory or
light green, each 100.00
Salad fork, green 35.00
Salad spoon, red (ILLUS. bottom) 50.00
Salt & pepper shakers, cobalt blue,
grey or yellow, each pr. 8.00
Soup plate w/flange rim, cobalt blue,
ivory, turquoise or yellow, 8" d.,
each 12.00
Soup plate w/flange rim, chartreuse,
forest green, grey or medium green,
8" d., each . . . . .17.00 to 19.00
Syrup pitcher w/original lid, ivory 90.00
Syrup pitcher w/original lid, red 150.00
Teapot, cov., chartreuse or rose,
medium, each 110.00
Teapot, turquoise or yellow, large,
each 50.00
Tom & Jerry set: master bowl & 6
mugs; ivory, "Tom & Jerry" in gold
lettering, 7 pcs. 210.00
Tumbler, juice, medium green or red,
5 oz., each 23.50
Tumbler, juice, turquoise or yellow,
5 oz., each 15.00
Tumbler, water, cobalt blue or ivory,
10 oz., each .23.00
Tumbler, water, medium green,
turquoise or yellow, 10 oz., each 19.00
Tumbler, water, red, 10 oz. 35.00
Utility tray, yellow 14.00
Vase, 8" h., yellow 95.00
Vase, 10" h., light green 250.00
Vase, 10" h., red 130.00
Vase, 12" h., cobalt blue 180.00
Vase, 12" h., ivory 125.00
Vase, bud, cobalt blue, ivory,
turquoise or yellow, each . . . .24.00 to 28.00
Vegetable bowl, turquoise, 8½" d. 15.00

FLOW BLUE

*Flowing Blue wares, usually shortened to
Flow Blue, were made at numerous
potteries in Staffordshire, England, and
elsewhere. They are decorated with a blue
that smudged lightly or ran in the firing.
The same type of color flow is also found on
certain wares decorated in green, purple and
sepia. Patterns were given specific names,
which accompany listings here. The
standard reference for collectors of this ware
is* Flow Blue China, *a series of three books
by Petra Williams.*

ALASKA (W. H. Grindley, ca. 1891)
Bowl, cereal, 8" d. $30.00
Bowl, 10" d. 50.00
Creamer (tiny flake). 50.00
Cup & saucer .60.00
Plate, 9" d. 31.00
Platter, 12" l. 60.00
Relish dish, 6" l. 24.00
Sauce dish 8.50
Vegetable bowl, cov., 12" d. 120.00

AMOY (Davenport, ca. 1844)
Cup, handleless, round or octagonal . . .62.00
Plate, 6" to 7" d. . . . . .35.00 to 40.00
Plate, 9" d. 60.00
Plate, 10½" d. .78.00
Sauce dish 39.00
Saucer 45.00
Vegetable bowl, open, 8½" 125.00

ARGYLE (W. H. Grindley, ca. 1896)

Argyle Pattern Cup & Saucer

Butter pat. 22.00
Cup & saucer (ILLUS.) 44.00
Plate, 8" d. 35.00
Plate, 10" d. 48.00
Platter, 13 x 9" 75.00
Platter, 15½ x 11" 112.00
Platter, 19 x 13½" 160.00
Soup plate w/flange rim 30.00
Vegetable bowl, open, 10 x 7" oval 40.00

ASHBURTON (W. H. Grindley, ca. 1891)
Bowl, 6½" d. . . . . .25.00 to 35.00
Bowl, 8" d. 45.00
Creamer & cov. sugar bowl, pr. 125.00
Gravy boat. 68.00
Plate, 7" d. 23.00
Plate, 8" to 9" d. . . . . .34.00 to 40.00
Plate, 10" d. 65.00
Platter, 15" to 16" l. . . . . .78.00 to 85.00
Soup tureen, 12½" d., w/ladle 195.00
Vegetable tureen, cov. 95.00

BEATRICE (J. Maddock & Son, ca. 1896)
Platter, 14¼" oval (ILLUS.) 58.00
Platter, 16" l. 90.00

Beatrice Pattern Platter

Vegetable bowl, cov. 85.00

BEAUFORT (W. H. Grindley, ca. 1903)
Plate, dinner 57.00
Platter, large .120.00
Sauce dish 9.00

BLUE ROSE (W. H. Grindley, ca. 1900)
Bowl, 6" d. 35.00
Plate, 6" d. 22.00
Sauce dish 16.50

BURLEIGH (Burgess & Leigh, ca. 1903)
Plate, 9½" d. 27.00
Platter, 16 x 12" 90.00
Soup plate w/flange rim 25.00

CASHMERE (Ridgway & Morley, G.L. Ashworth, et. al., 1840s and on)
Creamer. 195.00
Plate, 12" d. 45.00
Soup plate w/flange rim, 12" d. 60.00

CELTIC (W. H. Grindley, ca. 1897)

Celtic Pattern Bone Dish

Bone dish (ILLUS.) 45.00
Cup & saucer, large 85.00
Platter, 12½ x 8½" . . . . .70.00 to 75.00

CHAPOO (John Wedge Wood, ca. 1850)
Butter dish, cov. 215.00
Plate, 8½" to 10½" d. . . . . .75.00 to 95.00
Platter, 14" l. .185.00
Sauce tureen, small 165.00

CHISWICK (Ridgways, ca. 1900)
Bowl, soup 15.00
Gravy boat w/underplate 100.00
Plate, 6" to 7" d. ....16.00 to 18.00
Relish dish, 9" l. 27.50

CHUSAN (J. Clementson, ca. 1840)
Cup, handleless 60.00
Plate, 10½" d. 95.00
Platter, octagonal, 12 x 9" 200.00
Relish dish, shell-shaped 65.00

CHUSAN (Francis Morley & Co., ca. 1850)
Plate, 9" d. 50.00
Relish dish ....85.00 to 95.00
Soup tureen, open, pedestal base 460.00
Vegetable bowl, open, 10" d. 125.00

CIRCASSIA (J. & G. Alcock, ca. 1840)

Circassia Pattern Plate

Coffee pot 350.00
Cup plate 50.00
Plate, 8" d. (ILLUS.)................54.00
Soup plate w/flange rim, 10½" d. 67.00
Teapot, cov. 195.00
Tureen & underplate, cov., small 125.00

CLAYTON (Johnson Bros., ca. 1902)

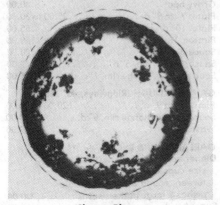

Clayton Plate

Nappy, oval 40.00
Plate, 7" d. (ILLUS.)................22.00
Platter, 14" l. 95.00
Sauce dishes, set of 6................96.00
Soup plates w/flange rim, 9" d.,
    set of 4 ....135.00

CLOVER (Josiah Wedgwood & Sons, ca. 1860)
Plate, dinner 50.00
Platter, 13" l. 85.00
Platter, 16" l. 100.00

COBURG (John Edwards, ca. 1860)
Plate, 9" to 10" d. ....45.00 to 65.00
Platter, 16 x 12" 160.00
Sugar bowl, cov. (professional repair
    to finial) 100.00

COLONIAL (J. & G. Meakin, ca. 1891)
Bone dish 50.00
Plate, 7" d. 20.00
Relish dish 45.00
Vegetable bowl, cov., round 140.00

CORAL (Johnson Bros., ca. 1900)
Plate, 9" d. 30.00
Platter 45.00
Relish dish 45.00

COUNTRY SCENES (E. Wood & Sons, ca. 1891)
Berry set, master bowl & 6 sauce
    dishes, 7 pcs. 225.00
Plate, 7" d. 22.00

CRUMLIN (Myott, Son & Co., ca. 1900)
Creamer, 9¾" h. 76.00
Gravy boat w/underplate 86.00
Soup plate w/flange rim 35.00

DAINTY (John Maddock & Son, ca. 1896)
Bone dish 45.00
Bowl, 6" d. 25.00
Bowl, 8" d. 35.00
Cake plate w/shaped handles, 10" 85.00
Plate, 6" to 8" d. 30.00
Plate, 9" d. 35.00
Platter, 10½" l. 55.00
Vegetable bowl, 9½" oval 55.00

DAISY (Burgess & Leigh, ca. 1897)
Bone dish 27.00
Butter pat, 3" d. 19.00
Creamer & cov. sugar bowl, pr. 195.00
Cup & saucer, demitasse 37.50
Cup & saucer 42.00

DEL MONTE (Johnson Bros., ca. 1900)
Bowl, soup, 7½" d. 35.00
Dinner service for 6, 42 pcs. 1,260.00
Plate, 8" d. 30.00
Plate, 9" d. 35.00

DEVON (Alfred Meakin, ca. 1907)
Cheese dish, cov. 175.00

Knife rest 90.00
Teapot, cover & stand, 3 pcs. 195.00
Vegetable bowl, open, 9½ x 7½" oval . .70.00
Vegetable bowl, open, round 75.00

DIANA (J. & G. Meakin, ca. 1907)
Celery tray, 10 x 6" 38.00
Gravy boat 40.00
Pickle dish, 8 x 5" 23.00
Plate, 9" d. 19.50
Platter, 16 x 12½" 48.00
Vegetable bowl, cov., handled, 8½ x
    6½" 55.00

DRESDEN (Villeroy & Boch, ca. 1900)
Bowl, cereal, 5¾" d. 26.00
Butter pats, set of 6 . . . . .60.00
Sauce dish, 5¼" d. 14.00

DUCHESS (W. H. Grindley, ca. 1891)
Bowl, oval 38.00
Butter pat, 3¼" d. 20.00
Gravy boat w/underplate . . . .86.00 to 100.00
Pitcher 120.00
Plate, 7" d. 22.00
Plate, 9" d. 25.00
Plates, 10" d., set of 10 . . . . .280.00
Saucer, 6" d. 15.00
Soup plate w/flange rim, 9" d. 45.00
Vegetable bowl, cov., oval . .110.00 to 125.00

DUNBARTON (New Wharf Pottery, ca. 1891)
Bone dishes, set of 8 . . . . .190.00
Soup plate w/flange rim, 9" d. 27.00
Sugar bowl, cov. 68.00

EASTERN FLOWERS (Mellor, Venables & Co., ca. 1845)
Plate, 10" d. 25.00
Soap dish w/drain insert, cov. 120.00
Toothbrush holder, cov. 185.00

EXCELSIOR (Thomas Fell, ca. 1850)

Excelsior Pattern Plate

Plate, 9" d. (ILLUS.) 67.00
Soup tureen & underplate, cov., large,
    2 pcs. 900.00

FAIRY VILLAS - 3 styles (W. Adams, ca. 1891)

Fairy Villas III Plate

Butter pat, 3" d. .14.00
Creamer, 4¾" h. .75.00
Gravy boat w/pedestal base 55.00
Pitcher, 9" h. 185.00
Plate, 7" to 9" d. . . . . .30.00 to 40.00
Plate, 10" d. (ILLUS.) 45.00
Sauce dish 35.00
Saucer, 6" d. 16.00
Soup plate w/flange rim, 9" d. 40.00
Soup tureen, 12" d., 7" h. (2 tiny
    flakes) 295.00

FLORAL (Thomas Hughes & Son, ca. 1895)
Butter pat 15.00
Gravy boat w/undertray 76.00
Soup plate w/flange rim 35.00

FLORIDA (W. H. Grindley, ca. 1891)
Bowl, 8" d. 35.00
Gravy boat 40.00
Platter, 10" l. 40.00
Sauce dish 18.00

FLORIDA (Johnson Bros., ca. 1900)
Bone dish 20.00
Cup 30.00
Gravy boat 40.00
Plate, 7" to 9" d. . . . . .25.00 to 30.00
Plate, 10" d. 55.00
Platter, 16½" l. .150.00
Sauce dish 28.00
Saucer, gold trim, 6" d. 7.00
Soup plate w/flange rim, 7½" d. 35.00

GAINSBOROUGH (Ridgways, ca. 1905)
Plate, 8" to 9" d. . . . . .20.00 to 25.00
Soup plate w/flange rim, 9" d. 38.00
Waste bowl 59.00

GARLAND (W. & E. Corn, ca. 1904)
Dinner service for six w/tea & coffee
    size cups & saucers, large soup
    tureen, round & oval vegetable
    dishes & large platter, set 1,200.00
Sugar bowl 65.00

GENEVA (Royal Doulton, dated 1906 & 1907)
Cheese dish, cov. 140.00
Pitcher, 1 qt. 125.00
Plate, 7½" d. .35.00

GEORGIA (Johnson Bros., ca. 1903)
Gravy boat. 75.00
Plate, 7" to 8" d. . . . . .28.00 to 32.00
Plate, 9" d. 38.00
Platter 95.00
Relish dish 60.00
Soup plate w/flange rim, 8¾" d. 40.00
Vegetable bowl, open, 8¾ x 7" oval 65.00
Vegetable tureen, cov. 150.00

GIRONDE (W. H. Grindley, ca. 1891)

Gironde Cup & Saucer

Bone dish 30.00
Bowl, soup, 7¾" d. 35.00
Bowl, 9" d. 35.00
Butter pat, 3 1/8" d. 19.00
Cup & saucer (ILLUS.) 45.00
Pitcher, milk, 8¾" h. 150.00
Plate, 7" to 9" d. . . . . .25.00 to 30.00
Platter, 15 x 10" . . . . .75.00 to 95.00
Platter, 19 x 13½" 150.00
Sauce dish, 5" d. 20.00
Saucer, 6" d. .15.00
Vegetable bowl, 9 x 6¾" oval 55.00

GLENWOOD (Johnson Bros., ca. 1900)

Glenwood Pattern Plate

Plate, 10" d. (ILLUS.). 25.00
Platter, 10½ x 7½" 28.00

GRACE (W. H. Grindley, ca. 1897)
Butter pat. 18.00
Gravy boat. 95.00
Plate, 8" d. 30.00
Platter, 21" l. 150.00

HAMILTON (John Maddock & Sons, ca. 1896)
Plate, 8" d. 20.00
Platter, 17 x 12" 75.00
Soup plate w/flange rim 26.00

HINDUSTAN (John Maddock, ca. 1855)
Plate, 7½" d. .45.00
Plate, 8½" d. .65.00
Plate, 9½" d. .70.00
Platter, 13½" l. 85.00
Platter, 16 x 12" 225.00

HOFBURG, THE (W. H. Grindley, ca. 1891)
Butter pat. 16.00
Celery tray 48.00
Dinner service for 4 w/cov. vegetable
    bowl, platter & cov. butter dish,
    19 pcs. .325.00
Gravy boat. 35.00
Pitcher, 6" h. .70.00
Plate, 9" d. 18.00
Plate, 10" d. .35.00
Platter, 13" l. 80.00
Sauce dish, 5" oval 25.00
Sugar bowl, cov. 82.50
Vegetable bowl, cov. 75.00

HOLLAND, THE (Alfred Meakin, ca. 1891)
Bone dish 34.00
Bowl, nappy. .30.00
Bowl, soup, 7¼" d. 35.00
Gravy boat w/underplate 95.00
Plate, 6" d. 20.00
Plate, 9" d. 35.00
Plate, 10" d. .37.50
Platter, 12½ x 8¾" 100.00
Soup tureen (tiny flake) 150.00
Vegetable bowl, cov., 12 x 7" 125.00

HOLLAND (Johnson Bros., ca. 1891)
Butter pat. 17.50
Plate, 6½" d. .15.00
Plate, 9" d. 30.00
Plate, 10" d. .47.50
Platter, 12½ x 9½" 50.00
Sugar bowl .115.00
Vegetable bowl, cov. . . . . .95.00 to 150.00

HONC (Petrus Regout, ca. 1858)
Bowl, 6" d., 3¼" h. 125.00
Plate, 8" d. 30.00
Plates, 9" d., w/copper lustre, set
    of 8 . . . . .270.00

HONG KONG (Charles Meigh, ca. 1845)
Cup plate, 4" d. 65.00
Honey dish, 5" d. 75.00
Plate, 10" d. 125.00
Platter, 18 x 14" 175.00
Relish dish 125.00
Sauce dish 25.00
Soup plate w/flange rim, 10½" d. 85.00

IDRIS (W. H. Grindley, ca. 1910)
Bouillon cup & saucer. 36.00
Cup & saucer 40.00
Plate, 8" to 9" d. . . . . .14.00 to 16.00
Plate, 10" d. 23.00
Soup plate w/flange rim 20.00
Vegetable bowl 65.00

INDIAN (possibly F. & R. Pratt, ca. 1840)
Cake plate 175.00
Honey dish, 5" d. 65.00
Plate, 7" to 8" d. . . . . .40.00 to 45.00
Plate, 9½" d. 80.00
Platter, 17" 295.00
Sauce dish, 5½" d. 40.00
Saucer, 6" d. 37.50
Sauce tureen & underplate,
  2 pcs. . . . . .135.00 to 150.00
Soup plate w/flange rim, 10¾" d. 85.00
Sugar bowl. 125.00
Teapot, cov. 275.00
Vegetable bowl, cov. 105.00

INDIAN JAR (Jacob & Thos. Furnival, ca. 1843)
Cup, handleless .60.00
Cup & saucer 70.00
Honey dish, 5" d. 65.00
Plate, 7½" d. 34.00
Plate, 10½" d. 80.00
Platter, 18 x 14" 295.00
Sauce dish, 5" d. 20.00
Saucer, 6" d. 27.50
Tray. 150.00

IVANHOE (Wedgwood, ca. 1901)
Butter pat. 27.00
Plate, 10¼" d., "Extorting Silver From
  Isaac" center .75.00
Plate, 10¼" d. "Friar Tuck Entertains
  the Black Knight" center 75.00
Plate, 10¼" d., "Ivanhoe & Rowena"
  center 75.00
Plate, 10¼" d., "Wamba & Garth the
  Swineherd" center 75.00
Saucer, 6¼" d. 30.00

JANETTE (W. H. Grindley, ca. 1897)
Bone dish 32.00
Plate, 8½" d. 30.00
Platter, 15" 75.00
Sugar bowl, cov., 6½" h. (ILLUS.) 90.00

Janette Pattern Sugar Bowl

JAPAN (Thos. Fell & Co., ca. 1860)
Pitcher, 1½ qt. .295.00
Plate, 6½" d. 35.00
Vegetable tureen, cov., octagonal
  (professional repair to finial) 175.00

JEWEL (Johnson Bros., ca. 1900)
Cup & saucer 45.00
Plate, 8" d. 30.00
Platter, 14" l. 85.00

KELVIN (Alfred Meakin, ca. 1891)
Bowl, 7" d. 48.00
Creamer. 85.00
Plate, 9½" d. 40.00
Vegetable bowl, cov., oval 165.00

KENWORTH (Johnson Bros., ca. 1900)
Butter pat. 25.00
Cup & saucer 60.00
Plate, luncheon 35.00
Plate, salad 30.00
Posset cup 75.00
Relish tray, 8" l. .49.00
Sauce dish 23.00
Vegetable bowl, open, 9" oval 48.00

KIN SHAN (Edward Challinor, ca. 1855)
Cup & saucer (professional repair to
  cup base) 70.00
Mug. 145.00
Plate, 7 5/8" d. 90.00

KIRKEE (John Meir & Son, ca. 1861)
Creamer. 120.00
Platter, 15 x 12" 200.00
Platter, 16" oblong, cut corners 295.00

KYBER (John Meir & Son, ca. 1870; W. Adams & Son, ca. 1891)
Cup & saucer, handleless (Meir) 85.00
Plate, 6" d. 25.00
Plate, 7" d. (Adams). 32.00
Plate, 7" d. (Meir) 38.00
Plate, 8" d. (Adams). 35.00
Plate, 8" d. (Meir) 50.00
Plate, 9" d. (Adams). 45.00
Plate, 9" d. (Meir) 60.00

Kyber Pattern Plate

Plate, 10" d., Adams (ILLUS.) 65.00
Plate, 12" d. (Adams) 45.00
Platter, 10 x 7½" (Adams) 110.00
Platter, 17" l. (Adams) 295.00
Sauce dish (Adams) 15.00
Saucer, 6" d. (Adams) 22.50
Saucer (Meir) 38.00
Soup plate w/flange rim, 9" d.
   (Adams) 40.00
Soup tureen, footed, 10" d. (Adams) . . .275.00
Vegetable bowl, open, 7½ x 5½"
   (Adams) 115.00
Vegetable bowl, open, 10½ x 7¾"
   oblong (Adams) 165.00
Vegetable tureen 245.00
Waste bowl 65.00

LA BELLE (Wheeling Pottery, ca. 1900)

La Belle Creamer

Banana boat 225.00
Bon bon dish, ornate feet, everted
   rim w/gold trim, 8 x 7 x 4½" 145.00
Bowl, 9½ x 8" 40.00
Bowl, 10½" d., floral handle 130.00
Bowl, cereal 45.00
Bread platter, pierced handles, 12 x
   9" 135.00

Butter pat 22.00
Cake plate 65.00
Charger, 11¼" d. 150.00
Coffee server w/hinged silverplate
   lid, large 250.00
Cookie jar, cov. .110.00
Creamer, individual, 3½" h. 60.00
Creamer (ILLUS.) 135.00
Fruit bowl, loop handle 235.00
Jardiniere, 10" d., 8½" h. 175.00
Pitcher, hot water 185.00
Pitcher, milk 125.00
Plate, 7½" d. 20.00
Plate, 8½" d. 40.00
Plate, 9½" d. 50.00
Plate, 10½" d. .110.00
Plate, chop, 13" d. 80.00
Plate, chop, 15" d. 85.00
Platter, 17 x 12½" 140.00
Relish 65.00
Sauce dish 23.00
Saucer 20.00
Soup plate w/flange rim, 7" d. 45.00
Sugar bowl, cov. 95.00
Syrup pitcher w/original brass lid,
   bulbous 120.00
Teacup & saucer 95.00
Vegetable bowl, cov., 7¾" d. 145.00
Waste bowl 55.00

LAHORE (Thos. Phillips & Son, ca. 1840)
Cup plate, 4" d. 65.00
Plate, 7½" d. 40.00
Platter, 16½ x 12½" 275.00

LAKEWOOD (Wood & Sons, ca. 1900)
Cup, demitasse 25.00
Platter, 12 x 9" .75.00
Soup plate w/flange rim, 9" d. 35.00

LANCASTER (New Wharf Pottery, ca. 1891)
Butter dish, cov. .40.00
Cup & saucer 55.00
Plate, 8" d. 32.50
Plate, 9" d. 36.00
Plate, 10" d. 47.00
Soup plate w/flange rim 38.00

LINDA (John Maddock & Sons Ltd., ca. 1896)
Bowl, 9" d. 45.00
Butter pat 16.00
Creamer & cov. sugar bowl, pr. 195.00
Cup & saucer 55.00
Gravy boat w/underplate 86.00
Plate, 6" d. 16.00
Plate, 9" d. 38.00
Platter, 10 x 7½" 30.00
Platter, 11½ x 8¼" 55.00
Platter, 12½ x 9¼" 65.00
Platter, 17" l. 95.00
Sauceboat w/cover, footed, 8¼" l.,
   w/underplate & ladle, 3 pcs. 150.00
Saucer, 6" d. 7.00

Soup tureen w/slotted lid, 9½" d. 125.00
Teapot, cov. 150.00
Tea set, cov. teapot, creamer & cov.
   sugar bowl, 3 pcs. 250.00
Vegetable bowl, cov., 10" oval 135.00
Vegetable bowl, cov., 11 x 7" 65.00

LOIS (New Wharf Pottery, ca. 1891)
Bowl, 9" d. 55.00
Plate, 6" d. 25.00
Plate, 8" d. 35.00
Platter, 10½ x 9" 50.00
Sauce dish 24.00
Vegetable bowl, 9" d. 60.00

LONSDALE (Ridgways, ca. 1910)

Lonsdale Pattern Plate

Plate, 10" d. (ILLUS.) . . . . .47.50 to 65.00
Plate, salad 15.00
Platter, 11½" l. 50.00
Platter, 13" l. 68.00
Platter, 15" l. 75.00
Vegetable bowl, cov. 165.00
Vegetable bowl, open 59.00

LORNE (W.H. Grindley, ca. 1900)
Bowl, cereal 37.50
Cup, demitasse 25.00
Egg cup 34.00
Gravy boat. 59.00
Plate, 10" d. 37.50
Platter, 10" l. 75.00
Platter, 14" l. 85.00
Relish dish 75.00
Sauceboat 60.00
Sauce dish, 5½" d. 15.00
Soup plate w/flange rim, 9" d. 25.00
Soup tureen, cov., 12½" d. 95.00
Vegetable bowl, cov., round 110.00
Vegetable bowl, open 48.00

LOTUS (W. H. Grindley, ca. 1910)
Bowl, 10½" d. 160.00
Butter pat. 17.00
Cup & saucer 40.00
Gravy boat. 40.00

Sauce dish 15.00
Soup ladle, 12" l. 100.00
Vegetable bowl, open, 11" oval 75.00

LUGANO (Ridgways, ca. 1910)
Bowl, small, oblong 35.00
Gravy boat. 40.00
Sauce dish 10.00
Soup plate w/flange rim 44.00
Vegetable bowl 55.00

MADRAS (Doulton & Co., ca. 1900)
Bowl, 8¼" d., 3" h. 55.00
Butter pat. 12.00
Creamer, 5½" h. .79.00
Cup & saucer 57.00
Gravy boat. 55.00
Pitcher, milk, 6½" h. 130.00
Pitcher, 8" h. 165.00
Plate, 9½" d. 30.00
Plate, 10½" d. 48.00
Platter, 10" l. 45.00
Platter, 11" l. 55.00
Platter, 16" l. 130.00
Relish dish, handled 65.00
Sauce dish, 5 3/8" d. 25.00
Saucer 17.00
Soup plate w/flange rim, 10" d. 45.00
Soup tureen w/cover, underplate &
   ladle, 3 pcs. 675.00
Vegetable bowl, cov., oval 260.00
Waste bowl, 7" d., 3" h. 50.00

MANHATTAN (Henry Alcock, ca. 1900)
Butter pat, 3 3/8" d. 20.00
Creamer. 145.00
Gravy boat w/attached underplate. 86.00
Plate, 8" d. 18.00
Sauce dish 16.00
Shaving mug 65.00
Waste bowl, 5¾" d., 3¼" h. 50.00

**MANILLA (Podmore Walker, ca. 1845; J.
Ridgway or Samuel Alcock, ca. 1845)**
Creamer (Podmore Walker) 275.00
Cup (Podmore Walker) 45.00
Cup & saucer, handleless (Podmore
   Walker) 128.00
Pitcher, water, 11" h. (handle
   repaired) 255.00
Plate, 6" to 8" d. (Podmore Walker) 48.00
Plate, 9½" to 10½" d. (Podmore
   Walker) . . . . .75.00 to 95.00
Platter, 13½ x 10½" 135.00
Relish dish. . . . . .98.00 to 110.00
Sauce dish 30.00
Soup plate w/flange rim, 9½" d. 95.00
Sugar bowl. 70.00
Vegetable bowl, cov. (Podmore
   Walker) 450.00

MARECHAL NIEL (W. H. Grindley, ca. 1895)
Butter pat. 20.00
Cup & saucer 30.00

Gravy boat 60.00
Plate, 9" d. 32.00
Plate, 10" d. . . . . .35.00 to 55.00
Platter, 16" 145.00
Saucer, 6½" d. 16.00
Sugar bowl, cov. 97.50
Teapot, cov. 250.00
Vegetable bowl, cov. 155.00

MARGUERITE (W. H. Grindley, ca. 1891)
Gravy boat w/underplate 55.00
Plate, 8" d. 27.50
Plate, 10" d. 30.00
Sauce dish 21.00
Soup tureen 295.00
Sugar bowl, cov. 82.50
Vegetable bowl, cov. 125.00

MARIE (W. H. Grindley, ca. 1891)
Compote 150.00
Pitcher, 6" h. 95.00
Pitcher, 8" h. 125.00
Plate, 8¾" d. 25.00
Plate, 10" d. 42.00
Sauce dish, 5" d. 20.00
Soup plate w/flange rim, 9" d. 34.00

MARQUIS, THE (W. H. Grindley, ca. 1906)
Bowl, cereal, 6" d. 30.00
Plate, 6" d. . . . . .20.00 to 25.00
Sauce dish 19.00

MARTHA (Bridgett & Bates, ca. 1896)
Bone dish .28.00
Pitcher, water, 9" h. 245.00
Plate, 7" d. 25.00
Plate, 10" d. 35.00
Platter, 16 x 12" 50.00
Soup plate w/flange rim 35.00
Vegetable bowl, 9" d. 46.00

MARTHA WASHINGTON (Unknown, English, ca. 1900)
Cup & saucer 50.00
Plate, 9" d. 47.50
Saucer, 6" d. 20.00

MATLOCK (F. Winkle & Co., ca. 1890)
Gravy boat w/attached underplate,
   cov., 8" l. 35.00
Plate, 9½" d. 15.00
Plate, 10½" d. 18.00
Platter, 16 x 12½" 75.00
Platter, 17¾ x 14" 95.00
Vegetable bowl w/cover & underplate,
   12" l. 65.00

MELBOURNE (W. H. Grindley, ca. 1900)
Bowl, 5¾" d., footed 70.00
Bowl, 9" oval 55.00
Bowl, fruit, 12" d. 145.00
Butter dish w/cover & drain insert 150.00
Butter pat, 3¼" d. 25.00
Creamer .85.00

Cup & saucer . . . . .35.00 to 50.00
Gravy boat w/underplate . . . .95.00 to 125.00
Plate, 6½" to 8½" d. . . . . .35.00 to 55.00
Platter, 10" 54.00
Platter, 11" to 12". . . . . .70.00 to 80.00
Platter, 14" to 16". . . . . .95.00 to 110.00
Relish dish 75.00
Sauce dish 25.00
Soup plate w/flange rim, 9" d. 30.00
Sugar bowl, cov. 95.00
Vegetable bowl, cov., 9" d. 150.00
Vegetable bowl, cov., 10"
   oval . . . . .135.00 to 150.00
Vegetable bowl, open, 9" to 10"
   oval . . . . .60.00 to 70.00
Waste bowl, 5¾" d. 75.00

MELROSE (Doulton, ca. 1891)
Plate, 9" to 10" d. . . . . .35.00 to 45.00
Platter, 11" l. 50.00
Platter, 16" to 18" l. . . . . . . .75.00 to 100.00
Sauce tureen w/cover & underplate . . .175.00
Vegetable bowl, cov., oval . . .90.00 to 110.00

MONGOLIA (Johnson Bros., ca. 1900)
Creamer & open sugar bowl, pr. 110.00
Cup 20.00
Plate, 9¼" d. 47.50
Vegetable tureen, cov. (hairline in
   cover) .125.00

MOREA (J. Goodwin, ca. 1878)
Cup plate .55.00
Plate, 7½" d. 35.00
Relish dish 65.00

MURIEL (Upper Hanley Potteries, ca. 1895)
Creamer .75.00
Gravy boat 45.00
Sugar bowl 100.00

NANKIN (Possibly T. Walker or Mellor Venables & Co., ca. 1845)
Plate, 8" d. 45.00
Plate, 9½" d. 60.00
Vegetable bowl, open, 10" d. 140.00

NAVY (Thos. Till & Son, ca. 1891)
Cup & saucer 52.00
Sauce dish 15.00
Soup plate w/flange rim 26.00
Vegetable bowl, cov. 145.00

NING PO (R. Hall & Co., ca. 1845)
Plate, 8½" to 9½" d. . . . . .50.00 to 60.00
Platter, 10 x 7" 85.00
Platter, 15¾ x 12" 185.00

NON PAREIL (Burgess & Leigh, ca. 1891)
Bone dish .45.00
Bowl, cereal, 6" d. 28.00
Butter pat .18.00
Cake plate . . . . .50.00 to 85.00
Creamer .125.00

Cup & saucer . . . . .50.00 to 60.00
Dish, handled, 7 x 6" 40.00
Plate, 7" d. .32.00
Plate, 8" to 9" d. . . . . .40.00 to 45.00

Non Pareil Plate

Plate, 10" d. (ILLUS.). 50.00
Platter, 12 x 10" 90.00
Platter, 13½ x 11½" 120.00
Platter, 15½ x 12½" 195.00
Platter, 17½ x 15" 175.00
Relish dish 66.00
Sauce dish, 5½" d. 22.00
Saucer, demitasse 25.00
Saucer, 6" d. 17.50
Soup plate w/flange rim, 9" d. 44.00
Spoon rest 65.00
Vegetable bowl, oval. 60.00
Vegetable tureen, cov. . . . . . .150.00 to 255.00
Waste bowl 60.00

NORMANDY (Johnson Bros., ca. 1900)
Bowl, 9" d. 55.00
Butter pat 29.00
Cup & saucer 55.00
Plate, 7" to 8" d. . . . . .20.00 to 25.00
Plate, 10" d. 42.00
Platter, 10½" oval 50.00
Platter, 14 x 10½" 98.00
Platter, 16 x 12" 90.00
Relish dish 23.00
Sauceboat 67.50
Sauce dish, 5" d. 16.00
Soup plate w/flange rim 42.50
Sugar bowl 125.00
Vegetable bowl, 10 x 7½" 55.00
Vegetable tureen, cov. 90.00
Waste bowl 55.00

OLD CURIOSITY SHOP (Ridgways, ca. 1910)
Plate, 8" d. 20.00
Plate, 9" d. 25.00
Tray, pierced handles 40.00

OLYMPIA (W. H. Grindley, ca. 1894)
Bone dish 25.00
Bowl, 9" d. . . . . .30.00 to 38.00
Cup & saucer 42.50

Gravy boat. 55.00
Plate, dinner 17.00
Platter, 14" l. 65.00
Platter, 16" l. 75.00
Soup plate w/flange rim, 8¾" d. 30.00

OREGON (Johnson Bros., ca. 1900)
Bowl, cereal, 7½" d. 35.00
Plate, 8¾" d. 49.00
Vegetable bowl, open, 9" to 10" oval . . .48.00

OREGON (T. J. & J. Mayer, ca. 1845)

Oregon Sauce Tureen

Pitcher, water, 13" h. 395.00
Plate, 6¼" d. 40.00
Plate, 7½" d. 60.00
Plate, 9½" d. 83.00
Platter, 13½" l. 225.00
Platter, 18 x 14" 325.00
Saucer, 6" d. 40.00
Sauce tureen, cover, underplate &
    ladle, 6" l., 3 pcs. (ILLUS.) 415.00
Sugar bowl, cov. 275.00
Teapot, cov. 415.00

ORIENTAL (Ridgways, ca. 1891)
Butter pat, 3¼" d. 20.00
Compote, 10 x 5½", handled 225.00
Plate, 5¾" d. 25.00
Platter 275.00
Relish tray, oval . . . . .45.00 to 58.00
Sauce dish . . . . .12.00 to 18.00
Soup plate w/flange rim, 9" d. 25.00
Soup tureen, cov., 12 x
    8½" . . . . .250.00 to 295.00
Teapot, cov. 350.00
Vegetable bowl, open, 8" to 9½"
    oval . . . . .90.00 to 125.00

ORMONDE (Alfred Meakin, ca. 1891)
Platter, 12½ x 9" 70.00
Platter, 18 x 15" 160.00
Soup plate w/flange rim 60.00

OSBORNE (W. H. Grindley, ca. 1900)
Creamer & cov. sugar bowl, pr. 285.00
Plate, 7" to 8" d. . . . . .20.00 to 27.00
Plate, 10" d. 34.00
Sauce dish 17.00
Vegetable bowl, open, oval 60.00

OSBORNE (Ridgways, ca. 1905)

Bone dish 30.00
Butter pat 18.00
Creamer & sugar bowl, pr. 145.00
Gravy boat 65.00
Saucer, 6¼" d. 15.00
Soup plate w/flange rim, 8¾" d. 35.00
Vegetable bowl, cov., cloverleaf-
  shaped 185.00
Vegetable bowl, cov., oval 135.00
Vegetable bowl, open, 10 x 7½" oval . . .40.00

OVANDO (Alfred Meakin, ca. 1891)

Butter pat 26.00
Gravy boat 62.50
Plate, 7" d. 26.00

OXFORD (Ford & Sons, ca. 1900)

Candy dish, handled, 12 x 10" 200.00
Gravy boat 59.00
Platter, 14 x 11" 125.00

OXFORD (Johnson Bros., ca. 1900)

Creamer 95.00
Plate, 9" d. 30.00
Plate, 10" d. 44.00

PAISLEY (Mercer, ca. 1890)

Creamer, 4¾" h. 66.00
Cup & saucer 50.00
Gravy boat w/underplate 95.00
Plate, 8" d. 25.00
Platter, 15½" l. 60.00
Sauceboat w/underplate 45.00
Sauce dish, 5½" d. 20.00
Sugar bowl, cov. 55.00
Vegetable dish, individual size,
  5¾ x 4¼" 30.00

PARIS (New Wharf Pottery and Stanley Pottery Co., 1890s)

Bowl, 9" d. 35.00
Butter pat 18.50
Plate, 9¼" d. 30.00
Platter, 14" l. 97.50
Vegetable bowl, cov., oval 125.00

PEACH or PEACH ROYAL (Johnson Bros., ca. 1891)

Bone dish 35.00
Plate, 9" d. 35.00
Plate, 10" d. 49.00
Soup plate w/flange rim 45.00
Spooner 75.00
Vegetable bowl, cov. 125.00
Vegetable bowl, open 58.00

PELEW (E. Challinor, ca. 1840)

Creamer 100.00
Cup & saucer, handleless 98.00
Plate, 7½" d. 50.00
Plate, 9½" to 10½" . . . . .78.00 to 95.00
Platter, 11" l. 120.00
Platter, 13 x 10" 190.00

Platter, 15½ x 12" 350.00
Sauce dish 37.00
Saucer, 6" d. 40.00
Soup plate w/flange rim, 10½" d. 110.00

PERSIAN (Johnson Bros., ca. 1902)

Bone dish 45.00
Bowl, 9½ x 7", handled 95.00
Plate, 7" to 9" d. . . . . .25.00 to 35.00
Platter, 14½ x 10½" . . . . .75.00 to 110.00
Vegetable bowl, cov., handled, 8" d.,
  3" h. 85.00
Vegetable bowl, open, 10" oval 42.00

PERSIAN MOSS (Utzschneider & Co., ca. 1891)

Bowl, cereal, 6" d. 30.00
Cup & saucer, demitasse 14.00
Cup & saucer 20.00
Vegetable dishes, open, 8" d., pr. 50.00

POPPY (W. H. Grindley, ca. 1891)

Gravy boat 40.00
Plate, 9" d. 35.00
Platter, 18" l. 125.00

PORTMAN (W. H. Grindley, ca. 1891)

Bowl, footed 75.00
Butter pat 17.50
Cup & saucer, demitasse 45.00
Cup & saucer 42.50
Sauce dish 21.00
Soup plate w/flange rim, 8" d. 23.00

PRINCETON (Johnson Bros., ca. 1900)

Bowl, soup, 7¾" d. 35.00
Butter pat 17.50
Cup & saucer 40.00
Gravy boat 55.00
Pitcher, 2-qt. 165.00
Plate, 9" d. 25.00
Sauce dish 24.00
Vegetable bowl, cov. 110.00
Vegetable bowl, open, oval 90.00

RALEIGH (Burgess & Leigh, ca. 1906)

Butter pat 14.00
Cup & saucer 30.00
Gravy boat 39.00
Sauce dish, 5" d. 20.00
Sauce tureen w/underplate & ladle 150.00
Vegetable bowl, cov., 11 x 7" 120.00

REGENT (Alfred Meakin, Ltd., ca. 1897)

Cup & saucer 75.00
Sugar bowl 90.00
Platter, 12 x 9¼" .65.00

RHINE (Thomas Dimmock, dated May 7, 1844)

Cup 35.00
Cup plate 48.00
Plate, 9" d. 50.00
Plate, 10" d. 75.00
Platter, 15 x 12" 130.00

Vegetable bowl, cov.,
  octagonal . . . . .100.00 to 150.00
Vegetable bowl, open, 9 x 6½" 98.00

RICHMOND (Alfred Meakin, ca. 1891)
Bread tray, handled 75.00
Cake plate, handled. 70.00
Platter, 16" l. 115.00

**ROCK or ROCK AND ROSE A LA CHINOISE
(Challinor, ca. 1850 or Mason)**
Cup & saucer, handleless 95.00
Plate, 9½" d. 60.00
Platter, 14 x 10" 125.00
Soup plate w/flange rim, 9½" d. 75.00
Teapot, cov. 275.00

ROSE (W. H. Grindley, ca. 1893)
Plate, 7" d. 12.00
Plate, 8" to 9" d. . . . . .28.00 to 37.00
Soup plate w/flange rim 35.00
Vegetable bowl, cov., oval 110.00

ROSEVILLE (John Maddocks, ca. 1891)

Roseville Soup Plate

Plate, 7" d. 25.00
Plate, 9" to 10" d. . . . . .32.00 to 40.00
Platter, 16 x 11½" 115.00
Sauce dish 15.00
Soup plate w/flange rim, 8½" d.
  (ILLUS.) 40.00
Soup tureen 225.00
Sugar bowl, cov. 49.00
Vegetable bowl, open, oval 55.00

**SABRAON (Maker unknown, probably Eng-
lish, ca. 1845)**
Creamer. 195.00
Gravy boat. 185.00
Punch bowl, footed, applied leaf form
  handles, gold trim, 10½" d.,
  6¼" h. 225.00
Soup plate w/flange rim, 8" d. 58.00

ST. LOUIS (Johnson Bros., ca. 1900)

St. Louis Sugar Bowl

Bone dish 32.50
Butter pat 15.00
Plate, 9" d. . . . . .30.00 to 35.00
Platter, small. 45.00
Platter, large. 60.00
Sugar bowl, cov. (ILLUS.) 60.00

SAVOY (Johnson Bros., ca. 1900)

Savoy Plate

Plate, 10" d. (ILLUS.). 40.00
Platter, 14½ x 10½" 115.00
Soup plate w/flange rim 36.00

**SCINDE (J. & G. Alcock, ca. 1840 and Thomas
Walker, ca. 1847)**
Bowl, soup, 9" d. 75.00
Chamber pot, cov. (minor handle
  repair) 285.00
Cup & saucer, handleless 110.00
Cup & saucer .120.00
Cup plate 75.00
Gravy boat, cov. 175.00
Honey dish, 5" d. 75.00
Pitcher, water, 12" h. (minor repair) . . .300.00
Plate, 6" to 7" d. . . . . .40.00 to 52.00

Plate, 8½" d. 62.00
Plate, 10½" d. 90.00
Platter, 11 x 8½" 175.00
Platter, 12 x 10" 200.00
Platter, 15½" l. 275.00

Scinde Relish Dish

Relish dish, shell-shaped (ILLUS.) 85.00
Sauce dish, 5" d. 47.50
Sauce tureen, cover & underplate,
  7½" w. . . . . .225.00 to 295.00
Soap dish w/cover & original insert
  (minor flakes) 295.00
Soup plate w/flange rim, 10½" d. 90.00
Sugar bowl. 175.00
Teapot, cov. (flake on spout) 325.00
Vegetable bowl, cov., 11 x
  9" . . . . .300.00 to 385.00
Vegetable bowl, open 165.00
Wash basin & pitcher, 2 pcs. 1,250.00

SEAWEED (Maker unknown, brush-painted)
Creamer, footed 190.00
Cup & saucer 75.00
Plate, 8½" d. 56.00

SEVILLE (New Wharf Pottery, ca. 1891)
Bowl, 6" d. 20.00
Gravy boat. 45.00
Plate, 9½" d. 55.00
Platter 115.00
Vegetable bowl, cov. 220.00

SHANGHAE (J. Furnival, ca. 1860)
Cup & saucer 58.00
Plate, 8" d. 45.00
Plate, 9" d. 75.00
Plate, 10" d. 95.00
Platter, 15½ x 12" 140.00
Sauce dish, 5" d. 28.00
Saucer 27.50
Vegetable bowl, cov., oblong
  (hairline) 145.00

SHANGHAI (W. H. Grindley, ca. 1891)
Cups & saucers, set of 4 . . . . .280.00
Plate, 5¾" d. 28.00
Plate, 10" d. 50.00
Sauce dish, 5" d. 20.00
Saucer, 6" d. 20.00
Vegetable bowl, open, 9" oval 60.00

SHAPOO (T & R Boote, ca. 1842)
Cup & saucer .120.00
Plate, 7" d. 55.00
Plate, 9" to 10" d. . . . . .85.00 to 95.00
Platter, 12½ x 9½" 225.00
Soup plate w/flange rim, 9½" d. 110.00

SHELL (Wood & Challinor, ca. 1840 & E. Challinor, ca. 1860)
Plate, 8" d. 32.00
Plate, 9½" d. 75.00
Sauce dish, 5" d. 32.50
Wash basin & pitcher 525.00

SIMLA (Elsmore & Forster, ca. 1860)
Coffee pot, cov. (small chip on spout) . .125.00
Possett cup 70.00
Sugar bowl, cov. 150.00

SOBRAON (Maker unknown, English, ca. 1850)
Cup & saucer 95.00
Honey dish, scalloped rim, 4" d. 65.00
Plate, 6½" d. 44.00
Plate, 8" d. 50.00
Plate, 9½" d. 60.00
Platter, 11" to 12" l., scalloped
  corners . . . . .145.00 to 160.00
Teapot, cov. (repair to spout tip &
  cover edge) .225.00
Vegetable bowl, cov. 375.00
Vegetable bowl, open, 10½" d. 120.00

SOMERSET (W. H. Grindley, ca. 1910)
Butter pat, 3½" d. 19.00
Cup & saucer 38.00
Plate, 10" d. 39.00
Sauce dish, 5" d. 25.00

SPINACH (Libertas, ca. 1900, brush-painted)

Spinach Pattern Bowl

Bean pot. 75.00
Bowl, 8" d. (ILLUS.) 40.00
Bowl, 10" d. . . . . .45.00 to 55.00
Cup & saucer, demitasse 55.00
Cup & saucer. . . . . .65.00 to 95.00
Plate, 7" to 8" d. 40.00

STANLEY (Johnson Bros., dated November 7, 1898)
Butter pat...........................14.00
Cup, demitasse.....................25.00
Sauce dish 15.00

SYDNEY (New Wharf Pottery, ca. 1891)
Butter pat...........................17.00
Cup & saucer 48.00
Sauce dish 14.00

SYLVIA (Joseph Clementson, ca. 1850)
Plate, 8½" d........................35.00
Wash basin & 12½" h. pitcher 325.00

TEMPLE, THE (Podmore Walker, ca. 1850)
Chamber pot 450.00
Creamer 250.00
Cup & saucer, handleless .....85.00 to 95.00
Pitcher, 6" h. 265.00
Plate, 7" to 8" d............57.00 to 70.00
Plate, 9" d..........................85.00
Plate, 10" d. ....80.00 to 100.00
Platter, 13" l.......................150.00
Platter, 16 x 12", cut corners.........295.00
Wash basin & pitcher 1,250.00
Waste bowl 165.00

TOGO (F. Winkle, ca. 1900)

Togo Pattern Plate

Bowl, 9" to 10" d. ....35.00 to 45.00
Cup & saucer 35.00
Plate, 7" d.........................29.00
Plate, 8" to 9" d............30.00 to 35.00
Plate, 10" d. (ILLUS.)...............45.00
Plate, 12" d........................125.00
Platter, 16" l.......................65.00
Soup plate w/flange rim 25.00
Soup tureen, round 125.00

TONQUIN (W. Adams & Son, ca. 1845)
Creamer...........................275.00
Plate, 6" d.........................45.00
Plate, 8½" to 9½" d...........65.00 to 85.00
Sauce dish 50.00
Saucer, 6" d. 40.00

Soup plate w/flange rim, 10½" d......125.00
Syllabub cup (pedestal base &
   handle), pr........................125.00
Toddy plate, 5" d....................75.00
Vegetable bowl, cov., octagonal 385.00

TONQUIN (Joseph Heath, ca. 1850)
Cup plate 58.00
Cup & saucer, handleless 95.00
Gravy boat.........................195.00
Honey dish, 4" d. 85.00
Plate, 7½" d........................70.00
Plate, 8½" to 9½" d.........75.00 to 95.00
Plate, 10½" d.......................125.00
Platter, 13½ x 11½"..................350.00
Soup plate w/flange rim, 12" d........75.00
Vegetable bowl, cov., 9" hexagon 395.00

TOURAINE (Henry Alcock, ca. 1898 and Stanley Pottery Co., ca. 1898)

Touraine Covered Vegetable Bowl

Bone dish..................40.00 to 50.00
Butter pat..........................35.00
Creamer ....135.00 to 150.00
Creamer & sugar bowl, pr. 250.00
Cup & saucer, demitasse ......55.00 to 65.00
Cup & saucer.............60.00 to 70.00
Gravy boat........................105.00
Pitcher, water..............385.00 to 425.00
Plate, 6½" d........................27.00
Plate, 7½" to 8½" d..........36.00 to 48.00
Plate, 9" to 10" d..............45.00 to 55.00
Platter, 10½" oval ....75.00 to 95.00
Platter, 12½ x 8½" 115.00
Sauce dish, 5" d....................26.00
Soup plate w/flange rim, 9" d........55.00
Sugar bowl, cov., large 150.00
Teapot, cov........................240.00
Vegetable bowl, cov., 9" oval
   (ILLUS.)..........................225.00
Vegetable bowl, open, 9½" d.........85.00
Waste bowl 85.00

TROY (Charles Meigh, ca. 1840)
Cup, handleless 24.00
Plate, 7" d.........................45.00
Plate, 8" d.........................50.00
Vegetable bowl, cov.................325.00

TULIPS - PITCHER (Maker unknown, probably mid-Victorian)
Pitcher, 5½" h., 3¾" d., gold trim......75.00

Pitcher, milk, 7½" h. 95.00
Pitcher, 8¾" h. 120.00

VERMONT (Burgess & Leigh, ca. 1895)
Butter pat, 3" d. 20.00
Gravy boat. 50.00
Pitcher, water .135.00
Platter, 12" l. 75.00
Platter, 16 x 11½" 100.00
Sauce dish, 5" d. 20.00
Soup plate w/flange rim, 9" d. 52.00
Teapot, cov., 8" h. 210.00
Vegetable bowl, cov.,
　11½" oval . . . . .98.00 to 125.00

VERONA (Ford & Sons, Ltd., ca. 1908)
Egg cup 40.00
Gravy boat w/underplate 95.00
Platter, 17" l. .150.00
Sauce tureen w/underplate 150.00

VERONA (Wood & Son, ca. 1891)
Gravy boat. 80.00
Plate, 8" d. 58.00
Vegetable bowl, open, round. 75.00

VERSAILLES (Furnival, ca. 1894)
Butter pat. 14.00
Creamer. 50.00
Cup & saucer. .80.00
Soup plate w/flange rim, 9" d. 45.00
Soup tureen, cov. 68.00
Vegetable bowl, cov., oval 110.00
Waste bowl 90.00

VIRGINIA (John Maddock & Sons, ca. 1891)
Plate, 9½" d. 35.00
Saucer, 6" d. 20.00
Soup plate w/flange rim, 8" d. 35.00
Vegetable bowl, open, 9½ x 7" oval 60.00

WALDORF (New Wharf Pottery, ca. 1892)

Waldorf Pattern Cup & Saucer

Bowl, 8" d. 70.00
Bowl, 9" to 10" d. . . . . .75.00 to 85.00
Creamer, 4" h. 100.00

Cup & saucer (ILLUS.). . . . . .50.00 to 65.00
Plate, 6" d. 30.00
Plate, 9" d. 35.00
Plate, 10" d. . . . . .50.00 to 65.00
Platter, 12" l. 50.00
Sauce dish 28.00
Vegetable bowl, open, 7" d. 58.00
Vegetable bowl, open, 9" d. . . .85.00 to 95.00
Waste bowl . . . . .40.00 to 55.00

WARWICK PANSY (Warwick China Co., ca. 1900)
Cake plate, handled, 10" d. 55.00
Creamer. 95.00
Syrup pitcher w/original lid 135.00

WATTEAU (Doulton, ca. 1900)
Bowl, 4" d., 2½" h. 40.00
Creamer, individual size 65.00
Dish, 8½" sq. .85.00
Gravy boat. 57.50
Jug, 8" w., 7" h. 125.00
Mug, 2-handled, 4" h. 125.00
Pitcher, 5¼" h. 100.00
Plate, 7½" d. .25.00
Plate, 10½" d. 80.00
Platter, 10½" l. 100.00
Tureen, cov., pedestal base,
　round . . . . .250.00 to 265.00
Vegetable bowl, cov., 10" 165.00
Vegetable bowl, open, 11 x 9" 95.00
Waste bowl & insert, 2 pcs. 425.00

WATTEAU (New Wharf Pottery, ca. 1891)
Platter, 16 x 12" 185.00
Vegetable bowl, open, 9" d. 60.00
Vegetable bowl, open, 10 x 7" 115.00

WAVERLY (W.H. Grindley, ca. 1891)
Bone dish, large 48.00
Bowl, soup, 7¾" d. 30.00
Cup & saucer .60.00
Plate, 6" to 7" d. . . . . .20.00 to 25.00
Plate, 9" d. 30.00
Platter, 14 x 10" 100.00
Relish dish, 9 x 5" 58.00
Sauce dish, 5½" d. 20.00
Vegetable bowl, cov. 115.00
Waste bowl, 5¾" d., 3" h. 50.00

WHAMPOA (Mellor & Venables, ca. 1840)
Cup & saucer .45.00
Plate, 7½" d. .50.00
Plate, 9½" d. .80.00
Plate, 10½" d. 115.00

WHEEL (Maker unknown, brush-painted)
Creamer & sugar bowl, child's, pr. 95.00
Mug. 75.00
Pitcher, tankard 135.00

WILLOW (Doulton & Co., ca. 1891)
Bowl, 7" d. . . . . .75.00 to 95.00
Bowl, fruit, 8" d. 85.00
Compote, low stand. 127.50

FRANKLIN MAXIM WARES

Franklin Maxim Staffordshire Plate

Statesman, diplomat, scientist and inventor---Benjamin Franklin (1706-90) is one of America's best-loved historical figures. He was also a printer and publisher who wrote and issued "Poor Richard's Almanac" each year from 1733 to 1758. Filled with wise and witty sayings expounding on the values of industry and thrift, these adages made the Almanac famous and have come to be known as "Franklin Maxims." Some were a shrewd observation of mankind: "He that falls in love with himself will have no rivals." Plates, bowls and mugs bearing "Franklin Maxims" are very collectible today.

Mug, "For age and want...Save while you may...No morning sun lasts all the day," pearlware w/black transfer, 2½" h. $145.00

Mug, "Idleness brings disgrace," soft paste porcelain w/rust transfer & copper lustre, 2 1/8" h. 150.00

Mug, "Little strokes fell great oaks," black transfer w/polychrome scene, 2½" h. 80.00

Plate, "Creditors have better memories than debtors," 5¼" d. 50.00

Plate, "Dost thou love life...Then do not squander time...There will be sleeping enough in the grave," black transfer w/polychrome enamel, Staffordshire, 1840-50, 6" d. (ILLUS.) . .85.00

Plate, "Employ time well if thou meanest to gain leisure," transfer of mother w/workbag on lap seated between babe in cradle & beehive, 6½" d. 58.00

Plate, "Keep thy shop and thy shop will keep thee," light blue transfer scene, embossed floral border w/polychrome enameling, 8¼" d. . . .40.00

Plate, "Keep within compass...And you shall be sure...To avoid many troubles...Which others endure," brown transfer of man within compass, scenery & beehives, embossed border w/multicolored enameling, 4¾" d. 110.00

Plate, "Silks and Satins...Scarlets and Velvets...Put out the kitchen fire," creamware w/green transfer of lady admiring herself in mirror & children raising havoc, embossed floral border w/mulitcolored enameling, 4¾" d. 85.00

FRANKOMA POTTERY

John Frank began producing and selling pottery on a part-time basis during the summer of 1933 while he was still teaching art and pottery classes at the University of Oklahoma. In 1934, Frankoma Pottery became an incorporated business that was successful enough to allow him to leave his teaching position, in 1936, and devote full time to its growth. The pottery was moved to Sapulpa, Oklahoma in 1938 and a full range of art pottery and dinner wares were eventually offered. Since John Frank's death in 1973, the pottery has been directed by his daughter, Joniece. The early wares and limited editions are becoming increasingly popular with collectors today. Also see COMMEMORATIVE PLATES.

Ash tray, "Anniv. of Okla. Natural Gas Co.". $20.00

Bookends, model of a bucking bronco kicking cactus, pr. 30.00

Bottle-vase, blue-green glaze 55.00

Bowl, 6" d., Indian-type design, dark brown glaze, Ada clay (pre-1954) 47.00

Candle holders, square form, green glaze, 1942, pr. 25.00

Christmas card, 1959 . . . . .58.00

Cornucopia vase, green glaze, Ada clay (pre-1954) .25.00

Creamer & sugar bowl, Wagon Wheel patt., pr. 22.00

Dealer's sign, 3rd-style, green glaze. . . .60.00

Figure of a fan dancer, designed by Joseph Taylor .100.00

Figure of a farm boy in bib overalls, 1950 . . . . .110.00

Honey pot, model of a beehive, green glaze 16.00

Model of a Dutch shoe, black glaze, 8½" l. 8.50

Model of an elephant, walking, green glaze, 1¾" l. 48.00

Model of a puma, seated, black onyx glaze, 7" l. 37.50

Model of a swan, moss green glaze,
12" l. 45.00
Mug, green & brown glaze, 4½" h. 6.00
Mug, figural (Democratic) donkey,
1978 . . . . .9.00
Mug, figural (Republican) elephant,
1968 . . . . .59.00
Mug, Uncle Sam decor on blue ground . .10.00
Pitcher, prairie green glaze, 2-qt. 8.50
Plate, 1968 limited edition Christmas
Plate 25.00
Plate, 1969 limited edition Christmas
Plate 23.00
Plate, 1970 limited edition Christmas
Plate 23.00
Plate, 1972 limited edition "Teenagers
of the Bible" series - "Jesus the
Carpenter," 7" d. 50.00
Sugar bowl, Mayan-Aztec patt. 7.00
Vase, 4½" h., rose-toned glaze 15.00
Vase, 15" h., bottle-shaped, green
w/black base 75.00

FULPER

Fulper Jardiniere

*The Fulper Pottery was founded in
Flemington, N.J., in 1805 and operated
until 1935, although operations were
curtailed in 1929 when its main plant was
destroyed by fire. The name was changed in
1929 to Stangl Pottery, which continued in
operation until July of 1978, when Pfaltz-
graff, a division of Susquehanna Broad-
casting Company of York, Pennsylvania,
purchased the assets of the Stangl Pottery,
including the name.*

Ash tray, lava green glaze $50.00
Basket, hand-thrown, blue & green
glaze basket w/rose-pink handle,
7" l. 48.00
Bookends, lion's mask, pr. 195.00
Bowl, 8" d., 3½" h., 2-handled, blue
drip on rose glaze. 65.00
Bowl, 9" d., 2½" h., royal blue glaze,
vertical ink stamp mark. 50.00

Bowl, 9" d., green w/brown "flambe"
glaze. 65.00
Bowl, 9½" d., 2" h., curled edge,
"flambe" glaze interior, purple drip
over rose matte exterior 45.00
Bowl, 13" d., rose glaze 75.00
Bowl, footed, green "flambe" glaze,
unmarked Vasekraft line 75.00
Bowl, hammered finish, "verte
antique" green glaze 115.00
Candlestick, cobalt blue "flambe"
glaze, 6" h. (single) 40.00
Candlesticks, green drip glaze over
rose, pr. 70.00
Chamberstick, hooded-type, purple
"flambe" glaze 65.00
Chamberstick, powder blue glaze 58.00
Console bowl, olive green crystalline
glaze, 16" l. 115.00
Console bowl w/flower frog, rose
glaze. 55.00
Decanter, bulbous w/narrow neck,
handled, black shaded to green
"flambe" glaze, 10" h. 145.00
Flower frog, figural white nude,
seated on green base w/yellow
florals, 5½" h. 85.00
Flower frog, model of a mushroom,
high brown glaze 22.00
Flower frog, model of a penguin 185.00
Flower frog, model of a scarab 45.00
Jar, tan w/black "flambe" glaze,
5½" h. 60.00
Jardiniere, bulbous w/waisted neck &
flaring rim, side handles, pale green
crystalline glaze, 12½" h. (ILLUS.) . . .200.00
Jardiniere, blue "flambe" glaze. 80.00
Jardiniere, green & rose glaze 70.00
Lamp base, 3-handled urn shape,
turquoise crystalline glaze, 8" h. 85.00
Lamp base, curled handles, green &
blue glaze, 11" h. 100.00
Mug, green glaze 35.00
Mug, stoneware, "Class Reunion -
1914," vertical ink stamp. 32.00

Fulper Pottery Perfume Lamp

Perfume night lamp, figural
ballerina, yellow dress
(ILLUS.) . . . . .135.00 to 195.00
Perfume lamp, figural parrot,
12½" h. 500.00
Pitcher, 4" h., bulbous w/scrolling
handle, butterscotch w/turquoise
highlights. 45.00
Pitcher, 5½" h., squat form, green
& black mottled glaze 85.00
Pitcher, 9" h., streaked purple semi-
glossy finish. 125.00
Powder jar, figural Art Deco lady
cover, ivory lustre finish . . .135.00 to 165.00
Urn, footed, crystalline glaze,
7½" h. 110.00
Vase, 2¾" h., blue glaze. 25.00
Vase, 4" h., brown, grey & yellow
"flambe" glaze 44.00
Vase, 4½" h., elephant handles,
mustard yellow glaze. 54.00
Vase, 5 x 6", handled, gunmetal
leopard skin glaze 115.00
Vase, 6½" h., blue volcanic glaze 65.00
Vase, 8" h., 7" w., octagonal, tan
leopard skin crystalline glaze. 285.00
Vase, 8" h., 2-handled, turquoise
& green high gloss finish 68.00
Vase, 8½" h., 2-handled, turquoise &
tan glaze 60.00
Vase, 9" h., 2-handled, black
"mirror" & crystalline glaze 175.00
Vase, 10" h., blue "flambe" glaze 225.00
Vase, 12" h., classic shape, irides-
cent smoky black glaze w/speckles .145.00
Vase, 12½" h., Vasekraft line, green
leopard skin crystalline glaze,
vertical ink stamp mark. 315.00

Fulper Vase

Vase, 18" h., 2-handled, coiled technique, slightly iridescent mottled
glaze (ILLUS.). 325.00
Wall pocket, green crystalline glaze,
8½" h. 95.00

GALLE' POTTERY

Grasshopper Ewer

*Fine pottery was made by Emile Galle'
the multi-talented French designer and
artisan, who is also famous for his glass and
furniture. The pottery is relatively scarce.
Also see the FURNITURE section for Art
Nouveau style pieces designed by Emile
Galle' and GLASS - Galle'.*

Centerpiece bowl, double-lobed vessel
formed as 2 ducks, whole glazed in
pale blue & heightened in darker
blue, red & gilt, ca. 1900, signed,
15¼" l. $660.00
Dish, modeled as 2 ducks w/heads
forming center handle, blue, white
& rusty orange, signed, 12½" l.,
7" h. 1,450.00
Ewer, modeled as a grasshopper
wearing a crown & regal attire, blue
& rust heightened w/gilding &
Japanese-inspired motifs, ca. 1885,
15 3/8" h. (ILLUS.) 1,980.00
Vase, 4½" h., floral pattern & gold
highlights on pale blue ground,
signed. 225.00

Galle' Pottery Vase

Vase, 6½" h., spherical w/flaring lip, enameled lavender, ochre, red & gilt butterflies in flight above cat- tails & other grasses on pale blue & avocado ground w/inscription (chip at base & burst glaze bubble at neck), late 19th c. (ILLUS.) 660.00

Vase, 11" h., flattened cylinder w/pinched points at rim, graceful handles, raised white florals & trailing grey leaves on glossy brown ground, signed 1,250.00

Wall pocket, fan-shaped, butterflies & bows decor, sky blue & brown w/touches of gold & black, pro- truding bow on side, 14" h. 695.00

GAUDY DUTCH

Gaudy Dutch Grape Pattern Plate

This name is applied to English soft paste and ironstone wares with designs copied from Oriental patterns. Production began in the 18th century. These copies flooded into this country in the early 19th century. The incorporation of the word "Dutch" derives from the fact that it was the Dutch who first brought these Oriental wares into Europe. The ware was not, as often erroneously reported, made specifically for the Pennsylvania Dutch.

Plate, 7" d., War Bonnet patt. $575.00
Plate, 7¼" d., Urn patt. 205.00
Plate, 8½" d., Grape patt. (ILLUS.) 400.00
Plate, 8½" d., Oyster patt., Ridgway border 675.00
Plate, 10" d., Double Rose patt. 325.00
Tea bowl & saucer, Double Rose patt. 395.00
Tea bowl & saucer, Grape patt. (small flakes on table ring) 200.00
Tea bowl & saucer, Oyster patt. ....395.00 to 450.00

Tea bowl & saucer, Single Rose patt. 350.00
Tea bowl & saucer, War Bonnet patt. ...475.00
Waste bowl, Double Rose patt., 5 3/8" d., 2¾" h. 325.00

GAUDY WELSH

Gaudy Welsh Pitcher

This is a name for wares made in England for the American market about 1830 to 1845. Decorated with Imari-style flower patterns, often highlighted with copper lustre, it should not be confused with Gaudy Dutch wares whose colors differ somewhat.

Bowl, 4¾" d., 2 5/8" h., footed, florals in typical colors $60.00
Creamer, mask spout, 2¼" h. 45.00
Creamer, Oyster patt., 3½" h. 65.00
Creamer, Tulip patt. 50.00
Cup, Wagon Wheel patt. 50.00
Cup & saucer, Flower Basket patt. 45.00
Cup & saucer, Oyster patt. 35.00
Cup & saucer, Pennant patt. (minor stains). 25.00
Cup & saucer, Poppy patt. 75.00
Cup & saucer, Tulip patt. 47.50
Cup & saucer, Wagon Wheel patt. 50.00
Mustard jar, 3" 40.00
Pitcher, 4½" h., Oyster patt. 50.00
Pitcher, 5" h., Sunflower patt., snake handle (ILLUS.) 150.00
Pitcher, 5½" h., Oyster patt. 75.00
Pitcher, 7½" h., w/pewter cover, cobalt blue, gold & orange decor 110.00
Pitcher, milk, 8½" h., Wagon Wheel patt. 175.00
Plate, 6" d., Oyster patt. 19.00
Plate, 6" d., Tulip patt. ....30.00 to 40.00
Plate, 7½" d., Wagon Wheel patt. 35.00
Plate, 8½" sq., Flower Basket patt. ....35.00 to 50.00
Plate, 8¼" d., Wagon Wheel patt. 75.00
Plate, 9" d., Tulip patt. 65.00

Grape I Pattern Plate

Plate, Grape I patt. (ILLUS.) 75.00
Soup plate w/flange rim, Oyster patt.
   w/pink border, 10" d. 75.00
Teapot, cov., Tulip patt., ca. 1840 .....145.00
Tea tile 70.00

GEISHA GIRL WARES

The beautiful geisha, a Japanese girl specifically trained to entertain with singing or dancing, is the featured decoration on this Japanese china which was cheaply made and mass-produced for export. Now finding favor with collectors across the United States, the ware varies in quality. The geisha pattern is not uniform--Butterfly, Paper Lantern, Parasol, Sedan Chair and other variations are found in this pattern that is usually colored in shades of red through orange but is also found in blue and green tones. Collectors try to garner the same design in approximately the same color tones.

Berry set: footed master bowl & 4
   footed sauce dishes; orange trim,
   5 pcs. $45.00
Bone dish, red trim....................4.50
Bowl, 10" d., red trim.................25.00
Butter pat, red trim 8.50
Cake plate, 2-handled, red trim
   w/heavy gold, 10" d. 125.00
Chocolate cup & saucer, red trim........7.50
Chocolate pot, cov., red trim . . .50.00 to 75.00
Chocolate pot, cov., blue trim . .65.00 to 90.00
Chocolate set: cov. chocolate pot &
   4 c/s; red trim, 9 pcs.......110.00 to 125.00
Chocolate set: cov. chocolate pot &
   5 c/s; Parasol patt., red-orange
   trim, 11 pcs.......................125.00
Chocolate set: cov. chocolate pot &
   5 c/s; red trim, 11 pcs. 95.00

Chocolate set: cov. chocolate pot &
   6 c/s; blue trim, 13 pcs. 175.00
Chocolate set: cov. chocolate pot &
   6 c/s; rust-red trim, 13 pcs.........125.00
Cookie jar, cov., blue trim ....70.00 to 100.00
Cookie jar, cov., red-orange trim, tall . .48.00
Creamer, individual size, red-orange
   trim, 2¼" h........................5.50
Creamer, orange trim, 3¾" h. 8.50
Cup & saucer, demitasse, red-orange
   trim 25.00

Geisha Girl Cup & Saucer

Cup & saucer, Paper Lantern patt.,
   orange trim (ILLUS.) 12.50
Cup & saucer, red trim w/gold...7.00 to 12.00
Dessert set: sugar shaker, 4 bowls &
   4 plates; red trim, 9 pcs. 95.00
Dish, 2-handled, red-orange trim 15.00
Hair receiver, red trim ....15.00 to 18.00
Hair receiver & cov. powder dish,
   red trim, matching pr. 38.00
Hatpin holder, 3-footed hexagon, red
   trim ....45.00 to 65.00
Match holder, wall-type, red trim 26.00
Nut dish, footed, red trim, marked
   "Nippon," 7" d......................14.00
Nut set: master bowl & 6 individual
   nut cups; red trim, 7 pcs. ....30.00 to 45.00
Pitcher, milk, 6" h., red trim ...50.00 to 65.00
Pitcher, milk, 10" h., red trim 75.00
Plate, 7½" d. ....4.00 to 7.50
Powder dish, cov., orange trim 28.00
Rice bowl, orange trim, 4" d. .....4.00 to 12.00
Salt & pepper shakers, cobalt blue
   trim, 3¼" h., pr. 20.00
Salt & pepper shakers, orange trim,
   pr..........................15.00 to 22.00
Salt & pepper shakers, red trim,
   pr..........................10.00 to 15.00
Sugar bowl, cov. child's playtime item ...6.50
Sugar bowl, cov., red trim ......8.00 to 10.00
Teapot, cov., orange trim, individual
   size, 1-cup 30.00
Teapot, cov., orange trim, regular
   size ....35.00 to 45.00
Tea set: cov. teapot, creamer & sugar
   bowl; red trim, 3 pcs. ....60.00 to 85.00
Tea set: cov. teapot & 4 c/s; red
   trim, 9 pcs........................110.00
Toothpick holder, red trim .....10.00 to 20.00
Toothpick holder, blue trim 30.00

PLATES

GIBSON GIRL PLATES

She is Disturbed by a Vision

The artist Charles Dana Gibson produced a series of 24 drawings entitled "The Widow and Her Friends," and these were reproduced on plates by the Royal Doulton works at Lambeth, England. The plates were copyrighted by Life Publishing Company in 1900 and 1901. The majority of these plates now sell for over $70.00.

A Message from the Outside World
(No. 1) $75.00
And Here Winning New Friends (No. 2) .82.50
A Quiet Dinner with Dr. Bottles (No. 3)..85.00
Failing to Find Rest and Quiet in the
Country She Decides to Return Home
(No. 4) 75.00
Miss Babbles Brings a Copy of the
Morning Paper (No. 5) 75.00
Miss Babbles, the Authoress, Calls and
Reads Aloud (No. 6) 82.50
Mrs. Diggs is Alarmed at Discovering...
(No. 7) 80.00
Mr. Waddles Arrives Late and Finds
Her Card Filled (No. 8) 80.00
She Becomes a Trained Nurse (No. 9) ...80.00
She Contemplates the Cloister (No. 10) .85.00
She Decides to Die in Spite of Dr.
Bottles (No. 11) 80.00
She Finds Some Consolation in Her
Mirror (No. 12) 87.50
She Finds That Exercise Does Not
Improve Her Spirits (No. 13) 87.50
She Goes into Colors (No. 14) ..55.00 to 80.00
She Goes to the Fancy Dress Ball as
"Juliet" (No. 15) ....55.00 to 70.00
She is Disturbed by a Vision (No. 16)
(ILLUS.) 80.00
She is Subject to More Hostile
Criticism (No. 17) 70.00
She Longs for Seclusion (No. 18) 85.00
She Looks for Relief Among Some of the
Old Ones (No. 19).................80.00

Some Think that She has Remained in
Retirement Too Long (No. 20) 77.50
The Day after Arriving at Her Journey's
End (No. 21) 77.50
They All Go Skating (No. 22)..........85.00
They All Go Fishing (No. 23) 87.50
They Take a Morning Run (No. 24).....72.50

GOLDSCHEIDER

"Bon Voyage"

The Goldscheider firm manufactured porcelain and faience in Austria between 1885 and 1953. Founded by Friedrich Goldscheider and carried on by his widow, the firm came under the control of his sons, Walter and Marcell, in 1920. Fleeing their native Austria at the time of World War II, the Goldscheiders set up an operation in the United States. They were listed in the Trenton, New Jersey City Directory from 1943 through 1950 and their main production seems to have been art pottery figurines.

Bust of a Chinese man & woman,
artist-signed, 7" h., pr. $75.00
Figure of "Blanche," artist-signed,
5½" h. 55.00
Figure of a "Lady Caller," artist-signed,
5½" h. 50.00
Figure of a Madonna, pink garments,
5½" h. 22.00
Figure of "Yankee Doodle Dandy,"
artist-signed, 5½" h. 55.00
Figure of a Colonial lady, black & blue
dress, artist-signed, 7" h. 50.00
Figure of a chorus girl, Art Deco style,
plum dance skirt w/florals, 7½" h. ...175.00
Figure of a lady, wearing a green
ruffled dress & holding a yellow hat,
8½" h. 62.00
Figure of a lady, holding a fan, marked
"U.S.A.," 9½" h..................125.00
Figure of a man, wearing a cape &
holding a bouquet, 9½" h. 75.00
Figure of a lady, wearing a gold dress

& holding a fan, on black base,
12¼" h. 225.00
Model of a dog, Spaniel seated on a
suitcase, "Bon Voyage," artist-
signed, 4½" h. (ILLUS.) 55.00
Model of a dog, German Shepherd in
recumbent position, 8" l. 52.50
Model of a dog, Wolfhound, artist-
signed, 11" h. 155.00

GOUDA

Gouda Jardiniere

*While tin-enameled earthenware has been
made in Gouda, Holland, since the early
1600s, the productions of modern factories
are attracting increasing collector attention.
The art pottery of Gouda is easily
recognized by its brightly colored peasant-
style decoration with some types having
achieved a "cloisonne" effect. Pottery work-
shops located in, or near, Gouda include
Regina, Zenith, Plazuid, Schoonhoven,
Arnhem and others. Their wide range of
production included utilitarian wares, as
well as vases, miniatures and large outdoor
garden ornaments.*

Ash tray, green & cobalt blue colorful interior decor, Anne Royal
house mark, 4 1/8" d., 1¼" h. $38.00
Basket w/rope-twist handle & flower
frog, multicolored decor, Regina
house mark, overall 8" h. 150.00
Bowl, cov., 6" d., floral decor, Anjer
mark 60.00
Bowl, 18¼" d., 5" h., colorful
peacock decor 300.00
Candle holders, black, blue, rust &
mustard yellow on ivory ground,
house mark, 4" h., pr. 35.00
Chamberstick, Art Deco gold & white
panels w/blue & green florals on
black matte ground, 5 3/8" d.,
3" h. (single) 75.00
Creamer, burnt orange & brown
decor, 2½" 38.00
Dish, cov., Art Nouveau shaded green
& bronze decor, signed, 6 x 4" 110.00

Flower holder w/brass top, shaded
blue & turquoise, gold trim, house
mark & numbers 85.00
Humidor, cov., tan, blue & green
designs on matte finish, house
mark 145.00
Inkwell w/cover & attached underplate,
multicolored decor, Kelat house
mark 150.00
Jardiniere, colorful stylized florals &
diapered reserves on black ground
(ILLUS.) 165.00
Pitcher, 2½" h., red dots on black
matte finish & high glaze tur-
quoise w/gold trim, Zenith 22.00
Powder box, cov., high glaze, 5" d.,
2" h. 110.00
Tea caddy, cov., glossy multicolored
decor, 4" h. 60.00
Tobacco jar, cov., melon-ribbed, h.p.
multicolored decor, 5½" w.,
6½" h. 130.00
Vase, 4¼" h., souvenir-type,
windmill scene & figure w/wheel-
barrow decor, Zenith 85.00
Vase, 5¼" h., 6" d., 2-handled,
colorful wide band w/cobalt blue
on black matte finish, Blareth
house mark 48.00
Vase, 5¾" h., Art Nouveau decor 95.00
Vase, 8 1/8" h., 4¾" d., Art Deco
royal blue, black, gold, red, green
& brown decor on matte finish,
house mark 88.00

Gouda Vase

Vase, 9¾" h., open handles, pastel
Art Deco designs on black ground,
Plazuid house mark (ILLUS.) 160.00
Vase, 10½" h., stylized florals, Regina
& Bochara crown mark 125.00
Vase, 11" h., vivid blues & yellow
decor, Zuid Royal Pottery house
mark 125.00
Wall pocket, scalloped mold, multi-
colored decor 65.00

GRUEBY

Grueby Pottery Vase

Some fine art pottery was produced by the Grueby Faience and Tile Company, established in Boston in 1891. Choice pieces were created with molded designs on a semi-porcelain body. The ware is marked and often bears the initials of the decorators. The pottery closed in 1907. Also see TILES.

Bowl, 8" d., low, swirl design,
  green high glaze $365.00
Vase, 4½" h., 4" d., yellow buds
  extending from green leaf-molded
  body 425.00
Vase, 5" h., flattened globular form,
  molded upright leaves on sides,
  thick green glaze (ILLUS.) 465.00
Vase, 6" h., 7½" w., sunburst design
  top, black drip on thick matte
  green glaze 425.00
Vase, 6½" h., green pebble-grain
  glaze 275.00
Vase, 7½" h., ovoid, molded flattened
  wide leaves & tall stems w/buds,
  mottled matte green glaze 465.00
Vase, 8½" h., bulbous melon-ribbed
  base, straight "stove-pipe" neck,
  stretchy green glaze 395.00

Vase with Lotus Leaves

Vase, 9½" h., cylindrical, molded
w/upright lotus leaves in low
relief, thick green glaze, 1894-99
  (ILLUS.) 660.00
Vase, 13" h., molded leaves in low
  relief, green glaze 475.00
Vase, 21¼" h., molded upright leaves
  & buds on sides, cucumber green
  glaze (drilled for lamp base) 1,980.00

HAMPSHIRE POTTERY

Hampshire Pottery Vase

Hampshire Pottery was made in Keene, N.H., where several potteries operated as far back as the late 18th century. The pottery now known as Hampshire Pottery was established by J.S. Taft shortly after 1870. Various types of wares, including Art Pottery, were produced through the years. Taft's brother-in-law, Cadmon Robertson, joined the firm in 1904 and was responsible for developing over 900 glaze formulas while in charge of all manufacturing. His death in 1914 created problems for the firm and Taft sold out to George Morton in 1916. Closed during part of World War I, the pottery was later reopened by Morton for a short time and manufactured white hotel china. From 1919 to 1921, mosaic floor tiles became the main production. All production ceased in 1923.

Berry dish, shell-shaped w/twig feet,
  h.p. fruit decor on cream ground,
  signed F.L. Gillride, 4½" d. $125.00
Bowl, shell-shaped, cobalt blue high
  glaze 65.00
Candle holder, handled, green matte
  finish 60.00
Chocolate pot, cov., souvenir, transfer
  print "Clinton Massachusetts
  Library" scene on ivory Royal
  Worcester-type finish, 9" h. 55.00

Coffee set: cov. coffee pot & 6 demitasse c/s; ivory Royal Worcester-
type finish w/green & gold highlights, artist-signed, 13 pcs. 175.00
Dish, heart-shaped, h.p. pink & blue
florals on ivory Royal Worcester-
type finish, artist-signed 135.00
Mug, souvenir, transfer print "Waynes-
ville, North Carolina" scene on ivory
Royal Worcester-type finish 40.00
Pin dish, souvenir, transfer print
"North Conway, New Hampshire"
scene on ivory Royal
Worcester-type finish 22.50
Pitcher, 8" h., relief-molded leaves on
green-glazed snakeskin ground 85.00
Pitcher, souvenir, transfer print
"Landing of the Pilgrims" scene on
Royal Worcester-type finish 95.00
Planter, bowl-shaped artichoke form,
green glaze 55.00
Stein, transfer print sailing ships on
ivory Royal Worcester-type finish,
5½" h. 35.00
Tumbler, green glaze, 5" h. 35.00
Vase, 3¼" h., green matte finish 40.00
Vase, 4½" h., maroon on light green
glaze............................45.00
Vase, 5½" h., bulbous, blue mottled
glaze............................50.00
Vase, 6" ., blue "volcanic" glaze 60.00
Vase, 7" h., relief-molded vertical
designs, green matte finish 75.00
Vase, 8" h., 6" d., 2-handled, stylized
leaf designs, green matte finish 110.00
Vase, 9" h., green matte finish 60.00
Vase, 9½" h., low relief-molded iris
leaves, green matte finish 90.00
Vase, 11" h., bow-tied throat, green
matte finish (ILLUS.)..............175.00

HAVILAND

Haviland China

Haviland porcelain was originated by
Americans in Limoges, France, shortly
before mid-19th century and continues in
production. Some Haviland was made by
Theodore Haviland in the United States
during the last World War. Numerous other

factories also made china in Limoges. Also
see OYSTER PLATES.

Bon bon, pierced handles, Marseille
blank, yellow floral decor $70.00
Bone dish, Ranson blank, all white 15.00
Bowl, 10 x 9½", pedestal base,
realistic dark blue & purple
grapes, artist-signed 185.00
Butter pat, pink, blue & yellow floral
decor, Theodore Haviland, Limoges ...6.50
Butter pat, Ranson patt. ....6.00 to 10.50
Butter pat, pale blue florals & green
leaves decor, Haviland, Limoges 7.00
Chocolate pot, cov., scalloped top &
base, small roses & other floral
decor, gold trim, overall 11½" h. ...100.00
Creamer & cov. sugar bowl, Plain
blank, pink rose spray decor,
gold trim, pr......................70.00
Cup & saucer, Moss Rose patt. on
Plain blank, H. & Co., Limoges 20.00
Cup & saucer, Rosalinde patt.,
Theodore Haviland, Limoges 22.00
Cup & saucer, demitasse, Drop Rose
patt., Haviland & Co. 39.00
Cups & saucers, demitasse, Ranson
patt., gold trim, set of 4............92.50
Cups & saucers, demitasse, red & gold
encrusted decor, Haviland & Co., set
of 9 ....135.00
Dessert set: master cake plate,
creamer, sugar bowl, eight 7½" d.
plates & 8 c/s; Moss Rose patt.
on Plain blank, 27 pcs..............250.00
Dinner service, Chenoneaux patt. on
Pilgrim blank, Theodore Haviland,
Limoges, 1920-36, 76 pcs. 600.00
Dinner service, unknown pattern on
Plain blank, 100 pcs. (ILLUS.
of part) 750.00
Dresser tray, Baltimore Rose patt.,
Haviland & Co., 12" 55.00
Fish set: platter & 12 dinner plates;
h.p. underwater scenes w/varied
fish species, 13 pcs. 425.00
Game set: platter & 12 plates; h.p.
game birds in natural habitat, gold
trim, signed L. Martin, 13 pcs. 450.00

Haviland Game Set

Game set: 18½" oblong platter, pr.
8¼" oblong platters, & twelve 7½"
sq. plates; h.p. game birds within
cobalt blue borders enriched

w/silver, bronze & gilt Japanese-
inspired floral motifs, ca. 1910,
15 pcs. (ILLUS. of part) 880.00
Nut cup, gold Greek Key rim,
Haviland & Co. 35.00
Pin tray, 3 large red cabbage roses
center, gold scrollwork sides,
Theodore Haviland, Limoges, 5" l.....22.50
Place setting: cup, saucer, bread &
butter, dinner & salad plates; Rosalinde patt. on Pilgrim blank,
Theodore Haviland, France, 5 pcs. ..105.00
Plate, 7" d., Ranson blank, floral
border w/single pink roses accented
w/white & green lacy foliage decor ..10.00
Plate, 7¼" d., Ranson blank, tiny pink,
blue & yellow floral border & pink
& green floral center 10.00
Plate, 7½" d., pale blue florals
w/green leaves decor, Haviland,
Limoges 9.00

Hand-Painted Haviland Plate

Plate, 8½" d., realistic red raspberries
& blossoms on rainbow pastel ground,
artist-signed (ILLUS.) 55.00
Plate, 8½" d., Autumn Leaf patt........13.00

Haviland & Co. Princess Patt.

Plate, 8½" d., Princess patt., Star
blank (ILLUS.) 17.50
Plate, 10" d., Ranson patt. 14.00
Plate, 10" d., Silver Anniversary patt.,
Haviland & Co. 12.00
Plate, chop, 12½" d., Princess patt.
on Star blank 67.50
Plate, salad, Chantilly patt. on Ranson
blank 15.00
Platter, 10" l., pale blue florals
& green leaves decor, Haviland &
Co., Limoges 32.50
Platter, 16" l., Garden Flowers patt. on
Plain blank, Theodore Haviland......45.00
Platter, 18" l., Ranson blank, blue
florals & green leaves decor,
Haviland & Co. 95.00
Ring tree, blue forget-me-not decor 35.00
Sauce dish, Ranson patt...............8.00
Sauce dish, Silver Anniversary patt. 8.00
Tea set: cov. teapot, creamer & cov.
sugar bowl; h.p. butterflies on one
side & blooming Lavender reverse,
gold handles, rims & center design,
Haviland & Co., Limoges, 3 pcs. 225.00
Vase, 11½" h., ovoid, 3 applied
handles, realistic yellow roses on
shaded brown, blue & green ground,
artist-signed & dated 1910..........600.00
Vegetable dish, cov., Newark patt. on
Plain blank, Theodore Haviland,
Limoges, ca. 1903, 10½" l. 45.00
Vegetable dish, cov., honeysuckle in
shades of pink & lavender, pale
green leaves, gold trim, Charles
Field Haviland, 10½" oval...........48.00
Vegetable dish, cov., Autumn Leaf
patt., round 30.00
Vegetable dish, cov., Princess patt.
on Silver blank, round 65.00
Vegetable dish, open, Princess patt.,
oval............................35.00

HISTORICAL & COMMEMORATIVE

*Numerous potteries, especially in Eng-
land and the United States, made various
porcelain and earthenware pieces to
commemorate persons, places and events.
Scarce English historical wares with
American views command high prices.
Objects listed here are alphabetically by
title of views.*

Arms of New York plate, flowers &
vines border w/spoked wheels
equidistant around, dark blue,
10" d. (Mayer) $495.00
Bakers Falls, Hudson River plate,
birds, flowers & scrolls border,
black, 9" d. (Clews) 100.00

Bakers Falls, Hudson River plate, birds, flowers & scrolls border, brown, 9" d. (Clews) 37.50

Battery, New York (Flagstaff Pavilion) bowl, shallow, entwined vine border, dark blue, 6½" d. (Stevenson, Stevenson & Williams) 950.00

Boston State House plate, flowers & leaves border, medium blue, 10" d. (Rogers) 150.00

Capitol, Washington plate, vine border of R. Stevenson w/portrait medallions of Washington & Clinton, dark blue, 10" d. (Stevenson & Williams) 425.00

Capitol, Washington Platter

Capitol, Washington platter, flowers within medallions border, dark blue, 20½" l., J. & W. Ridgway (ILLUS.)....625.00

Castle Garden, Battery, New York cup plate, shells border, circular center w/trailing vine around outer edge of center, dark blue, 3 5/8" d. (Wood) 145.00

Catholic Cathedral, New York plate, flowers between leafy scrolls border, dark blue, 6" d. (Andrew Stevenson) 1,000.00

Chief Justice Marshall, Troy plate, shell border, irregular opening to center giving "grotto" effect, dark blue, 10" d. (Enoch Wood & Sons)........650.00

Christianburg, Danish Settlement on the Gold Coast, Africa platter, shell border w/irregular opening to the center gives a "grotto" effect, dark blue, 20" (Enoch Wood & Sons)......550.00

City of Albany - State of New York plate, shell border, dark blue, 10" d. (Enoch Wood) 415.00

Commodore MacDonnough's Victory coffee pot & cover, shell border, dark blue, 11¼" h. (Enoch Wood & Sons) 1,100.00

Commodore MacDonnough's Victory plates, shell border, dark blue, 7½" d., pr. (Enoch Wood & Sons) 385.00

Commodore MacDonnough's Victory plate, shell border, dark blue, 10" d. (Wood) 425.00

Constitution and the Guerriere (so-called) plate, shell border w/irregular opening to the center gives a "grotto" effect, dark blue, 10" d. (Enoch Wood & Sons) 900.00

The Dam and Water Works, Philadelphia (sidewheel steamboat) plate, fruits, flowers & leaves border, blue, 10" d. (Henshall, Williamson & Co.)................365.00

Faneuil Hall, Boston, From the Harbor plate, fruits & flowers border, dark blue, 10" d. (Rowland & Marsellus)................25.00 to 40.00

Fort Edward, Hudson River toddy plate, birds, flowers & scrolls border, black, 5½" d. (Clews) ....100.00 to 135.00

General Jackson, Hero of New Orleans cup plate, single red line border, carmine, 3¾" d. (Wood) 650.00

Hancock House, Boston plate, long-stemmed roses border, pink, 8" d. (Jackson) 95.00

Hartford, Connecticut, plate, long-stemmed roses border, black, 10½" d. (Jackson) 85.00

Hartford, Connecticut plate, long-stemmed roses border, pink, 10½" d. (Jackson) 97.50

Harvard College plate, acorn border, blue, 10" d. (Clews) 185.00

Hendrick Hudson plate, rolled edge, vignettes border, dark blue, 10½" d. (Rowland & Marsellus).............40.00

Hope Hotel, Pittsburgh plate, black, 10½" d. (Bell Pottery) 750.00

Hudson, Hudson River platter, birds, flowers & scrolls border, purple, 13½" l. (Clews)..................115.00

Junction of the Sacandaga & Hudson Rivers plate, birds, flowers & scrolls border, brown, 7" d. (Clews) ....100.00 to 125.00

Lafayette at Franklin's Tomb pitcher & bowl, floral border, dark blue (minor imperfections), 9 1/8" h. pitcher & 12¼" d. bowl, pr. (Wood) 1,450.00

Landing of Lafayette at Castle Garden

Landing of General Lafayette at Castle Garden, New York, 16 August, 1824, platter, floral & vine border, dark blue, 17" l., Clews (ILLUS.) 690.00

Lewis & Clark Centennial plate, rolled edge, vignettes border, dark blue, 10½" d. (Rowland & Marsellus) 40.00

Library, Philadelphia plate, flowers within medallions border, medium blue, 8" d. (Ridgway) 225.00

Marine Hospital, Louisville, Kentucky plate, shell border, dark blue, 9" d. (Wood) 300.00

Miles Standish Monument plate, rolled edge, vignettes border, dark blue, 10" d. (Rowland & Marsellus) 45.00

Mount Vernon plate, fruits & flowers border, dark blue, 10" d. (Rowland & Marsellus) 35.00

Mount Vernon, The Seat Of The Late Gen'l. Washington cov. sugar bowl, rectangular w/domed lid, 2 scrolled handles, floral border, dark blue, 6½" h. 420.00

Near Fishkill, Hudson River plate, birds, flowers & scrolls border, light blue, 7½" d. (Clews) 85.00

Near Fort Miller, Hudson River soup plate, birds, flowers & scrolls border, brown, 9" d. (Clews) 98.00

Newburgh, Hudson River platter, birds, flowers & scrolls border, black, 15½" l. (Clews) 255.00

Residence of the Late Richard Jordon, New Jersey platter, floral border, mulberry, 9½" l. (J. Heath & Co.) . . . 390.00

Ship-Anchored cup plate, shell border w/irregular opening to center giving a grotto effect, dark blue (Enoch Wood & Sons) 325.00

State House, Hartford cup & saucer, flowers & leaves border, medium blue (Stevenson, Stevenson & Williams) 1,400.00

Table Rock, Niagara plate, shells border, circular center w/trailing vines around outer edge of center, dark blue, 10" d., Wood (ILLUS.) 350.00

Texian Campaign plate, battle scene center, symbols of war & a "goddess-type" seated border, blue, 9½" d. (Shaw) 65.00

Thousand Islands plate, rolled edge, vignettes border, dark blue, 10½" d. (Rowland & Marsellus) 40.00

Transylvania University, Lexington plate, shell border, dark blue, 9" d. (Wood) 250.00

Trenton Falls plate, fruit & floral border, dark blue, 7½" d. (Wood) . . . 250.00

Troy, N.Y. plate, rolled edge, vignettes border, dark blue, 10½" d. (Rowland & Marsellus) 40.00

View Near Conway, N. Hampshire, U.S. plate, flowers, shells & scrolls border, pink, 9" d. (Adams) 70.00

Wadsworth Tower creamer, shell border, dark blue (Enoch Wood & Sons) 350.00

Washington At Prayer, Valley Forge plate, fruits & flowers border, dark blue, 10" d. (Rowland & Marsellus) . . . 50.00

Washington Crossing the Delaware plate, fruits & flowers border, dark blue, 10" d. (Rowland & Marsellus) . . . 40.00

West Point, Hudson River plate, birds, flowers & scrolls border, black, 8" d. (Clews) 85.00

Worcester, Mass. plate, rolled edge, vignettes border, dark blue, 10½" d. (Rowland & Marsellus) 45.00

HULL

Little Red Riding Hood Butter Dish

This pottery was made by the Hull Pottery Company, Crooksville, O., beginning in 1905. Art Pottery was made until 1950 when the company was converted to utilitarian wares.

Table Rock, Niagara Plate

Ale set: 9½" h. tankard pitcher & six
  6½" h. steins; stoneware, relief
  molded Alpine scenes, 7 pcs. $145.00
Bank, Little Red Riding Hood patt. 215.00
Basket, circular handle, Dogwood
  patt., turquoise shaded to peach,
  7½" h. 75.00
Basket, Parchment & Pine patt.,
  beige ground, 8 x 7 x 5" 15.00
Basket, Serenade patt., blue matte
  finish, 6¾" h. 20.00
Basket, Tulip patt., blue shaded to
  cream, 6" h. . . . . 36.00 to 58.00
Basket, Water Lily patt., shaded
  turquoise through yellow to pink,
  10½" h. 70.00
Butter dish, cov., Little Red Riding
  Hood patt. (ILLUS.) 135.00
Candle holders, Serenade patt., blue
  matte finish, pr. 21.50
Candle holders, Water Lily patt.,
  brown shaded to beige, pr. 21.50
Console bowl, Wildflower patt.,
  blue shaded to pink, 12" w. 26.00
Console set: console bowl & pr.
  candle holders; Magnolia patt.,
  pink matte finish, 3 pcs. 50.00
Cookie jar, Little Red Riding Hood
  patt. 80.00
Cornucopia-vase, double, Bow Knot
  patt., pink top shading to white then
  to blue base, 13" h. 65.00
Cornucopia-vase, Parchment & Pine
  patt., beige ground, 7¾" h. 75.00
Cornucopia-vase, Poppy patt., cream
  shaded to pink, 8" h. 40.00
Creamer & sugar bowl, Magnolia
  patt., pink shaded to green, pr. 22.00
Ewer, Ebb Tide patt., aqua shaded to
  peach, 14" h. 45.00
Ewer, Parchment & Pine patt., beige
  ground, 14½" h. 35.00
Ewer, Royal Woodland patt., turquoise
  w/grey accents, 13½" h. 35.00

Wildflower Pattern Ewer

Ewer, Wildflower patt., blue shaded to
  pink, 8½" h. (ILLUS.) 47.50

Flower pot w/attached saucer, Sueno
  Tulip patt., blue shaded to yellow,
  6" h. 40.00
Grease bowl & cover, Sun Glow patt.,
  yellow glossy finish 7.00
Jardiniere, Iris patt., blue shaded to
  rose, 5½" h. 28.00
Jardiniere, handled, Woodland patt.,
  yellow matte finish, 5½" h. 23.00
Match holder, Little Red Riding Hood
  patt. 340.00
Model of a dancing girl, 7" h. 17.00
Mustard jar w/ladle, Little Red Riding
  Hood patt. 130.00
Pitcher, 7" h., side-pour, Little Red
  Riding Hood patt. 132.50
Planter, figural Bandana Duck, 5 x 7" . . . 35.00
Planter, figural parrot w/blooming
  flower, 9½ x 6" 18.00
Planter, twin geese 18.00
Planter, Woodland patt., 10½" l. 30.00
Rose bowl, Iris patt., blue shaded to
  pink, 4" d. 35.00
Salt box, Little Red Riding Hood patt. . . . 275.00
Salt & pepper shakers, Little Red Riding
  Hood patt., 3½" h., pr. 16.00
Table set: creamer, cov. sugar bowl,
  salt & pepper shakers, cov. butter
  dish & cov. teapot; Little Red Riding
  Hood patt., 6 pcs. 275.00

Blossom Flite Pattern Teapot

Teapot, Blossom Flite patt., black on
  glossy pink ground, 8" h. (ILLUS.) 35.00
Tea set: cov. teapot, creamer & sugar
  bowl; Magnolia Gloss patt., blue
  flowers on pink ground, 3 pcs. 55.00
Tea set: cov. teapot, creamer & sugar
  bowl; Parchment & Pine patt.,
  3 pcs. 65.00
Tea set: cov. teapot, creamer & sugar
  bowl; Woodland patt., pink shaded
  to green matte finish, 3 pcs. 85.00
Vase, 5" h., Bow Knot patt., footed,
  blue top shading to white then to
  pink bow on foot 25.00
Vase, 6" h., Orchid patt., blue matte
  finish. 23.00

Vase, 6" h., Tulip patt., blue shaded
to pink .... 20.00 to 39.00
Vase, 6½" h., Open Rose patt., pink
matte finish .... 18.00 to 25.00
Vase, 7" h., Ebb Tide patt., upright sea
shell, pink shaded to green 18.00
Vase, 8½" h., Magnolia patt., 2-handled,
shaded yellow to pink matte finish ... 25.00

Woodland Pattern Vase

Vase, double bud, 8½" h., Woodland
patt., glossy (ILLUS.) 22.00
Vase, 10½" h., Iris patt., shaded blue
to rose matte finish 35.00
Vases, 12½" h., Wildflower patt.,
blue shaded to pink matte finish,
pr. .... 40.00 to 50.00
Wall pockets, Little Red Riding Hood
patt., pr. 375.00

HUMMEL FIGURINES

The Goebel Company of Oeslau, Germany, first produced these porcelain figurines in 1934 having obtained the rights to adapt the beautiful pastel sketches of children by Sister Maria Innocentia (Berta) Hummel. Every design by the Goebel artisans was approved by the nun until her death in 1946. Though not antique, these figurines, with the "M.I. Hummel" signature, especially those bearing the Goebel Company factory mark used from 1934 and into the early 1940s, are being sought by collectors though interest may have peaked about 1980.

"Accordion Boy," stylized bee mark,
1956-68, 5" h. $88.00
"Accordion Boy," crown mark, 1934-49,
5" h. 275.00
"Accordion Boy," full bee mark, 1940-
57, 6" h. 115.00
"Angel Serenade," last bee mark used,
1972-79, 5½" h. 80.00

"Angel with Lute," three line mark,
1963-71, 2" h. 30.00
"Angel with Lute," 1956-68, 2" h. 26.00
"Angel with Trumpet," 1972-79, 2" h. ... 18.50
"Angelic Song," 1972-79, 4" h. 47.00
"Angelic Song," 1940-57, 4" h. 155.00
"Apple Tree Boy," 1972-79, 4" h. 50.00
"Apple Tree Boy," 1956-68, 4" h. 66.00
"Apple Tree Girl," 1940-57, 4" h. 108.00
"Apple Tree Girl," 1972-79, 6" h. 84.00
"Apple Tree Girl," 1956-68, 6" h. 132.00
"Artist" (The), 1972-79, 5½" h. 66.50
"Auf Wiedersehen," 1956-68, 5" h. 97.00
"Auf Wiedersehen," 1972-79, 7" h. 100.00
"Autumn Harvest," 1972-79, 4¾" h. 67.50
"Band Leader," 1972-79, 5" h. 67.00
"Barnyard Hero," 1963-71, 5½" h. 100.00
"Barnyard Hero," 1940-57, 5½" h. 246.00
"Bashful," 1972-79, 4¾" h. 65.50
"Be Patient," 1972-79, 4¼" h. 65.00
"Be Patient," 1963-71, 4¼" h. 82.00
"Begging His Share," 1972-79, 5½" h. ... 70.00
"Begging His Share," 1956-68,
5½" h. 166.00
"Bird Duet," 1972-79, 4" h. 55.00
"Birthday Serenade," 1972-79, 4¼" h. .. 62.00
"Book Worm," 1940-57, 4" h. 160.00
"Book Worm," 1940-57, 4¾" h. 260.00
"Book Worm," 1956-68, 8" h. 448.00
"Book Worm," 1972-79, 9" h. 558.00

"Boots"

"Boots," 1956-68, 5½" h. (ILLUS.) 78.00
"Boots," 1940-57, 5½" h. 135.00
"Boy with Toothache," 1972-79,
5½" h. 64.00
"Brother," 1956-68, 5½" h. 70.00
"Builder," 1972-79, 5½" h. 76.00
"Busy Student," 1972-79, 4¼" h. 60.00
"Busy Student," 1963-71, 4¼" h. 85.00
"Celestial Musician," 1972-79, 7" h. 95.00
"Chick Girl," 1956-68, 3½" h. 83.00

"Chimney Sweep," 1940-57, 4" h. 79.00
"Culprits," 1956-68, 6¼" h. . .125.00 to 150.00
"Doll Mother," 1956-68, 4¾" h. 140.00
"Duet," 1956-68, 5" h. . . . . . .110.00 to 120.00
"Farewell," 1972-79, 4¾" h. 88.00
"Farewell," 1956-68, 4¾" h. 140.00
"Farewell," 1940-57, 4¾" h. 210.00
"Farm Boy," 1956-68, 5" h. 130.00
"Favorite Pet," 1972-79, 4½" h. 76.00
"Favorite Pet," 1963-71, 4½" h. 127.00
"Feeding Time," 1972-79, 4¼" h. 76.00
"Feeding Time," 1972-79, 5½" h. 78.00
"Feeding Time," 1934-49,
    5½" h. . . . . .425.00 to 450.00
"Flower Vendor," 1972-79, 5¼" h. 76.00
"Follow the Leader," 1972-79, 7" h. 375.00
"For Father," 1972-79, 5½" h. 64.00
"For Father," 1956-68, 5½" h. 93.00
"For Mother," 1972-79, 5" h. 53.00
"Friends," 1972-79, 5" h. 72.00
"Friends," 1956-68, 10¾" h. 490.00
"Gay Adventure," 1972-79, 5" h. 58.00
"Globe Trotter," 1956-68, 5" h. 96.00
"Going to Grandma's," 1972-79,
    4¾" h. 93.00
"Going to Grandma's," 1940-57,
    4¾" h. 195.00
"Good Friends," 1940-57, 4" h. 150.00
"Good Friends," 1934-49, 4" h. 278.00
"Good Hunting," 1972-79, 5" h. 78.00
"Good Hunting," 1963-71, 5" h. 116.00
"Good Shepherd," 1956-68,
    6¼" h. . . . . .100.00 to 150.00
"Good Shepherd," 1940-57, 6¼" h. 145.00
"Goose Girl," 1972-79, 4" h. 56.00
"Goose Girl," 1956-68, 4" h. 83.00
"Goose Girl," 1972-79, 4¾" h. 78.00
"Goose Girl," 1956-68, 4¾" h. 114.00
"Goose Girl," 1940-57, 4¾" h. 168.00
"Goose Girl," 1956-68, 7½" h. 283.00
"Goose Girl," 1940-57, 7½" h. 337.00

"Happiness," 1956-68, 4¾" h. (ILLUS.) . .68.50
"Happiness," 1934-49, 4¾" h. 225.00
"Happy Birthday," 1972-79, 5½" h. 75.00
"Happy Days," 1972-79, 4¼" h. 68.00
"Happy Days," 1956-68, 4¼" h. 92.00
"Happy Days," 1972-79, 6¼" h. 155.00
"Happy Pastime," 1972-79, 3½" h. 57.00
"Happy Pastime," 1934-49, 3½" h. 255.00
"Happy Traveler," 1956-68, 5" h. 75.00
"Happy Traveler," 1940-57, 5" h. 112.00
"Happy Traveler," 1956-68, 7½" h. 305.00
"Hear Ye, Hear Ye," 1956-68, 5" h. . . .100.00
"Hear Ye, Hear Ye," 1940-57, 5" h. 170.00
"Heavenly Angel," 1956-68, 4¾" h. 83.00
"Heavenly Angel," 1956-68, 6¾" h. 108.00
"Heavenly Angel," 1972-79, 8¾" h. 140.00
"Heavenly Lullabye," 1972-79,
    3½ x 5". 70.00
"Heavenly Protection," 1956-68,
    9" h. . . . . .360.00 to 570.00
"Home From Market," 1940-57,
    4¼" h. 188.00
"Homeward Bound," 1972-79, 5¼" h. . .140.00
"Joyful," 1956-68, 4" h. 58.50
"Joyous News," 1972-79, 4¼ x 4¾" . . .110.00
"Just Resting," 1940-57, 4" h. 116.00
"Just Resting," 1956-68, 5" h. 112.00
"Kiss Me," 1963-71, 6" h. 98.00
"Knitting Lesson," 1972-79, 7½" h. 162.00
"Latest News," 1956-68, 5" h. 200.00
"Latest News," 1940-57, 5" h. 233.00
"Let's Sing," 1956-68, 3" h. 80.00
"Let's Sing," 1972-79, 4" h. 55.00
"Letter to Santa Claus," 1972-79,
    7¼" h. 122.00
"Little Bookkeeper," 1963-71, 4¾" h. . . .120.00
"Little Cellist," 1956-68, 6" h. 112.00
"Little Drummer," 1972-79, 4¼" h. 42.50
"Little Fiddler," 1934-49, 4¾" h. 190.00
"Little Fiddler," 1972-79, 6" h. 72.50
"Little Fiddler," 1956-68, 7½" h. 177.00
"Little Fiddler," 1972-79, 12¼" h. 475.00

"Happiness"

"Stitch in Time"

"Stitch in Time," 1963-71, 6¾" h.
(ILLUS.) 108.00
"Stormy Weather," 1972-79, 6¼" h. . . .165.00
"Stormy Weather," 1940-57, 6¼" h. . . .356.00
"Street Singer," 1956-68, 5" h. 70.00
"To Market," 1956-68, 4" h. 70.00
"To Market," 1940-57, 4" h. 122.50
"To Market," 1972-79, 5½" h. 85.00
"To Market," 1956-68, 5½" h. 95.00
"To Market," 1940-57, 5½" h. 150.00
"To Market," 1934-49, 5½" h. 245.00
"Trumpet Boy," 1972-79, 4¾" h. 45.00
"Trumpet Boy," 1940-57, 4¾" h. 85.00
"Tuneful Goodnight," 1972-79,
4¾" h. 250.00
"Umbrella Boy," 1956-68, 8" h. 585.00
"Umbrella Boy," 1940-57, 8" h. 800.00
"Umbrella Girl," 1963-71, 4¾" h. 235.00
"Umbrella Girl," 1956-68, 4¾" h. 350.00
"Umbrella Girl," 1972-79, 8" h. 470.00
"Umbrella Girl," 1963-71, 8" h. 495.00
"Umbrella Girl," 1956-68, 8" h. 550.00
"Umbrella Girl," 1940-57, 8" h. 600.00
"Volunteers," 1956-68, 5" h. 110.00
"Volunteers," 1940-57, 5" h. 210.00
"Waiter," 1972-79, 6" h. 70.00
"Wash Day," 1963-71, 6" h. . . . .85.00 to 100.00
"Wash Day," 1956-68, 6" h. 110.00
"Watchful Angel," 1972-79, 6¾" h. 105.00
"Watchful Angel," 1963-71, 6¾" h. 162.50
"Worship," 1956-68, 5" h. 90.00
"Worship," 1940-57, 5" h. 115.00

HUTSCHENREUTHER

The Hutschenreuther family name is associated with fine German porcelains. Carl Magnus Hutschenreuther established a factory at Hohenberg, Bavaria and was succeeded in this business by his widow and sons, Christian and Lorenz. Lorenz later established a factory in Selb, Bavaria (1857) which was managed by Christian and his son, Albert. The family later purchased factories near Carlsbad (1909), Altwasser, Silesia (1918) and Arzberg, Bavaria and, between 1917 and 1927, acquired at least two additional factories. The firm, noted for the fine quality wares produced, united all these branches in 1969 and continues in production today.

Cake plate, 2-handled, floral decor &
encrusted gold decor on green
ground $68.00
Dish, double-handled, heavy gold
decor on cobalt blue, 13" l. 85.00
Figure of Mephistopheles w/sword &
scissors at hip, 6" h. 130.00
Figure group, dancing girls (2), all
white, 1920, 9" h. 150.00

Model of a Boston Bulldog. 80.00
Model of a sailfish, 5" l. 125.00
Painting on porcelain, "Ruth," artist-
signed & numbered, ormolu frame,
4 x 6". 750.00
Plate, 7¾" d., h.p. pink & yellow rose
sprays on shaded green ground,
ca. 1910 . . . . .19.00
Plate, 9½" d., portrait of the Duchess
of Devonshire, wearing a large
feathered hat, rim w/lustrous green-
ground border panels of gilt foliate
scrolls & wildlife vignettes, artist-
signed, ca. 1900 . . . . .660.00
Plate, 9½" d., portrait of Helene
Sedlmayer, wearing traditional
Slavic costume w/red scarf & blue
bodice, rim w/gilt swags strung from
baskets & medallions between acid-
etched leaf & berry bands, artist-
signed, ca. 1900 . . . . .825.00
Plate, 10" d., h.p. portrait of maiden
w/four cherubs pulling her cart 115.00
Teapot, Blue Onion patt. 68.00

IMARI

Large Imari Dish

This is a multicolor ware that originated in China but was imitated and made famous by the Japanese and subsequently copied by English and European potteries. It was decorated in overglaze enamel. Made in the Hizen and Arita areas of Japan, much of it was exported through the port of Imari. Arita Imari often has brocade patterns. Imitative wares made elsewhere are now usually lumped together under the generic term Imari. It is currently being reproduced.

Barber's bowl, underglaze-blue w/iron-
red & green overglaze chrysanthemums, grapes & vines, underside

w/enameled plum blossom spray,
18th c., 9½" d. $440.00
Bowl, 7 x 3", scalloped rim, underglaze-blue & overglaze enameled
butterflies & floral decor 95.00
Bowl, 9 5/8 x 7 5/8" oval, underglaze-
blue w/orange overglaze florals 135.00
Bowl, 11" d., deep, underglaze-blue
floral panels, ca. 1890 ....85.00
Bowl, 11" d., underglaze-blue &
overglaze enameled landscape
scene w/bridge, 18th c.............140.00
Censer, globular on 3 columnar
supports, high angled handles, floral
medallions on a brocade ground
below a frieze of stylized dragons,
domed cover pierced w/cloud
patterns surmounted by a seated
Immortal, underglaze-blue & overglaze enamels & gilt, ca. 1860,
16½" h. 825.00
Charger, scalloped rim w/panels of
birds & flowers, center w/basket of
flowers, underglaze-blue & typical
colored overglaze enamels, 12" d. ...180.00
Charger, typical Imari colors w/scenes
of people on white ground, overall
gold tracery, 16" d................985.00
Charger, underglaze-blue decor, ca.
1800, 16" d. 200.00
Charger, underglaze-blue center scene
of child holding a dipper & fan standing before a bamboo lattice screen
through which is seen a floral
arrangement, late 19th c., 20½" d. ...210.00
Charger, large underglaze-blue flower-
shaped medallions reserved on a
diapered ground centering a large
underglaze-blue roundel of lotus
blossoms, ca. 1870, 24½" d. 660.00
Cup, underglaze-blue & rust overglaze
enameling, ca. 1850 ....25.00
Cup & saucer, underglaze-blue & multicolored overglaze enameling w/gilt
trim, ca. 1890.....................45.00
Dish, shell-shaped, ribbed oval well
w/underglaze-blue, iron-red & gold
central floral medallion surrounded
by sprays of peonies & chrysanthemums, squared handle w/floral
spray, gilt-edged rim w/iron-red
trellis diaper border interrupted
w/demiflowerheads, underside
mostly unglazed, 1705-20, 7½" w....550.00
Dish, scalloped rim, underglaze-blue &
red overglaze Hawthorne decor,
ca. 1880, 8½" w....................75.00
Dish, underglaze-blue central monogrammed roundel & exotic birds
amidst florals & fruit & rim w/six
panels of flowering plants, Arita,
1660-90, 14½" d. (ILLUS.) 7,150.00
Dish, underglaze-blue, iron-red & gold
flowering chrysanthemums behind a

fence in the center & w/buds &
flowering sprays around the rim,
early 18th c., 17" d. 990.00
Plate, 8½" d., scalloped rim, underglaze-blue & green overglaze dragon
decor, gilt trim, ca. 1860 ....185.00
Plate, 9 1/8" d., center w/iron-red,
salmon, brown, black, green & gold
scene of Dutch couple strolling
w/their dog in a garden, rim
w/underglaze-blue, iron-red, brown,
black & gold vases & other objects
between floral clusters within an
underglaze-blue border heightened
w/gilt trelliswork, underside w/two
flowering branches, 1720-30 ......2,420.00
Platter, fish-shaped, 19th c. 235.00
Tea set: cov. teapot & 4 c/s; Arita
Imari, ca. 1890, 9 pcs. 295.00
Tray, corner panels of underglaze-
blue stylized florals & birds,
10 x 8½".......................125.00

Imari Covered Tureen

Tureen & cover w/fruit knop, canted
rectangle, painted each side in
underglaze-blue w/pavilions on a
river landscape, cover w/foliate &
floral design, gilt highlighting &
overall floral decor in iron-red, gilt
animal head handles, ca. 1800,
14" l. (ILLUS.) 1,100.00

19th Century Imari Vase

Vase, 18 1/8" h., baluster-shaped
w/flaring rim, underglaze-blue tree
peonies, finches & decorative bands
at neck & base w/iron-red & gold
accents, late 19th c. (ILLUS.) 440.00
Vase, 23¼" h., high-shouldered ovoid
w/long cylindrical neck, typical
Imari colors w/large landscape panels
panels above a formal foliate border,
shoulder & neck w/ruyi collar of
stylized chrysanthemums,
ca. 1870 . . . . .1,760.00

IRONSTONE

Ironstone Fruit Bowl

*The first successful ironstone was
patented in 1813 by C.J. Mason in England.
The body contains iron slag incorporated
with the clay. Other potters imitated
Mason's ware and today much hard, thick
ware is lumped under the term ironstone.
Earlier it was called by various names,
including graniteware. Both plain white and
decorated wares were made throughtout the
19th century. The Tea Leaf Lustre ironstone
was made by several firms and is included
at the end of this listing.*

GENERAL
Bone dish, all white, Meakin $17.00
Bowl, 9" d., 5½" h., footed, all white
(ILLUS.) 60.00
Bowl, 9 7/8" d., all white, Davenport . . .12.00
Bowl, fruit, 10½" d., President shape,
all white, J. Edwards, 1855 . . . . .45.00
Bowl, 11" d., all white, Meakin 65.00
Bowl, collared base, deep, all white,
Burgess, 1864-92 . . . . .55.00
Butter dish, cov., square, Moss Rose
patt., copper lustre trim, Grindley,
1880-1900 . . . . .65.00
Cake stand, pedestal base, Chinese
shape, all white, T. & R. Boote,
1842-1906 . . . . .65.00
Cake stand, pedestal base, all white . .105.00

Cake stand, scalloped flange rim, all
white 80.00
Chamber pot, cov., child's, Gothic
shape, all white, Meigh, 1850s 88.00
Coffee pot, cov., Baltimore shape,
all white, Brougham & Mayer,
1853-55 . . . . .115.00

Ceres Shape Wheat Pattern

Coffee pot, cov., Ceres shape, Wheat
patt., Turner, Goddard & Co.,
1867-74 (ILLUS.) 165.00
Coffee set: cov. coffee pot, sugar
bowl, 6 c/s & 6 luncheon plates;
Ceres shape, white w/copper lustre
decor, Elsmore & Forster, 1853-71,
20 pcs. 540.00
Cookie plate, low pedestal, all white,
Henry Alcock & Co., 1861-1910 . . . . . .20.00
Creamer, Grenade shape, all white,
T.R. Boote, 1842-1906 . . . . .54.00
Creamer, Lily-of-the-Valley patt., all
white 195.00
Creamer, Memnon shape, all white,
John Meir & Son, 1857 . . . . .52.00
Cups, handleless, Huron shape, all
white, Adams, set of 4 . . . . .48.00
Cup & saucer, Chinese shape 45.00
Cup & saucer, Lily-of-the-Valley patt.,
all white 85.00
Cup & saucer, Wheat patt., all white,
Adams 15.00
Cup & saucer, flow blue-type florals 55.00

Ironstone Cuspidor

Cuspidor, faint Venetian Diamond-
type molding, h.p. florals (ILLUS.) 45.00
Feeding dish, blue numerals on side 30.00
Gravy boat, Corn & Oats patt., all
white, Davenport & Wedgwood,
1863 . . . . .20.00
Gravy boat, Fuchsia shape, all white . . .30.00
Gravy boat, Full Ribbed patt., all white,
J.W. Pankhurst, 1850-51 . . . . .32.00
Gravy boat, octagonal, all white,
Anthony Shaw & Son, 1860-1900. . . . . .34.00
Gravy boat, cov., Sydenham shape, all
white, T. & R. Boote, 1842-1906 . . . . .135.00
Gravy boat w/underplate, all white,
James Edwards, 1842-51, 2 pcs. 55.00
Gravy boat w/underplate, all white,
Wedgwood & Co. 32.00
Hot toddy bowl, cov., Lily-of-the-Valley
shape, all white, Anthony Shaw,
1851-56 . . . . .195.00
Hot toddy cup, Little Palm patt., all
white 15.00
Hot water pitcher, Prize Bloom patt.,
all white, T. J. & J. Mayer, 1843-55 . .165.00
Hot water pitcher, Wheat patt., all
white, Turner, Goddard & Co.,
1867-74 . . . . .78.00
Luncheon set: cov. coffee pot, sugar
bowl, 6 luncheon plates & 6 c/s;
Ceres shape, all white w/copper
lustre trim, Elsmore & Forster,
1853-71, 20 pcs. 540.00

"Gaudy" Ironstone Pitcher

Pitcher, 5¾" h., jug-type w/sea
serpent handle, "gaudy," multi-
colored floral decor (ILLUS.) 125.00
Pitcher, 6" h., bulbous, blue transfer
pastoral scene decor, Mason's 50.00
Pitcher, 6" h., hexagonal jug-type,
embossed florals & birds overall,
Mason's Patent 65.00
Pitcher, 6" h., octagonal, Mandarin
patt., w/blue & orange floral decor,
Mason's Patent 70.00
Pitcher, 6¼" h., Regency patt.,
Mason's 50.00

Pitcher, milk, Lily shape, all
white, Henry Burgess, 1860s. 95.00
Pitcher, milk, Panelled Grape patt.,
all white, Meakin 65.00
Plate, 8" d., Venus patt. transfer
decor, Podmore, Walker & Co.,
1834-59 . . . . .38.00

Ironstone Plate

Plate, 8" d., transfer decorated,
Mason's Patent, after 1891 (ILLUS.) . . .16.00
Plate, 8" d., Scalloped Decagon shape,
all white, John Wedge Wood,
1841-60 . . . . .16.00
Plate, 8½" d., "gaudy," underglaze-
blue leaf & berry design border
w/red & yellow overglaze enameling & copper lustre trim, E. Walley,
1845-46 . . . . .45.00
Plate, 8½" d., Columbia shape, all
white 25.00
Plate, 8½" d., 10-sided, "gaudy," floral
decor, impressed "Pearl White". 30.00
Plate, 8½" d., Canella patt. transfer
decor, Challinor, 1862-91 . . . . .30.00
Plate, 8½" d., Indian patt., decorated,
Livesley, Powell & Co., 1851-66 . . . . . .40.00
Plate, 8½" d., Laurel Wreath patt.,
all white, Elsmore & Forster, 1864 . . . .15.00
Plate, 8¾" d., all white, Henry Alcock
& Co., 1861-1910 . . . . .11.00
Plate, 8¾" d., Canella shape, multi-
colored transfer on brown ground,
Challinor 28.00
Plate, 9¾" d., cobalt blue & iron-red
flowering tree, birds & swan decor . . .75.00
Plate, 10¼" d., 10-sided, all white,
Davenport, 1850-87 . . . . .46.00
Plate, dinner, Corn & Oats patt., all
white, Davenport, 1863 . . . . .30.00
Plate, dinner, Trent shape, all white,
Alcock, 1854 & 1855 . . . . .18.00
Plates, dinner, Wheat patt., all white,
Meakin, pr. 30.00
Plate, luncheon, Corn & Oats patt., all
white, Davenport, 1863 . . . . .14.50
Plate, luncheon, Wheat patt., all white,
Meakin 26.00

Platter, 12 x 8 7/8", all white,
Davenport 10.00
Platter, 12" oval, Ceres shape,
all white 25.00
Platter, 13½ x 10 5/8" oval, Prairie
shape, all white, Clementson Bros.,
1865-1916 . . . . .22.00
Platter, 14½" l., Boote's 1851 Octagon
patt., all white 30.00
Platter, 14½ x 10 7/8" oval, Wheat
patt., all white, Meakin 25.00
Platter, 15¼" l., Fig shape, all white . . .35.00
Platter, 16½ x 11½", white, Meakin . . .125.00
Platter, 16¾ x 12½" oval, Bordered
Hyacinth patt., all white, W. Baker
& Co., 1839-1932 . . . . .35.00
Platter, 16¾ x 13", orange & pink
floral decor, Adams Tunstall, 1796 to
present 105.00
Punch bowl, handled, Loop & Line
patt., all white, Pankhurst, 1850-82 . .100.00

Berlin Swirl Pattern

Sauce tureen, cover & undertray, Berlin
Swirl patt., Mayer Bros. & Elliot,
1856 (ILLUS.) 250.00
Soup plate w/flange rim, Ceres shape,
all white 22.00
Soup plate w/flange rim, Corn & Oats
patt., all white, Davenport,
1793-1887 . . . . .14.00
Soup plate w/flange rim, Ivy Wreath
patt., all white, John Meir, 1857,
9¾" d. 16.00
Soup plate w/flange rim, Penang patt.,
Imari colors w/Oriental figures,
10½" d. 45.00
Soup plate w/flange rim, Ribbed
Raspberry w/Bloom patt., all white,
J. & G. Meakin, 1860s 18.00
Soup plate w/flange rim, Wheat
w/Blackberry patt., all white,
Thomas Hughes, 1860-94 . . . . .17.00
Soup tureen, cover, underplate &
ladle, Twin Leaves patt., all white,
James Edwards, 1851, 4 pcs. 270.00
Syllabub bowl, all white 35.00
Syrup pitcher & pewter top w/swan
finial, all white 57.50
Toddy cup, Wheat & Blackberry patt.,
all white, Meakin 30.00

Toothbrush holder, Oriental patt.,
brown transfer, 4½" h. 25.00
Toothbrush holder, Wheat & Blackerry
patt., all white, Meakin 30.00
Vegetable dish, cov., Trent shape, all
white, Samuel & John Alcock, 1854
& 1855 . . . . .35.00
Vegetable dish, cov., Wheat patt.,
all white, Meakin 65.00
Vegetable dish, cov., Wheat &
Blackberry patt., all white,
Meakin 77.50
Waste bowl, Lily-of-the-Valley patt.,
all white 75.00

TEA LEAF LUSTRE

Meakin Tea Leaf Lustre Ironstone

Coffee pot, cov., Bamboo shape,
Alfred Meakin, from 1875 on
(ILLUS.) 125.00
Cup & saucer, W. H. Grindley, from
1880 on 50.00
Cup & saucer, Mellor, Taylor & Co.,
1880-1904 . . . . .55.00
Cup & saucer, Wedgwood & Co., from
1860 on 45.00
Gravy boat, Wedgwood & Co. 30.00
Mush bowl, Bamboo shape, Alfred
Meakin, from 1875 on 30.00
Pitcher, 7" h., Henry Burgess,
1864-92 . . . . .110.00
Pitcher, 7" h., Wedgwood & Co. 90.00
Pitcher, 7 1/8" h., Bamboo shape,
Alfred Meakin 150.00
Pitcher, 8" h., Bamboo shape,
Meakin . . . . .195.00 to 250.00
Pitcher, 8" h., Cable shape, Anthony
Shaw, 1850-90 . . . . .195.00
Pitcher, 12" h., Bishop & Stonier,
1878-91 . . . . .75.00
Plate, 7¾" d. 15.00
Plate, 8½" d., Anthony Shaw 12.50
Plate, 9½" d., Anthony Shaw 16.50
Platter, 14" oval, Anthony Shaw 47.50
Platter, 14 x 10¼", Alfred Meakin
(ILLUS.) 50.00
Platter, 15 5/8 x 11 3/8" 65.00
Platter, 17¾ x 13¾", Arthur J.
Wilkinson, from 1879 on 60.00
Sauce dishes, square, Arthur J.
Wilkinson, set of 3 . . . . .54.00

Sauce tureen & cover, Alfred Meakin . . .75.00
Sauce tureen, cover, ladle & under-
    tray, Fish Hook shape, Meakin,
    4 pcs. 360.00
Sauce tureen, cover, ladle & under-
    tray, Cable shape, Anthony Shaw,
    4 pcs. 300.00
Shaving mug, Alfred Meakin 48.00
Shaving mug, Chinese shape, Anthony
    Shaw 130.00
Soap dish & cover, Powell & Bishop
    (no drain insert) 35.00
Soap dish, cover & drain insert,
    Alfred Meakin .75.00
Vegetable dish, cov., square, Bamboo
    shape, Alfred Meakin 70.00
Vegetable dish, cov., square, Powell &
    Bishop, 1876-91 . . . . .85.00
Wash basin, Alfred Meakin (chip at
    bottom edge) .85.00
Waste bowl 30.00

JASPER WARE

*Jasper ware is fine-grained exceedingly
hard stoneware made by including barium
sulphate in the clay and was first devised by
Josiah Wedgwood, who utilized it for the
body of many of his fine cameo blue-
and-white and green-and-white pieces. It
was subsequently produced by other
potters, notably William Adams & Sons,
and is in production at the present.*

WEDGWOOD

Jasper Ware Cheese Dish

Bowl, 4 7/8" d., 2 3/8" h., white
    relief leaf bands & classical figures
    on light blue, marked Wedgwood
    only, ca. 1862 . . . .$245.00
Candlestick, white relief decor on
    sage green, 7" h. (single) 225.00
Cheese dish w/dome lid, white relief
    classical figures & borders on deep
    blue, dated 1879, 9½" d. under-
    plate, overall 5" h. (ILLUS.) 450.00

Cookie jar, white relief classical ladies
    & cupids on sage green center
    band, lavender top & bottom bands,
    silverplate cover, rim & handle,
    marked Wedgwood only, 4¾" d.,
    5½" h. 750.00
Cookie jar, white relief classical ladies
    & cupids on black central band,
    gold top & bottom bands, silverplate
    cover, rim & handle, marked
    Wedgwood only, 5¼" d., 6" h. 695.00

Jasper Ware Cookie Jar

Cookie jar, white relief hunting scene
    on sage green, silverplate cover,
    rim & bail handle, 5½" h. (ILLUS.) . . .525.00
Cookie jar, black relief garlands,
    lion masks & classical figures on
    gold, black relief grapevine around
    base, silverplate cover, rim & handle,
    marked Wedgwood only, 5¾" d.,
    6½" h. 575.00
Cookie jar, white relief classical
    figures on deep blue, silverplate
    cover, rim & bail handle,
    dated 1882 . . . . .250.00
Creamer, jug-type, white relief classi-
    cal figures on crimson red, 3½" h. . .450.00
Creamer & cov. sugar bowl, white
    relief classical ladies on sage green,
    marked Wedgwood England, pr. 130.00
Cup & saucer, white relief berried
    laurel branches between vertical
    rows of white squares w/yellow
    florettes alternating w/green
    squares, all within foliate borders on
    green dip, ca. 1790 . . . . .1,650.00
Cup & saucer, white relief border
    bands & classical figures on light
    blue, marked Wedgwood only,
    ca. 1860 . . . . .245.00
Cup & saucer, white relief classical
    mythological figures on sage green,
    marked Wedgwood England. 100.00
Dish, heart-shaped, white relief on
    dark green, marked Wedgwood
    England, small 40.00

Flower pot & stand, engine-turned ridged squares alternating w/white relief florettes below a border of anthemia & lilies on blue, everted rim w/acanthus leaves, stand w/border of stiff leaves, late 18th c., 3 7/8" h. 935.00

Model of a drum, white relief classical ladies on black, marked Wedgwood only, 3 7/8" d., 4 5/8" h. 155.00

Pin tray, white relief classical figures on deep blue, marked Wedgwood only, 8½" l. 125.00

Pitcher, 5¼" h., white relief scene of children playing Blindman's Buff & w/grapevine border on blue, marked Wedgwood only 135.00

Pitcher, 7" h., white relief classical figures on crimson red, marked Wedgwood England 395.00

Wedgwood Jasper Pitcher

Pitcher, tankard, 7¼" h., rope handle, white relief classical figures & cherubs below grapevine border on sage green, marked Wedgwood only (ILLUS.). 180.00

Pitcher, 7½" h., white relief vintage grape borders & classical figures on dark blue, marked Wedgwood only 195.00

Pitcher, tankard, 8" h., white relief on crimson 475.00

Plaque, white relief bust portrait of the Duke of Edinburgh on deep blue, 3 x 2¼" oval, ogee-molded ebony frame, ca. 1915, overall 5 3/8 x 5 1/8" 475.00

Plaque, central white relief Madonna figure & laurel leaf rim on lilac, 10 x 7" oval 325.00

Plaque, white relief scene of Heracles in the Garden of Hesperides on green, mounted in gilt frame, 48 x 18" 425.00

Plate, 8" d., white relief center design & classical figures around edge on dark blue 185.00

Portland Vase Replica

Portland vase replica, white relief continuous frieze of classical figures said to represent the myth of Pelius & Thetis on dark blue, ca. 1840, 10½" h. (ILLUS.) 2,100.00

Potpourri vase, vertical rows of alternating blue & white squares applied w/mustard yellow florettes between bands of white arabesques on blue dip, pierced cover (glued on) w/mustard yellow anthemia & white billing doves knop, interior w/sunk box, ca. 1790, 4¾" h......1,760.00

Salt shaker, white relief figures on blue (single) 85.00

Spill vase, white relief floral garlands pendant from ram's heads & 3 small lavender & white oval medallions w/scenes on sage green, marked Wedgwood only, 2" d., 3 1/8" h. 406.00

Sweetmeat jar, white relief cupids & classical ladies on center sage green band, lavender top & bottom bands, silverplate cover, rim & bail handle, marked Wedgwood only, 3½" d., 4½" h. 550.00

Tea kettle, cov., white relief alternating florals & leaves on deep blue, wicker-wrapped metal handle, marked Wedgwood only, 6¼" d., 7½" h. 650.00

Teapot, cov., white relief medallions of classical ladies & white bands on light blue, marked Wedgwood only, dated 1862, 3 3/8" d., 3 5/8" h.......460.00

Teapot, cov., white relief classical ladies on sage green, 4 5/8" d., 4¼" h. 175.00

Urn, 2-handled, white relief ram's head, trophies & garlands on black, marked Wedgwood only, ca. 1840, 6" h. 475.00

Vase, 4¾" h., 3 5/8" d., white relief classical ladies & cupid on deep blue, marked Wedgwood only 125.00

Vase, 10 1/8" h., 4½" d., 2-handled,
pedestal base, white relief classical
figures, leaves & florettes on
black, marked Wedgwood only 475.00
Vase, 11 5/8" h., 5" d., footed, white
relief classical ladies on light blue,
dated 1865 . . . . .510.00

ADAMS & OTHERS

Jasper Ware Pitcher

Box & cover w/pink crown finial,
pale pink relief bust portrait of
Queen Alexandra on white, 3 x 3" . . .55.00
Box, cov., white relief nymph & cupid
on blue, Shafer & Vater, 5" oval 55.00
Candlesticks, white relief classical
figures on dark blue, brass trim,
w/English registry mark (1842-83),
pr. 395.00
Coffee pot, cov., white relief dancing
maidens on blue, Copeland-Spode,
8½" h. 85.00
Coffee pot, cov., white relief hunting
scene on blue, Copeland-Spode,
10½" h. 135.00
Cookie jar, white relief classical ladies
on deep blue, silverplate cover, rim
& bail handle, Adams, 5¾" d.,
6¾" h. 115.00
Cookie jar, white relief hunting
scene on blue, silverplate cover,
rim & bail handle 175.00
Creamer & sugar bowl, w/applied
busts of Clowes, Bourne & Wesley,
1910 centenary item, pr. 55.00
Dish, white relief full figure Indian
w/shield & hatchet & wheat sheaf
border on green, Heubach, 4¼" d. 58.00
Jardiniere, white relief on blue, ca.
1850, 8½" h. . . . . .175.00 to 200.00
Pitcher, 6¼" h., applied rope handle,
white relief classical figures on
green 295.00
Pitcher, 7" h., tankard, rope-twist
handle, white relief classical lady

& other designs on deep lilac
(ILLUS.) 100.00
Pitcher, 7" h., white relief vintage
grape border, classical figures,
cupid, dog, trees & florals on blue,
sterling silver hinged cover 300.00
Planter, white relief of Apollo & 4
Muses on blue, ca. 1850, large 225.00
Plaque, white relief cherub & goddess
surrounded by florals on green,
Germany, 5¾" d. 89.00
Plaque, white relief boy w/net & girl
w/jug on green, Germany, 6" 38.00
Plaque, white relief cherubs (3)
dancing within florals on green,
Germany, 7½ x 5" 115.00
Plaque, white relief classical gentle-
man holding mask in left hand &
walking stick in other on blue,
7½" oval 297.00
Plaque, white relief cherubs & goddess
on green, Germany, 8¼ x 3"
oblong 115.00
Spill vase, white relief florals, trees
& muses representing poetry &
drama on deep blue 110.00
Teapot, cov., cream relief "Dancing
Hours" figures & garlands on blue,
cream spout & handle, Copeland-
Spode, 4 1/8" d., 4½" h. 95.00
Toothpick holder, 3-handled, white
relief children (2) kissing on blue 38.00
Tyg (large 3-compartment mug),
3-handled, white relief bust
portraits of Washington & Franklin
on blue, 1876, 5" h. 175.00
Urn, cov., white relief "Dancing
Hours" figures on black 225.00
Wall pocket, white relief classical lady
& bow-tied garlands on green,
7½" h. 30.00

JEWEL TEA AUTUMN LEAF PATTERN

Autumn Leaf Salad Bowl

*Though not antique, this ware has a
devoted following. The Hall China Company of East Liverpool, Ohio, made the first
pieces of Autumn Leaf pattern ware to be
given as premiums by the Jewel Tea
Company in 1933. The premiums were an
immediate success and thousands of new
customers, all eager to acquire a piece of the*

durable Autumn Leaf pattern ware, began purchasing Jewel Tea products. Though the pattern was eventually used to decorate linens, glasswares and tinwares, we include only the Hall China Company items in our listing.

Bean pot, cov., 2-handled....	$75.00 to 110.00
Bowl, 5" d.	3.00
Bowl, 9" oval	15.00
Bowl, salad, 9" d. (ILLUS.)	18.00
Bowls, stacking-type, 18 oz., 24 oz. & 34 oz. bowls (3) & single cover, set	30.00
Butter dish, cov., ¼ lb.	125.00 to 165.00
Butter dish, cov., 1 lb.	185.00
Cake plate w/"Goldenray" metal base	90.00 to 110.00
Candy dish w/"Goldenray" metal base	95.00
Clock, electric	260.00 to 375.00
Coffee pot, cov., drip-type, w/metal insert	47.00
Coffee pot (or casserole) warmer, round	86.00
Coffee server, 7½" h.	38.00
Cookie jar, cov., tab handles	78.00
Creamer & cov. sugar bowl, 1940, pr.	18.00
Cup & saucer	7.00
Custard cup	4.00
Gravy boat	16.50
Irish coffee mug	45.00
Marmalade jar w/underplate & ladle, 3 pcs.	45.00

Autumn Leaf Pattern Mixing Bowl

Mixing bowl, 7" d. (ILLUS.)	12.00
Mixing bowls, nesting-type, set of 3	35.00
Mug, 6" h.	48.00
Mustard jar, cover, ladle & under-plate, 3 pcs.	50.00
Pickle dish, oval	12.00
Pie baker, 9½" d.	14.00
Pitcher, water, jug-type w/ice lip	20.00
Plate, 6" d.	3.50
Plate, 7" d.	5.50
Plate, 8" d.	4.50
Plate, 9" d.	6.50
Plate, 10" d.	9.50
Platter, 11½" l.	12.00
Platter, 13½" l.	16.00
Range top set, cov. grease jar & salt & pepper shakers, 3 pcs.	30.00

Salt & pepper shakers, bell-shaped, small, pr.	12.50
Salt & pepper shakers, large, pr.	18.50
Sauce dish	4.00
Souffle-casserole, 10 oz. individual size	21.50
Souffle-casserole, 1-qt.	60.00
Soup plate w/flange rim	8.50
Sugar bowl, cov., small	8.00
Sugar bowl, cov., large	20.00
Teapot, cov., Aladdin lamp shape w/long spout	42.50
Teapot, cov., square	75.00 to 125.00
Tidbit tray, 3-tier	55.00
Vegetable bowl, cov., handled, 10½" oval	42.50
Vegetable bowl, divided, 10½ x 8" oval	60.00 to 75.00

Autumn Leaf Pattern Vegetable Bowl

Vegetable bowl, 10½ x 8" oval (ILLUS.)	18.00

KAUFFMANN, ANGELIQUE

Cup & Saucer with Kauffmann Decor

Angelica Kauffmann (Marie Angelique Catherine Kauffmann) was an accomplished Swiss artist, who lived from 1741 until 1807. Paintings copied from her original work often embellish porcelain and those signed with her name have attracted collectors.

Bowl, 9½" d., classical scene after Kauffmann w/sleeping warrior & maiden center, cobalt blue border w/gilt tracery & gilt rim	$55.00
Box w/hinged lid, classical scene	

after Kauffmann on lid, 2" base,
1½" h. 55.00
Box, cov., scene of woman & cherub
signed "Kauffmann" on cover, red
& green ground w/gold tracery,
Royal Vienna round blank..........125.00
Bulb bowl, classical scene of 3 ladies
& cupid reserved on brown shaded
to white ground, highlighted w/gilt
florals, Victoria, Austria blank,
6½" d., 2½" h. 125.00
Cup, demitasse, footed, gold handle,
typical Kauffmann scene interior,
burgundy w/gold tracery exterior,
E.S. Prov. Saxe blank..............82.00
Cup & saucer, pedestal foot, typical
Kauffmann scene within heavy
gold borders (ILLUS.) 95.00
Perfume bottle w/ornate gilt stopper
w/cork, classical scene of women
after Kauffmann reserved on deep
rose, green & cream, gold trim,
2 5/8" d., 6½" h..................95.00
Plate, 8" d., reticulated rim, classical
scene w/two figures center, cobalt
blue border 55.00
Plate, 9¼" d., classical scene
w/chariot, ladies & cupid after
Kauffmann center, maroon & green
border, scalloped rim, E.S. Germany
Prov. Saxe blank..................55.00
Plate, 10" d., footed, classical scene
w/two maidens & cupid center,
green & cream border w/gilt roses,
pseudo beehive mark blank 85.00

Tea Set with Classical Decor

Tea set: cov. teapot, creamer, cov.
sugar bowl & 4 c/s; various
classical scenes after Kauffmann
reserved on cobalt blue ground
highlighted w/gold tracery & raised
enamel dots, Royal Vienna blanks,
11 pcs. (ILLUS. of part) 2,500.00
Tray, large reserve portrait of classical
figures, signed "Kauffmann," pseudo
beehive mark blank, 16½" d........175.00
Urn, pierced gold handles, typical
classical scenes after Kauffmann
decor, Royal Vienna blank, 7" h. 95.00

Vase, 16" h., 2-handled, reserve portrait of classical couple on cobalt
blue ground 195.00
Vase, classical portrait reserved on
cobalt blue ground, Royal Bonn
blank, large......................285.00

KOCH

Koch Chocolate Set

*Joseph Anton Koch was an Austrian
painter and etcher (1768-1839) whose work
has often been copied on porcelain. These
reproductions appear on the ceramics of
various factories and all carry the artist's
signature leading some collectors to lump
them together as "Koch" porcelain.*

Bowl, 6" d., apples decor $24.00
Bowl, 9" d., apples or grapes decor,
each ....68.00 to 75.00
Bowl, 10" d., grapes decor, J.C. Louise,
Bavaria blank 47.50
Celery tray w/pierced handle, apples
decor, 11½ x 5¼" 40.00
Celery tray, purple & green grapes
decor, 11½" l.....................38.00
Chocolate set: cov. chocolate pot & 6
c/s; grape clusters on dark green,
brown & yellow shading to cream
ground, 13 pcs. (ILLUS.) 640.00
Pancake dish w/dome cover, grapes
decor, 9½" d., 4½" h. 250.00
Plate, 6" d., grapes decor, J.C.
Louise, Bavaria blank 18.00
Plate, 7½" d., grapes on soft yellow
to brown & green ground, scalloped
gold edge.........................35.00
Plate, 8" d., gooseberries decor 24.00
Plate, 8½" d., apples or grapes decor,
J.C. Louise, Bavaria blank, each 40.00
Platter, 12", grapes decor............95.00

KUTANI

*This is a Japanese ware from the area of
Kutani, a name meaning "nine valleys,"
where porcelain was made as early as 1644*

by potters returning from the kiln center of
Arita who established a factory in the area.
The early wares, which were a heavy
porcelain approaching stoneware, are referred to as "Ko-Kutani" (old Kutani) to distinguish them from the "Ao-Kutani" (new
Kutani), the 19th century revival of the
wares.

Beaker, h.p. orange & gold florals
   & birds on white ground, Ao-Kutani,
   4½" h. $55.00
Bowl, 5" d., 1½" h., h.p. scene of
   women beside lake, in shades of
   green & red-orange w/green & gold
   borders, Ao-Kutani 67.50
Bowl, 7¼ x 3½", figures, florals &
   landscape decor on red ground,
   ca. 1900 ....250.00
Creamer & sugar bowl, h.p. scene
   of man & woman beside lake &
   large birds reserved on cobalt blue
   ground, gold trim, pr. 200.00
Model of a sleeping cat in curled
   position, ornate enameling in relief
   on coffee brown to black ground,
   11½" l.............................145.00
Pitcher, 9½" h., baluster-shaped,
   alternating panels of birds, flowers
   & Oriental performers, 19th c. 40.00
Plate, 8½" d., h.p. rooster decor,
   ca. 1900 ....250.00
Plate, fluted rim, h.p. florals & flying
   birds, Ao-Kutani 80.00
Teapot, cov., bulbous, One Thousand
   Faces patt., 4¼" d., 6" h. 190.00

Kutani Teapot

Teapot, cov., bamboo-molded handle,
   h.p. florals & diapered borders,
   Ko-Kutani (ILLUS.)................250.00
Tea set: cov. teapot, tea caddy &
   4 c/s; melon-ribbed, h.p. reserves
   w/children, diapered borders, ornate
   gold trim, 10 pcs. 185.00
Tea set: 8¼" h. cov. teapot, creamer,
   sugar bowl & 8 c/s; 6 h.p. figures on
   larger pieces & 3 figures on c/s,
   gold trim, 19 pcs. 395.00

Vase, 7" h., stick-type, bittersweet
   red & gold birds & florals in fan-
   shaped reserve on white ground,
   Ao-Kutani 125.00
Vase, 9¾" h., stick-type w/long
   cylindrical neck & ball-shaped base,
   h.p. reserve of florals on dark
   ground 200.00
Vases, 11" h., baluster-shaped, oval
   reserves w/family scenes & floral
   bouquets each side, pr.............155.00
Vases, 19½" h., yellow floral decor on
   white ground, 20th c., pr. 195.00

LEEDS

Leeds Pearlware Teapot

The Leeds Pottery in Yorkshire, England,
began production about 1758. It made,
among other things, creamware that was
highly competitive with Wedgwood's. In
the 1780s it began production of reticulated
and punched wares. Little of its production
was marked. Most readily available Leeds
ware is that of the 19th century during
which time the pottery was operated by
several firms.

Basket-dish, creamware, openwork
   stave sides molded w/entwined
   reedwork banding, 1790-1810,
   10" oval $265.00
Bowl & reticulated cover w/flower
   finial, 4¾" h., quatrefoil form,
   creamware, embossed base,
   impressed "Leeds Pottery" (fine
   crazing) 155.00
Cake stand, creamware, reticulated
   rim & foot, impressed "Leeds
   Pottery," 9" d., 4 3/8" h. (small
   chips on foot).....................165.00
Mug, creamware, engine-turned,
   ca. 1800 ....45.00
Pitcher, jug-type, "Farmer's Arms"
   decor 285.00
Plate, 8¾" d., creamware, scalloped
   blue border, blue flowers & leaves
   center............................120.00

Teapot & cover w/floral knop,
entwined strap handle, foliate-
molded spout, underglaze-blue
"chinoiserie" decor heightened in
iron-red & gilding, ca. 1790
(ILLUS.)...........................425.00

LENOX

Lenox Ming Pattern

*The Ceramic Art Company was estab-
lished at Trenton, New Jersey, in 1889 by
Jonathan Coxon and Walter Scott Lenox.
In addition to true porcelain, it also made a
Belleek-type ware. Re-named Lenox Com-
pany in 1906, it is still in production today.
Also see BELLEEK, AMERICAN and
TOBY MUGS & JUGS.*

Bouillon cup & saucer, 2 gold handles
& gold band w/monogram, made
for Tiffany & Co. $25.00
Bowl, 7½" d., 4½" h., lotus leaf
form 135.00
Bowl, salad, 10" d., 4" h., crimped
rim, sculptured sides, ivory glaze ...125.00
Bowl, 12" d., 5½" h., shell-shaped,
scalloped rim, pale pink decor.......45.00
Bust of Art Deco woman, creamy
white bisque finish, 3½ x 3½".......125.00
Cake set: 10½" d. footed master
cake plate & six 7¼" d. serving
plates; Mimosa patt., 7 pcs. 160.00
Candy dish & cover w/bird finial, coral
pink & white, round 115.00
Coaster, cobalt blue w/gold-washed
sterling silver overlay decor 50.00
Compote, cov., 7½" d., 6½" h., Art
Deco style, gold decor on white 85.00
Creamer, cobalt blue w/sterling silver
overlay...........................65.00

Cups, demitasse, ivory w/gold bands,
in sterling silver holders marked
Meriden, set of 6...................225.00
Cup & saucer, demitasse, h.p. colorful
bird on branch, artist-signed 55.00
Dish, shell-shaped, 3½" w. 25.00
Egg cup, double, Ming patt. 25.00
Fish plate, "Brook Trout" or "Pike,"
embossed gold border, signed W.
Morley, made for Ovington Bros.,
N.Y., 9" d., each..................100.00
Honey jar, cov., model of a beehive,
relief-molded bees w/sterling silver
overlay...........................135.00
Model of a bird, white, 6½" h.........75.00
Model of a swan, 11" l................150.00
Mug, inebriated man in Colonial attire
holding up bottle of wine, mono-
chromatic blue, artist-signed,
5½" h. 100.00
Pitcher, mask spout, textured ground,
creamy glaze......................95.00
Plate, 6" d., Washington-Wakefield
patt.................................10.00
Plate, 8" d., colorful fruit center,
signed Morley 85.00
Relish jar, cov., ivory & gold decor,
in sterling silver holder marked
Wallace, 4½" h....................85.00
Salt dip, model of a swan 30.00
Tea set: cov. teapot, sugar bowl &
creamer; deep brown glaze
w/ornate sterling silver overlay,
3 pcs. 275.00
Vase, 10" h., applied handles at
shoulders, h.p. orange poppies
w/gold trim 300.00
Vase, 14" h., h.p. cabbage roses
decor 595.00

Lenox Vase

Vase, 16½" h., h.p. scene of child
watching woman knit on flowing
blue ground (ILLUS.)...............800.00

LIMOGES

Limoges Game Plate

Numerous factories produced china in Limoges, France, with major production in the 19th century. Some pieces listed below are identified by the name of the maker or the mark of the factory. Although the famed Haviland Company was located at Limoges, wares bearing their marks are not included in this listing. Also see HAVILAND, OYSTER PLATES and SHAVING MUGS.

Asparagus set: platter w/drain insert, sauceboat w/underplate & six 7" plates; h.p. mauve-tinted asparagus on shaded ground, 10 pcs., L.D. & C. $450.00

Basket, h.p. pink & yellow roses w/green leaves & gold trim on multicolored pastel ground, 5½ x 5½", 13½" h. 100.00

Berry set: 9½" d. 3-footed master bowl & 8 sauce dishes; h.p. purple berries exterior, white blossoms interior, 9 pcs., T. & V. (Tressemann & Vogt) 245.00

Bon bon, pierced handles, white w/wide coin gold scalloped rim, 6½" l. 27.00

Bowl, fruit, 8¾ x 4½", 3-footed, large pink, purple & yellow asters & foliage on shaded green & cream ground, gold rim & feet, artist-signed, W.G. & Co. (Wm. Guerin & Co.) 69.00

Cache pot, gold handles, fox chasing rabbit amidst evergreen forest, artist-signed, 9 x 5" oval, 12¾" h. 850.00

Chocolate set: 15½" d. tray, cov. chocolate pot & 6 c/s; relief-molded poppies & scrollwork w/h.p. variegated pink & white roses & lacy green leaves on white ground, gold trim, dated 1906, 14 pcs., J.P.L. (J. Pouyat)............................445.00

Cider set: cider pitcher & 4 mugs; crab apples decor w/gold trim, artist-signed & dated 1907, 5 pcs. 255.00

Creamer & open sugar bowl, ruffled rims, h.p. Art Nouveau style florals, buds & leaves on shaded orange ground, gold interiors, pr., Elite (Bowo & Dotter) 120.00

Dreser set: tray, hair receiver, pin tray, hatpin holder & ring tree modeled as a hand; h.p. white violets decor on blue ground w/white beading, 5 pcs., G.D.A. (Gerard, Dufraisseix & Abbot) 165.00

Ewer, h.p. violets decor, gold trim, 6" h. 65.00

Fish set: 10½ x 6½" gilt-handled tray, 24" l. platter & twelve 8½" d. plates; various fish in h.p. underwater scene w/shells & seaweed, muted pastels, gold borders, 14 pcs..........................1,025.00

Game plaque, pierced to hang, pheasant decor, gold rim, artist-signed, 9½" d., Coronet (George Borgfeldt importer) 50.00

Game plaques, pierced to hang, grouse decor in earth tones of grey, tan, brown & light orange, artist-signed, 9½" d., pr...........................150.00

Game plaque, pierced to hang, ornate gold scalloped border, colorful quail on pastel ground, artist-signed, 10 1/8" d. 175.00

Game plate, scalloped edge, pr. brown, grey & yellow birds on green & pink ground, artist-signed, 10¾" d. (ILLUS.) 135.00

Limoges Game Plate

Game plate, gold rococo border, partridges (2) at lake shore w/trees in background, artist-signed, pierced to hang, 12¼" d. (ILLUS.) 250.00

Hair receiver, small blue flowers & white butterflies on creamy ivory ground, gold trim, J.P.L. 65.00

Humidor, cov., h.p. bust of Indian
    smoking pipe on gold shaded to
    orange ground 465.00
Ice cream set: 16 x 9" open handled
    tray & eight 6½" d. plates; dainty
    sprays of pink & blue florals &
    foliage, scalloped gold edges,
    9 pcs., Elite (Bowo & Dotter
    importer) 165.00
Ice cream set: 16 x 10½" tray & eight
    6¼" dishes; molded scalloped rims
    w/gold trim, roses & lilacs decor,
    artist-signed, 9 pcs., L.D. & C. 175.00

![Limoges Jardiniere]

Limoges Jardiniere

Jardiniere, ornate gold handles &
    feet, h.p. rose sprays on pastel
    ground, large (ILLUS.) 600.00
Mug, gold handle, h.p. strawberry
    decor, 3¾" h. 65.00
Oyster plate, scalloped edge, garlands
    of pink roses w/green leaves & blue
    ribbons on white ground, gold trim,
    8½" d. 50.00
Pitcher, 5" h., bulbous, beaded
    handle, h.p. waterlilies, gold trim,
    J.P.L. (Jean Pouyat) 125.00
Pitcher, tankard, 13" h., h.p. red
    cherries on shaded lavender to
    purple ground, D. & C. (R.
    Delinieres)........................225.00

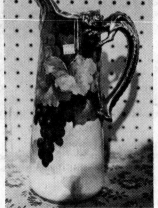

Limoges Tankard Pitcher

Pitcher, tankard, 14" h., stalk handle,
    h.p. grapes & leaves on shaded
    pastel ground, J.P.L. (ILLUS.) 225.00
Plaques, pierced to hang, ornate
    irregular rim, h.p. purple grapes,
    green pears, realistic peaches &
    red persimmons on shaded ground,
    11 3/8" d., pr. 275.00
Plaques, pierced to hang, gold
    rococo rim, h.p. winter country
    scene w/white & gold floral spray
    on shaded blue ground, gold
    trim, 11½" d., pr. 350.00
Plaque, pierced to hang, Dutch scene
    w/people on wharf, sailing ships
    & sea, artist-signed 85.00
Plaques, pierced to hang, gold rococo
    rims, h.p. winter & summer scenes
    of cottage beside a pond, 14 1/8" d.,
    pr................................465.00
Plate, 7½" d., scalloped rim, h.p.
    florals, gold trim, A.K. (Kittel &
    Klingenberg importer)..............48.00
Plate, 8½" d., stippled gold rim,
    h.p. gooseberries, T. & V. (Tresse-
    mann & Vogt) 45.00
Plates, 8½" d., ornate shell & scroll-
    molded rim, cupid scene decal on
    pink & on blue, matching pr.,
    A.L. (Lanternier) double mark 45.00
Plates, 8½" d., scalloped rim, h.p.
    florals & birds, gold trim, ca. 1895,
    set of 6 ....120.00
Plate, 10" d., rococo-molded rim,
    kitten portrait center, artist-
    signed, Coronet 76.00
Plate, 12½" d., h.p. ships at sea
    & women & children on shore,
    T. & V............................95.00
Powder box, cov., h.p. violets decor....50.00
Powder box, cov., pink florals &
    heavy gold paste decor, M.R.
    (Martial Redon)....................30.00
Punch bowl, collared base, ornate
    scroll-molded gold rim, h.p. multi-
    colored grapes & foliage interior
    & exterior decor, 13½" d., 6" h......385.00
Punch set: 13" d. punch bowl & 5 cups;
    h.p. fruit decor, 6 pcs. 285.00
Rose bowl, ruffled rop w/gold trim, 3
    gold feet, h.p. roses on deep pink
    ground, 8" d., 5¾" h...............55.00
Snuff box, h.p. wildflowers & gold
    tracery on pink ground, metal
    mounts, artist-signed & dated 1800 ..190.00
Tea set: cov. teapot, creamer & cov.
    sugar bowl; gold wishbone handles,
    h.p. dogwood decor, 3 pcs..........185.00
Vase, 7½" h., handled, reticulated
    band at neck, man & woman in
    meadow scene on front, relief-
    molded florals & scrollwork high-
    lighted w/gold reverse, M.R.
    Limoges (M. Redon) 100.00

Vase, 12½" h., oval portrait of
"Contemplation" reserved on pale
green lustrous ground w/gilt
details, artist-signed, ca. 1900 ...... 440.00
Vase, 13" h., 10" d., double-twist
handles, narrow neck, wide gold
band at base & brick red band
at neck, autumn florals on body 125.00
Vase, 15½" h., h.p. red poppies &
green leaves & wide gold border
top, artist-signed, T. & V. 250.00
Vase, 15½" h., cylindrical w/flared
base, gold handles, overall wisteria
blossoms w/gold trim on shaded
lavender ground, T. & V. 320.00

LIVERPOOL

Liverpool Creamware Jug

*Liverpool is often used as a generic term
for wares made by numerous potteries in
this English city during the 18th century.
Many wares are unmarked.*

Jug, creamware, transfer-printed in
black w/star-bordered roundel of
patriotic poem flanked by scene of
felling of trees & shipbuilding above
& below on one side & w/American
ship under full sail reverse, compass
beneath spout, rim w/cold-gilded
double-line-enclosed border of
circlets, ca. 1800, 8" h. $550.00
Jug, creamware, transfer-printed in
black w/scene of naval engage-
ment beneath banner inscribed
"Commodore Prebles Squadron
Attacking the City of Tripoli" above
account of battle on one side &
w/classical figures inspecting a
"Plan of the City of Washington"
reverse, cluster of war trophies beneath spout, 1805-10, 9" h.
(ILLUS.) 1,045.00
Jug, creamware, transfer-printed in
black one side w/oval map of the
East Coast flanked by figures of

George Washington & "Liberty"
beneath trumpeting angel of Fame
on left & "Wisdom" & "Justice"
standing behind seated Benjamin
Franklin on the right & w/black &
yellow sailing ship flying a red,
white & blue American flag above
a green sea reverse, oak wreath
inscribed "Success To The Infant
Navy of America" above an embla-
zoned eagle & 15 stars beneath
spout, rim w/cold-gilded border of
patterned panels & tassels, w/traces
of worn cold gilding overall, ca.
1812, 10¼" h. 1,870.00
Jug, creamware, transfer-printed in
black w/American ship inscribed
"Boston Frigate" one side &
w/Washington, "Fame," "Liberty,"
Franklin, "Wisdom" & "Justice" on
reverse, w/grapevine cartouche
w/initials below spout, all highlighted in green, iron-red, blue &
yellow enamel, ca. 1805, 10½" h.
(discolored & hairline below
spout) 1,980.00
Jug, creamware, swelling body
transfer-printed in black w/portrait
medallions of Samuel Adams & John
Hancock below monument inscribed
"The Memory of Washington and
the Proscribed Patriots of America"
one side & w/Continental soldier beneath American flag within husk-
bordered oval reverse, American
eagle below spout, all highlighted in
green, blue, yellow & russet enamel,
dated "1802," 10 7/8" h. (restored
spout) 990.00
Mug, creamware, transfer-printed in
black w/census figures for 1790 ... 3,080.00
Soup plate w/flange rim, transfer-
printed in black w/coat-of-arms
bearing motto "Let Wisdom Unite
Us" in center, black enamel rim,
9 7/8" d. (small edge flakes) 80.00

LLADRO

*Spain's famed Lladro porcelain manu-
factory creates both limited and non-limited
edition figurines as well as other porcelains.
The classic simple beauty of the figures and
their subdued coloring makes them readily
recognizable and they have an enthusiastic
following of collectors.*

Baby Sitter, No. 5083 .... $410.00
Boy Yawning, No. 4870 .... 22.00
Cinderella, No. 4828 .... 90.00
Courtship, No. 5072 .... 275.00

Debbie & Her Doll, No. 1379	85.00
Don Quixote, No. 4854	105.00
Don Quixote, No. 1030, w/stand	580.00
Ducks, No. 4895	26.00
Embroiderer, No. 4865	310.00
Flower Peddler, No. 5029	735.00
Gentle Kiss, No. 2086	210.00
Girl with Calla Lilies, No. 4650	57.00
Girl with Guitar, No. 4871	25.00
Graceful Duo, No. 2073	840.00
Ironing Time, No. 4981	93.00
Lady Tennis Player, No. 4798	100.00
My Dog, No. 4893	66.00

Napping

Napping, No. 5070 (ILLUS.)	200.00
Naughty Dog, No. 4982	140.00
Nostalgia, No. 5071	155.00
Portrait, No. 4942	735.00
Reminiscing, No. 1270	870.00
Rickshaw Ride, No. 1383	1,275.00
Rosita, No. 2085	190.00
Swinging, No. 1366	900.00
Tenderness, No. 2094	110.00
Thai Dancer, No. 2069	375.00
Waiting In The Park, No. 1374	230.00
Wedding, No. 4808	105.00
Wildflower, No. 5030	395.00

LONGWY

This faience factory was established in 1798 in the town of Longwy, France and is noted for its enameled pottery which resembles cloisonne. Utilitarian wares were the first production here but by the 1870s, an oriental style art pottery that imitated "cloisonne" was created through the use of heavy enamels in relief. By 1912, a modern

Art Deco style became part of Longwy's production and these wares, together with the oriental style pieces, have made this art pottery popular with collectors today. As interest in Art Deco has soared in recent years, values of Longwy's modern style wares have risen sharply.

Bowl, 3¾" d., enameled colorful florals on blue interior & light blue exterior	$38.00
Bowl, 5½" d., overall enameled colorful florals on burgundy red interior & blue exterior	55.00
Compote, 10" d., enameled multicolored decor on brilliant blue ground	295.00
Tile, footed, enameled ornate coat-of-arms center & deep pink, blue & yellow geometric design overall, 8¼" sq.	125.00
Vase, 4" h., 3" w., bulbous opening, narrow base, incised & enameled gold, blue & black geometric decor on eggshell "crackle" ground	95.00
Vase, 4½" h., 2" d., cylindrical, enameled colorful florals on deep purple ground	55.00
Vase, 6½" h., 3" d., cylindrical, enameled colorful floral on vivid blue ground w/white reserve of colorful bird w/outstretched wings perched on branch of pink apple blossoms	160.00
Vase, 7¼" h., 3" d., cylindrical, enameled top border & colorful florals on blue ground	155.00
Vase, 10¼" h., baluster-shaped, enameled florals on yellow ground	195.00

LOTUS WARE

Sugar Bowl with Fishnet Decor

Avidly sought by many collectors are these exquisite bone china wares made by Knowles, Taylor & Knowles, of East Liverpool, Ohio, in the last decade of the 19th

*century and into the 20th. The firm also
produced ironstone and hotel china.*

Creamer, plain, shaded to lemon
    yellow...........................$95.00
Creamer, violets decor, artist-signed . .125.00
Pitcher, 3½" h., twig handle & rim
    w/gold trim, white, fishnet panels
    separated by plain panels w/h.p.
    yellow & purple florals............295.00
Sugar bowl, cov., white, fishnet panels
    separated by plain panels w/h.p.
    florals (ILLUS.)...................700.00
Vase, 4¼" h., 5" d., beaded & ruffled
    rim w/band of beading extending
    ½" down neck, h.p. wild roses
    decor, gold trim...................325.00
Vase, 6" h., jardiniere shape, h.p.
    florals on body, heavy gold trim at
    ruffled rim........................600.00
Vase, 8" h., 5" d., straight-sided
    cylinder w/ball feet, white, fishnet
    panels separated by panels of h.p.
    orange & green florals.............520.00

LUSTRE WARES

"General Jackson" Commemorative Pitcher

*Lustred wares in imitation of copper,
gold, silver and other colors were produced
in England in the early 19th century and onward. Gold, copper or platinum oxides were
painted on glazed objects which were then
fired, giving them a lustred effect. Various
forms of lustre wares include plain lustre--
with the entire object coated to obtain a
metallic effect, bands of lustre decoration
and painted lustre designs. Particularly
appealing is the pink or purple "splash
lustre" sometimes referred to as "Sunderland" lustre in the mistaken belief it was
confined to the production of Sunderland
area potteries. Objects decorated in silver
lustre by the "resist" process, wherein parts
of the objects to be left free from lustre
decoration were treated with wax, are referred to as "silver resist."*

COPPER

Bowl, 2 5/8" h., copper lustre body
    w/cobalt blue band & floral decor . . .$35.00
Coffee pot, cov., copper lustre body
    w/scenes in pink lustre...........250.00
Goblet, copper luster body w/wide
    cream band filled w/pink lustre
    sprigs.............................75.00
Mug, copper lustre body w/blue band
    decor, 2¾" h.......................45.00
Mug, copper lustre body w/yellow cen-
    ter band & teal blue stripes decor,
    purple lustre interior rim, 2¾" h. 25.00
Mugs, copper lustre body w/wide blue
    band highlighted w/enameled
    florals, 3" h., pr..................95.00
Mug, coppper lustre body w/blue &
    green bands decor..................42.00
Pitcher, 3" h., copper lustre body
    w/cobalt blue band decor...........35.00
Pitcher, 3 1/8" h., copper lustre body
    w/purple transfer-printed scenes in
    white reserves & enameled "Hope,"
    purple lustre trim.................85.00
Pitcher, 4½" h., copper lustre body
    w/wide canary yellow band transfer-
    printed in rust w/scenes of classical
    lady playing badminton highlighted
    in green & blue enamels............45.00
Pitcher, 5" h., copper lustre body
    w/wide embossed band decor.......95.00
Pitcher, 5" h., jug-type, copper lustre
    body w/enameled floral decor.......75.00
Pitcher, 5¼" h., copper lustre body
    w/wide blue center band...........65.00
Pitcher, 5¾" h., jug-type, embossed
    horizontal reeding on neck & base
    flanking tomato red band reserved
    on each side w/oval panel transfer-
    printed in black w/bust portrait of
    "General Jackson," & w/oval panel
    of fruit under spout, all edged in
    black enamel & flanked by foliate
    sprays, ca. 1828.................1,045.00
Pitcher, 6" h., copper lustre body
    w/wide blue band embossed
    w/dancing figures.................65.00
Pitcher, 6 3/8" h., jug-type, copper
    lustre body w/embossed horizontal
    reeding on neck & base flanking
    tomato red band reserved w/oval
    panels transfer-printed in black
    w/portrait inscribed "Lafayette" one
    side & w/military scene inscribed
    "Cornwallis Resigning his Sword at
    York Town Oct. 1781" reverse,
    w/cluster of fruit within black-
    enameled borders w/foliate sprays
    beneath spout, Staffordshire,
    1825-30............................715.00
Pitcher, 7" h., jug-type, copper lustre
    body w/embossed dancing figures . . .95.00
Pitcher, 7" h., copper lustre body
    w/yellow band decor................80.00

Pitcher, 7¾" h., jug-type, copper lustre
body w/embossed beading around
rim, wide blue center band transfer-
printed in black on each side w/bust
portrait of "General Jackson The
Hero of New Orleans" & w/cluster
of fruit beneath spout, ca. 1828
(ILLUS.) 1,100.00
Pitcher, copper lustre body w/relief-
molded stag scene 80.00

Copper Lustre Teapot

Teapot, cov., griffin handle, copper
lustre body, ca. 1840, 6" h. (ILLUS.) . .180.00
Teapot, cov., copper lustre body
w/enameled blue & yellow florals,
8" h. 110.00
Teapot, cov., flattened globular form
w/domed lid, gooseneck spout,
C-scroll handle & scrolling feet,
copper lustre body w/white
enameled floral decor 195.00

SILVER & SILVER RESIST

Jug with Silver Lustre Trim

Pitchers, jug-type: 5¾" h. "silver
resist" lustre w/spotted dog one
side & bird perched amidst flowering shrubbery reverse beneath border of horizontal silver lustre lines;
5 5/8" h. transfer-printed in black
& enameled in iron-red, purple,
yellow, black & green on each side
w/pr. of birds perched on thistle
plant within silver lustre foliate

roundel, w/silver lustre borders on
rims, Leeds & Staffordshire, 1810-15,
pr. 440.00
Pitcher, 6" h., octagonal jug-type,
early 20th c. 58.00
Pitcher, 6 3/8" h., jug-type, "silver
resist" lustre floral ground reserved
w/roundel transfer-printed in black
& enameled in iron-red, blue, black,
yellow & green w/robin on oak
branch each side, ca. 1815, minute
chips at neck (ILLUS.) 715.00
Tea set: cov. teapot, creamer & sugar
bowl; silver lustre bands & ivory
classical figures on dark brown
ground, Gibsons, England, 1909-30,
3 pcs. 275.00

SUNDERLAND PINK & OTHERS

Pink Lustre Jug dated 1817

Bowl, 5 7/8" d., 2 7/8" h., pink lustre
band of florals & leaves interior
rim, medallions of pink lustre birds
& floral exterior 65.00
Bowl, 6" d., 2½" h., pink lustre House
patt. 58.00
Creamer, pink lustre scenic decor,
2½" h. 45.00
Cup, handleless, pink lustre House
patt. 25.00
Cup & saucer, handleless, h.p. pink
lustre florals . . . . .55.00 to 60.00
Cup & saucer, handleless, h.p. pink
lustre foliate scrolls decor, ca. 1850 . .45.00
Cup & saucer, pink lustre House patt. . . .40.00
Cup & saucer, wishbone handle, trans-
fer-printed in black w/scene of
Moses in Bulrushes, painted blue
clouds & pink lustre leaves border
on white ground 55.00
Goblet, straight sides, pink splash
lustre ground, attributed to
Sunderland 185.00
Mug, 2-handled, h.p. pink lustre sea-
shells decor 62.50
Pitcher, 6¾" h., jug-type, pear-shaped

body w/pale buff ground transfer-
printed in black each side w/roman-
tic view of figures on river bank (one
identified as "Kirkham River") &
inscribed "R & J Jackson - Strand,
1817, London" beneath spout,
w/wide blue border at neck w/pink
lustre & enameled green florals
within pink lustre borders &
w/foliate-molded spout, handle &
rim in pink lustre, Staffordshire,
dated 1817 (ILLUS.) 550.00
Pitcher, 8½" h., jug-type, transfer-
printed in black w/verse "Success to
All Sailors" & "A West View of the
Iron Bridge at Sunderland" & highlighted w/polychrome enameling on
pink splash lustre ground (some
edge wear) 175.00
Pitcher, 9 1/8" h., jug-type, transfer-
printed in black w/view of the Iron
Bridge & w/sailor's rhyme one side &
version of "Sailor's Farewell" reverse,
all within pink splash lustre borders,
Sunderland, ca. 1830 . . . . 385.00
Pitcher, 9 3/8" h., jug-type, transfer-
printed in brown & enameled in
brown, green, ochre & blue w/three
children inscribed "Jane," "Richard"
& "James" above their heads one
side & w/a rhyme within border of
Masonic devices below inscription
"Elizabeth Stroud, 1828," w/maiden
near temple & additional Masonic
emblems reverse, all within purple-
pink lustre bands, Staffordshire,
dated 1828 . . . . 770.00
Plaque, pierced to hang, inscribed
"The Rev. John Wesley, A.M. Wes-
leyan Methodist Society Established
1739. The Best of All God is With
Us" on white ground center, pink
splash lustre borders, 7½" w. 225.00
Plaque, pierced to hang, transfer-
printed in black w/nautical scene
center, pink splash lustre borders,
ca. 1830 . . . . 375.00
Plaque, pierced to hang, inscribed
"Prepare to Meet Thy God" in black
on white center, pink splash lustre
borders w/copper lustre edges 225.00
Plate, 7" d., pink splash lustre 15.00
Plate, 7¼" d., h.p. pink lustre florals
& scrolls 20.00
Salt dip, pedestal base, pink splash
lustre 75.00

MAJOLICA

*Majolica, a tin-enameled-glazed pottery,
has been produced for centuries. It*
*originally took its name from the island of
Majorca, a source of figuline (potter's clay).
Subsequently it was widely produced in
England, Europe and the United States.
Etruscan majolica, now avidly sought, was
made by Griffen, Smith & Hill, Phoenix-
ville, Pa., in the last quarter of the 19th
century. Most majolica advertised today is
19th or 20th century. Once scorned by most
collectors, interest in this colorful ware so
popular during the Victorian era has now
revived and prices have risen dramatically
in the past two years. Also see MINTON,
OYSTER PLATES and SARREGUE-
MINES.*

ETRUSCAN

Etruscan Daisy Pattern Compote

Bowl, salad, 8¼" d., footed, Shell
patt. w/molded small shells at foot-
rim, pink lining $300.00
Bowl, 8½" d., Shell & Seaweed
patt. 125.00 to 225.00
Bowl, 9¾" d., Classical Series patt.,
low relief mythological figures
center & grapevine border, overall
brown glaze . . . . 75.00 to 80.00
Bowl,, 9¾" d., Classical Series patt.,
low relief mythological figures
center & grapevine border, green &
pink on white 110.00
Bread tray, Oak patt., 12 x
9½" . . . . 85.00 to 125.00
Butter pat, Begonia Leaf patt., 3¾" l. . . . 24.00
Butter pat, Pansy patt. 20.00
Cake stand, footed, Maple Leaves
patt., tree trunk foot . . . . . . 135.00 to 195.00
Compote, 9" d., 5½" h., Grape Leaf
patt. 145.00
Compote, 9½" d., Grape Leaf patt. on
pink ground 140.00
Compote, Classical Series patt., sepia . . 70.00
Compote (or centerpiece), tall pedestal
Shell & Seaweed patt. 750.00
Compote, salad, 9" d., 5" h., Daisy
patt. (ILLUS.) 130.00
Creamer, Albino Shell & Seaweed
patt., pink lining, 4" h. 295.00
Creamer, Corn (or Maize) patt., model
of ear of corn, pink lining 80.00
Creamer, Shell & Seaweed patt.,
pink . . . . 125.00 to 225.00

Creamer & cov. sugar bowl, Shell &
 Seaweed patt., pr. 475.00
Cup & saucer, Shell & Seaweed patt. . . . 190.00
Dish, leaf-shaped, 9" l. . . . . 40.00 to 47.00
Humidor, cov., Shell & Seaweed
 patt. 950.00
Mug, Acorn patt., acorn branch on
 yellow basketweave w/brown edges
 & lavender lining, 3½" h. 125.00
Pitcher, 8" h., Corn (or Maize) patt.,
 model of ear of corn, pink lining 145.00
Pitcher, milk, Shell & Seaweed patt. . . . 275.00
Pitcher, water, Shell & Seaweed
 patt. 450.00
Pitcher, Wild Rose patt. w/butterfly
 lip 125.00
Plate, 7" d., Albino Shell & Seaweed
 patt. 95.00
Plate, 7" d., Cauliflower patt. 70.00
Plate, 7" d., Rose patt. 55.00
Plate, 7¾" d., Leaf on Plate patt.,
 green leaf on yellow basketweave . . . 45.00
Plate, 8" d., Bamboo patt. 75.00
Plate, 8¼" d., Blackberry & Basket-
 weave patt. . . . . 55.00 to 70.00
Plate, 8¾" d., Leaf on Plate patt.,
 green leaf on yellow basketweave . . . 65.00
Plate, 9" d., Begonia Leaf patt.,
 5 overlapping Begonia leaves 100.00
Plate, 9" d., Classical Series patt.,
 low relief mythological figures in
 green center, grey border. 45.00
Plate, 9" d., Maple Leaves patt.,
 sprigs of leaves on pink ground 175.00
Plate, 9" d., Strawberry patt. on white
 ground . . . . 75.00 to 90.00
Sauce dish, Daisy patt. 125.00
Sauce dish, Smilax patt. 80.00
Syrup pitcher w/pewter lid, Bamboo
 patt. 395.00
Syrup pitcher w/pewter lid, Coral
 patt. 375.00
Syrup pitcher w/pewter lid, Shell &
 Seaweed patt., 7" h. 145.00

Etruscan Sunflower Pattern Syrup

Syrup pitcher w/pewter lid, Sunflower
 patt. on pink ground (ILLUS.) 250.00
Teapot, cov., Bamboo patt. 198.00
Tea set: 6¾" teapot, 4½" h. creamer
 & 6" h. cov. sugar bowl; Bamboo
 patt., 3 pcs. . . . . 295.00 to 335.00

Begonia Leaf Tray

Tray, Begonia Leaf patt., leaf-shaped
 w/yellow edge, 9" l.
 (ILLUS.) . . . . 45.00 to 55.00
Tray, Begonia Leaf patt., leaf-shaped,
 green w/pink-yellow edges,
 12 x 9¼". 69.00

GENERAL

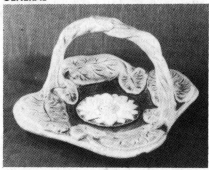

Magnolia Basket

Basket, twisted stalk handle, sunflower centered on cobalt blue,
 green leaves border, 8 x 8"
 (ILLUS.) 150.00
Bottle, model of a beige barrel
 w/brown staves, branch forming
 spout w/cork stopper at side,
 figural humped cat atop, numbered
 on base, 4¼" w., 6" h. 65.00
Bowl, 6" d., Begonia Leaf patt. 25.00
Bowl, 11" d., 5¼" h., pink & yellow
 florals, green leaves & brown
 branches on light green stippled
 ground 95.00
Bowl, 11" d., handled, yellow daisies
 & green leaves on turquoise ground,
 Germany 78.00

Bowl, 11" d., 2-handled, multicolored leaves, squash blossoms
& vines decor......................70.00
Bowl, 11" d., footed, Pond Lily
patt. by J. Holdcroft, white lilies
& buds on turquoise green pads.....130.00
Bowl, fruit, 12 x 9½", 4" h.,
shell-shaped w/three applied
shell feet, light blue exterior,
lavender interior 85.00
Bread plate, Pineapple patt., round 85.00
Bread tray, Corn (or Maize) patt.,
12" long 145.00
Butter dish, cov., Bamboo & Basketweave patt., 8" d., 4" h. 225.00
Butter dish, cov., Shell, Seaweed &
Waves patt., 7" d..................150.00
Butter pats, Leaf patt., set of 4........78.00
Butter tub & cover w/recumbent cow
finial, mottled green & yellow on
brown, marked "Royal Art Pottery,
England," 4" d., 3" h..............35.00
Butter tub & cover w/recumbent cow
finial, fence w/leaves on bucket-
type sides, Germany 70.00
Cake plates, berries, blossoms &
leaves outlined in gold & green on
cream ground, "Avalon Faience,"
Chesapeake Pottery Co., Baltimore,
set of 8 ....150.00
Cake set: master cake plate & 6 serving
plates; red cherry clusters, green
leaves & brown branches on blue-
green ground, Czechoslovakia,
7 pcs. 75.00
Cake stand, geranium blossoms &
leaves decor, greens & deep yellow
gold...............................85.00
Cake stand on low foot, Leaf on Plate
patt., green maple leaf on sky blue
ground w/yellow edge, 9" d. 135.00
Carafe, water, bulbous, Pineapple
patt. 345.00
Cheese dish, cov., blackberry blossoms
& branches on mottled ground,
large, 2 pcs.......................350.00

Cigarette holder, figural Elephant,
English, overall 8" h. (ILLUS.) 250.00
Compote, 9½" d., 5¼" h., Bellflower
patt. w/leaves on cobalt blue
ground 150.00
Chocolate set: cov. chocolate pot,
creamer, cov. sugar bowl & 4 mugs;
pedestal footed items, green
orchids & leaves decor on brownish
yellow ground, unmarked, ca. 1930,
7 pcs. 85.00
Cookie jar & cover w/twig finial,
wicker bail handle, red apples
w/green & yellow leaves decor
on green basketweave ground,
unmarked 58.00
Creamer, Basketweave & Floral patt.,
pale green w/brown & cream,
5".......................27.00 to 35.00
Creamer, Corn (or Maize) patt.,
3½" h. 70.00
Creamer, Pineapple patt., pink
interior, 2½" h....................125.00
Creamer, Wild Rose on Tree Bark
patt., blue ground, 4½" h. 65.00
Creamer & cov. sugar bowl, Blackberry patt. on turquoise ground,
creamer w/lavender lining, English
registry mark, pr..................75.00
Creamer & cov. sugar bowl, Fern &
Bamboo patt., green & brown,
Wardle & Co., Hanley, England,
large, pr. 115.00
Creamer & open sugar bowl, Picket
Fence patt., pr. 80.00
Cup & saucer, Bird & Fan patt.,
Shorter & Boulton, English registry
mark ....110.00 to 125.00
Cup & saucer, Bird & Fan patt.,
Wardle & Co., Hanley, England,
large 175.00
Cup & saucer, Pineapple patt. 45.00
Cup & saucer, Shell & Seaweed patt.
w/figural fish handle, yellow &
brown shells on cobalt blue 135.00
Cuspidor, lady's, Treebark patt.,
6½".............................125.00
Dish, fan-shaped, Fan & Bow patt.,
blended brown, yellow & lavender,
6½" l.............................65.00
Dish, Fern Leaf patt., 7" l..............29.00

Elephant Cigarette Holder

Fish Dish

Dish, fish-shaped, green, black, cream
  & brown, 7" l. (ILLUS.) 35.00
Dish, Begonia Leaf patt., rose, 7½" l....35.00
Dish, large pink roses on cobalt blue
  ground, 8" l. 50.00
Dish, Begonia Leaf patt., white w/blue,
  8½" l..............................27.00
Flower pot, birds & florals on turquoise
  ground, England, 6" h...............32.00
Humidor & cover w/pipe finial,
  bulbous, scalloped foot, portrait of
  man smoking pipe on basketweave
  ground, Germany, numbered on
  base, 6" d., 7" h....................70.00
Humidor, cov., "Sunny Bank" (tobacco),
  "Spaulding & Merrick, Chicago,"
  berries, blossoms & leaves on
  white, marked "Avalon Faience,"
  Chesapeake Pottery, Baltimore.....135.00
Jardiniere, florals & leaves decor,
  10½ x 9½"...........................120.00
Match holder, model of a green apple
  atop a basketweave plate w/leaves
  & branch, apple lifts to expose cobalt
  blue match holder, marked "Boch-
  Luxembourg" 165.00
Match & cigar holder, figural boy
  w/basket of fish, multicolored......110.00
Mug, Corn (or Maize) patt., 5" h. 35.00
Mustache cup, floral & leaf on brown
  shaded to tan w/blue center band....65.00
Pitcher, 4" h., brown handle & base,
  pink flowers on blue ground.........45.00
Pitcher, 4½" h., Aster patt. 60.00
Pitcher, 4½" h., Blackberry Fence
  patt., unmarked 40.00
Pitcher, 6" h., Fish on Waves patt.,
  Shorter & Boulton,
  England ....110.00 to 165.00
Pitcher, 6" h., angular squared body
  w/square top, yellow daisy on white
  mid-banding of soft blue ground 70.00
Pitcher, 6" h., Hawthorne patt., green ..75.00
Pitcher, 6¼" h., sheaf of wheat on
  cobalt blue ground 78.00
Pitcher, 6½" h., Blackberry patt.......100.00
Pitcher, 6½" h., triangular body, Owl
  & Fan patt................85.00 to 110.00

Majolica Monkey Pitchers

Pitchers, 6 5/8 to 8 7/8" h., each
  modeled as a monkey seated before

bundle of bamboo leaves, realisti-
  cally colored, lavender linings,
  Staffordshire, ca. 1880, graduated
  set of 3 (ILLUS. of pr.) 3,520.00
Pitcher, 9" h., Fern & Bamboo patt.,
  Wardle & Co., England............140.00
Pitcher, 9½" h., Wild Rose on Tree
  Bark patt........................85.00
Pitcher, 10½" h., Blossoms & Berries
  on Tree Bark patt., Holdcroft,
  England 75.00
Pitcher, 10½" h., colorful figural fish
  w/leaves at base 130.00
Pitcher, 11¼" h., figural white swan
  forms top, green & brown cattails
  on turquoise ground at base.......275.00
Pitcher, 12¾" h., figural duck w/cat-
  tail handle, marked "St. Clement
  France"...........................90.00
Planter, Leaves & Fern patt., 12" 90.00
Planter, Shell & Seaweed patt.,
  England, 6" 80.00
Plate, 5½" d., Begonia Leaf patt. 45.00
Plate, 6" d., Snail Shell patt., Fielding
  & Co., English registry mark 30.00
Plate, 7" d., Maple Leaf patt. 45.00
Plate, 7" d., Sunflower patt............32.50
Plate, 7½" d., Blackberry & Basket-
  weave patt., mottled center decor,
  white ground ....35.00 to 40.00
Plate, 7¾" d., cherries decor, brown
  glaze, marked "Sarreguemines" 22.00
Plates, 8¼" d., green leaves on ivory
  ground, French, set of 4...........100.00
Plate, 9" d., Pond Lily patt.............50.00

Majolica Plate

Plate, 10" d., multicolored florals
  & bamboo leaves on basketweave
  ground (ILLUS.) 55.00
Plate, 10½" d., Blackberry & Basketweave patt., mottled center,
  turquoise ground 65.00

Plate, 10½" d., brewmaster on keg
decor, pink & brown 40.00
Plate, 10¾" d., strawberries decor on
ribbed ground, Clifton-Avalon,
Chesapeake Pottery, Baltimore 105.00
Plate, 11½" d., Shaggy Dog & Dog-
house patt. 75.00
Platter, 9½" l., twig handles, over-
lapping leaves edged in brown, red
& blue floral decor on buff ground 65.00
Platter, 9¾" oval, Blackberry patt.,
"Clifton" Chesapeake Pottery,
Baltimore 60.00
Platter, 12 x 8¼", Begonia Leaf patt.,
mottled brown w/yellow & green
w/white edge 58.00

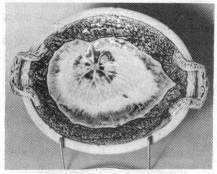

Begonia Leaf on Bark Platter

Platter, 12½" l., Begonia Leaf on Bark
patt. (ILLUS.) .95.00
Platter, 13" l., pierced handle, Acorn
patt. 85.00
Platter 13¼" oval, Fan & Butterfly
patt., blue ground 135.00
Platter, 14 x 11", Begonia patt., rope
trim on basketweave ground 125.00
Platter, 14" oval, Mottled Center
patt. 125.00
Platter, Wild Rose patt. w/eyelet
handles 65.00
Punch bowl, Blackberry patt., "Avalon
Faience," Chesapeake Pottery,
Baltimore 95.00
Sardine box & cover w/fish finial,
attached underplate, Pineapple
patt., 9½" l 185.00
Sardine box, cover w/realistic fishes &
undertray, upright acanthus leaves on
pale turquoise sides, George Jones,
England, 3 pcs. 750.00
Sauce dish, Bird & Fan patt., cobalt
or turquoise blue ground, Shorter &
Boulton, England, each 50.00
Sauce dish, Pineapple patt., mottled
brown & beige center, 5" d. 85.00
Syrup pitcher w/original lid, Maple
Leaf patt. 130.00
Syrup pitcher w/pewter lid, Pineapple
patt., 4 3/8" 125.00

Syrup pitcher w/pewter lid, Raspberry &
Foliage patt., signed "Bennett's Jan.
23, 1873 Patent" printed on base 135.00
Syrup pitcher w/pewter lid, brown twig
handle, daisies decor on tan, blue
lining 140.00
Syrup pitcher w/pewter lid, Birds on
Holly patt., "Bennett's Jan. 23, 1873
Patent" stamped on base 85.00
Teapot, cov., Bird & Fan patt., Wardle
& Co., England, 4½" h. 105.00
Teapot, cov., Pineapple patt., white
lining 300.00
Teapot, cov., bamboo-molded handle,
blue, yellow & pink bird decor,
English registry mark 145.00
Vases, 7" h., figural boy & girl
standing beside wicker-encased
bottle-vases, pr. 90.00
Vase, 8½" h., Art Nouveau style,
ornate handles, Iris decor 65.00

MARBLEHEAD POTTERY

Marblehead Pottery Mark

*This pottery was organized in 1904 by Dr.
Herbert J. Hall as a therapeutic aid to
patients in a sanitarium he ran in
Marblehead, Massachusetts. It was later
separated from the sanitarium and directed
by Arthur E. Baggs, a fine artist and
designer, who bought out the factory in
1916 and operated it until its closing in
1936. Most wares were hand-thrown and
decorated and carry the company mark of a
stylized sailing vessel flanked by the letters
"M" and "P."*

Basket, hanging-type, blue glaze $65.00
Bowl, 4" d., melon-ribbed, mottled
brown glaze .95.00
Bowl, 6½" d., low, blue glaze 45.00
Bowl w/flower frog, pink glaze, small . .58.00
Candle holder, chamberstick-type
w/ring handle, blue glaze 65.00
Creamer, mottled blue glaze, 3" h. 60.00
Lamp base, mustard yellow glaze,
impressed mark & original paper
labels, 12" h. base (fitted w/two-
bulb attachment & harp for shade) . .450.00

Marblehead Pottery Tile

Tile, 6" sq. (ILLUS.) 250.00
Vase, 2¾" h., inverted bell form,
  cobalt blue glaze 75.00
Vase, 3½" h., dark green glaze 45.00
Vase, 3½" h., squat form, cobalt blue
  glaze. 75.00
Vase, 3½" h., mottled brown glaze . . .125.00
Vase, 4" h., grey & blue speckled
  glaze . . . . 65.00 to 70.00
Vase, 4 x 6½", turquoise blue
  glaze. 105.00
Vase, 4¼" h., 5" d., inverted bell
  shape, 2" incised neck border w/red,
  orange & green berries on dark blue
  ground w/bright blue interior 675.00
Vase, 4½" h., wide cylindrical form,
  cobalt blue glaze 85.00
Vase, 4¾" h., slender cylinder, cobalt
  blue glaze 65.00
Vase, 5" h., grey designs on matte
  blue ground 60.00
Vase, 5½" h., wisteria decor 95.00
Vase, 6" h., 7¼" w., fan-shaped,
  dark blue glaze 48.00
Vase, 9" h., mottled lavender glaze . . .115.00
Vase, 12" h., stem & leaf in relief,
  tan on grey granulated ground,
  signed Hannah Tutt 425.00
Wall pocket, bean-shaped w/fine-
  ribbed horizontal lines & scalloped
  top, pink glaze, 5" h. 88.00
Wall pocket, incised decor of bird
  sitting in tree, 5" w., 7" h. 400.00

MARTIN BROTHERS POTTERY

*Martinware, the term used for this
pottery, dates from 1873 and is the product
of the Martin brothers--Robert, Wallace,
Edwin, Walter and Charles Martin, often
considered the first British studio potters.*

*From first to final stages, their hand-thrown
pottery was completely the work of the
team. The early wares may be simple and
conventional, but the Martin brothers built
up their reputation by producing ornately
engraved, incised or carved designs on their
wares. The amusing face-jugs are considered some of their finest work. After
1910, the work of the pottery declined and
can be considered finished by 1915, though
some attempts were made to fire pottery as
late as the 1920s.*

Ewer, squared sides, loop handle
  molded w/seaweed continuing to
  meet neck at one corner, incised
  wriggling sea & shellfish on body,
  olive & grey-blue glaze w/touches
  of ochre, dated 1897, 10 5/8" h. . .$1,650.00
Model of a Chimpanzee on pedestal,
  5" h. 200.00

Martin Brothers Stoneware Birds

Model of a grotesque bird w/remov-
  able head, stoneware, olive, grey,
  sapphire, green & beige glaze, on
  circular wooden base, 1904, 9" h.
  (ILLUS. left) .3,410.00
Model of a grotesque bird w/remov-
  able head, stoneware, blue, grey-
  blue, olive & beige glaze, on circular
  wooden base, 9¾" h. (ILLUS.
  right) 3,410.00
Pitcher, 10" h., incised birds decor 175.00
Spoonwarmer, stoneware, modeled as
  a globular grotesque reptilian
  creature w/wide gaping mouth &
  applied w/C-scroll handle at one
  side, mottled olive brown glaze
  w/blue highlights, dated October,
  1889 (ILLUS. left) 880.00
Stein, blue foliage & monogram decor,
  5" h. 105.00
Vase, 5" h., incised floral decor 90.00
Vase, 5" h., 7" d., squashed form, red
  & brown streaked lustre glaze 175.00

Vase, 6" h., squashed form, red &
  brown streaked glaze 140.00
Vase, 8" h., ovoid, modeled w/various
  underwater fishes swimming in
  luminous waters, glazed in tones of
  blue, mauve, burgundy & green,
  dated November, 1906 ....880.00

Martin Brothers Spoonwarmer & Vase

Vase, 9" h., globular w/simple reeded
  neck, incised birds & dragonfly
  amidst profusion of summer
  blossoms, deep & light blue, pink,
  burgundy, white & green on
  speckled tan ground, dated April,
  1889 (ILLUS. right)...............660.00
Vase, 9¾" h., cylindrical neck incised
  & glazed w/overlapping leafage in
  olive & blue, ovoid body incised
  w/dragonflies & a butterfly hovering
  above spring flowers, muted green &
  blue glaze on cream ground, dated
  September, 1883.................440.00

MASSIER (Clement) POTTERY

Clement Massier Vase

*Clement Massier was a French artist
potter who worked in the late 19th and early
20th centuries creating exquisite earthenware items with lustre decoration.*

Jardiniere, fruit-laden vines decor, iridescent green, aqua, burgundy &
  rose glaze, 12" h. $575.00
Jug, handled, Persian-style decor,
  iridescent gold glaze, signed
  "Clement Massier - Golfe-Juan,"
  12" h. 350.00
Toothpick holder, iridescent glaze,
  signed..........................125.00
Vase, 3½" h., iridescent red & gold
  glaze, signed "C.M., G.J.," 1889 ....100.00
Vase, 4¾" h., pinched form in metal
  floral mount, purple-blue iridescent
  glaze, signed "C. Massier Golfe-
  Juan" 400.00
Vase, 9" h., double gourd form,
  berries & vines decor, iridescent
  green & gold lustre glaze, signed
  "C.M. Golfe-Juan" (ILLUS.) 450.00

MC COY

Caboose Cookie Jar

*Collectors are now beginning to seek the
art wares of two McCoy potteries. One was
founded in Roseville, O., in the late 19th
century as the J.W. McCoy Pottery, subsequently becoming Brush-McCoy Pottery
Co., later Brush Pottery. The other was
founded also in Roseville in 1910 as Nelson
McCoy Sanitary Stoneware Co., later becoming Nelson McCoy Pottery. In 1967 the
pottery was sold to D.T. Chase of the
Mount Clemens Pottery Co., who sold his
interest to the Lancaster Colony Corp. in
1974. Productions of this company are still
marked McCoy and Nelson McCoy, Jr. is
President of the company known yet as the
Nelson McCoy Pottery Co.*

Ale set: tankard pitcher & 6 mugs;
  relief-molded buccaneer figure
  on sides, green glaze, ca. 1926,
  set.............................$125.00

Basket, Rustic line, pinecone decor,
  1945-47 . . . . .25.00
Basket, hanging-type, cherries &
  leaves motif, green matt glaze,
  Nelson-McCoy, 1935 . . . . .35.00
Bowl, Mont Pelee, lava-type w/char-
  coal iridescence, 1902 . . . . .325.00
Casserole, cov., cherries decor on
  ivory ground, square, Brush McCoy . . .14.00
Cookie jar, Animal Crackers, 1959-60 . . .25.00
Cookie jar, Apple, 1950-64 . . . . .16.00
Cookie jar, Banana Bunch, 1950-52 . . . . .24.00
Cookie jar, Barrel, 1971-72 . . . . .20.00
Cookie jar, Bean Pot, black, 1939-43 . . . .20.00
Cookie jar, Bobby Baker, 1974-75 . . . . . .22.00
Cookie jar, Bugs Bunny, 1971-72 . . . . . . .25.00
Cookie jar, Caboose, 1961 (ILLUS.) 50.00
Cookie jar, Coalby Cat, 1967 . . .65.00 to 75.00
Cookie jar, Coffee Mug, 1965 . . . . .18.00
Cookie jar, Ear of Corn, 1959 . . . . .60.00
Cookie jar, Fireplace, 1967 . . . . .28.00
Cookie jar, Green Pepper, 1972-75 . . . . .19.00
Cookie jar, Hamm's Beer, 1972 . . . . .55.00
Cookie jar, Humpty Dumpty, 1970 . . . . .42.00
Cookie jar, Kittens (Three) & Ball of
  Yarn, 1954-55 .20.00
Cookie jar, Locomotive Engine,
  1963-64 . . . . .45.00
Cookie jar, Love Birds (Kissing
  Penguins), 1945 . . . . .27.00
Cookie jar, "Mac" Dog, 1967 . . .35.00 to 40.00
Cookie jar, Monk, 1970 . . . . .20.00
Cuspidor, lady's, Nurock line, mottled
  yellow & brown Rockingham-type
  glaze, 3½" h., 1916 . . . . .22.50
Jardiniere, underglaze slip-painted
  tulips, brown glaze, marked
  Loy-Nel-Art 75.00
Jardiniere & pedestal base, diamond-
  quilted w/molded leaves at rim,
  celadon green glaze, 1950s, 2 pcs. . . .75.00
Mug, 3-handled, underglaze slip-
  painted florals, brown glaze,
  marked Loy-Nel-Art 110.00
Mug, barrel-shaped, brown glaze,
  Nelson McCoy 8.50
Pitcher, model of a chicken, creamy
  white glaze, 1943 . . . . .16.00
Pitcher, tankard, Corn line, 1910 . . . . . . .50.00

Bird Dog Planter

Planter, Bird Dog before a fence
  w/"No Hunting" sign, 1954, 12" l.,
  8½" h. (ILLUS.) 35.00
Planter, Chinese Man w/Wheelbarrow,
  yellow, 1950 . . . . .20.00
Planter, Frog w/Umbrella, 1954 . . . . .35.00
Planter, Poodle Dog, 1956 . . . . .10.00
Planter, Rocking Chair, 1954 . . . . .15.00
Planter, Rooster, 1941 . . . . .8.00
Soup tureen w/sombrero cover, El
  Rancho Bar-B-Que, 1960 . . . . .55.00
Tea set: teapot, creamer & sugar bowl;
  Pinecone patt., 1946, 3 pcs. 36.00
Vases, 8" h., blue hyacinths & green
  leaves, 1950, pr. 20.00
Vase, 10" h., figural lizard handles,
  Nelson McCoy Sanitary Stoneware
  Co., 1926 . . . . .22.00
Vase, 10½" h., 2-handled, underglaze
  slip-painted berries & leaves, brown
  glaze, Loy-Nel-Art 170.00
Wall pockets, fan-shaped, Blossom-
  time patt., 1947, pr. 18.00
Wall pocket, model of a mail box,
  green, 1951 . . . . .15.00

Cornucopia Wall Pocket

Wall pocket, cornucopia-shaped, beige
  on green basketweave, 1956, 8" l.
  (ILLUS.) 22.50

MEISSEN

   *The secret of true hard-paste porcelain,
known long before to the Chinese, was "discovered" accidentally in Meissen, Germany,
by J.F. Bottger, an alchemist, working with
E.W. Tschirnhausen, and the first European true porcelain was made in the
Meissen Porcelain Works organized about
1709. Meissen marks have been widely
copied by other factories. Some pieces listed
here are recent.*

Beaker, flaring rim painted in gilt
w/interlocking scrolls, flowerheads &
foliage, lower part molded in high
relief w/band of acanthus leaves,
gilt interior, ca. 1720 (minute foot
rim chips) $715.00
Box & cover, model of a small chick
w/head turned back, by Johann
Joachim Kaendler, painted black &
orange eyes, iron-red comb, sepia
beak, tan feet & w/tan & white
plumage delineated in sepia,
1740-48, 3 3/8" l. 2,200.00
Butter dish, cov., Blue Onion patt.,
ca. 1920 . . . . 85.00
Cache pot w/underplate, Blue Onion
patt., 7" h. 350.00
Coffee pot & cover w/knob finial,
"Hausmaler" decor, coat of arms
beneath a crown flanked by 2
flowering branches, rim & foot rim
w/scrolls & foliage in iron-red &
blue, domed cover painted w/dif-
ferent coat of arms & flower spray,
ca. 1730, 9" h. 2,420.00
Cup & saucer, cup painted w/eques-
trian figure in an extensive landscape, the saucer w/figures in a
boat in a river landscape, within
gilt "Laub-und-Bandelwerk"
(elaborate scrollwork) cartouches,
w/gilt scroll & foliage rims,
ca. 1730 . . . . 660.00
Cup & saucer, h.p. floral sprigs & gold
decor, ca. 1850 . . . . 90.00
Cups & saucers, quatrefoil, each
painted in a Kakiemon palette of
iron-red, turquoise-green, blue &
gold w/three branches bearing
pomegranates, prunus or other
blossoms, center w/small flowerhead, scalloped & barbed rim
edged in brown, 1730-35, pr. 1,650.00
Dinner service: 12 each dinner plates,
soup plates, salad/dessert plates,
bread & butter plates, teacups &
saucers & 1 each 14" oval platter,
11¾" oval cov. vegetable dish,
22 5/8" fish platter, 17" oval platter,
9" oval vegetable dish & sauceboat on attached stand; abstract
celadon green panels outlined in
underglaze-blue reserved on white
ground, ca. 1901, 78 pcs. 12,100.00
Dish, molded as a gilt-edged peony
blossom overlapping a leaf, painted
in iron-red, blue, yellow, puce, black
& green w/bouquet & 2 sprigs of
"deutsche Blumen," superimposed
w/another leaf veined in puce,
edged in green shading to yellow &
issuing from the yellow & green
stem handle opposite a shaded puce
bud, 1760-70, 7 3/8" l. 2,200.00

Meissen Leaf Dish

Dish, leaf-molded w/stem handle,
shaded green w/veins in puce,
ca. 1765, 9¾" l. (ILLUS.) 660.00
Figure of a woman oyster seller,
holding shell & w/covered tray on
her head, green & white dress
w/print skirt, purple & yellow
top, white apron, gold trim, 6" h. . . . 550.00
Figure of "Art," maiden naked but for
a pale blue drape falling about her
waist, w/objects emblematic of
Painting, Sculpture, Architecture &
Music, late 19th c., 18¾" h. 1,210.00
Figure of Ceres, standing beside a
flower-filled cornucopia & flanked
by cupids, late 19th c., 20 3/8" h. . . . 1,210.00
Funnel, Blue Onion patt., 4¾" h. 85.00

Lion by J.J. Kaendler

Model of a lion, mouth open & looking
to left, by J.J. Kaendler, ca. 1750,
repair to tip of tongue & firing
crack in one leg, 4½" l. (ILLUS.) . . . 1,650.00
Model of a lioness, head turned to the
left & seated on her haunches
w/open mouth, oval base applied
w/foliage, modelled by J.J.
Kaendler, ca. 1750, 2¾" h. (minor
repair to base & ears) 1,100.00
Model of a Dutch shoe, Blue Onion
patt., 7 x 2¼" 95.00
Monkey band figures, conductor & 7
musicians, 8 pcs. 2,900.00
Pitcher, water, 7" h., rococo-molded,
Blue Onion patt., ca. 1860 . . . . 225.00

Meissen Plaque

Plaque, the Presentation at the Temple, the Christ Child flanked by Mary & Joseph, Anne & 2 men by their side, 20th c., framed, 9 7/8 x 14¼" (ILLUS.) 1,320.00

Plates, 8" d., lace border, center bouquet bordered w/floral medallions, butterflies & bees decor, set of 10 . . . 600.00

Plates, 8" d., reticulated borders, Blue Onion patt., set of 6 . . . . 300.00

Plate, 10½" d., Blue Onion patt. 70.00

Platter, 10½" d., gold scalloped rim, rose center surrounded by rose buds on white ground 93.00

Platter, 11½" l., Blue Onion patt. 150.00

Sauceboat w/attached underplate, Blue Onion patt., 2-handled 190.00

Sauce ladle, Blue Onion patt., 4" l. 135.00

Snuff box, cov., rectangular, cover & exterior of box painted in shades of brown, green, iron-red & blue w/vignettes of chickens & songbirds within turquoise green trellis diaper panels edged in iron-red, blue, yellow, puce & salmon feathery C-scrolls & floral sprays, underside of box w/further bird vignette (rubbed), interior of cover w/hen, duck & 2 doves in a landscape, rims w/contemporary hinge & chased copper-gilt mount, mid-18th c., 3 5/8" l. 2,970.00

Meissen Tankard with Silver Cover

Tankard, painted w/bouquets of "deutsch Blumen" & scattered flowersprays, w/hinged silver lid w/seated dog thumbrest & inset w/coin bearing date "1621," ca. 1745, overall 7" h. (ILLUS.) 1,045.00

Teabowl & saucer, exterior of teabowl w/continuous scene of 3 travelers pausing in a river landscape, interior w/two peasants conversing, interior of saucer of quay scene, all within iron-red double lines, interior rim w/gilt border of floral scrollwork, brown, green, purple, blue, grey & iron-red, ca. 1740 . . . . 1,100.00

Teapot, Blue Onion patt., 6-cup size . . 235.00

Tea strainer, Blue Onion patt., handled, 5" l. . . . . 55.00 to 70.00

Tray, double handled, rococo gold border, "deutsche Blumen" decor, 11½ x 6" 189.00

Tureen, cov., "Fliegender Hund" patt., painted in a Kakiemon palette either side w/winged kylin, bird in flight, insects, flowering shrubbery & sprigs, double scroll handles heightened in puce & iron-red & tied w/yellow bowknots, brown-edged cover w/pierced green & yellow artichoke-form knop, ca. 1740, 11 3/8" d. 2,090.00

Meissen Covered Tureen & Stand

Tureen, cover surmounted w/figure of a putto supporting cornucopia & stand, shepherd tending various animals in a bucolic setting, whole later mounted w/elaborate gilt-bronze mask handles raised on 2 scrolling feet, Marcolini Period, overall 15¼" h. (ILLUS.) 3,025.00

Vase, 8¾" h., double handled, deep pink decor 245.00

Vases, 15 3/8" h., ovoid, deep cobalt blue body w/gilt decor, white coiling serpent handles w/details picked out in gilding, late 19th c., pr. 522.00

METTLACH

Etched Mettlach Plaque

Ceramics with the name Mettlach were produced by Villeroy & Boch and other potteries in the Mettlach area of Germany. Villeroy and Boch's finest years of production are thought to be from about 1890 to 1910. Also see STEINS.

Bowl, 9" d., etched Art Nouveau decor, No. 3364 . . . . $65.00
Coasters, printed under glaze gnome & German verse, No. 1032, set of 6 . . 400.00
Mug, advertising, "Hire's Root Beer," printed under glaze Hire's Kid w/mug, No. 2327, ¼ liter 135.00
Mug, advertising, "Bartholmay's Brewing," printed under glaze, No. 1909 . . . . . . 110.00
Pitcher, cameo relief brown branches & leaves on slat grey 245.00
Plaque, pierced to hang, "phanolith" cameo relief figure of maiden on blue-green ground, No. 7072, 6 x 8", framed 375.00
Plaque, pierced to hang, etched cavalier musician w/mandolin, No. 2625, 7½" d. 265.00
Plaque, pierced to hang, etched knight w/banner over his shoulder, No. 1384, 14¼" d. 495.00
Plaques, pierced to hang, etched portrait of Art Nouveau maiden picking white daisies on one & portrait of Art Nouveau lady eating cherries on other, No. 2596 & No. 2597, 15" d., pr. 1,595.00
Plaque, pierced to hang, etched black & white center scene of king meeting bishop & attendants, cream, brown & blue border, No. 1048, 16" d. . . . . 575.00 to 600.00
Plaque, pierced to hang, cameo relief figures of Trojan warriors in boat on sage green ground, No. 2442, 19" d. 1,100.00
Plaque, pierced to hang, etched sailing ship, No. 2750, 19" d. (ILLUS.) 1,000.00

Mettlach Punch Bowl

Punch bowl, cov., footed, open handles, etched floral reserves on lid (w/chip) & shoulders, body w/etched continuous scene of musicians, dancers & sidewalk parade, No. 2843, 12" d., 13½" h. (ILLUS.) 500.00
Vase, 11" h., footed, straight-sided cylinder, inlaid mosaic florals on white ground, No. 1289 . . . . 275.00
Vase, 13" h., etched w/reserve scenes of maiden picking flowers, No. 1749 . . . . 300.00 to 390.00
Vase, 14" h., elephant head handles, swollen cylinder, gold & red Art Nouveau designs on cobalt blue ground, No. 2851 . . . . 495.00
Vase, 14" h., etched Art Nouveau florals, shades of rust-red & green, No. 2909 . . . . 550.00
Vases, 14" h., 5½" d., 4 panels etched w/cherubs depicting the Four Seasons, pink lining, No. 1537, pr. 765.00

MINTON

The Minton factory in England was established by Thomas Minton in 1793. The factory made earthenware, especially the blue-printed variety and Thomas Minton is sometimes credited with invention of the blue "Willow" pattern. For a time majolica and tiles were also an important part of production, but bone china soon became the principal ware. Mintons, Ltd., continues in operation today. Also see OYSTER PLATES, RING TREES and TILES.

Bird bath on stand, majolica, molded as a large shell supported on the wings of a crane standing amidst calla lilies on a water lily molded base, dated 1872, overall 38¾" h. (ILLUS.) $2,860.00

Majolica Bird Bath

Cabaret set: cov. teapot, creamer,
  sugar bowl, tray & 2 c/s; Willow
  patt. in rust w/gold trim, 1880,
  8 pcs. 325.00
Cup & saucer, demitasse, Bird of
  Paradise & turquoise band decor
  (made for Tiffany's, New York) 32.00
Dessert plates, h.p. red roses & other
  florals on wide border, 9" d., set
  of 12 . . . . .235.00
Foot bath, blue transfer decor,
  ca. 1845 . . . . .1,500.00
Mug, Genevese patt., medium dark
  blue transfer 55.00
Plates, 8½" d., shaded pink, green &
  yellow florals highlighted
  w/enameling on cream ground,
  set of 6 . . . . .72.00
Plates, 10¼" d., pate-sur-pate, 3
  roundels on the border depicting
  classical profiles in white slip
  reserved on a deep teal ground
  within gilt borders, each further
  reserved on a white ground w/pale
  yellow panels enriched overall by
  gilding, artist-signed & dated
  1916, set of 15 . . . . .1,760.00
Plate, h.p. roses center, wide tur-
  quoise blue border w/ornate gold. . .265.00
Platter, 15 x 8", majolica, cupid
  between water lilies 250.00
Soup plates w/flange rims, enameled
  aqua & gilt decor, dated 1893,
  set of 12 . . . . .300.00
Soup tureen, cov., peach tree decor,
  dated 1878 . . . . .90.00
Tea & coffee set: cov. teapot
  w/stand, milk jug, 8 tea cups, 6
  coffee cups & 8 saucers; underglaze-
  blue entwined vines w/iron-red
  overglaze dashes flanked by gilt

foliate & blue band borders, gilt
  edge rims, 1811-14, 25 pcs. 770.00
Vase, 8" h., rosebuds, jeweling & gilt
  swags within turquoise reserves 175.00

Pilgrim Flask Vase

Vases, 14¼" h., Pilgrim Flask form,
  slip-painted realistic orchid spray
  on turquoise ground w/simulated
  cloisonne borders in shades of turquoise, cobalt blue, iron-red, green,
  white & gold, scroll-molded foot
  simulating carved wood base, dated
  1873 (crack in body of one), pr.
  (ILLUS. of one) 1,650.00
Wash basin & pitcher, child size,
  ivy leaves decor on cream ground,
  gold trim, 2 pcs. 250.00

MOCHA

Mocha Mug

*Mocha decoration is found on basically
utilitarian creamware or yellowware articles
and is achieved by a simple chemical*

reaction. *A color pigment of brown, blue, green or black is given an acid nature by infusion of tobacco or hops. When this acid nature colorant is applied in blobs to an alkaline ground color, it reacts by spreading in feathery seaplant designs. This type of decoration is usually accompanied by horizontal bands of light color slip. Produced in numerous Staffordshire potteries from the late 18th until the late 19th centuries, its name is derived from the similar markings found on mocha quartz.*

Bowl, 8" d., w/large pouring spout at rim, exterior w/wide white slip band w/blue feathering seaplants & brown striping on yellowware (minor edge wear) $180.00
Bowl, 9 1/8" d., 4" h., exterior w/white slip band w/blue feathering seaplants & brown striping on yellowware (wear, stains & minor flakes) 80.00
Chamberpot, exterior w/wide white slip band w/blue feathering seaplants & black striping on yellowware, 2 5/8" d., 2" h. miniature (small flakes) 45.00
Chamberpot, exterior w/wide white slip band w/blue feathering seaplants & brown striping on yellowware, 8" d., 5¾" h. 60.00
Mixing bowl, exterior w/white slip band w/dark brown-black feathering seaplants & blue striping on yellowware, 10" d., 5" h. (minor wear) 95.00
Mixing bowl, exterior w/wide white slip band w/blue feathering seaplants & brown striping on yellowware, 12¼" d., 5 5/8" h. (minor wear & chips).....................115.00
Mug, wide mocha band w/black sponge-like trees & black & blue bandings, 3" d., 3¾" h. 58.00
Mug, marbleized blue, brown & tan sides, zig-zag & dark brown band borders (w/repaired chip at rim), Staffordshire, ca. 1830, 4¼" d., 4½" h. (ILLUS.) 440.00
Mug, circle designs in mottled colors, Staffordshire 800.00
Mugs, one w/green feathering seaplants & dark green borders on tan & other w/blue feathering seaplants on wide white slip band on yellowware, pr.................495.00
Pepper pot, chocolate brown, blue, orange & white stripes, 3¾" h. 195.00
Pepper pot, Earthworm patt. in blue, white, black & brown, 4½" h........165.00
Pepper pot, Earthworm patt., pale blue & white w/chocolate brown & blue designs & brown striping 245.00
Pitcher, 5 1/8" h., straight sides,

wide mocha band w/black sponge-like trees & blue & black striping 85.00
Pitcher, 5¼" h., bulbous w/narrow top & embossed rim w/green stripe, green feathering seaplants & brown striping.........................325.00
Pitcher, 7" h., Earthworm patt. w/wavy lines in blue, black, white & brown on wide center band, embossed green rim (stains & hairline on side & small base flakes) 275.00

Mocha Mug & Pitcher

Pitchers & mug, Earthworm patt. pitchers & Cat's Eye patt. mug, late 19th c., 3 pcs. (ILLUS. of part) 220.00

MOORCROFT

Moorcroft Cookie Jar

This ware is made in a pottery established at Cobridge, England, in 1913, by William Moorcroft and now headed by his son Walter. Several marks have been used through the years. Earlier pieces bring the higher prices.

Bowl, 4" d., interior w/orchid blossom on indigo blue ground $70.00
Bowl, 6" d., 2-handled, Aurelian Ware,

ornate silver cover, Moorcroft-
Macintyre........................200.00
Bowl, 9" d., wisteria decor, 1930.......80.00
Bowl, 10" d., footed, orchids & white
floral decor, 1928-45 ....125.00
Bowl, 11" d., wisteria decor 175.00
Coffee pot, cov., Sicilian patt., Moor-
croft-Macintyre....................250.00
Cookie jar, Florian Ware, royal blue &
white florals on lighter blue ground,
in silverplate frame & w/silverplate
drop-in lid & swing handle, Moor-
croft-Macintyre, 1897-1913, 7" h.
(ILLUS.)..........................610.00
Creamer & sugar bowl, pansies on
cobalt blue ground, ca. 1916, pr. 80.00
Ginger jar, red & yellow pomegranates
on cobalt blue ground, Moorcroft-
Macintyre, 1897-1913, 8" h..........95.00
Goblet, 18th Century patt., Moorcroft-
Macintrye, 7" h. 150.00
Vase, 7" h., baluster-shaped,
pomegranate decor, Moorcroft-
Macintyre..........................90.00
Vase, 7¾" h., pansies on cobalt blue
ground 105.00
Vase, 8" h., Aurelian Ware, cobalt
blue, gold & orange Art Nouveau
style decor on cream ground,
Moorcroft-Macintyre, 1897-1913 ....295.00
Vase, 8" h., Florian Ware, cornflowers
on blue ground, 1897-1913 ....275.00
Vase, 8" h., pomegranate decor 95.00
Vase, 8" h., roses decor, gold trim,
Moorcroft-Macintyre, 1897-1913 ....165.00
Vase, 9" h., baluster-shaped, pansies
decor on "flambe" glaze 300.00
Vase, 9" h., shaded light to dark blue
florals, Moorcroft-Burslem,
1913-21 ....325.00
Vase, 10" h., Florian Ware, floral decor
outlined in cobalt blue, pale blue
ground, Moorcroft-Macintyre,
1897-1913 ....425.00
Vase, 11" h., Florian Ware, blue &
green floral decor, Moorcroft-
Macintyre, 1897-1913 ....350.00
Vase, 12" h., Florian Ware, anemones
w/ivy decor 350.00
Vase, 13" h., Florian Ware, poppies on
blue ground, 1897-1913 ....300.00
Vase, 13" h., large dahlias decor......120.00

MOORE (Bernard)

Initial Mark of Bernard Moore

*Bernard Moore, associated with Moore
Bros. St. Mary's Works until this
Staffordshire pottery was sold in 1905,
established his own firm at Wolfe St.,
Stoke-on-Trent the same year. He specialized in fine glaze-effects on the wares
produced until 1915.*

Bowl, 3¼" d., "flambe" glaze........$50.00
Bowl, 11" d., white "flambe" glaze
w/motto decor 115.00
Vase, 1½" h., onion form, "flambe"
glaze.............................40.00
Vase, 2½" h., baluster-shaped, dark
glaze.............................55.00
Vase, 3½" h., dragon decor, blue
"flambe" glaze, 1905 ....105.00
Vase, 5" h., double gourd form,
"flambe" glaze 65.00

NEWCOMB COLLEGE POTTERY

Newcomb College Vase

*This pottery was established in the art
department of Newcomb College, New
Orleans, La., in 1897. Each piece was hand
thrown and bore the pottery's mark and
decorator's monogram on the base. It was
always a studio business and never operated
as a factory and its pieces are therefore
scarce, with the early wares being eagerly
sought. The pottery closed in 1940.*

Bowl, 8" d., 3¾" h., florals at top
edge, dark blue ground..........$500.00
Candlestick, h.p. magnolias on blue
ground (single) 400.00
Ink stand: base, well & cover; signed
Sadie Irvine, 3 pcs................575.00
Mug, yellow-orange pansies w/deep
blue stripes on grey-blue high
glaze ground, artist-signed
(hairline) 525.00
Vase, 2¾" h., ovoid, 4 pendant floral
cartouches, soft rose & green glaze
on misty blue ground, 1895-1910 ....137.00
Vase, 3¼" h., 3" d., overall Art

Nouveau pink blossoms & green leaves
on ultramarine blue ground, signed
Sadie Irvine 375.00
Vase, 3¼" h., 5" d., holly berries &
leaves on matte blue ground, artist-
signed. 295.00
Vase, 3 3/8" h., bulbous, sides
w/verdant landscape at sunset in
shades of blue, green, lavender
& pink, signed Sadie Irvine,
1895-1910 . . . . .440.00
Vase, 3½" h., buttressed sides, incised
geometric decor, soft green
crystalline glaze 260.00
Vase, 3½" h., floral decor on blue
ground, artist-signed 475.00
Vase, 4" h., bulbous, blue flowers
w/yellow centers & green leaves at
rim, signed Sadie Irvine 325.00
Vase, 5" h., Art Nouveau geometric
decor in shades of blue & grey,
artist-signed (ILLUS.) 695.00
Vase, 5" h., bulbous, lily clusters (3)
on blue shaded to green ground,
artist-signed 635.00
Vase, 5¾" h., sunset scene decor,
artist-signed 700.00
Vase, 6" h., green drip glaze over
red clay, artist-signed 725.00
Vase, 6" h., incised florals on blue-
green ground, signed Sadie Irvine,
1910 . . . . .500.00
Vase, 6" h., white floral decor on
misty blue ground 425.00
Vase, bud, 8" h., open lily decor,
artist-signed 425.00
Vase, 10½" h., yellow-centered iris
decor & yellow tracery, artist-
signed. 700.00

NILOAK

Niloak Hywood Line Cornucopia

*This pottery was made in Benton,
Arkansas, and featured hand-thrown vari-
colored swirled clay decoration in objects of
classic forms. Designated Mission Ware,
this line is the most desirable of Niloak's*
*production which was begun early in this
century. Less expensive to produce, the cast
Hywood line, finished with either high gloss
or semi-matte glazes, was introduced during
the economic depression of the 1930s. The
pottery ceased operation about 1946.*

Ash tray, model of frog, Hywood line,
green $30.00
Ash tray, Mission Ware, brown, blue,
cream & rouge marbleized swirls,
5" d. 45.00
Bowls, 4" d., 1" h., Mission Ware,
brown, blue, cream & rouge
marbleized swirls, set of 4 . . . . .95.00
Bowl, 6" d., 2" h., Mission Ware,
marbleized swirls 24.00
Candlestick, Mission Ware, marbleized
swirls, 6" h. (single) 90.00
Candlestick, Mission Ware, marbleized
swirls, 6" base d., 10" h. (single) 135.00
Candlesticks, Mission Ware, marble-
ized swirls, 8½" h., pr. 195.00
Compote, 6½" h., Hywood line, 2-tone
matte finish 35.00
Cornucopia-vase, footed, Hywood line,
yellow glaze, 3" h. 7.50
Cornucopia-vase, Hywood line, powder
blue glossy glaze, 7" h. (ILLUS.) 12.50
Creamer, Hywood line, blue shading to
rose semi-matte glaze, 4" h. 13.00
Creamer & sugar bowl, Hywood line,
rose glaze, pr. .15.00
Ewer, winged eagle molded on sides,
Hywood line, green semi-matte
glaze 17.00
Lamp, Mission Ware, brown & cream
marbleized swirls, 20½" h. (factory
drilled) 125.00
Model of a bullfrog, Hywood line 20.00
Model of a Dutch shoe, Hywood line,
rose matte glaze 20.00
Mug, embossed floral decor, Hywood
line 10.00
Pitcher, cov., flat-sided, Hywood line,
raspberry shaded to green glaze 20.00
Pitcher, water, w/ice lip, Hywood line,
green 15.00
Pitcher, water, molded geometric
floral design, Hywood line, white
glaze 35.00
Planter, model of bunnies, Hywood
line, rose shading to green semi-
matte glaze 18.50
Planter, model of a camel, Hywood
line 40.00
Planter, model of a duck, Hywood
line 15.00
Planter, model of a fox reclining,
Hywood line 21.50
Planter, model of a frog w/open
mouth, Hywood line 30.00
Planter, model of a kangaroo,
Hywood line 15.00

Squirrel Planter

Planter, model of a squirrel, Hywood
line, blue shading to rouge, 6" h.
(ILLUS.) 22.50
Strawberry jar, Hywood line, light
blue. 7.00
Toothpick holder, Mission Ware,
marbleized swirls 35.00
Vase, 1" h., salesman's sample,
Mission Ware, marbleized swirls 40.00
Vase, 3½" h., Mission Ware, marble-
ized swirls 40.00
Vase, 4" h., Mission Ware, blue &
brown marbleized swirls . . . . 30.00 to 40.00
Vase, 5½" h., Mission Ware, marble-
ized swirls 40.00
Vase, 6½" h., Mission Ware, marble-
ized swirls . . . . 50.00 to 60.00
Vase, 7½"h., 2½" w., bulbous, tapered
neck, Mission Ware, brown, blue &
rust marbleized swirls 45.00
Vase, 8" h., Mission Ware, marble-
ized swirls 80.00
Vase, 9" h., Mission Ware, marble-
ized swirls 87.00
Vase, 9¾" h., Mission Ware, marble-
ized swirls 85.00
Vase, 12" h., Mission Ware, marble-
ized swirls 230.00
Vase, pillow-shaped, Mission Ware,
marbleized swirls 40.00

NIPPON

*This colorful porcelain was produced by
numerous factories in Japan late last
century and until about 1921. There are
numerous marks on this ware, identifying
the producers or decorating studios. The
hand-painted pieces of good quality have
shown a dramatic price increase within the
past three years. Also see NORITAKE,
PHOENIX BIRD and RING TREES.*

Ash bowl on base, 3 cigarette rests,
relief-molded pipe & matches
decor, 5" d. $350.00
Ash bowl on base, 3 cigarette rests,
Wedgwood jasper-type decor w/white
floral relief on blue (green "M" in
Wreath mark) 275.00
Ash tray, leaf-shaped, scenic decor
w/turquoise jeweling & brown
enameled beading (green "M" in
Wreath mark) .48.00
Ash tray, round w/protruding cigarette
rests, h.p. lion on tan ground center,
brown borders w/enameled beading
(green "M" in Wreath mark) 65.00
Ash tray, triangular w/three cigarette
rests, h.p. horse head center, Art
Deco border . . . . 85.00 to 125.00
Ash tray, h.p. deer scene &
enameled beading decor, 5" d.
(green "M" in Wreath mark) 95.00
Ash tray, relief-molded Betty Boop
type girl's face (Rising Sun mark) 125.00
Asparagus set: 12 x 7½" tray & six
7½" serving plates; ornate blue &
gold border, 7 pcs. (green Wreath
mark) 360.00
Basket, h.p. purple florals
w/"moriage" leaves, 5" h. 140.00
Berry bowl & underplate, 3-footed bowl
w/scalloped edge, lavish gold decor
on cream border, 8¾" d. under-
plate (Maple Leaf mark) 90.00
Berry set: master bowl & 5 sauce
dishes; cobalt blue & gold roses
on white ground, 6 pcs. 125.00
Bowl, 5½" d., 3-footed, Azalea patt. . . .40.00

Nippon Bowl

Bowl, 7" d., 2-handled, h.p. sailboat
scene w/gold palm trees in foreground, green Wreath mark (ILLUS.) . .22.50
Bowl, 7" d., ruffled rim, overall
"moriage" Aztec Indian type decor . .125.00
Bowl, 7½" d., 4½" h., 3 gold feet,
h.p. Bird of Paradise & tropical
florals interior, lavish gold interior
& exterior rim borders (red & green
R.C. Nippon mark) 80.00

Bowl, 7½" d., h.p. seascape & windmill interior & enameled designs exterior decor .55.00

Bowl, 8" w., diamond-shaped w/open handles, h.p. scene of Indian in canoe (green "M" in Wreath mark) . .105.00

Bowl, 8¼" d., h.p. stylized Egyptian symbols decor (green "M" in Wreath mark) 110.00

Bowl, 8½" d., gold scalloped rim, h.p. lilies interior & exterior decor 80.00

Bowl, 9¼" d., tab handles, Gouda-type decor w/colorful stylized florals on dark green ground (green "M" in Wreath mark) 90.00

Bowl, 9½" d., gold handles & gold Greek Key border, 6 panels of h.p. pink roses & blue daisies w/gold trim 70.00

Bowl, 10" d., scalloped rim, pink & red roses interior & exterior decor, heavy gold trim (blue Maple Leaf mark) 160.00

Bowl, 10" d., "gaudy," h.p. floral reserves w/ornate gold trim on cobalt blue ground 185.00

Bread tray, "gaudy" pink asters on shaded green ground, heavy gold trim 225.00

Butter tub, cover & drain insert, overall small pink roses decor w/gold trim 22.00

Cake set: 10" d. master cake plate w/pierced handles & five 5" d. plates; Art Deco style floral decor w/gold trim, geometric border, 6 pcs. 75.00

Cake plate, pierced handles, h.p. Egyptian war ship, mountains, oasis & tall palm trees outlined in gold, matte finish, 11" d. 80.00

Cake set: 12½" handled platter & four 6¼" d. plates; lavish gold on snow white ground, 5 pcs. 125.00

Cake set: master cake plate & 6 serving plates; h.p. pink & blue flowers outlined in gold, 7 pcs. (green "M" in Wreath mark) .75.00

Candlestick, hexagonal, Gouda-style decor w/stylized Art Deco florals on dark green, 8" h. (single) . . .85.00 to 100.00

Candlestick, 3-sided, h.p. desert scene w/Arab on camel in autumn colors & black enameled beading, bisque finish, 8" h. (single) 79.50

Candlestick, h.p. florals & delicate "moriage" decor on lavender & turquoise blue ground, 9" h. (single) 169.00

Celery set: 12" l. celery tray & 6 individual salt dips; h.p. scene of sailing ships w/trees in foreground, 7 pcs. 125.00

Cheese dish w/slant lid, h.p. dainty

bands of flowers & foliage on shaded creamy ground .55.00

Cheese & cracker dish, 2-tiered, pink & gold roses decor 42.00

Chocolate pot, cov., h.p. yellow florals, gold trim, 9" h. (Rising Sun mark) 60.00

Chocolate pot, cov., h.p. roses in oval reserve on cobalt blue ground, gold trim (Maple Leaf mark) 175.00

Chocolate pot, cov., h.p. pink & blue cherry blossoms & gold tracery decor (green "M" in Wreath mark) . .100.00

Chocolate set: cov. chocolate pot & 4 c/s; h.p. pink & green florals outlined in gold & ornate gold beading & tracery decor, 9 pcs. (green "M" in Wreath mark) 150.00

Chocolate set: cov. chocolate pot & 4 c/s; scalloped & fluted bodies w/h.p. rose clusters & lavish gold trim & borders, 9 pcs. (Maple Leaf mark) . . .195.00

Nippon Chocolate Set

Chocolate set: cov. chocolate pot & 6 c/s; ornate mold, h.p. iris decor, gold beading & trim, 13 pcs. (ILLUS. of part) 375.00

Chocolate set: cov. chocolate pot & 6 c/s; white w/lavish gold overlay, 13 pcs. 160.00

Chocolate set: cov. chocolate pot & 12 angular fluted cups; Art Deco style blue, black & white striped decor, 13 pcs. .275.00

Chocolate set: cov. chocolate pot, creamer, sugar bowl & 5 c/s; large coral roses over trailing green leaves on creamy yellow ground, 13 pcs. 250.00

Cigarette holder, bisque, trees & house decor, 3½" h. .75.00

Coaster, birds decor (M in Wreath mark) 12.50

Cologne bottle w/matching stopper, yellow floral decor w/gold trim 45.00

Compote, 7½" w., 3½" h., triangular base supported by 3 Egyptian winged

lions, bowl w/panels of stylized
tulips & birds (green M in Wreath
mark) 160.00
Condensed milk can holder, cover &
underplate, h.p. violets w/enamel
highlights 50.00
Console bowl, 2-handled, pedestal base,
h.p. florals & lavish gold decor,
10½" d., 3½" h. 110.00

Nippon Cookie Jar

Cookie jar, cov., melon-ribbed, 3-footed,
h.p. florals & lavish gold trim &
beading on white ground shaded to
cobalt blue, overall 7¾" h.
(ILLUS.) 400.00
Cookie jar, cov., h.p. ship decor on
cobalt blue ground, gold border,
8½" d. 125.00
Cookie jar, cov., 3-handled & 3-footed,
h.p. pink & rose florals on white 85.00
Cookie jar, cov., h.p. violets & roses
on green & cream ground, gold
trim 125.00
Cookie jar, cover & underplate, 3-footed
jar, h.p. red poppies & green leaves,
gold trim, 2 pcs. 95.00
Creamer, "googlie-eyed" Doll Face mold
(Rising Sun mark) 55.00
Cup & saucer, child's, pink, blue &
green florals w/gold trim on white
ground 18.00
Cup & saucer, relief-molded child's
face decor 65.00
Dish, handled, jasper-type, white
relief decor on soft blue ground,
9¼" l. 150.00
Dresser tray, h.p. orange poppies on
cream ground, 9½ x 6¾" (blue Rising
Sun mark) 45.00
Egg cup, double, h.p. violets w/green
leaves & gold trim, 3½" h. (blue
Maple Leaf mark) 35.00
Ferner, triangular, h.p. woodland
scene w/gold beading, 5" h. (green
M in Wreath mark) 195.00

Marmalade jar w/underplate, h.p.
leaves & vines w/gold tracery, 2 pcs.
(green "M" in Wreath mark) 75.00
Matchbox holder, h.p. horse head &
riding crop decor on shaded green
ground w/black enameled beading
& jeweling 75.00
Mayonnaise dish, underplate & ladle,
h.p. purple pansies & green leaves
w/gold trim, 3 pcs. 45.00

Nippon Mugs

Mug, relief-molded & h.p. stag scene,
5" h., green "M" in Wreath mark
(ILLUS. left) 310.00
Mug, h.p. fox hunt scene, 5" h.
(ILLUS. right) 200.00
Nut set: master nut bowl & 4 individ-
ual nut cups; diamond-shaped, h.p.
Indian w/canoe decor, 5 pcs. 145.00

Nippon Pancake Server

Pancake dish & dome cover, h.p. roses
& leaves, stylized gold borders
w/gold beading, blue Maple Leaf
mark (ILLUS.) 95.00
Pitcher, 5" h., squatty, "moriage"
dragon decor on grey ground 85.00
Pitcher, water, 8" h., h.p. red & white
floral decor w/gold trim on cobalt
blue ground .150.00
Pitcher, tankard, 13" h., red & green
chrysanthemums on green ground
(Royal Nishiki mark) 265.00
Plaque, pierced to hang, relief-molded
& h.p. child's face, 6" d. (Rising Sun
mark) 45.00
Plaque, pierced to hang, h.p. portrait
of a dog, stylized floral border,
7¾" d. 250.00

Plaque, pierced to hang, h.p. moose
(2) in forest setting center within
6-pointed star, gold border
w/Indian-type design, 8¾" d. 160.00
Plaque, pierced to hang, h.p. Dutch
windmill on river shore scene,
9" d. .135.00 to 165.00
Plaque, pierced to hang, relief-mold-
ed & h.p. portrait of a Bulldog, Art
Deco border, 10" d. 295.00
Plaque, pierced to hang, relief-mold-
ed & h.p. lion & lioness, 10½" d. 600.00
Plate, 4½" d., h.p. ducks decor (Rising
Sun mark) 30.00
Plate, 7½" d., h.p. Indian in canoe
decor (green "M" in Wreath mark) . . .75.00
Plate, 7½" d., white daffodils on
pastel ground, artist-signed 60.00
Plate, 7½" d., h.p. brilliant orange
poppies & foliage against pale green
ground, gold trim ("M" in Wreath
mark) 12.00
Plates, 7½" d., h.p. floral on white
center, cobalt blue borders w/lavish
gold tracery, set of 6 . . . . .240.00
Plate, 7¾" d., h.p. desert scene
w/Arab & palm trees decor 150.00
Plate, 8½" d., h.p. pink & white apple
blossoms center, ornate gold
border 45.00
Plate, 8½" d., h.p. portrait of lady
holding a dog, "gaudy" roses
w/lavish gold trim on dark green
border (Maple Leaf mark) 145.00
Plate, 9" d., gold & orange nasturtiums & green leaves on soft blue
ground, gold beaded border 36.00
Plate, 9¼" d., h.p. yellow & pink roses
w/gold leaves on pink ground,
scalloped border w/lavish gold trim
(blue Maple Leaf mark) 45.00
Plate, 9½" d., cluster of pink tea roses
within ornate gold framed medallion
center, magenta border w/rose-
filled medallions, heavy gold rim 75.00
Plate, 10" d., h.p. roses decor center,
ornate gold trim 120.00
Potpourri jar w/cover & inner lid,
Gouda-type decor w/colorful
stylized florals on creamy white
ground, 5½" h. ("M" in Wreath
mark) 115.00
Powder jar, cov., 3 gold feet, Art
Nouveau style floral decor 55.00
Punch bowl & base, lake scene w/trees
& house & large spray of red & pink
roses w/green & pink jeweling,
ornate gold trim, 2 pcs. (green "M"
in Wreath mark) 325.00
Salt dips, open, h.p. pink floral decor
w/gold trim, set of 6 . . . . .90.00
Shaving mug, h.p. roses & bands of
ornate gold beading (green "M" in
Wreath mark) 120.00

Syrup pitcher w/underplate, h.p. pink
roses w/ornate gold trim, 2 pcs. 50.00

Vanity Organizer

Vanity organizer, combination
hatpin holder, ring tree & pin tray,
h.p. decor, gold trim, 4¼" h.
(ILLUS.) 125.00

Nippon Vase

Vase, 9" h., 5¾" w., gold handles at
shoulders, cobalt blue ground
reserved w/colorful boat scene each
side, lavish gold trim, green "M" in
Wreath mark (ILLUS.) 175.00
Vase, 10" h., 2-handled, pedestal base,
large h.p. purple florals on soft yellow
ground, gold trim 125.00
Vase, 10½" h., magenta roses on
green ground, lavish raised gold
trim 125.00
Vase, 10½" h., melon-ribbed, h.p. pink
& blue peonies decor (blue "M" in
Wreath mark) .75.00
Vase, 10¾" h., gold handles at
shoulders, h.p. wild roses & blue
starflower spray on shaded green
ground, enameled floral "brocade"
borders (green "M" in Wreath
mark) 350.00

Vase, 12" h., 3 gold handles & 3 gold
feet, h.p. Art Nouveau florals
w/trailing leaves & gold outlined stems,
wide gold band top & bottom
borders w/floral medallions (green
"M" in Wreath mark) 250.00
Vase, 12" h., h.p. purple florals
w/trailing long green leaves &
"moriage" slip decor 175.00
Vase, 12½" h., h.p. woodland scene
w/"moriage" trees & florals 250.00
Vase, 13" h., ovoid w/narrow neck &
open handles at shoulders, h.p.
chrysanthemums reserved on pale
green ground overlaid w/lavish
gold (blue Maple Leaf mark).......210.00
Vase, 14" h., h.p. clusters of purple
grapes w/jeweling & gold tracery ...435.00
Vase, 15" h., h.p. pink & purple
orchids against dark green foliage,
ornate gold handles, rim & base 310.00

NORITAKE

Noritake Creamer

*Noritake china, still in production in
Japan, has been exported in large quantities
to this country since early in this century.
Though the Noritake Company first registered in 1904, it did not use "Noritake" as
part of their backstamp until 1918. Interest
in Noritake has escalated as collectors now
seek out pieces made between the "Nippon"
era and World War II (1921-41). The Azalea
pattern is also popular with collectors. Also
see PHOENIX BIRD and "Special Focus"
on SUGAR BOWLS.*

Ash tray, figural Pierrot, 5" w........$240.00
Ash tray, playing cards decor, 5½".....30.00
Bowl, 5" d., 3-footed, lake scene in
sunset colors 30.00
Bowl, 5¾" d., Azalea patt. 12.00
Bowl, 6¾" d., 2-handled, h.p. medallion
of dragons reserved on pebbled

jade green ground interior, Art Deco
designs exterior 35.00
Bowl, 7" d., 4" h., h.p. pink & red
roses, green leaves & heavy gold
florals 60.00
Bowl, 7½" sq., pierced handles,
scalloped silver rim, pink shaded
to peach waterlily decor w/black
accents 28.00
Bowl, 10" d., pierced gold handles,
h.p. scenic decor..................40.00
Bowl, footed, blue lustre finish,
1921-41...........................18.50
Cake plate, h.p. cobalt grape clusters
& white & gold roses on cream
ground, 9½" d. 55.00
Cake plate, Azalea patt., 9¾" d. 38.00
Cake plate, pierced handles, Tree in
Meadow patt. 20.00
Cake set: master cake plate & 8 serving
plates; blue border w/floral decor,
9 pcs. 75.00
Candlesticks, h.p. scenic decor, heavy
gold trim, 1921-41, pr. 60.00
Candy dish & cover w/figural Buddha
finial, tall Art Deco style 75.00
Candy dish, open, 2-compartment,
2-handled, h.p. floral cluster on
turquoise shaded to cream 25.00
Celery tray, Azalea patt..............30.00
Chocolate pot, cov., burnt orange spout,
handle & base on cream ground......15.00
Cookie jar, cov., floral decor, lustre
finish.............................40.00
Creamer, gold handle & rim, lavish
gold band on white, 5¾" h. (ILLUS.) ..20.00
Creamer & cov. sugar bowl, Tree in
Meadow patt., pr. 35.00
Creamer & sugar bowl, blue lustre
finish, 1921-41, pr. 9.00
Creamer & sugar shaker, h.p. gondola
scene on shaded ground, gold trim,
2 pcs. 32.00
Cruet w/stopper, Azalea patt.........155.00
Demitasse set: tray, cov. coffee pot,
creamer, cov. sugar bowl & 3 c/s;
windmill decor, 10 pcs. (green "M"
in Wreath mark) 235.00

Noritake Scenic Dish

Dish, pierced handles, h.p. flowering tree & house scene on orange ground, blue lustre border, gold trim, 6" w. (ILLUS.) 40.00

Dish with Art Deco Cat Handle

Dish w/figural Art Deco cat center handle, lustre finish w/scalloped border design, 9" d. (ILLUS.) 100.00

Dish w/ring handle, h.p. buildings & trees in autumn colors center, enameled arabesques & beaded border 25.00

Dresser set: dresser tray, 2 cov. boxes, hair receiver, ring tree, pin tray & pr. candlesticks; pink floral decor on shaded green ground, 8 pcs. 145.00

Egg cup, Azalea patt. 42.00

Feeding dish, h.p. teddy bear, dog, etc. decor 38.00

Flower holder, figural bird 95.00

Honey pot & cover w/bee finial, model of a beehive, applied bees on pink & blue ground, 4" base d., 4½" h. 35.00

Humidor & cover, Art Deco style silhouette scene of lady & man smoking, 6¾" h. (green "M" in Wreath mark) 275.00

Noritake Humidor

Humidor & cover, relief-molded owl on a branch decor, 7" h., green "M" in Wreath mark (ILLUS.) 600.00

Lemon dish, orange floral decor on blue lustre ground, 1930s 18.00

Marmalade jar, cover w/Bird of

Paradise finial, underplate & ladle, 3 pcs. 135.00

Mayonnaise bowl, underplate & ladle, cream & gold decor on white ground, 3 pcs. 25.00

Napkin ring, clown decor, 2¼" w 18.00

Pitcher, milk, Azalea patt. 140.00

Plaques, pierced to hang, relief-molded squirrels, 10½" d., pr. 550.00

Plate, 9½" d, Art Deco style scene of of man & lady fishing 50.00

Platter, 16 x 12", Azalea patt. 280.00

Salt dip, individual size, h.p. orchids decor on white ground 11.00

Salt & pepper shakers, bulbous, Tree in Meadow patt., pr. 12.00

Spooner, pagoda & willows decor, gold trim ("M" in Wreath mark) 32.00

Syrup pitcher w/underplate, Art Deco style decor, red & black 58.00

Tea set: cov. teapot, creamer, cov. sugar bowl & 6 c/s; Tree in Meadow patt., 15 pcs. 135.00

Toast rack, 2-slice, blue lustre finish 35.00

Toast rack, 4-slice, figural bird center .. 55.00

Toothpick holder, Tree in Meadow patt. 55.00

Vase, 6½" h., fan-shaped, floral decor 65.00

Vase, 7¼" h., pink & white roses on shaded brown ground 75.00

Vase, 11" h., pedestal base, h.p. red florals on dark blue ground, gold trim 155.00

Vase, 12" h., cobalt blue top & base, scene of cascading stream & trees in autumn colors, ornate gold trim, satin finish (Spoke mark) 300.00

Vegetable bowl, Azalea patt., 9½ x 7½" oval 70.00

Vegetable bowl, Tree in Meadow patt., 9¼" oval 28.00

Wall pocket, relief-molded floral top, applied figural bumblebees (2) on black ground, 2¼" w., 5" h. 45.00

Wall pocket, h.p. multicolored parrot decor, 8" h. 40.00

Wall pocket, h.p. red poppy on white & blue lustre ground, 8½" h. 40.00

Wall pocket, h.p. Art Deco scene of Cleopatra sailing the Nile 95.00

NORTH DAKOTA SCHOOL OF MINES POTTERY

All pottery produced at the University of North Dakota School of Mines was made from North Dakota clay. In 1910, the University hired Margaret Kelly Cable to teach pottery making and she remained at the school until her retirement. *Julia Mattson and Margaret Pachl were other instructors between 1923 and 1970. Designs and glazes varied through the years ranging from the Art Nouveau to modern styles. Pieces were marked "University of North Dakota - Grand Forks, N.D. - Made at School of Mines, N.D." within a circle and also signed by the students until 1963. Since that time, the pieces bear only the students' signatures. Items signed "Huck" are by the artist Flora Huckfield and were made between 1923 and 1949. We list only those pieces made prior to 1963.*

North Dakota School of Mines Pottery

Bowl, 3" d., blue drip glaze on green . . $60.00
Bowl, squeeze bag decor, artist-
   signed, small 85.00
Bowl-vase, 5½" d., 3½" h., carved
   designs, green glaze, artist-signed
   (ILLUS.) 55.00
Creamer & sugar bowl, turquoise, pr. . . . 63.00
Custard cup, 6 colored bands decor 60.00
Ewer, green drip glaze, 7" h. 28.00
Pot, orange bear track decor, artist-
   signed, 2" h. 40.00
Rose bowl, inscribed & carved "North
   Dakota-North Dakota Wheat" on
   beige matte ground, attributed to
   Margaret Kelly Cable, 4½" d.,
   3" h. 350.00
Rose bowl, Art Deco black Indian
   design, bentonite glaze, 4½" d.,
   3½" h. 375.00
Tile, carved scene, colorful, Julia
   Mattson, 1928 . . . . 450.00
Vase, 3" h., dark blue 70.00
Vase, 3" h., yellow matte finish 60.00
Vase, 5" h., incised wheat shocks,
   signed Huck (Flora Huckfield) 175.00
Vase, 5¾" h., bulbous, buff shaded to
   blue-grey 65.00
Vase, bud, 6" h., aqua, artist-signed . . . 45.00
Vase, 7" h., incised green rings decor,
   signed Cable (Margaret Kelly
   Cable) 115.00
Vase, 7¼" h., light moss green,
   signed Julia Mattson 100.00
Vase, 7½" h., 6½" d., incised leaves
   decor 250.00

Vase, 7½" h., incised turquoise rings
   decor, signed Cable (Margaret Kelly
   Cable) 115.00
Vase, 8½" h., brown & tan decor,
   signed Julia Mattson 115.00
Vase, 9" h., carved Indians on horse-
   back decor, signed Julia Mattson . . . 375.00

NYMPHENBURG

Nymphenburg Ring Box

A hard-paste porcelain factory that was to become world-famous was founded in Nymphenburg, Bavaria, Germany, in 1753, flourished under royal patronage until the late 18th century when it was taken over by the state, and was leased again to private interests in 1862. This factory is still in production making modern porcelains. The early productions are quite high-priced.

Bowl, oval form w/ornate pierced
   handles, h.p. floral bouquets &
   gold scrolls decor $225.00
Coffee pot, cov., one side w/blue &
   iron-red costumed minuet dancer
   within iron-red & green foliate
   scroll-work before a puce "camaieu"
   landscape, reverse w/a puce
   "camaieu" vignette of a memorial
   monument, ca. 1765, 6½" h. 495.00
Figurine, "Crinoline Lady," after
   Bustelli, Shield mark, 7" h. 250.00
Model of a Great Dane dog in recum-
   bent position, white, 10½" l., 3" h. . . 140.00
Plate, 10" d., h.p. scene w/figures in
   an extensive rocky river landscape
   w/buildings & trees within a floral
   scroll cartouche, shaped rim
   w/foliate garlands in green & gilt,
   1763-67 (minor foot rim chip) 495.00
Ring box & cover w/pear & leaf finial,
   h.p. roses & gold trim, 3¾" d.,
   3¼" h. (ILLUS.) 250.00
Vase, 5" h., cupids depicting the Four
   Seasons decor 200.00

OLD IVORY

Old Ivory Creamer & Sugar Bowl

Old Ivory china was produced in Silesia in a great diversity of table pieces, most of which bear pattern stock numbers.

Berry set: master bowl & 6 sauce
  dishes; No. 84, 7 pcs. $340.00
Bon bon, No. 75, 6½" 95.00
Bouillon cup & saucer, No. 75 . . . . .90.00
Bowl, 6" d., tab handle, No. 84 . . . . .55.00
Bowl, 6½" d., No. 16 . . . . .35.00
Bowls, salad, 6½" d., No. 28, set of 6 . .160.00
Bowl, master berry, 9" d., No. 16 . . . . . . .75.00
Bowl, master berry, 9½" d., No. 15 . . . . .60.00
Bowl, 10¼" d., No. 84 . . . . .78.00
Cake plate, pierced handles, No. 16,
  10" d. . . . . .45.00 to 82.50
Cake plate, pierced handles, No. 22,
  10" d. 225.00
Cake plate, pierced handles, No. 11,
  10½" d. 85.00
Cake plate, pierced handles, No. 84 . . . .57.50
Celery tray, No. 11, 11½" l. 75.00
Celery tray, No. 16 . . . . .70.00
Celery tray, No. 75, 11½ x 5½" 85.00
Chocolate cup & saucer, No. 84 . . . . .45.00
Chocolate cups & saucers, No. 16,
  set of 6 . . . . .275.00
Chocolate pot, cov., No. 75 . . . . .300.00
Creamer, No. 16 . . . . .45.00
Creamer, No. 84 . . . . .45.00
Creamer & cov. sugar bowl, No. 11,
  pr. 75.00
Creamer & cov. sugar bowl, No. 15,
  pr. 100.00
Creamer & cov. sugar bowl, No. 16,
  pr. 155.00
Creamer & cov. sugar bowl, No. 39,
  pr. 75.00
Creamer & cov. sugar bowl, No. 84,
  pr. . . . . .95.00 to 115.00
Creamer & cov. sugar bowl, No. 200,
  pr. (ILLUS.) 100.00
Cup & saucer, demitasse, No. 11 . . . . . .30.00
Cup & saucer, demitasse, No. 15 . . . . . . .45.00
Cup & saucer, No. 16 . . . . .39.00
Cup & saucer, No. 84 . . . . .55.00
Cup & saucer, No. 200 . . . . .38.00
Dresser tray, No. 84,
  12 x 7" . . . . .110.00 to 145.00
Nappy, handled, No. 7 . . . . .45.00
Nappy, No. 15 . . . . .47.50
Nappy, No. 16 . . . . .52.50
Nappy, No. 84 . . . . .47.50

Pickle dish, No. 84, 7¾" l. 80.00
Plate, 6" d., No. 10 . . . . .25.00
Plate, 6" d., No. 11 . . . . .15.00 to 20.00
Plate, 6" d., No. 16 . . . . .17.50
Plate, 6" d., No. 84 . . . . .25.00
Plate, 6" d., No. 200 . . . . .15.00
Plate, 6½" d., No. 75 . . . . .27.00
Plate, 6¾" d., No. 16 . . . . .20.00
Plate, 7" d., No. 14 . . . . .35.00
Plate, 7¼" d., No. 11 . . . . .20.00

Old Ivory Pattern No. 16

Plate, 7¾" d., No. 16 (ILLUS.) 26.00
Plate, 7¾" d., No. 28 . . . . .23.00
Plate, 7¾" d., No. 75 . . . . .23.00
Plate, 7¾" d., No. 82 . . . . .45.00
Plate, 7¾" d., No. 84 . . . . .41.50
Plate, 8½" d., No. 11 . . . . .30.00
Plate, 8½" d., No. 16 . . . . .40.00
Plate, 9¾" d., No. 28 . . . . .130.00
Platter, 11½" l., No. 22 . . . . .98.00
Platter, 13½" l., No. 84 . . . . .150.00
Salt & pepper shakers, No. 16, pr. 72.50
Salt & pepper shakers, No. 84, pr. 105.00
Toothpick holder, barrel-shaped,
  No. 16 . . . . .195.00
Toothpick holder, No. 75 . . . . .200.00
Vegetable bowl, No. 11, 10½" d. 35.00
Vegetable bowl, No. 16 . . . . .75.00

OLD SLEEPY EYE

Sleepy Eye, Minn., was named after an Indian Chief. The Sleepy Eye Milling Co. had stoneware and pottery premiums made at the turn of the century first by the Weir Pottery Company and subsequently by Western Stoneware Co., Monmouth, Ill. On these items the trademark Indian head was signed beneath "Old Sleepy Eye." The colors were Flemish blue on grey. Later pieces by Western Stoneware to 1937 were not made for Sleepy Eye Milling Co. but for other businesses. They bear the same

Indian head but "Old Sleepy Eye" does not appear below. They have a reverse design of teepees and trees and may or may not be marked Western Stoneware on the base. These items are usually found in cobalt blue on cream and are rarer in other colors.

Bowl (salt bowl), 6½" d., 4" h., Flemish blue on grey stoneware, Weir Pottery, 1903 ....$415.00

Butter jar, Flemish blue on grey stoneware, Weir Pottery, 1903 ....450.00

Mug, cobalt blue on white, small Indian head on handle, Western Stoneware Co., 1906-37 ....185.00

Pitcher, 4" h., cobalt blue on white, w/small Indian head on handle, Western Stoneware Co., 1906-37 (half-pint)........................140.00

Pitcher, 4" h., all yellow, w/small Indian head on handle, Western Stoneware Co., World War I era, 1914-18 (half-pint) 950.00

Pitcher, 5¼" h., cobalt blue on grey, w/small Indian head on handle, Western Stoneware Co., World War I era, 1914-18 (pint) 170.00

Pitcher, 6¼" h., cobalt blue on white, w/small Indian head on handle, Western Stoneware Co., 1906-37 (quart) 175.00

Pitcher, 6¼" h., all yellow, w/small Indian head on handle, Western Stoneware Co., World War I era, 1914-18 (quart) 985.00

Pitcher, 7¾" h., cobalt blue on white, w/small Indian head on handle, Western Stoneware Co., 1906-37 (half-gallon) 195.00

Old Sleepy Eye Pitcher

Pitcher, 8½" h., cobalt blue on white, w/small Indian head on handle, Western Stoneware Co., 1906-37 (ILLUS.)........................225.00

Pitcher, "Standing Indian," Flemish blue on grey stoneware 900.00

Stein, all blue, Western Stoneware Co., 7¾" h. 560.00

Stein, blue on white, Western Stoneware Co., 1906-37, 7¾" h. 435.00

Stein, all brown or all green, Western Stoneware Co., 7¾" h., each.........................1,140.00

Stein, brown on white, Western Stoneware Co., 7¾" h. 790.00

Stein, brown on yellow, Western Stoneware Co., 7¾" h. 785.00

Stein, chestnut brown, 1952, 22 oz. size 375.00

Stein, chestnut brown, 1952, 40 oz. size 440.00

Stein, Flemish blue on grey stoneware, Weir Pottery Co., 1903 ....425.00

Sugar bowl, cobalt blue on white, Western Stoneware Co., 1906-37, 4" h. 390.00

Vase, 9" h., Flemish blue on grey stoneware, Indian head signed, dragonfly, frog & bullrushes reverse, Weir Pottery Co., 1903 .....275.00

Vase, 9" h., grey stoneware, molded w/cattails & dragonfly each side 195.00

OWENS

Owens Utopian Bottle-Vase

Owens pottery is the product of the J.B. Owens Pottery Company, which operated in Ohio from 1890 to 1929. In 1891 it located in Zanesville and produced art pottery from 1896, introducing "Utopian" wares as its first art pottery. The company switched to tile after 1907. Efforts to rebuild after the factory burned in 1928 failed and the company closed in 1929.

Bottle-vase, Utopian, underglaze slip-painted florals, standard brown glaze, 6" h. (ILLUS.) $120.00

Honey jug w/handle, Utopian, underglaze slip-painted Indian portrait, standard brown glaze, 7" h. 675.00

Humidor, cov., Utopian, underglaze slip-painted pipe, cigar & matches, standard brown glaze, artist-signed......................195.00

Jardiniere, Utopian, underglaze slip-painted florals, standard brown glaze..........................125.00

Jug, Utopian, underglaze slip-painted currants, standard brown glaze, artist-signed, 5½" h. 145.00

Lamp, Soudanese line, gold & red Art Nouveau decor on glossy black ground, 14" h. 165.00

Mug, Utopian, underglaze slip-painted currants, standard brown glaze, artist-signed, 5" h. 135.00

Mug, Utopian, underglaze slip-painted grapes, standard brown glaze, 5" h. . . .90.00

Mug, Utopian, underglaze slip-painted cherries, standard brown glaze 110.00

Pitcher, tankard, 12" h., Matt Utopian, underglaze slip-painted floral decor, light matte finish, artist-signed 185.00

Pitcher, tankard, 12" h., Utopian, underglaze slip-painted cherries, standard brown glaze 110.00

Pitcher, Lotus line, underglaze slip-painted sandpiper standing on one leg on shaded light ground 295.00

Vase, 5" h., Utopian, underglaze slip-painted clover, standard brown glaze..........................85.00

Vase, 5" h., Utopian, spiral-molded form, underglaze slip-painted violets decor, standard brown glaze, artist-signed..........................95.00

Vase, 6" h., 2-handled, Feroza Faience line, violet-black metallic lustre glaze..........................135.00

Utopian Vase

Vase, 7½" h., Utopian, underglaze slip-painted orange wild rose w/green leaves, standard brown glaze, artist-signed (ILLUS.) 250.00

Vase, 8½" h., Matt Utopian, under-

glaze slip-painted roses, light matte finish..........................125.00

Vase, 9½" h., 6½" d., 2-handled, Henri Deux line, incised Art Nouveau decor filled w/color.......450.00

Vase, 13½" h., Utopian, underglaze slip-painted florals, standard brown glaze..........................285.00

Water set: 12" h. tankard pitcher & 3 mugs; Utopian, underglaze slip-painted florals, standard brown glaze, 4 pcs.....................400.00

OYSTER PLATES

Oyster Plate by the Union Porcelain Works

Oyster plates intrigue a few collectors. Oysters were shucked and the meat served in wells of these attractive plates specifically designed to serve oysters. During the late 19th Century, they were made of fine china and majolica. Some plates were decorated in the realistic "trompe l'oeil" technique while others simply matched the pattern of a dinner service. Following is a random sampling of oyster plates that were sold in the past eighteen months.

Austrian china, 6 wells, yellow florals & brown leaves decor $55.00

Austrian china, lavender florals & gold outlining on white ground, marked "Carlsbad-Victoria," pr. 95.00

German porcelain, "trompe l'oeil" technique w/realistic oyster wells, 9¼" d. 90.00

German porcelain, pink & yellow florals w/green leaves on oyster wells & sauce dips, ornate gold rim 35.00

German porcelain, enameled pink florals & gold trim, set of 4 ....70.00

German porcelain, white w/gold trim, marked "Weimar," 8¼" d., set of 8...95.00

Haviland china, 5 wells, dark green, brown & gold trim on salmon pink ground, 8 5/8" d. 55.00

Haviland china, 6 wells, yellow & brown

decor on yellow ground, ornate gold
trim, 8¾" d........................48.00
Haviland china, realistic shell-shaped
wells outlined w/h.p. marine life,
9" d., set of 6 ....260.00
Limoges china, scalloped gold edges,
rust or green ground, set of 6 ......210.00
Limoges china, white w/ornate gold
trim, 8" d., set of 7 ....325.00
Majolica, 6 realistic shell-molded wells
& 6 shaded brown, green & yellow
reversed shells, burgundy shaded to
light blue ground, marked "E," star,
"B. Napoli," 8½" d. 45.00
Majolica, depressed shells & molded
seaweed, cream & coral pink,
impressed "Minton" mark.........178.00
Majolica, turquoise, yellow &
brown fishscale ground, marked
"Wedgwood".......................65.00
Union Porcelain Works, Brooklyn, New
York, china, "trompe l'oeil" technique
w/four realistic clam form wells &
single seashell sauce well separated
by molded shellfish & seaweed,
dated 1881, 8½ x 6¾" (ILLUS.)......80.00
Union Porcelain Works, Brooklyn, New
York, china, "trompe l'oeil" technique
w/shell form wells & embossed
shellfish & seaweed, 8¾ x 6¾",
set of 6 ....480.00

PAIRPOINT - LIMOGES

The Pairpoint Manufacturing Company of New Bedford, Massachusetts, producers of fine plated silver, as well as glass items, had china especially made in Limoges, France for a short period of time. These tastefully decorated porcelains, often enhanced with plated silver, are in short supply. Also see PAIRPOINT under Glass and METALS - Plated Silver.

Charger, h.p. shorebirds (2) standing
in tall grass before barren tree at
seashore, relief-molded border
w/heavy gold trim, 16½" d. $1,500.00
Cookie jar w/silverplate rim, cover &
bail handle, relief-molded & h.p.
florals on burnt orange ground,
signed, overall 9½" h..............295.00
Cup & saucer, demitasse, h.p. pansies
on pink ground 85.00
Ewer, football-shaped, applied gold
lotus branch handle & triangular
spout, ridged body w/lotus leaf
depressions outlined in gold
enameling & shaded green leaves
decor, signed & numbered, 9"
across, 6¼" h......................750.00

Vase, applied openwork handles, h.p.
pink & yellow chrysanthemums,
leaves & buds decor, signed 425.00

PARIAN

Large Parian Figure

Parian is unglazed porcelain in the biscuit stage, and takes its name from its resemblance to Parian marble used for statuary. Parian wares were made in this country and abroad through much of the last century and continue to be made. Also see RING TREES.

Bust of Apollo, Germany, early 20th c.,
5" w. at shoulders, 7" h. $75.00
Bust of Shakespeare, signed "Robinson
& Leadbeater," 7¾" h..............125.00
Bust of a Grecian lady wearing
laurel wreath in her hair,
10½" h. 60.00
Figure of the Greek goddess Psyche,
seated & holding Cupid's quiver &
arrow while Cupid reaches for his
tools from behind her, 9" h. 165.00
Figure of a semi-nude partially draped
woman w/flowers in her hair, standing
beside a garland-draped pillar &
holding a flame aloft, with Cupid
hovering over her left arm, 6" w.
square base, 9" h. 145.00
Figure of a woman wearing draped
gown & pearl necklace, seated on
vine-covered stump & gazing at bird
perched on her shoulder, impressed "Copeland," 7" oval base,
13¼" h. 285.00
Figure of a little girl carrying basket
of flowers, pretty flesh tone features,
pastel pink & blue garments w/white,
signed "Robinson & Leadbeater,"
6¼" d., 16" h. 275.00

Figure of Little Red Riding Hood wearing cloak, w/basket at her feet, impressed "Minton," dated 1853 . . . . .115.00

Figures of little girls kneeling: one bowing her head & clutching a Bible; other w/hands clasped in her lap & staring into space; impressed "Minton," late 19th c., 9" & 9¾" h., pr. 165.00

Figure of a classical lady, 19" h. (ILLUS.) 425.00

Figure group, man seated on rock & holding birds overhead, hunting dogs seated at his side, 9½" h. 135.00

Plaque, pierced to hang, 3 figures of winged Cupid in high relief, self-framed, impressed "Enoret - B. & G.," 13" d. 160.00

Spillholder, babes in woods scene in relief on sage green ground, ca. 1850 . . . . .50.00

Vase, 5½" h., bust of Grecian woman wearing laurel wreath in low relief each side 35.00

Vase, bud, 6" h., relief-molded bird in swing, florals & leaves decor 50.00

Parian Vase

Vase, 9" h., applied white grape clusters at shoulders, florals, leaves & medallions on blue body (ILLUS.) 65.00

Vases, 10" h., applied white monkey-like creatures front & reverse & grape clusters at shoulders on blue body, ca. 1850, pr. 245.00

PARIS & OLD PARIS

China known by the generic name of Paris and Old Paris was made by several Parisian factories from the 18th through the 19th century; some of it is marked and some is not. Much of it was handsomely decorated.

Old Paris Tea & Coffee Service

Cup & saucer, handleless, h.p. pink floral decor, early 19th c. $175.00

Cup & saucer, 12-panel form, cobalt blue w/gold roses decor, late 19th c. 58.00

Garniture set: D-shaped bough pot & pr. square orange tubs; sides painted w/colorful birds perched on or near small trees in slightly recessed rectangular panels within gilt chain or vine & zig-zag borders, corners w/stop-fluted columns heightened in gilding & terminating in pine cone finials, now mounted w/tall stems of white bisque flowers & green leaves, 1790-1810, 15½" to 16½" h., 3 pcs. 4,125.00

Tea & coffee service: cov. coffee pot, cov. teapot, cov. sugar bowl, milk jug, waste bowl & 6 c/s; each painted w/realistic scene of animals in natural habitat within wide gold borders, mark of Marc Schoelcher (1820-28) in gold, 17 pcs. (ILLUS. of part) 1,430.00

Tea set: cov. teapot, creamer, cov. sugar bowl, waste bowl, 14 plates & 12 c/s; paneled sides w/regularly spaced blue & gold floral sprigs, ca. 1840, 30 pcs. (2 saucers w/chips) 192.50

Vase, 8¾" h., pedestal base, coral & gold bands at top & base, body w/portrait of French lady w/binoculars gazing out to sea reserved within panel 90.00

Vases, 13" h., baluster-shaped, h.p. floral medallion on pale green ground w/gilt highlights, ca. 1900, pr. 165.00

Vases, 14½" h., 7" d., ovoid w/tall flaring neck, tall loop handles at shoulders, turquoise blue ground reserved w/portrait medallion of children in landscape setting, pr. . . .450.00

Vases, 18" h., campana-shaped, each front w/panel depicting Napoleon & his troops in military campaign & w/rustic cottage in woodland setting reverse within gilt borders, the neck, rim, handles & base further enriched w/gilding, pr. 1,100.00

PATE-SUR-PATE

Taking its name from the French phrase meaning "paste on paste," this type of ware features designs in relief, obtained by successive layers of thin pottery paste, painted one on top of the other. Much of this work was done in France and England, and perhaps the best-known wares of this type from England are those made by Minton, which see.

Box, cov., footed, blue w/white "pate-sur-pate" cherubs & lion pulling chariot, gold trim, marked Limoges, 3¾" d. $119.00
Box, cov., blue w/white "pate-sur-pate" cupids decor, artist-signed, Limoges, 4¼ x 4" 190.00
Pitcher, 8" h., bearded head mask at handle terminal, pink w/white "pate-sur-pate" mythological figures 225.00
Plate, 9" d., blue w/white "pate-sur-pate" roses decor, gilt trim at edges . . 40.00
Vase, 9½" h., amphora-style, celadon green w/white "pate-sur-pate" medallion of Diana in flowing chiffon robe on mauve ground, Schultz-Marke.......................474.00
Wall pocket, deep olive green w/white "pate-sur-pate" figure of maiden wearing diaphanous gown & cupid w/harp, attributed to George Jones, 9 x 6½"........................585.00

PAUL REVERE POTTERY

Paul Revere Bread Plate

This pottery was established in Boston, Mass., in 1906, by a group of philanthropists seeking to establish better conditions for underprivileged young girls of the area. Edith Brown served as supervisor of the small "Saturday Evening Girls Club" pottery operation which was moved, in 1912, to

a house close to the Old North Church where Paul Revere's signal lanterns had been placed. The wares were mostly hand decorated in mineral colors and both sgraffito and molded decorations were employed. Although it became popular, it was never a profitable operation and always depended on financial contributions to operate. After the death of Edith Brown in 1932, the pottery foundered and finally closed in 1942.

Bread plate, "Eate Thy Breade In Joye And Thankfulnesse" inscribed on white border, yellow center, 9¾" d. (ILLUS.) $440.00
Creamer, blue, marked "S.E.G." (Saturday Evening Girls), 3" h........45.00
Flower pot, blue, marked "S.E.G." 55.00
Mug, yellow.........................43.00
Pitcher, 3½" h., mountains, sky & trees decor, marked "S.E.G" 285.00
Pitcher, 4" h., blue 50.00
Plate, 7½" d., decorated, marked "S.E.G." 200.00
Vase, 4" h., mustard yellow 50.00
Vase, 7" h., blue speckled glaze, artist-signed & dated 1923 ....52.50
Vase, 10" h., blue, marked "S.E.G." 95.00
Vase, 10" h., black glaze, w/label......75.00

PETERS & REED

Peters & Reed Flower Bowl

In 1897, John D. Peters and Adam Reed formed a partnership to produce flower pots in Zanesville, Ohio. Formally incorporated as Peters and Reed in 1901, this type of production was the mainstay until after 1907 when they gradually expanded into the art pottery field. Frank Ferrell, a former designer at the Weller Pottery, developed the "Moss Aztec" line while associated with Peters and Reed and other art lines followed. Though unmarked, attribution is not difficult once familiar with the various lines. In 1921, Peters and Reed became Zane Pottery which continued in production until 1941.

Basket, hanging-type w/chains, Moss Aztec line, floral decor $28.00
Bowl, 9" d., Pereco Ware, laurel branches & berries in relief, matte finish............................60.00
Cuspidor, Moss Aztec line, florals in relief.............................57.00
Flower bowl w/flower frog, dark blue glaze, plain (ILLUS.) 25.00
Jardiniere, Moss Aztec line, full figure women in relief around sides, 9" h....65.00
Jug, sprigged on single ear of corn, brown high glaze, 5½" d., 5½" h. 95.00
Jug, ball-shaped, handled, sprigged on grapevine & grape cluster, brown high glaze, 5½" d., 6¼" h. 75.00

Peters & Reed Art Pottery Pitcher

Pitcher, tankard, 13½" h., sprigged on grapevine & grape clusters, brown high glaze (ILLUS.) 135.00
Vase, 3½" h., 5½" d., sprigged on floral decor, brown high glaze 15.00
Vase, 6½" h., Moss Aztex line, florals in relief 35.00
Vase, 10" h., Moss Aztec line, pine-cones decor 55.00
Vase, 10½" h., Landsun line, blended glaze...........................40.00
Vase, 11¾" h., corset-shaped, Pereco Ware, florals in relief at top, semi-matte finish.......................36.00
Vase, 12" h., Moss Aztec line, flowers & berries decor 65.00
Vase, 12½" h., sprigged on wreath & cherubs, standard brown glaze 45.00
Wall pocket, Egyptian Ware, profile of Pharaoh decor....................39.00
Wall pocket, cone-shaped, Moss Aztec line, floral decor, signed Ferrell 50.00
Window box, Moss Aztec line, musician beside reclining couple in relief exterior, glossy terra cotta w/green highlights interior, signed Ferrell, 13" l., 5½" h.............115.00

PEWABIC POTTERY

Mary Chase Perry (Stratton) and Horace J. Caulkins were partners in this Detroit, Michigan pottery. Established in 1903, Pewabic Pottery evolved from their Revelation Pottery --- "Pewabic" meaning "clay with copper color" in the language of Michigan's Chippewa Indians. Caulkins attended to the clay formulas and Mary Perry Stratton was the artistic creator of forms & glaze formulas, eventually developing a wide range of colors for her finely textured glazes. The pottery's reputation for fine wares and architectural tiles enabled it to survive the depression years of the 1930s. After Caulkins died in 1923, Mrs. Stratton continued to be active in the pottery until her death, at age ninety-four, in 1961. Her contributions to the art pottery field are numerous.

Ash tray, mottled red over blue-green iridescent glaze, 5" d. $75.00
Bowl, 4½" d., green drip glaze 135.00
Bowl, 5½" d., 1 5/8" h., flared lip, iridescent mauve & green glaze, signed.........................220.00
Cup & saucer, Tiffany-type iridescent glaze ....150.00 to 200.00
Dish, round, mottled turquoise over yellow iridescent high glaze 125.00
Dish, scalloped rim, turquoise over lime iridescent glaze 125.00
Planter-vase, mottled green on brown matte ground, impressed decor at rim, Maple Leaf mark, artist-signed, 7 x 6"............................375.00
Vase, 4½" h., royal blue matte finish ..300.00
Vase, 7¾" h., bulbous base, florals & stems in relief, green matte finish...325.00

PHOENIX BIRD or FLYING TURKEY

Phoenix Bird Bowl

The phoenix bird, a symbol of immortality and spiritual rebirth, has been handed down through Egyptian mythology as a bird that consumed itself by fire after 500 years and then rose again, renewed from its ashes. This bird has been used to decorate

Japanese porcelain, designed for export, for more than 100 years. The pattern incorporates a blue design of the bird, variously known as the "Flying Phoenix," the "Flying Turkey" or the "Ho-o," stamped on a white ground. It became popular with collectors because there was an abundant supply since the ware was produced for a long period of time. Pieces can be found marked with Japanese characters, with a "Nippon" mark, or a "Made in Japan" or "Occupied Japan" mark. Though there are several variations to the pattern and border, we have lumped them together since values seem to be quite comparable. A word of caution to collectors, Phoenix Bird pattern is still being produced.

Bowl, 5" d., Phoenix Bird, marked
  "Made in Japan" (ILLUS.)...........$15.00
Bowl, 7¼" d., Phoenix Bird...........18.00
Coffee pot, demitasse, Flying Turkey ...45.00

Phoenix Bird Creamer

Creamer, Phoenix Bird, 3" h. (ILLUS.) 9.00
Creamer & sugar bowl, Phoenix Bird,
  3½", pr.........................35.00
Cup & saucer, Flying Turkey, marked
  "Noritake".......................11.00
Cup & saucer, Phoenix Bird............12.00
Egg cup, Flying Turkey...............10.00
Egg cup, double, Phoenix Bird, marked
  "Made in Japan"...................12.00
Ginger jar, cov., Phoenix Bird,
  marked "Made in Japan" 20.00
Nappy, Phoenix Bird, 5" d. 12.00
Pitcher, Phoenix Bird, small..........22.50
Plates, 6" d., Flying Turkey, set of 6 ....35.00
Plate, 7¼" d., Phoenix Bird, marked
  "Nippon" 6.00
Plate, 8½" d., Phoenix Bird 12.00
Plate, 9½" d., Phoenix Bird 15.00
Plate, 9¾" d., Flying Turkey..........65.00
Plate, 9¾" d., Phoenix Bird 18.50
Ramekin, Flying Turkey, marked
  "Noritake".......................12.50
Relish, Flying Turkey, 7" l. 20.00
Salt shaker, Flying Turkey.............8.50
Salt & pepper shakers, Phoenix Bird,
  pr. (ILLUS.) 20.00

Phoenix Bird Salt & Pepper Shakers

Teapot, cov., demitasse, stick handle,
  Phoenix Bird, 6" h. 140.00
Teapot, cov., Phoenix Bird 45.00
Tea tile, Flying Turkey 25.00

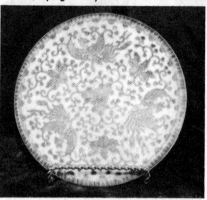

Phoenix Bird Tea Tile

Tea tile, Phoenix Bird (ILLUS.) 65.00
Toothpick holder, Flying Turkey.......18.00
Tumbler, juice, Phoenix Bird 15.00
Tumbler, Flying Turkey, 2½" h. 10.00
Vegetable bowl, cov., Flying Turkey,
  oval...........................80.00
Vegetable bowl, open, Flying Turkey,
  9" oval 35.00

PICKARD

Pickard, Inc., making fine hand-decorated china today in Antioch, Ill., was founded in Chicago in 1894 by Wilder A. Pickard. The company now makes its own blanks but once bought them from other potteries, primarily from the Havilands and others in Limoges, France.

Bon bon, ovoid, scalloped rim,
  garden scene w/roses, 1912, 7".....$75.00
Bowl, 6" d., 3" h., h.p. strawberries
  decor 75.00

Bowl, 6¾" d., scenic exterior w/matte finish, gold interior, signed E. Challinor 295.00

Bowl, 8" d., gold rococo rim, strawberries, white blossoms & gooseberries on cream shaded to apricot ground, 1905, signed Challinor, Bavarian blank 125.00

Bowl, 9" octagon, Enchanted Garden patt., artist-signed 150.00

Bowl, fruit, 9½" d., 4¼" h., gold scalloped rim & feet, deep yellow shaded to deep tan w/gold scrolling exterior, h.p. red cherries & gold branches on lemon yellow ground interior, 1905.....................175.00

Pickard Fruit Bowl

Bowl, fruit, 10½" across handles, 5" h., Seville patt., gold w/wide floral borders, artist-signed, 1919-22 (ILLUS.) 265.00

Cake plate, handled, fruit decor on blue & gold center, artist-signed 110.00

Candle holders, overall gold-etched florals, 2½" h., pr. 25.00

Candy dish, handled, wide gold rim, h.p. pink clover decor, Limoges blank, 5½" l......................60.00

Chocolate pot, cov., gold handle, pink sweet clover decor, artist-signed ....275.00 to 325.00

Compote, 6" d., 3" h. overall gold-etched decor, 1940s 40.00

Compote, 9¼" d., 2½" h., h.p. fruit decor, 1905-10 ....195.00

Creamer & cov. sugar bowl, angular gold handles, h.p. Deserted Garden patt., pr......................250.00

Creamer & cov. sugar bowl, stylized reddish leaves & green foliage on cream ground, heavy gold trim, artist-signed, 1898 mark, pr. 195.00

Creamer & open sugar bowl, large gondola form, ornute gold handles & rims, violets decor, Limoges blank, artist-signed, 1898, pr. 100.00

Cups & saucers, demitasse, band of fruit & blossoms, set of 6 ....185.00

Demitasse set: cov. coffee pot, sugar bowl & creamer; faceted, paneled shape tapering to hexagonal foot,

gold elongated spout & handle, polychrome oriental style florals, ca. 1920, 3 pcs. 175.00

Dish, 2-compartment w/ring handle, gold-etched, 6½" d.................20.00

Dish, irregular form, h.p. violets & daisies decor, 6¾ x 5¼" 75.00

Pitcher, 7 3/8" h., gold handle, top & bottom bands, h.p. fruit & blossoms decor 225.00

Pitcher, 8" h., ornate handle, Aura Argenta Linear patt., gold & platinum trim, artist-signed, 1905-10, Limoges blank....................395.00

Pitcher, 8" h., wide gold band & h.p. floral decor, 1898 ....295.00

Pitcher, cider, crab apples & heavy gold decor, artist-signed 395.00

Plate, 6" d., scalloped gold rim, h.p. violets w/swirling stems center, 1898, Limoges blank...............65.00

Plate, 8" d., painted lavender & blue ivy leaves w/enameled gold outlining on ecru ground, wide border of dainty fruit, 1912 ....55.00

Plate, 8" d., wide scalloped coin gold rim, strawberries & pink blossoms w/white enameled dots, artist-signed, 1898, Limoges blank........85.00

Plate, 8½" d., h.p. foliage & shelled peanuts w/raspberry-red highlights on beige shaded to soft brown ground, ca. 1900 ....68.00

Plate, 8¾" d., blended blue moonlight scene w/matte finish, artist-signed...........................195.00

Plate, 9" d., h.p. waterlilies & cattails decor 65.00

Plate, 9½" d., heavy gold florals on creamy white, artist-signed 95.00

Plate, 9¾" d., deep green border w/gold leaves, bust portrait of beautiful brunette w/lilacs in hair on shaded ground center 155.00

Vase, 10" h., Deserted Garden patt., artist-signed 275.00

Pickard Vase

Vase, 10¼" h., 2-handled, Fruit Panels patt., large medallions of fruit front & reverse on gold ground, artist-signed, 1912-19 (ILLUS.) 400.00

Vase, 12¾" h., Italian garden scene, semi-matte glaze, Nippon blank, signed E. Challinor, 1912-19 . . . . 595.00

PICTORIAL SOUVENIRS

Souvenir of Lake City, Minnesota

These small ceramic wares, expressly made to be sold as a souvenir of a town or resort, are decorated with a pictorial scene which is usually titled. Made in profusion in Germany, Austria, Bavaria, and England, they were distributed by several American firms including C.E. Wheelock & Co., John H. Roth (Jonroth), Jones, McDuffee & Stratton Co., and others. Because people seldom traveled in the early years of this century, a small souvenir tray or dish, picturing the resort or a town scene, afforded an excellent, inexpensive gift for family or friends when returning from a vacation trip. Seldom used and carefully packed away later, there is an abundant supply of these small wares available today at moderate prices. Their values are likely to rise. Also see HAMPSHIRE POTTERY.

Ash tray - matchbox holder, "Washington, D.C." scene, Nippon spoke mark $35.00

Creamer & cov. sugar bowl, "Niagara Falls" scene, marked "Bavaria," pr. . . 22.00

Dish, leaf-shaped, "Railroad Station, Waldoboro, Maine" scene, ornate gold trim, 4½" d. 25.00

Dish, pierced handle, "City Hall, Lake City, Minnesota" scene, gold trim, 5¼" sq. (ILLUS.) 18.50

Mug, "City Hall, Elgin, Illinois" scene, gold trim 15.00

Pitcher, "City Park, Jamestown, North Dakota" scene, marked "Bavaria" 25.00

Plate, 8" d., Congregational Church,

Eldora, Iowa" scene, marked "Wheelock" 15.00

Plate, 8" d., "The Portage, Akron, Ohio," Indian carrying canoe scene, marked "Syracuse China" 24.00

Plate, "Arcade Hotel, Newton, Kansas" scene, marked "Wheelock," small . . . 25.00

Plate, "Beaverhead Rock, Dillon, Montana" scene, marked "Wheelock," small 18.00

Plate, "View of Fifth Avenue, Moline, Illinois" scene, marked "Bavaria," small 20.00

Salt dip, 2-handled, "Capitol Building, Washington, D.C." scene, marked "Nippon," 2½" l. 90.00

Sauce dish, "Bunker Hill Monument, Boston, Massachusetts" scene, 5" d. 16.00

Sauce dish, "City Hall, Boston, Massachusetts," 5" d. 16.00

Sauce dish, "Bank & Library, Eastport, Maine" scene 20.00

Sauce dish, "Public School, Friend, Nebraska" scene 16.00

Vase, 4" h., 2-handled, "St. Anthony Hospital, Hays, Kansas" scene 5.00

Vase, 5½" h., "Court House, Lincoln, Kansas" scene 17.50

Vase, 5½" h., "Horseshoe Curve, Altoona, Pennsylvania" scene 9.50

Whimsey, model of a shoe, "Washington, D.C." scene, pink & white w/gold bow, 6¼" l. 40.00

PILKINGTON'S POTTERY

Royal Lancastrian Ware

Pilkington's Tile & Pottery Company was established in Lancashire, England, in 1892 for the manufacture of tiles. Eventually expanding, they introduced molded vases and other wares. Discovery of an opalescent glaze in 1903 led to the production of fine glazed earthenware which was marketed as

Lancastrian pottery. In 1928 they intro-duced Lapis Ware, distinguished by painted decoration of foliage, etc., under a matte glaze which became mottled and blurred during firing. The manufacture of pottery ceased in 1937 although decoration was continued for about another year. Pilking-ton's subsequently reopened in 1948 and again operated until August, 1957.

Tiles, 3 w/white stylized tulips on blue
   ground & single plain tile, in
   original box $300.00
Vase, 3¼" h., green matte finish 40.00
Vase, 6" h., Royal Lancastrian, blue &
   gold fleur-de-lis decor on gold ground,
   iridescent glaze, artist-signed,
   1924 . . . . .400.00
Vase, 7½" h., 4½" top d., Royal
   Lancastrian, cobalt blue matte
   finish, artist-signed (ILLUS.) 125.00
Vase, 8" h., Royal Lancastrian,
   molded orange mermaids decor,
   artist-signed .165.00
Vase, 10" h., globular, Lapis Ware 65.00

PISGAH FOREST

Walter Stephen experimented with making pottery shortly after 1900 with his parents in Tennessee. After their deaths, in 1910, he eventually moved to the foot of Mt. Pisgah in North Carolina where he became a partner of C. P. Ryman. Together they built a kiln and a shop but this partnership was dissolved in 1916. During 1920, Stephen again began to experiment with pottery and, by 1926, had his own pottery and equipment. Pieces are usually marked and may also be signed "W. Stephen" and dated. Walter Stephen died in 1961 but work at the pottery still continued, although on a part time basis.

Bowl, 4" h., turquoise glaze, signed
   "Stephen - 1946" $55.00
Bowl, 8 5/8" d., 2¾" h., turquoise
   glaze, pink glaze interior, dated
   1938 . . . . .35.00
Creamer, cameo-like relief equestrian
   figures decor, signed & dated 1942,
   5" h. 325.00
Creamer, turquoise crackle glaze,
   signed "Stephen - 1946" 17.00
Creamer & sugar bowl, cameo-like
   relief wagons, riders & etc. decor,
   signed "Stephen," pr. 375.00
Jar, cov., turquiose glaze, signed
   "Stephen - 1948," 4" h. 40.00
Pitcher, 9½" h., turquoise glaze,
   dated 1915 . . . . .45.00

Teapot, cov., turquoise glaze, dated
   1941 . . . . .65.00
Teapot, cov., cameo-like relief decor
   of covered wagon team 550.00
Vase, 3½" h., moss green glaze, pink
   interior, dated 1950 . . . . .30.00
Vase, 4" h., 5" d., collared neck,
   applied white cameo-like relief
   scene of covered wagon team &
   riders on green, signed "Stephen -
   1951" 90.00
Vase, 4½" h., beige & green crystal-
   line glaze, after 1926 . . . . .145.00
Vase, 7" h., cobalt blue matte finish,
   dated 1940 . . . . .75.00
Vase, 8" h., bulbous, turquoise crackle
   glaze w/maroon accents, creamy
   ivory interior, dated 1933 . . . . .50.00
Vase, 9" h., 7" widest d., trumpet-
   shaped, blue w/pink lining, signed
   "Stephen - 1948" 80.00
Vase, 13½" h., 3-handled, green
   exterior, pink interior 195.00

PRATT WARES

Pratt "Coiled" Pipe & Foxhead Sauceboat

The earliest ware now classified as Pratt ware was made by Felix Pratt at his pottery in Fenton, England from about 1810. He made earthenware with bright glazes, relief sporting jugs, toby mugs and commercial pots and jars whose lids bore multicolored transfer prints. The F. & R. Pratt mark is mid-19th century. The name Pratt ware is also applied today to mid and late 19th century English ware of the same general type as that made by Felix Pratt. Also see TOBY MUGS & JUGS.

Compote, 12½" 2-handled oval,
   color-printed scenic decor $295.00
Creamer, relief-molded peacocks
   w/multicolored enameling, 5¼" h.
   (hairlines in rim & handle) 135.00
Cup & saucer, child size, color-printed
   scene of Queen Victoria's children
   in goat-drawn open carriage

before Windsor Castle, yellow lustre
rims.............................150.00
Figure of "Hope," ca. 1800, 7" h. 125.00
Mush cup, color-printed pastoral
scene 55.00
Mustard jar, printed hunt scene on
blue ground, 1856 registry mark 55.00
Pipe, "coiled" construction, hollow
coiled body w/ochre, yellow & blue
stripes & leaf-molded bowl & mouthpiece washed in pale green,
8 1/8" l. (ILLUS. left) 1,210.00
Pitcher, 5½" h., color-printed classical
Greek figures on black ground 85.00
Pitcher, 6½" h., jug-type, handle
w/mask terminal, color-printed
hunting scene on blue, gold trim,
1856-60.........................150.00
Plaque, relief-molded scene of blacksmith shoeing horse w/lady, gentleman & groom observing, w/multi-
colored enameling, 9 x 8" oval
(minor edge wear & chip on inside
border ring).....................250.00
Plate, 8½" d., color-printed Snow
Owl & 2 chicks, blue & gold border,
mid-19th c.......................110.00
Plate, 9" d., color-printed "Wellington's Castle" scene center..........60.00
Platter, 4 1/8" oval, relief-molded fish,
w/multicolored enameling (hairline
& small edge flakes)..............125.00
Sauceboat, molded as a fox's head
w/ochre glaze & w/swan-form
handle, ca. 1800, repairs, 6 3/8" l.
(ILLUS. right) 1,320.00
Tea caddy, relief-molded comical
figures of 2 men & a lady in
exaggerated 18th c. finery, w/multi-
colored enameling, 5" h. (no lid) 325.00
Tea set: cov. teapot, creamer & sugar
bowl; color-printed florals on black
ground, 1860s, 3 pcs. 135.00

QUIMPER

HB HB

1882 & 1883 Marks of Grande Maison HB

*This French earthenware pottery has
been made in France since the end of the
17th century and is still in production
today. Because the colorful decoration on
this ware, predominently of Breton peasant
figures, is all hand painted and each piece is
unique, it has become increasingly popular*

*with collectors in recent years. Most pieces
offered today date from about the mid-19th
century to the present. Modern potteries
continue to operate today and contemporary examples are available in gift shops.*

Ash tray, Breton peasant woman
decor $45.00
Box, cov., Odetta line, portrait of
Breton peasant man w/wide
brim hat, H.B. Grande Maison,
1920-30, 5½ x 3½ x 1½"..........235.00

**HB
QuiMPER**

Grande Maison HB Mark 1883-1910

Butter pat, bird decor, H.B. Quimper,
1883-1910.......................27.00
Candlesticks, model of horse, Henriot
Quimper, after 1922, 7" l., pr. 125.00
Chamberstick, leaf-shaped base
w/handle, H.R. Quimper,
pre-1920........................200.00
Chocolate cups & saucers, peasants
decor, early 20th c., pr. 70.00
Creamer, crimped spout, peasant
woman decor, Henriot Quimper,
after 1922, 4" h. 65.00
Cream soup bowl & underplate, H.B.
Quimper, 1943 mark...............28.00
Cruet, double gemel-type, w/original
stoppers, peasant decor, Henriot
Quimper, after 1922,
7½" l....................125.00 to 140.00
Cup & saucer, octagonal, H.B. Quimper,
1943 mark 45.00
Cup & saucer, floral decor, large 75.00
Custard cup, handled, peasant decor,
Henriot Quimper, after 1922........35.00

Henriot Quimper Deep Dish

Deep dish, peasant man, yellow
ground, 8¼" d. (ILLUS.) 35.00
Dish, 3-compartment w/handles,
yellow & blue decor, large, H.B.
Quimper, 1883-1910 . . . . .118.00
Figure of St. Jean holding book
w/lamb, H.B. Quimper, 1943 mark,
13" h. 325.00
Figure group, male & female dancers
in Breton attire, signed Michaeu-
Vernex, Henriot Quimper, pre-1940,
10" h. 165.00
Figure group, mother & child, "First
Step," after Berthe Savigney, H.B.
Grande Maison 375.00
Flower holder, 5-finger, peasant
woman decor, Henriot Quimper,
after 1922 . . . . .110.00
Inkwell, Breton peasant couple &
Crest of Brittany decor, H.B.
Quimper, 1883-1910 mark 650.00
Inkwell, model of a hat, Henriot
Quimper, after 1922 . . . . .175.00
Inkwell, model of a pig, yellow
w/mottled green spots, brown ears
& snout, H.B. Quimper, 1943 mark,
4" l., 3" h. 85.00
Knife rest, peasant woman decor,
Henriot Quimper 37.50
Letter rack, 4-compartment, "decor
riche" trim w/elaborate borders,
H.B. Quimper, 1930s, 8 x 4½",
5" h. 325.00
Pitcher, 5" h., 5" d., left-handed,
peasant man decor on yellow
ground, Henriot Quimper, after
1922 . . . . .85.00
Pitcher, 5" h., 6" d., rope-twist han-
dle, peasant man decor, orange &
blue trim, Henriot Quimper,
1930s 85.00
Plates, 10½" d., peasant man &
woman decor, H.B. Quimper,
1883-1910, pr. .95.00
Plate, 10½" d., peasant decor,
Henriot Quimper, after 1922 . . . . .26.00
Plate, peasant woman decor, brown
ground, H.R. Quimper, pre-1922 . . . . .95.00

H.B. Quimper Porringer

Porringer, multicolored floral decor,
predominantly green trim, H.B.
Quimper, 1883-1910 (ILLUS.) 38.00

Salt dip, double, models of swans
attached to center ring, peasant
man interior of one & florals in other,
blue-sponged trim, Henriot Quimper,
France, w/pr. wooden salt spoons . . .45.00
Salt dip, double, model of Dutch
wooden shoes, H.R. Quimper 50.00
Salt & pepper shakers, figural bust
of peasant woman, pr. 95.00
Serving dish (or tray), Breton peasants
& floral decor, 15 x 9" 165.00
Vase, 6" h., floral decor, H.B.
Quimper 65.00
Vase, 8" h., double-handled, bulbous,
blue decor on white 95.00
Vase, 9" h., octagonal, peasant woman
decor, H.R. Quimper, 1886-1913 . . . .185.00
Vase, 10½" h., long side handles,
portrait decor, Henriot Quimper,
after 1922 . . . . .295.00
Wall pocket, bagpipe form, peasant
lady decor 110.00

REDWARE

Redware Covered Jar

Red earthenware pottery was made in the
American colonies from the late 1600s.
Bowls, crocks and all types of utilitarian
wares were turned out in great abundance to
supplement the pewter and handmade
treenware. The ready availability of the
clay, the same used in making bricks and
roof tiles, accounted for the vast production.
The lead-glazed redware retained its reddish
color, though a variety of colors could be
obtained by adding various metals to the
glaze. Interesting effects occurred accidentally through unsuspected impurities in the
clay or uneven temperatures in the firing
kiln which sometimes resulted in streaks or
mottled splotches. Also see SHENAN-
DOAH VALLEY POTTERY and SLIP
WARE.

Apple butter jar w/side handle, clear
lead glaze exposing clay shading

from yellow-red to russet-red
w/(replaced) wooden cover,
5½" top d., 5¼" h. $95.00
Apple butter jar, brown glaze, 7" h. 27.50
Bottle, straight sides w/sloping
shoulders, black matte glaze
w/incised wavy lines, 5¼" h. 35.00
Bowl, 4 1/8" d., 2½" h., yellow slip
glaze. 325.00
Bowl, 6" d., greenish amber interior
glaze. 40.00
Bowl, 8¼" d., 5" h., flared sides,
greenish interior glaze 45.00
Bowl, 9 7/8" d., 3¼" h., clear glaze
w/brown daubing at rim & into
bowl 315.00
Creamer, bulbous bottom, applied
strap handle, mottled dark brown
& amber glaze, 3 1/8" h. (edge
wear & minor glaze flakes) 85.00
Creamer, bulbous, dark brown
glaze, 4" h. 50.00
Crock, straight sides, earred handles,
tooled lip, incised stripes, simple
swags & tassels decor, greenish
glaze w/brown flecks, 16" d.,
14½" h. 450.00
Cup, canted sides w/incised hori-
zontal lines, applied handle, dark
brown glaze. .145.00
Cuspidor, lady's, handled, molded
scroll decor, clear lead glaze,
5" d., 2 3/8" h. 110.00
Flower pot w/saucer, crimped lip,
sponged on slip decor 195.00
Jar & cover w/coggled edge, incised
American Eagle & shield above
another flying American Eagle in
profile, chips on finial & jar, cream &
russet glaze w/running green,
American, 19th c., 9½" h. (ILLUS.). . .990.00
Jar, ovoid, clear lead glaze mottled
w/dark brown, 4¼" h. 85.00
Jar, ovoid w/flaring lip, earred
handles, clear lead glaze w/brown
splotches, 5½" h. 145.00

Redware Jar

Jar, ovoid, clear lead glaze w/green
splotch burnt through in firing,
9" d., 8" h. (ILLUS.) 115.00
Jug, ovoid w/strap handle, greenish
amber glaze w/orange spots & brown
brown flecks, probably Maine,
10½" h. 350.00
Jug, ovoid w/applied handle, clear
lead glaze exposing shaded russet-
red clay, qt. 135.00
Jug w/pouring lip & applied handle,
mustard yellow slip glaze, w/New
York advertising, 1-gal. 130.00
Milk cooling basin, amber glaze
w/red slip crow's foot & wavy line
decor, 8½" d., 2¾" h. (interior glaze
wear) 135.00

Milk Cooling Basin

Milk cooling basin, olive amber glaze
w/center flake, 12½" d., 2½" h.
(ILLUS.). 75.00
Mug, applied strap handle, ovoid,
dark speckled glaze, 3¾" h.
(minor hairline in base) 105.00
Mug, applied strap handle, 2 bands
of incised line decoration, greenish
glaze, 4 1/8" h. (minor edge wear
& small flakes) 410.00
Mug, applied strap handle, straight
sides w/slightly flaring base, black
shiny glaze, 5¼" h. . . . . . . .200.00 to 275.00
Pitcher, 3¾" h., squatty, applied
handle, clear glaze over yellow
slip top, dark brown glazed
bottom 105.00
Pitcher, 4 1/8" h., slightly bulbous
body w/high flaring spout, amber
glaze with running brown flecks 115.00
Pitcher, milk, light greenish glaze
w/splotches of orange-brown,
Western N.Y., qt. 495.00
Salt dip, master size, canted sides,
greenish glaze w/brown flecks,
3¼" d., 1¼" h. (old rim & foot
chips) 115.00
Sugar bowl, modeled as a tree trunk &
cover w/acorn finial, mottled
dark brown & amber glaze 220.00

RED WING STONEWARE

by Gail DePasquale

For many years now, decorated stoneware made in the eastern United States has been highly prized by collectors. Interest in it has, in fact, caused it to be synonomous with the word "stoneware" in general. Midwesterners who preferred stoneware products which were manufactured in their own region were thought to have inferior taste. It has only been in the last eight years (with the formation of the Red Wing Collectors' Society) that collectors of midwestern stoneware in general and of stoneware produced in Red Wing, Minnesota, specifically, have begun to take pride in their collections and to share their knowledge of Red Wing products with others. Consequently, Red Wing stoneware collecting has seen a remarkable and exciting growth which has expanded beyond the midwest and has become nation-wide in its appeal.

Many of the same factors that led to the collecting of eastern stoneware contributed to the popularity of collecting Red Wing today, i.e., beauty; affordability; uniqueness in function and design; and investment possibilities. The appeal for collectors of Red Wing products, however, transcends even these obvious reasons.

Because Red Wing stonewares combine eye appeal and are utilitarian, they are ideal to help achieve the popular "country look" as decorative adjuncts to one's home and since literally hundreds of types of items in various styles were produced, the variety alone provides the key ingredient to an enjoyable hobby.

History

The stoneware industry came to Red Wing, Minnesota because the right conditions existed. Glaciers had deposited perfect clay in the area, there were capital and manpower in the town, and there was a functional need for the product at that time in history. It was only when the Red Wing Stoneware Company began producing stoneware on a large scale in 1878, however, that the product became known beyond the local area. The Red Wing Stoneware Company was later joined by two other stoneware manufacturers---the Minnesota Stoneware Company and the North Star Stoneware Company, and products of all three companies are collected by Red Wing enthusiasts.

From these three independent manufacturers, various mergers and unions developed in order to weather the economic difficulties and to form a united front in order to meet increasing competition from outside the Red Wing area. An understanding of these various Red Wing companies and dates of their operations is important in putting their products in context.

1877-1906 - Red Wing Stoneware Company

1883-1906 - Minnesota Stoneware Company

1892-1896 - North Star Stoneware Company

1894-1906 - Union Stoneware Company (the joining ofthe 3 above stoneware companies for economic efficiency; each retaining its own identity, however)

1906-1936 - Red Wing Union Stoneware Company (the remaining 2 companies, Red Wing Stoneware and Minnesota Stoneware, united to form new company)

1936-1967 - Red Wing Potteries

Buying, Dating and Valuing Red Wing Stoneware

The earliest products produced by the Red Wing Stoneware companies were either hand-turned, hand-decorated salt-glazed items or were small brown-glazed molded pieces. White ware was not introduced until the mid-to-late 1890s. Stamped leaf designs were used as company markings on white ware until 1908 or 1909 when the familiar red "wing" was introduced as the Red Wing Union Stoneware Company trademark.

The importance of buying pieces signed with a company mark cannot be overstated.

A company signature adds to the value of any piece but other factors such as rarity, condition and desirability must also be considered. Eye appeal, decorating possibilities and personal taste very often determine the selling price of a particular piece.

It is important for collectors to buy only the pieces that have personal appeal. The uniqueness and variety of wares produced during the Red Wing clay industry's 90-year-long history provides something for everyone, and is the main reason that collecting Red Wing wares is such a popular hobby today.

(Editor's Note: *Gail DePasquale, a longtime collector of Red Wing stoneware, is a charter member of the Red Wing Collectors' Society and has written numerous articles on stoneware. Together with her husband, Dan, and fellow collector, Larry Peterson, she is the author of the book,* Red Wing Stoneware, *which serves as a general reference to the various product lines made by the Red Wing stoneware companies.*)

* * * * *

Red Wing Pottery Ash Tray

Ash tray, model of a wing, deep red glaze, marked "Red Wing Potteries" on underside (ILLUS.) ....$25.00 to 30.00
Batter bowl w/pouring lip & bail handle, spongeband decor on grey 250.00
Bean pot w/cover & bail handle, brown glaze, marked "Minnesota Stoneware Co.," ½ gal......................75.00
Bean pot w/cover & bail handle, brown & white glaze, "Red Wing Union Stoneware," ½ gal. 50.00

Red Wing Beater Jar

Beater jar, white glaze, blue bands & lettering "Red Wing Beater Jar, Eggs - Cream, Salad Dressing" (ILLUS.) ....70.00 to 85.00
Beater jar, white glaze, blue bands, w/various Iowa or Wisconsin merchants advertising reverse ....55.00 to 85.00
Beater jar, ribbed sides, white glaze, blue stripe bands ....45.00 to 67.50
Beater jar, ribbed sides, spongeware, blue & russet red daubing on tan 135.00
Beater jar, ribbed sides, spongeband decor on grey ....90.00 to 100.00
Beater jar, ribbed sides, yellowware ...65.00

Red Wing Spongeware Bowl

Bowl, 5" d., paneled sides, spongeware, blue & russet red daubing on tan (ILLUS.) 100.00
Bowl, 6" d., saffron ware w/blue & pink bands 35.00
Bowl, 6" d., paneled sides, spongeware, blue daubing on tan 100.00
Bowl, 7" d., saffron ware, blue & red sponge daubing on yellowware 48.00
Bowl, 7" d., ribbed sides, spongeware, blue & russet red daubing on tan, marked "Red Wing Ovenware" on underside........................55.00

Red Wing Spongeware Bowl

Bowl, 7" d., paneled sides, spongeware, blue & red daubing on tan (ILLUS.) 55.00
Bowl, 7" d., brown glaze, "RWSCo." mark on underside 25.00
Bowl, 7" d., spongeband decor, w/advertising 75.00
Bowl (nappie or pudding pan), 8" d., blue & white glaze w/picket fence design around rim ....65.00 to 80.00

Greek Key Pattern Bowl

Bowl, 8" d., Greek Key patt., light blue
around top fading to grey (ILLUS.) 55.00
Bowl, 8" d., saffron ware, sponge-
daubed blue & red on yellowware 45.00
Bowl, 8" d., spongeware, blue & red
daubing on tan, w/adver-
tising .60.00 to 70.00
Bowl, 10" d., paneled sides, sponge-
ware, blue & red daubing on
tan . . . . .75.00 to 95.00
Bowl w/bail handle (sometimes called
cooking pot or roaster), 10½" d.,
"Minnesota Stoneware Co." on base.125.00
Bowl, 11" d., spongeware, blue & red
daubing on tan . . . . .80.00 to 95.00
Butter crock, brown glaze, "Red Wing
Stoneware Co." on base, 2-lb. 30.00
Butter crock, white glaze, w/adver-
tising. 50.00
Butter crock, white glaze, lettered "20
lb." in blue 95.00

Red Wing 20 Lb. Butter Crock

Butter crock, white glaze, large (4")
red "wing" mark, 20 lb. (ILLUS.) 275.00
Butter jar, low style, white glaze, "Red
Wing Stoneware Co.," 3-lb. 25.00
Butter jar, spongeband decor on grey,
w/Iowa advertising, 3-lb. 225.00
Casserole dish, cov., saffron ware,
sponge-daubed blue & red on
yellowware, 7" d. 160.00
Casserole dish, cov., spongeband
decor on grey, w/advertising,
7" d. 135.00
Casserole dish, cov., spongeband
decor on grey, 8½" d. . . . . .125.00 to 150.00
Casserole dish, cov., white glaze, blue
bands, 7" d. . . . . .85.00 to 100.00

Covered Casserole Dish

Casserole dish, cov., yellowware
w/white & blue band, 7" d. (ILLUS.) . . .65.00

"Christmas Tree Holder"

Christmas tree holder, white glaze
(ILLUS.) 275.00

Red Wing Union Stoneware Churn

Churn w/lid, white glaze w/blue birch
leaves & oval stamp "Red Wing
Union Stoneware Co.," 2-gal.
(ILLUS.) 145.00
Churn w/lid, white glaze, large (4")
red "wing" signature, dated Decem-
ber 21, 1915, 2-gal. . . . . . .125.00 to 150.00
Churn, salt-glazed stoneware, blue
slip-quilled "lazy 8" decor, 3-gal.
(no lid) 140.00
Churn, white glaze, large (4") red
"wing" signature, 3-gal. (no lid). 100.00
Churn, white glaze, small (2") red

"wing" signature, dated 1915, 3-gal.
(no lid) 60.00
Churn w/lid, white glaze, large (4")
red "wing" signature, 4-gal. 125.00
Churn w/lid, white glaze, large (4")
red "wing" signature,
5-gal. . . . . .150.00 to 185.00

Early Salt-Glazed Churn

Churn, salt-glazed stoneware, hand-
decorated slip-quilled butterfly &
floral, impressed mark on side,
6-gal. (ILLUS.) .550.00

Early Red Wing Cookie Jar

Cookie jar, cov., "Cookies" & cattails
in relief on stippled ground, yellow-
orange glaze (ILLUS.) 100.00
Cookie jar, cov., spongeband decor,
"Cookies" in blue script on side 300.00
Crock, salt glaze w/Albany slip
interior, "Minn. Stoneware, Red
Wing, Minn." on bottom, 1-gal. 45.00
Crock, white glaze, small (2") red
"wing" & oval stamp "Red Wing
Union Stoneware Co., Red Wing,
Minn.," 2-gal. .25.00
Crock, white glaze, large (4") red
"wing" & oval stamp "Red Wing
Union Stoneware Co., Red Wing,
Minn.," 2-gal. (ILLUS.) 35.00

Red Wing Union Stoneware Crock

Crock, white glaze, large (4") red
"wing" & oval stamp "Red Wing
Union Stoneware Co.," 3-gal. 35.00

Crock with Nebraska Advertising

Crock, white glaze, Nebraska
advertising stamped in oval, 3-gal.
(ILLUS.) 125.00
Crock, salt-glazed, cobalt blue slip-
quilled target, impressed mark on
side, 4-gal. . . . . .150.00 to 175.00

Minnesota Stoneware Crock

Crock, salt-glazed, cobalt blue slip-
quilled birch leaf, impressed mark
on side, 5-gal. (ILLUS.) 250.00
Crock, salt-glazed, cobalt blue slip-
quilled birch leaf, unmarked, 5-gal. . .75.00

Crock, salt-glazed, cobalt blue slip-
quilled leaves, unmarked, 6-gal 95.00
Crock, white glaze, large (4") red
"wing" & oval stamp "Red Wing
Union Stoneware Co.," w/wire bail
handles & wooden grips at sides,
6-gal. 50.00
Crock, white glaze, large (4") red
"wing" & oval stamp "Red Wing
Union Stoneware Co.," 15-gal........60.00
Crock, white glaze, blue birch leaves
& oval stamp "Minnesota Stoneware
Co.," 20-gal. 200.00
Crock, white glaze, large (4") red
"wing" & oval stamp "Red Wing
Union Stoneware Co.," 30-gal.......100.00

"German" Cuspidor

Cuspidor, "German" style, white glaze
w/incised designs & blue bands,
unmarked (ILLUS.) 200.00
Fruit (or canning) jar, "Stone Mason
Fruit Jar, Union Stoneware Co., Red
Wing, Minn." printed in either black
or blue, qt. ....90.00 to 115.00

Red Wing Fruit Jar

Fruit (or canning) jar, "Stone Mason
Fruit Jar, Union Stoneware Co., Red
Wing, Minn.," ½ gal. (ILLUS.).......125.00
Fruit (or canning) jar, "Stone Mason
Fruit Jar, Union Stoneware Co., Red
Wing, Minn.," 1-gal...............250.00
Fruit (or canning) jar, "dome-top"
w/rounded shoulders, "Stone Mason
Fruit Jar, Union Stoneware Co., Red
Wing, Minn.," ½ gal..............475.00

Fruit (or canning) jar, wax sealer,
brown glaze, qt. 37.50
Fruit (or canning) jar, wax sealer,
brown glaze, "Minnesota Stoneware
Co." on base, ½ gal. 30.00
Fruit (or canning) jar, wax sealer,
white glaze, ½ gal. 40.00
Fruit (or canning) jar w/spring-type
(ball-lock) clamp on lid & bail
handle, white glaze, red "wing" &
oval stamp "Red Wing Union Stoneware Co., Red Wing, Minn.,"
3-gal. 100.00
Fruit (or canning) jar w/spring-type
(ball-lock) clamp on lid & bail
handle, white glaze, red "wing" &
oval stamp "Red Wing Union Stoneware Co., Red Wing, Minn.,"
5-gal. 120.00

Hot Water Bottle

Hot water bottle, molded leaf
designs, brown glaze, signed "Red
Wing" on bottom (ILLUS.) 200.00

Miniature Red Wing Union Stoneware Jug

Jug, brown-glazed shoulder, "Red
Wing Union Stoneware Co., Red
Wing, Minn." in oval, 3¼" h.
(ILLUS.)..........................300.00

Jug, beehive shape, brown glaze,
"Minnesota Stoneware Co."
impressed on base, ½ gal. 50.00

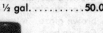

Red Wing Liquor Co. Jug

Jug, brown-glazed shoulder, white-
glazed base, advertising, "Red Wing
Liquor Co. Wholesale Wines and
Liquors, etc." in oval, ½ gal.
(ILLUS.) 150.00

Jug with Red "Wing"

Jug, brown-glazed shoulder, white-
glazed base, small (2") red "wing"
mark, 1-gal. (ILLUS.) 150.00

North Star Jug

Jug, brown-glazed shoulder, salt-
glazed base, North Star Pottery
mark on base, 1-gal. (ILLUS.) 175.00

Minnesota Stoneware Jug

Jug, wide mouth, brown glaze,
"Minnesota Stoneware Co." on
bottom, 1-gal. (ILLUS.) 60.00

Beehive Shape Jug

Jug, beehive shape, white glaze, red
"wing" & oval "Red Wing Union
Stoneware Co.," 3-gal. (ILLUS.) 150.00
Jug, beehive shape, brown glaze,
impressed "Red Wing Stoneware
Co." on side, 5-gal. 500.00
Jug, beehive shape, salt-glazed stone-
ware, blue slip-quilled leaf, impressed letters for "Red Wing
Stoneware Co." on handle, 5-gal. .1,000.00
Jug, beehive shape, salt-glazed
stoneware, blue slip-quilled leaf,
unmarked, 5-gal. 250.00
Jug, plain shoulders, white glaze, red
"wing" & oval "Red Wing Union
Stoneware Co.," 5-gal. 50.00
"Koverwate" (crock cover-weight
designed to hold pickles under
brine), 10-gal. (crock) size 80.00
Mixing bowls, spongeware, blue &
russet red daubing on grey, nested
set of 7 . . . . .400.00 to 500.00

Model of a pig, tail pinched in making,
  brown glaze, 6" l. 225.00
Model of a football w/figure of gopher
  on top, Red Wing Potteries,
  1939 .95.00 to 110.00
Mugs, brushed ware, green stain, set
  of 4 . . . . .110.00
Pantry jar, cov., white glaze, blue
  bands, red "wing" mark,
  1-lb. . . . . .225.00 to 250.00
Pantry jar, cov., white glaze, blue
  bands, red "wing" mark, 3-lb. 400.00

Red Wing Panty Jar

Pantry jar, cov., white glaze, blue
  bands, red "wing" mark, 5-lb.
  (ILLUS.) 250.00
Pantry jar, cov., white glaze, blue
  bands, red "wing" mark, 10-lb. 600.00
Pie plate, white glaze, "Minnesota
  Stoneware Co." mark on bottom 100.00
Pitcher (so-called Russian milk pitcher
  without pouring spout), brown glaze,
  ½ gal. 50.00
Pitcher, 6½" h., spongeband decor,
  w/Iowa advertising 175.00
Pitcher, 7½" h., spongeband decor,
  w/Minnesota advertising 145.00
Pitcher, 7½" h., saffron ware w/brown
  stripe bands. 75.00
Pitcher, 7½" h., saffron ware, yellow-
  ware w/band, w/Minnesota adver-
  tising. 100.00
Pitcher, 7¾" h., embossed irises,
  brown glaze, Red Wing Potteries,
  ca. 1940 . . . . .57.50 to 75.00
Pitcher, 8" h., brushed ware, gothic
  columns & Greek Key designs, green
  stain 75.00
Pitcher, 8¼" h., Cherry Band patt.,
  blue at borders fading to white,
  w/advertising. 150.00
Pitcher, 8¼" h., spongeband on grey,
  w/advertising. . . . . .95.00 to 150.00
Pitcher, 9¼" h., Cherry Band patt.,
  blue at borders fading to white
  (ILLUS.) . . . . .90.00 to 100.00

Cherry Band Pattern Pitcher

Poultry drinking fountain, "Korec"
  style, 1-gal. size w/original bottom
  plate. . . . . .35.00 to 55.00

"Eureka" Poultry Drinking Fountain

Poultry drinking fountain, "Eureka"
  style, marked "Pat'd April 7, 1885"
  & w/"Red Wing Stoneware Co."
  mark on bottom (ILLUS.) . . . . .75.00 to 85.00
Refrigerator jar, stacking-type, white
  glaze, blue bands, "Red Wing
  Refrigerator Jar," 5½" d. . .85.00 to 100.00

Hanging Salt Box

Salt box, cov., wall-type, spongeband
  decor (ILLUS.) 450.00

Snuff jar, cov., white glaze, qt. 75.00
Snuff jar, cov., brown glaze, "Minnesota Stoneware Co.," 1-gal. 75.00
Umbrella stand, straight-sided cylinder, spongeware, blue & russet
  red daubing on tan, 18" h...........500.00
Urn, brushed ware, cherubs in relief,
  green stain, "Red Wing Union Stoneware Co." ....60.00 to 80.00
Vase, 7¼" h., brushed ware, "Red
  Wing Union Stoneware Co." 35.00
Vase, 10" h., brushed ware, relief-
  molded decoration, green stain......60.00

Lily Pattern Wash Basin & Pitcher

Wash basin & pitcher, Lily patt.,
  light blue fading to white (ILLUS.) ...400.00

Water Cooler

Water cooler, cov., white glaze, blue
  bands, lettered "Water Cooler" in
  blue, large (4") red "wing" & oval
  stamp "Red Wing Union Stoneware
  Co.," original spigot, 3-gal.
  (ILLUS.)...........................275.00
Water Cooler, cov., white glaze, blue
  bands, small (2") red "wing" & oval
  stamped "Red Wing Union Stoneware
  Co.," 5-gal. 175.00
Water cooler, cov., white glaze, blue
  bands, large (4") red "wing" & oval
  stamp "Red Wing Union Stoneware
  Co.," 10-gal. 300.00

(End of Special Focus)

RIDGWAY

Wm. Ridgway Platter

*There were numerous Ridgways among
English potters. The firm J. & W. Ridgway
operated in Shelton from 1814 to 1930 and
produced many pieces with scenes of
historical interest. William Ridgway operated in Shelton from 1830 to 1865. Most
wares marked Ridgway that have been
offered in this country were made by one of
these two firms, or by Ridgway Potteries,
Ltd., still in operation. Also see FLOW
BLUE.*

Bowl, 4¾" d., 2¾" h., Coaching Days &
  Ways series, black transfer on
  caramel ground, silver lustre rim ...$45.00
Bowl, 9" d., Coaching Days & Ways
  series - "Eloped"....................75.00
Cider set: 9¾" h. tankard pitcher &
  six half-pint mugs; Coaching Days
  & Ways series, 7 pcs. 275.00
Mug, Coaching Days & Ways series,
  black transfer on caramel ground,
  silver lustre top & bottom bands &
  handle, 4¾" d., 5" h...............30.00
Pitcher, 3½" h., 3½" d., Coaching
  Days & Ways series 49.00
Pitcher, tankard, 6" h., 4" d., Coaching
  Days & Ways series, black transfer
  scenes on caramel ground, silver
  lustre rim & handle................65.00
Pitcher, 7" h., cobalt blue, gold, red
  & green floral decor 75.00
Pitcher, 8¾" h., jug-type, salt glaze
  stoneware, Jousting Knights patt.,
  light grey, dated Sept. 1, 1840 .....148.00
Plaque, pierced to hang, Coaching Days
  Days & Ways series - "In a Snow-
  drift," yellow ground, silver lustre
  rim, 12" d. 100.00
Plate, 9" d., Niagara patt., brown
  transfer 22.50
Platter, 11" l., Neva patt., Wm.
  Ridgway (ILLUS.)...................70.00
Platter, 17 x 13 3/8", Oriental Sports
  patt., men on elephant & horses
  w/dogs after large bear, w/animals
  & birds border, ca. 1840...........172.00
Platter, 18 x 14½", blue transfer scenic

river landscape center, wild rose
border, ca. 1840 ....140.00
Soap dish, cover & drain insert, blue,
3 pcs. 95.00
Teapot, cov., Coaching Days & Ways
series - "Walking Up the Hill," black
transfer on caramel ground, silver
lustre handle & trim, 5" d., 5" h.......95.00

ROCKINGHAM

Rockingham Glazed Milk Pan

*An earthenware pottery was first estab-
lished on the estate of the Marquis of
Rockingham in England's Yorkshire district about 1745 and occupied by a suc-
cession of potters. The famous Rockingham glaze of mottled brown, somewhat
resembling tortoise shell, was introduced
about 1788 by the Brameld Brothers, and
was well received. During the 1820s,
porcelain manufacture was added to the
production and fine quality china was
turned out until the pottery closed in 1842.
The popular Rockingham glaze was subsequently produced elsewhere, including
Bennington, Vt., and at numerous other
U.S. potteries. We list herein not only wares
produced at the Rockingham potteries in
England, but also items from other
potteries with the Rockingham glaze.*

Baker, mottled brown glaze, 12½ x
9½" oval $225.00
Bowl, 7½" d., 2 1/8" h., canted sides,
mottled brown glaze 65.00
Bowl, 7¾" d., 3¼" h., panel-molded
sides, smooth flaring rim, mottled
brown glaze.......................80.00
Bowl, 10¾" d., 3" h., mottled brown
glaze............................55.00
Bowl, 12½" oval, mottled brown
glaze...........................105.00
Cookie mold, eagle on rose & thistle
perch, mottled brown glaze, 5½ x
8 1/8" oval 550.00
Cuspidor, leaves in relief on sides,
mottled brown glaze, 8" d., 5½" h....35.00
Cuspidor, shell-shaped molded top,
mottled brown glaze 40.00

Custard cup, mottled brown
glaze ....10.00 to 15.00
Milk cooling basin, mottled brown
glaze, 11½" d., 3" h. (ILLUS.) 95.00
Model of a Spaniel dog seated,
mottled brown glaze 365.00
Models of lions in recumbent position,
yellowware, faces, manes & oval
bases w/streaky mottled brown
glaze, 1850-90, 14¾" l., pr.........990.00
Mug, waisted cylinder w/strap handle,
mottled brown glaze, 3½" h. 50.00
Mug, large applied handle, embossed
band around rim, mottled brown
glaze, 3½" h. 80.00
Pie plate, mottled brown glaze, 10" to
11" d., each...............85.00 to 125.00
Pitcher, milk, 6½" h., squat form,
mottled brown glaze 75.00
Pitcher, 7½" h., relief-molded vintage
& cherubs, mottled light brown
glaze............................95.00
Pitcher, 9" h., applied twig handle,
embossed arm w/hammer & "Protection to American Industry,"
mottled brown glaze 165.00
Pitcher, 9" h., twig handle, mask
spout, relief-molded American Eagle
on Liberty Bell one side, mottled
brown glaze.....................210.00
Plate, 7 7/8" d., scalloped rim, deeply
molded rayed center, mottled brown
glaze...........................155.00
Platter, 12¾" octagon, mottled brown
glaze............................95.00
Salt box, cov., hanging-type, relief-
molded pea fowls, mottled brown
glaze, 6½" w., 6" h...............115.00
Serving dish, mottled brown glaze,
9¾ x 7¼" oval, 1 7/8" h............75.00
Shaving mug, embossed Toby figures
on sides, mottled brown glaze,
impressed label "E. & W. Bennett,
Canton Avenue, Baltimore,"
4 1/8" h. 125.00

Rockingham Glaze Teapot

Teapot, cov., Rebecca at Well patt.,
mottled brown glaze, 10" h. (ILLUS.) . .88.00
Wash basin & pitcher, octagonal, mottled brown glaze, 10¼" h. pitcher &
13" d. bowl, pr. 180.00

ROOKWOOD

Rookwood Mark of 1900

*Considered America's foremost art pot-
tery, the Rookwood Pottery Company was
established in Cincinnati, Ohio in 1880, by
Mrs. Maria Longworth Storer. To accurately record its development, each piece
carried the Rookwood insignia, or mark, is
dated and, if individually decorated, is
usually signed by the artist. The pottery
remained in Cincinnati until 1959 when it
was sold to Herschede Hall Clock Company
and moved to Starkville, Mississippi, where
it continued in operation until 1967. Also
see TILES.*

Ash tray, figure of nude lady, green
or brown glaze, 4½" h., each $65.00
Ash tray, w/advertising, light brown
glaze, 1944 . . . . .26.00
Ash tray, fish-shaped, ivory high
glaze, 1945 . . . . .85.00
Bookend, model of a panther, green
high glaze, 1949, William Purcell
McDonald (single) 60.00
Bookends, Dutch boy & girl, Sara Alice
(Sallie) Toohey (1887-1931), pr. 155.00
Bookends, model of an elephant
w/trunk uplifted, ivory glaze, 1957,
pr. 150.00
Bookends, model of a Rook, green
high glaze, 1922, William Purcell
McDonald, 5½" h., pr. 185.00
Bowl, 4" d., simple molded design,
green Vellum glaze, 1907 . . . . .25.00
Bowl, 5" d., bulbous, floral garden
scene, Vellum glaze, 1930, Edward
T. Hurley 650.00
Bowl, 6" d., 3" h., molded classical
figures & stylized trees decor on
ivory shaded to chartreuse matte
glaze, 1919, Arthur P. Conant 190.00
Bowl, 6 x 5", band of blue violets
& geometric motifs, Vellum glaze,
1930, Edward G. Diers 425.00
Bowl, 6" octagon, 1½" h., underglaze
slip-painted floral spray, orange

shaded to brown standard glaze,
1894 . . . . .290.00
Bowl, 6½ x 3½", underglaze slip-
painted poppies decor, standard
brown glaze, 1903, Edith Regina
Felton 275.00
Bowl, 7½" d., 5" h., dogwood
blossoms, blue glaze, 1928, Sallie
Toohey 350.00
Bowl, 8½" d., 1¾" h., ruffled rim,
underglaze slip-painted brown &
white chrysanthemums, caramel
glaze, 1889, Amelia B. Sprague 250.00
Candle holders, floral decor w/tur-
quoise highlights, light turquoise
glaze, 1921, pr. 60.00
Candlesticks, green matte glaze, 1922,
6" h., pr. 45.00
Candlesticks, water lily decor, rose
glaze, 1927, pr. 65.00
Cheese dish, irregular fluted rim,
slip-painted interior scene of long-
tailed yellow rat on dark green
shaded to brown ground, olive green
standard glaze exterior, 1888,
artist-signed, 7¼" d., 1" h. 575.00
Creamer & sugar bowl, crimped rims,
underglaze slip-painted autumn
leaves, standard glaze, 1899, Clara
Christiana Lindeman, pr. 550.00
Creamer & sugar bowl, floral decor,
rose & blue Wax Matte glaze,
Elizabeth Neave Lincoln (1892-1931),
pr. 275.00
Ewer, underglaze slip-painted nastur-
tiums, standard glaze, 1899, William
Klemm, 6¾" h. 295.00
Ewer, underglaze slip-painted
berries & leaves decor, standard
glaze, 1892, Edith Regina Felton 400.00
Ewer, bulbous w/curled spreading lip,
underglaze slip-painted brown, green
& gold-green chrysanthemums,
standard glaze, 1895, Anna Marie
Bookprinter 385.00
Flower pot, flat form, lavender & green
blossoms & leaves decor, shaded
white to shell pink ground, 1906,
Lenore Asbury, 5" d., 2" h. 450.00
Honey pot, Limoges-type, h.p. dragon-
fly decor, 1884, 5" h. 360.00
Inkwell w/insert, brown matte glaze,
1923, 4½" d., 2½" h. 125.00
Jug, underglaze slip-painted portrait
of Chief "Rain-in-the-Face," green &
brown standard glaze, 1897,
Frederick Sturgis Laurence,
10" h. 4,675.00
Jug w/stopper, underglaze slip-painted
currants decor, standard glaze,
1899, Lenore Asbury 375.00
Loving cup, 3-handled, underglaze
slip-painted portrait of an Indian
w/feathers in his long hair & knotted

scarf around his neck in ochre,
brown, green & yellow, shaded
green & brown standard glaze, 1898,
Harriet E. Wilcox, 6" h. 1,870.00
Mug, underglaze slip-painted bust portrait of Indian "Standing Bear,"
shaded green & brown standard
glaze, 1900, Frederick Sturgis
Laurence, 5¼" h. 1,320.00
Mug, deeply incised black grapes
decor, green matte finish, 1905,
Sara Elizabeth (Sallie) Coyne,
6½" h. 120.00
Paperweight, figure of a nude lady,
seated, green high glaze, 1928,
Edward Abel 95.00
Paperweight, model of a bird perched
atop clump of flowers, grey-brown
glaze, 1946, 5½ x 6". 115.00
Paperweight, model of a chick, yellow
glaze, 1937, Louise Abel 95.00
Paperweight, model of a wolf,
reclining, blue glaze, 1934 . . . . .125.00
Pitcher, 6¼" h., in the Japanese taste,
underglaze slip-painted white-
breasted bird in flight over bamboo,
standard glaze, 1886, Anna Marie
Bookprinter .450.00
Pitcher, tankard, 7½" h., bisque,
sculptured cherub decor, "Cincinnati
Cooperage Co.," raised Ribbon mark
(1881-82) 795.00
Pitcher, water, incised Arts & Crafts
style designs, green matte finish,
1904 . . . . .260.00
Plaque, "The Evening," by Lorinda
Epply (1904-48), 8 x 5" tile
w/original frame, backing &
labels 1,450.00
Plaque, "The Edge of the Lake," under-
glaze slip-painted snow scene in
deep grey-blue, blue-tinged green &
white, Vellum Glaze, 1919, Sallie E.
Coyne, 8 x 6", original frame &
label w/title 880.00
Plaque, underglaze slip-painted pastel
leafless trees by a lakeside, Vellum
glaze, 1916, Charles Schmidt,
9¼ x 7¼" .1,210.00

Plaque by Lorinda Epply

Plaque, underglaze slip-painted pastel
blue, green, blue-green & pink scene
of trees by water's edge, Vellum
glaze, 1916, Lorinda Epply, framed,
12 3/8 x 9 3/8" (ILLUS.) 1,430.00
Plate, 10" d., mermaids decor, William
E. Hentschel (1907-39) 240.00
Teapot, cov., blue glossy glaze,
1915 . . . . .125.00
Tea set: cov. teapot, cov. creamer &
cov. sugar bowl; green shaded to
pink decor, ca. 1918, 3 pcs. 495.00
Tea tile, footed, fern decor, 1926,
6" sq. 85.00
Tray, Rook decor on blue matte
crystalline glaze, 1933 . . . . .145.00
Vase, 3" h., 5" d., underglaze
slip-painted florals, standard glaze,
1893, Sadie Markland 225.00
Vase, 4" h., urn-shaped, coral pink
matte glaze w/minute touches of
turquoise at rim, 1913, William E.
Hentschel 120.00

Rookwood Vase

Vase, 5" h., blue molded design
highlighted in white, Vellum glaze,
1929 (ILLUS.) 70.00
Vase, 5½" h., 4" base d., bulbous,
incised floral & foliage decor at base,
blue matte glaze, Sallie Toohey
(1887-1931) 400.00
Vase, 5½" h., purple to maroon yucca
leaves on sea green ground, 4-color
matte glaze, 1928, Margaret Helen
McDonald. .240.00
Vase, 6" h., dark blue & brown leaves
on turquoise ground, William E.
Hentschel (1907-39) 475.00
Vase, 6" h., cobalt blue florals in upper
portion & cobalt blue snails at base
on turquoise ground, 1920, Lorinda
Epply 395.00
Vase, 6" h., blue, tan & rose
abstract floral decor, 1921, Charles
Todd 175.00
Vase, 6" h., 3¾" d., white tulips
w/yellow centers & green leaves,
brown Wax Matte glaze, black lustre
glaze interior, 1934, Jens Jensen 425.00

Vase, 6½" h., bulbous base, flying
Rooks decor on rose & blue ground,
Iris glaze, 1904 . . . . .670.00
Vase, 6¾" h., 3¾" d., red maple
leaves at mouth, dark green crackle
glaze shading to dark red, matte
glaze, 1904, Olga Geneva Reed 375.00

Vase for Pan-American Exposition

Vase, 7" h., ovoid, underglaze slip-
painted peonies, Iris glaze, 1900,
Sara Sax, w/printed Rookwood label
"U.S.A./Pan-American Exposition/
Buffalo/1901" (ILLUS.) 825.00
Vase, 7½" h., tulips in relief,
aqua glaze, Charles S. Todd
(1911-20) 125.00
Vase, 7¾" h., iris spray decor on
blended green, blue & rose ground,
Vellum glaze, Frederick Rothenbusch
(1863-1931) .375.00
Vase, 8" h., scenic decor, Vellum
glaze, 1915, Lorinda Epply 695.00

Rookwood Iris Glaze Vase

Vase, 8" h., 6" d., creamy ivory
unfolding blossom on dark grey

ground, Iris glaze, Sallie Coyne,
1892-1931 (ILLUS.) 475.00
Vase, 8½" h., underglaze slip-painted
grey & white scene, Vellum glaze,
1910, Frederic Rothenbusch 700.00
Vase, 8½" h., floral decor, yellow
Wax Matte glaze, 1925, Katherine
Jones 425.00
Vase, 8½" h., 4½" d., underglaze slip-
painted orange carnations, shaded
orange to dark green standard
glaze, 1893, Emma D. Foertmeyer . . .550.00
Vase, 8¾" h., ovoid, continuous view
of city, including San Giorgio
Maggiore, w/boats sailing in the
foreground, shaded ice blue & ochre
high glaze, 1902, Charles
Schmidt 1,430.00
Vase, 9" h., scenic decor, Vellum
glaze, Frederick Rothenbusch
(1896-1931) .925.00
Vase, 9 1/8" h., cylindrical w/flared
base, winter scene w/trees, blue
Vellum glaze, 1914, Lenore Asbury . .525.00
Vase, 9½" h., chimney-shaped, blue-
grey floral decor, Vellum glaze,
1914, Edward George Diers 350.00
Vase, 9¼" h., underglaze slip-painted
florals, Vellum glaze, 1918, Edward
Diers 695.00
Vase, 10" h., tapering cylinder,
impressionistically painted
w/muted grey, green, beige & black
continuous scene of tall elegant
trees by a river bank, Vellum glaze,
1908, Edward T. Hurley 770.00
Vase, 10" h., slender neck, glossy
light caramel glaze, 1946 . . . . .55.00
Vase, 11 x 5", stylized floral decor,
blue shaded to green Wax Matte
glaze, 1920, Elizabeth Neave
Lincoln 325.00
Vase, 11½" h., primitive figures &
large Ostrich among scattered
foliage decor on butterscotch ground,
cobalt blue interior, 1930, Jens
Jensen 750.00
Vase, 12" h., Iris decor, blue to cream
matte finish, ca. 1943, Kataro
Shirayamadani 675.00
Vase, 12½" h., black aventurine
w/golden rooks, moon & clouds
decor, 1899, Kataro Shirayamadani
& Mathew Daly 3,500.00
Vase, 13½" h., slip-painted florals,
bisque finish, 1886, Albert R.
Valentien 1,290.00
Vase, 14¾" h., ovoid w/short neck,
underglaze slip-painted green &
charcoal group of 3 birds amidst
bamboo branches on pale sea green
ground, Vellum glaze, 1908, Kataro
Shirayamadani 1,100.00
Wall pocket, blue glaze, 1919, 9½" h. . .90.00

ROSEMEADE POTTERY

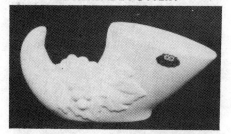

Rosemeade Cornucopia Vase

Laura Taylor was a ceramic artist who supervised Federal Works Projects in her native North Dakota during the Depression era and later demonstrated at the potter's wheel during the 1939 New York World's Fair. In 1940, Laura Taylor and Robert J. Hughes opened the Rosemeade-Wahpeton Pottery, naming it after the county and town of Wahpeton where it was located. Rosemead Pottery was made on a small scale for only about twelve years with Laura Taylor designing the items and perfecting colors. Wildlife animals and birds are popular among collectors. Hughes and Taylor married in 1943 and the pottery did a thriving business until her death in 1959. The pottery closed in 1961 but stock was sold from the factory salesroom until 1964.

Ash tray, souvenir of "Bismark,
 "N.D.," w/pheasant $32.00
Console set, bowl, leaping fawn
 figural flower frog & pr. candlesticks,
 4 pcs. 55.00
Cornucopia-vase, grape cluster & leaf
 in low relief, eggshell white matte
 finish, original paper label, 8 x 4"
 (ILLUS.) 18.00
Creamer & sugar bowl, modeled as
 ears of corn, pr. 10.00
Flower frog, model of a bird 14.00
Model of African Wolfhound dog 80.00

Rosemeade Buffalo

Model of a buffalo, brown finish,
 original label, 6" l., 6" h. (ILLUS.) 95.00
Model of a coyote on rock 28.00
Model of an elephant, sitting, rose
 matte finish, 4" h. 42.50
Model of a frog 25.00
Model of a horse, 6 x 6" 40.00
Model of a pheasant, 13" l., 7" h. 165.00
Pitcher, 5¾" h., incised rearing
 horse decor, tan high glaze 26.00
Planter, model of a swan, rose
 matte finish, 5" l. 12.00
Planter, model of an open rose,
 shaded pink matte finish 22.00
Salt & pepper shakers, figural black
 bear, original label, pr. 15.00
Salt & pepper shakers, figural cat, pr. . .13.00
Salt & pepper shakers, figural Paul
 Bunyan & Babe the Blue Ox, pr. 14.00
Salt & pepper shakers, figural
 pelican, pink finish, pr. 9.50
Salt & pepper shakers, figural
 pheasant, pr. .14.50
Salt & pepper shakers, model of
 tulip bud, decorated, pr. 9.50
Whimsey, model of a boot, black
 matte finish, 5¼" h. 27.00
Whimsey, model of a Victorian lady's
 shoe, blue finish 10.00

ROSE MEDALLION & ROSE CANTON

Rose Medallion Wares

This Chinese ware, made through last century and in the present one, features alternating panels of people and of flowers, birds or insects. Most pieces have four to six medallions, and colors utilized are appealling. The ware is called Rose Canton if flowers fill all the panels. Unless otherwise noted, our listing is for Rose Medallion wares. Also see "Special Focus" on SUGAR BOWLS.

Bowl, 8" d. $125.00
Bowl, 8½" d., 3¼" h. 195.00
Bowl, 10" d., 1¾" h. 75.00
Bowl, 14½ x 12" oval, 3½" h.,
 pedestal base 185.00

Butter pat, 2 7/8" sq. 45.00
Butter pat, 3" d. 60.00
Creamer...........................135.00
Cup & saucer, demitasse.............45.00
Cup & saucer, monogram in gilt
   medallion........................105.00
Cup & saucer, wishbone handle,
   unmarked 75.00
Cup & saucer, marked "China"........35.00
Cup & saucer, 12-sided 50.00
Dessert & tea set: pr. kidney-shaped
   dishes, 8 dessert plates, 10 teacups &
   8 saucers; ca. 1875, 28 pcs. (ILLUS.
   of part) 1,100.00
Dinner set: oval soup tureen &
   cover, 18 3/8" oval platter, 11¾"
   oval platter, 6 dinner plates, 3
   pudding plates & 9 berry dishes;
   ca. 1875, 21 pcs.................1,760.00
Dish, reticulated sides, "orange peel"
   glaze, 11 x 9¾"..................250.00

Rose Medallion Garden Seat

Garden seats, barrel-shaped, gold
   ground embellished w/flowers, fruit
   & butterflies, top w/central pierced
   cash medallion & sides w/further
   pierced cash medallions, 1 damaged
   & riveted, both w/smoke damage,
   18½" h., pr. (ILLUS. of one) 2,200.00
Jar, cov., hexagonal 125.00
Plate, 6" d........................40.00
Plate, 7" d........................45.00
Plate, 7" hexagon, marked "Made
   in China" 45.00
Plate, 7½" d., marked "Made in
   China" 32.00
Plate, 7½" sq., cut corners 35.00
Plate, 8½" d.......................35.00
Plate, 8½" d., Rose Canton...........93.50
Plate, 9¼" octagon 65.00
Plate, 9½" d. (ILLUS.)..............60.00
Plate, 9¾" d., Rose Canton..........82.50
Platter, 10 x 7½" oval (slight rim
   roughness)........................125.00

Rose Medallion Plate

Platter, 14" l., Rose Canton 250.00
Punch bowl, 11" d., 5" h. 295.00
Punch bowl, 14" d., 19th c..........1,400.00
Rice bowl, marked "China" 45.00
Rice server, oval scalloped rim, high
   footed base, China, 19th c.,
   10 x 13½"......................192.50
Soup tureen, cov., large 900.00
Sugar bowl, cov., marked "China" 65.00
Sugar bowl & cover w/fruit finial,
   intertwined handles, 4 1/8" h. 105.00
Teacup & saucer 28.00
Teapot, cov., individual size, 3¼" h.....85.00
Teapot w/dome lid, marked "Made in
   China," 6½" h.....................75.00
Tea set, cov., teapot & 2 tea cups,
   3 pcs. 350.00
Tea set: cov. teapot & 2 cups in wicker
   basket; brass fittings, ca. 1890,
   4 pcs. 375.00
Tray, marked "China," 5½ x 8" oval 25.00
Tray, reticulated rim, "orange peel"
   glaze underside, 9 x 7¾" 150.00
Vase, 3" h., ca. 1850...............90.00
Vase, 6" h., cylindrical w/collared
   neck 90.00
Vase, 7¼" h., stick-type 118.00

Rose Medallion Vases

Vases, 8" h., applied handles &
  salamander decor, pr. (ILLUS.) 500.00
Vase, 10" h., applied animal handles . .175.00
Vase, 11¾" h., cylindrical w/waisted
  throat, applied w/gilt lions &
  dragons, w/wooden base 350.00
Vegetable dish, cov., 10 x 9" 345.00

ROSENTHAL

Rosenthal Compote

*The Rosenthal porcelain manufactory has
been in operation since 1880 when it was
established by P. Rosenthal in Selb,
Bavaria. Tablewares and figure groups are
among its specialities. Also see COMMEM-
ORATIVE PLATES.*

Bowl, 6" d., ornate gold rim, h.p.
  orange poppies & green leaves
  outlined in gold on pale yellow
  ground $75.00
Bowl, fruit, 9½" d., pine cones decor,
  fall colors, artist-signed 55.00
Bowl, 13 x 8¾" oblong, ornate scroll-
  ed rim, blue Delft-type decor 150.00
Charger, Delft-type scenic decor,
  15" d. 160.00
Compote, 12" d., h.p. fruits & foliage,
  gold trim, gold handles w/women's
  heads (ILLUS.) 95.00
Figure of a dancer, polychrome enam-
  el & gilt brocade skirt, 6" h. 225.00
Figure of a small child holding a
  bouquet of flowers w/spotted fawn
  standing in front, 6½" h. 185.00
Figure of Cupid w/bow & arrow
  kneeling in a bed of roses, artist-
  signed, 7½" w. base, 8" h. 135.00
Figure of a naked child holding baby
  goat, 8" h. 125.00
Figure of a semi-nude harem dancer
  w/arms extended, on plinth base,
  polychrome enamel & gilt decor,
  artist-signed, 8¼" h. 325.00
Figure of a naked young boy seated
  on a grey goat, on pedestal base,
  12" h. 200.00
Model of a Boston Terrier dog, black
  & white, 7½ x 3½" 115.00
Model of a Dachshund puppy sitting
  on 1 haunch, 6" h. 125.00

Model of a German Short-haired
  Pointer dog, grey & white, 11½" l. . .250.00
Model of a Russian Wolfhound in
  recumbent position w/head raised,
  grey, black & white, 3¼ x 5½" 240.00
Model of a snail w/fairy rider, Art
  Deco styling, 3½ x 3½" 215.00
Mug, wreath of purple grape clusters
  around top w/trailing vines to base,
  5" h. 40.00
Nappy, handled, ruffled rim, brown
  nuts & foliage decor on autumn gold
  ground 54.00
Plate, 8" d., strawberries decor, artist-
  signed & dated 1908 . . . . .50.00
Plate, 10" d., portrait of young lady
  w/long, curly hair on dark green
  shaded to pale yellow ground, gold
  trim 70.00
Plates, 10¾" d., cobalt blue & gold
  border, multicolored rose decor on
  ivory ground center, ca. 1920, set
  of 12 . . . . .250.00
Vase, 8" h., Delft-type scenic decor 80.00
Vase, 9½"h., tulip-shaped, flaring
  base handles, h.p. floral decor 125.00

ROSEVILLE

*Roseville Pottery Company operated in
Zanesville, O., from 1898 to 1954 after
having been in business for six years prior
to that in Muskingum County, Ohio. Art
wares similar to those of the Owens and
Weller Potteries were produced. Items
listed here are by patterns or lines.*

ANTIQUE MATT GREEN (pre-1916)
Bowl, 4" d., handled, matt green
  glaze w/burnished highlights $19.00
Cuspidor, matt green glaze
  w/burnished highlights, 8 x 6½" 85.00
Jardiniere, matt green glaze
  w/burnished highlights, 12" h. 75.00
Wall pocket, matt green glaze
  w/burnished highlights 135.00

APPLE BLOSSOM (1948)
Basket w/circular branch handle,
  apple blossoms in relief on brown or
  pink, 8" h., each 45.00
Basket, hanging-type, apple blossoms
  in relief on pink 100.00
Bookends, apple blossoms in relief
  on blue, green or rose, each
  pr. . . . . .65.00 to 85.00
Candle holders, apple blossoms in
  relief on blue, 2" h., pr. 30.00
Cornucopia vase, apple blossoms in
  relief on green, 6" h. 25.00

Jardiniere, apple blossoms in relief
on blue, 8" h. 115.00
Vase, bud, 7" h., apple blossoms in
relief on pink .35.00
Vase, 10" h., apple blossoms in relief
on green 65.00
Vase, 12" h., apple blossoms in
relief on green 45.00

Apple Blossom Wall Pocket

Wall pocket, apple blossoms in relief
on blue, green or rose, 8" h., each
(ILLUS.) . . . . .55.00 to 75.00
Window box, apple blossoms in relief
on blue or rose, 12" l.
plus twig handles, each 42.00

AZTEC (1916)
Vase, 10" h., white slip geometric
designs on various shades of blue
or grey, each .200.00
Vase, tall pyramid form, white slip
geometric designs 270.00

AZUREAN (1902)
Mug, underglaze blue & white scenic
decor on blended blue ground,
4" h. . . . . .400.00 to 450.00

BANEDA (1933)

Baneda Vase

Jardiniere, band of embossed pods,
blossoms & leaves on raspberry
pink, 7" h. 135.00
Vase, 5½" h., band of embossed
pods, blossoms & leaves on green
(ILLUS.) 35.00
Vase, 6" h., band of embossed pods,
blossoms & leaves on blue . . .60.00 to 80.00
Vase, 6" h., band of embossed
pods, blossoms & leaves on green or
raspberry pink, each . . . . .35.00 to 55.00
Vase, 7½" h., cone-shaped, band of
embossed pods, blossoms & leaves
on green 75.00
Vase, 9½" h., double-handled, band of
embossed pods, blossoms & leaves
on green 72.50
Vase, 12" h., band of embossed pods,
blossoms & leaves on raspberry
pink 155.00

BITTERSWEET (1940)
Basket, overhead branch handle, orange
bittersweet pods & green leaves on
green bark-textured ground, 6" h. . . .42.50
Bookends, orange bittersweet pods
& green leaves on yellow bark-
textured ground, pr. 72.50
Creamer & cov. sugar bowl, orange
bittersweet pods & green leaves
on green bark-textured ground, pr. . .35.00
Ewer, orange bittersweet pods & green
leaves on yellow bark-textured ground,
8" h. 58.00
Jardiniere & pedestal base, orange
bittersweet pods & green leaves
on grey bark-textured ground, overall
24" h., 2 pcs. 375.00
Planter, 2-handled, orange bittersweet
pods & green leaves on green bark-
textured ground, 8" l. 32.00
Vase, 6" h., double bud, 2 columns
rising from stepped base joined by
spray of relief-molded leaves,
orange bittersweet pods on grey
bark-textured ground 32.00
Vase, 16" h., 2-handled, bulbous
w/slender neck & flaring mouth,
orange bittersweet pods & green
leaves on grey bark-textured
ground . . . . .125.00 to 175.00
Wall pocket, orange bittersweet pods
& green leaves on grey or yellow
bark-textured ground, each . .45.00 to 75.00

BLACKBERRY (1933)
Basket, hanging-type, band of blackberries & leaves in relief
on green textured ground, 6½" d. . .300.00
Bowl, 4" to 6" d., band of blackberries & leaves in relief on green
textured ground, each . . . . .90.00 to 100.00
Bowl, 10 x 6", 3½" h., band of
blackberries & leaves in relief on
green textured ground 125.00

Jardiniere, band of blackberries &
leaves in relief on green textured
ground, 9" h. . . . . .200.00 to 250.00
Jardiniere & pedestal base, band of
blackberries & leaves in relief on
green textured ground, overall 28" h.,
2 pcs. 600.00
Vase, 6½" h., 2-handled, band of
blackberries & leaves in relief on
green textured ground . . . .110.00 to 125.00
Vase, 8" h., bulbous base & wide
straight neck, 2 small open handles,
band of blackberries & leaves in
relief on green textured ground 170.00
Vase, 12" h., band of blackberries &
leaves in relief on green textured
ground 450.00
Wall pocket, cluster of blackberries
& leaves on green textured
ground . . . . .335.00 to 400.00

BLEEDING HEART (1938)

Bleeding Heart Jardiniere & Pedestal

Basket w/circular handle, pink blossoms
& green leaves on shaded pink,
9½" h. 72.50
Bowl, 10" d., pink blossoms &
green leaves on shaded pink 40.00
Ewer, pink blossoms & green leaves
on shaded blue, 10" h. 65.00
Jardiniere & pedestal base, pink blossoms
& green leaves on shaded green,
25" h. (ILLUS.) 325.00
Vase, 3½" h., pink blossoms & green
leaves on shaded green 22.50
Vase, 6" h., pink blossoms & green
leaves on shaded pink 38.00
Vase, 15" h., pink blossoms & green
leaves on shaded pink 125.00
Wall pocket, pink blossoms & green
leaves on shaded blue, 8" h. 50.00

BURMESE (1950s)

Bookend, figural bust of Burmese
woman, green or white, 8" h.
(single) . . . . .55.00 to 70.00
Bookends, figural busts, white glaze,
pr. . . . . .165.00 to 175.00
Candle holder-bookends, figural bust of
Burmese man, black glaze, pr. 125.00
Planter, green glaze, 10" l. 30.00
Wall pocket, figural bust of Burmese
man or woman, black glaze, 7½" h.,
each 150.00

BUSHBERRY (1948)

Ashtray, berries & leaves on russet
bark-textured ground . . . . . . .40.00 to 48.00
Basket, hanging-type, berries & leaves
on blue or green bark-textured
ground, 7" d., each . . . . .60.00 to 85.00
Bookends, berries & leaves on blue or
russet bark-textured ground, each
pr. . . . . .95.00 to 125.00
Bowl, fruit, 10" d., berries & leaves
on blue bark-textured ground 47.50
Cider set: pitcher & 6 mugs; leaves
& berries on russet bark-textured
ground, 7 pcs. 375.00
Console set: 10" d. bowl & pr.
2" h. candlesticks; berries & leaves
on blue or russet bark-textured
ground, 3 pcs., each set . . .75.00 to 95.00
Cornucopia vase, berries & leaves on
blue or russet bark-textured ground,
6" h., each. . . . . .35.00 to 55.00
Ewer, berries & leaves on green or
russet bark-textured ground, 10" h.,
each .75.00 to 90.00
Jardiniere, berries & leaves on russet
bark-textured ground, 8" h. 175.00
Pitcher w/ice lip, berries & leaves
on green bark-textured ground 90.00
Planter, berries & leaves on green or
russet bark-textured ground, 6½" l.,
each .22.00 to 30.00
Sugar bowl, open, berries & leaves on
russet bark-textured ground 15.00
Vase, 9" h., berries & leaves on
blue bark-textured ground 48.00
Vase, 14" h., flaring twig handles,
berries & leaves on blue bark-
textured ground 135.00
Wall pocket, berries & leaves on green
bark-textured ground 95.00

CAMEO (1920)

Jardiniere & pedestal base, border
of trees & maidens in flowing gowns
on ivory matte ground, overall
34" h., 2 pcs. 600.00

CARNELIAN I (1910-15)

Bowl, 4½" d., turquoise blue drip
glaze on aqua blue 25.00
Bowl, 8" d., medium blue drip glaze
on light blue .30.00

Candle holders, antique gold drip glaze
  on green, 2½" h., pr................24.00
Candle holders, dark green drip glaze
  on light green, 3" h., pr. 32.00
Ewer, medium blue drip glaze on light
  blue, 12½" h. 125.00
Vase, 5" h., dark blue drip glaze on
  light blue.................25.00 to 35.00
Vase, 15½" h., cobalt blue drip glaze
  on light blue 125.00
Vase, 18" h., medium blue drip glaze
  on light blue ....165.00 to 195.00

Carnelian I Wall Pocket

Wall pocket, dark green drip glaze on
  light green, 7½" h. (ILLUS.) 42.00
Wall pocket, medium blue drip glaze
  on light blue, 8" h. 47.50

CARNELIAN II (1915)
Bowl, 9" w., 3" h., handled, intermingled shades of green............30.00
Candle holders, intermingled shades
  of raspberry, pr....................30.00
Vase, 5" h., 7" w., fan-shaped, intermingled shades of blue 18.00
Vases, 7" h., 2-handled, intermingled
  pink & blue glaze, pr...............70.00
Vase, 7" h., intermingled shades of
  raspberry.........................38.00
Vase, 7½" h., 2-handled, bulbous
  bottom w/short cylindrical neck,
  intermingled olive green & turquoise
  blue glaze.........................40.00
Vase, 10" h., handled, intermingled
  shades of raspberry 80.00
Wall pocket, intermingled blue &
  green glaze, 8" h..................72.00

CHERRY BLOSSOM (1933)
Bowl, 6½" d., 5" h., earred
  handles, bulbous, cherry blossoms &
  ivory fencework against brown
  combed ground....................92.00
Candle holders, cherry blossoms & pink
  fencework against blue combed
  ground, pr. 180.00
Console set: bowl & pr. candle

holders; cherry blossoms & ivory
  fencework against brown combed
  ground, 3 pcs. 295.00
Jardiniere, cherry blossoms & pink
  fencework against blue combed
  ground, 9" d., 8" h. .....340.00 to 400.00
Lamp, cherry blossoms & ivory fencework against brown combed
  ground 175.00
Vase, 4" to 5" h., cherry blossoms &
  ivory fencework against brown
  combed ground, each ......85.00 to 105.00
Vase, 7" h., jug-type, 2-handled, cherry
  blossoms & ivory fencework against
  brown combed ground..............135.00
Vase, 7" h., expanding cylinder, cherry
  blossoms and pink fencework against
  blue combed ground 110.00
Vase, 12" h., cherry blossoms & pink
  fencework against blue combed
  ground 275.00
Wall pocket, cherry blossoms & pink
  fencework against blue combed
  ground 315.00

CHLORON (1907)
Mug, green matte finish ......90.00 to 110.00
Planter, footed, green matte finish,
  4½ x 5".........................92.50
Sconce, relief-molded figure of a
  warrior w/shield & staff, green
  matte finish, 17" h. (small chip) 450.00
Umbrella stand, green matte finish....350.00
Vase, 12½" h., 3-footed, green
  matte finish 137.50

CLEMATIS (1944)

Clematis Vase

Basket, hanging-type, clematis blossoms
  on blue, brown or green textured
  ground, each ....45.00 to 65.00
Bookends, model of stacked books
  w/clematis blossoms on blue or
  brown textured ground, each pr......45.00
Bowl, 4" d., clematis blossoms on blue
  textured ground 30.00

Candle holders, clematis blossoms on
   blue textured ground, 4½" h.,
   pr. . . . . 35.00 to 50.00
Console bowl, clematis blossoms on
   blue textured ground, 14" d. 38.00
Cookie jar, cov., clematis blossoms
   on blue textured ground, 10" h. 150.00
Cornucopia-vase, clematis blossoms on
   blue textured ground, 8" h. 40.00
Ewer, clematis blossoms on green
   textured ground, 6" h. 45.00
Ewer, clematis blossoms on brown
   textured ground, 15" h. 145.00
Jardiniere & pedestal base, clematis
   blossoms on blue textured ground,
   2 pcs. 240.00
Tea set: cov. teapot, creamer & sugar
   bowl; clematis blossoms on green
   textured ground, 3 pcs. 145.00
Vase, 4½" h., 3-prong, 2 handles at
   base, clematis blossoms on brown or
   green textured ground, each 19.00
Vase, 7½" h., 2-handled, clematis
   blossoms on green textured ground . .28.00
Vase, 9" to 10" h., handled,
   clematis blossoms on brown textured
   ground, each (ILLUS.) 52.00
Wall pocket, clematis blossoms on blue,
   brown or green textured ground,
   8" h., each . . . . .45.00 to 65.00
Window box, handled, clematis
   blossoms on blue textured ground,
   10½" l. 35.00

COLUMBINE (1940s)

Columbine Vase

Basket, fan-shaped w/overhead
   handle, columbine blossoms in relief
   on shaded blue, pink or tan ground,
   7" h., each . . . . .45.00 to 55.00
Bowl, 3" h., 2-handled, squatty,
   columbine blossoms in relief on
   shaded blue, pink or tan ground,
   each . . . . .30.00 to 37.00

Candle holders, columbine blossoms in
   relief on shaded tan ground, 7" h.,
   pr. 65.00
Ewer, columbine blossoms in relief
   on shaded pink or tan ground,
   7" h., each 45.00
Vase, 4" h., columbine blossoms in
   relief on shaded pink ground 20.00
Vase, 6" h., handled, columbine
   blossoms in relief on shaded pink
   ground (ILLUS.) . . . . .25.00 to 35.00
Vase, bud, 7" h., columbine blossoms
   in relief on shaded blue or tan
   ground, each . . . . .35.00 to 42.00
Vase, 14" h., columbine blossoms in
   relief on shaded pink ground 150.00
Wall pocket, columbine blossoms in
   relief on shaded blue ground 150.00

CORINTHIAN (1923)

Corinthian Vase

Bowl, 6½" d., 3¼" h., fluted body
   w/embossed fruit & floral band,
   green & ivory .47.50
Bowl, 8" d., fluted body w/embossed
   fruit & floral band, green & ivory 35.00
Candlestick, fluted body w/embossed
   fruit & floral band on foot, 8" h.
   (single) 25.00
Jardiniere, fluted body w/embossed
   fruit & floral band at shoulder,
   8" d., 6" h. 75.00
Jardiniere, fluted body w/embossed
   fruit & floral band at shoulder,
   12" d., 9" h. .160.00
Vase, 8½" h., bulbous, fluted body
   w/embossed fruit & floral band at
   shoulder (ILLUS.) 45.00
Vase, 10" h., cylindrical, fluted body
   w/embossed fruit & floral band at
   rim 72.50
Wall pocket, fluted body w/embossed
   fruit & floral band at rim, 12½" h. . . .125.00

COSMOS (1940)

Cosmos Vase

Basket, pedestal base, overhead
handle, realistic cosmos blossoms in
relief on blue band, shaded green
ground, 12" h. 95.00
Bowl, 6" d., handled, realistic cosmos
blossoms in relief on green band,
shaded blue ground 60.00
Candlesticks, open handles at base,
realistic cosmos blossoms in relief on
shaded green or tan ground, 4½" h.,
each pr. . . . . .35.00 to 40.00
Ewer, realistic cosmos blossoms in
relief on green band, shaded blue
ground, 10" h. .55.00
Jardiniere, realistic cosmos blossoms
in relief on green band, tan ground,
4" h. 27.50
Vase, 5" h., open handles at base,
realistic cosmos blossoms in relief
on green band, tan ground 27.50
Vase, 10" h., realistic cosmos blossoms
in relief on green band, blue ground
(ILLUS.) 95.00
Vase, 18" h., realistic cosmos blossoms
in relief on green band, blue
ground 150.00
Window box, realistic cosmos blossoms
in relief on blue ground, 11" l. 50.00

CREMONA (1927)

Console bowl, relief-molded small
floral cluster, mottled green, 11" d.,
2½" h. 40.00
Vase, 4" h., footed, relief-molded
small floral cluster, mottled green . . .22.50
Vase, 6" h., 2-handled, relief-molded
small floral cluster & leaves, mottled
light blue & green 28.00
Vase, 8" h., trumpet-shaped, relief-
molded small floral cluster, mottled
ivory 40.00
Vase, 10½" h., baluster-shaped,

flaring mouth, relief-molded small
floral cluster, mottled pink 42.00
Vase, 12" h., relief-molded small floral
cluster, mottled green 50.00

DAHLROSE (1924-1928)

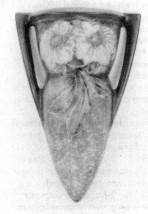

Dahlrose Wall Pocket

Bowl, 8½ x 5½", 2-handled, footed,
ivory blossoms in relief on mottled
tan shaded to green 35.00
Candlesticks, shaped base w/angular
handles, ivory blossoms in relief on
mottled tan shaded to green, 3½" h.,
pr. 56.00
Console bowl, handled, ivory blossoms
in relief on mottled tan shaded to
green, 10" oval, 4" h. 41.00
Flower holder, bud vase rising from
mound base w/adjoining stylized
handles, 8" h. .45.00
Vase, double bud, 6½" h., gate form . . .34.00
Vase, 10" h. 63.00
Vase, 12" h., square 120.00
Wall pocket, elongated handles, 10" l.
(ILLUS.) 82.50

DAWN (1937)

Bookends, incised florals w/slender
petals, pink or yellow matte finish,
5" h., each pr. . . . . .105.00 to 135.00
Bowl, 4" d., square base, tab handles,
incised florals w/slender petals,
pink matte finish 22.00
Candle holders, square base, incised
florals w/slender petals, pale yellow
matte finish, pr. 20.00
Flower frog, incised florals w/slender
petals, green matte finish, 4 x 3" 15.00
Vase, 6" to 7" h., incised florals
w/slender petals, pale yellow matte
finish, each . . . . .24.00 to 35.00

DELLA ROBBIA, ROZANE (1906)

Console bowl, overall incised design,
high-gloss glaze 725.00

Ewer, inscribed "You rising moon that
looks for us again. . . .," 5½" h. 950.00
Teapot, cov., footed, disc-shaped body
w/incised rooster & rising sun,
6½" h. 1,275.00

Della Robbia Rozane Vase

Vase, 9½" h., double gourd form, grey
penguins & pine trees on blue
textured ground, artist-signed
(ILLUS.) 725.00

DOGWOOD I (1916-1918)
Basket, hanging-type, dogwood
blossoms on textured green
ground 175.00
Jardiniere, dogwood blossoms on
textured green ground, 11" h. 45.00
Vase, bud, 8½" h., dogwood blossoms
on textured green ground 35.00
Vase, 10" h., dogwood blossoms on
textured green ground 65.00
Wall pocket, dogwood blossoms on
textured green ground, 9½" l. 145.00

DOGWOOD II (1928)

Dogwood II Basket

Basket, dogwood blossoms on matte
green ground, 6" h. (ILLUS.) 52.50
Jardiniere, dogwood blossoms on

matte green ground, 8" to 9" h.,
each .65.00 to 85.00
Planter, tub-shaped, rim handles,
8" d., 5" h. 35.00
Vase, 8" h., bulbous 57.00
Vase, bud, 8½" h. 40.00

DONATELLO (1915)

Donatello Double Bud Vase

Ash tray, cherubs in light relief on tan
band, green & ivory fluted body,
3" d. 62.50
Basket, hanging-type, cherubs in light
relief on wide tan band, green &
ivory fluted neck & base, w/original
chains, 7¾ x 5" 185.00
Bowl, 6" to 7" d., frolicking cherubs
in light relief on tan band, green &
ivory fluted body, each . . . . . .35.00 to 47.50
Bowl, 9½" d., shallow, cherubs in light
relief on tan band, green & ivory
fluted body 60.00
Candlesticks, 10" h., pr. 185.00
Compote, 7¼" d., 9½" h. 90.00
Console bowl w/flower frog, 7½" d.,
2 pcs. 50.00
Cuspidor. 125.00
Flower frog, 3½" d. 9.50
Flower pot w/saucer, 6½" h., 2 pcs. . . .110.00
Jardiniere, 4" to 5" h., each . . . .38.00 to 55.00
Jardiniere, 9½" h. 150.00
Jardiniere & pedestal base, overall
28" h., 2 pcs. 490.00
Umbrella stand 350.00
Vase, double bud, 5" h., 8" w., gate
form (ILLUS.) 40.00
Vase, bud, 10" h. 45.00
Vase, 12" h., cylindrical. 110.00
Vase, 14½" h. 225.00
Wall pocket, 9" to 10" h.,
each .65.00 to 95.00
Window box, 12 x 6" 115.00

DUTCH (pre-1916)
Ale set: tankard pitcher & 6 mugs;
creamware w/varied Dutch decals,
7 pcs. . . . . .435.00 to 525.00
Chamber pot, child's, creamware
w/Dutch decals 190.00
Creamer, creamware w/Dutch decals . .75.00

Mug, creamware w/decal of Dutch boy
  && girl fishing, 5" h. 65.00
Pitcher, 7½" h. .97.50
Pitcher, tankard, 11½" h., creamware
  w/decal of 2 Dutchmen 295.00
Soap dish w/cover 130.00
Sugar bowl, cov. 55.00
Teapot, cov. 125.00
Water set: pitcher & 1 tumbler;
  creamware w/decal of Dutch
  children, 2 pcs. 165.00

EARLAM (1930)
Bowl, 10" d., 4" h., handled, mottled
  green glaze 45.00
Candle holders, mottled green & blue
  glaze, 1½" h., pr. 42.00
Candle holders, mottled blue & green
  glaze, 5" w., 3" h., pr. 95.00
Planter, handled, green shading to
  mottled blue & apricot, 10½ x 5½" . . .40.00
Vase, 4½" h., bulbous w/small open
  handles at shoulder, mottled blue &
  green glaze 34.00
Vase, 7" to 9" h., mottled green glaze,
  each . . . . .55.00 to 78.00
Wall pocket, mottled blue & green
  glaze, 7" h. 65.00

EARLY EMBOSSED PITCHERS (pre-1916)

Embossed Tulip Pitcher

"The Boy," w/horn 145.00
"The Bridge," 5½" h. . . . . .35.00 to 40.00
"The Cow," green & yellow decor,
  8" h. 72.50
"The Grape" 60.00
"Landscape" 55.00
"The Owl," 6½" h. 225.00
"Tulip," 7" h. (ILLUS.) 52.00
"Wild Rose" 45.00

EGYPTO (1905)
Console bowl, 3-handled, shades of
  deep green matt glaze, 9" d., 3" h. . .100.00
Pitcher, 3½" h., w/applied ceramic
  seal, shades of deep green matt
  glaze 235.00
Vase, 5½" h., relief-molded decor,

w/applied ceramic seal, shaded dark
  green matt glaze 235.00
Vase, 12½" h., w/applied ceramic
  seal, shades of dark green matt
  glaze 180.00

FALLINE (1933)
Candlesticks, impressed triangles &
  peapod decor on base, brown,
  pr. . . . . .175.00 to 185.00
Lamps, impressed triangles & peapod
  decor, brown, brass base, 7" h.,
  pr. 275.00
Urn-vase, 2-handled, impressed
  triangles at shoulders, peapod
  shapes on body, blue shaded to
  green & tan, 6" h. 178.00
Vase, 6" h., 2-handled, ovoid body
  w/impressed triangles at shoulders,
  peapod shapes below, brown 125.00
Vase, 7½" h., handled, globular body
  w/impressed triangles & peapod
  decor, blue shaded to green & tan . . .150.00
Vase, 14" h., impressed triangles &
  peapod decor, brown shaded to
  tan 550.00

FERRELLA (1930)
Bowl, 12" d., reticulated base
  w/molded shells, flaring sides &
  pierced rim w/impressed shell
  design, mottled red & turquoise 230.00
Console set: 12" d. bowl w/reticulated
  base & rim & pr. candlesticks;
  mottled red & turquoise, 3 pcs. 445.00
Vase, 4" h., angular handles, reticulated base w/molded shells &
  pierced rim, mottled brown 125.00
Vase, 8" h., ovoid, pierced shell-
  molded base & rim, mottled brown . .215.00
Vase, 9" h., 2-handled, pierced shell-
  molded decor, mottled red &
  turquoise 250.00
Vase, 10" h., pierced shell-molded
  foot, expanding body w/side handles
  & reticulated flaring rim, mottled
  brown 260.00
Wall pocket, pierced shell-molded
  rim, mottled red & turquoise,
  6½" h. 425.00

FLORANE (1920s)
Bowl, 8½" d., shaded rust 45.00
Vase, 6" h., angular handles at
  shoulder, shaded rust to green 45.00
Vase, 7" h., shaded rust 35.00
Vase, double bud, shaded rust. 32.00
Wall pocket, shaded rust to green,
  10" h. 115.00

FLORANE II (late 1940s)
Bowl, 6" d., scalloped rim, soft blue
  w/tan lining. .16.00

Bowl, 8" d., soft green w/tan lining 20.00
Planter, oblong, molded comet-type
    design, soft blue, 4" l. 15.00
Planter, oblong, molded comet-type
    design, soft green, 10" l. 18.00
Vase, 7" h., crumpled shape, soft tan
    w/dark tan lining 30.00

FLORENTINE (1924-28)

Florentine Vase

Ash tray, bark-textured panels alter-
    nating w/embossed floral garlands,
    brown tones 35.00
Basket, bulbous w/flaring rim, bark-
    textured panels alternating w/em-
    bossed berries & foliage, tan & green
    tones, 8" h. 125.00
Basket, hanging-type, bark-textured
    panels alternating w/embossed
    garlands of cascading fruit & florals,
    dark brown tones, 8" 83.00
Bowl, 8¼" d., 3" h., bark-textured
    panels alternating w/berries &
    foliage, brown tones 50.00
Candle holders, bark-textured panels
    alternating w/berries & foliage,
    brown tones, 2½" h., pr...........35.00
Candlesticks, bark-textured panels
    alternating w/embossed pendant
    garlands of fruit & florals, brown
    tones, 10½" h., pr................58.00
Console set: 7" d. bowl & pr. low
    candle holders; bark-textured panels
    alternating w/floral garlands, brown
    & green tones, 3 pcs. 60.00
Jardiniere, handled, bark-textured
    panels alternating w/garlands of
    cascading florals & fruit, brown
    tones, 5" h. 36.00
Jardinere & pedestal base, bark-
    textured panels alternating w/gar-
    lands of cascading fruit & florals,
    brown tones, overall 28" h., 2 pcs. ..400.00
Umbrella stand, bark-textured panels

alternating w/garlands of cascading
    fruit & florals, brown tones 260.00
Vase, 6" h., 2-handled, bark-textured
    panels alternating w/floral
    garlands.........................35.00
Vase, 8" h., 2-handled, bark-textured
    panels alternating w/pendant gar-
    lands of fruit & florals, brown
    tones............................45.00
Vase, 10" h., bark-textured panels
    alternating w/embossed fruit &
    foliage (ILLUS.) 57.00
Wall pocket, central bark-textured
    panel flanked by pendant floral
    garlands, 7" h. 50.00
Wall pocket, loop handle, bark-tex-
    tured panel flanked by pendant floral
    garlands, brown tones, 8½" h. 55.00

FOXGLOVE (1940s)

Foxglove Cornucopia

Basket w/overhead handle, white fox-
    glove spray on shaded blue or green
    ground, 12" h., each ....95.00 to 125.00
Basket, hanging-type, white foxglove
    spray on shaded blue ground 96.00
Candlesticks, flat base, pierced
    handles, white foxglove spray on
    shaded blue ground, 5" h., pr. 35.00
Console bowl, white foxglove spray on
    shaded blue ground, 14 x 3".........55.00
Cornucopia-vase, white foxglove spray
    on shaded green or rose ground,
    6½" h., each (ILLUS.)........32.00 to 38.00
Ewer, white foxglove spray on shaded
    blue or pink ground, 10" h.,
    each ....55.00 to 75.00
Ewer, white foxglove spray on shaded
    blue or green ground, 15" h.,
    each ....100.00 to 135.00
Flower pot w/saucer, white foxglove
    spray on shaded blue ground, 5" h....45.00
Jardiniere, handled, white foxglove
    spray on shaded pink ground, 6" h....40.00
Jardiniere & pedestal base, white fox-
    glove spray on shaded blue ground,
    overall 30½" h., 2 pcs..............650.00
Rose bowl, 2-handled, white foxglove
    spray on shaded pink ground, 6" d. ...39.00
Tray, open handles, white foxglove

spray on shaded blue or green
ground, 8½" w., each ......35.00 to 45.00
Tray, open handles, white foxglove
spray on shaded green ground,
15" w............................75.00
Vase, 3" h., handled, white foxglove
spray on shaded blue ground 22.00
Vase, 6" h., white foxglove spray on
shaded blue or pink ground, each 18.00
Vase, 10" h., white foxglove spray on
shaded green or rose ground,
each ....45.00 to 65.00
Vase, 16" h., white foxglove spray on
shaded blue ground 165.00
Wall pocket, white foxglove spray on
shaded blue ground 48.00

FREESIA (1945)

Freesia Console Bowl

Basket w/overhead handle, white
blossoms & green leaves in relief on
shaded blue or brown textured
ground, 10" h., each...............60.00
Basket, hanging-type, white to yellow
blossoms & green leaves in relief on
shaded brown textured ground, 5" ...65.00
Bowl, 6" d., handled, white blossoms
& green leaves in relief on shaded
blue or green textured ground,
each 25.00
Candle holders, angular pierced
handles, domed base, white to
lavender blossoms & green leaves
in relief on shaded green textured
ground, 2" h., pr. 28.00
Console bowl, handled, white to yellow
blossoms & green leaves in relief on
shaded brown textured ground,
14" w. (ILLUS.)....................65.00
Creamer, white to yellow blossoms &
green leaves in relief on shaded
brown textured ground 30.00
Ewer, squatty, white to yellow blossoms & green
leaves in relief on shaded brown,
green or tangerine textured ground,
6" h., each.................40.00 to 50.00
Ewer, white blossoms & green leaves
in relief on shaded brown or green
textured ground, 15" h.,
each ....85.00 to 120.00
Jardiniere & pedestal base, white to
yellow blossoms & green leaves in
relief on shaded brown textured
ground, overall 24½" h., 2 pcs. 465.00
Pitcher, 10" h., white blossoms & green
leaves in relief on shaded blue,

brown, green or tangerine textured
ground, each ....55.00 to 75.00
Sugar bowl, white to yellow blossoms
& green leaves in relief on shaded
brown textured ground 30.00
Teapot, cov., white to lavender
blossoms & green leaves in relief on
shaded blue textured ground 60.00
Vase, 6" h., white to lavender blossoms
& green leaves in relief on shaded
green textured ground 35.00
Vase, 9" h., angular base handles,
white blossoms & green leaves in
relief on shaded blue, brown or
green textured ground,
each ....38.00 to 50.00
Vase, 12" h., white blossoms & green
leaves in relief on shaded blue or
green textured ground, each 75.00
Wall pocket, white blossoms & green
leaves in relief on shaded blue,
brown or green textured ground,
8½" h., each...............48.00 to 56.00
Window box, white blossoms & green
leaves in relief on shaded blue or
brown textured ground, 8" l.,
each ....40.00 to 50.00

FUCHSIA (1939)

Fuchsia Cornucopia

Basket w/overhead handle, pendant
fuchsia blossoms on brown w/cream
highlights, 7" d., 10½" h. 140.00
Basket, hanging-type, pendant fuchsia
blossoms on green w/tan highlights,
5"...............................110.00
Bowl, 5" d., handled, pendant fuchsia
blossoms on brown or green
w/cream highlights, each 45.00
Candle holders, base handles, pendant
fuchsia blossoms on tan w/cream
highlights, 2" h., pr...............35.00
Candlesticks, domed base, tubular
form raised on ring, pendant fuchsia
blossoms on blue or tan w/cream
highlights, 5½" h., each pr. ...78.00 to 85.00
Cornucopia-vase, pendant fuchsia
blossoms on blue w/cream highlights (ILLUS.) 45.00

Ewer, pendant fuchsia blossoms on
green w/tan highlights, 10" h. 67.00
Flower frog, pendant blossoms on blue
or green w/cream highlights, 5 x 3",
each 42.00
Flower pot w/saucer, pendant
blossoms on blue or brown w/cream
highlights, 5" h., each 93.00
Pitcher w/ice lip, 8" h., pendant
blossoms on tan w/cream high-
lights. 90.00
Vase, 6" h., handled, ovoid w/collared
neck, pendant blossoms on green
w/tan highlights 46.00
Vase, 12" h., 2 handles rising from
low foot to slightly flared rim,
pendant blossoms on brown
w/cream highlights 100.00
Vase, 18" h., pendant blossoms on
green or tan w/cream highlights,
each 195.00
Wall pocket, pendant blossoms on blue
or tan w/cream highlights, 8" h.,
each 125.00

FUTURA (1928)
Basket, hanging-type w/chains,
modernistic shape, shaded pink to
grey, 5" h. 140.00
Bowl, 8" oval stepped base, sharply
flared sides w/molded stylized
design, blended brown glaze 85.00
Candlesticks, shaped square base
rising to square candle nozzle, relief-
molded stylized green vine & foliage
on cream ground, 4" h., pr. 135.00
Flower pot, square base, canted sides,
relief-molded branch & foliage on
blended blue & green glaze, 3½" h. . .85.00
Jardiniere, expanding body w/angular
handles at shoulder, stylized design
on shaded terra cotta to green
glaze, 6" h. .110.00
Jardiniere & pedestal base, stylized
leaf design, blended brown glaze,
overall 29" h., 2 pcs. 600.00
Vase, 6" h., fan-shaped, blended blue
& white glaze 125.00
Vase, 8½" h., beehive-shaped, blue-
green leaves on blended tan glaze . .265.00
Vase, 10" h., bulbous base w/square
flaring sides, green design on
shaded blue ground 250.00
Wall pocket, geometric design,
blended green & cream on terra
cotta, 8" h. 145.00

GARDENIA (1940s)
Basket w/circular handle, white gardenia blossom on shaded green or
tan, 10" h., each . . . . .65.00 to 80.00
Bowl, 6" d., white gardenia blossom
on shaded grey 25.00

Gardenia Console Bowl

Console bowl, white gardenia blossom
on shaded brown, 12" l., 3" h.
(ILLUS.) 52.00
Cornucopia-vase, white gardenia
blossom on shaded green, 6" h. 30.00
Ewer, white gardenia blossom on
shaded grey or tan, 10" h.,
each . . . . .55.00 to 65.00
Planter, white gardenia blossom on
shaded grey, 4" sq. 22.00
Spooner, white gardenia blossom on
shaded green .25.00
Tray, white gardenia blossom on
shaded tan, 15" l. 52.50
Vase, 8" h., flared top, white gardenia
blossom on shaded grey 35.00
Vase, 12" h., base handles, white
gardenia blossom on shaded green . .68.00
Wall pocket, 2-handled, white gardenia
blossom on shaded green or grey,
8½" h., each . . . . .80.00 to 100.00
Window box, white gardenia blossom
on shaded grey, 12" l. 32.50

IMPERIAL I (1916)

Imperial I Basket

Basket w/overhead handle, pretzel-
twisted vine & grape leaves in relief
on green & brown textured ground,
6" h. (ILLUS.) .55.00
Basket, hanging-type, pretzel-twisted
vine & grape leaves in relief on
green & brown textured ground 68.00
Bowl, 6" d., 2" h., 2-handled, pretzel-
twisted vine & grape leaves in relief
on green & brown textured ground . . .45.00
Bowl, 8½" d., 4" h., pierced rim
handles, pretzel-twisted vine & grape
leaves in relief on green & brown
textured ground 55.00

Compote, 10" d., 6½" h., pierced
handles, pretzel-twisted vine &
grape leaves in relief on green &
brown textured ground 50.00
Jardiniere, pretzel-twisted vine &
grape leaves in relief on green &
brown textured ground, 7" h. 42.50
Vase, 6" h., pretzel-twisted vine &
grape leaves in relief on green &
brown textured ground 38.00
Vase, 10" h., 8" d., 2-handled, pretzel-
twisted vine & grape leaves in relief
on green & brown textured ground . . .85.00

IMPERIAL II (1924)
Basket, splotched blue & yellow tex-
tured matte glaze 85.00
Bowl, 8" d., mottled blue or yellow
glossy finish, each 100.00
Candlesticks, splotched orange & green
matte glaze, pr. 135.00
Pitcher, 12" h., mottled green glaze 75.00
Vase, 5" h., turquoise blue drip on
green glaze 150.00
Vase, 8½" h., semi-ovoid, relief-
molded floral design around neck,
cream drip on pink beige glaze 195.00
Vase, 11" h., splotched blue & yellow
textured matte glaze 375.00
Wall pocket, 3-compartment, splotched
orange & green textured matte
glaze. 200.00

IRIS (1938)

Iris Vase

Basket w/overhead handle, iris &
leaves on shaded blue ground, 8" to
10" h., each. . . . . .65.00 to 75.00
Basket, hanging-type, iris & leaves
on shaded tan ground, 5" h. 90.00
Bookends, iris & leaves on shaded
green to pink ground, pr. 65.00
Candlesticks, pierced handles rising
from flared base, iris & leaves on
shaded blue ground, pr. 45.00

Console bowl, 2-handled, iris & leaves
on shaded tan ground, 10" l., 3" h. . . .45.00
Ewer, iris & leaves on shaded green
to pink ground, 10" h. 65.00
Jardiniere, iris & leaves on shaded blue
ground, 4" to 6" h., each . . . . .27.00 to 35.00
Vase, 4" h., iris & leaves on shaded
blue, pink or tan ground,
each . . . . .20.00 to 25.00
Vase, 5" h., iris & leaves on shaded
green to pink ground (ILLUS.) 32.00
Vase, 15" h., iris & leaves on shaded
blue ground 115.00
Wall pocket, iris & leaves on shaded
blue ground, 8" h. 98.00

IVORY (Old Ivory - pre-1916)
Jardiniere, footed, relief-molded
Roman scene w/Gladiator, horses,
woman, etc., 10 x 8½" 145.00
Vase, 5" h., relief-molded grape leaf
design 20.00
Vase, 6" h., relief-molded florals &
designs 25.00

IVORY II (1940)
Bowl, 7" d., white matte glaze 35.00
Cornucopia-vases, Pine Cone patt.,
white matte glaze 55.00
Vase, 7" h., 2 handles rising from
stepped shoulders to rim of cylindrical neck, expanding body, white
matte glaze 45.00
Vase, 7½" h., Russco patt., white
matte glaze 40.00
Vase, 14" h., Velmoss II patt., white
matte glaze 95.00

IXIA (1930s)

Ixia Centerpiece

Basket w/angular overhead handle,
floral cluster on shaded green or
yellow, 10" h., each 65.00
Basket, hanging-type, pink floral
cluster on shaded yellow. 110.00
Bowl, 6½" d., handled, pink floral
cluster on shaded green 47.00
Candle holders, 2-light, pink floral
cluster on shaded pink, 3" h., pr. 52.00
Candlesticks, pink floral cluster on
shaded green, 4½" h., pr. 32.50
Centerpiece, 1-piece console set
w/candle holders attached to center
bowl, floral cluster on shaded pink,
13" l. (ILLUS.) .97.50

Console bowl, floral cluster on shaded
yellow, 12" d. 52.00
Flower frog, floral cluster on shaded
yellow. 30.00
Jardiniere, pink floral cluster on
shaded green, 4" h. 34.00
Vase, 6" to 7" h., floral cluster on
shaded green, pink or yellow,
each .32.00 to 45.00
Vase, 12" h., floral cluster on shaded
pink. 95.00

JONQUIL (1931)
Basket w/overhead handle, jonquil
blossoms & leaves in relief against
textured tan ground, 9" h. 190.00
Basket, hanging-type w/original chains,
jonquil blossoms & leaves in relief
against textured tan ground. 145.00
Bowl, 3" to 4" d., handled, jonquil
blossoms & leaves in relief against
textured tan ground, each . . .35.00 to 45.00
Candlesticks, domed base, jonquil
blossoms & leaves in relief against
textured tan ground, 4" h., pr. 105.00
Console bowl w/attached flower frog,
jonquil blossoms & leaves in relief
against textured tan ground,
10" d. 110.00
Jardiniere, jonquil blossoms & leaves
in relief against textured tan ground,
10" to 11" h., each . . . . .215.00 to 260.00
Vase, 4" to 5" h., jonquil blossoms &
leaves in relief against textured tan
ground, each . . . . .50.00 to 60.00
Vase, 7" h., jonquil blossoms & leaves
in relief against textured tan
ground 58.00
Wall pocket, jonquil blossoms & leaves
in relief against textured tan ground,
8½"h. 210.00

JUVENILE (1916 on)
Bowl, cereal, 4¾" d., green band
w/rabbits decor 35.00
Bowl, 6" d., duck w/hat decor 55.00
Bowl & mug, Sunbonnet girl decor,
2 pcs. 90.00
Chamber pot w/lid, rabbits decor 130.00
Creamer, bears decor, 4" h. 80.00
Creamer, grey band w/dog decor,
3½" h. 75.00
Creamer, fat puppy decor, 3½"h. 35.00
Creamer, Sunbonnet girl decor 35.00
Cup & saucer, chicks decor 60.00

Custard cup, ducks decor 35.00
Egg cup, rabbit decor, 3½" h. 85.00
Feeding dish, "Baby's Plate" on rolled
edge, chicks decor, 8" d. 43.00
Feeding dish w/rolled edge, duck
w/hat decor, 8" d. 40.00

Feeding dish w/rolled edge, nursery
rhyme "Little Bo Peep," 8" d. 45.00
Feeding dish w/rolled rim, nursery
rhyme "Old Woman, Old Woman,"
8" d. 45.00

Standing Rabbits Feeding Dish

Feeding dish w/rolled edge, rabbits
decor, 8" d. (ILLUS.) 45.00
Feeding dish w/rolled edge, Sun-
bonnet girl decor, 8" d. 48.00
Mug, 2-handled, chicks decor. 42.00
Mug, dog decor, 3" h. 60.00
Mug, rabbits decor 52.00
Mug, Sunbonnet girl decor 57.00
Pitcher, dog decor, 3½" h. 47.50
Plate, 7" d., rabbits decor 38.00
Plate, 8" d., dog decor 40.00
Pudding dish, chicks decor, 4" d. 48.00

LANDSCAPE (1910)
Custard cup, creamware w/windmill
decal decor 35.00
Pitcher, 7" h., creamware w/sailboats
decal decor 65.00
Teapot, cov., creamware w/sailboats
decal decor 115.00
Tea set: cov. teapot, creamer & sugar
bowl; creamware w/windmill decal
decor, 3 pcs. .250.00

LA ROSE (1924)
Basket, hanging-type, draped green
leaves & red roses on creamy ivory,
6" h. 110.00
Bowl, 9" d., 3" h., draped green leaves
& red roses on creamy ivory 60.00
Candle holders, 2 handles rising from
circular base to rim, draped green
leaves & red roses on creamy ivory,
4" h., pr. 32.50
Vase, 4" h., urn-shaped, draped green
leaves & red roses on creamy ivory . . .40.00
Vase, 5½" h., draped leaves & red
roses on creamy ivory 36.00
Vase, bud, 8" h., draped leaves & red
roses on creamy ivory 42.50
Wall pocket, draped leaves & red
roses on creamy ivory, 12" h. 85.00

LAUREL (1934)

Laurel Vase

Bowl, 8" d., 3¼" h., laurel branch &
berries in low relief, reeded panels
at sides, deep yellow 65.00
Console bowl, laurel branch & berries
in low relief, reeded panels at sides,
green, 13 x 8½" 70.00
Vase, 6" h., angular handles at
shoulder, laurel branch & berries in
low relief, reeded panels at sides,
brown or green, each 50.00
Vase, 8" h., footed, laurel branch &
berries in low relief, reeded panels
at sides, green (ILLUS.) 55.00
Vase, 12" h., 2-handled, laurel branch
& berries in low relief, reeded
panels at sides, brown 125.00

LOMBARDY (1924)

Bowl, 5½" d., 2" h., melon-ribbed,
turquoise blue matt glaze 60.00
Jardiniere, 3-footed, bulbous, melon-
ribbed, turquoise blue matt glaze,
14¾" d., 12¼" h. 225.00
Vase, 6" h., 3-footed, melon-ribbed,
blue-grey matt glaze 135.00
Wall pocket, melon-ribbed, blue matt
glaze, 8" h. 150.00
Wall pocket, melon-ribbed, turquoise
blue high-gloss glaze, 8" h. 200.00

LOTUS (1952)

Bowl, 9" d., 3" h., stylized lotus petals
in relief, blue & white high-gloss
finish. 70.00
Candle holders, footed, stylized lotus
petals in relief, blue & white high-
gloss finish, 2½" h., pr. 60.00
Planter, stylized lotus petals in relief,
tan & green high-gloss finish, 4" sq. . .72.50
Vase, 10½" h., pillow-shaped, stylized
lotus petals in relief, blue & yellow
or brown & tan high-gloss finish,
each . . . . .98.00 to 120.00
Wall pocket, stylized lotus petals in
relief, brown & tan high-gloss finish,
7½" h. 145.00

LUFFA (1934)

Bowl, 4" d., relief-molded ivy leaves
& blossoms on shaded green wavy
horizontal ridges 30.00
Candle holders, high domed base,
angular handles, relief-molded ivy
leaves & blossoms on shaded brown
& green wavy horizontal ridges,
5" h., pr. 100.00
Jardiniere, relief-molded ivy leaves &
blossoms on shaded brown & green
wavy horizontal ridges, 7" h. 95.00
Lamp, relief-molded ivy leaves &
blossoms on shaded brown & green
wavy horizontal ridges, 9½" h. 150.00
Vase, 6½" to 7½" h., relief-molded
ivy leaves & blossoms on shaded
green wavy horizontal ridges,
each . . . . .45.00 to 55.00
Vase, 15½" h., handled, relief-molded
ivy leaves & blossoms on shaded
green wavy horizontal ridges 325.00
Wall pocket, relief-molded ivy leaves
& blossoms on shaded brown &
green wavy horizontal ridges 225.00

LUSTRE (1921)

Basket w/angular overhead handle,
glossy orange, 6" h. 165.00
Basket w/angular overhead handle,
glossy pastel blue, 8" h. 200.00
Basket w/angular overhead handle,
glossy pink, 9" h. 235.00
Compote, 6" d., glossy silver grey 40.00
Console bowl, footed, glossy pink,
10" d. 75.00
Console bowl, footed, glossy orange,
13½" d. 300.00

MAGNOLIA (1943)

Magnolia Jardiniere & Pedestal

Ash tray, handled, magnolia blossoms
on textured blue or green ground,
each 45.00

Basket w/overhead handle, magnolia blossoms on textured blue, green or tan ground, 12" h., each . . . . . 65.00 to 75.00

Basket, hanging-type w/chains, magnolia blossoms on textured green or tan ground, each 65.00

Bookends, magnolia blossoms on textured blue ground, pr. 42.00

Bowl, 6" d., 2-handled, magnolia blossoms on textured blue ground . . . 25.00

Candle holders, domed base w/wide angular handles, magnolia blossoms on textured blue ground, 2½" h., pr. 25.00

Cider set: pitcher & 6 mugs; magnolia blossoms on textured blue ground, 7 pcs. 300.00

Cookie jar, cov., magnolia blossoms on textured blue or tan ground, each . . . . 120.00 to 145.00

Cornucopia-vase, magnolia blossoms on textured green or tan ground, 8" h., each . . . . 28.00 to 35.00

Ewer, magnolia blossoms on textured green ground, 6" h. 37.00

Ewer, magnolia blossoms on textured blue or tan ground, 15" h., each . . . . 125.00 to 160.00

Flower frog, angular side handle, magnolia blossoms on textured blue or green ground, 5" h., each 35.00

Flower pot w/saucer, magnolia blossoms on textured blue, green or tan ground, 2 pcs., each set . . 35.00 to 45.00

Jardiniere & pedestal base, magnolia blossoms on textured tan ground, overall 24½" h., 2 pcs. (ILLUS.) 360.00

Model of a conch shell, magnolia blossoms on textured blue or green ground, 6" w., each 35.00

Rose bowl, magnolia blossoms on textured green ground, 4" d. 30.00

Tea set: cov. teapot, creamer & sugar bowl; magnolia blossoms on textured blue, green or tan ground, 3 pcs., each set . . . . 125.00 to 150.00

Vase, 6" h., magnolia blossoms on textured green or tan ground, each . . 26.00

Vase, 9" to 10" h., magnolia blossoms on textured blue ground, each . . . . 42.00 to 50.00

Vase, 18" h., magnolia blossoms on textured blue ground 130.00

Wall pocket, magnolia blossoms on textured blue, green or tan ground, 8½" h., each . . . . 48.00 to 60.00

MATT COLOR (1920s)

Basket, hanging-type, pink or turquoise matt finish, 4½" h., each . . . . 55.00 to 65.00

Bowl, 5" d., blue matt finish 22.00

Flower pot, embossed geometric design, turquoise matt finish, 4" h. 15.00

Jardiniere, 2-handled, rose or royal blue matt finish, 4" h., each 22.50

Vase, 4" h., 2-handled, embossed geometric design, blue or turquoise matt finish 22.00

Vase, 6" h., lightly embossed horizontal ridges, rose matt finish 28.00

MATT GREEN (pre-1916)

Basket, hanging-type, dark green matt glaze, 9" 55.00

Jardiniere, dark green matt glaze, 4" d. 30.00

Jardiniere, dark green matt glaze, 6" d., 4" h. 70.00

Vase, double bud, 4" h., 8" w., 2 fluted columns joined by gate, dark green matt glaze 42.50

Wall pocket, dark green matt glaze, 8" h. 65.00

MAYFAIR (late 1940s)

Basket, tan glaze, 10" h. 36.00

Console set: bowl & pr. 4½" h. candle holders; shell-shaped, brown & pink glaze, 3 pcs. 35.00

Cornucopia-vases, brown glaze, 6" h., pr. 60.00

Pitcher, 6" h., brown glaze 40.00

Teapot, cov., cylindrical w/short spout, green glaze, 5" h. 20.00

Vase, 10½" h., brown glaze 25.00

Wall pocket, corner-type, brown or green glaze, 8" h., each . . . . . 40.00 to 48.00

MEDALLION (pre-1916)

Creamer, oval cameo decal decor w/gold floral swags on creamware, 3½" h. 46.00

Dresser tray, oval cameo decal decor w/gold floral swags on creamware, 10" oval 50.00

Powder box, cov., oval cameo decal decor w/gold floral swags on creamware 60.00

Ring tree, oval cameo decal decor w/gold floral swags on creamware . . . 70.00

MING TREE (1949)

Basket w/overhead handle, oriental branches in relief on blue or green ground, 14" h., each . . . . . . 110.00 to 125.00

Bookends, oriental branches in relief on blue ground, 5½" h., pr. 75.00

Bowl, 9" d., footed, oriental branches in relief on green ground 45.00

Console set: 10" d. bowl & pr. candle holders; oriental branches in relief on blue ground, 3 pcs. . . . . 65.00 to 75.00

Ewer, angular branch handle, oriental branches in relief on blue or white ground, 10" h., each 75.00

Model of a conch shell, on low

molded base, shaded green,
8½" w. 45.00
Planter, oriental branches in relief on
white ground, 8½ x 4". 25.00
Vase, 6" h., cylindrical, handled,
oriental branches in relief on green
ground 35.00
Vase, 14½" h., high domed base
w/cylindrical neck & flared mouth,
handled, oriental branches in relief
on green ground 165.00
Wall pocket w/overhead branch
handle, oriental branches in relief
on green ground, 8½" h. 195.00
Window box, oriental branches in
relief on green or white ground,
11 x 4", each . . . . .55.00 to 75.00

MOCK ORANGE (1950)

Mock Orange Planter

Basket, white blossoms & green leaves
on yellow ground, 6" h. 48.00
Bowl, 12" d., white blossoms & green
leaves on green ground. 65.00
Coffee pot, cov., white blossoms &
green leaves on yellow ground 50.00
Ewer, white blossoms & green leaves
on pink ground, 6" h. 38.00
Jardiniere & pedestal base, white
blossoms & green leaves on yellow
ground, overall 31" h., 2 pcs. 360.00
Planter, oblong base, cluster of white
blossoms & green leaves at base of
handle, green body, 7" l., 4" h.
(ILLUS.) 35.00
Vase, 7" to 8" h., white blossoms &
green leaves on pink ground, each . . .40.00
Vase, 18" h., white blossoms & green
leaves on pink ground 225.00

MODERNE (1930s)

Bowl, 10" d., turquoise blue w/deep
gold highlights 45.00
Compote, 6" h., white w/rose high-
lights. 40.00
Vase, 6" h., white w/rose highlights
(ILLUS.) 38.00
Vase, 9" h., low foot, cone-shaped
w/base handles, turquoise blue
w/deep gold highlights 65.00

Moderne Vase

MONTACELLO (1931)

Basket, white stylized trumpet flowers
w/black accents on band, mottled
tan ground, 6½" h. 200.00
Console bowl, white stylized trumpet
flowers w/black accents on band,
turquoise shaded to tan ground,
13¼" oval . . . . .95.00 to 135.00
Vase, 4" h., pierced side handles,
white stylized trumpet flowers
w/black accents on band, mottled
blue & tan ground 56.00

Montacello Vase

Vase, 7" h., white stylized trumpet
flowers w/black accents on band,
mottled tan ground (ILLUS.) 68.00
Vase, 9" h., pierced side handles,
white stylized trumpet flowers
w/black accents on band, mottled
green ground 95.00

MORNING GLORY (1935)

Bowl-vase, stylized pastel morning
glories in low relief on green
ground, 4" h. 195.00
Candlesticks, high domed base, styl-
ized pastel morning glories in low
relief on green ground, 5" h., pr. 275.00

Flower pot, stylized pastel morning
glories in low relief on white
ground, 5" h. 110.00
Vase, 6" h., handled, stylized pastel
morning glories in low relief on
white ground 150.00
Vase, 10" h., stylized pastel morning
glories in low relief on green
ground 275.00
Wall pocket, double, stylized pastel
morning glories in low relief on
white ground .335.00

MOSS (1930s)

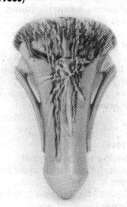

Moss Wall Pocket

Basket, hanging-type, pendant moss on
pink shaded to blue ground, 5" 130.00
Bowl, 8" d., handled, pendant moss on
pink shaded to green ground 38.00
Candlesticks, triple, pendant moss on
pink shaded to blue ground, 7" h.,
pr. 65.00
Flower pot w/saucer, pendant moss
on pink shaded to blue ground,
5" h., 2 pcs. 55.00
Jardiniere & pedestal base, pendant
moss on pink shaded to blue
ground, 2 pcs. . . . . 325.00 to 395.00
Vase, 6" h., urn-shaped, pendant moss
on pink shaded to green ground 55.00
Vase, 8" h., pillow-shaped, pendant
moss on pink shaded to green
ground 65.00
Wall pocket, pendant moss on pink
shaded to blue or green ground,
8" h., each (ILLUS.) 120.00

MOSTIQUE (1915)

Jardiniere, glossy designs in brown,
yellow, blue & green on pebbled
grey ground, 12" d., 9½" h. (ILLUS.) . .75.00
Jardiniere & pedestal base, glossy
designs on pebbled tan ground,
overall 28" h., 2 pcs. 290.00
Umbrella stand, glossy geometric
designs on pebbled grey ground 190.00

Mostique Jardiniere

Basket, hanging-type, glossy stylized
rose blossom designs on pebbled
grey ground, 10" d. 65.00
Bowl, 6¾" d., glossy designs on
pebbled grey ground 60.00
Console bowl, glossy stylized floral
designs on pebbled tan ground,
9½" d., 3" h. 75.00
Vase, 6" h., corset-shaped, handled,
glossy arrowhead motif on pebbled
tan ground 22.00
Vase, 12½" h., glossy green bandings
& stylized yellow & orange floral
designs on pebbled grey ground 55.00
Vase, 15" h., glossy arrowhead motif
on pebbled grey ground 110.00
Wall pocket, glossy stylized yellow
floral design on pebbled grey
ground, 10½" h. 60.00

NORMANDY (1924)

Normandy Hanging Basket

Basket, hanging-type w/original
chains, ribbed body & band of grapevines & clusters, green & ivory
w/brown ground band, 7" d.
(ILLUS.) 170.00
Jardiniere, ribbed body & band of
grapevines & clusters, green & ivory
w/brown ground band, 9" h. 155.00
Jardiniere & pedestal base, ribbed
body & band of grapevines &

clusters, green & ivory w/brown
ground band, overall 28" h., 2 pcs. . .500.00
Sand jar, ribbed body & band of grapevines & clusters, green & ivory
w/brown ground band, 14" h. 225.00

ORIAN (1935)
Candlesticks, glossy brown, 4½" h.,
pr. 85.00
Compote, 10½" d., 4½" h., pedestal
base, glossy turquoise interior &
burgundy exterior 85.00
Rose bowl, handled, glossy tan, 6" h. . . .55.00
Vase, 7½" h., squatty base & short
wide neck w/side handles, glossy
turquoise w/brown lining 120.00
Vase, 10½" h., 2-handled, glossy
brown, burgundy or turquoise,
each . . . . .90.00 to 110.00
Vase, 12" h., glossy yellow w/green
lining 185.00
Wall pocket, double, glossy turquoise,
8" h. 325.00

PEONY (1930s)

Peony Double Candle Holders

Ash tray, peony blossoms in relief
against textured gold ground 60.00
Basket w/overhead handle, peony
blossoms in relief against textured
gold, green or pink ground, 8" h.,
each .40.00 to 50.00
Basket, hanging-type w/original
chains, peony blossoms in relief
against textured gold, green or pink
ground, 5", each . . . . .65.00 to 85.00
Bowl, 11" oval, 2-handled, peony
blossoms in relief against textured
pink ground 45.00
Candle holders, double, peony
blossoms in relief against textured
gold shaded to green ground, 8½" l.,
5¾" h., pr. (!LLUS.) 60.00
Cornucopia-vase, peony blossoms
against textured pink ground, 8" h. . .38.00
Flower frog, 2-handled, peony
blossoms against textured gold or
pink ground, 4" h., each 30.00
Flower pot w/saucer, peony blossoms
against textured gold, green or
pink ground, 5" d., each 30.00
Jardiniere & pedestal base, peony
blossoms against textured green or
pink ground, overall 24½" h., 2 pcs.,
each set . . . . .375.00 to 450.00

Lemonade set: 7½" h. pitcher & 6
mugs; peony blossoms against textured gold or green ground, 7 pcs.,
each set . . . . .250.00 to 300.00
Model of a conch shell, peony blos-
soms against textured gold or green
ground, 9½" l., each . . . . .60.00 to 75.00
Rose bowl, peony blossoms against
textured green ground, 6" d. 32.00
Tea set: cov. teapot, creamer & open
sugar bowl; peony blossoms against
textured gold, green or pink ground,
3 pcs., each set . . . . .115.00 to 180.00
Vase, 4" h., angular base handles,
peony blossoms against textured
green or pink ground, each 22.00
Vase, 10" h., peony blossoms against
textured gold or pink ground,
each . . . . .38.00 to 45.00
Vase, 15" h., peony blossoms against
textured gold ground 115.00
Wall pocket, peony blossoms against
textured green ground,
8" h. .75.00 to 95.00

PERSIAN (1916)
Basket, hanging-type w/original
chains, colorful geometric motif on
creamware 130.00
Bowl, 7" d., 3½" h., 3-handled, red &
yellow water lily motif on
creamware 90.00
Candlesticks, flared base, pierced
handles rising from midsection to
rim, red & yellow water lily motif on
creamware, 8½" h., pr. 255.00
Jardiniere, colorful geometric motif on
creamware, 7" h. 180.00
Jardiniere, footed, colorful stylized
floral motif on creamware, 8" h. 195.00
Jardiniere, colorful geometric motif on
creamware, 14" d., 15" h. 400.00
Wall pocket, stylized floral motif on
creamware, 11" h. 235.00

PINE CONE (1931)

Pine Cone Pitcher

Ash tray, realistic pine cones in relief
on shaded blue, brown or green,
5 x 2½", each . . . . .48.00 to 65.00

Basket w/overhead branch handle,
shaped oblong, realistic pine cones
in relief on shaded brown or green,
10 x 9", each . . . . .95.00 to 125.00

Basket, hanging-type w/original
chains, realistic pine cones in relief
on shaded blue or brown,
each . . . . .125.00 to 155.00

Bookends, realistic pine cones in relief
on brown or green, each
pr. . . . . .135.00 to 155.00

Bowl, 5" d., 4" h., realistic pine cones
in relief on green 40.00

Candle holders, side handle, pine
cones on blue ground, 2½" h., pr. 47.50

Candle holders, triple, pine cones on
blue, brown or green ground,
5½" h., each pr. . . . . .135.00 to 145.00

Centerpiece, 1-piece console set w/six
candle holders attached to center
bowl, pine cones on green ground,
6" h. 140.00

Cornucopia-vase, pine cones on blue,
brown or green ground, 6" h.,
each . . . . .38.00 to 45.00

Flower pot w/saucer, pine cones on
blue or green ground, 5" d., each 85.00

Jardiniere & pedestal base, pine cones
on blue or brown ground, overall
30" h., 2 pcs., each set . . . .575.00 to 750.00

Mug, pine cones on brown or green
ground, 4" h., each. 80.00

Pitcher w/ice lip, 9" h., pine cones
on blue ground (ILLUS.) 125.00

Planter, handled, pine cones on blue or
green ground, 5", each 37.00

Rose bowl, pine cones on blue or
brown ground, 4" d., each . . .45.00 to 55.00

Tray, pine cones on brown or green
ground, 12" l., each 52.00

Tumbler, pine cones on blue, brown or
green ground, 5" h., each. . . .65.00 to 85.00

Vase, 6" h., fan-shaped, pine cones on
blue ground 45.00

Vase, 8" h., 10" w., pillow-shaped,
pine cones on brown ground 110.00

Vase, 10" h., bucket-shaped, pine
cones on green ground 65.00

Vase, 15" h., pine cones on blue or
brown ground, each . . . . .275.00 to 315.00

Wall pocket, double, pine cones on
brown or green ground, 8½" h.,
each 110.00

Wall shelf, pine cones on brown
ground . . . . .165.00 to 185.00

POPPY (1930s)

Basket w/overhead handle, yellow
poppies on turquoise blue shaded to
white ground, 10" h. 75.00

Basket, hanging-type w/original
chains, pink poppies on yellow
shaded to pink ground, 8½" 70.00

Ewer, pink poppies on yellow shaded
to pink ground, 10" h. 65.00

Flower pot w/saucer, poppies on turquoise blue shaded to white ground,
5" d. 65.00

Jardiniere & pedestal base, yellow
poppies on turquoise blue shaded to
white ground, 2 pcs. 550.00

Rose bowl, poppies on shaded pink
ground, 4" d. 25.00

Vase, 6" h., poppies on shaded pink
or turquoise blue ground,
each .30.00 to 40.00

Poppy Vase

Vase, 7" h., yellow poppies on shaded
pink & green ground (ILLUS.) 47.50

Wall pocket, triple, yellow poppies on
turquoise blue shaded to white
ground, 8½" h. 145.00

ROSECRAFT (1916-19)

Bowl, 8" d., 3" h., glossy black 35.00

Candlesticks, glossy black, 8½" h.,
pr. 90.00

Ginger jar, cov., glossy black 165.00

Rose bowl, glossy yellow, 6" d., 4" h. . . .20.00

Vase, double bud, 5" h., gate-form,
glossy blue or yellow, each. 70.00

Vase, 8" to 10" h., glossy black,
each . . . . .125.00 to 175.00

Wall pocket, glossy black, 9" h. 130.00

Wall pocket, glossy blue or yellow,
10" h., each .115.00

ROSECRAFT HEXAGON (1924)

Bowl, 4" d., 2" h., bleeding hearts
on dark teal blue glossy finish 32.50

Bowl, 7½" d., bleeding hearts on dark
brown or green matte finish,
each .75.00 to 90.00

Candlestick, flared base, bleeding
hearts on dark brown matte finish,
8" h. (single) .75.00

Vase, 5" h., bleeding hearts on dark
brown matte finish 52.00

Vase, 6" to 8" h., bleeding hearts on
   dark brown matte finish,
   each ....115.00 to 135.00
Vase, 10½" h., bleeding hearts on dark
   brown matte finish 160.00
Wall pocket, bleeding hearts on dark
   brown matte finish, 8½" h..........120.00

ROYAL CAPRI (late 1940s)

Ash tray, w/advertising, textured gold
   finish............................250.00
Dish, 9" w., irregular form, textured
   gold finish 225.00
Planter, mottled gold finish, 7" l.......215.00
Vase, bud, 7" h., textured gold finish ..195.00
Vase, 7" h., textured gold finish 250.00

ROZANE (1900s)

Rozane Portrait Vase

Candlestick, underglaze slip-painted
   floral decor, standard brown glaze,
   signed H. Pillsbury, 9½" h. (single) ..275.00
Ewer, ruffled rim, underglaze slip-
   painted floral decor, standard brown
   glaze, artist-signed, 7½" h. 150.00
Ewer, long slender neck w/low pointed
   double handle, underglaze slip-
   painted floral decor, shaded brown,
   tan & green standard glaze, artist-
   signed, 9½" h. 345.00
Letter holder, underglaze slip-painted
   floral decor, standard glaze, artist-
   signed, 3½" h. 225.00
Loving cup, 3-handled, underglaze
   slip-painted floral decor, standard
   glaze............................220.00
Mug, underglaze slip-painted blackberries decor, standard glaze, signed
   M. Timberlake....................225.00
Paperweight, underglaze slip-painted
   pansy decor, standard glaze, artist-
   signed............................260.00
Pitcher, tankard, 14" h., underglaze
   slip-painted corn decor, standard
   glaze, artist-signed 875.00
Vase, 3¾" h., underglaze slip-
   painted violets decor, standard
   glaze, artist-signed 135.00
Vase, 5" h., 6" widest d., 2-handled,
   bulbous base, underglaze slip-

painted pansy decor, shaded brown
   to black standard glaze 155.00
Vase, 7¼" h., underglaze slip-painted
   holly decor, standard glaze, artist-
   signed............................275.00
Vase, 9" h., pillow-shaped, underglaze
   slip-painted portrait of dog
   w/pheasant, standard glaze
   (ILLUS.) 1,450.00
Vase, 14" h., underglaze slip-painted
   portrait of an Indian, standard glaze,
   signed A. Williams 1,975.00

SILHOUETTE (1940s)

Silhouette Fan-shaped Vase

Ash tray, silhouette floral panel,
   shaded rust 25.00
Basket w/overhead handle rising from
   base to top of shaped rim, silhouette
   floral panel, white w/turquoise,
   8" h. 45.00
Basket, hanging-type w/original
   chains, silhouette floral panel,
   shaded rust or white w/turquoise,
   5" h., each................55.00 to 65.00
Candle holders, silhouette floral panel,
   shaded turquoise, 3" h., pr. 30.00
Cigarette box, cov., silhouette floral
   panel, shaded turquoise 47.00
Cornucopia-vase, silhouette floral
   panel, shaded turquoise or white
   w/turquoise, 6" h., each 28.00
Ewer, silhouette floral panel, shaded
   rust or turquoise, 10" h.,
   each ....50.00 to 65.00
Planter, silhouette floral panel, shaded
   rust, 15" l.........................38.00
Rose bowl, handled, silhouette panel
   of a nude, shaded rust or white
   w/turquoise, 6" h., each...115.00 to 130.00
Vase, 5" h., silhouette floral panel,
   shaded rust 22.00
Vase, 7" h., 8" w., fan-shaped, silhouette panel of a nude, shaded rust
   (ILLUS.) 95.00
Wall pocket, silhouette floral panel,
   shaded rust or white w/turquoise,
   8" h., each.................50.00 to 60.00

SNOWBERRY (1946)

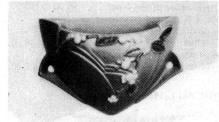

Snowberry Wall Pocket

Basket w/overhead handle, snowberry
branch in relief on shaded green or
rose ground, 10" h., each . . . . 48.00 to 55.00
Basket, hanging-type w/original
chains, snowberry branch in relief on
shaded blue, green or rose ground,
each . . . . 60.00 to 75.00
Bookends, snowberry branch in relief
on shaded blue, green or rose
ground, each pr. . . . . 65.00 to 85.00
Candle holders, 2-handled, bulbous,
snowberry branch in relief on
shaded blue, green or rose ground,
2" h., each pr. 20.00
Cornucopia-vase, snowberry branch in
relief on green or rose ground, 8" h.,
each 26.00
Ewer, snowberry branch in relief on
shaded blue, green or rose ground,
10" h., each. . . . . 60.00 to 70.00
Flower pot w/saucer, snowberry
branch in relief on shaded rose
ground, 5½" h. 25.00
Jardiniere & pedestal base, snowberry
branch in relief on shaded blue or
rose ground, overall 25" h., 2 pcs.,
each set . . . . 375.00 to 450.00
Tea set: cov. teapot, creamer & sugar
bowl; snowberry branch in relief on
shaded blue, green or rose ground,
3 pcs., each set . . . . 95.00 to 120.00
Vase, 6½" h., pillow-shaped,
snowberry branch in relief on shaded
green or rose ground, each 35.00
Vase, bud, 7" h., angular side handle
above flaring base, snowberry branch
in relief on shaded blue or rose
ground, each 28.00
Vase, 10" h., 2-handled, snowberry
branch in relief on shaded rose
ground 50.00
Wall pocket, snowberry branch in
relief on shaded green ground,
8" w., 5" h. (ILLUS.). 47.00
Window box, snowberry branch in
relief on shaded blue or green
ground, each 27.00

SUNFLOWER (1930)

Basket, hanging-type w/original
chains & liner, chrysanthemum-type
yellow sunflowers on mottled green
ground, large 265.00
Bowl-vase, chrysanthemum-type yel-
low sunflowers on mottled green
ground, 8" d., 7" h. 140.00
Candlesticks, curved handles rising
from flared base, chrysanthemum-
type yellow sunflowers on mottled
green ground, 4½" h., pr. 195.00
Jardiniere, chrysanthemum-type yel-
low sunflowers on mottled green
ground, 9" d. 65.00
Vase, 5" h., cylindrical, angular rim
handles, chrysanthemum-type yellow sunflowers on mottled green
ground 55.00

Sunflower Vase

Vase, 6" h., chrysanthemum-type
yellow sunflowers on mottled green
ground (ILLUS.) 60.00
Vase, 9" to 10" h., 2-handled, chrysanthemum-type yellow sunflowers on
mottled green ground,
each . . . . 135.00 to 150.00
Wall pocket, chrysanthemum-type
yellow sunflowers on mottled
green ground, 7½" h. 225.00

TOURMALINE (1933)

Bowl, 8" to 9" d., mottled turquoise
blue, each . . . . 35.00 to 40.00
Bowl-vase, mottled turquoise blue,
4" h. 38.00
Candlesticks, flaring ribbed base,
streaked powder blue, 4½" h., pr. . . . 40.00
Planter, ribbed sides, streaked powder
blue, 11" l. 48.00
Urn, ridged lines around upper half,
mottled turquoise blue, 5½" h. 35.00
Vase, 5½" h., handled, mottled
turquoise blue 42.00
Vase, 6" h., mottled tan 30.00
Vase, 8" h., pedestal base, ridged
lines at neck, streaked powder blue . . 45.00

VELMOSS (1934)

Bowl, 5" d., band of wavy horizontal
lines w/cluster of pendant leaves on
mottled green 35.00

Cornucopia-vase, band of wavy
horizontal lines w/cluster of pendant
leaves on mint green, 7" h. 30.00
Vase, 6" h., cylindrical, angular
handles, band of wavy lines
w/cluster of pendant leaves on
mottled blue or raspberry red, each . .45.00
Vase, double bud, 8" h., band of wavy
horizontal lines w/cluster of pendant
leaves on mint green. . . . . . . .40.00 to 55.00
Vase, 14" h., expanding cylinder,
2-handled, band of wavy horizontal
lines w/cluster of pendant leaves on
mottled blue or raspberry red,
each .120.00 to 145.00
Wall pocket, double, band of wavy hori-
zontal lines w/cluster of pendant
leaves on raspberry red, 8½" h. 275.00

VISTA (1920s)
Basket w/overhead handle, flaring
rim, embossed green coconut palm
trees & lavender-blue pool against
grey ground, 9½" h. 115.00
Basket w/overhead handle, expanding
cylinder, embossed green coconut
palm trees & lavender-blue pool
against grey ground, 12" h. 155.00
Bowl, 7" d., 3" h., embossed green
coconut palm trees & lavender-blue
pool against grey ground 65.00
Jardiniere, embossed green coconut
palm trees & lavender-blue pool
against grey ground, 8½" h. 125.00
Umbrella stand, embossed green
coconut palm trees & lavender-blue
pool against grey ground . .265.00 to 350.00
Vase, 10" h., expanding cylinder
w/flared foot, embossed green
coconut palm trees & lavender-blue
pool against grey ground 90.00
Wall pocket, embossed green coconut
palm trees & lavender-blue pool
against grey ground, 9½" h. 225.00

WHITE ROSE (1940s)
Basket w/circular handle, white roses
in relief on blue or pink, 10" h.,
each .60.00 to 75.00
Basket, hanging-type w/original
chains, white roses in relief on
brown or pink, each 85.00
Bowl, 3" d., handled, white roses in
relief on blue or pink, each. 20.00
Cornucopia-vase, double, white roses
in relief on pink shaded to green,
8" h. 45.00
Flower frog w/overhead handle, white
roses in relief on blue or pink, each . .24.00
Jardiniere & pedestal base, white
roses in relief on pink, large,
2 pcs. 550.00
Tea set: cov. teapot, creamer & sugar

bowl; white roses in relief on pink
shaded to green, 3 pcs. . . . . . .95.00 to 125.00
Vase, 8" h., pillow-shaped, angular
pointed handles, white roses in
relief on brown or pink, each 48.00
Wall pocket, white roses in relief on
blue, brown or pink, 6" h., each. 58.00

WINCRAFT (1948)

Wincraft Cornucopia-Vase

Basket w/overhead handle, florals in
relief on glossy lime green ground,
8" h. . . . . .45.00 to 55.00
Basket, hanging-type w/original
chains, florals in relief on glossy
lime green ground 70.00
Bookends, florals in relief on glossy
brown or lime green ground, each
pr. 45.00
Bowl, 8" d., blossoms in relief on
glossy apricot or lime green ground,
each 25.00
Candle holders, mottled glossy blue
ground, 2½" h., pr. 28.00
Console set: 14" l. bowl & pr. candle
holders; blossoms in relief on glossy
blue ground, 3 pcs. 70.00
Cornucopia-vase, blossoms in relief on
glossy shaded brown ground, 8" h.
(ILLUS.) 45.00
Ewer, foliage & berries in relief on
glossy yellow ground, 19" h. 225.00
Flower pot, florals in relief on glossy
blue, green or tan ground,
each . . . . .35.00 to 40.00
Planter, canoe-shaped, mottled glossy
blue ground, 10" l. 45.00
Tea set: cov. teapot, creamer & sugar
bowl; florals in relief on glossy
shaded blue or tan ground, 3 pcs.,
each set . . . . .85.00 to 125.00
Vase, 6" h., pillow-shaped, pine cones
& needles in relief on glossy tan
ground 30.00
Vase, 8" h., circular w/molded tree
branches in open center, mottled
glossy blue ground 50.00
Vase, 16" h., cylindrical w/shaped
flaring mouth, florals & foliage in

relief on mottled glossy blue
ground 110.00
Wall pocket, globular, florals in relief
on mottled glossy blue ground,
5" h. .... 75.00 to 95.00

WINDSOR (1931)
Bowl, 10" d., 3" h., angular side
handles, stylized yellow florals &
green foliage against mottled blue
ground 150.00
Candlesticks, curved handles rising
from flared base to drip tray,
geometric design on terra cotta
shaded to dark brown, 4½" h.,
pr......................150.00 to 190.00
Vase, 5" h., 2-handled, geometric
design on terra cotta shaded to dark
brown ....65.00 to 80.00
Vase, 6" h., geometric design on
mottled blue ground 110.00
Vase, 7½" h., 5¾" widest d.,
expanding cylinder, 2-handled,
geometric design on mottled blue
ground 105.00
Vase, 8" h., stylized ferns against
mottled blue or terra cotta ground,
each ....135.00 to 150.00

WISTERIA (1933)
Basket, hanging-type w/original chains,
lavender wisteria & vines on textured blue to brown ground, 7½" ...250.00
Bowl, 4" d., squatty, angular rim
handles, lavender wisteria & vines
on textured blue to brown
ground ....55.00 to 65.00
Bowl, 9 x 5", lavender wisteria &
vines on textured blue to brown
ground 70.00
Candlesticks, lavender wisteria & vines
on textured blue to brown ground,
4" h., pr........................105.00
Console bowl, handled, lavender
wisteria & vines on textured blue to
brown ground, 12 x 5½" oval 90.00
Jardiniere, wisteria & vines on
textured brown to blue ground,
5" h. 72.00
Vase, 4" h., wisteria & vines on textured blue to brown ground 60.00
Vase, 7" h., handled, wisteria & vines
on textured brown to blue ground....80.00
Vase, 8" h., wisteria & vines on textured brown ground 105.00
Wall pocket, wisteria & vines on textured brown ground, 8" h..........300.00

WOODLAND (1905)
Vase, 8" h., ovoid, small neck, incised
chrysanthemums & leaves in shades
of yellow, rust & green high gloss
enamel on stippled bisque
ground................325.00 to 395.00

Vase, 9" h., incised florals & foliage
enameled in dark green, pink &
white on stippled bisque ground 500.00
Vase, 9½" h., incised tulips decor on
stippled bisque ground 225.00
Vase, 10" h., incised poppy blossom
& bud w/stylized leaf in shades of
orange, yellow & dark green on
stippled bisque ground 600.00
Vase, 11" h., incised floral decor on
stippled bisque ground 690.00
Vase, 12" h., incised floral decor on
stippled bisque ground 950.00

ROYAL BAYREUTH

*Good china in numerous patterns and
designs has been made at the Royal
Bayreuth factory in Tettau, Germany, since
1794. Listings below are by the company's
lines, plus miscellaneous pieces. Interest in
this china remains at a peak and prices
continue to rise. Pieces listed carry the
company's blue mark except where noted
otherwise.*

CORINTHIAN
Creamer, white classical figures on
black ground $62.50
Creamer & cov. sugar bowl, white
classical figures on black ground,
pr.............................125.00
Creamer & open sugar bowl, white
classical figures on black ground,
pr.............................85.00
Mustard pot, cov., white classical
figures on black ground............75.00
Pitcher, 8" h., white classical figures
on black ground, w/salmon throat ..130.00
Plate, 7½" d., white classical figures
on black ground 95.00

DEVIL & CARDS

Devil & Cards Items

Ash tray 100.00
Candle holder, 3½ x 6" 265.00
Cup & saucer, demitasse, Devil &
Dice.............................160.00
Dresser tray......................475.00
Humidor, cov. 450.00

Match holder 350.00
Pitcher, 4½" h. 160.00
Pitcher, 5¼" h., 5¾" d., marked
  "Bermuda" . . . . .190.00 to 250.00
Pitcher, 5½" h. (green mark) 225.00
Pitcher, water, 7¾" h. . . . . . .325.00 to 380.00
Salt dip, master size, figural devil
  handle 195.00
Sugar bowl, cov. 175.00

MOTHER-OF-PEARL FINISH

Grape Cluster Bowl

Ash tray, Murex Shell patt., 4½" l. 35.00
Bowl, 9½ x 5½", grape cluster mold
  w/stem handle, pearlized lustre
  (ILLUS.) 250.00
Cake plate, pierced handles, poppy-
  molded, pearlized lavender & green
  shadings, 10½" d. 195.00
Chamberstick, Murex Shell patt. 145.00
Creamer, Murex Shell patt. w/coral
  handle . . . . .45.00 to 75.00
Creamer, Oyster & Shell patt. 125.00
Creamer, poppy-molded, pearlized
  lavender finish . . . . .145.00 to 160.00
Creamer & cov. sugar bowl, grape
  cluster mold, pearlized white w/pink
  leaves, pr. 210.00
Creamer & open sugar bowl, poppy-
  molded, pearlized white, pr. 145.00
Ladle, poppy-molded, unmarked 60.00
Match holder, Murex Shell patt. 75.00
Mustard jar, cover & ladle, grape
  cluster mold, pearlized white
  w/yellow, 3 pcs. 128.00
Nut set: master bowl & 4 serving
  dishes; poppy-molded, pink, 5 pcs. . .250.00
Pitcher, water, Murex Shell patt. 300.00
Plate, 7" d., oak leaf molded 55.00
Plate, 8" d., pansy-molded 100.00
Powder jar, cov., poppy-molded 175.00
Salt & pepper shakers, Murex Shell
  patt., pr. 50.00
Teapot, cov., Murex Shell patt.
  (unmarked) 195.00
Toothpick holder, Murex Shell patt. 75.00
Toothpick holder, 3-handled, Oyster &
  Pearl patt. 195.00

ROSE TAPESTRY
Basket, braided handle, 3-color roses,
  5 x 5" . . . . .250.00 to 300.00

Candlestick, 3-color roses (single) 650.00
Creamer, straight sides, 3-color roses,
  3" h. 115.00

Rose Tapestry Hair Receiver

Hair receiver, cov., gold footed,
  3-color roses, 4" d.
  (ILLUS.) . . . . .200.00 to 265.00
Hatpin holder, 3-color roses
  (unmarked) 225.00
Match holder 250.00
Nut cup 95.00
Pin box, cov., pinched-in sides,
  pink roses 165.00
Pitcher, 4" h., pinched spout, gold
  rim & handle, 3-color roses 240.00
Planter, 2 gold handles at base,
  fluted rim, 3-color roses, 3¼" d.,
  2¾" h. 150.00
Plate, 9½" d., ornate gold border,
  3-color roses .325.00
Powder box, cov., 3-color roses 175.00
Ring box, pink roses, 2¼" sq., 1¼" h. . .175.00
Salt & pepper shakers, 3-color roses,
  pr. 325.00
Sugar bowl, open, 3-color roses 125.00
Toothpick holder, 2-handled, 3-color
  roses 275.00
Trinket box, cov., square, 3-color
  roses 125.00
Vase, 5½" h., 3-color roses 250.00
Wall pocket, 3-color roses, 9" l. 425.00

SAND BABIES

Sand Babies Creamer

Bowl, small 125.00
Chamberstick, shield-back style 165.00

Creamer, 3" h. (ILLUS.) 90.00
Cup & saucer, child size . . . . . . .65.00 to 85.00
Feeding dish, 7" d. 95.00
Inkwell, cov., large 395.00
Planter, 2-handled, 3" h. 110.00
Vase, 3 5/8" h., 3-handled . . . .90.00 to 110.00

SNOW BABIES
Box, piano-shaped, 4" h. 95.00
Chocolate pot, cov., 6" h. . . . .190.00 to 225.00
Creamer & cov. sugar bowl, pr. 185.00
Dresser tray, ruffled rim 135.00
Flower pot 80.00
Inkwell (no insert) 95.00
Pitcher, 6" h. . . . . .145.00 to 185.00
Plate, 6" d., babies playing 62.00
Tea tile 175.00

SUNBONNET BABIES

Sunbonnet Babies Milk Pitcher

Ash tray, tricornered, babies ironing,
  5" w. 110.00
Bell, babies washing 325.00
Bowl, 7½" d., babies cleaning 325.00
Box, cov., babies cleaning, 2½ x 2" . . .175.00
Candy dish, boat-shaped, scalloped
  rim, 2-handled, babies fishing,
  9½ x 4¼" 195.00
Chamberstick, shield-back type,
  babies cleaning 325.00
Cup & saucer, babies cleaning 180.00
Mush set: creamer, bowl & plate;
  babies washing, 3 pcs. 310.00
Nut bowl, fluted gold rim, 3-footed,
  babies sweeping interior, shaded
  green exterior, 4¾" d., 2½" h. 130.00
Pitcher, milk, bulbous, babies mending
  (ILLUS.) 210.00
Plate, 9" d., babies washing 150.00
Rose bowl, babies cleaning 215.00
Tea tile, round, babies washing &
  ironing 120.00
Toothpick holder, 3-compartment,
  babies washing dishes & cleaning . . .275.00

Wash set, 1½" d. bowl, 2¾" h. pitcher,
  2 pcs. 300.00

TOMATO ITEMS

Tomato Mustard Pot

Tomato Creamer. 40.00
Tomato creamer & cov. sugar bowl,
  footed, pr. 70.00
Tomato dish, cov., 4½" d. 50.00
Tomato mustard pot, cover & lettuce
  leaf underplate, 3" d., 3 pcs.
  (ILLUS.) 60.00
Tomato pitcher, water, large 300.00
Tomato plate 40.00
Tomato sugar bowl, cov. . . . . . .45.00 to 67.50

MISCELLANEOUS

Lobster Bowl

Ash tray, figural elk's head. 110.00
Ash tray w/cigarette rests, scenic
  pastoral decor w/cows & trees. 50.00
Bowl, 7¾" d., 2½" h., poppy-molded,
  together w/poppy-molded ladle, pr.
  (ILLUS. w/wall pocket) 110.00
Bowl, 8" d., figural lobster (ILLUS.) 125.00
Bowl, 10" d., poppy-molded 165.00
Candle holder, figural bellringer 150.00
Candle holder, figural clown 175.00
Candlestick, girl w/dog decor, 4" h.
  (single) 85.00
Candlestick, Little Bo Peep decor,
  4" h. (single) . . . . .95.00 to 115.00
Candlestick, Little Jack Horner decor
  (single) 150.00

Chamberstick, saucer base, ring
handle, scenic pastoral decor
w/cows & trees 100.00
Chamberstick, saucer base, ring
handle, roses, pansies & forget-me-
nots decor .45.00
Chamberstick, shield-back type, fox
hunting scene decor 145.00
Chocolate set: chocolate pot & 4 c/s;
barnyard scene decor, 9 pcs. 550.00

Girl & Dog Creamer

Creamer, girl & dog decor (ILLUS.) 65.00
Creamer, fishing scene decor, 2½" h. . .45.00
Creamer, "tapestry," portrait of
beautiful lady decor, 2¾" h. 215.00
Creamer, sailboat in storm decor,
3" h. 80.00
Creamer, Dutch girl & cat decor,
3 3/8" h. 48.00
Creamer, pinched spout, Goose Girl
decor, 3½" h. 95.00
Creamer, "tapestry," pinched spout,
man tending turkeys decor, 3½" h. . . .175.00
Creamer, pinched spout, boy &
donkeys decor, 3 5/8" h. 120.00
Creamer, American flag & American
sports decor, 3¾" h. . . . . .75.00 to 90.00
Creamer, corset-shaped, farm scene
decor, 4" h. .52.50
Creamer, bulbous, Jack & the Bean-
stalk decor, 4" h. 95.00
Creamer, Little Boy Blue decor 90.00
Creamer, figural apple 75.00
Creamer, figural bellringer 175.00
Creamer, figural bull, brown, tan &
grey 137.50
Creamer, figural bull, black & brown
w/red horns 130.00
Creamer, figural cat, black 115.00
Creamer, figural chamois 118.00
Creamer, figural clown 140.00
Creamer, figural coachman 170.00
Creamer, figural cow, brown 145.00
Creamer, figural crow, black, 4¾" h. . .100.00
Creamer, figural duck . . . . . . .125.00 to 195.00
Creamer, figural frog,
green . . . . .110.00 to 125.00
Creamer, figural geranium 175.00
Creamer, figural lemon 65.00
Creamer, figural lobster . . . . . . .48.00 to 75.00

Creamer, figural maple leaf 145.00
Creamer, figural monk 250.00
Creamer, figural orange 105.00
Creamer, figural owl 185.00
Creamer, figural pansy 130.00
Creamer, figural pelican,
unmarked . . . . .55.00 to 75.00
Creamer, figural pheasant 210.00
Creamer, figural pig 250.00
Creamer, figural poodle, black 190.00
Creamer, figural poppy, yellow 95.00
Creamer, figural robin 135.00
Creamer, figural strawberry 135.00
Creamer, figural water buffalo, black
w/red horns 130.00
Cup & saucer, demitasse, ornate gold
handle, pink roses decor, gold trim . . .35.00
Dresser tray, scenic decor w/men
fishing, 11 x 8" 195.00
Dresser tray, "Ring Around the Rosie"
decor 125.00
Feeding dish, cherubs decor 125.00
Feeding dish, Little Boy Blue decor 80.00
Hatpin holder, pink roses & yellow &
white floral decor 225.00
Humidor, cov., hunting scene decor . . .195.00
Humidor, cov., stork decor on yellow
ground . . . . .85.00 to 100.00

Royal Bayreuth Clown Match Holder

Match holder, figural reclining clown,
red, late 19th c., 4 3/8" l., 3" h.
(ILLUS.) 240.00
Mug, handled, Nursery Rhyme decor,
2" h. miniature 55.00
Mush set: creamer, bowl & underplate;
girl w/dog decor on creamer &
underplate & "Ring Around the
Rosie" decor on bowl, 3 pcs. 125.00
Mustard jar, cov., figural grape
cluster, yellow . . . . .90.00 to 125.00
Mustard jar, cov., figural strawberry,
3¾" h. 75.00
Nappy, handled, Little Boy Blue decor . .95.00
Pin box, cov., pink & white florals
outlined in gold, 2½" sq. 48.00
Pitcher, milk, 6" h., Arab horseman &
palm tree decor (green mark) 135.00
Pitcher, 6" h., tavern scene

w/cavaliers decor on green
ground 125.00
Pitcher, 6" h., "tapestry," women
bathing by castle decor 425.00
Pitcher, 6¾" h., roses & ornate gold
decor 86.00
Plate, 6" d., Goose Girl decor 55.00
Plate, 6" d., Little Bo Peep decor 68.00
Plate, 6" d., "Ring Around the Rosie"
decor 75.00
Plate, 9" d., scenic decor w/sailboats
& fisherman 75.00
Powder jar, cov., Little Bo Peep
decor 150.00
Teapot, cov., scenic decor w/Dutch
boy flying kite & dog at heels on
blue & brown ground, gold trim,
3½" d., 4" h. 95.00
Tea tile, girl & dog decor 85.00
Toothpick holder, Brittany Girl decor . . . 95.00
Toothpick holder, figural elk 110.00
Vase, 4½" h., 2-handled, scenic
pastoral decor w/cows & trees 75.00

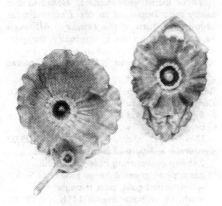

Poppy-Molded Bowl & Wall Pocket

Wall pocket, poppy-molded, 9½" h.
(ILLUS. right) 165.00
Whimsey, model of a lady's high-laced
shoe w/high heel, tan,
unmarked . . . . 70.00 to 80.00
Whimsey, model of a lady's high-laced
shoe w/high heel, black exterior,
cream interior 100.00

ROYAL BONN & BONN

*Bonn and subsequently Royal Bonn china
were produced in Bonn, Germany, in a
manufactory established in 1755. Later
wares made there are often marked Mehlem
or bear the initials FM or a castle mark.
Most wares were of the hand-painted type.
Clock cases also were made in Bonn.*

One of the Royal Bonn Marks

Bowl, 10 x 11½" oblong, h.p. blue
& gold floral decor $45.00
Cheese dish w/slant lid, overall pink
& yellow roses decor, 8 x 6½",
4½" h. 38.50
Cookie jar, pink & lavender florals &
green foliage w/ornate relief
gold trim on beige satin ground,
silverplate cover, rim & handle,
5 5/8" d., 6½" h. 100.00
Ewer, scenic decor, 14½" h. 150.00
Plate, 8" d., scalloped rim, purple
& gold floral decor 25.00
Plate, 9" d., majolica, red florals on
moss green ground 38.00
Plate, h.p. green, brown, lavender &
orange floral decor, blue castle
mark 185.00
Stein, Scottish golf scene, blue &
white, early 19th c. 1,000.00
Vase, 6" h., 2-handled, portrait of a
cavalier 145.00
Vase, 7" h., urn-shaped, berries &
foliage decor w/ornate gold trim . . . 127.00
Vase, 7½" h., gilt collar & side ring
handles, deep pastel florals w/gilt
tracery on ivory ground 225.00
Vase, 8" h., bust of peasant girl
one side, landscape reverse,
maroon & apple green ground
w/gilding, artist-signed 95.00
Vases, 8" h., 4" d., white & pink
orchids on green ground w/blue
bands & gold trim, pr. 225.00
Vase, 10" h., scenic decor, artist-
signed 175.00
Vases, 10¾" h., 8½" w., rectangular
rim on 4-sided form tapering towards
base, flowering cactus & blossoms
on cream ground, ca. 1900, pr. 330.00
Vase, 11" h., thistles on light satin
ground 195.00
Vase, 14" h., red & yellow florals
on brown shaded to soft green
ground 175.00
Vase, cov., 42" h., portrait of Jane,
Countess of Harrington, w/young
Lord Viscount Petersham &
the Honorable Lincoln Stanhope,
reserved on brilliant pink ground
w/gilt details, artist-signed, mid-
19th c. 4,400.00

ROYAL COPENHAGEN

"Rosenborg Castle" Bottle

This porcelain has been made in Copen-hagen, Denmark, since 1715. The ware is hard-paste. Also see COMMEMORATIVE PLATES.

Basket & stand, Flora Danica patt., reticulated, botanical specimen within border heightened by pink enamel & gilding, oval basket, 10½" l. stand $1,100.00

Bottle, Rosenborg Castle decor, 9" h. (ILLUS.) 65.00

Figure of Pan riding on the back of a turtle, 3¾" h. 130.00

Figure of a Dutch girl seated, wearing a hat & knitting, 6" h. 185.00

Figure of a nude infant, lying on back & holding sock, 6½" l. 200.00

Figure of a mermaid reclining 275.00

Figure of a young girl cradling a doll, 1938 . . . . .115.00

Model of a Boxer dog standing, tan, 5½ x 5½" 190.00

Model of a fox seated, w/head held high, 5½" h. .135.00

Model of a polar bear cub lying on back w/paws in air, 2¼ x 4¼" 145.00

Model of a pony, dappled coat, 4 x 6" 75.00

Monteith, Flora Danica patt., various botanical specimens within border heightened by pink enamel & gilding, 13" l. 1,760.00

Plaques, bisque, relief-molded classical figures, artist-signed, 5½" d., pr. 110.00

Vase, 5½ x 5½", grey flowers on white ground 65.00

Vase, 12 x 7½", gold fish & ship on crackle-glazed ground 345.00

Vase, 13½" h., swollen cylinder tapering towards base, horse chestnut blossoms on pale blue ground, 20th c. 253.00

Vase, bud, white florals w/mulberries on shaded ground 48.00

ROYAL DUX

Figure of a Bather

These wares were made in Bohemia and many were imported to the United States around the turn of the century. Although numerous pieces were originally inexpen-sive, collectors have taken a fancy to the ware and the prices of the better pieces continue to rise.

Basket, bullet-shaped, green glaze $85.00

Centerpiece, figure of maiden kneeling & gazing in pond lily form pool, beige tints, 11" w. base, overall 11½" h. 525.00

Centerpiece, figure of a shepherdess & 2 sheep at watering hole on mound base, pink, green & beige tones w/burnished gold, pink triangle mark, 14" w. base, overall 14" h. 795.00

Centerpiece, modeled as a group of Art Nouveau maidens standing w/bodies entwined, 18" w., 20" h. . . 600.00

Centerpiece, shell-form bowl raised on swelling wave awash w/flowers & foliage, one side w/semi-draped maidens, green, pink & beige tones burnished in gold, early 20th c., 16½" w. 715.00

Figure of a bathing beauty, pink bisque w/"pebbled" bisque cap & suit, 4" h. 45.00

Figure of a girl dressed in a sailor suit, gold-brushed clothing, ca. 1915, 7" h. 130.00

Figure of a lady reclining on a shell holding a cluster of grapes in her hand w/two doves at her side, matte finish, 8 x 9" .350.00

Figure of a boy carrying a basket of fish, 10" h. 200.00

Figure of an Art Deco semi-nude dancer, wearing cobalt blue drapery w/gold trim, 9¾" h. 375.00

Figure of a "flamenco" dancer
w/swirling skirt, shaded green
garments, shaded pink skin tones,
gold trim, pink triangle mark,
10¾" h. 125.00
Figure of a gypsy maiden holding a
tambourine, 14" h.........200.00 to 225.00
Figure of a gentleman in 18th c. garb
playing the violin, 16" h. 500.00
Figure of a classical maiden carrying
a water jug in one hand & a bowl in
the other, flesh tones w/beige &
green gown burnished in gold, satin
finish, 6 3/8" d., 20" h............575.00
Figure of a bather, young girl dressed
in a green & peach swimsuit
w/green scarf on her head & peach
towel over her lap, ca. 1910,
21¾" h. (ILLUS.)...............1,320.00
Figure group, Art Nouveau maiden
filling a lamp & companion holding
an hourglass, 15" h. 700.00
Figure group, mother standing behind
2 "toddler" boys, beige & green
tones w/burnished gold, satin finish,
pink triangle mark, 9½" base d.,
overall 16¼" h....................695.00
Model of an Irish Setter dog w/bird
in mouth, 18" l., 9" h..............125.00
Model of a rearing stallion, cream
matte finish w/burnished gold on
base, pink triangle mark, 16" l.,
15" h. 195.00
Vase, 5" h., applied floral & fruit decor
on orange & brown ground 95.00
Vase, 11½" h., reticulated rim, molded
w/two full-figure maidens in seated
position, grey ground 285.00
Vase, 14" h., ovoid w/ruffled rim,
applied open branch handles at
sides, blue-green glaze w/applied
white relief figure of young maiden
w/bow & arrow....................389.00
Vase, 17" h., full figure Dutch girl
beside tree in high relief, shades of
beige, gold & green matte finish 425.00

Royal Dux Vases

Vases, 20½" h., floral & leaf-molded
bodies, open branch handles, one
applied w/grape clusters & other
w/fruit & nut clusters, ivory bisque
finish heightened in gilt, ca. 1900,
pr. (ILLUS.) 770.00

ROYAL RUDOLSTADT

Royal Rudolstadt Berry Set

This factory's wares came from Thuringia, Germany, where a faience factory was established in 1720. E. Bohne, made hard paste porcelain here from 1854, and most wares found today date from the late 19th century.

Berry set: master berry bowl & 4
sauce dishes; beaded & scalloped
gilt rims, fruit decor, 5 pcs.
(ILLUS.)..........................$125.00
Bowl, 10" d., gold rim, h.p. pink,
green & white floral decor 75.00
Chocolate set: cov. chocolate pot & 6
c/s; orchid floral decor on shaded
ground w/gold tracery, 13 pcs. 250.00
Creamer & sugar bowl, h.p. pansies
on cream ground, pr................75.00
Dish, shell-shaped, h.p. floral
decor on ivory satin ground, gilt
trim, 10½ x 10½" 70.00
Hatpin holder, h.p. floral decor 28.00
Lamp, urn-shaped, embossed top & base
trim, purple & pink clover blossoms
w/gold accents on cream ground,
20½" h. 95.00
Pitcher, 5½" h., floral decor on cream
ground, gold trim 35.00
Pitcher, 8" h., 5" d., grey & gold
bird amidst coral & pink leaves
on cream ground 80.00
Plate, 6" d., h.p. lilies decor 22.50
Plate, 8" d., h.p. roses decor 25.00
Plate, 8¼" d., shaded lavender
asters decor, signed F. Kahn,
Prussia 42.00
Plate, 8½" d., forget-me-nots decor 35.00
Relish dish, h.p. floral decor, 8¾" l. 20.00
Tea set: cov. teapot, creamer & cov.
sugar bowl; h.p. pink & purple
pansies, ornate gold trim, 3 pcs. 95.00
Tray, portrait of mother & child,
oblong 155.00

Vase, 7" h., gold handles, enameled
floral medallion each side on cobalt
blue ground 159.00
Vase, 8½" h., "chinoiserie" decor 100.00
Vase, 8½" h., 2-handled, scene
entitled "Melitta at the Well"
reserved on wine ground, artist-
signed 395.00
Vase, 11" h., 2-handled, h.p. floral
decor 79.00
Whimsey, shoe, blue & gold floral
decor on white ground 25.00

ROYAL VIENNA

Royal Vienna Charger

*The second factory in Europe to make
hard-paste porcelain was established in
Vienna in 1719 by Claud Innocentius de Pa-
quier. The factory underwent various
changes of administration through the
years and finally closed in 1865. Since then,
however, the porcelain has been reproduced
by various factories in Austria and Germany, many of which have reproduced also
the early beehive mark. Early pieces, naturally bring far higher prices than the later
ones or the reproductions.*

Charger, center scene w/Napoleon &
Princess Louise in the company of 2
officers within gilt borders &
reserved on pale pink ground
w/gilt details, signed Wagner,
late 19th c., 14¼" d. (ILLUS.) $1,210.00
Charger, "The Rape of the Daughters
of Leucippus," depicting Castor &
Pollux attacking Phoebe & Clara
amongst rearing horses w/a cupid
looking on, painted after Rubens,
reserved on an etched gilt ground
w/details picked out in blue enamel,
artist-signed, late 19th c.,
16¼" d. 2,310.00
Chocolate pot, cov., violets decor on

yellow ground, ornate gold trim,
12" h. 160.00
Chocolate pot, cov., bust portrait of
beautiful lady reserved on burgundy
ground, gilt trim 145.00
Cup & saucer, gilt motifs on green
metallic exterior, interior w/scene
of snowy Alpine village, artist-
signed 165.00
Cup & saucer, cup w/gilt serpent
handle & 3 paw feet, scene w/color-
fully dressed figures in an open
square before red-roofed buildings
within a gilt panel on front, reverse
w/iron-red neoclassical foliate &
floral motifs highlighted w/gilt on
wide black border above a tooled gilt
band, borders repeated on saucer
around a central gilt flowerhead,
dated 1811 . . . . .7,420.00
Dish, center scene w/nymphs making
a sacrifice to cupid, lavender border
w/green vines & gilt highlights, late
19th c., 14½" oval 880.00
Figure group, Venus riding in a shell-
molded chariot supported by 2 sea
nymphs & attended by a cupid, on
stand molded w/water cascading
over rockwork, late 19th c., overall
12½" h. 990.00
Fruit set: 18" l. platter & eight 9" d.
fruit plates; h.p. various fruits
center, lavish gold trim, 9 pcs. 235.00
Plate, 9½" d., portrait of beautiful
woman center, lavish gold border,
signed Wagner 550.00
Plates, 9½" d., young Napoleonic
fisherboy (after Murillo) on one &
the maiden, "Libelle," wearing coral
pink gown & w/her transparent
wings barely visible in the afternoon
sky on other, each within green,
claret, pale blue & lilac paneled
borders enriched w/gilding, artist-
signed, late 19th c., pr. 550.00
Plates, 9¾" d., various allegorical
maidens within a lustrous chocolate
brown ground enriched w/blue or
green details & gilding, signed
Wagner, ca. 1900, set of 4 . . . . .1,650.00
Plate, 10" d., portrait of "Echo" center,
lustrous borders w/lavish gold,
signed Wagner 300.00
Platter, 19¾" oval, "Flirtation," center
scene w/scantily-clad classical
maiden reclining on the banks of a
river w/three musical cupids enter-
taning her, cobalt blue border
heightened w/gilding, ca. 1900 . . .1,540.00
Ramekin & cover w/floral finial, h.p.
Chintz patt. in puce, green, blue &
brown, turned wood handle, ca.
1775, 7½" l. (ILLUS.) 440.00

Chintz Pattern Ramekin

Tray, reticulated rim, center panel depicting the "Rape of Europa," maiden seated astride docile animal w/numerous attendants & cupids nearby, within gilt band & vivid pink border set w/claret red roundels between pale green bands, all highlighted w/gilt, dated 1806 tray w/late 19th c. decoration, 15 3/8" oblong 605.00

Vase, 5" h., expanding cylinder w/small neck, bust portrait of beautiful woman reserved on claret ground, gold trim 450.00

Vases painted by Wagner

Vases, 5¾" h., w/portraits of Mignon & Clematis with "Mignon" & "Clematis" within elaborate gilt borders reserved on lustrous brown or pale green ground, signed Wagner, ca. 1910, pr. (ILLUS.) 1,100.00

Vase, 7" h., bottle-shaped, bust portrait of "Teresita" reserved on lustrous brown & blue ground w/overall gilt highlights, signed Wagner 595.00

Vase, cov., 10¾" h., center portrait of a duchess wearing a bright blue gown w/red shawl & holding a piece of ripened fruit aloft, reserved on lustrous pale green ground enriched w/gilding, ca. 1910 . . . . .330.00

Vase, 12" h., three-quarter length portrait of "Unsohuld" reserved

Portrait Vase

within gilt borders on lustrous brown ground enriched w/gilding, artist-signed, ca. 1910 (ILLUS.) 770.00

Vase, 13½" h., each side w/portrait of a fair-haired maiden reserved on a lustrous brown ground within scrolling gilt border, ca. 1900 . . . . .1,210.00

Vase, 15½" h., oval panel depicting the Duchess of Devonshire w/a band of colorful flowers reverse, reserved on a gilt & jeweled ground, late 19th c. 1,430.00

Vase, cov., 23 5/8" h., scene of a maiden seated on a garden wall w/a playful cupid reserved on ivory ground enriched w/gilt motifs, artist-signed, ca. 1900 . . . . .2,640.00

ROYAL WORCESTER

This porcelain has been made by the Royal Worcester Porcelain Co. at Worcester, England, from 1862 to the present. For earlier porcelain made at Worcester, between 1751 and 1862, see WORCESTER.

Centerpiece bowl, circular bowl supported above 3 lion's masks, each issuing a cornucopia-form vessel, central bowl w/h.p. floral panels on blushed ivory ground heightened w/gilding, dated 1904, 8¾" h. $522.00

Cologne bottle w/silverplate top, lavender, rust, pale yellow & green pansies & leaves decor, dated 1887, 3¾" h. 220.00

Compote, figural Kate Greenaway type girl stem, oval bowl, ca. 1885 . . . . . .265.00

Cookie jar, h.p. pink daisies, pink fuchsias, yellow florals & green

leaves on beige satin ground, silverplate rim, cover & bail handle 270.00

Cornucopia-vase, h.p. lavender &
yellow florals, green leaves & small
pink florettes on beige matte finish
ground, 1898, 6½ x 4½" base,
7 1/8" h........................335.00

Creamer & cov. sugar bowl, h.p. gold
decor on ivory matte finish ground,
1886, pr........................125.00

Royal Worcester Ewer

Ewer, gilt lizard handle molded about
neck, blue florals & tan leaves
w/gold outlining on cream satin
ground, 1887 (ILLUS.)..............435.00

Figure, "The Scotsman," beige, soft
green, tan & burnished gold, satin
finish, dated 1903, 2 5/8" d., 6" h....435.00

Figure, "The Yankee," beige, soft
green, tan & burnished gold, satin
finish, dated 1906, 2 5/8" d.,
6¾" h..........................435.00

Figure, "Cairo Water Carrier," shaded
ivory w/details picked out in pastel
tones, gilt trim, dated 1888, 9" h.....385.00

Figures, "Joy" & "Sorrow," each
wearing pale yellow gown w/overall
dainty floral decor & gold trim, one
holding live bird & the other holding
dead bird, dated 1896, 3¼" d., 9" h.,
pr.............................875.00

Figure of a Kate Greenaway type boy
carrying basket, cream & beige
w/blue details & gold trim, satin
finish, dated 1893, 4¼" d., 9" h. 540.00

Figure, "Against the Wind," white,
1870, 12" h. 475.00

Flower pot, gadroon-molded edge,
h.p. red roses at green top & footed
base, gold trim, w/original brass
wire flower insert, 1909, 5 1/8" d.,
5" h. 325.00

Model of a frog, white, pre-1891 date
mark, 2½ x 3", 1½" h.............185.00

Model of a rabbit w/basket on his
back, beige matte finish
w/burnished green trim on basket,
1911 date mark, 2¼" d., 4¾" h. 455.00

Pitcher, 4¼" h., h.p. multicolor florals
on beige matte finish w/teal blue &
gold handle, 1899 ....175.00

Pitcher, 6" h., 2 1/8" d., h.p. rose &
yellow florals, green leaves & gold
trim on beige matte finish, 1902.....140.00

Pitcher, 7" h., 3¾" d., tan & green
leaf forms in body & leaf frond
handle, heavily burnished w/dull
gold on matte finish, 1903 ....230.00

Plates, 10½" d., enameled turquoise
stylized leaf & dart border, dated
1885, set of 12 ....240.00

Sugar shaker, figural Kate Greenaway
type girl wearing large hat (w/holes
in crown), beige matte finish, gold
trim, 7½" h......................458.00

Teapot, cov., bulbous, gold spout,
handle, base & finial, h.p. florals &
leaves on cream ground, dated 1867,
5½" h. 300.00

Tureen, cover & matching 15" l. ladle,
brown & gold molded elephant head
handles, overall brown ivy decor,
ca. 1880, 14½ x 8 x 8" 250.00

Vase, 5½" h., 3¼" d., basket form
w/ornate rope handle, h.p. multicolored florals on beige matte finish
ground, 1893 ....225.00

Vase, 6½" h., 4¼" d., shell-molded on
base surrounded w/small shells, gold
gold highlights on beige matte finish
ground, 1903 ....175.00

Vase, 8¼" h., 3 7/8" d., 2-handled,
h.p. pink, blue, yellow & lavender
florals & green foliage w/gold trim
on beige matte finish ground, 1902 ..210.00

Vase, 8½" h., 5½" d., shell-shaped,
dull heavy Roman gold & burnished
gold on glossy cream ground, 1888 ..405.00

Vase, 8¾" h., 6 5/8" d., gilt bronze
serpentine handles, enameled gold
& silver florals, gold heron in flight
over gold bamboo on gold-spattered
glossy cream ground, pre-1890 .....498.00

Pilgrim Flask Vases

Vases, 19½" h., "Pilgrim Flask" form, decorated in the Japanese taste w/flock of geese soaring above stylized oriental foliage one side & w/dragonflies & butterflies amidst chrysanthemums & peonies reverse, w/overall gilt, bronzed & silvered details, 1878, pr. (ILLUS.) 2,310.00

Vase, 23 5/8" h., applied at sides w/elaborate scrolling griffin handles & supported on base w/similarly molded figures, peacocks (3) perched in a gnarled tree w/garden ornaments nearby, plumage of central bird picked out in gilt, reserved on blue matte ground, artist-signed & dated 1901 . . . . 1,100.00

SALTGLAZED WARES

Saltglazed Waste Bowl & Teapot

This whitish ware has a pitted surface texture, which resembles an orange skin as a result of salt being thrown into the hot kiln to produce the glaze. Much of this ware was sold in the undecorated state, but some pieces were decorated. Produced during the last century in England, the United States and elsewhere, most pieces are unmarked. Also see STONEWARE.

Creamer w/original hinged pewter lid, melon-ribbed, relief-molded vintage, English registry mark (1842-83), 4 5/8" h. $55.00

Pitcher, 4" h., relief-molded cattails on pale green ground, English registry mark 55.00

Pitcher, 5" h., twisted serpentine handle, mask spout, relief-molded hunters, horses, hounds & stags 125.00

Pitcher, 6¾" h., hexagonal jug-type, relief-molded cupids & ornate leaves 118.00

Pitcher, 7" h., relief-molded storks standing in cattails & feeding on acorns 75.00

Pitcher, 7¼" h., 4¼" d., jug-type, relief-molded soldiers (3) & phoenix birds, marked "Published by E. Ridgway & Abington, Hanley, August 1, 1856" on base 125.00

Pitcher w/original hinged pewter lid,

7 3/8" h., relief-molded scene "Julius Caesar" on buff ground, marked "Published by C. Meigh, Nov. 1, 1839, Hanley" on base 195.00

Pitcher, 7¾" h., relief-molded Scottish tavern scene, Scotsman on galloping horse & thistle on dark olive green ground, marked "W. Ridgway & Co., 1885" 70.00

Pitcher, 7 7/8" h., 3¾" d., jug-type, relief-molded grey designs on blue, Dudson, late 19th c. 80.00

Pitcher, 8¼" h., relief-molded profile of Napoleon on each side 125.00

Pitcher, 9¾" h., bulbous, relief-molded decor entitled "Gypsy," marked "Published 1842 by Jones & Walley Cobridge" 115.00

Pitcher, 10½" h., octagonal, relief-molded Apostle patt., marked "Charles Meigh, Hanley, March 17th, 1842" on base 235.00

Pitcher, relief-molded cobalt blue floral bouquet within broken line oval front & reverse on white w/overall molded scallops, 1-gal. . . . 325.00

Teapot, cov., molded crabstock spout, painted rose, green, turquoise, yellow, iron-red & black scene of amorous couple on one side & house & distant buildings in landscape reverse, Staffordshire, ca. 1760, w/repairs to minor chips (ILLUS. right) 467.00

Waste bowl, painted pink, green, iron-red, yellow, turquoise & black scene of lady playing lute at front & floral spray reverse, pink-edged green trellis diaper border on rim interior, Staffordshire, ca. 1760, repaired chip, 5½" d. (ILLUS. left) 302.00

SAN ILDEFONSO (Maria) POTTERY

Created by a Pueblo Indian woman, Maria Montoya Martinez, and her husband, Julian, this glossy and matte glaze black pottery was always fired in a primitive manner. After 1923, Maria began to sign items, "Marie," "Maria," or "Marie and Julian." San Ildefonso pottery items also might carry the signatures of other village potters of that era, "Rosalia," "Tonita," and others. Popovi Da was Maria's son who worked with her after 1956 until his death and items signed "Maria and Popovi Da" can be so dated. Considered a true artistic achievement, early items signed by Maria, or her contemporaries, command good prices.

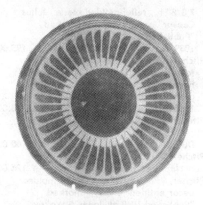

Plate signed Marie & Santana

Bowl, 5½" d., glossy & matte black
on black decor, signed Marie $700.00
Jar, ridged body w/slightly indented
base & tapering shoulder, 3 bird's
wing devices between vertical
rows of dots, glossy & matte black
on black, signed Marie & Julian,
5" d. 605.00
Jar, globular w/tapering neck, narrow
band enclosing serrated wings alternating w/scalloped diagonals at midsection, glossy & matte black on
black, signed Marie, 8" h. 1,650.00
Jar, flared body w/small base & tall
tapering neck, parallel bands surmounted by frieze of feathers, glossy
& matte black on black, signed Marie
& Santana, 9¼" d. 2,200.00
Plate, 5½" d., feather design, glossy
& matte black on black, signed Marie
& Santana. 475.00
Plate, 10¾" d., feather motifs bor-
dered by parallel lines below the
rim, glossy & matte black on black,
signed Marie & Santana
(ILLUS.) 1,760.00
Plate, 10¾" d., glossy & matte black
on black w/four terraced hook
devices at the rim, signed Marie &
Julian 880.00
Plate, 10 7/8" d., "negative" quatrefoil
w/scalloped rain clouds & dotted
details at rim, glossy & matte black
on black, signed Marie & Julian 880.00
Vase, 7" h., bulbous base w/sloped
shoulder & tapering neck, feather
design on upper half w/parallel lines
at neck, glossy & matte black on
black, signed Blue Fawn 580.00
Vase, 11¼" h., flaring rounded body
w/tall tapering neck, scalloped band
of triangular devices at rim above
narrow band enclosing Avanyu (water
serpent) and rain clouds on sides,
glossy & matte black on black,
signed Marie 2,310.00

SARREGUEMINES

Sarreguemines Character Jug

*This factory was established in Lorraine,
France, about 1770. Subsequently Wedg-
wood-type pieces were produced as was
Mocha ware. In the 19th century, the
factory turned to pottery and stoneware.*

Character jug, majolica, beige & brown
flesh tones w/rosy cheeks, nose &
mouth, blue interior, 4" d., 5¼" h.
(ILLUS.) $68.00
Pitcher, 8¼" h., majolica, rooster, hen
& chicks w/attacking hawk in relief
on green ground, light blue interior . . 48.00
Plates, 6½" d., floral border, castle
scene decor, artist-signed, set of 8 . . . 60.00
Plate, 7½" d., majolica, apples decor. . . 25.00
Plate, 7¾" d., majolica, pomegranates
decor 22.00
Plate, 8" d., majolica, embossed straw-
berries decor on blue ground 58.00
Plates, 8" d., wide etched lacy gold
border & center design on cobalt
blue ground, set of 6 . . . . 95.00
Plate, 8½" d., boy & girl in doorway
decor 35.00
Plates, 8½" d., pink latticework
edge, green fern fronds on white
basketweave center, set of 6 . . . . 45.00
Plate, 12" d., majolica, strawberries,
plums & grapes decor 85.00
Plates, "Foreign Legionnaires," humor-
ous military scene, pr. 50.00
Plates, scenes from the life of St. Joan,
set of 4 . . . . 85.00

SATSUMA

*These wares have been made in Japan for
centuries, and the early pieces are scarce*

and high-priced. But mass-produced Satsuma-type ware is plentiful and has been turned out for the past century and a quarter. The so-called "Thousand Faces" design is considered desirable by collectors and all Satsuma prices have escalated in the last decade. Also see BUTTONS.

Late 19th Century Satsuma Bowl

Bottle, baluster-shaped w/narrow neck, enameled scene of figures strolling in garden on body, diapered pattern at shoulder, neck & base, late 19th c., 3 3/8" h. (ILLUS. w/plate below) $176.00

Bowl, 3¾" d., lotus blossom form, interior w/enameled scene of procession of ladies w/noblewoman seated in sedan chair, exterior & edges w/gold diaper patterns & floral scrolls on royal blue ground, Kinkozan, late 19th c. (ILLUS. w/plate below) 275.00

Bowl, 4¾" d., center scene w/detailed landscape & figures surrounded by border of circle, floral & geometric designs, late 19th c., minute rim nick (ILLUS.).....................632.50

Bowl, 5 1/8" d., low foot, interior w/enameled polychrome scene of 12 personages & an elephant w/raised gold & white enamel accents, exterior w/floral & geometric border, late 19th c. 176.00

Bowl, 6" d., 2½" h., interior w/enameled scene of procession leaving temple w/nine men walking & single equestrian figure, pagoda, trees & mountains, exterior w/trees, leaves & border design, ornate gold trim, Shimazu mark in red & gold on base, Meiji period, 1880 ....195.00

Bowl, 7¼" d., overall enameled chrysanthemums w/fan-shaped reserves of genre scenes, 19th c............125.00

Bowl, 12" d., 2¼" h., wide nishikide diaper border, enameled Samurai warriors decor, ornate gold trim, Meiji period, ca. 1885 ....250.00

Box, cov., rectanuglar w/canted corners, cover w/scene of children & swans, scenic decor interior, gold highlights, 3½" l..............330.00

Chalice, interior w/butterfly decor & exterior w/overall multicolored floral decor, cup set in sterling silver Art Nouveau base, marked "Made for Shreve & Company, San Francisco," 5" w., 6¼" h.........1,500.00

Coffee pot, cov., flared feet, mirrored gold reserve of Mandarins w/overall encrusted gold & jeweling decor on cobalt blue shaded to dark green ground 195.00

Creamer & cov. sugar bowl, 3 scroll feet, Geisha & War Lord scene w/overall enameled jeweling, pr.....60.00

Cup & saucer, dragon handle on cup & scalloped rim on saucer, h.p. Arhats (elderly male disciples of Buddha, usually w/haloes about head) decor, late 19th c........................165.00

Flask, moon-type flattened disc shape, enameled scene of women in interior setting one side & procession of immortals reverse, late 19th c., 4" h. 475.00

Incense burner w/heart-pierced cover, globular vessel on tripod base, pointed handles, enameled figures in fan, floral & diamond-shaped reserves, late 19th c., 3" h.........250.00

Jar, cov., bulbous, enameled flying birds & insects at shoulders, peonies, vines & pleated drapery w/multi-colored designs in relief on body, Edo period, 1860 ....195.00

Pitcher, tankard, 8" h., scroll handle, colorful "nishikide" diapering & enameling w/Samurai warriors front & scholars reverse, encrusted gold trim, Meiji period, ca. 1885 ....155.00

Plate, 7½" d., wisteria decor, ca. 1920 ....200.00

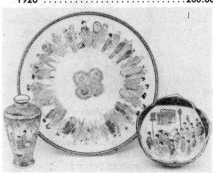

Satsuma Wares

Plate, 7¼" d., low ring foot, 4 central
chrysanthemums surrounded by
large procession of people, geometric rim border, Kenzan, late
19th c. (ILLUS. center) 302.50
Plate, 8½" d., 2 Samurai warlords
decor w/gilt & diapered patterns,
Meiji period, ca. 1890..............110.00
Plate, 9½" d., enameled birds, people
& mountain decor 65.00
Potpourri (rose petal) jar w/pierced
metal domed cover, ovoid, enameled
florals on deep blue ground, late
19th c., 4 5/8" h. 247.50
Salt dip, Samurai warriors decor 65.00
Tea caddy, enameled panels (2)
of children, surrounded by nishikide
diapering, heavy gold trim, 5" h. 115.00
Teapot, cov., enameled chrysanthemums & butterflies decor, ca. 1880 ...75.00
Teapot, cov., reeded handle, overall
brown enameled decor, ca. 1900.....45.00
Tea set: cov. teapot, cov. sugar
bowl, cov. creamer & 6 c/s; 8
Arhats & dragon on gold ground,
coiled dragon finials, handles &
spouts, ca. 1900, 15 pcs. 357.00
Tea set: cov. teapot, 6 c/s, 6
dessert plates; hanging wisteria
decor, 19 pcs. 325.00
Urn & domed cover w/knob finial,
baluster-shaped on square base
w/cut corners, enameled overall
florals & 3 reserves of children at
play, late 19th c., 4 1/8" h. 350.00
Vases, 2¼" h., Thousand Flowers patt.,
pr...............................150.00

Satsuma Vase

Vase, 3½" h., tapered bulbous form,
figural & chrysanthemum reserves
flanked by oval floral & butterfly
reserves on diapered ground,
late 19th c. (ILLUS.)................275.00

Vase, 4¼" h., tapered bulbous form
w/flared rim, floral & decorative
borders flanking scene of women
w/parasols in a landscape, late
19th c...........................250.00
Vase, 8¾" h., baluster form, pagoda
& mountains decor 90.00
Vase, 16" h., Samurai warriors decor,
ca. 1875 ....167.50

SCHLEGELMILCH

*Handpainted china marked "RS Ger-
many" and "RS Prussia" continues to
grow in popularity. According to Clifford J.
Schlegelmilch in his book "Handbook of
Erdmann and Reinhold Schlegelmilch—
Prussia—Germany and Oscar Schlegelmilch—Germany," Erdmann Schlegelmilch
established a porcelain factory in the Germanic provinces at Suhl, in 1861. Reinhold,
his younger brother, worked with him until
1869 when he established another porcelain
factory in Tillowitz, upper Silesia. China
bearing the name of this town is credited to
Reinhold Schlegelmilch. It customarily
bears also the phrase "RS Germany." Now
collectors seek additional marks including
E.S. Germany, R.S. Poland and R.S. Suhl.
Prices are high and collectors should beware
the forgeries that sometimes find their way
to the market. Also see SHAVING MUGS
and "Special Focus" on SUGAR BOWLS.*

R.S. GERMANY

R.S. Germany Creamer & Sugar Bowl

Ash tray, Dutch scene decor $35.00
Berry set: master bowl & 6 sauce
dishes; pink roses decor, 7 pcs. 90.00
Bowl, 3¼" oval, shell-molded rim,
floral decor 16.00
Bowl, 6½" d., shallow, 3-handled,
leaves outlined in black on gold
banded rim, salmon-color roses
decor 66.00
Bowl, 9" d., pastel florals w/touches
of orange on forest green shaded
to cream ground 75.00
Bowl, 9¼" d., cabbage leaf molded,
white interior, green-tinted pearlized exterior 155.00

Bowl, 10" d., scalloped rim, large
pink roses on shaded grey ground 42.50
Bowl, 10½" d., iris-molded rim, floral
decor, satin finish 38.00
Bowl, 11" d., ornate florals in relief
& gold decor, iridescent Tiffany
border 110.00
Cake plate, pierced handles, white
Azalea blossoms on shaded pale
green ground, 9¾" d. 35.00
Cake plate, Art Nouveau border, large
white poppies w/gold trim, 10" d. 39.00
Cake plate, tulips on green ground,
10" d. 69.00
Cake set: master cake plate & 6
individual plates; yellow roses decor,
7 pcs. 65.00
Candy dish, pierced handles, wide
scalloped rim, orange roses on grey-
green ground, 7" square 35.00
Candy dish, handled, white florals on
green ground, 8" l. 35.00
Celery tray, Bird of Paradise patt.,
11" l. 165.00
Chocolate pot, cov., floral decor,
9½" h. 155.00
Compote, pedestal base, windmill
scene w/mill & boat, large 275.00
Cookie jar, cov., 2-handled, pink roses
decor 90.00
Creamer & cov. sugar bowl, pansies
decor, artist-signed, pr. (ILLUS.) . . 55.00
Creamer & cov. sugar bowl, chickadee
& bluebirds decor, pr. 90.00
Cup & saucer, iris decor 35.00
Cup & saucer, swirl-molded, white
dogwood blossoms on light brown
glossy ground 35.00
Dresser set: hair receiver, cov. powder
bowl & dresser tray; blue & white Art
Nouveau decorative band, 3 pcs. 100.00
Ferner, white tulips on green ground . . 125.00
Hair receiver, overall roses & gold
leaves decor 58.00
Hatpin holder, calla lilies decor 67.50
Hatpin holder, orange poppies decor . . . 50.00

R.S. Germany Hatpin Holder

Hatpin holder, floral decor on shaded
ground, 4½" h. (ILLUS.) 60.00
Inkwell, cov., handled, pink roses
decor, 3" d., 2¾" h. 72.00
Marmalade jar w/underplate, morning
glories decor 55.00
Match box holder, blue 35.00
Match holder, figural pipe on tray 36.00
Mustard jar, cov., dogwood decor on
green shaded to white ground,
3" h. 65.00
Mustard jar, cover & spoon, roses
decor 58.00
Mustard jar, cover & spoon, pine cone
decor on cream ground 50.00
Napkin ring, pink roses & snowballs on
green ground 45.00
Nut cups, plain white w/gold trim, set
of 6 . . . . 100.00
Nut set: master nut bowl & 4 individual
nut cups; footed, magnolias & gold
decor, satin finish, 5 pcs. 75.00
Pitcher, milk, 5¾" h., chrysanthemums
& roses decor on light blue ground . . . 65.00
Pitcher, 6 3/8" h., pink roses decor,
gold trim 200.00
Pitcher, tankard, 11½" h., relief-
molded rim, poppies & pansies on
dark green shaded to pale yellow
ground, ornate gold trim 250.00
Pitcher, cider, roses decor 90.00

R.S. Germany Plate

Plate, 6½" d., orchid decor, green
border w/gilt trim (ILLUS.) 12.50
Plate, 6½" d., white floral decor on
pale green ground 14.00
Plate, 8" d., large pink roses decor,
gold trim 28.00
Plate, 8¼" d., Cottage Scene, w/rider
& 2 horses . . . . 135.00 to 185.00
Plate, 8½" d., pink & yellow carnations
decor on shaded ground 35.00
Plate, 8½" d., roses & gold leaves
decor, satin finish 42.00
Plate, 9½" d., large white tulips &
ornate gold leaves decor on shaded
green ground 45.00

Plate, 10½" d., icicle mold, floral
  decor 95.00
Powder box, cov., calla lily decor 35.00
Powder box, cov., green poppies
  decor 48.00
Relish tray, multicolored poppies &
  daisies decor on ivory to yellow
  ground 25.00
Salt & pepper shakers, peach florals
  w/gold highlights on green tinted
  ground, pr. 45.00
Sauce bowl & underplate, yellow roses
  decor on green ground 37.50
Sauce dish, calla lily decor, 5" d. 15.00
Syrup pitcher w/underplate, pink
  floral decor, gold trim 65.00
Teapot, cov., shaded pink full-blown
  roses on blue to cream ground 65.00
Teapot, cov., scenic decor. 129.00
Toothbrush holder, floral decor, gold
  trim 35.00
Toothpick holder, 2-handled, peach-
  pink florals w/gold highlights on
  green-tinted ground. 60.00
Toothpick holder, 3-handled, roses
  decor 65.00
Toothpick holder, 3-handled, violets
  decor, gold trim 38.00
Vase, 3½" h., bulbous, cherry blossom
  decor 35.00
Vase, 3½" h., bulbous, peacocks
  decor 65.00
Vase, bud, 6" h., floral decor on soft
  green ground .27.50

R.S. PRUSSIA

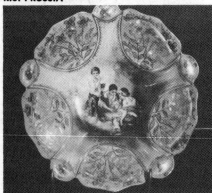

Dice Players Scene Bowl

Berry set: master bowl & 6 sauce
  dishes; bowl-in-bowl mold, poppies
  decor on blue shaded to beige
  ground, 7 pcs. 395.00
Bowl, 5" d., 3-footed, tiny roses decor . .65.00
Bowl, 5" d., scalloped & ruffled rim,
  Stag Scene decor 295.00
Bowl, 6½" d., footed, iris mold,
  lavender, pink & white lilies on
  shaded pastel satin finish 165.00

Bowl, 9¼' d., iris mold, mauve shaded
  to crimson roses w/green foliage &
  stems on shaded Nile to moss green
  ground, gold trim 260.00
Bowl, 9½" d., carnation mold, pink &
  white roses decor 187.00
Bowl, 9½" d., daisy mold, Madame
  Recamier portrait & roses decor. 595.00
Bowl, 9½" d., iris mold, Winter Season
  portrait . . . . .950.00 to 1,000.00
Bowl, 10" d., Victorian Lady feeding
  Chickens, bronze iridescent Tiffany
  finish. 595.00
Bowl, 10" d., bowl-in-bowl w/grape
  cluster mold, floral decor on white
  ground . . . . .150.00 to 200.00
Bowl, 10" d., beaded mold, roses decor
  on white ground, gold trim 135.00
Bowl, 10" d., carnation mold, overall
  poppies decor, gold trim 165.00
Bowl, 10" d., iris mold, poinsettias
  on satin finish ground 265.00
Bowl, 10" d., shell mold, scalloped rim,
  purple & blue florals w/gold-outlined
  leaves. 150.00
Bowl, 10" d., swag & tassel mold,
  Sheepherder scene 525.00
Bowl, 10½" d., Tiger & Tigress decor
  (minor hairline on rim) 2,950.00
Bowl, 10½" d., acorn mold, floral
  decor 215.00
Bowl, 10½" d., bowl within bowl mold,
  Summer Season portrait decor 875.00
Bowl, 10½" d., Dice Players Scene
  decor (ILLUS.) . . . . .700.00 to 1,500.00
Bowl, 10½" d., iris mold, pink poppies
  & shadow flowers on chartreuse
  ground 275.00
Bowl, 10½" d., iris mold, Winter
  Season portrait, satin finish 895.00
Bowl, 10½" d., 6-point clover mold
  w/raised jewels, roses decor on
  green shaded to yellow lustre
  finish. 180.00
Bowl, 10½" d., pink roses & snowballs
  on green & cream-tinted ground 195.00

R.S. Prussia with Swans

Bowl, 10¾" d., icicle mold, Swan on
Lake (ILLUS. center) 500.00
Bowl, 10¾" d., sawtooth mold, Canal
Scene w/Swans & Pine Trees, green
& blue. . . . . .600.00 to 625.00
Bowl, 10¾" d., 3" h., lilacs on shaded
cream to white ground, gold trim . . .175.00
Bowl, 10¾" d., lily pad molded rim,
Chinese Pheasant Scene decor. 600.00
Bowl, 11" d., icicle-molded rim, Man of
the Mountain (or Quiet Cove) Scene
decor 700.00
Bowl, 11" d., 3" h., Pond Lilies re-
flected in Water & Bluebirds decor . .375.00
Bowl, 11" d., floral-molded rim, Swan
Scene w/Bluebirds 475.00
Bowl, 13 x 8½" oval, jewel mold,
floral decor on white shaded to red
at border 250.00
Box, cov., scalloped mold, roses decor,
gold trim, 4" w. 210.00
Bun tray, 6-medallion mold, pink &
white roses decor, 11 x 7". 125.00
Bun tray, pierced handles, irregular
rim, roses decor on green shaded to
blue ground, gold trim, 12" l. 110.00
Bun tray, icicle mold, Swan on Lake
scene (ILLUS. left) 425.00
Bun tray, Melon Eaters 600.00
Bun tray, Mill scene 495.00
Bun tray, Ostriches in Desert scene . . 1,200.00
Butter dish w/cover & drain insert,
pink roses on shaded cream ground,
gold trim 695.00
Butter pat, floral decor 40.00
Butter pat, Melon Boys decor 65.00
Cake plate, pierced handles, point &
clover mold, shaded pink roses on
shaded green to grey ground, gold
trim, 9¾" d. 85.00
Cake plate, pierced handles, Castle
scene, brown tones, 10" d. 595.00
Cake plate, pierced handles, Tiger &
Tigress decor, 10½" d. 2,700.00
Cake plate, pierced handles, iris mold,
Winter Season portrait decor,
10½" d. 925.00
Cake plate, pierced handles, icicle
mold, Swan Scene decor, 11" d. 395.00
Cake plate, plume mold, yellow,
lavender & pink florals & fronds,
yellow & light turquoise border
w/gold trim, 11½" d. 217.00
Cake plate, pierced handles, fleur-de-
lis mold, multicolored roses on
shaded green ground, 11½" d. 145.00
Cake plate, huge poppies & green leaves
on muted green & gold ground,
11½" d. 185.00
Cake plate, pierced handles, icicle
mold, Old Man in Mountain (Quiet
Cove) decor .690.00
Cake plate, pierced handles, Spring
Season portrait decor 1,300.00

R.S. Prussia Summer Season Chocolate Set

Chocolate set: cov. chocolate pot &
2 c/s; Summer Season portrait
decor, 5 pcs. (ILLUS.). 3,200.00

R.S. Prussia Coffee Pot

Coffee pot, cov., octagonal, vertical
floral sprays decor on shaded
ground, gold trim (ILLUS.) 450.00
Creamer, Castle Scene decor,
3½" h. . . . . .150.00 to 225.00
Creamer, scalloped feet, Mill Scene,
green tint . . . . .130.00 to 150.00
Creamer, Parrots decor. 750.00
Creamer, Quiet Cove Scene decor. 150.00
Creamer, pink roses & gold tracery
on green ground. 65.00
Creamer, footed, scalloped rim,
lavender & yellow florals w/gold
trim decor, 4" h. 105.00

Bluebird Pattern Creamer & Sugar Bowl

Creamer & cov. sugar bowl, pedestal
base, jewel mold, Bluebird patt.,
pr. (ILLUS.) 575.00

Melon Boys Demitasse Cup & Saucer

Cup & saucer, demitasse, jewel mold,
Melon Boys decor, each (ILLUS. of
pr.) 450.00

Fall Season Portrait Dresser Tray

Dresser tray, carnation mold, Fall
Season portrait (ILLUS.) 1,650.00
Dresser tray, daisy mold, pink & laven-
der orchids on cream center, sky
blue border w/gold tracery & shadow
leaves, 12 x 8". 185.00
Dresser tray, iris mold, large red & yel-
low roses decor, 11¾ x
7½" .140.00 to 155.00
Dresser tray, jewel mold, Dice Boys &
florals gold edge, 11½ x 7½" 1,245.00
Dresser tray, plain mold, roses
decor . . . . .100.00 to 125.00
Dresser tray, point & clover mold, yel-
low roses decor, turquiose & gold
border, 12 x 8" 240.00
Dresser tray, 6-circle mold w/Bluebirds
in gold-edged circles, basket of
peach roses decor 275.00
Hatpin holder, octagonal, Pond Lilies
reflecting in Water 115.00
Hatpin holder w/attached pin tray,
white roses, daisies on yellow
ground, gold trim 175.00
Hatpin holder, Admiral Perry patt.
w/quotation "Midst Snow and Ice"
(ILLUS.) 800.00

Admiral Perry Hatpin Holder

Mustard jar, cov., green & white
florals on satin finish ground 95.00
Mustard pot, cov., pedestal base,
basket of roses decor on shaded
blue to white .125.00
Pin tray, iris mold, roses decor on
shaded strawberry red to mauve,
gold trim, 5½" l 120.00
Pitcher, 6" h., 4 molded feet, lavender
& white lilacs decor on purple
shaded to lavender satin finish, gold
trim 195.00
Pitcher, lemonade, 8½" h., white &
pink carnations & roses decor on
dark green shaded to white 590.00
Pitcher, tankard, 9½" h., jewel mold,
pink roses decor on green tinted
ground, gold trim 400.00
Pitcher, tankard, 11" h., purple floral
decor on pink shaded to white
ground 595.00
Pitcher, tankard, 11½" h., acorn mold,
Mill Scene, shaded brown to tan . . .1,700.00
Pitcher, tankard, 11½" h., Schooner
Scene 1,650.00
Pitcher, tankard, 13½" h., beaded
mold, roses decor 550.00
Pitcher, tankard, 14" h., double por-
trait, Victorian Lady Watering
Flowers one side & Victorian Lady
with Dog opposite, Tiffany-type
iridescent ground 2,200.00
Pitcher, tankard, 15" h., floral mold,
Madame Recamier portrait
decor 3,000.00
Plate, 6" d., Castle Scene decor, brown
tones 225.00
Plate, 6¼" d., Cottage Scene decor,
green tones w/green shadow
flowers, gold trim 60.00
Plate, 7½" d., scroll mold, multi-
colored florals & raspberry cluster
decor on cobalt blue ground 265.00
Plate, 7¾" d., carnation mold, pink
floral decor on blue ground 135.00

Plate, 8" d., scalloped rim, pink floral
decor on grey-green pearlized
ground 75.00
Plate, 8" d., 6 medallion mold, multi-
colored floral decor center, green
Tiffany-type iridescent border 179.00
Plate, 8¼" d., Castle Scene . .650.00 to 850.00
Plate, 8½" d., jewel mold, Melon Boys
in Keyhole, green tones 850.00
Plate, 8½" d., Mill Scene decor on
green shaded to yellow ground 650.00
Plate, 8½" d., Snowbirds decor on
shaded orange, yellow & cream
ground 950.00
Plate, 8¾" d., Spring Season or Winter
Season portrait in Keyhole decor,
each 800.00
Plate, 8¾" d., Swans (2), Temple &
Pine Trees decor, satin finish 300.00
Plate, 9" d., Dice Players Scene 395.00
Plate, 9½" d., iris mold, Mill Scene
decor on pink satin finish 550.00
Plate, 9½" d., fleur-de-lis mold, pink
poppies decor on dark green
ground 145.00
Plate, 10¼" d., Quiet Cove Scene,
blue-grey tones. 450.00
Plate, 10½" d., 5-circle mold w/Blue-
birds in gold-edged circles, shadow
flowers center. 450.00
Plate, 10" d., iris mold, Winter Season
portrait, satin finish 800.00
Plate, 10" d., iris mold, pink poppies
on shaded soft yellow to light green
ground, gold trim 185.00
Plate, 10½" d., iris mold, Fall Season
portrait on rust & cream ground . . .1,050.00
Plate, 10½" d., point & clover mold,
Dice Players. . . . . .950.00 to 1,000.00
Powder box, cov., footed, jewel mold,
Madame Recamier portrait decor . . .950.00
Relish, Swan on Lake w/Temple & Pine
Trees (ILLUS. w/bowl & bun tray) 180.00
Relish tray, pierced handles, Castle
Scene w/Bluebirds decor on green,
lavender & turquoise ground, 8" l. . . .175.00
Relish tray, red roses decor, 9½" l. 65.00
Relish tray, jewel mold, Melon Boys
Scene, green tones, 9¾" l. 600.00
Sauce dishes, Mill Scene & Castle
Scene, brown & yellow tones, 3 of
each pattern, set of 6 . . . . .1,500.00
Sauce dishes, roses & snowballs decor,
5½" d., set of 6 . . . . .240.00
Stickpin holder, scalloped rim & feet,
Castle Scene, brown tones, 3" h. 90.00
Sugar shaker, pink roses decor on
cream shaded to green ground 125.00
Syrup pitcher, cover & matching under-
plate, dainty floral decor on cream
to white ground 145.00
Teapot, cov., Castle Scene 550.00
Teapot, cov., footed, fleur-de-lis mold,
pink roses decor 265.00

Toothpick holder, 2-handled, sawtooth
mold, pink roses decor, 3" h. 125.00
Toothpick holder, 3-handled, scalloped
rim, floral decor on shaded green
ground, 2¼" h. 275.00
Vase, 4½" h., bottle-shaped, Castle
Scene on shaded green ground 300.00
Vase, 6½" h., bottle-shaped, Mill
Scene decor on shaded brown & yel-
low ground .400.00
Vase, 8" h., Sheepherders Scene. 350.00
Vase, 9" h., 2-handled, jeweled, Dice
Players Scene decor 1,800.00

Tiger and Tigress Vase

Vase, 9" h., Tiger & Tigress (ILLUS.) . .1,200.00
Vase, 10" h., 2-handled, Madame
Lebrun portrait 695.00
Vase, 10½" h., Art Nouveau style
handles, portrait of Countess
Potaka 350.00
Vase, 10½" h., 2 ornate handles,
Melon Boys decor w/jeweling. 1,075.00

OTHER MARKS
Berry set: master bowl & 6 sauce
dishes; Christmas Poinsettia decor,
7 pcs. (R.S. Tillowitz) 185.00
Bowl, 6¼" d., 2½" h., 4 molded
feet, ruffled rim, lily-of-the-valley
decor, pink, yellow & white border
(R.S. Tillowitz) 52.00
Bowl, 7¾" d., open handles, 4 leaf-
molded feet, roses & violets on soft
green ground, gold floral border
(R.S. Tillowitz) 95.00
Bowl, fruit, 10½" d., 2¾" h.,
scalloped rim, salmon pink roses on
beige, tan & green ground, gold trim
(R.S. Poland) 110.00
Cake plate, pierced handles, roses
decor, watered silk finish (R.S.
Poland). 135.00
Candle holder, floral decor, R.S. Poland
(single) 115.00

Celery tray, birds decor (E.S. Prov.
  Saxe) 63.00
Chocolate pot, cov., roses decor,
  9½" h. (E.S. Prov. Saxe) 135.00
Dresser tray, green oak leaves &
  acorns decor on cream ground, gilt
  rim, 12 3/8 x 9" (R.S. Poland) 118.00
Dresser tray, roses decor (E.S.
  Germany) 55.00
Mug, pink floral decor (R.S. Poland) 75.00
Sugar shaker, pink roses decor, gold
  trim (R.S. Tillowitz) 46.00
Syrup pitcher, pastel pink snowballs
  decor (R.S. Tillowitz) 35.00
Toothpick holder, Indian Chief decor
  (E.S. Germany) 95.00
Vase, 4" h., "Night Watch" scene
  after Rembrandt (R.S. Poland) 100.00
Vase, 6" h., Lady with Doves portrait
  decor on gold ground w/raised
  turquoise beading (E.S. Germany) ..195.00
Vase, 7½" h., "Night Watch" scene
  after Rembrandt in shades of
  medium to dark brown (R.S. Suhl) ...395.00
Vase, 8"h., pheasants (4) decor (R.S.
  Suhl) 265.00
Vase, 12" h., 2-handled, anemonies
  decor on peach shaded to white
  ground (R.S. Poland) 120.00

SEVRES

Sevres Cache Pots

*Some of the most desirable porcelain ever
produced was made at the Sevres factory,
originally established at Vincennes, France,
and transferred through permission of Madame de Pompadour, to Sevres as the Royal
Manufactory about the middle of the 18th
century. King Louis XV took sole responsibility for the works in 1759 when production of hard paste began. Between 1850 and
1900, many biscuit and soft-paste porcelains
were again made. Fine early pieces are
scarce and high-priced. Many of those available today are late productions. The various
Sevres marks have been copied.*

Busts of a young girl & boy, bisque,
  each on a "bleu-du-roi" (cobalt blue)
  waisted socle edged in gilding,
  16" h., pr.......................$522.00
Cache pots, square, each w/panel

after Boucher depicting shepherd
  lovers relaxing in a field & 3 panels
  of full-blown sprays of summer
  flowers within narrow "Bleu Celeste"
  (sky blue) borders enriched w/gild-
  ing, gilt-bronze mounts & 4 scrolling
  feet, lae 19th c., 9¾" h., pr.
  (ILLUS.) 1,980.00

Sevres Centerpiece Bowl

Centerpiece bowl, oval, reserved
  w/oval panel of full-blown summer
  flowers within gilt borders each side
  on "Bleu Celeste" ground exterior
  & w/garland of colorful florals
  entwined by purple ribbon around
  inside rim, w/gilt-bronze mounts
  w/curving handle & 4 feet joined by
  draped foliate swags, late 19th c.,
  17¼" across handles (ILLUS.) 715.00
Creamer, jug-type, h.p. portrait of a
  lady within a border of turquoise
  jewelling on blue ground enriched
  w/gilt diamond pattern enclosing
  white enamel fleur-de-lis, w/inter-
  laced floral initials on spout, branch
  handle & 3 branch feet, 18th c.,
  4" h. 660.00
Figure group, bisque, mother in
  peasant clothing carrying child on
  her back, circular base, ca. 1760,
  5½" h. 495.00
Plate, 7¾" d., h.p. cherubs, 1846 ......95.00
Plates, 9¼" d., shaped rim, h.p.
  bouquets & scattered flower sprays
  within blue-line & gilt-dash borders,
  1765, set of 12 ....1,320.00
Plate, 10" d., portrait of beautiful lady
  w/roses, artist-signed, 1850........100.00

Cabinet Plates with Portraits

Plates, 10¼" d., each w/different
  center portrait of court beauty or

Louis XIV or Louis XVI within white
band & wide "bleu-du-roi" border
enriched w/gilding, artist-signed, set
of 12 (ILLUS. of pr.) 2,310.00
Plate, center portrait of Mme.
De Lamballe, ivory & emerald green
border w/heavy raised gold trellis,
dots & floral swags, artist-signed,
19th c.........................225.00

18th Century Sevres Teapot

Teapot, cov., ovoid body, painted floral
wreath in shades of rose, purple,
iron-red, yellow, blue & green within
scalloped oval panel w/tooled gold
border each side on "bleu-du-roi"
ground, the cover w/yellow
ranunculus sprig knop, 1767,
4 1/8" h. (ILLUS.).................880.00
Tray, h.p. floral bouquet in shades of
pink, yellow, blue & green center,
"Rose Pompadour" (salmon pink)
border enriched w/gilt flowering
foliage, line & scroll motifs, gilt
dentil rim, 1757, 5¾" sq. 2,200.00

Sevres Covered Urns

Urns, cov., continuous frieze after
Boucher depicting 2 lovers relaxing
on an embankment near a river on
one, the other w/a scene of the two
lovers near a rustic cottage, within
"bleu-du-roi" borders, gilt-bronze

mounts, artist-signed, ca. 1910,
31" h., pr. (ILLUS.) 4,620.00
Vases, 18¼" h., elongated neck,
reserved w/panel of shepherd lovers
relaxing in pastoral setting & landscape scene reverse, "Bleu Celeste"
ground, late 19th c., pr. (now
mounted as table lamps) 1,980.00
Vases, cov., 21" h., reserved w/oval
panel of maiden wearing flowing
classical drapery & attended by a
cupid front & landscape scene reverse, lustrous pink, blue & green
paneled ground heightened
w/gilding, gilt-bronze mounts, artist-
signed, ca. 1900, pr. 2,970.00
Vases, cov., 23¾" h., campana-
shaped, continuous frieze w/rustic
maidens & their swain within
scrolling gilt borders, apple-green
ground, gilt-bronze mounts, late
19th c., pr. 1,650.00
Vases, cov., 27¼" h., painted
w/maiden wearing diaphanous pastel gown & attended by putto in
spring landscape on front & w/land-
scape scene on reverse, within
lustrous peach borders heightened
w/claret red & blue borders & gilding, gilt bronze mounts, artist-
signed, ca. 1900, pr. 3,850.00
Vases, 37" h., oval panel depicting
a colorfully clad hunting party of
ladies & gentleman on horseback,
reverse w/oval panel of a landscape,
each within scrolling gilt borders &
reserved on a "bleu-du-roi" ground,
gilt-bronze mounts, ca. 1900, pr. ...6,600.00
Vase, 47" h., reserved w/genre scene
of young women ironing & folding
laundry in rustic interior on front &
landscape vignette reverse within
"bleu-du-roi" borders heightened
w/gilt scrollwork gilt-bronze mounts,
ca. 1900......................9,900.00

SHAWNEE

*The Shawnee Pottery operated in Zanes-
ville, Ohio, from 1937 until 1961. Much of
the early production was sold to chain
stores and mail order houses including
Sears Roebuck, Woolworth and others.
Planters, cookie jars and vases, along with
the popular "Corn King" oven ware line, are
among the collectible items which are
plentiful and still reasonably priced.*

Bowl, 5" d., "Corn Queen" line........$9.00
Bowl, fruit, 6" d., "Corn Queen" line....16.00
Butter dish, cov., "Corn Queen" line....30.00

Cookie jar, "Corn King" line 62.50
Cookie jar, Little Chef, yellow 75.00
Cookie jar, Octagon 18.00
Cookie jar, figural Clown w/seal,
   gold trim . . . . .75.00 to 125.00
Cookie jar, figural Drummer Boy 85.00
Cookie jar, figural Dutch Boy 30.00

Shawnee Dutch Girl Cookie Jar

Cookie jar, figural Dutch Girl, marked
   "Great Northern" (ILLUS.) 105.00
Cookie jar, figural Lucky Elephant,
   gold trim 100.00
Cookie jar, figural Owl, gold
   trim . . . . .80.00 to 97.00
Cookie jar, figural Puss 'n Boots, gold
   trim 45.00
Cookie jar, figural Sailor Boy 30.00
Cookie jar, figural Smiley Pig
   w/shamrocks, gold trim 105.00
Cookie jar, figural Winnie Pig, coral
   collar 55.00

"Corn King" Line Creamer

Creamer, "Corn King" line, 4¾" h.
   (ILLUS.) 14.00
Creamer, figural elephant w/tusks 12.50
Creamer, figural Puss 'n Boots 15.00
Creamer, figural Smiley Pig 16.00
Creamer & cov. sugar bowl, "Corn
   Queen" line, pr. 20.00
Cup & saucer, "Corn King" line 22.50
Mixing bowl, "Corn Queen" line, 6" d. . . .12.50

Mug, "Corn King" line 20.00
Pitcher, 7½" h., figural Little Bo Peep . . .25.00
Pitcher, water, 8" h., "Corn King"
   line . . . . .25.00 to 32.50
Pitcher, figural Little Boy Blue, red
   pants 25.00
Planter, figural cherub 6.00
Planter, figural doe & fawn 10.00
Planter, figural Dutch Boy or Dutch
   Girl, each 12.00
Planter, model of a birdhouse w/birds . . .9.00
Planter, model of bridge 10.50
Planter, model of a clock, maroon face,
   gold trim 10.00
Planter, model of a cradle 6.50
Planter, model of doghouse w/dog 10.00
Planter, model of a grist mill, gold
   trim 12.50
Planter, model of water pump &
   trough 8.00
Planter, model of wishing well 10.00
Plate, 10" d., "Corn King" line 17.50
Platter, "Corn Queen" line 22.50
Relish tray, "Corn Queen" line, 6¼" l. . .10.00
Salt & pepper shakers, "Corn Queen"
   line, 3¼" h., pr. . . . . .8.00 to 12.00
Salt & pepper shakers, "Corn Queen"
   line, 5½" h., pr. 15.00
Salt & pepper shakers, figural Chanti-
   cleer Rooster, small, pr. 10.00
Salt & pepper shakers, figural Little Bo
   Peep, small, pr. 8.00
Salt & pepper shakers, figural Mugsy,
   5" h., pr. 24.00
Salt & pepper shakers, figural Winnie
   Pig, pr. 12.50
Spooner, "Corn King" line 17.00
Teapot, cov., "Corn King" line 42.50
Teapot, cov., "Corn Queen" line 37.50
Teapot, cov., "Corn Queen" line, 1-cup
   individual size 70.00
Teapot, cov., figural Granny Ann 40.00

Tom the Piper's Son Teapot

Teapot, cov., figural Tom the Piper's
   Son, 7" h. (ILLUS.) 27.50
Vegetable bowl, oval, "Corn King"
   line 26.00

SHENANDOAH VALLEY POTTERY

Shenandoah Valley Stoneware Crocks

The pottery of the Shenandoah Valley in Maryland and Virginia, turned out an earthenware pottery of a distinctive type. It was the first earthenware pottery made in America with a varied, brightly colored glaze. The most notable of these potters, Peter Bell, Jr., operated a pottery at Hagerstown, Maryland and later at Winchester, Virginia, from about 1800 until 1845. His sons and grandsons carried on the tradition. One son, John Bell, established a pottery at Waynesboro, Pennsylvania in 1833, working until his death in 1880, along with his sons who subsequently operated the pottery a few years longer. Two other sons of Peter Bell, Jr., Solomon and Samuel, operated a pottery in Strasburg, Virginia, a town sometimes referred to as "pot town" for six potteries were in operation there in the 1880s. Their work was also continued by descendants. Shenandoah Valley redware pottery, with its colorful glazes in green, yellow, brown and other colors, and the stoneware pottery produced in the area, is eagerly sought by collectors. Some of the more unique forms can be considered true American folk art and will fetch fantastic prices.

Butter crock, straight sides, earred handles, salt-glazed stoneware w/brushed brown floral motif, impressed mark & "D" on one shoulder, Samuel & Solomon Bell, Strasburg, Virginia, repaired crack, 8" d., 6" h. (ILLUS. right) $198.00

Crocks: first cylindrical w/incised ring at shoulder & molded rim; second cylindrical w/incised ring at shoulder & flaring rim; salt-glazed stoneware w/brushed cobalt blue decor, each impressed "Samuel, Richard and Charles Bell, Strasburg, Virginia," 1882-1908, 1-gal. & 1½ gal., pr. 330.00

Crock, cylindrical w/flaring rim, salt-glazed stoneware w/brushed band of cobalt blue florals at shoulder, impressed mark & "1½" at shoulder, John Bell, Waynesboro, Pennsyl-

vania, 1½ gal., 10¾" h. (ILLUS. left) 462.00

Crock, cylindrical w/molded flaring rim, salt-glazed stoneware w/brushed cobalt blue floral sprays, impressed "Samuel and Solomon Bell, Strasburg, Virginia," 1834-82, 1½ gal., 11 3/8" h. 220.00

Crocks, vasiform, redware: first w/dark brown glaze; second w/red-brown glaze; each impressed "John Bell, Waynesboro, Pennsylvania," 1833-80, 5¼" & 5½", pr. 176.00

Cuspidor, sides w/molded panels, redware w/white slip & clear glaze streaked w/running brown & green, 7" d. (edge chips) 275.00

Flower pot, tapering cylinder w/molded & dished foot, redware w/manganese glaze, impressed "Upton Bell, Waynesboro, Pennsylvania," 1881-99, 6½" w., 5¾" h. 418.00

Shenandoah Jar & Jug

Jars, cylindrical w/flaring rim: first of stoneware w/green lead glaze & impressed mark on shoulder; second of redware w/brown glaze & impressed mark on body; both by John Bell, Waynesboro, Pennsylvania, 1833-70, 6" h., pr. (ILLUS. of one left) 220.00

Jug, slightly ovoid w/applied strap handle, redware w/pale green lead glaze, impressed mark on shoulder, John Bell, Waynesboro, Pennsylvania, 1833-80, 7½" h. (ILLUS. right) 220.00

Jug, typical shape w/double-molded rim & applied strap handle, salt-glazed stoneware, impressed "Samuel and Solomon Bell, Strasburg, Virginia," 1834-82, 8¾" h. 220.00

Jug, cylindrical w/rounded shoulder & molded rim, salt-glazed stoneware w/brushed cobalt blue decor on shoulder, impressed "John Bell, Waynesboro, Pennsylvania," 1833-80, 9" h. 198.00

Pitcher, 9" h., cylindrical body

w/incised shoulder, flared, pinched
rim & applied handle, redware
w/yellow, brown & green mottled
glaze, Bell Pottery, Strasburg, Va.,
mid-19th c. 418.00
Wall pocket, applied w/bird & flowers
& scrolled hanger, white clay
w/clear glaze running w/brown &
green, 6½" h. (chip on end of
hanger, bird's beak repaired) 585.00

SLIP WARE

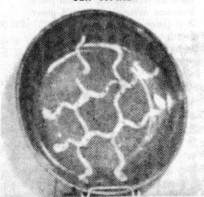

Slip Ware Pie Plate

*This term refers to ceramics, primarily
redware, decorated by the application of
slip, or semi-liquid paste made of clay. Such
wares were made for decades in England
and Germany and elsewhere on the Continent, and in the Pennsylvania Dutch
country and elsewhere in the United States.*

Charger, coggled edge, yellow slip
4-line straight & wavy designs on
redware, 11½" d., 1 5/8" h. $825.00
Charger, coggled edge, yellow slip
3-line designs on redware, 12¼" d.,
2" h. 750.00
Dish, coggled edge, yellow slip wavy
lines on redware, 5 5/8" d. 1,400.00
Jar, applied handle, white slip wavy
lines on green glaze, 3½" d. 265.00
Pie plate, coggled edge, yellow slip
squiggles on redware, 7 3/8" d.
(hairlines) .495.00
Pie plate, coggled edge, yellow slip
3-line design on redware, 8" d. 390.00
Pie plate, yellow slip lattice design
w/green speckles on redware,
8¼" d. (ILLUS.) 225.00
Pie plate, coggled edge, yellow slip
tree design on redware, clear glaze
w/puddled green glaze on tree,
8 7/8" d. (rim repair) 375.00
Pie plate, coggled edge, yellow slip

3-line crow's foot design on redware,
9" d. (old edge chips) 275.00
Pie plate, coggled edge, 3-line yellow
slip design on redware, clear lead
glaze, 11½" d. 425.00
Plate, 8½" d., coggled edge, yellow
slip initials on redware 280.00
Platter, 15½ x 10½", 2 3/8" h.,
coggled edge, yellow slip 4-line
crow's foot design on redware (old
edge chip & hairline) 575.00
Platter, 15½ x 12¼" oval, coggled
edge, 3 rows of yellow slip 3-line
designs on redware (old rim chips) . .500.00

SPATTERWARE

Spatterware Schoolhouse Pattern

*This ceramic ware takes its name from
the "spattering" of designs on it in color
with rustic decor and flowers, houses and
eagles and the like. Much of that now available in this country was imported from
potteries in England last century.*

Creamer, blue & green rainbow
spatter on white, 4½" h. (minor
stains) $195.00
Cup & saucer, handleless, Peafowl
patt., free-hand red, blue, green &
black peafowl, blue spatter borders,
impressed "W. Adams & Sons" (both
pieces w/rim wear & small chips) . . .165.00
Cup & saucer, handleless, Peafowl
patt., free-hand red, green, blue &
black peafowl, green spatter
borders 255.00
Cup & saucer, handleless, Schoolhouse
patt., free-hand red, ochre, green &
brown schoolhouse, blue spatter
borders (ILLUS.) 575.00
Cup & saucer, handleless, Thistle patt.,
free-hand red & green thistle,
yellow spatter borders 500.00
Cup & saucer, miniature, Tulip patt.,
free-hand red, blue, green & black

tulip, blue spatter borders (minor
stains & rim wear) 245.00
Cup & saucer, handleless, Tulip patt.,
free-hand red, blue, green & black
tulip center, brown & black rainbow
spatter borders 300.00

Spatterware Pitcher

Pitcher, 8 5/8" h., jug-type, red, green,
yellow, black & blue rainbow
spatter, ca. 1845 (ILLUS.) 750.00
Plate, 8¼" d., Schoolhouse patt., free-
hand red, black & green school-
house, green spatter border. 625.00
Plate, 8 3/8" d., Tulip patt., free-hand
red, blue, green & black tulip
center, blue spatter border. 250.00
Plate, 8½" d., Tulip patt., free-hand
red, blue, green & black tulip center,
black & purple rainbow spatter
border 475.00
Plate, 9¾" d., Schoolhouse patt., free-
hand red schoolhouse by green
spatter tree w/brown trunk, blue
spatter border. 550.00
Plate, 10 5/8" d., Tulip patt., free-hand
red, blue, green & black tulip center,
red spatter border 400.00
Platter, 13½" l., Peafowl patt., free-
hand red, green, blue & black
peafowl center, blue spatter back-
ground (rim repair) 300.00
Soap dish, green stick spatter on
white 105.00
Teapot, cov., child's, Peafowl patt. 375.00
Teapot, cov., yellow & red rainbow
spatter, 5¼" h. 750.00
Teapot, cov., bulbous, Peafowl patt.,
free-hand peafowl on green spatter
ground, 1-cup size 310.00
Sugar bowl, cov., red, yellow, green &
black rainbow spatter, 5 3/8" h.
(stains & hairlines & edge chip on
lid). 285.00
Sugar bowl, cov., Peafowl patt., free-
hand red, blue, green & black peafowl on blue spatter ground, 7¾" h.
(stains, wear & hairlines) 175.00

SPONGEWARE

Spongeware Cup & Saucer

*Spongeware's designs were spattered or
daubed on in colors, sometimes with a piece
of cloth. Blue and blue-and-white ware
predominated. Some collectors lump Spatterware and Spongeware into a single category,
but dealers offer them as separate wares. Also
see "Special Focus" on RED WING.*

Batter pitcher, 2-spout, bulbous, green
& brown daubing on yellowware $85.00
Bean pot, cov., brown & green daub-
ing on cream, 6" h. 90.00
Bowl, 6" d., blue daubing on yellow-
ware 45.00
Bowl, 6½" d., 4" h., blue & rust
daubing on tan 45.00
Bowl, 7" d., 3" h., blue daubing on
white 155.00
Bowl, 7" d., blue & rust daubing on
cream, w/Iowa advertising 46.50
Bowl, 8" d., blue & rust daubing on
cream, w/Iowa advertising 55.00
Bowl, 8" d., blue & rust daubing on
tan. 55.00
Bowl, 9" d., blue & rust daubing on
grey 65.00
Bowl, 11½" d., 6" h., blue daubing on
tan. 185.00
Bread plate, open handles, blue
daubing on white, 10¼" d 95.00
Butter dish, cov., blue daubing on
white, w/"Butter" on top. 115.00
Casserole, cov., green & brown
daubing on cream. 55.00
Cheese crock, highly molded, vented
cover w/10-petal flower form knob,
green & brown daubing on yellow-
ware 135.00
Cup & saucer, handleless, blue daub-
ing on white, ca. 1840 . . . . .130.00
Cups & saucers, blue daubing on
white, pr. (ILLUS. of one set). 230.00
Cuspidor, corset-shaped, blue daubing
on white, 8" d., 6" h. . . . . . .100.00 to 130.00
Cuspidor, oblong w/deeply ribbed
convex sides, green, grey & brown
daubing on yellowware. 135.00
Cuspidor, brown daubing on tan 65.00

Cuspidor, blue daubing on grey 125.00
Custard cup, band of brown daubing
   on yellowware, 3" d. 20.00
Custard cup, melon-ribbed, green &
   brown daubing on cream 42.00
Dish, blue daubing on creamy white,
   12½ x 9¾" oval 165.00
Funnel, wide mouth, handled, green
   daubing, 19th c., 5" d., 3" h. 65.00
Hot water pitcher, bulbous, blue
   daubing on white, 11 1/8" h. 160.00
Hot water pitcher, pear-shaped body,
   scalloped rim, blue daubing & center
   blue band on white, 11¾" h.
   (interior lime deposits) 175.00
Inkwell, green daubing on white,
   2 pcs. 85.00
Jardiniere, blue daubing on white &
   brown band around top & bottom,
   12" d., 9" h. 130.00
Milk cooling basin, blue daubing on
   white 175.00
Mixing bowl, blue & rust daubing on
   grey, 10" d. .75.00

Spongeware Mixing Bowl

Mixing bowl, blue & rust daubing on
   grey, 10½" d., 6" h. (ILLUS.) 95.00
Nest of bowls, brown daubing on
   yellowware, 4½", 5½" and 7" d.,
   from 1¾" to 2 1/8" h., set of
   3 . . . . .75.00 to 95.00
Pitcher, 9" h., molded design at base &
   top, shaded blue & brown horizon-
   tal daubing on tan 145.00
Pitcher, 9¼" h., molded diamond &
   acorn decor, brown & blue daubing
   on yellowware w/gilt trim 95.00
Pitcher, tankard, 12" h., blue daubing
   on white w/blue stripe . . . .165.00 to 195.00
Salt box, wall-type, relief-molded
   wildflower design, blue daubing on
   white 105.00
Serving dish, blue daubing on white,
   11½ x 8". 175.00
Soap dish, blue daubing on white 95.00
Teapot, pewter lid, wooden handle,
   brown daubing on white 125.00
Toothbrush holder, blue daubing on
   white 45.00
Wash basin & pitcher, blue daubing
   on white w/blue band, pr. 400.00

STAFFORDSHIRE FIGURES

Staffordshire Rooster Circa 1800

*Small figures and groups, made of pot-
tery were produced by the majority of the
Staffordshire, England, potters in the 19th
century and were used as mantel decorations or "chimney ornaments," as they were
sometimes called. Pairs of dogs were favo-
rites and were turned out by the carloads,
and 19th century pieces are still available.
Well-painted reproductions also abound and
collectors are urged to exercise caution
before investing.*

Dogs, Greyhound in seated position on
   molded base w/dead rabbit at feet,
   polychrome enameling, 8½" h.,
   pr. $260.00
Dog, Scotch Shepherd seated, 8" h. 165.00
Dogs, Spaniel in seated position, white
   coat w/copper lustre spots, black
   muzzle, 5 3/8" h., pr. 150.00
Dog, Whippet in recumbent position,
   russet coat, blue base, 6½" l.,
   4½" h. 70.00
Equestrian figure, Prince Albert on
   horseback, ca. 1840, 8" h. 165.00
Equestrian figure, William III on horse-
   back, 14" h. 115.00
Figure of a boy w/lamb, ca. 1840,
   4" h. 95.00
Figure of Tam O'Shanter in seated
   position, ca. 1830, 5" h. 100.00
Figure of a girl w/flowers, ca. 1830,
   6" h. 50.00
Figure of the Prince of Wales w/toy
   yacht, 6" h. .115.00
Figure of the Princess Royal, w/parrot,
   1845, 6" h. .115.00
Figure of an actress playing the banjo,
   wearing flowing plaid scarf, white
   w/gilt trim, ca. 1847, 6 5/8" h. 110.00
Figure of "The Woman of Samaria,"
   ca. 1850, 7" h. 120.00
Figures, man holding violin & woman

w/castenets, multicolored costumes,
  8" h., pr. 125.00
Figure of cupid in seated position,
  ca. 1850, 10" h. 75.00
Figure of John Wesley in the pulpit,
  ca. 1850, 11" h. 145.00
Figure of Elijah, w/ravens & tree, ca.
  1800, 12" h. 225.00
Figure of the goddess Diana w/bow,
  12" h. 145.00
Figure of Prince Albert standing,
  ca. 1840, 12" h. 170.00
Figure of Garibaldi, left hand on
  sword & right hand holding
  "Liberte" flag, 13" h. 95.00
Figure group, girls (3) clad in blue
  plaid dresses, standing on grassy
  base, 7½" h. 325.00
Figure group, Queen Victoria, Prince
  Albert & baby, ca. 1840, 8" h. 185.00
Figure group, Savoyard & his dancing
  bear, pearlware, mustachioed
  trainer wearing iron-red turban &
  cape lined in yellow, grey-dashed
  pink jacket & pale blue trousers,
  holding a stick in his right hand &
  rearing brown bear's ochre lead-
  rope in his left hand, standing
  before colorful flowering tree w/yel-
  low & ochre lion at their feet on a
  green & brown mottled base molded
  at front w/blue foliate scrolls,
  1820-30, 8¾" h. 1,980.00
Figure group, Uncle Tom & Little Eva,
  10" h. 450.00
Figure group, Princess Helena & Prince
  Christian of Schleswig-Holstein,
  porridge-glazed, 1866, 12" h. 75.00
Figure group, Robert Burns & Highland
  Mary in bower, green & brown
  enameling, gilt trim, 12" h. 90.00
Figure group w/tree trunk spillholder
  at rear, black & white dog w/his
  master wearing a cobalt blue jacket
  & deep orange cape, 9½" w. base,
  13" h. 495.00
Figure group, Thomas Smith & William
  Collier in "Mortal Combat," ca. 1860,
  13" h. 180.00
Figure group, Queen Victoria, King of
  Sardinia & dog, 14" h. 160.00
Figure group, shepherd & shepherd-
  ess w/spillholder vase, 14½" h. 225.00
Lions in recumbent position, brown,
  12" l., pr. 195.00
Lion in standing position, glass eyes
  & free-standing legs, 13" l. 200.00
Match holder w/striker, Colionial lady
  beside dresser w/mirror frame 65.00
Mountain goat w/curved horns &
  beard, creamware, incised hair
  markings splashed in brown, ca.
  1790, 6½" l. (repair to one ear &
  horn) 770.00

Rooster, incised feathering enriched in
  green, blue, ochre & yellow, on circular grass mound base highlighted
  w/blue & green, ca. 1800, 7¾" h.
  (ILLUS.) 3,080.00

Staffordshire Watch Holder

Watch holder, girl in red cape at top,
  3" w., 4¼" h. (ILLUS.) 200.00

STANGL POTTERY BIRDS

Pair of Love Birds

  *Johann Martin Stangl, who first came to
work for the Fulper Pottery in 1910 as a
ceramic chemist and plant superintendent,
acquired a financial interest and became
president of the company in 1926. The name
of the firm was changed to Stangl Pottery in
1929 and at this time much of the production was devoted to a high grade dinnerware to enable the company to survive the
depression years. Around 1940 a very
limited edition of porcelain birds, patterned
after the illustrations in John James
Audubon's "Birds of America," were is-*

sued. *Stangl subsequently began production of less expensive ceramic birds and these proved to be popular during the war years, 1940-46. Each bird was hand-painted and each was well marked with impressed, painted or stamped numerals which indicated the species and the size. Collectors are now seeking these ceramic birds which we list below.*

Allen Hummingbird, No. 3634,
  3½" h. $52.50
Bird of Paradise, No. 3408, 5½" h. 63.00
Blue Bird, No. 3276, 5" h.............60.00
Bluebird, No. 3276-S, 5" h. 48.00
Bluebird (Double), No. 3276-D,
  8½" h. 110.00
Blue-Headed Vireo, No. 3448, 4¼" h. ...47.00
Broadbill Hummingbird, No. 3629,
  6½" l., 4½" h....................95.00
Cardinal, No. 3444, 6" h. 68.00
Cerulean Warbler, No. 3456, 4¼" h. 42.50
Chat, No. 3590, 4¼" h. 60.00
Chestnut-Backed Chickadee, No. 3811,
  5" h. 55.00
Chestnut-Sided Warbler, No. 3812......55.00
Cockatoo, No. 3405-S, 6" h. 40.00
Cockatoo, medium No. 3580, 8 7/8" h. ..95.00
Cockatoo, No. 3484, 11 3/8" h.........185.00
Cock Pheasant, No. 3492, 6¼ x 11".....120.00
Drinking Duck, No. 3250-E, 3¾" h......36.50
Feeding Duck, No. 3250-C, 1¾" h.......40.00
Flying Duck, No. 3443, 9" h. 220.00
Gazing Duck, No. 3250-D, 3¾" h. 45.00
Grey Cardinal, No. 3596, 4¾" h. 40.00
Grosbeak, No. 3813, 5" h..............90.00
Hen, No. 3446, 7" h. 72.50
Kentucky Warbler, No. 3598, 3" h.......30.00
Key West Quail Dove, No. 3454, 9" h. ..255.00
Kingfisher, No. 3406-S, 3½" h. 50.00
Painted Bunting, No. 3452, 5" h. 87.50
Pair of Cockatoos, No. 3405-D, 9½" h. ..87.00
Pair of Hummingbirds, No. 3599,
  8 x 10½"........................180.00
Pair of Love Birds, No. 3404-D, 4½" h.
  (ILLUS.)...........................95.00
Pair of Orioles, No. 3402-D, 5½" h......95.00
Pair of Parakeets, No. 3582, 7" h......130.00
Pair of Redstarts, No. 3490-D, 9" h. ...125.00
Pair of Wrens, No. 3401-D, 8" h........72.50
Paraquet, No. 3449, 5½" h. 92.50
Preening Duck, No. 3250-B, 2¼" h......35.00
Rieffers Hummingbird, No. 3628,
  4½" h. 90.00
Rivoli Hummingbird, No. 3627, 6" h. ...125.00
Rooster, grey, No. 3445, 9" h..........92.50
Rufous Hummingbird, No. 3585, 3" h. ...42.50
Running Duck, No. 3432, 5" h. 300.00
Scissor-Tailed Flycatcher, No. 3757,
  11" h. 295.00
Standing Duck, No. 3431, 8" h.........80.00
Summer Tanager, No. 3868, 4" h. 100.00
Titmouse, No. 3592, 2½" h. 30.00

White Headed Pigeon (Double), No.
  3518-D, 12½ x 7½" 430.00
Wilson Warbler, No. 3597, 3½" h.......42.00
Wren, No. 3401-S, 3½" h. 38.00
Wren (Double), No. 3401-D, 8" h........73.50
Yellow Warbler, No. 3447, 5" h.........46.50

STONEWARE

"Somerset Potters Works" Crock

Stoneware is essentially a vitreous pottery, impervious to water even in its unglazed state, that has been produced by potteries all over the world for centuries. Utilitarian wares such as crocks, jugs, churns and the like, were the most common productions in the numerous potteries that sprang into existence in the United States during the 19th century. These items were often enhanced by the application of a cobalt blue oxide decoration. In addition to the coarse, primarily salt-glazed stonewares, there are other categories of stoneware known by such special names as basaltes, jasper and others. Also see ADVERTISING ITEMS, BENNINGTON, RED WING and SHENANDOAH VALLEY POTTERY.

Batter jug, bulbous, brushed cobalt
  blue leaf decor around spout on
  grey-blue, w/wire bail handle $260.00
Batter pitcher, bulging ovoid
  w/waisted neck, brushed cobalt blue
  floral & foliate swags on grey,
  9" h. 450.00
Butter churn, brushed cobalt blue wild
  flowers on grey, impressed "Ottman
  Bros. & Co., Fort Edward, N.Y.,"
  4-gal., 16½" h. (interior lime
  deposits) ....115.00 to 265.00
Butter churn, semi-ovoid, earred handles
  at sides, brushed cobalt blue flourish
  & "6" on grey, 6-gal., 16¾" h.
  (surface & edge wear) 85.00
Butter churn, semi-ovoid, earred
  handles, splashed w/cobalt blue on

grey at shoulders & over impressed
"4", 4-gal., 17½" h. (replaced
wooden lid & dasher) 130.00
Butter jar, slip-quilled cobalt blue ferns
& ribbon on grey, impressed "Burger
& Lang, Rochester, N.Y.," 2-gal. 120.00
Crock, straight sides, slip-quilled cobalt
blue stylized flower & stem on grey,
impressed "Woodruff, Cortland"
(Madison Woodruff), 1849-90,
half-gal. 260.00
Crock, straight sides, earred handles,
slip-quilled peacock & branch on
grey, impressed "Fort Edward
Pottery Co., Fort Edward, N.Y.,"
1870-80, 1-gal. 260.00
Crock, straight sides, earred handles,
cobalt blue slip-quilled "polka
dot" bird on grey, impressed "S.
Hart, Fulton," 2-gal., 9" h. 215.00
Crock, straight sides, earred handles,
stenciled cobalt blue "handshake"
on grey, impressed "Somerset
Pottery Works," ca. 1875, 2-gal.,
9½" h. (ILLUS.) 110.00
Crock, cobalt blue slip-quilled flower
on grey, impressed "F.B. Norton &
Co., Worcester," ca. 1865,
2-gal. . . . . .180.00 to 235.00
Crock, wide mouth, cobalt blue slip-
quilled parrot & branch on grey,
impressed "New York Stoneware
Co., Fort Edward, N.Y.," 1861-91,
2-gal. 350.00
Crock, straight sides, earred
handles, brushed cobalt blue wreath
encircling "2" on grey, impressed
"Burger Bros. & Co., Rochester,
N.Y.," 2-gal. 100.00
Crock, straight sides, cobalt blue slip-
quilled florals & leaves on grey,
impressed "Harrington, Lyons,"
1867-72, 2-gal. 220.00

Stoneware Crock by "P. Cushman"

Crock, slightly ovoid, applied handles,
wide rim w/incised line, brushed
cobalt blue floral on grey, impressed
"P. Cushman" (Albany, N.Y.),
1807-33, 3-gal., 13½" h. (ILLUS.) 440.00
Crock, straight sides, earred handles,
slip-quilled cobalt blue stylized floral
on grey, impressed "R.O.
Whittemore, Havanna, N.Y.,"
1860-80, 3-gal. 165.00
Crock, straight sides, earred handles,
slip-quilled cobalt blue bird & stump
on grey, unmarked, 3-gal. 395.00
Crock, straight sides, earred handles,
slip-quilled cobalt blue fish (speckled
trout?) above seaplants & "3"
w/flourishes on grey, unmarked,
3-gal. (some discoloration) 1,200.00
Crock, straight sides, earred handles,
slip-quilled bird & stump on grey &
impressed "4," unmarked, 4-gal.,
11" h. . . . . .300.00 to 375.00

Crock by "Burger Bros. & Co."

Crock, straight sides, earred handles,
slip-quilled cobalt blue floral &
foliage & "4" on grey, impressed
"Burger Bros. & Co., Rochester,
N.Y.," 4-gal. (ILLUS.) 235.00
Crock, straight sides, stenciled cobalt
blue floral & "Western Stoneware"
on light grey, 20th c., 4-gal. 40.00
Crock, straight sides, earred handles,
brushed cobalt blue flowers, leaves
& wavy lines on grey, zig-zag stripe
at rim, impressed "E. Fowler,
Beaver, Pa." & "5," 5-gal., 13¾" h. . .250.00
Crock, slip-quilled large cobalt blue
tree on front & blue script "H.
Loundes Manufactor, Petersburg,
Va." reverse on grey, 6-gal. 1,000.00
Crock, straight sides, earred handles,
slip-quilled cobalt blue poodle carrying basket in mouth on grey,
impressed "Clark & Fox, Athens,
N.Y.," 1829-38, 6-gal. 1,265.00

Crock, straight sides, earred handles,
slip-quilled cobalt blue fat chicken
pecking corn on grey, unmarked,
11½" h. 700.00

Jar, ovoid, applied loop handles,
incised lines w/cobalt blue slip &
impressed mark "Clarkson Crolius,
Manhattan" encircled in blue on grey
& w/incised lines at base, 1794-1838,
1-gal., 11" h. 880.00

Jar, brushed blue-green dashes &
stenciled "Hamilton & Jones,
Greensboro, Pa." on dark grey,
ca. 1870, 1-gal. ....95.00 to 110.00

Jar, semi-ovoid, brushed cobalt blue
designs & stenciled label "Williams &
Reppert, Greensboro, Pa." & "1½" on
grey, 1½ gal., 8¾" h. 145.00

Jar, ovoid, earred handles, brushed
cobalt blue primitive decor on grey,
impressed "Havens" (Putnam, Ohio,
1836-46), 2-gal., 11½" h. (minor rim
chips) 195.00

Jar, slightly ovoid, earred handles,
slip-quilled bird & branch on grey,
impressed "J.A. & C.W. Underwood,
Fort Edward, N.Y.," 1870-80, 2-gal.,
11¾" h. 250.00

Jar, stenciled cobalt blue label "T.F.
Reppert - Successor to Jas. Hamilton
& Co., Greensboro, Pa." on dark
grey, 2-gal., 11¾" h. 105.00

Jar, earred handles, brushed cobalt
blue vine, wavy line & stripe under
rim & stenciled label "Williams &
Reppert, Greensboro, Pa." on dark
grey, 3-gal., 14" h. 175.00

Jar, semi-ovoid w/flared rim, earred
handles, slip-quilled cobalt blue
polka-dot flowers & leaves
w/swirling flourishes on grey,
impressed "Ballard & Brothers,
Burlingon, V.T. 4," 1856-72, 4-gal.,
12½" h. (glaze wear w/surface &
edge chips) 275.00

Jar, slightly ovoid, earred handles,
slip-quilled stylized floral on grey,
impressed "Fort Edward Pottery
Co.," 1861-91, 4-gal., 14" h. 225.00

Jar, earred handles, brushed cobalt
blue wavy lines & stripes & stenciled
florals, foliage & label "From James
Hamilton & Co., Greensboro, Pa.,"
5-gal., 15½" h. 210.00

Jar, ovoid, brushed cobalt blue flower
on grey, impressed "Sipe, Nichols &
Co., Williamsport, Pa.," 7¾" h. 85.00

Jar, ovoid, earred handles, impressed
"L. Seymour, Troy," & 5 stars brushed
over in cobalt blue on grey,
9 1/8" h. 95.00

Jar, ovoid, earred handles, brushed
cobalt blue tulip on grey, impressed
"S.S. Perry, Troy, N.Y.," 1831-65 .....155.00

Ovoid Jug

Jug, ovoid, brushed cobalt blue
foliage on grey, 17" h. (ILLUS.) 140.00

Jug, straight sides, cobalt blue slip-
quilled florals on grey, impressed
"Whites, Utica," 2-gal. 145.00

Jug, straight sides, brushed & slip-
quilled blue bird & branch on grey,
impressed "Satterlee & Mory, Ft.
Edward, N.Y.," 4-gal. 375.00

Jug, cobalt blue slip-quilled tulips &
leaves on grey, impressed "C.H.
Smith & Bro., Flemington, N.J.,"
5-gal. 350.00

Preserving jar, stenciled cobalt blue
decorative diagonal band on grey,
9½" h. 60.00

Preserving jar, brushed cobalt blue leaf
band between incised lines on grey,
9½" h. 85.00

TECO POTTERY

Teco Pottery Marks

*Teco Pottery was actually the line of art
pottery introduced by the American Terra
Cotta and Ceramic Company of Terra Cotta
(Crystal Lake), Illinois in 1902. Founded by
William D. Gates in 1881, American Terra
Cotta originally produced only bricks and
drain tile. Because of superior facilities for
experimentation, including a chemical labo-*

ratory, the company was able to develop an
art pottery line, favoring a matte green
glaze in the earlier years but eventually
achieving a wide range of colors including a
metallic lustre glaze and a crystalline glaze.
Though some hand-thrown pottery was
made, Gates favored a molded ware because
it was less expensive to produce. By 1923,
Teco Pottery was no longer being made and
in 1930 American Terra Cotta and Ceramic
Company was sold.

Vase, 4½" h., bulbous, triangular top
  opening, crystaline glaze $100.00
Vase, 5" h., matte green
  finish . . . . 95.00 to 125.00
Vase, bud, 5½" h., bulbous w/narrow
  neck, matte green finish . . . . 75.00 to 100.00
Vase, 7" h., 7½" d., bulbous, matte
  green finish 225.00
Vase, 8" h., 2-handled, silvery green
  glaze . . . . 150.00 to 165.00
Vase, 10¾" h., 2-handled, matte green
  finish 110.00
Wall pocket, decorated, 8 x 10" 265.00

TEPLITZ

Teplitz Vase

*This ware was produced in numerous
potteries in the vicinity of Teplitz in the
Bohemian area of what is now Czechoslovakia during the late 19th and early 20th
centuries. Vases and figures, of varying
quality, were the primarily productions and
most were hand decorated. These items
originally retailed in gift shops at prices
from 25 cents to around $2. Now collectors
are searching out these marked items and
prices for finer examples are soaring.*

Centerpiece, molded waterlilies
  applied w/black berries, marked
  "Amphora-Teplitz," 13½" l. $145.00

Ewer, inlaid cameo portrait of bride
  & groom & overall mosaic stars &
  jeweling, marked "Teplitz-Austria"
  w/crown, 8½" h. 175.00
Ewer, gold handle & reticulated gold
  top, yellow florals & green leaves
  outlined in gold on off-white ground,
  gold trim, 11¼" h. 195.00
Figure of a girl selling roses, marked
  "Amphora-Teplitz," 8" h. 89.00
Figure of a girl supporting her market
  basket on a tree stump, 19th
  century attire, 12½" h. 345.00
Figure of an Art Novueau lady,
  applied grape wreath in her long
  flowing hair, wearing green gown
  applied w/fruit & holding grape
  clusters in her hands, artist-signed,
  15" h. 595.00
Pitcher, 4" h., warrior on horseback
  decor 95.00
Pitcher, 6½" h., goose girl decor,
  marked "Stellmacher" 70.00
Vase, 4¾" h., 2-handled, h.p. colorful
  drummer boy on dark green ground,
  marked "Stellmacher-Teplitz" 95.00
Vase, 5½" h., enameled portrait of
  woman carrying water on bronze-
  colored ground, marked "Teplitz-
  Stellmacher" 65.00
Vase, 5½" h., 2-handled, bulbous,
  applied large iridescent gold
  dandelions, orange oak leaves
  w/gold relief veining on cobalt
  blue shaded to light blue ground,
  gold trim, marked "Teplitz-
  Amphora" 195.00
Vase, 6" h., bulbous, h.p. colorful
  scene of child pointing toward
  moon on charcoal grey ground 75.00
Vase, 6 7/8" h., bulbous, h.p. orchid
  poppies & green leaves on creamy
  ivory ground, applied rigaree of 3
  mistletoe branches on body curve
  upward to neck to form overlapping
  collar of branches, leaves & berries,
  gold accents, marked "RStK,"
  ca. 1900 . . . . 90.00
Vase, 7" h., relief-molded contin-
  uous scene of infants & goats around
  body, cobalt blue, marked "Stellmacher-Teplitz" 325.00
Vase, 18" h., baluster-shaped, incised
  low relief pendant blossoming
  wisteria in shades of emerald green,
  olive green, sky blue & dusty rose
  on olive green ground, ca. 1900
  (ILLUS.) 660.00
Vase, 20¼" h., baluster-shaped
  w/reticulated rim, ferocious
  dragon coiling around body, pale
  green & ochre slightly iridescent
  glaze, marked "Turn-Teplitz-
  Bohemia-RStK," ca. 1900 . . . . 990.00

TERRA COTTA

Terra Cotta Teapot

This is redware or reddish stoneware, usually unglazed. All kinds of utilitarian objects have been made for centuries as have statuettes and large architectural pieces. Also see WEDGWOOD.

Bust of the goddess Diana, ca. 1892, 11" h. $550.00

Bust of a child w/head turned right & wearing a ruffled collar, inscribed "Rolland - 1772," 17" h...........1,700.00

Bust of Lafayette, painted to resemble stone, on a pedestal base, 19" h.....275.00

Bust of Madame Recamier, late 19th c., 23" h. 550.00

Figure of a bearded Roman robed sculptor w/tools in hand, artist-signed, 20" h. 148.00

Figure of a beautiful Grecian lady playing a mandolin, ca. 1870 ....450.00

Figure group, fisherman w/net & woman beside him w/basket on shoulder, signed, small 65.00

Medallion, portrait of Benjamin Franklin wearing fur hat, as he was observed in Paris in 1777, molded w/inscription "B. Franklin American," signed "Nini" & dated 1777, self-framed, 4½" d..........605.00

Plaque, relief figures of man & woman in wine cellar, marked "Muster-schutz," 13¼" d.................225.00

Roof tile finial, in the form of a cat, animal w/white glaze running w/brown & amber on green-glazed base, 21" l., 22" h. 375.00

Sugar bowl, cover & undertray, unglazed body w/enameled poly-chrome floral decor, impressed "Spode," 4½" h. 195.00

Teapot & cover w/foo dog finial, melon-ribbed body, straight spout, 4" h. (ILLUS.) 47.50

Teapot, cov., branch handle, bamboo-molded spout, enameled floral decor 35.00

Vases, 11½" h., flying dragons in relief, pr. 135.00

TIFFANY POTTERY

Tiffany Pottery Vases

In 1902 Louis C. Tiffany expanded Tiffany Studios to include ceramics, enamels, gold, silver and gemstones. Tiffany pottery was usually molded rather than wheel-thrown, but it is of the craftsman-type carefully finished by hand. A limited amount was produced until about 1914. It is scarce. Also see TIFFANY under Glass and METALS - Bronze.

Vase, 6¼" h., reticulated waisted cylinder w/incurved upper section pierced w/upright leafage & pendant pods, dense black glaze, signed "L.C.T." monogram, 1902-14 (hairline crack) $660.00

Vase, 6 3/8" h., waisted cylinder, pendant milk pods molded in medium relief, mustard exterior, green-glazed interior w/ochre drippings, signed, 1904-14 ....330.00

Vase, 9½" h., square form w/incised lip & undulating neck, lower body molded w/abstract stellate devices, honey brown glaze, signed, 1902-14 (ILLUS. right) 495.00

Vase, 10" h., cylindrical w/pinched lip, unglazed sides molded w/fruit-laden peach branches, green-glazed interior, signed, 1902-14 (ILLUS. left) 440.00

Vase, 11¼" h., waisted cylinder, molded on lower half w/four graduated rows of artichoke leaf-age below grasses, cream matte glaze exterior heightened w/avo-cado green, mottled blue & green interior glaze, signed, 1904-14 ....1,100.00

Vase, 20½" h., baluster-shaped, molded arrowroot leafage, mottled slightly iridescent lime green glaze, signed 2,090.00

TILES

American Encaustic Tiling Co.

Tiles have been made by potteries in the United States and abroad for many years. Apart from small tea tiles used on tables, there are also decorative tiles for fireplace, floors and walls and this is where present collector interest lies, especially in the late 19th century American-made art pottery tiles. Also see MARBLEHEAD, PHOENIX BIRD and PILKINGTON POTTERY.

American Encaustic Tiling Co., Zanesville, Ohio, maple leaf in relief, dark green glaze, 3 x 3" $25.00

American Encaustic Tiling Co., Zanesville, Ohio, winged bat in relief, glossy green glaze, 6 x 6" 90.00

American Encaustic Tiling Co., Zanesville, Ohio, geometric, glossy olive green glaze, 6 x 6" 14.00

American Encaustic Tiling Co., Zanesville, Ohio, bust portrait of child in low relief, green glaze, 6 x 6", framed 145.00

American Encaustic Tiling Co., Zanesville, Ohio, relief portraits of work-worn peasant man & woman, mustard yellow glaze, 6 x 6", pr. (ILLUS.) 425.00

American Encaustic Tiling Co., Zanesville, Ohio, "L'Automne," relief bust portrait of woman w/grapes in hair, 8½ x 8½" 125.00

American Encaustic Tiling Co., Zanesville, Ohio, 2 bird dogs in wooded area in relief, blue, brown & ivory, 18 x 6" tile in carved pine frame, overall 23 x 11 3/8" 195.00

Batchelder Tile Company, California, incised Aztec mask & symbols, yellow glaze, 4 x 4" 25.00

Beaver Falls Art Tile Company, Beaver Falls, Pennsylvania, lady in feathered hat, green, 3" d. 20.00

Boch Freres Pottery, Belgium, geometric design, grey matte glaze, 6 x 6" 15.00

California Art Tile Co., Richmond, Virginia, 5-color mission scene, matte finish, 8 x 4" 90.00

Copeland-Spode, h.p. colorful contin-

uous landscape, 19th c., pr., overall 12 x 6" 150.00

Delft Faience

Delft faience, scenic, blue & white, Holland, 19th c., 3 x 3" (ILLUS.) 20.00

Delft faience, Spanish Armada scene, blue & white, Holland, 19th c., framed, 12 x 4" 150.00

Delft faience, each w/small whale: 2 within "oxhead" corners; 1 within "spider's head" corners; 1 without corner decor; blue & white, Holland, late 17th c., 5" to 5 1/8" sq., set of 4 . . . . 302.00

Enfield Pottery & Tile Works, Enfield, Pennsylvania, blue intaglio bumble-bee, dark red clay, 3 x 3" 80.00

Enfield Pottery & Tile Works, Enfield, Pennsylvania, bold blue-green wave in low relief on white, 4 x 4" 30.00

Enfield Pottery & Tile Works, Enfield, Pennsylvania, monk bowling scene, unglazed buff-colored clay, 4 x 4" 65.00

Grueby Faience & Tile Company, Boston, Massachusetts, sailing ship, 4 x 4" 85.00

Grueby Faience & Tile Company, Boston, Massachusetts, plain, mottled green glaze, 6 x 2" 45.00

Grueby Faience & Tile Company, Boston, Massachusetts, waterlilies, green glaze, 6 x 6" 250.00

Grueby Faience & Tile Company, Boston, Massachusetts, cherubic figure w/ball in each hand, tan on blue ground, 6 x 6" 175.00

Grueby Faience & Tile Company, Boston, Massachusetts, grapes, tan glaze, 6 x 6" 335.00

Low (J. & J.G.) Art Tile Works, Chelsea, Massachusetts, geometric design, dark blue & grey glaze, dated 1881, w/tin frame, 6 x 3" 22.00

Low (J. & J.G.) Art Tile Works, Chelsea, Massachusetts, bust of beautiful woman, dated 1886, 4¼ x 4¼" 90.00

Mintons China Works

Mintons China Works, Stoke-on-Trent, Staffordshire, England, black farm- yard scene on white, artist-signed, 6 x 6" (ILLUS.) 85.00

Mintons China Works, Stoke-on-Trent, Staffordshire, England, geometric florettes, fleur-de-lis & Roman key transfer, gold & silver on black, 6 x 6"................................25.00

Mintons China Works, Stoke-on-Trent, Staffordshire, England, stylized floral, green, blue & yellow on white, 6 x 6" 45.00

Mintons China Works, Stoke-on-Trent, Staffordshire, England, brown Japanese-type floral motif, brown on beige, 6 x 6" 30.00

Moravian Pottery & Tile Works, Doyles- town, Pennsylvania, "Mayflower" ship, 4 x 4" 47.50

Moravian Pottery & Tile Works, Doyles- town, Pennsylvania, whaling ship "Bounty," tan & blue glaze, 4 x 4" 65.00

Mosaic Tile Co., Zanesville, Ohio, General Pershing, white bust on blue basalt ground; reverse "Zanesville Post No. 29 American Legion Home Building Fund Mfg. by the Mosaic Tile Co., Zanesville, Ohio," 5 x 3¼" oval...................................50.00

Mosaic Tile Co., Zanesville, Ohio, blue & rose birds & flowers, 6 x 6" 15.00

Mosaic Tile Co., Zanesville, Ohio, map of Mt. Desert Island, Maine, 6 x 6"..............................12.00

Mosaic Tile Co., Zanesville, Ohio, monkeys & owls in tree, 6 x 6" 25.00

Mosaic Tile Co., Zanesville, Ohio, black bear, 9 x 5" 110.00

Pardee (C.) Works, Perth Amboy, New Jersey, sailing ships.................55.00

Roblin Pottery, San Francisco, Cali- fornia, green.......................95.00

Rookwood Pottery, Cincinnati, Ohio, incised & underglaze slip-painted grape cluster, 6 x 6" 90.00

Rookwood Pottery, Cincinnati, Ohio, underglaze slip-painted Dutch figures, matte finish, 6 x 6"........185.00

Rookwood Pottery, Cincinnati, Ohio, underglaze slip-painted windmill scene, 6 x 6" 90.00

Rookwood Pottery, Cincinnati, Ohio, red apples in high relief on green leaves, 8 x 8"....................175.00

Rookwood Pottery, Cincinnati, Ohio, underglaze slip-painted dog portrait...........................975.00

Trent Art Tile Co., Trenton, New Jersey, profile portrait of man & woman, signed Isaac Broome, 1883-86, pr. 175.00

United States Encaustic Tile Co., Indianapolis, Indiana, King Lear type man in high relief, blue glaze, 6 x 6".............................75.00

United States Encaustic Tile Co., Indianapolis, Indiana, profiles of aged man & woman, shaded glossy brown tones, 6¼ x 6¼", pr. 175.00

TOBY MUGS & JUGS

Copeland Toby

The Toby is a figural jug or mug usually delineating a robust, genial drinking man. The name has been used in England since the mid-18th century. Copies of the English mugs and jugs were made in America.

Beswick "Micawber" Toby, 1930s, 8¾" h. $125.00

Copeland-Spode "Winston Churchill" Toby, 8½" h.......................110.00

Copeland-Spode Toby, seated &

holding a foaming pitcher, painted
florals on coat, purple pants & hat,
yellow stockings, gilt trim, made for
Ovington's, New York, 5½" h.
(ILLUS.) 110.00
Copper Lustre Toby, full seated figure
holding mug & pipe, wearing cobalt
blue coat, 4½" h. 125.00
Lenox "George Washington" Toby,
11" h. 395.00
Lenox "William Penn" Toby, Indian
head handle, white, 7" h. . .145.00 to 175.00
Lenox "William Penn" Toby, yellow
w/white handle 215.00
Lenox "William Penn" Toby, poly-
chrome 275.00
Occupied Japan "Street Vendor" Toby,
full figure w/doll in one hand & tray
of miscellaneous items in other,
7½" h. 50.00
Pearlware "Squire" Toby, sponged
brown tricorn, clothing w/additional
sponged devices, holding jug of ale,
seated on a corner chair, chamfered
rectangular base, ca. 1800, 11½" h.
(minor imperfections) 1,320.00
Prattware Toby, streaky brown tricorn,
brown shoes & ochre breeches,
long coat sponged in ochre,
(chipped) church warden pipe at his
side, holding foaming jug of ale,
chamfered square (repaired) base
covered in streaky green glaze,
ca. 1790, 9¾" h. 467.00
Rockingham glaze Toby, mottled
brown, 9 3/8" h. 185.00
Royal Doulton "Cap'n Cuttle" Toby,
full seated figure . . . . .150.00 to 190.00
Royal Doulton "Dick Turpin" Toby, full
seated figure, large 120.00
Royal Doulton "Fat Boy" Toby, full
seated figure 175.00
Royal Doulton "Johnny Appleseed"
Toby, large 260.00
Royal Doulton "Jolly Sailor" Toby 525.00
Royal Doulton "Mr. Pickwick" Toby, full
seated figure 200.00
Royal Doulton "Old Charley" Toby,
full seated figure, 6" h. 125.00
Royal Doulton "Sairy Gamp" Toby, full
seated figure . . . . .140.00 to 165.00
Royal Doulton "Sam Weller" Toby, full
seated figure, "A" mark,
4½" h. . . . . .150.00 to 195.00
Royal Doulton "Winston Churchill"
Toby, 1940s, 4½" 75.00
Shorter & Son "Beefeater" Toby, 1930s . .55.00
Shorter & Son "Coachman" Toby,
1930s. 60.00
Shorter & Son "Guardsman" Toby,
1930s. . . . . . : 50.00
Shorter & Son "HMS Old Salt" Toby,
1930s, 6½" h. 80.00
Shorter & Son "Pensioner" Toby, 1930s . .50.00

Staffordshire Toby, seated & holding
foaming glass of ale, polychrome
colors, 8½" h. 155.00
Staffordshire Toby, pearlware, brown-
streaked tricorn, breeches & shoes,
blue-washed waistcoat & streaky
green coat, holding brown jug of
foaming ale, seated on blue &
brown-edged Chippendale chair
issuing a handle (cracked) w/foliate
decor, chamfered rectangular base,
ca. 1790, 9 5/8" h. 715.00
Staffordshire Toby, transfer-printed in
Blue Willow patt., 1820s 350.00
Wedgwood "Coachman" Toby, 6" h. 110.00
Wedgwood "Town Crier" Toby,
ca. 1900 . . . . .67.00
Wood (Ralph) Toby, black (damaged)
tricorn, streaky green coat, white
waistcoat & pale yellow breeches,
church warden pipe between his
legs, holding brown-glazed foaming
beaker in one hand & a lighter
brown-glazed jug on his left knee,
seated on olive green-glazed chair
w/tall back curving to form a handle,
chamfered square base, ca. 1780,
9¾" h. 1,210.00

Pearlware Toby Jug

Yorkshire Toby, pearlware, crimson-
sponged cheeks, nose & chin &
brown hair, wearing green-scalloped
tricorn sponged on interior in rose,
yellow & brown, white waistcoat,
black- and yellow-sponged terra
cotta-colored coat, yellow breeches
& black shoes w/crimson bows,
seated on green chair above oblong
base sponged in green, brown &
crimson & w/caryatid handle affixed
to his back, ca. 1820, 9 5/8" h.
(ILLUS.) .1,430.00
Yorkshire Toby, pearlware, tricorn (rim

repaired) sponged on interior
w/stripes of blue, ochre, black &
rose, a rose stock tucked into his
white waistcoat, blue coat & ochre
breeches, holding an empty Toby jug
in his left hand & a (repaired) beaker
in his right, a pipe on his lap, seated
on green-glazed chair affixed w/a
figural handle, blue, black, ochre &
manganese dotted chamfered rectangular base, 1800-20, 10¼" h....1,045.00

VAN BRIGGLE

Van Briggle Console Bowl

*The Van Briggle Pottery was established
by Artus Van Briggle, who formerly worked
for Rookwood Pottery, in Colorado Springs,
Colo., at the turn of the century. He died in
1904 but the pottery was carried on by his
widow and others. From 1900 until 1920, the
pottery was dated. It remains in production
today, specializing in Art Pottery.*

Bookends, model of owl on base,
   Persian Rose (maroon to blue-green)
   glaze, 5" h., pr............$145.00
Bookends, model of squirrel, Persian Rose
   glaze, 6½", pr............85.00 to 100.00
Bookends, model of peacock on base,
   Persian Rose glaze, pr. 125.00
Bowl, 4" d., light green glaze, dated
   1905 ....225.00
Bowl, 4½" d., dragonflies in relief,
   black trailings over maroon
   glaze, dated 1917 ....95.00
Bowl, 5" d., light purple glaze,
   dated 1907 ....195.00
Bowl, 6" d., 3" h., leaf-molded rim,
   Turquoise Ming (royal blue over
   turquoise) glaze, after 1920 ....45.00
Bowl, 6" d., leaves & florals in relief,
   sky blue glaze, dated 1905 ....295.00
Bowl, 9" d., brown glaze, dated 1915 ...95.00
Bowl, 9" d., grey glaze, dated 1916 ....165.00
Bowl, 11" d., green glaze, dated
   1906 ....375.00
Bowl, medium green over cobalt
   blue glaze, 1907-12................135.00
Candle holders, 2-light, Persian Rose
   glaze, pr. 50.00

Chamberstick w/ring handle, maroon
   glaze, dated 1919, 7" h............150.00
Console bowl, relief-molded dragonflies, maroon glaze, 9" d. 125.00
Console bowl w/flower frog, green
   glaze, dated 1916, 13" d. bowl,
   2 pcs. (ILLUS.) 200.00
Console bowl w/large kneeling nude
   beside goose as flower holder,
   Turquoise Ming glaze, 15 x 10" bowl,
   2 pcs. 235.00
Console set: 9 x 4" shell-shaped bowl
   & pr. candlesticks molded as 3
   upright shells; blue glaze, 3 pcs. 65.00
Cup & saucer, hexagonal, blue glaze ...35.00
Flower bowl w/flower frog, Kelly green
   glaze, 1920s, 6" d., bowl, 2 pcs......150.00
Flower bowl w/figural duck flower
   frog, relief-molded stylized leaves,
   blue glaze, 6½" d. bowl, 2 pcs. 60.00
Flower frog, model of a turtle, Persian
   Rose glaze, dated 1914 ....75.00
Lamp w/original shade, model of a
   Cocker Spaniel dog, Persian Rose
   (rose to maroon) glaze 195.00
Lamp w/original shade, model of a
   squirrel, Turquoise Ming glaze......125.00
Model of a donkey, Persian Rose glaze,
   1923 ....65.00
Model of an owl, Turquoise Ming glaze,
   9¼" h. 85.00
Model of a Scotty dog, blue glaze,
   ca. 1940 ....65.00
Night light, model of an owl, Persian
   Rose glaze, yellow & black glass
   eyes, 9½" h. (electrified) 340.00
Paperweight, model of a rabbit
   w/pointed ears, Persian Rose glaze,
   3½" l. 90.00
Pitcher, 9" h., turquoise glaze,
   ca. 1930 ....35.00
Plaque, pierced to hang, relief bust
   of Indian maiden "Little Star,"
   Turquoise Ming glaze, 6"...........45.00
Plate, 8½" d., relief-molded poppy
   blossom & foliage, royal blue,
   maroon, white & blue-green matte
   glaze, dated 1902 ....1,760.00
Rose bowl, green glaze, dated 1916,
   4" h. 100.00
Tile, floral decor, 6" sq., dated 1908 ...350.00
Tiles, poppy pods in relief on grey-
   blue ground, 6" sq., pr. 275.00
Vase, 3" h., relief-molded butterflies,
   Turquoise Ming glaze..............30.00
Vase, 4½" h., relief-molded leaves on
   tan shaded to green glaze, dated
   1917 ....125.00
Vase, 5" h., cobalt blue w/brown
   highlights over chocolate brown
   glaze, dated 1905 ....225.00
Vase, 6¼" h., relief-molded yucca
   pods & leaves on blue glaze,
   1908-11..........................135.00

Vase, 7" h., cylindrical, relief-molded
leaves, Turquoise Ming glaze.......120.00
Vase, 8½" h., 2-handled, bulbous,
long-stemmed flowers in relief, blue
glaze, dated 1914 ....250.00

Indian Head Vase

Vase, 11" h., 3 Indian heads in relief,
Turquoise Ming glaze (ILLUS.) 135.00
Vase, 13" h., green butterflies in
relief, Mountain Craig (green & brown)
glaze, 1920s......................225.00
Vase, 15" h., cobalt blue over light
blue glaze, 1920 ....295.00
Vase, 16" h., "Despondency," Turquoise
Ming glaze, after 1920 ....200.00
Vase, 16" h., Yucca leaves in relief,
plum glaze, dated 1916 ....475.00

WARWICK

Warwick Portrait Vase

*Numerous collectors have turned their
attention to the productions of the Warwick
China Manufacturing Company that operated in Wheeling, West Virginia, from 1887
until 1951. Prime interest would seem to lie
in items produced before 1914 that were*
*decorated with decal portraits of beautiful
women, monks and Indians. Fraternal
Order items, as well as floral and fruit decorated items are also popular with collectors.
Also see FRATERNAL ORDER COL-
LECTIBLES.*

Cake plate, white w/roses decor,
gold edge, large $48.00
Cheese dish & dome lid, white
w/pink & white floral sprays & gold
scrollwork, gold-flecked ornate
handle & scalloped rim 52.00
Chocolate pot, cov., white w/lavender
roses decor 89.00
Creamer & sugar bowl, white w/gold
trim, pr. 40.00
Creamer & sugar bowl, floral decor
on brown ground, pr................50.00
Jardiniere, blue & white w/gold
decor, 7" d., 7" h. 65.00
Jardiniere, floral decor on deep red ...100.00
Mug, fruit decor on dark ground 20.00
Mug, portrait of Indian 75.00
Pitcher, cider, 7¾" h., bulbous,
portrait of monk on dark ground 150.00
Pitcher, tankard, Shrine emblem decor,
dated 1909 ....150.00
Pitcher, tankard, monk portrait.......250.00
Pitcher w/ice lip, 10½" h., floral decor
on ivory ground....................85.00
Plate, 6½" d., white w/wild roses
decor 35.00
Plate, child's nursery rhyme decor 50.00
Vase, 8" h., pillow-shaped, portrait
of beautiful woman on yellow
(ILLUS.).........................165.00
Vase, 10" h., 8" d., gold berry decor
on brown ground, loga mark 110.00
Vase, 10½" h., twig handles, stork
decor on white ground............150.00
Vase, 11½" h., portrait of beautiful
woman on red ground 185.00
Vase, 12" h., portrait of beautiful
woman on brown ground 250.00
Vase, twig handles, portrait of
Gypsy woman...........125.00 to 185.00

WEDGWOOD

*Reference here is to the famous pottery
established by Josiah Wedgwood in 1759 in
England. Numerous types of wares have been
produced through the years to the present.
Also see COMMEMORATIVE PLATES,
FLOW BLUE and JASPER WARE.*

BASALTES
Bust of Matthew Prior, wearing
tasseled cap & cloak over an
embroidered waistcoat, on circular
socle, ca. 1780, 7 1/8" h. $660.00

Bust of John Locke

Bust of John Locke, head turned to
the right & w/drapery over his
shoulders, on a "stovepipe" support, on circular socle w/laurel
leaf border, Wedgwood & Bentley,
1769-80, 8¼" h. (ILLUS.) 1,870.00
Candlesticks, triangular base, shaft
w/three sphinx caryatids supporting
a candle nozzle w/engine-turned
vertical flutes, ca. 1805, 6 1/8" h.,
pr. 715.00
Figure of a nymph, nude figure seated
on a high rockwork base molded
w/foliage & pierced w/aperatures,
11¼" h. 550.00
Model of a bulldog, white glass
eyes w/brown centers, marked
Wedgwood only, 2 x 5", 2¾" h. 350.00
Vase, 4½" h., bulbous, ca. 1880 . . . . . . 125.00
Vases, 7" h., ovoid, gilt floral diaper
ground decorated in bronzed & gilt
relief w/four classical medallions
flanked by floral garlands pendant
from rams' heads, foot & base
w/floral, foliate, egg-and-tongue
& cable borders, late 19th c., pr. . . . 1,100.00

CALENDAR TILES

1892 "1744 Mount Vernon - 1892," blue-
grey 65.00
1896 Trinity Church, Boston, brown or
blue, each 65.00
1897 Old Federal Street Theatre 65.00
1899 Washington Elm, "Under this
tree — Washington took command
of the American Army,"
brown . . . . 45.00 to 65.00
1902 Old North Church, Boston, brown . . 60.00
1903 Elmwood — Home of James
Russell Lowell, brown 60.00

1904 United States Frigate "Constitution" (Old Ironsides), brown 60.00
1905 The Stephenson & Twentieth
Century Locomotives, brown 45.00
1906 Jones, McDuffee & Stratton Co.
Store, Franklin St., printing at top &
bottom, brown . . . . 55.00 to 65.00
1907 Harvard Stadium, description
below picture in lower right corner,
light brown . . . . 55.00 to 60.00
1908 Harvard Medical School,
brown . . . . 55.00 to 62.50
1909 New Museum of Fine Arts, Boston,
brown 60.00
1911 U.S. Frigate "Constitution" & U.S.
Battleship "Florida," 5 lines printing
under each picture, brown . . . 45.00 to 58.00
1912 Cunard Line Dock (New) Boston,
6 descriptive lines, brown 35.00
1915 Boston Custom House Tower, 28
stories high, brown 60.00
1916 Massachusetts Institute of Tech-
nology, light brown 58.00
1917 Section of U.S. Navy Yard,
Boston, light brown 60.00
1918 Boston Lighthouse & 3 lines of
description, brown 60.00
1922 Cathedral Church of St. Paul -
erected 1820, brown . . . . 55.00 to 65.00
1923, The Minute Man, Concord,
Massachusetts, brown 55.00
1926 Coolidge Homestead, brown 57.50
1927 Longfellow's Wayside Inn,
Sudbury, brown 55.00
1928 Plymouth Rock, brown 60.00
1929 House of Seven Gables, Salem,
brown 42.50

CREAMWARE

Plate with Garibaldi Portrait

Compote, 8¼" d., 4¾" h., rope-twist
rim handles, reticulated foliate
scroll & basketweave bowl 175.00
Dish, shell-shaped, shaded brown,
green, yellow, orange, grey & blue
scene of mother seated between 2
small children & nursing her infant in

a hilly landscape, rim edged in ochre, signed Emile Lessore & dated 1861, 8 3/8" w. 412.00

Fruit stand, central roundel w/grey, maroon, green, yellow & salmon scene of couple seated beneath a tree, underside transfer-printed in brown & colorfully enameled w/butterfly & 3 sprigs, 3 applied green & ochre acanthus-molded S-scroll feet, signed E. Lessore, ca. 1864, 9¼" d...550.00

Model of a polar bear, ca. 1927, 10 x 4 1/8", 7" h. 395.00

Plate, 13" d., h.p. inscribed sepia portrait of Garibaldi within ochre rim, impressed mark & dated 1887 (ILLUS.) 425.00

Tray, brown, blue, mauve, olive green & yellow interior scene of mother & 2 children building a house of cards, rim edged in gold & brown, signed E. Lessore & dated 1864, 16 5/8" l....825.00

Tumblers, embossed hunting scene w/silver lustre sky, 9 oz., set of 8 ...150.00

Vase, 5 5/8" h., brown, blue, grey, yellow & orange flautist seated between his sweetheart & a dog at front & young shepherd playing a bagpipe & seated between a reclining shepherdess & goat reverse, ochre-edged rim w/foliate border, signed E. Lessore & dated 1861 ....385.00

DRABWARE

Dessert service: pr. circular sauce tureens w/covers & stands, ladle & pierced ladle, oval dish, oblong dish & 8 plates; each printed in black & enameled in rose, yellow, blue, iron-red & shades of green w/floral sprays, rims edged in blue enamel, ca. 1820, 16 pcs................1,210.00

Game pie dish & cover w/rabbit finial, hunting scenes & pendant game on sides, 8½" d.....................235.00

Jug, white cherubs in relief on glazed buff ground, ca. 1830, 7" h.........200.00

Jug, panels w/classical ladies in relief, ca. 1820, marked Wedgwood only, 5¾" d., 8" h. 230.00

Vase, 10" h., swan-form handles, 3-section, blue & white, ca. 1785 ....400.00

ROSSO ANTICO

Candlesticks, enameled Capri decor, marked Wedgwood only, 6" h., pr. ..495.00

Milk jug, redware decorated in black relief w/band of hieroglyphs including winged discs, sphinx, Apis & a canopic urn above strapwork border, interior glazed, ca. 1810, 2¾" h. 357.00

Rosso Antico Teapot

Teapot, cov., squat cylindrical redware body w/Egyptian inspired motif, fluted cover w/crocodile knop, short spout, angular handle (ILLUS.) 650.00

TERRA COTTA

Creamer & cov. sugar bowl, raised black jasper Egyptian motifs on terra cotta, marked Wedgwood England, pr....................................250.00

Vase, 2 1/8" h., 1½" d., 2 handles w/mask terminals, enameled pink florals & green foliage on brick red terra cotta ground, marked Wedgwood only 180.00

MISCELLANEOUS

Fairyland Lustre Bowl

Bowl, 6½" octagon, Dragon Lustre, interior w/fruit, marked Wedgwood, England 375.00

Bowl, 7" octagon, 3½" h., Butterfly Lustre, interior & exterior decor, marked Wedgwood, England 495.00

Bowl, 9 5/8" octagon, Fairyland Lustre, exterior w/"Dana-Castle on a Road" within "Cobble Bead" borders, interior w/"Fairy in a Cage," Portland vase mark, ca. 1917 (ILLUS.) 1,100.00

Bowl, 11 3/8" d., Dragon & Butterfly Lustre, mottled crimson-orange exterior w/three gold dragons chasing the sacred pearl, blue & red mother-of-pearl lustre interior w/five gold butterflies & a central medallion, Portland vase mark, ca. 1920 ....440.00

Box & cover w/widow finial, Dragon
Lustre, deep mottled green exterior
w/gold dragons & trim, mother-
of-pearl lustre interior, 5 7/8" d.,
5" h. 495.00

Box, cov., hexagonal, Insect Lustre,
cover w/gold spider in his web,
interior w/captive flies & other
insects, mother-of-pearl lustre
w/blue, red & brown stainings,
Portland vase mark, ca. 1920,
3¾" w. 440.00

Bulb planter, hedgehog form, light
blue glaze, 9" l. 450.00

Coffee service: cov. coffee pot, cov.
sugar bowl, milk jug & coffee can &
saucer; porcelain, powdered-ruby
ground reserved w/colorful butterflies, outlines & borders w/gold-
printed decor, ca. 1920, 5 pcs. 550.00

Compote, 6" d., 3½" h., ram's heads
& pendant grapes on lilac ground ...150.00

Dish, Fairyland Lustre, mottled blue
exterior, pale green interior w/foo
dog decor & gold trim, 2½" d. 75.00

Dish, majolica, leaf-shaped, dated Oct.
1867, 8¼ x 8½" 105.00

Figure of "Psyche" seated on rock,
majolica, modeled after Falconet,
deep blue, 19th c., 8" h. 1,150.00

Flower holder, salt-glazed, dark blue
florals & leaves in relief on light
grey ground, marked Wedgwood
only, 3¾" d., 5½" h. ......275.00 to 300.00

Match holder w/striker on base,
majolica, greens & browns, 4¾" d.,
3½" h. 85.00

Melba cup, Butterfly Lustre, pearlized
exterior w/three lustred butterflies,
spattered orange lustre interior
w/gold butterflies, 4" d., 3" h. 295.00

Mug, 3-handled, Butterfly Lustre,
mottled orange & blue w/gilt butterflies, 2¼" h. 145.00

Plate, 9½" d., commemorative, "Birth-
place of Longfellow, Portland,
Maine," blue transfer on white
(ILLUS.) 38.50

Plate, 9½" d., commemorative, "Old
North Church, Boston," dark blue
transfer on white 40.00

Plate, 10" d., commemorative,
"Bennington Battlefield Monument
1887-1891," blue transfer on white ...38.00

Plate, 10¼" d., Month series,
"August," brown transfer of girl
feeding chickens, green, yellow &
pink trim 135.00

Plate, 10¼" w., shell-shaped,
Moonlight Lustre.................425.00

Plate, 14" d., commemorative, "State
House, Boston 1900," blue transfer
on white..........................45.00

Sauce tureen, cov., Fallow Deer
patt., blue transfer on white,
7 x 4¼" 85.00

Sweetmeat jar, tan soldiers, elephants
& chariots in relief at bottom &
multicolored florals w/gold trim
above, silverplate cover, 4" h. 125.00

Wedgwood-Whieldon Cauliflower Ware

Tea caddy & pr. milk jugs, Cauliflower
ware, molded cream-colored cauliflower florettes above green leaves,
Wedgwood-Whieldon, ca. 1765,
w/tiny hair crack & spout chip in
one jug, 3¾" h. tea caddy &
4½" h. jugs, 3 pcs. (ILLUS.) 880.00

Vase, 4¼" h., 2½" d., Hummingbird
Lustre, h.p. colorful hummingbirds in
flight w/gold trim on mottled blue
ground exterior, mottled flame
lustre interior, gold trim 175.00

Vase, 9" h., Fairyland Lustre "Candle-
mass" vase, candles w/human heads
& pixies climbing bell ropes in
panels, all outlined in gold, Portland
vase mark........................1,195.00

Vase, 9 5/8" h., 4 5/8" w. across
ornate gold handles, overall h.p.
pink roses & green foliage, w/cobalt
blue & ornate gold trim, ca. 1900 ....398.00

Vase, 9¾" h., 4¾" d., Dragon Lustre,
mottled blue lustre exterior
w/dragon outlined in gold, ornate
design at top, base & neck interior ..465.00

Vase, 15" h., flow blue Ferara Harbor
scene decor, dated 1880 ....165.00

Wedgwood Commemorative Plate

WELLER

This pottery was made from 1872 to 1945 at a pottery established originally by Samuel A. Weller at Fultonham, Ohio, and moved in 1882 to Zanesville. Numerous lines were produced and listings below are by the pattern or lines. Most desirable is the Sicardo line. Also see "Special Focus" on SUGAR BOWLS.

ALVIN (1928)

Alvin Bud Vase

Vase, bud, 8½" h., tree trunk
w/realistically molded & colored
apples (ILLUS.) $62.00
Vase, 12" h., twig handles, tree
trunk w/realistically molded &
colored apples 65.00

ARDSLEY (1920-28)

Bulb bowl, handled, water lily form,
5" ....55.00 to 80.00
Candle holders, water lily form,
green matte glaze, 3" h., pr. 50.00
Candlestick, lily pad form base, green
matte glaze, 3" h. (single)...........35.00
Console set: 16½" d., 3½" h. bowl,
9½" h. Kingfisher flower frog & pr.
candlesticks; molded cattails &
grasses, green matte glaze, 4 pcs. ..275.00
Vase, 7" h., globular sides of sword-
shaped green leaves forming irregular
rim interspersed w/purple iris
blossoms 75.00
Vase, 9" h., molded water lily at
base, cattails & grasses body,
green matte glaze 35.00

Vase, double, 9½" h., molded water
lily at base, cattails & grasses body,
green matte glaze 62.50

ATLAS (1934-40)

Bowl, 4" d., rounded sides, star-
shaped opening, creamy ivory
interior & powder blue exterior 32.00
Candle holders, downward curving star
shape, powder blue & creamy ivory,
pr..............................25.00
Vase, 6" h., star-shaped, creamy ivory
interior & powder blue exterior 38.00

AURELIAN (1898-1910)

Ewer, 3-footed, slip-painted florals,
glossy brown glaze, 8" h. 250.00
Jardiniere & pedestal base, slip-
painted chrysanthemums, glossy brown
glaze, artist-signed, overall 39" h.,
2 pcs...........................1,500.00
Pitcher, tankard, 12" h., slip-painted
boysenberries & green leaves,
glossy brown glaze, artist-
signed.........................310.00
Vase, 6" h., footed, slip-painted
florals, glossy brown glaze,
artist-signed 175.00
Vase, 13" h., slip-painted florals,
glossy brown glaze, artist-signed ...350.00
Vase, 18" h., slip-painted chrysanthemums, glossy brown glaze,
artist-signed 595.00

AURORO (ca. 1900)

Vase, 4¾" h., 3¼" d., slip-painted
daisies on mottled light blue &
white ground, high gloss glaze 425.00
Vase, 8 3/8" h., mottled grey, pink
& pastels, high gloss glaze 195.00

BALDIN (1915-20)

Baldin Jardiniere & Pedestal

Bowl, 7" d., tan apples & branches molded in low relief against midnight blue 75.00

Jardiniere & pedestal base, realistically painted apples & branches molded in low relief against earth tones, overall 34" h., 2 pcs. (ILLUS.) 585.00

Umbrella stand, realistically painted apples & branches molded in low relief against earth tones 360.00

Vase, bud, 5" h., realistically painted apples & branches molded in low relief against earth tone browns 45.00

Vase, 9½" h., cylindrical, w/band of realistically painted apples & branches molded in low relief against brown earth tones 95.00

Vase, 12½" h., realistically painted apples & branches molded in low relief against midnight blue 125.00

BARCELONA (1920s)

Barcelona Vase

Basket, hanging-type, cone-shaped w/rounded bottom, ridged body w/colorful floral medallion decor .85.00 to 120.00

Candle holders, ridged body w/stenciled stylized florals, pr. 72.50

Vase, 9" h., 2-handled, ridged body w/colorful floral medallion decor (ILLUS.) 100.00

BESLINE (1920-25)

Console bowl, tan lustre decor against orange ground 65.00

Vase, 8" h., tan lustre woodbine decor against orange ground 400.00

BLOSSOM (mid-late 1930s)

Basket, rounded sides, irregular scalloped rim, molded pink flowers & green leaves, blue matte glaze, 6" h. 25.00

Cornucopia vase, flaring scalloped rim,

molded pink flowers & green leaves, green matte glaze, 6" h. 16.00

Cornucopia vase, molded pink flowers & green leaves, blue matte glaze, 8½" h. 20.00

Vase, 7½" h., molded pink flowers & green leaves, blue or green matte glaze, each 14.00

BLUE DRAPERY (1915-20)

Candle holders, clusters of roses pendant from nozzle, vertical folded blue matte drapery ground, 9" h., pr. 80.00

Jardiniere, clusters of roses pendant from rim, vertical folded blue matte drapery ground, 5½" h. 60.00

Planter, clusters of roses pendant from rim, vertical folded blue matte drapery ground, 12" l. 45.00

Vases, 6½" h., clusters of roses pendant from rim, vertical folded blue matte drapery ground, pr. 75.00

Vase, 8" h., clusters of roses pendant from rim, vertical folded blue matte drapery ground 44.00

Wall pocket, clusters of roses pendant from rim, vertical folded blue matte drapery ground, 9" h. 45.00

BLUE WARE (pre-1920)

Jardiniere, 3-footed, ivory relief of classical ladies against deep blue ground, 9" h. 130.00

Vase, 7½" h., ivory relief of classical lady against deep blue ground 125.00

Vase, 10" h., ivory relief of classical lady against deep blue ground 115.00

Vase, 13" h., ivory relief of classical lady holding grapes against deep blue ground 210.00

BONITO (1927-33)

Weller

Weller Pottery

Incised Weller Marks - 1927-1930s

Bowl, 5" d., florals & foliage on cream ground, artist-signed 40.00

Bowl, 6½" d., wildflowers & leaves on cream ground, artist-signed 50.00

Flower pot, h.p. blue, green & brown floral decor on cream ground, 4¾" h. 65.00

Flower pot, h.p. flowers & leaves w/multicolor stripes on cream ground 55.00

Vase, 6" h., colorful flowers on cream
  ground, signed Pillsbury 90.00
Vase, 10" h., 8½" d., h.p. florals
  on cream ground 117.00
Vase, 12" h., handled, h.p. florals &
  foliage on cream ground 150.00

BOUQUET (1930s)

Bouquet Vase

Pitcher, 9½" h., straight handle,
  bulbous base, yellow jonquil blossom
  & bud in relief on slate blue matte
  finish ground 46.00
Vase, 5½" h., white dogwood blossoms
  in relief on soft green matte
  finish ground (ILLUS.) 37.50
Vase, 12" h., white lily-of-the-valley
  blossoms in relief on slate blue
  matte finish ground 55.00

BRETON (1920s)

Bowl, 4" d., bands of florals in low
  relief at shoulder, brown matte
  finish. 35.00
Vase, 6" h., band of florals in low
  relief at shoulder, green matte
  finish. 18.00
Vase, 9" h., band of florals in
  low relief at shoulder, brown
  matte finish 45.00

BRIGHTON (1915)

Flower frog, model of a Flamingo on
  leafy base, 6"h. 110.00
Flower frog, model of a Swan, 5" 145.00
Flower frog, model of a Woodpecker . . . 70.00
Model of a Bluebird, 3½" h. 65.00
Model of a Kingfisher on a tree stump,
  9" h. 155.00
Model of Penguins (2) on textured
  base, 5" h. 140.00
Model of a Woodpecker, 6" h. 111.50

BURNTWOOD (1910)

Plate, 11" d., etched fish, creamy tan
  to brown w/brown border bands 45.00
Urn, etched birds & stylized florals on
  stippled creamy tan to brown
  w/brown border bands, 6½" 80.00

Vase, 8" h., hexagon-shaped, etched
  grape clusters, vines & leaves,
  creamy tan to brown w/brown border
  bands 115.00

CAMEO (1935-39)

Basket, white relief florals on matte
  powder blue, 7½" h. 32.50
Bowl, 4" d., 3-footed, white relief
  florals on matte coral 25.00
Console bowl, white relief florals on
  matte powder blue, 15" l., 3" h. 47.50
Cornucopia-vases, white relief florals
  on soft green, 6¾" h., pr. 22.00
Umbrella stand, white relief florals on
  matte coral 350.00
Vase, 7" h., white relief florals on
  matte powder blue 20.00
Vase, 9¾" h., handled, white relief
  florals on matte powder blue or
  coral, each 25.00
Vase, 13" h., bulbous w/reticulated
  handles at shoulder, white relief
  florals on matte powder blue 57.00

CHASE (late 1920s)

Vase, 5½" h., bulbous, white relief
  fox hunt scene on deep blue 165.00
Vase, 8¾" h., flask-shaped w/three
  neck openings, white relief fox hunt
  scene on deep blue 225.00
Vase, 10½" h., white relief fox
  hunt scene on deep blue 135.00

CLAYWOOD (1910)

Bowl, 6½" d., 2" h., incised stylized
  floral panels, tan to dark brown
  matte finish 45.00
Humidor, cov., incised stylized
  floral panels, tan to dark brown
  matte finish, 5" d., 4" h. 65.00
Mug, stylized florals on stippled
  ground, tan to dark brown matte
  finish. 60.00
Vase, 3" h., semi-ovoid, incised butter-
  flies against stippled ground, tan
  to dark brown matte finish 42.50
Vase, 8½" h., cylindrical w/flaring
  base, creamy tan pine cone & branch
  against dark brown matte finish 50.00

CLINTON IVORY (pre-1914)

Jardiniere & pedestal, florals in relief
  & highlighted in brown on ivory,
  matte finish, overall 27½" h.,
  2 pcs. 320.00
Planter, 4-footed, ladies' heads,
  poppies & foliage in relief & highlighted in brown on ivory, matte
  finish. 65.00
Umbrella stand, florals in relief & high-
  lighted in brown on ivory, matte
  finish, 19½" h. 80.00

COPPERTONE (Late 1920s)

Coppertone Vase

Bowl w/figural frog seated on rim,
blothcy semi-gloss green over
brown glaze, 6" d. 78.00

Candle holder, model of a turtle
w/pond lily candle nozzle on back,
blotchy semi-gloss green over brown
glaze, 3" h. . . . . .90.00 to 110.00

Console bowl w/figural frog seated on
rim, w/flower holder, blotchy semi-
gloss green over brown glaze,
10½" w., 2" h. 185.00

Flower holder, figural frog w/pond
lily 110.00

Model of a frog, 4½" h. 90.00

Model of a turtle, 4" l. 75.00

Model of a turtle, 6" l. 80.00

Vase, 6½" h., cylindrical w/flaring
top, blotchy semi-gloss green over
brown glaze. 20.00

Vase, 8" h., frog handles, lily pads
on sides, blotchy semi-gloss green
over brown glaze (ILLUS.) 160.00

Vase, 9" h., figural frog on side,
blotchy semi-gloss green over
brown glaze. 85.00

Vase, 12" h., frogs seated on lily
pad base, semi-gloss green over
brown glaze. .165.00

CORNISH (1933)

Candle holders, molded spray of
leaves w/pendant berries, brown
semi-gloss finish, pr. 30.00

Vase, 6" h., small closed
handles, canted sides, molded
spray of leaves w/pendant berries,
blue semi-gloss finish 45.00

Vase, 10" h., closed handles, cylindrical w/flaring base, molded spray
of leaves w/pendant berries, blue
semi-gloss finish. 43.00

DARSIE (1935)

Flower pot, cord & tassels molded in
relief, ivory glaze, 3" h. 17.50

Vase, 6½" h., cord & tassels molded
in relief, pale blue glaze 30.00

Vase, 9" to 10" h., cord & tassels
molded in relief, turquoise glaze,
each .25.00 to 30.00

Wall pocket, cord & tassels molded in
relief, ivory glaze, 8¾" h. 48.00

DELSA (1930s)

Ewer, embossed pansies on stippled
white ground, 7" h. 25.00

Vase, 6" h., embossed rose florals on
stippled blue ground 20.00

Vase, 9" h., embossed florals on
stippled white ground 15.00

DICKENSWARE 1ST LINE (1897-98)

Honey jug, gold-flecked handle, slip-
painted flowering shrub in autumnal
colors, glossy brown glaze, 5½" h. 85.00

Mug, slip-painted bust portrait of an
Indian Chief in full headdress, glossy
brown glaze . . . . .495.00 to 575.00

Letter holder, slip-painted clover blossoms, glossy brown glaze, artist-
signed. 82.00

Pitcher, tankard, 12" h., slip-painted
cherries & foliage, glossy brown
glaze. 450.00

Vase, 9½" h., slip-painted berries &
leaves, deep brown glossy glaze 135.00

Vase, 11½" h., double gourd form,
slip-painted thistle decor, glossy
brown glaze. .425.00

DICKENSWARE 2ND LINE TOBACCO JARS (1900-05)

Turk Tobacco Jar

Captain. 550.00

Chinaman 475.00

Irishman 550.00

Turk (ILLUS.) 550.00

DICKENSWARE 2ND LINE (1900-05)

Ewer, sgraffito fish, shaded grey matte
finish, artist-signed, 11½" h. 450.00

Jug, sgraffito portrait of monk 375.00

Lamp base, sgraffito portrait, "Dombey and Son" 650.00
Mug, sgraffito full-length portrait of monk drinking from stein, artist-signed 275.00

Dickensware 2nd Line Pitcher

Pitcher, tankard, sgraffito bust portrait of Indian in full headdress, "Chief Hollowhorn Bear," artist-signed (ILLUS.) 1,150.00
Vase, 6 x 4", pillow-shaped, sgraffito portrait of Dutch girl 425.00
Vase, 6¾" h., sgraffito stag's head 425.00
Vase, 7½" h., sgraffito portrait of Indian "Ghost Bull," shaded russet to green matte finish 1,150.00
Vase, 7½" h., sgraffito seagulls 500.00
Vase, 8" h., sgraffito full-length portrait of lady golfer . . . . . 475.00 to 550.00
Vase, 9½" h., sgraffito full-length portrait of gentleman & boy, "Dombey & Son" 700.00
Vase, 10" h., 2-handled, sgraffito portrait of Indian, shaded tan to green matte finish, artist-signed 875.00
Vase, 10½" h., sgraffito bust portrait of cavalier, artist-signed & dated 1901 . . . . 450.00
Vase, 16" h., sgraffito scene inscribed "Don Quixote and Sancho Setting Out," after G. Dore, artist-signed 1,500.00

DRESDEN (ca. 1905)
Mug, slip-painted windmills & water scene, blue matte finish . . . 295.00 to 325.00
Vase, 7" h., slip-painted windmills & boats scene, blue matte finish, artist-signed 400.00

EOCEAN (1898-1918)

Eocean Vase

Jardiniere, slip-painted purple & white iris on cream shaded to grey-green ground, 10½ x 8" 165.00
Mug, 2-handled, slip-painted purple plums on shaded grey ground, artist-signed, 4" h. 330.00
Mug, slip-painted cherries decor, 6" h. 275.00
Pitcher, tankard, 10½" h., slip-painted plums decor 150.00
Pitcher, tankard, slip-painted grapes decor, artist-signed, large 450.00
Umbrella stand, cylindrical w/ruffled rim, slip-painted iris blossoms in delicate shades of pink, ochre, orange & green on cream shaded to grey-green ground, ca. 1910, 21¼" h. 465.00
Vase, 3½" h., slip-painted blackberries decor 52.00
Vase, 8" h., slip-painted pansy decor on shaded light to deep grey ground (ILLUS.) 250.00
Vase, 9½" h., 4-handled, slip-painted stork decor on cream shaded to dark grey ground 715.00
Vase, 12" h., slip-painted raspberries decor 190.00
Vase, 13" h., 8¼" d., slip-painted pink & white roses on cream shaded to green ground, artist-signed 375.00

ETCHED MATT (1905-10)
Vase, 6½" h., etched stylized florals & leaves, shades of orange & tan, matte finish 350.00
Vase, 8" h., etched yellow roses on thorny branches, green matte finish 135.00
Vase, 10" h., waisted, stylized florals & leaves, shades of bittersweet red, orange & tan, matte finish 155.00

Etched Matt Vase

Vase, 15¼" h., etched portrait of a
woman w/wind-blown hair, matte
finish (ILLUS.) 625.00

ETNA (1906)
Jardiniere, relief-molded & painted
realistic red roses on shaded light to
dark grey, 10½ x 8½" 90.00
Mug, relief-molded & painted realistic
thistle decor on shaded grey 75.00
Vase, 6" h., bulbous, relief-molded &
painted realistic pansies on
shaded grey.....................75.00
Vase, 8½" h., relief-molded & painted
realistic grape cluster on shaded
light to dark grey 75.00
Vase, 8½" h., relief-molded & painted
realistic pink floral decor on shaded
grey 95.00

FLEMISH (1915-28)

Flemish Jardiniere

Basket, hanging-type, florals in relief
on light-colored basketweave matte
finish ground.....................75.00
Compote & cover w/floral finial,

8½" h., band of pink florals in relief
on foot, cream matte finish ground ..125.00
Ink well, robins seated on top beneath
rose encrusted arch, tan & cream
matte finish ground, 7 x 4½" 125.00
Jardiniere, panels of cream-colored
florals in relief on stippled ground,
7" h. (ILLUS.) 42.50
Jardiniere & pedestal base, cream-
colored florals in relief on tan
ground, overall 40" h., 2 pcs. 625.00
Tub, handled, roses in relief on tan
basketweave ground, 3½" h.........30.00
Vase, 8½" h., cylindrical, pink rose in
relief on basketweave ground 35.00
Vase, 14" h., waisted cylinder,
magnolia blossom in relief on brown
ground 150.00

FLORETTA (1904)
Jug, slip-painted grapes in low relief,
brown glaze......................65.00
Mug, slip-painted grapes in low relief,
on shaded brown ground, 5½" h. ...110.00
Pitcher, tankard, 12" h., slip-painted
clusters of grapes in low relief on
brown ground 90.00
Vase, 6" h., slip-painted clusters of
grapes in low relief on shaded brown
ground 40.00
Vase, 7½" h., slip-painted purple
grapes in low relief on oatmeal grey
ground 79.00
Vase, 9" h., slip-painted cherries in low
relief on grey ground...............67.50

FOREST (1915)

Forest Planter

Basket, hanging-type, realistically
molded & colored forest scene,
10" d. 175.00
Jardiniere & pedestal base, realistically
molded & colored forest scene,
12½" d., overall 29" h., 2 pcs. 650.00
Pitcher, realistically molded & colored
forest scene, high gloss glaze 150.00
Planter, tub-shaped, realistically
molded & colored forest scene,
4" h. 50.00
Planter, realistically molded & colored
forest scene, 22" l., 11" w., 11" h.
(ILLUS.).........................650.00

Umbrella stand, realistically molded &
  colored forest scene 425.00
Vase, 8" h., realistically molded &
  colored forest scene 62.00
Vase, 12" h., realistically molded &
  colored forest scene 145.00

GLENDALE (1920s)
Candle holders, birds & nest w/eggs
  in low relief, subdued colors 75.00
Flower frog, florals & foliage in low
  relief, shades of blue, tan & deep
  grey 25.00
Plate w/flower frog in the form of
  bird's nest w/eggs, seagulls & waves
  in low relief, shades of blue, white,
  & tan & deep grey, 15" d. 265.00
Vase, 4" h., nesting bird in low relief,
  shades of deep grey, tan & yellow . . .105.00
Vase, 8½" h., slightly ovoid, lovebirds
  seated on branch in low relief, blue,
  pink, yellow & tan 240.00
Vase, 12" h., baluster form, bird seated
  on branch amidst daisies & leaves
  w/hovering butterfly, tan, blue &
  yellow 350.00
Wall pocket, double, 2 flower holders
  in the form of tree trunks flanking
  pocket w/bird & nest of eggs in low
  relief, shades of blue, tan & russet,
  7" h. 185.00

HOBART (1920s)
Console bowl & flower frog in the form
  of 2 nude ladies rising from the sea,
  turquoise blue matte finish, 12" d.,
  2½" h., 2 pcs. 140.00
Figure of an Art Deco girl, standing
  w/outstretched arms & grasping
  the hem of her long skirt, pastel pink
  matte finish, 7½" h. 68.00
Flower frog, figure of a nude lady in
  classical pose on pedestal base
  pierced for flowers on outside edge,
  white matte finish, 8" h. 75.00
Flower holder, figure of an Art Deco
  girl w/outstretched arms grasping
  the hem of her long skirt, 2 tubular
  vases concealed by skirt, soft green
  matte finish, 8¼" w., 11" h. 98.00
Wall pocket, Art Deco girl standing
  w/outstretched arms & grasping the
  hem of her long skirt, turquoise blue
  matte finish 85.00

HUDSON (1920s-1935)
Vase, 5½" h., underglaze slip-painted
  pansies, deep blue matte glaze 145.00
Vase, 6" h., 2-handled, underglaze
  slip-painted florals, grey shaded to
  pink matte glaze, signed Hester
  Pillsbury 175.00
Vase, 9" h., underglaze slip-painted

pair of large bluebirds chasing a
  dragonfly over a lily covered pond,
  green shaded to pink matte glaze,
  signed Sara Reid McLaughlin 975.00

Hudson Vase

Vase, 9¾" h., underglaze slip-painted
  pink & yellow blossoms, pink shaded
  to blue-grey matte glaze (ILLUS.) 265.00
Vase, 10" h., underglaze slip-painted
  raspberries, blue matte glaze 130.00
Vase, 12" h., underglaze slip-painted
  flying geese, signed Hester
  Pillsbury 1,500.00
Vase, 18" h., underglaze slip-painted
  coral pink blossoms & green foliage,
  pastel matte glaze 800.00

IVORY (pre-1914)
Jardiniere, panels of florals & foliage
  in low relief, 5" h. 15.00
Jardiniere, scrollwork & florals in low
  relief, 8½" d., 7" h. 105.00
Jardiniere & pedestal base, scrollwork
  & blossoms in low relief, small,
  2 pcs. 185.00
Vase, 10" h., octagonal, nude maidens
  & floral garlands in low relief 95.00

JAP BIRDIMAL (1904)
Pedestal base, incised & slip-painted
  landscape scene w/moon shining
  through trees on grey-blue ground,
  glossy finish, 20" h. 275.00
Pitcher, 4" h., incised & slip-painted
  Viking ship 695.00
Pitcher, tankard, incised & slip-painted
  white storks on light grey ground . . .450.00
Urn, incised & slip-painted blue trees
  on white ground, 9" h. 235.00
Vase, 4" h., incised & slip-painted
  geese on lavender ground 255.00

KENOVA (pre-1920)
Urn, Art Nouveau style florals
w/trailing stems in low relief on dull
green ground, 9" h. 150.00
Vase, 8" h., morning glory vine in low
relief on matte ground............110.00
Vase, 9" h., 4" d., cylindrical, pink
florals in low relief on dull green
ground 115.00

KLYRO WARE (1920s)
Planter, pseudo corner posts & fence-
like rim w/cluster of florals & foliage
against white ribbed ground, 4" h. ...85.00
Vase, bud, 8½" h., tapering hexagon,
pendant blossoms & foliage against
tan ribbed ground................30.00
Wall pocket, cluster of pink florals &
pendant berries against ribbed
ground, 7½" h. 45.00

KNIFEWOOD (1915-20)
Bowl, 3" h., canted sides, swans
swimming amidst marsh grasses in
low relief 70.00
Jardiniere, trees & robins in low
relief, 6½" d., 6" h. 110.00
Vase, 4" h., molded & painted daisies
& butterflies in low relief...........50.00
Vase, 5" h., swans on lake & trees
scene, glossy brown ground 75.00
Vase, 7" h., molded & painted daisies
& butterflies in low relief on russet
ground 105.00
Wall pocket, multicolored daisies in
low relief, 9" h...................100.00

L'ART NOUVEAU (1903-04)

L'Art Nouveau Umbrella Stand

Jardiniere, relief-molded orange
florals w/trailing green stems, ivory
matte finish, 9" h..................65.00

Pitcher, tankard, 11" h., relief-molded
grape clusters, matte finish 130.00
Umbrella stand, 22" h. (ILLUS.).......495.00
Vase, 9" h., relief-molded decor,
matte finish 125.00

LA SA (1920-25)

La Sa Vase

Vase, 5" h., scenic decor w/palm trees,
iridescent gold, red & silver glaze
(ILLUS.).........................175.00
Vase, 7½" h., 2¼" d., scenic decor
w/lakeshore, trees & mountains,
iridescent pink & gold glaze 195.00
Vase, 8½" h., scenic decor, iridescent
glaze............................330.00
Vase, 10½" h., scenic decor, iridescent
glaze............................355.00

LOUELLA (1915)
Jar, cov., multicolored floral spray on
drapery effect mold, bluish cast,
9½" h. 110.00
Vase, 6½" h., multicolored floral spray
on drapery effect mold, bluish cast ...48.00
Vase, 8¾" h., applied ring handles,
flared & fluted top, painted floral
on drapery effect mold, bluish cast ...85.00

LOUWELSA (1896-1924)
Bowl, 13" d., 6½" h., slip-painted red
apples, standard brown glaze, artist-
signed...........................240.00
Clock, mantel-type, slip-painted
florals, standard brown glaze,
11" h. 750.00
Ewer, slip-painted ferns, standard
brown glaze, 3" d., 4½" h. 95.00
Ewer, slip-painted cherries & leaves,
standard brown glaze, 7" h. 105.00
Fern stand, slip-painted yellow chrysanthemums, green stems & foliage,
standard brown shaded to orange
glaze, 22" h. 200.00

Jardiniere, slip-painted pansies,
standard brown glaze, 12" d.,
10" h. 250.00
Jardiniere, slip-painted portrait of a
Cavalier, artist-signed, 16¼" d.,
12" h...........................1,400.00

Louwelsa Jug

Jug, slip-painted golden wheat,
standard brown glaze, 3½" h.
(ILLUS.) 100.00
Mug, slip-painted cluster of red
cherries & green leaves, standard
brown glaze, 6" h. 140.00
Mug, tankard, slip-painted hummingbirds, standard brown glaze, artist-
signed, 6½" h. 450.00
Pitcher, 5" h., 3-footed, slip-painted
pansies, standard brown glaze,
artist-signed 165.00
Pitcher, tankard, 12" h., slip-painted
grape clusters, standard brown
glaze...........................225.00
Pitcher, tankard, 12" h., slip-painted
Indian portrait, standard brown
glaze, artist-signed.............1,250.00
Vase, 2" h., squatty, slip-painted
berries & leaves, standard brown
glaze............................50.00
Vase, 6¼" h., slip-painted yellow
florals, standard brown shaded to
green glaze 115.00
Vase, 8½"h., slip-painted holly decor,
shaded blue ground 485.00
Vase, 9½" h., bottle-shaped, slip-
painted rose blossom, shaded brown
standard glaze, artist-signed 160.00
Vase, 11" h., slip-painted raspberries,
shaded blue glaze 860.00

MALVERN (Late 1920s)
Bowl, 11" l., 5½" h., open handles,
boat-shaped, molded w/buds &
leaves in relief on swirl-textured
green, mauve & ochre-brown
ground 75.00
Console set: 11" oval console bowl
w/flower frog & pr. candle holders;
relief-molded leaf & bud forming

bowl edge, swirl-textured green
body w/mauve interior, 4 pcs. 95.00
Planter, relief-molded leaf & bud on
swirl-textured green to ochre-brown
ground, 10" l., 4" h. 45.00
Vase, 6" to 7" h., relief-molded leaf &
bud on swirl-textured green to ochre-
brown ground, each ....40.00 to 55.00
Vase, 13½"h., relief-molded leaf &
bud on swirl-textured green to
ochre-brown ground 60.00

MAMMY LINE (1935)
Batter bowl 250.00
Cookie jar, cov., figural Mammy
w/watermelon, 11" h. 600.00
Syrup pitcher, cov., figural Mammy,
6" h. ....300.00 to 325.00
Teapot, cov., figural Mammy, 8" h. 450.00

MARVO (mid-1920s)

Marvo Jardiniere

Candlesticks, molded leaves &
berries, tan matte finish, pr. 35.00
Jardiniere, molded palm leaves &
fronds, tan matte finish, 7" h.
(ILLUS.)..........................48.00
Planter, model of a log, footed,
molded ferns & fronds, green matte
finish, 9" l. 37.50
Vase, 7" h., molded palm leaves &
fronds, green matte finish 37.00
Wall pocket, molded leaves & berries,
green matte finish 35.00

PATRICIA (early 1930s)
Vase, 4" h., bulbous w/narrow neck
& swan handles, embossed leaves,
pale green matte finish 26.00
Vase, 6" h., swan handles, embossed
leaves, creamy white matte finish....35.00
Vase, 8½" h., bulbous, high curving
swan handles, embossed leaves,
creamy white matte finish 65.00
Vase, 18" h., swan handles, embossed
leaves, mottled tan & green matte
finish.............................160.00

PEARL (1917-19)
Basket, footed, molded beads draped
from rosettes, cream lustre ground,
6½" h. 90.00
Bowl, 6" d., molded beads draped
from rosettes, cream lustre ground...32.00
Vase, 7¾" h., molded beads draped
from rosettes, cream lustre ground...85.00

PERFECTO (1907)
Vase, 13" h., 7" d., delicate pink roses
& green leaves against pink shaded
to grey ground, bisque finish, artist-
signed.........................550.00
Vase, 16" h., h.p. floral decor on
shaded ground, bisque finish.......775.00

ROCHELLE (early 1920s-35)
Vase, 7" h., 7" d., slip-painted orange
tulips & green leaves on shaded
brown ground, artist-signed.......425.00

ROMA (1914 - late 1920s)

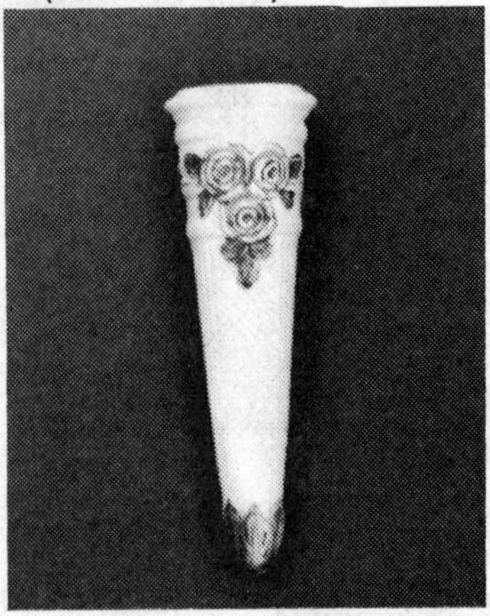

Roma Wall Pocket

Bowl, 2" h., footed, relief-molded &
tinted garlands of red roses & green
foliage on ivory ground 20.00
Compote, 11" d., stepped base, reeded stem, flared bowl w/relief-mold-
ed & tinted red & green floral band
on ivory ground 75.00
Console bowl, shell feet, relief-molded
& tinted red roses & green foliage
on ivory ground,
10½ x 4½" ....90.00 to 115.00
Planter, square, relief-molded & tinted
florals on ivory ground, 3½" h. 15.00
Planter, square, relief-molded & tinted
red & green floral band on ivory
ground, 6½" h....................40.00
Vase, 5" h., pedestal base, relief-
molded & tinted red roses on ivory
ground 23.00
Vase, triple bud, 8" h., cylindrical
flower holders w/horseshoe-shaped

band of relief-molded & tinted red
roses on ivory ground 25.00
Wall pocket, relief-molded & tinted red
roses & green foliage on ivory
ground, 7" h. (ILLUS.) 35.00
Window box, relief-molded & tinted
stylized pink florals & beige leaves
against tan & beige geometric
design ground, 13½ x 5½"........100.00

ROSEMONT (1920s)
Bowl, 9½" d., 2½" h., single stylized
flower & narrow band on glossy
black ground 25.00
Jardiniere, bird amidst flowering
branches on cream ground,
7½" h. ....225.00 to 295.00
Vase, 9" h., colorful bird in tree on
glossy black ground 110.00

SABRINIAN (late 1920s)
Ash tray, lavender, pink & blue shell-
molded body 95.00
Bowl, 9 x 6", 2½" h., irregular sea
shell form, lavender shaded to pink
w/turquoise sea plant 65.00
Console set: footed bowl & pr. candle
holders; lavender, pink & blue shell-
molded body, 3 pcs. 75.00
Vase, 9½" h., shell-molded body
w/seahorses at base, lavender,
pink & blue.......................95.00
Wall pocket, lavender, pink & blue
shell-molded body w/turquoise &
brown sea plants at top & base,
8½" h. 35.00
Window box, lavender, pink & blue
shell-molded body, 9 x 3½" 150.00

SICARDO (1902-07)

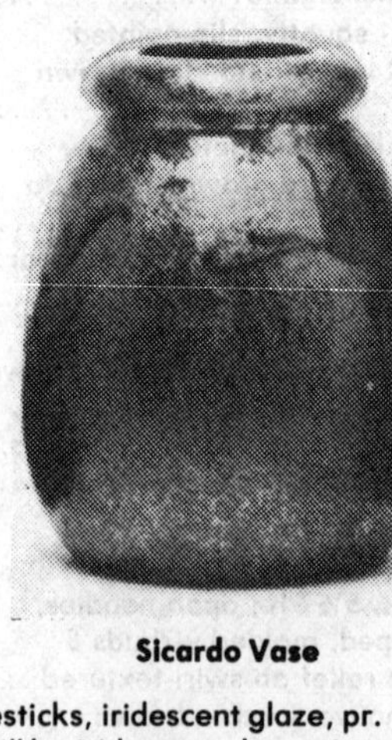

Sicardo Vase

Candlesticks, iridescent glaze, pr. 350.00
Vase, 4" h., iridescent glaze, signed...325.00
Vase, 6" h., triangular, iridescent
purple orchids & iris on shaded
blue-green ground 295.00

Vase, 7" h., thistle design on
iridescent ground 435.00
Vase, 7¼" h., ovoid w/bulging neck,
asters & foliage design in iridescent
green to copper lustre glaze, signed
(ILLUS.) 495.00
Vase, 15" h., iridescent
glaze . . . . .850.00 to 925.00

SILVERTONE (1925-29)

Silvertone Vase

Candle holder, relief-molded florals
against textured ground, shaded
pastel blue & grey (single) 18.00
Console bowl w/flower frog, relief-
molded florals against textured
ground, shaded pastel lavender &
blue, 12" d. . . . . .100.00 to 125.00
Vase, 6" h., squatty, relief-molded
florals against textured ground,
shaded pastel lavender & blue 85.00
Vase, 9½" h., handled, relief-molded
florals against textured ground,
shaded pastel tones (ILLUS.) 125.00
Vase, 10" h., stick-type w/tall angular
handles, relief-molded florals
against textured ground, shaded
pastel blue & grey 120.00
Wall pocket, relief-molded florals
against textured ground, shaded
pastel tones, 11" h. 65.00

SOUEVO (1910)

Basket, hanging-type w/chains, redware w/tan band of chocolate
brown geometric Indian motifs,
11" 100.00
Jardiniere, redware w/tan band of
black geometric Indian motifs, 7" h. . .75.00
Umbrella stand, redware w/tan band
of chocolate brown arrowheads . . .258.00
Vase, 8½" h., ovoid, redware w/tan
band of geometric Indian motifs at
shoulder 75.00
Wall pocket, fluted base w/bulging
neck, redware w/cream band of
chocolate brown geometric Indian
motifs at neck, 9½" h. 55.00

SYDONIA (late 1920s)

Console set: 17 x 6" bowl & pr. 7" h.
candlesticks; stylized shell form,
splotched blue glaze, 3 pcs. 85.00
Cornucopia-vase, stylized shell shape
on oval base, splotched green glaze,
8½" h. 45.00
Vase, 9" h., stylized shell shape,
splotched blue glaze w/deep green
base 30.00
Wall pocket, double, splotched blue
glaze 25.00

TURADA (1897-98)

Bowl, 8¼ x 3¼", blue & white lace-
like trim on glossy
brown . . . . .125.00 to 165.00
Humidor, cov., blue & tan lace-like
trim on glossy brown 275.00
Jardiniere, white & blue lace-like trim
on glossy black, 8" h. 150.00
Letter holder, 4-footed, white lace-
like trim on glossy cobalt blue,
8 x 3", 4½" h. . . . . .325.00 to 375.00
Mug, blue & tan lace-like trim on
glossy brown, 6" h. 145.00
Vase, 4¼" h., 5" w., pillow-shaped,
white & blue lace-like trim on glossy
black . . . . .175.00 to 200.00

TURKIS (late 1920s-1933)

Strawberry pot, brownish yellow drip
on deep red 40.00
Vase, 4" h., handled, brownish yellow
drip on deep red 27.50
Vase, 6½" h., brownish yellow drip on
deep red 65.00
Vase, 14" h., ovoid w/short collared
neck, 2-handled, brownish yellow
drip on deep red 95.00

TUTONE (late 1920s)

Basket, flowers, berries & arrowhead
leaves in relief on rose shaded to
green matte finish, 9 x 7" 45.00
Vase, 4" to 6" h., flowers, berries &
arrowhead leaves in relief on rose
shaded to green matte finish,
each . . . . .35.00 to 42.00
Vase, 7" h., crescent moon shape
w/candle holder at top, flowers,
berries & arrowhead leaves in relief
on rose shaded to green matte
finish 40.00
Wall pocket, flowers, berries & arrow-
head leaves in relief on rose shaded
to green matte finish, 10½" h. 45.00

WARWICK (late 1920s)

Basket w/overhead branch handle,
cylindrical w/ruffled rim, molded
tree bark ground w/green leaves &
red florals in relief, 7" h. 80.00
Vase, double bud, 4½" h., molded tree

bark ground w/branch of green
leaves & red florals in relief 45.00
Vase, 10" h., 6" w., rim handles,
molded tree bark ground w/branch
of green leaves & red florals in
relief . . . . 50.00 to 65.00
Wall pocket, molded tree bark ground
w/branch of leaves & florals in
relief, 11½" h. 75.00

WILD ROSE (1930s)

Wild Rose Ewer

Basket, hanging-type, open wild rose
decor, shaded pink matte finish 40.00
Candle holders, three-light, open wild
rose decor, shaded pink matte
finish, pr. 45.00
Console bowl, open wild rose decor,
shaded green matte finish 47.00
Ewer, open wild rose decor, shaded
pink matte finish, 6½" h. (ILLUS.) 45.00
Vase, 6½" h., open wild rose decor,
shaded green or pink matte finish,
each 25.00
Vase, 10" h., open wild rose decor,
shaded pink matte finish 36.00

WOODCRAFT (1920-33)

Basket, hanging-type w/chains, bark-
textured ground w/three foxes
peering from den in low relief,
8½" d., 4½" h. . . . . 150.00 to 195.00
Bowl, 6" d., 3½" h., squirrel seated on
branch eating a nut in low relief,
brown earthtones 95.00
Bowl, 9" sq., 4" h., footed, pierced
woven twig sides, brown earth-
tones 55.00
Candlesticks, twisted tree trunk form
w/figural owls, brown earthtones,
14" h., pr. . . . . 325.00 to 375.00
Jardiniere, bark-textured ground
w/branch of red fruit & green leaves
in low relief, 9½" d., 8" h. 225.00
Planter, upright log w/three foxes
peering from side, 5½" h. 100.00
Planter, log-shaped w/stump feet,
bark-textured ground w/oak leaves
in low relief, 9" l. . . . . 40.00 to 50.00

Vase, 7" h., fan-shaped, flowering tree
in low relief 25.00
Vase, 18" h., tree trunk w/owl &
squirrel, earthtones . . . . . 275.00 to 350.00
Wall pocket, bark-textured ground
w/branches & fruit in low relief &
figural squirrel at base, 9" h. 110.00
Wall pocket, cone-shaped tree limb
w/owl peering from knothole,
10" h. . . . . 110.00 to 135.00

ZONA (1915-20)

Zona Pitcher

Cup, saucer & 8" d. plate, tinted red
apples w/stems & leaves on creamy
white ground, 3 pcs. 55.00
Pitcher, 6" h., tinted red apples
w/stems & leaves on creamy white
ground . . . . 45.00 to 60.00
Pitcher, 7" h., tinted red apples & stems
in panels on cream ground
(ILLUS.) . . . . 65.00 to 75.00
Pitcher, 8" h., molded branch handle,
Kingfisher & cattails in low relief on
sides, deep pink 145.00
Platter, 12" l., tinted red apples
w/stems & leaves on creamy white
ground 32.00
Umbrella stand, ladies in long white
dresses holding garlands of roses
w/further garlands of ivy around
rim, white high-gloss glaze,
20½" h. 325.00
Wall pocket, panel w/stylized blos-
soms & foliage on creamy white
ground, 8½" h. 28.00

WOOD, ENOCH

*Enoch Wood established a pottery in Bur-
slem, England, about 1784, which continued
in business after 1790 as Wood & Caldwell
and in 1818 as Enoch Wood & Sons. The
last named company exported large quantities of ceramics to this country.*

Plate with Chinoiserie Decor

Bust of George Washington, yellowware, w/head turned slightly to the
left, his hair "en queue" & wearing
lace jabot & open coat, reverse
w/inscribed medallion above applied
eagle, dated 1818, w/another
Staffordshire bust of George
Washington inspired by the 1st but
painted in different colors, on
painted bases marbleized in grey,
ochre & green, 8¼" h., 2 pcs. $1,210.00

Creamer, blue scenic countryside
transfer, 1818-46, 5" h. 150.00

Plate, 6" d., dark blue chinoiserie
decor, ca. 1825 (ILLUS.) 65.00

Plate, 8½" d., red transfer center,
molded acanthus border, yellow
glaze, signed 275.00

Plate, 9½" d., dark blue transfer of
Cupid in a cage, impressed
"Wood" 100.00

Plate, 10½" d., medium blue Grecian
scene transfer, rope edge 75.00

WORCESTER

Worcester Circular Basket

The famed English Worcester factory was
established in 1751 and produced porcelains. Earthenwares were made in the 19th
century. Its first period is known as the
"Dr. Wall" period; that from 1783 to 1792
as the "Flight" period; that from 1792 to
1807 as the "Barr and Flight & Barr"
period. The firm became Barr, Flight & Barr
from 1807 to 1813; Flight, Barr & Barr from
1813 to 1840; Chamberlain & Co. from 1840
to 1848, and Kerr and Binns from 1852 to
1862. After 1862, the company became the
Worcester Royal Porcelain Company, Ltd.,
known familiarly as Royal Worcester, which
see.

Basket, center w/colorful floral spray
surrounded by smaller sprigs on
rim, sides of interlocking circlets
studded at intersections of the pale
yellow exterior w/green-centered
rose-petaled florettes, Dr. Wall
period, 1765-70, 7 7/8" d. $1,870.00

Basket, reticulated, center transfer-
printed in black w/two soldiers
conversing near a statue & ruins,
sides of interlocking circlets studded
at intersections of the exterior
w/flowerheads, gilt-edged rim &
rope-twist handles w/gilt-edged
floral terminals, Dr. Wall period,
ca. 1765, 8" oval 770.00

Basket, Pine Cone patt., transfer-
printed in underglaze-blue w/clusters
of flowers & rim, sides of interlocking circlets studded at intersections,
of exterior w/blue florettes,
trellis diaper scrollwork at rim,
Dr. Wall period, ca. 1775,
11 1/8" d. (ILLUS.) 880.00

Coffee pot, cov., "chinoiserie" decor,
transfer-printed in black & colorfully enameled w/Mandarin gentleman seated at a table, holding a
teabowl & surrounded by 3 admiring
ladies & a child, rims w/iron-red
& gold scallop-and-dot border, Dr.
Wall period, ca. 1770, 8¾" h. 1,650.00

Cup & saucer, colorful floral garlands
interrupting gilt scrolls issuing
from C-scroll-edged "gros bleu"
border around the rim, central
saucer depression & base of cup
w/turquoise "caillote" border
edged in gilt C-scrolls, Dr. Wall
period, 1775-80 . . . . 770.00

Dish, lozenge-shaped, Old Mosaick
Japan patt., underglaze-blue, iron-
red & gold prunus branch within
gilt-flowered iron-red border on
the cavetto & fan-shaped panels
on the rim patterned in underglaze-
blue & gilt or iron-red, rose, green
& turquoise floral sprays or diaper-
work & superimposed w/"mons"

Old Mosaick Japan Pattern Dish

Dr. Wall period, 1765-70, 10 3/8" l.
(ILLUS.) 1,540.00
Dish, duodecagonal form, Bengal Tiger
patt., iron-red, green, yellow, rose,
blue & gold panels of beasts or
vases on tables surrounding an iron-
red & blue-centered rose chrysanthemum reserved on grey-stippled
green ground, gilt-edged rim
w/iron-red & green cell diaper
border, Dr. Wall period, ca. 1770,
11 7/8" l. 2,145.00
Dishes, shell-shaped, Japan patt.,
iron-red, green, turquoise, pink,
underglaze-blue & gold central
floral patera surrounded by panels
of oriental gardens separated by
iron-red floral zones & underglaze-
blue & gilt diaper panels, Barr,
Flight & Barr period, ca. 1804,
7 5/8" & 8" l., pr. (one cracked) 1,100.00
Dishes, kidney-shaped, 3 rose, yellow,
orange, blue, purple & brown
exotic birds on a plateau before
others perched in a small tree in a
river landscape w/distant buildings
& purple hills, cavetto w/small
birds & insects in flight, basket-
molded rim w/gilt dentil edge,
Dr. Wall period, ca. 1770, 10¼" l.,
pr. 2,530.00
Fruit stand, lozenge-shaped,
spirally-fluted dish & foot, interior
& exterior w/blue vines issuing
iron-red blossoms & bright green
leaves, center w/blue roundel
depicting an iron-red & gilt stylized
kylin amidst vines, worn gilt-edged
rim w/six floral vignettes, Chamber-
lain period, ca. 1840, 12½" l. 550.00
Tea bowl & saucer, Dr. Wall period 110.00
Teapot, cov., Mansfield patt., painted
in underglaze-blue either side & on
cover w/stylized floral spray within
a "pineapple" & scrollwork border,
Dr. Wall period, 1765-75, 3¾" h. 550.00
Teapot, cov., Queen Charlotte patt.,
underglaze-blue, iron-red &

rose spiraling bands of stylized
flowers & foliage, rims w/iron-red
floral vine borders repeated on
handle & spout, Dr. Wall period,
ca. 1770, 5¼" h. 715.00
Teapot liner, Spiral Flute patt., cobalt
blue & gold trim, Barr, Flight &
Barr period, 1793 . . . . .125.00

YELLOWWARE

Yellowware Mixing Bowl

*Yellowware is a form of utilitarian ware
produced in the United States from the
1850s onward. Its body texture is less dense
and vitreous (impervious to water) than
stoneware. Most, but not all, yellowware is
unmarked and its color varies from deep
yellow to pale buff. In the late 19th and
early 20th centuries, bowls in graduated
sizes were widely advertised. Still in production, yellowware is plentiful and still
reasonably priced. Also see FOOD, CANDY
& MISCELLANEOUS MOLDS and MINI-
ATURES (Replicas).*

Beater jar, white slip pin stripes
decor, w/advertising $50.00
Bedpan . . . . .16.00 to 20.00
Bowl, 5¾" d., 3" h., collared base,
embossed exterior decor 25.00
Bowl, 6" d., blue pin stripe bands
decor 18.00
Bowl, 7" d., brown pin stripe bands
decor, w/advertising 20.00
Bowl, 8" d., 6 blue pin stripes decor 28.00
Bowl, 8½" d., brown pin stripe bands
decor .17.00 to 20.00
Bowl, 9" d., relief-molded exterior
decor 30.00
Bowl, 10½" d., 3-stripe white slip band
decor 28.00
Canister, cov., lettered "Sugar" 70.00
Chamber pot, applied handle, band of
5 white slip pin stripes near rim,
7" d., 4¾" h. 45.00
Mixing bowl, brown pin stripe bands
decor, 7½" d. 30.00
Mixing bowl, 10" d., 4½" h. (ILLUS.) 35.00
Mug, blue checkerboard design decor,
2 7/8" h. 32.50
Rolling pin, w/turned wood handles,
15" l. 100.00

ZSOLNAY

Zsolnay Bison & Polar Bears

This pottery was made in Pecs, Hungary, in a factory founded in 1855 by Vilmos Zsolnay. Currently Zsolnay pieces are being made in a new factory.

Bowl, 6" sq., reticulated, rose glaze
w/gold Persian motif decor $175.00
Bowl, 8" l., 4" h., heart-shaped, high
glaze w/small curls of gold, Art
Nouveau-type swimming fish &
twisted blossoming red, blue & green
florals on rich ground 410.00
Celery tray, reticulated border, floral
decor on pastel lustre ground,
13 x 7½" 175.00
Figure of a classic nude maiden
standing beside pedestal w/vase &
removing her garments, iridescent
blue, green & gold glaze, 4½" w.
plinth base, 11" h. 265.00
Model of a dog in standing position,
iridescent bronze & gold glaze, 7" h. . . 85.00
Model of a charging bison & model of
pr. walking polar bears, iridescent
yellow & blue-green glazes, 1920s,
6 1/8" & 4¾", pr. (ILLUS.) 176.00
Plate, 8½" d., shell-shaped w/reticu-
lated rim, red & gold florals on beige
ground 179.00

Zsolnay Urn

Urn, cylindrical, molded hunt scene in
wooded landscape in low relief,
iridescent green, ochre & brown on

cream, ca. 1900, 20½" h.
(ILLUS.) 4,510.00
Vase, 4½" h., iridescent glaze 50.00
Vase, 5½" h., iridescent green glaze . . . 40.00
Vase, 5½" h., ovoid, irregular flag-
stones in relief, iridescent red glaze
w/deeper tones in crevices 95.00
Vase, 8" h., reticulated double-walled
body, cream w/iridescent multi-
colored highlights 495.00
Vase, 11" h., scalloped rim, iridescent
cobalt blue w/panels of dark red
leaves at base 115.00
Vase, 13" h., lustred butterflies &
dragons in high relief, ca. 1880 . . . . . 250.00
Vase, 13½" h., relief-molded tadpole-
like creatures, iridescent metallic
blue-green glaze 145.00
Vase, 14½" h., closed top w/opening
at each side, reticulated designs in
red, gold & light green on light
blue ground 575.00

Zsolnay Wall Bracket

Wall brackets, reticulated Persian-type
floral & foliate devices overall, iridescent pale yellow & cobalt blue
glaze w/gilt details, ca. 1910,
repaired rim, 8¼" h., pr. (ILLUS. of
one) 385.00

(End of Ceramics Section)

CHALKWARE

So-called chalkware available today is actually made of plaster-of-paris, much of it decorated in color and primarily in the form of busts, figurines and ornaments. It was produced through most of the 19th century, and the majority of pieces were quite inexpensive when originally made.

Bank, model of a cat smoking a
pipe, 10" h., 19th c. $100.00
Beeswax mold, deeply carved cornu-
copia, 4 x 3½" 50.00
Bust of Hiawatha, 1890s, 20" h. 115.00

Bust of Indian brave, signed Sam
  Lord Wise, 1901 copyright 125.00
Mantel garniture, fruit arrangement
  in footed compote, white compote
  & original polychrome decorated
  fruit, 8½" d., 9" h. 400.00
Mantel garnitures, fruit arrangement in
  hour-glass form compotes, original
  polychrome paint, 11" h., pr. 800.00
Model of a cat seated, original
  brown paint w/features picked out in
  black, red & yellow, 9" h. (old
  paint touch up) 300.00
Model of a dog seated, white
  w/black spots & yellow collar, 8" h. . 160.00
Model of a parrot, original green,
  yellow & red paint w/wear, 9" h. 410.00

19th Century Chalkware Stag

Model of a stag in recumbent position on oblong base, olive-amber &
  black spots & features picked out in
  red & black, 5 3/8" h. (ILLUS.) 290.00

CHARACTER COLLECTIBLES

*Numerous objects made in the likeness of
or named after movie, radio, television, comic strip and comic book personalities or
characters abounded from the 1920s
through the 1940s. Scores of these are now
being eagerly collected and prices still vary
widely. Also see ADVERTISING ITEMS,
BANKS, BIG LITTLE BOOKS, CHRIST-
MAS TREE LIGHTS, COMIC BOOKS,
DISNEY COLLECTIBLES, DOLLS,
SHEET MUSIC and TOYS.*

Amos & Andy ash tray - matchbox
  holder combination, chalkware,
  "I'se Regusted" $74.00

Andy Gump brush, comb & mirror set,
  3 pcs. 35.00
Baby Sandy pull toy, wooden,
  w/goose 65.00
Barney Google pinback button,
  Kellogg's Pep Cereal premium 4.00

Barney Google & Spark Plug by Schoenhut

Barney Google & Spark Plug figures,
  wood-jointed, painted eyes, original
  felt & cloth garments on Barney
  & original blanket for Spark Plug,
  Schoenhut, ca. 1924, 7" & 6" h.,
  pr. (ILLUS.) 615.00
Batman bank, china 20.00
Batman mask 6.00
Batman night light 25.00
Batman pen 18.00
Batman shooting arcade 35.00
Beatles coloring book, 1964 . . . . 25.00
Beatles head scarf, 1964 . . . . 35.00
Beatles "Ringo" pinback button 10.00
Betty Boop ash tray, lustre ware,
  1930s 100.00
Betty Boop buckle, celluloid, small 35.00
Betty Boop buckle, celluloid, large 50.00
Betty Boop figure, chalkware, 18" h. 57.50
Betty Boop pin, enameled metal, on
  original Fleischer Studios card, 1½" . . 40.00
Betty Boop pocket watch 150.00
Betty Boop wall pocket, china, Betty
  w/cat on front, stamped on back
  "Betty Boop by Fleischer Studios,
  Japan" 110.00
Betty Boop & Bimbo ash tray, ceramic,
  Fleischer Studios 100.00
Blondie paint book, Whitman No. 605,
  1941 . . . . 15.00
Blondie paint box, tin, 1946,
  5¾ x 4½" . . . . 15.00 to 25.00
Buck Jones pin, horseshoe 12.50
Buck Jones rifle, compass & sun dial,
  Daisy, 3 pcs. 40.00
Buck Rogers Atomic Pistol, U-238,
  w/holster & box, Daisy Mfg. Co.,
  1948 . . . . 65.00 to 85.00
Buck Rogers badge, "Solar Scout,"
  Cream of Wheat premium, 1934 . . . . . 26.00
Buck Rogers Battle Cruiser Rocket
  Ship, red & yellow, Tootsietoy,
  Dowst Mfg. Co., 1937, 4¾" l.
  (ILLUS.) 42.00

Buck Rogers Battle Cruiser

Buck Rogers book, pop-up type, "A
    Dangerous Mission" 75.00
Buck Rogers Disintegrator pistol,
    XZ-38, Daisy Manufacturing Co.,
    1936 . . . . .105.00

Buck Rogers Liquid Helium Pistol

Buck Rogers Liquid Helium Water
    pistol, Daisy Mfg. Co., 1936
    (ILLUS.) 125.00
Buck Rogers paint book, 1935
    (unused) 95.00
Buck Rogers pencil box, American
    Lead Pencil Co., 1934 . . . . .32.50
Buck Rogers "pop" pistol, metal, Daisy
    Mfg. Co., ca. 1934 . . . . .45.00 to 60.00
Buck Rogers Rocket Pistol, XZ-31,
    Daisy Manufacturing Co., 1934 . . . . . . .53.00
Buck Rogers telescope 185.00
Buck Rogers Venus Duo Destroyer
    Rocket Ship, Tootsietoy, 1937 . . . . . . .115.00
Bugs Bunny mug, plastic 22.50
Captain America wrist watch, Fawcett
    Co., 1948 . . . . .300.00
Captain Marvel pinback button 10.00
Captain Marvel shirt, child size, 1940s . .45.00
Captain Marvel wrist watch, Fawcett,
    1948 . . . . .148.00
Captain Midnight decoder, 1940, radio
    premium 35.00
Captain Midnight decoder, 1947,
    Whistling Code-O-Graph, Ovaltine
    premium . . . . .28.00 to 35.00
Captain Midnight mug, Ovaltine
    premium 20.00
Captain Midnight stamp album, "Air
    Heroes," w/sixteen stamps, 1940 . . . .25.00
Captain Video ring, metal, w/space-
    ship & whistle 39.00

Charlie Chaplin stickpin, metal, 1920s,
    2" 30.00
Charlie Chaplin teaspoon, silverplate . . .10.00
Charlie Chaplin whistle, lithographed
    tin 45.00
Charlie McCarthy book, "Charlie
    McCarthy Meets Snow White," soft
    cover, Whitman, 1938 . . . . .45.00

Charlie McCarthy Figure

Charlie McCarthy figure, chalkware,
    14½" h. (ILLUS.) 35.00
Charlie McCarthy hand puppet, compo-
    sition head, 1930s 62.50
Charlie McCarthy "Radio Party" game,
    21 pcs. complete w/spinner &
    envelope, Chase & Sanborn Coffee
    premium, 1938 . . . . .33.00
Charlie McCarthy teaspoon, silver-
    plate 10.00
Chester Gump nodding figure, bisque,
    German, 2½" h. 50.00
Dagwood figure, King Features
    Syndicate, 1944 . . . . .35.00
Dale Evans hat, cowgirl style 25.00
Dale Evans wrist watch, Ingraham,
    1951 . . . . .39.00
Daniel Boone knife, w/store display
    card 9.00
Davy Crockett bank, metal 15.00
Davy Crockett night light 24.00
Davy Crockett pencil case 18.00
Dick Tracy badge,
    "Lieutenant" . . . . .35.00 to 65.00
Dick Tracy badge, "Sergeant" 37.50
Dick Tracy book, "Secret Service Patrol
    Secret Code," 1938, 12 pp. 50.00
Dick Tracy camera, Seymore Products
    Co., Chicago, Ill., 5" l., 2¾" h. 32.00
Dick Tracy flashlight, original box 20.00
Dick Tracy pinback button, "Secret
    Service Patrol" (ILLUS.) 20.00

Dick Tracy Pinback Button

Dick Tracy pistol, Tip-Top Bread
   premium 25.00
Dick Tracy wrist watch, New Haven
   Clock Co., 1937, original box 130.00
Dionne Quintuplets book, "We're Two
   Years Old," Whitman Publishing
   Co., 1936 . . . . .19.00
Dionne Quintuplets book, "We're Three
   Years Old," 1937 . . . . .18.50
Dionne Quintuplets book, "We Were
   Five," 1964 . . . . .15.00
Dionne Quintuplets bowl, chrome,
   5" d. 28.00
Dionne Quintuplets calendar,
   1936 . . . . .12.00 to 15.00
Dionne Quintuplets calendar, 1937,
   playing house w/ironing board &
   kitchen utensils. 18.50
Dionne Quintuplets calendar, 1946,
   12 x 15". 10.00
Dionne Quintuplets calendar, 1949,
   the Quints 15 years old, painted
   by Andrew Loomis, 29 x 42" 13.50
Dionne Quintuplets fan, cardboard,
   Quints playing in sand, 1936. . . . . .17.50
Dionne Quintuplets fan, 1938 . . . . .9.00
Dionne Quintuplets paper dolls, uncut,
   "All Aboard for Shut-Eye Town,"
   1937, original mailing envelope 45.00
Dionne Quintuplets photograph, glossy
   print, framed, 1937. . . . . .20.00
Dionne Quintuplets photographs,
   individual close-ups, Quaker Oats
   premium, 7 x 9", set of 5 w/original
   letter & mailing envelope 135.00
Dionne Quintuplets teaspoons, silver-
   plate, full figure handles w/names,
   set of 5 . . . . .88.00
Ed Wynn Fire Chief board game 35.00
Ed Wynn mask, Texaco premium given
   at Chicago World's Fair 35.00
Ella Cinders doll, boudoir-type, cloth
   w/molded buckram face, painted
   features, 28" .150.00
Elmer Fudd bank, cast white metal,
   Elmer beside barrel, "W.B.C.,"
   5½" h. 50.00
Farina (Our Gang) plate, portrait
   decor, Hal Roach Studio. 45.00

Fatty Arbuckle mirror, pocket-type 22.00
Felix the Cat figure, wood-jointed,
   Schoenhut, 1925, 4" h. 100.00
Felix the Cat figure, wood-jointed, copy-
   right 1922-24 by Pat Sullivan, pat.
   June 23, 1925, Schoenhut, 6" h. 120.00
Foxy Grandpa bookmark, celluloid 30.00
Foxy Grandpa puppet, papier mache,
   Germany 125.00
Gene Autry bicycle horn 52.50
Gene Autry lunch box & bullet-shaped
   thermos bottle, in original box. 38.00
Gene Autry song book, 1938, 88 songs,
   95 pp. 17.50
Gene Autry thermos bottle, w/tin cap,
   1949 . . . . .18.00
Gene Autry wrist watch, his gun
   indicating seconds, back die-bossed
   "Always Your Pal, Gene Autry,"
   green radium hands, brown leather
   band, copyright 1948 . . . . .164.00
Green Hornet playing cards,
   1966 . . . . .5.00 to 7.50
Hopalong Cassidy badge, "Sheriff,"
   star-shaped 7.00
Hopalong Cassidy bedspread, chenille . .96.00
Hopalong Cassidy book, "Hopalong
   Cassidy Returns," 1923 . . . . .15.00
Hopalong Cassidy breakfast set: bowl,
   cup & plate; milk white glass, 3 pcs. . .60.00
Hopalong Cassidy dental kit, original
   box. . . . . .55.00 to 75.00
Hopalong Cassidy drum, Rubbertone
   Corp., 1950 . . . . .35.00
Hopalong Cassidy field glasses, ca.
   1950 . . . . .20.00
Hopalong Cassidy lamp, wall-type, gun
   in holster, Alacite glass, Aladdin. . . .115.00

Hopalong Cassidy Lunch Box

Hopalong Cassidy lunch box w/thermos
   bottle, Aladdin Industries, 1950
   (ILLUS.) 27.00
Hopalong Cassidy mug, opaque white
   glass w/color decal picture. 12.50
Hopalong Cassidy mug, ceramic, multi-
   color bust of Hoppy, backstamped
   "Hopalong Cassidy by W.S. George"
   in gold, 3" h. (ILLUS.) 15.00

Hopalong Cassidy Mug

Hopalong Cassidy pocket knife,
　Imperial Knife Co., 1950s 28.00
Hopalong Cassidy pyrographic (wood
　burning) set......................125.00
Hopalong Cassidy thermos bottle,
　picture of Hoppy, Aladdin ...15.00 to 22.50
Hopalong Cassidy tumbler, milk white
　glass.............................10.50

Hopalong Cassidy Wallet

Hopalong Cassidy wallet, vinyl, picture
　of Hoppy & Topper on front (ILLUS.)...18.00
Howdy Doody bubble bath set, box
　pictures the gang giving Flub-A-Dub
　a bath............................30.00
Howdy Doody cookie jar.....150.00 to 225.00
Howdy Doody hand puppet,
　composition.......................75.00
Howdy Doody tumbler, Howdy &
　friends on picnic, Welch's Grape
　Juice premium, 1953...............20.00
Jack Armstrong (Frank Buck) explorer's
　sun watch w/sundial face, Post
　Cereal premium, World War II era....40.00
Jack Armstrong ring, "Secret Egyptian"
　w/code siren......................32.50
Jack Armstrong telescope 20.00
Jack Webb (Dragnet) cuff links, badge,
　holster & gun set.................45.00
Jack Webb (Dragnet) whistle 5.50
Jackie Coogan figure, chalkware,
　18" h.............................95.00
Jackie Coogan pencil box, tin,
　8½ x 2"...........................22.00
Jiggs ash tray & match holder, floor

model, wooden figure of Jiggs
　holding tray, 1930s...............225.00
Joe Palooka lunch box, 1946..........42.50
Joe Palooka punching bag, 16".......55.00
Kayo figure, wood jointed, 4" h.......62.00
Lil Abner wrist watch, animated,
　New Haven Clock Co., 1947 ....155.00
Little Henry figure, bisque, marked
　"Carl Anderson," copyright 1934,
　3½" h.............................37.50
Little Henry figure, bisque, movable
　arms, marked "Anderson,"
　6¼" h..................125.00 to 165.00
Little King pocket watch & wrist
　watch, pr.........................250.00
Little Lulu book, "Little Lulu Plays
　Pirate," hard cover...............20.00
Lone Ranger badge, "Deputy,"
　w/secret compartment.............16.00
Lone Ranger booklet, "How the Lone
　Ranger Captured Silver," Silver Cup
　Bread premium.....................95.00
Lone Ranger "First Aid" kit, tin,
　w/contents, ca. 1938..............34.00

Lone Ranger "Target" Game

Lone Ranger game, "Target," tin,
　Louis Marx & Co., 1938, w/stand,
　16 x 27" (ILLUS.)................175.00
Lone Ranger harmonica, Magnus, 1950,
　w/original box 18.00
Lone Ranger jigsaw puzzle, Clayton
　Moore, Jay Silverheels & Silver 9.00
Lone Ranger paperweight, "Round-Up,"
　snow-type........................28.00
Lone Ranger pencil box, 1940s, 8 x 4"...20.00
Lone Ranger pocket watch, New Haven
　Clock Co., 1939 ....135.00
Lone Ranger rifle, w/scope, Louis Marx
　& Co.............................55.00
Lone Ranger ring, "Atom Bomb,"
　w/instructions...................32.50
Lone Ranger ring, "Six-Shooter,"
　Cheerios premium, 1940s 44.00

Maggie & Jiggs figures, wood-jointed bodies & papier mache heads, Jiggs w/original "Corned Beef & Cabbage" pail & Maggie w/rolling pin, Schoenhut, copyright 1924, International Feature Service, 8" & 9" h., pr. 700.00

Mary Marvel wrist watch, depicting Mary flying, green radium hour & minute hands, blue patent leather band, copyright 1948, Fawcett Pub. Inc. 65.00

Mortimer Snerd jack-in-the-box toy 90.00

Mortimer Snerd marionette 35.50

Mutt & Jeff figures, celluloid, pr. 80.00

Olive Oyl pin, enameled 30.00

Orphan Annie & Sandy ash tray, bisque, 1930s 63.00

Orphan Annie book, "Little Orphan Annie, The Haunted House" by Harold Grey, first edition, 1928 . . . . . .50.00

Orphan Annie book, "Little Orphan Annie in Cosmic City," 1933 . . . . .18.00

Orphan Annie book, "Little Orphan Annie vs. Commandos," 1943 . . . . .13.00

Orphan Annie booklet, "Secret Society Membership," 1930s, 12 pp. 28.00

Orphan Annie decoder, 1936, Ovaltine premium 21.50

Orphan Annie game, "Treasure Hunt," Ovaltine premium, 1933 . . . . .25.00

Orphan Annie "ID" bracelet, 1930s 23.00

Orphan Annie mug, creamware pottery w/picture of Annie & Sandy, Ovaltine premium, signed Harold Grey . . .33.00

Orphan Annie Plastic Mug

Orphan Annie mug, plastic, Ovaltine premium, 3" h. (ILLUS.) 35.00

Orphan Annie & Sandy figures, wood-jointed, pr. 120.00

Our Gang pencil box, w/pictures of Jackie, Chubby, Farina & dog 20.00

Popeye animated alarm clock, by Smith, made in Great Britain 245.00

Popeye bank, dime register, copyright 1929 . . . . .34.00

Popeye Big Big Book, "Thimble Theater," 1935 .55.00

Popeye figure, chalkware, dated 1933, stamped "K.F.S. Inc.," 10" h. 76.00

Popeye figure, rubber, King Features Syndicate, 1935, 7" h. 85.00

Popeye figure, wood-jointed, 5½" h. 50.00

Popeye game, "Pipe Toss," 1935, original box 25.00

Popeye game, "Shipwreck," 1933 . . . . .23.00

Popeye paint set, 1933 . . . . .20.00

Popeye pistol, "Popeye Pirate Pistol," tin, by Marx Toy Co., King Features Syndicate, ca. 1935, 9½" l. 120.00

Popeye Plate

Popeye plate, w/picture & "I yam so strong 'cause I eats my spinach," King Features Syndicate, 7½" d. (ILLUS.) 15.00

Popeye soap figure, 1930s, 5" h. 29.00

Popeye song folio, 1936, 32 pp. 45.00

Popeye toy, battery-operated "Bubble Blowing Popeye," lithographed tin, Linemar, 12" h. 450.00

Popeye & Olive Oyl figures, rubber, 9" h., pr. 85.00

Porky Pig pencil holder, metal, Porky by tree trunk 35.00

Raggedy Ann bean bag 20.00

Red Ryder BB gun, Daisy Mfg., 1930s. . . .31.00

Red Ryder coloring book, 1952 (unused) 12.00

Roy Rogers binoculars 16.00

Roy Rogers camera, Herbert George Co., original box 24.50

Roy Rogers cap gun, cast iron w/black plastic grips 28.00

Roy Rogers gloves, gauntlet-type, leather, pr. 29.00

Roy Rogers guitar, composition board . .60.00

Roy Rogers harmonica, on original card 23.50

Roy Rogers lamp, table model 35.00

Roy Rogers neckerchief slide 22.00

Roy Rogers ring, branding iron 25.00

Roy Rogers thermos bottle, "Double R Bar Ranch" 18.50

Sergeant Preston distance finder 75.00

Sergeant Preston whistle, 1949 . . . . .17.50

Shield G-Man pistol, tin, w/trigger-
winding siren, made in U.S.A.,
1940s, 8" l. 18.00
Shield G-Man ring, 1940 ....14.00
Shirley Temple book, "How I Raised
Shirley Temple," by her mother,
40 pp. 20.00
Shirley Temple book, "The Little
Colonel" 16.00
Shirley Temple book, "The Little
Stowaway," Saalfield..............25.00
Shirley Temple book, "The Littlest
Rebel"............................15.00
Shirley Temple book, "Poor Little Rich
Girl," 1936 ....25.00
Shirley Temple book, "Shirley Temple
at Play," Saalfield, 1935, 8 full page
color illustrations, 18 pp.,
10 x 12½".........................30.00
Shirley Temple book, "Shirley Temple's
Storybook," Random House, first
printing, 1958 ....11.50
Shirley Temple book, "Spirit of Dragon-
wood," w/dust jacket 7.50
Shirley Temple book, "Thru the Day,"
1936 ....21.50
Shirley Temple book, "Wee Willie
Winkie," 1937 ....15.00

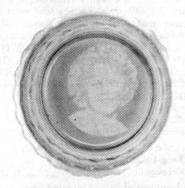

Shirley Temple Cereal Bowl

Shirley Temple (cereal) bowl, cobalt blue
glass w/decal portrait of Shirley
(ILLUS.) 44.00
Shirley Temple figure, salt-glazed
pottery, 6" h......................23.50
Shirley Temple magazine, "Life,"
February 3, 1958, cover illustration
& article 7.00
Shirley Temple mirror, pocket-type,
photo on pink ground, dated
1935, 1¾" d. 35.00
Shirley Temple mug, cobalt blue glass
w/decal portrait of Shirley 41.50
Shirley Temple pitcher, cobalt blue
glass 32.00
Shirley Temple poster, "Young People,"
27 x 41"..........................35.00
Shirley Temple scrapbook, 1936,

Saalfield No. 1722, 39 pp. of early
pictures 50.00
Shirley Temple sheet music, "At the
Codfish Ball," framed..............12.00
Shirley Temple sheet music, "Poor
Little Rich Girl" 10.00
Shirley Temple trunk for doll clothes....65.00
Skeezix bank, 1926................40.00
Skippy cereal bowl, Beetleware, raised
figure of Skippy at bottom, 1933 ....22.50
Skippy figure, bisque, movable arms,
1930s, 6" h. 50.00
Sky King Spy Detecto Writer 40.00
Smitty Christmas tree light bulb.......27.50
Smitty drawing & tracing book,
McLoughlin Bros., No. 526..........35.00
Smitty ring, Post Raisin Bran
premium, 1948 ....10.00
Smitty & Herbie jigsaw puzzle, fishing
in boat w/whale approaching,
framed, 1932 ....20.00
Spark Plug figure, wood-jointed,
Schoenhut, 9" l., 6¼" h............300.00
Spike Jones toy saxophone, w/box.....44.00
Superman animated alarm clock,
1940 ....550.00
Superman bank, dime register, 1940s...76.00
Superman card game, Ideal, 1966 ......10.00
Superman coloring book, 1940.........40.00
Superman figure, chalkware 60.00
Superman ring, "Crusader" 93.00
Superman swimming fins, "Official
Kiddie," original box 25.00
Superman swimming goggles, 1940s ...40.00
Terry & the Pirates coloring book, 1946
(unused)..........................18.00
Tess Truehart (Dick Tracy) pinback
button, Kellogg's Pep Cereal
premium 4.00
Tom Corbett Space Cadet belt 30.50
Tom Corbett gun, "Sparkling Space
Cadet" 110.00
Tom Mix arrowhead, "glow-in-dark" ...30.00
Tom Mix Big Big Book, "Tom Mix
and the Scourge of Paradise
Valley," 1937 ....85.00 to 95.00
Tom Mix compass & magnifying
glass, "Straight Shooter," Ralston
premium, 1930s 30.00
Tom Mix decoder badge, 1941 ....50.00
Tom Mix decoder manual, 1933 ....50.00

Tom Mix Hobby Horse

Tom Mix hobby horse, "Tony,"
  wooden, 40" l. (ILLUS.)............185.00
Tom Mix "ID" bracelet 30.00
Tom Mix periscope 38.50
Tom Mix pinback button, w/horse
  Tony, Ralston premium 31.50
Tom Mix ring, "Magnet," Ralston
  premium, 1930s-40s 35.00
Tom Mix ring, "Sliding Whistle,"
  Ralston premium, 1930s-40s 45.00
Uncle Walt doll, oilcloth, 1930s 58.00

Uncle Walt Picture

Uncle Walt picture, tin, Cracker Jack
  premium, 2" h. (ILLUS.) 25.00
Uncle Walt & Skeezix toothbrush
  holder, bisque....................70.00
Uncle Wiggily mug, china, Ovaltine
  premium, embossed "1924 Fred A.
  Wish Inc., Sebring Pottery Co.,
  manufactured for The Wonder Co.,"
  3" h. 32.00
Uncle Willie & Emma toothbrush
  holder, bisque, 1930s..............70.00
W.C. Fields teaspoon, silverplate 15.00
Wimpy doll, rubber head.............15.00
Wimpy figure, rubber, King Features
  Syndicate, 8½" h..................45.00
Wizard of Oz tumbler, pictures
  Judy Garland, Toto, Scarecrow,
  Tinman & Lion, 1939 ....20.00
Woody Woodpecker animated alarm
  clock, w/box............150.00 to 175.00
Woody Woodpecker mug, plastic 22.50
Woody Woodpecker teaspoon, silver-
  plate 10.00
Yellow Kid book, "movie-flip" type,
  dated 1895 ....125.00
Yellow Kid figure, papier mache 210.00
Yellow Kid paperweight, cast iron.....375.00
Yellow Kid pinback button No. 7 ....12.00
Yellow Kid sheet music, 1887, matted
  & framed 90.00
Zorro charm bracelet, 1957...........18.00
Zorro game, target board, gun &
  darts, T. Cohn 30.00

CHILDREN'S BOOKS

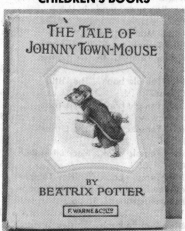

Child's Book by Beatrix Potter

*The most collectible children's books
today tend to be those printed after the
1850s and while age is not completely irrel-
evant, illustrations play a far more important role in determining the values. While
first editions are highly esteemed, it is the
beautifully illustrated books that most collectors seek. The following books, all in
good to fine condition, were sold within the
past twelve months. Also see ADVERTIS-
ING ITEMS, BIG LITTLE BOOKS,
BROWNIE, BUSTER BROWN, CHAR-
ACTER, DISNEY and GREENAWAY
COLLECTIBLES.*

"ABC Birds Book," published by
  McLoughlin, 1885, linen...........$25.00
"A Child's Garden of Verse," a "Jolly
  Jump-Up Book," published by
  McLoughlin, 1946 ....15.00
"Adventures of Peter Cottontail," by
  Thornton Burgess, 1914 ....22.00
"Adventures of Poor Mrs. Quack," by
  Thornton Burgess, 1918 ....12.00
"The Adventures of Tom Sawyer," by
  Mark Twain (Samuel Clemens), 1936
  edition w/eight color illustrations by
  Norman Rockwell 25.00
"Aesop's Fables," illustrated by John
  Tenniel, published by Phil, Porter &
  Coates, 1848 ....65.00
"Alice's Adventures in Wonderland,"
  by Lewis B. Carroll, 42 illustrations
  by John Tenniel, published by
  McLoughlin Bros. 70.00
"Alice in Wonderland in Words of One
  Syllable," published by Saalfield,
  1908 ....10.00
"A Little Child's Book of Stories," by
  Cornelia Otis Skinner, illustrated by

Jessie Wilcox Smith w/nine color plates 15.00

"All the Way to Fairyland," 8 color illustrations, 1897 ....7.50

"An Elephant Up a Tree," by H.W. Van Loon, 1933 ....10.00

"Animal Mother Goose Story," by Ruth E. Newton, published by Whitman, 1945 ....10.00

"Animated Animals," illustrated by Julian Wehr, 1945 ....15.00

"Around the World in An Automobile," chromolithograph scenes from Niagara Falls to Mt. Vesuvius, published by McLoughlin, 1907.......55.00

"Around the Zoo," color illustrations, 1910 ....20.00

"At the Back of the North Wind," illustrated by Jessie Wilcox Smith........55.00

"Aunt Jo's Scrap Bag," by Louisa Mae Alcott, 1893 ....14.00

"A Woe Begon Little Bear," by Thornton Burgess, 1929 ....15.00

"Baby's First Book," 6 color animal plates, published by McLoughlin, 1896 ....12.00

"Baby's First Christmas," by Eloise Wilkin, Little Golden Book of 1940's & 50's, 8 x 6" 3.75

"Baby's Opera," illustrated by Walter Crane, w/color plates, published by McLoughlin Bros., 1877 ......25.00 to 30.00

"Bambi," by Felix Salten, illustrated by Kurt-Wise, 1929, dust jacket illustrated by John Galsworthy 30.00

"Beauty & The Beast," published by Raphael Tuck, diecut outlines, 1900 ..20.00

"Billy Whiskers at the Fair," by Frances Montgomery, 1909 ....9.00

"Billy Whiskers - Tourist," 1929 ....10.00

"Billy Whisker's Vacation," 1908 ....18.00

"The Birds Christmas Carol," color plates by Helen Mason Grose, 1929 ...8.50

"Black Beauty," published by Saalfield Co., 1905 ....10.00

"Bobbsey Twins" series, each ....2.00 to 5.00

"Boys & Girls of Bookland," illustrated by Jessie Wilcox Smith..............65.00

"Chatterer the Red Squirrel," by Thornton Burgess, 1915 ....17.00

"The Cherry Scarecrow," by Johnny Gruelle, 1929.....................10.00

"Christmas Sunshine," published by McLoughlin Bros., 1905, linen cover ..10.00

"Christmas Time in Action," pop-up-type, 1949 ....10.00

"The Clown's Acrobatic Alphabet," 1928 ....20.00

"The Cruise of Rickety-Tobin," by Johnny Gruelle 20.00

"Doctor Doolittle's Zoo," by Hugh Lofting, illustrated, 1925, 1st edition 60.00

"The Emerald City of Oz," by L. Frank Baum, illustrated by J.R. Neill, ca. 1917 ....15.00

"The Fairy Caravan," by Beatrix Potter, 6 full color pages of illustrations, 1929, colored pictorial cover, 214 pp. 50.00

"Father Christmas," color illustrations, published by Raphael Tuck, 1903 .....22.00

"Father Goosey Gander," by Blanche Hule, color illustrations, published by Donahue, 1898 ....20.00

"Father Tuck's Fairy Tale Series - Little Red Riding Hood," 4 pp. color illustrations, published by Raphael Tuck 25.00

"Five Little Pepper's Little Brown House," by Margaret Sidney, Boston, 1907 ....12.50

"Freckles," by Gene Stratton Porter, illustrated by E. Stetson Crawford, 1904 ....13.00

"Fun for Tiny Tots," illustrated by Palmer Cox 10.00

"Funny Animals," by Palmer Cox, illustrated 25.00

"Little Black Sambo," New York, 6 full page color illustrations by Fern Peat, 1931, 10 x 13" 35.00

"Sleeping Beauty," pop-up edition, illustrated by H. Lentz, 1933 ....85.00

"The Tale of Johnny Town-Mouse," by Beatrice Potter, published by F. Warne & Co., 1918, 4 x 5¾" (ILLUS.).............................25.00

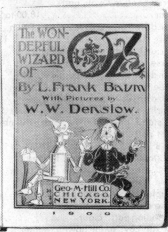

"The Wonderful Wizard of Oz"

"The Wonderful Wizard of Oz," by L. Frank Baum, illustrated by W.W. Denslow, published by George M. Hill Co., 1900, 1st edition (ILLUS.) 1,430.00

CHILDREN'S DISHES

Menagerie Pattern Table Set

During the reign of Queen Victoria, doll houses and accessories became more popular and as the century progressed, there was greater demand for toys which would subtly train a little girl in the art of homemaking.

Also see ABC PLATES, BROWNIE COLLECTIBLES, BUSTER BROWN COLLECTIBLES, CAMPBELL KID COLLECTIBLES, AKRO AGATE and PATTERN GLASS.

Berry set: master berry bowl & 6
   sauce dishes; pressed glass, Lacy
   Daisy patt., clear, 7 pcs. $45.00
Bowl, graniteware, grey, monkey
   riding elephant .25.00
Bowl, master berry, pressed glass,
   Oval Star patt., Northwood Glass
   Co., clear 25.00
Butter dish, cov., pressed glass,
   Arrowhead in Ovals patt.,
   clear. .18.00 to 28.00
Butter dish, cov., pressed glass, Drum
   patt., clear 125.00
Butter dish, cov., pressed glass,
   Nursery Rhymes patt., clear 75.00
Butter dish, cov., pressed glass,
   Sweetheart patt., clear 35.00
Butter dish, cov., pressed glass,
   Whirligig patt., clear 25.00
Cake stand, pressed glass, Baby Thumb-
   print patt., clear, 3 x
   4 1/8" . . . . .110.00 to 125.00
Cake stand, pressed glass, Rexford
   patt., clear. 25.00
Cheese dish, cov., pressed glass,
   Stippled Vine & Beads patt., clear 28.00
Cheese dish, cov., pressed glass,
   Threading patt., clear 45.00
Table set: cov. sugar bowl, creamer &
   spooner; pressed glass, Paneled
   Diamond Block patt., clear, 3 pcs. 38.00
Table set: cov. butter dish, cov. sugar
   bowl, creamer & spooner; pressed
   glass, Drum patt., clear, 4 pcs. 285.00
Table set: cov. butter dish, cov. sugar
   bowl, creamer & spooner, pressed
   glass, Menagerie patt., clear, 4 pcs.
   (ILLUS.) 2,100.00

Table set: cov. butter dish, open sugar
   bowl, creamer & spooner; pressed
   glass, Stippled Vine & Beads
   patt., clear, 4 pcs. 60.00
Teapot, cov., china, Blue Willow patt. . . .12.00
Teapot, cov., china, girl feeding
   teddy bear, marked "Germany" 15.00
Tea set: cov. teapot, cov. sugar
   bowl & 3 c/s; china, Granny Goose
   patt., 8 pcs. 18.00
Tea set: cov. teapot, sugar bowl, 4
   c/s & 4 plates; china, circus clowns
   & animals decor, marked "Germany,"
   ca. 1900, 14 pcs. 165.00
Tray, pressed glass, Doyle's 500 patt.,
   amber. 35.00
Tumbler, pressed glass, Patee Cross
   patt., clear . . . . .8.00 to 12.00
Tureen, cov., china, Blue Willow patt.,
   6 x 3" . . . . .15.00 to 22.50

Frances Ware Water Set

Water set: pitcher & 6 tumblers;
   Frances ware, frosted hobnail
   w/amber rim, 7 pcs. (ILLUS. of
   part) 250.00
Water set: pitcher & 6 tumblers; pressed
   glass, Patee Cross patt., clear
   7 pcs. 75.00
Water set: pitcher, 6 tumblers & tray;
   pressed glass, Oval Star patt.,
   clear, 8 pcs. .165.00
Wine jug, pressed glass, Wheat Sheaf
   patt., Cambridge Glass Co., clear 80.00

CHILDREN'S MUGS

The small size mug used by children first attempting to drink from a cup, appeals to many collectors. Because they were made of china, glass, pottery, graniteware, plated silver and silver, the collector is given the opportunity to assemble a diversified collection or to single out one particular type of decoration, such as Franklin Maxims, or a specific material, such as glass, around which to base his collection. Also see BABY

MEMENTOES, FRANKLIN MAXIM WARES, CARNIVAL, CUSTARD, DEPRESSION and PATTERN GLASS.

"A Good Girl" Glass Mug

China, alphabet-type, transfer & gold
  trim, Germany, 2¾" h. $25.00
China, circus clowns decal, pink lustre
  trim, Germany, late 19th - early
  20th c., 2" h. 18.00
China, transfer print of "Little Bo Peep"
  w/rhyme & scene, 3½" h. 67.50
China, transfer print of "Little Boy Blue"
  w/rhyme & scene, England, late
  19th - early 20th c. 45.00
China, scene of "Santa Claus Examin-
  ing His Record" decor. 60.00
China, orange & white elephant parade
  in relief, early Goebel mark,
  Germany 60.00
China, ironstone, all white, 1½" h. 8.00
Coin silver, bright-cut decor, Wood &
  Hughes, ca. 1846 .... 210.00
Coin silver, gadroon border, Eoff &
  Connor, ca. 1833 .... 275.00
Pressed glass, embossed alphabet, log
  handle, clear 55.00
Pressed glass, footed, "A Good Girl"
  within floral wreath, green, 3¾" h.
  (ILLUS.) 22.50
Pressed glass, Butterfly & Spray patt.,
  amber 45.00
Pressed glass, Ceres patt., amber 38.00
Pressed glass, Cupid & Venus patt.,
  clear, 2" h. 35.00
Pressed glass, Dahlia patt., clear 28.00
Pressed glass, Dog & Bird patt.,
  beaded handle, clear .... 30.00 to 40.00
Pressed glass, Heron & Peacock patt.,
  blue opaque or cobalt blue, each 40.00
Pressed glass, Heron & Peacock patt.,
  clear 30.00
Pressed glass, Hobnail patt., blue 25.00
Pressed glass, "Humpty Dumpty" patt.,
  w/"Tom Thumb" reverse, clear
  (ILLUS.) .... 32.00 to 45.00

"Humpty Dumpty" Mug

Pressed glass, Liberty Bell patt.,
  clear .... 95.00 to 135.00
Pressed glass, Monkey patt., clear 65.00
Pressed glass, Oval Medallion patt.,
  clear 20.00
Pressed glass, Owl & Bird patt., clear ... 40.00
Pressed glass, Rose in Snow patt.,
  clear 22.00
Pressed glass, Shell & Tassel patt.,
  blue, 2½" h. 38.00
Pressed glass, Sporting Bears patt.,
  clear 55.00
Pressed glass, Standing Dog patt.,
  black amethyst 125.00
Pressed glass, Standing Dog patt.,
  clear 55.00
Pressed glass, Thousand Eye patt.,
  vaseline 25.00
Staffordshire pottery, canary yellow
  lustre w/silver lustre rim &
  black transfer w/initial "E" within
  rayed circle, early 19th c., 2" h.
  (interior hairline) 300.00
Staffordshire pottery, canary yellow
  printed in black w/rabbit in a garden & inscribed "A Rabbit For
  William" within floral vine, ca.
  1820, 2 5/8" h. 412.00
Staffordshire pottery, canary yellow &
  pink lustre printed in black w/"A
  Trifle For Daniel" within border of
  acorns & oak leaves below a pink
  lustre rim band, ca. 1820, 2¼" h. 110.00
Staffordshire pottery, copper lustre
  w/blue band decor exterior & pink
  lustre interior rim 45.00
Staffordshire pottery, blue transfer "A
  Present for Sarah," brown base & rim
  stripes, 2 7/8" h. 175.00
Staffordshire pottery, black transfer
  scene of mother cat & kittens,
  2¼" h. 70.00
Staffordshire pottery, black transfer
  bust portraits of men w/inscription
  "We be Loggerheads Three - a Point
  of honour," 2½" h. (minor stains) 50.00
Staffordshire pottery, brown transfer of
  child skipping rope, 2½" h. (minor
  stains) 40.00
Staffordshire pottery, red transfer of

American Eagles shields & "The Land of Liberty," 2½" h. (stains & base flakes) 260.00

Staffordshire pottery, rose-red transfer of "The Actors" w/two children on stage 35.00

Staffordshire pottery, barrel-shaped, soft blue transfer "The Sisters," 1860s, 1860s, 4¼" d., 3¼" h. 125.00

Sterling silver, "Old Mother Hubbard" & "Sing a Song of Sixpence" decor, monogrammed initials, Gorham 225.00

CHRISTMAS TREE LIGHTS

Along with a host of other Christmas-related items, early Christmas tree lights are attracting a growing number of collectors. Comic characters seem to be the most popular form among the wide variety of figural lights available, most of which were manufactured between 1920 and World War II in Germany, Japan and the United States. Figural bulbs listed are painted clear glass unless otherwise noted.

Andy Gump $25.00
Angel in flower 37.00
Aviator, milk white 25.00
Banjo 20.00
Basket of flowers, milk white 25.00
Bear in suit, milk white 30.00
Bell w/embossed Santa faces 9.00
Bird, blue, pink, or red, each 8.00
Bird in cage 12.00
Boy, milk white 24.00
Boy holding airplane 38.00
Candle, milk white . . . . 10.00 to 15.00
Cat, milk white 10.00
Cat in boot 32.00
Cat & the fiddle, milk white, 4" h. 15.00 to 22.00
Choir girl, milk white 20.00
Clown's head 21.50
Cross 13.00
Dick Tracy 45.00
Dirigible, milk white, w/painted American flags each side, 3" l. 34.00
Dog in basket 24.00
Dog with bandage 42.00
Dog wearing hunting clothing 25.00
Duckling 22.00
Dunce's head 37.00
Dwarf (from Snow White & Seven Dwarfs) 32.00
Elephant, seated, milk white 22.00
Father Christmas, double-sided 18.00
Fish 25.00
Frog 12.00
Girl w/muff, milk white 20.00

Grapes 8.00
House, snow-covered 6-sided cottage, milk white w/orange & red paint, 2¾" . . . . 10.00 to 14.00
House w/Santa at chimney 35.00
Humpty Dumpty 35.00
Jack-O-Lantern 30.00
Japanese lantern, 3" . . . . 10.00 to 15.00
Kayo 35.00
Kewpie 45.00
Lion w/tennis racket 15.00
Little Red Riding Hood 30.00
Mickey & Minnie Mouse, pr. 48.00
Moon Mullins, milk white 45.00
Mother Goose 35.00
Orphan Annie or Sandy, each 45.00
Pagoda 6.50
Parrot . . . . 7.00 to 12.00
Parrots in birdcage, milk white 20.00
Pig 35.00
Pinecone 9.00
Red Riding Hood 52.00
Rosebud, milk white 16.50
Santa Claus w/bag, double-sided, milk white, 3" . . . . 14.00 to 22.00
Santa Claus, 3" . . . . 11.00 to 16.00
Santa Claus, double-sided, 4" 30.00
Santa Claus, 6" 95.00
Skull & crossbones 15.00
Smitty 35.00
Snowflake, tin w/pink bulb, Nippon 13.00
Snowman 12.00
Snowman w/bag, milk white w/painted bag, 3" . . . . 15.00 to 20.00
Star w/face 26.00
Teddy bear 40.00
Three Men in a Tub 35.00

CHRISTMAS TREE ORNAMENTS

Embroidered Christmas Tree Ornament

The German blown glass Christmas tree ornaments and other commercially-made ornaments of wax, cardboard and cotton batting, were popular from the time they were first offered for sale in the United

States in the 1870s. Prior to that time, Christmas trees had been decorated with homemade ornaments that usually were edible. Now nostalgic collectors who seek out ornaments that sold for pennies in stores across the country in the early years of this century, are willing to pay some rather hefty prices for those ornaments considered to be an unusual or of an artistic form.

Angel, tree-top figure, embossed litho-
  graphed paper w/gilt highlights,
  spun glass wings, 9" h. $40.00
Angel, wax w/spun glass wings 85.00
Angel, blown glass, spring clip 85.00
Baby bunting, blown glass, large. 85.00
Ball, candy container type, papier
  mache w/children decor, ca. 1910,
  3" d. 38.00
Bear w/muff, blown glass. 75.00
Bear w/stick, blown glass. 55.00
Bell, cotton batting. 28.00
Bell, crepe paper, w/Santa's face 85.00
Bird, blown glass, clear, tin clip
  marked "Germany" 25.00
Bird, hand-embroidered, separately
  attached wings & tail, ecru w/muted
  olive green stitching, 6" l., 4½" h.
  (ILLUS.). 6.00
Bugle, blown glass 20.00
Bust of baby Jesus, blown glass 75.00
Bust of Santa, blown glass, 3" h. 40.00
Cat in shoe, blown glass, silvered 55.00
Christmas stocking, blown glass 65.00
Christmas tree, blown glass, spring
  clip 45.00
Clown's head, blown glass, silver
  w/red, black & yellow, 3¾" h. 45.00
Clown w/banjo, blown glass, 4½" h. . . .45.00
Crown, blown glass 55.00
Cuckoo clock, blown glass 30.00
Disney characters, ball-shaped, Donald
  Duck, Mickey Mouse, Minnie Mouse
  or Pluto, each . . . . .15.00 to 20.00
Dog on ball, blown glass, large 80.00
Eagle, Dresden-type cardboard, glass
  eyes, large. .250.00
Ear of corn, blown glass 42.50
Elephant, blown glass 90.00
Elk, Dresden-type cardboard, small . . .125.00
Father Christmas, cotton batting 125.00
Father Christmas, papier mache,
  yellow, 8" h. 285.00
Fish, blown glass, 6" l. 70.00
Girl in rose, blown glass, 3" h. 80.00
Girl's head w/bows in hair, blown
  glass. 80.00
Gnome on a tree stump, blown glass . .145.00
Graf Zeppelin, blown glass. 225.00
Grape cluster, blown glass, red
  w/silver leaves, 2¼" w., 3½" l.
  (ILLUS.) . . . . .50.00 to 60.00

Blown Glass Christmas Tree Ornament

Happy Hooligan standing, blown
  glass. 160.00
Heart, blown glass, 3" 30.00
Horse, Dresden-type cardboard. 165.00
Hot air balloon, blown glass 30.00
Ice skater, blown glass, magenta
  costume trimmed w/cotton fur &
  glitter, 6" h. .40.00
Icicle, cotton batting 12.00
Insect on flower, blown glass 65.00
Kugel (blown glass ball), light green
  exterior w/silvered interior, brass
  top. 35.00
Man, blown, glass, 3" h. 105.00
Man-in-the-moon, blown glass 40.00
Monkey, blown glass, clear, tin clip
  marked "Germany" 125.00
Moose, Dresden-type cardboard 145.00
"Old Lady Who Lived in a Shoe," die-
  cut lithographed paper, dated 1885. . .65.00
Owl on ball, blown glass, pink, 3" 85.00

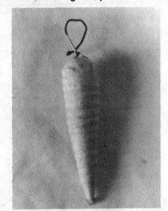

Papier Mache Christmas Tree Ornament

Parsnip, papier mache, 3½" l. (ILLUS.) . . .3.00
Peacocks, mother & baby, blown glass,
  spring clip 30.00
Pear, cotton batting 15.00
Pocket watch, blown glass 55.00
Revolver, blown glass, pink & blue 110.00
Rose, blown glass, spring clip 45.00
Sailboat, gold mesh & braid 150.00
Santa Claus holding tree, blown glass,
  3" h. (ILLUS.) .25.00

Santa Claus Christmas Tree Ornament

Santa Claus, papier mache & felt,
4" h. 25.00
Santa Claus, full figure w/plaster face,
fur beard & wire legs, holding goose
feather tree, German, 6" h. 85.00
Santa Claus seated in decorated
wreath, papier mache 45.00
Skier w/bisque face & cotton batting
body 95.00
Snowman, blown glass 15.00
Squirrel w/nut, blown glass 75.00
Stag leaping, blown glass, blue 40.00
Stork, Dresden-type cardboard 200.00

Wooden Christmas Tree Ornament

Violin, hand-carved walnut, 4¼" l.
(ILLUS.) 35.00
Zeppelin, "Los Angeles," w/American
flag, blown glass 200.00

CIGAR & CIGARETTE CASES, HOLDERS & LIGHTERS

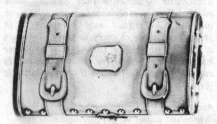

Silver-Gilt Cigar Case

Cigar case, silver-gilt, oblong trunk
form w/straps, carrying handle &
riveted borders, w/applied monogram cartouche on lid, St. Petersburg, Russia, 1866-69, 5½" l.
(ILLUS.) $990.00
Cigar case, silverplate, hinged 3-com-
partment case w/three cigars in
relief, early 20th c. 80.00
Cigar case, silverplate, olbong
w/rounded corners, 3-compartment,
gold-washed interior 28.00
Cigar case, sterling silver & bakelite,
torpedo-shaped telescopic model
that collapses when empty, made to
hold "White Dot" cigar made for the
French market, 1920s. 85.00
Cigar holder, amber w/gold "pique" &
intaglio-carved nudes 60.00
Cigar holder, amber w/gold mounts,
in silver case, 1905 . . . . .65.00
Cigar holder, ivory, in original plush-
lined case, 3¾" l. 25.00
Cigar holder, meerschaum, carved
buxom lady seated on lounge,
w/amber mouthpiece, 3¾" l. 65.00
Cigar holder, meerschaum, carved
w/three dogs, original case 50.00
Cigar holder, mother-of-pearl, 3" l. 45.00
Cigar lighter, counter-type w/adver-
tising for "El Pricipe de Gales
Havana Cigars," equestrian figure
on base 310.00
Cigar lighter, counter-type kerosene
model, "Rosa," w/original globe 290.00
Cigar lighter, desk or table model,
English bulldog wearing a Derby hat,
seated & w/cigar in mouth, 4" h. 125.00
Cigarette case, brass w/cobalt blue
enameled lid, original box, 1950s 22.50
Cigarette case, gold, tubular, engine-
turned w/bands of reeding converg-
ing in a single point on each side,
w/sapphire thumbpiece, original
fitted case, signed "Cartier," Lon-
don, 3 1/8" l. .715.00
Cigarette case, 18k gold, oblong,
hinged cover engraved w/mytho-
logical figure leaning against pedes-

tal, geometric borders w/foliate leaf-tips, Switzerland, ca. 1820, 3½" l. 825.00

Cigarette case, silver, oblong, hinged cover enameled w/a nude maiden reclining on bed, Continental, 1910-20, 3¾" l. 440.00

Cigarette case, silver-gilt & shaded enamel, oblong, hinged cover enameled "en plein" w/central oval reserve depicting peasant woman & her son crossing a river, borders w/stylized birds & scrolling florals & foliage, Moscow, 1879, 4½" l. ... 1,980.00

Cigarette case, silver-gilt, oblong, hinged cover "repousse" & chased w/an Art Nouveau flowering plant, cabochon sapphire thumbpiece, signed "Faberge," Moscow, ca. 1890, 3 5/8" l. 1,980.00

Cigarette case, silverplate, engraved scene of caddy & golfer wearing knickers on lid, enameled rust accents on stockings & sweater, gold-washed interior, "Evans" 48.00

Cigarette case, sterling silver, oblong w/rounded corners, hand-hammered, 4½ x 3" 95.00

Cigarette case, sterling silver, oblong, "repousse" decor, ca. 1895 . . 60.00 to 70.00

Cigarette case, sterling silver, w/gold-washed bands, oblong, marked "Elgin" 49.00

Cigarette case, gold-washed sterling silver w/enameled Art Nouveau pheasant on lid 165.00

Cigarette holder, carved ivory 35.00

Cigarette holder, meerschaum, carved w/dog, original case 38.00

Cigarette holder, silver, Russian hallmark 100.00

Cigarette lighter, brass, model of revolver, "Bully," dated 1914 ...... 30.00

Cigarette lighter, celluloid, bowling pin shape 30.00

Cigarette lighter, chrome w/enameled Art Deco "Jesters" decor, marked "Zenith" 40.00

CIGAR & TOBACCO CUTTERS

Counter-type, cast iron, advertising, "Arrow-Cupples Co." $45.00

Counter-type, cast iron, advertising, "Brown's Mule Tobacco, R.J. Reynolds Tobacco Co.," by "Enterprise Mfg. Co., No. 5837," 8½ x 8" 72.50

Counter-type, cast iron, advertising, "Five Bros. Tobacco Works, John Finzer & Bros., Louisville, Ky.,"

ornate & w/original painted pin-striping .... 65.00 to 85.00

Counter-type, cast iron, advertising, "Hulman & Co. Wholesale Grocers, Terre Haute, Ind." 75.00

Counter-type, cast iron, advertising, "Imperial Cigars," w/"Home Trade - Peace & Plenty - Charles Schiller, Duluth" 135.00

Counter-type, cast iron, advertising, "Red Seal Cigars" 85.00

"Reliance Cigar" Counter Model

Counter-type, advertising, "Reliance Cigars," cast iron, designed to dispense, cut & light cigars, base (held cigar boxes) w/cigars molded in relief & top w/gilt figure of boy leaning against lion w/lamp to rear & wick & cutter at front, by "Nosch & Co., New York," ca. 1880, 11" sq. base, overall 17" h. (ILLUS.) 1,430.00

Counter-type, cast iron, advertising, "Sailor's Pride Tobacco" 125.00

Counter-type, cast iron, "Standard Cutter" by "Reading Hardware Co." . . 47.50

Counter-type, cast iron, advertising, "Star Brand Tobacco," Jan. 29, 1885 patent 55.00

Counter-type, cast iron, "The Champion Knife Improved," by "Enterprise Mfg. Co., Philadelphia," original paint & pinstriping 45.00

Counter-type, cast iron, Greek woman in running position, original paint ... 650.00

Desk model, cast metal model of a monkey, holding decorative brass cutter overhead, creamy onyx base, 5½" h. 175.00

Desk model, silverplate, model of horse's head w/bridle & flowing mane, 5¾" l. 95.00

Pocket-type, advertising, "Havana

Cigars," silverplate w/etched
florals 30.00
Pocket-type, advertising, "Lord Closter
Cigars," metal, model of a pipe
tamper 15.00
Pocket-type, 10k gold, Masonic
emblem decor 48.00
Pocket-type, 14k gold, heart-shaped,
1¼ x 1" 85.00
Pocket-type, gold-plated oval slide-
type, 1916 patent 35.00
Pocket-type, mother-of-pearl & brass,
scissors-type 34.00
Pocket-type, nickel-plated brass,
scissors-type . . . . .12.00 to 15.00

Scissors-Style Cigar Cutter

Pocket-type, sterling silver, scissors-
type (ILLUS.) 35.00
Pocket-type, sterling silver, slide-type
w/chased designs 25.00

CLOCKS

*Also see ADVERTISING ITEMS,
AUTOMOBILE ACCESSORIES, ART
DECO, ART NOUVEAU, BREWER-
IANA, CHARACTER COLLECTIBLES
and DISNEY COLLECTIBLES.*

Alarm, Ansonia Clock Co., Ansonia,
Connecticut, "Simplex" model, 30-
hour time & alarm movement $50.00
Alarm, "Big Ben," nickelplate case,
black dial, alarm repeat movement,
1919 . . . . .30.00
Animated, Lux Clock Co., Waterbury,
Connecticut, "Black Cat" 90.00
Animated, Lux Clock Co., Waterbury,
Connecticut, "Spinning Wheel" 85.00
Animated, Lux Clock Co., Waterbury,
Connecticut, "Steamboat" (show-
boat) . . . . .75.00 to 110.00
Animated, Lux Clock Co., Waterbury,
Connecticut, "Woody Wood-
pecker" 200.00

Banjo Clock by Aaron Willard

Banjo, Aaron Willard, Boston, Massachusetts, brass 8-day time & strike
movement, drum clock w/white-painted
dial & seconds register surmounted
by giltwood acorn finial, mahogany
case w/"eglomise" panel in throat
painted w/grapes flanked by brass
fillets & geometric "eglomise" panel
in lower door w/spherule-mounted
acorn pendant below, ca. 1825,
41" h. (ILLUS.) 2,750.00
Banjo, E. Howard & Co., Boston,
drum clock w/white-
painted dial w/minute register &
inscribed w/maker's name,
mahogany case w/"eglomise" panel
in throat & shaped door below
w/oval "eglomise" panel
exposing pendulum bob, ca.
1850, 51½" h 1,870.00
Banjo, New Haven Clock Co., New
Haven, Connecticut, drum clock
w/white-painted dial, brass bezel,
mahogany case w/gilt metal eagle
finial, "eglomise" panel in throat
flanked by brass fillets &
w/transfer of Mount Vernon in
lower door, ca. 1930 . . . . .300.00
Banjo, Simon Willard & Son, drum
clock w/white-painted dial signed
by maker, mahogany case
w/"eglomise" panel in throat &
oblong "eglomise" panel in lower
door, 1815-25 (restored acorn
finial) 2,640.00
"Blinking Eye," cast iron figure of
Sambo, wearing green-painted hat,
brown & green vest over yellow
shirt & striped trousers, ca. 1860,
16" h. (ILLUS.) 1,320.00

"Blinking Eye" Clock

Carriage, Ansonia Clock Co., Ansonia, Connecticut, double-faced porcelain dial, brass case w/beveled glass sides, 10" h. 599.00

Carriage, Waterbury Clock Co., Waterbury, Connecticut, 4½" d. white enamel dial, brass case w/beveled glass sides, dated "Jan. 15, 1878" on rear door 325.00

China case, Ansonia Clock Co., Ansonia, Connecticut, Royal Bonn china case w/floral decor, boudoir size 300.00

China case, Ansonia Clock Co., Ansonia, Connecticut, Royal Bonn china case w/scroll-molded florals shaded deep rose to pink, 14" h. 500.00

China case, Gilbert Clock Co., Winsted, Connecticut, china case w/relief-molded Art Nouveau woman to the side of clock-face, large size 350.00

Double Dial Waterbury Calendar Clock

Double dial calendar, Waterbury Clock Co., Waterbury, Connecticut, double dials in die-pressed oak case w/free-standing reeded columns, molded base, ca. 1890, 29" h. (ILLUS.) .... .700.00 to 1,200.00

Double dial calendar, Ithaca Calendar Clock Co., Ithaca, New York, Model No. 9 .... .850.00

Double dial calendar, Seth Thomas Clock Co., Thomaston, Connecticut, "Office Model No. 7," 8-day time & strike movement, 10" time dial & 8" calendar dial, walnut case, overall 26½" h. 875.00

Double dial calendar, Waterbury Clock Co., Waterbury, Connecticut, 8-day time & strike movement, white-painted dial, oak case, late 19th c., 24" h. 605.00

Gallery, Gilbert Clock Co., Winsted, Connecticut, ornate oak case, ca. 1910 .... .200.00

Grandfather, unknown maker, white-painted dial w/painted floral & bird spandrels, cherrywood hooded case w/three brass finials, dial & door flanked by free-standing columns, waist w/shaped door flanked by fluted columns, molded base, bracket feet, New England, ca. 1800, 17" w., 80" h. 2,530.00

Pennsylvania Tall Case Clock

Grandfather, Jacob Godshalk, Philadelphia, Pennsylvania, brass dial w/sunburst design above maker's name & date register, Queen Anne walnut case w/flat-top hood above door flanked by turned columns, waist w/arched door on shaped iron hinges, molded base, ca. 1760, 22" w., 81" h. (ILLUS.) 5,500.00

Grandfather, Adam Brant, New Hanover, Pennsylvania, engraved brass dial w/maker's name, Queen Anne style walnut hooded case w/molded cornice above door flanked by turned columns, waist w/shaped door, molded base, ogee bracket feet, 19¾" w., 83" h. (some alteration to hood & repair to door) 4,950.00

Grandfather, Timothy Chandler, Concord, New Hampshire, white-painted dial w/minute & date registers above maker's name, maple hooded case w/pierced crest centering 3 brass ball finials, waist w/molded door, molded base, bracket feet, ca. 1815, 17¼" w., 89" h. 6,600.00

Grandfather, John Bailey, Hanover, New Hampshire, white-painted dial w/minute & date registers centering maker's name, cherry-wood hooded case in the Chippendale style w/swan's neck cresting ending in carved rosettes & brass urn finials at sides, waist w/molded arch door flanked by fluted pilasters, molded base, ogee bracket feet, ca. 1780, 21" w., 89" h. 6,050.00

Grandfather, William Mitchell, Jr., Richmond, Virginia, painted concave dial inscribed w/maker's name enclosed in door w/"eglomise" red, green & gilt spandrels, case w/flat top & w/free-standing columns flanking door exposing face, waist & w/door & mirror enclosed within gilt liner & free-standing columns w/gilt capitals, plain base w/applied half-round moldings at sides on cut-out feet, interior of case stenciled "Henry Williard Clock Case Manufacturer, 843 Washington St." & stamped "1601," w/weights, pendulum & key, ca. 1840, 91" h. 3,740.00

Grandfather, Frederick Dominick, Philadelphia, brass & silvered dial w/engraved roundel above centering a white owl, gilt metal spandrels & engraved w/maker's name below, walnut hooded Chippendale-style case w/swan's neck cresting centering 3 finials above the arched door, waist w/molded arch-top door, base w/applied scalloped panel, (replaced) ogee bracket feet, ca. 1770, 18¼" w., 94" h. 4,400.00

Grandfather, Joseph Thomas, Norristown, Pennsylvania, white-painted dial w/phases of the moon, minute & date registers, cherrywood hooded case w/swan's neck cresting ending in carved rosettes & centered w/turned finial above the arched dial door flanked by turned columns, waist w/paneled door, plain base on flaring bracket feet, ca. 1820, 101" h. 3,850.00

Kitchen, Gilbert Clock Co., Bristol & Winsted, Connecticut, "Boston" model, 8-day time & strike movement w/alarm, gingerbread-carved oak case 130.00

Kitchen, Ingraham Clock Co., Bristol, Connecticut, 8-day time & strike movement, white enamel dial, gingerbread-carved oak case 120.00

Kitchen, New Haven Clock Co., New Haven, Connecticut, 8-day time, strike & calendar movement, gingerbread-pressed oak case w/morning glory motif in shaped crest, late 19th c., restored, 23" h. 165.00

Kitchen, E.N. Welch Manufacturing Co., Bristol, Connecticut, 8-day time & strike movement w/alarm, ornate gingerbread-carved case, brass pendulum embossed "Colby Wringer Co" & inset w/colored glass center 195.00

Kitchen, Waterbury Clock Co., Waterbury, Connecticut, gingerbread-carved oak case, 22" h. . . . . 175.00 to 225.00

Rare Lighthouse Clock

Lighthouse, Simon Willard, Roxbury, Massachusetts, original blown clear glass dome w/knob finial & applied swirling rigaree enclosing the white porcelain dial inscribed "Simon Willard's Patent" surrounded by cast ormolu florals below a bell w/anthemion-chased finial on mahogany veneered tapering cylindrical case w/ormolu bandings & mounted w/ormolu crossed arrows, torches & swags on octagonal base, brass hairy paw feet, ca. 1825, 25" h. (ILLUS.)................286,000.00

Schoolhouse, Ansonia Clock Co., Ansonia, Connecticut, 8-day time & strike movement, octagon-top oak case w/short drop, late 19th c., 25" h. ....175.00 to 300.00

Schoolhouse, Ansonia Clock Co., Ansonia, Connecticut, 8-day time movement only, round-top black mahogany case, short drop, late 19th c........................260.00

Schoolhouse, Seth Thomas Clock Co., Thomaston, Connecticut, time & strike movement, mahogany case, short drop 250.00

Schoolhouse, Waterbury Clock Co., Waterbury, Connecticut, oak case, short drop 175.00

Schoolhouse, Waterbury Clock Co., Waterbury, Connecticut, pressed pattern oak case w/long drop 325.00

Case-on-Case Shelf Clock

Shelf clock, case-on-case, Benjamin Morril, Boscowen, New Hampshire, white-painted dial signed by maker in kidney-shaped opening, cherrywood case w/checkered-line inlay, upper case w/shaped crest & gilt metal American eagle finial, lower case w/bird's eye maple inlaid diamond reserve, bracket feet, ca. 1815, 12¾" w., 45" h. (ILLUS.) 11,000.00

Shelf, or mantel, Pillar & Scroll case, Eli Terry, Plymouth, Connecticut, wooden works movement, white-painted dial w/floral scroll

spandrels, mahogany & mahogany veneer case w/replaced urn finials, "eglomise" panel in lower door, 31¼" h........................1,000.00

Shelf, or mantel, Pillar & Scroll case, Mark Leavenworth & Son, Waterbury, Connecticut, white-painted dial w/floral spandrels, mahogany case w/scrolling crest & vigorously carved columns w/pineapple finials flanking door, animal paw feet, early 19th c. 1,650.00

Shelf, or mantel, Pillar & Scroll case, Wadsworth, Lounsbury & Turner, Litchfield, Connecticut, 30-hour wooden works movement, white-painted wooden dial, mahogany case w/scrolling crest & brass urn finials, free-standing columns flanking door w/restored "eglomise" panel in lower part, w/original label, ca. 1830, 29" h............632.50

Shelf, or mantel, Steeple case, Brewster & Ingraham, Bristol, Connecticut, 8-day time & strike movement, mahogany veneer case w/turned spires & 4 free-standing columns, 19" h....................475.00

Shelf, or mantel, Steeple case, A.G. Brown, Forestville, Connecticut, white-painted dial, steeply gabled crest flanked by turned tapering finials over 2-panel glazed door w/stenciled floral design in lower door flanked by ripple-carved columns, ripple-carved base, ca. 1845, 16" h. 990.00

Shelf, or mantel, Ansonia Clock Co., Ansonia, Connecticut, 8-day time & strike movement, white enamel dial, cast iron case w/applied lion's mask & drop ring handles at sides ...145.00

Shelf, or mantel, Ansonia Clock Co., Ansonia, Connecticut, 8-day time & strike movement, white enamel dial, cast iron case w/cherubs 325.00

European Shelf Clock

Shelf, or mantel, European maker, bronze case w/ornate design, early 1900s, 10" w., 13" h. (ILLUS.).........75.00

Shelf, or mantel, E. Ingraham & Co., Bristol, Connecticut, "Venetian" model, 30-hour time & strike movement, round-top rosewood case w/reverse painting of hot air balloon in lower door, ca. 1880.....125.00

Shelf, or mantel, E. Ingraham & Co., Bristol, Connecticut, "Ionic" model, 8-day movement..................315.00

Shelf, or mantel, Sessions Clock Co., Bristol & Forestville, Connecticut, white enamel dial, "Camel-back" walnut case, 1930s............125.00

Ship's, Chelsea Clock Co., Chelsea, Massachusetts, w/ship's bells, 6" d. dial, brass case.............225.00

Ship's, Seth Thomas Clock Co., Thomaston, Connecticut, w/exposed ship's bell, silvered dial, brass case..........................450.00

Statue, Ansonia Clock Co., Ansonia, Connecticut, white metal case mounted w/figures of "Superba" & "LaSourse," green onyx base, large...........................850.00

"Swinging Doll" Clock

"Swinging Doll," Ansonia Clock Co., Ansonia, Connecticut, white enamel dial, round brass case attached to cast metal tree trunk hung w/bisque (repaired) figure of a child seated in swing, ca. 1890, overall 8" h. (ILLUS.).........................550.00

Wag-on-wall, M. Donald, Bridgeton, brass keywind movement, white-painted dial w/corner spandrels representing the four continents, complete w/painted bracket, weights & pendulum, ca. 1810, 20¼" h. dial..................550.00

Wall regulator w/calendar, Ansonia

Clock Co., Ansonia, Connecticut, "Regulator Model A," 8-day time & calendar movement, 12" dial, octagon-top walnut case w/long drop, 32" h. 425.00

Wall regulator, Ansonia Clock Co., Ansonia, Connecticut, "Santa Fe" model, 8-day time & strike movement, black walnut case, 10" d. dial, 52" h. 1,250.00

Wall regulator, E. Ingraham & Co., Bristol, Connecticut, Ionic model, brass 8-day time & strike movement w/alarm, rosewood figure-8 case w/gilt lip liner, ca. 1880, 22" h. 395.00

Wall regulator, Gilbert Clock Co., Winsted, Connecticut, time movement w/calendar, oak box-shaped case 275.00

Seth Thomas Wall Regulator

Wall regulator, Seth Thomas, Plymouth Hollow, Connecticut, 8-day movement, white-painted dial, round-top rosewood veneer case w/reverse-painted black & gilt lower door, ca. 1860, 31¼" h. (ILLUS.).........................605.00

Wall regulator, E.N. Welch Manufacturing Co., Bristol, Connecticut, time movement w/calendar, round top oak case, short drop 400.00

CLOISONNE

Cloisonne work features enameled designs on a metal ground. There are several types of this work, the best-known utilizing cells of wire on the body of the object into which the enamel is placed. In the plique-a-jour form of

*cloisonne, the base is removed leaving trans-
lucent enamel windows. "Pigeon Blood"
cloisonne is a pseudo-cloisonne with foil enclosed within clear glass walls. Cloisonne is
said to have been invented by the Chinese and
brought to perfection by the Japanese.*

Bowl, multicolored hanging wisteria
vines, variegated green fern, butterflies & chrysanthemums on charcoal
grey ground, grey florals & foliage
center, ornate gold interior rim,
4 1/8" h., 8½" d. $725.00
Box, cov., round cushion shape,
scattered maple leaves outlined in
silver & gold on navy blue ground,
Japanese, late 19th c., 2 7/8" d. 200.00
Charger, scalloped rim w/detailed
border, blue florals & green leaves
w/two birds in flight & another
perched in a bush on turquoise blue
ground, 12" d. 435.00

Cloisonne Ginger Jar

Ginger jar, cov., scaly dragon in
search of the flaming pearl decor,
mid-19th c., 6½" h. (ILLUS.) 425.00
Incense container, coiling dragon on
cover, blue, red, brown & green
enhanced w/goldstone, 2¾" d.,
1 3/8" h. 115.00
Jar, cov., aqua, white, green & deep
red lacy floral & scrolling decor on
pink ground, 3 3/8" d., 3¾" h. 235.00
Plate, profuse florals & a bluebird in
flight against a river & mountain
landscape, vivid colors enhanced
w/goldstone, soft pink border,
8¼" d. 425.00
Plique-a-jour vase, ovoid, pastel
hydrangea blossoms on soft green
ground, 5¼" h. 790.00
Rose petal jar, cov., light blue, navy
blue, green & goldstone panels
filled w/birds, flowers & butterflies,
4¾" d., 4" h. 275.00

Salt dip, individual size, squatty,
florals on blue fishscale ground 30.00
Teapot, cov., multicolored florals &
6 butterflies on royal blue ground,
2¼ x 4" 245.00
Urns, cov., multicolored florals on turquoise shaded to green ground,
marked "China," 10" h., pr. 285.00

Cloisonne Vase

Vase, butterflies & florals on dark
blue, black & green ground, brass
rim, 3¼" h. (ILLUS.) 115.00
Vase, blooming prunus trees w/pair of
colorful birds on cobalt blue ground,
diapered collar & base borders,
7½" h. 380.00
Vase, white florals, green branches &
birds on deep red ground,
11¾" h. .1,100.00

COCA-COLA ITEMS

*Coca-Cola promotion has been achieved
through the issuance of scores of small
objects through the years. These, together
with trays, signs, and other articles bearing
the name of this soft drink, are now sought
by many collectors.*

Bag rack, metal, w/"Boy Sprite" $85.00
Billfold, pigskin, pictures gold
Coca-Cola bottle & "Have a Coke" 25.00
Blotter, 1904, red & white "Pure and
Healthful - Drink Coca-Cola, etc."
in oval flanked by straight-sided
bottles 100.00
Blotter, 1937, large bottle before
"icy" lettering of "Cold" 12.00
Blotter, pin-up girl at beach, 1940s 8.00
Blotter, 1951 . . . . .6.00

Blotter, 1953, Sprite Boy, "Good".......5.50
Blotter, 1954 ....4.00
Blotter, 1956, Santa, "Twas the Coke
    before Christmas" 5.00
Blotter, Andrews Sisters pictured 8.00
Booklet, "The Truth about Coca-Cola,"
    1912 ....31.50

Bottle Carrying Case

Bottle carrying case, wooden w/wooden
    slat handle, 1920s (ILLUS.)..........46.00
Bottle carrying case, cardboard,
    6-pack, 1937 ....17.50
Bottle carrying case, aluminum, 24-
    bottle 49.00
Bottle opener, 1909 ....16.00

1918 Calendar

Calendar, 1918, Distributor's, w/June
    Caprice (ILLUS.)...................110.00
Calendar, 1921, Summer Girl at
    Ballpark (no pad) 175.00
Calendar, 1926, girl seated on picnic

table holding glass of Coca-Cola
    w/tennis racket, tennis balls & bottle
    of Coca-Cola beside her, complete
    w/pads..........................235.00
Calendar, 1932, Norman Rockwell
    illustrations 180.00
Calendar, 1944, 6 pp.................20.00
Calendar, 1956, 6 pp.................25.00
Calendar, 1959, girl w/bottle of Coca-
    Cola at basketball game front page,
    6 pp. 25.00
Counter display, Santa Claus, color-
    printed cardboard, 18" h. 17.50
Coupon for complimentary drink, Lillian
    Russell, 1905 ....90.00 to 135.00
Doll, stuffed plush Santa Claus,
    18" h. 50.00
Door lock, Kam Indore Lock Co.,
    ca. 1910 ....32.00
Door pull plate, bottle-shaped 98.00
Door push plates, tin, "Refresh Your-
    self - Drink Coca-Cola in Bottles,"
    one says "Push," other says "Pull,"
    1940s, 3 x 6", pr..................85.00
Fan, Geisha girl pictured, 1911 ......122.00
Fan, woven palm reeds, 1915-20 ......40.00
Knife, pocket-type w/corkscrew,
    ornately embossed silverplate
    handle, 1906 ....275.00
Knife, pocket-type, bone handle, 1908 ..87.50
Knife, pocket-type, Remington, bottle-
    shaped when open 100.00
Lamp, hanging fixture, Tiffany-type
    leaded glass, "Coca-Cola 5 cents,"
    1910..........................3,500.00
Mirror, pocket-type, 1911, Coca-Cola
    Girl....................175.00 to 220.00
Mirror, pocket-type, 1914,
    Betty...................190.00 to 225.00
Nature Study Cards, "Birds of
    America" series, 1928, set of 14......10.00
Needle case, w/"Party Girl," on heavy
    paper cover, 1924-25, 2 x 3" 28.00

Convention Token

Token, souvenir of 1915 convention,
    in original presentation box,
    3½ x 2½" (ILLUS.) 65.00

Toy circus, cardboard cut-out set,
  uncut, 1930s......................42.00
Toy drink dispenser, red plastic,
  w/original box, 1960..............170.00
Toy frisbee, 1970...................40.00
Toy truck, metal, "Buddy L," 1960,
  10½" l..........................50.00
Toy wagon, wooden, Atlanta Wagon
  Co., 1940s, 18" l................145.00

1905 Juanita Change Tray

Tray, change, 1905, Juanita (ILLUS.)...225.00

1906 Change Tray

Tray, change, 1906, Relieves Fatigue
  (ILLUS.)................195.00 to 220.00
Tray, change, 1909, Coca-Cola Girl....135.00
Tray, change, 1912, Hamilton King
  Girl....................125.00 to 165.00
Tray, change, 1914, Betty, oval.......100.00
Tray, change, 1917, Elaine, oval......105.00
Tray, change, 1920, Garden Girl,
  oval....................135.00 to 155.00
Tray, 1909, Coca-Cola Girl, oval......425.00
Tray, 1914, Betty, oval...............260.00
Tray, 1917, Elaine, rectangular,
  19 x 8½"........................165.00

Tray, 1921, Summer Girl..............265.00
Tray, 1922, Autumn Girl....240.00 to 300.00
Tray, 1923, Flapper Girl.............145.00
Tray, 1925, Girl at Party............130.00
Tray, 1927, Curb Service.....195.00 to 260.00
Tray, 1930, Bathing Beauty...........130.00
Tray, 1930, Girl with
  Telephone..............80.00 to 120.00
Tray, 1932, Girl in Yellow Swimsuit....240.00
Tray, 1934, Maureen O'Sullivan &
  Johnny Weissmuller (Tarzan &
  Jane)..................275.00 to 350.00
Tray, 1935, Madge Evans.............110.00
Tray, 1936, Hostess.................80.00
Tray, 1937, Running Girl............65.00
Tray, 1938, Girl in the Afternoon.......40.00
Tray, 1939, Springboard Girl...50.00 to 70.00
Tray, 1940, Sailor Girl.............55.00
Tray, 1941, Girl Ice Skater.....45.00 to 65.00
Tray, 1942, Two Girls at Car.........55.00
Tray, 1943, Girl with Wind in Her
  Hair............................40.00
Tray, 1950, Girl with Menu..........27.50
Tray, 1961, Pansy Garden w/"Fishtail"
  emblem on sides..................16.00
Tray, 1972, Duster Girl Reproduction...12.00
Vending machine, red, "10 cents".....190.00
Vendor's bottle holder, wire, holds
  1 dozen.........................43.00
Vendor's apron, cloth, tan w/green
  pin stripes & red patch.............35.00
Vendor's suit & cap, man's, green
  w/red dome-cap, medium size......65.00
Vienna Art tin plate, beautiful lady
  w/flowing brown hair, red dress &
  hoop earrings, dated 1905, ornate
  gilt frame......................185.00
Watch fob, brass, girl w/glass in
  hand, 1908, 1¾ x 1½"............250.00
Watch fob, brass, "Coca-Cola" in
  oval, 1908, w/strap..............145.00
Watch fob, celluloid & metal,
  w/Gibson-type girl, 1906, 1¾ x
  1¼" oval.......................375.00
Watch fob, metal, girl in large hat
  drinking bottle of Coca-Cola in
  relief, 1917, 1½ x 1¼"...........175.00
Yo-yo, wooden, "Drink Coca-Cola".....25.00

COFFEE GRINDERS

Most coffee grinders collected are lap or table and wall types used in many homes in the late 19th and early 20th centuries. However, large store-sized grinders have recently been traded.

Lap-type, advertising, "None-Such,"
  printed tin w/wooden base, by
  the Bronzon Walton Co., Cleveland,

"None-Such" Lap Grinder

Ohio, w/printed directions on
side, 1890s, 5" sq., 8" h. (ILLUS.) . . .$150.00
Lap-type, cast iron base w/drawer,
iron hopper w/handle, dated 1873 . . .75.00
Lap-type, cherrywood base w/machine
dovetailing & drawer, cast iron
hopper & handle 75.00
Lap-type, oak base w/machine
dovetailing & drawer, cast iron
hopper & handle, "Imperial" by
Arcade 65.00
Lap-type, pine base w/machine
dovetailing & drawer, tall-style
w/handle at side, cast iron hopper
& handle w/wooden knob 85.00
Lap-type, tin, "Elma," 35.00
Store counter model w/crank handle,
cast iron, "Enterprise No. 1,"
12½" h. 165.00
Store counter model, single wheel,
cast iron, "Enterprise No. 2,"
w/iron hopper & drawer in base,
12½" h. . . . . .150.00 to 300.00
Store counter model, 2-wheel, cast iron,
"Enterprise No. 5," original paint,
w/patent date of 1878, 15½" d.
wheels, overall 17½" h. 285.00
Store counter model, 2-wheel, cast iron,
"Enterprise No. 7," w/patent
date of 1873, 17" d.
wheels . . . . .425.00 to 450.00
Store counter model, 2-wheel, cast iron,
"Landers, Frary & Clark," original
paint, 10" d. wheels 550.00
Store floor model, 2-wheel, cast iron,
"Enterprise," w/patent date of
1898, original red paint & brass
hopper w/eagle finial 3,000.00
Store floor model, 2-wheel, cast iron,
"Star Mill, Philadelphia," ornamental
base centering pierced star designs,
painted red w/gilt highlights &
stenciled inscription "Henry

"Star Mill"

"Troemner Maker, Philadelphia,"
ca. 1885, 61" h. (ILLUS.) 880.00
Table model, advertising, "Grand Union
Tea Co.," cast iron 175.00
Table model, cast iron, "Favorite Mill -
Arcade Manufacturing Co." 75.00
Wall-type, advertising, "Golden Rule
Coffee the finest Blend in the
World," cast iron, wood & tin,
overall 17" h. .165.00
Wall-type, cast iron w/glass jar,
"Kitchen Aid," by Hobard Mfg. Co. . . .22.00
Wall-type, cast iron & sheet iron,
"Mystic," V-shaped 15.00
Wall-type, cast iron w/red glass jar
marked "Koffie," crank handle at
side, measuring cup at base, mounted
on wooden board 75.00
Wall-type, cast iron w/glass jar,
"Steinfield No. 17," ornate 32.00
Wall-type, cast iron, "Telephone Mill -
Arcade Manufacturing Co.," w/patent
date of 1893, 13" h. 325.00
Wall-type, cast iron & sheet iron,
"Universal," 13¼" h. 95.00
Wall-type, cast iron w/blue & white
"Delft" faience jar 195.00

COMIC BOOKS

*Comic books, especially first, or early
issues of a series, are avidly collected today.
Prices for some of the scarce ones have
reached extremely high levels. Prices listed
below are for copies in fine to mint
condition.*

Dell Comics

Abbott & Costello, No. 16	$10.00
Action, No. 30, 1940	40.00
Avengers (The), No. 93, 1971	20.00
Barney Google & Sparkplug, No. 1, 1923	35.00
Barney Google & Sparkplug, No. 4, 1926	38.00
Beverly Hillbillies, No. 18	1.75
Blondie Comics, No. 38	1.50
Blue Bolt, No. 107, 1950	10.00
Bob Colt Western, No. 4	10.00
Bonanza, No. 21	1.50
Boy Comics, No. 26, 1945	20.00
Brave & the Bold (The), No. 52	5.00
Bringing Up Father, No. 15, 1929	25.00
Bugs Bunny, No. 8, 1942	65.00
Captain Marvel in St. Paul, Minn., Vol. 7, No. 42, 1945	36.00
Charlie Chaplin, No. 318, 1917	45.00
Daniel Boone, No. 7	1.00
Donald Duck, No. 238, 1949	23.00
Fairy Tale Parade, No. 69, 1945	18.00
Famous Feature Stories, Vol. 1, No. 1, 1938	140.00
Fantastic Comics, No. 6, 1941	40.00
F Troop, No. 3	1.75
Ghost Rider, No. 4, 1951	20.00
Great Comics, No. 1	27.00
Green Lantern, No. 81	10.00
Hit Comics, No. 2, 1940	120.00
Hogan's Heroes, No. 1	2.50
Hopalong Cassidy, No. 89, 1954	3.00
I Spy, No. 1	3.50
Jimmy Wakely, No. 4	20.00
Joe Palooka, No. 57, 1951	9.00
King Comics, No. 14, 1937	30.00
Lancer, No. 2	2.25
Lassie, No. 65	.75
Legend of Custer (The), No. 1	2.50
Lone Ranger (The), Vol. 1, No. 17	7.50
Lone Ranger (The), Vol. 1, No. 60	7.50
Lone Ranger (The), Vol. 1, No. 141, 1961	4.00
Mad, No. 3	80.00

Mad, No. 5, 1953	25.00
Man from U.N.C.L.E. (The), No. 18	1.50
Master Comics, No. 4, 1940	45.00
Mission Impossible, No. 3	4.50
Mod Squad, No. 1	2.25
More Fun Comics, No. 58, 1940	180.00
Mutt & Jeff, No. 7	46.00
Mutt & Jeff, No. 14, 1929	45.00
Nyoka The Jungle Girl, No. 30	15.00
Pep Comics, No. 9, 1940	40.00
Pep Comics, No. 12, 1942	60.00
Rat Patrol (The), No. 2	3.00
Secret Agent, No. 1	2.75
Star Ranger, No. 3, 1937	28.00
Superman, No. 4	400.00
Superman, No. 36	50.00
Superman, No. 74	25.00
Target Comics, No. 3, 1940	70.00
Tillie the Toiler, No. 5, 1930	15.00
Tillie the Toiler, No. 8, 1933	20.00
Tom Mix Western, 1949	15.00
Two-Fisted Tales, No. 24, 1951	12.00
Uncle Wiggily Helps Jimmy, 1946	6.50
Walt Disney's Comics & Stories, Vol. 28, No. 1	5.00
Western Roundup, No. 1	15.00
X-Men (The), No. 1, 1963	150.00

COMMEMORATIVE PLATES

Limited edition commemorative and collector plates rank high on the list of collectible items. The oldest and best-known of these plates, those of Bing & Grondahl and Royal Copenhagen, retain leadership in the field, but other companies are turning out a variety of designs, some of which have been widely embraced by the growing numbers who have made plate collecting a hobby. Plates listed below are a representative selection of the fine porcelain and glass plates available to collectors.

ANRI

1971 Christmas, St. Jakob In Groden	$76.50
1972 Christmas, Pipers At Alberobello	85.00
1973 Christmas, Alpine Horn	335.00
1974 Christmas, Young Man & Girl	79.00
1975 Christmas, Christmas in Ireland	70.00
1976 Christmas, Alpine Christmas	170.00
1977 Christmas, Legend Of Heiligenblut	125.00
1978 Christmas, The Klockler Singers	70.00
1979 Christmas, The Moss Gatherers of Villnoess	70.00
1980 Christmas, Wintry Churchgoing in Santa Christina	92.00
1981 Christmas, Santa Claus in Tyrol	105.00
1982 Christmas	125.00
1983 Christmas	124.00

BAREUTHER

1971 Bareuther Christmas Plate

1967 Christmas, Stiftskirche 110.00
1968 Christmas, Kappelkirche 35.00
1969 Christmas, Christkindlesmarkt 22.00
1970 Christmas, Chapel in Oberndorf ...18.50
1971 Christmas, Toys for Sale (ILLUS.)...29.50
1972 Christmas, Christmas in Munich ...37.00
1973 Christmas, Sleigh Ride 26.00
1974 Christmas, Black Forest Church....25.50
1975 Christmas, Snowman 24.00
1976 Christmas, Chapel in the Hills 20.00
1977 Christmas, Story Time...........22.50
1978 Christmas, Mittenwald 24.00
1979 Christmas, Winter Day 21.00
1980 Christmas, Mittenberg 21.50
1981 Christmas, Walk in the Forest 20.00
1982 Christmas, Bad Wimpfen 22.00
1983 Christmas 20.00
1969 Father's Day, Castle Neuschwan-
   stein 36.50
1970 Father's Day, Castle Pfalz........16.00
1971 Father's Day, Castle Heidelberg ...18.50
1972 Father's Day, Castle Hohen-
   schwangau 20.00
1973 Father's Day, Castle Katz 26.00
1974 Father's Day, Castle Wurzburg 27.50
1975 Father's Day, Castle Lichtenstein ..23.50
1976 Father's Day, Castle Hohenzol-
   lern 22.00
1977 Father's Day, Castle Eltz.........21.00
1978 Father's Day, Castle Falkenstein...21.50
1979 Father's Day, Castle Rheinstein....21.00
1980 Father's Day, Castle Cochum 22.50
1981 Father's Day, Castle Gutenfels ...22.50
1982 Father's Day, Castle Zwingen-
   berg 22.50
1983 Father's Day, Castle Lauenstein ...23.50
1969 Mother's Day, Dancing 29.00
1970 Mother's Day, Mother & Children ..16.00
1971 Mother's Day, Doing the Laundry ..17.00
1972 Mother's Day, Baby's First Step 18.00
1973 Mother's Day, Mother Kissing
   Baby 21.00

1974 Mother's Day, Musical Children ...19.00
1975 Mother's Day, Spring Outing 21.00
1976 Mother's Day 18.00
1977 Mother's Day 18.00
1978 Mother's Day 16.50
1979 Mother's Day 16.00
1980 Mother's Day 20.00
1981 Mother's Day 18.50
1982 Mother's Day 20.50
1983 Mother's Day 21.00

BELLEEK

1970 Belleek Christmas Plate

1970 Christmas, Castle Caldwell
   (ILLUS.)..........................89.00
1971 Christmas, Celtic Cross..........41.00
1972 Christmas, Flight of the Earls......45.00
1973 Christmas, Tribute to Yeats 60.00
1974 Christmas, Devenish Island 185.00
1975 Christmas, The Celtic Cross 56.00
1976 Christmas, Dove of Peace 54.00
1977 Christmas, Wren 54.00
1978 Wildlife Christmas, A Leaping
   Salmon 60.00
1979 Wildlife Christmas, Hare at Rest ...59.00
1980 Wildlife Christmas, The Hedgehog 58.00
1981 Wildlife Christmas, Red Squirrel ...60.00
1982 Wildlife Christmas, Irish Seal......78.00

BING & GRONDAHL

1895 Christmas 2,610.00
1896...........................1,170.00
1897............................685.00
1898............................400.00
1899............................870.00
1900............................530.00
1901............................215.00
1902............................185.00
1903............................155.00
1904.............................65.00
1905.............................78.50
1906.............................44.00
1907.............................58.50

1908 ....36.50
1909 ....43.50

1910 Bing & Grondahl Plate

1910 (ILLUS.) 43.00
1911 ....36.00
1912 ....36.00
1913 ....36.50
1914 ....36.00
1915 ....62.00
1916 ....34.00
1917 ....34.50
1918 ....35.00
1919 ....33.50
1920 ....32.50
1921 ....29.50
1922 ....27.00
1923 ....30.50
1924 ....31.00
1925 ....30.00
1926 ....33.00
1927 ....40.50
1928 ....25.50
1929 ....34.00
1930 ....39.50
1931 ....32.50
1932 ....36.00
1933 ....29.50
1934 ....33.50
1935 ....32.50
1936 ....35.00
1937 ....33.00
1938 ....49.00
1939 ....72.00
1940 ....76.50
1941 ....120.00
1942 ....79.50
1943 ....76.50
1944 ....40.00
1945 ....57.00
1946 ....32.00
1947 ....39.00
1948 ....26.00
1949 ....28.50
1950 ....58.00
1951 ....38.00
1952 ....42.00

1953 ....33.00
1954 ....47.00
1955 ....41.00
1956 ....52.00
1957 ....60.00
1958 ....42.00
1959 ....59.00
1960 ....92.00
1961 ....51.00
1962 ....32.00
1963 ....56.00
1964 ....26.00
1965 ....30.50
1966 ....23.50
1967 ....24.50
1968 ....20.50
1969 ....15.50
1970 ....14.50
1971 ....10.00
1972 ....9.50
1973 ....16.00
1974 ....11.00
1975 ....10.50
1976 ....10.00
1977 ....11.00
1978 ....13.50
1979 ....15.00
1980 ....17.50
1981 ....20.50
1982 ....21.50
1983 ....24.50
1969 Mother's Day, Dog & Puppies.....285.00
1970 Mother's Day, Birds & Chicks 25.50
1971 Mother's Day, Cat & Kitten 8.00
1972 Mother's Day, Mare & Foal 8.00
1973 Mother's Day, Duck & Ducklings ...8.00
1974 Mother's Day, Bear & Cubs........13.00
1975 Mother's Day, Doe & Fawns 9.00
1976 Mother's Day, Swan Family 9.50
1977 Mother's Day, Squirrel & Young ..12.00
1978 Mother's Day, Heron 10.00
1979 Mother's Day, Fox & Cubs........14.00
1980 Mother's Day, Woodpecker &
    Young...........................15.50
1981 Mother's Day, Hare & Young 16.50
1982 Mother's Day, Lioness & Cubs 19.00
1983 Mother's Day, Raccoon & Young ...19.00
1960 Jubilee, Kronborg Castle 74.50
1965 Jubilee, Churchgoers 43.00
1970 Jubilee, Amalienborg Castle 14.00
1975 Jubilee, Horses Enjoying Meal 19.50
1980 Jubilee.........................22.50

FRANKOMA
1965 Christmas, Goodwill Towards
    Men...........................190.00
1966 Christmas, Bethlehem Shep-
    herds 99.00
1967 Christmas, Gifts for the Christ
    Child..........................72.50
1968 Christmas, Flight into Egypt.......15.50
1969 Christmas, Laid in a Manger 10.00
1970 Christmas, King of Kings 8.00
1971 Christmas, No Room in the Inn 10.00

1972 Christmas, Seeking the Christ
    Child 8.00
1973 Christmas, The Annunciation 6.00
1974 Christmas 6.00
1975 Christmas 6.00
1976 Christmas 4.00
1977 Christmas 7.00
1978 Christmas 7.50
1979 Christmas 8.00
1980 Christmas 8.00
1981 Christmas 7.50
1982 Christmas 6.00

GORHAM - NORMAN ROCKWELL
1971 Four Seasons, Boy & His Dog,
    set of 4 . . . . .355.00
1972 Four Seasons, Young Love, set
    of 4 . . . . .115.00
1973 Four Seasons, Ages of Love, set
    of 4 . . . . .215.00
1974 Four Seasons, Grandpa & Me, set
    of 4 . . . . .110.00
1975 Four Seasons, Me & My Pal, set
    of 4 . . . . .125.00
1976 Four Seasons, Grand Pals, set
    of 4 . . . . .235.00
1977 Four Seasons, Going on Sixteen,
    set of 4 . . . . .160.00
1978 Four Seasons, The Tender Years,
    set of 4 . . . . .87.50
1979 Four Seasons, A Helping Hand,
    set of 4 . . . . .57.50
1980 Four Seasons, Dad's Boy, set of 4 . .83.00
1981 Four Seasons, Old Timers, set
    of 4 . . . . .76.50
1982 Four Seasons, Life with Father,
    set of 4 . . . . .60.00

HAVILAND & CO.
1970 Christmas, Partridge in a Pear
    Tree 100.00
1971 Christmas, Two Turtle Doves 29.00
1972 Christmas, Three French Hens 13.00
1973 Christmas, Four Colly Birds 16.50
1974 Christmas, Five Golden Rings 15.00
1975 Christmas, Six Geese A' Laying 15.00
1976 Christmas, Seven Swans A'
    Swimming 20.50
1977 Christmas, Eight Maids A'
    Milking 29.00
1978 Christmas, Nine Ladies Dancing . . .33.00
1979 Christmas, Ten Lords A' Leaping . . .19.50
1980 Christmas, Eleven Pipers Piping . . .30.50
1981 Christmas, Twelve Drummers
    Drumming 35.50

HUMMEL (Goebel Works)
1971 Christmas .610.00
1972 Christmas 49.00
1973 Christmas .115.00
1974 Christmas 58.00
1975 Christmas 55.00
1976 Christmas 50.00
1977 Christmas 65.00

1978 Christmas .50.00
1979 Christmas .35.00
1980 Christmas .42.00
1981 Christmas .49.00
1982 Christmas .72.00
1983 Christmas 100.00
1975 Mother's Day, Rabbits 40.00
1976 Mother's Day, Cats 43.00
1977 Mother's Day, Panda 42.00
1978 Mother's Day, Doe & Fawn 42.00
1979 Mother's Day, Long Eared Owl 46.00
1980 Mother's Day, Raccoon & Baby 47.00
1981 Mother's Day, Ringed Seal 48.00
1982 Mother's Day, Swan 50.00
1983 Mother's Day 72.00

KAISER
1970 Christmas .18.50
1971 . . . . .15.50
1972 . . . . .13.50
1973 . . . . .32.00
1974 . . . . .22.00
1975 . . . . .17.00
1976 . . . . .17.00
1977 . . . . .14.00
1978 . . . . .17.00
1979 . . . . .18.50
1980 . . . . .27.00
1981 . . . . .42.00
1982 . . . . .40.00

LALIQUE (GLASS)

1968 Lalique Annual Plate

1965 Annual 1,585.00
1966 Annual 150.00
1967 Annual 135.00
1968 Annual (ILLUS.) 65.00
1969 Annual 71.00
1970 Annual 54.00
1971 Annual 58.50
1972 Annual 48.00
1973 Annual 40.00
1974 Annual 43.50
1975 Annual 46.00
1976 Annual 90.00

LENOX BOEHM

1970 Wood Thrush 198.00
1971 Goldfinch 63.00
1972 Mountain Bluebird...............45.00
1973 Young American Bald Eagle.......61.00
1973 Meadowlark 43.00
1973 Mute Swans 195.00
1974 Rufous Hummingbirds...........54.50
1975 American Redstart 39.00
1976 Cardinals......................37.00
1977 Robins 34.00
1978 Mockingbirds 45.00
1979 Golden-crowned Kinglets 49.00
1980 Black-throated Blue Warblers 60.00
1981 Eastern Phoebes 71.00
1973 Wild Life - Raccoons............50.00
1974 Wild Life - Red Fox 33.00
1975 Wild Life - Rabbits.............50.00
1976 Wild Life - Chipmunks 51.00
1977 Wild Life - Beaver.............43.00
1978 Wild Life - Whitetail Deer 48.50
1979 Wild Life - Squirrels 51.00
1980 Wild Life - Bobcats 61.00
1981 Wild Life - Martens 73.00
1982 Wild Life - Otter 77.50

ORREFORS (Glass)

1970 Annual, Notre Dame Cathedral ...34.00
1971 Annual, Westminster Abbey 34.00
1972 Annual, Basilica Di San Marco.....33.50
1973 Annual, Cologne Cathedral 61.00
1974 Annual, Rue De La Victoire 42.00
1975 Annual, Basilica Of San Peitro,
     Rome 40.00
1976 Annual, Christ Church, Philadel-
     phia...........................39.50
1977 Annual, Mazjuid-E-Shah 81.00
1978 Annual, Santiago de Compostela .61.00

PORSGRUND

1971 Porsgrund Christmas Plate

1968 Christmas, Church Scene 148.50
1969 Christmas, Three Kings..........13.50
1970 Christmas, Road to Bethlehem 8.50
1971 Christmas, A Child is Born
     (ILLUS.).........................10.00

1972 Christmas, Hark the Herald
     Angels Sing 14.00
1973 Christmas, Promise of the Savior ..16.00
1974 Christmas, The Shepherds 24.00
1975 Christmas, Road to Temple 12.50
1976 Christmas, Jesus & the Elders 14.00
1977 Christmas, Draught of the Fish 14.00
1978 Christmas, Guests are Coming 14.00
1979 Christmas, Home for Christmas ...16.00
1980 Christmas, Preparing for Christ-
     mas............................18.00
1981 Christmas, Christmas Skating 20.00
1982 Christmas, White Christmas 22.00
1971 Father's Day, Fishing............6.00
1972 Father's Day, Cookout 4.50
1973 Father's Day, Sledding 5.50
1974 Father's Day, Father & Son with
     Wheelbarrow 6.00
1975 Father's Day, Skating 5.50
1976 Father's Day, Skiing 4.50
1977 Father's Day, Soccer 7.50
1978 Father's Day, Canoeing 7.50
1979 Father's Day, Father & Daughter...11.00
1980 Father's Day, Sailing 11.00
1981 Father's Day 11.50
1982 Father's Day 13.00
1970 Mother's Day, Mare & Foal 5.50
1971 Mother's Day, Boy & Geese 5.00
1972 Mother's Day, Doe & Fawn 5.00
1973 Mother's Day, Cat & Kittens 7.50
1974 Mother's Day, Boy & Goats.......7.50
1975 Mother's Day, Dog & Puppies 7.50
1976 Mother's Day, Girl & Calf 7.50
1977 Mother's Day, Boy & Chickens 10.00
1978 Mother's Day, Girl & Pigs 10.00
1979 Mother's Day, Boy & Reindeer 10.00
1980 Mother's Day, Girl & Lambs 11.00
1981 Mother's Day, Boy & Birds 11.00
1982 Mother's Day, Child with Rabbit ...12.00

RED SKELTON PLATES

1976 Freddie 340.00
1977 W.C. Fields 67.00
1979 Freddie in Bath Tub 196.00
1980 Freddie's Shack 80.00
1981 Freddie on the Green 68.50
1982 Love That Freddie 57.00

RORSTRAND

1968 Christmas, Bringing Home the
     Tree 299.00
1969 Christmas, Fisherman Sailing
     Home 46.00
1970 Christmas, Nils with His Geese
     (ILLUS.).........................17.00
1971 Christmas, Nils in Lapland 15.50
1972 Christmas, Dalecarlian Fiddler ...12.50
1973 Christmas, Farm in Smaland 65.50
1974 Christmas, Vadstena.............52.00
1975 Christmas, Nils in Vastmanland ...15.00
1976 Christmas, Nils in Uppland.......11.00
1977 Christmas, Nils in Varmland 11.00
1978 Christmas, Nils in Fjallbacka 17.00

1970 Rorstrand Christmas Plate

1979 Christmas, Nils in Vaestergoet-
land.............................18.00
1980 Christmas, Nils in Holland 26.00
1981 Christmas, Nils in Gotland........23.00
1982 Christmas, Nils at Skansen 29.00
1983 Christmas 32.00

ROSENTHAL

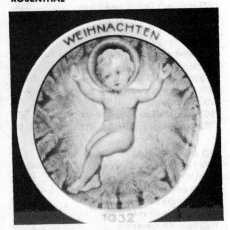

1932 Rosenthal Christmas Plate

1910-1967 Christmas, German Christmas scenes, each (ILLUS. of 1932
issue) 156.00
1968 Christmas, Bremen 72.00
1969 Christmas, Rothenburg on the
Tauber 52.00
1970 Christmas, Cologne on the Rhine ..31.00
1971 Christmas, Garmisch - Parten-
kirchen.........................56.00
1972 Christmas, Franconia 69.00
1973 Christmas, The Gates of Lubeck ...86.00
1974 Christmas, Wurzburg 61.00
1975 Christmas, City of Freiburg 70.00
1976 Christmas, Burg Cochem 47.00
1977 Christmas, Hanover Town Hall 91.00

1978 Christmas, Cathedral at Aachen ..100.00
1979 Christmas, Cathedral in Luxem-
burg 100.00
1980 Christmas, Brussels.............130.00
1981 Christmas, Trier................120.00
1982 Christmas, Milan Cathedral 120.00
1971 Wiinblad Christmas, Maria &
Child.........................1,310.00
1972 Wiinblad Christmas, King
Caspar 540.00
1973 Wiinblad Christmas, King
Melchior.......................415.00
1974 Wiinblad Christmas, King
Balthazar 290.00
1975 Wiinblad Christmas, The Annunciation 145.00
1976 Wiinblad Christmas, Angel with
Trumpet 130.00
1977 Wiinblad Christmas, Adoration of
the Shepherd....................190.00
1978 Wiinblad Christmas, Angel with
Harp 125.00
1979 Wiinblad Christmas, Exodus from
Egypt..........................160.00
1980 Wiinblad Christmas, Angel with
Glockenspiel....................145.00
1981 Wiinblad Christmas, Christ Child
Visits Temple....................190.00
1982 Wiinblad Christmas, Christening
of Christ 150.00
1983 Wiinblad Christmas.............130.00

ROYAL COPENHAGEN

1916 Royal Copenhagen Christmas Plate

1908.........................1,165.00
1909 ....97.00
1910 ....66.50
1911 ....82.00
1912 ....79.00
1913 ....69.50
1914 ....67.00
1915 ....74.50
1916 (ILLUS.) 47.00
1917 ....47.00
1918 ....48.00
1919 ....48.00
1920 ....46.00

1921	43.00
1922	39.00
1923	37.00
1924	55.00
1925	47.00
1926	48.00
1927	77.00
1928	45.00
1929	45.00
1930	56.00
1931	50.00
1932	47.00
1933	67.00
1934	62.00
1935	81.00
1936	82.00
1937	86.00
1938	155.00
1939	165.00
1940	250.00
1941	195.00
1942	225.00
1943	285.00
1944	120.00
1945	210.00
1946	90.00
1947	125.00
1948	98.00
1949	105.00
1950	115.00
1951	210.00
1952	74.50
1953	66.00
1954	80.00
1955	115.00
1956	105.00
1957	60.50
1958	72.00
1959	76.00
1960	98.00
1961	100.00
1962	135.00
1963	48.00
1964	45.00
1965	37.00
1966	31.00
1967	29.00
1968	18.00
1969	19.50
1970	20.50
1971	14.00
1972	11.00
1973	12.00
1974	12.00
1975	10.00
1976	19.00
1977	12.00
1978	13.00
1979	36.00
1980	19.50
1981	20.00
1982	21.00
1983	21.00
1971 Mother's Day, American Mother	10.00

1972 Mother's Day, Oriental Mother	6.00
1973 Mother's Day, Danish Mother	7.00
1974 Mother's Day, Greenland Mother	7.50
1975 Mother's Day, Bird in Nest	8.00
1976 Mother's Day, Mermaids	7.50
1977 Mother's Day, The Twins	8.50
1978 Mother's Day, Mother & Child	8.50
1979 Mother's Day, A Loving Mother	9.50
1980 Mother's Day, An Outing with Mother	11.50
1981 Mother's Day, Reunion	13.00
1982 Mother's Day, Children's Hour	13.00

ROYAL DOULTON

1972 Christmas, Christmas in England	33.00
1973 Christmas, Christmas in Mexico	22.00
1974 Christmas, Christmas in Bulgaria	27.00
1975 Christmas, Christmas in Norway	51.00
1976 Christmas, Christmas in Holland	37.00
1977 Christmas, Christmas in Poland	31.00
1978 Christmas, Christmas in America	21.00

SCHMID HUMMEL

1971 Christmas Angel	32.50
1972 Christmas, Angel with Flute	21.00
1973 Christmas, The Nativity	140.00
1974 Christmas, The Guardian Angel	17.00
1975 Christmas, Christmas Child	16.00
1976 Christmas, Sacred Journey	21.50
1977 Christmas, Herald Angel	14.00
1978 Christmas, Heavenly Trio	17.00
1979 Christmas, Starlight Angel	16.00
1980 Christmas, Parade into Toyland	32.00
1981 Christmas, A Time to Remember	25.50
1982 Christmas, Angelic Procession	27.00
1983 Christmas	24.00
1972 Mother's Day, Playing Hooky	17.50
1973 Mother's Day, Little Fisherman	48.50
1974 Mother's Day, Bumblebee	14.50
1975 Mother's Day, Message of Love	15.00
1976 Mother's Day, Devotion for Mother	21.00
1977 Mother's Day, Moonlight Return	24.50
1978 Mother's Day, Afternoon Stroll	16.00
1979 Mother's Day, Cherub's Gift	17.00
1980 Mother's Day, Mother's Little Helpers	22.00
1981 Mother's Day, Playtime	23.00
1982 Mother's Day, The Flower Basket	28.00
1983 Mother's Day, Spring Bouquet	26.00

SPODE

1970 Christmas, Partridge	46.50
1971 Christmas, Angels Singing	28.00
1972 Christmas, Three Ships A-Sailing	28.00
1973 Christmas, Three Kings of Orient	45.00
1974 Christmas, Deck the Halls	44.00
1975 Christmas, Christbaum	22.50
1976 Christmas, Good King Wenceslas	21.00
1977 Christmas, Holly & Ivy	33.00
1978 Christmas, While Shepherds Watched	22.00
1979 Christmas, Away in a Manger	29.00

1980 Christmas, Bringing in the Boar's
    Head 27.00
1981 Christmas, Make We Merry 46.50

WEDGWOOD

1970 Wedgwood Christmas Plate

1969 Christmas, Windsor Castle 195.00
1970 Christmas, Trafalger Square
    (ILLUS.) 27.00
1971 Christmas, Picadilly Circus 25.00
1972 Christmas, St. Paul's Cathedral 25.00
1973 Christmas, Tower of London 24.00
1974 Christmas, Houses of Parliament . . 22.00
1975 Christmas, Tower Bridge 25.00
1976 Christmas, Hampton Court 22.00
1977 Christmas, Westminster Abbey 23.00
1978 Christmas, Horse Guards 25.50
1979 Christmas, Buckingham Palace 31.00
1980 Christmas, St. James Palace 33.00
1981 Christmas, Marble Arch 37.00
1982 Christmas, Lambeth Palace 49.00
1983 Christmas 41.00

(End of Commemorative Plate Section)

COOKBOOKS

Cookbook collectors are usually good cooks and will buy important new cookbooks as well as seek out notable older ones. Many early cookbooks were published and given away as advertising premiums for various products used extensively in cooking. While some rare, scarce first edition cookbooks can be very expensive, most collectible cookbooks are reasonably priced. Also see ADVERTISING ITEMS and CAMPBELL KID COLLECTIBLES.

Advertising, "N.K. Fairbank & Co's
    Cottolene Shortening," copyright
    1882, 5 x 7" (ILLUS.) $7.50

Advertising Cookbook

Advertising, "Pillsbury Cookbook," 1914,
    illustrated, 122 pp. 25.00
Advertising, "Preserving with Karo,"
    1912 . . . . 5.00
Advertising, "Royal Baking Powder,"
    1942 . . . . 7.00
"American Family Cook Book," 1954,
    Wallace, 831 pp. 10.00
"Art of Good Cooking," 1966, Peck 10.00
"Atlanta Woman's Club," 1921 . . . . 10.00
"Good Housekeeping Cookbook," 1944,
    illustrated, 981 pp. . . . . 5.00 to 10.00
"Jolly Times," 1934, juvenile recipes 8.00
"Let's Cook It Right," by Davis, 1947,
    hardbound 6.00
"Luchow's German Cookbook," by
    Jan Mitchell 5.50
"The New American Cookbook," 1946 . . 10.00
"The New Butterick Cookbook," 1924 . . . 14.50
"New Columbian White House
    Cookery Book," 1893 . . . . 17.00
"New England Cookbook," 1906 . . . . 17.00
"The Practical Cookbook," by Mrs.
    Bliss, 1887, 1000 recipes 25.00
"Round the World Cookbook," by Ida
    Bailey Allen, 1934, hardbound 10.00
"St. John's Episcopal Church
    Cookbook," 1891, Chicago, 78 pp. 10.00
"Savannah Cookbook," by Harriet
    Ross Colquitt w/introduction by
    Ogden Nash, 1933 . . . . 10.00
"The Tonawanda Review Cookbook,"
    1883, recipes of 500 women 25.00
"Vegetarian Cookbook," 1922 . . . . 3.00
"Vitamin Cook Book," 1941, 319 pp. 8.00
"White House Cook Book," 1911 . . . . 25.00
"White House Cookbook," 1924 . . . . 20.00
"Wise Encyclopedia of Cookery," 1949,
    Wise Co., 1329 pp. 10.00
"Women's Institute Library of Cookery,"
    1919, hard cover, set of 5 . . . . 25.00

COOKIE CUTTERS

Bird in Flight

Recently there has been an accelerated interest in old tin cookie cutters. For the most part, these were made by tinsmiths who shaped primitive designs of tin strips and then soldered them to a backplate, pierced to allow air to enter and prevent a suction from holding the rolled cookie dough in the form. Sometimes an additional handle was soldered to the back. Cookie cutters were also manufactured in great quantities in an outline form that could depict animals, birds, star and other forms, including the plain round that sometimes carried embossed advertising for flour or other products on the handle. Aluminum cookie cutters were made after 1920. Only tin cutters are listed below. Also see ADVERTISING ITEMS.

Basket, flat backplate pierced w/single hole, 4¼" h. $25.00
Bird in flight, flat backplate pierced w/single hole, 3" l. (ILLUS.) 23.00
Boot, flat backplate, 3" h. 55.00
Cat, flat backplate, 3½" h. 29.00
Chick outline, w/brace handle 8.00
Christmas tree, flat backplate pierced w/two holes, 5¾" h. 27.50
Circle outline w/scalloped edge, 4¼" d. 7.00
Cow, flat backplate 36.00
Deer leaping, flat backplate pierced w/single hole, 4½" l...............20.00
Diamond, flat backplate, w/strap handle 15.00
Dog, Setter standing, flat backplate pierced w/single hole, 3"l. 12.00
Dog, flat backplate pierced w/single hole, 4¾" l. 15.00
Dutch lady, flat backplate pierced w/single small hole, 5¼" h. (handle missing) 20.00
Dutchman, flat backplate pierced w/single hole, 4 3/8" h...............15.00
Eagle, flat backplate pierced w/single hole, w/strap handle, 1 7/8" w. 15.00
Elephant, flat backplate, 4½" l. (ILLUS.) 55.00

Elephant Cutter

Heart w/crimped edge, flat backplate...........................8.00
Heart, flat backplate, w/cylindrical handle, 3" h. 37.50
Heart & diamond outlines, w/strap handles, 2¾" & 4¼", pr............8.00
Horse, flat backplate pierced w/two small holes, 6" l. (some rust) 65.00
Horse prancing, flat backplate pierced w/four holes, 7" l. 35.00
Horse standing, flat backplate pierced w/two holes, 5 3/8" l. 20.00
Horse w/rider, flat backplate pierced w/single hole, 14½" w., 10" l. 295.00
Multiple-type, round dish w/hearts, leaf designs, etc., cuts 12 cookies at once, 9½" d., pr. 80.00
Pennsylvania hat, flat backplate, large..............................22.50
Squirrel, flat backplate, 4" h. 25.00

CORKSCREWS

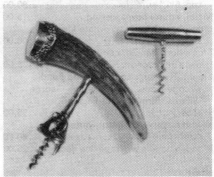

Pair of Corkscrews

More corkscrews should be available to collectors in years to come since wine sales in the United States have shown a profound increase within the past decade. The corkscrew is virtually an essential adjunct to wine since the cork closure adheres tightly to the glass wine bottle and without the pointed spiral shaft of the corkscrew to remove it, the wine could remain bottled forever. Today corkscrew collectors seek out those with unique form, with early patent dates, or with desirable handles that are made from a wide variety of materials. Also see *BOTTLE OPENERS* and *BREWERIANA.*

Advertising, chrome-plated, bottle-
shaped, "Anheuser Busch," brass
plate w/logo & emblem, dated
1897 ....$32.00
Advertising, wooden, "Penmar Distill-
ing, Norfork"........................14.00
Boar's tusk handle w/sterling silver
animal head mount & steel spiral
worm shaft, 4" l. shaft, overall
8" l.................................150.00
Brass, anchor form, souvenir, "Cypress
Gardens" 10.00
Brass, figural cat w/corkscrew in tail,
3¾" l................................45.00
Brass, figural Cheshire cat 110.00
Bronzed steel, concertina mechanism,
Wier's patent of 1884, James Heeley,
Birmingham, England 195.00
Cast iron, bar-mount type, "Cham-
pion," w/brass merchant's label,
Michael Redlinger's patent of 1897,
Arcade Manufacturing Co., Freeport,
Ill....................................200.00
Cast iron, bar-mount type, "Daisy,"
Charles Morgan's patent of 1895,
Burley & Co., Chicago 195.00
Cast iron, bar-mount type, "Yankee
No. 7," R. B. Gilchrest's patent of
1913 ....200.00
Chrome-plated brass cylinder (ILLUS.
right)................................20.00
Ivory handle w/scrolled sterling silver
cap, 5¼" w., 6" l. 80.00
Metal, figural doves kissing 15.00
Stag's horn handle w/ornate sterling
silver cap (ILLUS. left) ......85.00 to 100.00
Stag's horn handle, carved in the form
of an alligator 175.00
Steel, "The Surprise," T-shaped handle
w/cage frame, registered by George
Willetts, Birmingham, England,
1884 ....95.00
Wooden, carved, figural waiter,
removable head w/corkscrew 40.00
Wooden handle w/grapevine decor 25.00

CORONATION ITEMS

Items commemorating the coronation of English monarchs have been produced for

many years. Listed in chronological order according to reign, the following items have been sold, or offered for sale, in recent months. The spectacular 1981 Royal Wedding, uniting Charles, the Prince of Wales, and Lady Diana Spencer in matrimony, has created new interest in this area of collecting.

Edward VII (1901-10) box, printed tin,
portrait of Edward & Alexandra on
red ground, 4½ x 3½"............$22.50
Edward VII cup & saucer, demitasse,
china, portrait of Edward & Alexandra, heavy gold trim, Royal
Doulton 70.00
Edward VII dish, English silver, Indian
rupee w/bust portrait of Edward
center, beaded rim, 4" d. 55.00
Edward VII jug, stoneware, portrait of
Edward & Alexandra on brown & tan
ground, dated 1902, Royal Doulton,
8" h.................................145.00
Edward VII mug, china, Royal Doulton,
3" h. 75.00
Edward VII pitcher, china, portraits of
Edward & Alexandra on blue & green
ground, Royal Doulton.............295.00
Edward VII plate, china, portrait of
Edward & Alexandra & royal crest
center, flow blue edge, Royal
Doulton, 8" d. 65.00
Edward VII plate, china, portrait of
Edward & Alexandra & "June 26,
1902" center, 9" d. 75.00
Edward VII plate, china, portrait of
Edward & Alexandra center, flow
blue edge, 10" d. 72.50
Edward VII tumbler, glass, enameled
portrait of Alexandra, Russian......125.00

Edward VII & Alexandra

Edward VII & Alexandra woven silk
portraits by W.H. Grant, black &
white portraits w/flags & coat-of-
arms in red, blue & gold thread,
original mattes, pr. (ILLUS.) 400.00
George V (1910-36) beaker, china,
portrait of George & Mary of Teck
on flow blue ground, Wedgwood.....57.50
George V cup & saucer, porcelain, h.p.
decor 65.00

George V mug, china, portrait of
  George & Mary of Teck ......45.00 to 55.00
George V pitcher, stoneware, portrait
  of George & Mary, dated 1911, Royal
  Doulton, 6" h.............120.00 to 135.00
George V plate, china, portrait of
  George & Mary center, flow blue
  border, 7" d. 40.00
George V plate, lithographed tin,
  portrait of George & Mary..........95.00
George V playing cards, portrait of
  George, 1911, in original box........18.00
George V tea tile, portraits of George
  & Mary, blue & white decor, 10"......45.00

George V Wine Bottle

George V wine bottle, salt-glazed
  stoneware, crown stopper & relief-
  molded white standards w/oval
  reserve portraits of George & Mary
  on dark ground, Copeland-Spode,
  9½" h. (ILLUS.) 125.00
Edward VIII (January 1936 - December
  1936) beaker, china, portrait of
  Edward, Royal Doulton 65.00
Edward VIII candy tin, "Cremonia
  Toffee," w/portrait photograph of
  Prince of Wales in lounging suit......55.00
Edward VIII candy tin, "Riley's Toffee" ..25.00
Edward VIII creamer, blue & white
  Wedgwood Creamware..............60.00
Edward VIII cup, china, Royal Doulton ..45.00
Edward VIII cup & saucer, china,
  Grindley..........................25.00
Edward VIII cup & saucer, china, Royal
  Albert............................45.00
Edward VIII mug, china, designed by
  Dame Laura Knight.................30.00
Edward VIII mug, china, portrait, flags,
  lion & unicorn 35.00
Edward VIII mug, china, Wedgwood 30.00
Edward VIII pitcher, china, portrait of
  Edward, Aynsley...................15.00
Edward VIII plate, china, Meakin,
  8½" d. 35.00

Edward VIII plate, china, 10" d. 22.00
Edward VIII plate, china, bust portrait
  in relief ....20.00 to 30.00
Edward VIII postcard, portrait of
  Edward wearing lounge suit,
  unused 10.00
Edward VIII sugar bowl, jasper ware,
  white relief portrait of Edward on
  dark blue ground, Wedgwood 85.00
Edward VIII tea towel, cloth, embroidered w/cypher surmounted by
  crown 35.00

COW CREAMERS

Early 20th Century Cow Creamer

*These silver and earthenware cream jugs
were modeled in the form of that beautiful
bovine animal, the original source of their
intended contents. The most desirable
versions are the early silver and Dutch Delft
faience creations turned out in the 18th
century, as well as those produced in the
Staffordshire potteries before the mid-19th
century. However, traditional style cow
creamers, made in the late 19th or in the
20th centuries, are also deemed collectible.
The following group of cow creamers were
offered for sale, or sold at auction, within
recent months.*

Pottery, Delft faience, cow standing on
  base, blue-and-white, sailboats
  decor, 20th c......................$68.00
Pottery, Jackfield, cow in standing
  position on oval base, black glaze,
  gold trim, late 19th c., 7¼" l.,
  5½" h. 110.00
Pottery, Rockingham-glazed, cow in
  standing position, w/lid, mottled
  brown, 19th c., 5½" h..............200.00
Pottery, Staffordshire, cow standing
  on base, orange & white cow on
  green base w/purple lustre stripe,
  w/lid, early 20th c., 4¾" h..........90.00
Pottery, Staffordshire, cow standing,
  brown & white running glaze, w/lid
  intact, early 19th c., 6" l. (tips of
  horns chipped) 245.00

Pottery, Staffordshire, cow standing,
pink floral transfer on white, early
20th c., 7½" l., 5" h. (ILLUS.) 75.00
Silver, long-horned cow standing,
w/insect engraved on lid, 4½" l.,
2½" h. 180.00
Silver, horned cow standing, embossed
insect on lid, hand-chased "poll" &
coat, 7" l., 4½" h. 590.00

CURRIER & IVES

The Assassination of President Lincoln

*This lithographic firm was founded in
1835 by Nathaniel Currier with James M.
Ives becoming a partner in 1857. Current
events of the day were portrayed in the
early days and the prints were hand-colored.
Landscapes, vessels, sport, and hunting
scenes of the west all became popular subjects. The firm was in existence until 1906.
All prints listed are hand-colored unless
otherwise noted.*

Abraham Lincoln - The Nation's
Martyr, medium folio, black &
white $145.00
Adeline, small folio, N. Currier,
1849, framed .55.00
American Scenery, Palenville, N.Y.,
small folio 168.00
Assassination of President Lincoln
(The), small folio, 1865 (ILLUS.) 67.00
Autumn Fruits, medium folio,
framed 175.00
Base Hit (A), small folio, 1882. . . . . .185.00
Battle at Cedar Mountain (The), small
folio 165.00
Battle of Baton Rouge, La., small
folio 195.00
Battle of Mill Spring, Ky., small folio . . .140.00
Battle of Murfreesboro, Tenn., large
folio, 1862 . . . . .175.00
Birthplace of Washington (The), small
folio, framed .198.00
Blue Fishing, small folio, framed 310.00
Bouquet of the Vase (The), small
folio, 1870 . . . . .80.00

Brave Wife (The), small folio, framed . .100.00
Brer Thuldy's Statue; "Liberty Frightenin
De World," small folio 225.00
Brig, small folio, N. Currier. 650.00
Broadway Belle (A), small folio 60.00
Bull-dozed, small folio, 1875 . . . . .175.00
Burial of the Bird (The), small
folio .60.00 to 75.00
Burning of Chicago (The), small folio,
1871, framed 85.00
Bustin' A Picnic, small folio 175.00
Catterskill Fall (The), small folio 165.00
Chappaqua Farm, Westchester County,
N.Y., small folio, 1872 . . . . .160.00
"Charley Ford," small folio, 1880 . . . . . .115.00
City Hall, New York, small folio,
N. Currier. 225.00
Col. Michael Corcoran at the Battle
of Bull Run, Va., small folio 145.00
Darktown Fire Brigade; "A Prize
Squirt," small folio . . . . .60.00 to 120.00
Darktown Lawn Party (A); "A Bully
Time," small folio, 1888 . . . . .175.00
Darktown Opera - The Serenade, small
folio, 1886 . . . . .200.00
Darktown Tournament - Close Quarters,
small folio, 1890 . . . . .175.00
Death Bed of the Martyr President,
Abraham Lincoln, small folio,
black & white, 1865 . . . . .60.00
Death of Major Ringgold, small
folio, N. Currier, 1846 . . . . . .85.00 to 115.00
Death of President Lincoln, small
folio, 1865 . . . . .65.00
Death Shot (The), small folio 200.00
De Boss Rooster, small folio, 1882 . . . . .175.00
Declaration (The), small folio, N.
Currier, 1846 .250.00
Deer Shooting in the Northern Woods,
small folio 185.00
Dwight L. Moody, small folio,
black & white .30.00
Evangeline, small folio 60.00
Falls of Niagara From Clifton House,
small folio, N. Currier 145.00
Favorite Horse (The), small folio,
framed 55.00
Flower Vase (The), small folio, N.
Currier, 1848 . . . . .95.00
Flower Vase (The), medium folio,
framed 20.00
Fort Pickens, Pensacola, Florida,
small folio 165.00
Friend in Need (A), small folio, black
& white, framed 45.00
Fruit Girl (The), small folio, framed. 40.00
Fruits of the Season, small folio, 1870 . . .85.00
Gems of American Scenery, small
folio 200.00
Genl. Taylor at the Battle of Palo Alto,
small folio, N. Currier, 1846 . . . . .105.00
Gen. U.S. Grant - The Nation's Choice
for President, small folio, black &
white 50.00

Glimpse of the Homestead (A),
  medium folio, 1863 . . . . .300.00
Grand Horse "St. Julien," "The King of
  Trotters," small folio, 1880 . . . . . .215.00
Halt by the Wayside (A), small folio . . .145.00
Harvest Field (The), medium folio, N.
  Currier, oval .295.00
Home of Washington, Mt. Vernon,
  medium folio, C. Currier, 1852 . . . . . .185.00
Horse Car Sports - Going To A Chicken
  Show, small folio, 1886 . . . . .250.00
Ice Cream Bucket - Thawing Out, small
  folio, 1889 . . . . .200.00
In the Mountains, small folio 225.00
In the Woods, small folio 145.00
Indian Lake - Sunset, large folio,
  1860 . . . . .635.00
James Monroe - 5th President, small
  folio, N. Currier 150.00
Just Caught - Trout and Pickerel, small
  folio, 1872 . . . . .125.00
Kiss Me Quick, small folio, N. Currier . . .60.00
Lake George, N.Y., small folio 165.00
Last Ditch of the Chivalry (The),
  medium folio .135.00
Life of a Fireman - The Night Alarm,
  large folio, N. Currier, 1854 . . . . . . .2,300.00
Little Belle (The), small folio 40.00
Little Cherubs (The), small folio,
  framed 75.00
Little Flower Girl (The), small folio,
  1852 . . . . .52.00
Little Snowbird, small folio, framed . . .150.00
Love is the Lightest, small folio, N.
  Currier, 1847 .48.00
Magic Lake, medium folio 75.00
Maiden Rock, Mississippi River, small
  folio 300.00
Mammoth Iron Steamship "Great
  Eastern," small folio, framed 110.00
Moss Rose (The), small folio, N.
  Currier, 1847 .145.00
Mountain Spring, West Point, Near
  Cozzen's Dock (The), medium folio,
  1862 . . . . .695.00
Mountaineer's Home (The), medium
  folio 325.00
My Little White Kittie after the Gold-
  fish, small folio, framed 105.00

New York Bay from Bay Ridge, L.I.

New York Bay from Bay Ridge, L.I.,
  large folio, 1860 (ILLUS.) 875.00

Niagara Falls from Goat Island,
  medium folio .220.00
Nip and Tuck!, small folio, 1878 . . . . . . .150.00
Old Farm House (The), small folio, N.
  Currier 500.00
Prairie Fires of the Great West, small
  folio, 1871, framed 510.00
Queen of the Turf, "Maud S.," Record
  2:10, large folio, 1880 . . . . .950.00
Rocky Mountains (The), small folio 395.00
Santa Ana's Messengers Requesting
  Genl. Taylor to Surrender, small
  folio, N. Currier, 1847 . . . . .115.00
Scales of Justice (The), small folio, N.
  Currier 200.00
Spaniel (The), small folio, N. Currier,
  1848 . . . . .215.00
Squirrel Shooting, small folio 400.00
Style Ob De Road (De), small folio,
  1884 . . . . .225.00
True Yankee Sailor (The), small folio,
  N. Currier 185.00
Two Little Fraid Cats, small folio 85.00
View on the Rondout, medium folio . . .325.00
View on the St. Lawrence - Indian
  Encampment, small folio 250.00
Washington - First in War, First in
  Peace, small folio, C. Currier 65.00
Washington at Valley Forge, small
  folio, N. Currier, framed . . .185.00 to 220.00
Washington Crossing the Delaware,
  small folio, N. Currier, framed 325.00
Washington Family (The), small folio,
  framed 145.00
Washington's Reception on the Bridge
  at Trenton in 1789, small folio,
  framed 88.00
Water Rail Shooting, small folio, N.
  Currier, 1855 . . . . .350.00 to 375.00
Widow's Treasure (The), small folio,
  N. Currier 45.00

Wild Duck Shooting

Wild Duck Shooting, large folio,
  N. Currier, 1852, framed (ILLUS.) . .5,500.00
Wound Up, small folio, 1877, framed . .115.00
Year After Marriage (A), small folio,
  N. Currier, 1847 . . . . .60.00

DECOYS

Group of Decoys

Decoys have been utilized for years to lure flying water fowl into target range. They have been made of carved and turned wood, papier mache, canvas and metal, and some are in the category of outstanding folk art and command high prices.

Black Duck, Mason, wooden, glass eyes, old worn repaint, branded w/owner's name on base, 16" l. (age crack in block) $185.00

Black Duck, carved wood, worn original paint, attributed to Soug Jester, Virginia, ca. 1935, 16¼" l. ...115.00

Black Duck, carved wood w/relief-carved wings, tack eyes, worn original paint, Upper St. Lawrence River area, 17¾" l.........160.00

Bluebill Drake, Wildfowler Factory, New York, balsa wood & pine, glass eyes, original paint, 13½" l.....50.00

Bluebill Drake, carved wood, glass eyes, original paint, by Charles Mallette, Chippewa Bay, New York, ca. 1940, 13¾" l. 75.00

Bluebill Drake, Mason Standard Grade, wooden, replaced glass eyes, 14" l.............................125.00

Bluebill Drake, carved wood, glass eyes, from Saginaw Bay area, 16" l. ...35.00

Bluebill Hen, Herter's Factory, pine head, printed canvas body, 1930s 65.00

Bluebill Hen, Mason Premier Grade, wooden 150.00

Mason Detroit Grade Blue Wing Teals

Blue Wing Teal Drake, Mason Premier Grade, carved wood, slightly turned head, hollow construction (minor restoration to bill) 3,850.00

Blue Wing Teal, carved wood w/simple relief carving, old worn working repaint, northern Wisconsin or Canada area, 12¾" l..........35.00

Bufflehead Duck, carved wood, painted, glass eyes, St. Lawrence Seaway, Long Point area..................175.00

Bufflehead Hen, Mason Standard Grade.........................750.00

Canada Goose Preening

Canada Goose in preening position, carved wood, ca. 1950 (ILLUS.)......650.00

Canada Goose, flat sheet iron stick-up type, painted, 17 x 26" 150.00

Canada Goose, carved wood, hollow construction, by George Warin, St. Clair Flats, Strawberry Island, Michigan.......................2,860.00

Canvasback Drake, carved wood, glass eyes, by Jaspar Dodge, ca. 1890, 13¾" l................105.00

Canvasback Drake, carved wood, glass eyes, old worn repaint, 14¾" l.............................65.00

Canvasback Drake, carved wood, old worn paint, North Carolina, ca. 1910, 17¼" l. (age cracks & weathering in block) 65.00

Canvasback Drake, carved wood, by Capt. Otis Bridges, Choptank River, ca. 1927...................85.00

Canvasback Drake, carved wood, glass eyes, old working repaint (age cracks in block) 70.00

Canvasback Hen & Drake, Mason Premier Grade, hollow construciton w/inletted weight, original paint, pr. 550.00

Canvasback Hen & Drake, carved wood, by John Schweikart, St. Clair Flats, Strawberry Island, Michigan, pr.........................9,900.00

Crow, carved wood, worn black paint, 1 eye missing & 1 replaced, 15" h. on driftwood base 425.00

Fish, "Pike," carved wood w/metal fins & glass eyes, vivid paint, 10" l...............................55.00

Fish, carved wood w/metal fins, 11½" l. 125.00

Fish, "Rainbow Trout," carved wood w/metal fins, original paint, 13¾" l. 45.00

Fish, carved wood, tack eyes, weighted belly, worn old black & yellow paint, 15½" l. (glued repair to tail)........85.00

Fish, carved wood w/metal fins & tack eyes, original white & red paint, Michigan, 18" l...................55.00

Fish, "Sturgeon," carved wood w/copper fins, 24" l. 65.00

Laughing Gull, carved wood, hollow
    construction, glass eyes, old "blistered"
    paint, by Charles Wilbur, Island
    Heights, New Jersey, ca. 1920,
    14½" l. 140.00
Loon, carved w/root head & tack
    eyes, old black repaint, 12" l. 135.00
Mallard Drake, carved wood, worn
    original paint, glass eyes, stamped
    "Evans Decoy," 15¼" l. (age
    cracks) 105.00

Mason Standard Grade Mallard Drake

Mallard Drake, Mason Standard
    Grade, original paint (ILLUS.) 300.00
Mallard Hen "sleeper," carved wood,
    by Robert Ellison, Bureau,
    Illinois 16,500.00
Mallard Hen, Mason Detroit Grade 100.00
Merganser Hen, carved wood, by Keyes
    Chadwick, Oak Bluffs, Martha's
    Vineyard, Massachusetts.........3,025.00
Pigeon, carved wood, original paint,
    signed by owner 40.00
Redhead Drake, carved wood, hol-
    low construction, glass eyes, worn
    original paint, by Otto Misch, Bay
    City, Michigan, ca. 1930, 15" l. 95.00
Robin Snipe, carved wood, by John
    Dilley of Quogue, Long Island
    (replaced bill & lightly hit by
    shot) 3,075.00
Shorebirds, tin folding-type, original
    paint w/some minor touchup,
    stenciled interior label w/patent
    date of 1874, set of 3 ....180.00
Turkey, wood & composition, original
    glass eyes, (restored) original paint &
    some repair, North Carolina,
    27½" h. 800.00
White Swan in preening position, carved
    hollow cedar, original paint, by
    George Cook, Island Heights,
    New Jersey 880.00
Widgeon Drake "sleeper," carved
    wood, Illinois River style hollow
    body, glass eyes, repainted, 12" l. ..105.00
Widgeon Drake, carved pine, hollow
    construction, original paint, glass
    eyes, original paint, by
    Wildfowler, Old Saybrook,
    Connecticut, branded owner's mark,
    ca. 1940, 13½" l. 95.00

DISNEY (Walt) COLLECTIBLES

Cinderella Planter

*Scores of objects ranging from watches to
dolls have been created in imitation of Walt
Disney's copyrighted animated cartoon
characters, and an increasing number of
collectors are now seeking these, made
primarily by licensed manufacturers. Also
see BIG LITTLE BOOKS, CHRISTMAS
TREE ORNAMENTS and SHEET
MUSIC.*

Alice in Wonderland paint set, tin $18.00
Alice in Wonderland planter...........25.00
Bambi card game 10.00
Bambi planter, ceramic, 9½" l., 7" h. ...17.50
Cinderella planter, ceramic, pastel blue,
    pink, green & yellow, impressed WDP,
    6½" l., 6½" h. (ILLUS.)..............17.50
Cinderella wrist watch, w/glass slipper,
    U.S. Time, 1950, boxed set 140.00
Disney characters rug, Mickey & Minnie
    on train, Pluto, Bambi & others,
    1960 copyright, 5½ x 4' 250.00
Disney characters toy, windup tin
    "Disneyland Express" train, characters
    pictured, original box 78.00
Donald Duck carpet sweeper,
    lithographed tin 50.00
Donald Duck figurine, bisque, Donald
    on scooter 45.00
Donald Duck hand puppet, rubber head,
    cloth body, marked Walt Disney
    Productions 9.00
Donald Duck sand pail, printed tin,
    Ohio Art Co., 1939 ....52.50
Dumbo the Elephant celluloid, circus
    clowns riding a fire engine,
    applied to airbrushed background,
    1941, 10¼ x 7½" 165.00
Dumbo the Elephant figure, rubber, Sun
    Rubber Co........................22.00
Dumbo the Elephant pitcher, ceramic,
    2-qt. 28.50
Dwarf Dopey soap figure, "Castile,"
    w/box............................25.00

Dwarf Sneezy figurine, bisque, 4½" h. . .85.00
Ferdinand the Bull book, Whitman No.
  842, 1938, 36 pp. 35.00
Ferdinand the Bull figure, composition,
  Knickerbocker. 110.00
Goofy blotter, Sunoco premium, 1939. . .15.00
Goofy toy, windup tin Goofy on uni-
  cycle, Linemar. 210.00
Jiminy Cricket celluloid, leaning over
  the side of the table grabbing hold
  of his umbrella hooked on the handle
  of a tankard, applied to original
  watercolor background, 1939, 9¾ x
  7½". 825.00
Jiminy Cricket wrist watch, U.S. Time,
  1948 . . . . .100.00
Lady & The Tramp song book,
  illustrated, 1955 . . . . .15.00
Mickey Mouse alarm clock, full figure
  on face, Ingersoll, 1934 . . . . .275.00
Mickey Mouse bank, Thrift Book 58.00
Mickey Mouse book, "The Adventures of
  Mickey Mouse, Book No. 1," published
  by David McKay Co., Philadelphia,
  ca. 1931 . . . . .78.50
Mickey Mouse book, "Mickey Mouse
  Presents Walt Disney's Nursery
  Stories from Walt Disney's Silly
  Symphony," Whitman, 1937, 212 pp. . .95.00
Mickey Mouse bracelet, die-cut figure of
  Mickey center, 1930s 70.00
Mickey Mouse clock radio, General
  Electric 57.50
Mickey Mouse figure, rubber, Sun
  Rubber Co., 10½" h. 25.00
Mickey Mouse figurine, bisque, w/sword,
  3½" h. 50.00
Mickey Mouse hair brush, sterling
  silver. 40.00
Mickey Mouse handkerchief, Mickey
  playing football, 8½" sq. 8.00
Mickey Mouse party horn, Louis Marx,
  1930s, 7" l. 41.50
Mickey Mouse planter, lustre ware,
  Mickey playing saxophone, 1930s,
  4" l. 50.00
Mickey Mouse sheet music, "Mickey
  Mouse's Birthday Party," 1936 . . . . . . .15.00
Mickey Mouse sled, "Flexible Flyer,"
  1930s. 170.00

Mickey Mouse Toy

Mickey Mouse toy, pull-type, wooden,
  Mickey Mouse Choo-Choo 485, W.D.P.,
  made by Fisher Price, 4 x 8½ x 7"
  (ILLUS.) 75.00
Mickey Mouse toy, windup tin
  drummer 545.00
Mickey Mouse toy, windup tin "Mickey
  Mouse Express," Louis Marx & Co. . .300.00
Mickey Mouse toy, windup tin Mickey
  playing xylophone, Linemar. 315.00
Mickey Mouse watering can, tin, 1935,
  Ohio Art, 6" h. 34.00
Mickey Mouse wrist watch, round,
  yellow-gloved minute & hour hands
  & 3 Mickey figures on subsidiary
  seconds dial, metal band w/Mickey
  figures, Ingersoll, 1933 . . . . .340.00
Mickey Mouse & Donald Duck toy,
  Mickey & Donald riding fire truck,
  Sun Rubber Co., 6½" l. 26.00
Mickey & Minnie Mouse bracelet,
  bangle-type, 1932. . . . . .25.00
Mickey & Minnie Mouse cookie jar,
  "turnabout" 55.00

Minnie Mouse Book

Minnie Mouse book, "pop-up," 1933
  (ILLUS.) 140.00
Minnie Mouse fork & spoon, sterling
  silver, pie-eyed, cut-out handles,
  S.H. & Miller International Sterling,
  set 125.00
Minnie Mouse Halloween costume,
  original box says "Mickey & Minnie
  of Radio Fame," Wornova Play
  Clothes, early 1930s 175.00
Minnie Mouse handkerchief, Minnie
  serving tea, 8½" sq. 8.00
Minnie Mouse teaspoon, silverplate 15.00
Peter Pan sheet music, "The Second
  Star To The Right" 20.00
Pinocchio bank, composition,
  1930s. 66.00
Pinocchio book, "Pinocchio's Christmas
  Party," 1939, premium for Blooming-
  dale's Toy Department. 24.00
Pinocchio celluloid, Pinocchio sur-
  rounded by Cossack marionettes,
  entitled "There are no strings on
  me," applied to airbrushed ground,
  1939, 8½ x 8½" 935.00

Pinocchio paint book, Whitman No.
573, 1939 copyright by Walt
Disney Productions, 11 x 15"........60.00
Pluto planter, ceramic, Pluto w/wheel-
barrow 20.00
Pluto salt & pepper shakers, china,
marked Walt Disney, pr............13.00
Pluto toy, "Pop-Up Critter," wooden,
Fisher Price, Disney Enterprises,
1936 ....32.00
Snow White bracelet, enameled metal,
1938 ....42.50

Snow White Cut-out Figure

Snow White cut-out figure, paper,
copyright 1938, Walt Disney Enter-
prises (ILLUS.) 6.00
Snow White pencil sharpener.........20.00
Snow White & Seven Dwarfs bank,
dime register, 1938 ....39.00
Snow White & Seven Dwarfs paper
doll book, 1938, 11½ x 17" 250.00
Three Caballeros sheet music, "You
Belong To My Heart" 15.00
Three Little Pigs figurines, bisque,
set of 3 ....75.00
Three Little Pigs mug, Patriot china.....35.00
Thumper (from Bambi) cookie jar,
ceramic 50.00
Thumper (from Bambi) planter, marked
Disney 20.00

DOLL FURNITURE & ACCESSORIES

Armoire, Victorian, Eastlake substyle, bamboo-turned details,
ca. 1885 ....$225.00

Baking set, aluminum, "Mirro,"
21 pcs. 23.00
Bassinet, wicker, woven white oak
splint, looped handles, 13 x 9½".....24.00

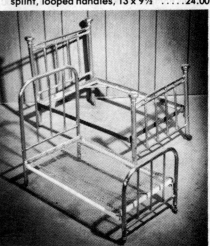

Brass Beds

Bed, brass (ILLUS.) ....100.00 to 150.00
Bed, cast iron, headboard w/cherubs,
late 19th c., 19½" l. 99.00
Bed, walnut, simplified Eastlake style,
applied relief decor, w/slats, 16" w.,
28" l., 19" h. headboard............195.00
Bed, walnut, carved Jenny Lind portrait top, 26½" h. headboard,
w/original straw mattress, bolster
& pillows, 15" w., 34" l. 295.00
Bed, wrought iron, scrolled headboard
& footboard w/brass finials, early
20th c., 11" w., 24" l., 18" h. 95.00
Bed, folding-type, oak, 5¾" w., 14" l.,
8¼" h. headboard 28.00
Butter bucket, cov., graniteware, grey
mottled..........................25.00
Carpet sweeper, wooden, Bissell 50.00
Carriage, metal, Marklin-type, ivory
w/pink-gold trim, w/silk parasol,
12" l., 7½" h......................600.00
Carriage, wicker, Whitney Carriage
Co., Leomister, 1930 ....110.00
Carriage, wicker, 4-wheeled, w/pivot-
mounted cotton parasol, 28" l.......247.00
Carriage w/hood, tin, Wyandotte,
1930 ....49.00
Cart, wooden, 2-wheel type, worn red
paint w/"PET" stenciled in black,
9 x 5", 23" tongue 105.00
Chair, ladder-back, 2-slat back, black
paint w/floral decor on slats, original
woven rush seat, 14½" h...........100.00
Chair, white wicker, 27" h. 35.00
Chest of drawers, Victorian, walnut,
pr. short step-back drawers on top
over 3 long drawers, w/attached

mirror in cut-out frame, old dark
varnish finish, 10¾" w., overall
18¾" h. 75.00
Clothes hamper, wicker ....15.00 to 30.00
Coal bucket & scoop, tin, 6 x 4½"
bucket 50.00

Coffee Grinder

Coffee grinder, lap-type, cast iron &
wood, 4 x 2½" (ILLUS.) 75.00
Cookie pan, aluminum, picture of girl
rolling dough w/wood rolling pin 15.00
Cook stove, "Creston," cast iron,
w/oven, 4 lids & lifter, bean pot,
coal scuttle & water kettle,
11 x 11".........................155.00
Cook stove, wood burning type, cast
iron, stamped "IXL" on oven door 60.00
Cradle, pine, slat sides & bottom, solid
ends, rockers, w/mattress, 8 x 16" ...12.00
Cradle, suspended-type, wicker, 18" l.
cradle suspended from 16" h. stand ..85.00
Cradle, wood w/grain-painted tin
hood, square nail construction,
heart-shaped end, early 19th c. 195.00
Cupboard, painted pine, 1-piece construction, pewter-type cupboard
w/open top w/three shelves &
squared opening for storage at
bottom, painted red, 14" w.,
25¾" h. 100.00
Cupboard, stepback-type, golden oak, 2
doors, 2 shelves at top, 2 doors
below, pot rack inside 1 door,
16½" w., 17½" h...................85.00

Cutlery Tray

Cutlery tray, 3½" w., 4" l. (ILLUS.)......55.00
Dining suite: round-top table & 4 chairs;
walnut, ca. 1930, 5 pcs. 335.00
Dish draining rack, wire 5.00
Dish pan, graniteware, salem blue 6.00
Doll house, Schoenhut, 1-room
bungalow w/side opening,
w/Schoenhut round table, desk,
chairs, bed & cast iron stove,
11 x 14 x 11½"....................225.00
Doll house, Schoenhut, 6-room cottage
w/red shingled roof & front opening,
original furniture, lighted, w/table
stand............................550.00
Doll house, 7-room Queen Anne style
w/tower, 2 bay windows, porch,
stained glass windows & wood
shingled roof, "gingerbread" trim,
interior w/lace curtains, wallpaper
& carpeting, ½" scale, late 19th c....275.00
Doll house bedroom furniture: twin bed,
chest & mirrored vanity; Renwal,
3 pcs. 17.50
Doll house chest of drawers, walnut,
4 x 6 x 7".........................42.00
Doll house dining room furniture: dining
table, 9 chairs, cov. hutch, buffet
& tea wagon; metal, Tootsietoy,
13 pcs. 100.00
Doll house doll, celluloid Negro
child, Germany, 1" h...............14.00
Doll house doll, celluloid baby,
moveable arms, legs & eyes, 3" h.....18.00
Doll house doll, bisque head, arms &
legs, cloth body, molded blonde
hair, original clothes, marked
Germany, 4½" h. 150.00
Doll house doll, all bisque, jointed,
painted features, shoes & socks,
h.h. wig, 5" h. 100.00

Doll House Highchair

Doll house highchair, 5" h. (ILLUS.) 8.00
Doll house kitchen set: table & 4
chairs; painted black, Renwal, 5 pcs. .15.00
Doll house letter rack, hanging-type,
petit-point & red silk w/"Truth,"
1¾" w., 3¼" l. 45.00

Doll house living room furniture: couch, chair, radio, lamp, table, foot stool & piano, upholstered, Germany, 7 pcs. 35.00

Doll house pitcher, ironstone, 1" h......5.00

Doll house radio, walnut, Strombecker .10.00

Doll house radio w/pull-out phonograph, Renwal....................30.00

Doll house settee, cast iron, Arcade, 1880s............................75.00

Doll house sewing machine, celluloid, lift top, 3¼"........................9.00

Doll house vanity w/three-way mirror, metal, Tootsietoy 18.00

Dresser, oak, 2-drawer, w/mirror......38.00

Dresser, walnut, 3-drawer, plain, 12" w., 10½" h. 75.00

Dresser, Victorian, Eastlake substyle, w/candle shelves flanking mirror plate, 12" w., 20" h. 90.00

Dust pan, graniteware, black..........20.00

Dust pan, tin, blue 9.00

Egg beater, tin, 1920, 5½" 10.00

Fainting couch, oak w/velvet cushions, 15½" l. 65.00

Flatware, aluminum, service for 6 w/serving pieces, ca. 1920 ....20.00

Food grinder, cast iron 30.00

Foot Warmer

Foot warmer, w/hand-crocheted cover, 2¼" (ILLUS.) 10.00

Griddle, cast iron, "Wagner," 4½" d. ...35.00

Hat, brown velvet....................3.50

High chair, Mission style, oak, 30½" h. ....35.00 to 45.00

Ice cream freezer, "White Mountain Jr." 159.00

Ironing board, tin, embossed children, Wolverine 15.00

Kitchen cabinet, oak, w/shelves, doors & pull out bread board, 15½" h. ....55.00 to 75.00

Kitchen cabinet, tin, red & white, Wolverine 15.00

Kitchen utensils: spatula, potato masher, ladle, strainer & serving spoon; metal w/red wooden handles, 1930s, 5 pcs....................20.00

Laundry set: wash stand w/tub & wash board, wringer & drying rack; wood, 5 pcs. 150.00

Parasol, cream w/lace trim, wooden handle, 15¾" l....................85.00

Plate, graniteware, grey mottled, 2½" d. 12.00

Potato masher, wooden handle w/wire masher............................6.75

Refrigerator, "Wizard," 1940s, 13" h. ...37.00

Refrigerator, white, Wolverine, 13½" h. 22.50

Rocking chair, ladder-back type w/rush seat, original red paint 45.00

Rolling pin, maple, lathe-turned, 9" l....40.00

Sad iron, "A-Best-O" 30.00

Sad iron, "Dover Dolly Iron," 2-pc......................25.00 to 35.00

Scales, balance-type, cast iron, red, w/two pans & weights 65.00

Sewing basket, wicker 25.00

Sewing table, folding-type, pine, ornate legs, 21 x 13" 47.50

Sprinkling can, lithographed, tin, Dutch children decor, Ohio Art 17.00

Stroller, lithographed tin, children playing decor, Ohio Art, 20"........25.00

Stroller, wicker, high wheels, original paint & upholstery 495.00

Table, oak, round w/turned legs, 20" d., 18" h. 135.00

Table, walnut, dropleaf, oval, 8½" h....35.00

Tea kettle & cover w/porcelain knob, cast iron, Wagner Ware............95.00

Tea kettle, graniteware, gooseneck spout, mustard & russet.............25.00

Paper-covered Wood Trunk

Trunk, paper-covered wood, leather side straps, 2 wooden slats on cover, die-cut Santa Claus on inside of lid, w/tray (ILLUS.)...............45.00

Trunk, dome-top, tin w/oak stripes, red floral decor....................65.00

Utensil set: egg beater, spatula, slotted spoon & ladle; "Mother's Little Helper," A & J, 1923, original box w/colorful pictures & rhymes, 4 pcs. 45.00

Waffle iron, cast iron, "Stover, Jr.......................75.00 to 100.00

Wash basin, graniteware, blue, 5" 10.00

CHINA HEADS

by Sybill McFadden

A charmer in the world of antiques is the serene and lovely china doll of great grandmother's day.

Her head and often her limbs are of shiny glazed porcelain. (Doll collectors apply the term "bisque" to dolls made of *unglazed* porcelain.)

China dolls appeared first in Germany as long ago as the late 18th century. However, the earliest ones which are still in existence today were crafted in the 1830s and '40s. These early chinas seem to have come from the fine porcelain factories of Meissen, Berlin, and Nymphenberg. They evolved, no doubt, from the early glazed porcelain figurines from which they took their inspiration. They are so finely modelled, exquisite and aristocratic, that if any are found other than in museums today they draw prices high in the four-figure bracket. They nearly always depict ladies and gentlemen and were sometimes reputed to be portraits of royalty and important personages. Hands were molded with individual fingers as in figurines, and faces were truly lifelike, conceived in creamy china and finished in the finest glazes. It is hard to imagine that such workmanship was lavished on a plaything for a child and it is thought they were originally intended for adults, but no one knows for sure. They appear today, usually in pristine condition, in museums and a few fine collections, most often in their original Edwardian-type clothing.

The china play dolls, with which this article is concerned, were manufactured mainly in the rich clay districts of Thuringia in Germany. They were turned out for export in astronomical numbers and became popular in America in the early 1860s. This was the type of doll great grandmother cuddled and treasured and often retired finally to a trunk in the family attic.

She is not what we call rare today, though she was loved no less fiercely for that. She has molded china hair, usually black, painted eyes, usually blue, and a tiny rosebud mouth, often heart-shaped. Her gaze was no-nonsense, direct and straightforward. She did not smile. Still she has an aesthetic beauty all her own - a simple and unique purity of design.

Some of these chinas, intended to represent children, have round faces, short necks, and short molded hairstyles. Grandmother may have chosen to dress her child-type in children's clothing or yet again, as a lady in floor-length gown. However, appearing at the same time were lady-type chinas with slim faces on long slim necks, also popular in America during and after the Civil War years. These lady dolls featured intricate hairdos with curls, ringlets, braids and buns decorated with combs, snoods, applied flowers and sometimes high-lustre glazing, often in gold. Although finer examples of the china doll, these ladies were also intended as children's play dolls and, as could be expected, were a bit more expensive. For collectors today, they are the most desirable, but alas, are difficult to find and considerably more expensive than the more common examples.

China dolls were often sold as heads only, sometimes with matching arms and legs. The shoulder plates had two or three sew-holes for attaching to home-made cloth bodies.

Since these dolls' heads were sent from Germany largely before the 1891 law which designated all imported merchandise must be marked with the country of origin, very few of them have any marks. Some exceptions are the *Kling* and the rare *Conte-Boehme*, both stamped inside the shoulder plate, and the *Charles T. Dotter* which is incised on the back of the shoulder plate "Patented Dec. 7/'80." Some few others are incised on the back shoulder plate with numbers or letters.

Of interest to china doll collectors is the great variety of molded hair styles. Colors were painted, with overall evenness, in black or blonde, with black hair predominating, perhaps because it contrasted better with the white china. Blondes are less frequently seen; in a ratio to the black heads of about one in three, or one in five. Only a very few rare early chinas have brown hair.

A popular early head is one with a molded dome over which went a wig. These are known as *Biedermeier* chinas, bald heads, or wigged chinas. The Biedermeier often has a black painted spot on the dome thought to indicate where the wig went. Better china heads have brushmarks around the hairline, usually at temples or sides of the face.

The names of a number of famous ladies of history eventually began to be popularly used for certain china dolls, mainly to designate hairstyles, as none of these types were portraits of actual personages. Nevertheless, some dolls have become known as Jenny Lind, Dolley Madison, Empress Eugenie, Mary Todd Lincoln, Princess Alexandra, Adelina Patti or Queen Victoria, to name a few. These titles are not, however, approved by knowledgeable doll collectors who consider them unreliable and confusing.

While the china doll is a treasure today, one wonders how satisfactory these unyielding dolls on ladies' bodies could have been to little girls of grandmother's day. (Baby dolls were as yet a half century in the future.) England's Queen Victoria was at the height of her reign, and her influence had spread to America as well, affecting American styles and mores. Little girls were expected to be prim and proper. Their toys were ladylike and designed to instruct. Fun for the sheer sake of it was still a long way off. The china doll was a truly Victorian concept.

However, loved and played-with she was indeed, as evidenced by the wear shown on many hard-glazed faces, often scuffed and scratched, and sometimes battered and broken, especially about the shoulder plates. Evidence of coddling and treasuring is apparent, too, in the myriad examples available to collectors in perfect condition!

A few points to look for in china dolls may here be helpful.

China heads and shoulder plates are either pink-tinted to simulate flesh-color, or are pure white. The pink-toned heads, sometimes called "pink lustre" are preferred, and are more expensive. Painting of the face and features should be studied. The better dolls have red eyelines about the eye denoting lids, and sometimes red dots in the corners of the eye. Scratches on the face are undesirable, and cracks - even hairlines - devalue the doll by half. Modelling of the old heads is important. Some have clearly and deeply etched curls and hairstyles. Others have obviously ill-defined, rounded hairstyles with little or no detail. "Pet Name" dolls, with a name molded into the pseudo dress yoke of the shoulder plate and highlighted in gilt, are quite common.

These features are rare on old chinas: glass eyes, swivel necks, pierced ears and pegged wooden bodies. Not rare, but seldom seen, are domed heads, wigs, hairstyles with applied flowers, ornaments, snoods, painted ribbons, bands, or combs, lustre trimming,

molded fancy hairstyles and boy or young man dolls.

As with all collectibles, buy the best one can afford, even if it means passing up a few tempting dolls in less fine condition at attractive lower prices.

Plain or fancy, the antique china doll brings with her all the nostalgia of a lost era while retaining a quiet charm and dignity. Little wonder, then, that she has been cherished for more than a century, and today may claim her rightful place of honor in museums and doll collections around the world.

(Editor's Note: *Sybill McFadden, who displays 29 china dolls in her Museum of Antique Dolls and Toys in Lakewood, New York, writes with the authority of 25 years of collecting, writing and lecturing in the doll and toy world.*)

* * * * *

The china head dolls have been arranged according to size.

Small "Frozen Charlotte"

"Frozen Charlotte," pink lustre china 1-piece doll w/extended arms & stiff legs, painted black "covered wagon" hairstyle, painted blue eyes & red eyelines, 4" (ILLUS.) $80.00

Miniature China Head Dolls

Common hairstyle china head dolls,
  molded & painted black common
  hairstyle, blue eyes, cloth bodies
  w/china arms & legs, dressed,
  6" each (ILLUS. of pr.)..............50.00

China Head Doll with Pegged Wooden Body

Pegged wooden body china head doll,
  painted black "covered wagon" hairstyle w/center part, pink lustre
  cheeks, articulated wooden body
  w/china arms & legs w/red-painted
  shoes & red ribbon garters, ca. 1840,
  7½" (ILLUS.)....................1,000.00

China Head "Peddler"

Common hairstyle china head doll
  dressed as "Peddler," painted black
  hair & blue eyes, wearing wine red
  cape & straw bonnet & carrying basket of flowers & toys, 8" (ILLUS.) 200.00

"Snood-and-Scarf" hairstyle china head
  lady, molded & painted blonde hair

China Head Lady with "Snood"

w/pink scarf, black snood w/pink
ribbons at sides, painted blue eyes
w/red eyelines, shaded pink taffeta
& silk dress, 11" (ILLUS.) 600.00

"Biedermeier" Lady

"Biedermeier" china head lady,
  w/black tonk mark on bald head,
  original blonde mohair wig, painted
  blue eyes & red eyelines, original
  straw-filled cloth body w/replaced
  china arms & legs, wearing original
  bonnet, 12" (ILLUS.) 400.00
Japanese china head lady w/pierced
  ears & pearl earrings, painted black
  hairstyle w/curls molded at forehead & ribbon over crown, painted

Japanese China Head Doll with Pierced Ears

brush strokes at temples, blue eyes
& red eyelines, original pink lace-
trimmed dress, ca. 1918, 13"
(ILLUS.) 250.00

China Head Boy

China head boy (or young man),
painted black wave-molded hair
w/brush strokes around forehead &
sides, painted blue eyes, teal blue
wool suit, beige shirt w/knitted
buttons, 14" (ILLUS.) 500.00

"Frozen Charlie" or "Badekinder"

"Frozen Charlie" or "Badekinder"
(bathing child) 1-piece china doll
w/extended arms & stiff legs, pink
lustre head, painted black hair
w/feathered brush strokes, brown
eyes, 14" (ILLUS.) 350.00

"Biedermeier" Lady

"Biedermeier" china head lady, bald
head w/brown human hair wig,
painted blue eyes & red eyelines,
pink blush cheeks, cloth body
w/replaced china arms & legs, lace
& net dress, 15" (ILLUS.) 400.00

"Covered Wagon" Hairstyle

"Covered wagon" hairstyle china head
doll, painted black hairstyle
w/center part & molded vertical
sausage curls, painted brown eyes &
red eyelines, original cloth body
w/china arms & legs, 15" (ILLUS.) . . .550.00

China head lady w/slim face,
elaborate hairstyle & long slim neck,
painted black hair, blue eyes & red
eyelines, cloth body w/china arms &
legs, wearing dress copied from the

China Head Lady in Godey Attire

1860s Godey fashion print behind,
15" (ILLUS.) .1,200.00

"Pet Name" Dolls

"Pet Name" china head dolls, molded
common hairstyles & each
w/"Marion" molded in china
shoulder plate dress yoke & highlighted in gilt: 8" black-haired version, $100; 16" blonde (ILLUS.) 200.00

Blonde China Head

Blonde china head doll w/common
hairstyle, painted blonde hair, blue
eyes & red eyelines, original cloth
body w/china arms & legs, blue
chiffon & velvet costume w/hat, 17"
(ILLUS.) 300.00

"Conte-Boehme" China Head Lady

"Conte-Boehme" marked china head
lady, painted black molded ornate
hairstyle w/coronet braid around
head & brush strokes at temples,
painted blue eyes & red eyelines,
original body w/china arms & legs
w/painted pink ribbon garters &
green shoes, marked inside the head
w/Conte-Boehme mark of raised
arm & shield w/incised "V" below &
number "37," cream satin dress
w/green velvet ribbons, 17"
(ILLUS.) 1,500.00

China Head Lady with Elaborate Hairstyle

Elaborate hairstyle china head lady,
painted black molded hairstyle incorporating braids pulled to back of
head & 7 long drop curls w/brush
strokes at temples, early 1860s,
17" (ILLUS.) .1,000.00
"Huret" china head doll, cork pate
w/brown mohair wig, pink lustre
head, artistically painted blue eyes,

French "Huret" China Head Doll

original kid body w/kid arms & legs,
wearing original hand-loomed linen
redingote tunic & pleated skirt, lace
& flower-trimmed hat, 17"
(ILLUS.) 3,000.00

China Head with "Corkscrew" Curls

Elaborate hairstyle china head doll,
    painted black hair molded w/bangs
    at forehead & "corkscrew" curls over
    shoulders & down back of neck,
    painted blue eyes & red eyelines,
    china hands & legs, redressed in
    pink & brown cotton apron-style full-
    length dress, 1860s, 21" (ILLUS.) 400.00

China Head with Exposed Ears

Blonde china head doll w/finely
    molded & painted blonde hairstyle
    w/ears exposed, painted blue eyes
    & red eyelines, cloth body w/china
    arms & legs, ca. 1860, 22" (ILLUS.) . . .300.00

Charles T. Dotter Doll with Patent Date

Blonde china head doll by Charles T.
    Dotter, finely molded & painted
    blonde hair, painted blue eyes & red
    eyelines, incised "Dec. 7, '80" on
    back of shoulder plate, cloth body
    w/china arms & legs, redressed in
    brown chiffon & velvet w/ecru lace
    collar, 22" (ILLUS.) 400.00

Large "Biedermeier" China Head Doll

"Biedermeier" china head doll, solid
    dome head w/blonde mohair wig,
    painted blue eyes & red eyelines,
    original blue dress w/lace trim, 24"
    (ILLUS.) 600.00

(End of China Head Dolls Section)

*   *   *   *   *

DOLLS

Bisque Head Dolls

Also see ADVERTISING ITEMS, BASE-BALL MEMORABILIA, BILLIKEN COL-LECTIBLES, CAT COLLECTIBLES and DOLL FURNITURE & ACCESSORIES.

A.B.G. (Alt, Beck & Gottschalk)
  bisque head character baby marked
  "1322. 34," "flirty" sleep eyes,
  open mouth, bent limb composition
  body, dressed, 13½" $247.50
Adolf Hulss bisque head character
  toddler, dressed, 23" (ILLUS. front) . . 675.00
Alexander (Madame) Cornelia,
  dressed . . . . 395.00 to 425.00
Alexander (Madame) Dionne Quintuplet
  "Annette," w/pin, dressed, 18" 350.00
Alexander (Madame) Little Shaver,
  vinyl, dressed 225.00
Alexander (Madame) Princess Eliza-
  beth, composition, dressed, 24" 300.00

Alexander Sonja Henie

Alexander (Madame) Sonja Henie,
  composition, dressed & w/trunk &
  wardrobe (ILLUS.) 475.00

Alexander (Madame) Presidents'
  Wives, 1st series . . . . . . 1,400.00 to 1,800.00
Alexander (Madame) Presidents'
  Wives, 2nd series . . . . 650.00 to 850.00
Alexander (Madame) Princess Eliza-
  beth, composition, blue sleep eyes,
  1937, original dress, 14" 225.00
A.M. (Armand Marseille) bisque head
  girl marked "390-A-2m," blue-grey
  sleep eyes, brown h.h. (human hair)
  wig, ball-jointed composition body,
  dressed, 8" 275.00
A.M. bisque socket head Negro girl
  marked "AM Germany 353," brown
  sleep eyes, composition body,
  dressed in Christening gown, 10" . . . 475.00
A.M. bisque head character baby
  marked "985," brown sleep eyes,
  original blonde mohair wig, 5-piece
  composition body, dressed, 15" 375.00
A.M. bisque head girl marked "1894,"
  blue sleep eyes, blonde h.h. wig,
  ball-jointed composition body,
  dressed, 15" 695.00

Armand Marseille Bisque Head Girl

A.M. bisque head girl marked "Alma
  2/0," brown sleep eyes, open mouth,
  brown h.h. wig, kid body, legs cloth
  below knee, dressed, 19" (ILLUS.) . . . 300.00
A.M. bisque head girl marked "390-
  246-1," blue sleep eyes, original
  brown h.h. wig, ball-jointed composition body, dressed, 26" 295.00
Arranbee "Nancy," composition, orig-
  inal clothes, 20" 100.00
Bahr & Proschild bisque head
  character baby, blue sleep eyes,
  open-closed mouth, 5-piece
  body, dressed, 14" 850.00

Bahr & Proschild bisque head character baby, brown sleep eyes, blonde mohair wig, bent limb body, dressed, 15" 330.00

Barbie (by Mattel), No. 1, vinyl plastic, movable head, painted eyes w/white irises, heavy eyeliner, pointed "Oriental" eyebrows, rooted saran hair, metal cylinders in both legs w/openings in feet to fit on round "posing" stand, 1959, 11½" 725.00

Barbie, hard plastic, titian bubble cut hair, 1961.........................95.00

Barbie, hard plastic, blonde bubble cut hair, 1961.........................75.00

Barbie, hard plastic, bubble cut hair, 1962 ....13.50

Barbie, hard plastic, bubble cut hair, 1963 ....35.00

Barbie, hard plastic, bubble cut hair, bendable legs, 1965 ....150.00

Belton bisque head girl marked "0," blue paperweight eyes, outlined open-closed mouth, pierced ears, ball-jointed wood & composition body, dressed, 13" 770.00

Belton bisque head girl marked "4," brown paperweight eyes, (replaced) h.h. wig, wood & papier mache body, straight wrists, dressed, 13" 1,250.00

Belton bisque head girl, blue threaded paperweight eyes, closed mouth, original ball-jointed composition body, straight wrists, dressed, 12½" 1,400.00

Bergmann (C.M.) bisque head child, blue eyes, ball-jointed composition body, dressed, 29"..........850.00

All Bisque Girl

Bisque girl, all bisque, h.p. features, movable arms, Occupied Japan, undressed, 4" (ILLUS.) 40.00

Bisque head girl marked "F.G." (F. Gaultier), brown stationary eyes, closed mouth, composition body, straight wrists, dressed, 11".......995.00

Bisque head girl marked "E.D." (E. Denamur), blue stationary eyes, open mouth w/upper row of teeth, dark brown h.h. wig, ball-jointed composition body, straight wrists, dressed, 11½" 562.00

Bisque Head Character Child

Bisque head character child marked "165-1," grey glass "googlie" side-glance eyes, ball-jointed composition body, dressed, 13" (ILLUS.) ...1,540.00

Bisque head girl marked "F 4/0 G" (F. Gaultier), brown almond-shaped inset paperweight glass eyes, closed mouth, pierced ears, blonde mohair wig, jointed wood & composition body, straight wrists, dressed, 13"....................2,300.00

Bisque "bonnet head" girl, molded blonde hair & yellow bonnet, gold trim on shoulders, cloth body, china hands & feet, dressed, 14" ....350.00 to 380.00

Bisque head girl marked "L (anchor) C" (possibly Lanternier), brown glass eyes, open mouth, face painted like a clown, composition body, painted bisque hands, dressed as a clown, 15" 440.00

Bisque head girl marked "R.D." (Rabery & Delphieu), blue stationary glass eyes, closed mouth, pierced ears, brown h.h. wig in long curls, ball-jointed composition body, jointed wrists, dressed, 19" 1,995.00

Bisque head character baby marked "L.W.C. 152 11" (Louis Wolf), grey threaded sleep eyes, open mouth w/four upper inset teeth, 5-piece bent limb body, dressed, 19½" 467.00

Bisque head girl marked "Eden Bebe Paris 9," brown stationary glass eyes, open mouth w/upper row of teeth, pierced ears, original brown h.h. wig, ball-jointed composition body, dressed, 21½" 1,095.00

Bisque Head Girl

Bisque head girl marked "Paris 95," blue paperweight eyes w/brushed brown eyebrows, open-closed mouth, pierced ears, wood & composition body, dressed, 22½" (ILLUS.) 2,475.00

Bisque head girl marked "E.D." (E. Denamur), brown paperweight eyes, open mouth, ball-jointed composition body, dressed, 24" 1,495.00

Bisque dome head baby marked "241-9-Germany," blue sleep eyes, open mouth w/two lower porcelain teeth, jointed composition body, dressed in Christening gown, 25" ...750.00

Boudoir doll, "Flapper," composition body, black hair, ca. 1920, 23½" 215.00

Bru Bisque Head Girl

Bru bisque head girl marked "Jne 2," brown paperweight eyes, closed mouth, jointed kid-over-wood body, bisque arms, wooden legs, dressed, 12½" (ILLUS.) 3,520.00

Bru bisque head girl, blue stationary paperweight glass eyes, closed mouth, pierced ears, original blonde h.h. wig, original jointed wood body, jointed wrists, dressed, 14" ....6,765.00 to 7,500.00

Bru bisque head girl, blue paperweight eyes w/blushed eyelids, pierced ears, delicately painted facial details, kid body, bisque lower arms, wood lower legs, dressed, 33" 9,350.00

Buddy Lee (trademark doll for H.D. Lee Co.), composition, dressed as a cowboy ....115.00 to 145.00

Bye-lo Baby, bisque head marked "Grace S. Putnam," blue sleep eyes, cloth body, curved legs, celluloid hands, dressed, 14" head circumference 495.00

Chad Valley (stiffened) cloth girl, blue glass eyes, dressed, 16" 255.00

Charlie McCarthy, composition, dressed, 20" 275.00

Charlie McCarthy

Charlie McCarthy, composition, dressed, 25" (ILLUS.) 149.00

Chase (Martha) stockinette girl, blonde bobbed hair, dressed, 15½" 495.00

Chase (Martha) stockinette child, dressed, 29" 825.00

Creche woman, Neopolitan, gesso over wood head & hands, glass eyes, original silk costume, early 18th c., 14" 250.00

Composition head Negro girl, painted eyes, closed mouth, straw-filled body, composition hands, dressed, 17" 125.00

Composition head baby, cloth body, composition arms & legs, ca. 1935, dressed, 18" (ILLUS.) 50.00

Composition Head Baby

Doll house girl, all bisque, blue eyes,
molded hair, jointed arms & legs,
3¼".............................65.00
Doll house doll, Gibson-type girl,
molded blonde hair, original Victorian
lady costume w/black shoes, 7" 135.00
Doll house grandma, all bisque 75.00

Door of Hope Mission Dolls

Door of Hope Mission maidservant
(amah) carrying child on back,
carved wooden head, cloth body,
dressed, 11" maidservant (ILLUS.) ...310.00
Door of Hope Mission Buddhist
Priest, carved "shaved" wooden
head, China, ca. 1920, dressed,
12"............................177.00
Door of Hope Mission bridegroom,
carved wooden head w/long h.h.
pigtail, China, ca. 1920, dressed,
12¼"...........................275.00

Door of Hope Mission chief mourner,
carved wooden head, cloth body,
China, ca. 1920, dressed, 12¼" 275.00
Door of Hope Mission farmer, carved
wooden head, cloth body, wooden
hands w/rake, dressed 275.00
Effanbee "Baby Tinyette," composition,
dressed 165.00

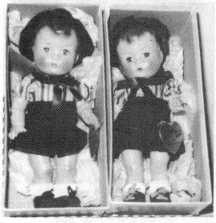

Effanbee "Candy Kids"

Effanbee "Candy Kids," composition,
dressed, pr. (ILLUS.)...............350.00
Effanbee "Little Lady," composition,
dressed, 18" 115.00
Effanbee "Patsy Ann," composition,
1936, dressed ....175.00 to 195.00
Effanbee "Patsy Ruth," composition
head, cloth body, composition arms
& legs, dressed, 27" 475.00
Effanbee "Skippy," dressed 265.00
Emma Clear George & Martha Washington, parian, original clothes, 19"
& 21", pr. 900.00

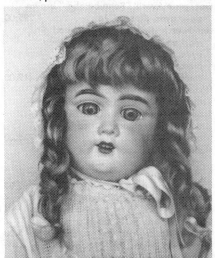

Bisque Head Florodora

Florodora (Armand Marseille) bisque
head girl, blue sleep eyes, open
mouth w/teeth, blonde mohair
wig in braids, dressed, 26" (ILLUS.) . . 500.00

French Fashion

French Fashion, bisque dome head,
glass eyes, kid body, dressed
(ILLUS.) 1,000.00
French Fashion, bisque head, blue
feathered paperweight glass eyes,
closed mouth, pierced ears, brown
h.h. wig, kid leather body, bisque
arms, dressed & carrying umbrella,
15½" 1,940.00
French Fashion, bisque swivel head
marked "3," blue glass eyes,
outlined closed mouth, pierced ears,
gusseted kid body, individually
stitched fingers, dressed, 16" 825.00
Frozen Charlie, brown eyes w/molded
eyelids, pink-toned flesh tint, 11" . . . 300.00
Frozen Charlotte, pink-toned flesh tint,
15" 725.00
Georgene Averill "Bonnie Babe," brown
sleep eyes, dressed, 16" 1,295.00
Handwerck (Heinrich) bisque head girl
marked "69-6 O 1 2," brown sleep
eyes, open mouth w/teeth,
pierced ears, ball-jointed wood &
composition body, dressed, 15½" . . . 412.00
Handwerck (Heinrich) bisque head girl
marked "69-12x 4," blue sleep eyes,
open mouth w/teeth, pierced ears,
ball-jointed composition body,
dressed, 24" 715.00
Handwerck (Heinrich) bisque head girl
marked "109," blue sleep eyes,
pierced ears, ball-jointed composition
sition body, dressed, 25" 595.00
Handwerck (Heinrich) bisque head girl
marked "109," brown sleep eyes,
pierced ears, ball-jointed composi-
tion body, dressed, 28" 615.00
Handwerck (Heinrich) - Simon & Halbig
bisque head girl, brown sleep eyes,
pierced ears, blonde h.h. wig in

long curls, ball-jointed composi-
tion body, dressed, 21" 525.00
Handwerck (Heinrich) - Simon & Halbig
bisque head girl, blue sleep eyes,
original h.h. wig, dressed, 36" 1,500.00

Happifats

Happifats, all bisque, 4" (ILLUS.) 220.00
Hendren (Madame) composition head
character girl, original cloth body,
dressed, 17½" head circum-
ference 195.00
Heubach (Ernst) - Koppelsdorf bisque
head baby marked "339," blue glass
sleep eyes, closed mouth, cloth
body, celluloid hands, dressed in
Christening gown, 15" 587.00
Heubach (Ernst) - Koppelsdorf bisque
dome head Negro baby marked
"399," sleep eyes, pierced ears,
curved limb composition body,
dressed, 15" (circular crack on top of
head) 278.00

Heubach - Koppelsdorf Character Baby

Heubach (Ernst) - Koppelsdorf bisque head character baby marked "342.6," blue sleep eyes, open mouth w/two upper inset teeth & tongue, 5-piece bent limb body, dressed, 20" (ILLUS.) 330.00

Heubach (Ernst) - Koppelsdorf bisque shoulder head girl marked "275.1," blue threaded sleep eyes, open mouth w/inset teeth, kid body, wood & composition arms & legs, dressed, 22" 165.00

Heubach (Gebruder) bisque head girl marked "9573," "googly side glancing eyes, watermelon mouth, chunky body, painted shoes & socks, dressed, 8" 750.00

Heubach (Gebruder) bisque head "whistling" boy, intaglio eyes, molded hair, cloth body, composition arms, original clothes, 11½" ...750.00

Heubach (Gebruder) bisque head boy marked "7602," blue intaglio eyes, "pouty" expression, molded hair, bent limb composition body, dressed, 13½" (toe chipped) 350.00

Horsman "Baby Bumps," composition head, pink sateen body stuffed w/cork, dressed, 18" 175.00

Horsman "Campbell Kids," composition, 1948, boy or girl, each ....150.00 to 185.00

Horsman "Poor Pitiful Pearl," vinyl head, plastic body, dressed, 12" 65.00

Ideal Novelty & Toy Co. "Baby Snooks" (Fanny Brice), composition head, hands & feet, dressed 200.00

Ideal Novelty & Toy Co. "Bonnie Braids," vinyl head, hard plastic body, dressed 100.00

Ideal Novelty & Toy Co. "Deanna Durbin," composition, original dress, 21" 400.00

Saucy Walker

Ideal Novelty & Toy Co. "Saucy Walker," hard plastic head, grey glass eyes, soft cloth body, w/voice-box, ca. 1953, dressed, 22" (ILLUS.)...65.00

Jumeau bisque socket head girl marked "Depose Tete Bte S.G.D.G. 6," blue inset paperweight glass eyes w/long painted lashes, closed mouth, pierced ears, blonde mohair wig, jointed wood & composition body, dressed, 15" 1,800.00

Jumeau Bisque Head Girl

Jumeau bisque head girl marked "Depose Tete Bte S.D.G.D. 7," closed mouth, dressed, 17" (ILLUS.) 1,400.00

Jumeau bisque head girl marked "E8J," brown paperweight eyes w/blushed eyelids, closed mouth, applied ears, blonde mohair wig, composition body, straight wrists, dressed, 18½" 4,125.00

Jumeau bisque head girl marked "1907," blue stationary glass eyes, open mouth w/molded upper row of teeth, pierced ears, original brown h.h. wig, ball-jointed composition body, dressed, 20½" 1,250.00

Jumeau bisque head girl marked "9," blue stationary paperweight glass eyes, open mouth w/upper row of teeth, pierced ears, original brown h.h. wig, ball-jointed composition body, jointed wrists, dressed, 22" 1,370.00

Jumeau bisque head girl marked "1907," brown glass sleep eyes, open mouth w/molded upper row of teeth, pierced ears, brown h.h. wig, ball-jointed composition body, jointed wrists, dressed, 22½" 1,250.00

Jumeau bisque head girl marked "DEP" & "12," blue glass sleep eyes, open mouth w/row of teeth, pierced ears, original brown h.h. wig, ball-jointed composition body, jointed wrists, dressed, 28" 1,050.00

K (star) R (Kammer & Reinhardt) bisque head Kaiser Baby marked "100," dressed, 11" 465.00

K (star) R bisque head character girl marked "114," painted blue eyes, closed "pouty" mouth, ball-jointed composition body, dressed, 10½" 1,320.00

K (star) R bisque head girl marked "122," blue eyes, open mouth w/wobbly tongue, w/dimples, baby body, jointed at shoulders & hips, dressed, 17" 695.00

Bisque Head Character Baby

K (star) R bisque head character baby marked "126," dressed, 19" (ILLUS.)............................460.00

K (star) R bisque head baby marked "121," blue sleep eyes, open mouth w/wobbly tongue, dressed, 25" ...1,150.00

K (star) R bisque head girl marked "117N," blue "flirty" eyes, original brown h.h. wig, original toddler body, original rubber hands, dressed, 27" 3,200.00

K (star) R bisque head baby marked "126," dressed, 28" (ILLUS. w/Adolf Hulss toddler) 800.00

K (star) R - Simon & Halbig bisque head character toddler marked "126 32," brown sleep eyes, open mouth w/two inset teeth & tremble tongue, 5-piece composition body, dressed, 14" 330.00

K (star) R - Simon & Halbig bisque head character baby marked "121,"

blue sleep eyes, open mouth w/two inset teeth & tongue, w/dimples, 5-piece composition body, dressed, 15"............................715.00

K (star) R - Simon & Halbig bisque head character baby marked "126 42," blue sleep eyes, open mouth w/two inset teeth & tremble tongue, 5-piece composition body, dressed, 16".....302.00

K (star) R - Simon & Halbig bisque head girl marked "70," brown sleep eyes, open mouth w/inset teeth, pierced ears, ball-jointed composition body, dressed, 26" 550.00

Kathe Kruse baby, chemically treated muslin (plastic) head, muslin body, dressed, 14" 350.00

Kathe Kruse boy, muslin, all original, tagged & signed on foot, dressed, 14½"............................650.00

Kathe Kruse girl, molded muslin, painted features, h.h. wig, jointed cloth body, dressed, 21" 450.00

Kestner (J.D.) bisque head girl marked "3 134," brown glass eyes, open mouth w/molded teeth, jointed wood & composition body, dressed, 10".....302.00

Kestner (J.D.) bisque head girl marked "A 5 J.D.K. 221," brown "googly" slide glancing eyes, ball-jointed wood & composition body, undressed, 11½"................1,650.00

Kestner (J.D.) bisque head character baby marked "152 5," brown sleep eyes, open mouth w/two upper inset teeth, 5-piece bent limb composition body, dressed, 13" 412.00

Kestner (J.D.) bisque head girl marked "136," brown sleep eyes, open mouth, brown h.h. wig, jointed composition body, dressed, 19".....350.00

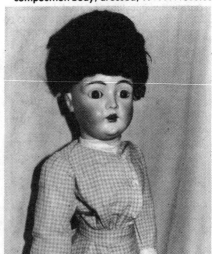

Kestner "Gibson Girl"

Kestner (J.D.) bisque head "Gibson Girl" marked "162," open mouth, original h.h. wig, dressed, 20" (ILLUS.) 600.00

Kestner (J.D.) bisque head girl marked "164," brown sleep eyes w/molded brows, ball-jointed composition body, dressed, 26" 695.00

Kestner (J.D.) bisque head girl marked "192," "oily" bisque, blue sleep eyes, brown h.h. wig in ringlets, dressed, 30" 800.00

Kestner (J.D.) bisque head girl marked "146," brown sleep eyes, h.h. wig, dressed, 32" . . . . .795.00 to 995.00

Kewpie, bisque, 5" 95.00

Kewpie, composition, 27" 200.00

Kley & Hahn bisque solid dome head toddler, blue eyes, open-closed mouth, 5-piece bent limb body, dressed, 17" 675.00

Kley & Hahn Bisque Head Girl

Kley & Hahn bisque head character girl marked "520 8½," painted brown eyes, closed mouth, ball-jointed composition body, dressed, 21" (ILLUS.) 2,640.00

Kley & Hahn bisque head girl marked "Walkure Germany," blue eyes, open mouth, pierced ears, blonde h.h. wig, jointed composition body, dressed, 28½" 750.00

Lenci child, felt, painted blue eyes, dressed as a Scottish boy, 16½" 990.00

Lenci child, felt, painted brown eyes, w/paper tag, dressed as an Eastern European boy & holding a whip, 17" 440.00

Milliner's model, papier mache, painted blue eyes, molded black hair w/high Apollo's knot & clusters of 5 curls over each ear, aquiline nose,

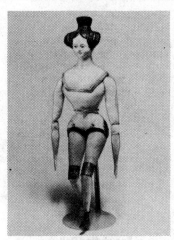

Milliner's Model

cloth over wood body, jointed wood legs, minor repainting around edge of shoulderplate, ca. 1835, undressed, 22" (ILLUS.) 3,410.00

Minerva tin head girl, open mouth, h.h. wig, cloth body, wooden hands, dressed, 22" 140.00

Nancy Ann Storybook "Beauty" (from Beauty & the Beast), bisque, mohair wig, dressed, 5½" 33.00

Nancy Ann Storybook "June" - "A Rosebud Girl to Love Me Through the June Days," bisque, jointed head & arms, dressed in long dress w/underslip & pantaloons, 6" 50.00

Nancy Ann Storybook "Little Bo Peep," bisque, mohair wig, dressed, 5½" . . .20.00

Nancy Ann Storybook "Little Red Riding Hood," bisque, mohair wig, dressed, 5" 20.00

Nancy Ann Storybook "Queen of Hearts," bisque, jointed arms & legs, mohair wig, dressed, 5½" 42.00

Parian head lady, glass eyes, molded chestnut brown hair w/ribbon insert, original clothes, 17" 1,150.00

Queen Louise (Armand Marseille) bisque head marked "15," blue stationary eyes, open mouth, pierced ears, ball-jointed composition body, dressed & w/accessories, 30" 715.00

Rag-stuffed (J.B. Sheppard & Co., Philadelphia) girl, oil-painted features, ca. 1900, dressed 950.00

Rag-stuffed cloth doll, white face & hands w/embroidered features & black legs made to resemble stockings, wearing turkey red clown-type short-legged suit, 15" 35.00

Rag-stuffed Negro child, embroidered features, appliqued eyes, mouth & clothing, ca. 1940, 16" (ILLUS.) 50.00

Rag-stuffed Doll

Rag-stuffed (Izannah Walker) girl,
painted brown eyes & corkscrew
curls, painted arms, legs, w/but-
toned boots, ca. 1873, dressed,
18" 5,225.00
Rag-stuffed (Izannah Walker) girl, oil-
painted cloth face & hair, 1880s,
20" 6,000.00
Schmidt (Bruno) bisque head boy
known as "Tommy Tucker" marked
"2096," blue sleep eyes, open mouth
w/two inset teeth, molded & painted
hair, ball-jointed composition body,
dressed, 12½" 770.00
Schmidt (Bruno) bisque head girl
known as "Wendy" marked "2033
BSW (within a heart) 537," blue glass
eyes, closed mouth, pierced ears,
blonde mohair wig, ball-jointed
toddler body, original dress, 13" ..3,575.00
Schoenau & Hoffmeister bisque head
girl marked "1909," blue sleep eyes,
original h.h. wig, ball-jointed
composition body, dressed, 23" 495.00
Schoenhut baby, wooden, original
paint, dressed, 15" 395.00
Schoenhut boy, wooden, "pouty" expression,
molded hair, original military outfit,
16" 1,075.00
Schoenhut girl, wooden, intaglio
eyes, "pouty" expression, original
h.h. wig, dressed, 16" 650.00
S.F.B.J. (Societe Francaise de Fabri-
cation de Bebes et Jouets) bisque
head girl marked "4," brown glass
sleep eyes, open mouth w/molded
teeth, pierced ears, wood & composition body, dressed, 13½".........165.00
S.F.B.J. bisque head girl marked
"301 Paris 8," blue sleep eyes, open
mouth, pierced ears, wood &
composition body, dressed, 21" 275.00
S.F.B.J. bisque head girl marked "301,"
dressed, 28" (ILLUS.) 800.00

S.F.B.J. Bisque Head Girl

S.F.B.J. bisque head girl, blue glass
eyes, open mouth w/upper row of
teeth, pierced ears, dark blonde h.h.
curly wig, ball-jointed composition
body, jointed wrists, dressed,
35½" 2,000.00

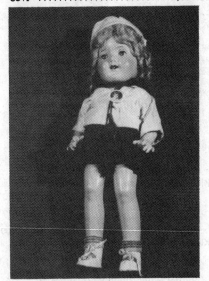

Shirley Temple

Shirley Temple, composition, marked
"E.G." (Goldberger), blue glass eyes,
blonde h.h. wig, button says "Everybody Loves Me Little Miss Movie,"
1930s, original clothes & box, 18"
(ILLUS.) 400.00
Simon & Halbig bisque head girl
marked "719," blue eyes, open
mouth, ball-jointed composition
body, dressed, 12" 350.00

Simon & Halbig bisque head baby
marked "1428 6," blue sleep eyes,
open-closed mouth, composition
body, dressed, 14" 1,320.00
Simon & Halbig bisque head girl
marked "1078," blue "flirty" eyes, open
mouth w/upper row of teeth, blonde
h.h. wig, ball-jointed composition
body, jointed wrists, dressed,
24½" 668.00
Simon & Halbig - Bergmann (C.M.)
bisque head child, brown glass sleep
eyes, open mouth w/inset teeth,
pierced ears, ball-jointed wood &
composition body, dressed, 21¼" ...330.00
Skeezix, oil cloth ....45.00 to 75.00
Steiner (Bourgoin) bisque head girl,
green glass wire-operated eyes,
closed mouth, pierced ears, original
brown h.h. wig, ball-jointed
composition body, dressed, 29" ...6,000.00
Steiner (Jules) bisque head girl,
blue stationary glass eyes, closed
mouth, pierced ears, original brown
h.h. wig, jointed composition body,
straight wrists, dressed, 12¼" 1,995.00
Steiner (Jules) bisque dome head
walking girl, grey threaded glass
eyes w/blushed eyelids, open mouth
w/teeth, blushed ears, composition
& kid arms & legs, clockwork
mechanism in torso, moving arms &
legs & crying "Mama," dressed,
20" 1,375.00
Steiner (Jules) bisque head girl, blue
glass stationary paperweight eyes,
closed mouth, pierced ears, brown
h.h. wig in long curls, ball-jointed
composition body, dressed,
24½" 3,500.00
UNIS (Union Nationale Inter Syndicale)
bisque head girl marked "301," blue
eyes, ball-jointed composition body,
dressed, 24" 700.00
Wax (poured) head girl, glass eyes,
inserted hair, ca. 1790, dressed,
10"..............................575.00
Wax (poured) head girl (unmarked
Pierotti), blue glass eyes, closed
mouth, individually inserted hair, cloth
body, poured wax hollow arms &
legs, dressed, 25"................895.00
Wooden lady, Queen Anne type, black
pupilless eyes, dressed & w/trunk
& other clothes, 13½"............3,800.00
Wooden lady, Queen Anne type,
painted features, pierced ears, hair
pulled up into a "tuck" comb, brush
marks at temple, jointed body,
dressed, 15" 660.00

(End of Doll Section)

DOOR KNOCKERS

Brass, lady's head..................$32.50
Brass, shield w/American Eagle atop,
early 20th c., 7½" h. 35.00
Brass, devil's head w/serpent-form
striker ring.......................35.00
Bronze, horseshoe & boot w/detailed
spur & stars, ca. 1900 ....35.00
Cast iron, acanthus leaf, 7¼" h. 25.00
Cast iron, basket of flowers, indoor
model 22.50
Cast iron, lady's head, ca. 1870 ....75.00
Cast iron, Quaker man's head 28.00

DOOR STOPS

Conestoga Wagon Door Stop

*All door stops listed are flat-back cast
iron unless otherwise noted. Also see
WOODENWARES.*

Alligator, original paint, 16½" l. $110.00
Basket of flowers, original paint,
10½" h. 65.00
Basket of fruit, original paint, marked
"Albany Fdy. Co.," 10½" h. 85.00
Basket of 5 colorful tulips in full bloom,
original paint, marked "Albany
Foundry," ca. 1870, 9 x 7½" 110.00
Bear, full figure......................75.00
Bird drinking at fountain, long-necked
bird at ewer-shaped vessel, on
stepped oblong base, old worn black
repaint, 10 7/8" h. 95.00
Camel, full figure, old worn white
repaint over beige, 5¾" h. 110.00
Cat w/arched back, old black repaint
w/green eyes & red mouth,
10¾" h. 95.00
Clown, original paint 125.00
Cockatoo, full figure on round base,
old colorful repaint, 14" h. 155.00
Conestoga wagon, 11" l., 8½" h.
(ILLUS.)..........................125.00

Cornucopia w/fruit, old polychrome
  paint, 7½" h. 45.00
Cottage w/picket fence . . . . . . 45.00 to 55.00
Dog, Boston Bulldog in standing
  position, original paint, 7½" h. . . .65.00
Dog, Boston Terrier facing left, full
  figure, original paint 70.00
Dog, English Setter, black & white,
  15½". 97.50
Dog, Russian Wolfhound, Hubley. 125.00

Scottie Door Stop

Dog, Scottie, original paint (ILLUS.) 75.00
Draft (or dray) horse w/bridle &
  harness, old worn red & black paint
  w/yellow striping on black base,
  8¼" h. 135.00
Dutch girl, 13" h. 100.00
Elephant, Hubley 150.00
Frog, original yellow paint 55.00
George Washington 135.00
Golfer in knickers & cap, original
  colorful paint, 1920s 125.00
Heron w/crest, original paint 60.00
Humpty Dumpty, white, 5" h. 75.00
Kitten w/bow tie, black, 8" h. 85.00
Lady w/scarf, green, 7" h. 120.00
Lighthouse & keeper's house, original
  paint 125.00
Lion in standing position w/tail curled
  over back, well-defined mane, on
  oblong base, 10¾" l. 135.00
Monkey in seated position, full figure,
  old worn repaint, 6¾" h. 85.00
Mule kicking 45.00
Owl, original black paint, 6¾" h. 72.50
Parrot on rockwork base, old poly-
  chrome repaint, 11" h. 85.00
Peter Rabbit wearing red sweater,
  blue pants, 8¼" h. 80.00
Rabbit, full figure, white 185.00
Salem witch (brass) 125.00
Soldier in Colonial uniform, original
  paint, 7½" h. .55.00
Squirrel seated on a log & eating a nut,
  original brown paint, ca. 1920,
  9" h. 180.00
Stagecoach, ca. 1930 . . . . .90.00
Stork, worn blue repaint over gold,
  7½" h. 65.00

Swan, full figure, white 150.00
Vase of poppies & daisies 42.00
Victorian lady 65.00
Windmill. 42.00

ENAMELS

Russian Enamel Sugar Shovels

    *Enamels have been used to decorate a
variety of substances, particularly metals.
The best-known small enameled wares such
as patch and other small boxes and napkin
rings are the Battersea Enamels made by
the Battersea Enamel Works in the last half
of the 18th century. However, the term is
often loosely applied to other English
enamels. Russian enamels, usually on a
silver or gold base, are famous and
expensive. Early 20th century French
enamel on copper wares and those items
produced in China at the turn of the century
in imitation of the early Russian style, are
also drawing dealer and collector attention.
Also see FABERGE.*

Battersea box w/hinged lid, enameled
  lamb pictured above "Innocence,"
  1¼ x 1¾". $495.00
Battersea box w/hinged lid, oval,
  copper, enameled light blue & white
  & lettered "Have Communion with
  Few, Be Familiar with One, Deal
  Justly with All, Speak Evil of
  None," ca. 1800 . . . . .295.00
Battersea patch box w/hinged lid,
  copper, enameled colorful laurel
  wreath, crown, eagle & crossed
  standards on white top, mottled
  green base, 1 5/8" d., 1" h. 145.00
Bell push, silver-gilt, enameled translucent pink over a "guilloche"
  ground & applied w/gilded leaf,
  w/pink hardstone cabochon thumb-

piece, Russian, The Third Artel, St. Petersburg, ca. 1900, 2½" d.......1,650.00

Bowl, copper, enameled rose & blue chrysanthemums, yellow, rose & blue blue anemone sprays & 2 butterflies on chartreuse ground, marked "China," 3" d. 30.00

Bowl, silver-gilt, enameled multicolor florals & foliage on lobed panels & upper border w/turquoise between filigree scrolls, set w/red hardstone cabochons, Russian, Maria Semyenova, Moscow, ca. 1900, 3 5/8" d. 1,760.00

Demitasse spoons, silver-gilt, backs of fig-shaped bowls enameled w/stylized flower within borders of white beads, Russian, Nicholai Zverev, Moscow, ca. 1910, 4 1/8" l., set of 12 ....990.00

Kovsh, silver-gilt, enameled multi-color florals & scrolling foliage within borders of blue & white beads, cartouche-shaped handle w/conforming enamel, Russian, Cyrillic maker's mark, St. Petersburg, ca. 1890, 4¾" l....................605.00

Plaque, copper, enameled scene of 2 colorfully dressed couples courting in a landscape setting, Limoges, France, late 19th-early 20th c., framed, 8 5/8 x 7" 1,100.00

Snuff box in the form of a quail, copper, enameled in realistic hues w/pink feathers & lying on grassy mound, hinged cover w/interior hunting scene of gentlemen, South Staffordshire, ca. 1770, 3" l. 1,540.00

Sugar shovels, silver-gilt, enameled w/vivid florals & foliage within geometric reserves, w/monograms in bowls, Russian, artist-signed, Moscow, ca. 1900, 5 3/8" l., pr. (ILLUS.).........................825.00

Russian Enamel Tea Glass Holder

Tea glass holder, silver-gilt, enameled multicolored scrolling foliage

centered w/oval "niello" plaque w/view of the Moscow Kremlin within blue bead borders, Russian, artist-signed, Moscow, ca. 1900, 4½" h. (ILLUS.) 880.00

Teaspoons, silver-gilt, back of fig-shaped bowls enameled w/stylized florals & geometric forms, Russian, The Eleventh Artel, Moscow, ca. 1910, 5¼" l., set of 12 in fitted case........................1,760.00

Vase, baluster-shaped, copper, enameled ruby red w/high relief pink & green stylized florals over silver foil, signed "Faure-Limoges-France" in gilt, 3¾" h. 325.00

Faure Limoges Enamel Vases

Vase, inverted pyriform, copper, emerald green, ochre & rust pendant flowering trumpet vines & leafage reserved against emerald green, sapphire blue & sky blue ground, ca. 1920, signed "Faure-Marty-Limoges" in in gilt, ca. 1920, 9½" h. (ILLUS. left)......................1,320.00

Vase, bulbous, enameled salmon pink, yellow, white, cranberry & ochre medium & low relief irregular panels of chevrons, ca. 1925, signed "C. Faure-Limoges-France" in gilt, w/dent to base, 9¾" h. (ILLUS. right).........................2,200.00

EPERGNES

Epergnes were popular as centerpieces on tables of last century. Many have receptacles of colored glass for holding sweetmeats or other edible items or for flowers or fruits. Early epergnes were made entirely of metal including silver.

Blue Opalescent Epergne

Blue glass, 4-lily, w/applied spiraling
   rigaree, in 9" d. bowl, 16" h.......$260.00
Blue opalescent glass, single lily in
   bowl w/crimped rim, 10½" h.
   (ILLUS.).........................175.00
Blue Satin glass, single lily
   w/enameled birds & flowers, in
   fluted bowl, 18" h. 250.00
Blue Satin glass, single lily, shaded
   light to deeper blue Drape patt. lily
   in ruffled bowl raised on footed
   silverplate domed base, overall
   19" h. 245.00
Cased glass, single lily, shaded aqua
   cased in creamy white w/applied
   clear rim & enameled decor, 12" d.
   ruffled bowl in silverplate on copper
   holder marked "WMF" (Wurttember-
   gishe Metallwarenfabrik), 19½" h...795.00
Cased glass, 4-lily, pink cased in
   white w/ruffled rims & w/applied
   spiraling vaseline rigaree trim,
   bowl resting on mirrored ormolu
   plateau w/applied ormolu leaves,
   7 7/8" d. base, overall 14¼" h. 335.00
Cranberry to vaseline opalescent glass,
   4-lily, center lily & 3 smaller lilies,
   vertical opalescent threading &
   applied vaseline rigaree, probably
   Webb, bowl resting on faceted
   mirrored plateau, overall 15" h. 239.00
Cranberry opalescent to peach
   opalescent glass, 4-lily, in 12" d.
   bowl, 17½" h. 185.00
Cranberry glass, 3-lily, center lily & 2
   smaller lilies applied w/clear spiral
   twist rigaree in 10 1/8" d. ruffled
   bowl, 22¼" h. 345.00
Pink shaded to opalescent to clear
   glass, 3-lily, lilies w/squared tops
   & applied clear spiraling rigaree, in
   13" sq. bowl w/folded over rim,
   21¼" h. 295.00
Purple mother-of-pearl glass, 4-bowl,

Diamond Quilted patt., center bowl
   above 3 bowls amidst stylized glass
   leaves, on beveled mirrored
   plateau, 8¾" h..................1,000.00
Rose pink mother-of-pearl glass
   w/creamy white lining, 4-bowl,
   Diamond Quilted patt., center bowl
   on frosted stem above 3 rose bowl
   shaped flower holders on frosted
   knopped stems, resting on mirrored
   plateau, 10" d., 8¾" h...........1,800.00
Silver, 3-bowl, formed as an openwork
   stand on 3 slender supports conjoined by a scrolled stretcher w/urn
   finial, holding 3 circular sweetmeat
   dishes w/raised centers & tendril
   handles, all centered by a maenad
   finial, w/frosted surfaces, borders of
   interlaced ribbonwork enclosing
   flowerheads, Tiffany & Co., New
   York, ca. 1870, 10¼" h...........1,100.00
Vaseline glass, single lily, applied
   cranberry ruffled rim, in ornate
   brass holder 95.00
White opaque glass, single lily, wide
   cranberry rim, in bowl w/ruffled
   hobnail rim, 9¼" h. 120.00

FABERGE

Faberge Silver-Gilt & Enamel Bowl

   *Carl Faberge (1846-1920) was goldsmith
and jeweler to the Russian Imperial Court,
and his creations are recognized as the
finest of their kind. He made a number of
enamel fantasies, including Easter eggs, for
the Imperial family and utilized precious
metals and jewels in other work.*

Belt buckle, silver-gilt & translucent
   enamel, elongated quatrefoil form,
   enameled translucent salmon pink
   over "guilloche" ground, reeded gold
   mounts, signed in Cyrillic,
   workmaster Michael Perchin, St.
   Petersburg, ca. 1900, 2¾" l. $1,650.00

Bowl, silver-gilt & shaded enamel,
domed foot, lobed sides, enameled
multicolored stylized florettes &
foliage on pink, pale blue, pale
yellow, emerald green, slate blue &
Chinese red grounds, signed in
Cyrillic, workmaster Fyodor Ruckert,
Moscow, ca. 1900, 5" d. (ILLUS.) ...9,900.00
Box, cov., silver-gilt & enamel, circular,
enameled in the old Russian style in
muted shades of green, brown &
purple, Moscow, ca. 1910, 2" d. ...2,310.00
Brooch, beetle-form, gold & garnet
body & diamond head w/two garnet
eyes, workmaster August Holstrom,
St. Petersburg, ca. 1900, 1 1/8" l. ...2,860.00
Cigarette case, gold, oblong w/round-
ed sides, stippled finish, applied
w/two-color gold monogram, cabochon
cabochon sapphire thumbpiece,
Moscow, ca. 1900, 3 5/8" l. 2,640.00
Cigarette case, silver-gilt & translucent
enamel, oblong, enameled translucent royal blue over a "guilloche"
ground, center of hinged lid applied
w/medallion of St. George slaying
the Dragon within diamond-set
borders, diamond thumbpiece, workmaster August Hollming, St. Petersburg, ca. 1900, 3¾" l. 3,850.00

Faberge Silver Cigarette Case

Cigarette case, silver, hinged cover
applied w/central monogram beneath coronet within ribbon-tied
reeded border & w/ribbon-tied
branches below, reverse w/presen-
tation inscription, cabochon sapphire
thumbpiece, signed in Cyrillic, 4" l.
(ILLUS.) 1,650.00
Cuff links, mother-of-pearl circular
discs set w/central pearl surrounded
by circle of diamonds in gold chain,
gold shanks, workmaster August
Hollming, St. Petersburg, ca. 1910,
pr. 2,200.00
Desk clock, silver & translucent

enamel, square, enameled translucent red over a sun-ray ground,
border of clock reeded & applied
w/ribbon bows between crossed
arrows, outer border chased w/leaf-
tips, raised on 2 toupie feet, w/strut
support, workmaster Michael
Perchin, St. Petersburg, ca. 1900,
4" h..........................19,800.00
Etui (case for small articles), gold-
mounted silver-gilt & translucent
enamel, oval, enameled translucent
pink over a "guilloche" ground, gold
borders chased w/leaf-tips, border
of hinged cover set w/seed pearls,
moonstone thumbpiece, back w/band
of plain silver applied w/stylized
gilded flowers & foliage, workmaster
Henrik Wigstrom, St. Petersburg,
ca. 1910, 3 3/8" l................5,775.00
Fish slice, silver, pierced blade, foliate
scroll handles, w/monogram, ca.
1900, 13 1/8" l. 880.00
Kovsh, silver-gilt & shaded enamel, old
Russian style enameled blue, red,
yellow & green scrolls & stylized
grape clusters on cream ground,
upper border & high handle enameled black, Fyodor Ruckert, Moscow,
ca. 1900, 4 1/8" l................1,760.00
Letter opener, tortoise shell blade
mounted w/silver-gilt handle
enameled in the old Russian style in
shades of green, orange, blue &
white, Moscow, ca. 1910,
12¾" l. 2,970.00
Napkin ring, silver & translucent
enamel, central vacant circular
reserve on enameled translucent
lime green over a "guilloche"
ground, workmaster Anders John
Nevalainen, St. Petersburg, ca. 1900,
2" d..........................1,100.00
Teapot, cov., silver, slightly bombe
form w/geometric angular handle,
cover w/ivory finial, signed in
Cyrillic, ca. 1910, 7 1/8" w. 1,100.00

FAIRY LAMPS

*These are candle burning night lights of
the Victorian era. Best known are the Clarke
Fairy Lamps made in England, but they
were also made by other firms. They were
produced in two sizes, each with a base and
a shade. The Fairy Pyramid Lamps listed
below all have a clear glass base and are
approximately 2 7/8" d. and 3¼" h. The
Fairy Lamps are usually at least 4" d. and*

5" h. when assembled and these may or may not have an additional saucer or bottom holder to match the shade in addition to the clear base.

FAIRY PYRAMID LAMPS

Amber opalescent glass shade, Swirl patt., marked Clarke clear glass base, 2 7/8" d., 3¼" h. $88.00

Amber "overshot" glass shade, Swirl patt., marked Clarke clear glass base 100.00

Burmese glass shade, salmon pink shaded to yellow, acid finish, marked Clarke clear glass base ....195.00 to 275.00

Cranberry glass shade, Diamond Quilted patt., marked Clarke clear glass base 95.00

Cranberry "overshot" glass shade w/embossed ribs, marked Clarke clear glass base 105.00

Lemon yellow satin glass shade, marked Clarke clear glass base 115.00

Rose mother-of-pearl satin glass shade w/white lining, Diamond Quilted patt., marked Clarke clear glass base 150.00

Vaseline glass shade, marked Clarke clear glass base 85.00

Verre Moire (Nailsea) glass shade, cranberry w/white opaque loopings, marked Clarke clear glass base 235.00

Yellow opaque "overshot" glass shade, Swirl patt., marked Clarke clear glass base, 2 7/8" d., 3½" h. ...125.00

FAIRY LAMPS

Baccarat "Rose Tiente" Fairy Lamp

Baccarat glass shade & matching base, Rose Tiente Pinwheel (or Sunburst) patt., 5¼" d. base (ILLUS.) ....195.00 to 245.00

Blue opalescent satin glass shade & matching ruffled base, Swirl patt., blue candle cup, 5¾" sq. base, 6½" h. 495.00

Blue (royal) "overshot" crown-shaped glass shade (made for Victoria's

1887 Jubilee), marked Clarke clear glass base, 3" d., 4½" h. 195.00

Blue-tinted clear glass shade w/six-acid-etched alternating oval reserves w/female figures & bust portraits within lacy frames, marked Clarke clear glass base, unmarked clear candle cup, 4½" h. 335.00

Brass openwork shade set w/multi-colored glass jewels, square brass base, clear glass candle cup, 4½" w., 3¾" h. 165.00

Burmese glass shade, salmon pink shaded to yellow, acid finish, pressed Burmese glass base marked Clarke, clear glass candle cup, 3 7/8" d., 5" h. 398.00

Burmese glass shade & matching ruffled base, salmon pink shaded to yellow, acid finish, signed Thomas Webb Queen's Burmese Ware, pressed Burmese glass insert marked Clarke & marked Clarke clear glass inner candle cup, 6¾" d., 5¾" h. 650.00

Burmese glass shade & matching base w/fold-over sides, salmon pink shaded to yellow, acid finish, marked Clarke clear glass candle cup insert, 6" h. 535.00

Burmese glass shade & matching footed base, salmon pink shaded to yellow w/yellow feet, acid finish, Webb, marked Clarke pressed Burmese glass insert & clear glass candle cup, 4¼" d., 6½" h. 735.00

Fairy Lamp-Epergne

Burmese glass fairy lamp-epergne, salmon pink shaded to yellow, acid finish, pr. lamps on clear bases & three flower holders on stand (ILLUS.) 625.00

Cranberry frosted glass shade w/etched florals & leaves, marked Clarke clear glass base, 4" d., 4¾" h. 175.00

Green overlay glass shade w/white
  lining, marked Clarke clear glass
  base & candle cup, 3 7/8" d.,
  4 3/8" h. 100.00
Green & opaque white striped acid
  finish glass shade, attributed to
  Stevens & Williams, marked Clarke
  clear glass base, 4" d., 5¼" h. 175.00
Pink "candy stripe" overlay glass
  shade w/embossed ribs & white
  lining & ruffled base w/applied clear
  feet, matching pink-striped candle
  cup, 4 3/8" d., 5¼" h. 350.00
Pink satin glass shade w/embossed
  stars & crimped base w/pink interior
  cased in white, marked Clarke clear
  glass insert, 6¼" d., 5" h. 435.00
Pink, white & clear swirl stripe acid
  finish shade, marked Clarke clear
  ruffled base w/frosted wafer foot,
  attributed to Stevens & Williams,
  5¼" d. base, 6" h. 560.00
Verre Moire (Nailsea) glass shade &
  matching ruffled base, frosted
  heavenly blue w/white opaque
  loopings, marked Clarke clear
  glass candle cup, 6 1/8" d.,
  4 7/8" h. 425.00
Verre Moire (Nailsea) glass shade
  & matching ruffled base, chartreuse
  w/white opaque loopings, marked
  Clarke clear glass candle cup, 7" d.,
  6¼" h. 450.00

FIGURAL FAIRY LAMPS
Bisque, cat's head, green glass eyes,
  grey coat, blue collar, 3½" h. 145.00
Bisque, dog's head, amber glass eyes,
  shaded brown & tan coat, blue collar,
  3" d., 3½" h. 145.00
Bisque, owl, amber & black glass eyes,
  shaded grey feathers, blue ribbon at
  neck, 3½" h. 145.00
Glass, emerald green double baby face
  shade on frosted clear shoulders,
  4 3/8" d., 4¼" h. 195.00
Porcelain, lighthouse, pink w/green
  roof, white & gold trim, 3¼" d.,
  7¾" h. 165.00

FANS

*Also see ADVERTISING ITEMS,
BREWERIANA and COCA-COLA
ITEMS.*

Celluloid, folding-type, h.p. swans,
  11" l. $40.00
Ivory "brise," folding-type, painted

& varnished w/scene of Europa & the
  Bull surrounded by trellis-like frame,
  "chinoiserie" on lower portion of
  sticks, France, 19th c., 7¼" l. 150.00
Ivory "brise," folding-type, painted &
  varnished w/scenes of pr. lovers
  & lady in landscape, abstract
  florals on lower portion of sticks,
  19th c., 5¼" l. 135.00
Ivory "brise," folding-type, engraved
  macaques (short-tailed monkeys)
  playing w/tiny dragonflies, each
  guard w/four monkeys, Japan,
  late 19th c., 10" l. 1,700.00
Lace, "needle" lace depicting lady
  in robed gown flanked by large
  scrolled flowers & 2 coat-of-arms,
  mother-of-pearl sticks w/gold foil
  accents, Europe, late 19th c.,
  10½" 400.00
Lace, "point d'angleterre," tortoise
  shell sticks w/gold monogram,
  late 19th c., 13½" 325.00

"Mourning Fan"

Mourning fan, black silk, ebony
  sticks, 1870s, opening to 18"
  (ILLUS.) 55.00
Ostrich feather, black, tortoise shell
  sticks inlaid w/"Gerry" in diamond
  chips, 20" l. 400.00
Painted paper, 10 small overlapping
  reserves w/landscapes, European
  figures, "chinoiserie" & "trompe
  l'oeil," France or Netherlands,
  ca. 1765, 11½" 280.00
Painted paper, 13 overlapping "trompe
  l'oeil" panels of ephemera including
  map, jack of clubs, notices, etc.,
  ivory sticks, Italy or France, ca. 1770,
  11" l. 750.00
Painted & embroidered satin, bride in
  pale blue gown on ivory ground,
  surrounded by Brussels lace frame,
  mother-of-pearl sticks, Europe,
  ca. 1890, 10" l. 125.00
Painted silk, Venus & attendants in
  landscape, pierced ivory sticks,
  ca. 1800, 9", framed 275.00

Fan with Ballooning Scenes

Painted silk, 3 vignettes of
ballooning scenes w/Montgolfier
& Roberts Brothers, France, ca. 1784,
11" l., framed (ILLUS.) 950.00
Painted silk, draped lady leans on
floral swag while 4 cherubs hover
nearby, w/"point de gaze" floral
lace border, blonde tortoise
shell sticks, ca. 1890, 13½".........200.00
Painted silk, ladies in garden
w/swan, edged by pastel blue,
pink & white lace, carved ivory
sticks w/gilding, opens to 26" 125.00
Painted vellum, center w/scenes of
nymphs, satyrs & cupids, different scene each side, pierced
& carved ivory sticks, opens to
20", framed 895.00
Sandlewood "brise," pierced fretwork
painted w/rose garlands & swags
surrounding musical emblems,
ca. 1840 ....175.00
Silver "brise" filigree, folding-type,
scrolled floral motif, Europe,
19th c., 8"......................475.00

Silver "Brise" Fan

Silver "brise" filigree, cloisonne
enameled vignettes in blue & green
on filigree ground, China, mid-19th c.,
8" l. (ILLUS.).................450.00
Voile & lace, h.p. florals & butterflies on white & silver, wooden
sticks, Victorian, 13½" l., opening to
25".............................50.00

FARM COLLECTIBLES

Corn Sheller

*Early agricultural tools, implements and
other adjuncts of farm life in America are
being collected today. Many are preserved
in museums. Most 19th century implements
remain fairly inexpensive and have been
used extensively by interior decorators as a
theme for restaurants, lounges and other
businesses.*

Barn lantern, brass, 1886 patent $75.00
Barn lantern, tin & glass 12.00
Barn roof ornament, 5-sided star,
wrought iron, Pennsylvania, 1830s ..100.00
Beehive, woven rye straw, dome-
shaped, w/round wooden base,
18th c., 3 pcs.....................400.00
Branding irons, various letters,
w/plain or twisted details on
handle, about 16" l., each ...10.00 to 20.00
Bull whip, heavy leather, 10' l..........25.00
Calf weaner, cast iron, "Daisy,"
w/sharp spikes....................15.00
Cheese curd knife, wooden, pistol
grip handle, sword shaped blade 75.00
Corn husking peg 6.00
Corn husking thumb guard, leather
w/iron points 9.00
Corn knife, wooden handle, steel
blade 20.00
Corn planter, wood, iron & tin,
original red paint & stencilling, 1893 ..25.00
Corn sheller, cast iron, 1859 patent
date, 40" h. 200.00
Corn sheller, small hand-type, cast
iron, 1873 patent date 19.00
Corn sheller, "Corn King," hardwood
frame, cast iron sheller parts 115.00
Corn sheller, hardwood frame, cast
iron sheller mechanism & crank,
original paint (ILLUS.) 65.00
Cranberry rake, wooden w/steel
tines, refinished, large 135.00

Egg carrier, wooden, "Star," holds
    4 dozen..........................45.00

Iron Wire Egg Basket

Egg gathering basket, iron wire, 6" h.
    (ILLUS.)...........................20.00
Egg gathering basket, iron wire
    folding-type...............14.50 to 25.00
Egg scale, "Farm Master"............15.00
Farmyard bell, cast iron, "Crystal
    Metal Upright No. 1," w/yoke......195.00
Flax hatchel, cherrywood w/wrought
    iron spikes, cov., 5½ x 23 x 5".......65.00
Goose yoke, wooden.................25.00
Grain bin, walnut & other wood,
    hinged slant lid opening to bin,
    1-board ends w/cut-out feet, old
    worn green paint, 40" w.,
    17" deep, 37½" h. 95.00
Grain flail, hardwood,
    52" l......................15.00 to 45.00
Grain measure, bentwood round,
    original stenciled label "Shaker
    Society, Sabbathday Lake, Me.,"
    11¼" d., 5¼" h. (replaced bottom)...55.00
Grain measure, bentwood round
    w/metal rim, old red painted
    finish, 11¾" d., 5½" h......35.00 to 40.00
Grain measure, bentwood round
    w/applied shaped handles each
    side, never had finish, 13½" d.,
    9¼" h. 100.00
Grain measure, bentwood round
    w/cast iron handles & band, 15" d. ...26.50
Grain measures, bentwood rounds,
    old green paint, graduated sizes of
    5½" d., 7" d., & 8½" d., set of
    3 ....115.00
Grain scoop, copper, 6" l.............12.00
Grain scoop, oak, hand-hewn.........32.00
Grain shovel, hewn from single piece
    of wood, iron re-inforcing band at
    front edge of blade, refinished,
    some age cracks, 55" l. 85.00
Grain shovel, hand-hewn wood, nice
    form, 1-piece....................120.00
Grain sieve, bentwood round w/woven
    horsehair sieve, 12½" d............150.00

Hay fork, all wood, 3-tine w/bentwood
    bracing, 60" l..............90.00 to 110.00
Implement seat, cast iron, "Champion" .30.00
Implement seat, cast iron, "Jones
    Rake" 60.00
Milking stool, wooden, 3-legged w/side
    handle 40.00
Ox yoke, single, oak, scrubbed
    white finish, 35" l. (age cracks &
    wear) 65.00
Ox yoke, double, carved pine &
    wrought iron, w/bentwood neck
    noose 110.00
Oxen shoes, pr. 16.00
Pitch fork, wrought iron, 2-tine,
    w/wooden handle, 80" l...........20.00
Potato digging fork, 4-tine, "Keen
    Kutter"..........................27.50
Sap carrying yoke, wooden, w/original
    wooden carrying hooks............35.00

Scythe with Grain Cradle

Scythe w/mortised wooden grain
    cradle (ILLUS.) ....75.00 to 90.00
Seed dispenser, poplar, hanging-type,
    slanted lid w/five interior bins & dis-
    pensing opening in base w/hinged
    flap, old dark finish, w/small tin
    scoop, 24½" w., 6¼" deep, 14½" h...65.00
Seed sowing device, wooden trough
    to be hung over the shoulder,
    w/hand operated lever to regulate
    the flow of seeds, old red paint,
    attributed to the Shakers, 116½" l...105.00
Sheep herder's poke, hand-hewn
    bentwood bow w/cross-piece 57.00

FIREARMS

Sharps 1852 Model Carbine

Automatic shotgun, Browning Belgian-
    made 1931 model, 16 gauge $550.00

Boot pistol, muzzle-loading, single
barrel 125.00
Carbine, Sharps 1852 model, by Robins
& Lawrence, Windsor, Vermont,
No. 2169, brass butt plate, patch box
& barrel band, traces of original
blueing, ca. 1854, 37¾" l. (ILLUS.) . . .550.00
Carbine, Springfield 1873 Trapdoor
model 325.00
Carbine, Winchester 1895 model, .30-06
caliber 450.00
Derringer, Eclipse model by James
Brown & Son, Pittsburgh, ca. 1880,
.30 caliber, 5½" l. 135.00
Derringer, Elliot's 1865 patent "over &
under" model .395.00
Musket, flintlock, tiger stripe maple
full stock, American Revolutionary
War era 450.00
Musket, U.S. Springfield 1864 model,
.58 caliber 375.00
Pistol, Colt 1873 model, single action . .525.00
Revolver, Allan & Thurber 1837 model,
drop-hammer percussion-type,
etched florals, 7¾" l. 195.00
Revolver, Colt 1851 Navy model,
w/Hartford address & matching
serial numbers, .36 caliber 465.00

1860 Colt Army Model Revolver

Revolver, Colt 1860 Army model,
matching serial numbers, 8" barrel
(ILLUS.) 605.00
Revolver, Colt 1861 Navy model,
matching serial numbers,
.36 caliber 550.00
Revolver, Smith & Wesson No. 1,
second issue, nickel-plated brass
frame & nickel-plated steel barrel,
rosewood grips, .22 caliber,
1860-68 . . . . .185.00
Rifle, Henry "repeating" (cartridge
magazine) rifle, "Henry's Patent,
Oct. 16, 1860," brass frame, .44
caliber, 43½" l. 4,000.00
Rifle, Kentucky full stock, curly maple
stock, percussion lock marked "J.
Tarratt & Sons," barrel w/brass inlay
initialed "J.N.D.," 36¼" barrel, overall 52" l. (minor damage to stock &
hammer screw replaced) 375.00
Rifle, Kentucky full stock, flintlock-
type, maple stock w/incised carving
& brass inlays, brass patch box,
attributed to Adam Angstadt of
Reading, Pennsylvania, ca. 1810,

45¾" barrel, overall 61" l. (13" of
forestock replaced) 1,025.00
Rifle, Kentucky full stock, curly maple
stock, signed "B.H. Burden" & dated
1855 on barrel, .38 caliber, 43" l.
barrel 850.00
Rifle, Kentucky full stock, curly maple
stock w/brass patch box, 12
engraved silver inlays & simple
carved detail on butt of stock,
octagonal barrel engraved "F.
Allison," 43" l. barrel, overall
58" l. 1,000.00
Rifle, Kentucky full stock, curly maple
stock, w/brass patch box & trim of 6
inlaid brass fish, 5 silver inlays & oval
engraved w/eagle & "Ohio," flintlock marked "M.M. Marlin, Warrant-
ed," 42" l. barrel, overall 58" l. 900.00
Rifle, Kentucky half-stock, maple stock
w/inlaid silver diamonds & stars,
percussion lock, 36 3/8" l. barrel,
overall 52" l. .275.00
Rifle, Kentucky half-stock, maple
(refinished) stock, percussion lock
signed "Joseph Golcher," 36½" l.
barrel, overall 53" l. 150.00
Rifle, Kentucky (Jaeger) half-stock,
black walnut stock w/deer carving
behind cheek area, flintlock, patch
box w/wooden cover, brass trigger
guard & trim, Lancaster County,
Pennsylvania, ca. 1760, 26" l. barrel,
overall 40" l. (2" of fore end restored
where wood had been split out from
front sling swivel) 900.00
Rifle, U.S. Model 1841, Robbins,
Kendall & Lawrence so-called "Mississippi" model, w/brass patch box,
.58 caliber 250.00

Civil War Rifle-Musket

Rifle-musket, Springfield 1861 model,
full stock, semi-octagonal bands,
varnished stock, dated 1862, 56" l.,
w/steel ramrod (ILLUS.) 495.00
Shotgun, double-barrel, walnut half-
stock w/checkering & carved rosette,
brass trim, buck & ball rifle converted from flintlock to percussion,
ca. 1830, 25" barrels, overall
40½" l. 150.00
Shotgun-rifle, "over-and-under model,"
curly maple half-stock w/silver inlay
& engraved patch box, barrel signed
"Amos Benfer 1878," double loading
rods w/resoldered mounting loops,
30" barrels, overall 47½" l. 850.00

FIRE EXTINGUISHERS

Harden's Hand Grenades

*Various types of small glass fire extin-
guishers intended primarily for use in
extinguishing small fires, were made in the
19th and early in the 20th centuries and are
now being collected.*

Amber glass grenade, canteen-
shaped $200.00
"Harden's Hand Grenade," blue glass,
quilted design, footed 70.00
"Harden's Hand Grenade," cobalt blue
glass, bulbous w/vertical ribbing &
embossed star, 6½" h., each (ILLUS.
of pr.) 58.00
"Harden's Hand Grenade," cobalt blue
glass, bulbous .45.00
"Hayward's Hand Fire Grenade," clear
glass, pleated 110.00
"Hayward's Hand Fire Grenade," cobalt
blue glass, bulbous w/panelling 150.00
"Hayward's Hand Fire Grenade," cobalt
blue glass, pleated 185.00
"Marvel Kill-Fyr Extinguisher," glass . . .30.00
"Phoenix," tin, tubular-type, salmon-
colored, marked "patented April 25,
1899, Norwich, Conn.," 2½" d.,
15" l. 35.00
"Red Comet," set of 8 transparent
red glass balls w/instructions, in
original red box w/decal 160.00
"Red Comet," hanging-type 17.50

FIRE FIGHTING COLLECTIBLES

Badge, "Pres. Norwood Vol. Fire Co.,
No. 1," brass, ornate w/old fire truck
pictured $30.00
Book, "Our Firemen," Baltimore,
1898 . . . . .100.00
Bucket, galvanized tin, wire bail
handle, painted red w/"Fire" in black
lettering, ca. 1890 . . . . .85.00

Fire Fighting Equipment

Bucket, leather, eagle & shield &
"Mechanic Fire Society" in banner,
original red paint, 11½" h. (hole in
bottom & handle missing) 1,250.00
Fire alarm box, cast iron, "Gamewell,"
17" h. 140.00
Fire alarm rattle, wooden 50.00
Fire house alarm bell, "New Haven
Clock Co.," 1886 . . . . .350.00
Fire house slide pole, brass, 2" d.,
20' l. 250.00
Fireman's (dress) coat, full-length,
navy blue wool w/30 brass buttons,
w/matching cap, ca. 1900 . . . . .50.00
Fireman's helmet, leather, w/gilded
eagle crest, "Verona F.D.," old black
& red paint, labeled "John Olson Co.,
188 Grand St., N.Y. City," 14¾" 140.00
Firemen's helmet, leather, original
liner, "Claremont Fire Dept., Engine
No. 1," metal maker's seal "Cairns
& Bros., Clifton, N.J.," dated 1932 . . . .80.00
Fireman's helmet, metal, h.p. front-
piece & lettered "Chief" 65.00
Fireman's trumpet horn, presentation
piece, brass, engraved "Tempest
Engine Co. No. 1, A.F.D.," 12½" l. . . .550.00
Fireman's trumpet horn, brass, ca.
1870, 18½" l. 340.00
Fireman's trumpet horn, presentation
piece, silverplate, engraved
w/name, hose company & dated
1862, 17" l. 495.00
Fireman's parade uniform: long parade
coat, shirt w/gold buttons, leather
belt & high leather helmet w/eagle
on front metal shield; ca. 1890,
4 pcs. 325.00
Fireman's uniform buttons, brass
w/embossed trumpets, set of 20 . . . . .15.00
Fire mark, cast iron, "United Fireman's
Insurance Co." 145.00
Fire pumper truck, American LaFrance
800 gallon pumper, 6-cylinder Buda

engine, chemical tank, brass bell &
siren, 1918 . . . . .25,000.00
Fire pumper-wagon bell (from horse-
drawn vehicle), foot pedal-operated
nickel-plated brass gong, "New
Departure," ca. 1902, 15" d. 495.00
Hose nozzle, brass, "Elkhart," 10" l. 40.00
Hose nozzle, handled, brass, marked
"Poweron P-4-A American LaFrance
Corp.," 10" l. 25.00

Fireman's Lantern

Lantern, "Dietz," brass, 1907, 15" h.
(ILLUS.) 160.00
Photograph, 1915 American LaFrance
truck in front of Chicago fire house,
framed, 37 x 27" 75.00
Print, 2 engines surrounded by flames,
advertising, "Cole Bros., Pawtucket,
R.I.," horse-drawn steamers, original
frame, 1870, 33 x 27" 2,100.00
Program, "Firemen's Memorial Fund,"
Sousa Band Concert, Metropolitan
Opera House, Nov., 1, 1908 . . . . .15.00
Watch fob, embossed truck, axes &
hats 35.00

FIREPLACE & HEARTH ACCESSORIES

Also see ART NOUVEAU and METALS.

Andirons, brass, Federal, ball tops,
ring-turned standards, spurred
arch supports, ball feet, w/conform-
ing log guards, ca. 1800, 10" h.,
pr. $275.00
Andirons, brass, Federal, turned oval

finials, hexagonal upper sections
on turned narrow standards above
hexagonal plinths, spurred arch
supports, shod slipper feet,
w/brass gallery & ball-turned log
guards, Boston, 1800-30, 18½" h.,
pr. 440.00
Andirons, brass, Federal, turned finials
& standards, scrolling arch supports,
ball feet, w/conforming log guards,
stamped "Rostand," late 19th c.,
19" h., pr. 200.00
Andirons, brass, Federal, ball tops,
baluster standards, spurred arch
supports, slipper feet,
w/matching log guards, ca. 1820,
20" h., pr. 302.50
Andirons, brass, Federal, double lemon
tops w/ring-turned mid-bands,
columnar standards, spurred arch
supports, ball feet, 1800-20, 20" h.,
pr. 660.00
Andirons, brass, Federal, octagonal
finials, ring- and octagonal-turned
standards, spurred arch supports,
ball feet, w/matching log guards,
ca. 1810, 25" h., pr. 275.00

Federal Andirons

Andirons, brass, Federal, urn-form
finials, reeded columnar standard,
spurred arch supports, ball feet,
w/iron log support at rear, New
York, ca. 1800, 28" h., pr.
(ILLUS.) 3,630.00
Andirons, brass, ball finials, scrolling
feet, Bradley & Hubbard, 20th c.,
pr. 150.00
Andirons, brass & wrought iron,
Federal, shaped brass finials,
baluster-turned iron standards,
spurred arch supports, ball feet,
stamped "R. Wittingham," New
York, early 19th c., 21" h., pr. 1,320.00
Andirons, cast iron, figural head &

torso of lady w/scalloped skirt,
12½" h., pr.....................230.00

Andirons, wrought iron, tooled heart
finials, crooked necks, chamfered
standards, arch supports, penny
feet, Pennsylvania, 18½" h., pr. 474.00

Andirons, wrought iron, models of cats
w/amber glass eyes, pr............175.00

Bellows, painted & decorated wood,
turtle-back style, free-hand
orange, green, black & gold fruit
& foliage on yellow ground, brass
nozzle, 17¼" l. (poorly releather-
ed)................................137.50

Bellows, poplar, worn leather sides,
tin nozzle, 22¾" l..................35.00

Clock jack, meat roasting rack on
clockwork mechanism, brass w/cast
iron ring to hang meat, embossed
"Salter's Economical Warrented,"
15½" h............................250.00

Coal hod, cast iron, ornate...........137.50

Coat scuttle (or hod), copper, cylindrical w/one open side, flaring
cylindrical foot, brass bail handle
& grip, 19th c., 18" h..............308.00

Ember carrier, sheet iron pan w/wrought
iron handle, 9½ x 8¾" pan,
17¾" l. handle.....................30.00

Ember shovel, flaring sheet iron
blade w/wrought iron handle,
11¾" l.............................15.00

Ember tongs, wrought iron, 26¾" l. 75.00

Fire dogs (log guards), cast iron,
"Haven & Co., Cincinnati," ca. 1862,
9½" h., pr.........................20.00

Victorian Fire Grate

Fire grate, Victorian, brass & cast
iron, shaped iron backplate cast
w/figure of standing man, projecting
center section mounted w/brass
urn finials above serpentine pierced
brass grill w/elaborate dragon &
foliate motifs flanked by elaborate
standards w/ball finials, England,
mid-19th c., 31" w., 31½" h.
(ILLUS.).........................550.00

Fire grate, Federal, brass & cast iron,
shaped iron backplate & sloping
sides w/scrolled terminals & brass
urn finials centering 4 iron bars
above an outwardly curving base
w/pierced brass scrolling skirt flanked
by brass urn finials on scrolled
legs & ring-turned brass feet,
1810-30, 28¼" w., 32½" h.........935.00

Fireplace fender, brass, pierced &
applied w/gadrooning, foliate
feet, Victorian, 45½" w...........880.00

Fireplace fender, brass, D-shaped,
pierced overall w/stylized crosses
& circles, flaring stepped base,
paw feet, England, 1810-20, 47" w. ..330.00

Fireplace fender, wrought iron,
alternating wavy & twisting spindles
in frame, scrolled feet, ball finials,
41" w., 11" h.....................225.00

Hearth broiler, rotary-type, wrought
iron, square rack (or grid)..........50.00

Hearth broiler, rotary-type, wrought
iron, alternating wavy & straight
bars on grid, rattail handle, 9" w.
broiler, overall 23" l..............175.00

Hearth broiler, stationary-type,
wrought iron, 9 bars across iron
rod legs, 10¼" sq. grid rack,
8½" l. handle......................40.00

Hearth broiler, stationary-type, wrought
iron, 10 bars across legs, 13 x 12"
rack, 19" l. handle.................55.00

Hearth broom, birch splint, turned
wood handle, early 19th c., 56" l. ...160.00

Hearth crane, wrought iron, 30 x 13" ...80.00

Hearth crane, wrought iron, w/twisted
diagonal brace, 41 x 19"...........35.00

Hearth crane hook, wrought iron,
S-hook, 18th c., 8" l...............10.00

Hearth griddle w/rim, hanging-type,
wrought iron, 18th c., 13" d. pan 192.50

Hearth Skillet

Hearth skillet, wrought iron, long
handle w/side braces, 11½" d.
skillet pan, 20½" l. handle
(ILLUS.).........................210.00

Hearth toaster, rotary-type, wrought
iron w/four twisted wire arches,
ring handle, late 18th c...........325.00

Hearth toasting fork, wrought iron, front-
footed, shank handle w/hanging
loop in end, 14½" l................210.00

Hearth toasting fork, wrought iron,
3-tine, arched shank & faceted handle,
signed & dated "1839," 20" l. 165.00

Oven peel, wrought iron, shaped
blade, short handle w/twisted detail,
20¾" l. 70.00

Oven peel, wrought iron, flat blade,
leaf form centered on long handle
w/bold heart finial, 18th c., 42" l. 90.00

Posnet pan, cast iron, shallow
bowl on 3 feet, long handle,
overall 18¼" l. 38.00

Potato rake, wrought iron, flattened
scrolling end w/long shaft &
hanging ring at end 65.00

Skewer holder & pr. skewers,
wrought iron, 11" l. 45.00

Trammel, brass, sawtooth-type,
adjusts up from 11½" 65.00

Trammel, wrought iron, sawtooth-
type, adjusts up from 34" 85.00

Trammel, wrought iron, sawtooth-
type, adjusts up from 40½" 125.00

Sawtooth Trammel

Trammel, wrought iron, sawtooth-
type w/notched sliding hook &
scrolling terminals, early 19th c.,
41" l. (ILLUS.) 495.00

Trammel chain, wrought iron links,
extends to 30" 12.50

Trammel chain, wrought iron links,
w/twisted details, extends to 51" 45.00

Waffle iron, cast iron 45.00

Waffle iron, wrought iron 67.50

FISHER (Harrison) GIRLS

The Fisher Girl, that chic American girl whose face and figure illustrated numerous magazine covers and books at the turn of the century, was created by Harrison Fisher. A professional artist who had studied in England and was trained by his artist father, he was able to capture an element of refined, cultured elegance in his drawings of beautiful women. They epitomized all that every American girl longed to be and catapulted their creator into the ranks of success. Harrison Fisher, who was born in 1877, worked as a commercial artist full time until his death in 1934. Today collectors seek out magazine covers, prints, books and postcards illustrated with Fisher Girls.

"Sweetheart"

Book, "A Dream of Fair Women," 20
color illustrations, 1907 ....$150.00

Book, "A Garden of Girls," 1910 ......135.00

Book, "American Belles," 1911........250.00

Book, "A Song of Hiawatha," by Henry
Wadsworth Longfellow, illustrations
by Fisher, 1906 ....70.00 to 85.00

Book, "Fair Americans," 1911........215.00

Book, "The Little Gift Book," 30 color
illustrations, 1913 ....190.00

Book, "Maidens Fair," 1912..........285.00

Magazine cover, Cosmopolitan, August
1910 ....10.00

Postcard, "The Only Pebble," 1915,
matted 45.00

Postcards, "The Greatest Moments of a
Girl's Life" series, set of 6, original
gilt frame, overall 28 x 10" ...80.00 to 95.00

Postcards, "The Senses" series, set of
6, original gilt frame, overall 27½ x
9"..................................75.00

Print, "Sweetheart," 1909, 13 x 17"
(ILLUS.) 32.50

FOOD, CANDY & MISC. MOLDS

Also see BUTTER MOLDS and METALS.

Beeswax, wooden, 5-compartment,
carved floral pattern w/ribbed sides,
handled, 10 x 2" $130.00

Cake, rabbit, cast iron, marked "Griswold," 2-part, 12 x 11"...........150.00

Candle, 24 pewter tubes in original
pine frame, 19½ x 7", 16½" h.......650.00

Chocolate, boy in tuxedo & top hat,
tin, 7½" h. 32.50

Tin Chocolate Mold

Chocolate, chickens (3) on nest,
tin (ILLUS.) 62.50
Chocolate, cupid, tin, large 95.00
Chocolate, duck, tin 55.00
Chocolate, eggs (6) w/embossed
rabbits, tin, marked "Made in
Germany," 6½" l. 20.00
Chocolate, egg w/embossed grapes,
tin, large 68.00
Chocolate, girl wearing fashionable
hat, dress & high button shoes,
nickel-plated sheet iron, marked
"Elegante" & "Letang Fils, Paris,"
ca. 1900, 6¾ x 3¾ x ½" 75.00
Chocolate, heart w/embossed cupid,
tin, double hinged 58.00
Chocolate, horse standing, tin,
2-piece w/hinge at top, 5¼" l. 87.00
Chocolate, Kewpie, tin, 8" h. 150.00
Chocolate, lady finger shape
w/embossed cats (6), tin, hinged,
6¼ x 8". 20.00
Chocolate, lamb, tin, small 45.00
Chocolate, lamb, tin, large 125.00
Chocolate, lion, tin, small 45.00
Chocolate, owl, tin, large 68.00
Chocolate, penguin w/top hat &
glasses, tin, hinged, marked
"Anton Reiche, Dresden" 45.00
Chocolate, rabbit, tin, marked
"Germany," 7" h. 50.00
Chocolate, rabbit in seated position,
tin, hinged, 10" h. 75.00
Chocolate, rabbits (6), tin, marked
"Germany," 8" l. 40.00
Chocolate, rooster, tin, 2-part,
6¼" h. . . . . .40.00 to 45.00
Chocolate, rooster, tin, 10" h. 135.00
Chocolate, roosters (4), tin, hinged,
marked "T.C. Wegandt," 4" h. 55.00
Chocolate, Santa Clauses (3), tin,
marked "Dresden," 2½ x 6¾" 20.00
Chocolate, squirrel w/acorn & large
bushy tail, tin, 15" h. 175.00
Chocolate, turkey, tin, 4½ x 4½" 30.00
Chocolate, witch, tin 25.00
Food, asparagus, ironstone 42.00
Food, cauliflower, ironstone, Alcock . . .50.00

Food, crown, ironstone china, large 54.00
Food, ear of corn, ironstone,
medium 53.00
Food, ear of corn, ironstone, large 70.00
Food, ear of corn, yellowware 75.00
Food, fish, copper, marked
"Kreamer," 9½" l. 45.00
Food, fish, ironstone, medium
size. . . . . .40.00 to 55.00

Redware Pottery Fish Mold

Food, fish, redware, amber glaze
w/brown splotches, 11¾" l.
(ILLUS.) 150.00
Food, fish, redware, interior glaze,
12¼" l. 65.00
Food, fish, yellowware, brown
sponged Rockingham glaze, 7½ x
5¾" oval 95.00
Food, grape cluster center, ironstone,
small. 36.00
Food, grape cluster center, ironstone,
medium 40.00
Food, pineapple center, fluted sides,
yellowware, 7 x 4 7/8" oval 65.00
Food, poinsettia center, ironstone 52.00
Food, rabbit, yellowware, 9 x 6", 4" h. . .50.00
Food, shell, ironstone, Edge Malkin,
small. 40.00
Food, swirled sides, redware, clear
interior glaze w/brown exterior
sponging, impressed "John Bell,
Waynesboro," 8½" d., 4" h. 255.00
Food, turk's turban, copper, 9¾" d. 75.00
Food, turk's turban, redware, clear
glaze w/brown splotches, 6½" d. 55.00
Food, turk's turban, redware, scalloped
edge, greenish glaze w/orange
spots, w/tin center upright, 11" d.,
3½" h. 195.00
Food, turk's turban, mottled brown
Rockingham glaze pottery, 8¼" d. . . .40.00
Ice cream, asparagus, pewter 40.00
Ice cream, automobile, pewter 85.00
Ice cream, boy on bike, pewter 60.00

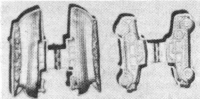

Pewter Ice Cream Molds

Ice cream, cabin cruiser, pewter,
5½" l. (ILLUS. left) 50.00

Ice cream, camel, pewter, 5" l. 20.00

Ice cream, candle embossed "Jack Be Nimble," pewter 130.00

Ice cream, candlestick, pewter 45.00

Ice cream, cauliflower, pewter, 3¾" l. 27.50

Ice cream, chick emerging from shell, pewter, 3½" h. 27.50

Ice cream, chick, pewter, marked "E & Co. N.Y.," 3½" h. . . . . . . .15.00 to 25.00

Ice cream, Chinaman, pewter . .60.00 to 75.00

Ice cream, Christmas tree, pewter 50.00

Ice cream, convertible automobile, pewter, marked "E & Co., N.Y.," 4¾" l. (ILLUS. right) 55.00

Ice cream, cornucopia, pewter. 27.50

Ice cream, dahlia, pewter, marked "E. & Co." 37.50

Ice cream, dog in shoe, pewter 50.00

Ice cream, donkey, pewter 45.00

Ice cream, eagle, pewter 85.00

Ice cream, grape cluster, pewter. 55.00

Ice cream, lamb, pewter, marked "E & Co. N.Y.," 3¼" l. 20.00

Ice cream, liberty bell, pewter, 3½" h. 32.50

Lily Ice Cream Mold

Ice cream, lily, 3-part, pewter (ILLUS.) . . . . .50.00 to 60.00

Ice cream, locomotive, pewter, 5½" l. . .60.00

Ice cream, lovebirds, pewter, 5" l. 35.00

Ice cream, loving cup, pewter 35.00

Ice cream, mandolin, pewter 90.00

Ice cream, Masonic emblem, pewter . . .16.00

Ice cream, pear, pewter, 4" h. 32.50

Ice cream, pick-up truck, pewter, 1930s, 6½" l. .135.50

Ice cream, pig seated, pewter, 3½" h. . . .60.00

Ice cream, pineapple, pewter, marked "Brevete," 3 1/8" h. 42.00

Ice cream, potato, pewter. 35.00

Ice cream, pumpkin, pewter . . .30.00 to 40.00

Ice cream, Puss 'n Boots, pewter 42.00

Ice cream, raspberries, pewter, marked "E. & Co., N.Y.," 4" l. 25.00

Ice cream, rooster, pewter, small 160.00

Ice cream, Santa Claus w/basket & backpack, pewter, marked "S. & Co.," 4 3/8" h. .95.00

Ice cream, shell, pewter, marked "C.C.," 4" l. 35.00

Ice cream, snowman, pewter, 4 7/8" h. 35.00

Ice cream, squirrel, pewter 140.00

Ice cream, stork, pewter 75.00

Ice cream, top hat, pewter 38.00

Ice cream, turkey, pewter, 4¾" h. 37.00

Ice cream, wedding bells, pewter 80.00

Ice cream, witch on broomstick, pewter, 5½" l. .62.50

Jelly, hen on nest, ironstone 32.00

Jelly, grape cluster, tin, 1870s 50.00

Maple sugar, Three Heart patt., wooden, 14 x 3½" 85.00

Maple sugar candy, fluted, tin, 3½" d., 1¼" h., set of 4 . . . . .20.00

Maple sugar candy, house w/windows, door & chimney, 6-compartment, carved pine, 26½ x 5 x 4" 140.00

Maple sugar candy, heart, carved birch w/initials, ca. 1810, 8 x 4 x 1½" 190.00

Pudding, fluted sides, tin, w/locking cover, marked "Kreamer," 6½" h. . . .35.00

Pudding, geometric top, copper w/tin lining, 5 x 3¼" oval 105.00

Pudding, rose center, copper w/tin lining 60.00

Pudding, spiral cone, tin, 6¾" d., 8" h. 15.00

Pudding, swirled top, copper w/tin lining, 4 1/8" oval, 4 1/8" h. 150.00

FOOT & BED WARMERS

19th Century Brass Bed Warmer

Bed warmer, brass pan w/simple floral engraving on lid, turned wood handle, 33" l. $245.00

Bed warmer, brass pan w/pierced & engraved foliate design, ring-turned wood handle, 18th c., 42" l. 330.00

Bed warmer, brass pan w/engraved floral design on lid, turned wood handle w/worn original grain-painted finish, 42½" l. 375.00

Bed warmer, brass pan w/engraved bird & tulip tree design on lid, turned wood handle, 43½" l. 235.00

Bed warmer, brass pan w/engraved star design on lid, wrought iron handle, 18th c., 44" l. 660.00

Bed warmer, brass pan w/pierced & engraved floral design on lid, turned fruitwood handle, early 19th c., 45" l. (ILLUS.) 285.00

Bed warmer, cast iron pan w/pierced
brass lid & iron rat-tail handle 195.00

Bed warmer, copper pan w/hinged
domed lid engraved w/foliate
design, turned wood handle, late
18th c., 40" l. (minor dents) 195.00

Bed warmer, copper pan w/engraved
floral design on lid, turned wood
handle, 12¼" d., 44" l. 300.00

Bed warmer, copper pan w/engraved
floral & scrolling design on lid,
turned wood handle, 18th c. 295.00

Bed warmer, copper pan w/pierced
floral design on lid, turned maple
handle w/black-painted finish,
18th c. 295.00

Foot warmer, carpet-covered tin
w/brass ends, marked "Lehmans,"
14 x 8" 40.00

Foot warmer, carpet-covered tin,
marked "Clark Heater No. 2" 17.50

Carpet-Covered Foot Warmer

Foot warmer, carpet-covered tin,
w/charcoal drawer (ILLUS.) 50.00

Foot warmer, pierced tin box w/per-
forated heart & circle designs, in
mortised walnut frame w/turned
corner posts, wire bail handle,
8" sq., 6" h. 155.00

Foot warmer, pierced tin box in
mortised wood frame w/turned
corner posts, 8¾ x 8", 6" h. 65.00

Foot warmer, pierced tin box w/per-
forated geometric designs, in
mortised wood frame w/turned
corner posts, metal ember pan,
11 x 10", 5¾" h. 145.00

Foot warmer, stoneware pottery,
dome-shaped, vent hole w/ring cap,
brown Albany slip glaze, marked
"C.J. Jager Co.," 9 x 7" 220.00

Foot warmer, stoneware pottery,
model of a pig, marked "George L.
Starks & Co., Saranac Lake, N.Y." 90.00

Foot warmer, stoneware pottery,
marked "Doulton Lambeth" 65.00

Foot warmer, stoneware pottery,
marked "Henderson Foot
Warmer" 105.00

FOOT & BOOT SCRAPERS

Cast Iron Foot Scraper

Cast iron, flat bar w/conical finials at
ends, mortised construction,
18th c. $95.00

Cast iron, flat bar w/figural griffins at
ends, reticulated foliate base, 15" d.
(ILLUS.) 400.00

Cast iron, model of a Dachshund dog,
advertising "Alabama Pipe Co.,"
11" l. 85.00

Cast iron, pot of stylized scrolling
foliage set in oblong pan w/gadroon
edge, 14½ x 12" 90.00

Cast iron, scalloped footed pan
centered w/scraping bar, 11 x 10",
8" h. 95.00

Wrought iron, bar w/exaggerated
ram's horn curls at ends, set in
stone base, 12 x 8" 225.00

Wrought iron, simple scrolled ends,
trestle base, 12" w., 6" h. 75.00

Wrought iron, stylized cut out model of
a dog w/simple tooled ears & eyes,
11¾" l. 525.00

Wrought iron, sweeping twisted arm
rising to scraper blade & continuing
to scrolling top, hole at bottom of
arm & butterfly at end of blade to
attach to porch, 6" blade, 14" arm ...110.00

FRACTURS

*Fractur paintings are decorative birth
and marriage certificates of the 18th and
19th centuries and also include family registers and similar documents. Illuminated
family documents, birth and baptismal
certificates, religious texts and rewards of
merit, in a particular style, are known as
"fractur" because of the similarity to the
16th century type-face of that name. Gay
watercolor borders, frequently incorporating stylized birds, angels, animals or
flowers surrounded the hand-lettered
documents, which were executed by local
ministers, school masters or itinerant
penmen. Most are of Pennsylvania Dutch
origin.*

Fractur Dated 1851

Birth & Baptismal record for Zachariah
Thomas, vital statistics in ornamental
calligraphy above figures of a dark-
haired lady holding hands over a tea
table w/a dark-haired gentleman
holding a brightly colored bouquet of
flowers, executed in red, yellow,
green, blue & black watercolor
w/gilt highlights, attributed to
Reverend Henry Young, Centre
County, Pennsylvania, dated 1851,
framed, 8½ x 6½" (ILLUS.) $4,400.00
Birth record for Christina Frantz, vital
statistics in ornamental German
calligraphy surrounded by paired
cornucopiae overflowing w/enormous
garden bouquet of blossoms,
pendant from bow-knotted spray,
executed in shades of yellow, rose,
green & blue, signed Karl E. Munch,
Dauphin County, Pennsylvania,
dated 26 January 1818, framed,
7½ x 11¾" 2,640.00
Birth record for Elizabeth Mosser, vital
statistics in ornamental calligraphy
w/paired spindly-crested birds
perched in a flowering tulip plant,
in shades of orange, green & blue,
Southeastern Pennsylvania, dated
1830, framed, 9½ x 7½" 550.00
Birth record for Lucinda Boston, vital
statistics in ornamental calligraphy
w/stylized pots of flowers, hearts,
stars & vining foliage within border
stripe w/invected corners, executed
in watercolors, recording birth in
1834, New Salem, Ohio, by M.S.,
1844, framed, 15¼" sq. (some tears
& professional edge repair) 400.00
Birth record, printed & hand-colored
vital statistics & deer, birds on
branches & tulips, recording birth in

1778, Lancaster County,
Pennsylvania, beveled pine frame,
19½ x 16½".....................350.00
Bookplate in pen & ink, inscribed for
Peter Miller, Lebanon County,
w/simple trees at sides, red & black,
old frame, 7 7/8 x 5" (stains) 150.00
Certificate, German script legend
centralized between floral motifs,
in shades of red, yellow & green,
original beveled wood frame
(refinished), overall 12¼ x 10¼" (ink
faded & paper darkened) 115.00
Vorschrift (writing specimen), for Jacob
Beitler, ornamental German
calligraphy w/strapwork lettering
enclosing flowers & birds, Southeastern Pennsylvania, dated 1782,
framed, 8 x 13" 1,980.00
Vorschrift (writing specimen),
strapwork lettering enclosing
flourishes & scrolls & pendant
flowers, bird perched above &
below, in red, yellow, green &
brown, probably Lancaster County,
Pennsylvania, dated 1793, framed,
8 x 13".........................1,540.00

Vorschrift Dated 1810

Vorschrifts (writing specimens), large
strapwork lettering enclosing scrolls
& flourishes, borders w/large tulips
sprouting from checkered pots,
in shades of red, yellow & green,
Southeastern Pennsylvania, dated
1810, 8 x 10¼", pr. (ILLUS. of one)...770.00

FRAMES

*Also see BROWNIE COLLECTIBLES,
CELLULOID and ROYCROFT ITEMS.*

Bird's eye maple, box-style, 2¼" deep
ogee-molded framework, 24" w.,
28" h. $150.00

Small Brass Frame

Brass square w/round opening, beaded
edges & applied scrolls in corners,
3" sq. (ILLUS.) 15.00
Brass, easel-type, ornate, cast
w/woman's head at top & cherub
each side, 9½" w., 12" h. 75.00
Brass-plated cast iron, easel-type, cast
w/dogwood blossoms & flowing
vines, oblong w/oval 3 x 5½"
opening, overall 5½" w., 8" h........45.00
Cast iron, easel-type, rococo-style cast
w/openwork leaves & scrolls, gilt
finish, oblong w/oval 4 x 5½"
opening, overall 8½" w., 11" h.......35.00
Celluloid, oval, 5 7/8" w., 8" h. 20.00
Gilt gesso on wood, 2" w. ornately
molded framework, overall 17¾" w.,
22¼" h. 65.00
Golden oak, plain, 12" w., 15" h., pr. ...38.00
Painted pine, 1 5/8" w. beveled framework, painted yellow & black
graining w/black corner blocks,
overall 10 7/8" w., 12¾" h.........155.00
Painted poplar, beveled framework
w/original red-painted flame
graining, 16½" w., 14½" h. 120.00
Pine, canted framework, refinished,
11" w., 12½" h., pr. 75.00

English Silver Frame

Silver, "repousse" floral bouquet
design alternating w/cartouches, on
blue velvet backing, w/English hallmarks, 13½" h. (ILLUS.) 1,045.00
Sterling silver, easel-type, engraved
floral garlands, marked "Lullaby
1909 Sterling," 4" d. 65.00
Sterling silver, easel-type, "repousse"
work overall, Gorham, 5" oval......65.00
Walnut, box-style, w/gilt inner liner,
11" w., 13" h......................20.00
Walnut, box-style, w/gilt inner liner,
17" w., 15" h......................35.00
Walnut, box-style, 29" w., 35" h. 50.00
Walnut, cross-bar, applied carved
leaves at corners, 12" w., 14" h. 24.00
Walnut, cross-bar, applied carved
leaves at corners, w/gilt inner liner,
14" w., 16" h......................50.00
Walnut, oval, deep ogee-molded
framework, 12" h. 60.00
Walnut, round, deep ogee-molded
framework, 17" d. 145.00

FRATERNAL ORDER COLLECTIBLES

B.P.O.E. Mug

American Legion cane, marked "Paris
1927"...........................$35.00
B.P.O.E. (Benevolent & Protective
Order of Elks) card holder, sterling
silver, ornate, ca. 1800 ....55.00
B.P.O.E. demitasse spoon, sterling
silver, elk on handle, reverse
w/clock & "Muncie, Indiana, 1899" ...28.00
B.P.O.E. mug, china, brown elk & clock
emblems, Warwick China, 4½" h.
(ILLUS.) ....45.00 to 55.00
B.P.O.E. print, sepiatone, "Oh, How I
Love An Elk," young lady w/elk
pictured, 1907, oak frame...........35.00
B.P.O.E. ring, 10k green gold band
w/white gold elk's head & red,
white & blue enamel emblems 129.00
G.A.R. (Grand Army of the Republic)
book, "Official Souvenir 31st

Encampment, 1897, Buffalo, N.Y.,"
die-cut buffalo head shape, 50 pp. ...47.50
I.O.O.F. (International Order of Odd
Fellows) graveside flag holder, cast
iron, heart in hand emblem, back
impressed "Pat'd. Sep. 17, 1901,
G. H. Dawson, Rockford, Ill.," worn
white metal plating, 28½" h. 115.00
I.O.O.F. wall hanging, leather
w/symbols, fringed, 18 x 18" 40.00
Knights of Columbus ceremonial sword
w/sheath, name engraved 75.00
Knights of Pythias medal, brass on
silver, dated 1874 ....12.50
Knights of Pythias sword, etched
blade, Pettibone Bros. Mfg., Cinn.,
Ohio 90.00
Knights Templar watch fob, gold,
large 300.00

Masonic Locket

Masonic locket, gold, hinged lid
engraved w/sunburst & triangle,
inscribed "Hiram Lodge No. 7" in
banner at top & "John Dean" in
banner below, all on a reeded
ground flecked w/ermine, back
dated 1798, 2¾" oval (ILLUS.) 2,200.00
Masonic pitcher, tankard, china,
cobalt blue & silver lustre, "Northern
No. 25 -- 60th Anniversary, 1853-
1913," 12" h. 115.00
Masonic vase, cut glass, strawberry
diamond & thumbprint cutting &
"Zenobia, Toledo, Ohio," signed
Libbey, 2½" d., 5" h. 78.00

Order of the Eastern Star cup, saucer,
creamer & sugar bowl, china, 4 pcs. ..25.00
Shrine 1898 spooner, clear glass,
3-handled, "Pittsburgh"............70.00
Shrine 1900 chalice, clear glass,
"Washington, D.C." 52.00
Shrine 1906 cup & saucer, clear glass,
"Pittsburgh".......................55.00
Shrine 1907 toothpick holder, pot-
shaped, clear glass w/ruby-flashed
band, "Pittsburgh" & "Los Angeles" ..90.00
Shrine 1908 wine, ruby-flashed glass

w/gilt sabres, "St. Paul, Minn,"
5" h. 70.00
Shrine 1909 goblet, clear glass,
"Louisville" 75.00
Shrine 1911 champagne, clear glass,
"Rochester," "New York" &
"Pittsburgh".......................90.00
Shrine 1915 tumbler, milk white glass,
"Pittsburgh".......................55.00
Shrine badge, "Supreme Council,
Springfield, Mass.," 1913 ....35.00
Shrine knife, embossed figure of
draped nude, "Medinah Shrine,
Chicago, New Orleans," ring-pull
blades, Germany, 1910 ....32.00
Shrine paperweight, spelter, figural
Shriner wearing fez, tie & coat,
w/brass plate advertising "Moore's
Metal," 1930 ....32.00
Shrine plaque, "Crescent Temple,
Atlantic City," 1927................65.00

FRUIT JARS

Ball Ideal

Air-Tight, clear, qt. $45.00
Amazon Swift Seal within circle,
aqua, qt. 5.50
American Porcelain Lined, w/mono-
gram, aqua, ½ gal. 25.00
Atlas E-Z Seal, aqua, pt. ....2.00 to 3.50
Atlas E-Z Seal, amber, qt. 27.00
Atlas Good Luck, w/large embossed
four-leaf clover, clear, qt.............3.00
Atlas Strong Shoulder Mason, green,
qt. 20.00
Ball Ideal, aqua, qt., in wire holder
(ILLUS.) 8.00
Ball Perfect Mason, olive green, pt. 35.00
Ball Standard, aqua, ½ gal. 8.50
Ball Sure Seal, aqua, ½ gal. 4.50
Beaver, w/embossed beaver chewing
log, aqua, ½ gal. 20.00

Boyd Mason, olive green, qt. 45.00
Canadian King, Made In Canada, Wide
   Mouth, clear, qt. 22.00
Canton (The) Domestic Fruit Jar,
   clear, qt. 60.00
Clarke Fruit Jar, Cleveland, O., aqua,
   ½ gal. 55.00
Crystal Mason, clear, pt. 7.50
Dandy (The) Trade Mark, clear, qt. 40.00
Eagle, aqua, qt. .80.00
Electric Fruit Jar, aqua, qt. 30.00
Gem, aqua, qt. 5.00
Globe, amber, qt. 45.00
Glocker Sanitary Trade Mark, Pat.
   1911, Others Pending, aqua, qt. 20.00
Ideal (The), clear, midget 75.00
Independent Jar, clear, pt. 38.00
Knowlton Vacume Fruit Jar, w/star,
   blue, ½ gal. 24.50
Knox Mason, clear, ½ pt. 5.00
Leotric, aqua, pt. 5.00
Lightning, aqua, ½ pt. 12.00
Lightning, amber, qt. 35.00
Lightning Trade Mark, amber, pt. 45.00

Lockport Mason

Lockport Mason, clear, ½ gal. (ILLUS.) . .11.00
Lustre, R.E. Tongue & Bros. Co.,
   Phila. within circle, aqua, qt. 7.00
Mansfield Improved Mason, aqua, pt. . .12.00
Marion (The) Jar, Mason's Patent
   Nov. 30th, 1858, aqua, ½ gal. 12.00
Mason (The) Jar of 1872, aqua, qt. 32.50
Mason's Improved, w/Hero Cross,
   aqua, ½ gal. .2.50
Mason's Patent Nov. 30th, 1858, amber,
   ½ gal. 60.00
Millville Atmospheric Fruit Jar, aqua,
   qt. 40.00
Myers Test Jar, aqua, ½ gal. 125.00
New Paragon, aqua, ½ gal. 100.00
Patent Sept. 18, 1860, aqua, qt. 45.00
Pearl (The), clear, qt. 30.00

Peerless, aqua, qt. 100.00
Peoria Inspected Pottery on base,
   groove ring wax seal, qt. 23.00
Perfect Seal, Made in Canada, Wide
   Mouth Adjustable, clear, ½ gal. 1.00
Pine Deluxe Jar, clear, ½ gal. 4.00
Porcelain Lined, aqua, ½ gal. 18.00
Potter & Bodine, Philadelphia in script,
   blue, qt. 100.00
Presto, clear, ½ pt. 8.00
Princess, clear, qt. 15.00
Protector, paneled, aqua, qt. 22.50
Queen Wide Mouth Adjustable, clear,
   ½ gal. 6.00
Reliable Home Canning Mason, clear,
   qt. 2.00
Root Mason, aqua, pt. 3.00
Safety, amber, qt. 100.00
Selco Surety Seal with circle, aqua,
   qt. 5.75
Standard, underlined w/shepherd's
   crook, wax seal, aqua, ½ gal. 35.00
Standard Mason, aqua, qt. 6.00
Sun (in circle) Trade Mark, aqua,
   qt. 45.00
Sure Seal, 2 lines in script within
   circle, aqua, qt. 3.00
Swayzee's Improved Mason, aqua, qt. . . .3.50
Swayzee's Improved Mason, olive green,
   qt. 24.50
Telephone Jar (The), green, qt. 7.00
Veteran, w/bust of Veteran within
   circle in frame, clear, pt. 17.50
Wan-Eta Cocoa Boston, aqua, pt. 12.50
Wears, clear, pt. .8.00
Wears, clear, qt. .14.00

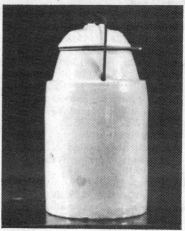

Weir Stoneware Jar

Weir (The) Patented March 1st, 1892,
   stoneware, qt. (ILLUS.) . . . . . .26.00 to 50.00
Woodbury, aqua, qt. 30.00

FURNITURE

Furniture made in the United States during the 18th and 19th centuries is coveted by collectors. American antique furniture has a European background, primarily English, since the influence of the Continent usually found its way to America by way of England. If the style did not originate in England, it came to America by way of England. For this reason, some American furniture styles carry the name of an English monarch or an English designer. However, we must realize that, until recently, little research has been conducted and even less published on the Spanish and French influences in the areas of the California missions and New Orleans.

After the American Revolution, cabinetmakers in the United States shunned the prevailing styles in England and chose to bring the French styles of Napoleon's Empire to the United States and we have the uniquely named "American Empire" style of furniture in a country that never had an emperor.

During the Victorian period, quality furniture began to be mass-produced in this country with its rapidly growing population. So much walnut furniture was manufactured, the vast supply of walnut was virtually depleted and it was of necessity that oak furniture became fashionable as the 19th century drew to a close.

For our purposes, the general guidelines for dating furniture will be:
Pilgrim Century - 1620-85
William & Mary - 1685-1720
Queen Anne - 1720-50
Chippendale - 1750-85
Federal - 1785-1820
   Hepplewhite - 1785-1800
   Sheraton - 1800-20
American Empire - 1815-40
Victorian - 1840-1900
   Early Victorian - 1840-50
   Gothic Revival - 1840-90
   Louis XV (rococo) - 1845-70
   Louis XVI - 1865-75
   Eastlake - 1870-95
   Renaissance - 1860-85
   Jacobean & Turkish Revival -
   1870-90
Art Nouveau - 1890-1918
Turn-of-the-Century - 1895-1910
Mission (Arts & Crafts movement) -
1900-15
Art Deco - 1925-40
All furniture included in this listing is American unless otherwise noted. Also see MINIATURES (Replicas).

ARMOIRES & WARDROBES
Armoire, Louis XV Provincial, cherrywood, oblong top w/molded cornice above frieze w/three short reeded panels over pr. paneled cupboard doors separated by panel w/reeded inset, scalloped apron, short cabriole legs, scrolled feet, France, 19th c. $2,500.00

Louis XV Provincial Armoire

Armoire, Louis XV Provincial, pine, molded cornice above pr. fielded cupboard doors fitted w/wrought iron lock plates, now on bun feet of later date, France, 65" w., 89½" h. (ILLUS.)................4,950.00

Kas (American version of the Netherlands' *Kast* or wardrobe), cherrywood, molded cornice above case w/rounded corners & removable door w/four raised panels opening to shelf & brackets for clothes rod, molded base, (replaced) large ball feet, Zoar, Ohio, 48" w., 78¼" h. ...675.00

Kas, cherrywood, molded cornice above cupboard door w/raised panels carved w/fan details at corners, molded base, squared feet, Ohio, large.................950.00

Schrank (Pennsylvania-Germany version of a massive wardrobe), walnut, 3-part construction: removable molded cornice; center w/pr. hinged cupboard doors opening to coat rack; lower section w/pr. short drawers on (now reduced) ogee bracket feet, Pennsylvania, ca. 1790, 59" w., 84½" h. 3,575.00

Schrank, Chippendale, walnut, 3-part construction: upper part w/removable projecting cornice; arch-top double-paneled cupboard doors; lower section w/pr. thumb-molded drawers, molded base, ogee bracket feet, Pennsylvania, ca. 1780, 65" w., 93" h. (minor restoration to feet) ..9,075.00

Chippendale Schrank

Schrank, Chippendale, walnut, 3-part
construction: bold removable cornice; center w/pr. paneled cupboard
doors opening to red-painted
shelved interior; base w/three short
thumb-molded drawers, (restored)
bracket feet, Pennsylvania, ca. 1770,
81½" w., 99½" h. (ILLUS.) 6,600.00
Schrank, walnut, projecting molded
cornice above single double-paneled
cupboard door opening to hanging
pegs, cut-out bracket feet, dated
1848, refinished & w/traces of old
salmon paint .985.00

American Empire Wardrobe

Wardrobe, American Empire,
mahogany, wide overhanging cornice above frieze w/inset arch
w/gilt-stenciled fruit above pr. cupboard doors, w/black & gilt stripe
outlining, flanked by free-standing
ebonized columns w/Ionic capitals,

on winged animal paw feet, New
York state, some repairs, 54" w.
flaring to 66" w. at projecting cor-
nice, 91" h. (ILLUS.) 1,950.00
Wardrobe, American Empire country-
style, grain-painted finish in
imitation of bird's eye & tiger stripe
maple, coved cornice, pr. raised
panel cupboard doors, single long
drawer in base w/original turned
wood pulls, bun feet 850.00

Victorian Wardrobe

Wardrobe, Victorian, walnut, shaped
molded cornice above pr. paneled
cupboard doors, scalloped apron
w/applied central carving continuing
to bracket feet (ILLUS.) 675.00
Wardrobe, Victorian (late), walnut,
sections can be dismantled &
reassembled, large (needs some
repair) 250.00

BEDS
Child's bed, American Empire country-
style, painted maple, bulbous-turned
head & foot rails on baluster-turned
uprights w/"turnip" feet, plain side
rails, worn dark red paint exposing
old red beneath, ca. 1845, 25½" w.,
55" l., 24" h. (split in one post &
no bed slats) .250.00
Trundle bed, painted birch, rope-type,
heavy square posts, red paint,
ca. 1850 . . . . .325.00
Youth's bed, country-style, painted
finish, shaped head & footboards
flanked by short square posts &
enhanced w/applied "picture frame"
molding at ends, plank sides, old
red paint 450.00

American Empire country-style poster
bed, maple, plain paneled headboard flanked by bulbous-turned &
blocked posts w/ball finials, shaped
footboard flanked by conforming
posts, three-quarter size..........485.00

American Empire country-style tall
poster bed, poplar headboard
w/"rolling pin" crest & shaped
poplar footboard flanked by maple
vase- and ring-turned posts, original
rope-type side rails, 52½" w.,
71½" l., 79" h. posts..............325.00

Art Nouveau Bed

Art Nouveau bed, mahogany, headboard carved w/clematis blossoms,
vines & leaves on intersecting openwork bands above veneered panels,
attributed to Louis Majorelle, Nancy,
France, ca. 1910, queen size,
66¾" w. (ILLUS.) 5,280.00

Brass beds, tubular, rounded head &
foot above 5 vertical rods headed
by solid brass balls, single size, pr...600.00

Brass Bed

Brass bed, tubular, double size
(ILLUS.)........................850.00

Brass tester bed, crown canopy,
elaborate details & finials on tubular
posts, 19th c., 108" h. to canopy top,
double size....................1,400.00

Federal tall poster bed, curly maple,
shaped headboard flanked by square
tapering posts w/urn-shaped finials,
squared footrail flanked by reeded &
ring-turned posts on turned feet,
New England, ca. 1815, 55½" w.,
80" h........................2,860.00

Federal tester bed, curly maple,
shaped headboard flanked by vase-
and ring-turned posts & footrail
flanked by conforming posts, on
ring-turned feet, w/tester, New
England, ca. 1830, 54" w., 83" l.,
67" h. (restoration to side rails) ...1,320.00

Federal tester bed, inlaid mahogany,
shaped headboard flanked by vase-
and ring-turned posts & w/reeded-
and ring-turned footposts on fan- and
line-inlaid tapering legs ending in
cross-banded cuffs, w/tester, Salem,
Massachusetts, ca. 1805, 59" w.,
78" l., 62½" h. posts (some
restoration to top of posts) 6,875.00

Federal Country-style Tester Bed

Federal country-style tester bed,
painted poplar, shaped headboard
flanked by baluster-shaped posts,
plain footrail w/conforming posts,
original (lengthened) rope-pegged
side rails, 1825-50, 55" w., 76" l.,
65" h. posts, replaced tester
(ILLUS.)........................600.00

Federal country-style poster bed,
cherrywood, shaped headboard
flanked by turned posts w/vase-
shaped finials & turned footrail
flanked by conforming posts,
19th c., 41" w., 77" l., 60" h. 1,210.00

Federal country-style low poster bed, painted pine, shaped head & footboards flanked by bulbous-turned low posts w/flattened mushroom finials, rope-type, early red-painted finish, three-quarter size 800.00

"Cannonball" Poster Bed

Federal country-style low poster bed, painted pine, "rolling pin" crest on boldly shaped head & footboards flanked by ring- and baluster-turned posts w/"cannonball" finials, original rope-pegged side rails, original painted red & brown flame graining on pumpkin-colored ground, 52½" w., 69½" l., 43½" h. (ILLUS.) 650.00

Federal-style "pencil post" bed, cherry-wood, shaped headboards between chamfered tapering headposts supporting a half-tester, footrail flanked by low footposts w/acorn finials, 20th c., 60" w., 81½" l., 77" h. 495.00

Shaker bed, birch, maple & pine, plain slightly rounded headboard flanked by square posts w/flattened mushroom finials, square footrail, original side rails altered for mattress, 36½" w., 70½" l., 34" h. posts 350.00

Victorian half-tester bed, rococo sub-style, rosewood, ornately carved, attributed to the workshop of Prudent Mallard, 64" w., 78" l., 96" h. 3,500.00

Victorian tester bed, walnut, ornate crest, double oval in headboard, in the manner of Prudent Mallard, New Orleans 4,100.00

Victorian poster bed, walnut, early spool-turned style, shaped head-board w/applied spool-turned rail at crest & scalloped footrail flanked by blocked- and spool-turned posts, side rails w/conforming scallops, 56" w., 72" l., 53" h. headposts 300.00

Victorian (late) bed, cast iron, rod-like framework cast w/plumes above heart-form silhouettes in head & footboards w/detailed ornamentation, painted white, ca. 1890, double size 450.00

Victorian (late) bed, cast iron w/brass trim, overall circle details & ornate C-scrolls incorporated into design, ca. 1890, double size 1,300.00

Zoar, Ohio bed, cherrywood, plain crestrail above solid headboard flanked by square posts w/ball finials, spool-turned legs, "sleigh" shaped side rails .... 450.00 to 1,500.00

BEDROOM SUITES (Victorian)

Bed in the Bamboo Taste

Bamboo taste: bed, chest of drawers, dressing table & occasional table; maple & bird's eye maple, w/label of "R.J. Horner & Co., 63-65 West 23rd Street, N.Y., Furniture Makers," 4 pcs. (ILLUS. of bed only) 5,225.00

Cottage-style: bed, chest w/mirror & commode stand; oak, bed w/oblong headboard applied w/leaf carvings & chest & commode w/applied conforming carvings, late 19th c., 3 pcs. 1,100.00

Cottage-style: bed, chest w/mirror & commode stand; painted & deco-rated birch or maple, late 19th c., 3 pcs. 700.00

Eastlake substyle: bed (headboard only), drop-front chest w/mirror, tall chest & commode stand; cherry-stained maple w/rose marble tops on case pieces, typical incised carvings, Grand Rapids, Michigan, 4 pcs. 5,300.00

Renaissance substyle: bed & drop-front chest w/mirror; walnut w/burl wal-nut panels & w/applied cabochon carvings at crests, ca. 1870, 2 pcs. 1,100.00

Renaissance substyle: bed & drop-front chest w/mirror; walnut w/burl wal-

Renaissance Substyle Bedroom Suite

nut panels & applied carvings at crest
of high-back bed & on chest w/white
marble top & w/candle shelves
flanking mirror, ca. 1870, 2 pcs.
(ILLUS.) 1,540.00

BENCHES

Wagon Bench

Child's Hitchcock-type bench, painted
& decorated, 2-slat back, woven
rush seat, painted green w/gilt
stenciling decor, 39" w. 418.00
Church pew, oak, short 90.00
Church pew, oak, long, various styles,
each . . . . 200.00 to 325.00
Cobbler's bench, pine, maple & other
hardwoods, oblong work tray
w/plain three-quarter gallery &
drawer below opposite round seat,
"pencil post" legs, refinished 1,550.00

Cobbler's bench, primitive pine, oblong
floor-standing bench w/numerous
small & medium drawers w/original
pulls, seat w/drawer beneath &
backrest on turned legs to the
side of bench 315.00
Deacon's bench, painted hardwood &
pine, plain crestrail above turned
spindles, shaped arms on turned
supports, plank seat, turned legs,
worn old mustard yellow paint,
Pennsylvania, ca. 1840 . . . . 495.00
Kneeling (prayer) bench, Victorian,
walnut, upholstered oblong slip top,
plain apron, short turned legs,
overall 8" h. 215.00
Mammy's bench, painted finish, plain
crestrail over 9-spindle back, shaped
arms on turned supports, plank seat
w/cradle guard, turned legs w/flat-
tened frontal stretcher on rockers,
original painted finish . . . . . 695.00 to 975.00
Wagon bench, painted hardwood,
2-chairback style, straight slats
joined to 3 turned legs,
(replaced) paper rush seat, worn
original red paint w/yellow striping,
polychrome florals & oval scene in
crest, possibly Alpine, 34¾" l.
(ILLUS.) 355.00
Water bucket bench, primitive poplar,
2-tier, oblong top w/raking three-
quarter gallery, sides form cut-out
feet, weathered scrubbed finish,
26" w., 17" deep, 31" to top of
gallery 425.00
Water bucket bench, primitive pine,
2-tier, single board sides form cut-
out feet, refinished, 42" w., 16"
deep, 33" h. 225.00
Window bench, Louis XVI, painted &
upholstered, oblong seat w/green &
brown flame-stitch needlepoint
raised on circular tapering stop-
fluted legs, now painted grey &
highlighted w/green, France, late
18th c., 35" l. 990.00

American Empire Country Style Bench

American Empire country-style bench,
painted hardwood & pine, plain
crestrail above 18 arrow-form
spindles & 4 uprights, shaped arms
on ball-turned support, wide plank
seat, bulbous-turned legs, ball feet,

black repaint over worn &
weathered surface, 75½" l.
(ILLUS.)..........................325.00

Federal "fancy" bench, painted &
decorated, plain crestrail above 18
arrow-form spindles & 4 uprights,
plank seat, shaped arms on shaped
supports, turned legs w/stretchers,
free-hand & stenciled florals on
smoked red-painted ground......5,250.00

Mission-style (Arts & Crafts movement)
bench, oak, plain crestrail above 4
vertical slats joined to square corner
posts w/chamfered tenons, single
slat side, w/drawer under seat,
branded "L. & J.G. Stickley," 42" l...950.00

Primitive pine bench, mortised &
square nail construction, 1-board
oblong top, shaped apron, cut-out
sides mortised through top,
weathered white finish, 47¾ x 13¼"
seat, 18¾" h. 75.00

Primitive pine bench, oblong top,
plain apron, cut-out sides forming
feet, old worn green paint, early
20th c..........................95.00

Primitive pine bench, plain crestrail
above solid back, shaped downswept
sides forming armrests & continuing
to cut-out feet, plank seat, layers of
white paint 270.00

Primitive poplar bench, 1-board top,
plain apron, cut-out sides form
feet, stripped of finish & w/traces
of old red remaining, 49 x 14½"
seat, 18" h. 45.00

Primitive poplar bench, 1-board top
w/rounded extension at one end,
plain apron, cut-out sides forming
feet, old worn dark green paint
over yellow, 70 x 11¾" seat,
16½" h. 65.00

Queen Anne style bench, mahogany,
oblong top, plain apron, cabriole
legs, pad feet, old finish & some
repairs, England, 65" l., 21" deep,
15½" h. (w/three tops including
slip seat covered in white duck,
mahogany & white marble tops for
coffee table use)..................750.00

Windsor Bench

Windsor bench, bamboo-turned,
bowed crestrail over 29 spindles,
shaped arms on baluster-turned
upright & spindles, shaped plank
seat w/incised detail, bamboo-
turned legs w/stretchers, repairs
& replacements, 68½" l. (ILLUS.)..2,400.00

Windsor "arrow-back" bench, painted
finish, plain crestrail above 29 arrow-
form uprights flanked by arms on
turned spindles, plank seat, bamboo-
turned legs w/conforming stretchers,
worn & weathered old green
repaint, branded "L. Allwine,
Philada" on underside of seat,
75" l. 4,250.00

Windsor bench, pine & maple, plain
crestrail above 27 turned spindles,
shaped arms on turned supports,
plank seat, turned & tapering legs
w/flattened frontal stretcher, old
refinishing 825.00

BOOKCASES

Biedermeier Bookcase

Biedermeier bookcase, maple, stepped cornice above pr. glazed
doors opening to shelves, Germany, early 19th c., 46" w.,
71" h............................2,640.00

Biedermeier bookcase, stained maple,
stepped cornice above pr. glazed
& paneled doors opening to shelves,
block feet, Germany, early 19th c.,
44" w., 72" h. (ILLUS.) 2,750.00

Mission-style (Arts & Crafts movement)
bookcase, oak, flat three-quarter
gallery above oblong top over case
w/pr. 6-pane glazed doors opening
to shelves, solid sides w/four

chamfered tenons in each, attributed
to Gustav Stickley, ca. 1912,
44" h..............................1,430.00
Mission-style (Arts & Crafts movement)
bookcase, stained oak, oblong top
w/low three-quarter gallery above
pr. 12-pane glazed doors opening to
shelves, hammered metal hardware
& keyhole escutcheons, attributed
to L. & G.J. Stickley, early 20th c.,
48" w., 54½" h.................1,210.00
Turn-of-the-Century bookcase, golden
oak, plain oblong top above 4
beveled glass-fronted doors,
63½" w., 55" h.................1,450.00
Turn-of-the-Century bookcase, golden
oak, 5-stack type w/glass-fronted
doors lifting to shelves, w/drawer
at base, original condition, 72" h. ...500.00
Turn-of-the-Century bookcase, mahogany, molded cornice above pr.
beveled glass-fronted 2-pane doors
opening to 7 adjustable shelves
over 3 short drawers in base,
overall 96" h. 1,000.00
Victorian bookcase, Eastlake substyle,
bird's eye maple in the "Bamboo"
taste, oblong top w/three-quarter
"bamboo-turned" spindle gallery
above 4 open shelves flanked by
"bamboo-turned" columns, single
drawer at base, turned legs on
casters, w/label of "R.J. Horner,"
ca. 1890, 31½" w., 56" h.........1,045.00
Victorian bookcase, Eastlake substyle,
mahogany, molded cornice above glazed
spiral-molded details over glazed
doors w/molded frames flanked by
free-standing reeded columns, 2
drawers at molded base, ca. 1870,
49½" w., 75" h...................475.00
Victorian bookcase, Renaissance
Revival substyle, walnut & burl
walnut, molded cornice centered
w/ornately carved pediment above
pr. glazed cupboard doors opening
to 7 shelves flanked by stiles
w/applied carvings, base w/pr.
drawers w/carved pulls, ca. 1870..2,200.00
Victorian bookcase, oak w/ornate
carvings, central section w/pr.
glazed cupboard doors opening to
shelves above frieze drawers over
cupboard doors & flanking conforming side sections, ca. 1874,
large 4,200.00

BOXES

Bible box, painted pine, slightly
slanting hinged lid on original brass
hinges opening to well, rosehead
nail construction, old blue paint,
late 18th c., 18 x 17 x 10"..........395.00
Bible box, pine, hinged lid opening to

well, rosehead nail construction,
incised compass design & tombstone
carving on front, worn brown
patina, 23½" w., 8¼" h. 1,250.00

Hanging Candle Box

Candle box, hanging-type, inlaid
mahogany, scroll-carved pierced
crest above molded hinged lid
opening to paper-lined well, case
w/inlaid oval reserve & borders,
probably Maryland, early 19th c.,
21" h. (ILLUS.) 660.00
Candle box, hanging-type, pine, sides
w/scalloped edges, old green paint,
12½" l..........................80.00
Candle box, hanging-type, poplar,
scalloped crest above 2 open compartments in case w/square nail
construction, old worn green paint,
12 x 4¾", overall 16" h............210.00
Desk-top box, curly maple veneer,
dovetail construction, hinged lid
opening to well, w/applied chip-
carved details at lid molding &
base molding, ivory keyhole
escutcheon 400.00
Desk-top box, poplar, dovetail construction, slant-top lifting to simple
interior fitted w/two shelves, old
worn refinishing w/hasp removed &
holes plugged, 21 x 18½", 10¼" h. ...75.00
Desk-top box, painted finish, dovetail
construction, slant-top lid forming
writing surface w/low molding as
gallery, applied molding at base,
original brass keyhole escutcheon,
original finish 295.00
Hat box, cov., pine bentwood oval 450.00
Knife box, Federal, mahogany
w/satinwood inlay, late 18th c.,
15" h..........................1,000.00
Knife boxes, Federal, inlaid mahogany, shaped lid w/cross-banded
border & shaped front opening to
fitted interior of conformingly
shaped case w/bookend-inlaid

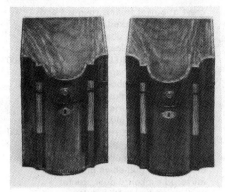

Federal Knife Boxes

panels & light & dark wood &
diamond-inlaid border, engraved
silver handle & keyhole escutcheon,
ca. 1790, 14½" h., pr. (ILLUS.) 2,970.00
Knife boxes, George III, mahogany,
hinged slant lid opening to fitted
interior, England, ca. 1790, 15" h.,
pr. 1,430.00
Knife boxes, George III, inlaid
mahogany, hinged slant lid w/bow
front opening to fitted interior, conformingly shaped case, England,
ca. 1800, 15½" h., pr. 1,210.00
Storage box w/hinged lid, Shaker,
painted poplar, oblong lid w/bread-
board ends lifting to compartment,
w/traces of original red stain, Mt.
Lebanon, New York, ca. 1860,
13½ x 7", 5" h. 330.00
Storage box w/lift-off lid, bentwood
oval w/laced seams, original rose-
mahling on orange ground &
w/"decoupage" print on lid, 18 x
11½" oval 425.00
Storage box w/domed lid, original
painted graining in imitation of
curly maple, 24 x 11¾", 10¼" h. 450.00
Storage box w/domed lid, poplar,
original brush stroke painted
graining & black edge stripe on red
ground, original lock, 28½ x 13",
12" h. (hasp missing) 200.00
Storage box w/hinged lid, Chippen-
dale, pine, lid w/molded edge lifting
to case w/false facade of 4 small
cockbeaded drawers above 2
working drawers, ca. 1780, 31 x
18", 27½" h. .495.00

BUREAUS PLAT

Continental bureau plat, giltwood,
leather-inset oblong top w/outset
rounded corners, shaped frieze
w/two drawers one side &
w/reverse decorated to match
w/central carved shell surrounded
by floral wreaths, sides w/carved
scrolls & floral branches, cabriole
legs headed by alternating fully
carved male & female busts &
ending in hairy hoof feet, Continental, early 18th c., 65" w.,
31½" h. 33,000.00
Directoire bureau plat, mahogany
w/ormolu mounts, leather-inset
oblong top w/slightly rounded outset corners, frieze w/four drawers
surrounding a kneehole at front &
conforming false facade opposite,
circular fluted legs ending in ormolu
thimble "sabots," France, late
18th c., 50" w., 30" h. 3,410.00
Louis XV bureau plat, kingwood par-
quetry w/ormolu mounts, gilt-tooled
leather-inset oblong top within
ormolu rim, shaped frieze w/three
drawers fitted w/ormolu foliate
handles at front & w/conforming
false facade opposite, sides centered w/ormolu foliate cabochon
mounts, cabriole legs fitted w/ormo-
lu foliate "chutes" ending in ormolu
hoof "sabots," France, ca. 1780,
62¾" w., 30¾" h. 17,600.00

Louis XV Style Bureau Plat

Louis XV style bureau plat, marquetry
& kingwood parquetry w/ormolu
mounts, gilt-tooled leather-inset
oblong top fitted w/ormolu rim,
frieze w/three shaped drawers
w/floral marquetry against kingwood ground within cross-banded
borders & w/ormolu keyhole escutcheons & mounts, cabriole legs
w/ormolu foliate "chutes" & scrolled
ormolu "sabots," in the manner of
Bernard Van Risamburgh, France,
late 19th c., 52" l., 30½" h.
(ILLUS.) 13,200.00
Louis XV-XVI transitional bureau plat,
purplewood & fruitwood cube
pattern parquetry w/ormolu mounts,
tooled leather-inset serpentine top

fitted w/ormolu rim, frieze w/four
drawers at front, cabriole legs
w/ormolu "chutes" ending in ormolu
scrolled toes, France, late 19th c.,
73" w., 31½" h. 3,300.00

CABINETS

Turn-of-the-Century China Cabinet

Barber shop mug cabinet, oak, open
front w/segmented compartments
for mugs, 24" w., 36" h. 850.00
Barber shop mug cabinet, painted
finish, cupboard door w/adjustable
mirror opening to compartments for
mugs & shelf for towels 290.00
Cane cabinet, Victorian, oak & glass,
tall oblong form w/hinged slant-top
& front, late 19th c., 19½" w.,
18½" deep, 47" h. 330.00
China cabinet, Mission-style (Arts &
Crafts movement), oak, oblong top
w/inset oblong backrail above
glazed door w/twelve-panel grid
opening to shelves, glazed sides
w/further grids, square straight legs,
w/paper label of Gustav Stickley, ca.
1910, 36" w., 62¾" h. 825.00
China cabinet, Turn-of-the-Century,
golden oak w/bent glass door & bent
glass sides, animal paw feet,
refinished 995.00
China cabinet, Turn-of-the-Century,
golden oak, shaped top w/inset oval
mirror in shaped backrail above bent
glass door flanked by columns,
curved glass sides, carved lion's paw
feet 1,200.00
China cabinet, Turn-of-the-Century,
golden oak, shaped top w/carved

crest at outset front & rounded ends
above mirror-backed open shelf
above bent glass door flanked by
columns & bent glass sides, carved
animal paw feet (ILLUS.) 1,350.00
Dental cabinet, mahogany, oblong top
w/molded edge above pr. cupboard
doors w/frosted glass panes,
porcelain work surface above 16
drawers w/clear glass knobs &
porcelain dividers, refinished 1,750.00
Dental cabinet, oak, 3-part: upper part
w/three-quarter gallery over 7 short
drawers, pr. pull-down bins &
mirrored cupboard door; center
section w/six graduated drawers &
cupboard door; base w/drawer over
pr. cupboard doors, short legs 1,600.00

Dental Cabinet

Dental cabinet, painted hardwood,
oblong top w/mirrored backrail
above arrangement of 11 drawers &
2 small cupboard doors flanked by
turned columns over arrangement of
5 drawers & single cupboard door,
shaped apron, square legs,
w/numerous coats of creamy ivory
paint (ILLUS.) 550.00
Hardware store bolt cabinet, oak,
50-drawer 450.00
Hardware store bolt cabinet, oak,
72-drawer hexagonal
shape . . . . 875.00 to 975.00
Hardware store bolt cabinet, oak,
80-drawer octagonal shape swiveling on base, original white porcelain drawer pulls,
refinished . . . . 1,200.00 to 1,450.00
Jeweler's cabinet, oak, glass-inset
hinged top w/sections for rings, 2
drawers below, 16 x 8", 5" h. 250.00

"Hoosier" Cabinet

Kitchen cabinet, Turn-of-the-Century
"Hoosier" style, oak, plain top above
"flour bin" cupboard door & short
cupboard doors over tambour slide
raising to storage compartment,
white graniteware work surface
above 3 graduated drawers & cupboard door, refinished
(ILLUS.) ....425.00 to 550.00
Library (index card) file cabinet, oak,
4-drawer, 10 x 14 x 16" 95.00
Medicine cabinet, corner-type, oak,
plain, refinished 90.00
Medicine cabinet, pine, plain, w/green
glass towel bar below 75.00
Printer's type cabinet, oak 110.00
Sheet music cabinet, Queen Anne
revival style, rosewood, ca. 1900,
20" w., 37" h.....................300.00
Side cabinet, Art Deco style, rosewood
w/ivory inlay, stepped oblong top
above cabinet door inlaid w/two
graduated bands of circles centering
an oval ivory medallion opening to
fitted interior w/two shelves above
pr. drawers w/ivory pulls, raised on
ivory ball feet on socle form base,
1928-29, 24½" w., 45½" h. 8,800.00
Side cabinet, primitive pine, plain open
top w/shelves above 9-drawer base,
overall 67½" h...................550.00
Side cabinet, Victorian Eastlake substyle, inlaid & ebonized wood, coved
crest w/incised carving above half-
round mirror plate framed by inlaid
florals, foliage & birds above
partially galleried open shelf raised
on supports above base w/central
floral & foliate-inlaid cupboard door
flanked by paneled cupboard doors,
plinth base, New York, ca. 1885,
48" w., 63" h. 1,320.00

Victorian Cabinet by Herter Brothers

Side cabinet, Victorian Eastlake substyle, walnut, 2-part construciton:
upper part w/molded cornice above
open shelves flanked by carved &
paneled cupboard doors within
fluted columns above gadroon
molding raised on turned & carved
columns; lower section w/marble
slab top above arrangement of 6
drawers & pr. cupboard doors,
overall machine-carved details,
stamped "Herter Bro's," 1880s,
93" w., 90" h. (ILLUS.) 1,320.00
Side cabinet, Victorian Renaissance
substyle, walnut & burl walnut,
2-part construction: upper part
w/elaborate arched crest w/urn
finial above fully carved bust above
pr. glazed doors opening to shelves;
lower section w/oblong top
w/molded edge above 4 graduated
long drawers w/elaborately carved
pulls & applied burl panels, molded
base, 37" w., 94" h..............2,090.00
Vitrine cabinet, Louis XV style, decorated in the "Vernis Martin" (imitation oriental lacquer) technique
and w/ormolu mounts, early 20th c.,
overall 57" h. 1,045.00

CANDLESTANDS
American Empire country-style tilt-top
candlestand, cherrywood, 1-board
round top, ring- and baluster-turned
heavy standard on cruciform cross-
member base w/scrolling toes,
19¼" d., 29¾" h. (top is early
replacement).....................225.00
Chippendale tilt-top candlestand, walnut, round dished top tilting & revolving above birdcage support, turned
standard, tripod w/cabriole legs,
pad feet, Pennsylvania, 1770-90,
24 3/8" top d., 28" h. (small patch
to rim) 3,080.00

Federal Inlaid Birch Candlestand

Federal tilt-top candlestand, inlaid birchwood, oblong octagonal top w/inlaid bird's eye maple diamond reserve & inlaid edge tilting above reeded & ring-turned urn-form standard, downswept tripod, spade feet, New Hampshire, ca. 1805, some repairs, 21 x 13½" top, 28½" h. (ILLUS.)...............3,410.00

Federal tilt-top candlestand, mahogany, shaped oblong top tilting above ring-turned & petal-carved standard, reeded scrolling downswept tripod, scrolled toes, 27¼ x 19½" top, 29½" h.......................1,540.00

Federal tilt-top candlestand, mahogany, oval top tilting above baluster- and vase-turned standard, arched tripod w/square tapering legs, spade feet, 1790-1810, 23½ x 17 1/8" top, 29" h..............1,045.00

Federal Mahogany Candlestand

Federal tilt-top candlestand, mahogany, oval top tilting above ring- and vase-turned standard, downswept cabriole tripod, pad feet, Eastern Massachusetts, ca. 1800, 24¾" l., 26¾" h. (ILLUS.)................1,650.00

Federal candlestand, inlaid cherrywood, round top w/line-inlaid star, urn-form standard, arched tripod, snake feet, New England, 1790-1810, 16¾" top d., 27¾" h..............660.00

Federal candlestand, mahogany, cloverleaf-shaped top, column- and vase-turned standard, arched tripod w/square tapering legs, Newport, Rhode Island, 1790-1810, 28¾" h.....................2,860.00

Federal candlestand, maple, square top, urn-form standard, downswept tripod w/cabriole legs, shod slipper feet, Massachusetts, 1790-1810, 27" h. 770.00

Federal candlestand, painted finish, oval top, baluster-turned standard, spider tripod, 1790-1810, painted black w/gilt stenciling & trim at later date, 20 1/8 x 16 5/8" top, 27¼" h. ..352.00

Federal country-style candlestand, cherrywood oval top, birch vase-turned standard, downswept tripod, snake feet, old dark finish, 22½ x 17" top, 27¼" h. 450.00

Fedral country-style candlestand, tiger stripe maple, oblong top w/cut-out corners, ring- and urn-turned standard, downswept tripod, curled feet 285.00

Hepplewhite candlestand, curly maple, square top w/cut-out corners, ring- and baluster-turned standard, spider legs, refinished, 19½ x 17¾" top, 27" h. 700.00

Hepplewhite country-style candlestand, maple, oblong top w/cut corners, baluster- and urn-turned standard, downswept tripod w/square legs, 18 x 12¾" top 375.00

Hepplewhite country-style candlestand, 1-board pine top w/ovolo corners, ring- and baluster-turned standard, downswept tripod, snake feet, refinished, 17 x 16¾" top 450.00

Queen Anne tilt-top candlestand, walnut, round top w/molded edge tilting & revolving above birdcage support, ring- and ball-turned standard, cabriole legs, snake feet, Philadelphia, ca. 1765, 21" top d., 28" h........................4,400.00

Queen Anne tilt-top candlestand, walnut, round top w/molded edge tilting & revolving above birdcage support, ring- and urn-turned standard, cabriole legs, snake feet,

Queen Anne Walnut Candlestand

Pennsylvania, ca. 1780, 21½" top d.,
  28½" h. (ILLUS.)................8,250.00
Queen Anne candlestand, cherrywood,
  square top w/shaped corners,
  baluster-turned standard, downswept tripod, snake feet, New
  England, ca. 1770, 14 x 15¼" top,
  25½" h. 660.00
Victorian candlestand, Egyptian Revival
  substyle, walnut w/round white
  marble inset top, molded apron,
  baluster-turned standard, 4 legs
  w/carved feet, 17½" top d., 28" h. ..165.00

CHAIRS

18th Century Child's Highchair

Child's "ladderback" armchair, 2-slat
  back between turned uprights,
  woven splint seat, spindle arms
  joined to frontal uprights, old black
  repaint w/red leaf stencil at crest,
  19½" h. 65.00

Child's swivel-seat desk chair,
  oak 80.00
Child's highchair, American Colonial
  period, maple, 3-slat back flanked by
  heavy turned uprights w/bulbous
  finials, sausage-turned arms joining
  uprights w/flattened ball handholds, ring-turned splayed legs
  w/stretchers, New England, 1720-60
  (ILLUS.)........................935.00
Child's highchair, Turn-of-the-Century,
  oak w/die-pressed pattern at
  crestrail above turned spindles,
  original darkened finish 110.00
Child's highchair, Victorian (early)
  cottage-style, painted & decorated,
  plain crestrail above 4 turned
  spindles flanked by thumb-back
  uprights & arms on spindle supports,
  plank seat, turned splayed legs
  w/stretchers, worn layers of paint,
  ca. 1850 ....100.00 to 125.00
Child's highchair, Windsor "bow-back"
  style, 7-spindle back, shaped seat,
  ring- and baluster-turned splayed
  legs, painted black & highlighted
  w/striping, ca. 1810 ....1,800.00
Child's highchair, Windsor (late) "low-
  back" style, hickory w/caned seat,
  ca. 1870 ....155.00

Highchair-Stroller

Child's highchair-stroller combination,
  Victorian patent-type, oak w/die-
  pressed pattern in back & caned
  seat (ILLUS.) ....270.00 to 450.00
Child's "Boston" rocker, painted &
  decorated 165.00
Child's rocker, bentwood w/cane seat
  & back, Thonet, Austria, ca. 1910 ...125.00
Child's rocker, golden oak w/die-
  pressed design in crest above
  spindled back, ca. 1910 ....135.00

Child's rocker, golden oak, caned seat
& back, ca. 1890 . . . . .165.00
Child's rocker w/arms, painted finish,
2-slat back between heavy turned
uprights, woven splint seat, painted
deep red. 105.00
Child's rocker w/arms, Victorian, so-
called Lincoln rocker w/upholstered
back & seat, scrolling arms w/heart
cut-outs, maple w/early red-painted
finish. 225.00

Child's Wicker Rocker

Child's rocker w/arms, loom-woven
wicker, original green paint, 1920s,
22" h. (ILLUS.) .90.00
Child's side chair, bentwood w/caned
seat, Thonet, Austria, early 1900s,
25" h. . . . . .70.00 to 85.00
Child's side chairs, Windsor "birdcage"
type, birdcage crest over 5-spindle
back, plank seat, turned tapering
legs w/stretchers, 19th c., set of 4. . .460.00

American Empire armchairs, mahogany,
molded oblong crestrail above
shaped & reeded splat flanked by
molded stiles, reeded scrolling arms
ending in carved volutes, trapezoidal
slip seat, reeded sabre legs,
probably New York, 1815-25, pr. . .3,960.00
American Empire wing armchair,
mahogany, upholstered back
w/shaped wings & roll-over arms,
seat w/loose cushion, bulbous-
turned legs on brass casters, red
& white floral upholstery. 500.00
American Empire desk chair, walnut,
shaped crestrail ending in roundels
above vase-form splat, swiveling
slip seat w/mechanism within urn-
form pedestal, cruciform base
w/scroll-carved flattened feet. 90.00
American Empire "gondole" chairs,
mahogany, shaped crestrail
w/rounded ears above vase-form
splat & sloping stiles, slip seat,
sabre legs, 1830-50, set of 4. . . . . . . .550.00

American Empire side chair, curly
maple, oblong roll-over crestrail
above bold vase-form splat,
(replaced) cane seat, sabre legs
w/flattened frontal stretcher, old
refinishing w/good color. 200.00
American Empire side chairs, mahog-
any, shaped crestrail over vase-form
splat, trapezoidal slip seat, cabriole
legs, 1830-50, pr. 275.00
American Empire side chairs, maple,
scrolling crestrail above lyre-form
splat flanked by chamfered stiles,
cane seat, turned legs w/stretchers,
Pennsylvania, ca. 1825, pr. 155.00
American Empire "cane-seat" side chair,
tiger stripe maple, roll-over crestrail above vase-form splat flanked
by uprights, square caned seat
w/roll-over frontal seatrail, turned
legs w/flattened frontal & turned
side stretchers 200.00
Barber's chair, "Koken," oak frame,
ca. 1885, unrestored condition. 500.00
Boston rocker, painted & decorated,
shaped crestrail above vase-form
splat, shaped arms on turned
supports, "roll-over" seat, turned
legs on rockers, repainted over
original graining. 125.00
Centennial (1876) corner armchair,
Queen Anne revival style, walnut,
horseshoe-shaped backrail w/cush-
ion-molded crest above 2 pierced
flattened splats & 3 baluster-turned
uprights, apron w/scalloped skirt,
ring-turned legs w/flattened ball
feet. 390.00
Centennial "1876" armchair, Queen Ann
revival style, painted finish, cupid's
bow crestrail over vase-form splat,
arms raised on baluster supports
continuing to turned legs w/bead-
and-reel frontal stretcher, worn
"alligatored" dark finish 175.00
Centennial "1876" side chairs, Chippendale revival style, mahogany, cupid's
bow crestrail above pierce-carved
splat, needlepoint-covered slip seat,
plain seatrail, cabriole legs w/carv-
ed knees, claw-and-ball feet, New
York, set of 6 . . . . .1,800.00
Chippendale corner chair, mahog-
any, horseshoe-shaped backrail
w/shaped handholds & cushion-
molded crest above 2 pierced vase-
form splats & 3 turned uprights,
slip seat, plain seatrail, stop-fluted
square legs, Newport, Rhode Island,
ca. 1770 (some restoration). 7,425.00
Chippendale corner armchair, red
cedar, horseshoe-shaped backrail
w/cushion-molded crest above 3 vase-

and ring-turned uprights & 2 vase-
form splats, shaped slip seat, plain
seatrail, cabriole legs w/acanthus-
carved knee on front leg, blocked
& turned cross-stretchers, claw-and-
ball feet, Bermuda, 1780-1800 . . . . . 7,700.00

Chippendale open armchair, walnut,
cupid's bow crestrail centering
fan-carved device above pierce-
carved beaker-form splat, shaped
arms w/scrolled handholds, plain
seatrail, cabriole legs, claw-and-
ball feet, Massachusetts, ca. 1775
(lacks slip seat) 2,750.00

Chippendale wing armchair, mahogany,
upholstered shaped back w/serpen-
tine crest flanked by ogival wings
& scrolling arms, seat w/loose
cushion, square molded legs w/H-
stretcher, Pennsylvania,
ca. 1775 . . . . 7,425.00

Chippendale "slipper" seat side chair,
cherrywood, cupid's bow crestrail
above pierced vase-form splat, rush
seat, square legs w/box stretcher,
Philadelphia, 1760-90 . . . . 440.00

Chippendale side chair, mahogany,
cupid's bow crestrail centering
carved fan above pierce-carved
voluted splat, slip seat, plain seatrail, cabriole legs w/block- and
vase-turned stretchers, shod pad
feet, Eastern Massachusetts,
ca. 1770 . . . . 2,750.00

Chippendale side chairs, mahogany,
cupid's bow crestrail above pierced
beaker-form splat, slip seat, cabriole
legs, claw-and-ball feet, Philadel-
phia, ca. 1770, pr. 3,575.00

Chippendale country-style side chair,
cherrywood, cupid's bow crestrail
above pierced vase-form splat, over-
upholstered (worn) leather seat,
square legs w/H-stretcher 1,050.00

Federal "Lolling" Armchair

Federal (Martha Washington) "lolling"
open armchair, upholstered back
w/shaped crest above double line-
inlaid downward curving arms,
upholstered seat, square tapering
legs w/cross-banded cuffs joined by
H-stretcher, ca. 1790 (ILLUS.) 19,800.00

Federal "lolling" open armchair, upholstered back w/shaped crest above
line-inlaid downswept arms & upholstered seat, square line-inlaid
tapering legs w/H-stretcher,
Massachusetts, ca. 1795 . . . . 8,250.00

Federal (Martha Washington) "lolling"
open armchair, maple upholstered
back w/serpentine crest & seat,
shaped line-inlaid arm supports,
line-inlaid square tapering legs w/H-
stretcher, Massachusetts, ca. 1795
(restored stretcher bar) 3,300.00

Federal "barrel-back" armchair,
mahogany, upholstered barrel-
shaped back w/shaped wings & outward scrolling arms, upholstered
bow-fronted seat w/loose cushion,
reeded turned tapering legs,
inverted urn shape feet on casters,
blue silk upholstery, Philadelphia,
1800-15 . . . . 4,400.00

Federal open armchair, mahogany,
shaped crestrail w/carved leaf above
conformingly carved stayrails,
reeded downswept scrolling arms on
turned supports, reeded seatrail,
ring-turned & reeded tapering
legs, ball feet, School of Duncan
Phyfe, New York, ca. 1810 (slight
repair to one leg) 3,080.00

Federal wing armchair, cherrywood,
upholstered shaped back flanked by
shaped wings & outward scrolling
arms, square tapering legs
w/stretchers, ca. 1800 (now on
casters & w/some restoration to one
front foot) 1,540.00

Federal "cane-seat" side chairs, curly
maple, oblong crestrail w/acanthus-
and volute-carved ends above
acanthus- and volute-pierce-carved
stayrail, caned seat, sabre legs
w/stretchers, New York, ca. 1820,
assembled set of 4 . . . . 990.00

Federal "cane-seat" side chairs, curly
maple, roll-over crestrail above
medial stayrail, caned seat, sabre
legs w/flattened frontal stretcher,
New York, ca. 1820, set of 8 . . . . . . 2.750.00

Federal "cane-seat" side chairs, tiger
stripe maple, plain crestrail over
pierce-carved scroll & flowerhead
stayrail, caned seat, ring-turned legs
w/flaring feet joined by stretchers,
New England, ca. 1820, set of 8
(ILLUS. of one) 5,500.00

Federal "Cane-Seat" Side Chair

Federal "fancy" side chairs, painted & decorated, oblong crestrail above medial stayrail flanked by baluster-turned uprights, trapezoidal caned seat w/roll-over front, ring-turned tapering legs w/stretchers, gilt-stenciled & painted decor on black ground retouched, Baltimore, Maryland, 1800-20, set of 6 . . . . .1,210.00

Federal "fancy" side chairs, painted & decorated, turned & scrolled crestrail above vase-form splat & chamfered uprights, trapezoidal rush seat, turned & tapering legs w/stretchers on ball feet, gilt-stenciled florals on black over red ground, New England, 1825-50, set of 6 . . . . .550.00

Federal "shield-back" side chairs, mahogany, shield-shaped back w/four fluted & scale-carved stiles emanating from carved shell, over-upholstered seat w/bowed front, square tapering legs, spade feet, New York, 1790-1810, pr. 2,420.00

Federal country-style "arrow-bdck" side chairs, plain crestrail over 4 arrow spindles flanked by "thumb-back" stiles, plank seat, turned tapering legs w/stretchers, refinished w/good color, pr. 170.00

Federal country-style "arrow-back" side chairs, painted & decorated, oblong panel in shaped crest above 3 arrow-form spindles flanked by "thumb-back" uprights, shaped plank seat, bamboo-turned legs w/stretchers, worn original yellow paint w/free-hand florals at crest & red & black striping, set of 3 . . . . .390.00

Federal country-style "balloon-back" side chairs, painted & decorated,

balloon-shaped back w/vase-form splat, shaped plank seat, turned legs, stenciled florals on dark ground, set of 6 . . . . .1,250.00

Federal "Spindle-Back" Chairs

Federal country-style "spindle-back" side chairs, painted & decorated, shaped crestrail above turned & shaped spindles flanked by "thumb-back" uprights, shaped plank seat, bamboo-turned legs w/stretchers, painted yellow w/gilt foliate motifs at crest & highlighted w/brown striping, ca. 1840, pr. (ILLUS. of one) 412.00

Federal country-style "spindle-back" sewing rocker, painted & decorated, plain crestrail above 5 tapering spindles flanked by "thumb-back" uprights, shaped seat, turned splayed legs on "carpet-cutter" rockers, black over red painted graining w/gilt stenciled fruit at crest & gilt striping 100.00

Federal-style dining chairs, mahogany, shield-shaped back w/pierced oval splat incorporating draped plumes & bellflowers, over-upholstered ser-pentine-fronted seat, square tapering legs w/relief-carved details, Marlborough feet, ca. 1900, 2 armchairs & 4 side chairs, set of 6 . . . . .1,400.00

French Empire armchair, mahogany w/ormolu mounts, angular crestrail w/ormolu mounts, upholstered back & bow-fronted seat, arms swept down in the form of dolphins, slightly flared square legs, France, 1800-25 style 2,310.00

Hitchcock-style side chair, painted & decorated, "pillow" crestrail over medial stayrail, rush seat, ring-turned tapering legs, button feet, original black paint w/worn gold

stenciling & yellow striping,
ca. 1840 . . . . .85.00
Louis XV "bergere en gondole"
(armchair w/upholstered inward
curving arms), painted & parcel
gilt, molded voluted frame carved
w/scrolls & flowerheads, cabriole
legs, painted beige & highlighted
w/gilding, floral silk upholstery,
France, mid-18th c. 3,850.00
Louis XV side chairs, walnut,
cartouche-shaped upholstered back
& serpentine-fronted seat, molded
cabriole tapering legs ending in
scrolled toes, signed "Blanchard,"
France, mid-18th c., set of 4 . . . . . .4,510.00
Mission-style (Arts & Crafts movement)
"Morris" reclining armchair, oak,
horizontal slats in adjustable back,
flat open arms, w/cushions, original finish, attributed to Gustav
Stickley. 400.00
Pennsylvania-decorated "plank-seat"
side chairs, angel-wing crestrail
above vase-form splat, plank seat,
turned legs, painted black & yellow
fruit, flower & shell decor on
brown ground highlighted
w/striping, ca. 1845, pr. 300.00
Pennsylvania-decorated "plank seat"
side chairs, shaped crestrail above
lyre-form splat, plank seat, turned
legs w/stretchers, painted polychrome foliage & fruit on peach-
pink ground, gilt trim, Pennsylvania, ca. 1840, set of 6 (minor
retouching) .825.00

Pilgrim Century Armchair

Pilgrim Century "rush-seat" armchair,
maple & ash, back w/turned crestrail over stayrails joined by reel-
turned spindles between heavy
uprights w/lemon-turned finials,
rush seat, turned legs (slightly

reduced in height) w/stretchers,
Massachusetts, 1670-90 (ILLUS.) 660.00
Queen Anne open armchair, maple,
pine & ash, yoked crestrail above
vase-form splat in "spooned" back,
arms w/scrolling terminals, woven
rush seat, turned & blocked legs,
brush feet, original finish,
1750-70 . . . . .4,600.00
Queen Anne open armchair, painted
finish, yoked crestrail above vase-
form splat in "spooned" back,
scrolled arms on vase-turned uprights, worn rush seat, blocked-and-
turned legs w/bead-and-reel frontal
stretcher, carved Spanish feet, old
worn black repaint 1,600.00
Queen Anne wing armchair,
mahogany, upholstered back
w/shaped crest flanked by ogival
wings & outward scrolling arms,
seat w/loose cushion, cabriole legs
w/blocked & turned stretchers, pad
feet, Massachusetts, ca. 1755 . . . .10,450.00
Queen Anne side chair, maple & birch,
yoked crestrail above vase-form
splat & ring- and baluster-turned
stiles, woven splint seat, ring- and
vase-turned legs, shod pad feet,
New York, ca. 1760 . . . . .605.00
Queen Anne side chair, maple,
yoked crestrail above vase-form
splat in "spooned" back, rush seat,
vase-turned & blocked stretchers
w/bead-and-reel frontal stretcher,
brush feet, New England,
1730-50 . . . . .1,045.00
Queen Anne side chair, maple, yoked
crestrail over vase-form splat in
"spooned" back, replaced rush
seat, turned & blocked legs w/bead-
and-reel frontal stretcher, Spanish
feet, old dark brown finish 800.00
Queen Anne side chair, maple, yoked
crestrail above vase-form splat in
"spooned" back, over-upholstered
seat, angular line-incised cabriole
legs w/blocked & turned stretchers,
squared pad feet, Connecticut,
ca. 1750 (repair to one foot) 2,420.00
Queen Anne side chair, walnut,
yoked crestrail above shaped vase-
form splat in "spooned" back, slip
seat, shaped seatrail, cabriole
C-scroll carved legs, pad feet, New
York, 1730-50 . . . . .2,420.00
Queen Anne side chair, walnut,
yoked crestrail centering a volute-
carved shell device above vase-form
splat in "spooned" back, slip seat,
cabriole legs w/ring- and block-
turned stretchers, pad feet,
Newport, Rhode Island, 1740-55
(minor repairs to crest) 2,640.00

Queen Anne Walnut Side Chair

Queen Anne side chair, walnut,
yoked crestrail above vase-form
splat in "spooned" back, slip seat,
molded seatrail, cabriole legs,
pad feet, New York, ca. 1740
(ILLUS.) 1,320.00

Shaker Rocker

Shaker rocker w/arms, 4-slat back
w/lemon-form finials on turned
stiles, woven splint seat, rockers
fitted w/metal bottoms, painted
black over old red, Union Village,
Ohio, mid-19th c. (ILLUS.) 1,320.00
Shaker rocker (No. 3 size) w/arms,
woven tape seat & back, attributed
to Mt. Lebanon, New York
community. 400.00

Shaker rocker (No. 6 size) w/arms,
4-slat back w/lemon-form finials on
turned uprights & mushroom finials
on arms, woven tape seat, original
finish. . . . . .925.00 to 1,175.00
Shaker rocker (No. 7 size) w/arms,
4-slat back w/cushion bar, shaped
arms, woven tape seat 700.00
Shaker "tilting" side chair, maple &
other hardwoods, 3-slat back,
woven tape seat, turned legs fitted
w/tilters on rear legs. 525.00
Turn-of-the-Century dining chairs,
golden oak, plain crestrail above
turned spindles, caned seat
refinished & recaned 150.00
Victorian dining chair, Eastlake sub-
style, walnut .150.00
Victorian dining chairs, Eastlake sub-
style, walnut, typical scalloped
crest w/incised carvings above
stylized splat, demi-arms, caned
seat, turned legs, refinished, ca.
1890, set of 6 . . . . .575.00
Victorian "Hall" chair, Elizabethan
Revival substyle, rosewood, pierce-
carved foliate scrolling crest above
conforming splat flanked by turned
spindles & ring- and vase-turned
stiles w/mushroom finials, upholstered seat, turned legs, late
19th c. 137.50

Victorian "Stanton Hall" Armchairs by Meeks

Victorian parlor armchairs, rococo
substyle, pierce-carved laminated
rosewood, Stanton Hall patt. by John
& Joseph Meeks, New York, ca. 1855,
pr. (ILLUS.) .5,000.00
Victorian parlor gentleman's armchair,
rococo substyle, carved laminated
rosewood, upholstered balloon-
shaped back & finger-molded open
arms, attributed to John Henry
Belter, New York, ca. 1855 . . . . . . .1,210.00
Victorian parlor (lady's) armchair,
rococo substyle, walnut, finger-
molded frame, rounded upholstered
back, short padded arms, bowed

seat, semi-cabriole legs on casters,
late 19th c. 275.00

Victorian parlor lady's armchair,
rococo substyle, rosewood, upholstered oval back w/pierce-carved
crest centered w/carved grape
cluster, semi-cabriole legs, New
York, ca. 1855 . . . . 935.00

Victorian parlor side chairs, rococo
substyle, carved laminated rosewood, Rosalie patt. w/ornately
carved crest over upholstered
balloon-shaped back, semi-cabriole
legs, John Henry Belter, New York,
ca. 1855, pr. 3,500.00

Victorian parlor side chairs, rococo
substyle, carved laminated rosewood,
scrolling crest centering carved rose,
oval back & over-upholstered seat,
demi-cabriole legs, New York, ca.
1860, pr. 440.00

Victorian parlor side chairs, rococo substyle, pierce-carved laminated rosewood, upholstered back w/floral-
carved crest continuing to cornucopia, grapes & scrolls, floral-carved
seatrail & demi-cabriole legs, John
Henry Belter, ca. 1855, pr. 4,675.00

Belter "Slipper" Chairs

Victorian "slipper-seat" side chairs,
pierce-carved laminated rosewood,
shaped frame w/foliate crest above
pierced leaf-carved back, over-
upholstered seat, floral-carved
apron & demi-cabriole legs on
casters, attributed to John Henry
Belter, New York, ca. 1855, pr.
(ILLUS.) 1,210.00

Wallace Nutting signed Colonial
Revival style "ladder-back" armchair, rush seat, early 20th c.,
48" h. back 325.00

Wallace Nutting signed armchair,
Windsor "brace-back" style, fan-
shaped crest above 9-spindle back
w/braces to shaped seat & arm
w/shaped knuckles on arms, vase-

and ring-turned tapering legs
w/bobbin stretchers, early
20th c. 1,725.00

Wallace Nutting signed armchair,
Windsor "comb-back" style, shaped
crest on 5-spindle comb over
9-spindle bowed back w/shaped
knuckles on arms, shaped saddle
seat, vase- and ring-turned tapering
splayed legs, early 20th c. 990.00

Wallace Nutting signed side chairs,
Windsor "fan-back" style, shaped
crestrail above 8-spindle back &
vase- and ring-turned uprights, shaped
saddle-seat, vase- and ring-turned
tapering splayed legs w/bobbin
stretchers, Framingham, Massa-
chussets, early 20th c., pr. 550.00

Wicker rocking chair w/arms, woven
reed w/roll-over arms, cane seat
(no cushion) 195.00

William & Mary Armchair

William & Mary armchair, walnut,
pierce-carved crest above molded &
caned back flanked by baluster- and
ring-turned uprights w/shaped
finials, shaped arms w/acanthus-
carved terminals, trapezoidal seatrail, block- and ring-turned legs
w/ring- and vase-turned stretchers,
England, early 18th c. (ILLUS.) 1,155.00

William & Mary "banister-back" side
chair, scalloped crestrail above
split banister uprights flanked by
vase- and ring-turned stiles
w/shaped finials, (replaced) rush
seat, ca. 1715 . . . . 485.00

William & Mary "banister-back" side
chair, maple, scalloped crestrail
above 3 split banisters flanked by
vase- and ring-turned uprights,
rush seat, block- and vase-turned
legs w/stretchers, New England,
1750-75 . . . . 1,100.00

Windsor "bow-back" armchair, bowed crestrail above 7-spindle back, oval saddle seat, splayed legs w/H-stretcher, worn old black repaint w/yellow & white striping 2,675.00

Windsor "bow-back" armchair, bowed crestrail above 9-spindle back, arms w/shaped handgrips on vase-turned supports, shaped seat branded "I. Henzey" on underside, ring- and vase-turned tapering splayed legs w/"bobbin" stretchers 1,550.00

Windsor "comb-back" armchair on rockers, shaped crest over 5-spindle comb above 7-spindle back w/up-rights joined to curving arms, rounded seat, bamboo-turned legs w/conforming stretchers, on rockers, 1800-20 . . . . 418.00

Windsor "fan-back" side chair, shaped crestrail above 7-spindle back, narrow seat, splayed legs w/"bob-bin" stretchers, tapering feet, old black repaint 850.00

Windsor "fan-back" side chair, shaped crestrail w/scrolling ears above 9-spindle back, shaped saddle seat, vase- and ring-turned tapering legs w/stretchers, original painted finish, New England, late 18th c. 1,210.00

Windsor "Low-Back" Armchair

Windsor "low-back" armchair, painted finish, horseshoe-shaped backrail w/cushion-molded crest above 17 turned spindles & eliptical seat, baluster- and ring-turned legs, "blunt arrow" feet, painted brown, Pennsylvania, 1760-80, repair to arm & single replaced spindle (ILLUS.) 4,125.00

Windsor "step-down" side chair, bamboo-turned, shaped crestrail above 7-spindle back, shaped seat w/incised edge, splayed legs w/stretchers, (very worn) red painted finish w/white striping exposing old grey beneath 240.00

Windsor "step-down" side chairs, shaped crestrail above 7-spindle back, round seat w/incised edge, bamboo-turned splayed legs w/stretchers, old (repainted) black & red graining w/yellow striping & painted oblong seascapes at crest, pr. (minor damage) 520.00

Windsor "writing" armchair, hoop-back above 7 tapering spindles, shaped leather-upholstered writing surface w/short drawer below at arm to right, shaped seat fitted w/drawer below, baluster-turned tapering legs w/"bobbin" stretchers, painted cream highlighted w/green lines, New England, 1790-1810 . . . . 6,600.00

Windsor (late) low-back armchair (so-called Firehouse Windsor), bentwood backrail continuing to arms over turned spindles, shaped seat, turned legs, 1860-80, black repaint 45.00

CHESTS & CHESTS OF DRAWERS

Apothecary chest, pine, 27-drawer 375.00

Blanket chest, painted pine, oblong top w/molded edge lifting above case w/deep well, molded base, painted black w/white sponge-daubed reserves edged in white, probably Pennsylvania, late 18th c., 29½ x 14½", 13½" h. 440.00

Blanket chest, painted pine, oblong top w/molded edge lifting to deep well w/till in dovetailed case, applied molding at base, cut-out bracket feet, original brown-painted flame graining w/faint red & green striping, 38 x 18¾", 21½" h. (replaced hinges & worn feet) 225.00

Blanket chest, cherrywood, oblong top w/molded edge lifting to deep well w/till in case w/square corner posts continuing to turned feet, 44 x 19¾", 22¼" h. 300.00

Blanket chest, painted pine, oblong top w/molded edge lifting to deep well w/till in dovetailed case, applied molding at base, cut-out bracket feet, original red-painted flame graining, 44½ x 20¼", 23¼" h. 300.00

Blanket chest, red-stained pine, oblong top w/molded edge lifting to deep well w/two tills in dovetailed case, applied molding at base, large ball-turned front feet & cut-out back feet, New England, 18th c., 45 x 20", 25" h. 825.00

Blanket Chest dated "1781"

Blanket chest, Pennsylvania-decorated pine, oblong top w/molded
edge lifting to deep well w/till in
case above pr. short molded drawers,
molded base, ogee bracket feet,
green ground painted w/three
arched panels w/man on horse &
paired love birds flanked by urns of
tulips & w/yellow & red tulips on
drawers, Pennsylvania, dated "1781,"
(some paint restoration), 48 x 23½",
25" h. (ILLUS.)...................6,875.00

Blanket chest, walnut, oblong top
lifting to deep well w/till in
dovetailed case, cut-out bracket
feet, original wrought iron strap
hinges, marked "Salem, Ohio" in
lid, 49¾ x 19", 25¼" h............525.00

Blanket chest, Chippendale, painted &
decorated, oblong top w/molded
edge lifting to deep well w/till in
case w/applied mid-molding above
short central drawer flanked by
larger drawers, ogee bracket feet,
painted green ground w/red
oblong panels highlighted in
yellow, 50½" w., 29½" h........2,200.00

Blanket chest, Zoar (Ohio), painted
finish, oblong top lifting to deep well
in dovetailed case, ball feet, painted
blue-green......................650.00

Mule chest (box chest w/one or more
drawers below storage compart-
ment---forerunner of chest of
drawers), Queen Anne, painted pine,
oblong top w/molded edge lifting to
deep well in case w/two drawers
below, molded base, bracket feet,
(now) painted red, New England,
1750-70, 37" w., 42" h.............660.00

Mule chest, William & Mary, painted &
decorated pine, oblong top
w/molded edge lifting to deep well
in case faced to simulate 2 short
drawers over long drawer above pr.
long working drawers, all within
molded surrounds, molded base,
large ball feet, painted black w/yel-
low squiggles, New England, ca.
1725, 37" w., 37" h. (ILLUS.).......6,875.00

William & Mary Chest

Seed storage chest, 24-drawer, grain-
painted finish, 4 rows of 6 graduated
drawers w/original pulls & stenciled
identifications for various types of
seeds........................1,695.00

Sugar chest, Sheraton-style, cherrywood, oblong top lifting to deep
storage compartment above single
long drawer w/turned wood pulls,
ring- and baluster-turned legs,
tapering feet, 1810-25............900.00

Sugar chest, Sheraton country-style,
cherrywood, oblong top w/bread-
board ends lifting to deep storage
compartment, ring- and baluster-
turned legs, tapering feet, early
1800s........................1,800.00

Sugar chest, Sheraton country-style,
poplar, pegged construction,
oblong top lifting to deep compartment above single long drawer,
bulbous-turned tall legs, Tennessee
origins, 1840-50.................1,500.00

American Empire chest of drawers,
cherrywood, oblong top w/scrolling
backsplash above case w/deep
upper drawer over 3 slightly
recessed drawers flanked by bold
C-scrolls at stiles, C-scroll feet,
Zoar traditional design...........225.00

American Empire chest of drawers,
curly maple, oblong top above deep
upper drawer over 3 slightly
recessed & graduated long drawers
flanked by applied flattened
columns, C-scroll feet, original
pressed clear glass pulls, large
size.........................375.00

American Empire chest of drawers,
maple & mahogany veneer, oblong
top set w/pr. recessed short drawers
& w/scrolling backboard mounted
w/brass rosettes above case w/long
drawer over 3 slightly recessed

drawers flanked by ring-turned & acanthus-carved columns continuing to ring-turned feet, Pennsylvania, 1820-30 . . . . .715.00

American Empire chest of drawers, walnut w/burl veneer drawer fronts, oblong top above 5 long drawers flanked by half-round fluted columns w/Ionic capitals, 1845-50, 54" h. (restored). 595.00

Chippendale "bachelor's" chest of drawers, walnut, oblong top above pull-out writing slide over 4 long thumb-molded graduated drawers, bracket feet, Southern origin, ca. 1770, 32½" w., 32½" h. 7,150.00

Chippendale tall chest of drawers, cherrywood, oblong top w/molded projecting cornice above arrangement of central fan-carved drawer flanked by short drawers over 5 long graduated & thumb-molded drawers, bracket feet, Connecticut, ca. 1785, 40" w., 56½" h. 7,425.00

Chippendale tall chest of drawers, curly maple, oblong top w/line-inlaid edge above 2 short & 4 long graduated drawers w/replaced brass oval drop ring handles, line-inlaid base, bracket feet, ca. 1790, 36½" w., 47" h. 2,750.00

Chippendale tall chest of drawers, curly maple, oblong top w/applied molding above central fan-carved drawer over 5 long thumb-molded graduated drawers w/replaced brass bat's wing handles & keyhole escutcheons, cut-out bracket feet, New England, ca. 1780, 40¼" w., 59" h. 7,150.00

Chippendale tall chest of drawers, walnut, oblong top w/molded edge above 6 graduated thumb-molded drawers w/oval brass drop ring handles, bracket feet, Pennsylvania, 1780-1800, 39½" w., 55" h. 2,420.00

Chippendale tall chest of drawers, walnut, oblong top w/molded cornice above arrangement of 5 short drawers & 4 long graduated drawers, cut-out bracket feet, Pennsylvania, 1765-1800, 41" w., 58¼" h. 8,800.00

Chippendale "block-and-shell" carved chest of drawers, mahogany, oblong top w/molded edge above long drawer carved w/central concave shell & flanking convex shells w/stop-fluted center petals above pr. conformingly blocked long graduated drawers within cockbeaded surrounds, original brass bat's wing handles & keyhole

escutcheons, molded base, ogee bracket feet, Rhode Island or Connecticut, 1765-80, 37½" w., 33½" h. 63,250.00

Chippendale Blocked Serpentine-Front Chest

Chippendale "blocked serpentine-front" chest of drawers, mahogany, oblong top w/molded edge & serpentine front above case of conforming outline w/four graduated long drawers, molded base, short cabriole legs, claw-and-ball feet, Massachusetts, ca. 1770, 37¼" w., 32¾" h. (ILLUS.). 30,800.00

Chippendale "bow-front" chest of drawers, cherrywood, oblong top w/bowed front above case of conforming outline w/four long cockbeaded & graduated drawers w/brass oval drop ring handles, gadrooned skirt, ogee bracket feet, New York, 1780-1800, 47½" w., 37½" h. (some repairs to feet) 1,870.00

Chippendale "bow-front" chest of drawers, inlaid mahogany, oblong top w/inlaid edge above case of conforming outline w/four cockbeaded graduated long drawers w/brass drop ring handles, ogee bracket feet, Massachusetts, 1780-1800, 41½" w., 31½" h. 5,500.00

Chippendale "serpentine-front" chest of drawers, mahogany, oblong top w/serpentine front above case of conforming outline w/four cockbeaded & graduated long drawers w/original brass drop ring handles, molded base, ogee bracket feet, Salem, Massachusetts, 1770-90, 37½" w., 34" h. 19,800.00

Chippendale "serpentine-front" chest of drawers, mahogany, oblong top w/molded edge & serpentine front above conformingly shaped case w/four long graduated drawers within cockbeaded surrounds, molded base, shaped bracket feet,

Chippendale "Serpentine-Front" Chest

Massachusetts, ca. 1780, some
repairs, 40" w., 31" h. (ILLUS.) 4,950.00
Chippendale chest of drawers, cherrywood, oblong top w/molded edge
above 4 long thumb-molded &
graduated drawers w/original brass
drop ring handles flanked by stop-
fluted pilasters, New London,
Connecticut, 1780-1800, 38½" w.,
33" h. 10,175.00
Chippendale chest of drawers, curly
cherrywood, oblong top w/molded
edge above case w/four long thumb-
molded & graduated drawers flanked
by fluted quarter columns, ogee
bracket feet, Pennsylvania, ca. 1790,
38½" w., 35" h. (drawer bottoms
replaced) 15,950.00
Chippendale chest of drawers, walnut,
oblong top w/molded edge above
case w/two short & 3 long thumb-
molded & graduated drawers
w/original brasses flanked by fluted
quarter columns, ogee bracket feet,
Philadelphia, ca. 1765, 36¼" w.,
35½" h. 11,000.00
Chippendale country-style chest of
drawers, birch w/worn brown-red
finish, oblong top w/molded edge
above upper drawer faced to
resemble 3 short drawers w/con-
cave fan carving on central
drawer, fan-carved short drawer
flanked by short drawers over 4
long graduated drawers, original
brass bail handles, cut-out bracket
feet, 38" w., 50" h. 8,000.00
Federal tall chest of drawers, cherrywood, oblong top above case
w/two short drawers over 5 long
graduated drawers, 1780-1800
(ogee bracket feet of later date),
40½" w., 56½" h. 3,300.00
Federal tall chest of drawers, inlaid
walnut, molded cornice w/line-inlaid
edge above 6 long graduated

drawers within cockbeaded surrounds flanked by vine- and berry-
inlaid canted corners, bracket feet,
Pennsylvania, ca. 1800, 42½" w.,
67" h. (repairs to feet) 6,600.00

Federal Chest of Drawers

Federal "bow-front" chest of
drawers, inlaid birch & tiger stripe
maple, oblong top w/bowed front
& outset rounded corners & pattern-inlaid edge above conforming
case w/four maple-veneered &
mahogany banded drawers flanked
by ring- and spiral-turned columns,
pattern-inlaid apron, ring-turned
tapering feet, New Hampshire or
Massachusetts, 1800-20, 43" w.,
37¾" h. (ILLUS.). 1,650.00
Federal "bow-front" chest of
drawers, inlaid cherrywood, oblong
top w/bowed front above case of
conforming outline w/four inlaid,
cockbeaded & graduated long
drawers w/brass oval drop handles,
bracket feet, probably Connecticut,
ca. 1805, 41½" w., 38" h. 2,750.00
Federal "bow-front" chest of
drawers, inlaid mahogany, oblong
top w/bowed front & inlaid edge
above case of conforming outline
w/four graduated & cockbeaded
drawers, shaped skirt continuing to
flaring French feet, Northeastern
Massachusetts, 1790-1810, 39¼" w.,
37½" h. 1,760.00
Federal "serpentine-front" chest of
drawers, mahogany & cherrywood,
oblong top w/serpentine front above
conformingly shaped case w/deep
upper drawer centering an inlaid
oval reserve above 3 long cockbeaded & graduated drawers,
shaped skirt, bracket feet, ca. 1800,
39" w., 40" h. (repairs to feet).....2,090.00

Federal chest of drawers, birch & bird's
eye maple, oblong top above case
w/four long graduated drawers
w/bird's eye maple facade & birch
crossbanding, original brass oval
drop ring handles, apron w/inlaid
square central drop continuing to
cut-out bracket feet 3,520.00
Federal chest of drawers, bird's eye
maple, oblong top w/outset rounded
corners above case w/four long
drawers w/mahogany veneer
borders flanked by turned stiles
continuing to turned feet, Massachusetts or New Hampshire, 1800-20,
42½" w., 38½" h 770.00
Federal country-style chest of drawers,
grain-painted finsh, oblong top
above pr. short drawers over 3 long
drawers, all w/turned wood pulls,
cut-out bracket feet, New England,
ca. 1830 . . . . .625.00
Louis XV-XVI transitional "chiffonier"
(narrow tall chest of drawers),
inlaid fruitwood w/ormolu mounts,
oblong top w/rounded corners
above case w/six drawers, the
sides w/inlaid lozenge pattern on
cross-banded fruitwood ground,
slightly hipped cabriole legs
w/foliate sabots, France, 1750-75,
16½" w., 34" h. 2,750.00
Mission-style (Arts & Crafts movement)
chest of drawers w/mirror, stained
oak, oblong top set w/superstructure
holding swiveling oblong mirror
above case w/three long graduated
drawers w/turned wood pulls,
w/paper label of Gustav Stickley,
48" w., 33" h. plus mirror 1,430.00
Pilgrim Century "joined" chest, oak &
pine, oblong hinged top w/molded
edge lifting to case w/deep well &
three-panel front, the stiles continuing to form square legs, Upper
Connecticut River Valley, 1690-1720,
48½" w., 28¾" h. 1,670.00
Pilgrim Century chest, oak, oblong
top w/molded edge lifting to deep
well in case w/panels of incised
carvings of stylized tulips & centering the initials "W.B." & date
"1699," above long drawer w/incised
carving of meandering vine,
Connecticut River Valley, dated
1699, 55" w., 29½" h. (now
reduced in height at feet) 6,325.00
Queen Anne chest-on-frame, walnut,
2-part construction: upper part
w/projecting molded cornice above
arrangement of 5 short drawers over
3 long thumb-molded & graduated
drawers; lower section w/pr. thumb-
molded short drawers, shaped

skirt, cabriole legs, trifid feet,
w/original brasses, Pennsylvania,
ca. 1760, 40" w., 69½" h 7,700.00
Queen Anne "block-front" chest of
drawers, mahogany, oblong top
w/molded edge & blocked front
above case of conforming outline
w/four long graduated drawers
within cockbeaded surrounds,
blocked bracket feet, Boston,
Massachusetts, ca. 1750, 33½" w.,
29" h 28,600.00
Victorian "butler's" chest of drawers,
walnut, oblong top w/molded edge
above case w/fall-front upper
drawer opening to small compartments over 4 long drawers,
ca. 1850 . . . . .2,800.00

Victorian Tall Chest of Drawers

Victorian tall chest of drawers, walnut
w/burl walnut panels, oblong top
w/molded edge above case w/six
long graduated drawers w/burl
walnut panels & original wooden
pear-shaped pulls flanked by
chamfered stiles (ILLUS.) 1,200.00
Victorian chest of drawers, cottage-
style, walnut, oblong top above
case w/three drawers w/turned
pulls, original "alligatored" finish,
small commode-size 225.00
Victorian chest of drawers, early
style, walnut, oblong top set w/pr.
step-back short drawers recessed to
back above case w/three long
drawers, all w/turned mushroom
pulls, scalloped apron, bracket feet,
41¼" w., 45½" h 175.00
Victorian chest of drawers w/mirror,
Renaissance substyle, walnut & burl
walnut w/white marble top, superstructure w/shaped & carved crest
above mirror flanked by candle
shelves over chest w/white marble
slab top & 3 long drawers w/applied
burl panels, 46" w., overall 84" h. . . .800.00

Victorian "Drop-Front" Dresser

Victorian "drop-front" dresser w/mirror, Renaissance substyle, walnut & burl walnut, superstructure w/shaped crest w/applied rounded rosette carvings & shaped mirror plate flanked by candle shelves, white marble slab tops on "drop-front" drawers & flanking drawers w/columnar dividers & original pear-shaped wooden & brass handles, plinth base, on casters, 82" h. (ILLUS.) 1,400.00

William & Mary chest of drawers, oak, oblong top above case w/four long geometrically paneled drawers w/brass teardrop pulls, molded base, flattened bun feet, England, late 17th c., 39½" w., 38½" h. (restored) 1,210.00

William & Mary chest of drawers, oak, 2-part construction: upper part w/molded oblong top above 2 drawers w/geometric moldings; lower section w/two conforming drawers, molded base, large bun feet, England, late 17th c., 40" w., 38" h. (restored) 1,760.00

William & Mary chest of drawers, walnut, oak & pine, oblong top above paneled long drawer above 2 paneled deep drawers, w/applied moldings separating the drawers & forming panels at the flanking stiles, cove-molded base, stile feet, Boston, Massachusetts, 1690-1710, 42" w., 40" h. (restored feet).........................2,200.00

Zoar (Ohio) chest of drawers, cherrywood, oblong top w/molded edge set w/pr. handkerchief boxes to rear joined by shaped backboard over case w/deep upper drawer over 3 slightly recessed drawers flanked by vigorously carved double C-scrolls, drawers faced w/curly maple & sides w/curly maple panels, signed "George Ackerman" 4,000.00

COMMODES

Victorian Washstand Commode

Georgian commode, mahogany w/"verde antico" marble top, oblong marble slab top above case w/pr. short cockbeaded drawers over 3 long cockbeaded graduated drawers, w/brass pulls & keyhole escutcheons, canted corners w/pendant leaf & floral high relief carvings, plinth base, England, ca. 1750, 38½" w., 34½" h. (replaced backboard) 12,100.00

Louis XV commode, rosewood parquetry w/"breche d-Alep" marble top, oblong serpentine-fronted marble slab above case of conforming outline w/two short & 2 long drawers inlaid w/quartersawn rosewood panels within crossbanded borders, signed "Mignon," France, 1825-50 (fitted w/ormolu handles & keyhole escutcheons at later date), 49½" w., 34½" h......3,575.00

Louis XV commode, kingwood parquetry w/"breche d-Alep" marble slab top, oblong serpentine-fronted marble slab top above case of conforming outline w/three drawers fitted w/ormolu handles & keyhole escutcheons, cabriole legs fitted w/ormolu "chutes" & "sabots," France, 1825-50, 56¾" w., 39" h.........................33,000.00

Louis XVI Provincial commode, walnut, oblong top w/molded edge above case w/three long drawers flanked by stop-fluted columns continuing to form straight legs, late 18th c. (now fitted w/ormolu drawer pulls & keyhole escutcheons), 32½" w., 31½" h. 1,650.00

Victorian commode, Early Victorian style, walnut w/white marble slab top, single drawer over pr. cupboard doors, original finish, mid-19th c. . . . . 250.00 to 350.00

Victorian commode, Renaissance sub-style, walnut w/brown speckled marble slab top & shaped back-splash, single drawer over pr. cartouche-paneled cupboard doors w/applied carvings, plinth base (ILLUS.) 600.00

CRADLES

Country-Style Cradle on Rockers

Country-style low cradle on rockers, cherrywood, tombstone-type head & footboards & shaped canted sides pierced w/hand holds, ca. 1820 . . . . . 225.00

Country-style low cradle on rockers, curly maple, shaped head & foot-boards & shaped paneled sides w/applied pegs joined to corner posts w/flattened ball finials, ca. 1800 . . . . 925.00

Country-style low cradle on rockers, painted maple, shaped head & foot-boards, canted sides, old red paint . . 105.00

Country-style low cradle on rockers, painted pine, tombstone-type head & footboards pierced w/hand holds & shaped sides joined to short corner posts w/flattened ball finials, shaped rockers, red-painted finish, Pennsyl-vania, early 19th c. (ILLUS.) 345.00

Country-style low cradle on rockers, pine, shaped head & footboards, scrolling sides pierced w/heart-shaped hand holds 325.00

Country-style low cradle on rockers, poplar, rounded head & footboards,

canted & shaped sides pierced w/hand holds, heavy rockers, refinished, 37" l. 175.00

Country-style cradle on rockers, wal-nut, shaped head & footboards & paneled sides joined to squared corner posts w/turned finials, shaped rockers, 19th c., 41½" l. . . . 350.00

Country-style low cradle on rockers, woven splint on heavy wooden framework, shaped rockers, large size 325.00

Hooded cradle on rockers, painted pine, arched hood, canted & shaped sides, rounded footboard, old painted graining finish 250.00

Hooded Cradle

Hooded cradle on rockers, painted maple & pine, arched hood, canted sides, shaped footboard, painted finish, New England, ca. 1830 (ILLUS.) 450.00

Hooded cradle on rockers, pine & maple, arched hood, shaped & canted sides, scalloped footboard, shaped rockers, refinished 715.00

Platform-type cradle, Victorian Renaissance substyle, walnut, pierce-carved head & footboards & pierce-carved flattened spindle sides suspended from turned posts w/shaped finials on platform mounted w/applied turned roundels, w/pedal for rocking, ca. 1870 . . . . 595.00

Platform-type cradle, Victorian, wal-nut, machine-carved details in head & foot crestrails w/turned spindles below & at sides, late 19th c. 270.00

Spindle-sided crib on rockers, Victor-ian, walnut, plain rails above baluster-turned spindles w/ring- and baluster-turned corner posts w/shaped finials, late 19th c. 225.00

Spindle-sided crib on rockers, birch & oak, early 20th c., refinished (ILLUS.) 225.00

Spindle-Sided Cradle

Suspended-type cradle, Victorian, Renaissance-Rococo substyle, walnut, pierce-carved shaped head & footboards & pierce-carved flattened spindles at sides, scrolling framework w/applied roundels, 1870s............................595.00

Windsor-style cradle on rockers, painted finish, arrow-shaped spindles all sides w/thumb-back finials at corner head-posts ....395.00 to 550.00

CUPBOARDS

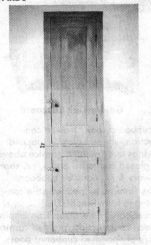

Shaker Chimney Cupboard

Chimney cupboard, pine & poplar, molded cornice above single 1-board cupboard door opening to single shelf, original dark paint w/yellow striping, 15¼" w., 10¾" deep, 68" h. (bread in side at one hinge) . . .850.00

Chimney cupboard, Shaker, painted pine, beveled top above 2 paneled cupboard doors, each opening to

shelves, molded base, original grey paint, w/two turned pegs mounted on left side of case, Hancock, Massachusetts, ca. 1830, 23½" w., 11½" deep, 84" h. (ILLUS.) 14,300.00

Chimney cupboard, pine, picture frame molding surround, single cupboard door w/two chamfered panels 1,600.00

Corner cupboard, cherrywood, Chippendale country-style, 2-part construction: upper part w/molded cornice above pr. paneled cupboard doors; lower section w/pr. paneled cupboard doors, shaped apron continuing to bracket feet, late 18th c., refinished, 78" h..........3,500.00

Corner cupboard, cherrywood, Federal country-style, 2-part construction: upper part w/molded cornice above double-paneled cupboard doors; lower section w/single drawer centered above pr. paneled cupboard doors, scalloped apron, bracket feet, old worn finish, 43½" w., 82½" h. 1,900.00

Corner cupboard, cherrywood & poplar, 1-piece construction, applied ogee-molded cornice above pr. 8-pane doors opening to shelves, medial molding above pr. paneled cupboard doors, scalloped apron, bracket feet, refinished, 55" w., 86" h. (one piece of cornice missing) 1,000.00

Corner cupboard, oak, 1-piece construction, plain crest above single cupboard door w/leaded glass panes over graduated drawers, ca. 1900...500.00

Corner cupboard, walnut, Federal, 2-piece construction: upper part w/molded swan's neck cresting ending in carved roundels & centering a turned finial above pr. arched & geometrically glazed cupboard doors flanked by fluted pilasters; lower section w/pr. short thumb-molded drawers over pr. paneled cupboard doors flanked by conforming pilasters, ogee bracket feet, probably Pennsylvania, ca. 1785, 54" w., 107" h. (missing parts of feet)........................3,080.00

Hanging cupboard, cherrywood, Chippendale style, stepped & shaped crest above molded cornice over paneled cupboard door w/shield-shaped ivory keyhole escutcheon, molded base, 25¼" w., 8" deep, 33½" h. 990.00

Hanging cupboard, walnut & poplar, molded cornice above paneled cupboard door opening to 3 removable shelves w/scalloped fronts, molded base, Zoar, Ohio, 27" w., 35" h.....900.00

Hanging cupboard, primitive pine,
  molded cornice above pr. 3-panel
  cupboard doors on iron H-hinges,
  late 18th c., 28" w., 12" deep,
  39" h. (split near one hinge) 220.00
Hanging cupboard primitive pine
  w/painted finish, plain top above
  paneled cupboard door w/turned
  wood pull, original green paint,
  small size 695.00
Linen press, walnut, Chippendale,
  2-part construction: upper part
  w/swan's neck crest centering
  urn-turned finial flanked by scalloped
  opening over arched cupboard
  doors opening to 4 sliding shelves;
  lower section w/pr. paneled
  cupboard doors opening to single
  shelf & single drawer, molded base,
  Pennsylvania, 1760-80, 44" w.,
  23" deep, 87" h. 22,000.00
Pewter cupboard, butternut, 1-piece
  construction, molded cornice above
  3 open shelves w/plate rails & center
  shelf w/spoon slots flanked by
  cut-out shaped sides over pr.
  paneled cupboard doors 4,250.00
Step-back wall cupboard, walnut,
  2-piece construction: upper part
  w/coved cornice above pr. double-
  paneled cupboard doors opening to
  shelves over open pie shelf; lower
  section w/oblong top above pr.
  double-paneled cupboard doors,
  cut-out bracket feet, 45" w.,
  85" h. 1,195.00

Step-Back Wall Cupboard

Step-back wall cupboard, butternut,
  2-piece construction: upper part

w/(replaced) cornice above detailed
  frieze over glazed 3-pane center
  panel flanked by pr. 6-pane glazed
  cupboard doors & open pie shelf;
  lower section w/oblong top above
  short center drawer flanked by
  drawers over pr. raised panel cupboard doors, cut-out bracket feet,
  55½" w., 22½" deep, 89½" h.
  (ILLUS.) 1,000.00
Step-back wall cupboard, pine, 2-piece
  construction: upper part w/molded
  cornice above pr. cupboard doors
  w/chamfered panels opening to
  shelves; lower section w/pr. cupboard doors w/conforming panels,
  all on rattail hinges, cut-out bracket
  feet, stripped & refinished 2,500.00

Golden Oak Cupboard

Wall cupboard, oak, 1-piece construction, shaped crest w/applied
  carvings over molded cornice above
  pr. glazed cupboard doors, pr. short
  drawers & pr. paneled cupboard
  doors flanked by beaded stile continuing to form feet (ILLUS.) 750.00
Wall cupboard, pine, American Empire,
  2-piece construction: molded cornice
  above pr. paneled cupboard doors
  flanked by fluted pilasters; lower
  section w/four drawers, Virginia,
  1830-50 . . . . .935.00
Wall cupboard, pine, Federal country-
  style, 2-piece construction: upper
  part w/molded cornice above pr.
  glazed doors opening to shelves;
  lower section w/pr. cupboard doors
  opening to shelves, bracket feet,
  early 19th c., 47½" w., 86" h.
  (some repairs) 1,210.00

DESKS

Clerk's desk, pine & poplar, mortised
& pinned construction, hinged
slanting top w/gallery lifting to 3
pigeonholes & storage above case
w/single drawer, pencil-post legs,
old yellow-green stained finish,
24¾" w., 19¼" deep, 34" h. plus
gallery 750.00

American Empire slant-front desk,
maple, hinged lid w/thumb-molded
edge lifting to fitted interior w/seven
drawers & 7 compartments above
case w/three graduated drawers
flanked by spirally-turned pilasters,
molded base, baluster-turned feet,
New England, 1820-40, 39" w.,
41" h. (one interior drawer
missing) 935.00

Biedermeier drop-front desk,
mahogany, oblong top w/molded
cornice above cyma-curved drawer
over drop-front writing surface
opening to central document drawer
flanked by short drawers above case
w/three graduated drawers, molded
bracket base, Germany, 1820-40 ..2,500.00

Chippendale "partner's" desk,
mahogany, oblong top w/molded
edge above arrangement of 3
shallow cockbeaded drawers (each
side) flanked by tier of 3 conforming
graduated drawers, paneled sides,
molded base, original brass drop
handles, England, ca. 1770, 72 x 31"
top, 31" h. 6,750.00

Chippendale "block-front" slant-front
desk, mahogany, hinged lid opening
to mirrored prospect door flanked by
column drawers w/spiral-twist finials
& scalloped pigeonholes over short
drawer & pr. concave-blocked short
drawers above case w/four graduated blocked drawers within cockbeaded surrounds, molded base
w/pendant fan, cabriole legs, claw-
and-ball feet, North Shore,
Massachusetts, 1760-80, 43½" w.,
45½" w. 55,000.00

Chippendale "serpentine-front" slant-
front desk, walnut, hinged lid
opening to fitted interior w/central
pull-out prospect section w/three
locking small drawers flanked by pr.
fan-carved drawers above plain
drawer over case w/four blocked
serpentine, graduated long drawers
within cockbeaded surrounds &
flanked by fluted quarter columns,
attributed to John Shearer, Martins-
burg, Virginia, ca. 1800, 46" w.,
48" h. 13,200.00

Chippendale slant-front desk, curly
maple, hinged lid opening to stepped

interior w/valanced pigeonholes
over small drawers & centering a
pinwheel-carved drawer above case
w/four graduated long drawers
within cockbeaded surrounds, skirt
w/fan-carved pendant, bracket feet,
stained red, original brass drop
handles, New Hampshire, 31" w.,
50½" h. 5,500.00

Chippendale slant-front desk, mahogany, hinged lid opening to central
blocked & shell-carved prospect
door over a short drawer flanked
by valanced pigeonholes & short
drawers above case w/four cockbeaded graduated long drawers,
ogee bracket feet, original brass
drop handles, signed "Rawson,"
Providence, Rhode Island, ca. 1775,
41" w., 43" h. 15,400.00

Chippendale Slant-Front Desk

Chippendale slant-front desk,
mahogany, hinged lid opening to
fitted interior w/scalloped pigeonholes over shaped short drawers &
blocked central prospect door opening to valanced pigeonhole over
concave short drawer w/pull-out
compartment & 2 secret drawers
above case w/four graduated long
drawers, claw-and-ball feet, New
York or Pennsylvania, 48" w.,
43½" h. (ILLUS.) 5,500.00

Chippendale slant-front desk, tiger
stripe maple, hinged lid w/thumb-
molded edge opening to fitted
interior w/arched & paneled prospect door flanked by pigeonholes
over short drawers above case
w/four cockbeaded & graduated
long drawers flanked by chamfered
fluted corners, bracket feet,
Pennsylvania, 1780-1800, 42½" w.,
36" h. 8,800.00

Chippendale slant-front desk, walnut,
hinged lid opening to fitted interior
w/pigeonholes over short drawers &

central prospect door opening to
small drawer flanked by document
drawers above case w/four long
graduated drawers flanked by fluted
quarter colums, ogee bracket feet,
Pennsylvania, 1780-95, 38" w., 44" h.
(lacks small pieces from rear
feet)...........................3,190.00

Federal "butler's" desk, mahogany,
oblong top over deep drawer hinged
at front to open & form writing surface & fitted w/pigeonholes, small
drawers & central prospect drawer,
above 3 cockbeaded & graduated
long drawers, arched & shaped
skirt, flaring French feet, New York,
1790-1815, 47" w., 45¾" h. 1,430.00

Federal lady's "tambour" desk, Hepplewhite style, cherrywood w/inlay,
2-piece: upper part w/flat top above
pr. tambour doors opening to 6 short
drawers above open cupboard;
lower section w/fold-out writing
surface above 4 graduated line-
inlaid long drawers, square tapering
legs, original oval brass drop ring
handles, ca. 1800, 39½" w.,
48½" h.........................2,600.00

Federal lady's desk, inlaid mahogany,
2-piece: upper part w/projecting
cornice above pr. inlaid cupboard
doors opening to marbleized paper-
lined interior w/two short drawers;
lower section w/hinged felt-lined
writing flap opening to well & fitted
w/three short drawers over single
long drawer, inlaid dies, square
double-tapering legs w/cross-banded
cuffs, New England, ca. 1800, 30" w.,
48¾" h.........................7,700.00

Federal lady's desk, mahogany,
2-piece: upper part w/oblong top
over pr. short drawers w/fall-front
writing surface opening to pigeonholes & 4 short drawers; lower
section w/single long drawer over
single cockbeaded drawer, shaped
apron, turned legs, bulb feet, New
York, ca. 1810, 31" w., 53½" h. ...3,575.00

Federal slant-front desk, tiger stripe
maple, hinged lid opening to fitted
interior w/valanced pigeonholes over
short drawers & centering prospect
drawer opening to 2 further drawers
above case w/four graduated long
drawers w/incised edges, bracket
feet, New England, ca. 1800,
40" w., 42¼" h...................3,850.00

Louis XV style lady's desk, fruitwood,
oblong top w/four small drawers
above pigeonholes, pull-out writing
surface over 3 small drawers &
single long drawer, cabriole legs,
early 20th c., 39" w., 39" h.........330.00

Mission-style (Arts & Crafts movement)
"chalet" desk, oak, slightly curving
crestrail w/two angular cut-outs at
corners above drop-front opening to
form writing surface & reveal
shelved interior w/further pierced
decoration, flaring sides joined by
lower shelf, continuing to shaped
feet, attributed to Gustav Stickley,
1900-02, 23½" w., 46" h. 1,430.00

Mission-style (Arts & Crafts movement)
drop-front desk, oak, crest w/three-
quarter gallery & top shelf above
drop-front writing surface on
hammered copper hinges & centering a 5-slat panel opening to several
pigeonholes & closed compartment,
the sides continuing to form feet
joined by 2 shelves, Gustav Stickley's
model No. 518, ca. 1902, 26" w.,
52" h...........................4,675.00

Mission-style (Arts & Crafts movement)
desk w/bookcase, oak, slant-front
opening to compartmented interior,
kneehole flanked by bookshelves
accessible from sides, square legs,
L. & J.G. Stickley.................375.00

Queen Anne Desk on Frame

Queen Anne desk-on-frame, maple,
2-piece: upper part w/hinged slant
lid opening to valanced pigeonholes
over 3 short drawers above single
long drawer in case; frame w/plain
frieze, circular tapering legs, pad
feet, New England, 1750-70, now
mounted w/brass plaque w/chrono-
logical listing of early owners,
30½" w., 36" h. (ILLUS.) 13,750.00

Queen Anne slant-front desk,
mahogany, hinged lid opening to
interior w/blocked & fan-carved
prospect door concealing secret
drawers & valanced pigeonholes over
over tiers of blocked small drawers

above case w/four graduated
thumb-molded long drawers, molded
base, ogee bracket feet, Newport,
Rhode Island, 1750-70, 36" w.,
42½" h. 16,500.00
Shaker "wagon" desk, painted pine,
plain top above pr. paneled cupboard doors hinged at base &
opening to cubby holes & 2 short
drawers, painted yellow, Harvard,
Massachusetts community, 26" w.,
27" h. (doors once hinged from
sides but now returned to original
state) 2,310.00
Turn-of-the-Century "partner's" desk,
golden oak, 66 x 53" top, kneehole
(each side) w/flanking drawers,
paneled ends, molded base 2,500.00
Turn-of-the-Century "roll-top" desk,
golden oak, S-roll opening to compartments & small drawers, kneehole w/drawers to one side,
paneled ends, 36" w. 795.00
Turn-of-the-Century "roll-top" desk,
golden oak, S-roll opening to small
drawers & pigeonholes above case
w/short drawer & bank of three
drawers to one side, paneled back
& sides, late 19th c.,
50" w. . . . . .935.00 to 1,320.00

Oak Roll-Top Desk

Turn-of-the-Century "roll-top" desk,
golden oak, S-roll opening to
numerous drawers & pigeonholes,
kneehole flanked by banks of
drawers, paneled sides & back,
molded base, 60" w.
(ILLUS.) . . . . .3,000.00 to 4,200.00
Victorian cylinder-roll desk, walnut
w/burl walnut panels, cylinder roll
opening to numerous compartments
& small drawers, kneehole flanked
by drawers, paneled sides. 4,250.00
Victorian "Davenport" desk, walnut,
slanting felt-covered writing surface
w/three-quarter pierced gallery,

Davenport Desk

four drawers at side, ca. 1870,
restored, 22" w., 36" h. (ILLUS.) 700.00
Victorian drop-front desk, Renaissance
Revival substyle, walnut w/burl
walnut panels, shaped pediment
above shaped molded top w/pr.
short drawers above drop-front
writing surface opening to bird's eye
maple central compartment flanked
by pigeonholes over pr. short
drawers above case w/pr. paneled
cupboard doors flanked by carved
pilasters, molded plinth base,
mid-19th c., 45" w., 54" h. 880.00
Victorian "partner's" desk, walnut,
60 x 48" oblong top w/central
drawer & pull-out slide (each side)
above kneehole flanked by banks
of drawers, 1880s, refinished 2,400.00
Victorian "patent" desk, Wooton
Standard Grade. . . . . . .4,000.00 to 12,000.00
Victorian "patent" desk, Wooton
Extra Grade, walnut w/bird's
eye maple drawers
interior . . . . .15,000.00 to 28,000.00
William & Mary desk-on frame, walnut,
2-piece: upper part w/slant lid on
wrought iron hinges opening to
fitted interior w/pigeonholes over
2 wells & w/two drawers below;
frame w/turned legs joined by box
stretchers, Southern, 1730-50,
43½" w., overall 39" h. (restored
stretchers) 1,540.00
William & Mary slant-front desk, pine,
hinged lid opening to central compartment flanked by drawers &
smaller compartments w/well in
work surface above case w/false
upper drawer over 3 working
drawers, massive ball feet, original

brass drop pulls & much original color & traces of red paint, Massachusetts, ca. 1730, 36¼" w., 45½" h. 12,000.00

DINING SUITES

Mission-style (Arts & Crafts movement) dining suite: 48" d. table, sideboard & 6 chairs; oak, all signed Gustav Stickley, 8 pcs. 6,000.00

Mission-style (Arts & Crafts movement) dining suite: 60" d. pedestal base table w/seven extension leaves, 72" l. sideboard, 2 arm & 10 side chairs; oak, w/label of L. & J.G. Stickley, 14 pcs. 4,500.00

Turn-of-the-Century (Empire Revival) dining suite: 60" d. pedestal base table w/griffin legs, 66" l. sideboard w/beveled mirror in superstructure, 78" h. china cabinet w/mirrored back, 2 arm & 4 side chairs w/leather seats; oak, ca. 1910, 9 pcs. 9,000.00

Turn-of-the-Century (Empire Revival) dining suite: 60" d. pedestal base table w/five extension leaves, "side-by-side" bookcase-desk, china cabinet & 10 chairs; oak w/ornate gargoyle carvings, 1890s, 13 pcs. 9,000.00

Twentieth Century Jacobean Revival dining suite: oblong table, 1 arm & 5 side chairs; walnut, carved baroque crests, finials, splats & stretchers, ca. 1930, 7 pcs. 330.00

Victorian dining suite, Eastlake substyle: table, sideboard & 6 "caneseat" side chairs; cherrywood, 8 pcs. 2,500.00

Victorian dining suite, Elizabethan Revival substyle: round extension table w/pedestal base, 66" h. sideboard w/two-tier superstructure, server w/scroll & leaf-carved backrail, 2 arm & 6 side chairs w/upholstered seats; mahogany w/ornate scroll & leaf carvings, table extending to 144" l., ca. 1880, 11 pcs. 10,200.00

DRESSING GLASSES

Federal dressing glass, inlaid mahogany, framed oblong mirror pivoting on upright supports w/line inlay above base w/bow-fronted central drawer flanked by small lineinlaid drawers, "toupie" feet, 1800-15 . . . . .715.00

Federal dressing glass, mahogany, framed shield-shaped mirror pivoting between shaped supports w/urn finials, oblong case w/bowed front & conforming single drawer,

Dressing Glass with Shield-Shaped Mirror

ogee bracket feet, ca. 1800, w/some repair to one support, 20" w., 27" h. (ILLUS.) 990.00

Federal dressing glass, mahogany, framed oblong mirror pivoting between square uprights flanked by S-scroll brackets above case w/four short drawers, brass ball feet, Boston, Massachusetts, 1810-20, 31½" w., 35" h. 385.00

Federal dressing glass, mahogany veneer on pine, framed oblong mirror pivoting between turned uprights above base w/two drawers faced w/crotch-grained mahogany veneer, ball feet, 1820-30, 32" w. 495.00

DRY SINKS

Cherrywood Dry Sink

Cherrywood dry sink, open work well above pr. paneled cupboard doors opening to shelves, 1-board sides, 65" l. (ILLUS.) 700.00

Chestnut dry sink, open work well above case w/two drawers & pr. paneled cupboard doors, paneled sides 400.00

Painted pine dry sink, open work well above pr. 1-board cupboard doors w/breadboard ends, plank sides, original red-painted finish 950.00

Painted pine dry sink, single shelf

above open work well of dovetail construction in case w/pr. short drawers above pr. paneled cupboard doors, paneled sides, old green paint, 1830-40, 33" w. 975.00

Painted pine dry sink, superstructure w/shaped sides supporting 2-tier shelf above open work well w/flat work surface to side above single drawer, case w/pr. paneled cupboard doors, cut-out bracket feet, old red paint, 56" w., 48" h. 475.00

Painted poplar dry sink, oblong work well above pr. short drawers over paneled cupboard doors, cut-out bracket feet, original dark brown grain-painted finish, Ohio origin 275.00

Primitive pine dry sink, zinc-lined open work well w/backsplash in case w/pr. raised panel cupboard doors, paneled sides, cut-out bracket feet, refinished 675.00

Primitive pine dry sink, zinc-lined open work well w/heart-shaped back splash in case w/pr. raised chamfered panel cupboard doors, original hardware 1,250.00

Primitive pine dry sink, open work well above 2 drawers & pr. paneled cupboard doors, scroll-cut apron continuing to bracket feet, 19th c., 48" w., 36" h. .365.00

Primitive Pine Dry Sink

Primitive pine dry sink, open work well w/narrow shelf raised at rear in case w/pr. 1-board cupboard doors opening to shelves, worn-down base, worn green paint, repairs & old replacement board at bottom, 37½" w., 49½" h. (ILLUS.) 435.00

Primitive pine dry sink, superstructure w/two drawers & open shelf raised above open work well in case w/pr. raised panel cupboard doors flanked

by stiles continuing to form feet, Pennsylvania, early 19th c., 55" w., overall 53" h. .660.00

Shaker dry sink, pine, wide board construction, removable well w/hinged 1-board lid above case w/pr. paneled cupboard doors, bracket feet, yellow washed over red stain, Mt. Lebanon, New York, 51" w., 37" h. (replaced wooden knobs on cupboard doors) 1,350.00

Shaker-style dry sink, pine w/original red-painted finish, open work well above case w/pr. single raised chamfered panel cupboard doors, bracket feet. .975.00

GARDEN & LAWN FURNITURE (Cast Iron)

Cast Iron Garden Armchair

Armchair, Victorian Renaissance substyle, ornate C-scroll grillwork back & geometric cast seat, scrolling foliate arms, stamped "Peter Timmes Son, Brooklyn, New York," ca. 1895 (ILLUS.) 400.00

Armchair, cast w/lacy vintage back & bold acanthus leaf legs, worn white repaint 500.00

Bench, cast w/bent rustic branches, late 19th c., 35" w. 605.00

Bench, cast w/ornate scrolling crest centered w/female mask above entwined openwork ovals, lacy cast seat, foliate cast legs, ca. 1870, 44½" l. 825.00

Bench, Victorian Renaissance substyle, cast three-chairback style of entwining scrolls beneath arched crests, lacy cast seat w/beaded apron hung w/pendant drops, X-form sides forming legs, "J.L. Mott, New York," ca. 1880, 45" l. 440.00

Bench, Victorian Renaissance substyle, cast ornate C-scroll grillwork back & geometric cast seat, scrolling foliate arms, stamped "Peter Timmes Son, Brooklyn, N.Y.," ca. 1895 ....880.00

Victorian Cast Iron Bench

Benches, cast scrolling ferns in shaped back continuing to scrolling arms, lacy cast seat, second half 19th c., large, pr. (ILLUS. of one) 9,075.00

Love seat, bent iron wirework lattice-woven back & shaped arms on cast rod legs joined by iron wirework braces, 36" w., pr. 635.00

Planter, 2 tiers of elongated oval baskets w/roll-over bent iron wire galleries raised on 4 legs w/C-scroll braces & scrolling feet, ca. 1850, 40" l., 37" h....................440.00

HALL RACKS & TREES

Bentwood Hall Rack designed by J. Hoffmann

Hall bench, Mission-style (Arts & Crafts movement), stained oak, raised panels in back & sides, hinged seat lifting to deep compartment for storage, w/decal mark "The Work of L. & J.G. Stickley," early 20th c., 55" w., 37" h. 2,860.00

Hall coat & hat rack, chamfered tapering post fitted w/sixteen pegs for hats, coats, baskets, etc., old worn red & white paint, 52" h. 470.00

Hall coat & hat rack, bentwood, center beveled edge rounded-top mirror plate above semi-circular drawer over shelves & umbrella pan flanked by vertical spindles surmounted by coat hooks, designed by Josef Hoffmann, executed by J.J. Kohn, ca. 1910, 41½" w., 81¾" h. (ILLUS.) 3,300.00

Hall tree, Turn-of-the-Century, golden oak, oblong mirror plate flanked by brass hanging hooks above seat w/lift-lid for storage ......450.00 to 525.00

Victorian Renaissance Hall Tree

Hall tree, Victorian, Renaissance substyle, walnut, pierce-carved crest over molded cornice w/shaped mirror within conforming framework flanked by pierce-carved wings, white marble slab shelf above drawer flanked by umbrella racks (missing drip pans), turned feet, ca. 1865 (ILLUS.) 385.00

Hall tree, Victorian, Renaissance sub-style, walnut, shaped crest centering carved cabochon above dentil-carved frieze over arch-top mirror plate flanked by pilasters hung w/pegs, white marble slab shelf w/drawer below flanked by umbrella racks complete w/pans, large..........1,600.00

Hall tree, Victorian, rococo substyle, walnut, round crest hung w/applied carved grape cluster above open-work molded frame hung w/turned

Victorian Rococo Hall Tree

pegs, shaped oblong mirror plate
pivoting within, white marble slab
shelf w/rounded corners above
drawer raised on ring- and baluster-
turned supports flanked by umbrella
rack, complete w/shell-shaped pans,
shaped base, turned feet (ILLUS.) ...975.00
Hat rack, Victorian, walnut, expand-
able-type w/turned pegs fitted
w/porcelain buttons & brass
rosettes, original finish......35.00 to 50.00
Umbrella stand, Mission-style (Arts &
Crafts movement), oak, 4 straight
supports joined at top by simple
stretchers & at base by oblong
copper-lined pan, early 20th c.,
19¾" w., 29½" h..................110.00

HIGHBOYS

Queen Anne bonnet-top highboy,
walnut, 2-piece: upper part
w/molded swan's neck crest
centering 3 urn & flame finials over
arrangement of 6 short drawers,
w/concave shell-carved upper central
drawer, over 3 long graduated
thumb-molded drawers flanked by
stop-fluted pilasters; lower section
w/long drawer over 3 short drawers
flanked by stop-fluted pilasters,
shaped apron centered w/concave-
carved shell, cabriole legs w/shell-
carved knees, attributed to Joseph
Armitt, Philadelphia, ca. 1755,
42" w., 86" h..................52,800.00
Queen Anne bonnet-top highboy,
cherrywood, 2-piece: upper part
w/molded swan's neck crest
centering 3 spirally-turned finials
above central fan-carved short

Queen Anne Bonnet-Top Highboy

drawer & flanking short drawers
over 4 graduated long thumb-molded
drawers; lower section w/long
shallow drawer over central fan-
carved drawer & flanking drawers,
shaped skirt w/pendant acorn drops,
cabriole legs, shod pad feet,
Connecticut, 1760-80, w/slight
repairs to drawers & crest, 39" w.,
88" h. (ILLUS.)..................23,100.00
Queen Anne flat-top highboy,
mahogany, 2-piece: upper part
w/molded cornice above 2 short &
3 long graduated thumb-molded
drawers; lower section w/long
drawer over central fan-carved
drawer & flanking drawers, shaped
skirt, cabriole legs, pad feet, Salem,
Massachusetts, 1755-75, 36" w.,
69" h. (some repairs to feet)......9,900.00
Queen Anne flat-top highboy, maple,
2-piece: upper part w/coved cornice
above 5 graduated thumb-molded
long drawers; lower section w/shal-
low long drawer above deep fan-
carved short drawer & flanking
drawers, scalloped skirt, cabriole
legs, shod pad feet, Connecticut,
1740-60, 38¾" w., 70 7/8" h.......8,800.00
Queen Anne flat-top highboy, maple,
2-piece: upper part w/molded cornice above 2 short & 4 long graduated thumb-molded drawers; lower
section w/long drawer over fan-
carved central drawer & flanking
drawers, shaped skirt w/acorn drop
pendants, cabriole legs, shod pad

feet, (most) original brass bat's wing
handles, New England, 1760-80,
38¾" w., 74" h. 11,000.00
Queen Anne flat-top highboy, tiger
stripe maple, 2-piece: upper part
w/molded cornice above arrangement of 3 short drawers & 4 long
graduated thumb-molded drawers;
lower section w/long thumb-molded
drawer over central concave fan-
carved drawer & flanking short
drawers, shaped skirt, cabriole legs,
pad feet, original brass bat's wing
handles, attributed to the Dunlap
School, New Hampshire, 1760-80,
38" w., 74" h. 22,000.00
Queen Anne flat-top highboy, walnut,
2-piece: upper part w/molded
cornice above pr. short drawers over
3 long graduated drawers; lower
section w/short central drawer
flanked by deeper drawers,
scalloped skirt w/bell-shaped drop
pendants, cabriole legs, pad feet,
original brass handles, New England,
1730-60, 39¼" w., 63¾" h. (small
patch to one drawer) 7,150.00

ICE BOXES

Oak Ice Box

Maple ice box, 2-door, applied ornate
carvings 475.00
Oak ice box, 2-door, original brass
hardware, small size ..... 300.00 to 400.00
Oak ice box, 3-door, original brass
hardware (ILLUS.) 650.00
Oak ice box, 4-door, 2 glass-fronted
& 2 all wood doors, 45" w., 64" h. ... 475.00
Oak ice box, 4-door, "McCray," 3 glass-
fronted doors & 1 door w/mirror,
55" w., 66" h. 450.00

ICE CREAM PARLOR SETS

Child's ice cream parlor chair, bent
iron frame, wooden seat
(ILLUS.) .... 80.00 to 110.00

Child's Ice Cream Parlor Chair

Child's ice cream parlor set: table
& pr. chairs; round wooden table
top & chair seats, bent iron
frames, 3 pcs. 200.00
Ice cream parlor chair, bent iron
frame w/heart design in back,
wooden seat 55.00
Ice cream parlor table, round black
opaque glass top, bent iron base 300.00
Ice cream parlor table, white opaque
marble glass top, bent iron base 150.00
base 150.00
Ice cream parlor set: table & 4
chairs; laminated wooden wooden
table top & seats, bent iron
frames, ca. 1890, 5 pcs..... 400.00 to 550.00
Ice cream soda fountain stool,
bent iron frame w/arms, wooden
seat .... 60.00 to 125.00

LOVE SEATS, SOFAS & SETTEES

William & Mary Day Bed

Child's settee, bentwood w/caned back
& seat, signed "Thonet-Austria" 450.00
Day bed, American Empire country-
style, maple & oak, "rolling pin"

crestrail at headboard above turned
spindles flanked by turned posts
w/mushroom finials, ca. 1850,
w/new upholstered mattress 1,150.00
Day bed, William & Mary, painted
finish, headboard w/shaped crest
above 5 flattened spindles flanked
by block- and ring-turned uprights,
molded seatrail, ring- and block-
turned legs joined by turned
stretchers, bulbous feet, painted
black w/gilt highlights, New
England, 1730-50, w/velvet-covered
cushion, 60" l. (ILLUS.) 3,300.00
Lounge (fainting couch), Victorian,
Eastlake substyle, oak, typical
machine carvings, 1880-1900 (now
w/blue velvet upholstery) 500.00
Lounge (fainting couch), Victorian,
Louis XV substyle, walnut, finger-
molded frame, ca. 1865 (now
w/tapestry upholstery) 450.00
Lounge (fainting couch), wicker, loom-
woven fiber, painted white, 1930s . . . 365.00
Love seat, Victorian, rococo substyle,
pierce-carved walnut frame, ca.
1860 (replaced upholstery) 3,000.00
Recamier, American Empire (classical
revival), mahogany w/brass inlay,
upholstered scrolled back & seat,
w/volute-carved molded sides,
intersecting line- and beaded brass-
inlaid seatrail, bulbous roundel-
carved legs on brass casters, Boston,
Massachusetts, ca. 1820, 79" l. 5,500.00

Victorian Recamier

Racamier, Victorian, rococo substyle,
carved laminated rosewood,
scrolling crestrail centered w/carved
florals above back w/"tufted" upholstery, serpentine-fronted seatrail,
demi-cabriole legs on casters, attributed to John Henry Belter, New
York, New York, ca. 1855
(ILLUS.) 2,200.00
Settee, American Empire, mahogany,
cylindrical crestrail w/scrolling
leaf-carved terminals above
upholstered back & seat, scrolled
arms faced w/carved swan's necks,

American Empire Mahogany Settee

molded apron, carved winged
animal paw feet, 19th c.,
65" l. (ILLUS.) 1,210.00
Settee, Federal, mahogany w/caned
back & seat, plain rolling crestrail
& high roll-over arms w/caned
panels, plain seatrail, tall animal
paw feet, New York, 1800-15 . . . . 77,000.00
Settee, Federal country-style "arrow-
back" type, poplar & pine, plain
crestrail above arrow-form spindles,
shaped arms on turned supports,
plank seat, turned legs w/stretchers,
early refinishing 1,000.00
Settee, Federal country-style, painted
& decorated, shaped crestrail above
3 wide vase-form splats & 2 turned
uprights flanked by scrolled arms,
seat w/roll-over front, bulbous-
turned legs w/flattened stretchers,
tapering feet, free-hand vintage
motif w/grapes & foliage in shades
of green, gold & brown on cream
ground, Pennsylvania, ca. 1840,
75" l. 770.00
Settee, Mission-style (Arts & Crafts
movement), "fumed" oak, plain
crestrail above upright splats, arms
w/three vertical uprights, plain
seatrail, square legs, 6 leather
cushions, Stickley Brothers "Quaint"
furniture, original finish 600.00
Settee, Victorian rococo substyle,
walnut, undulating finger-molded
frame w/rose-carved crest, upholstered back & serpentine-fronted
seat, ca. 1865, original finish &
upholstery, 66" l. 350.00
Settee, Victorian, rococo substyle,
pierce-carved laminated rosewood
frame, attributed to John Henry
Belter, New York, New York, ca.
1855 . . . . 1,760.00
Settee, Victorian, rococo substyle,
pierce-carved laminated rosewood
frame w/serpentine crest & serpentine-fronted seat, demi-cabriole
legs 2,500.00
Settee, wicker, loom-woven, 2-chair-
back style, upholstered cushions
(ILLUS.) 600.00

Wicker Settee

Settee, Windsor, maple & pine, plain
crestrail above 27 turned spindles,
shaped downswept arms on turned
supports, plank seat, bamboo-turned
legs w/flattened frontal stretcher,
refinished 825.00

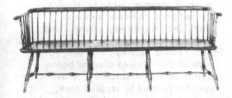

Windsor Settee

Settee, Windsor, shaped backrail continuing to scrolled knuckle handholds above 39 turned spindles,
plank seat, bamboo-turned legs
w/conforming stretchers (ILLUS.)..6,600.00
Settee, Windsor "bow-back," painted
black finish, arched crestrail above
30-spindle back, shaped arms on
shaped supports, plank seat, raking
turned legs w/stretchers, New
England, ca. 1800, 79½" l........3,300.00
Sofa, American Empire, mahogany,
scroll- and leaf-carved crestrail
above upholstered back & scrolling
arms, carved winged animal paw
feet, 1830s, 84" l................4,500.00
Sofa, American Empire, mahogany,
acanthus- and shell-carved crestrail
above upholstered back & scrolling
arms, stylized lyre-form feet,
w/fitted bolsters, Philadelphia,
ca. 1830, 81" l..................1,760.00
Sofa, Chippendale, mahogany, upholstered "camelback" & outward
scrolling arms, seat w/loose
cushion, carved cabriole legs, shod
pad feet, England, ca. 1745,
67¾" l..........................3,920.00
Sofa, Federal, mahogany, oblong crestrail w/central carved swag & tassel

reserve flanked by carved thunder-
bolts & bow-knots above upholstered
back & arms on reeded downswept
supports, reeded seatrail carved
w/flowerhead corners, round
reeded tapering legs on brass
casters, attributed to Duncan Phyfe,
New York, ca. 1810, 71" l.......13,200.00
Sofa, Federal, mahogany, oblong crestrail w/central carved bow-tied wheat
sheaf reserve panel flanked by
carved swags & tassels above
upholstered back & seat, arms
w/reeded incurvate armrails on
reeded baluster-turned supports,
reeded bowed seatrail, ring-turned &
reeded tapering legs w/brass
casters, attributed to Duncan Phyfe,
New York, ca. 1805, 80" l. (minor
repair to one arm)..............25,300.00
Sofa, Federal country-style, mahogany,
shaped upholstered back curving
into flattened arms continuing to
form bold C-scrolls, seat w/loose
cushion, vase- and ring-turned legs,
tapering feet, original finish &
upholstery......................550.00
Sofa, Federal country-style, walnut,
upholstered "camelback" & seat
flanked by scrolling arms, turned
legs, New England, ca. 1850, now
w/wool twill upholstery, 84" l.......990.00
Sofa, Victorian, rococo substyle,
walnut, serpentine crestrail centered
w/carved florals above "tufted"
upholstered back, finger-molded
seatrail, short demi-cabriole legs
(needs refinishing & upholstery)....460.00
Sofa, Victorian, rococo substyle, walnut, upholstered heart-shaped
medallion back in finger-molded
frame w/carved crest (refinished
& replaced upholstery)..........3,200.00

LOWBOYS

Chippendale Lowboy

Chippendale lowboy, cherrywood,
oblong top w/molded edge above

central short shallow drawer flanked
by deeper drawers w/original brass
bat's wing handles, shaped apron
w/two pendant drops, cabriole legs
w/bold shell-carved knees, claw-
and-ball feet, 35½" w.,
28 5/8" h. .10,000.00
Chippendale lowboy, mahogany,
oblong top w/molded edge &
notched corners above single long
drawer & 3 short drawers w/shell-
and acanthus-carved central drawer
& flanking drawers, acanthus-carved
cabriole legs, claw-and-ball feet,
Maryland, ca. 1770, restored,
33" w., 29" h. (ILLUS.) 13,750.00
Queen Anne lowboy, cherrywood,
oblong top w/wide overhang &
molded edge above long drawer
over shallow central & flanking
deeper drawers, original brass bat's
wing handles, fan-carved shaped
apron, cabriole legs, pad feet,
Connecticut, ca. 1750, 36" w.,
29½" h. 25,300.00
Queen Anne lowboy, curly maple,
oblong top w/molded edge above
case w/long drawer over 3 short
drawers, shaped skirt hung w/two
pendant drops, cabriole legs, pad
feet, Massachusetts, ca. 1760,
restored, 32" w., 28¾" h. 8,250.00
Queen Anne lowboy, walnut, oblong
top w/molded edge above case
w/three short thumb-molded drawers,
shaped apron, removable angular
cabriole legs, squared feet, Pennsylvania, ca. 1750, restored, 34" w.,
28½" h. 17,050.00

Queen Anne Lowboy

Queen Anne lowboy, walnut, oblong
top w/molded edge & notched
corners over case w/single long
drawer above 3 short drawers,
shaped skirt, cabriole legs, paneled
trifid feet, Pennsylvania, ca. 1750,
35" w., 30" h. (ILLUS.) 15,400.00

MANTELS

Federal mantel, painted pine,
molded mantelpiece above punch-
carved frieze over fluted panels,
the opening w/flower-carved
border flanked by fluted pilasters,
painted grey, New England,
ca. 1800, 80" w., 48½" h. 1,100.00
Federal mantel, pine, dentil molding
over raised panels w/applied
molding, the opening flanked by
applied moldings, New England,
ca. 1800, 74¾" w., 80½" h. 385.00
Federal country-style mantel, painted
pine, top shelf w/molded edge
above raised central panel section
flanked by wide reeded pilasters,
old worn white repaint, ca. 1840,
75" w., 52½" h. 200.00
Primitive pine mantel, plain shelf
w/applied moldings below, the
opening flanked by simple
pilasters, stripped of finish,
53½" w., 50" h. 85.00
Victorian cottage-style mantel, pop-
lar w/original brown & tan painted
graining on shelf, flattened
pilasters & undershelf frieze
against dark brown ground,
ca. 1865, 61¾" w., 50" h. 220.00

MIRRORS

American Empire "Cheval" Glass

American Empire "cheval" mirror,
mahogany, oblong mirror plate
within framework tilting between
tapering turned columns w/raking
crest above & flattened stretcher
below, on brass casters, New York,
ca. 1815, 44" w., 82" h. (ILLUS.) 2,530.00

American Empire over-mantel mirror,
giltwood, broken cornice hung
w/acorn-shaped spherules above
stylized egg-and-dart molding over a
frieze applied w/classical figures
above 3 panels of glass divided by
colonettes & flanked by fluted
pilasters w/Corinthian capitals over
acanthus-carved molding flanked by
applied carved fleur-de-lis &
garlands, 77½" w., 31" h. 1,320.00

American Empire country-style wall
mirror, painted pine, ogee-molded
framework grain-painted black over
red, original glass, 8" w., 10" h. 85.00

American Empire country-style wall
mirror, painted poplar, half-round
baluster-turned posts w/corner
blocks, worn original flame-painted
graining w/natural finish, applied
turnings trimmed in blue, green &
yellow, 13 x 11" 355.00

American Empire country-style 2-part
wall mirror, painted pine, fluted
framework enclosing mirror plate
below original reverse painted scene
of house & trees, 10½" w.,
16½" h. 145.00

American Empire country-style 2-part
wall mirror, painted pine, half-
round pilasters w/corner blocks,
upper section w/reverse painting now
replaced w/scenic print, original
"speckled" mirror plate below,
15¾" w., 39½" h. 175.00

Chippendale wall mirror, mahogany,
scroll-carved high crest w/scrolling
ears above original mirror plate,
w/conforming pendant below,
16½" w., 31½" h. 1,000.00

Chippendale wall mirror, mahogany,
giltwood & gesso, scroll-carved crest
w/scrolling ears centered w/applied
carved giltwood phoenix bird,
oblong mirror plate within gilt slip,
shaped pendant below, American,
18th c., 18¼" w., 34½" h. (some
restoration) 935.00

Chippendale wall mirror, walnut, giltwood & gesso, shaped crest w/scrol-
ling ears centering an applied
pierced shell-carved giltwood roundel,
acanthus-carved gilt slip centering
oblong mirror plate flanked by gilt
fillets, shaped pendant below,
ca. 1775, 19" w., 38" h. 4,950.00

"Courting" mirror, maple, cushion-
molded frame w/"eglomise" panel
at shaped top, oblong mirror plate
below, Continental, 18th c., 7" w.,
12" h. 605.00

"Courting" mirror, shaped crest, original (worn) mirror plate & traces of
old finish, 18th c., 11" w., 17¼" h. 775.00

Federal "convex" wall mirror, carved
giltwood, circular mirror plate within
egg-and-dart & ogee-molded framework w/carved spread-winged
American eagle finial & acanthus-
carved pendant, 1815-30, 31" d.,
overall 52" h. 880.00

Federal wall mirror, inlaid mahogany
& giltwood, molded swan's neck
crest ending in carved rosettes &
centering a gilt urn w/spray of
flowers over an inlaid oval shell,
2-part mirror plate w/"eglomise"
panel depicting compote of flowers
w/acanthus & flowerhead fillets
flanking, shaped pendant below,
New York, ca. 1795, 23" w.,
58" h. (some repairs) 3,300.00

Federal 2-part wall mirror, giltwood,
broken cornice w/molding hung
w/gilt spherules above molded
gilt slip frieze, "eglomise" panel
w/flower pot above oblong mirror
plate flanked by twisted columns
w/carved capitals, plain molded
base, 1800-20, 24" w., 41 5/8" h. 660.00

18th Century Pine Mirror

Painted pine dressing mirror, shaped
crest pierced w/hole for hanging,
carved & molded frame centering
oblong mirror plate, painted black,
18th c., 11¼" w., 19" h. (ILLUS.) . . . 1,210.00

Queen Anne over-mantel mirror, burl
walnut veneer cushion-molded
frame, beveled glass mirror plate,
probably England, ca. 1750,
47½" w., 19" h. 1,100.00

Queen Anne wall mirror, pine,
scalloped crest centering carved
shell above molded & carved frame
centering mirror plate, original dark

mahogany finish & original mirror
plate, small size 1,650.00

Queen Anne Wall Mirror

Queen Anne style wall mirror,
japanned finish w/gilt decor,
scroll-carved shaped crest above
convex-molded frame enclosing
beveled mirror plate, England, late
18th-early 19th c., 34" w., 54" h.
(ILLUS.) 3,575.00
Turn-of-the-Century hall mirror, golden
oak frame w/four brass hooks
centering beveled mirror plate,
original finish 45.00
Victorian pier mirror, rococo substyle,
carved giltwood, oval mirror plate
within elaborate bead, gadroon &
foliate scroll frame surmounted by
elaborate pierce-carved crest &
w/shaped half-round white marble
console shelf over elaborate giltwood pediment, ca. 1865, 37" w.,
108" h. 990.00
Victorian pier mirror, rococo substyle,
walnut, ornately carved rounded
crest & framework w/gilt gesso surrounding the mirror plate, white
marble slab shelf below, ca. 1850,
48" w., 108" h. 4,000.00
Victorian wall mirror, walnut, ogee-
molded frame, small size (replaced
mirror plate) 70.00

PARLOR SUITES (Victorian)

Eastlake substyle: sofa & pr. side
chairs; walnut, typical incised
carvings, maroon velvet upholstery,
1880s, 3 pcs. .800.00
Eastlake substyle: settee, pr. arm-
chairs & 6 side chairs; walnut,
typical incised carvings, original
finish & upholstery, 9 pcs. 1,300.00

Louis XV substyle: sofa & lady's
parlor armchair; walnut, finger-
molded frames & grape-carved
crests, demi-cabriole legs, medal-
lion-upholstered backs, 2 pcs. 1,100.00

Victorian Parlor Suite

Louis XV substyle: sofa & lady's &
gentleman's armchairs; rosewood,
finger-molded frames w/grape-carved
crests & "tufted" upholstery in ser-
pentine-back sofa & balloon-back
chairs, 3 pcs. (ILLUS. of part) 2,640.00
Louis XV substyle: medallion-back
sofa, lady's & gentleman's balloon-
back armchairs & 4 balloon-back
side chairs; walnut, finger-molded
frames & serpentine-fronted upholstered seats, 7 pcs. . . . .3,500.00 to 5,000.00
Louis XV substyle: love seat, lady's &
gentleman's armchairs & 4 side
chairs; walnut, plain finger-
molded frames, green velvet up-
holstery, 7 pcs. 1,900.00
Renaissance Revival substyle: settee
& armchair; rosewood, each
scrolled crestrail centered
w/circular painted plaque depicting
classical female & w/padded open
armrests ending in classical female
bust portrait & Egyptian heads,
fluted cylindrical legs, attributed
to Herter Brothers, New York,
ca. 1860, 49" l. settee, 2 pcs. 3,190.00
Renaissance Revival substyle: settee,
armchair & pr. side chairs; rosewood, carved in the manner of John
Jelliff w/portrait busts in relief at
crest, damask upholstery, ca.
1865, 4 pcs. .2,530.00
Rococo substyle: lady's & gentleman's
armchairs & 4 side chairs; pierce-
carved laminated rosewood in the
manner of Belter, New York, ca.
1855, 6 pcs. .7,500.00

SCREENS

Candle screen, Victorian, needlepoint canvas in rosewood frame
on tripod base w/scrolling feet,
62½" h. pole 495.00
Folding screen, 4-fold, painted wall-

paper, one side depicting harbor
scene & other side w/country cottage in pastoral landscape, late
18th c., each panel 20½" w.,
64" h. 3,410.00
Folding screen, 6-fold, Chinese
coromandel lacquer, presentation
piece w/names of high-ranking
official's grandsons & nephews on
reverse, early 19th c., each panel
15" w., 71" h. 3,850.00
Folding screen, 6-fold, Charles X,
painted paper, depicting boatmen,
equestrian figures on the banks
of the Seine, the Palais Royal,
Porte Saint-Denis & the Pantheon,
in shades of blue, ochre & red,
France, early 19th c., each panel
16" w., 84" h. 7,425.00
Folding screen, 6-fold, George III,
leather w/polychrome & gilt decor
in the chinoiserie taste w/scenes
of Chinese at various pursuits,
England, ca. 1760, each panel
22" w., 96" h. 9,900.00
Folding screen, 8-fold, painted
paper, depicting Chinese figures in
pavilions in landscape setting,
shades of red, salmon pink, blue &
green highlighted w/gilding, China,
late 18th c., each panel 21½" w.,
83" h. 13,200.00
Folding screen, 8-fold, black coro-
mandel lacquer, 1 side w/contin-
uous scene depicting court scene
bordered w/bat, mask & medallion
motifs & other side w/continuous
landscape scene w/birds bordered
by a bamboo motif above vase,
urn & censer motifs, brass-capped
arched feet, 20th c., each panel
18" w., 96" h. 2,200.00
Pole screen, Federal, mahogany,
shield-shaped embroidered screen
adjusting on turned standard,
cabriole legs, snake feet, New
England, ca. 1795, overall 54" h. 825.00
Pole screen, Queen Anne,
mahogany, oblong crewel-work
on canvas screen depicting a
branch sprouting w/variety of
berries, florals & leaves over hilly
landscape w/sheep, rabbit, deer,
fox & butterfly, adjusting on turned
standard w/shaped finial, cabriole
legs, shod slipper feet, Newport,
Rhode Island, 1740-70, 16¾ x 14¼"
panel, overall 45½" h. 1,870.00
Pole screen, Queen Anne, walnut,
embroidered needlework screen
w/urn of flowers adjustable on
standard, cabriole legs, pad feet,
New York, ca. 1785, 20½" w.
screen, overall 59½" h. (ILLUS.) . . .2,090.00

Queen Anne Pole Screen

Pole screen, Victorian, rococo
substyle, rosewood & mahogany,
Berlin woolwork in scrolling framework adjustable on standard w/urn
finial, tripod base w/reverse-scrolled
legs, ca. 1865 (replaced urn finial). . .275.00

SECRETARIES
American Empire "secretaire a
abattant" (w/fall-front), mahogany
veneer, attributed to the workshop
of Duncan Phyfe, New York,
1825-30 . . . . .17,600.00
American Empire "secretaire a
abattant" (w/fall-front), mahogany
w/ormolu mounts, attributed to
Anthony Quervelle, Philadelphia,
1820-30 . . . . .9,900.00
American Empire secretary table-desk,
tiger stripe maple, 2-part construction: upper part w/coved
cornice above pr. paneled cupboard
doors opening to shelves & flanked
by half-round turned & reeded
pilasters; desk-table w/single
drawer, ring- and vase-turned legs,
tapering feet 9,000.00
Biedermeier secretary-bookcase,
mahogany & birch, 2-part construction: upper part w/molded cornice
above central birch-faced cupboard
door flanked by pr. arch-paneled
cupboard doors faced in birch; lower
section w/fall-front writing surface
exposing central cupboard door
flanked by document drawers &
surrounded by small drawers above
case w/three long drawers, block
feet, Germany, 1800-25, 41½" w.,
78" h. 3,190.00
Chippendale secretary-bookcase, tiger
stripe maple, 2-part construction:
upper part w/swan's neck cresting

ending in carved rosettes above arched & geometrically glazed cupboard doors opening to shelves; lower section w/hinged slant-lid opening to valanced pigeonholes, central fan-carved drawer flanked by columnar document drawers & short drawers above case w/four thumb-molded & graduated long drawers, ogee bracket feet, New England, ca. 1780, 40" w., 80" h. (restorations to top & interior) 9,625.00

Federal secretary-bookcase, cherrywood, 2-part construction: upper part w/molded swan's neck cresting centering 3 spiral-carved wooden finials above frieze w/inlaid pinwheel device & pr. paneled cupboard doors opening to shelves & flanked by fluted quarter columns; lower section w/bellflower-inlaid slant-lid opening to fitted interior w/nine short drawers above case w/four graduated long drawers, flaring bracket feet, Vermont, ca. 1810, 38½" w., 89" h. 17,600.00

Federal Secretary-Bookcase

Federal secretary-bookcase, inlaid mahogany & curly maple, 2-part construction: upper part w/shaped crest centering a curly maple reserve & mounted w/three urn-form finials above pr. arch-top glazed & mullioned doors opening to shelves above pr. short cockbeaded drawers w/ivory keyhole escutcheons; lower section w/single long cockbeaded drawer above pr. cupboard doors, ring-turned circular tapering legs, New England, ca. 1810, some inlay repairs, 38" w., 76" h. (ILLUS.) 2,310.00

Federal secretary-bookcase, inlaid walnut, 2-piece construction: upper part w/molded cornice above bellflower-inlaid frieze & pr. paneled cupboard doors opening to shelves; lower section w/hinged slant-lid opening to central fan-inlaid prospect door flanked by valanced pigeonholes over short drawers above case w/four line-inlaid long drawers w/original brass drop ring handles, (replaced) oblong feet, Pennsylvania, ca. 1800, 42" w., 91" h. . . .4,950.00

Federal country-style secretary-bookcase, painted maple, 2-part construction: upper part w/molded coved cornice above pr. paneled cupboard doors opening to shelves; lower section w/hinged slant-lid lifting to storage space above 2 drawers w/turned pulls, square tapering legs, old red-painted finish, ca. 1840, small size 950.00

Federal country-style secretary tabledesk, primitive pine, 2-part construction: upper part w/steeply pitched raking cornice w/applied molding above pr. paneled cupboard doors opening to shelves; lower section w/hinged slant-lid lifting to storage space, square tapering legs w/chamfered corners, ca. 1850 . . . . .425.00

Turn-of-the-Century "side-by-side" secretary-bookcase, oak, drop-front desk w/compartmented interior above 3 drawers & surmounted by oval mirror beside glazed "curio" (or bookcase) cabinet, applied machine carvings to drop-front & drawers, brass handles, ca. 1910 . . . .450.00 to 595.00

Victorian drop-front secretary bookcase, walnut & burl walnut, 2-part construction: upper part w/arched crest centering urn-turned finial & frieze w/applied central roundel above pr. arch-top glazed cupboard doors opening to shelves; lower section w/drop-front opening to pigeonholes & small drawers above case w/two short drawers over 2 long drawers, all w/pear-shaped wooden drop handles, plinth base, ca. 1880 . . . . .2,100.00 to 2,500.00

Victorian (late) cylinder-roll secretary-bookcase, oak, 2-part construction: upper part w/molded cornice above pr. glazed doors opening to shelves; lower section w/cylinder rolling to expose numerous compartments above case w/long drawers, original finish 1,095.00

Victorian cylinder-roll secretary-bookcase, walnut & burl walnut, 2-part construction: upper part w/molded

Victorian Cylinder-Roll Secretary Bookcase

cornice & ornate crest above pr.
glazed cupboard doors; lower
section w/cylinder rolling to expose
numerous pigeonholes & small
drawers above case w/pr. cupboard
doors, plinth base (ILLUS.) 1,800.00

SHELVES

Victorian Shelves

Candle shelf, pine, D-shaped top
w/protruding ears supported on
gracefully curved center bracket,
square nail construction, ca. 1810,
15" w. at top, 10½" to top of
shelf 195.00
Clock shelf, oak, early 20th c. . . 22.00 to 30.00
Clock shelf, walnut, ornate, small,
late 19th c. . . . . .45.00 to 85.00

Clock shelf, Victorian, Eastlake
substyle, walnut, typical carvings,
w/drawer below shelf, small 70.00
Corner hanging shelf, walnut,
bracket supports w/carved rope
edge details, 12" w., 12" h. 45.00
Corner hanging shelves, walnut,
3-tier w/deepest shelf at center,
shaped sides, 13¼" w., 30" h. 115.00
Corner hanging shelves, tiger stripe
maple, 5-tier w/mirrored back, early
20th c. 225.00
Floor standing shelves, Victorian,
rosewood, 4-tier, shaped sides,
ca. 1850, 36" w., 50" h., pr.
(ILLUS. of one) 2,420.00
Hanging shelf w/mirror & lift-top
compartment, oak, scrolling &
pierced architectural round-top
mirror frame over lift-top compartment w/serpentine front, original
finish & decal label "Variety
Bracket Works, South Bend,
Indiana, Sept. 24, '72," 13¾" w.,
26¼" h. 145.00
Hanging shelves, 3-tier, graduated
shelves, scalloped ends, early 19th
c., 16½" w., 20½" h. 330.00
Hanging shelves, mahogany, 3-tier,
"whale" ends, old dark finish,
21¼" w., 26¾" h. (small old
repair to one tail) 450.00
Hanging shelves, cherrywood, 4-tier,
detailed cut-out shaped ends, nice
old finish, New England, early
19th c., 29½" w., 42¼" h. 775.00

SIDEBOARDS

Federal sideboard, Hepplewhite-style,
inlaid mahogany, oblong top w/ser-
pentine front above conforming case
w/central frieze drawer above pr.
cupboard doors flanked by cupboard
doors, all w/line inlay, square bellflower-inlaid tapering legs w/cross-
banded cuffs, Baltimore, Maryland,
ca. 1790, 72" w., 40" h. 7,425.00
Federal sideboard, Hepplewhite style,
inlaid mahogany, oblong top w/ser-
pentine front above conforming case
w/three short drawers over pr. cupboard doors & pr. bottle drawers,
square tapering legs w/cross-
banded cuffs, 1795-1810, 71" w.,
42" h. 4,125.00
Federal sideboard, Sheraton-style,
maple & tiger stripe maple, oblong
top w/bowed front above conforming case w/short drawer over
concave-carved drawer flanked
by bow-fronted cabinets, ring- and
baluster-turned legs, tapering feet,
ca. 1810, small size. 610.00
Federal sideboard, Sheraton-style,

brass-inlaid mahogany, oblong top w/rear splashboard flanked by brass side rails above case w/three brass-inlaid shallow drawers over pr. central cupboard doors & side cupboards separated by stop-fluted & acanthus-carved half colonettes, baluster-turned legs, brass animal paw feet, New York, ca. 1815, 73½" w., 50½" h. (repair to 2 feet).........................4,950.00

Federal country-style hunt board, cherrywood, oblong top, plain apron w/pr. short drawers w/turned mushroom pulls, square tapering legs ..9,500.00

Federal country-style hunt board, Southern pine, oblong top, mortised & pinned apron w/pr. short drawers, square tapering legs, 60" w., 42¼" h. (refinished & w/replaced brass oval drop ring handles) 1,800.00

Jacobean Revival sideboard, oak, 2-part construction: superstructure w/stepped cornice supported by caryatids over backboard w/geometric & floral carvings; lower section w/oblong top w/gadrooned edge over pr. short drawers centering grotesque mask pulls above pr. cupboard doors w/applied geometric carvings flanked by lion masks, late 19th-early 20th c., 60½" w., 72" h..................220.00

Mission-Style Sideboard

Mission-style (Arts & Crafts movement) sideboard, stained oak, backboard banded to form plate rack at rear of oblong top above pr. short drawers over single long drawer, original hammered metal pulls, in the manner of Gustav Stickley, early 20th c. (ILLUS.) ....385.00 to 550.00

Mission-style sideboard, oak, w/label of Charles P. Limbert Co............350.00

Mission-style sideboard, oak, oblong top above pr. central cupboard doors opening to shelves flanked by 3 short drawers w/single long drawer

below all, square legs, w/hammered copper handles & hinges, w/paper label of L. & J.G. Stickley, ca. 1905 ..440.00

Turn-of-the-Century sideboard, golden oak w/quarter-sawn oak veneer, 2-part construction: superstructure w/shaped top above cabinet doors w/bent glass panels flanked by mirror-backed open shelves; base w/convex split drawers over serpentine cabinet doors & long drawer flanked by fluted columns, flattened melon-shaped feet, ca. 1900, 51" w., 86" h. 650.00

Turn-of-the-Century Sideboard

Turn-of-the-Century sideboard, golden oak, 2-part construction: superstructure w/ornately carved crest over mirror-backed shelf arrangement on cornucopia-carved supports; base w/pr. short convex-fronted drawers over bow-fronted drawer & pr. paneled cupboard doors w/applied fruit carvings, molded base, C-scroll feet, 54" w., 84" h. (ILLUS.) 2,450.00

Turn-of-the-Century sideboard, golden oak, 2-part construction: superstructure centered w/beveled mirror plate & shelves on columnar supports headed by winged griffins; base w/arrangement of drawers & cupboard doors...................760.00

Victorian sideboard, Eastlake-eclectic style, walnut, 2-part construction: superstructure w/pierce-carved crest centering turned finial above mirror-backed 2-tier shelf arrangement on turned supports; base w/oblong top over 3 frieze drawers & 3 machine-carved cupboard doors w/pr. drawers below, plinth base, 61" w., 95" h. 1,650.00

Victorian Sideboard

Victorian sideboard, Renaissance substyle, walnut, 2-part construction:
superstructure w/ornate arched
crest w/applied carving of hanging
game above shelf over oval mirror
backing; base w/mottled pink marble
slab top above arrangement of short
drawers over pr. cupboard doors
also w/applied pendant game
carvings, plinth base (ILLUS.) 2,800.00

STANDS

Federal Basin Stand

Basin stand, Federal country-style,
painted & decorated, squared top
pierced for basin w/shaped back-
splash & three-quarter gallery,
plain frieze, turned legs joined by
medial shelf w/drawer below,

turned & tapering feet, free-hand
fruit & striping on yellow grain-
painted & swirled ground, ca. 1830
(ILLUS.) 725.00
Basin stand, Federal country-style,
painted & decorated, squared top
pierced for basin & 2 receptacles
w/shaped three-quarter gallery,
plain frieze, ring-turned legs joined
by medial shelf w/drawer below,
tapering turned feet, decorated
w/transfer scenes at shaped
gallery, apron & drawer front. 600.00
Basin stand, corner-type, Federal,
mahogany & bird's eye maple,
oblong top pierced for basin &
receptacles w/shaped backsplash
& shaped apron, square tapering
legs joined by medial shelf
w/drawer below & lower T-shaped
stretcher-shelf, flaring feet, Salem,
Massachusetts, 21½" w.,
38½" h. 4,950.00
Basin stand, corner-type, Federal,
inlaid mahogany, oblong top
pierced for basin & receptacles
w/shaped three-quarter gallery,
shaped apron, line-inlaid square
legs joined by medial shelf
w/line-inlaid drawer below, flaring
feet, New England, ca. 1815,
22½" w., 15" deep, 39" h. 2,090.00
Butler's tray-top stand, Federal
Sheraton style, curly maple,
dovetailed tray w/straight-sided
gallery pierced w/hand holds on
baluster-turned X-bar folding base
w/flattened stretchers, warm
brown finish, 30¼ x 20½" tray,
33½" h. 1,800.00
Crock stand, primitive pine, 3-tier,
dark green painted finish, 52" w.,
26" deep, 36½" h. 115.00
Plant stand, Victorian, Eastlake
substyle, oak, low style,
original finish 58.00
Sewing stand, American Empire, crotch
mahogany veneer, oblong top
w/molded edge flanked by
D-shaped drop leaves, case w/three
convex-molded short drawers
w/turned wood pulls over veneered
"sewing bag" between columnar
uprights on C-scroll feet joined by
turned stretcher 1,210.00
Sewing stand, American Empire
country-style, cherrywood, oblong
top flanked by D-shaped drop
leaves, case w/two short convex-
molded drawers w/turned pulls,
ring- and baluster-turned legs,
flattened ball feet, ca. 1840,
17¾" x 21" top plus drop leaves,
28" h. (ILLUS.) 600.00

American Empire Country-Style Stand

Sewing stand, Victorian, walnut &
burl walnut veneer, lobed top
lifting to fitted interior w/inlaid
compartments, conforming apron
w/single drawer, turned standard
w/carved lower section on scrolling
tripod base, England, late 19th c.,
21" w., 30½" h.....................302.50
Wash stand, Federal country-style,
cherrywood, poplar & other woods,
plain oblong top w/backsplash
flanked by towel bars, apron
w/single drawer, turned legs
joined by medial stretcher shelf,
worn old red finish, 31½" w.,
20" deep, 33¾" h. 250.00
Wash stand, Victorian cottage-style,
grain-painted finish, oblong top
w/backsplash flanked by towel
bars, apron w/single drawer,
turned legs joined by medial
stretcher-shelf 165.00

STOOLS

Early 19th Century Stool

Foot stool, oak, Mission-style (Arts &
Crafts movement), upholstered top,
refinished, 15 x 12¾" top, 9¾" h. 99.00
Foot stool, painted pine, oblong top
w/carved "pillow" center, turned
tapering splayed legs, old green
paint, 12½ x 6¾" top, 8¾" h. 95.00
Foot stool, painted finish, Hepplewhite
country-style, early 19th c. (ILLUS.) ...95.00
Foot stool, painted finish, Zoar-type,
2-board top w/shaped trestle-
type sides w/stretcher, original
brown paint......................75.00
Foot stool, pine & poplar, oblong top,
scalloped apron, cut-out sides
mortised through top, old worn blue
repaint w/traces of red & green
below, 15 x 7" top, 6 5/8" h. 65.00
Foot stool, tiger stripe maple, oblong
top, shaped apron, cut-out sides
forming feet, refinished, 14 x 6½"
top, 7" h. 225.00
Foot stool w/lift-top, walnut w/needle-
point upholstered cushion top, ogee-
molded frame, late 19th c., 20 x 16"
top, 10" h. 65.00
Milking stool, chestnut 25.00
Piano stool, oak or walnut, round
seat swiveling on column w/four
adjacent legs w/cast iron claw &
glass ball feet, each ....65.00 to 90.00
Weaver's stool, narrow semi-circular
seat, 3 "pencil post" legs, old red
repaint, 19 x 3½" seat, 27" h.
(damage to corner of seat) 95.00

American Empire Stools

American Empire stools, "classical,"
upholstered seat over cherrywood
curule base joined by ring-turned
medial stretcher, Massachusetts,
ca. 1820, 19½" l., 19" h., pr.
(ILLUS.) 2,090.00
Mission-style stool, oak, w/paper
label of "Gustav Stickley," Syracuse,
New York, ca. 1912, 20 x 15" seat,
15" h. 385.00
Victorian (late) stool, maple, caned
oval seat, turned splayed legs
w/stretchers, 13 x 10" oval seat,
17" h. 85.00
William & Mary stool, birch, square
seat, molded skirt, sausage-turned
legs w/medial H-stretcher, possibly
Canada, ca. 1700, 19 x 18" seat,
18" h. 412.50
Windsor "high" stool, shaped seat,
turned splayed legs w/stretchers,
early 19th c......................137.00

TABLES

American Empire Work Table

American Empire card table, mahogany, in the classical taste, oblong folding top w/canted corners above conformingly shaped apron, on acanthus-carved dolphin standard & acanthus-carved uprights, shaped plinth base on acanthus-carved gilt & "verte" painted dolphin feet on brass casters, New York, ca. 1820, 37" w., 29½" h. 3,850.00

American Empire drop-leaf table, cherrywood & mahogany, D-shaped top w/single oblong drop leaf, ogee-molded apron, bulbous ring-turned legs, turned feet, ca. 1835, top opening to 40" l., 29" h. 198.00

American Empire drop-leaf table, mahogany, oblong top w/shaped drop leaves on acanthus-carved pedestal continuing to tetrapod w/hairy paw feet, 38¾" x 22¾" top w/14¼" drop leaves, 27" h. (repairs to base & refinished) 375.00

American Empire work table, mahogany w/crotch mahogany veneer, oblong hinged top lifting to reveal mirror on underside above baize-lined surface also lifting to reveal fitted interior, case w/convex frieze drawer over deep concave-arched drawer over gadrooned edge, acanthus-carved urn-form standard on shaped oblong base w/acanthus-carved lion's paw feet on casters, attributed to Anthony Quervelle, Philadelphia, 1820-30, 22¾ x 17" top, 29½" h. (ILLUS.) 1,320.00

American Empire country-style Pem-

broke table, oblong top w/shaped drop leaves, plain apron, rope-carved & ring-turned legs w/ball feet on casters, 40 x 14½" top w/13" drop leaves, 30½" h. 550.00

Art Nouveau 2-tier table, fruitwood marquetry, shield-form top inlaid w/daisy garland raised on 3 twisted reeded legs joined by galleried stretcher-shelf near feet, branded "L. Majorelle," ca. 1900, 20" w., 29¾" h. 1,540.00

Chippendale drop-leaf dining table, mahogany, oblong top w/D-shaped drop leaves, shaped skirt, scroll- and bellflower-carved cabriole legs, claw-and-ball feet w/under-cut talons, Newport, Rhode Island, ca. 1765, w/some carvings of later date, 53 x 52" extended top, 29" h. 6,050.00

Chippendale drop-leaf dining table, maple, oblong top w/rounded ends flanked by half-round drop leaves, turned tapering legs, claw-and-ball feet, Northern New England, 1770-1800, 52 x 46" extended top, 28½" h. (some repairs) 2,310.00

Chippendale tilt-top tea table, cherrywood, square top tilting above baluster-turned standard, downswept tripod, elongated claw-and-ball feet, New England, 1770-90, 33" sq. top, 27" h. 1,210.00

Chippendale Tilt-Top Tea Table

Chippendale tilt-top tea table, mahogany, round dished top w/molded edge tilting & revolving above birdcage support, ring- and ball-turned standard, cabriole legs, claw-and-ball feet, Philadelphia, ca. 1770, 32¾" d., 28½" h. (ILLUS.) 10,450.00

Chippendale tilt-top tea table, walnut, round dished top tilting above birdcage support, baluster-turned standard, tripod cabriole legs, claw-and-ball feet, Pennsylvania, 1770-1790, 35" top d., 28" h. 1,870.00

Federal 2-part banquet table, inlaid mahogany, D-shaped end sections w/deep drop leaves, plain apron, reeded tapering legs on brass ball feet, New York, ca. 1810, 90 x 52" extended top, 28½" h...........14,300.00

Federal 3-part banquet table, inlaid mahogany, center section w/oblong top flanked by deep drop leaves & D-shaped ends w/drop leaves, apron w/inlaid stringing, ring-turned & reeded tapering legs, baluster- and ball-turned feet, 1810-20, 95½ x 48½" extended top, 28¼" h. (damage to one leaf).........................3,740.00

Federal card table, birch w/bird's eye maple inlay, oblong folding top above conformingly shaped frieze centering bird's eye maple inlaid reserve flanked by oblong inlaid dies, ring-turned & reeded tapering legs, turned feet, Dunlap School, New Hampshire, ca. 1810, 35 x 15½" folded top, 28" h. 3,410.00

Federal card table, inlaid mahogany, oblong folding top w/projecting center opening to felt-lined playing surface above conformingly shaped frieze centering inlaid oval floral reserve flanked by flower-inlaid dies, square tapering legs, cross-banded cuffs, Baltimore, Maryland, ca. 1800, 35¾ x 17" folded top, 29" h.......................7,150.00

Federal country-style drop-leaf dining table, cherrywood top & maple base, oblong top w/deep drop leaves, plain apron, turned legs, original flame-grain painted finish ..950.00

Federal Pembroke table, inlaid mahogany, oblong top flanked by short D-shaped drop leaves, apron w/single drawer, square tapering legs w/cross-banded cuffs, New England, ca. 1805, 37 x 34½" extended top, 29" h..............1,430.00

Federal Pembroke table, tiger stripe maple, oblong top w/rounded ends flanked by half-round drop leaves, plain apron w/drawer in one end, square chamfered legs w/cross-stretchers, New York, 1790-1810, 39 x 32¼" extended oval top, 27¾" h.......................3,300.00

Federal serving table, mahogany, oblong top w/outset rounded front corners & reeded edge, apron w/pr. paneled drawers flanked by reeded colonettes, baluster- and ring-turned

Federal Serving Table

legs joined by medial shelf, brass ball feet & brass casters, New York, ca. 1815, repairs to shelf & 1 leg, 36 x 18" top, 37" h. (ILLUS.) 3,300.00

Federal "reverse-serpentine" side table, inlaid walnut, oblong top w/reverse serpentine front edge above conformingly shaped apron w/single drawer, bellflower-inlaid dies above square tapering & line-inlaid, cross-banded cuffs, Maryland, ca. 1800, 41 x 22" top, 34½" h. 2,750.00

Federal side table, yellow pine, D-shaped top, square tapering legs, 1800-10, 40" w. 880.00

Federal work table, inlaid mahogany & curly maple, oblong top w/outset rounded corners above 2-drawer frieze flanked by ring-turned three-quarter columns continuing to ring-turned & reeded tapering legs, Eastern Massachusetts, ca. 1810, 19" sq. top, 28" h. 1,760.00

Federal country-style side table, curly maple, square top, plain apron, turned legs 350.00

Federal country-style work table, cherrywood & bird's eye maple, New England, ca. 1835, 19" w., 28" h. 605.00

Harvest table, primitive pine, oblong top w/single drop leaf, plain apron, turned tapering legs, turned feet, Pennsylvania, ca. 1830, 68 x 38" extended top, 26" h. 880.00

Hutch table, pine & birch, 2-board round pine top tilting on mortised & pinned birch frame w/nailed pine seat, 42" d., 29½" h. .800.00

Mission-style (Arts & Crafts movement) center table, stained oak, oblong top, apron w/single drawer, square legs joined by stretcher-shelf, w/remnants of Gustav

Mission Style Center Table

Stickley red decal mark, 36" w.,
30½" h. (ILLUS.) 605.00

Queen Anne Breakfast Table

Queen Anne drop-leaf breakfast-size
table, painted maple, narrow oblong
top w/rounded ends flanked by
D-shaped drop leaves, shaped
apron, cabriole legs, pad feet,
w/worn red-painted graining on
base, Massachusetts, ca. 1750, top
opening to 30" d., 27½" h.
(ILLUS.) 22,000.00
Queen Anne drop-leaf dining table,
mahogany, oblong top flanked by
oblong drop leaves, scalloped
skirt, cabriole legs, pad feet,
Massachusetts, 1740-60, 43 3/8 x
42½" extended top, 28" h. 2,860.00
Saloon table, round oak top, cast iron
base, w/patent of 1886 by Hinkel
of Milwaukee, 48" d. 385.00
Tavern table, maple & pine, oblong
2-board pine top, plain apron, ring-
turned legs w/box stretcher, New
England, 1760-80, 31 x 20" top,
25" h. 1,045.00
Tavern table, maple, oval top, plain
apron, turned & tapering legs,

button feet, New England, 1780-
1800, 32 x 23½" oval top, 27" h. 1,760.00
Tavern table, maple & pine, oblong
top w/breadboard ends, apron
w/single drawer, vase- and
ring-turned legs w/box stretcher,
painted red, New England, 1750-80,
37 x 22" top, 24¾" h. (feet
reduced in height) 660.00

Painted Pine & Maple Tavern Table

Tavern table, painted pine & maple,
oblong top w/breadboard ends,
apron w/single drawer, vase- and
ring-turned legs w/box stretcher, ball
feet, w/traces of old red paint on
base, ca. 1750, 44 x 23½" top, 26" h.
(ILLUS.) 7,425.00
Tavern table, walnut, oblong top
w/molded edge, plain apron,
baluster- and ring-turned legs w/box
stretcher, turned feet, Pennsylvania, 1780-1810, 43" w., 28" h.
(top reset) 770.00
Victorian card table, mahogany &
walnut, oblong folding top, apron
w/burl-inlaid panels & applied
carved garlands fitted w/drawer
at each end, turned tapering legs
on casters, 38¼ x 19½" folded top,
28¾" h. 1,430.00
Victorian drop-leaf dining table,
walnut, oblong extension-type top
w/rounded ends & half-round drop
leaves, plain apron, turned legs,
turnip feet on casters, ca. 1875,
w/three leaves 750.00
Victorian dining table, mahogany,
round extension-type top, plain
apron, reeded urn standard
w/massive shaped legs, claw-and-
ball feet, late 19th c., original
finish, 54½" d., w/four leaves 660.00
Victorian dining table, mahogany
& mahogany veneer, square
extension-type top w/gadrooned
border, plain conforming apron,
round pedestal w/acanthus-carved
band, curving legs w/acanthus-

carved knees & paw feet, late
19th c., 48" sq. top, 30" h.,
w/six leaves 550.00

Victorian Parlor Center Table

Victorian parlor center table, rococo
substyle, mahogany w/white
marble "turtle" top, shaped apron
w/boldly carved florals, semi-
cabriole legs w/carved bellflowers
at knees continuing to foliate-
carved toes, shaped X-stretcher
centered w/turned urn finial,
ca. 1860, 44 x 31" top, 31" h.
(ILLUS.) 1,320.00
Wicker oval-top table, painted white,
1920s. 285.00

WHATNOTS & ETAGERES

Art Nouveau Etagere

Etagere, walnut, 3-tier, w/inlaid floral
marquetry, signed Galle', France,
ca. 1900, 48" h. (ILLUS.) 4,500.00
Etagere, Victorian, rococo substyle,
walnut, superstructure w/3-mirror

back & ornately-carved crest over
serpentine-fronted quarter-round
shelves supported on S-scrolls above
base w/serpentine-fronted marble
slab over conformingly shaped
drawer, short scrolling feet, 63" w.,
99" h. 6,500.00

Victorian Etagere

Etagere, Victorian, rococo substyle,
pierced & scrolled crest w/urn-
shaped finial over central mirror
plate flanked by shaped side
mirrors & shelves on turned
supports, shaped white marble slab
shelf over conforming apron on
pierced & scrolled supports rising
from conformingly-molded serpentine base, ca. 1860, 50" w., 102" h.
(ILLUS.) 1,760.00
Etagere, Victorian, ornate wicker,
oval mirror at shaped crest above
long half-round shelf above arrangement of 4 half-shelves & long shelf
at base, wicker cabriole legs 1,700.00
Whatnot, corner-type, Victorian,
bamboo-turned & lacquer, wedge-
shaped rounded shelves randomly
placed between bamboo-turned
uprights, England, ca. 1870,
12" deep, 62" h. 160.00
Whatnot, Victorian, rococo substyle,
walnut, 4-tier, pierced & scrolled
crest above 4 serpentine shelves
w/molded edges, pierced & scrolled
fretwork-molded side supports,
molded feet, ca. 1865, 40" w.,
72" h. (minor damage to fretwork) . . 425.00
Whatnot, Victorian, rococo substyle,
walnut, 5-tier (needs refinishing) . . . 250.00
Whatnot, Victorian, cottage-style,
walnut, 5-tier, plain rounded shelves
on spool-turned uprights, ca. 1890,
original finish 150.00

WICKER FURNITURE

by Connie Morningstar

Although the first Wicker came to America on the *Mayflower*, it was not until the 1880s that the twins, Rattan and Reed, wove their way into American hearts and parlors. In the next generation, Willow, Raffia, the Grasses, and the adoptee Fiber, also were admired and popular members of the family.

The Wickers are of Scandinavian origin, their name a translation of the Swedish *vikker* meaning "willow" and *vika*, "to bend." The name is applied to any woven item--furniture, baskets, carriages, lamps, etc.

Cyrus Wakefield, Boston grocer-cum-entrepreneur, is credited with being the first to realize the potential of rattan. Once considered good only for packing the cargoes of ships in the China trade, rattan was routinely dumped on the docks when the ships were unloaded. Wakefield salvaged this material and sold it to local basketmakers who stripped the vine and used only the inner reed. The outer bark (cane) was then sold to chairmakers for seats.

In 1884, Wakefield established the Wakefield Rattan Company in South Reading (later re-named Wakefield), Mass. He had experimented with the idea of wrapping wooden chairs with rattan, but the process was tedious and his firm concentrated instead on the importing and wholesaling of rattan until about 1854 when one Sylvanus Sawyer perfected an automatic machine for trimming, splitting, and shaving rattan strips. In one day, this machine could do the work of 200 hand-strippers and did it infinitely better. Wicker furniture thus became commercially feasible.

But it was a tad slow to catch on. Pliable, paintable, stainable reed began to be used in the 1860s. Most of it was intended for garden furniture and was left in its natural state or only slightly stained. In keeping with the taste of the times, dark tones predominated in the parlor. By the 1870s, numerous items in several fancy patterns were available.

The Golden Age of Wicker arrived with the 1880s. In each of the first three years of the decade, wicker furniture production doubled that of the preceding year so that by 1884 Wakefield was turning out over $1,000,000 worth of goods annually. This was matched by the firm's chief competitor, Heywood Brothers and Company of Gardner, Mass.

The time was right. Victorian passion for elaborate over-decoration was in full swing. After-the-Fair fascination with oriental motifs continued, and the material, itself from the mysterious Orient, was inexpensive and easily worked into the curlicues and arabesques, hearts and fans that were so fashionable in the Victorian parlor.

Hardwoods were used for structural members and all but seat rims and rockers were wrapped in rattan. Seats usually were caned. A light varnish was the usual finish but colors were becoming popular and could range from white to red, green, lavender, gold, bronze or black.

New in 1884 was the chaise lounge with rattan frame and upholstered seat. Blue or crimson silk plush upholstery against yellow rattan was considered especially chic. In Chicago, a Wakefield spokesman noted that his firm had furnished an entire room in rattan using that material for all woodwork, doors, casings - even the mantel. Several patterns of chamber suites also were available.

Chicago led the world in the production of all parlor furniture in the 1880s. Major wicker manufacturers there included Charles W. H. Frederick, Western Rattan Company, Parthier & Greve, and George J. Schmidt & Brother. In order to meet this competition for the developing market in the western states, both Heywood and Wakefield established factories in the city. Heywood & Morrill Rattan Company was the western branch of the Gardner firm. In 1897, these furniture giants merged to form Heywood Brothers & Wakefield Company and became the country's largest importer of rattan and manufacturer of wicker products.

Wicker designs followed the trends of the Mission movement about the turn of the century and, by 1910, the elaborate curlicues and arabesques of the preceding generation were passe. Lines straightened and a man-made twisted paper product called fiber reed or art fiber largely replaced imported rattan.

Fiber furniture was turned out by most manufacturers and by the end of the 1920s, it accounted for about eighty percent of the nation's wicker production. Firms such as Grand Rapids Fibre Cord Company offered the material in kit form for home assembly. Although most furniture items were available in fiber, breakfast sets and radio tables were especially popular. Multicolored finishes were much in demand.

In 1917, Marshall B. Lloyd and Lewis Larsen invented the Lloyd Loom, a machine that wove a steel-cored fiber strand into a tight, reed-like cloth that was then fitted over bentwood frames to produce sturdy, comfortable wicker furniture and carriages.

The Lloyd Manufacturing Company quickly captured the public's fancy with the new material. Four years later, its Menominee, Mich., plant and patent were purchased by the Heywood-Wakefield Company, the corporate name adopted at that time. The Lloyd label continued to be used for many years thereafter, however, and the Menominee plant was, in 1982, the last of the Heywood-Wakefield organization to succumb to bankruptcy.

Changing fashions, particularly the emergence of Art Moderne, relegated wicker to the attic in the 1930s. Some forty years later, a revival of interest in things Victorian brought the survivors into favor again and encouraged a rash of reproductions. Although the fancy patterns of the 1880s seem to be preferred, fiber pieces (including a copy of a 1917 Lloyd Loom chair) are being reproduced.

The sixth annual all-wicker auction of the Montgomery Auction Exchange, Montgomery, N.Y., was held May, 1984 in which the highest price received for a single item was $1050 for a 19th-century, three-shelf stand with sheet music holder. A similar, fully-restored piece is listed at $2800 in the catalog of a New England dealer. An elaborate painted easel brought the highest price, $1400, at the Hidden Treasures auction in West Allis, Wis., in June, 1984.

Suites, of course, bring more. An ornate, turn-of-the-century painted wicker parlor suite consisting of settee, two rockers, and two armchairs went for $3575 in New Orleans in October, 1983. At the Montgomery auction, it was $1200 for a fancy 19th-century three-piece ensemble. And a 20th-century dining suite of round table and six chairs with upholstered seats brought $1700 at the Wisconsin auction.

A number of dealers currently specialize in old wicker furniture. They include Elizabeth & Richard King, Inc., Tracy Road, Northeast Harbor, ME 04662 (catalog, $5), The Wicker Garden, 1318 Madison Ave., New York, NY 10128 (catalog, $7.50), and A Summer Place, 1310 Boston Post Road, Guilford, CT 06437.

(Editor's Note: *Connie Morningstar is respected for her diligent furniture research. She delves into the records of early cabinetmakers, furniture shops and factories and writes with accuracy, authority and clarity about various American furniture styles. She is the author of several books on furniture, including* EARLY UTAH FURNITURE, *numerous articles for various periodicals and is a regular bi-monthly columnist for* THE ANTIQUE TRADER WEEKLY *newspaper.*)

*   *   *   *   *

BABY BASSINETS, CRADLES, ETC.

Wicker Bassinet

Bassinet on ornate base, w/mosquito netting hook at one end (ILLUS.) . . . $400.00

Buggy, loom-woven fiber, hood w/"opera" windows, spoke wheels . . . . 200.00 to 275.00

Buggy, loom-woven fiber, deluxe model w/teardrop-shaped "opera" windows in hood, wooden handle, hand brake, wooden spoke wheels w/rubber tires 275.00

Buggy for twins, loom-woven fiber, hood w/"opera" windows, spoke wheels 375.00

Carriage, push-type, red plush-lined interior & black parasol, wooden spoke wheels . . . . 400.00 to 600.00

Wicker Cradle

Cradle, platform-type, late 19th c.
(ILLUS.)..........................950.00

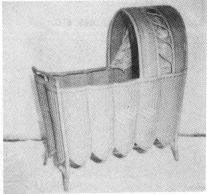

Hooded Crib

Crib, hooded-type, loom-woven fiber
(ILLUS.)..........................700.00
Stroller, 2-wheel rickshaw-type push
cart.....................200.00 to 400.00

CHAIRS

Ornate Wicker Chair

Armchair, curlicue trim, cane seat,
ca. 1905 (ILLUS.)..................275.00
Armchair, ornate scrollwork, roll-over
arms, Victorian, late 19th c........247.00

Painted White Wicker Chair

Armchair, C-scroll heart motif back,
roll-over crestrail continuing to
downswept arms, original cane seat
now w/upholstery, painted white,
Victorian, late 19th c. (ILLUS).......270.00

Heywood Brothers & Wakefield Chair

Armchair, rolled arms, attributed to
Heywood Brothers & Wakefield,
Wakefield, Massachusetts, ca. 1898,
36¾" h. at back (ILLUS.)...........995.00

Ornate Wicker Chairs

Armchair-divan, heart medallion &
curlicue back w/roll-over crest
continuing to roll-over arms, ca.
1899, 28″ w. seat (ILLUS. left) 400.00
Corner armchair, shaped back above
scrolling latticework continuing to
roll-over arms, ca. 1903 (ILLUS.
right)..........................300.00
Corner armchair, ornate, original cane
seat now replaced w/upholstery,
1899-1905......................130.00
Corner armchair, ornate, original
finish, Heywood Brothers & Wakefield, ca. 1897 ....450.00

Corner Armchair

Corner armchair, ornate, woven
rush seat, 1899-1905 (ILLUS.) 125.00

"Fancy" Wicker Chair

Photographer's studio prop "fancy"
chair, curlicue trim, stained finish
(ILLUS.)..........................375.00

Photographer's studio prop "fancy"
chair, curlicue trim, stained
finish, caned seats.......325.00 to 400.00
Platform rocker, attributed to
Heywood Brothers & Wakefield Co.,
natural finish...................375.00

Patented Wicker Chair

Platform rocker, "The Ordway Chair,"
by A.H. Ordway & Co., Framingham,
Massachusetts, 1890 & '93 patents,
natural finish (ILLUS.) 2,800.00
Platform rocker, "The Ordway Chair,"
1890 & '93 patents 375.00

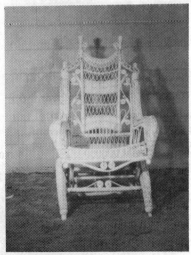

Wicker Platform Rocker

Platform rocker, painted white, ca. 1900
(ILLUS.)..........................350.00
Rocker w/arms, roll-over crest &
wrapped & scrolled uprights, cane
back & seat, wrapped cabriole legs,
ca. 1880 ....175.00

Lacy Wicker Rocker

Rocker w/arms, lacy back w/"fiddle" design, cane seat now w/upholstery, 1885-95 (ILLUS.)..................200.00

Ornate Wicker Rocker

Rocker w/arms, ornate w/numerous curlicues, cane seat, natural finish (ILLUS.)..........................500.00

Matching Wicker Rockers

Rockers w/arms, roll-over crestrail continuing to arms & ending in C-scrolls, late 19th c., pr. (ILLUS.) 600.00

White Wicker Rocker

Rocker w/arms, roll-over crestrail continuing to arms & shaped apron, painted white (ILLUS) 235.00

Rocker w/arms, ornate, roll-over crest continuing to roll-over arms, back w/variety of scroll & bobbin motifs, late 19th c. 275.00

Sewing rocker, oblong back w/lacy woven panel, cane seat, wrapped legs w/scrolling bentwood stretchers, late 19th c.............165.00

Victorian Wicker Side Chairs

Side chair, heart motif back w/curli-cues (ILLUS. left) 200.00

Side chair, curlicue back, cane seat, late 19th c. (ILLUS. center).........150.00

Side chair, cane seat & back (ILLUS. right).........................200.00

Side chair, ornate scrollwork & curli-cues, wrapped legs, late 19th c......165.00

Side chair, ornate, numerous curlicues, wrapped legs, late 19th c..........225.00

Side chair, roll-over balloon back, cane seat, elaborate curlicues, natural

Heywood Wakefield Chair

finish, Heywood Brothers & Wake-
field Company (ILLUS.) 500.00

Wicker Chair with Cane Back

Side chair, cane back, roll-over crestrail continuing to form side & seat
rails, wrapped legs, 1890s (ILLUS.) . .375.00

Early 20th Century Chair

Side chair, ornate back, round seat
w/deeply scalloped apron (ILLUS.) . .225.00

CHILDREN'S CHAIRS

Wicker Highchair

Highchair, ornate back, wrapped legs,
painted white (ILLUS.) 175.00
Highchair, various styles, painted
white, early 20th c. . . . . . . .150.00 to 225.00
"Potty" chair, loom-woven skirt,
w/original wooden lid to cover seat,
painted white . . . . .60.00 to 125.00
Rocker w/arms, high back, ornate,
painted white, 1890s 225.00
Rocker w/arms, loom-woven fiber,
roll-over crest continuing to arms,
painted white, 1920s . . . . . . .60.00 to 125.00
Side chair, ornate style, original brown
& green paint, 1890s. 140.00

DESKS

Wicker Desks

Lady's desk, kidney-shaped top
w/letter rack in three-quarter gallery,
single drawer in apron (ILLUS. left) . .350.00
Lady's desk, oblong top w/letter rack
in three-quarter gallery, wrapped
bentwood braces & legs w/stretchers
(ILLUS. right) 275.00
Lady's desk & chair, oblong top w/four-
drawer superstructure, single drawer
in apron, trestle base, w/matching chair,
painted white, late 19th c., 2 pcs. . . .247.50

Writing Table-Desk & Chair

Lady's writing table-desk & chair,
  oblong top w/rounded ends, loom-
  woven fiber, dark stain finish, 2 pcs.
  (ILLUS.)..........................290.00

DINING CHAIRS & SUITES
Dining chairs, loom-woven fiber,
  ornate, ca. 1917, restored & painted
  white, set of 4 ....700.00

Wicker Dining Suite

Dining table & 4 chairs, wooden round-
  top table w/woven apron & chairs
  w/wedge-shaped seats, 5 pcs.
  (ILLUS.)..........................750.00

Dining Table & Chairs

Dining table & 6 chairs, wooden
  round-top table w/loom-woven apron,
  square pedestal base & high-back
  chairs w/cushion seats, painted
  white, 7 pcs. (ILLUS.).............1,700.00

LAMPS

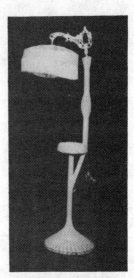

Wicker Floor Lamp

Floor lamp, so-called "Bridge" lamp
  w/ash tray holder fitted to standard (no glass insert), painted white
  (ILLUS.)..........................350.00
Floor lamp, domical lacy shade,
  tall square standard w/flaring base,
  30" d. shade, 67" h. 700.00

Floor Lamp with Fringed Shade

Floor lamp, domical shade w/original
  fringe, tall square standard w/flaring
  base (ILLUS.) 475.00
Floor lamps, various styles...175.00 to 600.00

Wicker Table Lamp

Table lamp, domical shade w/metal
cap, cylindrical standard w/expanding
base (ILLUS.) 140.00
Table lamp, domed shade & cylindrical
base .90.00 to 185.00

Wicker Table & Lamp

Table lamp on stand, complete
(ILLUS.) 850.00

LOUNGES, LOVE SEATS, SOFAS & SETTEES

Wicker Chaise Lounge

Chaise lounge, slanting back flanked by
wings continuing to arms, w/loose
cushion in seat, natural finish,
20th c. (ILLUS.) 375.00

1920s Wicker Chaise Lounge

Chaise lounge, loom-woven fiber,
w/upholstered loose cushion, 20th c.
(ILLUS.) 650.00
Chaise lounge, roll-over crest above
latticework back, oblong cane seat
w/single high scrolling end,
valanced apron, late 19th c., 74" l. . .385.00

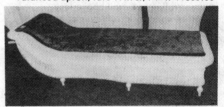

Lounge or Day Bed

Day bed or lounge, roll-over seat rail,
lattice-woven apron, wrapped legs,
upholstered velvet cushion (ILLUS.). .225.00

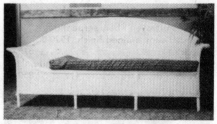

Wicker Day Bed

Day bed, loom-woven fiber, arched
back seat w/angled headrest,
plain apron, wrapped legs, 1930s
(ILLUS.) 300.00
Settee, arched crestrail above solid
cane back, oblong seat flanked by
scrolling arms, deep apron, complete
w/cushions, late 19th c., 73" l. 330.00
Settee, roll-over crestrail above tightly
woven back flanked by roll-over
arms, upholstered seat, tightly woven

Wicker Settee

apron, painted white, late 19th c.
(ILLUS.) 425.00

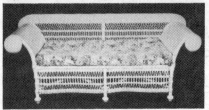

Attributed to Wakefield Rattan Co.

Settee, rolling crestrail above lacy
   latticework back, roll-over arms, seat
   w/loose cushions, lacy apron,
   wrapped legs, attributed to Wake-
   field Rattan Co., 1885 (ILLUS.) 950.00

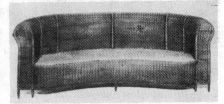

Loom-Woven Fiber Sofa

Sofa, loom-woven fiber, serpentine-
   fronted seat, stained finish, 1920-30
   (ILLUS.) 575.00
Sofa, loom-woven fiber, painted white,
   1920s 350.00

PORCH, PARLOR & VERANDA SUITES

Settee & Chairs

Suite: settee & pr. armchairs;
   double chairback settee & highback
   chairs w/curlicues below arms,
   painted white, upholstered seats,
   ca. 1900, 3 pcs. (ILLUS.) 675.00

Late 19th Century Suite

Suite: settee & pr. armchairs; roll-
   over crestrail & arms, back w/woven
   design incorporating spindles &
   curlicues, cane seats, legs joined
   by X-stretchers, late 19th c., 3 pcs.
   (ILLUS.) 1,100.00

Three Piece Suite

Suite: settee, armchair & rocker; latticework back w/roll-over crest continuing
   to arms, cane seats, shaped apron,
   natural finish, ca. 1900, 3 pcs.
   (ILLUS.) 750.00

Suite with Coil Spring Cushions

Suite: sofa, armchair & rocker; loom-
   woven fiber, painted white, w/loose
   coil spring cushion seats, 1925-35,
   3 pcs. (ILLUS.) . . . . 850.00 to 1,000.00

Upholstered Wicker Suite

Suite: sofa, armchair & rocker; loom-woven fiber, painted white, uphol-stered back & sides & coil spring cushions, 1925-36, 3 pcs. (ILLUS.) 450.00

Four-Piece Suite

Suite: settee, pr. armchairs & square table; natural finish, 1920s, 4 pcs. (ILLUS.) 750.00
Suite: sofa, low-back rocker w/arms, day bed & porch swing; loom-woven fiber, painted white, w/upholstered coil spring cushions, 4 pcs. 2,000.00

Five-Piece Suite

Suite: sofa, chaise lounge, pr. armchairs & oval-top table; loom-woven fiber, painted white, w/loose coil spring cushions, ca. 1930, 5 pcs. (ILLUS.) 1,100.00
Suite: sofa, armchair, rocking chair, table & floor lamp base; loom-woven fiber w/diamond design in backs & aprons, 1920s, 5 pcs. 650.00
Suite: settee, pr. armchairs, pr. end tables, coffee table & floor lamp w/shade; woven reed, Philippine Islands, 20th c., 7 pcs............1,045.00

STANDS

Fern Stand with Bird Cage Top

Fern stand, basket top, 3-legged base w/medial shelf, 33" h..............35.00
Fern stand, square container top w/bowed sides & woven accents, turned legs w/X-stretcher, ca. 1890, 10¼" sq. container, overall 36½" h. 70.00
Fern stand, oblong container on legs joined by X-stretcher, painted white, 1930s, 30 x 11", 31" h. ....60.00 to 75.00
Fern stand, oblong container w/bird cage top, painted white, 1920s (ILLUS.) ....275.00 to 375.00

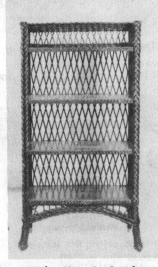

Wicker Magazine Stand

Magazine or book stand, 4-tier, 1920s (ILLUS.)...........................300.00

Wicker Music Stands

Sheet music stand, 2-tier (ILLUS. left) ..450.00
Sheet music stand, 3-tier (ILLUS. right) ....550.00 to 675.00
Sheet music stand, 4-tier (ILLUS. right) 1,050.00

Two-Tier Stand & Music Stand

Two-tier stand, curlicue trim at legs
(ILLUS. left) 300.00

Wicker Stands

Two-tier stand, oblong top, spingle
apron w/curlicue brackets,
wrapped legs (ILLUS. left) 300.00
Two-tier stand, oblong top, pendant
drop apron, D-shaped side shelves
raised on spindle supports above
bottom tier, wrapped legs (ILLUS.
right)............................375.00

Wicker Stands

Two-tier stands, oblong top, spindle &
curlicue apron, wrapped legs, ball
feet, matching pr. (ILLUS.) 350.00

TABLES

Drop-leaf table, loom-woven fiber
apron, wrapped legs joined by X-
stretcher 300.00

Large Wicker Table

Oblong-top table, wooden oblong top
w/braided wicker edge, woven
apron & corner brackets, lower
shelf w/woven apron, flaring feet
(ILLUS.) 550.00

Oval-Top Double Pedestal Table

Oval-top table, oval woven top & roll-
over apron, double pedestal on
shaped platform base on casters
(ILLUS.) ....400.00 to 600.00

Late Victorian Table

Round-top table, round bird's eye
maple top w/shaped edge,
woven apron, wrapped legs
w/ball details, X-braces &
stretcher, 1890s (ILLUS.) 600.00

Ornate Wicker Tables

Round-top table, round wooden
top, woven apron, shaped legs
w/curlicue details & medial
stretcher-shelf, Heywood Brothers,
1890s, 22" d. top, 29½" h.
(ILLUS. left) 575.00

Round-top table, round wooden top,
apron w/elaborate curlicue details,
legs joined by shaped stretcher
w/S-scroll details, 1890s (ILLUS.
right)........................... 350.00

Sewing table, lift-top, bamboo legs,
ca. 1885 .... 125.00

Elaborate Square Table

Square-top table, square wooden top
w/molded edge, woven apron, ornate
leg brackets & center shelf supported
on X-stretcher (ILLUS.)............. 575.00

MISCELLANEOUS WICKER ITEMS
Bed tray, reverse-painted blue bird
applied w/real feathers under glass
insert, 16 x 8" 15.00
Carpet beater................. 14.00 to 32.00
Clothes hamper, small size, painted
white 48.00
Clothes hamper, large size, painted
white 85.00

Ornate Easel with Mirror

Easel w/mirror, ornate heart motif
w/numerous curlicue details
(ILLUS.) 1,400.00

Invalid's Chair

Invalid's chair on wheels,
late 19th c. (ILLUS.)............... 252.00

Wicker Log Basket

Log basket, painted white (ILLUS.) 50.00

Ottoman

Ottoman, Chittenden & Eastman Co.,
  Burlington, Iowa, 1901-02, 16" sq.,
  16" h. (ILLUS.) 65.00

Wicker Phonograph Console

Phonograph, "Victrola," ca. 1915, 46" h.
  (ILLUS.) ....1,100.00 to 1,750.00
Picnic hamper, suitcase-type,
  20th c. ....20.00 to 35.00
Porch swing, loom-woven fiber,
  20th c...........................350.00

Wicker Screen

Screen, 3-fold, closely woven panels,
  curlicue trim at crest (ILLUS.) 375.00

Wicker Tea Cart

Tea cart, 2-tier w/removable
  glass-lined tray top, 14" d. wheels
  w/rubber tires, 1915-25
  (ILLUS.) ....450.00 to 650.00
Tray, serving-type, 18" d. 25.00
Tray, serving-type, w/butterfly &
  flower pressed under glass center ...55.00

Corner Whatnot

Whatnot, corner-type, 5-tier w/basket-
  shelf at base, ornate scrolling
  curlicues throughout, painted
  white (ILLUS.)...................2,000.00

*The illustrations in the "special focus"
section are through the courtesy of
Montgomery Auction Exchange, Inc.,
Montgomery, New York and Hidden
Treasures Auction and Appraisal Service,
Milwaukee, Wisconsin. The Montgomery
Auction Exchange held their seventh
annual wicker auction in May, 1985 and
Hidden Treasures inaugurated its first
annual all wicker auction in June, 1984.*

Wicker Glossary

Rush *is perhaps the oldest and most common member of the wicker family. Since very early times, the tall, wiry, pliable stems of various perennial marsh grasses have been woven for chair seats and backs.*

Rattan *has become the generic name for any number of vinelike, climbing palms native to Malaysia. It is left natural or varnished.*

Reed, *the strong, fibrous, pliable core of the rattan vine, has been used for furniture since the mid-19th century. Reed can be painted, stained, or varnished.*

Cane *is the hard outer layer or bark of the rattan vine that has been peeled off in long, narrow, glossy strips and woven for chair seats and backs. It was introduced into Europe in the mid-17th century and is still popular today.*

Raffia, *the coarse frond of a palm grown in Madagascar (now Malagasy Republic), was used to wrap post-Victorian wicker furniture.*

Sea Grass, *a product of China, was imported during the early 20th century. Dried sea weed was twisted by hand to make a ropelike material that was then hand woven over a metal-braced wooden frame. The natural color is variegated green and tan. Pieces usually are trimmed around the edges with contrasting colors.*

Prairie Grass *is an American twisted-straw product similar to sea grass. It was used about 1910-1930.*

Willow *as a wicker furniture material was in vogue between about 1900 and 1930. Unlike rattan and reed, willow provided its own support or frame and the pieces were woven much like a basket. Willow's strong, smooth, blond surface could easily be stained or enameled. Favored stains were grey, green, and brown. While many colors were used, pastels in pink, blue, and ivory were most popular in the mid-1920s.*

Fiber, *a machine-twisted wood pulp product, was developed about the time of World War I as a substitute for the more expensive and imported reed. It remained popular through the 1920s. Fiber is the only member of the wicker family that cannot tolerate being stripped or washed with water.*

(End of Furniture Section)

GAMES

Early Games, Puzzles & Books

Also see ADVERTISING ITEMS, AVIATION COLLECTIBLES, CHARACTER COLLECTIBLES and DISNEY COLLECTIBLES.

Above the Clouds, Milton Bradley $10.00
Alphabet Game, Parker Bros., 1893 . . . 115.00
Arithmetic Game, tin, Buffalo Toy & Tool Works. 20.00
Around the World with Nellie Bly, McLoughlin Bros., 1890 . . . . 65.00
Authors card game, McLoughlin Bros., 1902 . . . . 20.00
Candy Land, Milton Bradley, No. 4700, 1955, original box 19.50
Checkerboard, painted red & black squares within black border, applied molded edge, 10¾" sq. 235.00
Game of States, Milton Bradley, 1954 . . . 15.00
Game of Troublesome Pigs, McLoughlin Bros. 35.00
Going to the Fire, Parker Bros., early 1900s. 25.00
Going to Market card game, Willy's Overland Co., 1915. . . . . 45.00
Goldilocks & The Three Bears, McLoughlin Bros., 1890 . . . . 110.00
How Silas Popped the Question, Parker Bros., 1920s 15.00
In Dixie Land card game, Fireside Game Co., 1897 . . . . 65.00
Jolly Old Maid card game, Parker Bros. 25.00
Katch Dart, wooden paddles, suction cup darts, original box, 1930 . . . . 15.00
Lindy - The New Flying Game, Parker Bros., 1927 . . . . 18.50
Madame LeNormand's Gypsy Fortune Telling, 36 cards, w/instructions 12.00
Mah Jong, plastic tiles & counters in original wooden box 70.00
Meteor, clay marble game, ca. 1910 . . . 65.00
Shoot the Hat card game, McLoughlin Bros., 1892. . . . . 12.00
Snap card game, McLoughlin Bros. 12.00
Swinging 'round the Circle, McLoughlin Bros. 185.00
Walter Johnson Baseball 45.00

GLASS

ACORN

This pattern was made in a limited number of pieces in both opaque and translucent colored glass. Resembling the fruit of the oak tree, after which it is named, this glass is thought to have been first produced at Hobbs Glass Co., Wheeling, West Virginia, about 1890 and was later made by the Beaumont Glass Co., Martins Ferry, Ohio. Collectors are alerted to the fact that the more plentiful salt shakers are sometimes ground down and offered for sale as toothpick holders, somewhat scarcer in this pattern.

Salt shaker w/original top, blue
  opaque $25.00
Salt shaker w/original top, char-
  treuse opaque 55.00
Salt shaker w/original top, pink shading
  to white opaque 35.00
Salt shaker w/original top, white
  opaque 45.00
Salt & pepper shakers w/original tops,
  blue opaque, pr. 55.00
Sugar shaker w/original top, black
  amethyst 115.00
Sugar shaker w/original top, blue
  opaque, w/gold spattered decor 90.00
Sugar shaker w/original top, pink
  shading to white opaque 140.00
Syrup pitcher w/original top, emerald
  green translucent 125.00
Syrup pitcher w/original top, pink 160.00
Toothpick holder, pink shading to
  white opaque .65.00
Toothpick holder, pink shading to
  white opaque, w/enameled decor . . .75.00

AGATA

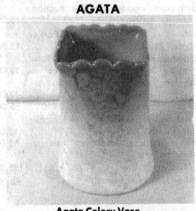

Agata Celery Vase

Agata was patented by Joseph Locke of the New England Glass Co., in 1887. The application of a mineral stain left a mottled effect on the surface of the article. It was applied chiefly to the Wild Rose (Peach Blow) line but sometimes was applied as a border on pale opaque green. In production for a short time, it is scarce. Items listed below are of the Wild Rose line unless otherwise noted.

Bowl, 5" d., crimped rim . . . . $550.00 to 975.00
Bowl, 9" d., 3 3/8" h., green
  opaque . . . . .1,475.00 to 1,550.00
Celery vase, 6¼" h. (ILLUS.) 1,300.00
Cruet w/replaced stopper. 800.00
Cruet w/original stopper, green
  opaque 1,000.00
Mustard pot w/silverplate top,
  3" h. 910.00
Pitcher, 6 3/8" h., crimped rim 1,650.00
Tumbler 540.00

AKRO AGATE

Child's Cup & Saucer

This marbled ware was made by the Akro Agate Company in Clarksburg, West Va., between 1932 and 1951 and most articles bear on the reverse side the likeness of a crow flying through a capital letter A. The majority of these pieces were small.

Ash tray, shell-shaped, marbleized
  blue swirls in white opaque $15.00
Bowl, 3 3/8" d., child's playtime
  item, Octagonal-O patt., marbleized
  lemonade & oxblood 30.00
Cigarette holder, green opaque 5.00
Creamer, child's playtime item,
  Octagonal-O patt., marbleized
  lemonade & oxblood 30.00
Creamer, child's playtime item, green
  translucent 8.00

Cup & saucer, child's playtime item,
Chiquita patt., Azure blue trans-
lucent (ILLUS.) 13.50

Cup & saucer, child's playtime item,
Octagonal-O patt., marbleized
lemonade & oxblood 32.00

Cup & saucer, child's playtime item,
Raised Daisy patt., green opaque cup
& yellow opaque saucer 35.00

Flower pot, marbleized orange swirls
in white opaque 12.00

Lemonade set, child's playtime item:
lemonade pitcher & 6 tumblers;
green translucent, 7 pcs. 50.00

Planter, pumpkin, 6" l. 7.50

Plate, 4¼" w., child's playtime item,
Octagon patt., lemonade & oxblood . . 17.50

Plate, child's playtime item, marbleized
lemonade & oxblood 15.00

Powder jar, Colonial lady cover, blue
opaque, 6" h. . . . . 48.50 to 65.00

Powder jar, Colonial lady cover, pink
opaque, 6" h. . . . . 35.00 to 48.00

Powder jar, Scottie dog cover, white
opaque 55.00

Shaving mug w/lid, blue opaque 15.00

Stippled Band Pattern Teapot

Teapot, cov., child's playtime item,
Stippled Band patt., Azure blue
transparent (ILLUS.) 15.00

Teapot, cov., child's playtime item,
pumpkin 125.00

Tea set, 8 pcs. in original "Little
American Maid" box 40.00

Tea set, child's playtime item:
cov. teapot, 6 tumblers, 2 plates
& 2 c/s; ultramarine, 13 pcs. 45.00

Tea set, child's playtime item:
creamer, sugar bowl, 4 plates &
4 c/s; amber translucent, 14 pcs. 65.00

Tea set, child's playtime item,
blue opaque, 15 pcs. 65.00

Tumbler, child's playtime item, white
opaque, 2" h. 3.00

Water set, child's playtime item:
pitcher & 4 tumblers; green opaque,
5 pcs. 25.00

Vases, marbleized green & tan swirls
in white opaque, pr. 10.00

ALEXANDRITE

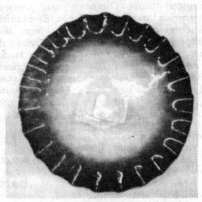

Alexandrite Bowl

This glass, shading from a yellowish color to rose to blue, was produced by Thomas Webb & Sons and Stevens & Williams of England. A somewhat similar ware was made by Moser of Carlsbad.

Bowl, 3¼" widest d., 3½" h., flared
rim $585.00

Bowl, 4½" w., 2" h., ruffled rim,
Honeycomb patt. (ILLUS.) 750.00

Bowl & underplate, crimped rim,
Thomas Webb & Sons, 5" d. bowl,
6½" d. plate, overall 2¼" h., pr. . . 1,085.00

Goblets, 16-optic bowl, polished
hexagonal clear stem, set of 10 . . . . . 200.00

Plate, 8" d. 75.00

Toothpick holder, hat-shaped,
2 7/8" d., 2" h. 905.00

Tumbler, juice, Honeycomb patt.,
2 3/8" d., 3 5/8" h. 345.00

Vase, 2 5/8" h., 2½" d., bulbous
w/fluted top 560.00

Vase, 3" h., 2½" d., folded over star-
shaped top, Honeycomb patt. 605.00

Vase, 4¼" h., 2½" d., Honeycomb
patt. 560.00

Wine, Baby Thumbprint patt., amber
stem & foot, Thomas Webb & Sons,
4½" h. 800.00

Wine, Honeycomb patt., 4½" h. 705.00

AMBERINA

Amberina Canoe Dish

Amberina was devised by the New England Glass Company, and pressed Amberina was made by Hobbs, Brockunier & Company (under a license from the former) and by other glass factories. A similar ware called Rose Amber was made by Mt. Washington Glass Works. The glass shades from amber to red. Cut and plated Amberina also were made. About the turn of this century and again in the 1920s, the Libbey Glass Co. made some Amberina.

Basket, waisted cylinder w/fan-shaped
    top, applied amber handle, signed
    Libbey, 7½" h. plus handle $1,500.00
Bowl, 5 3/8" d., 2¾" h., waisted
    sides, scalloped rim 175.00
Bowl, 6" w., 4¼" h., tricornered,
    3 applied clear scrolling feet, Swirl
    patt., enameled gold branches, leaves
    & white florals outlined in gold 200.00
Butter dish, cover & ice liner (few
    grains undissolved sand) 355.00
Celery vase, cylindrical w/square
    top & scalloped rim, Diamond Quilted
    patt., Mt. Washington, 6½" h. 250.00
Champagne, hollow stem, 6" h. 200.00
Creamer & open sugar bowl, Plated
    Amberina, squat form, New Eng-
    land Glass Co., 1886, pr. 5,500.00
Cruet w/original faceted stopper,
    applied amber handle, Reverse
    Amberina, Inverted Thumbprint
    patt., 6¾" h. 245.00
Cruet w/faceted amber stopper, ap-
    plied amber handle, Baby Thumb-
    print patt., New England Glass Co.,
    ca. 1880, 7¾" h. 275.00
Cruet w/original stopper, Venetian
    Diamond patt., Mt. Washington 285.00
Dish, canoe-shaped, pressed Daisy
    & Button (101) patt., Hobbs,
    Brockunier & Co., late 19th c.,
    8" l. (ILLUS.) . . . . 650.00 to 800.00
Ice cream dish, pressed Daisy & Button
    (101) patt., Hobbs, Brockunier & Co.,
    late 19th c., 5½" sq. 150.00
Mug, applied ribbed handle, Baby
    Thumbprint patt., 2½" h. 135.00

Amberina Mug

Mug, barrel-shaped, applied amber
    handle, Swirl patt., 3¾" h. (ILLUS.) . . 120.00
Pitcher, 4½" h., tricornered straight-
    sided neck w/rounded angles,
    bulbous body, applied reeded
    handle, polished pontil 105.00
Pitcher, tankard, 5" h., 3 3/8" d.,
    applied amber handle, Honeycomb
    patt., Thomas Webb & Sons 330.00

Amberina Pitcher

Pitcher, 7" h., squared rim, applied
    amber reeded handle, Inverted
    Thumbprint patt., New England
    Glass Co., 1883 (ILLUS.) 220.00
Pitcher, 7½" h., melon-ribbed, applied
    handle, Reverse Amberina, Inverted
    Thumbprint patt., signed Libbey 550.00
Pitcher, 8½" h., bulbous, applied
    handle, Inverted Thumbprint patt. . . 350.00
Pitcher, water, square top, applied
    reeded handle w/shell terminal,
    Coin Spot patt., Mt. Washington 375.00
Punch cup, applied amber reeded
    handle, Inverted Thumbprint patt.,
    2½" h. 110.00
Punch cup, applied amber reeded
    handle, paneled optic effect, New
    England Glass Co., 2½" d., 2¼" h. . . . 92.00
Rose bowl, egg-shaped, enameled
    pink & white florals on branch
    decor, 4½" d., 6" h. 216.00
Rose bowl, Hobnail patt., 6" h. 250.00
Salt shaker w/pewter top, Reverse
    Amberina, Inverted Baby Thumb-
    print patt. (single) 165.00
Salt & pepper shakers w/original tops,
    Baby Inverted Thumbprint patt.,
    Mt. Washington, 1880s, pr. 275.00
Salt & pepper shakers w/original tops,
    Diamond Quilted patt., pr. 175.00
Sauce dish, pressed Daisy & Button
    (101) patt., Hobbs, Brockunier & Co.,
    4 7/8" sq. 125.00
Spooner, Diamond Quilted patt., New
    England Glass Co., 1883, 3¼" w.,
    4¾" h. 285.00

Spooner, square top, Diamond
Quilted patt., Mt. Washington 310.00
Syrup pitcher w/original top, Honey-
comb patt., 8" h. 395.00
Toothpick holder, 3-legged, pressed
Daisy & Button (101) patt. Hobbs,
Brockunier & Co. 175.00
Toothpick holder, ribbon candy
pleated top, Tiny Thumbprint
patt. 225.00
Toothpick holder, urn-shaped,
Venetian Diamond patt. . . . . 175.00 to 235.00
Tumbler, Baby Inverted Thumbprint
patt. 65.00
Tumbler, Diamond Quilted patt., New
England Glass Co., 2½" d., 3¾" h. . . . 95.00
Tumbler, Inverted Thumbprint
patt. . . . . 65.00 to 95.00

Swirl Pattern Tumbler

Tumbler, Swirl patt. (ILLUS.) 85.00
Tumbler, signed Libbey 160.00
Vase, 6" h., 4 1/8" d., egg-shaped,
scalloped top, enameled tan
branches w/pink & white floral
decor 230.00
Vase, 7" h., lily form, fluted rim
tapering to stem, New England Glass
Co., late 19th c. . . . . 200.00 to 300.00
Vase, 8 1/8" h., 6 3/8" d., fan-
shaped top w/applied amber edging,
applied amber wishbone feet,
Swirl patt. 140.00
Vase, 9¼" h., 4½" d., satin finish
Reverse Amberina, Swirl patt.,
enameled lacy gold florals 1,112.00
Vase, 9½" h., 5½" widest d., 2
applied amber handles, signed
Libbey, ca. 1917 . . . . 445.00
Vase, 11¼" h., bulbous shoulder
continuing to tapering amber stem,
circular foot, Libbey 495.00
Vase, 11½" h., 5¾" d., jack-in-pulpit
type fluted top w/amber edging,
Swirl patt., ground pontil 194.00
Whiskey shot glass, Diamond Quilted
patt., 2½" h. 165.00

ANIMALS

Chinese Pheasant

*Americans evidently like to collect glass
animals and for the past fifty years,
American glass manufacturers have turned
out a wide variety of animals to please the
buying public. Some were produced for long
periods and some were later reproduced by
other companies, while others were made for
only a short period of time and are rare. We
have not included late reproductions in our
listings and have attempted to date the productions where possible. Evelyn Zemel's
book, "American Glass Animals A to Z,"
will be helpful to the novice collector.*

Airedale Dog, clear, A.H. Heisey &
Co., 1948-49, 6" h. $540.00
Angel Fish bookend, clear, American
Glass Co., 8½" h. (single) 45.00
Angel Fish bookends, clear, A.H.
Heisey & Co., 7" h., pr. 165.00
Baby Bear, clear, New Martinsville
Glass Mfg. Co. 40.00
Baby Seal candlestick, clear, New
Martinsville Glass Mfg. Co., 4¾" h. . . 45.00
Boston Terrier Dog covered dish,
clear, Co-Operative Flint Glass Co.,
1927-30, 7½" l., 5¼" h. 55.00
Bull, clear, A.H. Heisey & Co.,
1948-52, 4" h. 1,225.00
Chinese Pheasant, blue, Paden City
Glass Mfg. Co., 13¾" l., 5¾" h. 85.00
Chinese Pheasant, clear, Paden City
Glass Mfg. Co., 13¾" l., 5¾" h.
(ILLUS.) 66.50
Colt standing, clear, Fostoria Glass
Co., 1938-44, 4" h. 23.00
Cygnet (Baby Swan), clear, A.H. Heisey
& Co., 1947-49, 2¼" h. 155.00
Deer standing, clear, Fostoria Glass
Co., 4½" h. 30.00
Donkey standing, clear, A.H. Heisey
& Co., 1944-53, 6½" h. 170.00
Duck sitting, clear, Viking Glass Co.,
1960s, 5" h. 16.50
Ducks (3) swimming, clear, K.R.
Haley, 9½" l., 4" h. 40.00
Eagle bookend, clear, Cambridge
Glass Co., 1964-68, 4½" base d.,
6" h. (single) 82.00
Eagle bookend, clear, Fostoria Glass
Co., 1938-44, 7¼" h. (single) 85.00

Elephant w/trunk up & extended,
A.H. Heisey & Co., 1944-53, small
size, 5¼" l., 4½" h. 150.00

Elephant standing w/trunk raised
above head, clear, Steuben Glass
Works, 5½ x 7" . . . . .410.00 to 425.00

Fish match holder, clear, A.H. Heisey
& Co. 75.00

Gazelle, clear, A.H. Heisey & Co.,
1927-49, 11" h. 1,275.00

Gazelle bookend, clear, Steuben
Glass Works, 6¾" h. (single) 300.00

Gazelle bookend, clear, New Martinsville Glass Mfg. Co., 8¼" h. (single) . .42.00

Giraffe w/head turned, clear, A.H.
Heisey & Co., 1942-52, 11" h. 140.00

Giraffe w/head straight, clear, A.H.
Heisey & Co., 1942-52, 11¼" h. 133.00

Goose (Mallard) w/wings half up,
clear, A.H. Heisey & Co., 1942-53,
4½" h. 72.00

Goose (Mallard) w/wings down, clear,
A.H. Heisey & Co., 1942-53,
5¾" h. 290.00

Goose (Mallard) w/wings up, clear,
A.H. Heisey & Co., 1942-53, 6½" h. . . .87.50

Hen, clear, A.H. Heisey & Co., 1948-
49, 4½" h. 380.00

Hen, clear, New Martinsville Glass
Mfg. Co., 2¾" base d., 5" h. 45.00

Heron standing, clear, Duncan &
Miller Glass Co., 7¼" h. 112.00

Horse rearing bookends, clear, A.H.
Heisey & Co., 7¾" h., pr. 175.00

King Fish aquarium, green, L.E. Smith,
1920s, 15" l., 10" h. 250.00

Mama Pig, clear, New Martinsville
Glass Mfg. Co., 6½" l., 3¾" h. 225.00

Owl, dark forest green, Degenhart
Crystal Art Glass, 1947-78 . . . . .35.00

Papa Bear, clear, New Martinsville
Glass Mfg. Co., 6½" l., 4¾" h. 275.00

Pelican

Pelican, clear, Fostoria Glass Co.,
1938-44, 3" sq. base, 4½" w., 4½" h.
(ILLUS.) 50.00

Pheasant w/turned head, light blue,
Paden City Glass Mfg. Co., 2½ x
2¾" base, 12" l., 7" h. . . . . . .95.00 to 125.00

Pig & 3 piglets, clear, A.H. Heisey &
Co., 1948-49, 3 1/8" h. mother pig,
set of 4 . . . . .550.00

Piglet sitting, clear, A.H. Heisey & Co.,
1948-49, 1" h. .70.00

Piglet, clear, New Martinsville Glass
Mfg. Co., 2" l., 1¼" h. 45.00

Plug Horse Sparky, clear, A.H. Heisey
& Co., 1941-46, 3½" l., 4¼" h. 88.00

Plug Horse Sparky, cobalt blue, A.H.
Heisey & Co., 1941-46, 3½" l.,
4¼" h. 750.00

Police Dog (German Shepherd) bookend, clear, New Martinsville Glass
Mfg. Co., 1937-50, 2¼ x 5" base,
5 1/8" h. (single) 46.00

Pony, long-legged, clear, New Martinsville Glass Mfg. Co., 5¼ x 3¼" oval
base, 4¼" l., 12" h. 65.00

Pony kicking, clear, A.H. Heisey & Co.,
1941-45, 2¼ x 1½" base, 3" l.,
4" h. 160.00

Pony standing, clear, A.H. Heisey &
Co., 1940-52, 2¼ x 1½" base, 3" l.,
5" h. 77.00

Pony standing, clear, Paden City Glass
Mfg. Co., 5½ x 3" base,
12" h. .50.00 to 75.00

Poodle finial powder dish, marigold
sprayed-on finish, Jeannette Glass
Co., 6" h. 12.50

Pouter Pigeon, clear, Westmoreland
Glass Co., 2¼" h. 14.00

Pouter Pigeon, clear, A.H. Heisey &
Co., 1947-49, 6½" h. . . . . . .465.00 to 500.00

Pouter Pigeon bookends, clear, Paden
City Glass Mfg. Co., 3 x 3¾" base,
6½" h., pr. 70.00

Rabbit, clear, New Martinsville Glass
Mfg. Co., 3¼ x 1½" base, 5" l.,
3" h. 45.00

Ringneck Pheasant, clear, A.H. Heisey
& Co., 1942-53, 11" l., 4¾" h. 128.00

Ringneck Pheasant, clear, K.R. Haley,
1947, 5¼ x 3¾" base, 11½" l. 22.00

Rooster, clear, New Martinsville Glass
Mfg. Co., 8" l., 8" h. 50.00

Rooster bookend, clear, K.R. Haley,
5¼ x 4" oval base, 3¾" h. (single) . . .50.00

Rooster fighting, clear, A.H. Heisey &
Co., 1940-46, 8½" h. 125.00

Rooster muddler, clear, Cambridge
Glass Co., overall 5½" l. 15.00

Scottie Dog bookend, clear, A.H.
Heisey & Co., 1941-46, 3½" l., 5" h.
(single) 95.00

Scottie Dog bookend, clear, Cambridge
Glass Co., 6½" h. (single) 85.00

Sea Horse bookend, clear, Fostoria
  Glass Co., 1938-44, 8" h. (single) 75.00
Seal, clear, Fostoria Glass Co., 1938-44,
  3¼" sq. base, 3¾" h................87.50
Seal, frosted, Fostoria Glass Co.,
  1938-44, 3¼" sq. base, 3¾" h.......58.00
Seal, lilac, Fostoria Glass Co., 1938-44,
  3¼" sq. base, 3¾" h...............80.00
Seal w/ball, clear, New Martinsville
  Glass Mfg. Co., 7¼" h. 52.00
Sparrow, clear, A.H. Heisey & Co.,
  1942-45, 4" l., 2¼" h...............70.00
Squirrel bookends, clear, New Martins-
  ville Glass Mfg. Co., 6¼ x 2¼" base,
  5¼" h., pr........................78.00
Squirrel on log, clear, Paden City Glass
  Mfg. Co., 5¾ x 2½" base,
  5¼" h. ....30.00 to 45.00
Starfish bookends, clear, New Martins-
  ville Glass Mfg. Co., 6¼ x 2¾" base,
  7¾" h., pr........................88.00
Sword Fish, clear, Duncan & Miller
  Glass Co., 4 x 3¾" base, 5" h. 110.00
Tiger bookends, clear, New Martins-
  ville Glass Mfg. Co., 5¾ x 3¼" base,
  6¾" h., pr.......................195.00
Tropical Fish centerpiece, large & small
  angel fish w/coral, clear, A.H.
  Heisey & Co., 12" h. 1,050.00
Wolfhound (Russian) bookend, clear,
  New Martinsville Glass Mfg. Co.,
  1920s, 9" l., 7¼" h. (single).........58.00
Wood Duck, clear, A.H. Heisey & Co.,
  7" l., 5½" h.....................550.00

APPLIQUED

Vases with Appliqued Decoration

  Simply stated, this is an art glass form
with applied decoration. Sometimes master
glass craftsmen applied stems or branches
to an art glass object and then added
molded glass flowers or fruit specimens to
these branches or stems. At other times, a
button of molten glass was daubed on the

object and a tool pressed over it to form a
prunt in the form of a raspberry, rosette or
other shape. Always the work of a skilled
glassmaker, applied decoration can be found
on both cased (2-layer) and single layer
glass. The English firm of Stevens and
Williams is renowned for the appliqued
glass they produced.

Ewer, flattened bulbous form, vaseline
  opalescent Stripe patt. w/applied
  amber handle & applied amber
  leaves on body, 4 3/8" d., 8¼" h. ..$135.00
Ewers, ruffled rim, vaseline opalescent
  w/applied clear handle & clear petal
  feet, applied clear branches on body
  w/eight pink florettes, 4½" d.,
  13¼" h., pr....................665.00
Rose bowl, scissors-cut rim, cream
  opaque w/applied amber loop feet,
  applied amber, green & dusty rose
  leaves & clear flower prunt, pink
  lining, Stevens & Williams, 5" d.,
  5¼" h. 215.00
Tumbler, amber w/applied amber pear
  & apple, green leaves & amber
  branch, Stevens & Williams, 3¼" d.,
  3¾" h. 230.00
Vase, 4" h., 3 5/8" d., fluted top edge,
  amber w/applied amber thorny feet
  & applied green branch & leaves
  w/red strawberry on body, Stevens &
  Williams 215.00
Vase, 5 3/8" h., 4 3/8" d., opaque
  off white w/applied amber handles,
  amber top edging & applied ruffled
  amber & rose leaf on front 89.00
Vase, 6½" h., 3½" d., white opaque
  w/applied amber leaves & acorns ...110.00
Vase, 6 5/8" h., 3¼" d., jack-in-pulpit
  top w/applied amber edging, pink
  exterior w/applied white flower,
  amber branch & leaves, white lining,
  Stevens & Williams...............140.00
Vase, 7¼" h., 4" d., shaded pink
  w/applied amber plums, stems &
  branch w/green & amber leaves,
  amber edging, white lining, Stevens
  & Williams.....................332.00
Vase, 8¾" h., 4 3/8" d., pink w/applied
  clear flower, branch & base trim,
  white lining 118.00

BACCARAT

  Baccarat glass has been made by Cristaller-
ies de Baccarat, France, since 1765. The firm
has produced various glasswares of excellent
quality and paperweights. Baccarat's Rose
Tiente is often referred to as Baccarat's
Amberina. Also see FAIRY LAMPS and
PAPERWEIGHTS.

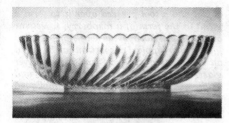

Baccarat Swirl Bowl

Bowl, 12" oval, Swirl patt., clear
(ILLUS.) $85.00
Card tray, fan-shaped, footed, opal-
escent w/enameled butterflies
decor, signed, 5" l. 85.00
Celery tray, Rose Tiente Swirl patt.,
3½" w., 9½" l. 49.00
Celery tray, cranberry, signed, 10" l. . . 150.00
Centerpiece bowl, scalloped rim,
Rose Tiente Sunburst Swirl patt.,
ormolu feet fastened to bowl,
10¾" d., 5½" h. 252.00
Cologne bottle w/matching stopper,
Rose Tiente Diamond Point Swirl
patt., 2¼" d., 5½" h. 65.00

Rose Tiente Swirl Cologne Bottles

Cologne bottle w/matching stopper,
Rose Tiente Swirl patt., 2" d., 5" h. . . . 55.00
Cologne bottle w/matching stopper,
Rose Tiente Swirl patt., 2½" d.,
6 5/8" h. 65.00
Cologne bottle w/matching stopper,
Rose Tiente Swirl patt., 3¼" d.,
8" h. 75.00
Cologne bottle w/matching stopper,
cobalt blue cut to clear 125.00
Flower center, two 12 x 5" horseshoe-
shaped pieces, Swirl patt., clear 45.00
Goblets, Perfection patt., clear,
set of 6 . . . . 150.00
Jar, Rose Tiente Swirl patt., 3" 28.00
Lamp, sapphire blue Sunburst patt.
base, frosted ball shade,
w/chimney, 2 1/8" d., 9½" h. 180.00
Powder dish, cov., Rose Tiente Swirl
patt., signed 42.50
Ring tree, Rose Tiente Swirl patt. 55.00

Ring tree, Swirl patt., vaseline
opalescent, 3¾" d., 2¾" h. 58.00
Sweetmeat jar, cranberry cut to clear
strawberries, blossoms & leaves on
fern-etched ground, silverplate
cover & handle 350.00
Toothbrush holder, Rose Tiente Swirl
patt. . . . . 50.00 to 75.00
Tumbler, flat, Rose Tiente Swirl
patt. 25.00 to 37.50
Tumbler, footed, Rose Tiente Swirl
patt. 45.00 to 52.00
Tumble-up (water carafe w/tumbler
lid), Swirl patt., blue, 7½" 165.00
Vase, 8½" h., cameo-carved tree
stump w/opalescent snake
w/enameled multicolored head
curled around body & w/enameled
multicolored insect at top,
signed 1,200.00
Vase, 14 5/8" h., 6½" d., trumpet-
shaped, Rose Tiente Swirl patt.,
in ornate ormolu base 225.00
Water set: 7" h. pitcher & six 4" h.
tumblers; Rose Tiente Thumbprint patt.,
7 pcs. 295.00

BLOWN THREE MOLD

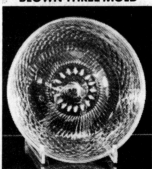

Blown Three Mold Deep Dish

*This type of glass was entirely or partially
blown in a mold from about 1820 in the
United States. The object was formed and the
decoration impressed upon it by blowing the
glass into a metal mold, usually of three but
sometimes more sections, hinged together.
Mold-blown glass actually dates back to ancient times. Recent research reveals that certain geometric patterns were reproduced in
the 1920s and collectors are urged to read all
recent information available. McKearin reference numbers are to George L. and Helen
McKearin's book, "American Glass."*

Decanter w/original Sunburst stopper,
geometric, clear, pt. (GI-7) $150.00
Decanter w/original Sunburst stopper,
geometric, clear, pt. (GII-7) 140.00

Decanter w/original stopper,
geometric, yellow-olive (GII-7) 3,100.00
Decanter w/(replaced) Sunburst
stopper, geometric, clear, qt.
(GIII-19) 150.00
Decanter w/(replaced) Diamond-
Quilted stopper (of same period),
baroque, clear, qt. (GV-10) 300.00
Dish, deep, geometric, clear, 8" d.,
GII-18 (ILLUS.) 120.00
Flip glass, geometric, clear w/applied
cobalt blue rim, 3 3/8" h. (GI-24) 300.00
Flip glass, geometric, clear, 4½" h.
(GIII-21) 150.00
Hat shape, folded rim, geometric,
clear, 2¼" h. (GIII-3) 100.00
Hat shape, folded rim, geometric,
clear, 2" h. (GIII-5) 70.00
Pitcher, 6" h., applied & crimped strap
handle, ribbed interior & exterior,
geometric, clear (GII-18) 575.00
Salt dip, geometric, purple-blue
(GIII-4) 375.00
Salt dip, geometric, clear, 2 7/8" d.,
2¾" h. (GIII-13) 225.00
Toilet water bottle w/drop nipple-
stopper, geometric, cobalt blue
(GI-7) 350.00

clear w/thumbprints & floral
clusters 85.00
Candlesticks, scalloped top, cut &
engraved Deer & Castle patt., olive
green, frosted & clear, 9" h., pr. 105.00
Candlesticks, stepped rings at base,
etched Deer in Forest patt., ruby,
frosted & clear, w/short prisms,
pr. 195.00
Cologne bottle w/original facet-cut
ruby stopper, ruby scallop-cut base,
frosted stem w/ruby circles & medallion w/etched deer scene, 2½" d.,
7 3/8" h. 135.00
Decanter w/stopper, flute-cut neck,
base & stopper, etched Deer &
Castle patt., ruby, frosted & clear,
3" d., 11" h. 70.00
Decanters w/original stoppers, clear
w/engraved duck in flight & cattails,
17" h., pr. 150.00
Finger bowl & underplate, etched
Vintage patt., ruby, pr. (ILLUS.) 90.00
Perfume bottle w/stopper, Lithyalin
glass, laminated dark red & black,
ca. 1830, 5" h. 1,250.00
Stein, applied handle, amber, etched
buildings on front, pewter lid
w/amber glass inset, 1¾" d.,
2¼" h. 125.00

BOHEMIAN

Vintage Pattern Finger Bowl & Underplate

Numerous types of glass were made in the once-independent country of Bohemia and fine colored, cut and engraved glass was turned out. Flashed and other inexpensive wares also were made and many of these, including ruby-shaded glass and etched ruby glass, were exported to the United States last century and in the present one. One favorite pattern in the late 19th and early 20th centuries was Deer and Castle. Another was Deer and Pine Tree.

Banana bowl, amber cut to clear, in
brass frame, 11 x 8" $375.00
Bowl, 6 5/8 x 4¾", pale amber cut to

Vintage Pattern Tumbler

Tumbler, footed, etched Vintage patt.,
ruby (ILLUS.) 85.00
Vases, 3½" h., white frosted ground
w/enameled colorful trees & black
deer decor, artist-signed, pr. 65.00
Vase, 6½" h., Bird & Castle patt., ruby,
frosted & clear 60.00

BREAD PLATES & TRAYS

Scores of special bread plates were produced last century and early in this one, of pattern glass and as commemorative pieces. Also see HISTORICAL & COMMEMORATIVE, IOWA CITY and PATTERN GLASS.

Nellie Bly Bread Tray

"A Good Mother Makes a Happy
   Home" plate, w/star rosettes,
   clear $60.00
American Flag tray, 38-star, frosted &
   clear 225.00
Beehive patt. platter, frosted center 49.00
Egyptian patt. platter, Cleopatra
   center, clear 50.00
Festoon patt. plate, clear, 9¼" d. 22.50
Garden of Eden plate, clear 35.00
Golden Rule plate, "Do Unto Others,"
   stars & bar border, clear . . . . .38.00 to 45.00
Horseshoe (Good Luck) patt. tray,
   single horseshoe handles, clear 33.50
"It is Pleasant to Labor for Those Whom
   We Love" plate, grapevine center,
   clear . . . . .38.00 to 45.00
Lotus & Serpent plate, clear 45.00
Nellie Bly tray, clear (ILLUS.) 165.00
Royal Crying Baby plate, clear 50.00
Scroll w/florals plate, clear, 12" d. 30.00
Sheaf of Wheat tray, "Give Us This
   Day," clear. 32.50
Tree of Life patt. plate, "Give Us This
   Day," etc., clear, extended handles . .28.50
Virginia Dare plate, clear 30.00
"Waste Not - Want Not" tray,
   clear . . . . .32.00 to 40.00

BRIDE'S BASKETS

*These are berry or fruit bowls, once
popular as wedding gifts; hence the name.*

Blue opalescent bowl w/crimped rim,
   silverplate frame marked "Walling-
   ford, Biggs & Rodger Co.," 9½" d. . . .$148.00
Blue opalescent bowl, Diamond
   Quilted patt. w/fluted edge, original
   black cast iron basket-form frame,
   13" d., overall 17¾" h. 235.00

Cased bowl, white interior, shaded
   pink exterior, 10¼" d. bowl
   w/enameled white & cream daisies
   & leaves, ornate silverplate frame
   w/embossed peaches, leaves &
   horses, overall 9¾" h. 305.00
Cased bowl, glossy white interior
   w/enameled pink florals & green
   leaves, soft beige satin exterior,
   on ornate silverplate compote stand
   w/figural Cupid holding bowl aloft,
   11 1/8" d. bowl, overall 11 3/8" h. 283.00
Cased bowl, blue interior w/enameled
   orange butterfly, blue & pink florals
   & orange berries highlighted w/gold
   trim, white exterior, in silverplate
   basket-frame, 11¼" d. bowl, overall
   11½" h. 243.00

Cased Glass Bride's Basket

Cased bowl, lime green interior
   w/enameled pink & white florals
   highlighted w/gold & citron
   scrolls, white exterior, ornate
   silverplate frame marked "Wilcox,"
   11½" d. bowl, overall 11½" h.
   (ILLUS.) 325.00
Cased bowl, white interior, 12½" d.
   fluted bowl w/mirrored gold hearts
   decor embellished w/scrolling &
   sprays of enameled blue forget-
   me-nots, pink exterior, ornate silver-
   plate frame 235.00
Cased bowl, apple green interior,
   raspberry shaded to white exterior
   w/enameled florals, fluted & ruffled
   rim, silverplate frame 225.00
Cased bowl, white interior, blue
   exterior w/enameled florals,
   silverplate frame 485.00
Cranberry shaded to pink bowl,
   applied ruffled rim binding, ornate
   footed silverplate frame, overall
   11¼" h. 150.00
Cream tinged w/pale green bowl
   w/enameled yellow florals, leaves &
   dot decor, ruffled rim, 10¼" d.,
   3¼" h. 232.00

Bride's Basket with Cherubs on Base

Pink, shaded from light to deep pink
   11½" d. bowl w/ruffled & crimped
   rim applied w/clear edging &
   enameled decor interior, silverplate
   footed stand w/three figural cherubs marked "Wm. A. Rogers Quad-
   ruple Plate," 12" h. (ILLUS.) 500.00
Pink opaque hobnail-type pattern
   bowl w/enameled purple florals,
   reticulated silverplate frame 200.00
Robin's egg blue bowl w/iridescent
   highlights, silverplate frame 165.00
Rubina Crystal shell-shaped bowl,
   enameled blue & white florals &
   gold leaves decor, silverplate frame
   w/figural cherub standard, 10" d.
   bowl, overall 11" h. 305.00

BRISTOL

Bristol Dresser Bottle

*While glass was made in several glass-
houses in Bristol, England, the generic*

*name Bristol glass is applied today by col-
lectors to a variety of semi-opaque glasses,
frequently decorated by enameling, and
made both abroad and in United States
glasshouses in the 19th and 20th centuries.*

Bobeche, blown, white $5.00
Butter tub, white opaque w/enameled
   cranes, ducks & trees decor, silverplate cover w/cow finial & overhead
   fixed handle, 5½" h. 295.00
Cake stand, Celadon green
   w/enameled herons in flight, gold
   trim 105.00
Cologne bottle w/original scalloped
   stopper, soft apple green satin
   w/applied green handles, gold trim,
   3 1/8" d., 9 3/8" h. 100.00
Compote, white w/enameled floral
   decor, small 45.00
Cookie jar, soft green opaque
   w/enameled pink, yellow & white
   florals & green leaves, silverplate
   rim, cover & bail handle, 5½" d.,
   6¾" h. 100.00
Cruet w/original ball-shaped stopper,
   sapphire blue translucent w/applied
   blue handle & enameled small white
   florals, yellow & gold leaves decor,
   2¼" d., 4¾" h. 92.50
Dresser bottle w/original stopper
   w/crimped edge, white opaque
   w/enameled floral & foliage decor,
   10" h. (ILLUS.) 57.00
Ewer, applied handle, bulbous base,
   white shaded to blue w/enameled
   birds & florals, 12" h. 160.00
Patch box w/hinged lid, turquoise blue
   w/gold decor, 1 5/8" d., 1 1/8" h. . . .100.00
Pitcher, 2 1/8" h., 1¾" d., gold
   trim on handle, gold bands around
   top, turquoise blue w/gold floral
   & leaves decor 75.00
Sweetmeat jar, pink w/enameled
   blue & white florals, green foliage
   & duck in flight, white lining,
   silverplate cover, handle & bottom
   rim, 3" d., 5" h. 100.00
Urn, cov., pink opaque w/overall
   enameled white dots & oval gold
   medallion w/young boy & girl
   w/lamb & florals within enameled
   white scrolls, 5 3/8" d., 17¾" h. 540.00
Vase, 4" h., light aqua w/enameled
   dots decor 26.00
Vases, 6" h., 5" d., French blue w/black
   & gold classic profile portrait decor,
   pr. 85.00
Vase, 6" h., threaded neck, crimped
   top, caramel w/enameled floral
   decor 65.00
Vase, 8" h., dove grey w/decal
   transfer of Greenaway-type children
   dancing on the green one side, h.p.

Bristol Vase

blossoming branches reverse
(ILLUS.) 125.00
Vases, 9½" h., blue w/enameled
white classical figures, gold trim,
pr. 195.00
Vase, 10¼" h., 2½ x 4¼", flattened
oval on pedestal base, turquoise
blue w/enameled grey, yellow &
purple bird on front, green leaves
& bug on reverse, white dots & gold
bands on pedestal base 180.00
Vase, 12½" h., soft yellow
w/enameled floral decor, gold
trim 72.50
Vase, 15" h., 5" d., scalloped top,
pedestal base, pink w/overall
enameled blue & white florals,
some orange florals, panel w/white
heron in marsh outlined in blue
dots, gold trim 195.00
Vase, 18" h., jug-type, green w/h.p.
roses decor 125.00
Vase, 24" h., white w/enameled
colorful birds & floral decor 450.00

BURMESE

Burmese is an homogeneous glass that shades from pink to pale yellow and was patented by Frederick S. Shirley and made by the Mt. Washington Glass Co. A license to produce the glass in England was granted to Thomas Webb & Sons, which called its articles Queen's Burmese. Gunderson Burmese was made briefly about the middle of this century. Also see FAIRY LAMPS.

Thomas Webb & Sons Bottle-Vase

Bottle-vase, acid finish, ivy leaves
decor, signed Thos. Webb & Sons,
Queens Burmese Ware, 4¼" d.,
7¾" h. (ILLUS.) $860.00
Bowl, 3" widest d., 3¼" h., flared
6-scallop rim w/traces of original
gold around edge, applied lemon
yellow rigaree collar around throat,
enameled white & bittersweet-red
floral decor, Mt. Washington 845.00
Bowl, 4" d., 2½" h., folded 5-point
star rim, acid finish, Mt.
Washington 275.00
Bowl, 4" d., 2½" h., crimped rim,
glossy, decorated 385.00

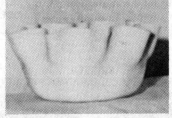

Bowl by Mt. Washington

Bowl, 6" d., 3" h., ruffled rim,
Mt. Washington Glass Co. (ILLUS.) . .600.00
Celery vase, Hobnail patt., acid finish,
Gunderson, 7" h. 195.00
Cookie jar w/silverplate rim, cover
& bail handle, enameled decor,
attributed to Thomas Webb, 5" d. . . .550.00
Creamer, acid finish, Mt. Washington,
3½" h. 240.00
Creamer & open sugar bowl, acid
finish, Mt. Washington, pr. 585.00
Creamer, ball-shaped w/ruffled collar,
applied lemon yellow handle,
enameled prunus blossom decor,
Thomas Webb & Sons 685.00
Cruet w/original ribbed stopper,
applied yellow handle, ribbed
body, acid finish, Mt. Washington,
3¾" d., 7" h. .825.00

Cruet w/original stopper, signed
Webb Queen's Ware 475.00
Cup, enameled blackberry decor,
3¼" h. (no saucer) 260.00
Marmalade jar w/silverplate cover
& silverplate base, acid finish,
attributed to Webb, 5¾" d.,
5½" h. 275.00
Pitcher, 9" h., applied handle, acid
finish, oak leaves & vines decor,
gold trim, Mt. Washington.......1,450.00
Rose bowl, 8-crimp top, acid finish,
lavender 5-petal flower w/green
& brown leaves decor, attributed
to Webb, 3½" d., 3 3/8" h. 345.00
Sugar shaker w/original top, acid
finish, enameled white & bittersweet-red dots form delicate
blossoms decor, Mt. Washington,
4½" h. 585.00
Toothpick holder, ball-shaped
w/collared 6-sided top, acid finish,
2½" d., 2 5/8" h................135.00
Toothpick holder, bulbous base
w/square top, Diamond Quilted
patt., glossy, Mt. Washington,
2 3/8" d., 2¾" h................245.00
Toothpick holder, bulbous w/square
top, acid finish, Mt. Washington,
2¾" h. ....175.00 to 225.00
Toothpick holder, bulbous w/square
top, acid finish, brown leaves &
blue & white floral decor, 3" h.......275.00
Toothpick holder, tricornered,
Venetian Diamond patt., glossy.....382.50
Tumbler, whiskey, Diamond Quilted
patt., acid finish, reheated yellow
top edge, Mt. Washington..........175.00
Tumbler, acid finish, Mt. Washington,
4¼" h. ....225.00 to 330.00
Tumbler, acid finish, ivy leaf decor,
Mt. Washington 300.00
Vase, 2¾" h., 2½" w., bulbous
w/pinched waist, square top, acorns
& oak leaves decor, Mt.
Washington 295.00

Vase attributed to Webb

Vase, 3 3/8" h., 3 1/8" d., ball-
shaped w/pinched rim, acid
finish, green ivy leaves & lavender
5-petal florals, attributed to
Webb (ILLUS.) 325.00

Vase, 4 3/8" h., 2½" d., acid finish,
green foliage w/red buds decor,
attributed to Webb.............345.00
Vase, 4½" h., 5" d., squat form, acid
finish, Mt. Washington.........285.00
Vase, 5½" h., 2 7/8" d., dimpled
sides, acid finish, red berries &
green leaves decor, attributed to
Webb 383.00
Vase, 6" h., lily form, Mt. Washington, original paper label 550.00

Mt. Washington Vase

Vase, 11¾" h., bottle-shaped, enameled
daisy-like florals & scrolls, Mt.
Washington (ILLUS.) ...1,400.00 to 1,600.00
Vase, 11¾" h., bulbous w/elongated
neck, painted daisies, butterfly
& verse by James Montgomery, Mt.
Washington, late
19th c. ....1,500.00 to 1,950.00
Water set: Egyptian-style squat
water pitcher & 6 tumblers; acid
finish, Mt. Washington, 1880s,
7 pcs........................2,275.00
Whimsey, hat, glossy, Gunderson,
2" h. 85.00

CAMBRIDGE

*The Cambridge Glass Company was
founded in Ohio in 1901. Numerous pieces
are now sought, especially those designed
by Arthur J. Bennett, including Crown
Tuscan, which is not included in this
particular issue. Other productions included*

crystal animals, "Black Amethyst," "blanc opaque," and other types of colored glass. The firm was finally closed in 1954, and should not be confused with the New England Glass Co., Cambridge, Mass. Also see ANIMALS under Glass.

Ram's Head Console Bowl

Bon bon, pressed Caprice patt., blue,
   4½ x 4"........................$18.00
Bowl, 7½" d., Azurite (dark opaque
   blue) w/black base 40.00
Bowl, 9½" d., low, Honeycomb patt.,
   Amberina (ruby top delicately
   blending off to amber).............95.00
Bowl, 10" d., 3" h., Jade (blue-green
   opaque) 40.00
Bowl, 12" d., Heliotrope (purple
   opaque) w/gold-encrusted daisies ...54.00
Bowl, 13" d., crimped, 2-handled,
   4-footed, pressed Caprice patt.,
   yellow...........................55.00
Brandy, amethyst bowl, clear Nude
   Lady stem........................80.00
Butter dish, cov., Colonial patt.,
   cobalt blue.......................55.00
Butter dish, cov., etched Rose Point
   patt., crystal 150.00
Candlesticks, pressed Caprice patt.,
   blue, 3½" h., pr..................32.00
Candlesticks, Azurite, 9" h., pr........65.00
Candy dish, cov., 4-footed, Diane
   patt., yellow 110.00
Centerpiece bowl, Azurite, 11½" w.,
   3¼" h............................55.00
Centerpiece bowl, Decagon patt.,
   Ebony (opaque black), 12" d. 45.00
Champagne, clear bowl, Carmen
   (clear brilliant ruby red) Nude Lady
   stem 140.00
Cocktail, canary yellow bowl, clear
   Nude Lady stem 75.00
Cocktail, Carmen bowl, clear Nude
   Lady stem.......................125.00
Cocktail, Dianthus (light transparent
   pink) bowl, clear Nude Lady stem ...150.00
Cocktail, Moonlight (delicate pastel
   blue) bowl, clear Nude Lady stem ...175.00
Console bowl, Ram's Head handles,
   Rubina (ruby top blending to green,
   then to blue), large (ILLUS.) 450.00

Ivory Console Set

Console set: Ram's Head bowl & pr.
   Doric Column candlesticks; Ivory
   (light cream opaque), 3 pcs.
   (ILLUS.).........................500.00
Cordial, etched Rose Point patt.,
   crystal, 1 oz. 100.00
Creamer, Colonial patt., cobalt
   blue.............................40.00
Crown Tuscan ash tray, 3-footed, h.p.
   decor 15.00
Crown Tuscan bowl, 8" d., 3-toed,
   Seashell patt. 65.00
Crown Tuscan bowl, 12" d., footed,
   gold-encrusted Rose Point patt......225.00
Crown Tuscan candlesticks, Nude Lady
   stems, pr. ....250.00 to 350.00
Crown Tuscan candy dish, cov., 3-com-
   partment, Seashell patt. 50.00
Crown Tuscan cigarette box, cov., shell
   feet, Seashell patt..................45.00
Crown Tuscan compote, 6" h., Nautilus
   design, floral decor................60.00
Crown Tuscan compote, 8", Seashell
   patt., Nude Lady stem, decorated ...170.00
Crown Tuscan cornucopia-vases,
   Seashell patt., 10" h., pr. ..245.00 to 300.00

Flower Center with Flying Nude Lady

Crown Tuscan flower or fruit center,
   Seashell patt. w/Flying Nude lady,
   enameled roses decor, gold trim
   (ILLUS.).........................350.00
Crown Tuscan ivy ball, keyhole stem ...42.50
Crown Tuscan plate, 7" d., Seashell
   patt., roses decor.................20.00
Crown Tuscan relish, 3-compartment,
   4-toed...........................58.00
Crown Tuscan salt dip, Mt. Vernon
   patt., w/gold......................35.00

Crown Tuscan swan, 3" 40.00
Crown Tuscan swan, 8½" . . . . .95.00 to 140.00
Crown Tuscan torte plate, Seashell
   patt., 14" d. 70.00
Crown Tuscan vase, 7½" h., Nautilus
   Shell 58.00
Crown Tuscan vase, 10" h., keyhole
   stem .55.00 to 75.00
Figure flower holder, "Bashful Char-
   lotte," crystal, 6½" h. 40.00
Figure flower holder, "Bashful Char-
   lotte," crystal, 11½" h. 100.00

Draped Lady Flower Holder

Figure flower holder, "Draped Lady,"
   apple green satin finish, 8½" h.
   (ILLUS.) 175.00
Figure flower holder, "Draped Lady,"
   light emerald green, 8½" h. 130.00
Figure flower holder, "Draped Lady,"
   Mandarin Gold (very light golden
   yellow), 8½" h. 235.00
Figure flower holder, "Draped Lady,"
   Moonlight (delicate pastel blue),
   8½" h. 325.00
Figure flower holder, "Draped Lady,"
   pink frosted, 8½" h. . . . . . .100.00 to 120.00
Figure flower holder, "Draped Lady,"
   crystal, 13" h. 150.00
Figure flower holder, "Draped Lady,"
   light emerald green, 13" h. 325.00
Figure flower holder, "Draped Lady,"
   Ivory, 13½" h. 800.00
Figure flower holder, "Rose Lady,"
   amber, 8½" h. 190.00
Figure flower holder, "Rose Lady,"
   green frosted, 8½" h. 175.00
Flower holder, Heron, crystal, 12" 65.00
Flower holder, Pouter Pigeon, crystal . . .88.00
Flower holder, Pouter Pigeon, frosted . .72.50
Flower holder, Sea Gull, crystal,
   8" h. . . . . .60.00 to 75.00
Ivy ball, Ebony 42.00

Sherbet, pressed Caprice patt.,
   Moonlight, 6 oz. 22.50
Swan, Carmen, 3½" l. 85.00
Swan, crystal, 3½" l. 22.50
Torte plate, Caprice Alpine patt.,
   blue, 14" d. .95.00
Tumbler, Tally Ho patt., amethyst,
   10 oz. 15.00
Tumbler, pressed Caprice patt., blue,
   12 oz. 37.50
Vase, 8" h., square mouth, Everglade
   patt., crystal 20.00
Vase, 12" h., keyhole stem,
   amethyst 40.00

CAMPHOR

Camphor Salt & Pepper Shakers

All types of objects were made in so-called Camphor glass, which has a cloudy appearance, somewhat resembling that of gum camphor, from whence it takes its name. It was pressed, blown and blown-molded.

Basket, flaring rim, applied braided
   handle, pink, 3½" w. $16.00
Bowl, 10" d., fluted, polished pontil . . .125.00
Card holder 35.00
Jars, cov., h.p. horses decor, 6" h.,
   pr. 40.00
Powder jar, cov., 2 nude ladies on
   lid, green 20.00
Powder jar, cov., relief-molded
   irregular pattern, elephant on lid,
   green, original green silk cord &
   tassel, 1930s 55.00
Ring tree, 4½" h. 12.50
Salt & pepper shakers w/original tops,
   hand holding torch, ca. 1876, 3½" h.,
   pr. (ILLUS.) 60.00
Salt & pepper shakers w/original tops,
   Swirl patt., blue, pr. 40.00
Vase, 8½" h., Art Deco nude decor 27.50

CARNIVAL GLASS

Earlier called Taffeta glass, the Carnival glass now being collected was introduced early in this century. Its producers gave it an iridescence that attempted to imitate that of some Tiffany glass. Collectors will find available books by leading authorities Donald E. Moore, Sherman Hand, Marion T. Hartung and Rose M. Presznick.

ACANTHUS

Acanthus Bowl

Bowl, 7" d., marigold $22.00
Bowl, 8" to 9" d., green 75.00
Bowl, 8" to 9" d., marigold (ILLUS.) 50.00
Bowl, 8" to 9" d., purple 58.00
Bowl, 8" to 9" w., tricornered, purple . . .75.00
Bowl, 8" to 9" d., smoky 65.00
Plate, 9" to 10" d., marigold 135.00
Plate, 9" to 10" d., smoky 175.00

ACORN (Fenton)

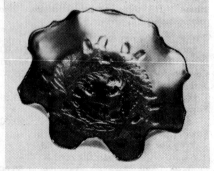

Acorn Bowl

Bowl, 5" d., aqua opalescent 60.00
Bowl, 5" d., blue 25.00
Bowl, 5" d., marigold 15.00
Bowl, 5" d., marigold over milk white. .300.00
Bowl, 7" d., aqua opalescent 80.00
Bowl, 7" d., blue 37.50

Bowl, 7" d., green 27.00
Bowl, 7" d., ice blue 100.00
Bowl, 7" d., marigold . . . . .25.00 to 30.00
Bowl, 7" d., marigold over milk white. .175.00
Bowl, 7" d., purple 55.00
Bowl, 7" d., red 380.00
Bowl, 7½" d., ruffled, vaseline 125.00
Bowl, 8" to 9" d., blue 60.00
Bowl, 8" to 9" d., green 35.00
Bowl, 8" to 9" d., marigold 22.50
Bowl, 8" to 9" d., ribbon candy rim,
  purple. 60.00
Bowl, 8" to 9" d., red (ILLUS.) 300.00
Compote, vaseline (Millersburg) 2,100.00

ACORN BURRS (Northwood)

Acorn Burrs Tumbler

Berry set: master bowl & 5 sauce
  dishes; marigold, 6 pcs. 225.00
Berry set: master bowl & 6 sauce
  dishes; green, 7 pcs. 315.00
Bowl, master berry, 10" d., marigold . . .68.00
Bowl, master berry, 10" d., purple 135.00
Butter dish, cov., marigold 140.00
Butter dish, cov., purple . . . . .185.00 to 200.00
Creamer, marigold. 75.00
Pitcher, water, marigold 375.00
Pitcher, water, purple 500.00
Punch bowl, marigold 400.00
Punch bowl base, ice blue. 175.00
Punch bowl base, ice green 100.00
Punch bowl & base, ice green,
  2 pcs. 1,800.00
Punch cup, blue. 36.50
Punch cup, green . . . . .30.00 to 35.00
Punch cup, ice blue 75.00
Punch cup, marigold 20.00
Punch cup, purple. 25.00
Punch cup, white 40.00
Punch set: bowl, base & 6 cups;
  green, 8 pcs. 700.00
Punch set: bowl, base & 6 cups;
  marigold, 8 pcs. 350.00
Punch set: bowl, base & 6 cups;
  purple, 8 pcs. 650.00
Sauce dish, amber 39.00
Sauce dish, green 30.00

Sauce dish, marigold . . . . 18.00 to 25.00
Sauce dish, purple 58.00
Spooner, green 93.50
Spooner, marigold 67.50
Spooner, purple 100.00
Sugar bowl, cov., marigold 95.00
Sugar bowl, open, purple 190.00
Table set: cov. sugar bowl, creamer,
   spooner & cov. butter dish; green,
   4 pcs. 450.00
Table set: cov. sugar bowl, creamer,
   spooner & cov. butter dish;
   marigold, 4 pcs. 395.00
Table set: cov. sugar bowl, creamer,
   spooner & cov. butter dish; purple,
   4 pcs. 500.00
Tumbler, green 60.00
Tumbler, marigold 45.00
Tumbler, purple (ILLUS.) 50.00
Water set: pitcher & 4 tumblers;
   green, 5 pcs. 500.00
Water set: pitcher & 6 tumblers;
   purple, 7 pcs. 735.00

ADVERTISING & SOUVENIR ITEMS

"Millersburg Courthouse" Bowl

Ash tray, souvenir, "Cleveland
   Memorial," purple (Millersburg) . . 1,400.00
Basket, "John H. Brand Furniture Co.,
   Wilmington, Del.," marigold 44.00
Bell, souvenir, BPOE Elks, "Atlantic
   City, 1911," blue 1,050.00
Bell, souvenir, BPOE Elks, "Parkers-
   burg, 1914," blue 1,250.00
Bowl, 6¼" d., "Isaac Benesch,"
   marigold (Millersburg) . . . . . 85.00 to 110.00
Bowl, 6¼" d., "Isaac Benesch," purple
   (Millersburg) 165.00
Bowl, "Burnheimer," blue 435.00
Bowl, "Central Shoe Store," purple 185.00
Bowl, "Horlacher," green 110.00
Bowl, "Horlacher," purple 60.00
Bowl, souvenir, BPOE Elks, "Atlantic
   City, 1911," blue, 1-eyed
   Elk . . . . 350.00 to 395.00

Bowl, souvenir, BPOE Elks, "Detroit,
   1910," purple, 1-eyed Elk . . 375.00 to 425.00
Bowl, souvenir, BPOE Elks, "Detroit,
   1910," purple, 2-eyed Elk (Millers-
   burg) . . . . 750.00 to 1,025.00
Bowl, souvenir, "Brooklyn Bridge,"
   marigold 285.00
Bowl, souvenir, "Millersburg Court-
   house," purple (ILLUS.) 435.00
Bowl, souvenir, Millersburg Court-
   house, unlettered, purple 1,050.00
Card tray, "Isaac Benesch," Holly
   Whirl patt., marigold 110.00
Paperweight, souvenir, BPOE Elks,
   purple (Millersburg) 875.00
Plate, "Ballard, California," purple
   (Northwood) 275.00
Plate, "Cambell & Beasley," w/hand-
   grip, purple 350.00
Plate, "Driebus Parfait Sweets,"
   6¼" d., purple 190.00
Plate, "Greengard Furniture Co.,"
   purple . . . . 375.00 to 400.00
Plate, "E.A. Hudson Furniture Co.,"
   7" d., purple (Northwood) 170.00
Plate, "Paradise Soda," purple (North-
   wood) 160.00
Plate, "Rhodes Chocolate, Pueblo,"
   purple 550.00
Plate, souvenir, BPOE Elks, "Atlantic
   City, 1911," blue 575.00
Plate, souvenir, BPOE Elks, "Parkers-
   burg, 1914," 7½" d., blue . . 625.00 to 700.00

AGE HERALD
Bowl, 8" to 9" d., collared base,
   straight edge, purple 500.00

APPLE BLOSSOMS

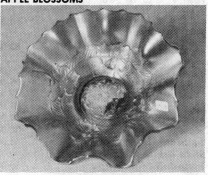

Apple Blossoms Bowl

Bowl, 7" d., collared base, marigold
   (ILLUS.) 20.00
Bowl, 7" d., collared base, peach
   opalescent 95.00
Bowl, 7" d., collared base, purple 60.00
Syrup pitcher, marigold 375.00

APPLE BLOSSOM TWIGS
Banana boat, ruffled, peach
   opalescent 135.00

Banana boat, ruffled, purple 60.00
Bowl, 5" d., marigold...............15.00
Bowl, 7" d., white 48.00
Bowl, 8" to 9" d., marigold 30.00
Bowl, 8" to 9" d., peach opalescent 130.00
Bowl, 8" to 9" d., purple 115.00
Bowl, 8" to 9" d., white 60.00
Plate, 9" d., blue...................140.00
Plate, 9" d., marigold ....100.00 to 120.00
Plate, 9" d., peach
    opalescent ....200.00 to 240.00
Plate, 9" d., purple ....160.00 to 190.00
Plate, 9" d., white...................75.00
Plate, 10" d., ruffled, white 100.00
Plate, chop, peach opalescent 225.00

APPLE TREE
Pitcher, water, marigold.............135.00
Pitcher, water, white...............550.00
Tumbler, blue 46.50
Tumbler, marigold...........25.00 to 37.50
Water set: pitcher & 6 tumblers;
    blue, 7 pcs. 460.00
Water set: pitcher & 6 tumblers;
    marigold, 7 pcs. 325.00

AUSTRALIAN
Bowl, 9" to 10" d., Emu, marigold 81.50
Bowl, 9" to 10" d., Kangaroo,
    marigold 88.00
Bowl, 9" to 10" d., Kingfisher,
    marigold 67.50
Bowl, 9" to 10" d., Kingfisher, purple ..105.00
Bowl, 9" to 10" d., Kookaburra,
    purple...........................105.00
Bowl, 9" to 10" d., Magpie, marigold ...95.00
Bowl, 9" to 10" d., Magpie, purple.....125.00
Bowl, 9" to 10" d., Swan, marigold 80.00
Bowl, 9" to 10" d., Swan, purple.......130.00
Bowl, 9" to 10" d., Thunderbird,
    marigold 70.00
Cake plate, Butterfly & Bells,
    marigold 80.00
Compote, Butterfly & Bush, marigold ..107.00
Compote, Ostrich, marigold.........110.00
Compote, Ostrich, purple 195.00
Sauce dish, Kangaroo, marigold 42.50
Sauce dish, Kangaroo, purple 70.00
Sauce dish, Kingfisher, marigold 38.00
Sauce dish, Magpie, marigold 38.00
Sauce dish, Magpie, purple 55.00
Sauce dish, Swan, marigold ....35.00 to 50.00
Sauce dish, Swan, purple 50.00

AUTUMN ACORNS
Bowl, 8" to 9" d., amber 65.00
Bowl, 8" to 9" d., blue 45.00
Bowl, 8" to 9" d., green 40.00
Bowl, 8" to 9" d., marigold 40.00
Bowl, 8" to 9" d., purple 47.50
Bowl, 8" to 9" d., red 425.00

AZTEC
Tumbler, marigold 450.00

BANDED DRAPE
Mug, marigold 23.50
Water set: pitcher & 6 tumblers;
    marigold, 7 pcs. 270.00

BASKET (Northwood)

Northwood's Basket

Aqua opalescent, 4½" d., 4¾" h. 260.00
Cobalt blue 100.00
Green.............................235.00
Ice blue............................330.00
Ice green 200.00
Marigold 65.00
Purple (ILLUS.).....................80.00
White 145.00

BASKETWEAVE VARIANT CANDY DISH
(Fenton's Hat)

Basketweave Variant Dish

Blue...............................29.00
Ice green 75.00
Marigold (ILLUS.)...................38.00
Red 225.00

BEADED CABLE (Northwood)
Bowl, 7" d., ruffled, marigold..........30.00
Candy dish, green 45.00
Candy dish, marigold................30.00
Candy dish, purple 50.00
Rose bowl, aqua opalescent 225.00

Rose bowl, blue .92.50
Rose bowl, green 85.00
Rose bowl, ice green 700.00
Rose bowl, marigold 50.00

Beaded Cable Rose Bowl

Rose bowl, purple (ILLUS.) . . . . .60.00 to 80.00
Rose bowl, white 475.00

BEADED SHELL

Beaded Shell Mug

Berry set: master bowl & 3 footed
  sauce dishes; purple, 4 pcs. 200.00
Bowl, master berry, marigold 54.00
Butter dish, cov., purple 160.00
Creamer, marigold. 60.00
Creamer, purple .70.00
Mug, blue. 85.00
Mug, marigold 145.00
Mug, purple (ILLUS.). 80.00
Mug, white . . . . .650.00 to 1,225.00
Pitcher, water, marigold 300.00
Sauce dish, marigold 20.00
Spooner, footed, marigold 45.00
Sugar bowl, cov., marigold. 50.00
Sugar bowl, open, marigold 45.00
Tumbler, marigold 47.50
Tumbler, purple 57.50

BEADS & BELLS

Bowl, 7" d., peach opalescent 50.00
Bowl, 7" d., purple 40.00

BEAUTY BUD VASE

Marigold, 8" h. . . . . .25.00 to 35.00
Purple, 8" h. . . . . .30.00 to 42.50

BIG FISH BOWL (Millersburg)

Green 325.00
Marigold, square 400.00
Purple, ice cream shape . . . . .475.00 to 500.00
Purple, round .267.00
Purple, square 307.00
Vaseline, crimped rim 5,300.00
Vaseline w/marigold, tricornered . . .2,250.00

BIRDS & CHERRIES

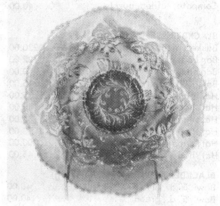

Birds & Cherries Chop Plate

Bon bon, blue .62.00
Bon bon, green . . . . .50.00 to 75.00
Bon bon, marigold 35.00
Bon bon, purple 49.50
Bowl, 8" to 9" d., blue 297.00
Compote, blue .65.00
Compote, green 42.00
Compote, marigold 55.00
Compote, purple . . . . .45.00 to 65.00
Plate, chop, blue (ILLUS.) 1,000.00

BIRD WITH GRAPES

Wall vase, marigold, 8" h., 7½" w. 49.00

BLACKBERRY

Blackberry Miniature Compotes

Basket, blue 40.00
Basket, red 260.00
Bowl, 5" d., purple 30.00
Bowl, 10" d., ruffled, green 125.00
Bowl, 10" d., ruffled, purple 125.00
Compote, miniature, blue. 72.50

Compote, miniature, marigold
(ILLUS.) 55.00
Compote, miniature, purple (ILLUS.) 66.50

BLACKBERRY BLOCK
Pitcher, water, marigold 285.00
Pitcher, water, purple 900.00
Tumbler, blue . . . . .55.00 to 65.00
Tumbler, green . . . . .100.00 to 245.00
Tumbler, marigold 50.00
Tumbler, purple . . . . .75.00 to 100.00

BLACKBERRY BRAMBLE
Compote, ruffled, green 38.00
Compote, ruffled, purple 40.00

BLACKBERRY SPRAY
Basket, medium, red 230.00
Bon bon, marigold 22.00
Bon bon, red 210.00
Bowl, 7" d., red 245.00
Hat shape, aqua 35.00
Hat shape, aqua opalescent 145.00
Hat shape, blue 35.00
Hat shape, marigold 30.00
Hat shape, red .200.00
Hat shape, vaseline 45.00

BLACKBERRY WREATH (Millersburg)
Bowl, 5" d., blue .40.00
Bowl, 5" d., green 40.00
Bowl, 5" d., marigold 25.00
Bowl, 5" d., purple 35.00
Bowl, 7" d., blue 350.00
Bowl, 7" d., green . . . . .45.00 to 55.00
Bowl, 7" d., marigold 47.50
Bowl, 7" d., purple 42.50
Bowl, 7" w., tricornered, purple 85.00
Bowl, 8" to 9" d., green 57.50
Bowl, 8" to 9" d., marigold 47.50
Bowl, 8" to 9" d., purple 65.00
Bowl, 10" d., blue 450.00
Bowl, 10" d., green 65.00
Bowl, 10" d., marigold 90.00
Bowl, 10" d., purple 115.00
Bowl, ice cream, large, blue 750.00
Bowl, triangular, large, marigold 125.00
Plate, 6" to 7½" d., marigold 410.00
Sauce dish, green 27.00
Sauce dish, marigold 25.00
Sauce dish, purple 40.00

BLOSSOM TIME
Compote, purple. 100.00

BLUEBERRY (Fenton)
Tumbler, blue 70.00
Water set: pitcher & 6 tumblers;
blue, 7 pcs. .1,050.00

BO PEEP
Mug, marigold .140.00
Plate, marigold .350.00

BOUQUET
Pitcher, water, blue 465.00
Pitcher, water, marigold 175.00
Tumbler, blue 40.00
Tumbler, marigold 28.00
Water set: pitcher & 4 tumblers;
blue, 5 pcs. 400.00
Water set: pitcher & 6 tumblers;
marigold, 7 pcs. 355.00

BROKEN ARCHES (Imperial)

Broken Arches Punch Set
Punch bowl & base, marigold,
12" d., 2 pcs. .245.00
Punch cup, marigold 14.50
Punch cup, purple 19.50
Punch set: bowl, base & 4 cups;
purple, 6 pcs. 550.00
Punch set: bowl, base & 8 cups;
marigold, 10 pcs. (ILLUS.) 400.00

BUTTERFLIES

Butterflies Bon Bon
Bon bon, blue . . . . .45.00 to 60.00
Bon bon, green . . . . .35.00 to 45.00
Bon bon, marigold 40.00
Bon bon, purple (ILLUS.) 47.50

BUTTERFLY & BERRY (Fenton)
Berry set: master bowl & 3 sauce dishes;
marigold, 4 pcs. 125.00
Berry set: master bowl & 4 sauce
dishes; blue, 5 pcs. 300.00
Berry set: master bowl & 4 sauce
dishes; marigold, 5 pcs. 130.00

Berry set: master bowl & 4 sauce
  dishes; purple, 5 pcs. 110.00
Berry set: master bowl & 6 sauce
  dishes; marigold, 7 pcs. 170.00
Bowl, 7" d., 3-footed, marigold 48.00
Bowl, 8" to 9" d., footed, blue 90.00
Bowl, 8" to 9" d., footed, green 86.00
Bowl, 8" to 9" d., footed, marigold 60.00
Bowl, master berry or fruit, 4-footed,
  blue 128.00
Bowl, master berry or fruit, 4-footed,
  green 120.00
Bowl, master berry or fruit, 4-footed,
  marigold 65.00
Bowl, master berry or fruit, 4-footed,
  purple 197.50
Butter dish, cov., blue 165.00
Butter dish, cov., marigold 100.00
Creamer, green .150.00
Creamer, marigold. 47.50

Butterfly & Berry Hatpin Holder

Hatpin holder, blue (ILLUS.) 475.00
Hatpin holder, marigold 700.00
Nut bowl, purple. 185.00
Pitcher, water, blue 375.00
Pitcher, water, marigold 165.00
Sauce dish, blue 32.50
Sauce dish, green 55.00
Sauce dish, marigold 22.50
Spooner, blue 95.00
Spooner, green .120.00
Spooner, marigold 62.50
Spooner, purple 90.00
Sugar bowl, cov., green 125.00
Sugar bowl, cov., marigold. 70.00
Table set, marigold, 4 pcs. 325.00
Tumbler, blue 32.50
Tumbler, green .72.50
Tumbler, marigold 30.00
Tumbler, purple 125.00
Vase, 7" h., blue. 45.00
Vase, 7" h., purple 36.50
Vase, 8" h., marigold 30.00
Vase, 9" h., blue 33.50
Vase, 9" h., marigold 25.00
Vase, 9" h., purple 55.00

Vase, 10" h., blue. 46.50
Vase, red 400.00
Water set: pitcher & 4 tumblers;
  blue, 5 pcs. .450.00
Water set: pitcher & 6 tumblers;
  green, 7 pcs. 665.00
Water set: pitcher & 6 tumblers;
  marigold, 7 pcs. 270.00
Water set: pitcher & 6 tumblers;
  purple, 7 pcs. 1,300.00

BUTTERFLY & FERN (Fenton)
Pitcher, water, blue . . . . .350.00 to 395.00
Pitcher, water, green. 450.00
Pitcher, water, purple 385.00
Tumbler, blue 62.50
Tumbler, green .40.00
Tumbler, marigold 32.50
Tumbler, purple .42.50
Water set: pitcher & 6 tumblers;
  blue, 7 pcs. .610.00
Water set: pitcher & 6 tumblers;
  green, 7 pcs. 695.00
Water set: pitcher & 6 tumblers;
  marigold, 7 pcs. 500.00
Water set: pitcher & 6 tumblers;
  purple, 7 pcs. 535.00

BUTTERFLY & TULIP

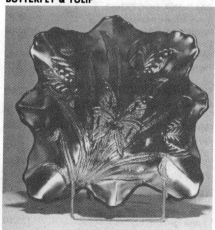

Butterfly & Tulip Bowl

Bowl, 9" w., 5½" h., footed, marigold .185.00
Bowl, 9" w., footed, purple (ILLUS.). . . .750.00
Bowl, 10½" square flat shape, footed,
  marigold 300.00
Bowl, 10½" square flat shape, footed,
  purple. 900.00

CAPTIVE ROSE
Bon bon, 2-handled, blue, 7½" d. 75.00
Bon bon, 2-handled, marigold, 7½" d. . .22.50
Bon bon, 2-handled, purple, 7½" d. 35.00
Bowl, 8" to 9" d., ribbon candy rim,
  blue. 48.00
Bowl, 8" to 9" d., green 46.00

Bowl, 8" to 9" d., ruffled rim,
   marigold 30.00

Captive Rose Bowl

Bowl, 8" to 9" d., ribbon candy rim,
   purple (ILLUS.). 42.50
Compote, clambroth 75.00
Compote, green 50.00
Compote, ice blue 89.00
Compote, marigold 40.00
Compote, purple. 47.50
Compote, white 68.00
Plate, 9" d., blue. 138.00
Plate, 9" d., green 178.00
Plate, 9" d., marigold 120.00
Plate, 9" d., purple 125.00

CAROLINA DOGWOOD
Bowl, blue opalescent 320.00
Bowl, marigold 40.00
Bowl, marigold on milk white 355.00
Bowl, peach opalescent. 110.00
Plate, 8 5/8" d., peach opalescent 295.00

CAROLINE
Basket w/applied handle, peach
   opalescent 335.00
Bowl, 8" to 9" d., peach opalescent 65.00
Bowl, 8" to 9" w., tricornered, peach
   opalescent 50.00
Bowl, 9" sq., peach opalescent 65.00
Plate, w/handgrip, peach opalescent . . 135.00

CATHEDRAL
Celery vase, chalice shape, footed,
   marigold 135.00

CHATELAINE
Pitcher, purple. 1,365.00
Tumbler, purple 295.00

CHECKERBOARD
Cordial, marigold 130.00
Pitcher, water, purple 1,750.00
Tumbler, purple 338.00

CHERRY
Berry set: master bowl & 3 sauce
   dishes; Jeweled Heart exterior,
   purple, 4 pcs. 175.00
Bowl, 7" d., 3-footed, crimped rim,
   peach opalescent 55.00

Bowl, 8" to 9" d., 3-footed, marigold 35.00
Bowl, 8" to 9" d., 3-footed, peach
   opalescent. 115.00
Bowl, 8" to 9" d., 3-footed, purple 61.50
Sauce dish, purple 37.00

CHERRY or CHERRY CIRCLES (Fenton)
Bon bon, 2-handled, blue 52.00
Bon bon, 2-handled, marigold 36.00
Bon bon, 2-handled, purple 50.00
Bon bon, 2-handled, red. 1,300.00
Bowl, 5" d., fluted, blue. 18.00
Bowl, 7" d., 3-footed, peach
   opalescent w/plain interior 41.50
Bowl, 8" to 9" d., white 70.00
Plate, 6" d., marigold. 42.00

CHERRY or HANGING CHERRIES (Millersburg)
Banana compote (whimsey), green. . . .715.00
Banana compote (whimsey), marigold .735.00
Banana compote (whimsey), purple . . .715.00
Bowl, 5" d., ruffled, blue satin 500.00
Bowl, 5" d., piecrust rim, purple 35.00
Bowl, 7" d., green. 115.00
Bowl, 7" d., marigold 60.00
Bowl, 7" d., purple 115.00
Bowl, 8" to 9" d., dome-footed,
   marigold 55.00
Bowl, ice cream, 10" d., green 125.00
Bowl, ice cream, 10" d., marigold 95.00
Bowl, ice cream, 10" d., purple 125.00
Bowl, ruffled, Hobnail exterior,
   marigold, large 485.00
Butter dish, cov., green 300.00
Butter dish, cov., marigold 150.00
Butter dish, cov., purple 180.00
Creamer, green 62.50
Creamer, marigold. 57.50
Creamer, purple. 77.50
Pitcher, water, purple 545.00
Plate, 7" d., marigold. 400.00
Plate, 7" d., purple 300.00
Powder jar, cov., green 850.00
Spooner, green 56.00
Spooner, marigold 65.00
Spooner, purple 82.50
Sugar bowl, cov., marigold . . . .60.00 to 75.00
Sugar bowl, cov., purple 125.00
Table set, marigold, 4 pcs. 375.00
Table set, purple, 4 pcs. . . . .500.00 to 700.00
Tumbler, green 220.00
Tumbler, marigold 225.00
Tumbler, purple 245.00

CHERRY CHAIN (Fenton)
Bon bon, 2-handled, blue 63.00
Bon bon, 2-handled, marigold 42.50
Bowl, 5" d., blue 28.00
Bowl, ice cream, 5" d., white 36.50
Bowl, 8" to 9" d., white 125.00
Bowl, 10" d., Orange Tree exterior,
   blue. 65.00
Bowl, 10" d., Orange Tree exterior,
   marigold 40.00

Bowl, 10" d., Orange Tree exterior,
white 153.00
Plate, 6" to 7" d., marigold 46.50

CHRISTMAS COMPOTE

Christmas Compote

Marigold.........................2,115.00
Purple (ILLUS.)....................2,800.00

CHRYSANTHEMUM or WINDMILL & MUMS

Bowl, 8" to 9" d., 3-footed, blue 92.50
Bowl, 8" to 9" d., 3-footed, green 80.00
Bowl, 8" to 9" d., 3-footed, marigold....42.50
Bowl, 10" d., 3-footed, blue.............75.00
Bowl, 10" d., 3-footed, green 150.00
Bowl, 10" d., 3-footed, marigold 55.00
Bowl, 10" d., 3-footed, purple 65.00
Bowl, 10" d., collared base, red 950.00

CIRCLED SCROLL

Circled Scroll Tumbler

Bowl, master berry, purple............75.00
Creamer, marigold...................57.50
Creamer, purple 65.00
Pitcher, water, marigold 950.00
Spooner, marigold 52.50

Tumbler, marigold (ILLUS.) 310.00
Vase, 7½" h., marigold..............50.00
Vase, 7½" h., purple 52.50

COBBLESTONES BOWL (Imperial)
Green, 9" d........................40.00
Purple, 9" d. ....50.00 to 60.00

COIN DOT

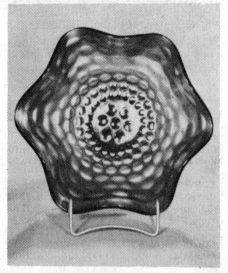

Coin Dot Bowl

Bowl, 7" d., ribbon candy rim, green....50.00
Bowl, 7" d., purple 27.50
Bowl, 7" d., red 450.00
Bowl, 8" to 9" d., stippled, aqua........50.00
Bowl, 8" to 9" d., green........25.00 to 30.00
Bowl, 8" to 9" d., marigold 27.50
Bowl, 8" to 9" d., peach opalescent ...195.00
Bowl, 8" to 9" d., purple (ILLUS.) 37.50
Pitcher, water, marigold 130.00
Rose bowl, green 65.00
Rose bowl, ice green 65.00
Rose bowl, marigold 50.00
Rose bowl, purple...................70.00
Tumbler, marigold 48.00
Water set: pitcher & 6 tumblers;
marigold, 7 pcs. 425.00

COIN SPOT
Compote, 7" d., marigold 25.00
Compote, 7" d., fluted, peach
opalescent.......................46.00
Plate, 9" d., purple..................35.00

COMET or RIBBON TIE (Fenton)
Bowl, 8" to 9" d., blue 50.00
Bowl, 8" to 9" d., green 51.50
Bowl, 8" to 9" d., marigold (ILLUS.) 33.50
Bowl, 8" to 9" d., purple 37.50
Plate, 9" d., ruffled, blue.............160.00
Plate, 9" d., ruffled, purple...........115.00

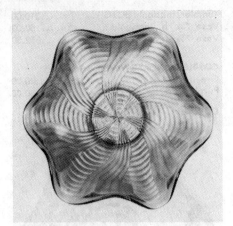

Comet Bowl

CONE & FLUTE
Creamer, marigold..................15.00
Pitcher, marigold 110.00

CONSTELLATION
Compote, marigold 52.50
Compote, white 72.50
Plate, 7" d., white.................32.50

CONTINENTAL BOTTLE
Marigold 25.00

CORAL (Fenton)
Bowl, 8½" d., collared base, green....120.00
Bowl, 9½" d., collared base,
  marigold ....55.00 to 70.00
Plate, 9" d., marigold...............695.00

CORN BOTTLE

Corn Bottle
Green............................225.00
Marigold 200.00
Smoky (ILLUS.) 210.00

CORN VASE (Northwood)
Green (ILLUS.)....................350.00

Corn Vase

Ice green 265.00
Marigold 400.00
Purple ....385.00 to 425.00
White 190.00

CORNUCOPIA
Candlestick, white (single) 85.00
Vase, 5" h., marigold...............34.00

COSMOS

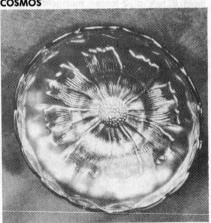

Cosmos Bowl

Bowl, 5" d., green..................40.00
Bowl, 9" d., green (ILLUS.) 70.00
Bowl, 9" d., marigold 27.50
Bowl, ice cream, 10½" d., marigold 88.00
Plate, 7" d., green 62.50
Plate, chop, 10½" d., marigold 115.00

COSMOS & CANE
Bowl, 10" d., white.................127.50
Butter dish, cov., white (ILLUS.) 300.00
Compote, marigold 60.00
Compote, white 180.00
Cuspidor, clambroth 675.00

Cosmos & Cane Butter Dish

Cuspidor, white 750.00
Pitcher, white 1,200.00
Rose bowl, Headdress interior,
   marigold 150.00
Spooner, 2-handled, marigold 65.00
Tumbler, amber 125.00
Tumbler, clambroth 110.00
Tumbler, marigold 78.50
Tumbler, marigold, w/advertising 120.00

COUNTRY KITCHEN (Millersburg)
Bowl, 5" d., ruffled, marigold......... .75.00
Spooner, marigold 100.00
Sugar bowl, cov., vaseline 550.00

CRAB CLAW

Crab Claw Water Set

Bowl, 8" to 9" d., fluted rim, smoky 50.00
Pitcher, marigold 220.00
Sauce dish, smoky 20.00
Tumbler, marigold 55.00
Water set: pitcher & 4 tumblers;
   marigold, 5 pcs. (ILLUS.) 250.00

CRACKLE
Automobile vases, marigold, pr.
   (no brackets)..................... .22.00
Candy jar, cov., marigold 15.00
Cuspidor, marigold 50.00
Plate, 9½" d., purple............... .40.00
Tumblers, dome-footed, marigold,
   set of 6 .... .80.00

Water set: cov. pitcher & 5 tumblers;
   marigold, 6 pcs. 90.00

CRUCIFIX
Candlesticks, marigold, pr. 400.00

CURVED STAR
Chalice, marigold................. .90.00
Epergne, 3-lily, marigold............ .190.00

CUT ARCS
Bowl, 9" d., marigold 20.00

DAHLIA
Berry set: master bowl & 5 sauce
   dishes; purple, 6 pcs.............. .275.00
Bowl, master berry, 10" d., footed,
   white 170.00
Creamer, marigold................. .80.00
Creamer, purple 125.00
Creamer & spooner, purple, pr....... .225.00
Pitcher, water, purple 595.00
Pitcher, water, white ...... .550.00 to 600.00
Sauce dish, white 50.00
Spooner, marigold 60.00
Sugar bowl, cov., purple 100.00
Table set, purple, 4 pcs. 825.00
Table set, white, 4 pcs. 650.00
Tumbler, marigold 82.50
Tumbler, purple 92.50
Tumbler, white 175.00
Water set: pitcher & 6 tumblers;
   marigold, 7 pcs.................. 1,025.00

DAISIES & DRAPE VASE (Northwood)
Aqua opalescent................... .325.00
Blue........................... .185.00
Marigold 135.00
Purple......................... .175.00
White 120.00

DAISY & LATTICE BAND
Pitcher, tankard, marigold.... 90.00 to 125.00
Tumbler, blue 50.00
Tumbler, marigold 22.50
Water set: pitcher & 6 tumblers;
   marigold, 7 pcs. 225.00

DAISY & PLUME
Bowl, 8" to 9" d., 3-footed,
   marigold 45.00
Candy dish, footed, green............ .48.00
Compote, green 37.50
Compote, marigold 32.50
Compote, purple.................. .45.00
Rose bowl, 3-footed, blue........... .50.00
Rose bowl, 3-footed, green........... .42.50
Rose bowl, 3-footed, ice green........ .625.00
Rose bowl, 3-footed, marigold 40.00
Rose bowl, 3-footed, purple (ILLUS.) 70.00

Daisy & Plume Rose Bowl

DAISY BLOCK ROWBOAT
Marigold, 12" l., 4" w., 3¼" h. 185.00
Purple. 215.00

DAISY WREATH
Bowl, 8" to 9" d., blue opalescent 265.00
Bowl, 8" to 9" d., milk glass
   w/marigold overlay 145.00
Bowl, 8" to 9" d., peach opalescent 60.00

DANDELION (Northwood)
Mug, aqua opalescent 450.00
Mug, blue. 385.00
Mug, ice blue. 625.00
Mug, green 650.00
Mug, marigold 265.00
Mug, purple. 280.00
Mug, Knight's Templar, ice blue 1,000.00
Mug, Knight's Templar, ice green 900.00
Mug, Knight's Templar, marigold 375.00
Pitcher, water, green. 750.00
Pitcher, water, marigold 325.00
Pitcher, water, purple 825.00
Tumbler, green. 87.50
Tumbler, ice blue 195.00
Tumbler, ice green 245.00
Tumbler, marigold 38.50
Tumbler, purple .55.00
Tumbler, white .135.00
Water set: pitcher & 6 tumblers;
   marigold, 7 pcs. 525.00
Water set: pitcher & 6 tumblers;
   purple, 7 pcs. 750.00

DANDELION, PANELED
Pitcher, water, blue 325.00
Pitcher, water, green (ILLUS.) 335.00
Pitcher, water, marigold 185.00
Pitcher, water, purple 385.00
Tumbler, blue 40.00
Tumbler, green . . . . .32.50 to 40.00
Tumbler, marigold 35.00
Tumbler, purple .27.50
Water set: pitcher & 6 tumblers;
   blue, 7 pcs. . . . . .500.00 to 650.00

Paneled Dandelion Pitcher

Water set: pitcher & 6 tumblers;
   green, 7 pcs. .735.00
Water set: pitcher & 6 tumblers;
   marigold, 7 pcs. 450.00
Water set: pitcher & 6 tumblers;
   purple, 7 pcs. 650.00

DIAMOND (Millersburg)
Pitcher, water, green. 215.00
Pitcher, water, marigold 237.00
Pitcher, water, purple 185.00
Punch bowl & base, purple, 2 pcs. 900.00
Tumbler, green 45.00
Tumbler, marigold 40.00
Tumbler, purple . . . . .35.00 to 45.00
Water set: pitcher & 5 tumblers;
   green, 6 pcs. .400.00
Water set: pitcher & 6 tumblers;
   marigold, 7 pcs. 390.00
Water set: pitcher & 6 tumblers;
   purple, 7 pcs. 475.00

DIAMOND CONCAVE
Tumbler, ice blue 27.50
Tumbler, vaseline. 210.00

DIAMOND LACE (Imperial)
Bowl, 5" d., purple 22.00
Bowl, 8" to 9" d., amber 48.00
Bowl, 8" to 9" d., clambroth 55.00
Bowl, 8" to 9" d., marigold 28.50
Bowl, 8" to 9" d., purple 62.50
Bowl, 10" d., purple. . . . . .40.00 to 70.00
Pitcher, water, purple 187.50
Tumbler, purple .42.50
Water set: pitcher & 6 tumblers;
   purple, 7 pcs. 430.00

DIAMOND POINT COLUMN
Vase, 6" h., marigold. 12.00
Vase, 8" h., green (ILLUS.) 30.00
Vase, 10" h., white 42.50

Diamond Point Column Vase

DIAMOND & RIB VASE
Vase, 8" h., green 22.00
Vase, 10" h., marigold..............22.00
Vase, 10" h., purple 29.00
Vase, 11" h., ice green 36.00
Vase, 12" h., purple 21.50
Vase, 19" h., purple 395.00

DIAMOND RING

Diamond Ring Bowl

Berry set: master bowl & 6 sauce
    dishes; marigold, 7 pcs.............40.00
Bowl, 8" to 9" d., marigold 27.50
Bowl, 8" to 9" d., smoky (ILLUS.) 38.50

DIAMOND & SUNBURST
Decanter w/stopper, marigold 60.00
Wine, marigold.....................28.50
Wine, purple 35.00
Wine set: decanter w/stopper & 6
    wines; marigold, 7 pcs............325.00
Wine set: decanter w/stopper & 6
    wines; purple, 7 pcs. 495.00

DIVING DOLPHINS FOOTED BOWL

Diving Dolphins Bowl

Marigold 160.00
Purple (ILLUS.)....................300.00

DOGWOOD SPRAYS
Bowl, 8" to 9" d., dome-footed, peach
    opalescent......................85.00
Bowl, 8" to 9" d., dome-footed, purple ..65.00

DOLPHINS COMPOTE (Millersburg)
Blue, Rosalind interior 2,500.00
Marigold, Rosalind interior..........168.00
Purple, Rosalind interior.....750.00 to 800.00

DOUBLE DUTCH BOWL
Marigold, 7" d. 20.00
Purple, 7" d. 42.00
Marigold, 8" to 9" d., footed........32.50
Purple, 8" to 9" d., footed 80.00

DOUBLE STAR or BUZZ SAW (Cambridge)
Cruet w/stopper, green, small, 4".....400.00
Cruet w/stopper, marigold, large, 6" ..241.00
Pitcher, water, green...............225.00
Pitcher, water, marigold............425.00
Tumbler, green 50.00

DOUBLE STEM ROSE
Bowl, 8" to 9" d., dome-footed,
    marigold 26.00
Bowl, 8" to 9" d., dome-footed,
    peach opalescent 55.00
Bowl, 8" to 9" d., dome-footed, purple ..50.00
Bowl, 8" to 9" d., dome-footed, white...77.50

DRAGON & LOTUS (Fenton)
Bowl, 7" d., 3-footed, blue .....50.00 to 65.00
Bowl, 7" d., 3-footed, purple 50.00
Bowl, 8" to 9" d., amber ......80.00 to 100.00
Bowl, 8" to 9" d., collared base,
    aqua opalescent..................650.00
Bowl, 8" to 9" d., 3-footed, blue
    (ILLUS.)........................60.00
Bowl, 8" to 9" d., 3-footed, green 62.50
Bowl, 8" to 9" d., collared base,
    lime green opalescent............590.00
Bowl, 8" to 9" d., 3-footed, marigold....40.00

Dragon & Lotus Bowl

Bowl, 8" to 9" d., milk glass
   w/marigold iridescence 695.00
Bowl, 8" to 9" d., 3-footed, peach
   opalescent.....................475.00
Bowl, 8" to 9" d., 3-footed,
   purple ....60.00 to 75.00
Bowl, 8" to 9" d., red .... 525.00 to 600.00
Bowl, 8" to 9" d., blue base
   w/marigold overlay 40.00
Bowl, ice cream shape, 10" d.,
   amber ....150.00 to 165.00
Bowl, ice cream shape, 10" d., blue 55.00
Bowl, ice cream shape, 10" d.,
   red ....475.00 to 550.00
Plate, collared base, blue 665.00
Plate, spatula footed, marigold 650.00

DRAGON & STRAWBERRY BOWL (Fenton)
Bowl, 9" d., blue 475.00
Bowl, 9" d., green....................400.00
Bowl, 9" d., marigold 315.00

DRAPERY (Northwood)
Candy dish, tricornered, ice
   blue ....90.00 to 115.00
Rose bowl, aqua opalescent 190.00
Rose bowl, blue 90.00
Rose bowl, ice blue opalescent 198.00
Rose bowl, marigold ....145.00 to 350.00
Rose bowl, purple ....160.00 to 195.00
Vase, 7" h., aqua opalescent 175.00
Vase, 7" h., blue.....................60.00
Vase, 8" h., ice green 100.00
Vase, 8" h., white...................45.00
Vase, purple 35.00

EMBROIDERED MUMS (Northwood)
Bowl, 8" to 9" d., amber 125.00
Bowl, 8" to 9" d., blue 115.00
Bowl, 8" to 9" d., ice blue 235.00
Bowl, 8" to 9" d., ice green 265.00
Bowl, 8" to 9" d., marigold 52.00
Bowl, 8" to 9" d., purple 85.00
Plate, ice green ....700.00 to 950.00

ESTATE
Creamer, marigold opalescent 45.00

Creamer, peach opalescent 75.00
Creamer & sugar bowl, aqua opal-
   escent, pr. 275.00
Creamer & sugar bowl, peach opal-
   escent, pr. 87.50
Mug, marigold 72.50

FANCIFUL (Dugan)
Bowl, 8" to 9" d., peach opalescent 155.00
Bowl, 8" to 9" d., purple 65.00
Bowl, 8" to 9" d., shallow, white 75.00
Plate, 9" d., blue ....120.00 to 150.00
Plate, 9" d., marigold................90.00
Plate, 9" d., peach opalescent 360.00
Plate, 9" d., purple ....225.00 to 250.00
Plate, 9" d., white ....95.00 to 125.00

FANTAIL
Bowl, 9" d., footed, blue 50.00
Bowl, 9" d., footed, w/Butterfly &
   Berry exterior, shallow, blue 95.00
Bowl, 9" d., footed, green 80.00
Bowl, 9" d., footed, marigold 50.00

FARMYARD BOWLS & PLATES

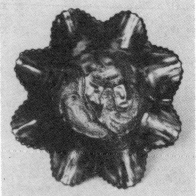

Farmyard Bowl

Bowl, purple (ILLUS.) 2,500.00
Plate, 10" d., purple 8,125.00

FASHION (Imperial)

Fashion Tumbler & Pitcher

Bowl, 9" d., marigold 20.00
Bowl, 9" d., ruffled, smoky 45.00
Compote, smoky 150.00
Creamer, purple 30.00
Creamer, breakfast size, smoky 50.00
Creamer & sugar bowl, marigold, pr. . . .60.00
Pitcher, water, marigold (ILLUS.
    right) . . . . .120.00 to 140.00
Pitcher, water, purple 750.00
Pitcher, water, smoky 332.50
Punch bowl & base, marigold, 12" d.,
    2 pcs. 72.50
Punch cup, marigold 12.50
Punch cup, smoky 30.00
Punch set: 12" d. bowl, base & 4
    cups; marigold, 6 pcs. 95.00
Rose bowl, marigold, 7" d. 42.50
Sugar bowl, marigold 20.00
Sugar bowl, smoky 90.00
Tumbler, marigold (ILLUS. left) 25.00
Tumbler, smoky 85.00
Water set: pitcher & 6 tumblers;
    marigold, 7 pcs. 235.00
Water set: pitcher & 6 tumblers;
    smoky, 7 pcs. 400.00

FEATHER & HEART

Feather & Heart Tumbler

Pitcher, water, green 550.00
Pitcher, water, marigold 395.00
Pitcher, water, purple 475.00
Tumbler, green 150.00
Tumbler, marigold . . . . .55.00 to 85.00
Tumbler, purple (ILLUS.) 115.00
Water set: pitcher & 1 tumbler;
    green, 2 pcs. 500.00
Water set: pitcher & 5 tumblers;
    marigold, 6 pcs. 500.00

FEATHER STITCH BOWL

Blue 55.00
Marigold 42.50

FEATHERED SERPENT

Berry set: master bowl & 6 sauce
    dishes; marigold, 7 pcs. 195.00
Bowl, 8" to 9" d., green 70.00
Bowl, 8" to 9" d., marigold 48.00
Bowl, 8" to 9" d., purple 47.50

Bowl, 10" d., ruffled, blue 63.50
Bowl, 10" d., fluted, green 45.00
Bowl, 10" d., flared, purple 62.50
Sauce dish, green 20.00
Sauce dish, marigold 16.50

FENTON'S BASKET

Aqua, 2 sides turned up 38.00
Blue 100.00
Ice blue w/three rows of lace 60.00
Ice green 85.00
Marigold 18.00
Purple 50.00
Red . . . . .195.00 to 300.00
Vaseline . . . . .40.00 to 58.00
White, square . . . . .45.00 to 85.00

FENTON'S FLOWERS

Rose bowl, blue 75.00
Rose bowl, green 56.50
Rose bowl, ice green opalescent 650.00
Rose bowl, marigold 58.00
Rose bowl, white 275.00

FENTONIA

Fentonia Water Set

Butter dish, cov., footed, marigold 120.00
Creamer, marigold 65.00
Pitcher, water, blue (ILLUS.) 375.00
Pitcher, water, marigold 230.00
Spooner, blue .85.00
Spooner, marigold 60.00
Table set, marigold, 4 pcs. 350.00
Tumbler, blue (ILLUS.) 57.50
Tumbler, marigold 40.00
Water set: pitcher & 6 tumblers;
    marigold, 7 pcs. 310.00

FERN

Compote, 6" d., 5" h., purple 39.50
Compote, w/Daisy & Plume exterior,
    purple 47.50
Dish, hat-shaped, red 375.00

FIELD FLOWER

Pitcher, water, green 185.00
Pitcher, water, marigold 90.00
Pitcher, water, purple 400.00
Tumbler, green 55.00
Tumbler, marigold 27.50

FIELD THISTLE (English)

Bowl, 10" d., marigold	.50.00
Compote, marigold	.195.00
Pitcher, water, marigold	.250.00
Plate, 6" d., marigold	.60.00
Plate, 9" d., marigold	.295.00
Spooner, marigold	.55.00
Table set: cov. butter dish, creamer & spooner; marigold, 3 pcs.	.170.00
Tumbler, marigold	.60.00
Vase, 7" h., marigold	.45.00
Water set: pitcher & 4 tumblers; marigold, 5 pcs.	.380.00

FILE & FAN

Compote, blue opalescent	.125.00
Compote, peach opalescent	.65.00 to 85.00

FINECUT & ROSES (Northwood)

Candy dish, 3-footed, amber	.55.00
Candy dish, 3-footed, green	.55.00
Candy dish, 3-footed, ice blue	.95.00
Candy dish, 3-footed, marigold	.30.00
Candy dish, 3-footed, purple	.45.00
Candy dish, 3-footed, white	.90.00
Rose bowl, aqua opalescent	.700.00
Rose bowl, green	.190.00
Rose bowl, ice blue	.215.00 to 250.00
Rose bowl, marigold	.65.00 to 90.00
Rose bowl, purple	.78.50

FINE RIB (Northwood & Fenton)

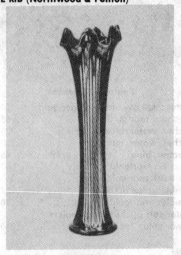

Fine Rib Vase

Vase, 6½" h., 5" d., squatty, marigold	.32.00
Vase, 9" h., scalloped rim, blue	.28.00
Vase, 9" h., fluted rim, ice green	.40.00
Vase, 9" h., 3½" d., marigold	.20.00
Vase, 9" h., red, Fenton	.160.00
Vase, 10" h., amber	.27.00
Vase, 10" h., flared top, ice green	.65.00
Vase, 11" h., blue (ILLUS.)	.40.00
Vase, 11" h., purple	.20.00

Vase, 12" h., red, Fenton	.215.00
Vase, 14" h., ice green	.225.00
Vase, 15" h., blue	.50.00
Vase, 15" h., marigold	.22.00

FISHERMAN'S MUG

Fisherman's Mug

Marigold	.195.00 to 235.00
Peach opalescent	.1,085.00
Purple (ILLUS.)	.87.50

FISHSCALE & BEADS

Bowl, 7" d., marigold	.15.00
Bowl, 7" d., ribbon candy rim, purple	.25.00
Plate, 7" d., ruffled rim, peach opalescent	.65.00
Plate, 7" d., white	.75.00
Plate, 8" d., clambroth	.49.50
Plate, 8" d., flat, marigold	.52.00

FLEUR DE LIS (Millersburg)

Fleur De Lis Bowl

Bowl, 10" d., green	.140.00 to 185.00
Bowl, 10" d., marigold	.145.00
Bowl, 10" d., purple (ILLUS.)	.175.00

FLORAL & GRAPE

Pitcher, water, blue	.175.00
Pitcher, water, marigold	.70.00 to 85.00
Pitcher, water, purple	.175.00
Pitcher, water, white	.237.50

Tumbler, blue ....25.00 to 35.00
Tumbler, marigold 16.00
Tumbler, purple 32.50
Water set: pitcher & 6 tumblers;
    blue, 7 pcs. 335.00
Water set: pitcher & 6 tumblers;
    marigold, 7 pcs. 210.00

FLORAL & WHEAT COMPOTE
Clambroth 35.00
Marigold 25.00
Peach opalescent 95.00
White 70.00

FLOWERS & FRAMES
Bowl, 7" d., dome-footed, purple 120.00
Bowl, 9" d., dome-footed, peach
    opalescent.......................97.50

FLUTE (Imperial)

Flute Punch Set

Berry set: master bowl & 6 sauce
    dishes; purple, 7 pcs..............250.00
Bowl, 8" to 9" d., green 40.00
Breakfast set: individual size
    creamer & sugar bowl; purple, pr....110.00
Creamer, clambroth.................15.00
Creamer, marigold.................29.00
Pitcher, water, clambroth............100.00
Pitcher, water, marigold.............175.00
Punch cup, green 15.00
Punch cup, marigold 30.00
Punch cup, purple..................28.00
Punch set: bowl, base & 5 cups;
    purple, 7 pcs. (ILLUS.) 535.00
Salt dip, footed, individual size,
    marigold 40.00
Sauce dish, marigold 25.00
Sauce dish, purple 26.00
Sugar bowl, breakfast size, purple 70.00
Sugar bowl, cov., green 20.00
Toothpick holder, green ....50.00 to 75.00
Toothpick holder, lavender...........125.00
Toothpick holder, marigold 60.00
Toothpick holder, purple.............60.00
Toothpick holder, vaseline w/marigold
    overlay.........................295.00
Tumbler, marigold 39.00

Tumbler, purple 60.00
Vase, 9" h., marigold................35.00

FLUTE & CANE
Goblet, marigold 85.00
Pitcher, milk, marigold .....110.00 to 125.00
Pitcher, tankard, marigold 365.00

FOUR SEVENTY FOUR
Goblet, water, marigold 125.00
Pitcher, milk, green 185.00
Pitcher, milk, marigold 85.00
Pitcher, milk, purple 200.00
Pitcher, water, green...............360.00
Pitcher, water, marigold ....125.00 to 190.00
Punch bowl & base, green, 2 pcs.......390.00
Punch bowl & base, marigold, 2 pcs.....65.00
Punch bowl & base, purple, 2 pcs. 900.00
Punch cup, green 25.00
Punch cup, marigold 18.00
Punch cup, purple..................45.00
Punch set: bowl, base & 2 cups;
    marigold, 4 pcs. 250.00
Punch set: bowl, base & 5 cups;
    green, 7 pcs. 350.00
Tumbler, marigold 32.50
Whiskey (or wine) decanter
    w/stopper 625.00

FROLICKING BEARS

Frolicking Bears Pitcher

Pitcher, green (ILLUS.) 3,000.00

FROSTED BLOCK
Bowl, scalloped & fluted, clambroth 26.50
Creamer, clambroth..................16.00
Plate, 7" sq., clambroth.............18.00
Plate, 9" d., clambroth..............28.50
Relish, marigold 37.50
Rose bowl, clambroth 60.00
Sugar bowl, clambroth 20.00

FRUIT SALAD
Punch bowl & base, purple, 2 pcs. 750.00

Punch cup, marigold 11.00
Punch cup, peach opalescent 90.00

FRUITS & FLOWERS (Northwood)
Berry set: master bowl & 4 sauce
   dishes; purple, 5 pcs..............150.00
Bon bon, stemmed, 2-handled, aqua
   opalescent......................375.00
Bon bon, stemmed, 2-handled, blue ..125.00
Bon bon, stemmed, 2-handled, green...55.00
Bon bon, stemmed, 2-handled, ice
   blue...........................260.00
Bon bon, stemmed, 2-handled,
   marigold ....36.00 to 40.00
Bon bon, stemmed, 2-handled, purple ..85.00
Bon bon, stemmed, 2-handled, white ..132.00
Bowl, 7" d., purple................125.00
Bowl, 8" to 9" d., aqua opalescent.....350.00
Bowl, master berry, 10" d., ice green ..750.00
Plate, 7" d., hand-grip, green........125.00
Plate, 7" d., hand-grip, marigold.......60.00
Plate, 7½" d., hand-grip, pastel
   marigold 185.00
Plate, 7½" d., hand-grip, purple ..87.50
Sauce dish, purple ....28.00 to 35.00

GARDEN PATH

Garden Path Chop Plate

Bowl, 8" to 9" d., marigold 36.50
Bowl, 10" d., ruffled, marigold........68.00
Plate, 7" d., peach opalescent 500.00
Plate, chop, 11" d., purple (ILLUS.)...1,775.00
Sauce dish, peach opalescent........165.00
Sauce dish, purple 75.00

GARLAND ROSE BOWL (Fenton)
Blue...............................60.00
Marigold 37.50

GAY NINETIES
Pitcher, green 5,550.00
Tumbler, purple...................1,000.00

GOD & HOME
Tumbler, blue.............175.00 to 190.00

Water set: pitcher & 6 tumblers;
   blue, 7 pcs......................2,400.00

GODDESS OF HARVEST

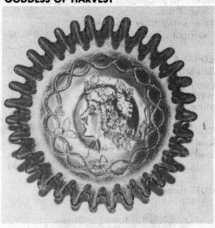

Goddess of Harvest Bowl

Bowl, marigold (ILLUS.) 4,200.00

GOLDEN HARVEST
Decanter w/stopper,
   marigold ....110.00 to 135.00
Wine, marigold.....................19.00
Wine, purple 30.00
Wine set: decanter & 6 wines;
   marigold, 7 pcs. 195.00
Wine set: decanter & 6 wines;
   purple, 7 pcs.....................340.00

GOOD LUCK

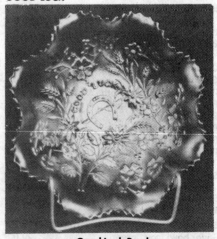

Good Luck Bowl

Bowl, 8" to 9" d., fluted, aqua
   opalescent......................635.00
Bowl, 8" to 9" d., fluted, blue 175.00
Bowl, 8" to 9" d., fluted,
   green ....125.00 to 225.00
Bowl, 8" to 9" d., fluted, marigold 100.00

Bowl, 8" to 9" d., fluted, purple
(ILLUS.) 125.00
Bowl, 8" to 9" d., fluted, teal blue 500.00
Plate, 9" d., green 400.00
Plate, 9" d., marigold. 220.00
Plate, 9" d., purple 175.00
Plate, 9" d., white 1,600.00
Plate, 9" d., w/Basketweave exterior,
purple. 375.00

GRAPE & CABLE
Banana boat, blue 235.00
Banana boat, green 235.00
Banana boat, ice blue . . . . . . .400.00 to 450.00
Banana boat, ice green 450.00
Banana boat, marigold 175.00
Banana boat, purple 200.00
Berry set: master bowl & 6 sauce
dishes; green, 7 pcs. 245.00
Berry set: master bowl & 6 sauce
dishes; purple, 7 pcs. 220.00
Bon bon, 2-handled, blue 75.00
Bon bon, 2-handled, green 55.00
Bon bon, 2-handled, marigold 42.50
Bon bon, 2-handled, purple 50.00
Bowl, 5" d., blue, Northwood 35.00
Bowl, 5" d., blue, Fenton. 25.00
Bowl, 5" d., marigold. 35.00
Bowl, 5" d., purple 30.00
Bowl, 7½" d., ball-footed, amber,
Fenton 100.00
Bowl, 7½" d., ball-footed, blue,
Fenton 30.00
Bowl, 7½" d., ball-footed, green,
Fenton 45.00
Bowl, 7½" d., ball-footed, marigold,
Fenton 27.50
Bowl, 7½" d., ball-footed, purple,
Fenton 57.50
Bowl, 7½" d., ball-footed, red,
Fenton 410.00
Bowl, 7½" d., ball-footed, vaseline,
Fenton 100.00
Bowl, 7½" d., flat, purple 27.50
Bowl, 7½" d., ruffled, ice blue 500.00
Bowl, 7½" d., spatula-footed, blue,
Northwood 60.00
Bowl, 7½" d., spatula-footed, green,
Northwood 45.00
Bowl, 7½" d., spatula-footed, mari-
gold, Northwood 30.00
Bowl, 7½" d., spatula-footed, purple,
Northwood 40.00
Bowl, 8" to 9" d., aqua opalescent,
Northwood 900.00
Bowl, 8" to 9" d., ball-footed, purple,
Fenton 42.50
Bowl, 8" to 9" d., ball-footed, red,
Fenton 425.00
Bowl, 8" to 9" d., spatula-footed,
green, Northwood 55.00
Bowl, 8" to 9" d., spatula-footed, mari-
gold, Northwood 52.50

Bowl, 8" to 9" d., spatula-footed,
ruffled, purple, Northwood 65.00
Bowl, 8" to 9" d., stippled, ice blue 600.00
Bowl, berry or fruit, 9" d., clambroth . . .50.00
Bowl, berry or fruit, 9" d., green 75.00
Bowl, berry or fruit, 9" d., stippled,
ice blue . . . . .475.00 to 800.00
Bowl, berry or fruit, 9" d., ice
green . . . . .650.00 to 750.00
Bowl, berry or fruit, 9" d.,
marigold . . . . .90.00 to 125.00
Bowl, berry or fruit, 9" d.,
purple . . . . .70.00 to 95.00
Bowl, orange, 10½" d., Persian
Medallion interior, blue, Fenton 300.00
Bowl, orange, 10½" d., footed,
Persian Medallion interior, green,
Fenton 245.00
Bowl, orange, 10½" d., footed,
Persian Medallion interior,
marigold, Fenton 75.00
Bowl, orange, 10½" d., footed, ice
blue. 825.00
Bowl, orange, 10½" d., footed,
marigold 110.00
Bowl, orange, 10½" d., footed,
purple. 225.00
Bowl, ice cream, 11" d., marigold 55.00
Bowl, ice cream, 11" d., white 195.00
Breakfast set: individual size creamer
& sugar bowl; green, pr. 150.00
Breakfast set: individual size creamer
& sugar bowl; marigold, pr. 77.50
Butter dish, cov., green 175.00
Butter dish, cov., marigold 150.00
Butter dish, cov., purple 180.00

Grape & Cable Candle Lamp

Candle lamp, green (ILLUS.) 585.00
Candle lamp, purple 475.00
Candle lamp shade, green 235.00
Candle lamp shade, marigold 210.00
Candle lamp shade, purple. 235.00
Candlestick, green (single) . . .80.00 to 110.00
Candlesticks, marigold, pr. 150.00
Candlesticks, purple, pr. 220.00

Centerpiece bowl, ice green 650.00
Centerpiece bowl, marigold 220.00
Centerpiece bowl, purple 250.00
Centerpiece bowl, white 350.00
Cologne bottle w/stopper,
  marigold . . . . .135.00 to 165.00
Cologne bottle w/stopper, purple 200.00
Compote, cov., purple, large 395.00
Compote, open, green, large 400.00
Compote, open, marigold, large 250.00
Compote, open, purple,
  large . . . . .365.00 to 400.00
Cookie jar, marigold 265.00
Cookie jar, purple . . . . .275.00 to 300.00
Creamer, purple 125.00
Creamer, individual size, green. 60.00
Creamer, individual size, marigold 75.00
Creamer, individual size, purple 67.50
Cup & saucer, green 425.00
Cuspidor, cov., purple 350.00
Decanter w/stopper, whiskey,
  marigold 650.00
Decanter w/stopper, whiskey,
  purple . . . . .700.00 to 900.00
Dish, blue, 6" d. 53.50
Dish, purple, 6" d. 90.00
Dresser tray, green 120.00
Dresser tray, marigold . . . . . .125.00 to 155.00
Dresser tray, purple 195.00
Fernery, ice blue 1,200.00
Fernery, purple 490.00
Fernery, white . . . . .1,400.00 to 2,000.00
Hatpin holder, green 185.00
Hatpin holder, marigold 150.00
Hatpin holder, purple . . . . . . .125.00 to 175.00
Hat shape, marigold 32.50
Hat shape, purple 50.00
Humidor, marigold 255.00
Nappy, single handle, marigold. 52.50
Nappy, single handle, purple 90.00
Pin tray, marigold . . . . .120.00 to 145.00
Pin tray, purple 165.00
Pitcher, water, 8¼" h., marigold. 200.00
Pitcher, water, 8¼" h., purple 250.00
Pitcher, tankard, 9¾" h.,
  marigold . . . . .435.00 to 500.00
Pitcher, tankard, 9¾" h.,
  purple . . . . .550.00 to 575.00
Plate, 7½" d., turned-up hand grip,
  marigold 55.00
Plate, 7½" d., turned-up hand grip,
  purple 65.00
Plate, 8" d., footed, purple 85.00
Plate, 9" d., green 83.50
Plate, 9" d., spatula-footed,
  green . . . . .85.00 to 110.00
Plate, 9" d., marigold. 75.00
Plate, 9" d., spatula-footed, marigold . .72.50
Plate, 9" d., purple 90.00
Plate, 9" d., spatula-footed, purple. . . .110.00
Plate, 9" d., w/Basketweave exterior,
  green . . . . .85.00 to 100.00
Plate, 9" d., w/Basketweave exterior,
  marigold 100.00

Plate, 9" d., stippled, blue 130.00
Plate, 9" d., stippled,
  green . . . . .200.00 to 300.00
Plate, 9" d., stippled, marigold 60.00
Plate, 9" d., stippled, purple. 100.00
Plate, 9" d., stippled, teal blue 1,100.00
Powder jar, cov., green 125.00
Powder jar, cov., marigold. . . . . .65.00 to 75.00
Powder jar, cov., purple . . . . .80.00 to 100.00
Punch bowl & base, blue, 11" d., 2 pcs. . .415.00
Punch cup, green . . . . .25.00 to 35.00
Punch cup, marigold . . . . .12.00 to 20.00
Punch cup, purple. 22.50
Punch set: bowl, base & 3 cups;
  purple, 5 pcs. 625.00
Punch set: 11" bowl, base & 6 cups;
  stippled, blue, 8 pcs. 395.00
Punch set: 11" bowl, base & 6 cups;
  marigold, 8 pcs. 350.00
Punch set: 14" bowl, base & 8 cups;
  marigold, 10 pcs. 700.00
Punch set: 14" bowl, base & 12 cups;
  purple, 14 pcs. 1,400.00
Punch set: 17" bowl, base & 8 cups;
  purple, 10 pcs. 1,550.00
Sauce dish, green . . . . .18.00 to 25.00
Sauce dish, marigold 19.00
Sherbet or individual ice cream dish,
  blue. 25.00
Sherbet or individual ice cream dish,
  ice green 120.00
Sherbet or individual ice cream dish,
  marigold . . . . .20.00 to 35.00
Sherbet or individual ice cream dish,
  purple. 45.00
Spooner, green 125.00
Spooner, marigold 62.50
Spooner, purple 105.00
Sugar bowl, cov., marigold. 75.00
Sugar bowl, cov., purple 110.00
Sugar bowl, individual size, green 85.00
Sugar bowl, individual size, marigold. . .60.00
Sugar bowl, individual size, purple 56.00

Grape & Cable Sweetmeat

Sweetmeat jar, cov., purple
  (ILLUS.) . . . . .185.00 to 225.00

Table set, purple, 4 pcs. . . . . . 450.00 to 575.00
Tumbler, green 40.00
Tumbler, marigold 35.00
Tumbler, purple . . . . .25.00 to 38.00
Tumbler, tankard, blue 79.00
Tumbler, tankard, green 175.00
Tumbler, tankard, marigold 40.00
Tumbler, tankard, purple 60.00
Water set: pitcher & 6 tumblers;
   green, 7 pcs. .435.00
Water set: pitcher & 6 tumblers;
   marigold, 7 pcs. 300.00
Water set: pitcher & 6 tumblers;
   purple, 7 pcs. . . . . .400.00 to 450.00
Whiskey set: whiskey decanter
   w/stopper & 1 shot glass; marigold,
   2 pcs. 750.00
Whiskey set: whiskey decanter
   w/stopper & 6 shot glasses; purple,
   7 pcs. 2,175.00
Whiskey shot glass,
   marigold . . . . .100.00 to 165.00
Whiskey shot glass, purple . .140.00 to 250.00

GRAPE & GOTHIC ARCHES (Northwood)

Grape & Gothic Arches Table Set

Bowl, master berry, marigold 35.00
Creamer, blue 46.00
Creamer & spooner, blue, 2 pcs. 90.00
Pitcher, water, blue . . . . .295.00 to 325.00
Pitcher, water, marigold 100.00
Sauce dish, marigold 15.00
Spooner, marigold 36.50
Sugar bowl, cov., green 75.00
Sugar bowl, cov., marigold 45.00
Table set, blue, 4 pcs. (ILLUS.) 350.00
Table set, marigold, 4 pcs. . . .175.00 to 195.00
Tumbler, blue 40.00
Tumbler, green 38.50
Tumbler, marigold 22.50
Water set: pitcher & 6 tumblers; blue,
   7 pcs. 425.00
Water set: pitcher & 6 tumblers;
   green, 7 pcs. 575.00
Water set: pitcher & 6 tumblers;
   marigold, 7 pcs. 270.00

GRAPE & LATTICE

Tumbler, blue 38.00
Tumbler, marigold 22.00

GRAPE ARBOR (Northwood)

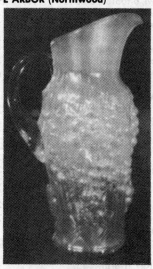

Grape Arbor Pitcher

Bowl, 10" d., footed, marigold 100.00
Bowl, orange, footed, marigold 85.00
Hat shape, blue .125.00
Hat shape, ice green 375.00
Pitcher, water, ice blue (ILLUS.) 710.00
Pitcher, water, marigold 240.00
Pitcher, water, white 495.00
Tumbler, blue 100.00
Tumbler, ice blue . . . . .115.00 to 135.00
Tumbler, marigold 20.00
Tumbler, purple .55.00
Tumbler, white .120.00
Water set: tankard pitcher & 1
   tumbler; ice blue, 2 pcs. 820.00
Water set: pitcher & 6 tumblers; ice
   green, 7 pcs. 8,500.00
Water set: pitcher & 6 tumblers;
   marigold, 7 pcs. 350.00
Water set: pitcher & 6 tumblers;
   purple, 7 pcs. 650.00

GRAPE DELIGHT

Grape Delight Rose Bowl

Nut bowl, 6-footed, blue 125.00
Nut bowl, 6-footed, marigold 47.50
Nut bowl, 6-footed, purple 72.50
Rose bowl, 6-footed, blue 55.00
Rose bowl, 6-footed, marigold 50.00
Rose bowl, 6-footed, purple 65.00
Rose bowl, 6-footed, white (ILLUS.) 65.00

GRAPEVINE LATTICE
Bowl, 7" d., ruffled, marigold 28.00
Bowl, 7" d., white 45.00
Pitcher, water, blue . . . . .225.00 to 410.00
Pitcher, water, marigold . . . .160.00 to 230.00
Pitcher, water, white 475.00
Plate, 6" to 7" d., marigold 36.00
Plate, 6" to 7" d., peach opalescent 130.00
Plate, 6" to 7" d., white 50.00
Tumbler, marigold 25.00
Tumbler, purple . . . . .60.00 to 75.00
Water set: pitcher & 6 tumblers;
    marigold, 7 pcs. 325.00

GREEK KEY (Northwood)

Greek Key Plate

Bowl, 8" to 9" d., fluted, green 58.00
Bowl, 8" to 9" d., ruffled, marigold 65.00
Bowl, 8" to 9" d., purple 70.00
Pitcher, water, marigold 700.00
Pitcher, water, purple 450.00
Plate, 9" d., marigold 300.00
Plate, 9" d., green (ILLUS.) 450.00
Tumbler, green . . . . .100.00 to 130.00
Tumbler, marigold . . . . .65.00 to 75.00
Tumbler, purple 82.50
Water set: pitcher & 6 tumblers;
    purple, 7 pcs. 895.00

HAMMERED BELL
Chandelier shade, white 77.00

HARVEST FLOWER
Pitcher, tankard, marigold 600.00
Tumbler, marigold 95.00

HATTIE (Imperial)

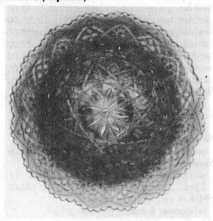

Hattie Bowl

Bowl, 8" to 9" d., marigold 50.00
Bowl, 8" to 9" d., purple 62.00
Bowl, 8" to 9" d., smoky (ILLUS.) 70.00
Plate, chop, green 275.00

HEADDRESS BOWL
Marigold 25.50
Compote, 6" d., 4¾" h., marigold 40.00

HEART & VINE (Fenton)

Heart & Vine Bowl

Bowl, 8" to 9" d., ribbon candy rim,
    blue (ILLUS.) 50.00
Bowl, 8" to 9" d., marigold 42.00
Bowl, 8" to 9" d., purple 45.00
Plate, 9" d., blue 220.00
Plate, 9" d., purple 130.00

HEARTS & FLOWERS (Northwood)
Bowl, 8" to 9" d., ruffled, blue 475.00
Bowl, 8" to 9" d., ruffled, green 180.00
Bowl, 8" to 9" d., ruffled, ice blue 225.00
Bowl, 8" to 9" d., ruffled, ice green 325.00

Bowl, 8" to 9" d., ruffled, marigold 43.50
Bowl, 8" to 9" d., ruffled, purple 69.00
Bowl, 8" to 9" d., ruffled, white 105.00

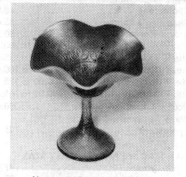

Hearts & Flowers Compote

Compote, 6¾" h., aqua opalescent
  (ILLUS.) ....300.00 to 350.00
Compote, 6¾" h., blue 145.00
Compote, 6¾" h., green 550.00
Compote, 6¾" h., ice blue 162.50
Compote, 6¾" h., marigold 75.00
Compote, 6¾" h., purple 175.00
Compote, 6¾" h., white 125.00
Plate, green......................300.00
Plate, ice green 1,000.00
Plate, purple 245.00

HEAVY GRAPE (Dugan)
Bowl, master berry, 10" d., peach
  opalescent.......................575.00
Bowl, master berry, 10" d., purple 175.00

HEAVY GRAPE (Imperial)
Berry set: master bowl & 6 sauce
  dishes; marigold, 7 pcs...........110.00
Bowl, 5" d., 2" h., marigold..........22.00
Bowl, 5" d., 2" h., purple 32.50
Bowl, 7" d., fluted, green 30.00
Bowl, 7" d., purple 50.00
Bowl, 8" to 9" d., marigold 26.50
Bowl, 10" d., marigold...............65.00
Bowl, 10" d., purple 55.00
Compote, green 300.00
Fruit bowl & base, marigold, 2 pcs.....250.00
Nappy, handled, green 25.00
Nappy, handled, marigold 18.00
Plate, 7" to 8" d., blue 65.00
Plate, 7" to 8" d., green 52.50
Plate, 7" to 8" d., marigold 40.00
Plate, 7" to 8" d., purple 70.00
Plate, chop, 11" d., amber 175.00
Plate, chop, 11" d., green 100.00
Plate, chop, 11" d., marigold 150.00
Plate, chop, 11" d., purple ...175.00 to 200.00

HOBNAIL (Millersburg)
Butter dish, cov., purple (ILLUS.) 550.00
Cuspidor, marigold 475.00
Cuspidor, purple....................600.00

Hobnail Butter Dish

Pitcher, water, blue 1,050.00
Pitcher, water, marigold 1,550.00
Pitcher, water, purple 1,500.00
Rose bowl, marigold 175.00
Rose bowl, purple...................220.00
Sugar bowl, cov., marigold..........400.00
Tumbler, blue 375.00
Tumbler, marigold 1,250.00
Water set: pitcher & 1 tumbler; blue,
  2 pcs........................2,350.00

HOBSTAR (Imperial)
Butter dish, cov., marigold 62.50
Compote, marigold 45.00
Creamer, marigold..................42.50
Spooner, marigold 40.00
Spooner, purple 85.00

HOBSTAR & FEATHER (Millersburg)

Hobstar & Feather Punch Set

Punch cup, green 28.50
Punch cup, marigold 22.50
Punch cup, purple..................80.00
Punch set: bowl, base & 12 cups;
  marigold, 14 pcs. (ILLUS.).........1,525.00
Rose bowl, green, 7½" top d.,
  13" h..........................2,000.00
Sauce dish, purple, 4" d. 190.00
Vase, purple 450.00

HOBSTAR BAND
Celery vase, 2-handled, marigold 75.00
Pitcher, marigold 150.00

Hobstar Band Tumbler

Tumbler, marigold (ILLUS.) 33.50
Water set: pitcher & 6 tumblers;
   marigold, 7 pcs. 285.00

HOLLY, HOLLY BERRIES & CARNIVAL HOLLY
Bon bon, 2-handled, blue 65.00
Bon bon, 2-handled, purple 60.00
Bowl, 5" d., marigold 20.00
Bowl, 7" d., fluted, peach opalescent . . .55.00
Bowl, 7" d., purple 48.00
Bowl, 8" to 9" d., blue 60.00
Bowl, 8" to 9" d., green 55.00
Bowl, 8" to 9" d., marigold 55.00
Bowl, 8" to 9" d., purple 50.00

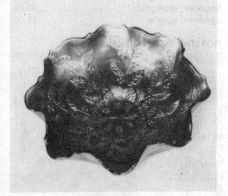

Holly Bowl in Red

Bowl, 8" to 9" d., red (ILLUS.) 650.00
Bowl, 10" d., fluted, green 77.50
Bowl, 10" d., fluted, marigold 150.00
Bowl, 10" d., purple 75.00
Compote, small, blue. 24.50
Compote, small, green 30.00
Compote, small, marigold 20.00
Compote, small, red 220.00
Compote, small, vaseline 48.00
Dish, hat-shaped, blue, 5¾" 25.00
Dish, hat-shaped, green, 5¾" 37.50
Dish, hat-shaped, marigold, 5¾" 22.50
Dish, hat-shaped, red, 5¾" 230.00
Dish, hat-shaped, red, 7" 215.00
Dish, hat-shaped, amber. 92.00

Dish, hat-shaped, vaseline 25.00
Goblet, marigold 30.00
Nappy, single handle, peach
   opalescent 48.00
Nappy, single handle, purple 35.00
Nappy, tricornered, green 80.00
Plate, 9" to 10" d., blue . . . . .120.00 to 200.00
Plate, 9" to 10" d., green 125.00
Plate, 9" to 10" d., marigold . . .65.00 to 100.00
Plate, 9" to 10" d., purple . . . .200.00 to 225.00
Plate, 9" to 10" d., white . . . . .90.00 to 165.00
Sauceboat, handled, purple 50.00
Vase, 6" h., pinched, peach
   opalescent .125.00

HOLLY STAR or PANELED HOLLY STAR
Bon bon, green 47.00
Bon bon, marigold 32.50

HOLLY WHIRL or HOLLY SPRIG (Millersburg & Fenton)
Bowl, 7" d., marigold 55.00
Bowl, 7" d., ruffled, purple 40.00
Bowl, 7" d., vaseline 650.00
Bowl, 7½" w., tricornered, purple 45.00
Bowl, 8" to 9" d., ruffled, blue 45.00
Bowl, 8" to 9" d., green 55.00
Bowl, 8" to 9" d., marigold . . . . .35.00 to 40.00
Bowl, 8" to 9" d., purple 75.00
Card tray, 2-handled, green 65.00
Card tray, 2-handled, purple 90.00
Nappy, green 38.00
Nappy, marigold. 60.00
Nappy, purple .55.00
Nappy, tricornered, purple 85.00
Nut dish, 2-handled, purple 60.00
Rose bowl, small, vaseline 400.00
Sauce dish, peach opalescent, 5½" d. . .38.00
Sauce dish, purple, 5½" d. 150.00

HOMESTEAD (Imperial)
Plate, amber 500.00
Plate, green. 525.00
Plate, marigold 325.00
Plate, purple 455.00
Plate, white 285.00

HONEYCOMB

Honeycomb Rose Bowl

Bon bon, marigold 30.00
Card tray, Beads & Flowers exterior,
    peach opalescent, 7" 65.00
Rose bowl, peach opalescent (ILLUS.) . .195.00

HORSEHEADS or HORSE MEDALLION (Fenton)

Horseheads Bowl

Bowl, 7" d., blue .93.00
Bowl, 7" d., green 128.00
Bowl, 7" d., marigold . . . . .50.00 to 60.00
Bowl, 8" d., marigold (ILLUS.) . .65.00 to 79.00
Bowl, 8" d., purple 125.00
Bowl, jack-in-the-pulpit shaped, blue . .125.00
Bowl, jack-in-the-pulpit shaped,
    marigold 75.00
Nut bowl, 3-footed, green 125.00
Nut bowl, 3-footed, marigold 82.50
Nut bowl, 3-footed, vaseline 110.00
Plate, 7" to 8" d., marigold 155.00
Rose bowl, blue 200.00
Rose bowl, marigold 95.00

ILLINOIS SOLDIER'S & SAILOR'S PLATE
Blue 665.00
Marigold 625.00

ILLUSION
Bon bon, 2-handled, blue 42.50
Bon bon, 2-handled, marigold 45.00

IMPERIAL GRAPE
Berry set: master bowl & 7 sauce
    dishes; green, 8 pcs. 65.00
Bowl, 7" d., 2½" h., green 36.50
Bowl, 7" d., 2½" h., marigold 15.00
Bowl, 8" to 9" d., clambroth 25.00
Bowl, 8" to 9" d., green 40.00
Bowl, 8" to 9" d., marigold 26.50
Bowl, 8" to 9" d., purple 50.00
Bowl, 8" to 9" d., white 69.00
Bowl, 10" d., clambroth 40.00
Bowl, 10" d., marigold 32.50
Bowl, 10" d., smoky 31.50
Compote, marigold 35.00
Cup & saucer, green 65.00
Cup & saucer, marigold 57.50
Decanter w/stopper, marigold 65.00
Decanter w/stopper, purple 165.00

Decanter w/stopper, smoky 100.00
Goblet, green 72.50
Goblet, marigold 32.50
Goblet, purple .62.50
Goblet, smoky .125.00
Pitcher, water, green 125.00
Pitcher, water, marigold 76.50
Pitcher, water, smoky 300.00
Plate, 6" d., green 50.00
Plate, 6" d., marigold 35.00
Plate, 6" d., purple 65.00
Plate, 9" d., ruffled, clambroth 35.00
Plate, 9" d., ruffled, green 147.50
Plate, 9" d., flat, marigold 85.00
Plate, 9" d., ruffled, marigold 47.50
Punch bowl, marigold 60.00
Punch bowl, purple 225.00
Punch bowl & base, marigold, 2 pcs. 140.00
Punch cup, green 25.00
Punch cup, marigold 10.00
Punch set: punch bowl, base & 6
    cups; green, 8 pcs. 257.50
Punch set: punch bowl, base & 9
    cups; marigold, 11 pcs. 245.00
Sauce dish, green 17.00
Sauce dish, ruffled rim, marigold 13.00
Sauce dish, smoky 32.50
Tumbler, green .27.50
Tumbler, marigold 18.00
Tumbler, purple 35.00
Water bottle, green 120.00
Water bottle, purple . . . . .120.00 to 165.00
Wine, green 32.00
Wine, marigold 17.50
Wine, purple 30.00
Wine set: decanter w/stopper & 6
    wines; green, 7 pcs. 225.00
Wine set: decanter w/stopper & 6
    wines; marigold, 7 pcs. 210.00

Imperial Grape Decanter & Wines

Wine set: decanter w/stopper & 6
    wines; purple, 7 pcs. (ILLUS. of
    part) 270.00

INVERTED FEATHER (Cambridge)

Inverted Feather Cookie Jar

Compote, jelly, marigold 55.00
Cookie jar, cov., green
  (ILLUS.) ....165.00 to 220.00
Creamer, marigold...................70.00
Parfait, marigold 50.00
Pitcher, water, tankard, marigold ...4,300.00
Tumbler, green ....450.00 to 500.00
Tumbler, marigold.........450.00 to 500.00

INVERTED STRAWBERRY (Cambridge)

Bowl, 7" d., green...................49.00
Bowl, 8" to 9" d., purple 150.00
Bowl, master berry, 10" d., purple 135.00
Candlesticks, marigold, 7" h., pr. 380.00
Compote, open, giant, marigold 100.00
Compote, open, giant, purple 250.00
Creamer, green 85.00
Creamer & sugar bowl, purple, pr. ...325.00
Cuspidor, green ....560.00 to 610.00
Cuspidor, marigold 500.00
Decanter, green, marked Near-Cut ..3,550.00
Pitcher, milk, purple...............1,500.00
Pitcher, tankard, green ....350.00 to 1,200.00
Pitcher, tankard, purple 800.00
Powder jar, cov., green..............110.00
Spooner, green.....................75.00
Sugar bowl, cov., green 100.00
Table set: creamer, sugar bowl &
  spooner; marigold, 3 pcs. 550.00
Tumbler, marigold 250.00
Tumbler, purple 215.00

INVERTED THISTLE (Cambridge)

Pitcher, water, purple 2,000.00
Tumbler, purple 310.00

IRIS

Compote, 6¾" d., blue 170.00
Compote, 6¾" d., green 62.50
Compote, 6¾" d., marigold 42.50
Compote, 6¾" d., purple 57.50
Goblet, buttermilk, green.............65.00
Goblet, buttermilk, marigold..........52.50
Goblet, buttermilk, marigold,
  souvenir........................69.00
Goblet, buttermilk, purple 55.00

IRIS, HEAVY (Dugan or Diamond Glass)

Heavy Iris Pitcher & Tumblers

Pitcher, water, marigold 295.00
Pitcher, water, white 1,000.00
Tumbler, marigold 47.50
Tumbler, purple 55.00
Tumbler, white 140.00
Water set: pitcher & 6 tumblers;
  purple (ILLUS.)...................865.00

JARDINIERE (THE)

Marigold 325.00
Purple.............................600.00

JEWELED HEART

Jeweled Heart Water Pitcher

Bowl, master berry, 10½" d., fluted,
  peach opalescent 140.00
Pitcher, marigold (ILLUS.) 650.00
Plate, 7" d., ruffled, peach opal-
  escent 38.00
Sauce dish, peach opalescent 22.50
Sauce dish, peach opalescent w/rayed
  interior..........................41.00
Sauce dish, purple 40.00
Tumbler, marigold..........80.00 to 100.00

KITTENS (Fenton)

Bowl, cereal, blue (ILLUS.) 200.00
Bowl, cereal, marigold (ILLUS.) 92.50

Kittens Pattern

Bowl, ruffled, marigold (ILLUS.) 120.00
Bowl, 4-sided, blue (ILLUS.) 225.00
Bowl, 4-sided, marigold . . . . . . .70.00 to 95.00
Bowl, 4-sided, purple 175.00
Bowl, 6-sided, marigold 80.00
Cup & saucer, marigold
  (ILLUS.) . . . . .180.00 to 225.00
Dish, turned-up sides, marigold
  (ILLUS.) . . . . .100.00 to 110.00
Dish, turned-up sides, purple 175.00
Plate, 4½" d., marigold 90.00
Saucer, marigold . . . . .90.00 to 110.00
Spooner, blue 200.00
Spooner, marigold 115.00
Toothpick holder, blue . . .150.00 to 190.00
Toothpick holder, marigold . .110.00 to 130.00
Vase, marigold .125.00

LATTICE & GRAPE (Fenton)

Pitcher, water, blue 250.00
Pitcher, water, marigold 115.00
Pitcher, water, white 510.00
Plate, 7" d., white 50.00
Tumbler, blue 45.00
Tumbler, marigold . . . . .18.00 to 25.00
Tumbler, white 85.00
Water set: tankard pitcher & 6
  tumblers; blue, 7 pcs. 715.00
Water set: tankard pitcher & 6
  tumblers; marigold,
  7 pcs. . . . . .200.00 to 225.00

LATTICE & POINSETTIA (Northwood)

Bowl, cobalt blue 175.00
Bowl, ice blue 305.00
Bowl, marigold 95.00
Bowl, purple 145.00

LEAF & BEADS (Northwood)

Nut bowl, handled, green 52.50
Nut bowl, handled, marigold 30.00
Rose bowl, aqua opalescent 235.00
Rose bowl, blue .85.00
Rose bowl, green 50.00
Rose bowl, ice blue opalescent 210.00
Rose bowl, lavender (ILLUS.) 130.00
Rose bowl, marigold 60.00
Rose bowl, purple 65.00
Rose bowl, white 425.00

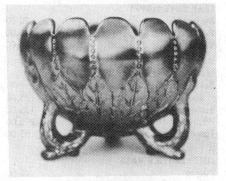

Leaf & Beads Rose Bowl

**LEAF & FLOWERS or LEAF & LITTLE FLOWERS
(Millersburg)**
Compote, green, miniature . .225.00 to 240.00
Compote, marigold, miniature 250.00
Compote, purple, miniature 250.00

LEAF CHAIN (Fenton)

Leaf Chain Bowl

Bowl, 7" d., aqua 150.00
Bowl, 7" d., blue .40.00
Bowl, 7" d., green 45.00
Bowl, 7" d., marigold 60.00
Bowl, 7" d., red .475.00
Bowl, 7" d., vaseline w/marigold
  overlay 50.00
Bowl, 7" d., white 62.50
Bowl, 8" to 9" d., aqua 120.00
Bowl, 8" to 9" d., clambroth 45.00
Bowl, 8" to 9" d., green (ILLUS.) 46.50
Bowl, 8" to 9" d., light blue 80.00
Bowl, 8" to 9" d., marigold 35.00
Bowl, 8" to 9" d., white 50.00
Plate, 7" to 8" d., blue 72.00
Plate, 7" to 8" d., marigold 37.50
Plate, 9" d., green 92.50
Plate, 9" d., marigold 85.00
Plate, 9" d., white 120.00

LEAF RAYS NAPPY
Marigold 20.00
Peach opalescent 35.00
White 30.00

LEAF TIERS
Berry set: 9" d. master bowl & 4
  sauce dishes; marigold, 5 pcs. 75.00
Butter dish, cov., marigold 135.00
Pitcher, footed, marigold 295.00
Tumbler, marigold 65.00

LINED LATTICE VASE
Purple.............................45.00
White, 10" h. 35.00

LION (Fenton)

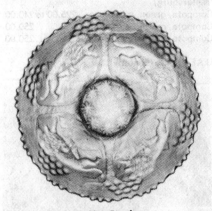

Lion Bowl

Bowl, 5" d., marigold 100.00
Bowl, 7" d., blue 235.00
Bowl, 7" d., marigold (ILLUS.) 115.00
Plate, 7½" d., marigold 350.00

LITTLE BARREL PERFUME

Little Barrel Perfume

Green (ILLUS.).......................80.00
Marigold 70.00
Smoky ....85.00 to 120.00

LITTLE FISHES

Little Fishes Bowl

Bowl, 6" d., 3-footed, marigold 45.00
Bowl, 6" d., 3-footed, purple 90.00
Bowl, 8" to 9" d., 3-footed, blue 160.00
Bowl, 8" to 9" d., 3-footed, marigold....95.00
Bowl, 10" d., 3-footed, blue (ILLUS.) ...165.00
Bowl, 10" d., 3-footed, marigold 125.00

LITTLE FLOWERS

Little Flowers Chop Plate

Berry set: master bowl & 3 sauce
  dishes; blue, 4 pcs.................100.00
Berry set: master bowl & 6 sauce
  dishes; green, 7 pcs. 270.00
Berry set: master bowl & 6 sauce
  dishes; marigold, 7 pcs.............195.00
Bowl, 5" d., aqua 100.00
Bowl, 5" d., blue 27.50
Bowl, 5" d., green..................25.00
Bowl, 5" d., marigold 20.00
Bowl, 5" d., purple 30.00
Bowl, 8" to 9" d., blue 60.00
Bowl, 8" to 9" d., marigold 70.00
Bowl, 8" to 9" d., purple ....50.00 to 65.00
Bowl, 8" to 9" d., red...............1,000.00
Bowl, 10" d., purple 75.00
Nut bowl, blue 75.00
Nut bowl, marigold 65.00
Plate, 6" d., marigold...............165.00
Plate, chop, marigold (ILLUS.) 600.00

LITTLE STARS BOWL (Millersburg)
Bowl, 7" d., green ....90.00 to 140.00

Bowl, 7" d., fluted rim, marigold 75.00
Bowl, 7" d., purple 70.00
Bowl, 8" d., green. 75.00
Bowl, 8" d., flat, ruffled rim, marigold . .80.00
Bowl, 8" d., flat, ruffled rim, purple . .95.00
Bowl, ice-cream, 9" d., marigold 265.00

LOGANBERRY VASE (Imperial)
Amber 400.00
Green. 195.00
Marigold 125.00
Purple. 195.00

LONG HOBSTAR
Bowl, 10" d., collared base, marigold . . .25.00

LONG THUMBPRINTS
Creamer, marigold. 20.00
Creamer & sugar bowl, marigold, pr. . . .25.00
Sugar bowl, marigold 20.00
Vase, 7" h., green 32.00

LOTUS & GRAPE

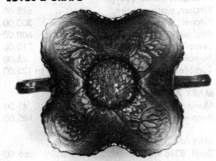

Lotus & Grape Bon Bon

Bon bon, 2-handled, blue 30.00
Bon bon, 2-handled, green 45.00
Bon bon, 2-handled, celeste blue
  (ILLUS.) 185.00
Bon bon, 2-handled, marigold 32.50
Bon bon, 2-handled, purple 50.00
Bowl, 5" d., footed, marigold 35.00
Bowl, 8" to 9" d., blue 55.00
Bowl, 8" to 9" d., green 53.00
Plate, 9" d., blue. 360.00
Plate, 9" d., green 625.00
Plate, 9" d., purple 360.00

LOUISA (Westmoreland)
Bowl, 8" to 9" d., 3-footed, peach
  opalescent 415.00
Bowl, 8" to 9" d., 3-footed, teal blue 40.00
Nut bowl, footed, blue. 35.00
Nut bowl, footed, purple 52.50
Plate, 9½" d., footed, aqua 325.00
Plate, 9½" d., footed, teal blue 98.00
Rose bowl, footed, amber 60.00
Rose bowl, footed, green (ILLUS.) 62.50
Rose bowl, footed, lavender. 85.00
Rose bowl, footed, marigold 60.00

Louisa Rose Bowl

Rose bowl, footed, purple 55.00
Salt & pepper shakers, marigold, pr. . . .22.50

LUSTRE FLUTE (Northwood)
Creamer, green .19.00
Creamer & sugar bowl, green, pr. 50.00
Creamer & sugar bowl, marigold, pr. . . .55.00
Hat shape, fluted, green, 5" d. 25.00
Hat shape, fluted, purple, 5" d. 32.50
Nappy, green 35.00
Nappy, marigold. 20.00
Punch cup, green 16.00
Sugar bowl, green 25.00
Sugar bowl, marigold 15.00

LUSTRE ROSE (Imperial)

Lustre Rose Flattened Fernery

Berry set: master bowl & 4 sauce
  dishes; marigold, 5 pcs. 140.00
Berry set: master bowl & 6 sauce
  dishes; marigold, 7 pcs. 90.00
Bowl, 7" d., green. 37.50
Bowl, 8" to 9" d., 3-footed, amber 45.00
Bowl, 8" to 9" d., 3-footed, green 40.00
Bowl, 8" to 9" d., 3-footed, marigold 30.00
Bowl, 8" to 9" d., 3-footed, purple 50.00
Bowl, 10½" d., 3-footed, clambroth 55.00

Bowl, 10½" d., 3-footed,
   marigold . . . . .40.00 to 55.00
Bowl, 10½" d., 3-footed, white 130.00
Butter dish, cov., green 30.00
Butter dish, cov., marigold 65.00
Creamer, marigold . . . . .30.00 to 40.00
Fernery, amber 60.00
Fernery, blue .50.00
Fernery, clambroth, 7½" d., 4" h. 42.50
Fernery, marigold 35.00
Fernery, flattened, purple (ILLUS.) 95.00
Pitcher, water, clambroth 80.00
Pitcher, water, 8" h., marigold 60.00
Plate, 9" d., amber 85.00
Plate, 9" d., green 75.00
Plate, 9" d., marigold . . . . .45.00 to 60.00
Plate, 9" d., purple 95.00
Rose bowl, amber 85.00
Rose bowl, green 30.00
Spooner, green 40.00
Spooner, marigold 35.00
Spooner, purple 25.00
Sugar bowl, cov., marigold 45.00
Table set, marigold, 4 pcs. 165.00
Tumbler, green 30.00
Tumbler, marigold 20.00
Tumbler, purple 35.00
Water set: pitcher & 6 tumblers;
   marigold, 7 pcs. 170.00
Water set: pitcher & 6 tumblers;
   purple, 7 pcs. 595.00

MANY FRUITS
Punch bowl, 9¾" d., marigold 180.00
Punch bowl, 9¾" d., purple 200.00
Punch bowl & base, marigold, 2 pcs. . .270.00
Punch bowl & base, purple, 2 pcs. 400.00
Punch cup, marigold 15.00
Punch cup, purple . . . . .10.00 to 15.00
Punch set: bowl & 5 cups; purple,
   6 pcs. 235.00
Punch set: bowl, base & 5 cups;
   purple, 7 pcs. 525.00
Punch set: bowl, base & 6 cups;
   blue, 8 pcs. 500.00
Punch set: bowl, base & 6 cups;
   marigold, 8 pcs. 375.00

MANY STARS (Millersburg)
Bowl, 8" to 9" d., green 300.00
Bowl, 10" d., green 200.00
Bowl, 10" d., marigold 235.00
Bowl, ice cream, 10" d., marigold 310.00
Bowl, 10" d., purple 235.00

MAPLE LEAF (Dugan)
Berry set: master bowl & 6 sauce
   dishes; marigold, 7 pcs. 150.00
Berry set: master bowl & 6 sauce
   dishes; purple, 7 pcs. 220.00
Bowl, master berry or fruit,
   purple . . . . .70.00 to 95.00

Bowl, ice cream, footed, large,
   purple 105.00
Butter dish, cov., purple 135.00
Creamer, marigold 45.00
Creamer, purple 60.00
Dish, ice cream, footed, marigold,
   4" d. 25.00
Dish, ice cream, footed, purple, 4" d. . . .30.00
Pitcher, water, purple 185.00
Sauce dish, marigold 12.00
Sauce dish, purple 22.50
Spooner, marigold 50.00
Spooner, purple 65.00
Table set, marigold, 4 pcs. 200.00
Tumbler, blue .50.00
Tumbler, marigold 25.00
Tumbler, purple 35.00
Water set: pitcher & 6 tumblers;
   marigold, 7 pcs. 175.00
Water set: pitcher & 6 tumblers;
   purple, 7 pcs. . . . . .275.00 to 400.00

MARILYN (Millersburg)
Pitcher, water, green 675.00
Pitcher, water, marigold 300.00
Pitcher, water, purple 600.00
Tumbler, green 210.00
Tumbler, marigold 45.00
Tumbler, purple . . . . .100.00 to 125.00

MARY ANN VASE
Marigold 45.00
Purple 105.00

MAYAN
Bowl, 8" to 9" d., green 65.00
Bowl, 8" to 9" d., purple 60.00

MEMPHIS (Northwood)

Memphis Punch Bowl & Base

Berry set: master bowl & 6 sauce
   dishes; marigold, 7 pcs. 145.00
Bowl, master berry, marigold 62.50
Punch bowl & base, green, 2 pcs. 175.00
Punch bowl & base, ice green,
   2 pcs. 2,950.00

Punch bowl & base, marigold,
   2 pcs. 180.00
Punch bowl & base, purple, 2 pcs.
   (ILLUS.) 340.00
Punch cup, green 30.00
Punch cup, ice blue. 55.00
Punch cup, ice green 50.00
Punch cup, marigold . . . . .15.00 to 25.00
Punch cup, purple . . . . .20.00 to 30.00
Punch cup, white 60.00
Punch set: bowl, base & 4 cups;
   ice blue, 6 pcs. 2,000.00
Punch set: bowl & 6 cups; purple,
   7 pcs. 625.00
Punch set: bowl, base & 6 cups;
   marigold, 8 pcs. . . . . .315.00 to 400.00
Punch set: bowl, base & 6 cups;
   white, 8 pcs. 500.00

MIKADO
Compote, 10" d., blue 280.00
Compote, 10" d., marigold . . .125.00 to 145.00

MILADY (Fenton)
Pitcher, water, marigold 475.00
Powder jar, cov., marigold 65.00
Tumbler, blue 60.00
Tumbler, marigold . . . . .70.00 to 90.00
Tumbler, purple .75.00
Water set: pitcher & 5 tumblers;
   blue, 6 pcs. .900.00

MILLERSBURG PIPE HUMIDOR
Green 3,375.00
Marigold 3,000.00

MIRRORED LOTUS
Bowl, 7" d., blue 55.00
Bowl, 7" d., ice green. 250.00
Bowl, 7" d., marigold 55.00
Rose bowl, white 525.00

MITERED OVALS
Vase, green 1,700.00

MORNING GLORY (Millersburg)

Pitcher, tankard, purple
   (ILLUS.) . . . . .6,350.00 to 7,500.00
Tumbler, green 1,150.00

MULTIFRUITS (Millersburg)
Punch bowl & base, purple, 2 pcs. 500.00
Punch cup, green 40.00

MULTIFRUITS & FLOWERS (Millersburg)
Pitcher, water, marigold 4,400.00
Punch bowl & base, green, 2 pcs. 1,000.00
Punch bowl & base, purple, 2 pcs. 350.00
Punch cup, purple 35.00
Punch set: bowl, base & 3 cups;
   purple, 5 pcs. 950.00
Punch set: bowl, base & 4 cups;
   marigold, 6 pcs. . . . . .680.00 to 700.00
Punch set: bowl, base & 8 cups;
   green, 10 pcs. 1,800.00
Punch set: bowl, base & 8 cups;
   tulip-shaped, marigold, 10 pcs. . . .1,425.00
Sherbet, green .600.00

NAUTILUS (Dugan)
Creamer, peach opalescent . .170.00 to 240.00
Sugar bowl, peach opalescent 275.00
Sugar bowl, purple . . . . .150.00 to 225.00
Vase, peach opalescent 195.00

NESTING SWAN (Millersburg)
Bowl, amber 225.00
Bowl, green . . . . .200.00 to 290.00
Bowl, marigold .175.00
Bowl, purple . . . . .225.00 to 285.00

NIPPON (Northwood)
Bowl, 8" to 9" d., 3" h., green 45.00
Bowl, 8" to 9" d., 2¼" h., ice blue 185.00
Bowl, 8" to 9" d., ice green 120.00
Bowl, 8" to 9" d., marigold 42.00
Bowl, 8" to 9" d., fluted,
   white . . . . .115.00 to 200.00
Plate, 9" d., green 150.00
Plate, 9" d., marigold. 195.00
Plate, 9" d., white. 600.00

NU-ART

Morning Glory Tankard Pitcher

Nu-Art Chrysanthemum Plate

Plate, Chrysanthemum, amber 750.00
Plate, Chrysanthemum, green 350.00
Plate, Chrysanthemum, marigold 550.00
Plate, Chrysanthemum, purple
  (ILLUS.)..........................700.00

OCTAGON (Imperial)

Octagon Wine & Decanter

Bowl, 12" sq., green..................49.00
Compote, jelly, green 75.00
Compote, jelly, marigold 50.00
Creamer, marigold...................38.00
Decanter w/stopper, marigold
  (ILLUS.).........................75.00
Goblet, water, marigold 37.50
Pitcher, milk, marigold 75.00
Pitcher, water, 8" h., marigold........70.00
Pitcher, water, 8" h., purple..........400.00
Pitcher, water, tankard, 9¾" h.,
  marigold 100.00
Pitcher, water, tankard, 9¾" h.,
  purple ....300.00 to 400.00
Sauce dish, marigold 17.00
Sugar bowl, cov., marigold...........41.50
Toothpick holder, marigold 170.00
Tumbler, green 85.00
Tumbler, marigold 25.00
Tumbler, purple 50.00
Water set: pitcher & 1 tumbler;
  purple.........................320.00
Water set: pitcher & 4 tumblers;
  marigold, 5 pcs. 225.00
Wine, marigold (ILLUS.)..............25.00
Wine set: decanter & 6 wines;
  marigold, 7 pcs. 215.00

OHIO STAR (Millersburg)

Compote, jelly, marigold 400.00
Vase, marigold 300.00
Vase, purple 375.00

OPEN ROSE (OLD) (Imperial)

Berry set: master bowl & 6 sauce
  dishes; marigold, 7 pcs. .....65.00 to 85.00
Bowl, 7" d., footed, green.............35.00
Bowl, 7" d., footed, purple 40.00

Bowl, 8" to 9" d., amber 55.00
Bowl, 8" to 9" d., aqua 52.00
Bowl, 8" to 9" d., green 55.00
Bowl, 8" to 9" d., marigold 30.00
Bowl, 8" to 9" d., purple 35.00
Bowl, 8" to 9" d., smoky 55.00
Bowl, 10" d., marigold...............45.00
Bowl, 10" d., smoky 52.50
Bowl, 10" d., fluted, white 65.00
Plate, 9" d., amber 100.00
Plate, 9" d., green 80.00
Plate, 9" d., marigold...............60.00
Plate, 9" d., purple 60.00
Plate, chop, purple 375.00
Rose bowl, amber....................40.00
Sauce dish, blue 30.00
Sauce dish, marigold 22.50
Spooner, marigold 29.00
Water set: pitcher & 6 tumblers;
  marigold, 7 pcs. 200.00
Water set: pitcher & 6 tumblers;
  purple, 7 pcs....................375.00
Whimsey, tricornered, purple 150.00

ORANGE TREE (Fenton)

Orange Tree Mug

Berry set: master bowl & 6 sauce
  dishes; marigold, 7 pcs............220.00
Bowl, 8" to 9" d., amber 65.00
Bowl, 8" to 9" d., blue 40.00
Bowl, 8" to 9" d., green 70.00
Bowl, 8" to 9" d., marigold .....35.00 to 40.00
Bowl, 8" to 9" d., purple 75.00
Bowl, 8" to 9" d., red 800.00
Bowl, 8" to 9" d., white 95.00
Bowl, 10" d., 3-footed, blue 170.00
Bowl, 10" d., 3-footed, green 295.00
Bowl, 10" d., 3-footed,
  marigold ....70.00 to 90.00
Bowl, 10" d., 3-footed, white 140.00
Bowl, ice cream, amber w/blue base ..155.00
Breakfast set: individual size creamer
  & cov. sugar bowl; blue, pr. 97.50
Breakfast set: individual size creamer
  & cov. sugar bowl; marigold, pr. 75.00
Breakfast set: individual size creamer
  & cov. sugar bowl; purple, pr. 110.00
Breakfast set: individual size creamer
  & cov. sugar bowl, white, pr. 125.00
Butter dish, cov., blue 225.00
Compote, 5" d., blue 65.00

Compote, 5" d., marigold 24.50
Compote, green 90.00
Creamer, footed, blue 62.50
Creamer, footed, marigold 37.50
Creamer, footed, purple 55.00
Creamer, individual size, blue 35.00
Creamer & cov. sugar bowl, footed,
  blue, pr. 140.00
Dish, ice cream, footed, blue 19.00
Dish, ice cream, footed, marigold 20.00
Goblet, blue 50.00
Goblet, green .75.00
Goblet, marigold 30.00
Goblet, marigold, w/advertising. 40.00
Hatpin holder, blue 180.00
Hatpin holder, green 335.00
Hatpin holder, marigold 155.00
Hatpin holder, purple 165.00
Loving cup, blue 225.00
Loving cup, green 225.00
Loving cup, marigold 125.00
Loving cup, purple 215.00
Loving cup, white 225.00
Mug, amber. .100.00
Mug, Amberina. 132.50
Mug, aqua 225.00
Mug, blue (ILLUS.) 42.50
Mug, green 225.00
Mug, marigold . . . . 20.00 to 35.00
Mug, marigold w/blue base. . .95.00 to 125.00
Mug, marigold w/green base. 120.00
Mug, marigold w/vaseline
  base . . . . .140.00 to 175.00
Mug, purple. 80.00
Mug, red 310.00
Mug, teal blue 175.00
Mug, vaseline 145.00
Pitcher, water, blue 325.00
Pitcher, water, marigold 275.00
Pitcher, water, white 470.00
Plate, 9" d., flat, blue. 145.00
Plate, 9" d., flat, clambroth . . .80.00 to 105.00
Plate, 9" d., flat, green 275.00
Plate, 9" d., flat, marigold 70.00
Plate, 9" d., flat, white 125.00
Powder jar, cov., blue 65.00
Powder jar, cov., green. 195.00
Powder jar, cov., marigold 45.00
Powder jar, open, peach opalescent . . .195.00
Punch bowl & base, blue,
  2 pcs. . . . . .225.00 to 275.00
Punch bowl & base, marigold, 2 pcs. . . .135.00
Punch bowl & base, white, 2 pcs. 250.00
Punch cup, blue. 26.50
Punch cup, marigold 11.50
Punch cup, purple. 20.00
Punch cup, white 31.50
Punch set: bowl, base & 5 cups; white,
  7 pcs. 500.00
Punch set: bowl, base & 6 cups; blue,
  8 pcs. 325.00
Punch set: bowl, base & 8 cups;
  marigold, 10 pcs. 210.00
Rose bowl, blue 50.00

Rose bowl, marigold 47.50
Rose bowl, purple. 37.50
Rose bowl, red 575.00
Rose bowl, white 250.00
Sauce dish, footed, blue 30.00
Sauce dish, footed, marigold 15.00
Sauce dish, footed, white 46.50
Shaving mug, amber 65.00
Shaving mug, blue 50.00
Shaving mug, marigold 37.50
Shaving mug, purple 275.00
Shaving mug, red 375.00

Orange Tree Spooner

Spooner, blue (ILLUS.) 75.00
Sugar bowl, blue 50.00
Sugar bowl, purple. 52.50
Sugar bowl, white 75.00
Sugar bowl, open, breakfast size,
  blue. 32.50
Sugar bowl, open, breakfast size,
  marigold 25.00
Sugar bowl, open, breakfast size,
  purple. 37.50
Sugar bowl, open, breakfast size,
  white 32.00
Tumbler, blue .50.00
Tumbler, marigold 45.00
Tumbler, white . . . . .85.00 to 110.00
Water set: pitcher & 6 tumblers;
  marigold, 7 pcs. 430.00
Wine, blue 45.00
Wine, green. .150.00
Wine, marigold 25.00
Wine, purple 35.00

ORANGE TREE ORCHARD (Fenton)
Pitcher, blue .330.00
Pitcher, marigold 185.00
Pitcher, white .500.00
Tumbler, blue .45.00
Tumbler, marigold 40.00
Tumbler, white 165.00
Water set: pitcher & 6 tumblers; blue,
  7 pcs. 750.00

ORANGE TREE SCROLL
Pitcher, marigold 130.00
Pitcher, white .325.00

Tumbler, marigold 50.00
Water set: pitcher & 6 tumblers; blue,
   7 pcs. 900.00

ORIENTAL POPPY (Northwood)

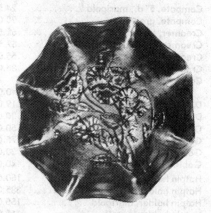

Oriental Poppy Tumblers

Pitcher, water, marigold 350.00
Pitcher, water, purple 465.00
Pitcher, water, white 675.00
Tumbler, ice blue 185.00
Tumbler, ice green 205.00
Tumbler, marigold 40.00
Tumbler, purple, each (ILLUS.) 40.00
Tumbler, white 120.00
Water set: pitcher & 6 tumblers;
   marigold, 7 pcs. 535.00
Water set: pitcher & 6 tumblers;
   purple, 7 pcs. 850.00
Water set: pitcher & 6 tumblers;
   white, 7 pcs. 925.00

PAINTED CHERRIES

Tumbler, blue 15.00
Water set: pitcher & 6 tumblers;
   blue, 7 pcs. .225.00

PALM BEACH (United States Glass Co.)

Butter dish, cov., white 210.00
Creamer, marigold 70.00
Creamer, white .82.50
Pitcher, water, white 725.00
Sauce dish, white 35.00
Spooner, marigold 85.00
Spooner, white .85.00
Tumbler, amber 80.00
Tumbler, marigold 210.00
Tumbler, white 155.00
Whimsey, banana boat, marigold,
   6" . . . . .75.00 to 110.00
Whimsey vase, white 250.00

PANSY (Imperial)

Bowl, 8" to 9" d., green 35.00
Bowl, 8" to 9" d., marigold 30.00
Bowl, 9" d., fluted, purple (ILLUS.) 37.50
Creamer, green .22.00
Creamer & sugar bowl, marigold, pr. . . .40.00
Dresser tray, marigold 33.00
Dresser tray, purple 65.00
Nappy, marigold 20.00
Pickle (or relish) dish, amber, 6 x 9" 32.50

Pansy Bowl

Pickle (or relish) dish, blue, 6 x 9" 25.00
Pickle (or relish) dish, clambroth,
   6 x 9" 10.00
Pickle (or relish) dish, green, 6 x 9" 25.00
Pickle (or relish) dish, marigold, 6 x 9" . .25.00
Pickle (or relish) dish, purple, 6 x 9" 35.00
Pickle (or relish) dish, smoky, 6 x 9" 73.00
Plate, 9" d., ruffled, purple 95.00
Sugar bowl, marigold 20.00

PANSY SPRAY

Pansy Spray Sugar Bowl

Bowl, 8" to 9" d., green 45.00
Bowl, 8" to 9" d., purple 50.00
Dresser tray, flat, oval, green 55.00
Dresser tray, flat, oval, marigold 45.00
Nappy, handled, green 15.00
Relish, marigold, 7½" 25.00
Sugar bowl, open, purple, 3½" h.
   (ILLUS.) 50.00

PANTHER (Fenton)

Berry set: master bowl & 6 sauce
   dishes; blue, 7 pcs. 700.00
Berry set: master bowl & 6 sauce
   dishes; marigold, 7 pcs. 400.00
Bowl, 5" d., footed, blue 85.00
Bowl, 5" d., footed, marigold 40.00
Bowl, 9" d., claw-footed, blue 265.00
Bowl, 9" d., claw-footed,
   marigold . . . . .90.00 to 110.00
Bowl, 9" d., claw-footed, white 625.00
Centerpiece bowl, blue 900.00

PEACH (Northwood)

Berry set: master bowl & 6 sauce
  dishes; white, 7 pcs..............310.00
Butter dish, cov., white 425.00
Sauce dish, white 58.50
Spooner, white 98.00
Sugar bowl, cov., white ......90.00 to 125.00
Table set, white, 4 pcs. 690.00
Tumbler, blue 72.50
Tumbler, marigold 2,100.00
Tumbler, white 60.00
Water set: pitcher & 6 tumblers;
  white, 7 pcs. 875.00

PEACH & PEAR OVAL FRUIT BOWL

Marigold 65.00
Purple............................80.00

PEACOCK, FLUFFY (Fenton)

Fluffy Peacock Water Set

Pitcher, water, blue 650.00
Pitcher, water, green...............585.00
Pitcher, water, marigold.............325.00
Pitcher, water, purple..............500.00
Tumbler, blue 65.00
Tumbler, green......................55.00
Tumbler, marigold 45.00
Tumbler, purple 68.00
Water set: pitcher & 6 tumblers;
  purple, 7 pcs. (ILLUS.) .....885.00 to 925.00

PEACOCK & DAHLIA (Fenton)

Bowl, marigold 65.00
Plate, 7½" d., marigold .....130.00 to 200.00

PEACOCK & GRAPE (Fenton)

Bowl, 8" to 9" d., 3-footed, amber 160.00
Bowl, 8" to 9" d., 3-footed, blue........50.00
Bowl, 8" to 9" d., 3-footed, green 70.00
Bowl, 8" to 9" d., 3-footed, ice green
  opalescent 595.00
Bowl, 8" to 9" d., 3-footed, marigold....45.00
Bowl, 8" to 9" d., collared base,
  peach opalescent 228.00
Bowl, 8" to 9" d., collared base,
  purple............................50.00
Bowl, 8" to 9" d., ruffled rim,
  3-footed, purple 50.00

Bowl, 8" to 9" d., 3-footed,
  red ....400.00 to 475.00
Bowl, 8" to 9" d., 3-footed, vaseline ...175.00
Bowl, 8" to 9" d., 3-footed, vaseline
  opalescent 400.00
Plate, 9" d., blue....................400.00
Plate, 9" d., marigold................180.00
Plate, 9" d., 3-footed, green 110.00
Plate, 9" d., 3-footed, marigold 130.00

PEACOCK & URN

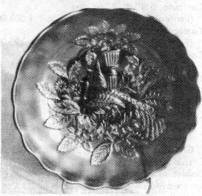

Peacock & Urn Plate

Berry set: master bowl & 4 sauce
  dishes; marigold, 5 pcs.............225.00
Berry set: master bowl & 6 sauce
  dishes; purple, 7 pcs. .....650.00 to 675.00
Bowl, 5" d., blue..............45.00 to 60.00
Bowl, 5" d., purple..................100.00
Bowl, 7" d., ruffled, green
  (Millersburg) 300.00
Bowl, 7" d., ruffled, marigold
  (Millersburg) 375.00
Bowl, 7" d., ruffled, purple
  (Millersburg) 285.00
Bowl, 8" to 9" d., blue (Fenton) 92.50
Bowl, 8" to 9" d., blue (Millersburg) ...600.00
Bowl, 8" to 9" d., green (Fenton) 180.00
Bowl, 8" to 9" d., green
  (Millersburg)............295.00 to 425.00
Bowl, 8" to 9" d., marigold (Fenton) 75.00
Bowl, 8" to 9" d., marigold
  (Millersburg) 130.00
Bowl, 8" to 9" d., purple (Fenton)......115.00
Bowl, 8" to 9" d., purple
  (Millersburg) 210.00
Bowl, 8" to 9" d., white (Fenton) 98.00
Bowl, ice cream, 10" d., blue
  (Northwood) 325.00
Bowl, ice cream, 10" d., green 340.00
Bowl, ice cream, 10" d., ice blue
  (Northwood) ....575.00 to 675.00
Bowl, ice cream, 10" d., ice green
  (Northwood) 575.00
Bowl, ice cream, 10" d., marigold 215.00
Bowl, ice cream, 10" d., purple 280.00
Bowl, ice cream, 10" d., white
  (Northwood) 350.00

Bowl, 10½" d., ruffled, blue
  (Millersburg) 1,325.00
Bowl, 10½" d., ruffled, green 220.00
Bowl, 10½" d., ruffled, marigold......110.00
Bowl, 10½" d., ruffled, purple 220.00
Compote, 5½" d., 5" h., aqua (Fenton)..90.00
Compote, 5½" d., 5" h., blue (Fenton) ..50.00
Compote, 5½" d., 5" h., marigold
  (Fenton) 36.50
Compote, 5½" d., 5" h., purple
  (Fenton) 55.00
Compote, 5½" d., 5" h., red
  (Fenton) 1,000.00
Compote, 5½" d., 5" h., vaseline
  (Fenton) 125.00
Compote, 5½" d., 5" h., white
  (Fenton) 75.00
Compote, blue (Millersburg Giant) 475.00
Compote, green (Millersburg
  Giant) ....895.00 to 950.00
Compote, marigold (Millersburg
  Giant)............................500.00
Compote, purple (Millersburg
  Giant) 845.00
Cuspidor, purple 4,168.00
Goblet, marigold (Fenton) 43.00
Ice cream dish, aqua opalescent,
  small 1,100.00
Ice cream dish, marigold, small 47.50
Ice cream set: large bowl & 4 small
  dishes; ice blue, 5 pcs..............950.00
Ice cream set: large bowl & 4 small
  dishes; marigold, 5 pcs.............395.00
Ice cream set: large bowl & 6 small
  dishes; purple, 7 pcs.
  (Northwood) ....550.00 to 625.00
Ice cream set: large bowl & 6 small
  dishes; purple, 7 pcs. (Dugan) 400.00
Plate, 6½" d., purple 235.00
Plate, 9" d., blue ....200.00 to 225.00
Plate, 9" d., marigold ....125.00 to 175.00
Plate, 9" d., purple 150.00
Plate, 9" d., white 195.00
Plate, chop, 11" d., marigold,
  Northwood (ILLUS.) 350.00
Plate, chop, 11" d., purple
  (Millersburg)...........510.00 to 700.00
Plate, chop, 11" d., purple
  (Northwood)......................325.00
Sauce dish, blue (Millersburg) 130.00
Sauce dish, blue (Northwood) 49.00
Sauce dish, ice green, 6" d.
  (Northwood)............170.00 to 200.00
Sauce dish, marigold (Millersburg) 70.00
Sauce dish, marigold (Northwood) 36.00
Sauce dish, purple
  (Millersburg)..........150.00 to 195.00
Sauce dish, purple
  (Northwood).............45.00 to 55.00
Sauce dish, white (Northwood) 125.00

PEACOCK AT FOUNTAIN (Northwood)
Berry set: master bowl & 4 sauce
  dishes; white, 5 pcs................175.00

Berry set: master bowl & 5 sauce
  dishes; marigold, 6 pcs............185.00
Berry set: master bowl & 6 sauce
  dishes; blue, 7 pcs................270.00
Berry set: master bowl & 6 sauce
  dishes; purple, 7 pcs..............205.00
Bowl, ice cream, ice blue 375.00
Bowl, ice cream, purple 250.00
Bowl, ice cream, white 225.00
Bowl, master berry, blue.............125.00
Bowl, master berry, ice blue.........100.00
Bowl, master berry, marigold,
  large...............75.00 to 100.00
Bowl, master berry, purple...........165.00
Bowl, orange, 3-footed, aqua
  opalescent.....................2,000.00
Bowl, orange, 3-footed,
  blue ....250.00 to 275.00
Bowl, orange, 3-footed, green 525.00
Bowl, orange, 3-footed, lavender 325.00
Bowl, orange, 3-footed,
  marigold...........150.00 to 195.00
Bowl, orange, 3-footed,
  purple ....240.00 to 285.00
Butter dish, cov., marigold 150.00

Peacock at Fountain Butter Dish
Butter dish, cov., purple (ILLUS.) 225.00
Butter dish, cov., white 275.00
Compote, blue ....450.00 to 550.00
Compote, ice blue ....700.00 to 775.00
Compote, ice green 650.00
Compote, marigold 355.00
Compote, purple.....................110.00
Creamer, blue.......................105.00
Creamer, marigold....................75.00
Creamer, purple......................87.50
Pitcher, water, blue .....400.00 to 425.00
Pitcher, water, green 1,600.00
Pitcher, water, marigold.............210.00
Pitcher, water, purple 360.00
Pitcher, water, white................675.00
Punch bowl, marigold 125.00
Punch bowl, purple 375.00
Punch bowl & base, blue, 2 pcs......365.00
Punch bowl & base, ice blue, 2 pcs. ..2,350.00
Punch bowl & base, marigold, 2 pcs....225.00
Punch bowl & base, purple,
  2 pcs. ....480.00 to 500.00
Punch cup, blue......................25.00
Punch cup, ice blue 95.00

Punch cup, marigold 30.00
Punch cup, purple 35.00
Punch cup, white 60.00
Punch set: bowl & 1 cup; marigold,
   2 pcs. 125.00
Punch set: bowl, base & 1 cup;
   green, 3 pcs. 2,250.00
Punch set: bowl, base & 4 cups;
   ice green, 6 pcs. 2,400.00
Punch set: bowl, base & 4 cups;
   marigold, 6 pcs. 400.00
Punch set: bowl, base & 4 cups;
   purple, 6 pcs. 675.00
Punch set: bowl, base & 6 cups;
   ice blue, 8 pcs. 2,650.00
Punch set: bowl, base & 6 cups;
   marigold, 8 pcs. 365.00
Sauce dish, blue 42.50
Sauce dish, marigold 20.00
Sauce dish, purple 25.00
Sauce dish, teal blue 125.00
Sauce dish, white 45.00
Spooner, blue 125.00
Spooner, marigold 65.00
Spooner, purple . . . . 95.00 to 115.00
Spooner, white .100.00
Sugar bowl, cov., blue 125.00
Sugar bowl, cov., ice blue 220.00
Sugar bowl, cov., marigold 85.00
Sugar bowl, cov., purple . . . . . . 80.00 to 100.00
Table set: cov. butter dish, sugar bowl
   & spooner; purple, 3 pcs. 350.00
Table set, marigold, 4 pcs. 350.00
Tumbler, blue 45.00
Tumbler, green .365.00
Tumbler, ice blue 275.00
Tumbler, marigold 35.00
Tumbler, purple .38.00
Tumbler, white .125.00
Water set: pitcher & 6 tumblers; blue,
   7 pcs. 525.00
Water set: pitcher & 6 tumblers;
   marigold, 7 pcs. 435.00
Water set: pitcher & 6 tumblers;
   purple, 7 pcs. 535.00

PEACOCK ON FENCE (Northwood Peacock)

Bowl, 8" to 9" d., aqua opalescent
   (ILLUS.) 530.00
Bowl, 8" to 9" d., fluted,
   blue . . . . 325.00 to 375.00
Bowl, 8" to 9" d., fluted, green 625.00
Bowl, 8" to 9" d., fluted, ice blue 375.00
Bowl, 8" to 9" d., fluted, ice green 375.00
Bowl, 8" to 9" d., fluted, marigold 85.00
Bowl, 8" to 9" d., fluted, peach
   opalescent 500.00
Bowl, 8" to 9" d., fluted, purple 195.00
Bowl, 8" to 9" d., fluted,
   white . . . . 275.00 to 350.00
Plate, 9" d., blue 335.00
Plate, 9" d., green 625.00
Plate, 9" d., ice blue 750.00
Plate, 9" d., ice green 260.00

Peacock on Fence Bowl

Plate, 9" d., lavender 395.00
Plate, 9" d., marigold 235.00
Plate, 9" d., purple 245.00
Plate, 9" d., white 275.00
Table set, purple, 4 pcs. 425.00

PEACOCK STRUTTING (Westmoreland)

Breakfast set: individual size cov.
   creamer & cov. sugar bowl; purple,
   pr. 72.50
Breakfast set: individual size creamer
   & open sugar bowl; purple, pr. 65.00
Creamer, cov., individual size, purple . .40.00
Sugar bowl, cov., individual size,
   purple 25.00

PEACOCK TAIL

Peacock Tail Plate

Bon bon, 2-handled, blue 35.00
Bon bon, 2-handled, footed, green 30.00
Bon bon, tricornered, marigold 16.00
Bon bon, tricornered, purple 40.00
Bowl, 5" d., ruffled, green 25.00
Bowl, 5" d., ruffled, marigold 22.50

Bowl, 5" d., ruffled, purple 30.50
Bowl, 7" d., purple 22.50
Bowl, 7" d., red 385.00
Bowl, 9" d., blue 47.50
Bowl, 9" d., green. 55.00
Bowl, 9" d., crimped, marigold 30.00
Bowl, 9" d., ribbon candy rim, purple . . .36.00
Bowl, 10½" d., marigold 47.00
Compote, 6" d., 5" h., blue 39.00
Compote, 6" d., 5" h., green. 38.00
Compote, 6" d., 5" h., marigold 45.00
Compote, 6" d., 5" h., purple . . .48.00 to 65.00
Plate, 6" d., marigold (ILLUS.) 28.00
Sauce dish, green 35.00
Sauce dish, purple 28.00
Whimsey, hat-shaped, blue 26.50

PERFECTION (Millersburg)

Perfection Water Pitcher

Pitcher, water, marigold 2,700.00
Pitcher, water, purple
  (ILLUS.) . . . . .2,000.00 to 3,000.00
Tumbler, green .500.00
Tumbler, purple 450.00

PERSIAN GARDEN (Dugan)
Berry set: master bowl & 6 sauce
  dishes; peach opalescent, 7 pcs. 450.00
Bowl, 5" d., white 50.00
Bowl, 9" d., ruffled, marigold. 50.00
Bowl, ice cream, 11" d., peach
  opalescent 350.00
Bowl, ice cream, 11" d., purple 275.00
Bowl, ice cream, 11" d., white 210.00
Fruit bowl (no base), marigold,
  11½" d. . . . . .70.00 to 85.00
Fruit bowl (no base), peach opalescent,
  11½" d. 195.00
Fruit bowl (no base), purple, 11½" d. . .135.00
Fruit bowl (no base), white, 11½" d. . . .180.00
Fruit bowl & base, peach opalescent,
  2 pcs. 385.00
Fruit bowl & base, purple, 2 pcs. 300.00
Fruit bowl & base, white, 2 pcs. 240.00

Ice cream dish, white, small 60.00
Ice cream set: 11" d. master ice cream
  bowl & 3 small dishes; white, 4 pcs. . .200.00
Plate, 6" to 7" d., blue 80.00
Plate, 6" to 7" d., marigold 40.00
Plate, 6" to 7" d., peach opalescent. . . .180.00
Plate, 6" to 7" d., purple 180.00
Plate, 6" to 7" d., white 97.50
Plate, chop, 11" d.,
  purple . . . . .1,400.00 to 2,000.00

PERSIAN MEDALLION (Fenton)

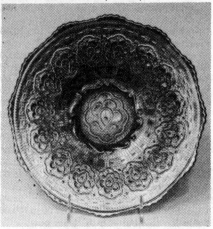

Persian Medallion Chop Plate

Bon bon, 2-handled, blue 45.00
Bon bon, 2-handled, green 60.00
Bon bon, 2-handled, marigold 25.00
Bon bon, 2-handled, purple 35.00
Bon bon, 2-handled, red 355.00
Bon bon, 2-handled, vaseline 60.00
Bowl, 5" d., green. 25.00
Bowl, 5" d., marigold 45.00
Bowl, 5" d., purple 35.00
Bowl, 7" d., pie crust edge, purple 75.00
Bowl, 8" to 9" d., fluted, blue 55.00
Bowl, 8" to 9" d., ribbon candy rim,
  blue. 90.00
Bowl, 8" to 9" d., marigold 40.00
Bowl, 8" to 9" d., ribbon candy rim,
  purple. 47.50
Bowl, 9½" d., footed, Grape & Cable
  exterior, blue .225.00
Bowl, ice cream, 10½" d., purple 55.00
Bowl, 10½" d., fluted, blue. 70.00
Compote, 6½" d., 6½" h., blue 70.00
Compote, 6½" d., 6½" h., green. 48.00
Compote, 6½" d., 6½" h., marigold 32.50
Compote, 6½" d., 6½" h., white 400.00
Hair receiver, blue 105.00
Hair receiver, marigold 32.50
Plate, 6½" d., blue. 60.00
Plate, 6½" d., green 115.00
Plate, 6½" d., marigold. 35.00
Plate, 6½" d., red slag 325.00
Plate, 6½" d., white. 95.00

Plate, 9" d., blue . . . . 100.00 to 150.00
Plate, 9" d., white 375.00
Plate, chop, 10½" d., blue (ILLUS) 300.00
Rose bowl, blue 65.00
Rose bowl, marigold 45.00
Rose bowl, white 135.00

PETAL & FAN
Berry set: master bowl & 6 sauce
   dishes; peach opalescent, 7 pcs. 250.00
Bowl, 5" d., peach opalescent 32.50
Bowl, 5" d., purple 30.00
Bowl, 11" d., peach
   opalescent . . . . .95.00 to 140.00
Plate, 6" d., ribbon candy edge,
   purple 105.00

PETER RABBIT (Fenton)
Bowl, 8" d., marigold 750.00
Plate, blue 1,450.00
Plate, green 2,400.00
Plate, marigold 1,200.00

PILLOW & SUNBURST
Bowl, marigold 25.00
Bowl, purple 40.00
Plate, 8" d., aqua 38.00
Wine, marigold 25.00
Wine, purple 50.00

PINEAPPLE
Bowl, 8" d., marigold 35.00
Creamer, marigold, 4½" h. 28.50
Creamer, purple .38.00
Plate, 8" d., purple 135.00
Sugar bowl, aqua 215.00

PINE CONE (Fenton)
Bowl, 5" d., blue .35.00
Bowl, 5" d., marigold 25.00
Bowl, 5" d., purple 35.00
Bowl, 7" d., ruffled rim, blue 75.00
Bowl, 7" d., marigold 26.50
Plate, 6½" d., blue 45.00
Plate, 6½" d., green 100.00
Plate, 6½" d., marigold 55.00
Plate, 6½" d., purple . . . . .85.00 to 100.00
Plate, 7½" d., blue 160.00

PODS & POSIES (Dugan)
Bowl, 10" d., peach opalescent 90.00
Bowl, 10" d., purple 140.00
Plate, 6" d., green 275.00
Plate, 6" d., peach opalescent 90.00
Plate, 6" d., purple 145.00
Plate, 9" d., green 525.00
Plate, 9" d., purple 360.00
Plate, chop, 11" d., peach opalescent . . 465.00

POINSETTIA (Imperial)
Pitcher, milk, amber 59.00
Pitcher, milk, green 100.00
Pitcher, milk, marigold 58.50
Pitcher, milk, smoky . . . . .70.00 to 85.00

POINSETTIA & LATTICE
Bowl, aqua opalescent . . .2,200.00 to 4,800.00
Bowl, ice blue 200.00
Bowl, marigold . . . . .90.00 to 110.00
Bowl, purple 160.00

PONY
Bowl, 8" to 9" d., marigold 65.00
Bowl, 8" to 9" d., marigold w/aqua
   base 200.00
Bowl, 8" to 9" d., purple 150.00
Plate, marigold 475.00

POPPY (Millersburg)
Compote, green 360.00
Compote, marigold 275.00
Compote, purple 325.00

POPPY (Northwood)
Pickle dish, blue 60.00
Pickle dish, marigold 50.00
Pickle dish, white 225.00

POPPY SHOW (Northwood)

Poppy Show Bowl

Bowl, 7" d., purple 38.00
Bowl, 8" to 9" d., blue (ILLUS.) 225.00
Bowl, 8" to 9" d., ice blue 400.00
Bowl, 8" to 9" d., ice green 495.00
Bowl, 8" to 9" d., marigold 125.00
Bowl, 8" to 9" d., purple 170.00
Bowl, 8" to 9" d., white 185.00
Plate, blue 425.00
Plate, green 1,000.00
Plate, ice blue .615.00
Plate, ice green 340.00
Plate, marigold . . . . .275.00 to 350.00
Plate, purple 450.00
Plate, white . . . . .285.00 to 325.00

POPPY SHOW VASE (Imperial)
Marigold 250.00
Purple (ILLUS.) .950.00
Smoky . . . . .550.00 to 625.00

Poppy Show Vase

PRIMROSE BOWL (Millersburg)
Green ....95.00 to 110.00
Marigold 75.00
Purple...............................80.00

PRISMS
Compote, 7¼" d., 2½" h., 2-handled,
   marigold 50.00
Compote, 7¼" d., 2½" h., 2-handled,
   purple............................55.00

QUESTION MARKS
Bon bon, footed, marigold, 6" d.,
   3¾" h. 23.50
Bon bon, footed, peach opalescent,
   6" d., 3¾" h. 55.00
Bon bon, footed, purple, 6" d., 3¾" h. ..26.50
Bon bon, footed, white, 6" d., 3¾" h. ...60.00
Plate, dome-footed, w/Georgia Peach
   exterior, purple 100.00

QUILL (Dugan or Diamond Glass Co.)

Quill Pitcher

Pitcher, water, purple (ILLUS.) 2,200.00
Tumbler, marigold..........275.00 to 325.00
Tumbler, purple 400.00

RAINDROPS (Dugan)
Bowl, 9" d., dome-footed, peach
   opalescent........................65.00

RAMBLER ROSE (Dugan)
Pitcher, water, purple 325.00
Tumbler, blue 37.50
Tumbler, marigold 21.50
Tumbler, purple 35.00

RANGER
Pitcher, milk, marigold 145.00
Sherbet, marigold 17.50
Tumbler, marigold 105.00

RASPBERRY (Northwood)
Pitcher, milk, green 185.00
Pitcher, milk, marigold 110.00
Pitcher, milk, purple ....160.00 to 215.00
Pitcher, water, green.................250.00
Pitcher, water, ice green 2,275.00
Pitcher, water, purple 235.00
Sauceboat, purple 75.00
Tumbler, green.......................50.00
Tumbler, ice blue 315.00
Tumbler, marigold 27.50
Tumbler, purple 35.00
Water set: pitcher & 2 tumblers; green,
   3 pcs. 290.00
Water set: pitcher & 4 tumblers; green,
   5 pcs. 360.00
Water set: pitcher & 5 tumblers;
   ice blue, 6 pcs...................2,250.00
Water set: pitcher & 6 tumblers;
   marigold, 7 pcs. 300.00
Water set: pitcher & 6 tumblers;
   purple, 7 pcs.....................425.00

RAYS & RIBBONS (Millersburg)
Banana boat, green 850.00
Bowl, 8" to 9" d., green 56.50
Bowl, 8" to 9" d., purple 75.00
Bowl, 10" d., marigold...............50.00
Bowl, 10" d., purple 80.00

ROBIN (Imperial)

Robin Mug

Mug, marigold (ILLUS.) 45.00
Pitcher, water, marigold 190.00
Tumbler, marigold 47.50
Water set: pitcher & 6 tumblers;
  marigold, 7 pcs. . . . . .365.00 to 400.00

ROCOCO VASE
Clambroth 40.00
Marigold 30.00
Smoky. 75.00

ROSALIND (Millersburg)
Bowl, 10" d., ruffled, green 150.00
Bowl, 10" d., marigold . . . . . . .75.00 to 100.00
Bowl, 10" d., purple 125.00
Compote, 6", small, ruffled, green 350.00
Compote, 6", small, ruffled, purple. . . .485.00
Compote, tall, ruffled, marigold 650.00
Plate, 9" d., green 575.00

ROSE COLUMNS VASE

Rose Columns Vase

Amethyst, experimental, w/factory-
  painted rose decoration (ILLUS.). . .3,250.00
Green 1,250.00
Marigold 1,200.00

ROSE SHOW
Bowl, 9" d., aqua opalescent 485.00
Bowl, 9" d., blue 150.00
Bowl, 9" d., green. 400.00
Bowl, 9" d., ice blue 300.00
Bowl, 9" d., ice green. 500.00
Bowl, 9" d., ice green opalescent 700.00
Bowl, 9" d., marigold 120.00
Bowl, 9" d., purple 210.00
Bowl, 9" d., teal blue 275.00
Bowl, 9" d., white 245.00
Plate, 9" d., blue (ILLUS.). 425.00
Plate, 9" d., ice blue. 625.00
Plate, 9" d., ice green 525.00
Plate, 9" d., marigold. 270.00
Plate, 9" d., purple. 350.00
Plate, 9" d., white. 235.00

Rose Show Plate

ROUND UP (Dugan)

Round Up Plate

Bowl, 9" d., low, fluted, blue 70.00
Bowl, 9" d., marigold 50.00
Bowl, 9" d., peach opalescent 250.00
Bowl, 9" d., purple 120.00
Bowl, 9" d., white. 95.00
Plate, 9" d., blue (ILLUS.). 165.00
Plate, 9" d., flat, peach opalescent 200.00
Plate, 9" d., ruffled, peach
  opalescent 325.00
Plate, 9" d., purple 195.00
Plate, 9" d., white 225.00

RUSTIC VASE
Blue, 9" h. 30.00
Blue, 19" h. 165.00
Green, 11" h. 32.00
Marigold, 11" h. 22.00
Marigold, 16" h. 125.00
Purple, 9" h. 37.50
Purple, 16" h. 100.00
White, 10" h. 50.00
White, 18" h. 225.00

SAILBOAT (Fenton)
Bowl, 5" d., aqua 80.00
Bowl, 5" d., ruffled, blue 55.00
Bowl, 5" d., ruffled, green 75.00
Bowl, 5" d., marigold 22.50
Bowl, 5" d., red 265.00
Compote, blue 100.00
Compote, marigold 45.00
Goblet, water, green 225.00
Goblet, water, marigold 160.00
Goblet, water, purple 350.00
Plate, 6" d., blue 425.00
Plate, 6" d., marigold 100.00
Wine, blue 28.00
Wine, marigold 30.00
Wine, vaseline 125.00

SCALE BAND
Pitcher, marigold 85.00
Plate, 6" d., flat, marigold 22.00
Tumbler, marigold 60.00

SCALES
Bowl, 7" d., peach opalescent 60.00
Bowl, 8" to 9" d., aqua opalescent 320.00
Bowl, 8" to 9" d., milk white
    w/marigold overlay . . . . . .150.00 to 200.00
Plate, 6½" d., purple . . . . .30.00 to 45.00

SCOTCH THISTLE COMPOTE
Green 75.00

SCROLL EMBOSSED
Bowl, 8" to 9" d., green 50.00
Bowl, 8" to 9" d., marigold 35.00
Bowl, 8" to 9" d., purple . . . . . . .35.00 to 45.00
Bowl, 8" to 9" d., smoky 35.00
Compote, green 35.00
Compote, marigold 30.00
Compote, purple 75.00
Plate, 9" d., green 67.50
Plate, 9" d., marigold 100.00
Plate, 9" d., purple 120.00
Sauce dish, purple, 5½" d. 11.50

SEACOAST PIN TRAY (Millersburg)
Green 280.00
Marigold 290.00
Purple 325.00

SEAWEED (Millersburg)
Bowl, 8" to 9" d., marigold 100.00
Bowl, 10" d., blue 900.00
Bowl, 10" d., ruffled, green . .200.00 to 235.00
Bowl, 10" d., ruffled, marigold 195.00
Bowl, 10" d., purple 255.00
Plate, 9" d., green 550.00
Plate, 9" d., marigold 500.00

SHELL & JEWEL
Creamer, cov., green 28.00
Creamer & cov. sugar bowl, marigold,
    pr .45.00 to 80.00

Sugar bowl, cov., green 28.00
Sugar bowl, cov., marigold 20.00

SHELL & SAND
Bowl, 8" to 9" d., ruffled, purple 50.00
Plate, green 80.00

SHIP & STARS PLATE
Marigold 25.00

SINGING BIRDS (Northwood)

Singing Birds Water Set

Berry set: master bowl & 6 sauce
    dishes; green, 7 pcs. 350.00
Bowl, master berry, purple 90.00
Butter dish, cov., green 285.00
Butter dish, cov., marigold 100.00
Butter dish, cov., purple 195.00
Creamer, marigold 55.00
Creamer, purple 77.50
Mug, aqua opalescent . . . . .875.00 to 1,000.00
Mug, blue 85.00
Mug, green 110.00
Mug, ice blue .775.00
Mug, lavender 125.00
Mug, marigold 65.00
Mug, stippled, marigold . . . . . .95.00 to 125.00
Mug, purple 68.00
Mug, purple, w/advertising, "Hotel
    Verdome" .135.00
Mug, white 725.00
Pitcher, green 275.00
Pitcher, marigold 210.00
Sauce dish, green 35.00
Sauce dish, marigold 30.00
Sauce dish, purple 25.00
Spooner, marigold 60.00
Spooner, purple 85.00
Sugar bowl, cov., marigold 80.00
Table set: cov. sugar bowl, creamer &
    spooner; marigold, 3 pcs. 225.00
Table set, purple, 4 pcs. 900.00
Tumbler, green 35.00
Tumbler, marigold 30.00
Tumbler, purple 50.00
Water set: pitcher & 5 tumblers;
    green, 6 pcs. 525.00

Water set: pitcher & 6 tumblers;
  green, 7 pcs. 600.00
Water set: pitcher & 6 tumblers;
  marigold, 7 pcs. 365.00
Water set: pitcher & 6 tumblers;
  purple, 7 pcs. (ILLUS. of part) 665.00

SIX PETALS
Bowl, 7" w., tricornered, peach
  opalescent.......................65.00
Bowl, 7" w., tricornered, purple 52.50
Bowl, 8" d., peach opalescent 62.50
Bowl, 8" d., white 60.00

SKI STAR (Dugan)
Banana bowl, peach
  opalescent ....95.00 to 120.00
Basket, peach opalescent 395.00
Berry set: master bowl & 2 sauce
  dishes; peach opalescent, 3 pcs. 165.00
Bowl, 5" d., fluted, peach opalescent ...60.00
Bowl, 5" d., ruffled, peach opalescent ..45.00
Bowl, 5" d., ruffled, purple 47.00
Bowl, 7" d., ruffled, purple 75.00
Bowl, 8" to 9" d., dome-footed, peach
  opalescent.......................87.50
Bowl, 8" to 9" d., dome-footed, purple ..70.00
Bowl, 10" d., peach opalescent 120.00
Bowl, 10" d., purple 120.00
Bowl, 11" d., peach
  opalescent ....95.00 to 115.00
Bowl, tricornered, peach opalescent ..130.00
Plate, 8½" d., dome-footed, w/hand-
  grip, peach opalescent ....125.00 to 160.00
Plate, 8½" d., dome-footed, w/hand-
  grip, purple 240.00
Sauce dish, purple 38.50

SODA GOLD (Imperial)

Soda Gold Water Set

Candlesticks, marigold, 7½" h., pr. 37.00
Cuspidor, marigold 35.00
Goblets, marigold, 8 oz., 4 5/8" h.,
  set of 6 ....60.00
Pitcher, milk, marigold 195.00
Pitcher, water, marigold 130.00
Pitcher, water, smoky 250.00
Tumbler, marigold 40.00
Tumbler, smoky 50.00

Water set: pitcher & 6 tumblers;
  marigold, 7 pcs. 295.00
Water set: pitcher & 6 tumblers;
  smoky, 7 pcs. (ILLUS.) 800.00

SOUTACHE
Bowl, 8¾" d., dome-footed, piecrust
  edge, peach opalescent 90.00
Plate, 9½" d., dome-footed, peach
  opalescent......................300.00

SPRINGTIME (Northwood)
Bowl, master berry, green 150.00
Butter dish, cov., green 400.00
Butter dish, cov., marigold 165.00
Butter dish, cov., purple 275.00
Creamer, marigold 85.00
Creamer, purple 135.00
Pitcher, green 495.00
Pitcher, marigold 310.00
Pitcher, purple ....600.00 to 750.00
Sauce dish, marigold 25.00
Sauce dish, purple 37.50
Spooner, green 150.00
Spooner, marigold 60.00
Spooner, purple 120.00
Sugar bowl, cov., purple 120.00
Table set, marigold, 4 pcs. 525.00
Tumbler, green 85.00
Tumbler, marigold 52.50
Tumbler, purple 95.00
Water set: pitcher & 4 tumblers;
  green, 5 pcs. 1,100.00
Water set: pitcher & 6 tumblers;
  marigold, 7 pcs. 690.00

"S" REPEAT
Punch bowl & base, purple, 2 pcs. 90.00
Punch cup, purple....................27.50
Punch set: bowl, base & 4 cups;
  purple, 6 pcs......................240.00

STAG & HOLLY (Fenton)

Stag & Holly Bowl

Bowl, 7" d., spatula-footed, blue 100.00
Bowl, 7" d., spatula-footed, green 125.00
Bowl, 7" d., spatula-footed, marigold . . .52.50
Bowl, 7" d., spatula-footed, red 1,050.00
Bowl, 8" to 9" d., spatula-footed,
   blue. 135.00
Bowl, 8" to 9" d., spatula-footed,
   green 165.00
Bowl, 8" to 9" d., spatula-footed,
   marigold .87.50
Bowl, 8" to 9" d., spatula-footed,
   purple . . . . .95.00 to 110.00
Bowl, 10" to 11" d., 3-footed, amber . . .475.00
Bowl, 10" to 11" d., 3-footed, blue
   (ILLUS.) 190.00
Bowl, 10" to 11" d., 3-footed,
   marigold . . . . .85.00 to 125.00
Bowl, 10" to 11" d., 3-footed, purple . . .195.00
Bowl, 10" to 11" d., 3-footed, red 850.00
Plate, 9" d., marigold. 325.00
Plate, chop, 12" d., 3-footed,
   marigold 535.00
Rose bowl, blue, large. 595.00
Rose bowl, marigold, large. 225.00

STAR & FILE
Bowl, 5" d., marigold 18.00
Bowl, 7" d., marigold 22.50
Bowl, 8" to 9" d., marigold 35.00
Card tray, 2 turned-up sides,
   marigold, 6¼" d. 22.50
Celery vase, 2-handled, marigold 27.50
Compote, jelly, clambroth 50.00
Compote, jelly, marigold 55.00
Compote, large, marigold. 37.50
Creamer, marigold. 20.00
Creamer & sugar bowl, marigold, pr. . . .50.00
Pitcher, milk, smoky 40.00
Pitcher, water, marigold 120.00
Plate, 6" d., marigold. 25.00
Relish tray, 2-handled, marigold 45.00
Rose bowl, marigold 52.50
Sugar bowl, marigold 15.00
Tumbler, marigold 50.00
Water set: pitcher & 6 tumblers;
   marigold, 7 pcs. 255.00
Wine, marigold 35.50
Wine decanter w/stopper, marigold 90.00
Wine set: decanter w/stopper & 6 wines;
   marigold, 7 pcs. 285.00

STAR MEDALLION
Bowl, 5" sq., marigold 25.00
Bowl, 7" d., smoky 22.50
Bowl, 8" d., marigold. 30.00
Bowl, 8" d., smoky. 26.50
Pitcher, milk, clambroth 37.50
Pitcher, milk, marigold 35.00
Pitcher, milk, smoky 40.00
Plate, 9" to 10" d., clambroth 45.00
Plate, 9" to 10" d., marigold 40.00
Punch cup, marigold 15.00
Sherbet, stemmed, marigold 25.00

Tumbler, marigold 22.50
Tumbler, tankard, marigold 25.00

STAR OF DAVID (Imperial)

Star of David Bowl

Bowl, 8" to 9" d., collared base, green
   (ILLUS.) 65.00
Bowl, 8" to 9" d., collared base,
   marigold 45.00
Bowl, 8" to 9" d., collared base,
   purple. 67.50
Bowl, 9" d., flat, ruffled, purple 90.00

STAR OF DAVID & BOWS (Northwood)
Bowl, 7" d., dome-footed, green 70.00
Bowl, 7" d., dome-footed, purple 60.00
Bowl, 8" to 9" d., dome-footed, fluted,
   purple. 70.00

STIPPLED PETALS
Bowl, peach opalescent. 58.50
Bowl, white 60.00

STIPPLED RAYS

Stippled Rays Bon Bon

Bon bon, 2-handled, green (ILLUS.) 40.00
Bon bon, 2-handled, marigold 45.00
Bon bon, 2-handled, purple 28.00
Bon bon, 2-handled, red 260.00

Bowl, 5" d., purple 29.50
Bowl, 5" d., red....................275.00
Bowl, 7" d., dome-footed, green 25.00
Bowl, 7" d., marigold................20.00
Bowl, 7" d., red............235.00 to 250.00
Bowl, 8" to 9" d., amber 97.50
Bowl, 8" to 9" d., green 29.00
Bowl, 8" to 9" d., marigold 36.00
Bowl, 8" to 9" d., purple 45.00
Bowl, 8" to 9" d., teal blue 20.00
Bowl, 8" to 9" d., ribbon candy rim,
    green 57.50
Bowl, 8" to 9" d., ribbon candy rim,
    purple..........................27.50
Bowl, 10" d., green.................55.00
Bowl, 10" d., ruffled, marigold........45.00
Bowl, 10" d., purple 27.50
Bowl, 10" d., red slag 450.00
Bowl, 10" d., white ....275.00 to 300.00
Creamer & sugar bowl, marigold, pr. ...30.00
Plate, 6" to 7" d., blue 40.00
Plate, 6" to 7" d., marigold 18.50
Sugar bowl, open, red 320.00

STORK & RUSHES (Dugan or Diamond Glass Works)
Basket, handled, marigold 90.00
Bowl, master berry or fruit, marigold ...40.00
Butter dish, cov., marigold 125.00
Creamer, marigold...................70.00
Hat shape, marigold 22.00
Mug, aqua base w/marigold overlay ..450.00
Mug, marigold 20.00
Mug, purple........................90.00
Pitcher, water, blue 375.00
Pitcher, water, purple 365.00
Punch cup, marigold 18.00
Punch cup, purple 18.50
Sauce dish, marigold 16.50
Sauce dish, purple 30.00
Spooner, marigold 60.00
Tumbler, blue 30.00
Tumbler w/lattice band, blue........55.00
Tumbler, marigold 20.00
Tumbler, purple 42.50
Vase, marigold 24.00
Water set: pitcher & 6 tumblers;
    blue, 7 pcs. 475.00
Water set: pitcher & 6 tumblers;
    marigold, 7 pcs. 320.00

STRAWBERRY (Fenton)
Bon bon, 2-handled, blue 45.00
Bon bon, 2-handled, green 20.00
Bon bon, 2-handled, marigold 22.50

STRAWBERRY (Millersburg)
Bowl, 5" d., green..................55.00
Bowl, 5" d., marigold................20.00
Bowl, 5" d., purple 50.00
Bowl, 7" d., green..................75.00
Bowl, 7" d., purple 105.00
Bowl, 8" to 9" d., purple 150.00
Bowl, 8" to 9" d., vaseline..........450.00

Compote, amber....................45.00
Compote, green 175.00
Compote, marigold 105.00
Compote, purple ....125.00 to 150.00
Compote, vaseline 640.00

STRAWBERRY & WILD STRAWBERRY (Northwood)

Northwood Strawberry Plate

Bowl, 5" d., marigold................27.50
Bowl, 5" d., fluted, purple............56.50
Bowl, 7" d., marigold................48.50
Bowl, 7" d., purple 30.00
Bowl, 8" to 9" d., stippled, blue 90.00
Bowl, 8" to 9" d., stippled, ribbon
    candy rim, green 150.00
Bowl, 8" to 9" d., ruffled, Basketweave
    exterior, green 62.50
Bowl, 8" to 9" d., marigold 40.00
Bowl, 8" to 9" d., purple 52.50
Bowl, 10" d., ice green..............575.00
Bowl, 10" d., marigold...............39.00
Bowl, 10" d., purple.................85.00
Plate, 6" to 7" d., w/handgrip,
    green 87.50
Plate, 6" to 7" d., w/handgrip,
    marigold 100.00
Plate, 6" to 7" d., w/handgrip,
    purple 125.00
Plate, 9" d., green 105.00
Plate, 9" d., lavender...............135.00
Plate, 9" d., marigold...............85.00
Plate, 9" d., purple (ILLUS.) 98.50

STRAWBERRY SCROLL (Fenton)
Pitcher, water, blue .....1,850.00 to 2,000.00
Tumbler, blue 235.00

STREAM OF HEARTS
Compote, marigold ....50.00 to 65.00

SUNFLOWER BOWL (Northwood)
Bowl, 8" d., footed, blue.....100.00 to 125.00
Bowl, 8" d., footed, clambroth 75.00
Bowl, 8" d., footed, green............48.00

Bowl, 8" d., footed, marigold 35.00
Bowl, 8" d., footed, purple 50.00

SUNFLOWER PIN TRAY (Millersburg)
Clambroth 195.00
Green 240.00
Marigold 350.00
Purple 250.00

SWAN PASTEL NOVELTIES
Salt dip, blue 10.00
Salt dip, ice blue .27.50
Salt dip, ice green .55.00
Salt dip, peach opalescent 200.00
Salt dip, pink 32.50
Salt dip, purple .160.00

SWIRL HOBNAIL (Millersburg)

Swirl Hobnail Cuspidor

Cuspidor, purple (ILLUS.) . . . .495.00 to 550.00
Rose bowl, marigold 185.00
Rose bowl, purple 280.00
Vase, green 250.00
Vase, marigold . . . . .220.00 to 250.00
Vase, purple . . . . .200.00 to 275.00

SWIRL RIB
Tumbler, marigold . . . . .20.00 to 25.00
Vase, 10½" h., peach opalescent 37.00
Vase, 14½" h., peach opalescent 48.00

TEN MUMS

Ten Mums Water Pitcher

Bowl, 8" to 9" d., ribbon candy edge,
  blue 87.50
Bowl, 10" d., footed, green 80.00
Bowl, 10" d., footed, marigold 195.00
Bowl, 10" d., ribbon candy edge,
  purple . . . . .80.00 to 110.00
Pitcher, water, marigold 375.00
Tumbler, blue . . . . .60.00 to 75.00
Tumbler, marigold 45.00
Water set: pitcher & 5 tumblers; blue,
  6 pcs. (ILLUS. of pitcher) 2,900.00
Water set: pitcher & 6 tumblers;
  marigold, 7 pcs. 850.00

TEXAS HAT
Marigold 25.00

THIN RIB VASE
7½" h., ice green (Northwood) 80.00
8" h., aqua 27.00
9" h., aqua opalescent 70.00
9½" h., aqua 30.00
11" h., aqua opalescent 130.00

THISTLE (Fenton)

Thistle Banana Boat

Banana boat, blue (ILLUS.) 210.00
Banana boat, green 185.00
Banana boat, marigold . . . . . .150.00 to 200.00
Banana boat, purple . . . . .165.00 to 200.00
Bowl, 8" to 9" d., ruffled, amber 125.00
Bowl, 8" to 9" d., ribbon candy edge,
  blue 45.00
Bowl, 8" to 9" d., flared, green 55.00
Bowl, 8" to 9" d., ribbon candy edge,
  green 40.00
Bowl, 8" to 9" d., ribbon candy edge,
  marigold 42.50
Bowl, 8" to 9" d., ribbon candy edge,
  purple 50.00
Compote, green (Scotch Thistle) 65.00
Compote, marigold (Scotch Thistle) 20.00
Plate, 9" d., green 1,200.00
Plate, 9" d., purple 1,250.00
Vase, 6" h., marigold 30.00

THISTLE & THORN (Sowerby's, England)
Bowl, 5" to 6" d., footed, marigold 25.00
Bowl, 9" d., footed, marigold 35.00
Creamer, marigold 30.00
Sugar bowl, footed, marigold, 5¼" h. . . .28.00

THREE FRUITS (Northwood)

Three Fruits Plate

Bowl, 9" d., dome-footed, basketweave & grapevine exterior, aqua
opalescent .... 425.00 to 475.00
Bowl, 9" d., dome-footed, basketweave & grapevine exterior, ice
green 750.00
Bowl, 9" d., dome-footed, basketweave & grapevine exterior,
purple 200.00
Bowl, 9" d., dome-footed, basketweave & grapevine exterior,
white 250.00
Bowl, 9" d., spatula-footed, aqua
opalescent 375.00
Bowl, 9" d., spatula-footed, ruffled,
green 85.00
Bowl, 9" d., spatula-footed, ice
green 385.00
Bowl, 9" d., spatula-footed, marigold ... 40.00
Bowl, 9" d., spatula-footed, pastel
marigold .... 40.00 to 60.00
Bowl, 9" d., spatula-footed, purple 70.00
Bowl, 9" d., spatula-footed, stippled,
purple 60.00
Bowl, 9" d., spatula-footed, stippled,
white 125.00
Plate, 9" d., aqua opal-
escent .... 825.00 to 1,000.00
Plate, 9" d., blue .... 90.00 to 110.00
Plate, 9" d., green .... 85.00 to 110.00
Plate, 9" d., lavender .... 135.00 to 175.00
Plate, 9" d., marigold .... 50.00 to 70.00
Plate, 9" d., stippled, marigold 80.00
Plate, 9" d., purple (ILLUS.) 115.00
Plate, 9" d., stippled,
purple .... 100.00 to 125.00
Plate, 9½" w., 12-sided, marigold
(Fenton) 105.00
Plate, 9½" w., 12-sided, blue (Fenton) . 105.00
Plate, 9½" w., 12-sided, green
(Fenton) .... 85.00 to 115.00
Plate, 9½" w., 12-sided, purple
(Fenton) .... 90.00 to 100.00

TIGER LILY (Imperial)

Pitcher, water, green 175.00
Pitcher, water, marigold .... 100.00 to 180.00
Tumbler, aqua 210.00
Tumbler, blue 100.00
Tumbler, green 27.50
Tumbler, marigold 26.50
Tumbler, purple 50.00
Water set: pitcher & 4 tumblers; mari-
gold, 5 pcs. 225.00

TORNADO VASE (Northwood)

Tornado Vase

Marigold 150.00
Purple (ILLUS.) 110.00

TOWN PUMP NOVELTY (Northwood)

"Town Pump"

Marigold 1,000.00
Purple (ILLUS.) 550.00

TREE TRUNK VASE (Northwood)

8" h., green 28.00
9" h., aqua opalescent 300.00
9" h., green 60.00

10" h., ice blue 150.00
10" h., purple 37.50
10" h., teal blue 100.00
12" h., ice blue 175.00
12" h., 5" d., ice green 125.00
15" h., purple, w/elephant
 foot....................325.00 to 375.00
18" h., ice green 750.00
18" h., purple 350.00

TROUT & FLY (Millersburg)
Bowl, ice cream, green 320.00
Bowl, ice cream, lavender 490.00
Bowl, ice cream, marigold 295.00
Bowl, ice cream, purple .....275.00 to 425.00
Bowl, ruffled, green ....300.00 to 350.00
Bowl, ruffled, lavender 950.00
Bowl, ruffled, marigold 250.00
Bowl, ruffled, purple 425.00
Bowl, square, marigold...............425.00
Bowl, square, purple.......425.00 to 450.00

TWINS (Horsehoe Curve)
Bowl, 6" d., marigold 19.00
Fruit bowl, marigold 50.00
Fruit bowl & base, marigold, 2 pcs. 75.00

TWO FLOWERS (Fenton)

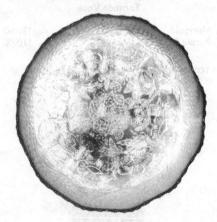

Two Flowers Bowl

Bowl, 6" d., footed, marigold 20.00
Bowl, 7" to 8" d., footed, blue 55.00
Bowl, 7" to 8" d., footed, marigold 38.00
Bowl, 10" d., footed, scalloped rim,
 blue..............................75.00
Bowl, 10" d., footed, scalloped rim,
 marigold (ILLUS.) 45.00
Bowl, 10" d., footed, scalloped rim,
 purple............................95.00
Bowl, 10" d., footed, aqua 225.00
Bowl, 10" d., footed, vaseline 225.00
Plate, 9" d., footed, marigold........340.00
Plate, chop, 11½" d., 3-footed,
 marigold 350.00

Plate, chop, 13" d., 3-footed,
 marigold 475.00
Rose bowl, 3-footed, blue 100.00
Rose bowl, 3-footed, marigold 100.00

VENETIAN GIANT ROSE BOWL (Cambridge)

Venetian Giant Rose Bowl

Green (ILLUS.).....................950.00

VICTORIAN
Bowl, 11" d., purple........110.00 to 200.00

VINEYARD
Pitcher, water, marigold .....75.00 to 110.00
Tumbler, marigold 37.50
Tumbler, purple 42.50
Water set: pitcher & 6 tumblers;
 marigold, 7 pcs. 200.00
Water set: pitcher & 6 tumblers;
 purple, 7 pcs......................475.00

VINTAGE

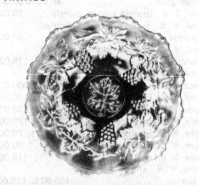

Vintage Plate

Berry set: master bowl & 5 sauce
 dishes; green, Fenton, 6 pcs. 130.00
Bon bon, 2-handled, marigold, Fenton ..30.00
Bowl, 7" d., fluted rim, green, Fenton...30.00
Bowl, 7" d., fluted rim, purple, Fenton ..33.00

Bowl, 8" to 9" d., footed, blue,
Fenton 55.00
Bowl, 8" to 9" d., green, Fenton 45.00
Bowl, 8" to 9" d., marigold, Fenton 28.00
Bowl, 8" to 9" d., footed, purple,
Fenton 40.00
Compote, 7" d., blue, Fenton 46.00
Compote, 7" d., fluted rim, green,
Fenton 35.00
Compote, 7" d., purple, Fenton 50.00
Epergne, blue, Fenton 110.00
Epergne, marigold, Fenton 80.00
Epergne, purple, Fenton 125.00
Fernery, footed, blue, Fenton 50.00
Fernery, footed, green, Fenton 50.00
Fernery, footed, marigold, Fenton 40.00
Fernery, footed, purple, Fenton........48.00
Fernery, footed, red,
Fenton ....275.00 to 350.00
Nut dish, footed, marigold, Fenton,
6" d. 50.00
Plate, 7" d., blue, Fenton ....115.00 to 165.00
Plate, 7" d., green, Fenton (ILLUS.) 110.00
Plate, 7" d., purple, Fenton ...90.00 to 140.00
Powder jar, cov., marigold, Fenton.....45.00
Powder jar, cov., purple, Fenton 100.00
Wine, marigold, Fenton...............18.00
Wine, purple, Fenton 25.00

VINTAGE BAND
Mug, marigold 30.00
Tumbler, marigold 500.00

WAFFLE BLOCK
Basket w/tall handle, clambroth,
10" h. ....40.00 to 65.00
Basket w/tall handle, marigold,
10" h. 55.00
Cuspidor, clambroth 195.00
Punch bowl & base, clambroth 165.00
Punch bowl & base, marigold 125.00
Punch cup, marigold 15.00

WATERLILY (Fenton)
Bon bon, marigold, 7½" d. 20.00
Bowl, 6" d., aqua ....95.00 to 145.00
Bowl, 10" d., footed, marigold 50.00
Sauce dish, footed, marigold 25.00
Tumbler, marigold 55.00

WATERLILY & CATTAILS
Banana boat, blue 130.00
Bon bon, 2-handled, marigold, large ...60.00
Dish, 3 turned up sides, marigold,
6" d. 17.50
Pitcher, water, marigold 575.00
Plate, 6" d., marigold.................60.00
Sauce dish, marigold.........15.00 to 25.00
Toothpick holder, marigold ....65.00 to 80.00
Tumbler, marigold 42.50
Whimsey, marigold ....30.00 to 55.00

WHIRLING LEAVES BOWL (Millersburg)
Green, 9" d............................55.00

Marigold, 9" d. ....45.00 to 50.00
Purple, 9" d. 85.00
Green, 9½" w., tricornered...90.00 to 150.00
Marigold, 9½" w., tri-
cornered ....85.00 to 150.00
Purple, 9½" w., tricornered 120.00
Green, 10" d. ....85.00 to 110.00
Marigold, 10" d. 65.00
Purple, 10" d. 95.00

WHITE OAK TUMBLERS
Tumbler, marigold 150.00

WIDE PANEL
Bowl, 12" d., marigold................45.00
Epergne, 4-lily, green ......425.00 to 700.00
Epergne, 4-lily, marigold............525.00
Goblet, red 100.00
Rose bowl, clambroth 12.00
Salt dip, marigold 40.00

WILD ROSE
Bowl, 7" d., 3-footed, open heart rim,
green, Northwood 50.00
Bowl, 7" d., 3-footed, open heart rim,
marigold, Northwood 35.00
Bowl, 7" d., 3-footed, open heart rim,
purple, Northwood................45.00
Bowl, 8" to 9" d., marigold,
Northwood 35.00
Lamp, 3-portrait medallions, w/orig-
inal burner & etched chimney
shade, green, small, Millersburg....625.00
Lamp, w/original burner & etched
chimney shade, purple, Millers-
burg 500.00
Syrup pitcher, marigold..............600.00

WILD STRAWBERRY (Northwood)
Bowl, 10" d., marigold................85.00
Plate, 8" d., w/handgrip, green.......105.00

WINDFLOWER
Bowl, 8" to 9" d., blue 42.50
Bowl, 8" to 9" d., ice green 275.00
Bowl, 8" to 9" d., marigold 27.50
Bowl, 8" to 9" d., purple 42.00
Plate, 9" d., blue ....120.00 to 160.00
Plate, 9" d., marigold 48.00
Sauceboat, marigold 40.00

WINDMILL or Windmill Medallion (Imperial)
Bowl, 7" d., green....................48.00
Bowl, 7" d., marigold.................36.50
Bowl, 7" d., purple...........50.00 to 75.00
Bowl, 8" to 9" d., ruffled, purple 42.50
Bowl, 8" to 9" d., ruffled, vaseline......95.00
Bowl, 10" d., purple 75.00
Dresser tray, oval, marigold..........40.00
Dresser tray, oval, purple............47.50
Pickle dish, green...................22.50
Pickle dish, marigold 40.00
Pickle dish, purple 45.00
Pitcher, milk, marigold 75.00

Pitcher, milk, purple 275.00
Pitcher, milk, smoky 140.00
Pitcher, water, marigold 90.00
Plate, 8" d., marigold. 20.00
Sauce dish, clambroth 30.00
Sauce dish, marigold 15.00
Sauce dish, purple 23.50
Tumbler, green . . . . .30.00 to 43.00

Windmill Tumbler

Tumbler, marigold (ILLUS.) 35.00
Tumbler, purple 72.50
Water set: pitcher & 1 tumbler; green,
    2 pcs. 150.00
Water set: pitcher & 2 tumblers;
    purple, 3 pcs. 1,200.00

WINE & ROSES
Pitcher, water, marigold . . . .285.00 to 425.00
Wine, blue 55.00
Wine, marigold 35.00
Wine set: decanter & 6 wines;
    marigold, 7 pcs. . . . . .325.00 to 390.00

WISHBONE (Northwood)

Wishbone Plate

Bowl, 8" to 9" d., footed, blue . .75.00 to 85.00
Bowl, 8" to 9" d., footed, green 75.00
Bowl, 8" to 9" d., footed, ice green 875.00
Bowl, 8" to 9" d., footed, lavender 185.00
Bowl, 8" to 9" d., footed, lime
    green .75.00 to 95.00
Bowl, 8" to 9" d., footed, marigold 60.00
Bowl, 8" to 9" d., footed, purple. 85.00
Bowl, 8" to 9" d., footed, white 425.00
Bowl, 10" d., piecrust rim, green 100.00
Bowl, 10" d., marigold . . . . .60.00 to 95.00
Epergne, marigold 250.00
Epergne, purple . . . . .325.00 to 450.00
Pitcher, water, purple 1,000.00
Plate, 8½" d., footed, marigold. 275.00
Plate, 8½" d., footed, purple (ILLUS.) . .225.00
Plate, chop, 11" d., marigold 450.00
Tumbler, marigold 100.00
Tumbler, purple . . . . .95.00 to 125.00
Water set: pitcher & 3 tumblers;
    marigold, 4 pcs. 375.00
Water set: pitcher & 4 tumblers;
    green, 5 pcs. 1,600.00

WISHBONE & SPADES
Banana bowl, ruffled, peach opal-
    escent, 10" l. 175.00
Bowl, 8" d., marigold 60.00
Bowl, 8" d., peach opalescent . .60.00 to 75.00
Plate, 6½" d., peach opalescent 60.00
Plate, 6½" d., purple . . . . . . .120.00 to 150.00
Plate, chop, 11" d., purple 650.00
Sauce dish, peach opalescent . .50.00 to 75.00
Sauce dish, purple 35.00

WREATH OF ROSES
Bon bon, 2-handled, green,
    8" d. .40.00 to 65.00
Bon bon, 2-handled, purple, 8" d. 45.00
Compote, 6" d., blue 30.00
Compote, 6" d., marigold 27.50
Compote, 6" d., fluted, green 30.00
Punch bowl, Persian Medallion in-
    terior, blue 200.00
Punch bowl & base, green, 2 pcs. 225.00
Punch bowl & base, Persian Medallion
    interior, marigold, 2 pcs. 225.00
Punch bowl & base, purple, 2 pcs. 255.00
Punch cup, Persian Medallion interior,
    blue. 40.00
Punch cup, Vintage interior, blue 20.00
Punch cup, green 25.00
Punch cup, Vintage interior, marigold . .60.00
Punch cup, purple . . . . .15.00 to 25.00
Punch set: bowl, base & 6 cups;
    Persian Medallion interior, purple,
    8 pcs. 375.00
Rose bowl, marigold . . . . .30.00 to 50.00
Rose bowl, purple . . . . .55.00 to 70.00
Whimsey, tricornered, marigold 45.00

WREATHED CHERRY (Dugan)
Berry set: master bowl & 6 sauce
    dishes; marigold, 7 pcs. . . .210.00 to 250.00

Bowl, berry, 12 x 9" oval, marigold 67.50
Bowl, berry, 12 x 9" oval, purple 120.00
Bowl, berry, 12 x 9" oval, white 220.00
Butter dish, cov., purple 250.00
Creamer, marigold..................45.00
Creamer, purple....................65.00
Creamer, white.....................80.00
Pitcher, water, purple 275.00
Pitcher, water, white w/red cherries ..350.00
Sauce dish, oval, blue 35.00
Sauce dish, oval, marigold 35.00
Sauce dish, oval, peach opalescent.....55.00
Sauce dish, oval, white 57.00
Spooner, marigold 55.00
Spooner, purple 75.00
Spooner, white 110.00
Tumbler, marigold 40.00
Tumbler, purple ....45.00 to 55.00
Tumbler, white 115.00

ZIG ZAG (Millersburg)
Bowl, 9½" d., marigold 125.00
Bowl, 9½" d., green................250.00
Bowl, 10" w., tricornered, piecrust
  rim, green 215.00
Bowl, 10" w., tricornered, purple 290.00

ZIPPERED HEART
Berry set: master bowl & 5 sauce
  dishes; purple, 6 pcs...............225.00
Sauce dish, purple, 5" d. 25.00

ZIPPERED LOOP LAMP (Imperial)

Zippered Loop Lamp

Lamp, hand, marigold, 4½" h.........650.00
Lamp, sewing, marigold, small 315.00
Lamp, sewing, marigold, large
  (ILLUS.).........................400.00

(End of Carnival Glass Section)

CHOCOLATE

Cactus Pattern Chocolate Glass

This glass is often called Caramel Slag. It was made by the Indiana Tumbler and Goblet Company of Greentown, Ind., and other glasshouses, beginning at the turn of this century. Various patterns were produced, highly popular among them being Cactus and Leaf Bracket. Also see GREENTOWN, MISCELLANEOUS.

Animal covered dish, Cat on Tall
  Hamper, Greentown $170.00
Animal covered dish, Dolphin, Green-
  town....................225.00 to 295.00
Berry set: 8" d. master bowl & 6
  sauce dishes; Leaf Bracket patt.,
  Greentown, 7 pcs......275.00 to 300.00
Bowl, master berry, 8" d., Leaf
  Bracket patt......................100.00
Bowl, 8¼ x 5¼" oval, Geneva patt. 65.00
Bowl, master berry, 9¼" d., Cactus
  patt............................75.00
Butter dish, cov., flat base, Cactus
  patt., Greentown 175.00
Butter dish, cov., pedestal base, Cac-
  tus patt., Greentown (ILLUS.
  center) 350.00
Butter dish, cov., Daisy patt., Green-
  town 175.00
Butter dish, cov., Dewey patt.,
  4" d. ....135.00 to 150.00
Butter dish, cov., Dewey patt.,
  5¼" d. 115.00
Celery tray, Leaf Bracket patt.,
  Greentown, 11" l. ....85.00 to 110.00
Celery vase, Fleur-de-Lis patt., Green-
  town, 5¾" h.....................180.00
Compote, 4½" d., 3½" h., Geneva
  patt............................130.00
Compote, jelly, 5¼" d., 5" h., Cactus
  patt., Greentown 125.00
Compote, 6", scalloped rim, Melrose
  patt., Greentown........225.00 to 285.00
Compote, 7¼" d., Cactus patt., Green-
  town (ILLUS. left)................90.00
Compote, 8¼" d., Cactus patt., Green-
  town 140.00
Creamer, Cactus patt., Greentown 75.00
Creamer, Leaf Bracket patt. 70.00
Creamer, Shuttle patt., Greentown,
  6" h. ....55.00 to 70.00

Creamer, tankard, Strigil patt., 6" h. . . .75.00
Cruet w/original stopper, Cactus patt.,
   Greentown 175.00
Cruet w/original stopper, Leaf Bracket
   patt., Greentown . . . . .150.00 to 165.00
Fernery, 3-footed, Vintage patt.,
   Fenton 160.00
Hatpin holder, Orange Tree patt. 235.00

Chocolate Glass Kerosene Lamps

Lamps, kerosene, Wild Rose with
   Festoon patt., Greentown, no
   burners or chimneys, each (ILLUS. of
   pr.) 425.00
Mug, Cactus patt. 65.00
Mug, Herringbone Buttress patt.,
   Greentown 57.50
Mug, Shuttle patt., Greentown 50.00
Nappy, triangular, handled, Leaf
   Bracket patt., Greentown 48.00
Nappy, handled, Masonic patt., Green-
   town 85.00
Pitcher, water, Heron patt., Green-
   town . . . . .200.00 to 300.00

Chocolate Glass Water Pitchers

Pitcher, water, Indiana Feather patt.
   (ILLUS. left) .550.00
Pitcher, water, scalloped rim, Racing
   Deer & Doe patt., Greentown 325.00
Pitcher, water, Ruffled Eye patt.,
   Greentown 300.00
Pitcher, water, Squirrel patt., Green-
   town 310.00
Pitcher, water, Wild Rose & Bow Knot
   patt., Greentown (ILLUS. right) 335.00

Relish, Leaf Bracket patt., 8 x 5" oval . . .65.00
Sauce dish, Cactus patt., Greentown . . .40.00
Sauce dish, Geneva patt. 40.00
Sauce dish, Leaf Bracket patt., 4¾" d. . .35.00
Sauce dish, Teardrop & Tassel patt.,
   Greentown, 4½" d. 140.00
Sauce dish, Wild Rose with Bowknot
   patt., Greentown 95.00
Spooner, Cactus patt., Greentown 85.00
Spooner, Dewey patt., Greentown 85.00
Spooner, Leaf Bracket patt.,
   Greentown 85.00
Spooner, Wild Rose with Bowknot
   patt., Greentown . . . . .95.00 to 125.00
Spooner, child's, pedestal base,
   Austrian patt. 165.00
Stein, Indoor Drinking Scene, Green-
   town, 8½" h. .210.00
Stein w/pouring spout, Outdoor
   Drinking Scene . . . . .110.00 to 165.00
Sugar bowl, cov., Cactus patt. 132.50
Sugar bowl, cov., Chrysanthemum Leaf
   patt. 325.00
Sugar bowl, cov., Leaf Bracket patt.,
   Greentown 100.00
Sweetmeat, cov., Cactus patt., Green-
   town (ILLUS. right) 350.00
Syrup pitcher w/original top, Cactus
   patt. 90.00
Syrup pitcher w/original top, Cord
   Drapery patt., Greentown 225.00

Picture Frame Toothpick Holder

Toothpick holder, model of a picture
   frame (ILLUS.) 650.00
Toothpick holder, Cactus patt., Green-
   town 65.00
Toothpick holder, Geneva patt.,
   Greentown . . . . .95.00 to 125.00
Tumbler, Cactus patt., Greentown 57.50
Tumbler, Leaf Bracket patt.,
   Greentown 57.50
Tumbler, Sawtooth patt. 70.00
Tumbler, Shuttle patt., Greentown,
   3¾" h. 75.00
Tumbler, Wild Rose with Bowknot
   patt., Greentown 105.00
Vase, Scalloped Flange patt., Green-
   town 55.00

CHRYSANTHEMUM SPRIG, BLUE

Blue Chrysanthemum Sprig Sauce Dishes

Some collectors of off-white to near yellow Custard Glass have referred to this blue opaque glass in the Chrysanthemum Sprig pattern as "blue custard." This misnomer is being replaced and this scarce glassware, produced by the Northwood Glass Company at the turn of the century, deserves a classification of its own. Also see CUSTARD GLASS.

Bowl, master berry or
   fruit . . . .$385.00 to 450.00
Butter dish, cov. . . . . .850.00 to 1,000.00
Celery vase 950.00
Compote, jelly . . . . .300.00 to 500.00
Creamer . . . . .300.00 to 350.00
Cruet w/original stopper 600.00
Pitcher, water. . . . . .550.00 to 800.00
Sauce dish, each (ILLUS. of pr.) 110.00
Spooner . . . . .225.00 to 300.00
Sugar bowl, cov. 425.00
Table set, cov. sugar bowl, creamer &
   spooner, 3 pcs. 1,000.00
Toothpick holder. 300.00
Tumbler 195.00

CORALENE

Coralene Seaweed on Blue Satin

Coralene is a method of decorating glass, usually Satin glass, with the use of a beaded-type decoration customarily applied to the glass with the use of enamels, which

were melted. Coralene decoration has been faked with the use of glue.

Pitcher, 6¼" h., 4" d., applied amber
   handle & rigaree around neck, white
   coralene water lilies & green leaves
   on orange satin $195.00
Pitcher, water, square mouth, applied
   blue reeded handle, yellow coralene
   seaweed on shaded blue satin, white
   lining (ILLUS.) 600.00
Rose bowl, yellow coralene seaweed
   on blue mother-of-pearl satin, white
   lining, 3½" h. 300.00
Toothpick holder, yellow coralene sea-
   weed on yellow-gold shaded to white
   satin 225.00
Vase, 5" h., yellow & green coralene
   beading on cocoa brown satin 189.00
Vase, 5" h., jack-in-pulpit type,
   shimmering blue coralene seaweed
   on white satin, blue lining, signed
   Webb 335.00
Vase, 5½" h., 2¾" d., yellow coralene
   stars & white enameled dots at rim
   on shaded pink mother-of-pearl
   Snowflake patt. satin, white lining . .425.00
Vase, 6 1/8" h., stick-type, yellow
   coralene seaweed on shaded aqua
   blue satin, signed Thomas Webb 450.00
Vase, 8¼" h., doughnut-shaped, large
   multicolor coralene florals & green
   leaves on shaded rose-amber satin,
   signed "Patent" 195.00
Vase, 8½" h., flared rim, yellow
   coralene seaweed on blue satin 290.00
Vase, 10¼" h., 4 5/8" d., 3 applied
   clear reeded scroll feet, scallop-cut
   rim w/gold edge, pink & blue
   coralene florals & green foliage
   on cranberry 295.00
Vase, 11" h., yellow coralene florals
   & stars on blue shaded to pink &
   rose satin, ca. 1880. . . . . .650.00
Vase, 13½" h., gold beaded handles,
   pink coralene florals & green leaves
   on shaded orange to rust ground 525.00

COSMOS

A pattern of Cosmos flowers applied to milk-white glass gives this ware its name. The flowers are stained with various colors.

Butter dish, cov., pink band
   decor . . . .$165.00 to 225.00
Cologne bottle w/original stopper,
   pink band decor . . . . .135.00 to 190.00
Condiment set: salt & pepper shakers
   & mustard pot; pink band decor,
   in Pairpoint silverplate stand 185.00

Creamer, pink band decor 140.00
Creamer & cov. sugar bowl, pink
    band decor, pr. 240.00
Pickle castor, pink band decor, in
    original footed silverplate
    frame . . . . .295.00 to 385.00
Pitcher, water, 9" h., pink band
    decor . . . . .175.00 to 225.00
Powder box, cov., decorated 195.00
Salt shaker w/original top (single) 50.00
Salt & pepper shakers w/original
    tops, pink band decor, pr. 85.00
Sugar bowl, cov. . . . . .145.00 to 185.00
Syrup pitcher w/original top 225.00
Table set: cov. butter dish, cov.
    sugar bowl & creamer; pink band
    decor, 3 pcs. 315.00
Table set: cov. butter dish, cov.
    sugar bowl, creamer & spooner;
    pink band decor, 4 pcs. . . . .465.00 to 525.00
Tumbler, pink band decor . . . . .35.00 to 50.00
Vase, 7½" h., pink band decor 95.00

Cosmos Water Set

Water set: pitcher & 4 tumblers; pink
    band decor, 5 pcs. (ILLUS.) 575.00

CRACKLE

Butter Dish with Silverplate Lid & Underplate

*Sometimes called Iced Glass and also
known by a trade name Craquelle, this type
of ware has been made for centuries by sub-
mersing hot glass in cold water, reheating it
and then blowing it to produce a crackled or
frosted effect on the outside of the articles,
or by other methods. The interior of the articles remains smooth. Also see FAIRY
LAMPS.*

Butter dish, cranberry, silverplate lid
    w/cow finial & underplate
    (ILLUS.) $275.00
Candy dish, cov., yellow base, blue lid
    w/floral knop, 5" h. 95.00
Cologne bottles w/original stoppers,
    cranberry w/applied clear rigaree
    trim, 9¾" h., pr. 450.00
Cruet w/original stopper, applied
    handle, clear, 8½" h. 65.00
Cruet w/clear faceted stopper, cran-
    berry w/applied clear handle 155.00
Pitcher, water, 7½" h., bulbous, cran-
    berry w/applied clear reeded
    handle 95.00
Pitcher, water, 7 5/8" h., 5¼" d.,
    bulbous w/round mouth, Amberina
    w/applied amber reeded handle,
    ground pontil 185.00
Pitcher, water, 7¾" h., 5½" d., round
    mouth, blue w/applied amber
    reeded handle 118.00
Pitcher, tankard, 11" h., cranberry
    w/applied clear reeded handle 165.00
Rose bowl, 8-crimp top, Rubina Crystal
    (cranberry shaded to clear), 4½" d.,
    3 5/8" h. 88.00
Vase, 5 7/8" h., 3½" d., cut scalloped
    rim, cranberry 75.00
Whipped cream bucket, cranberry,
    silverplate rim & handle 150.00

CRANBERRY

*Gold was added to glass batches to give
this glass its color on reheating. It has been
made by numerous glasshouses for years
and is currently being reproduced. Both
blown and molded articles were produced. A
less expensive type of cranberry was made
with the substitution of copper for gold.
Also see FAIRY LAMPS.*

Bowl, 7½" d., applied clear rigaree
    around top, enameled floral decor .$125.00
Box w/hinged lid, enameled decor on
    lid, 4" d. 95.00
Celery vase, Swirl patt., satin finish . . .100.00
Condiment set: salt, pepper & mustard
    pot; cut panels, in crescent moon-
    shaped holder, 5½" h. 150.00

Cranberry Cookie Jar

Cookie jar, enameled white florals &
ferns decor, silverplate rim, cover &
bail handle marked "Simpson, Hall &
Miller," 19th c., 5" h. (ILLUS.) 195.00
Creamer, applied clear handle, collar
& foot, 4¼" h. 85.00
Decanter w/original clear stopper,
applied clear handle, ribbed body,
10½" h. 195.00
Finger bowl, amber threading around
ruffled rim 70.00
Mug, applied clear handle, Baby
Inverted Thumbprint patt., 2 3/8" d.,
4" h. 60.00
Perfume bottle w/original stopper,
enameled colorful florals & leaves
decor, 3 1/8" h. ....60.00 to 80.00
Pitcher, 5¼" h., applied clear handle,
Hobnail patt. 65.00
Pitcher, 6" h., 3 5/8" d., round mouth,
applied clear reeded handle,
enameled blue-centered white
florals, gold bands w/white dots &
gold trim 110.00

Cranberry Glass Pitcher

Pitcher, water, 8" h., bulbous, Inverted Thumbprint patt. (ILLUS.) 110.00
Pitcher, tankard, 12¾" h., 6¼" d.,
applied clear handle, optic effect
panels............................275.00
Rose bowl, ruffled rim, threaded body,
gold trim, 3" h. 55.00
Salt & pepper shakers w/original tops,
satin finish, raised enamel floral
decor, pr.........................125.00
Salt dip, enameled blue & white florals
& green leaves decor, gold trim,
2¾" d., 1¾" h. 65.00
Salt dip, ribbed, 2 applied rows of
vaseline rigaree, in hallmarked
silver holder, 3" d., 1½" h. 100.00
Sugar shaker w/original top, cut panels
of block design around top, 2½" d.,
5½" h. 70.00
Sugar shaker w/hallmarked silver top,
Drape patt., 6½" h. 78.00
Toothpick holder, barrel-shaped,
Inverted Baby Thumbprint patt.
w/enameling, satin finish...........95.00
Tumbler, enameled overall vivid
florals, gold trim, 3¾" h. 47.50
Tumbler, Inverted Thumbprint patt.,
2 7/8" d., 4¼" h..................35.00
Vase, 5½" h., 4" d., applied clear
feet, clear top edging pulled to
points & clear leaves around
center 115.00
Vase, 7½" h., 2 7/8" d., enameled
white lily-of-the-valley & gold leaves
decor 70.00
Vase, 7½" h., fluted trefoil edge,
Inverted Thumbprint patt...........125.00
Vase, 8" h., 4¾" d., ruffled rim
w/applied clear edging, Inverted
Thumbprint patt...................98.00

Cranberry Glass Vase

Vase, straight-sided cylinder w/ap-
plied clear ruffled feet & clear twisting rigaree around body (ILLUS.) 125.00
Wines, clear stem & foot, 5 1/8" h.,
set of 6 ....145.00

CROWN MILANO

Crown Milano Vase

This glass, produced by Mt. Washington Glass Company late last century, is opal glass decorated by painting and enameling. It appears identical to a ware termed Albertine, also made by Mt. Washington.

Cup & saucer, handleless, h.p. overall
   gold floral & berry decor on Burmese-colored ground $1,200.00
Cookie jar, gold-outlined florals &
   leaves decor on Burmese-colored
   satin finish ground, silverplate rim,
   cover & bail handle marked "M.W.,"
   4 7/8" d., 6½" h. 625.00
Cookie jar, cov., h.p. apple blossoms &
   pink, rose & lavender daisies encircling jar, gold scrolling on lid, 8" h. ...850.00
Creamer & cov. sugar bowl, h.p. florals
   & gold scrolls on ivory ground,
   pr. 2,850.00
Decanter w/hollow stopper, bulbous
   base, enameled roses decor w/gold
   scrolls on neck & stopper, glossy
   finish, signed, 10" h. 1,250.00
Ewer, h.p. scene of a shepherd tending
   his flock by a country brook front &
   smaller scene of a country church
   reverse 2,450.00
Mustard pot, h.p. floral decor, silverplate lid signed "M.W." 575.00
Rose bowl, h.p. pansies & leaves on
   Burmese-colored ground,
   unsigned 375.00
Urn & crown-form lid, h.p. blossoms
   & foliage outlined in gold, signed,
   8" d., 16½" h. 2,950.00
Vase, 8" h., stick-type w/bulbous base,
   enameled gold florals & foliage
   decor, signed 1,200.00
Vase, 11" h., ovoid w/integral handles
   curling from rim, h.p. Canada geese
   in flight against gold sun & stars,
   signed (ILLUS.) 3,025.00

Vase, 14" h., enameled gold dragon,
   florals & scrolls on soft white ground
   w/gold shadow flowers 1,450.00
Vase, 17" h., enameled ducks (4) flying
   over a wheat field of raised gold,
   attributed to Frank Guba, glossy
   finish 3,750.00

CUP PLATES

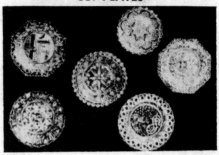

Lacy Cup Plates

Produced in numerous patterns for almost 150 years, these little plates were designed to hold a cup while the tea or coffee was allowed to cool in a saucer. Cup plates were also made of ceramics. Where numbers are listed below, they refer to numbers assigned these plates in the book "American Glass Cup Plates," by Ruth Webb Lee and James H. Rose. A number of cup plates have been reproduced. Also see STAFFORDSHIRE CUP PLATES under ceramics.

L & R No. 20 ....$39.50
L & R No. 25 ....17.50
L & R No. 41-A 25.00
L & R No. 47 ....18.50
L & R No. 52 ....9.50
L & R No. 55 ....25.00
L & R No. 56 ....15.00
L & R No. 72 ....25.00
L & R No. 79 ....10.00
L & R No. 89 ....45.00
L & R No. 89, fiery opalescent 70.00
L & R No. 127-A 30.00
L & R No. 134-A 30.00
L & R No. 147-A 25.00
L & R No. 149 ....25.00
L & R No. 159-B 10.00
L & R No. 162-A 32.50
L & R No. 165 ....30.00
L & R No. 174, opalescent 110.00
L & R No. 175 ....30.00
L & R No. 176-A 10.00
L & R No. 177 ....25.00
L & R No. 177-A 25.00
L & R No. 178-A 16.00
L & R No. 184 ....65.00

Lacy Sandwich Cup Plate

L & R No. 205	.55.00
L & R No. 209	.10.00
L & R No. 214	.45.00
L & R No. 233-A	.30.00
L & R No. 235	.16.00
L & R No. 255	.10.00
L & R No. 257	.18.00
L & R No. 262, grey-blue	.80.00
L & R No. 268, opalescent	.40.00
L & R No. 269-C	.15.00
L & R No. 272, opalescent	.55.00
L & R No. 279, amethyst	.200.00
L & R No. 280, clambroth	.10.00
L & R No. 285, opalescent	.70.00
L & R No. 289	.35.00
L & R No. 311	.12.00
L & R No. 311, lavender tint	.40.00
L & R No. 311, opalescent	.30.00
L & R No. 323, honey amber	.150.00
L & R No. 323, opalescent	.15.00
L & R No. 326, opalescent	.55.00
L & R No. 343-B	.26.00
L & R No. 412, dark sapphire blue	.65.00
L & R No. 441-A	.25.00
L & R No. 447-B	.10.00
L & R No. 459-F, opalescent	.42.50
L & R No. 465-F, opalescent	.47.50
L & R No. 465-J	.25.00
L & R No. 465-L, violet blue	.195.00
L & R No. 476	.11.00
L & R No. 479	.20.00
L & R No. 522, amethyst	.30.00
L & R No. 537, opalescent	.10.00
L & R No. 564	.30.00
L & R No. 565-A	.50.00
L & R No. 576, medium blue	.350.00
L & R No. 590	.20.00
L & R No. 595	.42.50
L & R No. 596	.55.00
L & R No. 615-A	.110.00
L & R No. 618	.25.00
L & R No. 619	.30.00
L & R No. 624	.30.00
L & R No. 625-A	.70.00
L & R No. 643	.20.00
L & R No. 655	.45.00
L & R No. 661	.23.50
L & R No. 667-A	.17.50

L & R No. 672	.40.00
L & R No. 675-B	.25.00
L & R No. 676-C	.40.00
L & R No. 679	.22.50
L & R No. 680	.11.00
L & R No. 686	.110.00
L & R No. 699	.10.00
L & R No. 802, blue	.180.00
L & R No. 807, blue	.110.00

CUSTARD GLASS

This ware takes its name from its color and is a variant of milk-white glass. It was produced largely between 1890 and 1915 by the Northwood Glass Co., Heisey Glass Company, Fenton Art Glass Co., Jefferson Glass Co., and a few others. There are 21 major patterns and a number of minor ones. The prime patterns are considered Argonaut Shell, Chrysanthemum Sprig, Inverted Fan and Feather, Louis XV and Winged Scroll. Most custard glass patterns are enhanced with gold and some have additional enameled decoration or stained highlights. Unless otherwise noted, items in this listing are fully decorated.

ARGONAUT SHELL

Argonaut Shell Butter Dish

Berry set, master bowl & 4 sauce dishes, 5 pcs.	$525.00
Bowl, master berry or fruit, 10½" l., 5" h.	175.00 to 195.00
Butter dish, cov. (ILLUS.)	215.00
Compote, jelly, 5" d., 5" h.	100.00 to 125.00
Creamer	110.00
Cruet w/original stopper	325.00 to 385.00
Pitcher, water	325.00
Salt & pepper shakers w/original tops, pr.	350.00
Sauce dish	65.00
Spooner	95.00 to 125.00
Sugar bowl, cov.	155.00
Table set, cov. butter dish, cov. sugar bowl, creamer & spooner, 4 pcs.	680.00
Toothpick holder	270.00

Tumbler 78.00
Water set, pitcher & 6 tumblers,
   7 pcs. 750.00

BEADED CIRCLE

Beaded Circle Pitcher

Bowl, master berry or fruit 225.00
Butter dish, cov. 235.00
Compote, jelly. 350.00
Creamer. 120.00
Cruet w/original stopper 650.00
Pitcher, water (ILLUS.) 475.00
Salt shaker w/original top (single) 200.00
Salt & pepper shakers w/original tops,
   pr. 255.00
Sauce dish 55.00
Spooner 115.00
Sugar bowl, cov. 165.00
Tumbler 75.00

BEADED SWAG

Beaded Swag Wine & Goblet

Goblet 52.50
Goblet, souvenir (ILLUS. right) 75.00
Pickle dish 250.00
Sauce dish, souvenir 45.00
Spooner 80.00
Toothpick holder. 145.00
Tumbler, souvenir 55.00
Water set, tankard pitcher & 4
   tumblers, 5 pcs. 500.00

Wine, w/advertising 75.00
Wine, souvenir (ILLUS. left). 70.00

CHERRY & SCALE (Fentonia)

Cherry & Scale Pattern

Berry set, master bowl & 6 sauce
   dishes, 7 pcs. .325.00
Bowl, master berry or fruit 125.00
Butter dish, cov. (ILLUS. center) 225.00
Creamer. 110.00
Pitcher, water .325.00
Spooner (ILLUS. right) 90.00
Sugar bowl, cov. (ILLUS. left) 125.00
Tumbler 60.00
Water set, water pitcher & 6 tumblers,
   7 pcs. 600.00

CHRYSANTHEMUM SPRIG

Chrysanthemum Sprig Pitcher & Tumbler

Berry set, master bowl & 5 sauce
   dishes, 6 pcs. .600.00
Bowl, master berry or fruit, 10½"
   oval. 175.00
Butter dish, cov. 255.00
Celery vase . . . . .595.00 to 625.00
Compote, jelly. .87.50
Compote, jelly (undecorated). 38.50
Condiment set, 4-footed tray, salt &
   pepper shakers w/original tops &
   toothpick holder, 4 pcs. 945.00
Condiment tray 650.00
Creamer. 110.00
Creamer & cov. sugar bowl, pr. 200.00
Creamer & open sugar bowl, pr. 150.00
Cruet w/original stopper . . . .240.00 to 300.00
Pin tray. 20.00
Pitcher, water (ILLUS.) . . . . . .255.00 to 280.00
Salt & pepper shakers w/original tops,
   pr. 175.00

Sauce dish 50.00
Spooner 90.00
Sugar bowl, cov. 165.00
Sugar bowl, cov. (undecorated) 110.00
Table set, 4 pcs. 650.00
Toothpick holder. 225.00
Tumbler (ILLUS.) . . . . .45.00 to 55.00
Water set, pitcher & 6 tumblers,
   7 pcs. 765.00

DIAMOND WITH PEG

Diamond with Peg Pattern

Berry set, master bowl & 6 sauce
   dishes, 7 pcs. 600.00
Bowl, master berry or fruit 225.00
Butter dish, cov. 200.00
Creamer. 75.00
Creamer, souvenir 55.00
Mug, souvenir 75.00
Napkin ring, souvenir (ILLUS. center) . .150.00
Pitcher, tankard, 7½" h. 125.00
Pitcher, water, tankard 375.00
Salt & pepper shakers w/original tops,
   souvenir, pr. 95.00
Sauce dish 50.00
Spooner 55.00
Sugar bowl, cov. 165.00
Toothpick holder (ILLUS. left) 80.00
Tumbler . . . . .40.00 to 65.00
Tumbler, souvenir 52.00
Vase, 6" h., souvenir 50.00
Vase, 8" h. 85.00
Water set, pitcher & 6 tumblers,
   7 pcs. 480.00
Whiskey shot glass, souvenir (ILLUS.
   right) . . . . .40.00 to 50.00
Wine 50.00

EVERGLADES (Carnelian)

Everglades Butter Dish

Bowl, master berry or fruit, footed
   compote 235.00
Butter dish, cov. (ILLUS.) 370.00
Compote, jelly. 350.00
Creamer. 135.00
Cruet w/original stopper 750.00
Pitcher, water 650.00
Salt shaker w/original top (single) 65.00
Salt & pepper shakers w/original tops,
   pr. 250.00
Sauce dish 65.00
Spooner 120.00
Sugar bowl, cov. 150.00
Tumbler 110.00

FAN (Northwood Fan)

Fan Creamer & Spooner

Berry set, master bowl & 6 sauce
   dishes, 7 pcs. 550.00
Bowl, master berry or fruit 180.00
Butter dish, cov. 215.00
Creamer (ILLUS.). 100.00
Pitcher, water 225.00
Sauce dish 55.00
Spooner (ILLUS.) 90.00
Sugar bowl, cov. 110.00
Table set, cov. butter dish, cov. sugar
   bowl & spooner, 3 pcs. 450.00
Table set, 4 pcs. 550.00
Tumbler 80.00
Water set, pitcher & 6 tumblers,
   7 pcs. 650.00

FENTONIA - See Cherry & Scales Pattern

FLUTED SCROLLS (Jackson)

Fluted Scrolls Tumbler & Pitcher

Bowl, master berry or fruit, footed 95.00
Creamer. 55.00
Cruet w/replaced stopper. 160.00
Pitcher, water, footed (ILLUS.) 180.00
Salt shaker w/original top (single) 40.00
Salt & pepper shakers w/original tops,
  pr. 125.00
Sauce dish 40.00
Sugar bowl, cov. 135.00
Spooner 50.00
Tumbler (ILLUS.) 37.50
Water set, pitcher & 6 tumblers,
  7 pcs. 400.00

GENEVA

Banana boat, 4-footed, 11" oval. 185.00
Berry set, oval master bowl & 6 sauce
  dishes, 7 pcs. .335.00
Bowl, master berry or fruit, 8½" oval,
  4-footed 95.00
Bowl, master berry or fruit, 8½" d.,
  3-footed 120.00
Butter dish, cov. 135.00
Compote, jelly. .75.00
Creamer. 70.00
Cruet w/original stopper 290.00
Pitcher, water 200.00
Salt & pepper shakers w/original
  tops, pr. 120.00

Geneva Oval Sauce

Sauce dish, oval (ILLUS.) 45.00
Sauce dish, round 42.00
Spooner 60.00
Sugar bowl, cov. 130.00
Syrup pitcher w/original top 250.00
Table set, 4 pcs. 395.00
Toothpick holder. 115.00
Tumbler 50.00
Water set, pitcher & 6 tumblers,
  7 pcs. 525.00

GEORGIA GEM (Little Gem)

Georgia Gem Breakfast Set

Berry set, master bowl & 6 sauce
  dishes, 7 pcs. .275.00
Bowl, master berry or fruit . . . .75.00 to 140.00
Butter dish, cov. . . . . .230.00 to 275.00
Celery vase 170.00
Creamer. 55.00
Creamer (undecorated) 40.00
Creamer & open sugar bowl, breakfast
  size, pr. (ILLUS.) 125.00
Cruet w/original stopper . . . .225.00 to 275.00
Hair receiver, souvenir 55.00
Pitcher, water 310.00
Powder jar, cov., souvenir 50.00
Salt & pepper shakers w/original tops,
  pr. 77.00
Sauce dish (undecorated) 27.50
Spooner 65.00
Sugar bowl, cov. 80.00
Sugar bowl, open, breakfast size,
  souvenir 42.50
Table set, 4 pcs. . . . . .375.00 to 425.00
Toothpick holder . . . . .45.00 to 60.00
Toothpick holder, souvenir 40.00
Tumbler, souvenir 45.00
Water set, pitcher & 4 tumblers,
  5 pcs. 435.00

GRAPE & GOTHIC ARCHES

Grape & Gothic Arches Sauce Dish

Berry set, master bowl & 6 sauce
  dishes, 7 pcs. .475.00
Bowl, master berry or fruit 175.00
Butter dish, cov. 200.00
Creamer. 90.00
Goblet 55.00
Pitcher, water 285.00
Rose bowl 75.00
Sauce dish (ILLUS.) 50.00
Spooner 85.00
Sugar bowl, cov. 110.00
Sugar bowl, open 55.00
Tumbler 50.00
Vase, 10" h. (made from goblet mold) . .65.00
Vase, ruffled hat shape 50.00
Water set, pitcher & 4 tumblers,
  5 pcs. 500.00

INTAGLIO

Berry set, 9" d. footed compote & 6
  sauce dishes, 7 pcs. 400.00
Bowl, fruit, 7½" d. footed compote 225.00
Bowl, fruit, 7½" d. footed compote
  (undecorated) 175.00

Bowl, fruit, 9" d. footed
   compote ....180.00 to 230.00

Intaglio Butter Dish

Butter dish, cov. (ILLUS.).....160.00 to 295.00
Compote, jelly ....90.00 to 125.00
Creamer ....75.00 to 115.00
Cruet w/original stopper ....275.00 to 325.00
Pitcher, water.............350.00 to 400.00
Salt & pepper shakers w/original tops,
   pr......................180.00 to 200.00
Sauce dish 50.00
Spooner...................75.00 to 110.00
Sugar bowl, cov....................120.00
Table set, 4 pcs. ....450.00 to 500.00
Tumbler....................40.00 to 70.00
Water set, pitcher & 6 tumblers,
   7 pcs. ....500.00 to 800.00

INVERTED FAN & FEATHER

Inverted Fan & Feather Cruet

Berry set, master bowl & 4 sauce
   dishes, 5 pcs......................570.00
Bowl, master berry or fruit, 10" d.,
   5½" h., 4-footed 180.00
Butter dish, cov. 255.00
Compote, jelly......................400.00
Creamer...........................135.00
Cruet w/original stopper (ILLUS.) 625.00
Pitcher, water 375.00
Punch bowl, footed 2,500.00
Punch cup.........................240.00
Salt & pepper shakers w/original tops,
   pr......................................425.00

Sauce dish 60.00
Spooner 115.00
Sugar bowl, cov......................175.00
Table set, 4 pcs. 800.00
Toothpick holder....................465.00
Tumbler 85.00
Water set, pitcher & 6 tumblers,
   7 pcs...............................750.00

IVORINA VERDE - See Winged Scroll Pattern

JACKSON - See Fluted Scrolls Pattern

LOUIS XV

Louis XV Pattern

Berry set, master bowl & 6 sauce
   dishes, 7 pcs......................400.00
Bowl, berry or fruit, 10½ x 7¾" oval ..120.00
Butter dish, cov. (ILLUS. right) 155.00
Creamer (ILLUS. left rear) 65.00
Creamer & cov. sugar bowl, pr. 150.00
Cruet w/original stopper 225.00
Pitcher, water (ILLUS.) 175.00
Salt & pepper shakers w/original tops,
   pr. (ILLUS.) 155.00
Sauce dish, footed, 5" oval 35.00
Spooner (ILLUS. left front) .....55.00 to 85.00
Sugar bowl, cov. (ILLUS.) .....85.00 to 100.00
Table set, 4 pcs. 475.00
Tumbler 50.00
Water set, pitcher & 6 tumblers,
   7 pcs. 575.00

MAPLE LEAF (Northwood)

Maple Leaf Butter Dish

Banana bowl 195.00
Bowl, master berry or fruit 380.00
Butter dish, cov. (ILLUS.) . . . . .175.00 to 235.00
Compote, jelly. 375.00
Creamer. 75.00
Creamer & open sugar bowl, pr. 175.00
Cruet w/original stopper 1,100.00
Pitcher, water 340.00
Salt & pepper shakers w/original tops,
    pr. 540.00
Sauce dish 90.00
Spooner 75.00
Sugar bowl, cov. 170.00
Table set, 4 pcs. . . . . .465.00 to 550.00
Toothpick holder. 550.00
Tumbler 78.00
Water set, pitcher & 6 tumblers,
    7 pcs. 750.00

NORTHWOOD GRAPE (Grape & Cable - Grape & Thumbprint)

Ruffled Master Berry Bowl

Bowl, 7½" d., ruffled rim 40.00
Bowl, master berry or fruit, 11" d.,
    flat rim, footed 270.00
Bowl, master berry or fruit, 11" d.,
    ruffled, footed (ILLUS.) 425.00
Butter dish, cov. 250.00
Cologne bottle w/original stopper 500.00
Creamer. 115.00
Creamer & open sugar bowl, breakfast
    size, pr. 125.00
Dresser tray . . . . .275.00 to 325.00
Fernery, footed, 7½" d., 4½" h. 150.00
Humidor, cov. 550.00
Nappy, 2-handled. 45.00
Pin dish. 110.00
Pitcher, water 385.00
Plate, 7" d. 40.00
Plate, 8" d. 65.00
Punch cup. 40.00
Sauce dish, flat 40.00
Sauce dish, footed . . . . .38.00 to 45.00
Spooner 95.00
Sugar bowl, cov. 125.00
Sugar bowl, open, breakfast
    size. .45.00 to 65.00
Tumbler 82.50
Vase, 3½" h. 46.00
Water set, pitcher & 5 tumblers,
    6 pcs. 700.00

PRAYER RUG

Nappy, 2-handled. 28.00
Nappy, ruffled, 6" d. 50.00
Plate, 7½" d. 16.00
Tumbler 80.00

PUNTY BAND

Punty Band Tumbler

Creamer, individual size, souvenir 37.00
Mug, souvenir. 42.50
Salt & pepper shakers w/original
    tops, souvenir, pr. 80.00
Toothpick holder, souvenir 60.00
Tumbler, floral decor, souvenir
    (ILLUS.) 55.00
Vase, 5½" h., souvenir 75.00
Wine, souvenir 50.00

RIBBED DRAPE

Ribbed Drape Pattern

Butter dish, cov. (ILLUS. left). 265.00
Compote, jelly. .180.00
Cruet w/original stopper 325.00
Pitcher, water 345.00
Salt & pepper shakers w/original
    tops, pr. 200.00
Sauce dish 40.00
Spooner (ILLUS. right) 100.00
Toothpick holder. 135.00
Tumbler 75.00

RING BAND

Bowl, master berry or fruit 115.00
Butter dish, cov. 220.00
Celery vase 300.00
Compote, jelly. .145.00

Condiment set, condiment tray, jelly
compote, toothpick holder & salt &
pepper shakers, 5 pcs............429.00
Condiment tray.....................175.00
Creamer...........................82.50
Cruet w/original stopper...........300.00
Mug...............................45.00
Pitcher, water.....................230.00
Punch cup..........................50.00
Salt & pepper shakers w/original tops,
souvenir, pr......................115.00
Sauce dish.........................42.50
Spooner...........................100.00
Sugar bowl, cov...................130.00
Syrup pitcher w/original
top.................245.00 to 320.00
Toothpick holder, 2½" h.............90.00

Ring Band Toothpick Holder

Toothpick holder, souvenir (ILLUS.).....55.00
Tumbler............................55.00
Tumbler, souvenir..................38.00
Water set, pitcher & 6 tumblers,
7 pcs............................580.00

VICTORIA (Tarentum's)

Tarentum's Victoria Pitcher & Tumblers

Berry set, master bowl & 5 sauce
dishes, 6 pcs....................575.00
Bowl, master berry or fruit..........175.00
Butter dish, cov...................285.00
Celery vase........................225.00
Creamer............................50.00
Pitcher, water (ILLUS.)............350.00
Sauce dish.........................55.00

Spooner............................85.00
Sugar bowl, cov...................165.00
Tumbler (ILLUS.)...................60.00

WINGED SCROLL (Ivorina Verde)

Winged Scroll Water Set

Berry set, master bowl & 6 sauce
dishes, 7 pcs....................500.00
Bowl, fruit, 8½" d.................170.00
Bowl, master berry, 11" l., boat-
shaped...........................100.00
Butter dish, cov.........150.00 to 175.00
Celery vase........................275.00
Cigar jar..........................165.00
Cigarette jar......................120.00
Cologne bottle w/original stopper....245.00
Creamer............................85.00
Creamer & cov. sugar bowl, pr.
(undecorated)...................125.00
Cruet w/original stopper...........170.00
Custard cup........................45.00
Dresser tray.......................150.00
Hair receiver......................125.00
Match holder.......................155.00
Nappy, folded side handle, 6".......55.00
Olive dish.........................45.00
Pickle dish........................45.00
Pitcher, water, 9" h., bulbous......255.00
Pitcher, water, tankard............225.00
Powder jar, cov....................80.00
Powder jar, cov., souvenir.........55.00
Salt & pepper shakers w/original tops,
pr...............................175.00
Sauce dish, 4½" d.........28.00 to 40.00
Spooner............................80.00
Sugar bowl, cov...................175.00
Syrup pitcher w/original top........335.00
Table set, 4 pcs...................580.00
Toothpick holder...................115.00
Tray for smoke set.................145.00
Tumbler............................75.00
Water set, tankard pitcher & 6
tumblers, 7 pcs. (ILLUS. of part).....650.00

(End of Custard Glass Section)

CUT GLASS

Cut glass most eagerly sought by collectors is American glass produced during the so-called "Brilliant Period" from 1880 to about 1915. Pieces listed below are by type of article in alphabetical order.

BASKETS

Cut Glass Basket

Brilliant Period cutting, notched
handle, 6" l., 4" h. $185.00
Harvard patt. & other cutting, applied
double-twisted handle, 9½" d.
(ILLUS.) 550.00
Harvard patt. variant band above
cornflowers & foliage, 8-petal blazed
flower center, double-twisted handle,
6½" d., overall 6½" h. 185.00
Hobstars, double-twisted handle, 8½" d.,
8½" h. 395.00

BOTTLES

Cut Glass Whiskey Bottle

Condiment, comet & cane, matching
stopper w/finial, 4½" h. 95.00
Condiment, chain of hobstars above
& below engraved flowers & fine

crosshatching w/single stars, sterling
silver top 60.00
Cordial, large 16-point hobstars (3)
alternating w/oval panels of five
8-point hobstars flanked by fans &
strawberry diamond hexagons, star-cut
base, lapidary-cut stopper, 4¾" d.,
7" h. 150.00
Cordial, checkerboard design of starred
blocks & flat X-cuts, panel-cut neck,
star-cut base, original lapidary-cut
stopper, 2¾" sq., 7½" h., pr. 250.00
Cordial, Hoare's Hindoo patt., corset-
shaped, 8" h. 185.00
Whiskey, chain of hobstars, diamond
point & fan, w/sterling silver whiskey
shot glass top, ca. 1900, 7¾" h.
(ILLUS.) 550.00
Whiskey, Hawkes signed, Strawberry
Diamond & Fan patt., sterling silver
shot glass form top 165.00
Whiskey jug w/handle, cranberry cut
to clear, Brilliant Period cutting,
matching stopper 485.00
Whiskey jug w/handle, Fry's Japan
patt., strap handle w/St. Louis
Diamond cutting, 5" d., 8" h. 825.00
Whiskey jug w/handle, Hawkes signed,
engraved log cabin in the woods
w/pine trees, large smiling sun
overhead, crescent moon on
stopper 225.00

BOWLS

Thistle Pattern Bowl

Banana, American Shield patt. 150.00
Bishop's hat shape, large hobstars,
cane & strawberry diamond, 13½" l.,
9" w. 250.00
Bishop's hat shape, Thistle patt.
w/deeply cut beading, blaze & straw-
berry diamond, overlap brim
(ILLUS.) 850.00
Fruit, Libbey signed, hat-shaped,
Thistle patt. 400.00
Ice, cradle-shaped, hobstars & fans,
7 x 5", 4½" h. 225.00

Orange, hobstars & other cutting,
9" d. 375.00
Orange, Straus' Corinthian patt., cut
stem, hobstar base, 10 x 7" oval
bowl, 9" h. 750.00
Butterfly & daisy, hobstar base, serrated rim, 9" d., 2½" h. 195.00
Chain of hobstars on sides, center
w/butterflies & circle of 4" diamond
vesicas, 10" d., 2½" h. 175.00
Clark signed, Huyler patt., 24-point
hobstar center, 7¾" d., 2" h. 195.00
Clark (T.B.) & Co., hobnail heart motif
alternating w/hobnail bands,
scalloped & serrated rim, 8" d.,
7 1/8" h. 195.00
Dorflinger's Prince of Wales Plumes
patt., knobbed stem, hobstar foot,
9" d., 7" h. 375.00
Egginton signed, Lotus patt., low,
7" d. 165.00
Expanding Star patt., 9" d., 4" h. 400.00
Festoon patt. variant, sterling silver
rim, 9½" d. 285.00
Harvard patt., large 24-point hobstar
center, scalloped & serrated rim,
7 7/8" d., 1 7/8" h. 160.00
Harvard patt. variant sides, large
quatrefoil & floral center,
10¼" octagon 150.00
Hawkes signed, chain of twenty-six
8-point hobstars above mitre cuts,
star-cut center, 7¾" d. 135.00
Hawkes signed, Kensington patt.,
9" d., 4" h. 450.00
Hawkes signed, fan, feather, hobstar &
strawberry diamond, 12 x 8" oval ...475.00
Hoare signed, Nassau patt., 8" d. 200.00
Hobstars, vesicas of tiny hobnail,
strawberry diamond, fan & single
stars, straight sides, scalloped &
serrated rim, 9¼" d., 3 7/8" h......225.00
Libbey signed, Colonna patt., 7" d. 160.00
Libbey signed, Sultana patt., 16-point
hobstar base, 10" d. 265.00
Libbey's Kimberly patt. variant, fluted,
10" d. 275.00
Libbey's Stratford patt., 10 1/8" d......450.00
Maple City Glass Co. signed,
hobstars, strawberry diamond
points & fans, serrated rim, 8" d. 165.00
Mt. Washington Glass Co.'s Butterfly &
Daisy patt., sterling silver pierced
rim marked "WSW" (Wilcox Co.),
8½" d. 450.00
Parisian patt. variant, hobstar base,
9" d. 275.00
Pitkin & Brooks signed, Korea patt.,
8" d. 200.00
Pitkin & Brooks' Roland patt., 8" d.,
3" h. 350.00
Ribbon Star patt. variant, scalloped &
serrated rim, 8¼" d. 235.00
Russian patt., low, 9½ x 7" oval 300.00

Cut Glass Bowl with Silver Rim

Star-filled vesicas against strawberry
diamond, pierced sterling silver
rim, 10¾" d. (ILLUS.) 425.00
Tuthill signed, Brilliant Period cutting,
8" d. 250.00
Tuthill signed, Rex patt., 8" d........1,800.00
Venetian patt., "repousse" sterling
silver rim, 10" d. 375.00

BOXES

Libbey's Florence Pattern Box

Dresser, central sunburst & hobstar
within band of vertical notched
prism on hinged lid, corresponding
sides, brass fittings, 4¼ x 3",
3¼" h. 140.00
Dresser, intaglio-cut daisies & leaves
on hinged lid, vertical prism sides,
silverplate fittings, 6" d. 300.00
Handkerchief, Brilliant Period cutting,
hinged lid, 7 x 7".................595.00
Handkerchief, intaglio-cut florals on
hinged lid, large 315.00
Jewelry, overall flashed hobstars,
hinged lid, 6" sq. base, 5½" sq. top .450.00
Pin, flute-cut sides, sterling silver lid

w/"repousse" flowers & leaves,
2" d. 50.00
Powder, 4 flashed stars w/fans
between, star-cut bottom, sterling
silver lid w/embossed & engraved
florals & lions, 3 7/8" d., 3½" h.......95.00
Powder, Libbey's Florence patt., hinged
lid, 6" d. (ILLUS.) 425.00
Powder, Pairpoint's Daisy patt., 32-point
star base, sterling silver rim, 6" d. ..300.00
Snuff, Harvard patt. 55.00

BUTTER DISHES & TUBS

Cut Glass Butter Tub

Covered dish, Arcadia patt. variant,
dome lid & underplate 375.00
Covered dish, Brilliant Period cutting,
dome lid & underplate 395.00
Covered dish, Harvard patt. alternating
w/floral panels, dome lid w/faceted
knob, 7" d. underplate............295.00
Covered dish, hobstars & other cutting,
dome lid & underplate 200.00
Covered dish, 16-point hobstars, cane
& fan, dome lid & underplate 335.00
Tub, hobstars, fan & diagonal slashes,
tab handles extending from scalloped
& serrated rim, 5" d., 3¾" h. plus
tab handles (ILLUS.) 170.00

CANDLESTICKS & CANDLE HOLDERS

Chain of hobstars in diamond field
w/flute motifs, teardrop stem,
24-point hobstar base, 9¼" h.,
pr..............................310.00
Hawkes signed, Delft Diamond patt.,
full teardrop stem, 9" h., pr.........310.00
Libbey, signed, plain flutes, teardrop
stem, 6" h., pr. 295.00
Pairpoint, green cut to clear, 10" h.,
pr..............................150.00

CARAFES

Brilliant Period cutting, notched neck,
24-point rayed base, bulbous, 6½" d.,
7½" h. 95.00
Clark signed, hobstar, fan & bull's
eye, 8" h. 135.00

Corinthian patt. variant...............80.00
Hoare signed, Comet patt., 6½" d.,
7½" h. 250.00
Hobstars, strawberry diamond &
notched prisms, panel-cut neck,
serrated rim, rayed base, 6¼" d.,
7¼" h. 95.00
Hobstars (3 large 8-point), strawberry
diamond, cross-cut diamond, fan &
other cutting, notched & paneled
step-cut neck, star-cut base, 6½" d.,
7" h. 75.00
Hobstars (4 large 16-point & 4 small
8-point), strawberry diamond & fan,
notched & paneled step-cut neck,
large 16-point hobstar base, 6½" d.,
7 5/8" h. 110.00
Stars & fans, notched flute-cut neck,
ball-shaped, 8" h. 85.00
Strawberry diamond & fan, panel-cut
neck w/serrated rim, rayed base,
5¾" d., 7¾" h. 80.00
Strawberry diamond & fan w/hobstars,
32-point star-cut base 110.00

CELERY TRAYS & VASES

Tray, boat-shaped, Russian patt.
w/strawberry diamond button, intaglio-
cut floral panel around sides,
horizontal step-cut back, 13¼ x
4¾"...........................125.00
Tray, boat-shaped, cane variant
w/band of intaglio-cut florals around
base, scalloped rim, 13½ x 4½",
2½" h. 125.00
Tray, Egginton signed, thistles & leaves
on sides, cane, strawberry diamond
& flashed fan, 12-point hobstar
center, 11¼" l. 125.00
Tray, Expanding Star patt. with
rolled rim 175.00
Tray, Harvard patt., 11½ x 4½".......165.00
Tray, hobnail, starred blocks, strawberry diamond & fan w/four 16-point
hobstars, 11 5/8" l................85.00
Tray, hobstar, diamond & prism,
10½ x 4½".......................125.00
Tray, Libbey signed, Gem patt., chain
of eight 12-point hobstars, cross-cut
diamond & fan, fan radiant center,
12 x 4 3/8" 125.00
Tray, Libbey's Lovebirds (Wisteria)
patt., 11¼ x 4½", 2" h. 1,095.00
Tray, Sinclaire's Adam patt., 10½" l. ..195.00
Vase, Brilliant Period cutting, scalloped & serrated rim, 6½" h. 245.00

CHAMPAGNES, CORDIALS & WINES

Champagne, Straus' Encore patt.,
teardrop stem, pr. 175.00
Champagne, Hoare signed, Monarch
patt., hollow stem, set of 4 ....395.00
Champagne, Libbey signed, engraved
florals & ferns, set of 9............275.00

Brilliant Period Champagne

Champagne, Brilliant Period cutting,
  notched stem (ILLUS.) 60.00
Cordial, cranberry, cobalt blue &
  green cut to clear, cut stem &
  base, assorted set of 6 . . . . .275.00
Cordial, Hoare's Monarch patt. 45.00
Cordial, Hobstar & Prism patt.,
  notched stem, rayed base, set of 6 . .185.00
Cordial, Libbey signed, Harvard
  patt., fluted stems w/large faceted
  knobs, 24-point rayed base, set of
  6 . . . . .385.00
Cordial, Russian patt. w/hobstar
  button, elongated teardrop in stem,
  4" h. 85.00
Wine, emerald green cut to clear,
  fan & panel-cut bowl, notched stem . .40.00
Wine, Hawkes' Louis XIV patt. 125.00
Wine, Hobnail patt. w/row of bull's
  eyes below rim, lapidary-cut knob,
  panel-cut teardrop stem, radiant
  star-cut base, set of 10 . . . . .295.00
Wine, Rhine-type, cranberry cut to
  clear, diamond design on bowl,
  clear stem & foot, 6¾" h., set of 4 . . .207.00
Wine, Russian patt. 90.00
Wine, Straus' Davies patt., pr. 100.00
Wine, cobalt cut to clear, Straw-
  berry Diamond & Fan patt. 150.00
Wine, Strawberry Diamond & Fan
  patt., notched stem, set of 12 . . . . . . .350.00

CLOCKS
Boudoir, Harvard patt. overall,
  petticoat base, 4" d. base, 6½" h. . . .450.00
Boudoir, roses, leaves & notching,
  4" w., 6" h. 150.00
Boudoir, Russian patt. w/starred
  buttons overall, 4" w., 6¼" h. 195.00

COMPOTES
Brilliant Period cutting on bowl & base,
  notched prism stem, 7" d., 9½" h. . . .237.00

Brilliant Period cutting, teardrop in
  stem, hobstar base, 8½" d.,
  9" h. 400.00
Bull's eye, hobstar & other cutting,
  prism & bevel-cut stem, rayed
  base, 6" d., 9¼" h. 185.00
Cane patt. w/strawberry hobs alter-
  nating w/panels of intaglio-cut
  florals, scalloped & serrated rim,
  panel-cut stem w/beaded edges,
  star-cut base, 7¼" d., 9" h. 135.00
Chain of hobstars, checkered diamond
  & other cutting, 8" d., 6½" h. 225.00
Clark signed, Cornflower patt., flashed
  star base, Pat. 1909, 7¼" d., 3" h. . . .275.00
Cobalt blue cut to clear, cov., clear
  pedestal, 17¼" h. 450.00
Cranberry cut to clear, intaglio florals
  & foliage, twisted stem, serrated
  rim, 7" d., 8¼" h., pr. 245.00
Hawkes signed, "gravic" Iris w/ball
  stem 250.00
Hobstars & other cutting, flared
  skirt, 7" d., 6" h. 125.00
Hobstars, etc., teardrop in stem,
  hobstar base, 7¼" d., 12½" h. 250.00
Pinwheel, hobstar & other cutting,
  notched prism stem, cut base, 7" d.,
  9" h. 225.00

Tuthill Compote

Tuthill signed, intaglio Vintage patt.,
  rolled rim (ILLUS.) 500.00

CREAMERS & SUGAR BOWLS

Heart Pattern Creamer & Sugar Bowl

Geometric cutting w/hobstar
  center, creamer w/tri-pour spout,
  pr. 385.00
Hawkes' "gravic" Strawberry, pr. 325.00

Hawkes signed, stars & other cutting,
pedestal base, 4½" & 4" h., pr. 175.00

Heart patt., flattened oval shape,
serrated rim, pr. (ILLUS.) 232.00

Hobstars, bonnet-shaped, pr. 175.00

Hobstars, fan & other cutting,
hobstar base, notched handles,
pr. 110.00

Hobstars, strawberry diamond, fan
& prism, 4" d., 3" h., pr...........165.00

Notched prism overall, sterling
silver rim w/embossed design, pr. ..190.00

Pinwheels & vesicas, star-cut
base, pr..........................117.50

Tuthill signed, Rosaceae patt., pr.....425.00

CRUETS

Cut Glass Cruets

Hawkes signed, Brilliant Period
cutting, sterling silver stopper 90.00

Hawkes signed, hobstars, original
stopper, pr. 250.00

Hobstars (2 large 8-point Florence
type & one 8-point hobstar), strawberry diamond & fan, pineapple-
shaped, original lapidary-cut
stopper, 7½" h. 75.00

Pinwheels w/raised hobstar
centers, crosshatching, fans, etc.,
panel-cut neck, rayed base, lapidary-
cut stopper, 6" h. 45.00

Pinwheels, faceted stopper 55.00

Strawberry Diamond patt., faceted
stopper...........................30.00

Strawberry Diamond & Fan patt.,
loop handle, ball-cut stopper,
19th c., 12½" h., pr. (ILLUS.)........335.00

DECANTERS

Cranberry cut to clear 259.00

Florals & foliage w/diamond-shaped
sections of Harvard patt., bowling
pin shape, 16-point rayed base,
large matching hollow stopper,
15" h., 5" widest d................450.00

Hawkes signed, hexagonal panels
of Brilliant Period cutting,
matching stopper w/teardrop,
13½" h. 195.00

Hobstars, fans & vesicas, original
lapidary-cut stopper, 9" h. 165.00

Hobstars (6 large & 6 small), strawberry diamond & star, panel- &
honeycomb-cut neck, triple
honeycomb-cut handle, star-cut
base, original lapidary-cut stopper,
pedestal foot, 5¼" d., 11½" h. 350.00

Intaglio-cut large 10-petal flowers
& leaves w/double row of
Harvard patt., step-cut neck,
notched handle, rayed base, faceted
stopper, 11¼" h. 225.00

Libbey's Corinthian patt., side
handle 280.00

Rye Pattern Decanter

Sinclaire signed, cut & engraved Rye
patt., original stopper, qt., 10½" h.
(ILLUS.) 1,250.00

DISHES, MISCELLANEOUS

Bon Bon Dish

Boat-shaped, divided, Clark signed,
etched flowers & leaves, chain of
stars border, serrated rim,
7½ x 5½"........................95.00
Bon bon, club-shaped, serrated
rim, 5" l. (ILLUS.)..................25.00
Bon bon, Hawkes' Pillars &
Diamonds patt., shell-shaped.......95.00
Candy, Averbeck's Star & Button
patt., 6" d.......................42.50
Candy, Egginton signed, diamonds
of hobstars & strawberry
diamond, 6" d. 65.00
Candy, Hawkes signed, "gravic" Strawberry, 5½" d. 160.00
Heart-shaped, sides w/panels of
beading, base cut in 8-point
hobstar within another 8-point hobstar surrounded by radiating
notched fan & splits, 5¼ x 5" 135.00
Ice cream, hobstar center & border,
4¾" d., set of 12 ....250.00
Ice cream, four 16-point hobstars,
cane, beading, hobnail & star,
5 7/8" d., set of 8 ....395.00
Olive, Tuthill signed, Phlox patt.,
8-point hobstar & fans center,
concave scalloped edge, 7¼" l.,
3 5/8" w., 1 5/8" h.................135.00
Oval, 2-handled, Hawkes signed,
roses, other florals & foliage, leaf
border, large daisy center,
handles cut in ferns over panel
cuts, 15¼" l. across handles,
8½" w., 6"h. 450.00
Oval centerpiece, Straus' Imperial
patt., folded over sides, 4 large
16-point hobstars, strawberry
diamond, beading & fan around
large 32-point hobstar center,
10½" l., 8½" w., 4" h. 350.00
Relish, Clark signed, pinwheels &
crosshatching, 8" l................60.00
Relish, Harvard patt. 80.00
Relish, Sinclaire signed, Stars &
Roses patt., 2-compartment,
14" l., 8" w. 140.00
Sauce, Brilliant Period cutting, 5" d.,
1¼" h. 35.00
Square, four 16-point hobstars,
hobnail, strawberry diamond, star
& fan, 24-point hobstar center,
5½" sq. 65.00
Square, shell & vesica, 5½" sq. 125.00
Square, Hawkes signed, Grecian
patt., 8¾" sq. 1,450.00
Tricornered, Fry signed, six 16-point
hobstars flashed fans, stars, etc.,
9¾" w., 1½" h....................375.00
Trowel-shaped, handled, Hunt's Royal
patt., 5½" w., 9" l. 285.00
Tuthill's intaglio grapes & chain of
hobstars, 6" d....................250.00

FERNERIES

Triangular Fernery

Hobstars & fluted fans, 7¾" d., 4" h.....85.00
Hobstars & fans overall, 3-footed,
8" d. 80.00
Intaglio-cut florals & polished leaves,
triangular, 3-footed (ILLUS.) 120.00
Tuthill signed, Primrose patt.........475.00

GOBLETS
Brunswick patt. variant, 3¾" d.,
6" h. 130.00
Cane patt. bowl, St. Louis cut stem
w/thirty-two point star base, set
of 4 ....200.00
Libbey signed, Cornucopia patt.,
7¼" h., set of 8 ....315.00
Libbey signed, knobbed teardrop
stem 95.00
Pluto patt. variant, knobbed teardrop
stem 95.00
Steuben signed, green bowl w/intaglio-
cut thistles & leaves, clear
knobbed stem & square double block-
cut base 250.00
Strawberry Diamond & Fan patt. 35.00
Venetian patt.......................115.00

ICE BUCKETS & TUBS
Bucket, Brilliant Period cutting,
7" d., 5" h. 295.00
Bucket, Dorflinger's Marlboro patt.,
tab handles, w/underplate 1,400.00
Bucket, King's patt., sunburst base 150.00
Bucket, large hobstars, checkered
diamonds, fans & other cutting,
2-handled.........................385.00
Tub, 16-point hobstars (4), hobnail,
strawberry diamond & fan, 16-point
hobstar base, 5½" d., 4¾" h.
including 1" tab handles 165.00

JARS & JARDINIERES
Cookie, panels of intaglio-cut flowers
& leaves, sterling silver "repousse"
cover w/flowers & leaves, 3 7/8" d.,
5 5/8" h.........................275.00
Cookie, prism & clear pillars, large
hobstar on cover & base, 4¾" d.,
7" h. 375.00

Horseradish, Elmira Cut Glass Co.'s
Pattern No. 33, hollow stopper,
5½" h. 295.00

Mount Washington Signed Jam Jar

Jam, strawberry diamond, hobstars
& slashes, cover marked "M.W.,"
Mount Washington (ILLUS.).........300.00
Mustard, 8 alternating columns of
beading & strawberry diamond &
star, star-cut base, cover w/lapidary-
cut knob, star-cut center &
beaded edge, 2¾" d., 4" h. 45.00
Powder, intaglio-cut grapes &
leaves, sterling silver cover w/Art
Nouveau floral design 135.00
Puff, bull's eye, zipper & vesicas,
beaded top 50.00

KNIFE RESTS

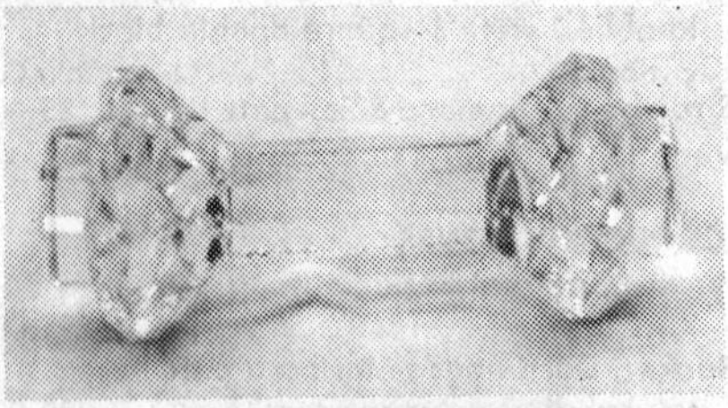

Cut Glass Knife Rest

Faceted ball ends, notched panel bar,
5½" l......................40.00 to 55.00
Hobstars, starred diamonds & other
cutting on ends, dumbbell shape 110.00
Prism-cut ball ends, notched panel bar,
4½" l. 30.00
Star-cut & faceted ends, notched bar,
5½" l. (ILLUS.).....................65.00

MISCELLANEOUS ITEMS

Ash tray, hobstars & fans, 6" d. 65.00
Ash tray, hobstars & fans w/deep
slashes, serrated edge, elongated
tab handle/rest....................87.50
Atomizer, Strawberry & Fan patt.,
5" h. 100.00

Bone dishes, crescent-shaped, Russian
patt., scalloped & serrated rims,
6¾" l., 4" w., set of 4 ....300.00
Cake plate, fans alternating w/cross-
hatching center, hobstar border,
scalloped & serrated rim, 12" d......450.00

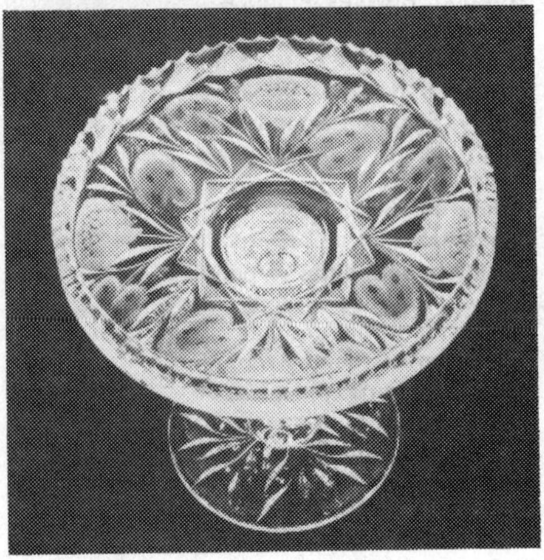

Lotus Pattern Cake Stand

Cake stand, Allen Cut Glass Company's Lotus patt., designed by
William Allen, patented July 15,
1913, 8" d. (ILLUS.) 950.00
Cake stand, pedestal base, Hoare's
Saturn patt., scalloped rim, 10" d.,
6" h. 800.00

Harvard Pattern Canoe

Canoe, Harvard patt., salesman's
sample, 3½" l. (ILLUS.) 125.00
Canoe, hobstars, diamond & fan, 9" l. ..110.00
Canoe, overall hobstars, 11" l.........235.00
Cheese & cracker server: 5" d. footed
cheese tray & 9¼" d. plate; Brilliant
Period cutting, 2 pcs. 195.00
Cheese & cracker server: 4½" d.
cheese tray & 9½" d. plate; Sin-
claire's Flute & Panel patt., 2 pcs. ...247.50
Cheese & cracker server, Double
Lozenge patt., 2 pcs. 190.00
Cocktail shaker, Hawkes signed,
overall Brilliant Period cutting,
silverplate top w/pouring spout 245.00
Cocktail shaker, Hawkes' Block &
Thumbprint patt., sterling silver rim,
strainer & top 155.00

Florence Pattern Coffee Pot

Coffee pot on standard, cov., Florence patt., matching cover w/lapidary-cut finial, 12" h. (ILLUS.) 5,600.00
Console set: 8" d., 4" h. centerpiece & pr. 10" h. candlesticks; Hawkes signed, centerpiece w/1" overlapping rim cut in chain of bull's eyes above strawberry diamond blocks & candlesticks w/2" overlapping rim cut in strawberry diamond blocks, almond-cut teardrop stem & base, 3 pcs. 450.00
Desk set: letter rack, cov. box & stamp box w/hinged sterling silver lid; Hawkes signed, Gracia patt., w/sterling silver trim, 3 pcs. 385.00
Finger bowl, cross-cut diamond, strawberry diamond, star & fan, star-cut center, 4½" d., 2 3/8" h. 25.00
Finger bowl, Clark signed, Winola patt., cross-cut diamond & fan, 16-point hobstar center, 5 1/8" d., 2 5/8" h. 55.00
Finger bowl, Hawkes' Chrysanthemum patt. 125.00
Finger bowl & underplate, Hawkes signed, Russian patt. 200.00
Flask, lady's, panel cutting alternating w/vertical notched prism, sterling silver screw-on cap, 3" w., 3 7/8" h. 100.00
Flask, lady's, geometric line & star cutting, sterling silver "repousse" screw-on cap, 3" w., 4¼" h. 95.00
Flask, each side w/large oval medallion of Cane patt., sterling silver screw-on cap, 3" w., 4¾" h. 155.00
Flower center, hobstars, cane & strawberry diamond, step-cut neck, large hobstar base, 8" d. 225.00
Flower center, footed, Hoare signed, eight 20-point hobstars, beading, strawberry diamond & fan, notched

panel-cut neck, 32-point hobstar foot, 9¾" d., 7½" h. 650.00
Flower center, 4 large 24-point hobstar rosettes separated by flashed stars, notched panel-cut neck w/lapidary-cut rim, 24-point hobstar base surrounded by 16-point hobstars, strawberry diamond & fan, 10" d., 4¾" h. 550.00
Flower center, Quaker City Cut Glass Co.'s Whirlwind patt., 10" d. 695.00
Flower center, Hawkes signed, engraved florals, 12" d., 7" h. 265.00
Hair receiver, Brilliant Period cutting, sterling silver top w/Art Nouveau type stylized floral decor 115.00
Hair receiver, vertical rows of cane outlined by notched prism, silver-plate cover w/Art Nouveau type floral design 100.00
Humidor, hobstars, strawberry diamond & fan, sterling silver cover marked "Tiffany," 3½" d., 4¾" h. 275.00
Humidor, barrel-shaped, prism notchings, hobstar bottom, "repousse" sterling silver cover, 6" d., 6½" h. 295.00
Humidor, overall hobstars, matching mushroom-shaped cover, 6½" h. . . .295.00
Humidor, alternating vertical panels of hobstar & zipper, hobstar bottom, matching cover, 4½" d., 9" h. . .475.00
Ice cream set: 14 x 8" tray & six 7" d. plates; blocks of strawberry diamond & flat hobstars, fan border, scalloped & serrated rim, 7 pcs. 550.00
Ice cream set: 15 x 7½" tray & eight 6" d. plates; Jubilee patt., 7 pcs. . . .1,250.00
Lemonade set: pitcher & 6 tumblers; Libbey signed, Scotch Thistle patt., 7 pcs. 500.00
Loving cup, 3-handled, notched prism, "repousse" sterling silver top, 3" h. 325.00

Brilliant Period Loving Cup

Loving cup, 3-handled, sterling silver rim, 6" h. (ILLUS.) 350.00
Mayonnaise bowl & underplate,

tapered sides, hobstars, strawberry
diamond & fan, scalloped & serrated
rims, 5" d. bowl, 6¼" underplate,
pr. 110.00

Mayonnaise bowl & underplate, intaglio-cut butterflies, crescent-cut
rims, pr. 125.00

Mayonnaise bowl & underplate, large
hobstars & other Brilliant Period
cutting, scalloped & serrated rims,
pr. 145.00

Mustard pot, cov., squatty, Notched
Prism patt., faceted ball finial, rayed
base, 3½" d., 3½" h. 45.00

Mustard pot, cov., large 8-point hobstars, beading & fans, star-cut base,
cover w/star center & lapidary-cut
finial, ridged edge w/spoon notch,
2¾" d., 4" h. 55.00

Mustard pot, open, handled, Mt.
Washington's Wheeler patt. 225.00

Paperweight, top w/engraved monogram surrounded by floral & foliage
motif continuing to sides, Russian
patt. w/hobstar & button base,
3¼ x 2¾", 2" h. 200.00

Planter, six 16-point hobstars, X-cuts
over beading & fan, beaded brass
rim & insert, 6½" d., 3" h. 125.00

Platter, Sinclaire's Diamonds & Silver
Threads patt., 14½ x 11½" 2,500.00

Punch ladle, Hawkes' Brazilian patt.,
notched panel-cut stem w/teardrop,
Gorham silverplate bowl, 13¾" l. 325.00

Punch ladle, Pairpoint signed, strawberry diamond, cross-cut diamond &
fan handle w/teardrop, shell-shaped
double spout bowl, 15" l. 350.00

Punch ladle, hobstar, strawberry diamond & fan handle w/teardrop,
Pairpoint silverplate bowl, 15" l. 250.00

Sauce boat & underplate, daisies &
leaves between panels of 8-point
hobstars, strawberry diamond &
beading, hobstar centers, 5 1/8" l.,
3¼" w. sauce boat & 6 7/8" oval
underplate, 2 pcs. 165.00

Sherbets, Harvard patt., star-cut
base, 3" d., 3½" h., set of 4 ....195.00

Sherbets & underplates, Tuthill
signed, swags of flowers & foliage
intertwined w/swagged line &
circles, set of 10 (20 pcs.) 1,250.00

Soap dish, cov., Sinclaire signed,
Rose patt. 150.00

Sugar bowl, Hoare's Hindoo patt.,
triple notched handles, four 16-point
hobstars, 20-point hobstar base,
2¾" h. 50.00

Sugar shaker, Straus' Encore patt.,
16-point hobstar base, silverplate
top & rim, 5" h. 150.00

Sugar shaker, fields of cross-cut &

clear diamonds, sterling silver top,
3" base d., 5" h. 150.00

Sugar shaker, egg-shaped, Mt.
Washington's Strawberry Diamond
& Fans patt. 375.00

Sugar shaker, corset-shaped, Brilliant
Period cutting, "repousse" sterling
silver top 190.00

Sugar shaker, geometric cutting,
rayed base, silverplate top 110.00

Syrup jug, Bergen's Glenwood patt. ...250.00

Teapot, cov., intaglio-cut poppies,
matching top w/bull's eye rim &
flute-cut knob, 16-point rayed base,
9½" across handle & spout,
8½" h. 2,000.00

Tumble-up (water carafe w/tumbler
top), bulbous, relief diamond,
panel-cut middle & shoulders,
wafer pedestal base 175.00

Whipped cream bowl, pedestal base,
2 large blazed hobstars, small
hobstars & vertical notch-cut prism,
scalloped & serrated rim, hobstar
foot, 6" d., 5¼" h. 650.00

Whiskey jug, Fry's Japan patt., St.
Louis Diamond strap handle, original stopper, 8" h. 725.00

Wine set: 12" h. handled decanter on
pedestal base & 6 wine glasses;
Persian patt., 7 pcs. 1,300.00

NAPPIES

Harvard Pattern Nappy

Egginton signed, Lotus patt., handled. ..80.00

Fans & crosshatching, ring handle,
7" w. 48.00

Feathered hobstar 65.00

Fry's Ceres patt. 150.00

Harvard patt., loop handle, 6" w.
(ILLUS.) 165.00

Hawkes signed, pinwheel, crosshatching, fan & other cutting, 5" d. 75.00

Hoare signed, Brilliant Period cutting,
7½" d. 125.00

Hobstars & fan sprays, star-cut base,
loop handle, 6" d. 65.00

Hobstars & strawberry diamond,
triangular, 6½ x 6" 75.00

Intaglio pears, cherries & leaves,
7½" w. 60.00

Notched prism, 6" d. 125.00
Russian patt. 85.00
Straus signed, Drape patt., honeycomb
    loop handle w/strawberry diamond
    thumbrest .125.00
Straus' Ulysses patt., tricornered,
    handled 75.00

PERFUME & COLOGNE BOTTLES

Hawkes Signed Cologne Bottle

Cologne, stars, diamond & fan, original
    faceted stopper, 6" h. 55.00
Cologne, bulbous, Brilliant Period
    cutting overall, St. Louis Diamond
    stopper, 12" widest d., 6½" h. 165.00
Cologne, vaseline cut to clear, faceted
    vaseline bubble stopper, 2½" d.,
    7" h. 95.00
Cologne, Pitkin & Brooks signed,
    Aurora Borealis patt., ball-shaped
    stopper, 7" h. 295.00
Cologne, Hawkes signed, copper
    wheel engraving, Verre de Soie
    finish, sterling silver stopper,
    7½" h. (ILLUS.) 90.00
Perfume, lay-down type, sapphire blue
    cut to clear, Cane patt., Gorham
    sterling silver screw-on lid, 7½" l. . .325.00

PITCHERS

Champagne, deep cut flowers &
    leaves, hobstar base, applied
    notched handle, 6½" d., 13½" h. . . .325.00
Cream, hobstars & cane, triple-
    notched handle, 4½" h. 295.00
Tankard, notched prism, ornate ster-
    ling silver collar & strap handle,
    7¾" h. 375.00
Tankard, hobstars & crosshatching,
    notched handle, 8½" h. 165.00
Tankard, pinwheels, hobstars & cane,
    serrated rim, star-cut base,
    10½" h. 175.00

Brilliant Period Tankard

Tankard, Libbey signed, hobnail,
    notched prism & other cutting, 1896-
    1906, 11½" h. (ILLUS.) 550.00
Tankard, overall swirled prism,
    sterling silver top marked "Tiffany,"
    12" h. 425.00
Water, Bergen's Sunflower patt.,
    bulbous, 7" h. 425.00
Water, Russian patt., bulbous, star-cut
    base, triple honeycomb handle,
    honeycomb neck, square mouth,
    6" d., 7 3/8" h. 425.00
Water, Dorflinger's Colonial patt.,
    7½" h. 185.00
Water, Hawkes signed, "gravic" Tiger
    Lily, bulbous, notched handle,
    7½" h. 285.00
Water, Hawkes signed, Juno patt.,
    corset-shaped, hollow triple-notch-
    ed handle, 7½" h. 195.00
Water, hobstars, pinwheels, straw-
    berry diamond & fan, bulbous,
    8" h. 185.00

Harvard Pattern Water Pitcher

Water, Harvard patt., 9" h. (ILLUS.)....300.00
Water, Hawkes signed, Brunswick
  patt., triple-notched handle, 9" h....500.00
Water, hobstars & fan, notched
  handle, 9" h. 175.00
Water, Lotus patt. variant, bulbous,
  hobstar base, 9½" d., 10" h........600.00
Water, elaborate starbursts & pinwheels, 10" h. 135.00
Water, Pinwheel patt., triple-notched
  handle, 7½" widest d., 13" h.......495.00
Water, Harvard patt. variant on body
  & base, double bull's eye handle,
  13½" h. 375.00

PLATES

Centauri Pattern Plate

6" d., Brilliant Period cutting 30.00
7" d., Hawkes signed, Centauri patt.
  (ILLUS.) 95.00
7" d., Hawkes signed, Hobstar &
  Silver Thread patt. 125.00
7" d., Tuthill's intaglio-cut grapes,
  oranges & pears 135.00
7" d., overall strawberry diamond &
  clear flat hobnail, fan cutting at rim ..50.00
7¾ x 6½", heart-shaped, large central
  hobstar surrounded by hobstars &
  fans, serrated & scalloped rim 325.00
8" d., Mt. Washington Glass Co's
  Butterfly & Daisy patt. 125.00
8" d., Tuthill signed, wide border of
  intaglio-cut flowers & deeply cut
  polished leaves, star-cut center.....270.00
9" d., Bergen's Bermuda patt. 145.00
10" d., Empire Cut Glass Company's
  Maynard patt......................125.00
10" d., Irving Cut Glass Company's
  White Rose patt. 150.00
10" d., Pairpoint's Urn & Flame patt. ...195.00
10" d., arches of cane over hobstars,
  notched prism fans & crosshatching .550.00
10" d., center handle, Harvard patt.,
  w/hobstars & cane 195.00

PUNCH BOWLS

Cut Glass Punch Bowl & Base

Dorflinger's Marlboro patt., chain of
  twelve 8-point hobstars, strawberry
  diamond & fan, 24-point hobstar
  center, w/matching base, 14 1/8" d.,
  11½" h., 2 pcs...................1,400.00
Elmira Cut Glass Co.'s No. 17 patt.,
  large 16-point & 25-point hobstars,
  cane, strawberry diamond & star,
  16-point hobstar knob, w/matching
  base, 11" d., 11¼" h., 2 pcs. 1,100.00
Harvard patt., w/matching base,
  14" d., overall 15½" h., 2 pcs......2,000.00
Hawkes signed, Albion patt.,
  14" d............................1,600.00
Hawkes signed, swirled panels of
  hobstar & fan, w/matching base,
  15" d., 13½" h., 2 pcs...........3,950.00
Hoare signed, Brilliant Period cutting ..850.00
Hobstars & cane, scalloped & serrated
  rim, matching flared base w/ringed
  neck, 2 pcs. (ILLUS.) 715.00
Hobstars & cross-cut diamond panels,
  scalloped & serrated rim, flaring
  base, 14¼" d., 13¾" h., 2 pcs.......735.00
Hobstars, comet & fan, serrated &
  scalloped rim, w/matching vase-
  shaped base, 11" d., overall 24" h.,
  2 pcs. (2 teeth on bowl & 1 on base
  chipped) 650.00

ROSE BOWLS
Cross-cut diamond & fan, 3½" d.,
  3¾" h. 95.00
Durand's Bridgeton Rose patt.,
  3-footed 400.00
Fry signed, Brilliant Period cutting,
  7" d., 6" h. including standard 250.00
Graduated cross-cut diamond w/fan
  border, serrated rim, 32-point rayed
  base, 5" d., 5½" h................130.00
Hobstars, strawberry diamond, fan &
  single stars, hobstar base, 4" d., 2"
  serrated opening, 3½" h. 140.00

SALT & PEPPER SHAKERS

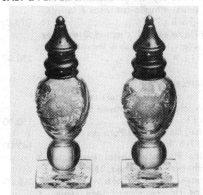

Hawkes Signed Salt & Pepper Shakers

Brilliant Period cutting, bulbous,
"repousse" floral sterling silver top,
2¾" h., pr. 38.00

Geometric cutting, pedestal base,
glass top, 6" h., pr. 42.00

Hawkes signed, Brilliant Period
cutting, pedestal base, square foot,
sterling silver top, pr. 135.00

Hawkes signed, Chrysanthemum patt.,
square base, sterling silver top,
5½" h., pr. (ILLUS.) 500.00

Pyramidal stars on pear-shaped body,
panel-cut & beaded stem, panel-cut
octagonal base, w/original top,
5" h., pr. 45.00

Straus' Imperial patt., 2¾" pepper
shaker w/silverplate top & 2¼ x
1¾" oval open salt dip w/serrated
rim & hobstar base, set of 6 pr. 700.00

Vertical splits intersected by 4 horizontal splits, International sterling silver
top, 1" d., 3" h., pr. 28.00

SALT DIPS

Brilliant Period Salt Dip

Brilliant Period cutting, individual size . .15.00

Brilliant Period cutting, ornate ruffled
sterling silver rim 45.00

Cross-cut diamond & fan, scalloped &
serrated rim, star-cut base, 2" d.,
set of 4 . . . . .55.00

Dorflinger's Parisian patt., paperweight-type, master size 85.00

Hobstars, heart-shaped, scalloped &
serrated rim, 2½" w. 70.00

Hobstars, canoe-shaped w/fan ends,
serrated rim, 3½ x 1½" 50.00

Hobstars (8) & strawberry diamond,
24-point hobstar base, 3 3/8" d.,
1 5/8" h. 95.00

Relief diamond, strawberry diamond &
fan, star-cut base, tapering sides,
1¾" sq. (ILLUS.) 20.00

Strawberry diamond & fan, 16-point
rayed base, scalloped & serrated
rim, 2" d. 10.00

Vertical notched prism, 1¼" sq., set of
8 . . . . .95.00

SPOONERS

Band of Harvard patt. variant w/hob-
star buttons below cornflowers &
leaves, star-cut base, corset-shaped,
3½" d., 4¾" h. 95.00

Brilliant Period cutting, corset-shaped . .95.00

Hobstars, cross-cut diamond, zipper &
other cutting, 25-point star base,
scalloped & serrated rim, 5¾" h. 195.00

Hobstars & fan, 4½" h. 85.00

Hobstars, hobnail & diamond point,
2 triple notch-cut handles, hobstar
base, 4¾" h. 475.00

Spoonholder tray, hobstars, strawberry
diamond & fan, serrated rim, 7¼ x
3¼", 2" h. 85.00

SYRUP PITCHERS & JUGS

Hawkes signed, Harvard patt. 85.00

Hobstars, silverplate beaded lid &
handle, 7" h. 165.00

Notched prism, ornate lid & handle 110.00

TRAYS

Brilliant Period Tray

Bread, 18- & 20-point hobstars w/cane,
strawberry diamond, flashed fan &
beading, 24-point hobstar base,
11¾ x 5½", 2 5/8" h. 295.00

Calling card, Sinclaire signed, Assyr-
ian patt., 7 x 6" 1,050.00

Calling card, Sinclaire signed,

Diamonds & Silver Threads patt.,
7¼ x 6¼"........................950.00
Dresser, Russian patt., w/cross-
hatched buttons, 11¼ x 6¼" 295.00
Dresser, Hawkes signed, large central
medallion of bird in flight among
branches surrounded by fine line
cutting, 12 x 8½", 1½" h. gallery ...245.00
Ice cream, Libbey's Kimberly patt.,
14 x 7½"........................250.00
Ice cream, Libbey signed, Ivernia
patt. variant w/deeply cut &
flashed flowers in the four
sections, 16 x 9¾" 795.00
Ice cream, hobstars & split vesicas of
checkered diamond, 17½ x 10½" ...750.00
Ice cream, Russian patt. w/vesicas &
hobstars, 18" l. 1,100.00
Chain of 8-point hobstars alternating
w/strawberry diamond centering
32-point hobstar surrounded by
notched prism radiants, 14" d. 1,800.00
Cluster-type patt., hobstars, cane,
strawberry diamond & other cutting,
scalloped & serrated rim, 18 x 10½"
(ILLUS.).........................850.00
Dorflinger's Parisian patt., 24-point
hobstar center, 11 1/8" d..........325.00
Hawkes signed, Classic patt., 10¼ x
7" oval 350.00
Hawkes signed, chain of 34 small
8-point hobstars beneath horizontally ridged edge, radiant star center
surrounded by 34 groups of mitre
cuts, 11" d., 1½" h. 175.00
Hawkes' Chrysanthemum patt., folded
corners, 14½ x 7½"...............750.00
Hawkes' Devonshire patt., 16 x
10½" oval 850.00
Hobstars (6) separated by X-cut hobnail vesicas, strawberry diamond,
star & fan, large 24-point hobstar
center, 11¾" d., 1½" h. 325.00
Hobstars alternating w/caning centering a waffled square, serrated
rim, ca. 1910, 13 x 7¼" 225.00
Libbey signed, four 16-point hobstars
separated by 4 sets of 4 blazed
almond cuts & strawberry diamond,
16-point hobstar center surrounded
by 4 Kohinoor triangles, fan &
strawberry diamond, 12" d. 795.00
Mt. Washington Glass Co.'s Ox Bow
patt., turned up rim, 12" d. 545.00
Pairpoint's Butterfly & Daisy patt., 3
panels each w/three daisies & a
butterfly, ridged ¼" h. star-cut foot,
pierced sterling silver rim marked
"Bailey, Banks & Biddle," 9½" d. 175.00
Russian patt. w/cut buttons, handled,
15" d. 575.00
Sinclaire signed, octagonal, intaglio-
cut grapes & leaves, chain of
leaves center, 9½ x 7½"...........225.00

Sinclaire signed, bracket-shaped
sides, intaglio-cut roses & leaves,
13 3/8 x 9¾" 275.00
Sinclaire signed, chain of Greek Key
w/engraved buds & leaves,
14 3/8" d........................250.00

TUMBLERS
Juice, chain of hobstars center
w/diamond fan, rayed base, set
of 6 ....150.00
Juice, Dorflinger's Parisian patt.,
3 7/8" h.........................145.00
Juice, Florence hobstar, single stars &
checkered diamond, 16-point rayed
base, 3½" h., set of 6.............155.00
Juice, Hawkes signed, fans, cross-
hatching, stars & other cutting 35.00
Juice, Hoare signed, Hindoo patt.,
3¾" h. 125.00
Juice, Hoare's Pluto patt., 3¾" h. 135.00
Juice, Libbey's Harvard patt. 35.00
Juice, Pairpoint's Butterfly & Daisy
patt., 3¼" h......................30.00
Juice, Straus' Drape patt., 3 7/8" h.....145.00
Juice, Tuthill signed, Vintage patt.,
3¾" h. 55.00
Lemonade, blaze w/strawberry
diamond band, blazed base, 4¾" h. ..25.00
Water, fan & zipper, 3¾" h., set of
10 in original leatherette box 475.00
Water, Hawkes' Louis XIV patt. 85.00
Water, Hoare signed, Heart patt.,
3 7/8" h.........................135.00
Water, Hoare's Carolyn patt. variant ...85.00
Water, Libbey signed, strawberry
diamond, set of 6 ....300.00
Water, pinwheel, strawberry diamond
& fan 30.00
Water, Pointed Loop patt.............100.00
Whiskey, Double Lozenge patt., set
of 4 ....140.00
Whiskey, Hoare's Monarch patt. 30.00

VASES

Brilliant Period Vase

Almy & Thomas signed, hobstars, cross-cut diamond, fan & other cutting, fan-shaped, long teardrop stem, pedestal base, 12" h. 350.00

Averbeck's Maud Adams patt., 16-point hobstars (6), beading, strawberry diamond, fan & flashed fan, trumpet-shaped, 20-point hobstar base, 5¼" d., 14" h. 225.00

Clark signed, Notched Prism patt., trumpet-shaped, ring- and notch-cut base & stem, scalloped & serrated rim, 6¼" d., 18" h. 375.00

Comet patt., bud, attributed to Hoare, 7 5/8" h. 255.00

Egginton signed, Creswick patt., hobstar, star & strawberry diamond, 5" h. 63.00

Florence hobstars, cane, strawberry diamond & fan, 24-point rayed base, scalloped & serrated rim, 8" d., 21" h. 1,350.00

Geometric cutting, sterling silver base w/"repousse" grapes & cornu-copia, 7½" top d., 15" h. 275.00

Harvard patt. fields alternating w/step cutting & graduated hobstars, lapidary-cut knob above base, scalloped pedestal foot w/hob-star, 10¼" h. 325.00

Hawkes signed, Easter patt., fan, flute & hobnail, scalloped pedestal foot w/hobstar, 13¾" h. 300.00

Hawkes signed, hobstar & radiating notched prism motifs, 14" h. (ILLUS.) 550.00

Hawkes' gravic "Iris" patt., sterling silver base, 17" h. 375.00

Libbey signed, Radiant patt., 12" h. 285.00

Sinclaire signed, panels of intaglio-cut roses & leaves alternating w/hob-stars & prisms, 7¾" h. 185.00

Straus signed, hobstars, cane & other cutting, scalloped & serrated rim, 24-point hobstar base, 14" h. (ILLUS.) 1,200.00

Strawberry diamond top & base, honeycomb center, hourglass-shaped, sterling silver top marked "Gorham," 5½" h. 58.00

Thistle patt., trumpet-shaped, 16" h. ..190.00

Tuthill signed, intaglio-cut grapes & chain of hobstars, square, 10" h. 575.00

Tuthill signed, Poppy patt., trumpet-shaped, 14" h. 1,100.00

Vesicas w/hobstar centers surrounded by cross-cut diamond & stars, corset-shaped, scalloped & serrated rim, rayed base, 6½" top d., 15¾" h. 295.00

Yellow cut to clear, geometric & floral cutting, flared mouth, 11" h.........595.00

Zipper, fan, strawberry diamond & flashed pinwheel, corset-shaped, 4" d., 9½" h. 240.00

WATER SETS

Tuthill Signed Water Set

Pitcher & 2 tumblers, Tuthill signed, hobstars & florals, 3 pcs. 475.00

Pitcher & 2 tumblers, Tuthill signed, Poppy patt., 3 pcs. (ILLUS.) 650.00

Pitcher & 4 tumblers, Brilliant Period cutting, 5 pcs. 245.00

Pitcher & 4 tumblers, intaglio-cut cosmos & hobstars, 5 pcs. 425.00

Pitcher & 4 tumblers, pinwheel, cross-cut diamond & fan, 5 pcs. 235.00

Pitcher & 5 tumblers, Fry signed, 6 pcs. 395.00

Pitcher & 6 tumblers, Brilliant Period cutting, 7 pcs. 600.00

Pitcher & 6 tumblers, Libbey signed, Scotch Thistle patt., 7 pcs..........500.00

Pitcher & 6 tumblers, pinwheel & cross-hatching, 7" h. pitcher w/honeycomb handle & shaped mouth, ca. 1920, 7 pcs. 355.00

Straus Signed Vase

(End of Cut Glass Section)

CUT VELVET

Cut Velvet Rose Bowl

Several glasshouses, including Mt. Washington, produced this two-layered glass with its velvety or acid finish and raised pattern. The inner casing is frequently white, and the pattern was developed by blowing into a mold.

Bottle-vase, Diamond Quilted patt.,
  green, white lining, 3¼" d.,
  5 7/8" h......................$115.00
Bottle-vase, Diamond Quilted patt.,
  rose-pink, white lining, 3 5/8" d.
  7 1/8" h.........................150.00
Bottle-vase, Diamond Quilted patt.,
  blue, white lining, 3 3/8" d.,
  7¼" h...........................120.00
Bottle-vase, ribbed, rose-pink, white
  lining, 4 1/8" d., 7 7/8" h..........150.00
Finger bowl, Diamond Quilted patt.,
  heavenly blue, white lining, 4½" d.,
  2½" h..................125.00 to 140.00
Pitcher, 3 3/8" h., 2¾" d., bulbous
  w/round mouth, applied opaque
  white satin handle, Diamond Quilted
  patt., rose-pink...................216.00
Pitcher, 4½" h., 5" w., applied amber
  handle, Honeycomb patt., rose-pink,
  white lining......................325.00
Punch cup, pink, white lining..........65.00
Rose bowl, 6-crimp top, Diamond
  Quilted patt., rose, white lining,
  3 3/8" d., 3¾" h. (ILLUS.) ..170.00 to 200.00
Vase, 4¾" h., 3½" d., ewer-shaped,
  applied frosted handle, Diamond
  Quilted patt., deep blue, white
  lining 135.00
Vase, 5 7/8" h., 3 1/8" d., slightly
  bulbous w/square top, Diamond
  Quilted patt., shaded heavenly
  blue, white lining................180.00
Vase, 6¼" h., Diamond Quilted patt.,
  green, white lining...............110.00
Vase, 7 1/8" h., 3¼" d., ruffled top,
  Diamond Quilted patt., heavenly
  blue, white lining................150.00
Vase, 7¼" h., 3¼" d., ruffled rim,

Diamond Quilted patt., rose, white
  lining 175.00
Vase, 8½" h., 4¼" d., ribbed,
  lavender-pink, white lining 158.00
Vase, 9½" h., bulbous w/narrow neck
  & flaring fluted rim, Diamond Quilted
  patt., green, white lining 325.00
Vase, 10 3/8" h., 4½" d., ruffled rim,
  Diamond Quilted patt., deep rose,
  white lining 275.00

CZECHOSLOVAKIAN

Iridescent Gold Czechoslovakian Glass Vase

At the close of World War I, Czechoslovakia was declared an independent republic and immediately developed a large export industry. Czechoslovakian glass factories produced a wide variety of colored and hand-painted glasswares from about 1918 until 1939, when the country was occupied by Germany at the outset of World War II. Between the wars, fine quality blown glasswares were produced along with a deluge of cheaper, vividly colored spatterwares for the American market. Subsequent production was primarily limited to cut crystal or Bohemian-type etched wares for the American market. Although it was marked, much Czechoslovakian glass is mistaken for the work of Tiffany, Loetz, or other glass artisans it imitates. It is often misrepresented and overpriced.

Basket, applied clear looped thorn
  handle, red & yellow spangle
  w/green Aventurine, 6½" h........$65.00
Basket, applied cobalt blue handle, expanded lavender millefiori in pale
  green ground, signed, 5" d., 7" h. 47.00
Bowl, cased, black exterior, bright
  yellow interior, polished pontil 45.00
Decanter w/cobalt blue tall steeple

stopper, clear w/applied cobalt blue elongated teardrop prunts, polished pontil, 5½" d., 15" h. 70.00

Decanters w/stoppers, green overlay cut to white opaque florals & panels, 14" h., pr. 150.00

Epergnes, single 10½" h. lily in 9" d. bowl, white opaline w/ruby-red trim, pr. 145.00

Liqueur set: pr. decanters & 5 liqueurs; clear to cranberry w/gold overlay rims & h.p. decor, 7 pcs. 750.00

Perfume bottle, black w/original clear stopper etched w/nude lady, signed, 5" h. 85.00

Perfume bottle w/fan-shaped stopper, blue cut glass 50.00

Puff box, cov., green 50.00

Rose bowl, "mercury" glass 35.00

Vase, 4" h., Loetz-type, iridescent multicolored shades, signed........70.00

Vase, 5¾" h., red marbled glass w/applied black legs & rim, signed . . .22.50

Vase, 6" h., 8" w., red & black spatter 40.00

Vase, 9" h., bottle-shaped, applied reeded handles at shoulders, iridescent gold, signed, ca. 1920 (ILLUS.)..........................145.00

Vase, 9" h., jack-in-pulpit type, jade green w/applied black top edge 27.50

Vase, 10" h., pinched sides, green w/yellow & white fused enamel decor 32.00

Vase, 11" h., multicolored swirl........55.00

Vase, 12¼" h., fluted rim, black opaque w/tango orange trim, signed...........................65.00

Water set: pitcher w/applied handle & 6 tumblers; cobalt blue & orange spatter in clear, signed, 7 pcs. 150.00

D'ARGENTAL

Glass known by this name is so-called after its producer, who fashioned fine cameo pieces in France late last century.

Cameo bowl-vase, 3 3/8" d., 3½" h., carved navy blue to yellow scene of laundress washing at river bank, w/boat at anchor & hills & trees on distant shore against frosted soft pink translucent ground, signed ...$585.00

Cameo vase, 3½" h., bulbous, carved black thistles & leaves against yellow ground, signed 348.00

Cameo vase, 6¾" h., 4 1/8" d., carved brown to rust scene w/house, shed & trees in foreground & hilltop chateau in background against

frosted white translucent ground, signed..........................650.00

Cameo vase, 7¾" h., 3½" d., carved deep purple statue-monument in foreground w/Venetian boats on water, moon & clouds in background against frosted ground, signed..........................662.00

D'Argental Cameo Vase

Cameo vase, 8" h., carved red-brown to rose medallions & line segments (ILLUS.)..........................450.00

Cameo vase, 8 5/8" h., 4 5/8" d., carved navy blue to yellow forest landscape w/lake & 2 deer against soft frosted pink translucent ground, w/band of ducks flying around top, signed..........................987.00

Cameo vase, 9½" h., 4 1/8" d., carved brown to rust & rose tree landscape w/bay & mountainous background against rich frosted blue ground, signed..........................962.00

Cameo vase, 9 5/8" h., 4¼" d., carved w/three ornately bordered panels reserved w/house & landscape scenes against brown-purple shaded to gold frosted ground, signed..........................750.00

Cameo vase, 11½" h., 5" d., carved dark brown to rust cottage scene w/stream, trees & hills against frosted white translucent ground, signed..........................962.00

Cameo vase, 13¾" h., swollen cylinder, carved pink & ochre medieval ruins above gorge waterfall surrounded by woodlands against pale yellow ground, ca. 1920, signed...................1,540.00

Cameo vase, 14" h., footed, carved deep brown florals against medium brown ground, signed 835.00

DAUM NANCY

Daum Nancy Cameo Vase with Daffodils

This fine glass, much of it cameo, was made by Auguste and Antonin Daum, who founded a factory in 1875 in Nancy, France. Most of their cameo and enameled glass was made from the final decade of last century. Also see ART DECO.

Cache pot, blue w/gold flecks, in wrought iron framework, signed, 7 7/8" d., 6¾" h. $950.00

Cameo bowl, 5¾" d., 2½" h., carved & enameled barren forest scene w/snow-laden trees & snow-covered ground against mottled gold frosted ground, signed 695.00

Cameo ewer, slender waisted cylinder w/flat shoulder, straight cylindrical neck, elongated spout, applied angular handle, carved deep purple to brilliant royal blue scrolling strapwork on neck & shoulder & lily blossoms & leafage on sides against hammered streaked burgundy ground, base w/a whiplash pattern, ca. 1900, signed, 16½" h. 9,350.00

Cameo liqueur, barrel-shaped, carved & enameled barren forest scene w/snow-laden trees & snow-covered ground against mottled gold ground, signed, 1 7/8" h. 395.00

Cameo perfume bottle, carved & enameled bachelor buttons against brown to yellow ground 1,195.00

Cameo rose bowl, carved & enameled barren forest scene w/snow-laden trees & snow-covered ground against rosy gold to mottled yellow satin finish ground, signed, 2¾ x 3", 2¾" h. 595.00

Cameo salt dip, carved & enameled leafy tree scene against pink opal-

escent frosted ground, signed, 1 7/8 x 1 3/8" oval, 1 1/8" h. 495.00

Cameo salt dip, carved red crocus against leafy green ground, signed, oval. 425.00

Cameo toothpick holder, carved maroon florals & blue fronds on gold-traced stems against pebbled blue ground, gold rim, signed 350.00

Cameo tumbler, carved & enameled autumn-colored florals, signed, 4¾" h. 450.00

Cameo tumbler, barrel-shaped, carved & enameled purple violets & green leaves against mottled white to blue satin ground, signed, 2¼" d., 5" h. 660.00

Cameo vase, 2½" h., 1" d., stick-type, carved & enameled blackbirds in snow scene, signed 600.00

Cameo vase, 3½" h., 2¾" w., flattened oval, carved & enameled leafy green forest trees against mottled chartreuse frosted ground, signed . .495.00

Cameo vase, 4 3/8" h., 6¼" d., carved & enameled barren forest scene w/snow-laden trees & snow-covered ground against mottled gold frosted ground, signed 875.00

Cameo vase, 5" h., bulbous w/tapering neck, carved lime green & lemon yellow wildflowers & leafage against pale grey to emerald green hammered ground, fire-polished, ca. 1900, signed. 1,870.00

Cameo vase, 8½" h., footed ovoid, carved light orange & green daffodils & leafage against hammered opalescent ground shaded to green at foot, signed (ILLUS.) 1,430.00

Cameo Vase with Continuous Scene

Cameo vase, 11 5/8" h., flaring circular form w/wide mouth, carved burgundy continuous riverbank scene w/wind-blown trees & mountains in distance against mottled yellow, apricot, salmon & rose ground, ca. 1912, signed (ILLUS.). 4,070.00

Cameo vase, 13" h., 9" w., carved
dark plum tiger lilies against soft
plum ground, signed.............1,600.00
Cameo vase, 13" h., 4 1/8" d., carved
landscape scene w/deep green
pine trees around lake & peach
mountains in background against
frosted mottled gold ground,
signed......................1,112.00
Cameo vase, 15" h., straight-sided
cylinder w/gilt cushion-molded
foot tooled w/strapwork, carved
& enameled dusty pink rose branches
& applied red, green & yellow random cabochons against frosted grey
ground, heightened w/gilding
overall, ca. 1910, signed.........1,210.00
Cameo vase, 16¼" h., ovoid w/tri-
angular neck & incurvate base,
carved grey & emerald green Queen
Anne's Lace & leafage against clear
mottled w/emerald green, deep
purple & grey ground, ca. 1910,
signed......................1,320.00

Large Cameo Vase

Cameo vase, 20½" h., carved rough-
skinned orange squash w/green
leafy vines & tendrils against partly
hammered mottled grey & purple
ground, ca. 1910 (ILLUS.).........1,760.00
Cameo vase, 21" h., carved green
continuous water landscape w/tall
trees in foreground against mottled
orange & yellow ground, ca. 1910,
signed......................2,640.00
Vases, 4 5/8" h., 7" l., modeled as
dove wings, turquoise blue mottled
w/yellow, signed, pr. 300.00
Vase, 5¾" h., 4½" d., mottled light
brown w/gold Aventurine flecks,
dark brown base, signed...........80.00
Vase, 10" h., variegated blues w/gold
flecks, signed 325.00
Vase, 12" h., lobed cadmium red vase

w/everted rim blown into wrought
iron ribbed skelton frame w/S-form
handles by Majorelle, ca. 1920,
signed......................825.00
Vase, 25" h., elongated cylindrical
neck, spreading foot, mottled
mustard, gold & orange shading to
deep blue-green at foot, ca. 1910,
signed......................770.00

DE LATTE

DeLatte Cameo Vase

*This ware, chiefly opaque and cameo
glass, was made by Andre de Latte in
Nancy, France, from 1921. His firm also
made light fixtures, but it is chiefly his
cameo glass that is now sought.*

Bottle w/matching stopper, enameled
yellow, black & white Art Deco
florals on mottled blue ground,
signed......................$460.00
Cameo vase, 6¾" h., spherical,
carved maroon trumpet flower
blossoms & leafage against grey
shading to maroon ground, ca.
1920, signed 550.00
Cameo vase, 7" h., pedestal foot,
carved light to midnight blue
florals against white ground,
signed......................675.00
Cameo vase, 8" h., globular w/small
neck & slightly flaring rim, carved
deep blue blossoming vine
w/tendrils aginst frosted white
ground, signed (ILLUS.)...........700.00
Cameo vase, 8¾" h., carved powder
blue to navy blue peacock
w/spreading tail against lemon
yellow ground, signed...........765.00
Cameo vase, 10" h., swollen cylinder
w/small neck, carved maroon to
rose landscape scene against
mottled frosted white ground,
signed......................995.00

DEPRESSION GLASS

The phrase "Depression Glass" is used by collectors to denote a specific kind of transparent glass produced primarily as tablewares, in crystal, amber, blue, green, pink, milky-white, etc., during the late 1920s and 1930s when this country was in the midst of a financial depression. Made to sell inexpensively, it was turned out by such producers as Jeannette, Hocking, Westmoreland, Indiana and other glass companies. We list all the major Depression Glass patterns.

ADAM (Process-etched)

Adam Pitcher

Ash tray, clear $10.50
Ash tray, 4½", green 14.50
Ash tray, 4½", pink 20.00
Bowl, nappy, 4¾" sq., green or pink 9.00
Bowl, nappy, 5¾" sq., green 20.00
Bowl, nappy, 5¾" sq., pink 22.00
Bowl, nappy, 7¾" sq., green 11.50
Bowl, nappy, 7¾" sq., pink 13.00
Bowl, cov., vegetable, 9" sq., green ... 56.00
Bowl, cov., vegetable, 9" sq., pink 36.00
Bowl, 9" sq., green 18.00
Bowl, 9" sq., pink 14.50
Bowl, 10" oval vegetable, green 17.00
Bowl, 10" oval vegetable, pink 16.50
Butter dish, cov., green 220.00
Butter dish, cov., pink 62.00
Cake plate, 10" sq., green 15.50
Cake plate, 10" sq., pink 13.50
Candlesticks, 4" h., green, pr. 66.00
Candlesticks, 4" h., pink, pr. 53.00
Candy jar, cov., green 75.00
Candy jar, cov., pink 49.00
Coaster, clear or green 10.00
Coaster, pink 13.50
Creamer, green 12.50
Creamer, pink 11.00
Creamer & cov. sugar bowl, green,
    pr. 39.50

Creamer & cov. sugar bowl, pink,
    pr. 30.00
Creamer & open sugar bowl, green,
    pr. 28.00
Creamer & open sugar bowl, pink, pr. .. 21.00
Cup & saucer, green 17.50
Cup & saucer, pink 20.00
Pitcher, jug, cone-shaped, 8" h.,
    32 oz., clear 17.00
Pitcher, jug, cone-shaped, 8" h.,
    32 oz., green (ILLUS.) 34.00
Pitcher, jug, cone-shaped, 8" h.,
    32 oz., pink 25.00
Plate, sherbet, 6" sq., green 4.50
Plate, sherbet, 6" sq., pink 4.00
Plate, salad, 7¾" sq., green 7.00
Plate, salad, 7¾" sq., pink 8.00
Plate, salad, round, pink 75.00
Plate, salad, round, yellow 120.00
Plate, dinner, 9" sq., green 13.00
Plate, dinner, 9" sq., pink 12.50
Plate, grill, 9" sq., green 11.00
Plate, grill, 9" sq., pink 11.50
Platter, 12" l., green 14.00
Platter, 12" l., pink 12.00
Relish dish, 2-part, oblong, 8", green ... 12.00
Relish dish, 2-part, oblong, 8", pink 10.00
Salt & pepper shakers, footed, 4" h.,
    green, pr. 72.50
Salt & pepper shakers, footed, 4" h.,
    pink, pr. 39.00
Sherbet, green 19.50
Sherbet, pink 14.00
Sugar bowl, cov., green 31.00
Sugar bowl, cov., pink 22.00
Sugar bowl, open, green 10.00
Sugar bowl, open, pink 13.00
Tumbler, cone-shaped, 4½" h., 7 oz.,
    green 15.50
Tumbler, cone-shaped, 4½" h., 7 oz.,
    pink 15.00
Tumbler, cone-shaped, 5½" h., 9 oz.,
    green 22.00
Tumbler, cone-shaped, 5½" h., 9 oz.,
    pink 38.00
Vase, 7½" h., green 35.00
Vase, 7½" h., pink 125.00
Water set: pitcher & six 4½" tumblers;
    pink, 7 pcs. 125.00

AMERICAN SWEETHEART (Process-etched)

Berry set: 9" bowl & 6 sauce
    dishes; Cremax, 7 pcs. 50.00
Bowl, berry, 3½" d., pink 23.00
Bowl, cream soup, 4½" d., Monax 40.00
Bowl, cream soup, 4½" d., pink 25.00
Bowl, cereal, 6" d., Cremax 8.00
Bowl, cereal, 6" d., Monax 10.00
Bowl, cereal, 6" d., pink 8.50
Bowl, 9" d., Cremax 29.00
Bowl, 9" d., Monax 36.00
Bowl, 9" d., pink 18.50
Bowl, 10" oval vegetable, Monax 42.50
Bowl, 10" oval vegetable, pink 26.00

Bowl, soup, rimmed, 10" d., Monax 37.00
Bowl, soup, rimmed, 10" d., pink.......26.00
Bowl, console, 18" d., Monax.........288.00
Bowl, console, 18" d., ritz blue.......802.00
Bowl, console, 18" d., ruby red 705.00
Creamer, Monax 7.00
Creamer, pink.......................8.50
Creamer, ritz blue 100.00
Creamer & cov. sugar bowl, Monax,
    pr.............................155.00
Creamer & open sugar bowl, Monax,
    pr..............................11.50
Creamer & open sugar bowl, pink, pr. ..14.50
Creamer & open sugar bowl, ritz
    blue, pr.........................172.00
Creamer & open sugar bowl, ruby
    red, pr..........................178.00
Cup & saucer, Monax 10.50
Cup & saucer, pink 11.50
Cup & saucer, ritz blue.............121.00
Cup & saucer, ruby red 97.00
Lamp shade, Monax.................385.00
Lazy Susan, 15½" plate on metal
    stand, Monax 200.00
Pitcher, jug, 7½" h., 60 oz., pink 421.00
Pitcher, 8" h., 80 oz., pink...........360.00
Plate, bread & butter, 6" d., Monax.....3.25
Plate, bread & butter, 6" d., pink 3.00
Plate, salad, 8" d., Monax or pink 6.00
Plate, salad, 8" d., ritz blue 82.50
Plate, salad, 8" d., ruby red 63.00
Plate, luncheon, 9" d., Monax 8.00
Plate, luncheon, 9" d., pink 10.00
Plate, luncheon, 9" d., ritz blue 78.00
Plate, luncheon, 9" d., ruby red 58.00
Plate, dinner, 10" d., Monax..........13.50
Plate, dinner, 10" d., pink............15.00
Plate, chop, 11" d., Monax...........11.00
Plate, chop, 11" d., pink 9.00
Plate, salver, 12" d., Monax..........11.50

American Sweetheart Salver

Plate, salver, 12" d., pink (ILLUS.) 10.50
Plate, salver, 12" d., ritz blue.........163.00

Plate, salver, 12" d., ruby red.........155.00
Plate, 15" d., w/center handle,
    Monax 155.00
Plate, 15½" d., Monax 160.00
Platter, 13" oval, Monax 37.00
Platter, 13" oval, pink 17.00
Platter, 13" oval, ritz blue 14.00
Platter, 13" oval, ruby red 90.00
Salt & pepper shakers, Monax, pr. 233.00
Salt & pepper shakers, pink, pr........285.00
Sherbet, footed, 4", Monax 13.00
Sherbet, footed, 4", pink.............10.50
Sherbet, low footed, 4¼", Monax 14.00
Sherbet, low footed, 4¼", pink 8.50
Sherbet, ice cream in metal holder,
    clear 3.00
Sherbet, ice cream in metal holder,
    Monax 6.00
Sherbet, ice cream in metal holder,
    pink..............................6.50
Sugar bowl, open, Monax 6.50
Sugar bowl, open, pink 8.00
Sugar bowl, open, ruby red 64.00
Tid bit set, 2-tier, Monax 39.00
Tid bit set, 2-tier, pink 71.50
Tid bit set, 2-tier, ruby red 247.00
Tid bit set, 3-tier, Monax 55.00
Tid bit set, 3-tier, pink 85.00
Tid bit set, 3-tier, ruby red 545.00
Tumbler, 3½" h., 5 oz., pink...........33.00
Tumbler, 4" h., 9 oz., pink............33.00
Tumbler, 4½" h., 10 oz., pink.........39.00

BLOCK or Block Optic (Press-mold)

Block Creamer & Sugar Bowl

Bowl, nappy, 4¼" d., green 4.00
Bowl, nappy, 5¼" d., green 6.00
Bowl, nappy, 7" d., green 12.50
Bowl, nappy, 8½" d., green 11.00
Butter dish, cov., oblong, green........31.00
Butter dish, cov., round, green 32.00
Candlesticks, green, pr. 42.50
Candlesticks, pink, pr................29.50
Candy jar, cov., low, 2¼" h., green 26.00
Candy jar, cov., low, 2¼" h., pink......27.50
Candy jar, cov., low, 2¼" h., yellow....38.00
Candy jar, cov., tall, 6¼" h., clear 18.00
Candy jar, cov., tall, 6¼" h., green.....27.00
Candy jar, cov., tall, 6¼" h., pink 49.00
Compote, 4" d., cone-shaped, green ...23.00

Compote, 4" d., cone-shaped, pink 17.00
Creamer, cone-shaped, green 6.00
Creamer, cone-shaped, pink 9.00
Creamer, round, footed, green 8.00
Creamer, round, footed, yellow 9.00
Creamer, straight sides, green 6.00
Creamer, straight sides, yellow 5.00
Creamer & open sugar bowl, green,
   pr. 15.00
Creamer & open sugar bowl, pink,
   pr. 14.50
Creamer & open sugar bowl, yellow,
   pr. 17.50
Creamer & open sugar bowl, cone-
   shaped, green (ILLUS.) 15.00
Creamer & open sugar bowl, cone-
   shaped, pink, pr. 14.00
Creamer & open sugar bowl, cone-
   shaped, yellow, pr. 24.00
Cup & saucer, clear 4.00
Cup & saucer, green 9.00
Cup & saucer, pink or yellow 7.00
Goblet, wine, 4" h., 2 oz., clear 7.50
Goblet, wine, 4" h., 2 oz., green 19.00
Goblet, wine, 4" h., 2 oz., pink 11.00
Goblet, 6" h., clear. 7.00
Goblet, 6" h., green 12.50
Goblet, 6" h., pink 13.00
Goblet, 6" h., yellow 11.00
Goblet, 7¼" h., clear. 8.50
Goblet, 7¼" h., green. 16.50
Goblet, 7¼" h., pink 11.00
Goblet, 7¼" h., yellow 17.00
Ice tub, clear 15.00
Ice tub, green 22.50
Ice tub, pink. 40.00
Mug (or cup), green 27.00
Nite set, 3" tumbler bottle & 6"
   tumbler, green 43.00
Nite set bottle, 3", green. 15.00
Nite set bottle, 3", pink. 17.50
Pitcher, 7 5/8" h., 68 oz., green 29.00
Pitcher, 8" h., 80 oz., clear 16.00
Pitcher, 8" h., 80 oz., green 35.00
Pitcher, 8" h., 80 oz., pink 37.00
Pitcher, 8½" h., 54 oz., clear 16.50
Pitcher, 8½" h., 54 oz., green 27.00
Pitcher, 8½" h., 54 oz., pink 32.00
Plate, 6" d., clear 1.00
Plate, 6" d., green or pink. 2.00
Plate, 6" d., yellow. 2.50
Plate, luncheon, 8" d., green 3.50
Plate, luncheon, 8" d., pink 3.00
Plate, luncheon, 8" d., yellow 4.00
Plate, dinner, 9" d., green 10.50
Plate, dinner, 9" d., yellow 14.50
Plate, grill, 9" d., clear 4.00
Plate, sandwich, 10" d., clear 5.50
Plate, sandwich, 10" d., green 11.00
Salt & pepper shakers, squat, green,
   pr. 28.50
Salt & pepper shakers, squat, pink,
   pr. 50.00

Salt & pepper shakers, footed, clear,
   pr. 25.00
Salt & pepper shakers, footed, green,
   pr. 21.00
Salt & pepper shakers, footed, pink,
   pr. 52.00
Salt & pepper shakers, footed, yellow,
   pr. 18.00
Sandwich server, center handle, green .31.50
Sandwich server, center handle, pink. . .37.00
Sherbet, round or V shaped, clear 2.50
Sherbet, round or V shaped, green 3.50
Sherbet, round or V shaped, pink 4.50
Sherbet, round or V shaped, yellow 6.00
Sherbet, stemmed, 5" h., clear 6.50
Sherbet, stemmed, 5" h., green. 4.50
Sherbet, stemmed, 5" h., pink 8.00
Sherbet, stemmed, 5" h., yellow 9.50
Sugar bowl, cone-shaped, clear. 4.00
Sugar bowl, cone-shaped, green 6.50
Sugar bowl, cone-shaped, pink 7.00
Sugar bowl, round, clear 3.25
Sugar bowl, round, green 6.00
Sugar bowl, round, pink 5.50
Sugar bowl, round, yellow 6.50
Sugar bowl, straight sides, green 6.50
Tumbler, whiskey, 2½" h., clear 6.50
Tumbler, whiskey, 2½" h., green 16.00
Tumbler, whiskey, 2½" h., pink 9.50
Tumbler, juice, 3" h., 5 oz., clear 3.75
Tumbler, juice, 3" h., 5 oz., green 10.50
Tumbler, juice, 3" h., 5 oz., pink 8.50
Tumbler, juice, footed, 3¼" h., 5 oz.,
   green 11.00
Tumbler, juice, footed, 3¼" h., 5 oz.,
   pink. 8.00
Tumbler, 9 oz., clear 4.00
Tumbler, 9 oz., green. 10.00
Tumbler, 9 oz., pink 9.00
Tumbler, 9 oz., yellow 8.00
Tumbler, footed, 9 oz., clear 8.50
Tumbler, footed, 9 oz., green 11.00
Tumbler, footed, 9 oz., pink 10.50
Tumbler, footed, 9 oz., yellow 12.00
Tumbler, iced tea, 10 oz., clear 5.50
Tumbler, iced tea, 10 oz., green 11.00
Tumbler, iced tea, 10 oz., pink 8.50
Tumbler, iced tea, footed, 6" h.,
   10 oz., green .15.00
Tumbler, iced tea, footed, 6" h.,
   10 oz., pink or yellow. 12.50
Tumbler, flat, 14 oz., green 16.00

BUBBLE (Press-mold)
Berry set: master bowl & 6 sauce
   dishes; white, 7 pcs. 12.50
Bowl, 4" d., blue 7.50
Bowl, 4" d., clear 2.00
Bowl, 4" d., pink 15.00
Bowl, 4" d., ruby red 4.50
Bowl, fruit, 4½" d., blue or green 5.00
Bowl, fruit, 4½" d., clear 2.00
Bowl, fruit, 4½" d., milk white. 3.00
Bowl, fruit, 4½" d., ruby red 4.00

Bowl, cereal, 5¼" d., blue 6.00
Bowl, cereal, 5¼" d., clear 4.00

Bubble Cereal Bowl

Bowl, cereal, 5¼" d., green (ILLUS.) 5.50
Bowl, soup, 7¾" d., blue 7.00
Bowl, soup, 7¾" d., clear 4.50
Bowl, soup, 7¾" d., green 15.00
Bowl, soup, 7¾" d., pink 4.75
Bowl, soup, 7¾" d., ruby red 5.75
Bowl, 8 3/8" d., blue or green 7.50
Bowl, 8 3/8" d., clear 4.00
Bowl, 8 3/8" d., milk white 3.50
Bowl, 8 3/8" d., pink 4.75
Bowl, 8 3/8" d., ruby red 8.00
Candlesticks, clear, pr. 12.00
Creamer, blue .16.00
Creamer, clear or green 5.00
Creamer, milk white 2.50
Creamer, ruby red 3.00
Creamer & open sugar bowl, blue, pr. . .27.00
Creamer & open sugar bowl, clear, pr. . . .6.50
Creamer & open sugar bowl, green,
    pr. 12.50
Cup & saucer, blue 4.50
Cup & saucer, clear 2.75
Cup & saucer, green 6.00
Cup & saucer, ruby red 6.50
Pitcher, ice lip, 64 oz., blue 35.00
Pitcher, ice lip, 64 oz., clear 50.00
Pitcher, ice lip, 64 oz., ruby red 33.00
Plate, bread & butter, 6¾" d., blue 2.00
Plate, bread & butter, 6¾" d., clear 1.50
Plate, bread & butter, 6¾" d., green 2.50
Plate, dinner, 9¼" d., blue 4.50
Plate, dinner, 9¼" d., clear 3.00
Plate, dinner, 9¼" d., green 5.50
Plate, dinner, 9¼" d., ruby red 6.00
Plate, grill, 9¼" d., blue 7.50
Plate, grill, 9¼" d., clear 4.00
Platter, 12" oval, blue 7.50
Platter, 12" oval, clear 7.00
Salt & pepper shakers, blue, small,
    pr. 10.00
Sugar bowl, open, blue 11.00
Sugar bowl, open, clear 4.50
Sugar bowl, open, green 6.50

Sugar bowl, open, milk white or ruby
    red 3.00
Tid bit server, blue 39.00
Tid bit server, ruby red 27.00
Tumbler, juice, 6 oz., clear or ruby
    red 6.00
Tumbler, old fashioned, 9 oz., clear 6.50
Tumbler, old fashioned, 9 oz., ruby red . .6.00
Tumbler, 12 oz., clear 5.50
Tumbler, 12 oz., green 6.00
Tumbler, 12 oz., ruby red 8.00
Tumbler, iced tea, 16 oz., clear 10.50
Tumbler, iced tea, 16 oz., ruby red 11.00
Tumbler, 7" h., footed, clear 8.00
Tumbler, 7" h., footed, green 6.00
Water set: pitcher & 6 tumblers;
    red, 7 pcs. 62.00
Water set: ice lip pitcher & 8
    tumblers; red, 9 pcs. 71.00

CAMEO (Process-etched)

Cameo Tumbler

Bowl, cream soup, 4¾" d., clear 2.50
Bowl, cream soup, 4¾" d., green 47.50
Bowl, nappy, 5½" d., clear 5.00
Bowl, nappy, 5½" d., green 20.00
Bowl, nappy, 5½" d., yellow 21.00
Bowl, nappy, 7" d., green 27.00
Bowl, nappy, 8¼" d., green 23.00
Bowl, nappy, 8¼" d., yellow 21.00
Bowl, 9" oval vegetable, green 14.00
Bowl, 9" oval vegetable, pink 125.00
Bowl, 9" oval vegetable, yellow 20.00
Bowl, soup, flanged rim, 9" d., green . . .28.00
Bowl, 3-footed console, 11" d., green . . .45.00
Bowl, 3-footed console, 11" d., pink 22.00
Bowl, 3-footed console, 11" d., yellow . .50.00
Butter dish, cov., green 127.00
Cake plate, flat, handled, 10½" d.,
    green 73.00
Cake plate, footed, 10" d., green 14.00
Candlesticks, 4" h., green, pr. 76.00
Candy dish, cov., low, green 39.00
Candy dish, cov., low, yellow 51.00
Candy jar, cov., 6½" h., green 89.00
Compote, cone-shaped, 4" h., green . . .18.50
Cookie jar, cov., green 35.00

Creamer, 3" h., green 15.50
Creamer, 3" h., yellow 12.00
Creamer, 4" h., green 15.00
Creamer, 4" h., yellow 15.50
Creamer & open sugar bowl, 3" h.,
  green, pr.........................25.00
Creamer & open sugar bowl, 3" h.,
  pink, pr..........................22.50
Creamer & open sugar bowl, 3" h.,
  yellow, pr........................24.00
Creamer & open sugar bowl, 4" h.,
  green, pr.........................30.00
Cup & saucer, green.................12.50
Cup & saucer, pink 7.75
Cup & saucer, yellow 8.50
Cup & saucer w/ring, green 95.00
Domino tray, 7" d., green 83.00
Goblet, wine, 4" h., green 43.00
Goblet, 6" h., green................33.00
Ice bowl, 3½" h., green.............97.50
Jar, cov., closed handles, 2", green 85.00
Mayonnaise bowl w/ladle, green,
  2 pcs. 18.50
Mayonnaise bowl w/underplate, green,
  2 pcs. 23.00
Mayonnaise set: bowl, underplate & ladle;
  green, 3 pcs. 35.00
Pitcher, syrup or milk, 5¾" h., 20 oz.,
  green 132.00
Pitcher, juice jug, 6" h., 36 oz., green ...44.00
Pitcher, jug, 8½" h., 56 oz., clear ...15.00
Pitcher, jug, 8½" h., 56 oz., green.....36.50
Plate, sherbet, 6" d., clear or yellow.....2.00
Plate, sherbet, 6" d., green 2.50
Plate, luncheon, 8" d., green 7.50
Plate, luncheon, 8" d., pink 18.00
Plate, luncheon, 8" d., yellow 6.00
Plate, salad, 8½" sq., green..........25.00
Plate, salad, 8½" sq., yellow..........5.50
Plate, dinner, 9½" d., clear 6.00
Plate, dinner, 9½" d., green 12.00
Plate, dinner, 9½" d., pink...........31.00
Plate, dinner, 9½" d., yellow 6.50
Plate, sandwich, 10" d., green 9.50
Plate, sandwich, 10" d., pink........32.00
Plate, dinner, closed handles, 10½" d.,
  green 10.00
Plate, grill, closed handles, 10½" d.,
  green 42.50
Plate, grill, closed handles, 10½" d.,
  yellow.............................6.00
Plate, grill, 10½" d., green...........7.00
Plate, grill, 10½" d., yellow..........5.50
Platter, 10½" oval, green 12.50
Platter, 10½" oval, yellow 20.00
Platter, closed handles, 12", green 13.00
Platter, closed handles, 12", yellow 5.50
Relish dish, 7½", green.............15.50
Salt & pepper shakers, green, pr. 47.00
Sandwich server, green..............10.50
Sherbet, 3", green 10.00
Sherbet, 3", pink...................39.00
Sherbet, 3", yellow.................19.00
Sherbet, thin, high stemmed, green 22.00

Sherbet, thin, high stemmed, yellow ...27.50
Sugar bowl, open, 3" h., green 10.00
Sugar bowl, open, 3" h., yellow 11.00
Sugar bowl, open, 4" h., green 14.00
Sugar bowl, open, 4" h., yellow 11.50
Tumbler, juice, footed, 3 oz., green 38.00
Tumbler, juice, 3" h., 5 oz., green 17.50
Tumbler, juice, 3" h., 5 oz., pink 61.00
Tumbler, juice, footed, 5 oz., green 37.50
Tumbler, 4" h., 9 oz., clear 4.00
Tumbler, 4" h., 9 oz., green (ILLUS.) 17.00
Tumbler, 4" h., 9 oz., yellow..........16.00
Tumbler, 4¾" h., 10 oz., green 19.00
Tumbler, 4¾" h., 10 oz., pink 60.00
Tumbler, 4¾" h., 10 oz., yellow 23.50
Tumbler, footed, 5" h., 9 oz., green ...18.50
Tumbler, footed, 5" h., 9 oz., yellow ...14.00
Tumbler, 5" h., 11 oz., green 21.00
Tumbler, 5" h., 11 oz., yellow.........36.00
Tumbler, 5¼" h., 14 oz., green 38.00
Tumbler, footed, 6" h., 11 oz., green ...29.00
Tumbler, footed, 6" h., 11 oz., yellow ...13.00
Vase, 5¾" h., green.................99.00
Vase, 8½" h., green.................18.50
Water bottle, no stopper, green 25.00
Water bottle w/stopper, green 80.00
Water bottle, 8½" h., green frosted 26.00
Water bottle, 8½" h., dark green
  "White House Vinegar" base 18.00
Wine, green........................40.00
Wine set: decanter & 5 wine goblets;
  green, 6 pcs. 275.00

CHERRY BLOSSOM (Process-etched)

Delfite Junior Pieces

Bowl, nappy, 4¾" d., Delfite 9.00
Bowl, nappy, 4¾" d., green 10.00
Bowl, nappy, 4¾" d., pink 8.50
Bowl, nappy, 5¾" d., Delfite 12.50
Bowl, nappy, 5¾" d., green or pink 20.00
Bowl, soup, 7¾" d., green 36.00
Bowl, soup, 7¾" d., pink.............35.00
Bowl, nappy, 8½" d., Delfite 35.00
Bowl, nappy, 8½" d., green 20.00
Bowl, nappy, 8½" d., pink 16.50
Bowl, handled, 9" d., Delfite 16.00
Bowl, handled, 9" d., green 18.50
Bowl, handled, 9" d., pink............17.00
Bowl, 9" oval vegetable, green 21.00
Bowl, 9" oval vegetable, pink..........19.50
Bowl, fruit, 3-footed, 10½" d., green ...42.00
Bowl, fruit, 3-footed, 10½" d., pink 37.00
Butter dish, cov., green.............79.00
Butter dish, cov., pink 61.00

Cake plate, 10¼" d., green 16.50
Cake plate, 10¼" d., pink 17.50
Coaster, green 8.50
Coaster, pink 10.50
Creamer, clear 9.50
Creamer, Delfite 15.00
Creamer, green 12.50
Creamer, pink 10.50
Creamer & cov. sugar bowl, green,
    pr. 29.00
Creamer & cov. sugar bowl, pink, pr. . . . 31.00
Creamer & open sugar bowl, Delfite,
    pr. 28.00
Creamer & open sugar bowl, green,
    pr. 19.50
Creamer & open sugar bowl, pink,
    pr. 18.00
Cup & saucer, Delfite 15.50
Cup & saucer, green 17.50
Cup & saucer, pink 16.00
Mug, 8 oz., green 151.00
Mug, 8 oz., pink 136.00
Pitcher, jug, overall patt., 6½" h.,
    36 oz., Delfite 70.00
Pitcher, jug, overall patt., 6½" h.,
    36 oz., green 37.50
Pitcher, jug, overall patt., 6½" h.,
    36 oz., pink 34.00
Pitcher, jug, cone-shaped, patt. top,
    8" h., 36 oz., Delfite 75.00
Pitcher, jug, cone-shaped, patt. top,
    8" h., 36 oz., green 35.00
Pitcher, jug, cone-shaped, patt. top,
    8" h., 36 oz., pink 38.00
Pitcher, straight side, patt. top, 8" h.,
    42 oz., Delfite 89.00
Pitcher, straight side, patt. top, 8" h.,
    42 oz., green 32.50
Pitcher, straight side, patt. top, 8" h.,
    42 oz., pink 34.00
Plate, sherbet, 6" d., Delfite 7.00
Plate, sherbet, 6" d., green or pink 5.00
Plate, salad, 7" d., green 13.00
Plate, salad, 7" d., pink 13.50
Plate, dinner, 9" d., Delfite 13.00
Plate, dinner, 9" d., green 15.00
Plate, dinner, 9" d., pink 12.00
Plate, grill, 9" d., green 15.00
Plate, grill, 9" d., pink 15.50
Platter, 11" oval, Delfite 34.00
Platter, 11" oval, green 19.00
Platter, 11" oval, pink 20.00
Platter, 13" oval, Delfite or green 36.00
Platter, 13" oval, pink 39.00
Platter, divided, 13" oval, green or
    pink 34.00
Sherbet, Delfite 12.50
Sherbet, green 11.50
Sherbet, pink 10.50
Sugar bowl, cov., clear 17.00
Sugar bowl, cov., green 21.00
Sugar bowl, cov., pink 20.00
Sugar bowl, open, Delfite 14.00
Sugar bowl, open, green 10.50

Sugar bowl, open, pink 9.00
Tray, sandwich, handled, 10½" d.,
    Delfite 15.00
Tray, sandwich, handled, 10½" d.,
    green 16.00
Tray, sandwich, handled, 10½" d., pink . 13.50
Tumbler, juice, footed, 3½" h.,
    4 oz., Delfite 15.00
Tumbler, juice, footed, 3½" h., 4 oz.,
    green 14.50
Tumbler, juice, footed, 3½" h., 4 oz.,
    pink 11.50
Tumbler, patt. top, 3½" h., 5 oz.,
    green 14.00
Tumbler, patt. top, 3½" h., 5 oz.,
    pink 12.00
Tumbler, patt. top, 4" h., 9 oz.,
    clear 9.00
Tumbler, patt. top, 4" h., 9 oz.,
    Delfite 17.50
Tumbler, patt. top, 4" h., 9 oz.,
    green 15.00
Tumbler, patt. top, 4" h., 9 oz., pink . . . 12.00
Tumbler, footed, 4½" h., 9 oz., clear . . . 10.00
Tumbler, footed, 4½" h., 9 oz., Delfite . . 16.00
Tumbler, footed, 4½" h., 9 oz., green . . . 23.00
Tumbler, footed, 4½" h., 9 oz., pink . . . 22.00
Tumbler, patt. top, 5" h., 12 oz.,
    Delfite 16.00
Tumbler, patt. top, 5" h., 12 oz.,
    green 46.50
Tumbler, patt. top, 5" h., 12 oz., pink . . . 33.00

JUNIOR SET:
Creamer, Delfite 27.00
Creamer, pink 26.00
Creamer & sugar bowl, Delfite, pr.
    (ILLUS) 45.00
Creamer & sugar bowl, pink, pr. 47.50
Cup, Delfite 26.00
Cup, pink 28.00
Cup & saucer, Delfite (ILLUS.) 25.00
Cup & saucer, pink 24.00
Plate, 6" d., Delfite 7.50
Plate, 6" d., pink 7.00
Saucer, Delfite 4.00
Saucer, pink 5.00
Sugar bowl, Delfite 24.00
Sugar bowl, pink 25.00
14 pc. set, Delfite 207.50
14 pc. set, pink 172.00

CLOVERLEAF (Process-etched)
Ash tray, 4", black 47.50
Ash tray, 5¾", black 68.00
Bowl, dessert, 4" d., green 12.50
Bowl, dessert, 4" d., pink 9.00
Bowl, dessert, 4" d., yellow 15.00
Bowl, nappy, 5" d., green 14.50
Bowl, nappy, 5" d., yellow 22.00
Bowl, deep, 7" d., green 26.00
Bowl, deep, 7" d., yellow 36.00
Bowl, deep, 8" d., green 38.00
Candy dish, cov., green 36.00
Candy dish, cov., yellow 86.50

Creamer, black 12.00
Creamer, green 7.50
Creamer, yellow 9.00
Creamer & open sugar bowl, black,
   pr. 21.00
Creamer & open sugar bowl, green,
   pr. 15.50
Creamer & open sugar bowl, yellow,
   pr. 24.00
Cup & saucer, black 13.00
Cup & saucer, clear 6.50
Cup & saucer, green 7.00
Cup & saucer, pink 6.00
Cup & saucer, yellow 12.00
Plate, sherbet, 6" d., black 22.00
Plate, sherbet, 6" d., green or yellow 4.50
Plate, salad, 8" d., black 10.50
Plate, salad, 8" d., green 4.50
Plate, salad, 8" d., pink 5.00
Plate, grill, 10" d., green or yellow 14.00
Salt & pepper shakers, black, pr. 67.00
Salt & pepper shakers, green, pr. 26.00
Salt & pepper shakers, yellow, pr. 82.00
Sherbet, black 12.50
Sherbet, clear 4.00
Sherbet, green 5.00
Sherbet, pink 4.50
Sherbet, yellow 7.50
Sugar bowl, open, black 10.50

Cloverleaf Sugar Bowl

Sugar bowl, open, green (ILLUS.) 8.00
Sugar bowl, open, yellow 9.00
Tumbler, 3¾" h., 10 oz., green 21.00
Tumbler, 3¾" h., 10 oz., pink 22.50
Tumbler, 4" h., 9 oz., green 24.50
Tumbler, 4" h., 9 oz., pink 17.00
Tumbler, footed, 5¾" h., 10 oz.,
   green 17.50
Tumbler, footed, 5¾" h., 10 oz.,
   yellow 19.00
Tumbler, footed, 6½" h., 13 oz.,
   green 18.50
Tumbler, footed, 6½" h., 13 oz.,
   yellow 21.00

COLONIAL or Knife & Fork (Press-mold)

Bowl, berry, 4" d., clear 4.00
Bowl, berry, 4" d., green 8.50
Bowl, berry, 4" d., pink 19.00
Bowl, cream soup, 4½" d., green 34.00

Bowl, cream soup, 4½" d., pink 26.00
Bowl, nappy, 4½" d., clear 7.50
Bowl, nappy, 4½" d., green 8.00
Bowl, nappy, 5½" d., green 7.50
Bowl, nappy, 5½" d., pink 22.50
Bowl, soup, 7" d., clear 8.00
Bowl, soup, 7" d., green 37.00
Bowl, soup, 7" d., pink 28.00
Bowl, 9" d., clear . . . . .7.00 to 9.50
Bowl, 9" d., green 17.00
Bowl, 9" d., pink 12.00
Bowl, 10" oval vegetable,
   clear . . . . .9.50 to 14.00

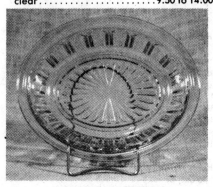

Colonial Vegetable Bowl

Bowl, 10" oval vegetable, green
   (ILLUS.) 19.00
Bowl, 10" oval vegetable,
   pink . . . . .15.00 to 22.00
Butter dish, cov., clear 26.00
Butter dish, cov., green 45.50
Butter dish, cov., pink 250.00
Celery or spooner, clear . . . . . . .35.00 to 50.00
Celery or spooner, green 105.00
Celery or spooner, pink 86.50
Cheese dish, wooden base, dome
   cover, clear 65.00
Creamer, clear 8.00
Creamer, green 14.50
Creamer, pink . . . . .6.00 to 10.00
Creamer & cov. sugar bowl, clear,
   pr. 21.50
Creamer & cov. sugar bowl, green,
   pr. 36.00
Creamer & cov. sugar bowl, pink,
   pr. 65.00
Creamer & open sugar bowl, clear,
   pr. 12.50
Creamer & open sugar bowl, green,
   pr. 23.50
Cup & saucer, clear 6.00
Cup & saucer, green 12.00
Cup & saucer, opaque white 14.00
Cup & saucer, pink 9.00
Goblet, cordial, 3¾" h., 1 oz., clear 14.00
Goblet, cordial, 3¾" h., 1 oz., green
   (ILLUS.) 22.00
Goblet, cordial, 3¾" h., 1 oz., pink 15.00
Goblet, cocktail, 4" h., 3 oz., clear 8.00
Goblet, cocktail, 4" h., 3 oz., green 17.00

Colonial Cordial & Wine

Goblet, wine, 4½" h., 2½ oz., green
  (ILLUS.) 19.00
Goblet, claret, 5" h., 4 oz., clear 11.00
Goblet, claret, 5" h., 4 oz., green 18.50
Goblet, 5¾" h., 8½ oz., clear 11.00
Goblet, 5¾" h., 8½ oz., green. 20.50
Pitcher, 7" h., 54 oz., clear 20.00
Pitcher, 7" h., 54 oz., green 38.00
Pitcher, 7" h., 54 oz., pink 33.00
Pitcher, 7½" h., 67 oz., clear 26.00
Pitcher, 7½" h., 67 oz., green or
  pink. 43.00
Plate, sherbet, 6½" d., clear 2.50
Plate, sherbet, 6½" d., green 3.50
Plate, sherbet, 6½" d., pink 3.00
Plate, luncheon, 8½" d., clear 4.00
Plate, luncheon, 8½" d., green 6.50
Plate, luncheon, 8½" d., pink 5.00
Plate, dinner, 10" d., clear 11.00
Plate, dinner, 10" d., green 40.00
Plate, dinner, 10" d., opaque white. 12.00
Plate, dinner, 10" d., pink 25.00
Plate, grill, 10" d., clear 8.00
Plate, grill, 10" d., green 18.00
Plate, grill, 10" d., pink 14.00
Platter, 12" oval, clear. 11.00
Platter, 12" oval, green 14.50
Platter, 12" oval, pink 17.00
Salt & pepper shakers, clear, pr. 43.00
Salt & pepper shakers, green, pr. 105.00
Sherbet, clear 5.00
Sherbet, green 9.50
Sherbet, pink. 6.00
Sugar bowl, cov., clear 14.50
Sugar bowl, cov., green 21.50
Sugar bowl, cov., pink . . . . .18.50 to 23.00
Sugar bowl, open, clear 6.00
Sugar bowl, open, green. 10.00
Tumbler, whiskey, 2½" h., 1½ oz.,
  clear 4.00
Tumbler, whiskey, 2½" h., 1½ oz.,
  green 10.00
Tumbler, whiskey, 2½" h., 1½ oz.,
  pink. 8.50
Tumbler, juice, 3" h., 5 oz., clear 4.00
Tumbler, juice, 3" h., 5 oz., green 18.00

Tumbler, juice, 3" h., 5 oz., pink 9.00
Tumbler, cordial, footed, 3¼" h., 3 oz.,
  clear 7.00
Tumbler, cordial, footed, 3¼" h., 3 oz.,
  green 17.00
Tumbler, cordial, footed, 3¼" h., 3 oz.,
  pink. 10.00
Tumbler, claret, footed, 4" h., 5 oz.,
  clear 7.00
Tumbler, claret, footed, 4" h., 5 oz.,
  green 18.00
Tumbler, claret, footed, 4" h., 5 oz.,
  pink. 13.00
Tumbler, 4" h., 9 oz., clear 6.00
Tumbler, 4" h., 9 oz., green 16.50
Tumbler, 4" h., 9 oz., pink 8.50
Tumbler, cordial, footed, 5¼" h.,
  10 oz., clear 7.00
Tumbler, cordial, footed, 5¼" h.,
  10 oz., green .25.00
Tumbler, cordial, footed, 5¼" h.,
  10 oz., pink 16.00
Tumbler, 10 oz., clear 12.00
Tumbler, 10 oz., green. 18.50
Tumbler, 10 oz., pink. 15.00
Tumbler, iced tea, 12 oz., green 33.50
Tumbler, iced tea, 12 oz., pink 21.00
Tumbler, lemonade, 15 oz., clear 10.50
Tumbler, lemonade, 15 oz., green. 67.00
Tumbler, lemonade, 15 oz., pink 30.00

COLUMBIA (Press-Mold)
Bowl, cereal, 5" d., clear. 8.50
Bowl, low soup, 8" d., clear 9.00
Bowl, salad, 8½" d., clear 10.50
Bowl, 10½" d., ruffled edge, clear 12.00
Bowl, 10½" d., ruffled edge, pink 14.00
Butter dish, cov., clear. 14.00
Butter dish w/metal lid, clear. 20.00
Cup & saucer, clear 5.50
Plate, bread & butter, 6" d., clear 1.50
Plate, luncheon, 9½" d., clear 4.00
Plate, luncheon, 9½" d., pink 9.50
Plate, chop, 11¾" d., clear 7.00

CUBE or Cubist (Press-mold)
Bowl, dessert, 4½" d., clear 1.00
Bowl, dessert, 4½" d., green or pink 4.00
Bowl, 4½" d., deep, clear. 3.50
Bowl, 4½" d., deep, green or pink 4.50
Bowl, salad, 6½" d., clear 4.00
Bowl, salad, 6½" d., green. 9.00
Bowl, salad, 6½" d., pink 6.50
Bowl, 7 3/8" d., scalloped edge,
  green or pink 9.00
Butter dish, cov., green 47.50
Butter dish, cov., pink 46.00
Candy jar, cov., green, 7½" h. 20.50
Candy jar, cov., pink, 7½" h. 18.50
Coaster, clear, 3¼" d. 18.00
Coaster, green, 3¼" d. 4.50
Coaster, pink, 3¼" d. 4.00
Creamer, clear, 2" h. 3.50
Creamer, green, 2" h. 4.00

Creamer, pink, 2" h. 3.00
Creamer, clear, 3" h. 2.00
Creamer, green, 3" h. 5.50
Creamer, pink, 3" h. 4.00
Creamer & cov. sugar bowl, green,
  3", pr. 18.50
Creamer & cov. sugar bowl, pink,
  3", pr. 12.50
Creamer & open sugar bowl, clear,
  2", pr. 2.50
Creamer & open sugar bowl, green,
  2", pr. 9.50
Creamer & open sugar bowl, pink,
  2", pr. 4.50
Creamer, open sugar bowl & tray,
  clear, 3 pcs. . . . . .6.00 to 10.00
Cup & saucer, green. 8.00
Cup & saucer, pink 6.00
Pitcher, 8¾" h., 45 oz., green 160.00
Pitcher, 8¾" h., 45 oz., pink 125.00
Plate, sherbet, 6" d., clear 1.00
Plate, sherbet, 6" d., green or pink 2.00
Plate, luncheon, 8" d., green 4.00
Plate, luncheon, 8" d., pink 3.50
Powder jar, cov., 3-legged, clear. 8.50
Powder jar, cov., 3-legged, green 14.00
Powder jar, cov., 3-legged, pink 12.00
Salt & pepper shakers, clear, pr. 12.50
Salt & pepper shakers, green, pr. 23.00
Salt & pepper shakers, pink, pr. 21.50
Sherbet, clear 2.00
Sherbet, green 5.00
Sherbet, pink. 4.50
Sugar bowl, cov., clear, 3" 3.00
Sugar bowl, cov., green, 3" 11.50
Sugar bowl, cov., pink, 3" 9.50
Sugar bowl, open, clear or pink, 2" 2.00
Sugar bowl, open, green, 2" 4.00
Sugar bowl, open, green or pink, 3" 5.00
Tray for 3" creamer & sugar, clear,
  7½". 3.50
Tumbler, 4" h., 9 oz., green 32.50
Tumbler, 4" h., 9 oz., pink . . . . .20.00 to 25.00

DAISY or Number 620 (Press-mold)

Bowl, berry, 4½" d., amber 5.50
Bowl, berry, 4½" d., clear 3.50
Bowl, cream soup, 4½" d., amber. 5.50
Bowl, cream soup, 4½" d., clear 3.50
Bowl, cereal, 6" d., amber 16.00
Bowl, cereal, 6" d., clear . . . . . . .9.50 to 15.00
Bowl, deep berry, 7 3/8" d., amber 13.50
Bowl, deep berry, 9 3/8" d., amber 18.00
Bowl, deep berry, 9 3/8" d., clear 7.00
Bowl, 10" oval vegetable, amber. 12.00
Bowl, 10" oval vegetable, clear 6.50
Creamer, footed, amber 5.00
Creamer, footed, clear 3.00
Creamer & sugar bowl, footed,
  amber, pr. 11.00
Cup & saucer, amber 5.00
Cup & saucer, clear 4.50
Plate, sherbet, 6" d., amber or clear 2.00
Plate, salad, 7 3/8" d., amber 6.00

Plate, luncheon, 8 3/8" d., amber 4.50
Plate, luncheon, 8 3/8" d., clear 2.50
Plate, dinner, 9 3/8" d., amber 4.50
Plate, dinner, 9 3/8" d., clear 3.00
Plate, grill, 10 3/8" d., amber 9.00
Plate, grill, 10 3/8" d., clear 4.00
Plate, cake or sandwich, 11½" d.,
  amber. 8.00
Plate, cake or sandwich, 11½" d.,
  clear 5.50
Platter, 10¾", amber. 10.00
Platter, 10¾", clear 5.50
Relish dish, 3-part, amber, 8 3/8" 13.50
Relish dish, 3-part, clear, 8 3/8" 7.50
Sherbet, amber. 5.00
Sherbet, clear 3.50
Sugar bowl, amber. 5.00
Sugar bowl, clear .3.50
Tumbler, 9 oz., footed, amber 13.50
Tumbler, 9 oz., footed, clear 7.00
Tumbler, 12 oz., footed, amber 27.00
Tumbler, 12 oz., footed, clear 15.00

DIAMOND QUILTED or Flat Diamond (Press-mold)

Bowl, cream soup, 4¾" d., blue. 11.00
Bowl, cream soup, 4¾" d., green 9.00
Bowl, cream soup, 4¾" d., pink. 7.50
Bowl, cereal, 5" d., pink 5.00
Bowl, single handle, 5½" d., black 15.00
Bowl, single handle, 5½" d., blue 11.00
Bowl, single handle, 5½" d., green. 9.00
Bowl, single handle, 5½" d., pink 8.00
Bowl, 7" d., black 22.50
Bowl, 7" d., blue 14.50
Bowl, 7" d., green. 9.50
Bowl, 7" d., pink .7.50
Candlesticks, low, black, pr. 25.00
Candlesticks, low, blue, pr. 23.00
Candlesticks, low, green, pr. 12.00
Candlesticks, low, pink, pr. 14.00
Coaster, pink, 3" d. 4.00
Console bowl, rolled edge, pink 25.00
Creamer, black 12.50
Creamer, blue or green. 8.50
Creamer, pink. 6.00
Creamer, red. 35.00
Creamer & sugar bowl, black, pr. 21.00
Creamer & sugar bowl, blue, pr. 20.00
Creamer & sugar bowl, green or pink,
  pr. 16.00
Cup & saucer, black 11.50
Cup & saucer, pink 8.00
Ice bucket, blue . . . . .25.00 to 32.00
Plate, sherbet, 6" d., black 5.00
Plate, sherbet, 6" d., green 2.50
Plate, sherbet, 6" d., pink 3.00
Plate, salad, 7" d., black or green 5.00
Plate, salad, 7" d., blue 5.50
Plate, luncheon, 8" d., black 10.50
Plate, luncheon, 8" d., blue 9.00
Plate, luncheon, 8" d., green 4.50
Plate, luncheon, 8" d., pink 5.00
Plate, sandwich, 14" d., green 40.00

Sherbet, black 8.00
Sherbet, blue or green 6.50
Sherbet, pink 5.50
Sugar bowl, blue 8.00
Sugar bowl, green or pink 6.50
Tumbler, whiskey, 1½ oz., green 7.50

DIANA (Press-mold)

Child's Cup & Saucer

Bowl, cereal, 5" d., amber or pink 4.00
Bowl, cereal, 5" d., clear 3.00
Bowl, cream soup, 5½" d., amber 6.00
Bowl, cream soup, 5½" d., clear 5.00
Bowl, cream soup, 5½" d., pink 3.00
Bowl, salad, 9" d., amber 7.00
Bowl, salad, 9" d., clear 5.50
Bowl, salad, 9" d., pink 8.50
Bowl, fruit console, 11" d., amber 8.50
Bowl, fruit console, 11" d., clear 4.00
Bowl, scalloped compote, 12" d., clear . . .7.00
Candy jar, cov., round, amber 26.00
Candy jar, cov., round, clear 13.00
Candy jar, cov., round, pink 22.00
Coaster - ash tray, 3½", amber 5.00
Coaster - ash tray, 3½", clear 3.00
Coaster - ash tray, 3½", pink 3.50
Creamer, oval, amber 5.50
Creamer, oval, clear 3.50
Creamer, oval, pink 6.50
Creamer & open sugar bowl, oval,
    amber, pr. . . . . .7.00 to 15.00
Creamer & open sugar bowl, oval,
    pink, pr. 5.00
Cup & saucer, demitasse, clear 4.50
Cup & saucer, demitasse, pink 12.50
Cup & saucer, amber 8.00
Cup & saucer, clear 5.00
Cup & saucer, pink 6.50
Plate, bread & butter, 6" d., amber 2.00
Plate, bread & butter, 6" d., clear 1.25
Plate, bread & butter, 6" d., pink 1.50
Plate, dinner, 9½" d., amber 6.50
Plate, dinner, 9½" d., clear 4.50
Plate, dinner, 9½" d., pink 7.00
Plate, sandwich, 11¾" d., amber 7.00
Plate, sandwich, 11¾" d., clear 4.50
Platter, 12" oval, amber 8.00
Platter, 12" oval, clear 6.50
Platter, 12" oval, pink 5.50

Salt & pepper shakers, amber, pr. 62.50
Salt & pepper shakers, clear, pr. 26.00
Salt & pepper shakers, pink, pr. 32.50
Sherbet, amber 7.00
Sherbet, pink 9.50
Sugar bowl, open, oval, amber 5.00
Sugar bowl, open, oval, clear 4.00
Tumbler, 4 1/8", 9 oz., clear 10.00
Tumbler, 4 1/8", 9 oz., pink 8.50
Water set: pitcher & 6 tumblers; green,
    7 pcs. 125.00
Junior set: 6 cups, saucer & plates
    w/round rack; clear (ILLUS. of cup &
    saucer) 38.00

DOGWOOD or Apple Blossom or Wild Rose (Process-etched)

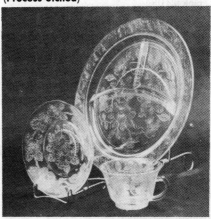

Dogwood Pattern

Bowl, cereal or dessert, 5½" d., clear . . .6.00
Bowl, cereal or dessert, 5½" d., green. .15.00
Bowl, cereal or dessert, 5½" d., pink . . .13.50
Bowl, nappy, 8½" d., Cremax 28.00
Bowl, nappy, 8½" d., green 55.00
Bowl, nappy, 8½" d., pink 32.00
Bowl, fruit, 10¼" d., Cremax 60.00
Bowl, fruit, 10¼" d., green 105.00
Bowl, fruit, 10¼" d., pink 130.00
Cake plate, 13" d., green 63.50
Cake plate, 13" d., pink 74.00
Creamer, thin, 2¾" h., green 36.00
Creamer, thin, 2¾" h., pink 11.50
Creamer, thick, 3¼" h., pink 13.00
Creamer & open sugar bowl, thin,
    2¾" h., green, pr. . . . . .50.00 to 75.00
Creamer & open sugar bowl, thin,
    2¾" h., pink, pr. 20.00
Creamer & open sugar bowl, thick,
    3¼" h., green, pr. 56.00
Creamer & open sugar bowl, thick,
    3¼" h., pink, pr. 23.00
Cup & saucer, Cremax 33.50
Cup & saucer, green 19.00
Cup & saucer, pink (ILLUS.) 10.00
Pitcher, jug, 8" h., green . . . . . .25.00 to 30.00
Pitcher, jug, 8" h., pink . . . . .30.00 to 45.00

Pitcher, jug, 8" h., hand-decorated,
  clear 185.00
Pitcher, jug, 8" h., hand-decorated,
  green 500.00
Pitcher, jug, 8" h., hand-decorated,
  pink. 120.00
Plate, bread & butter, 6" d., green 4.00
Plate, bread & butter, 6" d., pink 4.50
Plate, luncheon, 8" d., clear 2.50
Plate, luncheon, 8" d., green 5.00
Plate, luncheon, 8" d., pink 4.00
Plate, dinner, 9¼" d., pink 16.50
Plate, grill, 10½" d., overall patt.,
  green 18.00
Plate, grill, 10¼" d., overall patt.,
  pink 13.00
Plate, grill, 10½" d., border patt.,
  pink (ILLUS.) 13.00
Plate, salver, 12" d., Monax 23.00
Plate, salver, 12" d., pink 19.50
Platter, 12" oval, pink 265.00
Sherbet, low foot, pink 16.50
Sugar bowl, open, thin, 2½" h., green . .29.00
Sugar bowl, open, thin, 2½" h., pink 9.00
Sugar bowl, open, thick, 3¼" h.,
  green 30.00
Sugar bowl, open, thick, 3¼" h., pink . .10.00
Tid bit set, 8" & 12" plates
  w/center handle, pink 44.00
Tumbler, plain, 3½" h., 5 oz., pink 4.00
Tumbler, decorated, 4" h., 10 oz.,
  green 58.00
Tumbler, decorated, 4" h., 10 oz., pink . .21.50
Tumbler, plain, 4" h., 10 oz., green
  or pink 5.50
Tumbler, decorated, 4¾" h., 11 oz.,
  green 59.50
Tumbler, decorated, 4¾" h., 11 oz.,
  pink. 28.00
Tumbler, plain, 4¾" h., 11 oz., green . . .10.00
Tumbler, plain, 4¾" h., 11 oz., pink 7.00
Tumbler, decorated, 5" h., 12 oz., pink . .31.00
Tumbler, plain, 5" h., 13 oz., pink 13.50
Water set: 8" decorated pitcher & six
  4" h. decorated tumblers; pink,
  7 pcs. . . . . .225.00 to 300.00

DORIC (Press-mold)

Doric Sandwich Tray

Bowl, nappy, 4½" d., Delfite 6.00
Bowl, nappy, 4½" d., green 5.50
Bowl, nappy, 4½" d., pink 5.00
Bowl, cereal, 5½" d., green 24.50
Bowl, cereal, 5½" d., pink 21.00
Bowl, nappy, 8¼" d., clear 10.00
Bowl, nappy, 8¼" d., green 13.00
Bowl, nappy, 8¼" d., pink 9.50
Bowl, handled, 9" d., green . . . . . . .9.50 to 12.00
Bowl, handled, 9" d., pink. 9.00
Bowl, 9" oval vegetable, green 13.00
Bowl, 9" oval vegetable, pink 11.50
Butter dish, cov., green 76.50
Butter dish, cov., pink 58.00
Cake plate, 10" d., green 14.00
Cake plate, 10" d., pink 11.50
Candy dish, 3-section, 6", Delfite. 6.00
Candy dish, 3-section, 6", green 8.00
Candy dish, 3-section, 6", pink. 5.00
Candy jar, cov., 8" h., green or pink 28.00
Coaster, 3" d., green 10.50
Coaster, 3" d., pink 9.00
Creamer, green 10.50
Creamer, pink 8.50
Creamer & cov. sugar bowl, green,
  pr. 36.00
Creamer & cov. sugar bowl, pink, pr. . . .26.50
Cup & saucer, green. 9.50
Cup & saucer, pink 8.50
Pitcher, jug, 5" or 6" h., 36 oz.,
  green 29.50
Pitcher, jug, 5" or 6" h., 36 oz.,
  pink. 28.50
Pitcher, 7" h., 47 oz., pink 350.00
Plate, sherbet, 6" d., green 3.00
Plate, sherbet, 6" d., pink 2.50
Plate, salad, 7" d., green 12.50
Plate, salad, 7" d., pink . . . . .9.50 to 12.00
Plate, dinner, 9" d., green 10.00
Plate, dinner, 9" d., pink 7.50
Plate, grill, 9" d., green . . . . . . .10.00 to 15.00
Plate, grill, 9" d., pink 8.00
Platter, 12" oval, green or pink 13.00
Relish dish, 4 x 4", green. 7.50
Relish dish, 4 x 4", pink 6.00
Relish dish, 4 x 8", green 9.00
Relish dish, 4 x 8", pink 7.00
Relish dish, 8 x 8", green 16.00
Relish dish, 8 x 8", pink 10.00
Relish inserts in metal holder,
  sq., green 39.00
Relish inserts in metal holder, sq.,
  pink. 40.00
Relish tray, 4-part, handled, green 38.50
Relish tray, 4-part, handled,
  pink . . . . .35.00 to 40.00
Salt & pepper shakers, clear, pr. 22.00
Salt & pepper shakers, green, pr. 31.00
Salt & pepper shakers, pink, pr. 27.00
Sherbet, Delfite 4.50
Sherbet, green .9.00
Sherbet, pink. 7.00
Sugar bowl, cov., green 26.50
Sugar bowl, cov., pink 21.00

Tray, sandwich, handled, 10" d.,
  green or pink (ILLUS.) 10.00
Tumbler, footed, 4" h., 10 oz., green ...48.50
Tumbler, footed, 4" h., 10 oz., pink.....21.50
Tumbler, 4½" h., 9 oz., green 53.00
Tumbler, 4½" h., 9 oz., pink..........26.00
Tumbler, footed, 5" h., 13 oz., green ...51.50
Tumbler, footed, 5" h., 13 oz., pink.....35.50

DORIC & PANSY (Press-mold)

Doric & Pansy Cup & Saucer

Bowl, berry, 4½" d., clear or green 5.00
Bowl, berry, 4½" d., pink 6.00
Bowl, berry, 4½" d., ultramarine 10.50
Bowl, large berry, 8" d., clear 16.00
Bowl, large berry, 8" d., pink 22.00
Bowl, large berry, 8" d., ultra-
  marine...................45.00 to 60.00
Bowl, handled, 9" d., clear 16.50
Bowl, handled, 9" d., ultramarine 21.00
Butter dish, cov., ultramarine 600.00
Creamer, ultramarine 145.00
Creamer & open sugar bowl, ultra-
  marine, pr. ....300.00 to 325.00
Cup & saucer, clear 11.00
Cup & saucer, ultramarine (ILLUS.) 19.00
Plate, sherbet, 6" d., green 8.00
Plate, sherbet, 6" d., pink 5.50
Plate, sherbet, 6" d., ultramarine 7.00
Plate, salad, 7" d., ultramarine 26.00
Plate, dinner, 9" d., green 19.00
Plate, dinner, 9" d., ultramarine 20.00
Salt & pepper shakers, ultramarine,
  pr.................................380.00
Sugar bowl, open, pink 50.00
Sugar bowl, open, ultramarine 130.00
Tray, handled, 10", green 9.00
Tray, handled, 10", ultramarine........20.00
Tumbler, 4½", 9 oz., ultramarine 36.00

CHILDREN'S PRETTY POLLY PARTY DISHES
Creamer, pink.......................26.50
Creamer, ultramarine 31.00
Creamer & sugar bowl, pink, pr. 40.00
Creamer & sugar bowl, ultramarine,
  pr. ....55.00 to 70.00
Cup & saucer, pink 25.50
Cup & saucer, ultramarine 31.00
Plate, pink 6.00
Plate, ultramarine 7.50
Sugar bowl, pink....................25.50
Sugar bowl, ultramarine 27.00

14 piece set, pink 170.00
14 piece set, ultramarine 210.00

ENGLISH HOBNAIL (Handmade - not true Depression)

English Hobnail Nut Cup

Ash tray, 4½" d., clear 20.00
Ash tray, 4½" d., pink 26.00
Bowl, nappy, 4½" d., amber 7.50
Bowl, nappy, 4½" d., clear............4.25
Bowl, nappy, 4½" d., green 7.00
Bowl, nappy, 4½" d., pink 11.50
Bowl, cream soup, 4¾" d., clear 5.00
Bowl, cream soup, 4¾" d., pink 11.00
Bowl, mayonnaise, 6" d., green 10.00
Bowl, nappy, 6½" d., clear 6.50
Bowl, nappy, 6½" d., green 9.00
Bowl, nappy, 6½" d., pink 8.00
Bowl, 6½" d., turquoise 22.50
Bowl, fruit, 2-handled, footed, 8" d.,
  amber.............................35.00
Bowl, fruit, 2-handled, footed, 8" d.,
  clear..............................20.00
Bowl, fruit, 2-handled, footed, 8" d.,
  green 25.50
Bowl, fruit, 2-handled, footed, 8" d.,
  pink...............................22.00
Bowl, nappy, 8" d., green 26.00
Bowl, rounded & flared sides, 12" d.,
  blue...............................50.00
Bowl, rounded & flared sides, 12" d.,
  clear..............................14.00
Bowl, rounded & flared sides, 12" d.,
  green 23.00
Bowl, canted (bell) sides, 12" d., clear ..35.00
Bowl, canted (bell) sides, 12" d.,
  turquoise..........................77.00
Candlesticks, 3½" h., amber or clear,
  pr.................................20.00
Candlesticks, 3½" h., turquoise, pr.....67.50
Candlesticks, 9" h., amber, pr. 75.00
Candlesticks, 9" h., clear, pr..........30.00
Candlesticks, 9" h., green, pr..........75.00
Candlesticks, 9" h., pink, pr. 50.00
Candy dish, cov., amber 35.00
Candy dish, cov., clear 20.00
Candy dish, cov., green..............60.50
Candy dish, cov., pink 47.50
Celery tray, 12" l., clear 7.50

Cigarette jar & cover, clear 12.50
Cigarette jar & cover, pink 22.00
Coaster, clear, 5½" d. 4.50
Cologne bottle, blue 30.00
Cologne bottle, clear 23.50
Cologne bottle, green 28.00
Cologne bottle, pink 29.00
Cologne bottle, turquoise 31.00
Cologne bottles w/stoppers, turquoise,
   pr. 125.00
Compote, 5" d., rounded sides, clear . . .12.00
Creamer, clear 8.50
Creamer, pink. 17.00
Creamer, turquoise 33.75
Creamer & open sugar bowl, clear,
   pr. 14.50
Cruet, oil, 6 oz., clear 21.50
Cup & saucer, clear 6.00
Cup & saucer, green or pink 35.00
Dish, cov., 3-footed, clear. 35.00
Dish, cov., 3-footed, green 59.50
Dish, cov., 3-footed, pink 55.00
Egg cup, clear 12.00
Finger bowl, 4½" d., clear 4.50
Flip jar, cov., amber. 225.00
Goblet, cordial, 1 oz., clear 14.00
Goblet, wine, 2 oz., clear 10.00
Goblet, cocktail, 3 oz., clear. 6.50
Goblet, claret, 5 oz., clear 7.00
Goblet, claret, 5 oz., green 20.00
Goblet, claret, 5 oz., pink 12.50
Goblet, 6¼" h., 8 oz., clear 8.00
Goblet, 6¼" h., 8 oz., green . . .20.00 to 25.00
Goblet, 6¼" h., 8 oz., pink 19.50
Goblet, 6¼" h., 8 oz., topaz 12.00
Goblet, 6¼" h., 8 oz., turquoise 44.00
Ivy ball, clear. 10.00
Lamp, 6¼" h., clear. . . . . .24.00 to 36.00
Lamp, 6¼" h., green 70.00
Lamp, 6¼" h., pink 58.00
Lamp, 9¼" h., amber. 115.00
Lamp, 9¼" h., clear 34.50
Lamp, 9¼" h., green or pink 78.50
Lamp, 9¼" h., turquoise 125.00
Marmalade jar, cov., clear 16.00
Marmalade jar, cov., pink. 21.50
Nut cup, individual size, footed, amber . .4.00
Nut cup, individual size, footed, clear . . .5.50
Nut cup, individual size, footed,
   green 10.00
Nut cup, individual size, footed, pink
   (ILLUS.) .9.00 to 16.50
Nut cup, individual size, footed,
   turquoise 30.00
Pitcher, 38 oz., clear 38.00
Plate, sherbet underplate, 6" d., clear . . .2.00
Plate, sherbet underplate, 6" d., green . .4.00
Plate, sherbet underplate, 6" d., pink. . . .2.50
Plate, luncheon, 8" d., clear 5.00
Plate, luncheon, 8" d., green 7.50
Plate, luncheon, 8" d., pink 8.00
Plate, luncheon, 8" d., turquoise 15.50
Plate, luncheon, 8" sq., clear 5.00
Plate, luncheon, 8" sq., green 8.00
Plate, luncheon, 8" sq., turquoise 16.00

Plate, dinner, 10" d., clear 8.00
Plate, dinner, 10" d., green 16.50
Plate, dinner, 10" d., pink 18.50
Plate, sandwich, 10" d., clear 17.00
Puff box, cov., clear 35.00
Puff box, cov., green 31.00
Puff box, cov., pink 28.00
Puff box, cov., turquoise 43.50
Relish dish, 3-compartment, 8" d.,
   clear 18.00
Rose bowl, 4", clear 15.00
Salt & pepper shakers, amber, pr. 66.50
Salt & pepper shakers, clear, pr. 24.50
Salt & pepper shakers, green,
   pr. .65.00 to 70.00
Salt & pepper shakers, pink, pr. 63.50
Salt & pepper shakers, turquoise, pr. . . .135.00
Sherbet, low foot, clear 5.00
Sherbet, high foot, clear 6.50
Sugar bowl, open, clear . . . . .5.00 to 10.00
Sugar bowl, open, footed, clear. 6.00
Sugar bowl, open, footed, pink 12.50
Sugar bowl, open, footed, tuquoise 28.50
Tid bit tray, 2-tier, clear. 17.00
Tumbler, whiskey, 3 oz., clear 5.50
Tumbler, 3¾" h., 5 oz., clear 5.50
Tumbler, footed, 7 oz., clear 6.00
Tumbler, 3¾" h., 8 oz., clear 10.00
Tumbler, footed, 9 oz., clear 8.00
Tumbler, footed, 9 oz., green. 15.00
Tumbler, 4" h., 10 oz., clear 6.00
Tumbler, 5" h., 12 oz., clear 6.50
Tumbler, 5" h., 12 oz., pink. 15.50
Tumbler, footed, 12½ oz., clear 10.50
Urn, cov., 15½" h., clear. 75.00
Vase, 5¾" h., clear 20.00
Vase, 7¼" h., green 29.50

FLORAL or Poinsettia (Process-etched)

Floral Candy Jar

Bowl, berry, 4" d., green. 11.50
Bowl, berry, 4" d., pink 10.00
Bowl, nappy, 7½" d., green 12.50
Bowl, nappy, 7½" d., pink 11.50

Bowl, cov. vegetable, 8" d., green 29.00
Bowl, cov. vegetable, 8" d., pink.......24.50
Bowl, 9" oval vegetable, green 12.00
Bowl, 9" oval vegetable, pink.........10.50
Butter dish, cov., green 74.50
Butter dish, cov., pink 63.00
Candlesticks, green, pr. 62.00
Candlesticks, pink, pr................60.00
Candy jar, cov., green 28.00
Candy jar, cov., pink (ILLUS.) 25.00
Coaster, green, 3¼" d. 7.00
Coaster, pink, 3¼" d. 6.50
Creamer, green 9.50
Creamer, pink.........................8.00
Creamer & cov. sugar bowl, green, pr...26.00
Creamer & cov. sugar bowl, pink, pr. ...21.50
Creamer & open sugar bowl, green
  or pink, pr..........................15.00
Cup & saucer, green...................13.50
Cup & saucer, pink 12.00
Pitcher, 8" h., 32 oz., cone-shaped,
  green 26.00
Pitcher, 8" h., 32 oz., cone-shaped,
  pink 21.00
Pitcher, lemonade, 10¼" h., 48 oz.,
  jug-type, green 210.00
Pitcher, lemonade, 10¼" h., 48 oz.,
  jug-type, pink 160.00
Plate, sherbet, 6" d., green 3.00
Plate, sherbet, 6" d., pink............3.50
Plate, salad, 8" d., green 7.50
Plate, salad, 8" d., pink..............6.50
Plate, dinner, 9" d., green 11.50
Plate, dinner, 9" d., pink 10.00
Platter, 10¾" oval, green 11.00
Platter, 10¾" oval, pink 9.50
Refrigerator dish, cov., green 47.00
Refrigerator dish, cov., Jadite 19.00
Relish, 2-part, green 9.50
Relish, 2-part, pink..................9.00
Salt & pepper shakers, footed, green,
  4" h. pr...........................35.50
Salt & pepper shakers, footed, pink,
  4" h., pr..........................29.00
Salt & pepper shakers, green, 6" h.,
  pr.................................27.00
Salt & pepper shakers, pink, 6" h.,
  pr.................................33.00
Sherbet, green 10.50
Sherbet, pink........................9.00
Sugar bowl, cov., green 20.00
Sugar bowl, cov., pink 15.50
Sugar bowl, open, green or pink 7.50
Tray, handled, green, 6" sq...........14.00
Tray, handled, pink, 6" sq. 12.50
Tumbler, footed, green, 4" h., 5 oz. 11.50
Tumbler, footed, pink, 4" h., 5 oz. 10.50
Tumbler, footed, green, 4¾" h., 7 oz....13.00
Tumbler, footed, pink, 4¾" h., 7 oz.....10.00
Tumbler, footed, green, 5¼" h., 9 oz. ..27.50
Tumbler, footed, pink, 5¼" h., 9 oz....24.00
Water set: cone-shaped pitcher & 6
  footed tumblers; green, 7 pcs........90.00

(OLD) FLORENTINE or Poppy No. 1 (Process-etched)
Bowl, berry, 5" d., clear 6.25
Bowl, berry, 5" d., cobalt blue 15.00
Bowl, berry, 5" d., green or yellow 8.00
Bowl, berry, 5" d., pink 9.00
Bowl, nappy, 6" d., green 22.00
Bowl, nappy, 6" d., pink 14.00
Bowl, 8½" d., green...................20.00
Bowl, 8½" d., pink 26.00
Bowl, 8½" d., yellow 25.00
Bowl, cov. vegetable, 9½" oval, clear ..27.50
Bowl, cov. vegetable, 9½" oval,
  green 35.00
Bowl, cov. vegetable, 9½" oval, pink ...46.00
Bowl, 9½" oval vegetable, green 15.50
Bowl, 9½" oval vegetable, yellow......16.50
Butter dish, cov., clear...............115.00
Butter dish, cov., green 100.00
Butter dish, cov., pink 170.00
Butter dish, cov., yellow 110.00
Coaster-ash tray, green 20.00
Coaster-ash tray, pink 31.50
Coaster-ash tray, yellow 34.00
Creamer, plain rim, clear 6.50
Creamer, plain rim, green 7.50
Creamer, plain rim, pink or yellow 10.00
Creamer, ruffled rim, clear...........16.50
Creamer, ruffled rim, pink 20.00
Creamer & cov. sugar bowl, clear, pr. ..22.00
Creamer & cov. sugar bowl, green, pr...29.50
Creamer & cov. sugar bowl, pink, pr....36.50
Creamer & cov. sugar bowl, yellow,
  pr.................................24.00
Creamer & open sugar bowl, cobalt
  blue, pr............................12.00
Creamer & open sugar bowl, green,
  pr.................................13.50
Creamer & open sugar bowl, pink, pr. ..16.50
Creamer & open sugar bowl, yellow,
  pr.................................15.50
Cup & saucer, clear 6.00
Cup & saucer, green..................9.00
Cup & saucer, pink or yellow 9.50
Pitcher, 6½" h., 36 oz., jug-type, clear ..30.00
Pitcher, 6½" h., 36 oz., jug-type,
  green 32.50
Pitcher, 6½" h., 36 oz., jug-type, pink ..41.00
Pitcher, 6½" h., 36 oz., jug-type,
  yellow..............................40.00
Pitcher, 7½" h., 54 oz., clear 41.00
Pitcher, 7½" h., 54 oz., green 66.50
Pitcher, 7½" h., 54 oz., pink 98.00
Pitcher, 7½" h., 54 oz., yellow 125.00
Plate, sherbet, 6" d., clear 2.50
Plate, sherbet, 6" d., green, pink or
  yellow..............................4.00
Plate, luncheon, 8" d., clear 4.00
Plate, luncheon, 8" d., green 6.00
Plate, luncheon, 8" d., pink 7.50
Plate, luncheon, 8" d., yellow 7.00
Plate, dinner, 9¾" d., clear 6.50
Plate, dinner, 9¾" d., green 10.00
Plate, dinner, 9¾" d., pink or yellow ...12.00

Plate, grill, 9¾" d., green 8.50
Plate, grill, 9¾" d., pink 10.50
Plate, grill, 9¾" d., yellow 9.50
Platter, 11½" oval, clear 9.00
Platter, 11½" oval, green 11.00
Platter, 11½" oval, pink or yellow 12.00
Salt & pepper shakers, clear, pr. 24.00
Salt & pepper shakers, green, pr. 30.00
Salt & pepper shakers, pink, pr. 45.50
Salt & pepper shakers, yellow, pr. 42.50
Sherbet, clear .4.00
Sherbet, green 6.00
Sherbet, pink. 7.00
Sherbet, yellow. 8.00
Sugar bowl, cov., clear 18.50
Sugar bowl, cov., green 24.00
Sugar bowl, cov., pink 20.00
Sugar bowl, cov., yellow 23.00
Sugar bowl, open, clear 4.25
Sugar bowl, open, cobalt blue 37.00
Sugar bowl, open, green. 6.50
Sugar bowl, open, pink 12.50
Sugar bowl, open, yellow 8.00
Tumbler, juice, footed, clear, 3¼" h.,
   5 oz. 7.50
Tumbler, juice, footed, green, 3¼" h.,
   5 oz. 11.00
Tumbler, juice, footed, pink, 3¼" h.,
   5 oz. 12.00
Tumbler, juice, footed, yellow, 3¼" h.,
   5 oz. 12.50
Tumbler, water, footed, clear, 4" h.,
   9 oz. 6.75
Tumbler, water, footed, green, 4" h.,
   9 oz. 11.00
Tumbler, water, footed, pink, 4" h.,
   9 oz. 18.50
Tumbler, water, footed, yellow, 4" h.,
   9 oz. 14.00
Tumbler, iced tea, footed, clear, 5" h.,
   12 oz. 8.50
Tumbler, iced tea, footed, green, 5" h.,
   12 oz. 13.50
Tumbler, iced tea, footed, pink, 5" h.,
   12 oz. 21.00
Tumbler, iced tea, footed, yellow, 5" h.,
   12 oz. 18.50

FLORENTINE or Poppy No. 2 (Process-etched)

Florentine or Poppy No. 2 Pattern

Ash tray, clear, 2½" d. 11.00
Ash tray, green, 2½" d. 15.00
Ash tray, yellow, 2½" d. 20.00
Bowl, berry, 4½" d., clear 7.00
Bowl, berry, 4½" d., green 8.25
Bowl, berry, 4½" d., pink 6.00
Bowl, berry, 4½" d., yellow 13.00
Bowl, cream soup w/plain rim, 4¾" d.,
   clear 6.50
Bowl, cream soup w/plain rim, 4¾" d.,
   green 8.50
Bowl, cream soup w/plain rim, 4¾" d.,
   pink. 9.00
Bowl, cream soup w/plain rim, 4¾" d.,
   yellow. 12.50
Bowl, cream soup w/ruffled rim, 5" d.,
   clear 14.00
Bowl, cream soup w/ruffled rim, 5" d.,
   green 17.50
Bowl, cream soup w/ruffled rim, 5" d.,
   pink. 8.00
Bowl, cream soup w/ruffled rim, 5" d.,
   yellow. 19.00
Bowl, cereal, 6" d., clear or pink 10.00
Bowl, cereal, 6" d., green 15.50
Bowl, cereal, 6" d., yellow 27.50
Bowl, nappy, 8" d., green or pink 16.50
Bowl, nappy, 8" d., yellow 22.00
Bowl, cov. vegetable, 9" oval, clear 32.00
Bowl, cov. vegetable, 9" oval, green . . .31.50
Bowl, cov. vegetable, 9" oval, pink 28.75
Bowl, cov. vegetable, 9" oval, yellow . . .42.00
Bowl, 9" oval vegetable, clear or
   green 15.50
Bowl, 9" oval vegetable, yellow. 21.00
Butter dish, cov., clear. 87.50
Butter dish, cov., green. 85.50
Butter dish, cov., pink 45.00
Butter dish, cov., yellow 105.00
Candlesticks, clear or green, 3" h., pr. . . .45.00
Candlesticks, yellow, 3" h., pr. 41.00
Candy dish, cov., clear 66.00
Candy dish, cov., green. 94.50
Candy dish, cov., pink 92.50
Candy dish, cov., yellow 140.00
Celery, oval, clear 22.00
Coaster, clear, 3¼" d. 7.50
Coaster, green, 3¼" d. 8.50
Coaster, yellow, 3¼" d. 14.00
Coaster-ash tray, clear, 3¾" d. 6.50
Coaster-ash tray, green, 3¾" d. 18.00
Coaster-ash tray, yellow, 3¾" d. 14.50
Coaster-ash tray, green, 5½" d. 20.00
Coaster-ash tray, yellow, 5½" d. 26.50
Compote, 3½" d., blue 41.00
Compote, 3½" d., clear. 9.00
Compote, 3½" d., green 22.50
Compote, 3½" d., pink 10.00
Condiment set: creamer, sugar bowl,
   salt & pepper shakers & 8½" d.
   tray; yellow, 5 pcs. 124.00
Creamer, clear 5.00
Creamer, green or yellow. 7.50
Creamer, pink. .3.00

Creamer & cov. sugar bowl, green, pr. . .35.00
Creamer & cov. sugar bowl, yellow,
pr. 29.00
Creamer & open sugar bowl, clear, pr. .11.00
Creamer & open sugar bowl, green,
pr. 14.00
Creamer & open sugar bowl, pink, pr. . .50.00
Creamer & open sugar bowl, yellow,
pr. (ILLUS.) 14.00
Cup & saucer, clear 7.00
Cup & saucer, green 10.00
Cup & saucer, pink 9.00
Cup & saucer, yellow 9.50
Custard cup, clear 29.50
Custard cup, green 75.00
Custard cup, yellow 63.50
Gravy boat, yellow 35.50
Gravy boat w/platter, pink, 11½" oval .75.00
Gravy boat w/platter, yellow,
11½" oval 72.00
Nut dish, handled, ruffled rim, green . . .47.00
Nut dish, handled, ruffled rim, pink 8.50
Pitcher, 6" h., 24 oz., cone-shaped,
yellow 110.00
Pitcher, 7¼" h., 30 oz., cone-shaped,
clear 14.50
Pitcher, 7¼" h., 30 oz., cone-shaped,
green 22.50
Pitcher, 7¼" h., 30 oz., cone-shaped,
yellow 20.50
Pitcher, 7½" h., 36 oz., footed, cone-
shaped, clear 17.50
Pitcher, 7½" h., 36 oz., footed, cone-
shaped, green 29.00
Pitcher, 7½" h., 36 oz., footed, cone-
shaped, yellow 21.00
Pitcher, 7½" h., 54 oz., straight sides,
clear 42.50
Pitcher, 7½" h., 54 oz., straight sides,
green 50.50
Pitcher, 7½" h., 54 oz., straight sides,
yellow 137.00
Pitcher, 8" h., 76 oz., jug-type, clear 50.50
Pitcher, 8" h., 76 oz., jug-type, green . . .54.00
Pitcher, 8" h., 76 oz., jug-type, pink . . .225.00
Pitcher, 8" h., 76 oz., jug-type, yellow . .16.75
Pitcher, 80 oz., bulbous, pink 167.00
Plate, sherbet, 6" d., clear 2.00
Plate, sherbet, 6" d., green or yellow 3.00
Plate, sherbet, 6" d., pink 4.00
Plate, 6¼" d., w/indentation, clear 7.00
Plate, 6¼" d., w/indentation, green 3.00
Plate, 6¼" d., w/indentation, pink 4.00
Plate, 6¼" d., w/indentation, yellow 19.00
Plate, luncheon, 8½" d., clear 4.25
Plate, luncheon, 8½" d., green 5.00
Plate, luncheon, 8½" d., yellow 6.25
Plate, dinner, 10" d., clear 7.00
Plate, dinner, 10" d., green 9.50
Plate, dinner, 10" d., yellow 10.00
Plate, grill, 10½" d., clear 6.25
Plate, grill, 10½" d., green or yellow 8.50
Platter, 11" oval, clear 8.00
Platter, 11" oval, green 12.50

Platter, 11" oval, yellow 11.50
Relish, clear, 10" .10.00
Relish, green, 10" 12.00
Relish, yellow, 10" 15.50
Relish, 3-part, green or pink 16.00
Relish, 3-part, yellow 19.00
Salt & pepper shakers, clear, pr. 23.50
Salt & pepper shakers, green, pr. 30.50
Salt & pepper shakers, yellow, pr.
(ILLUS.) 36.00
Sherbet, clear or green 6.00
Sherbet, pink 5.75
Sherbet, yellow 8.00
Sugar bowl, cov., green 18.00
Sugar bowl, cov., yellow 22.50
Sugar bowl, open, clear 5.00
Sugar bowl, open, green 5.50
Sugar bowl, open, yellow 7.50
Tray, yellow, 8½" d., (ILLUS.) 65.00
Tumbler, clear, 3½" h., 5 oz. 5.50
Tumbler, green or pink, 3½" h., 5 oz. 8.50
Tumbler, yellow, 3½" h., 5 oz. 14.00
Tumbler, footed, clear, 3½" h., 5 oz. 6.00
Tumbler, footed, green, 3½" h., 5 oz. 8.00
Tumbler, footed, pink, 3½" h., 5 oz. 9.00
Tumbler, footed, yellow, 3½" h., 5 oz. . . .9.50
Tumbler, blue, 4" h., 9 oz. 39.50
Tumbler, clear, 4" h., 9 oz. 7.50
Tumbler, green or pink, 4" h., 9 oz. 8.50
Tumbler, yellow, 4" h., 9 oz. 13.00
Tumbler, footed, clear, 4½" h., 9 oz. 9.00
Tumbler, footed, green, 4½" h., 9 oz. . . .16.50
Tumbler, footed, pink, 4½" h., 9 oz. 9.25
Tumbler, footed, yellow, 4½" h., 9 oz. . .14.00
Tumbler, iced tea, clear, 5" h., 12 oz. . . .17.50
Tumbler, iced tea, green or pink,
5" h., 12 oz. .24.00
Tumbler, iced tea, yellow, 5" h., 12 oz. . .32.00
Tumbler, footed, clear, 5" h., 12 oz. 12.00
Tumbler, footed, green, 5" h., 12 oz. 19.00
Tumbler, footed, yellow, 5" h., 12 oz. . . .21.50
Vase (or parfait), 6" h., clear 17.00
Vase (or parfait), 6" h., green 38.50
Vase (or parfait), 6" h., yellow 44.50

GEORGIAN or Lovebirds (Process-etched)

(All items in green only.)

Bowl, berry, 4½" d. 5.00
Bowl, cereal, 5¾" d. 12.50
Bowl, 6½" d. 44.50
Bowl, berry, 7½" d. 38.00
Bowl, 9" oval vegetable 47.00
Butter dish, cov. .63.00
Creamer, footed, 3" h. 7.00
Creamer, footed, 4" h. 10.00
Creamer & cov. sugar bowl, 3" h.,
pr. 35.00
Creamer & cov. sugar bowl, 4" h., pr. . .25.00
Creamer & open sugar bowl, 3" or
4" h., pr. 15.50
Cup & saucer 9.50
Hot plate, center design, 5" d. 32.00
Plate, sherbet, 6" d. 3.00

Plate, luncheon, 8" d. 5.50
Plate, dinner, 9¼" d. 16.50
Plate, 9¼" d., center design only 15.00
Platter, 11" oval .42.00
Sherbet. 8.25
Sugar bowl, cov., footed, 3" h. 26.50
Sugar bowl, cov., footed, 4" h. 7.25
Sugar bowl, open, footed, 3" h. 7.75
Sugar bowl, open, footed, 4" h. 7.50
Tumbler, 4" h., 9 oz. 37.50
Tumbler, iced tea, 5¼" h., 12 oz. 64.00

HOBNAIL (Press-mold)

(*Also see Moonstone.*)

Bowl, nappy, 5½" d., clear 4.75
Cup, clear 3.00
Cup, pink 2.50
Cup & saucer, clear 4.25
Cup & saucer, pink 4.00
Decanter w/stopper, clear, 32 oz. 15.00
Goblet, clear, 10 oz. 5.00
Pitcher, milk, 18 oz., clear 13.00
Pitcher, 8" h., 55 oz., clear 16.00
Pitcher, 8" h., 55 oz., pink 16.50
Pitcher, 67 oz., jug-type, clear 14.50
Pitcher, 67 oz., jug-type, pink 15.50
Plate, sherbet, 6" d., clear 1.25
Plate, sherbet, 6" d., pink 1.75
Plate, luncheon, 8½" d., clear 2.50
Plate, luncheon, 8½" d., pink 3.50
Sherbet, clear 2.50
Sherbet, pink. 3.50
Tumbler, whiskey, clear, 1½ oz. 3.00
Tumbler, wine, footed, clear, 3 oz. 4.50
Tumbler, wine, footed, pink, 3 oz. 30.00
Tumbler, footed, clear, 5 oz. 4.25
Tumbler, clear, 9 oz. 4.00
Tumbler, pink, 9 oz. 5.00
Tumbler, clear, 10 oz. 4.75
Tumbler, clear, 15 oz. 6.00

HOLIDAY (Press-mold)

Holiday Creamer

(*All items in pink only. Later iridescent pieces not included.*)

Bowl, berry, 5 1/8" d. 6.00
Bowl, cereal or flat soup, 7¾" d. 26.00
Bowl, fruit, 8½" d. 16.00

Bowl, 9½" oval vegetable. 13.00
Butter dish, cov. .34.00
Cake plate, footed, 10½" d. 55.50
Candlesticks, 3" h., pr. 52.00
Console bowl, 10" d. 58.00
Creamer (ILLUS.). 5.50
Creamer & cov. sugar bowl, pr. 15.00
Cup & saucer, plain base 7.00
Cup & saucer, rayed base 7.50
Pitcher, milk, 4½" h., 16 oz. 43.00
Pitcher, 6¾" h., 52 oz. 25.00
Plate, sherbet, 6" d. 2.75
Plate, dinner, 9" d. 9.00
Plate, chop, 13 5/8" d. 64.00
Platter, 11 3/8 x 8" 10.50
Sandwich tray, 10½" d. 8.50
Saucer, plain or rayed base 3.00
Sherbet. 5.00
Sugar bowl, cov. 14.00
Sugar bowl, open 6.50
Tumbler, footed, 4" h., 5 oz. 23.50
Tumbler, footed, 6" h., 9 oz. 63.50
Tumbler, 4" h., 10 oz. 13.50
Water set, pitcher & 6 tumblers,
    7 pcs. 125.00

HOMESPUN or Fine Rib (Press-mold)

Bowl, 4½" d., closed handles, pink 4.50
Bowl, cereal, 5" d., clear. 5.00
Bowl, cereal, 5" d., pink 9.00
Bowl, berry, 8¼" d., pink 9.50
Butter dish, cov., clear. 29.00
Butter dish, cov., pink 42.00
Coaster-ash tray, pink 4.00
Creamer, footed, clear or pink. 7.00
Creamer & sugar bowl, footed, pink,
    pr. 15.50
Cup & saucer, pink 7.50
Pitcher, 96 oz., ball tilt type, pink 60.00
Plate, sherbet, 6" d., pink 2.00
Plate, dinner, 9¼" d., pink 8.00
Platter, 13", closed handles, pink 7.50
Sherbet, clear 4.00
Sherbet, pink. 5.00
Sugar bowl, footed, pink 5.50
Tumbler, juice, footed, clear, 4" h.,
    5 oz. 4.00
Tumbler, juice, footed, pink, 4" h., 5 oz. .5.50
Tumbler, water, pink, 4" h., 9 oz. 7.00
Tumbler, footed, pink, 6¼" h., 9 oz. 10.50
Tumbler, iced tea, clear, 5¼" h.,
    13 oz. 7.00
Tumbler, iced tea, pink, 5¼" h., 13 oz. . .13.50
Tumbler, footed, clear, 6½" h., 15 oz. . .12.00
Tumbler, footed, pink, 6½" h., 15 oz. . . .14.50

CHILD'S TEA SET
Cup & saucer, pink 28.00
Plate, clear 4.00
Plate, pink 7.00

IRIS or Iris & Herringbone (Press-mold)
Berry set: 11" d. flared fruit bowl &
    6 sauce dishes; clear, 7 pcs. 25.00

Bowl, fruit, 4½″ d., amber iridescent 5.50
Bowl, fruit, 4½″ d., clear 29.50
Bowl, nappy, 5″ d., amber iridescent 6.00
Bowl, nappy, 5″ d., clear 4.75
Bowl, nappy, 6″ d., clear 31.50
Bowl, soup, 7½″ d., amber iridescent . .21.50
Bowl, soup, 7½″ d., clear 66.50
Bowl, fruit, 8″ d., beaded rim, amber
    iridescent 11.00
Bowl, fruit, 8″ d., beaded rim, clear 67.00
Bowl, fruit, 8″ d., ruffled rim, amber
    iridescent or clear 8.50
Bowl, nappy, 9½″ d., amber iridescent
    or clear 8.00
Bowl, 11″ d., amber iridescent 8.00
Bowl, 11″ d., clear 27.00
Bowl, fruit, 11″ d., flared, amber
    iridescent 7.50
Bowl, fruit, 11″ d., flared, clear 9.50
Butter dish, cov., amber iridescent 31.00
Butter dish, cov., clear 27.50
Candlesticks, 2-branch, amber irides-
    cent, pr. 19.00
Candlesticks, 2-branch, clear, pr. 15.00
Candy jar, cov., clear 66.50
Coaster, clear 31.00
Creamer, amber iridescent 6.00
Creamer, clear 5.00
Creamer & cov. sugar bowl, amber
    iridescent, pr. .15.50
Creamer & cov. sugar bowl, clear, pr. . .16.50
Creamer & open sugar bowl, amber
    iridescent, pr. .15.00
Creamer & open sugar bowl, clear, pr. . .12.50
Cup & saucer, demitasse, amber
    iridescent 125.00
Cup & saucer, demitasse, clear 62.00
Cup & saucer, amber iridescent 10.50
Cup & saucer, clear 11.50
Goblet, wine, amber iridescent, 4″ h.,
    3 oz. 13.50
Goblet, wine, clear, 4″ h., 3 oz. 11.00
Goblet, wine, amber iridescent,
    4½″ h., 3 oz. 13.50
Goblet, wine, clear, 4½″ h., 3 oz. 11.00
Goblet, clear, 5¾″ h., 4 oz. 12.50
Goblet, clear, 5¾″ h., 8 oz. 13.00
Goblet, clear, 7″ h. 13.00
Nut bowl w/metal insert, frosted
    w/pink roses, 11½″ 24.00
Nut set: bowl w/metal holder, cracker
    & picks; clear, set 31.00
Pitcher, 9½″ h., jug-type, amber
    iridescent 22.00
Pitcher, 9½″ h., jug-type, clear 18.00
Plate, sherbet, 5½″ d., amber
    iridescent 4.50
Plate, sherbet, 5½″ d., clear 6.00
Plate, luncheon, 8″ d., clear 30.50
Plate, dinner, 9″ d., amber iridescent . . .18.50
Plate, dinner, 9″ d., clear 26.50
Plate, sandwich, 11¾″ d., amber
    iridescent 10.00
Plate, sandwich, 11¾″ d., clear 11.00

Sherbet, amber iridescent, 2½″ h. 7.00
Sherbet, clear, 2½″ h. 13.50
Sherbet, amber iridescent, 4″ h. 7.50
Sherbet, clear, 4″ h. 10.00
Sugar bowl, cov., amber iridescent 11.50
Sugar bowl, cov., clear 11.00
Sugar bowl, open, amber iridescent 4.75
Sugar bowl, open, clear 4.50
Tumbler, clear, 4″ h. 46.50
Tumbler, footed, amber iridescent,
    6″ h. 10.00
Tumbler, footed, clear, 6″ h. 9.50

Iris Tumbler

Tumbler, footed, clear, 7″ h. (ILLUS.) . . .12.50
Vase, 9″ h., amber iridescent 11.50
Vase, 9″ h., clear 12.00
Vase, 9″ h., pink .50.00
Water set: pitcher & 6 tumblers; amber
    iridescent, 7 pcs. 85.00

LACE EDGE or Open Lace (Press-mold)

Lace Edge Bowls

Bowl, cereal, 6½″ d., clear 5.50
Bowl, cereal, 6½″ d., pink (ILLUS.) 11.00
Bowl, nappy, 7¾″ d., plain or ribbed,
    pink 15.50
Bowl, 9½″ d., plain or ribbed, pink
    (ILLUS.) 11.75
Butter dish (bon bon or preserve),
    cov., pink 43.00

Candlesticks, pink, pr...............128.00
Candlesticks, pink frosted, pr..........39.00
Candy jar, cov., ribbed, pink, 4" h. 29.00
Compote, cov., 7" d., pink............27.00
Compote, open, 7" d., clear 11.50
Compote, open, 7" d., pink............14.00
Console bowl, 3-footed, pink,
    10½" d. 116.00
Console bowl, 3-footed, pink frosted,
    10½" d. 54.00
Cookie jar, cov., clear, 5" h. 25.00
Cookie jar, cov., pink, 5" h. 43.50
Creamer, pink........................13.50
Creamer & open sugar bowl, pink, pr. ..25.50
Cup & saucer, clear 17.50
Cup & saucer, pink 22.00
Fish bowl, pink, ½ gal. 20.00
Flower bowl w/crystal block, pink 18.00
Flower bowl w-o/crystal block, pink....12.50
Plate, bread & butter, 7¼" d., pink 12.00
Plate, salad, 8½" d., clear 3.25
Plate, salad, 8½" d., pink.............11.00
Plate, dinner, 10½" d., clear or pink....16.00
Plate, grill, 10½" d., pink 12.50
Platter, 12¾" oval, clear..............10.00
Platter, 12¾" oval, pink..............19.00
Platter, 12¾" oval, 5-part, pink 14.00
Relish, pink, 7½" d. 43.00
Relish, 3-part, clear, 10½" d. 12.00
Relish, 3-part, pink, 10½" d. 13.00
Relish, 4-part, pink, 13" d. 23.50
Sherbet, pink.......................52.00
Sugar bowl, open, clear 9.50
Sugar bowl, open, pink 13.00
Tumbler, pink, 4½" h., 9 oz...........8.50
Tumbler, footed, pink, 5" h., 10½ oz....40.00
Vase, 7" h., pink frosted 79.00

LORAIN or Basket or Number 615 (Process-etched)

Lorain Cup & Saucer

Bowl, cereal, 6" d., clear..............15.00
Bowl, cereal, 6" d., green 27.50
Bowl, cereal, 6" d., yellow 42.50
Bowl, salad, 7¼" d., green 27.50
Bowl, salad, 7¼" d., yellow 43.00
Bowl, berry, 8" d., green.............65.00
Bowl, berry, 8" d., yellow....130.00 to 145.00
Bowl, 9¾" oval vegetable, green 28.00
Bowl, 9¾" oval vegetable, yellow......40.00
Cake plate, yellow, 11½" d...........30.00

Creamer, footed, clear 11.00
Creamer, footed, green 13.00
Creamer, footed, yellow 17.00
Creamer & open sugar bowl, footed,
    clear, pr. 19.00
Creamer & open sugar bowl, footed,
    green, pr........................25.50
Creamer & open sugar bowl, footed,
    yellow, pr.......................36.50
Cup & saucer, clear 13.50
Cup & saucer, green 12.00
Cup & saucer, yellow (ILLUS.) 16.50
Plate, sherbet, 5½" d., clear or green ...4.00
Plate, sherbet, 5½" d., yellow 5.00
Plate, salad, 7¾" d., clear 6.00
Plate, salad, 7¾" d., green 7.00
Plate, salad, 7¾" d., yellow 9.50
Plate, luncheon, 8 3/8" d., green 10.00
Plate, luncheon, 8 3/8" d., yellow 18.00
Plate, dinner, 9 3/8" d., yellow 44.00
Plate, dinner, 10¼" d., green 35.50
Plate, dinner, 10¼" d., yellow 43.00
Platter, 11½", clear 8.75
Platter, 11½", green 18.00
Platter, 11½", yellow 30.00
Relish, 4-part, clear, 8" 11.00
Relish, 4-part, green, 8" 14.75
Relish, 4-part, yellow, 8" 20.50
Sherbet, green 13.00
Sherbet, yellow.....................24.00
Sugar bowl, open, footed, clear........9.75
Sugar bowl, open, footed, green 13.00
Sugar bowl, open, footed, yellow 17.00
Tumbler, footed, clear or green,
    4¾" h., 9 oz. 14.00
Tumbler, footed, yellow, 4¾" h., 9 oz. ...18.50
Tumbler, footed, green, 5 1/8" h.,
    12 oz. 18.50
Tumbler, footed, yellow, 5 1/8" h.,
    12 oz. 19.50

MADRID (Process-etched)

Madrid Candlestick

Ash tray, amber, 6" sq. 177.00
Ash tray, green, 6" sq................77.50
Bowl, cream soup, 4¾" d., amber.......9.00
Bowl, cream soup, 4¾" d., clear 7.00
Bowl, cream soup, 4¾" d., green 8.00
Bowl, nappy, 5" d., amber or pink 4.50
Bowl, nappy, 5" d., green 7.00
Bowl, soup, 7" d., amber or clear 7.50
Bowl, soup, 7" d., blue................10.00

Bowl, soup, 7" d., green 8.00
Bowl, 8" d., amber 10.50
Bowl, 8" d., blue 65.00
Bowl, 8" d., clear 8.50
Bowl, 8" d., green 15.00
Bowl, fruit, 9 3/8" d., amber.........14.50
Bowl, fruit, 9 3/8" d., green 19.00
Bowl, salad, 9½" d., amber 18.50
Bowl, salad, 9½" d., blue 69.00
Bowl, salad, 9½" d., green 20.00
Bowl, salad, 9½" d., pink 17.00
Bowl, 10" oval vegetable, amber......11.00
Bowl, 10" oval vegetable, blue........24.00
Bowl, 10" oval vegetable, clear 7.75
Bowl, 10" oval vegetable, green 13.50
Bowl, 11¾" d., blue 40.00
Bowl, 11¾" d., green................13.00
Bowl, 11¾" d., pink 20.00
Butter dish, cov., amber 54.00
Butter dish, cov., clear 125.00
Butter dish, cov., green 70.00
Cake plate, amber or clear, 11½" d.....11.25
Cake plate, pink, 11½" d..............9.25
Candlesticks, amber, 2" h., pr. (ILLUS.
  of one) 14.00
Candlesticks, carnival or pink, 2" h.,
  pr................................13.00
Console bowl, flared, amber, 11" d. 10.00
Console bowl, flared, carnival, 11" d.....9.75
Console bowl, flared, pink, 11" d. 8.75
Console set: bowl & pr. candlesticks;
  carnival, 3 pcs. 19.00
Console set: bowl & pr. candlesticks;
  pink, 3 pcs. 28.00
Cookie jar, cov., amber...............31.00
Cookie jar, cov., clear 27.50
Cookie jar, cov., pink 30.00
Creamer, amber 5.00
Creamer, blue.......................13.00
Creamer, carnival 15.00
Creamer, clear 4.75
Creamer, green 8.50
Creamer, pink.......................4.00
Creamer & cov. sugar bowl, amber,
  pr.................................35.00
Creamer & cov. sugar bowl, clear, pr. ..31.00
Creamer & cov. sugar bowl, green,
  pr.................................43.00
Creamer & open sugar bowl, amber,
  pr.................................11.00
Creamer & open sugar bowl, blue, pr. ..32.50
Creamer & open sugar bowl, clear, pr....9.00
Creamer & open sugar bowl, green,
  pr.................................13.50
Cup & saucer, amber 7.00
Cup & saucer, blue 19.00
Cup & saucer, clear 6.50
Cup & saucer, green 10.00
Cup & saucer, pink 7.25
Hot dish coaster, amber, 5" d. 28.00
Hot dish coaster, clear, 5" d. 24.00
Hot dish coaster, green, 5" d..........30.00
Hot dish coaster w/ring, amber 31.50
Hot dish coaster w/ring, clear 21.00

Hot dish coaster w/ring, green 30.00
Jam dish, amber, 7" d................13.50
Jam dish, blue, 7" d. 21.00
Jam dish, clear, 7" d. 11.75
Jello mold, amber, 2" h. 7.00
Pitcher, juice, 5" h., 36 oz., amber......28.00
Pitcher, 8" h., 60 oz., square, amber....31.00
Pitcher, 8" h., 60 oz., square, blue....140.00
Pitcher, 8" h., 60 oz., square, green ...105.00
Pitcher, 8" h., 60 oz., square, pink......28.00
Pitcher, 8½" h., 80 oz., jug-type,
  amber..............................44.50
Pitcher w/ice lip, 8½" h., 80 oz.,
  amber..............................47.50
Plate, bread & butter, 6" d., amber 2.75
Plate, bread & butter, 6" d., blue 6.50
Plate, bread & butter, 6" d., clear 1.50
Plate, bread & butter, 6" d., green 3.00
Plate, salad, 7½" d., amber 7.00
Plate, salad, 7½" d., blue 15.50
Plate, salad, 7½" d., clear 5.25
Plate, salad, 7½" d., green 7.50
Plate, luncheon, 9" d., amber 5.25
Plate, luncheon, 9" d., blue 15.75
Plate, luncheon, 9" d., clear 3.75
Plate, luncheon, 9" d., green 7.50
Plate, dinner, 10½" d., amber 24.00
Plate, dinner, 10½" d., blue 45.00
Plate, dinner, 10½" d., green 29.00
Plate, grill, 10½" d., amber 8.00
Plate, grill, 10½" d., clear 6.75
Plate, grill, 10½" d., green 13.50
Plate, grill, 10½" d., pink 9.00
Platter, 11½" oval, amber or pink......10.00
Platter, 11½" oval, blue 25.50
Platter, 11½" oval, green 14.00
Relish, amber, 10½" d. 9.50
Relish, pink, 10½" d. 8.25
Salt & pepper shakers, amber, 3½" h.,
  pr.................................34.00
Salt & pepper shakers, blue, 3½" h.,
  pr................................115.00
Salt & pepper shakers, clear, 3½" h.,
  pr.................................46.00
Salt & pepper shakers, green, 3½" h.,
  pr.................................53.50
Salt & pepper shakers, footed, amber
  or clear, 3½" h., pr................55.00
Salt & pepper shakers, footed, blue,
  3½" h., pr........................118.00
Salt & pepper shakers, footed, green,
  3½" h., pr.........................68.50
Sherbet, amber......................5.25
Sherbet, blue.......................10.00
Sherbet, clear 4.00
Sherbet, green......................6.50
Sherbet, pink.......................6.00
Sugar bowl, cov., amber 31.00
Sugar bowl, cov., blue 125.00
Sugar bowl, cov., green 47.00
Sugar bowl, open, amber 4.75
Sugar bowl, open, blue 11.00
Sugar bowl, open, clear 4.00
Sugar bowl, open, green...............8.00

Sugar bowl, open, pink 6.00
Tumbler, juice, amber, 3 7/8" h., 5 oz. . .11.75
Tumbler, juice, blue, 3 7/8" h., 5 oz. . . .18.00
Tumbler, juice, clear, 3 7/8" h., 5 oz. . . .12.50
Tumbler, juice, green, 3 7/8" h., 5 oz. . . .45.00
Tumbler, footed, amber, 4" h., 5 oz. 14.00
Tumbler, footed, green, 4" h., 5 oz. 25.50
Tumbler, amber or clear, 4½" h.,
 9 oz. 10.50
Tumbler, blue, 4½" h., 9 oz. 20.00
Tumbler, green, 4½" h., 9 oz. 17.00
Tumbler, pink, 4½" h., 9 oz. 11.00
Tumbler, footed, amber, 5¼" h.,
 10 oz. 15.50
Tumbler, footed, blue, 5¼" h., 10 oz. . . .21.00
Tumbler, footed, green, 5¼" h.,
 10 oz. 29.50
Tumbler, amber, 5½" h., 12 oz. 15.00
Tumbler, blue, 5½" h., 12 oz. 31.50
Tumbler, green, 5½" h., 12 oz. 27.50

MANHATTAN or Ribbed Horizontal (Press-mold)

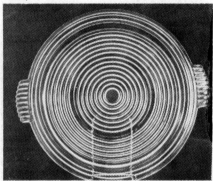

Manhattan Sandwich Plate

Ash tray, clear 5.50
Bowl, dessert, 4½" d., clear 4.25
Bowl, fruit, 5 3/8" d., handled, clear 4.50
Bowl, fruit, 5 3/8" d., handled, pink 8.00
Bowl, 7½" d., clear 7.00
Bowl, 7½" d., pink 5.50
Bowl, 8" d., 2-handled, clear 9.50
Bowl, 9" d., clear 13.50
Bowl, 9" d., pink 11.50
Bowl, fruit, 9½" d., clear 14.00
Bowl, fruit, 9½" d., pink 15.00
Candlesticks, double, square, clear,
 4¼" h., pr. 8.00
Candlesticks, double, square, pink,
 4¼" h., pr. 23.00
Candy dish, cov., clear 18.00
Candy dish, cov., pink 5.75
Candy dish, open, 3-legged, clear 19.00
Candy dish, open, 3-legged, pink 5.75
Coaster, clear, 3½" d. 3.00
Coaster, pink, 3½" d. 3.75
Compote, 5¾" h., clear 9.50
Compote, 5¾" h., pink 13.00
Cookie jar, cov., clear 25.00

Cookie jar, cov., pink 120.00
Creamer, clear 3.75
Creamer, pink 5.00
Creamer & open sugar bowl, clear, pr. . . .8.25
Creamer & open sugar bowl, pink, pr. . . .11.00
Cup & saucer, clear 10.50
Lazy Susan, 5 inserts, clear, 14" 14.75
Lazy Susan, 5 inserts, clear w/ruby
 inserts, 14" 30.00
Lazy Susan, 5 inserts, pink, 14" 28.50
Pitcher, juice, 42 oz., clear 15.00
Pitcher w/ice lip, 80 oz., ball tilt type,
 clear 20.00
Pitcher w/ice lip, 80 oz., ball tilt type,
 pink 32.00
Plate, sherbet, 6" d., clear 2.25
Plate, sherbet, 6" d., pink 7.50
Plate, salad, 8½" d., clear 5.75
Plate, dinner, 10½" d., clear 7.25
Plate, 14" d., clear (ILLUS.) 10.50
Relish, 4-part, clear, 14" 13.75
Relish, 4-part, pink, 14" 37.50
Salt & pepper shakers, round or
 square, clear, 2" h., pr. 12.00
Salt & pepper shakers, round or
 square, pink, 2" h., pr. 26.00
Sherbet, clear 4.75
Sherbet, pink. 6.00
Sugar bowl, open, clear 3.75
Sugar bowl, open, pink 5.50
Tumbler, footed, clear, 10 oz. 6.75
Tumbler, footed, pink, 10 oz. 8.50
Vase, 8" h., clear 8.00
Vase, 8" h., pink .5.00
Wine, clear 5.50

MAYFAIR or Open Rose (Process-etched)

Mayfair Juice Tumbler & Shakers

Bowl, cream soup, 5" d., blue 43.00
Bowl, cream soup, 5" d., pink 29.00
Bowl, fruit, 5½" d., blue 22.00
Bowl, fruit, 5½" d., pink 13.50
Bowl, nappy, 7" d., blue 37.00
Bowl, nappy, 7" d., pink 15.50
Bowl, 9½" oval vegetable, blue. 37.00
Bowl, 9½" oval vegetable, pink. 16.50
Bowl, cov. vegetable, 10" d., blue 83.00
Bowl, cov. vegetable, 10" d., pink 65.00
Bowl, 10" d., blue 39.00
Bowl, 10" d., pink 13.50
Bowl, 10" d., handled, blue. 33.50

Bowl, 10" d., handled, pink 13.50
Bowl, 11¾" d., blue 43.50
Bowl, 11¾" d., green 21.50
Bowl, 11¾" d., pink 36.50
Bowl, fruit, 12" d., flared, blue 51.00
Bowl, fruit, 12" d., flared, green 23.50
Bowl, fruit, 12" d., flared, pink 33.50
Butter dish, cov., blue 210.00
Butter dish, cov., pink 44.00
Cake plate, footed, blue, 10" d. 44.00
Cake plate, footed, green, 10" d. 18.00
Cake plate, footed, pink, 10" d. 19.00
Cake plate, handled, blue, 12" d. 47.50
Cake plate, handled, green, 12" d. 40.00
Cake plate, handled, pink or pink
    frosted, 12" d. 28.00
Candy jar, cov., blue 147.50
Candy jar, cov., pink 33.50
Celery dish, pink, 10" d. 20.00
Celery dish, 2-part, blue, 10" d. 31.00
Celery dish, 2-part, pink, 10" d. 69.00
Cookie jar, cov., blue 165.00
Cookie jar, cov., pink 30.00
Cookie jar, cov., pink frosted 32.50
Creamer, blue 46.50
Creamer, green 135.00
Creamer, pink 14.00
Creamer, pink frosted 7.50
Creamer & open sugar bowl, blue, pr. . .88.00
Creamer & open sugar bowl, pink or
    pink frosted, pr. 25.00
Cup & saucer, blue 41.00
Cup & saucer, pink 19.50
Decanter w/stopper, pink, 10" h. 105.00
Goblet, wine, pink, 4½" h., 3 oz. 52.50
Goblet, cocktail, pink, 4" h., 3½ oz. 53.00
Goblet, champagne, pink, 5¼" h.,
    4½ oz. 75.00
Goblet, water, pink, 5¾" h., 9 oz. 41.00
Goblet, water, thin, blue, 7¼" h.,
    9 oz. 95.00
Goblet, water, thin, pink, 7¼" h.,
    9 oz. 112.00
Pitcher, juice, 6" h., 37 oz., blue 76.00
Pitcher, juice, 6" h., 37 oz., clear 9.00
Pitcher, juice, 6" h., 37 oz., pink 30.00
Pitcher, 8" h., 60 oz., jug-type, blue 99.00
Pitcher, 8" h., 60 oz., jug-type, pink 33.00
Pitcher, 8½" h., 80 oz., jug-type,
    blue 129.00
Pitcher, 8½" h., 80 oz., jug-type, pink . .55.00
Plate, bread & butter, 6" w., blue 11.00
Plate, bread & butter, 6" w., pink 7.50
Plate, sherbet, 6½" d., blue 11.00
Plate, sherbet, 6½" d., pink 8.25
Plate, sherbet, 6½" d., off-center
    indentation, blue 16.00
Plate, sherbet, 6½" d., off-center
    indentation, pink 17.50
Plate, luncheon, 8½" d., blue 24.00
Plate, luncheon, 8½" d., pink 15.00
Plate, luncheon, 8½" d., yellow 85.00
Plate, dinner, 9½" d., blue 40.00
Plate, dinner, 9½" d., pink 36.00

Plate, dinner, 9½" d., yellow 6.75
Plate, grill, 9½" d., blue or pink 24.00
Plate, grill, 11½" d., yellow 87.50
Plate, 12" d., 2-handled, pink 20.00
Platter, 12" oval, pierced handles,
    blue 37.00
Platter, 12" oval, pierced handles,
    clear 15.00
Platter, 12" oval, pierced handles,
    pink 16.50
Relish, 2-part, blue 34.00
Relish, 4-part, blue 36.00
Relish, 4-part, pink 21.50
Relish, 4-part, pink frosted 17.00
Salt & pepper shakers, blue, pr. 205.00
Salt & pepper shakers, pink, pr.
    (ILLUS.) 42.00
Salt & pepper shakers, pink frosted,
    pr. 32.50
Salt & pepper shakers, footed, blue,
    pr. 165.00
Sandwich server w/center handle,
    blue, 12" 45.00
Sandwich server w/center handle,
    green, 12" 18.00
Sandwich server w/center handle,
    pink, 12" 25.00
Sandwich server w/center handle,
    pink frosted, 12" 22.00
Sherbet, blue, 2¼" h. 48.00
Sherbet, pink, 2¼" h. 130.00
Sherbet, pink, 3¼" h. 11.50
Sherbet, footed, blue, 4¾" h. 57.00
Sherbet, footed, pink, 4¾" h. 56.00
Sherbet w/underplate, blue, 2¼" h.
    sherbet 71.00
Sugar bowl, cov., blue 1,250.00
Sugar bowl, open, blue 43.00
Sugar bowl, open, pink 14.50
Tumbler, whiskey, green, 2¼" h.,
    1½ oz. 40.00
Tumbler, whiskey, pink, 2¼" h.,
    1½ oz. 52.00
Tumbler, juice, footed, pink, 3¼" h.,
    3 oz. 53.00
Tumbler, juice, blue, 3½" h., 5 oz. 70.00
Tumbler, juice, pink, 3½" h., 5 oz.
    (ILLUS.) 30.00
Tumbler, water, blue, 4¼" h., 9 oz. 65.00
Tumbler, water, pink, 4¼" h., 9 oz. 20.00
Tumbler, footed, blue, 5¼" h., 10 oz. . . .75.00
Tumbler, footed, pink, 5¼" h., 10 oz. . . .25.00
Tumbler, blue, 4¾" h., 11 oz. 90.00
Tumbler, pink, 4¾" h., 11 oz. 92.50
Tumbler, iced tea, blue, 5¼" h.,
    13½ oz. 110.00
Tumbler, iced tea, pink, 5¼" h.,
    13½ oz. 28.50
Tumbler, iced tea, footed, blue,
    6½" h., 15 oz. 105.00
Tumbler, iced tea, footed, pink,
    6½" h., 15 oz. 27.50
Vase, 5½ x 8½", sweetpea, hat-
    shaped, blue .75.00

Vase, 5½ x 8½", sweetpea, hat-
shaped, pink 105.00
Water set: pitcher & 6 tumblers; blue,
7 pcs. 695.00

MISS AMERICA (Press-mold)

Miss America Goblets

Bowl, nappy, 4½" d., green 7.25
Bowl, nappy, 4½" d., pink 12.00
Bowl, cereal, 6¼" d., clear. 5.50
Bowl, cereal, 6¼" d., green 8.00
Bowl, cereal, 6¼" d., pink 12.00
Bowl, fruit, 8" d., curved top,
clear 25.00
Bowl, fruit, 8" d., curved top, pink 41.50
Bowl, fruit, 8¾" d., deep, clear 22.00
Bowl, fruit, 8¾" d., deep, pink 42.00
Bowl, 10" oval vegetable, clear 10.00
Bowl, 10" oval vegetable, pink. 15.75
Butter dish, cov., clear. 160.00
Butter dish, cov., pink 298.00
Cake plate, footed, clear, 12" d. 13.75
Cake plate, footed, pink, 12" d. 25.00
Candy dish w/metal lid, clear, 6¼" d. . .22.50
Candy jar, cov., clear. 44.00
Candy jar, cov., pink 87.50
Celery tray, clear, 10½" oblong. 7.75
Celery tray, pink, 10½" oblong 13.75
Coaster, clear, 5¾" d. 10.75
Coaster, pink, 5¾" d. 16.75
Compote, 5" d., clear. 8.00
Compote, 5" d., pink 14.50
Creamer, clear 5.50
Creamer, pink 11.00
Creamer & open sugar bowl, clear,
pr. 12.00
Creamer & open sugar bowl, pink, pr. . .23.00
Cup & saucer, clear 8.75
Cup & saucer, pink 18.00
Goblet, wine, clear, 3¾" h., 3 oz.
(ILLUS.) 15.00
Goblet, wine, pink, 3¾" h., 3 oz. 45.50
Goblet, wine, red, 3¾" h., 3 oz. 175.00
Goblet, water, clear, 5½" h., 10 oz.
(ILLUS. center). 15.00
Goblet, water, pink, 5½" h., 10 oz. 35.00
Goblet, water, red, 5½" h., 10 oz. 150.00
Goblet, juice, clear, 4¾" h. 14.75

Goblet, juice, pink, 4¾" h. 47.00
Pitcher, 8½" h., 65 oz., clear 56.00
Pitcher, 8½" h., 65 oz., pink 88.00
Pitcher w/ice lip, 8½" h., 65 oz., clear . .50.00
Pitcher w/ice lip, 8½" h., 65 oz., pink. . .88.50
Plate, sherbet, 5¾" d., clear 2.50
Plate, sherbet, 5¾" d., pink 5.00
Plate, bread & butter, 6¾" d., clear 2.50
Plate, bread & butter, 6¾" d., green 6.00
Plate, bread & butter, 6¾" d., pink 9.75
Plate, salad, 8½" d., clear 4.50
Plate, salad, 8½" d., pink 12.50
Plate, dinner, 10¼" d., clear 9.00
Plate, dinner, 10¼" d., pink 17.00
Plate, grill, 10¼" d., clear 5.75
Plate, grill, 10¼" d., pink 11.75
Platter, 12" oval, clear. 10.00
Platter, 12" oval, pink 14.50
Relish, 4-part, clear, 8½" d. 6.75
Relish, 4-part, pink, 8½" d. 12.00
Relish, divided, clear, 12" d. 13.25
Relish, divided, pink, 12" d. 12.00
Salt & pepper shakers, clear, pr. 20.00
Salt & pepper shakers, green, pr. 198.00
Salt & pepper shakers, pink, pr. 40.00
Sherbet, clear 5.50
Sherbet, pink. 11.75
Sugar bowl, open, clear 6.00
Sugar bowl, open, pink 11.75
Tid bit server, 2-tier, clear 17.25
Tid bit server, 2-tier, pink 200.00
Tumbler, clear, 4" h., 5 oz. 12.50
Tumbler, pink, 4" h., 5 oz. 36.00
Tumbler, clear, 4½" h., 10 oz. 9.75
Tumbler, green, 4½" h., 10 oz. 12.00
Tumbler, pink, 4½" h., 10 oz. 23.00
Tumbler, clear, 6¾" h., 14 oz. 19.50
Tumbler, green, 6¾" h., 14 oz. 19.00
Tumbler, pink, 6¾" h., 14 oz. 43.00

MODERNTONE (Press-mold)

Blue Moderntone

Ash tray, blue, 5½" d. 11.50
Ash tray w/match holder, blue,
7¾" d. 140.00
Bowl, cream soup w/plain rim, 4¾" d.,
amethyst 6.50
Bowl, cream soup w/plain rim, 4¾" d.,
blue. 9.25
Bowl, nappy, 6½" d., blue 23.50
Bowl, soup, 7½" d., blue. 75.00
Bowl, nappy, 8¾" d., blue 27.50

Butter dish w/metal lid, blue 54.50
Creamer, amethyst 5.75
Creamer, blue. 6.75
Creamer & open sugar bowl, amethyst,
    pr.. . . . . .14.50
Creamer & open sugar bowl, blue, pr.
    (ILLUS.) 12.25
Creamer & sugar bowl w/metal lid,
    blue, pr.. . . . . .34.00
Cup & saucer, amethyst 7.25
Cup & saucer, blue 7.75
Custard or jello cup, amethyst 5.75
Custard or jello cup, blue 9.00
Nut bowl, handled, ruffled rim,
    amethyst, 5" d. 8.25
Nut bowl, handled, ruffled rim, blue,
    5" d. 15.00
Plate, sherbet, 5¾" d., amethyst 3.00
Plate, sherbet, 5¾" d., blue. 2.75
Plate, salad, 6¾" d., amethyst 4.25
Plate, salad, 6¾" d., blue 5.50
Plate, luncheon, 7¾" d., amethyst 5.25
Plate, luncheon, 7¾" d., blue 4.50
Plate, dinner, 8 7/8" d., amethyst 7.25
Plate, dinner, 8 7/8" d., blue 7.75
Plate, 10½" d., amethyst 16.00
Plate, 10½" d., blue. 19.50
Platter, 11" oval, amethyst 18.75
Platter, 11" oval, blue 17.75
Platter, 12" oval, amethyst 20.00
Platter, 12" oval, blue 26.50
Punch set: punch bowl in metal holder,
    8 cups & ladle w/blue knob; blue,
    11 pcs. 140.00
Salt & pepper shakers, amethyst, pr. . . .28.50
Salt & pepper shakers, blue, pr.
    (ILLUS.) 22.50
Sherbet, amethyst 5.25
Sherbet, blue. 6.50
Sugar bowl, open, amethyst. 5.50
Sugar bowl, open, blue 5.75
Sugar bowl w/metal lid, blue 20.00
Teapot, cov., "Little Hostess,"
    amethyst 31.50
Tumbler, whiskey, blue, 1½ oz. 13.50
Tumbler, blue, 5 oz.. . . . . .13.00
Tumbler, amethyst, 4" h., 9 oz. 12.25
Tumbler, blue, 4" h., 9 oz.. . . . . .14.50
Tumbler, amethyst, 12 oz.. . . . . .45.00
Tumbler, blue, 12 oz. 31.00

MOONSTONE (Press-mold)

(All items clear to opalescent only. Also see Hobnail.)

Bon bon, heart-shaped, 6½" w.. . . . . . . .7.25
Bowl, dessert, 5½" d., crimped 5.75
Bowl, 5½" d., straight 7.50
Bowl, cov., 6" d. 12.00
Bowl, 6½" d., handled, crimped 5.50
Bowl, 7¾" d. 7.25
Bowl, 9½" d., crimped 11.25
Candlesticks, 4¼" h., pr. (ILLUS.) 12.50

Moonstone Candlesticks

Candy jar, cov. .16.50
Cigarette box, cov.. . . . . .13.25
Creamer. 4.75
Cruet w/stopper 16.25
Cup & saucer 8.00
Dish, cloverleaf-shaped, 6" w. 7.25
Goblet, 10 oz. .12.00
Mustard jar, cov., w/spoon, 3" 16.00
Perfume bottle w/stopper, 5¼" h. 10.00
Plate, sherbet, 6¼" d. 2.75
Plate, luncheon, 8" d. 7.00
Plate, 10" d., crimped 14.00
Plate, 11" d. 12.50
Puff box, cov. 13.50
Relish, divided 6.75
Salt & pepper shakers, pr.. . . . . .31.00
Sherbet. 5.00
Sugar bowl. 4.75
Tumbler, 3½" h., 4 oz.. . . . . .8.50
Tumbler, footed, 5½" h. 13.00
Vase, 5" h. 8.25
Vase, 8" h. 16.00

NORMANDIE (Process-etched)

Normandie Cup & Saucer

Bowl, nappy, 5" d., amber 4.50
Bowl, nappy, 5" d., carnival 3.75
Bowl, nappy, 5" d., pink 5.25
Bowl, 6½" d., amber 7.75
Bowl, 6½" d., carnival 5.75

Bowl, nappy, 8½" d., amber 14.00
Bowl, nappy, 8½" d., carnival 10.75
Bowl, nappy, 8½" d., pink 15.50
Bowl, 9½" oval vegetable, amber. 11.50
Bowl, 9½" oval vegetable, carnival 12.50
Bowl, 9½" oval vegetable, pink. 25.00
Creamer, amber or carnival 5.50
Creamer, pink. 8.00
Creamer & cov. sugar bowl, amber,
    pr. 70.00
Creamer & open sugar bowl, amber,
    pr. 11.75
Creamer & open sugar bowl, carnival,
    pr. 10.50
Creamer & open sugar bowl, pink, pr. . .20.00
Cup & saucer, amber or pink 7.00
Cup & saucer, carnival (ILLUS.) 5.50
Pitcher, 8" h., 80 oz., amber 44.00
Pitcher, 8" h., 80 oz., clear 50.00
Pitcher, 8" h., 80 oz., pink 71.00
Plate, bread & butter, 6" d., amber 2.25
Plate, bread & butter, 6" d., carnival. 1.75
Plate, bread & butter, 6" d., pink 3.00
Plate, salad, 8" d., amber or pink 7.25
Plate, luncheon, 9¼" d., amber,
    carnival, or pink 7.75
Plate, dinner, 10½" d., amber 26.50
Plate, dinner, 10½" d., carnival. 9.75
Plate, dinner, 10½" d., pink 31.50
Plate, grill, 10½" d., carnival 5.75
Plate, grill, 10½" d., pink 22.00
Platter, 12" oval, amber 12.00
Platter, 12" oval, carnival 9.50
Platter, 12" oval, pink 13.75
Salt & pepper shakers, amber, pr. 32.00
Salt & pepper shakers, carnival, pr. 28.00
Salt & pepper shakers, pink, pr. 51.50
Sherbet, amber or pink 5.25
Sherbet, carnival 4.25
Sherbet, clear 3.25
Sugar bowl, cov., amber 66.00
Sugar bowl, open, amber 4.75
Sugar bowl, open, carnival 5.00
Tumbler, amber, 4" h., 5 oz. 11.00
Tumbler, pink, 4" h., 5 oz. 27.00
Tumbler, amber, 4½" h., 9 oz. 10.00
Tumbler, pink, 4½" h., 9 oz. 24.50
Tumbler, amber, 5" h., 12 oz. 13.50
Tumbler, pink, 5" h., 12 oz. 30.00

NUMBER 612 or Horseshoe (Process-etched)

Number 612 Sherbet

Bowl, berry, 4½" d., yellow 16.00
Bowl, cereal, 6½" d., green 14.50
Bowl, cereal, 6½" d., yellow 18.00
Bowl, salad, 7½" d., green 21.00
Bowl, salad, 7½" d., yellow 17.50
Bowl, berry, 9" d., green. 26.50
Bowl, berry, 9" d., yellow 28.50
Bowl, 10½" oval vegetable, green 12.75
Bowl, 10½" oval vegetable, yellow. 17.50
Butter dish, cov., green 650.00
Creamer, footed, green 10.50
Creamer, footed, yellow 12.50
Creamer & open sugar bowl, footed,
    green, pr. 19.50
Creamer & open sugar bowl, footed,
    yellow, pr. 26.50
Cup & saucer, green or yellow 10.00
Pitcher, 8½" h., 64 oz., green 170.00
Pitcher, 8½" h., 64 oz., yellow 267.00
Plate, sherbet, 6" d., green 3.00
Plate, sherbet, 6" d., yellow 3.50
Plate, salad, 8 3/8" d., green or
    yellow. 6.00
Plate, luncheon, 9 3/8" d., green or
    yellow. 7.50
Plate, dinner, 10 3/8" d., green 14.00
Plate, dinner, 10 3/8" d., yellow 10.00
Plate, 11¼" d., green 10.50
Plate, 11¼" d., yellow 12.00
Platter, 10¾" oval, green 13.00
Platter, 10¾" oval, yellow 14.50
Relish, 3-part, footed, green 15.50
Relish, 3-part, footed, yellow 19.50
Sherbet, green 9.50
Sherbet, yellow (ILLUS.) 12.00
Sugar bowl, open, footed, green 8.75
Sugar bowl, open, footed, yellow 9.50
Tumbler, footed, green or yellow,
    9 oz. 15.50
Tumbler, footed, green, 12 oz. 75.00
Tumbler, footed, yellow, 12 oz. 107.50

OLD CAFE (Press-mold)

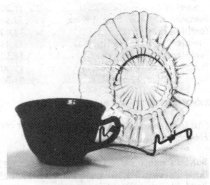

Old Cafe Cup & Saucer

Ash tray, red 3.50
Bowl, nappy, 3¾" d., clear 2.00
Bowl, nappy, 3¾" d., pink 3.00
Bowl, nappy, 5" d., handled, clear 5.00

Bowl, nappy, 5" d., handled, pink 3.50
Bowl, nappy, 5½" d., clear w/ruby
  cover. 10.00
Bowl, nappy, 5½" d., pink 7.00
Bowl, 9" d., handled, pink. 6.00
Bowl, 9" d., handled, red 7.50
Candy dish, cov., clear 3.50
Candy dish, cov., pink 4.50
Candy dish, cov., red 9.00
Cookie jar, cov., pink. 50.00
Cup & saucer, pink 8.00
Cup & saucer, red cup, clear
  saucer (ILLUS.) 8.50
Mint tray, low, flared, clear, 8" 3.50
Mint tray, low, flared, pink, 8" 4.50
Mint tray, low, flared, red, 8" 7.50
Olive dish, clear, 6" oblong 5.00
Olive dish, pink, 6" oblong 4.00
Pitcher, 8" h., 80 oz., pink 65.00
Plate, sherbet, 6" d., clear 4.00
Plate, sherbet, 6" d., pink 5.00
Plate, dinner, 10" d., pink 13.00
Sherbet, clear 3.00
Sherbet, pink. 4.00
Tumbler, juice, clear, 3" h. 4.00
Tumbler, juice, pink, 3" h. 5.00
Tumbler, clear, 4" h. 4.00
Tumbler, pink, 4" h. 7.00
Vase, 7¼" h., clear 5.00

OYSTER & PEARL (Press-mold)
Bowl, 5¼" heart shape, clear. 4.00
Bowl, 5¼" heart shape, pink 6.00
Bowl, 5¼" heart shape, red 10.00
Bowl, 5¼" heart shape, white
  w/green or w/pink 8.50
Bowl, 5¼" d., handled, clear 4.00
Bowl, 5¼" d., handled, pink. 5.00
Bowl, 5¼" d., handled, red 7.50
Bowl, 6½" d., handled, clear 4.00
Bowl, 6½" d., handled, pink. 8.00
Bowl, 6½" d., handled, red 9.50
Candlesticks, clear or pink, pr. 15.00
Candlesticks, green, pr. 8.00
Candlesticks, red, pr. 26.00
Candlesticks, white w/green or
  w/pink, pr. 16.00
Console bowl, clear, 10½" d. 14.00
Console bowl, pink, 10½" d. 15.50
Console bowl, red, 10½" d. 26.00
Console bowl, white, 10½" d. 10.00
Console bowl, white w/green or
  w/pink, 10½" d. 15.00
Plate, 13½" d., clear 11.50
Plate, 13½" d., pink. 16.00
Plate, 13½" d., red. 24.00
Relish, divided, clear or pink, 10¼"
  oval. 6.00
Vase, jadite. 8.50
Vase, white 14.50
Vase, white w/pink 13.00

PARROT or Sylvan (Process-etched)
Bowl, berry, 5" d., amber 13.00

Bowl, berry, 5" d., green. 15.00
Bowl, soup, 7" d., amber or green 22.00
Bowl, berry, 8" d., green. 49.00
Bowl, 8¼" sq., green. 64.00
Bowl, 10" oval vegetable, amber 37.50
Bowl, 10" oval vegetable, green 32.50
Butter dish, cov., green 235.00
Creamer, footed, green 18.00
Creamer & cov. sugar bowl, green,
  pr. 115.00
Creamer & open sugar bowl, amber,
  pr. 46.00
Creamer & open sugar bowl, green,
  pr. 38.00
Cup & saucer, amber 32.00
Cup & saucer, green 30.50
Jam dish, amber 24.00
Plate, sherbet, 5¾" d., amber 9.00
Plate, sherbet, 5¾" d., green 14.50
Plate, salad, 7½" d., green. 18.00
Plate, dinner, 9" d., amber 24.00
Plate, dinner, 9" d., green 28.50
Plate, grill, 10½" d., amber 15.50
Plate, grill, 10½" d., green 16.50
Platter, 11¼" oblong, amber 37.00
Platter, 11¼" oblong, green. 26.00
Salt & pepper shakers, green, pr. 195.00
Sherbet, cone-shaped, amber 13.00
Sherbet, cone-shaped, green 15.50
Sherbet, amber, 4¼" h. 12.00

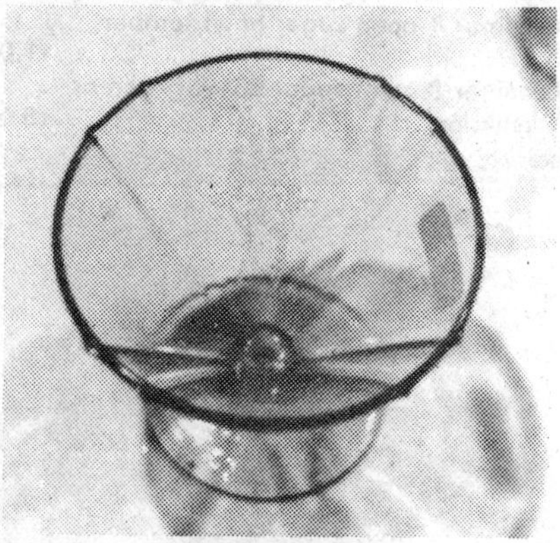

Parrot Sherbet

Sherbet, green, 4¼" h. (ILLUS.) 15.50
Sugar bowl, cov., green 98.00
Sugar bowl, open, amber 10.00
Sugar bowl, open, green. 16.00
Tumbler, green, 4¼" h., 10 oz. 110.00
Tumbler, green, 5½" h., 12 oz. 100.00
Tumbler, footed, cone-shaped, amber,
  5¾" h. 97.00
Tumbler, footed, cone-shaped, green,
  5¾" h. 120.00

PATRICIAN or Spoke (Process-etched)
Bowl, cream soup, 4¾" d., amber 9.00
Bowl, cream soup, 4¾" d., clear 6.00
Bowl, cream soup, 4¾" d., green 13.50
Bowl, cream soup, 4¾" d., pink. 14.00

Bowl, nappy, 5" d., amber 7.00
Bowl, nappy, 5" d., clear...............6.00
Bowl, nappy, 5" d., green 6.50
Bowl, nappy, 5" d., pink 8.50
Bowl, cereal, 6" d., amber 13.00
Bowl, cereal, 6" d., clear.............10.50
Bowl, cereal, 6" d., green 15.50
Bowl, nappy, 8½" d., amber 24.00
Bowl, nappy, 8½" d., clear 15.00
Bowl, nappy, 8½" d., green 22.00
Bowl, nappy, 8½" d., pink 14.00
Bowl, 10" oval vegetable, amber 17.00
Bowl, 10" oval vegetable, clear 12.50
Bowl, 10" oval vegetable, green 16.50
Bowl, 10" oval vegetable, pink........14.50
Butter dish, cov., amber 60.00
Butter dish, cov., clear...............61.50
Butter dish, cov., green 86.50
Butter dish, cov., pink 165.00
Cookie jar, cov., amber...............50.00
Cookie jar, cov., clear 65.00
Cookie jar, cov., green 117.00
Creamer, amber, clear or green 7.50
Creamer, pink.......................6.50
Creamer & cov. sugar bowl, amber,
   pr.................................42.00
Creamer & cov. sugar bowl, green,
   pr.................................57.50
Creamer & cov. sugar bowl, pink,
   pr.................................62.50
Creamer & open sugar bowl, amber,
   pr.................................11.00
Creamer & open sugar bowl, green or
   pink, pr..........................15.00

Patrician Cup & Saucer

Cup & saucer, amber or green (ILLUS.) ..11.50
Cup & saucer, clear 8.00
Cup & saucer, pink 12.00
Jam dish, amber, 6".................15.50
Jam dish, green, 6".................22.00
Pitcher, 8" h., 60 oz., amber 63.50
Pitcher, 8" h., 60 oz., clear 46.00
Pitcher, 8" h., 60 oz., green 88.00
Pitcher, 8" h., 60 oz., pink 135.00
Pitcher, 8½" h., 68 oz., clear 55.00
Pitcher, 8½" h., 80 oz., jug-type,
   amber.............................78.00
Pitcher, 8½" h., 80 oz., jug-type, clear ..75.00
Pitcher, 8½" h., 80 oz., jug-type,
   green 85.00

Plate, bread & butter, 6" d., amber 6.00
Plate, bread & butter, 6" d., clear or
   green 3.50
Plate, bread & butter, 6" d., pink 3.75
Plate, salad, 7½" d., amber, green or
   pink................................8.50
Plate, salad, 7½" d., clear 6.50
Plate, luncheon, 9" d., amber or green...6.00
Plate, luncheon, 9" d., clear 5.00
Plate, dinner, 10½" d., amber or clear 4.50
Plate, dinner, 10½" d., green or pink ...24.00
Plate, grill, 10½" d., amber 6.50
Plate, grill, 10½" d., clear 5.00
Plate, grill, 10½" d., green...........11.00
Plate, grill, 10½" d., pink 10.00
Plate, 11" d., amber 21.00
Platter, 11½" oval, amber 14.50
Platter, 11½" oval, clear............9.50
Platter, 11½" oval, green 12.50
Salt & pepper shakers, amber, pr......40.00
Salt & pepper shakers, clear, pr. 36.00
Salt & pepper shakers, green, pr. 46.00
Salt & pepper shakers, pink, pr......64.00
Sherbet, amber......................6.00
Sherbet, clear 5.00
Sherbet, green......................8.00
Sherbet, pink.......................7.50
Sugar bowl, cov., amber 40.00
Sugar bowl, open, amber 5.50
Sugar bowl, open, clear 5.00
Sugar bowl, open, green..............6.00
Sugar bowl, open, pink 7.00
Tumbler, amber, 4" h., 5 oz. 19.50
Tumbler, green, 4" h., 5 oz. 24.50
Tumbler, amber, 4½" h., 9 oz.........20.00
Tumbler, clear, 4½" h., 9 oz. 16.50
Tumbler, green, 4½" h., 9 oz.........22.00
Tumbler, pink, 4½" h., 9 oz..........17.00
Tumbler, footed, amber, 5" h., 10 oz. ...29.00
Tumbler, footed, clear, 5" h., 10 oz. 32.50
Tumbler, footed, green, 5" h., 10 oz. ...35.00
Tumbler, iced tea, amber, 5" h.,
   12 oz. 27.00
Tumbler, iced tea, amber, 5 3/8" h.,
   14 oz. 27.00
Tumbler, iced tea, clear, 5 3/8" h.,
   14 oz. 21.50
Tumbler, iced tea, green, 5 3/8" h.,
   14 oz. 29.50
Tumbler, iced tea, pink, 5 3/8" h.,
   14 oz. 46.00

PETALWARE (Press-mold)
Bowl, cream soup, 4½" d., clear 5.00
Bowl, cream soup, 4½" d., Cremax or
   Monax 7.00
Bowl, cream soup, 4½" d., pink.........6.50
Bowl, cereal, 5¾" d., clear 3.50
Bowl, cereal, 5¾" d., Cremax or
   Monax 5.00
Bowl, cereal, 5¾" d., pink 6.00
Bowl, 8¾" d., clear 12.00
Bowl, 8¾" d., Cremax 14.50
Bowl, 8¾" d., Monax.................12.50

Bowl, 8¾" d., pink 11.00
Bowl, 9¼" oval vegetable, Cremax 9.00
Bowl, 9¼" oval vegetable, pink 12.50
Creamer, Cremax or Monax 4.50
Creamer, pink 2.50
Creamer & open sugar bowl, Cremax
  or Monax, pr. 11.00
Creamer & open sugar bowl, pink, pr. . . .9.00
Cup & saucer, Cremax or pink 5.50
Cup & saucer, Monax 6.00
Lamp, clear 90.00
Lamp shade, Monax, 6" h. 7.50
Mustard jar w/metal cover, blue 10.50
Plate, bread & butter, 6" d., clear 1.00
Plate, bread & butter, 6" d., Cremax
  or Monax 2.00
Plate, bread & butter, 6" d., pink 1.75
Plate, salad, 8" d., clear 2.00
Plate, salad, 8" d., Cremax or
  Monax 3.50
Plate, salad, 8" d., pink 3.00
Plate, dinner, 9" d., clear 3.50
Plate, dinner, 9" d., Cremax, Monax
  or pink 5.00
Plate, salver, 11" d., Cremax 6.50
Plate, salver, 11" d., Monax or pink 7.00
Plate, salver, 12" d., Monax 10.00
Platter, 13" oval, clear 7.50
Platter, 13" oval, Cremax or Monax 10.00
Platter, 13" oval, pink 9.00
Sherbet, Cremax 5.00
Sherbet, Monax .7.00
Sherbet, pink 6.00
Sugar bowl, open, footed, Cremax,
  Monax or pink 4.50
Tid bit server, Monax 18.50

PINEAPPLE & FLORAL or Number 618 or Wild-flower (Press-mold)

Pineapple & Floral Plate

Ash tray, clear, 4½" 12.00
Bowl, berry, 4½" d., amber 19.50
Bowl, berry, 4½" d., clear 34.50
Bowl, cream soup, 4 5/8" d., amber 14.50
Bowl, cream soup, 4 5/8" d., clear 16.50

Bowl, cereal, 6" d., clear 16.50
Bowl, salad, 7" d., clear 4.00
Bowl, 10" oval vegetable, amber 13.00
Bowl, 10" oval vegetable, clear 16.50
Compote, diamond-shaped, amber 7.50
Compote, diamond-shaped, clear 2.00
Creamer, diamond-shaped, amber 8.00
Creamer, diamond-shaped, clear 5.50
Creamer & open sugar bowl, diamond-
  shaped, amber, pr. 12.00
Creamer & open sugar bowl, diamond-
  shaped, clear, pr. 10.50
Cup & saucer, amber or clear 9.00
Plate, sherbet, 6" d., amber (ILLUS.) 3.50
Plate, sherbet, 6" d., clear 3.00
Plate, salad, 8 3/8" d., amber 6.00
Plate, salad, 8 3/8" d., clear 4.50
Plate, dinner, 9 3/8" d., amber 12.00
Plate, dinner, 9 3/8" d., clear 9.00
Plate, grill, 10½" d., clear 12.50
Plate, 11½" d., amber 12.00
Plate, 11½" d., clear 10.50
Platter, 11", closed handles, amber 11.50
Platter, 11", closed handles, clear 8.00
Relish, divided, clear, 11½" 12.00
Sherbet, amber .10.00
Sherbet, clear 12.00
Sugar bowl, open, diamond-shaped,
  amber 7.00
Sugar bowl, open, diamond-shaped,
  clear 5.50
Tumbler, clear, 4" h., 9 oz. 21.00
Tumbler, iced tea, clear, 4½" h.,
  12 oz. 33.50

PRINCESS (Process-etched)

Princess Pattern Sugar Bowl

Ash tray, green, 4" 49.50
Bowl, nappy, 4½" d., green 16.00
Bowl, nappy, 4½" d., pink 11.50
Bowl, 5½" d., amber 18.00
Bowl, 5½" d., green 17.50
Bowl, 5½" d., pink 13.00
Bowl, 5½" d., yellow 22.00
Bowl, salad, 9" octagon, green or
  pink 22.00
Bowl, salad, 9" octagon, yellow 88.00
Bowl, 9½" hat shape, green 21.50
Bowl, 9½" hat shape, pink 24.00
Bowl, 10" oval vegetable, green 15.50
Bowl, 10" oval vegetable, pink 14.50
Bowl, 10" oval vegetable, yellow 44.50

Butter dish, cov., green 64.00
Butter dish, cov., pink 66.50
Cake stand, footed, green, 10" d. 14.50
Cake stand, footed, pink, 10" d. 13.50
Candy jar, cov., green or pink 35.00
Coaster, green, 4" 16.50
Cookie jar, cov., green 34.00
Cookie jar, cov., green frosted 28.00
Cookie jar, cov., pink. 40.50
Creamer, green .9.50
Creamer, pink 8.50
Creamer, yellow. 9.00
Creamer & cov. sugar bowl, green,
    pr.. . . . . .27.50
Creamer & cov. sugar bowl, pink or
    yellow, pr.. . . . . .30.00
Creamer & open sugar bowl, green,
    pr.. . . . . .16.00
Creamer & open sugar bowl, yellow,
    pr.. . . . . .18.50
Cup & saucer, amber or yellow 8.00
Cup & saucer, green. 11.00
Cup & saucer, pink 9.00
Pitcher, 6" h., 37 oz., jug-type,
    green 31.00
Pitcher, 6" h., 37 oz., jug-type, pink 27.00
Pitcher, 8" h., 60 oz., jug-type, green
    or pink 33.50
Pitcher, 8" h., 60 oz., jug-type, yellow . .64.50
Plate, sherbet, 6" d., amber 4.00
Plate, sherbet, 6" d., green 4.50
Plate, sherbet, 6" d., pink or yellow 3.00
Plate, salad, 8" d., amber, pink or
    yellow. 6.00
Plate, salad, 8" d., green 8.00
Plate, dinner, 9½" d., amber 8.00
Plate, dinner, 9½" d., green 17.00
Plate, dinner, 9½" d., pink 9.00
Plate, dinner, 9½" d., yellow 10.00
Plate, grill, 9½" d., amber or yellow 6.00
Plate, grill, 9½" d., green 10.00
Plate, grill, 9½" d., pink 7.00
Plate, grill, 11½" d., handled, green 8.50
Plate, grill, 11½" d., handled, pink or
    yellow. 6.50
Plate, 11½" d., handled, green 14.50
Plate, 11½" d., handled, pink 10.00
Platter, 12" oval, green 13.50
Platter, 12" oval, pink 12.00
Platter, 12" oval, yellow 32.50
Relish, divided, green 16.00
Relish, divided, pink 13.50
Salt & pepper shakers, green or pink,
    4½" h., pr.. .35.00
Salt & pepper shakers, yellow, 4½" h.,
    pr.. . . . . .64.50
Salt & pepper (or spice) shakers, green,
    5½" h., pr.. .31.00
Salt & pepper (or spice) shakers,
    yellow, 5½" h., pr.. . . . . .60.00
Sherbet, green .12.50
Sherbet, pink. 10.00
Sherbet, yellow. 22.50
Sugar bowl, cov., green (ILLUS.) 20.00

Sugar bowl, cov., pink 21.50
Sugar bowl, cov., yellow 22.00
Sugar bowl, open, amber 7.00
Sugar bowl, open, green or pink 8.00
Sugar bowl, open, pink frosted 2.75
Sugar bowl, open, yellow 7.50
Tumbler, green, 3½" h., 5 oz. 20.00
Tumbler, pink, 3½" h., 5 oz.. . . . . .13.50
Tumbler, yellow, 3½" h., 5 oz.. . . . . .18.50
Tumbler, green, 4" h., 9 oz. 17.00
Tumbler, pink, 4" h., 9 oz.. . . . . .12.00
Tumbler, yellow, 4" h., 9 oz.. . . . . .15.50
Tumbler, footed, green, 5¼" h.,
    10 oz. 20.00
Tumbler, footed, pink, 5¼" h.,
    10 oz. 14.50
Tumbler, footed, yellow, 5¼" h.,
    10 oz. 16.00
Tumbler, footed, green, 6½" h.,
    12 oz. 53.50
Tumbler, footed, pink, 6½" h., 12 oz. . . .26.00
Tumbler, footed, yellow, 6½" h.,
    12 oz. 19.00
Tumbler, green, 5" h., 12½ oz. 23.50
Tumbler, pink, 5" h., 12½ oz.. . . . . .17.00
Tumbler, yellow, 5" h., 12½ oz.. . . . . . . .20.00
Vase, 8" h., green or pink 20.00
Vase, 8" h., pink frosted 14.00

QUEEN MARY or Ribbed Vertical (Press-mold)

Queen Mary Cup & Saucer

Ash tray, oval, clear. 2.50
Ash tray, square, clear 4.00
Bowl, nappy, 4" d., clear or pink 2.50
Bowl, nappy, 4" d., handled, clear 2.50
Bowl, nappy, 4" d., handled, pink 3.25
Bowl, dessert, 4½" d., clear. 2.25
Bowl, dessert, 4½" d., pink 3.25
Bowl, 5½" d., 2-handled, clear 2.25
Bowl, 5½" d., 2-handled, pink 4.00
Bowl, 6" d., clear 3.25
Bowl, 6" d., pink 5.50
Bowl, nappy, 7" d., clear 5.50
Bowl, nappy, 7" d., pink 6.00
Bowl, 8¾" d., clear 8.50
Butter (or jam) dish, cov., clear 24.00
Butter (or jam) dish, cov., pink. 79.50

Candlesticks, clear, 4½" h., pr. 11.00
Candy jar, cov., clear. 14.00
Candy jar, cov., pink 22.00
Celery dish, oval, clear 5.50
Cigarette jar, clear, 2 x 3" oval 8.50
Coaster, clear, 3½" d. 2.50
Coaster, pink, 3½" d. 2.00
Coaster-ash tray, clear, 4¼" d. 3.00
Coaster-ash tray, pink, 4¼" d. 9.00
Compote, 5¾" d., clear. 6.00
Creamer, clear or pink 4.00
Creamer & open sugar bowl, clear, pr. . . . 6.50
Creamer & open sugar bowl, pink, pr. . . . 8.00
Cup & saucer, clear 4.50
Cup & saucer, pink (ILLUS.) 7.00
Pickle dish, clear 5.00
Plate, sherbet, 6" d., clear 2.00
Plate, sherbet, 6" d., pink 2.50
Plate, 6¾" d., clear 2.75
Plate, 6¾" d., pink. 4.00
Plate, salad, 8½" d., clear 4.00
Plate, salad, 8½" d., pink 5.50
Plate, dinner, 10" d., clear 10.00
Plate, dinner, 10" d., pink 19.00
Plate, 12" d., clear 7.00
Plate, 12" d., pink. 14.50
Plate, 14" d., clear 5.50
Punch cup, pink. 4.00
Punch set: punch bowl, 4 cups & ladle;
   clear, 6 pcs. 55.00
Relish, 3-part, clear, 12" d. 8.00
Relish, 4-part, clear, 14" d. 8.00
Salt & pepper shakers, clear, pr. 15.00
Salt & pepper shakers, clear w/red
   tops, pr. 20.00
Sherbet, clear 3.25
Sherbet, pink. 4.00
Sugar bowl, open, clear 4.50
Sugar bowl, open, pink 3.75
Tumbler, juice, pink, 3½" h., 5 oz. 5.00
Tumbler, water, pink, 4" h., 9 oz. 5.50
Tumbler, footed, clear, 5" h., 10 oz. . . . 11.00
Tumbler, footed, pink, 5" h., 10 oz. 15.50

RAINDROPS or Optic Design (Press-mold)

(All items listed are green.)

Bowl, berry, 4½" d. 4.00
Bowl, cereal, 6" d. 5.00
Creamer. 6.00
Cup & saucer 5.50
Plate, sherbet, 6" d. 1.75
Plate, luncheon, 8" d. 3.75
Sherbet. 4.25
Tumbler, whiskey, 1 7/8" h. 5.00
Tumbler, 3" h., 4 oz. 4.00
Tumbler, 11 oz. 7.50

RIBBON (Press-mold)

(While pattern was also made in black, all items listed are green.)

Bowl, 4" d. 12.00
Bowl, 8" d. 15.00
Candy dish, cov. 23.00
Creamer, footed 4.00
Creamer & open sugar bowl, footed,
   pr. 7.00
Cup & saucer 6.00
Plate, sherbet, 6¼" d. 1.75
Plate, luncheon, 8" d. 3.50
Salt & pepper shakers, pr. 15.50
Sherbet. 3.25
Sugar bowl, open, footed 3.75
Tumbler, 5½" h., 10 oz. 8.50
Tumbler, 6½" h., 13 oz. 14.00

RING or Banded Rings (Press-mold)

Bowl, 5" d., green. 3.25
Bowl, 8" d., green. 7.00
Butter tub or ice bucket, clear 7.50
Butter tub or ice bucket, green. 17.00
Cocktail shaker, clear 9.00
Cocktail shaker, green 12.00
Creamer, footed, clear 4.75
Creamer & open sugar bowl, footed,
   clear, pr. 7.50
Creamer & open sugar bowl, footed,
   green, pr. 11.00
Cup & saucer, clear or green 4.50
Decanter w/stopper, clear 13.00
Decanter w/stopper, green 18.50
Goblet, clear, 7" h., 9 oz. 5.00
Goblet, green, 7" h., 9 oz. 7.50
Pitcher, 8" h., 60 oz., clear 9.50
Pitcher, 8" h., 60 oz., green 10.00
Pitcher, 8½" h., 80 oz., clear 10.00
Pitcher, 8½" h., 80 oz., green 18.00
Plate, sherbet, 6¼" d., green 1.75
Plate, 6½" d., off-center ring, clear 1.75
Plate, 6½" d., off-center ring, green 3.25
Plate, luncheon, 8" d., clear 2.50
Plate, luncheon, 8" d., green 3.00
Salt & pepper shakers, clear, 3" h., pr. . . 20.00
Sandwich server w/center handle,
   clear 10.50
Sandwich server w/center handle,
   green 16.00
Sherbet, low, clear. 4.00
Sherbet, low, green 4.75
Sherbet, footed, clear, 4¾" 4.00
Sugar bowl, open, footed, clear or
   green 4.50
Tumbler, whiskey, clear, 2" h., 1½ oz. . . . 3.50
Tumbler, clear, 3½" h., 5 oz. 2.25
Tumbler, green, 3½" h., 5 oz. 4.00
Tumbler, clear, 4¼" h., 9 oz. 2.50
Tumbler, green, 4¼" h., 9 oz. 4.25
Tumbler, clear, 5 1/8" h., 12 oz. 3.50
Tumbler, green, 5 1/8" h., 12 oz. 4.50
Tumbler, cocktail, footed, clear, 3½" h. . . 3.25
Tumbler, water, footed, clear, 5½" h. . . . 3.75
Tumbler, iced tea, footed, clear,
   6½" h. 5.00
Tumbler, iced tea, footed, green,
   6½" h. 3.75

ROULETTE or Many Windows (Press-mold)

Bowl, fruit, 9" d., green 10.00
Cup & saucer, green 4.75
Pitcher, 8" h., 64 oz., green 22.50
Pitcher, 8" h., 64 oz., pink 21.00
Plate, sherbet, 6" d., green 2.00
Plate, luncheon, 8½" d., clear 3.00
Plate, luncheon, 8½" d., green 3.50
Plate, 12" d., green 8.00
Sherbet, green 3.75
Tumbler, whiskey, green, 2½" h.,
  1½ oz. 7.00
Tumbler, whiskey, pink, 2½" h.,
  1½ oz. 5.50
Tumbler, juice, pink, 3¼" h., 5 oz. 3.50
Tumbler, old fashioned, green, 3¼" h.,
  8 oz. 3.00
Tumbler, water, green, 4 1/8" h.,
  9 oz. 10.00
Tumbler, water, pink, 4 1/8" h.,
  9 oz. 9.00
Tumbler, footed, green, 5½" h.,
  10 oz. 12.00

ROYAL LACE (Process-etched)

Royal Lace Butter Dish

Bowl, cream soup, 5" d., blue 22.00
Bowl, cream soup, 5" d., clear 8.00
Bowl, cream soup, 5" d., green 20.50
Bowl, cream soup, 5" d., pink 11.00
Bowl, nappy, 5" d., blue 23.00
Bowl, nappy, 5" d., clear 11.50
Bowl, nappy, 5" d., green 18.50
Bowl, nappy, 5" d., pink 13.00
Bowl, nappy, 10" d., blue 33.50
Bowl, nappy, 10" d., green 19.50
Bowl, nappy, 10" d., pink 17.00
Bowl, 10" d., 3-footed, rolled edge,
  blue 42.00
Bowl, 10" d., 3-footed, rolled edge,
  pink 40.00
Bowl, 10" d., 3-footed, ruffled edge,
  blue 140.00
Bowl, 10" d., 3-footed, ruffled edge,
  clear 16.00
Bowl, 10" d., 3-footed, ruffled edge,
  pink 25.00
Bowl, 10" d., 3-footed, straight edge,
  blue 43.00
Bowl, 10" d., 3-footed, straight edge,
  clear 15.50

Bowl, 10" d., 3-footed, straight edge,
  pink 21.00
Bowl, 11" oval vegetable, blue 32.50
Bowl, 11" oval vegetable, clear 13.50
Bowl, 11" oval vegetable, green 19.50
Bowl, 11" oval vegetable, pink 17.00
Butter dish,, cov., blue 345.00
Butter dish, cov., clear (ILLUS.) 53.00
Butter dish, cov., green 195.00
Butter dish, cov., pink 115.00
Candlesticks, rolled edge, blue, pr. 90.00
Candlesticks, rolled edge, clear, pr. 35.00
Candlesticks, rolled edge, green, pr. . . .56.50
Candlesticks, rolled edge, pink, pr. 43.50
Candlesticks, ruffled edge, blue, pr. 95.00
Candlesticks, ruffled edge, clear, pr. 30.00
Candlesticks, ruffled edge, green, pr. . . .35.00
Candlesticks, ruffled edge, pink, pr. 38.00
Candlesticks, straight edge, blue, pr. 82.00
Candlesticks, straight edge, clear, pr. . . .27.00
Candlesticks, straight edge, green,
  pr. 57.50
Candlesticks, straight edge, pink, pr. . . .36.50
Cookie jar, cov., blue 210.00
Cookie jar, cov., clear 30.00
Cookie jar, cov., green 63.00
Cookie jar, cov., pink 37.00
Creamer, blue 25.00
Creamer, clear 7.50
Creamer, green .16.00
Creamer, pink 11.00
Creamer & cov. sugar bowl, blue, pr. . .125.00
Creamer & cov. sugar bowl, clear, pr. . .26.50
Creamer & cov. sugar bowl, pink, pr. . . .46.50
Creamer & open sugar bowl, blue, pr. . .47.50
Creamer & open sugar bowl, clear,
  pr. 13.00
Creamer & open sugar bowl, green,
  pr. 24.50
Creamer & open sugar bowl, pink,
  pr. 17.00
Cup & saucer, blue 27.00
Cup & saucer, clear 8.00
Cup & saucer, green 18.00
Cup & saucer, pink 13.00
Nut dish, pink, 5" d. 105.00
Pitcher, 54 oz., straight sides, blue 82.50
Pitcher, 54 oz., straight sides, clear 35.50
Pitcher, 54 oz., straight sides, green . . .72.50
Pitcher, 54 oz., straight sides, pink 46.50
Pitcher, 8" h., 68 oz., blue 105.00
Pitcher, 8" h., 68 oz., clear 39.00
Pitcher, 8" h., 68 oz., green 73.00
Pitcher, 8" h., 68 oz., pink 47.00
Pitcher, 8" h., 80 oz., blue 120.00
Pitcher, 8" h., 80 oz., clear 38.50
Pitcher, 8" h., 80 oz., green 67.50
Pitcher, 8" h., 80 oz., pink 52.50
Pitcher, 8½" h., 96 oz., blue 140.00
Pitcher, 8½" h., 96 oz., clear 43.00
Pitcher, 8½" h., 96 oz., green 105.00
Pitcher, 8½" h., 96 oz., pink 68.00
Plate, sherbet, 6" d., blue 8.00
Plate, sherbet, 6" d., clear 3.00

Plate, sherbet, 6" d., green 4.50
Plate, sherbet, 6" d., pink 4.00
Plate, luncheon, 8½" d., blue 22.00
Plate, luncheon, 8½" d., clear 5.00
Plate, luncheon, 8½" d., green 11.00
Plate, luncheon, 8½" d., pink 7.50
Plate, dinner, 10" d., blue 26.00
Plate, dinner, 10" d., clear 8.50
Plate, dinner, 10" d., green 15.50
Plate, dinner, 10" d., pink 10.00
Plate, grill, 10" d., blue 21.00
Plate, grill, 10" d., clear 8.50
Plate, grill, 10" d., green. 12.00
Plate, grill, 10" d., pink 9.00
Platter, 13" oval, blue 32.50
Platter, 13" oval, clear. 13.50
Platter, 13" oval, green 24.00
Platter, 13" oval, pink 16.00
Salt & pepper shakers, blue, pr. 185.00
Salt & pepper shakers, clear, pr. 35.50
Salt & pepper shakers, green, pr. 100.00
Salt & pepper shakers, pink, pr. 42.00
Sherbet, blue. 24.50
Sherbet, clear 7.50
Sherbet, green 17.00
Sherbet, pink. 9.00
Sherbet in metal holder, blue. 18.50
Sherbet in metal holder, clear 7.00
Sugar bowl, cov., blue 110.00
Sugar bowl, cov., clear 26.00
Sugar bowl, cov., green 45.00
Sugar bowl, cov., pink 32.00
Sugar bowl, open, blue 21.00
Sugar bowl, open, clear 6.50
Sugar bowl, open, green. 13.50
Sugar bowl, open, pink 8.00
Toddy set: cov. cookie jar, 8 tumblers,
 metal tray & ladle; blue, 11 pcs. 135.00
Tumbler, blue, 3" h., 5 oz. 23.50
Tumbler, clear, 3" h., 5 oz. 8.50
Tumbler, pink, 3" h., 5 oz. 13.50
Tumbler, blue, 4" h., 9 oz. 23.00
Tumbler, clear, 4" h., 9 oz. 8.00
Tumbler, green, 4" h., 9 oz. 16.00
Tumbler, pink, 4" h., 9 oz. 11.00
Tumbler, blue, 4¾" h., 12 oz. 36.50
Tumbler, green, 4¾" h., 12 oz. 34.00
Tumbler, pink, 4¾" h., 12 oz. 15.00
Tumbler, blue, 5 3/8" h., 13 oz. 42.50
Tumbler, green, 5 3/8" h., 13 oz. 45.00
Tumbler, pink, 5 3/8" h., 13 oz. 31.00

ROYAL RUBY (Press-mold)

(All items in ruby red.)

Ash tray, 4½" sq. 4.00
Bowl, berry, 4¼" d. 3.50
Bowl, 5¼" d. 6.50
Bowl, soup, 7½" d. 7.00
Bowl, 8" oval vegetable. 14.00
Bowl, berry, 8½" d. 10.00
Console bowl, 11½" d. 18.00
Creamer, flat. 5.00

Creamer, footed .4.50
Creamer & sugar bowl, flat, pr. 9.50
Creamer & sugar bowl, footed, pr. 15.00
Cup & saucer 4.50
Goblet, ball stem 7.00
Pitcher, 42 oz., tilted or upright 20.00
Pitcher, 3-qt., tilted or upright 26.00
Plate, sherbet, 6½" d. 3.00
Plate, salad, 7" d. 3.50
Plate, luncheon, 7¾" d. 3.25
Plate, dinner, 9" d. 6.00
Punch bowl 24.50
Punch bowl & base 45.00
Punch cup. 2.50
Salt & pepper shakers, pr. 60.00
Sherbet. 4.50
Sugar bowl, flat .4.25
Sugar bowl, footed 6.50
Tumbler, cocktail, 3½ oz. 5.50
Tumbler, juice, 5 oz. 3.50
Tumbler, water, 9 oz. 4.00
Tumbler, water, 10 oz. 4.00
Tumbler, iced tea, 13 oz. 5.50
Vase, 4" h., ball-shaped 4.00
Vase, bud, 5½" h., ruffled top 5.50
Vase, 6½" h., bulbous. 6.00
Wine, 2½ oz. 7.00

SANDWICH (Press-mold)

Desert Gold Cup & Saucer

Bowl, dessert, 4 7/8" d., amber or
 clear 3.00
Bowl, dessert, 4 7/8" d., desert gold 2.50
Bowl, dessert, 4 7/8" d., green 3.00
Bowl, dessert, 4 7/8" d., pink 3.50
Bowl, 6" d., clear 10.50
Bowl, 6" d., desert gold 6.00
Bowl, 6" d., pink 7.00
Bowl, salad, 6½" d., amber 6.50
Bowl, salad, 6½" d., clear 5.00
Bowl, salad, 6½" d., desert gold 5.50
Bowl, salad, 6½" d., green 20.00
Bowl, nappy, 7" d., clear 6.00
Bowl, nappy, 7" d., green 29.00
Bowl, 8" d., clear 6.50
Bowl, 8" d., desert gold 5.00

Bowl, 8" d., green 38.00
Bowl, 8" d., pink .11.50
Bowl, 8½" d., red 26.00
Bowl, 8½" oval vegetable, clear 4.00
Bowl, 8½" oval vegetable, green 35.00
Bowl, 9" d., clear 12.50
Butter dish, cov., amber 47.50
Butter dish, cov., clear 26.50
Cookie jar, cov., amber or clear 25.00
Cookie jar, cov., desert gold 23.50
Cookie jar, cov., green 15.00
Creamer, clear 3.50
Creamer, green .13.00
Creamer & cov. sugar bowl, clear, pr. . .14.00
Creamer & cov. sugar bowl, green,
    pr. 27.00
Creamer & open sugar bowl, clear, pr. . . .5.50
Creamer & open sugar bowl, green,
    pr. 23.00
Cup & saucer, amber 5.00
Cup & saucer, clear 3.00
Cup & saucer, desert gold 4.00
Cup & saucer, green 20.00
Custard cup, clear 2.25
Custard cup, green 2.00
Pitcher, juice, 6" h., 36 oz., clear 43.00
Pitcher, juice, 6" h., 36 oz., green 84.00
Pitcher w/ice lip, 2-qt., clear 44.00
Pitcher w/ice lip, 2-qt., green 175.00
Plate, 4½" d., amber or green 1.50
Plate, dessert, 7" d., amber 3.00
Plate, dessert, 7" d., clear 5.00
Plate, dessert, 7" d., desert gold 1.75
Plate, 8" d., clear 2.75
Plate, dinner, 9" d., amber 4.75
Plate, dinner, 9" d., clear 8.00
Plate, dinner, 9" d., desert gold 3.50
Plate, dinner, 9" d., green 39.00
Plate, snack, 9" d., clear 3.50
Plate, serving, 12" d., amber 8.00
Plate, serving, 12" d., clear 16.00
Punch bowl & stand, clear 25.00
Punch cup, clear .1.50
Punch set: punch bowl & 6 cups; clear,
    7 pcs. 23.50
Punch set: punch bowl & 8 cups; clear,
    9 pcs. 29.00
Punch set: punch bowl, base & 8 cups;
    clear, 10 pcs. .35.00
Punch set: punch bowl, base & 10 cups;
    clear, 12 pcs. .35.00
Punch set: punch bowl, base & 12 cups;
    clear, 14 pcs. .55.00
Sherbet, clear 3.50
Sugar bowl, cov., clear 12.50
Sugar bowl, cov., green 15.00
Sugar bowl, open, clear 2.50
Sugar bowl, open, green 12.50
Tumbler, clear, 5 oz. 3.75
Tumbler, green, 5 oz. 2.25
Tumbler, water, clear, 9 oz. 5.00
Tumbler, water, green, 9 oz. 2.75
Tumbler, footed, clear, 9½ oz. 12.50
Vase, green 14.00

Water set: small pitcher & 6 tumblers;
    green, 7 pcs. .100.00

SHARON or Cabbage Rose (Chip-mold)

Sharon Pattern Tumblers

Bowl, cream soup, 5" d., amber 18.00
Bowl, cream soup, 5" d., green 27.00
Bowl, cream soup, 5" d., pink 26.00
Bowl, nappy, 5" d., amber 5.00
Bowl, nappy, 5" d., green 7.50
Bowl, nappy, 5" d., pink 6.50
Bowl, cereal, 6" d., amber 10.50
Bowl, cereal, 6" d., green 16.00
Bowl, cereal, 6" d., pink 14.00
Bowl, soup, 7½" d., amber 25.50
Bowl, soup, 7½" d., green 27.00
Bowl, soup, 7½" d., pink 24.00
Bowl, nappy, 8½" d., amber 4.50
Bowl, nappy, 8½" d., green 16.50
Bowl, nappy, 8½" d., pink 15.00
Bowl, 9½" oval vegetable, amber 9.50
Bowl, 9½" oval vegetable, green or
    pink 14.00
Bowl, fruit, 10½" d., amber 14.00
Bowl, fruit, 10½" d., green or pink 20.00
Butter dish, cov., amber 35.50
Butter dish, cov., green 62.50
Butter dish, cov., pink 37.00
Cake plate, footed, amber, 11½" d. 18.50
Cake plate, footed, clear, 11½" d. 9.50
Cake plate, footed, green, 11½" d. 60.00
Cake plate, footed, pink, 11½" d. 22.00
Candy jar, cov., amber 32.00
Candy jar, cov., green 145.00
Candy jar, cov., pink 35.50
Cheese dish, cov., amber 155.00
Cheese dish, cov., pink 610.00
Creamer, amber .7.50
Creamer, green .12.50
Creamer, pink 9.50
Creamer & cov. sugar bowl, amber
    or pink, pr. 32.00
Creamer & cov. sugar bowl, green,
    pr. 40.00
Creamer & open sugar bowl, amber,
    pr. 13.00

Creamer & open sugar bowl, green,
 pr. 24.00
Creamer & open sugar bowl, pink, pr. . .16.00
Cup & saucer, amber 10.00
Cup & saucer, green or pink 14.00
Jam dish, amber, 7½" 23.00
Jam dish, green, 7½" 30.00
Jam dish, pink, 7½" 86.00
Pitcher, 9" h., 80 oz., amber 82.50
Pitcher, 9" h., 80 oz., pink 96.00
Pitcher w/ice lip, 9" h., 80 oz., amber . . .87.50
Pitcher w/ice lip, 9" h., 80 oz., clear 45.00
Pitcher w/ice lip, 9" h., 80 oz., green . .340.00
Pitcher w/ice lip, 9" h., 80 oz., pink. 98.00
Plate, bread & butter, 6" d., amber 2.50
Plate, bread & butter, 6" d., green 4.00
Plate, bread & butter, 6" d., pink 3.50
Plate, salad, 7½" d., amber 10.00
Plate, salad, 7½" d., green 12.50
Plate, salad, 7½" d., pink 17.00
Plate, dinner, 9¼" d., amber 8.50
Plate, dinner, 9¼" d., green or pink 11.00
Platter, 12¼" oval, amber 10.00
Platter, 12¼" oval, green or pink 14.00
Salt & pepper shakers, amber, pr. 30.00
Salt & pepper shakers, green, pr. 50.00
Salt & pepper shakers, pink, pr. 35.00
Sherbet, amber 8.00
Sherbet, green 18.00
Sherbet, pink 9.00
Sugar bowl, cov., amber 23.00
Sugar bowl, cov., green 38.00
Sugar bowl, cov., pink 28.00
Sugar bowl, open, amber 6.50
Sugar bowl, open, green 8.00
Sugar bowl, open, pink 7.50
Tumbler, amber, 4" h., 9 oz. 18.00
Tumbler, green, 4" h., 9 oz. 50.00
Tumbler, pink, 4" h., 9 oz. 21.00
Tumbler, amber, 5¼" h., 12 oz. (ILLUS.
 left) 29.00
Tumbler, green, 5¼" h., 12 oz. 47.50
Tumbler, pink, 5¼" h., 12 oz. 28.50
Tumbler, footed, amber, 6½" h., 15 oz.
 (ILLUS. right) .60.00
Tumbler, footed, pink, 6½" h., 15 oz. . . .32.00

SIERRA or Pinwheel (Press-mold)
Bowl, berry, 4" d., green or pink 6.00
Bowl, cereal, 5½" d., green or pink 6.00
Bowl, berry, 8½" d., green 12.50
Bowl, berry, 8½" d., pink 10.50
Bowl, 9½" oval vegetable, green 31.00
Bowl, 9½" oval vegetable, pink 29.50
Butter dish, cov., green or pink 46.00
Creamer, green .11.50
Creamer, pink 8.00
Creamer & cov. sugar bowl, pink, pr. . . .20.00
Cup & saucer, green 11.50
Cup & saucer, pink 9.50
Pitcher, 6½" h., 32 oz., green 58.00
Pitcher, 6½" h., 32 oz., pink 37.50
Plate, dinner, 9" d., green 10.50
Plate, dinner, 9" d., pink 9.00

Platter, 11" oval, green 25.00
Platter, 11" oval, pink 18.00
Salt & pepper shakers, green, pr. 28.00
Salt & pepper shakers, pink, pr. 24.50
Serving tray, 2-handled, green or pink . . .9.00
Sugar bowl, cov., green or pink 16.50
Tumbler, footed, green, 4½" h., 9 oz. . .37.00
Tumbler, footed, pink, 4½" h., 9 oz. 19.50

SPIRAL (Press-mold)

(All items in green only.)

Bowl, mixing, 7" d. 16.50
Bowl, berry, 8" d. 13.50
Candlesticks, low, pr. 15.00
Candy dish, cov. 18.00
Creamer, footed .5.50
Creamer & sugar bowl, flat or footed,
 pr. 15.00
Cup & saucer 4.75
Ice or butter tub 15.00
Mug. 35.00
Pitcher, 7 5/8" h., 58 oz. 20.00
Plate, sherbet, 6" d. 1.75
Plate, luncheon, 8" d. 2.50
Preserve, cov. 14.50
Salt & pepper shakers, pr. 21.50
Sandwich server w/center handle 18.50
Sherbet. 2.75
Sugar bowl, flat .5.50
Tumbler, water, 5" h., 9 oz. 8.00
Tumbler, iced tea, 5¼" h., 12 oz. 8.50

SWIRL (Press-mold)

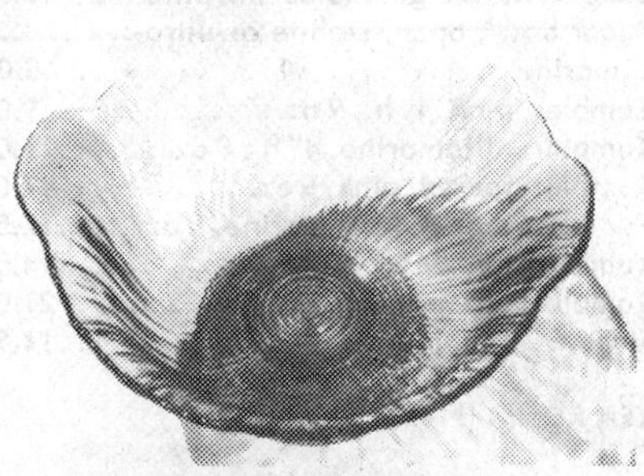

Swirl Pattern Fruit Bowl

Berry set: master bowl & 6 sauce
 dishes; Delfite, 7 pcs. 35.00
Bowl, nappy, 5¼" d., Delfite or ultra-
 marine 7.00
Bowl, nappy, 5¼" d., pink 5.00
Bowl, nappy, 9" d., Delfite or ultra-
 marine 14.00
Bowl, nappy, 9" d., pink 12.00
Bowl, fruit, 10" d., handled, footed,
 pink 11.50
Bowl, fruit, 10" d., handled, footed,
 ultramarine (ILLUS.) 20.00
Butter dish, cov., pink 110.00
Butter dish, cov., ultramarine 170.00
Candlesticks, double, ultramarine,
 pr. 22.00

Candy dish, cov., pink 71.50
Candy dish, cov., ultramarine 75.00
Candy dish, open, 3-footed, pink,
   5½" d. 10.00
Candy dish, open, 3-footed, ultra-
   marine, 5½" d. 9.00
Coaster, pink, 1 x 3¼". 6.00
Coaster, ultramarine, 1 x 3¼" 7.00
Coaster, pink (Goodyear Tire) 15.00
Console bowl, footed, ultramarine,
   10½" d. 15.00
Creamer, Delfite, pink or ultramarine . . .7.50
Creamer & open sugar bowl, pink, pr. . .11.00
Creamer & open sugar bowl, ultra-
   marine, pr. 14.50
Cup & saucer, Delfite 13.00
Cup & saucer, pink 7.00
Cup & saucer, ultramarine 8.00
Plate, sherbet, 6½" d., Delfite. 4.00
Plate, sherbet, 6½" d., pink 2.25
Plate, sherbet, 6½" d., ultramarine 3.00
Plate, salad, 7¼" d., ultramarine 9.00
Plate, 8" d., ultramarine 8.50
Plate, dinner, 9½" d., Delfite. 7.00
Plate, dinner, 9½" d., pink 6.00
Plate, dinner, 9½" d., ultramarine 8.50
Plate, 12½" d., pink. 8.50
Plate, 12½" d., ultramarine 12.00
Platter, 12" oval, Delfite 17.50
Salt & pepper shakers, ultramarine,
   pr. 26.00
Sherbet, pink. 5.00
Sherbet, ultramarine 9.00
Soup bowl w/lug handles, pink 10.00
Soup bowl w/lug handles, ultramarine .15.00
Sugar bowl, open, Delfite or ultra-
   marine 8.00
Tumbler, pink, 4" h., 9 oz. 9.00
Tumbler, ultramarine, 4" h., 9 oz. 11.00
Tumbler, footed, pink, 9 oz. 7.00
Tumbler, footed, ultramarine, 9 oz. 17.50
Tumbler, pink, 4¾" h., 12 oz. 14.50
Tumbler, ultramarine, 4¾" h., 12 oz. . . .21.00
Vase, 8½" h., pink or ultramarine 14.50

TEA ROOM (Press-mold)

Tea Room Tumbler

Banana split dish, green, 7½" 38.50
Bowl, salad, 8¾" d., green 57.50
Bowl, salad, 8¾" d., pink 47.00
Bowl, 9½" oval vegetable, green 46.00
Bowl, 9½" oval vegetable, pink. 42.00
Candlesticks, green, pr. 44.50
Candlesticks, pink, pr. 40.50
Celery or pickle dish, clear, 8½" 11.50
Celery or pickle dish, green, 8½" 19.00
Creamer, clear .10.50
Creamer, green .12.00
Creamer, pink. .12.50
Creamer & cov. sugar bowl, green or
   pink, pr. 23.00
Creamer & open sugar bowl on tray,
   green 45.50
Creamer & open sugar bowl on tray,
   pink. 49.00
Cup & saucer, green 36.00
Cup & saucer, pink 32.00
Goblet, green, 9 oz. 56.00
Goblet, pink, 9 oz. 51.50
Ice bucket, green 57.00
Ice bucket, pink 51.00
Lamp, electric, green, 9". 40.50
Lamp, electric, pink, 9" 33.00
Mustard, cov., clear 45.00
Mustard, cov., green or pink 125.00
Parfait, green 21.50
Parfait, pink 20.00
Pitcher, 64 oz., green 115.00
Pitcher, 64 oz., pink 90.00
Plate, sherbet, 6½" d., green 22.50
Plate, sherbet, 6½" d., pink 15.50
Plate, luncheon, 8¼" d., green 26.00
Relish, divided, clear or pink 10.50
Relish, divided, green 16.50
Salt & pepper shakers, clear, pr. 46.50
Salt & pepper shakers, green, pr. 42.00
Salt & pepper shakers, pink, pr. 44.00
Sandwich server w/center handle,
   pink. 92.50
Sherbet, footed, ice cream, green 25.00
Sherbet, low-footed sundae, green. 18.00
Sherbet, low-footed sundae, pink 13.00
Sherbet, tall-footed sundae, green 27.00
Sugar bowl, cov., green, 4" h. 12.50
Sugar bowl, cov., pink, 4" h. 10.00
Sugar bowl, cov., footed, green or
   pink, 4½" h. .11.00
Sugar bowl, open, oblong, pink 10.00
Tumbler, green, 8½ oz. 19.00
Tumbler, pink, 8½ oz. 16.00
Tumbler, footed, green, 9 oz. 22.00
Tumbler, footed, pink, 9 oz. (ILLUS.) 12.50
Tumbler, green, 11 oz. 28.50
Tumbler, pink, 11 oz. 25.00
Tumbler, clear, 12 oz. 17.00
Tumbler, green, 12 oz. 36.00
Tumbler, pink, 12 oz. 30.00
Vase, 6" h., ruffled rim, green 45.00
Vase, 6" h., ruffled rim, pink 35.00
Vase, 9" h., ruffled rim, clear. 18.00
Vase, 9" h., ruffled rim, green 37.00

Vase, 11" h., ruffled rim, clear 39.50
Vase, 11" h., ruffled rim, green 66.00
Vase, 11" h., ruffled rim, pink 62.00
Water set: pitcher & 5 tumblers; green,
  6 pcs. 160.00
Water set: pitcher & 6 tumblers; pink,
  7 pcs. 180.00

TWISTED OPTIC (Press-mold)
Bowl, cream soup, 4¾" d., green 7.00
Bowl, cereal, 5" d., green 7.50
Bowl, 9" d., pink 17.00
Candlesticks, amber, 3", pr. 16.00
Candlesticks, clear, 3", pr. 9.50
Candlesticks, green, 3", pr. 14.00
Candlesticks, pink, 3", pr. 11.00
Candlesticks, yellow, 3", pr. 22.50
Candy jar, cov., green 17.00
Coaster, pink. 2.00
Creamer, amber .8.50
Creamer, pink 5.50
Creamer, yellow .9.00
Creamer & open sugar bowl, green, pr. . .9.00
Creamer & open sugar bowl, pink, pr. . .11.00
Cup & saucer, green 11.00
Cup & saucer, pink 7.00
Olive dish, pink. .6.50
Plate, sherbet, 6" d., amber 2.50
Plate, sherbet, 6" d., green or pink 2.00
Plate, salad, 7" d., green 3.00
Plate, luncheon, 8" d., amber or pink 3.50
Plate, luncheon, 8" d., clear 3.00
Plate, luncheon, 8" d., green 4.00
Plate, luncheon, 8" d., yellow 6.50
Sandwich server w/center handle,
  amber or green 14.00
Sandwich server w/center handle,
  yellow. 30.00
Sherbet, green or pink. 4.25
Sugar bowl, open, amber 4.00
Sugar bowl, open, green 5.00
Sugar bowl, open, pink 6.00
Tumbler, pink, 4½" h., 9 oz. 7.00
Tumbler, green, 5¼" h., 12 oz. 4.00
Tumbler, pink, 5¼" h., 12 oz. 8.00
Vase, green. 22.50

WATERFORD or Waffle (Press-mold)
Ash tray, clear, 4" 3.50
Bowl, dessert, 4¾" d., clear 4.00
Bowl, dessert, 4¾" d., pink 6.00
Bowl, nappy, 5¼" d., clear 10.00
Bowl, nappy, 5¼" d., pink 16.00
Bowl, nappy, 8¼" d., clear 6.00
Bowl, nappy, 8¼" d., pink 11.00
Butter dish, cov., clear. 18.00
Butter dish, cov., pink 175.00
Cake plate, handled, clear, 10¼" d. 5.00
Cake plate, handled, pink, 10¼" d. 8.00
Coaster, clear, 4" 1.50
Coaster, pink, 4". 2.50
Creamer, clear 2.50
Creamer, pink. 8.00
Creamer & cov. sugar bowl, clear, pr. . . .8.50

Creamer & cov. sugar bowl, pink, pr. . . .26.50
Creamer & open sugar bowl, clear, pr. . . .5.00
Creamer & open sugar bowl, pink, pr. . .12.00
Cup & saucer, clear 5.50
Cup & saucer, pink 11.00
Goblet, clear, 5¼" h. 11.00
Goblet, clear, 6" h. 9.00
Lamp, clear, 4" h. 26.00
Pitcher, 42 oz., jug-type, clear 13.50
Pitcher w/ice lip, 80 oz., clear 20.00
Pitcher w/ice lip, 80 oz., pink 88.00
Plate, sherbet, 6" d., clear 2.00
Plate, sherbet, 6" d., pink 3.25

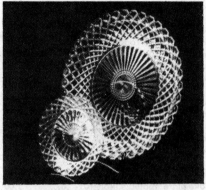

Waterford Pattern Plates

Plate, salad, 7½" d., clear (ILLUS.) 2.50
Plate, salad, 7½" d., pink 4.50
Plate, dinner, 9 5/8" d., clear 4.50
Plate, dinner, 9 5/8" d., pink 10.00
Plate, 10¼" d., handled, clear 4.50
Plate, 10¼" d., handled, pink 9.00
Plate, 13¾" d., clear (ILLUS.) 7.00
Plate, 13¾" d., pink. 10.00
Relish, 5-section, clear w/ruby inserts,
  13¾" d. 17.50
Relish, 5-section, green w/ivory
  inserts, 13¾" d. 33.00
Salt & pepper shakers, clear, short, pr. . .5.00
Salt & pepper shakers, clear, tall, pr. 6.00
Salt & pepper shakers, pink, tall, pr. 7.00
Sherbet, clear 2.50
Sherbet, pink. 6.50
Sugar bowl, cov., clear 5.50
Sugar bowl, open, clear 2.50
Sugar bowl, open, pink 6.50
Tumbler, footed, clear, 3½" h., 5 oz. 8.00
Tumbler, footed, pink, 3½" h., 5 oz. 12.00
Tumbler, footed, clear, 5" h., 10 oz. 7.00
Tumbler, footed, pink, 5" h., 10 oz. 8.50

WINDSOR DIAMOND or Windsor (Press-mold)
Ash tray, Delfite, 5¾" d. 32.00
Ash tray, green, 5¾" d. 37.50
Ash tray, pink, 5¾" d. 28.00
Bowl, nappy, 4¾" d., clear 3.25
Bowl, nappy, 4¾" d., green 5.75
Bowl, nappy, 4¾" d., pink 5.00
Bowl, cream soup, 5" d., green 14.50

Bowl, cream soup, 5" d., pink 12.50
Bowl, cereal, 5 1/8" d., green 13.50
Bowl, cereal, 5 1/8" d., pink 12.00
Bowl, 5 3/8" d., green 10.00
Bowl, 5 3/8" d., pink 12.00
Bowl, 7" d., footed, clear 5.50
Bowl, 7" d., footed, green 4.00
Bowl, 7" d., footed, pink 15.50
Bowl, 8" d., pink 21.50
Bowl, 8" d., 2-handled, pink 10.00
Bowl, nappy, 8½" d., clear or green 12.00
Bowl, nappy, 8½" d., pink 10.00
Bowl, 9½" d., handled, clear 9.50
Bowl, 9½" d., handled, green 13.50
Bowl, 9½" d., handled, pink 12.50
Bowl, 9½" oval vegetable, green 12.50
Bowl, 9½" oval vegetable, pink 10.50
Bowl, fruit, 10½" d., clear 15.50
Bowl, fruit, 10½" d., green 19.00
Bowl, fruit, 10½" d., pink, sharp
    points 125.00
Bowl, 11¾ x 7" boat shape, clear 15.00
Bowl, 11¾ x 7" boat shape, green or
    pink 20.00
Bowl, 12½" d., pink 63.50
Butter dish, cov., clear 18.50
Butter dish, cov., green 69.50
Butter dish, cov., pink 36.50
Cake plate, footed, clear, 10¾" d. 5.00
Cake plate, footed, green, 10¾" d. 17.00
Cake plate, footed, pink, 10¾" d. 12.00
Cake plate, green, 13½" d. 19.00
Candlesticks, clear, 3" h., pr. 12.00
Candlesticks, green, 3" h., pr. 21.00
Candlesticks, pink, 3" h., pr. 54.00
Candy jar, cov., clear 10.50
Coaster, clear, 3" d. 2.00
Coaster, green or pink, 3" d. 7.50
Creamer, flat, clear 4.00
Creamer, flat, green 7.50
Creamer, flat, pink 5.00
Creamer, footed, clear 2.25
Creamer, footed, green 10.00
Creamer, footed, pink 7.50
Creamer & cov. sugar bowl, footed,
    pink, pr. 21.00
Creamer & open sugar bowl, pink, pr. . .13.00
Cup & saucer, clear 4.25
Cup & saucer, green or pink 9.00
Pitcher, milk, 4½" h., 16½ oz., clear . . .13.50
Pitcher, milk, 4½" h., 16½ oz., green . .11.00
Pitcher, milk, 4½" h., 16½ oz., pink . . .83.00
Pitcher, juice, 5" h., 20 oz., clear 10.00
Pitcher, juice, 5" h., 20 oz., pink 17.00
Pitcher, 6¾" h., 52 oz., clear 15.00
Pitcher, 6¾" h., 52 oz., green 41.00
Pitcher, 6¾" h., 52 oz., pink 23.50
Plate, sherbet, 6" d., clear 1.50
Plate, sherbet, 6" d., green 4.00
Plate, sherbet, 6" d., pink 3.00
Plate, salad, 7" d., clear 3.75
Plate, salad, 7" d., green or pink 10.00
Plate, dinner, 9" d., clear 4.50
Plate, dinner, 9" d., green 10.00

Plate, dinner, 9" d., pink 9.00
Plate, chop, 13 5/8" d., clear 5.50
Plate, chop, 13 5/8" d., green or pink . . .14.50
Platter, 11½" oval, clear 4.25
Platter, 11½" oval, green or pink 10.00
Powder jar, cov., clear 7.50
Relish, divided, clear, 11½" 6.00
Relish, divided, green, 11½" 5.00
Salt & pepper shakers, clear, pr. 12.00
Salt & pepper shakers, green, pr. 33.50
Salt & pepper shakers, pink, pr. 26.00
Sandwich tray, handled, clear, 10¼" d. . .6.00
Sandwich tray, handled, green,
    10¼" d. 10.00

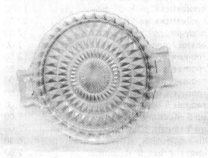

Windsor Diamond Sandwich Tray

Sandwich tray, handled, pink, 10¼" d.
    (ILLUS.) 9.00
Sherbet, clear 2.25
Sherbet, green 7.50
Sherbet, pink 6.00
Sugar bowl, cov., flat, clear 7.00
Sugar bowl, cov., flat, green or pink 13.00
Sugar bowl, cov., footed, clear 3.50
Sugar bowl, cov., footed, green 19.00
Sugar bowl, cov., footed, pink 14.00
Sugar bowl, open, clear 4.00
Sugar bowl, open, green 6.00
Sugar bowl, open, pink 5.50
Tray, green or pink, 4" sq. 12.00
Tray, pink, 8" sq. 50.00
Tray, green, 9 x 4 1/8" 16.00
Tray, pink, 9¾ x 8½" 29.00
Tray, handled, clear, 9¾ x 8½" 5.00
Tray, handled, green or pink, 9¾ x
    8½" 30.00
Tray, clear, 13½" 10.00
Tray, green or pink, 13½" 14.00
Tumbler, clear, 3¼" h., 5 oz. 4.00
Tumbler, green, 3¼" h., 5 oz. 20.00
Tumbler, pink, 3¼" h., 5 oz. 10.00
Tumbler, clear, 4" h., 9 oz. 3.00
Tumbler, green, 4" h., 9 oz. 15.00
Tumbler, pink, 4" h., 9 oz. 8.50
Tumbler, footed, clear, 4" h., 9 oz. 4.00
Tumbler, clear, 5" h., 12 oz. 5.50
Tumbler, green, 5" h., 12 oz. 20.00
Tumbler, pink, 5" h., 12 oz. 14.00
Tumbler, footed, clear, 7¼" h. 7.00

(End of Depression Glass Section)

DE VEZ & DEGUE

"Cristallerie de Pantin" Vase

Cameo glass with the name De Vez was made in Pantin, France, by Saint-Hilaire, Touvier De Varreaux and Company. Some pieces made by this firm were signed "Degue," after one of the firm's glassmakers. The official company name was "Cristallerie de Pantin."

Cameo vase, 4" h., 2 5/8" d.,
  carved purple scene of
  house, river & tree against soft
  frosted pink ground, signed
  DeVez.........................$395.00
Cameo vase, 5" h., 2 3/8" d., carved
  navy blue to rose to yellow island
  scene w/houses & mountainous background, leafy tree branches frame
  top of scene, signed DeVez.........475.00
Cameo vase, 6" h., 2 7/8" d., carved
  navy blue to yellow & soft pink
  scene of inlet w/islands, trees &
  mountainous background, tree
  branches frame top of scene,
  signed DeVez 550.00
Cameo vase, 6" h., 3" d., carved
  navy blue to rose scene of hunting
  dog w/bird in his mouth swimming to
  shore, thatched hunter's blind,
  grasses on shore & bird in sky
  against frosted gold ground, signed
  DeVez.........................750.00
Cameo vase, 6½" h., 2 7/8" d.,
  carved & enameled navy blue to
  yellow & pink scene of mountain
  lake, trees & foliage against shell
  pink satin ground, signed DeVez 595.00
Cameo vase, 8" h., 3" d., barrel-
  shaped, carved deep green to rose
  scene w/tree-lined shore in foreground, water, mountains & trees in
  distance against soft frosted gold
  ground, signed DeVez 595.00

Cameo vase, 8¼" h., 2¾" d., carved
  navy blue to rose scene of trees,
  island w/tower & clouds in sky againt
  frosted gold ground, pine cones
  framing top border, signed DeVez ..650.00
Cameo vase, 9 3/8" h., 2 5/8" d.,
  carved dark green to rose river
  landscape scene w/trees & hills
  against frosted gold ground, signed
  DeVez.........................605.00
Cameo vase, 9½" h., 3½" d.,
  bulbous base & tall slender neck,
  carved green to rose scene w/large
  swan & 3 small swans swimming in
  foreground against frosted gold
  ground, signed DeVez 875.00
Cameo vase, 9¾" h., 2½" d., carved
  brown to yellow to off white
  harbor scene w/two men in boat in
  foreground, other boats & house on
  shore, leafy branches frame top of
  scene, signed DeVez 650.00
Cameo vase, 11½" h., carved &
  enameled rose to purple irises,
  foliage & dragonfly against acid-
  cut frosted ground, signed "Pantin"
  (ILLUS.).........................650.00
Cameo vase, 13" h., carved forest
  green tranquil river scene w/moun-
  tains & grassy banks against
  pale blue ground, ca. 1910, signed
  DeVez.........................880.00

DUNCAN & MILLER

Duncan & Miller Opalescent Bowl

Duncan & Miller Glass Company, a successor firm to George A. Duncan & Sons Company, was operated by George A. Duncan and Edwin C. Miller in Washington, Pa., from the late 19th century and produced many types of pressed wares and novelty pieces, many of which are now eagerly sought by collectors. George A. Duncan was a pioneer glass manufacturer, associated earlier with several firms. Also see ANIMALS under Glass.

Basket, Canterbury patt., clear, 8" h. . .$45.00
Bowl, 3½" h., square w/flaring
  shaped rim, pink opalescent (ILLUS.) .27.50

Bowl, 11" d., Venetian patt., clear 25.00
Candlesticks, First Love patt., clear,
    pr. 65.00
Carafe, Mardi Gras patt., clear 35.00
Champagne, Teardrop patt., clear 8.00
Cocktail shaker, Chanticleer Rooster,
    ruby . . . . .210.00 to 245.00
Console set: bowl & pr. 2-light candle-
    sticks; First Love patt., clear, 3 pcs. . . . 95.00
Console set: bowl & pr. candlesticks;
    Hobnail patt., yellow, 3 pcs. 60.00
Cornucopia vase, First Love patt.,
    clear, 8" 46.00
Cornucopia vase, Cape Cod patt.,
    blue opalescent, 14" 95.00
Goblet, Hobnail patt., pink
    opalescent 30.00
Hat shape, Hobnail patt., pink opal-
    escent, small 40.00
Hat shape, Hobnail patt., pink opal-
    escent, large 88.00
Ice bucket, Nautilus patt., clear 95.00
Ice cream set: 8" master bowl & six
    4" matching bowls; Star in Square
    patt., ruby-stained, 7 pcs. 165.00
Mayonnaise bowl & underplate,
    Teardrop patt., clear 18.00
Punch bowl & base, Mardi Gras patt.,
    clear, 14" d., 11½" h. 250.00
Relish dish, divided cloverleaf shape,
    clear w/silver overlay, 8" d. 19.00
Relish, 3-handled, Canterbury
    patt. w/etched flowers & butter-
    flies, clear, 8" .21.00
Relish, Teardrop patt., clear, 12" 20.00
Swan, ruby, 3½" .65.00
Swan, blue opalescent, 6" 48.00
Swan, pink opalescent w/pink neck,
    6½" l. 65.00
Swan, clear, 7" l. . . . . .10.00 to 15.00
Swan, ruby w/clear neck,
    8" l. . . . . .26.00 to 40.00
Swan, chartreuse w/clear neck,
    12½" l. 75.00
Swan, clear, 12½" 40.00
Swan, emerald green w/clear neck &
    head, 13" 48.00
Tumbler, Canterbury patt., clear,
    13 oz. 14.00

Teardrop Pattern Short Tumbler

Tumbler, flat, scotch & soda, Teardrop
    patt. (ILLUS.) 8.00
Tumbler, iced tea, footed, Teardrop
    patt., clear, 6" h. 8.75
Vase, 3½" h., Chanticleer patt., blue
    opalescent satin 95.00

DURAND

Durand Perfume Bottle

*Fine decorative glass similar to that made
by Tiffany and other outstanding glasshouses of its day was made by the Vineland
Flint Glass Works Co. in Vineland, N.J.,
first headed by Victor Durand, Sr., and
subsequently by his son Victor Durand, Jr.,
in the 1950s. Also see SHADES under
Glass.*

Bowl-vase, bulbous rose bowl shape,
    iridescent peacock blue, signed,
    7½" d. $700.00
Box & cover w/star-cut lid,
    iridescent deep blue King Tut patt.,
    5½ x 3½" 875.00
Candlesticks, ruby peacock body,
    "saucer" rims & wafer attached to
    Spanish yellow bases, pr. 495.00
Compote, 7" d., 6¾" h., iridescent
    gold, signed & numbered 350.00
Luncheon set: 7 dinner plates, 15 lunch-
    eon plates, 6 bowls & underplates &
    5 similar bowls; translucent amber
    w/ruffled rims edged in green,
    unsigned, 39 pcs. 440.00
Perfume bottle w/original stopper,
    iridescent gold w/applied gold
    threading, 6" h. (ILLUS.) 550.00
Plate, 8" d., ruby w/white pulled
    feathering & faint pink concentric
    circles over the white feathers,
    "Bridgeton Rose" engraving by
    Charles Link on underside 300.00

Rose bowl, deep iridescent blue &
  silver King Tut patt., signed 510.00
Sherbet, blue w/white pulled
  feathering 225.00
Sherbet, green w/white pulled
  feathering, signed 225.00
Sherbet & underplate, King Tut patt....325.00
Vase, 4" h., iridescent amber engraved w/three thistle plants,
  signed..........................125.00
Vase, 6" h., iridescent amber,
  signed..........................145.00
Vase, 6¼" h., 5 3/8" d., iridescent
  blue w/applied random threading,
  signed..........................762.00
Vase, 6½" h., 5¼" d., iridescent
  butterfly blue w/random iridescent
  threading, signed 750.00
Vase, 6¾" h., silver lustre w/pulled
  green & opal decor, unsigned.......285.00
Vase, 7" h., bulbous, translucent
  green, brown, purple & yellow,
  unsigned 225.00
Vase, 7" h., iridescent deep blue,
  signed..........................350.00

Unsigned Covered Vase

Vase, cov., 7½" h., iridescent blue
  w/imbedded white hearts & clinging vines, unsigned (ILLUS.).......1,000.00
Vase, 7½" h., gold lustre w/trailing
  green lustre vine & leaves.........575.00
Vase, 7¾" h., globular w/narrow neck
  & flaring turned-down rim, iridescent
  gold w/medial banding of intaglio
  cut florals & foliage, signed.......1,350.00
Vase, 8" h., bulbous, iridescent green
  w/silver King Tut patt., signed 1,150.00
Vase, 9" h., baluster-shaped, iridescent gold w/gold & cream pulled
  feathering & applied w/green & gold
  "spider web" threading, signed &
  numbered........................308.00
Vase, 9" h., gold lustre & white King
  Tut patt., iridescent gold interior....550.00
Vase, 9" h., green & gold King Tut
  patt. (ILLUS.) 650.00

King Tut Vase

Vase, 9½" h., "crackle," iridescent
  blue & white exterior, gold interior,
  unsigned 395.00
Vase, 12" h., baluster-shaped, iridescent white w/imbedded amber & gold
  gold hearts & vines & applied
  threading, unsigned................308.00
ase, 12½" h., green & gold King Tut
  patt. w/pink & lavender highlights,
  signed..........................950.00
Wine, ruby w/white pulled peacock
  feathering, 5½" h. 425.00

FENTON

Dancing Ladies Vases

*Fenton Art Glass Company began
producing glass at Williamstown, West
Virginia, in January 1907. Organized by
Frank L. and John W. Fenton, the company
began operations in a newly built glass
factory with an experienced master glass
craftsman, Jacob Rosenthal, as their
factory manager. Fenton has produced a
wide variety of collectible glassware
through the years, including Carnival
(which see). Still in production today, their
current productions may be found at finer
gift shops across the country.*

Basket, Hobnail patt., plum opalescent,
4½" h. $65.00
Basket, Dot Optic patt., cranberry
opalescent, 7" h. 85.00
Basket, Hobnail patt., blue opalescent,
5" d., 7" h. .22.00
Basket, Hobnail patt., cranberry opal-
escent, 10". .60.00
Basket, Diamond Optic patt., black,
chrome handle, ca. 1931 . . . . .200.00
Candlestick, Venetian red (opaque),
ca. 1924, 10" h. (single) 67.50
Candy jar, cov., Jade green, 1925 . . . . . .45.00
Compote, 10" d., Mikado patt.,
Mandarin red (opaque), ca. 1934 . . . .275.00
Pitcher, 6" h., Diamond Optic patt.,
cranberry 75.00
Pitcher, Rib Optic patt., green opal-
escent, applied cobalt blue handle . . .85.00
Vase, 8" h., 6" w., bulbous melon
shape, ruffled rim, ruby 55.00
Vase, 8" h., peacock blue satin 30.00
Vase, 9" h., Dancing Ladies patt.,
periwinkle blue (ILLUS. center) 190.00
Vase, 9" h., Dancing Ladies patt.,
green (ILLUS. each side). . . .150.00 & 200.00
Vase, 9" h., 2-handled, "Hanging
Heart" art glass, Oriental Ivory,
ca. 1925 . . . . .175.00
Vase, footed, "Karnak Red" art glass
w/entwining loops & leaf forms,
ca. 1925 . . . . .400.00

FINDLAY ONYX

Findlay Onyx

*This ware was produced by Dazell, Gill-
more & Leighton Co., of Findlay, O., about
1889. Some pieces are layered glass and
other homogeneous with a molded raised
pattern. It was produced in several colors
with lustred patterns contrasting with the
body color.*

Celery vase, creamy ivory w/silver
(or platinum), 6½" h. $525.00
Creamer, raspberry red w/white
opalescent design 850.00
Salt shaker w/original top, cinnamon
w/silver, 2¾" h. (ILLUS. left) 165.00

Salt shaker w/original top, creamy
ivory w/silver, 2¾" h. (single) 125.00
Spooner, creamy ivory
w/silver. . . . . .250.00 to 395.00
Spooner, raspberry red w/white
opal. 665.00
Sugar bowl, cov., creamy ivory
w/silver, 4½" d., 6" h. (ILLUS.
center) 485.00
Sugar bowl, cov., raspberry red
w/white opal. 570.00
Sugar shaker w/original top, creamy
ivory w/silver, 5¾" h. (ILLUS.
right) . . . . .365.00 to 450.00
Vase, 4" h., creamy ivory
w/silver. . . . . .175.00 to 225.00

FLORETTE

*Florette was made by the Consolidated
Lamp & Glass Co. of Pittsburgh, Pennsylvania, from 1894. A variety of items were
made in white, soft blue, pink, soft green &
yellow opaque with both a glossy and a
satin finish. Less frequently encountered
are those items made in Pigeon Blood red
and apricot satin glass.*

Butter dish, cov., pink satin
finish . . . .$160.00 to 185.00
Condiment set: salt & pepper shakers
& mustard jar w/original tops in
handled holder; pink satin finish,
set 135.00
Condiment set: salt & pepper shakers
& mustard jar w/original tops in
handled stand; blue, glossy finish,
cased, set 115.00
Condiment set: salt & pepper shakers
& mustard jar w/original tops in
handled stand; pink, glossy finish,
cased, set. 150.00
Cookie jar w/original silverplate lid,
pink satin finish 185.00
Creamer, pink satin finish . . . .65.00 to 110.00
Pitcher, water, 7¼" h. pale blue
satin finish, applied camphor handle,
white lining .250.00
Pitcher, water, 7¼" h., blue, glossy
finish 195.00
Pitcher, water, 7¼" h., pink, satin
finish. 200.00
Salt shaker w/original top,
pale blue, glossy finish 50.00
Sugar shaker w/original top, pink
satin finish 115.00
Syrup pitcher w/original silverplate
top, pink satin finish, squat form 185.00
Table set: cov. butter dish, sugar
bowl, creamer & spooner; pink
satin finish, 4 pcs. 450.00

Toothpick holder, pale blue, glossy
finish...........................40.00
Toothpick holder, pink, glossy finish....45.00
Toothpick holder, yellow, glossy
finish...........................62.00
Tumbler, pink satin finish.............50.00
Vase, 5¾" h., pink, glossy finish,
cased...........................52.50

FOSTORIA

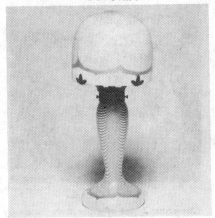

Fostoria Lamp

Fostoria Glass Company, founded in 1887, is still in operation today in Moundsville, West Va. It has produced numerous types of fine wares through the years, many of which are now being collected. Also see ANIMALS and SHADES under Glass.

Bouillon cup & saucer, June patt.,
pink...........................$45.00
Bowl, 6" d., Heirloom patt., pink
opalescent......................25.00
Bowl, 12" d., 3-footed, Versailles
patt., blue......................50.00
Butter dish, cov., Fairfax patt., green,
round...........................68.00
Butter dish, cov., Priscilla patt., green
w/gold..........................95.00
Candle holders, Chintz patt., clear,
4" h., pr........................28.00
Candle holders, Trojan patt., amber,
pr.............................37.50
Clarets, Buttercup patt., clear, set
of 8...........................128.00
Cocktail, Chintz patt., clear...........18.00
Cocktail, Navarre patt., clear.........15.00
Cocktail, Willowmere patt., clear......14.00
Compote, cov., 6¼" d., 8½" h.,
Vintage patt., clear..............40.00
Compote, open, 5" d., Navarre patt.,
clear...........................16.00
Console set: oval bowl & pr. candle
holders; Baroque patt., blue, 3 pcs...50.00

Console set: 11½" bowl & pr. double
candle holders; Meadow Rose patt.,
clear, 3 pcs.....................50.00
Cordial, Romance patt., clear.........20.00
Cordials, Beacon patt., clear, set
of 12..........................140.00
Creamer & sugar bowl, Romance patt.,
clear, pr........................20.00
Creamer & sugar bowl, footed, June
patt., yellow, pr.................46.00
Creamer & sugar bowl, Romance patt.,
clear, pr........................47.00
Cup & saucer, Navarre patt., clear.....16.00
Cup & saucer, Versailles patt., pink....32.50
Goblet, Chintz patt., clear............18.50
Goblet, Romance patt., clear.........11.75
Goblet, Vintage patt., clear..........12.00
Ice bucket, 2-handled, Versailles
patt., green.....................53.00
Lamp, cased domical shade, baluster
base, opalescent w/striated green
feathering edged in iridescent
amber, ca. 1912, 6 5/8" d.,
15¼" h. (ILLUS.).................880.00
Plate, 7½" d., Versailles patt., blue.....8.00
Plate, 9" d., Versailles patt., yellow....13.00
Rose bowl, Vesper patt., amber,
medium size.....................18.00
Sherbet, Chintz patt., clear...........14.50
Sherbet, Navarre patt., clear.........18.00
Sherbets, Trojan patt., topaz, set of 6...75.00
Torte plate, Romance patt., clear,
14" d...........................20.00
Tray w/center handle, Versailles
patt., topaz.....................30.00
Tumbler, iced tea, footed, Buttercup
patt., clear......................20.00
Tumbler, iced tea, footed, Navarre
patt., clear......................18.50
Tumbler, water, footed, Trojan patt.,
topaz, 5¾" h.....................18.00
Tumbler, whiskey, footed, June patt.,
yellow, 2 oz......................75.00
Vase, Oakwood Fan patt., Azure blue..75.00
Wine, Chintz patt., clear.............24.00
Wine, Trojan patt., yellow...........35.00

FRANCES WARE

This was made by Hobbs, Brockunier & Co., Wheeling, West Va., in the 1880s. It is frosted or clear glass with stained amber tops or rims and was both mold-blown and pressed. It usually has a pattern of hobnails or swirled ribs.

Berry set: 9" oval bowl & 12 sauce
dishes; frosted swirl w/amber
rims, 13 pcs.....................$375.00
Bowl, berry, 7½" sq., frosted
hobnail w/amber rim.......60.00 to 80.00

Bowl, berry, 9 x 7" oval, clear hob-
nail w/amber rim 65.00
Butter dish, cov., frosted hobnail
w/amber rim 95.00
Celery tray, frosted hobnail
w/amber rim, 12 x 7" 85.00
Celery tray, frosted swirl w/amber
rim, 12 x 7" . . . . .55.00 to 75.00
Creamer, clear hobnail w/amber rim . . .50.00
Creamer, frosted hobnail w/amber
rim 70.00
Creamer & cov. sugar bowl, frosted
hobnail w/amber rim, pr. 145.00
Finger bowl, frosted swirl w/amber
rim 25.00
Ice cream tray, frosted hobnail
w/amber rim, 14 x 9½" 225.00
Pitcher, milk, 5" h., clear hobnail
w/amber rim 165.00
Pitcher, milk, 5½" h., frosted
hobnail w/amber rim 185.00

Frances Ware Pitcher

Pitcher, water, frosted hobnail
w/amber rim (ILLUS.) . . . . .150.00 to 185.00
Pitcher, child's, clear hobnail w/amber
rim 125.00
Sauce dish, 4" sq., clear hobnail
w/amber rim .28.00
Sauce dish, 4" sq., frosted hobnail
w/amber rim . . . . .25.00 to 32.00
Spooner, clear hobnail w/amber rim . . .45.00
Spooner, frosted hobnail w/amber
rim 60.00
Sugar bowl, cov., frosted hobnail
w/amber rim .75.00
Sugar bowl, cov., frosted swirl
w/amber rim . . . . .85.00 to 110.00
Sugar bowl, open, frosted hobnail
w/amber rim .55.00
Syrup pitcher w/original lid, frosted
hobnail w/amber rim 125.00
Table set: cov. butter dish, cov. sugar
bowl, creamer & spooner; frosted
hobnail w/amber rim,
4 pcs. . . . . .290.00 to 360.00

Toothpick holder, frosted hobnail
w/amber rim .48.00
Toothpick holder, frosted swirl
w/amber rim .95.00
Tumbler, clear hobnail w/amber
rim 35.00
Tumbler, frosted hobnail w/amber
rim 42.50

FRY

Fry Foval Creamer

*Numerous types of glass were made by
the H.C. Fry Company, Rochester, Pa. One
type of its art line was called Foval (and also
Pearl Art Glass) and was blown in the
mid-1920s. Cheaper was its silky-opalescent
ovenware made for utilitarian purposes but
also now being collected. The company also
made fine cut glass.*

Bread pan, ovenware, opalescent $15.00
Candlesticks, Foval, blue-tinged white
opaline w/Delft blue spiral thread-
ing, 12" h., pr. 169.00
Casserole, cov., ovenware, oval 35.00
Creamer, Foval, pearly opaline
w/blue-tinted loopings, applied
Delft blue handle (ILLUS.) 135.00
Cup & saucer, Foval, opaline w/Delft
blue handle . . . . .75.00 to 85.00
Cup & saucer, Foval, opaline w/Jade
green handle .85.00
Lemonade pitcher & cover, clear
"crackle" w/Jade green
handle . . . . .85.00 to 95.00
Lemonade pitcher & cover, Foval, opal-
ine w/applied Delft blue handle &
finial, 10½" h. 165.00
Lemonade set: pitcher & 4 mugs; clear
"crackle" w/green handle on pitcher
& clear handles on mugs, 5 pcs. 115.00
Plate, grill, ovenware 20.00
Platter, 16½" l., ovenware 30.00
Vase, 11" h., jack-in-pulpit type, Foval,
opaline w/Delft blue spiral twist &
3 rows of blue at crimped rim 150.00

GALLE'

Galle' Cameo Bowl

Galle' glass was made in Nancy, France, by Emile Galle', a founder of the Nancy School and a leader in the Art Nouveau movement in France. Much of his glass, both enameled and cameo, is decorated with naturalistic motifs. The finest pieces were made in the last two decades of the 19th century and the opening years of the present one. Pieces marked with a star preceding the name were made between Galle's death in 1904 and 1914.

Bon bon dish, cover & underplate, clear w/enameled pastel ribbons, bows, flying insects & rows of dots, signed, 7¼" d. underplate, 5½" h. $950.00

Cameo bottle w/florette-form stopper, carved pale lavender poppy blossoms & leafage against grey ground streaked w/pale lavender, fire-polished, ca. 1900, signed, 5¼" h. 880.00

Cameo bowl, 4½" d., carved purple clematis blossoms & vines against grey ground, ca. 1900, signed 385.00

Cameo bowl, 4¼" h., conical w/incurved notched rim, carved dusty rose & lavender prunus blossoms, leafage & vines against clear "martele" surface, fire-polished, ca. 1900, signed 4,675.00

Cameo bowl, 14¾" d., raised on short yellow foot, carved crimson, deep pink & lavender waterlily pads, buds & blossoms against magenta to pale yellow ground, fire-polished interior, ca. 1900, signed (ILLUS.).........2,200.00

Cameo liqueur, spherical bowl carved w/dusty rose nasturtium blossoms & leafage against clear ground,

raised on short pale avocado cylindrical stem & circular foot, fire-polished, ca. 1900, 3" h. 1,980.00

Cameo perfume flacon, rectangular, carved amber kneeling figure one side, bear & figure on horseback reverse, against pale grey ground splashed w/oxblood red & cut & enameled in blue, white & rust w/Persian-inspired florettes & strapwork, ca. 1900, signed, w/gilt mounts of later date, 4½" h. 605.00

Cameo vase, 2½" h., 3" d., carved green leaves against frosted ground, signed..........................400.00

Cameo vase, 3" h., oval, carved & enameled cream, azure, rust, pink, green & brown blossoms & leafage w/gilt details against pale green ground, ca. 1900, signed 1,320.00

Cameo vase, 4¾" h., footed, carved lavender & plum nasturtium blossoms & leafage against pale grey ground splashed w/lavender, fire-polished, ca. 1900, signed 660.00

Cameo vase, 5" h., slightly waisted cylinder, carved olive green spiky leafage against grey & dusty rose ground, ca. 1900, signed 330.00

Cameo vase, 5½" h., pyriform, carved & enameled amber, mustard, oxblood red, pale green & deep brown fuchsia blossoms & leafage against pale amber ground, whole heightened w/gilding, ca. 1900, signed 1,980.00

Galle' Cameo Vases

Cameo vase, 5 7/8" h., tiered foot, carved cherry red poppy blossoms & leafage against grey & yellow ground, partially fire-polished, signed w/star, 1904-14 (ILLUS. right)..........................660.00

Cameo vase, 8¼" h., tapering cylinder w/collared neck, carved Chinese red & burgundy sprays of wild roses &

leafage against yellow ground, ca.
1900, signed (ILLUS. left) 1,210.00

Cameo vase, 9" h., flattened ovoid
w/waisted neck, carved ochre-
brown pendant pine boughs w/pine
cones against ice blue ground, neck
w/applied silver lip & pendant relief-
molded pine branch, foot applied
w/simple silver ring, ca. 1900,
signed 3,410.00

Cameo vase, 9" h., gourd-shaped,
carved amber oak leaves & acorns
against moss green ground internally
decorated w/gold inclusions, fire-
polished, signed 2,250.00

Galle' Mold-Blown Cameo Vase

Cameo vase, 9½" h., mold-blown &
cameo-carved bright green & brown
blossoming clematis vines against
yellow & grey ground, ca. 1925,
signed (ILLUS.) 3,025.00

Cameo vase, 9 5/8" h., expanding
cylinder, carved green & brown
river landscape w/trees on banks
against salmon pink & grey
ground, ca. 1900, signed 880.00

Cameo vase, 10½" h., Pilgrim flask
form, carved spray of crimson
hyacinth blossoms & leafage against
yellow ground, ca. 1900, signed ...1,430.00

Cameo vase, 13¼" h., globular,
carved lime to deeper green
pendant sycamore branches against
grey ground, ringed at neck
w/salmon, ca. 1900, signed 880.00

Cameo vase, 14" h., pedestal base,
carved dark to light blue florals
against frosted white ground,
signed 1,400.00

Cameo vase, 15¾" h., carved deep
cranberry red & green undulating
fern fronds & grasses against
pale grey & emerald green
ground, ca. 1900, signed 1,210.00

Wine jug w/original rigaree-trimmed
stopper, enameled thistles on
amber, signed..................945.00

GOOFUS

Goofus Bowl with Strawberries

*This is a name collectors have given a
pressed glass whose colors were sprayed on
and then fired. Most pieces have intaglio or
convex designs and were produced by the
Northwood Glass Co.*

Bowl, 7" d., 3½" h., footed, molded
strawberries & leaves, red & gold ...$27.50

Bowl, 9" d., molded cherries & leaves,
red & gold 20.00

Bowl, 9" d., red raspberries 21.00

Bowl, 9½" d., 3½' h., scalloped rim,
long stemmed red roses on gold 38.00

Bowl, 9½" d., pedestal base, crimped
& fluted rim, red & gold Greek Key
motif & floral & leaf center on
green ....30.00 to 38.00

Bowl, 10" d., pears & apples, red &
gold ....28.00 to 37.50

Bowl, 10" d., ruffled rim, red strawberries & gold leaves (ILLUS.) 26.00

Bread tray, "The Lord's Supper," red &
gold, w/clear grapes........30.00 to 45.00

Compote, 6½" d., cherries & leaves,
red & gold 17.50

Compote, 9½" d., ruffled rim, strawberries & leaves 47.50

Pickle jar, relief-molded ship in full
sail & seagulls, 9½" h...........25.00

Plate, 10½" d., red grape clusters on
gold w/iridescent pink
edge...................18.00 to 25.00

Plate, 10½" d., open roses, gold
w/iridescent pink edge 27.50

Plate, 10½" d., scalloped edge, 5 large
red iris on gold 15.00

Plate, 12" d., relief-molded red roses
on gold 28.00

Powder box, cov., relief-molded red
roses on gold......................30.00

Vase, 5½" h., bulbous, relief-molded
cabbage roses, white..............30.00

Vase, 7¼" h., relief-molded red grapes
on gold 20.00

Vase, 7¼" h., relief-molded red roses
on gold 20.00

Vases, 9½" h., floral & bird decor,
red & gold, pr.....................45.00

GREENTOWN

Austrian Pattern Butter Dish

Greentown glass was made in Greentown, Ind., by the Indiana Tumbler & Goblet Co. from 1894 until 1903. In addition to its famed Chocolate glass, which see, it produced other types of clear and colored glass. Miscellaneous pieces are listed here. Also see CHOCOLATE, HOLLY AMBER and PATTERN GLASS.

Bowl, 8" d., Dewey patt., amber $30.00
Bowl, 8" d., Leaf Bracket patt.,
   clear . . . . .25.00 to 38.50
Bowl, 10 x 4" oblong, Holly patt.,
   clear 135.00
Bowl, master berry, Teardrop & Tassel
   patt., cobalt blue 45.00
Bowl, "Mitted Hand," clear . . . .35.00 to 50.00
Butter dish, cov., Austrian patt.,
   clear (ILLUS.) .85.00
Butter dish, cov., Dewey patt.,
   amber . . . . .60.00 to 75.00
Butter dish, cov., Dewey patt.,
   emerald green 65.00
Butter dish, cov., Holly patt., clear 235.00
Compote, jelly, cov., Cord Drapery
   patt., clear. 45.00
Compote, 6", Pleat Band patt., clear. . . .15.00
Cordial, Shuttle patt., clear 30.00
Creamer, child's, Austrian patt.,
   clear. . . . . .30.00 to 50.00
Creamer, child's, Austrian patt.,
   canary yellow 50.00
Creamer, Austrian patt., clear. 35.00
Creamer, Dewey patt., amber 35.00
Creamer, Dewey patt., vaseline 35.00
Creamer, Overall Lattice patt., clear . . .17.00
Creamer & cov. sugar bowl, breakfast
   size, Dewey patt., vaseline, pr. 95.00
Cruet w/original stopper, Dewey patt.,
   amber 110.00
Goblet, Beehive (Pattern No. 32) patt.,
   clear. 65.00
Goblet, Brazen Shield patt., clear 35.00
Hair pin tray, in the form of a
   hair brush, clear, 3 9/16" w.,
   8 1/16" l. 60.00

Lamp, kerosene-type, Beaded Wild Rose
   patt., clear, 8" h. 150.00
Mug, Austrian patt., clear. 14.00
Mug, Dewey patt., clear 25.00
Mug, Elves patt., Nile green 60.00
Mug, Holly patt., clear, large. . .65.00 to 95.00
Mug, Serenade patt., blue 42.50
Mug, Serenade patt., custard. 45.00

Shuttle Pattern Mug

Mug, Shuttle patt., clear (ILLUS.) 22.50
Nappy, cov., handled, Austrian patt.,
   clear 55.00
Nappy, Leaf Bracket patt., clear 25.00
Pitcher, water, Cord Drapery patt.,
   amber. 165.00
Pitcher, water, Herringbone Buttress
   patt., clear. .145.00

Ruffled Eye Pattern Pitcher

Pitcher, water, Ruffled Eye patt.,
   amber (ILLUS.). 130.00
Pitcher, water, Teardrop & Tassel patt.,
   clear 65.00
Plate, 6" d., Serenade patt., milk
   white 35.00
Plate, 10" d., Pattern No. 11, clear 18.00
Plate, footed, Dewey patt., canary
   yellow 40.00
Punch cup, Austrian patt., clear, gilt
   trim. 18.00
Punch cup, Overall Lattice patt., clear . .17.00
Relish dish, Cord Drapery patt., clear,
   9½" oval 18.00

Relish dish, serpentine-shaped, Dewey
   patt., green 37.50

Relish dish, Teardrop & Tassel patt.,
   green, oval 40.00

Rose bowl, Pattern No. 11, clear 15.00

Salt dip, Pattern No. 11, clear 15.00

Sauce dish, Brazen Shield patt., blue . . .30.00

Sauce dish, Brazen Shield patt., clear 9.00

Sauce dish, Cord Drapery patt., clear 9.00

Sauce dish, Dewey patt., amber 7.00

Spooner, Austrian patt., clear, gilt
   trim 35.00

Spooner, Pattern No. 11, ruby-stained . .40.00

Stein, Elves patt., Nile green 50.00

Stein, Serenade patt., milk white 32.50

Stein, Serenade patt., Nile green 58.00

Sugar bowl, cov., Austrian patt., clear . .40.00

Sugar bowl, cov., Cord Drapery patt.,
   clear 35.00

Sugar bowl, cov., Herringbone But-
   tress patt., emerald green 135.00

Table set: cov. butter dish, cov.
   sugar bowl, creamer & spooner;
   Dewey patt., canary yellow, 4 pcs. . .225.00

Tray, serpentine, Dewey patt.,
   amber, small .38.50

Tumbler, Austrian patt.,
   clear .22.50 to 30.00

Tumbler, Brazen Shield patt., cobalt
   blue 45.00

Tumbler, Dewey patt., canary
   yellow . . . . .55.00 to 65.00

Tumbler, Fleur de Lis patt.,
   clear . . . . .25.00 to 35.00

Tumbler, Pattern No. 11, clear 14.00

Tumbler, Teardrop & Tassel patt.,
   cobalt blue 45.00

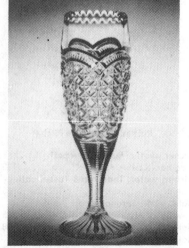

Austrian Pattern Vase

Vase, 8" h., Austrian patt., clear
   (ILLUS.) 50.00

Wine, Austrian patt., canary yellow . . .110.00

Wine, Austrian patt., clear . . . . .18.00 to 25.00

GUTTATE

Guttate Tumbler

*Guttate is a mold-blown glassware made
by the Consolidated Lamp & Glass Company at Fostoria, Ohio, during the late
1890s. A beautifully designed pattern, it
was made primarily in opaque pastel colors,
sometimes cased in clear to form a glossy
finish and sometimes in a satin finish with a
white lining. It is also found in transparent cranberry. Because of its appealing
design, it is popular and somewhat scarce.
Cased cranberry items available today are
new pieces currently being reproduced along
with a variety of tumblers. Collectors
should exercise caution.*

Butter dish, cov., white w/gold trim . . .$75.00

Cruet w/original stopper, white 155.00

Pitcher, water, white 70.00

Pitcher, water, white w/gold trim 85.00

Pitcher, yellow cased in clear 265.00

Salt & pepper shakers w/original tops,
   pink cased in clear, pr. 85.00

Salt & pepper shakers w/original tops,
   pink satin, pr. .68.00

Salt & pepper shakers w/original tops,
   white, pr. 35.00

Sugar bowl, cov., cranberry 125.00

Sugar shaker w/original top, pink
   cased in clear 150.00

Syrup pitcher w/original dated top,
   pink satin, tall 195.00

Syrup pitcher w/original top, pink
   cased in clear, tall 185.00

Tumbler, pink cased in clear (ILLUS.) . . .40.00

Water set: pitcher & 6 tumblers;
   white, 7 pcs. .285.00

HANDEL

*Lamps, shades and other types of glass
by Handel & Co., which subsequently became The Handel Co., Inc., were produced in Meriden, Connecticut, from 1893 to
1941. Also see LIGHTING DEVICES.*

Cake plate, 2-handled, reticulated
   rim, pink floral decor, gold edge,
   10" d. $75.00

Handel Tobacco Humidor

Humidor w/embossed metal lid, owl
on pine branch decor on green
shaded to russet opal ware, signed
& numbered, 5" h. (ILLUS.) 325.00
Humidor w/embossed metal lid, bears
climbing up tree decor on brown
opal ware ground, artist-signed 315.00
Humidor w/pewter lid & pipe finial,
horse & dog decor on brown & green
opal ware ground, signed Braun 345.00
Pitcher, tankard, 11" h., gold-trimmed
green fern fronds on satin finish opal
ware, artist-signed...............380.00
Vase, 10" h., "Teroma," overall woodland scene in realistic colors, artist-
signed 1,450.00
Vase, 12" h., palm leaf decor on opal
ware, signed & numbered.........600.00

HEISEY

Heisey Colonial Pattern

Numerous types of fine glass were made by
the A.H. Heisey Glass Co., Newark, O., from
1895. The company's trademark — an H enclosed within a diamond — has become
known to most glass collectors. The company's name and molds were acquired by Imperial Glass Co., Bellaire, O., in 1958, and

some pieces have been reissued. The glass listed below consists of miscellaneous pieces and
types. Also see ANIMALS under Glass,
CUSTARD and PATTERN GLASS.

Ash tray, Horse Head patt., clear,
4½" sq. $75.00
Banana split dish, Roman Key patt.,
clear 20.00
Basket, Lariat patt., clear, signed,
11" ....75.00 to 110.00
Bowl, 7¼" d., 3-footed, clear,
orchid-etched 35.00
Bowl, 8" d., Colonial patt., clear
(ILLUS.) 25.00
Bowl, fruit, 11" d., pedestal base,
Flamingo (pink), signed............55.00
Bowl, 12" d., Crystolite patt., clear 65.00
Candle holder, Lariat patt., clear
(single) 17.00
Candle holders, 3-light, Crystolite patt.,
pr.............................75.00
Candle holders, 2-light, Waverly patt.,
orchid-etched, clear, pr. 55.00
Candlesticks, Ridgeleigh patt., clear,
w/bobeche & prisms, 7" h., pr. 85.00
Candy dish, Crystolite patt., clear,
ornate metal holder 60.00
Celery tray, Pineapple & Fan patt.,
clear 35.00
Champagne, Oxford patt., clear,
6½ oz. 15.00
Cigarette box, cov., Horse Head patt.
w/horse head on lid, clear,
4¼ x 4" ....38.00 to 50.00
Cocktail shaker w/Rooster Head
stopper, clear 60.00
Console bowl, Empress patt., clear,
rose-etched, 12" d.................65.00
Console bowl, footed, Ipswich patt.,
clear, signed, 12" d. ....40.00 to 45.00
Cordial, Colonial patt., clear 15.00
Creamer & sugar bowl, Fandango patt.,
clear, pr.........................48.00
Creamer & sugar bowl, Greek Key
patt., clear, pr. 55.00
Creamer & sugar bowl, Lariat patt.,
clear, pr. 32.00
Creamer & sugar bowl on tray,
individual size, Crystolite
patt., 3 pcs......................30.00
Cruet w/original stopper, Colonial
patt., clear......................20.00
Cruet w/original stopper, Pineapple &
Fan patt., clear, 6 oz..............85.00
Cruet w/original stopper, Pleat & Panel
patt., clear.....................105.00
Cruet w/original stopper, Williamsburg
patt., clear......................35.00
Cruet w/original stopper, Yeoman
patt., clear......................30.00
Crushed fruit jar, cov., Flat Panel patt.,
clear, signed & dated 1908, 2-qt.
(ILLUS.) 147.50

Crushed Fruit Jar

Cup & saucer, Empress patt., clear 37.00
Cup & saucer, Empress patt., Sahara
(yellow) 27.50
Cups & saucers, Pleat & Panel patt.,
Flamingo (pink), set of 6 . . . . .80.00
Goblet, Barcelona patt., clear 22.00
Goblet, Carcassonne patt., Sahara
(yellow) 25.00
Ice bucket, Twist patt., Moongleam
(green). . . . . .85.00 to 95.00

Heisey Ice Bucket

Ice bucket, banded staves w/wire
bail handle, Flamingo (ILLUS.) 85.00
Mayonnaise bowl & underplate, Lariat
patt. w/etching, clear 60.00
Nut cup, individual size, Empress patt.,
clear 10.00
Nut cup, individual size, dolphin
footed, Flamingo (pink). 13.00
Parfait, Tyrolean patt., clear, 5 oz. 52.50
Pitcher, 6" h., Coarse Rib patt., clear . . .40.00
Pitcher, water, 8½" h., Colonial
patt., clear. 70.00
Pitcher, water, Crystolite patt., clear . .115.00

Pitcher, water, Greek Key patt., clear,
3-pt. 95.00
Pitcher, water, tankard, Narrow Flute
patt., clear, 3-pt. 65.00
Pitcher, water, Pinwheel & Fan patt.,
clear, 3-pt. 125.00
Tumbler, iced tea, footed, Crystolite
patt., 10 oz. 15.00
Tumbler, juice, footed, Crystolite patt. . . .10.00
Tumbler, juice, Twist patt., green 13.00
Tumbler, old fashioned, Tally Ho
patt., clear. 30.00
Tumbler, water, footed, Banded
Flute patt., clear, 7 oz. 18.00
Tumbler, water, Pineapple & Fan patt.,
clear w/gold 40.00
Vase, 4" h., Spiral Optic patt.,
Flamingo 32.50
Vase, 7" h., fan-shaped, Lariat patt.,
clear 40.00
Wine, Barcelona patt., clear. 30.00
Wine, Beaded Swag patt., white
opaque w/enameled decor 95.00

HISTORICAL & COMMEMORATIVE

Battleship Maine Plate

Reference numbers are to Bessie M. Lindsey's book, "American Historical Glass." Also see MILK WHITE GLASS and POLITICAL & CAMPAIGN ITEMS.

Admiral Dewey plate, bust portrait of
Dewey, clear, 5½" d., No. 392 . . . . .$22.50
Admiral Dewey tumbler, portrait of
Dewey within laurel wreath topped
by spread-winged eagle, flagship
"Olympia," ammunition, mounted
cannon, etc., stippled & clear, 4" h.,
No. 398 . . . . .42.50
Admiral Dewey water pitcher, portrait
of Dewey within laurel leaves,
"Gridley You May Fire When Ready,"
eagle, w/shield, etc., 9¼" h.,
No. 401 . . . . .93.00

Admiral Dewey water pitcher, bust
portrait of Dewey & flagship Olympia
reverse, w/mounted cannons,
crossed rifles, U.S. & Cuban flags & 4
stacks of cannon balls toward base,
clear, No. 400 . . . . .64.50

Atlantic Cable plate, clear, 9¾" d.,
No. 126 . . . . .30.00

Battleship Maine plate, picture of ship
center, pierced club & shell border,
milk white, 7¼" d., No. 463 (ILLUS.) . .32.50

Bible bread tray, open Bible center,
clear, 10½ x 7", No. 200 . . . . .55.00

Blaine - Logan tray, frosted bust
portraits center, stippled ivy border,
11½ x 8½", No. 315 . . . . .255.00

Bryan (William J.) covered cup, bust
portrait of Bryan, "The People's
Money" above, clear, No. 336 . . . . . . .51.50

Bunker Hill platter, "Prescott 1776
Stark - Warren 1876 Putnam," clear,
13½ x 9", No. 44 . . . . .60.00

Cleveland bottle, bust of Cleveland,
clear & acid finish, 10" h., No. 318 . . .187.00

Cleveland - Thurman tray, bust
portraits of Cleveland & Thurman
within ivy leaf borders, clear,
9½ x 8½", No. 325 . . . . .287.00

Columbia bread tray, shield-shaped,
Columbia superimposed against 13
vertical bars, blue, 11½ x 9½",
No. 54 . . . . .125.00

Columbia bread tray, shield-shaped,
Columbia superimposed against 13
vertical bars, clear, 11½ x 9½",
No. 54 . . . . .150.00

Columbus Plate

Columbus plate, bust portrait of
Columbus center w/dates "1492-
1892," pilot wheel border, clear,
9" d., No. 4 (ILLUS.) 45.00

Constitution platter, eagle & banner
center, clear, 12½" l., No. 43 . . . . .49.50

Corcoran whiskey tumbler, shield &

harp emblematic of the U.S. &
Ireland are framed by wreath of
laurel & oak leaves, clear, 3 1/8" h.,
No. 377 . . . . .225.00

Emblem container, tall Eagle bearing
a shield, ribbon inscribed "E Pluribus
Unum," milk white, 6¾" h., No. 55 . .165.00

Emblem pickle dish, eagle, shield,
arrows & olive branches, clear,
10 x 5¾", No. 58 . . . . .55.00

Emblem Centennial goblet, 2 shields
w/thirteen stars & keystones
inscribed "1776 July 4th 1876,"
"Centennial" on foot, clear, 5½" h.,
No. 61 . . . . .45.00

Eureka platter, Diagonal Band patt.
w/motto "Eureka," clear & stippled,
11½ x 9", No. 103 . . . . .26.00

Faith, Hope & Charity plate, maidens
posed as Three Graces center,
w/1875 patent date, clear, 10" d.,
No. 230 . . . . .50.00

Fitzhugh Lee (Major General) plate, bust
portrait transfer of the Major
General center, one-o-one border,
clear, 5½" d., No. 378 . . . . .20.00

Flaming Sword relish dish, sapphire
blue, 10 x 4¼", No. 209 . . . . .52.50

Flower Pot patt. bread tray, "In God
We Trust" in stippled lettering along
sides, 12 x 8", No. 202 . . . . .34.50

Garden of Eden platter, log handles,
clear, No. 207 . . . . .42.50

Garfield Memorial plate, Garfield
center, laurel wreath against stippled ground border, clear, 10" d.,
No. 302 . . . . .44.50

Garfield Star plate, frosted bust of
Garfield center, star border, clear,
6" d., No. 299 . . . . .30.00

Gladstone (William Ewart) plate, "In
Memory of England's Statesman,"
clear, 5 1/8" d., No. 442 . . . . .32.50

Grant Memorial plate, bust portrait of
Grant center, laurel wreath on
stippled border, amber, 10" d.,
No. 288 . . . . .65.00

Grant Memorial plate, bust portrait of
Grant center, laurel wreath on
stippled border, clear, 10" d.,
No. 288 . . . . .50.00

Grant Memorial plate, bust portrait of
Grant center, laurel wreath on
stippled border, vaseline, 10" d.,
No. 288 . . . . .75.00

Grant "Patriot and Soldier" plate, bust
portait of Grant center, decorative
border, deep rim, amber, 9½" sq.,
No. 291 . . . . .53.00

Grant "Patriot and Soldier" plate, bust
portrait of Grant center, decorative
border, deep rim, clear, 9½" sq.,
No. 291 . . . . .50.50

Independence Hall ABC plate, "1776-
1876," clear, 6¾" d., No. 33 . . . . . . .150.00
Independence Hall platter, "The
Nation's Birthplace," w/bear paw
handles, clear, No. 29 . . . . .95.00

Lincoln Logs Plaque

Lincoln Logs plaque, center relief
portrait of Lincoln framed within
openwork log rails stippled to
resemble tree bark, milk white,
8¼ x 6¾", No. 278 (ILLUS.) 210.00

Lord's Supper Bread Platter

Lord's Supper bread platter, clear,
11 x 7", No. 235 (ILLUS.) . . . . .35.00 to 45.00
Martyr's platter, Lincoln & Garfield
bust portraits & inscription, clear,
12½ x 7¾", No. 271 . . . . .350.00
McCormick reaper platter, clear,
13 x 8", No. 119 . . . . .85.00
McKinley Memorial platter, "It is God's
Way, etc.," clear, 10½ x 8", No. 356 . .37.50
McKinley Protection & Plenty plate,
portrait of McKinley center, star
border, clear, 7¼" d., No. 333 . . . . . . .38.00
McKinley tumbler, "Our President 1896
to 1900," clear, 3¾" h., No. 350 . . . . .35.00
Mitchell (John) bread tray, gilded
portrait of Mitchell center, "Leader,
Counsellor, Friend, President United

Mine Workers of America," clear,
10¾ x 6¾", No. 448 . . . . . .175.00 to 190.00
Mormon Temple bread tray, w/daily
bread motto, clear, No. 238 . . . . .310.00
Niagara Falls tray, frosted scene of
Niagara Falls from American side
center, clear, 11½ x 16", No. 489 . . .125.00
"Old Statehouse Philadelphia" tray,
amber, round, No. 32 . . . . .80.00
Preparedness toothpick holder, clear,
2¼" h., No. 483 . . . . .66.00
Railroad engine cov. container, clear,
6" l., 4½" h., No. 138 . . . . .150.00
Railroad train platter, Union Pacific
Engine No. 350, clear, 12 x 9",
No. 134 . . . . .70.00 to 85.00
Rock of Ages bread tray, clear
w/opaque white inlaid center,
No. 236 . . . . .143.00
Shakespeare statuette, frosted bust of
Shakespeare, marked "Gillinder &
Sons, Centennial Exhibition,"
5" h., No. 405 . . . . .175.00
Sir Moses Montefiore plate, portrait of
Jewish philanthropist center, ornate
inscribed border, clear, 10½" d.,
No. 239 . . . . .135.00
Three Presidents goblet, bust portraits
of Washington, Lincoln & Garfield
framed in medallion settings, 3" d.,
6¼" h., No. 250 . . . . .300.00
Three Presidents platter, bust portraits
of Garfield, Washington & Lincoln,
inscribed "In Remembrance," clear,
12½ x 10", No. 249 . . . . .56.00

Three President's Platter

Three Presidents platter, bust portraits
of Garfield, Washington & Lincoln,
inscribed "In Remembrance," clear
w/frosted center, 12½ x 10", No. 249
(ILLUS.) 110.00
Washington Bi-Centennial plate, por-
trait of Washington center, "G.
Washington 1732-1932," border of 13
stars, clear, 8" d., No. 258 . . . . .25.00
Washington Monument paperweight,
milk white, 2¾" square base,
5½" h., No. 255 . . . . .150.00

HOLLY AMBER

Holly Amber Compote & Sauce Dish

Holly Amber was produced by the Indiana Tumbler and Goblet Co. A molded glass, it is characterized by a glossy finish, shadings that range from opalescent to brownish amber, and holly leaf patterns. It is also called Golden Agate. It is scarce and therefore expensive. Collectors are alerted to the fact that the St. Clair Glass Company has reproduced some Holly Amber pieces.

Bowl, 7 3/8 x 4 5/8" oval $360.00
Bowl, berry, 8½" d., 3½" h. 600.00
Butter dish, cov. 1,000.00
Compote, jelly, cov., 4½" d. 975.00
Compote, cov., 6½" d. (ILLUS. left) . .1,100.00
Cruet w/original stopper 1,400.00
Mug, handled, 4" h. 395.00
Mug, handled, 4½" h. . . . . . . 450.00 to 475.00
Parfait, 6" h. .425.00
Pickle tray, 2-handled, 6½ x 4" 350.00
Sauce dish (ILLUS. right) 240.00
Syrup jug w/original tin lid 750.00
Toothpick holder. 275.00
Tumbler, 4" h. 350.00

HONESDALE

Honesdale Vase

This glass was made by the Honesdale Decorating Company, Honesdale, Pa., originally established to decorate glass for C. Dorflinger & Sons, but purchased in 1916 by C.F. Prosch, who operated it until its closing in the early 1930s. Some cameo pieces also were stained & gilded.

Cameo vase, 12" h., carved stylized
   yellow long-stemmed blooms &
   green leaves w/gold details against
   etched frosted ground, signed $350.00
Vase, 8" h., enameled gold swags
   & medallions on frosted ground,
   signed. 75.00
Vase, 11" h., enameled Art Nouveau
   decor in gold on green, signed. 110.00
Vase, 12½" h., etched border band
   & stylized florals & scrolling design
   in topaz over frosted crystal, signed
   (ILLUS.) 550.00
Vase, 17½" h., green cut to clear
   basketweave design which criss-
   crosses 4 single stars in a square,
   w/gold tracery 900.00

IMPERIAL

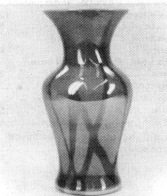

Free Hand Ware Vase

Imperial Glass Company, still operating in Bellaire, O., was a major producer of Carnival glass (which see) earlier in this century, but it also produced numerous other types including an Art Glass line called "Free Hand Ware" in about the 1920s and its "Jewels" beginning about 1916. The company owns the molds of a number of other earlier factories, and it has been reissuing some of these wares. Also see ANIMALS, SHADES and STRETCH under Glass.

Free Hand Ware vase, 5½"h., 6" d.,
   iridescent white trailing vines &
   leaves imbedded in cobalt blue $175.00
Free Hand Ware vase, 6½" h., blue

abstract drag on orange, orange
lustre throat (ILLUS.) 125.00
Free Hand Ware vase, 6½" h.,
orange lustre over white body
w/orange lustre throat 95.00
Free Hand Ware vase, 8" h., iridescent blue random pulls on frosted
ground 125.00
Free Hand Ware vase, 9" h., green
drag loops on opal 285.00
Free Hand Ware vase, 9½" h., top
pulled into 3 graceful handles,
iridescent green heart-shaped leaves
& vine imbedded in opal, orange
lustre throat interior 285.00
Free Hand Ware vase, 10" h., dark
blue pulled drag loops on light blue .200.00
Free Hand Ware vase, 10" h., blue
drag loops over opaque white 200.00
Free Hand Ware vase, 10" h., white
drag loops on dark cobalt blue
ground 115.00
Free Hand Ware vase, 10" h., glossy
Kelly green exterior, orange lustre
interior 110.00
Free Hand Ware vase, 11¼" h., orange
heart-shaped leaves & vines on
cobalt blue ....195.00 to 225.00
Free Hand Ware vase, 11½" h.,
bronze lustre exterior, iridescent
blue interior 138.50
Jewels bowl, 4½" d., pearl silver 59.00
Jewels bowl, 5" d., iridescent
marigold 45.00
Jewels bowl, 9" d., pedestal base,
green 35.00
Jewels candy dish, cov., pink, tall 30.00
Jewels vase, 8½" h., Pearl Ruby
lustre 50.00
Vase, 6" h., pink "NuCut" design.......65.00
Vase, 8½" h., fan-shaped, blue thread-
ing on pale cranberry..............90.00

IOWA CITY GLASS

*This ware, made by the Iowa City Glass
Manufacturing Co., Iowa City, Iowa, from
1880 to about 1883, was produced in many
shapes and patterns.*

Bread plate, "Be True," sleeping dog
center..........................$95.00
Bread plate, "Elaine" 50.00
Bread platter, Frosted Stork patt.,
1-0-1 border......................60.00
Cheese dish, cov., "Girl at Play" 155.00
Goblet, Deer patt. 135.00
Plate, 5½" d., "Be Playful," kitten
center, stippled bird handles 95.00
Plate, 6½" d., "Be True," sleeping
dog center 45.00

JACK-IN-PULPIT VASES

Jack-in-Pulpit Vase

*Glass vases in varying sizes and
resembling in appearance the flower of this
name have been popular with collectors
since the 19th century. They were produced
in various solid colors and in shaded wares.*

Amber, applied flower, leaf &
branch, Stourbridge, England,
19th c...........................$90.00
Amber, applied rigaree around body,
8" h. 65.00
Amethyst shading to vaseline, ribbed
body, 6" h........................57.00
Blue opalescent to clear blue,
6¾" h. 70.00
Blue opaque shaded to maroon top,
ruffled hobnail rim, 6¾" widest d.,
7" h. 110.00
Cased, cream exterior, white interior,
applied pink & white florettes &
amber branches & leaves, applied
amber edging, 6 7/8" h. 140.00
Cased, white exterior, celestial blue
interior, clear edging around
ruffle w/mica flecks, 5½" h. 100.00
Cased, white exterior, shaded rich
green interior, applied clear feet,
5½" d., 6 5/8" h..................100.00
Cased, white exterior, shaded
lavender interior, 7¼" h. 100.00
Green shaded to opaque yellow,
embossed pattern & ribs, dark green
edging at ruffle, 4½" across top,
9" h. 88.00
Green opalescent, ribbed body, applied pink florette & green leaf,
9" h. 88.00
Light green w/blue opalescent throat
& crimped edge, 13" h. (ILLUS.) 115.00
Pink opalescent shaded to vaseline,
5 1/8" w. at top, 11¼" h............110.00

Purple shading to pale green, 6¼" h. . . . 75.00
Rubina crystal, clear coiled stem on
  petal feet rising to cranberry
  ruffled edge, 9¼" h. 100.00
Rubina crystal, applied vaseline
  edging, 5¼" w. at top, 11" h. 130.00
Rubina Verde opalescent, applied
  vaseline feet, 4" widest d., 8¼" h. . . . 93.00

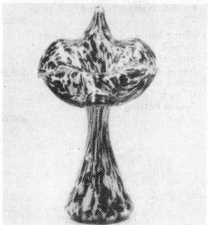

Jack-in-Pulpit Vase

Spangled, blue & beige spatter
  w/silver mica flecks, 7" h. (ILLUS.) . . . 85.00
Spangled, green w/maroon & white
  spatter & silver mica flecks,
  8" h. 110.00
Spatter, pink & white in clear, applied
  vaseline opalescent edging,
  5" widest d., 8" h. 80.00
Spatter, green, peach & white
  spatter, Diamond Quilted patt. in
  base, 9¼" h. 100.00
Vaseline opalescent, applied w/vaseline
  shell feet, ruffle & rigaree around
  center, 4¾" h. 55.00
Vaseline opalescent, Swirl patt.,
  applied pink spiral trim, 4¼" w. at
  top, 7¾" h. 90.00
White shaded to pink at top edge,
  applied feet, 6½" h. 85.00
White opalescent w/purple ruffle,
  7" h. 50.00

KELVA

Kelva was made early in this century by the C.F. Monroe Co., Meriden, Conn., and was a type of decorated opal glass very like the same company's Wave Crest and Nakara wares. This type of glass was produced until about the time of the first World War. Also see NAKARA and WAVE CREST.

Kelva Box

Box w/hinged lid, deep pink ground
  w/grey, blue & yellow floral decor,
  signed, 5½" d., 3½" h. $425.00
Box w/hinged lid, octagonal mold,
  moss green w/pink florals &
  daisies decor, signed (ILLUS.) 550.00
"Collars and Cuffs" box, signed, 7" d.,
  6" h. 725.00
Humidor, cov., dark green ground
  w/pink floral decor 625.00
Jewelry box w/hinged lid, embossed
  scrollwork, olive green w/colorful
  strawflowers decor, original
  lining, 8" d. 875.00
Jewelry box w/hinged lid, mottled
  green w/pink & white florals &
  leaves decor, signed, 8" d., 3¾" h.
  (no lining) 750.00
Jewelry box w/hinged lid, ormolu
  base, soft green ground w/shaded
  poppies decor w/enameled white
  beaded centers, round, small 425.00
Powder box w/hinged lid, blue ground
  w/pink floral decor, 4" d. 275.00
Sweetmeat bowl w/silverplate rim,
  cover & bail handle, mottled green
  w/colorful floral decor, 6" d.,
  4½" h. to top of lid 320.00
Vase, 14" h., silverplate ormolu feet,
  green ground w/pink floral decor,
  signed. 650.00

LALIQUE

Lalique Egg-Form Box

Fine glass, including numerous extraordinary molded articles, has been made by the glass house established by Rene' Lalique early in this century in France. The firm was carried on by his son, Marc, until his death in 1977 and is now headed by Marc's daughter, Marie-Claude. All Lalique glass is marked, usually on, or near, the bottom with either an engraved or molded signature. Unless otherwise noted we list only those pieces marked "R. Lalique" produced before the death of Rene' Lalique in 1945. Also see COMMEMORATIVE PLATES.

Ash tray, oblong w/frosted fan
   shapes & strutting peacock tails,
   4½ x 5" $75.00
Ash tray, "Antheor," frosted nude
   mermaid 325.00
Bowl, 7" d., 3" h., "Coquilles," clear
   & opalescent 350.00
Bowl, 9¼" d., molded parakeets on
   intricate floral ground, pale opalescence tinged w/blue, ca. 1925 ....660.00
Bowl, 11¾" d., 2" h., molded fish in
   bubbly water, clear & opalescent ...350.00
Box, cov., relief-molded floral top,
   narrower base, frosted, 3½"
   widest d., 2½" h. 275.00
Box, cov., "Oeuf Pervenches," egg-
   shaped, molded periwinkle
   blossoms, deep sapphire blue,
   w/ground inner lip of cover, 1925,
   4½" l. (ILLUS.) 604.00
Figure of Suzanne, nude but for
   drapery descending from her outstretched arms, opalescent, ca.
   1932, 9" h. 2,420.00
Figure of "Joueuse de Flute," oviform
   molded w/border of roses enclosing
   the draped figure of a maiden
   holding a double flute to her mouth
   & standing on a mound of overlapping petals, clear & frosted,
   14½" h. 2,250.00

"Epsom" Mascot

Mascots, "Epsom," realistic head of a
   horse w/stylized molded mane,
   frosted, chrome mount, black onyx
   base, ca. 1932, 6" l., pr. (ILLUS. of
   one) 2,530.00
Menu card holder, molded "Menu" &
   grapes on vine, frosted, 6" 350.00
Pendant, "Fioret," molded nude,
   frosted, original braided cloth chain,
   1¼" d. 295.00
Perfume bottle, "Couer Joie," heart-
   shaped, made for Nina Ricci, in
   original satin pink box w/white satin
   inside, 4" h. 235.00
Perfume bottle w/stopper, "Ambre
   D'Orsay," square w/molded female
   figures holding flowers, black,
   5" h. 450.00

Lalique Perfume Bottles

Perfume bottles w/stoppers, green
   glass cylinder w/ring-molded
   stopper & dusty midnight blue
   globular "Dans La Nuit," molded
   w/stars, 2½" & 3¼" h.
   respectively, pr. (ILLUS. right) 605.00
Perfume bottles w/stoppers,
   "Requette," clear flatted circular
   form w/scalloped edge enameled
   w/blue bands, made for Worth,
   ca. 1925, 11" h. footed display
   bottle & small 3 5/8" h. bottle, pr.
   (ILLUS. left) 770.00
Tumbler, "Hesperides," frosted swirling
   leaves on clear, 4" h. 95.00
Vase, 4¾" h., "Tournesol," sunflowers
   in relief, frosted 600.00
Vase, 5" h., "Bouchardon," spherical
   w/scrolling handles in the form of
   nude kneeling female figures
   holding floral festoons, grey,
   ca. 1932 ....880.00
Vase, 5" h., "Rampillon," molded high
   relief diamond forms on overall
   stylized floral ground..............200.00

"Formose" Vase

Vase, 6¾" h., "Formose," spherical,
footed, molded pattern of swimming fish in medium relief, clear
& opalescent (ILLUS.) 695.00

Lalique Serpent Vase

Vase, 9½" h., molded as a coiling
serpent, dark brown-amber, ca. 1925
(ILLUS.) 4,950.00
Vase, 9¾" h., "Aras," molded tropical
birds (macaws) & cherries, opales-
cent 2,100.00
Vase, 9¾" h., ovoid, molded panels
of long-stemmed roses, colorless,
ca. 1925 . . . . .880.00
Vase, 10" h., "Ceylon," intaglio-
molded leafy branches & medium
relief pairs of lovebirds, clear &
opalescent .1,750.00
Vase, 10¼" h., "Penthievre," molded
graduated bands of stylized fish
swimming at cross-currents to each
other in medium relief, frosted &
polished grey, ca. 1932 . . . . .1,045.00
Vase, 10¼" h., "Penthievre," spheri-
cal, molded graduated bands of
stylized fish swimming at cross-
currents to each other in medium
relief, frosted & polished sapphire
blue, ca. 1932 . . . . .3,410.00

LATTICINO

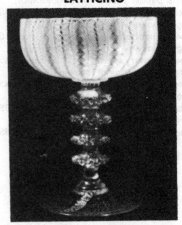

Latticino Champagne

*Latticino (or Latticinio) glass is charac-
terized by threads of colored glass imbedded
in clear glass in simple or intricate, interlacing patterns. It represents a revival of an
ancient technique that was popular in the
18th century and was revived again during
the 19th century and produced by numerous
glasshouses.*

Champagne, pink & white threading
in clear, rigaree at stem, 1875-80,
5" h. (ILLUS.) $165.00
Cup & saucer, demitasse, white
threading in pale yellow, ca. 1895 . . .160.00
Finger bowl, lavender & white
threading in clear 75.00
Vase, 3¼" h., 4¼" d., ruffled rim,
vertical bands of white & gold
threading & pink twisted ribbons 85.00
Wine, clear stem w/white threading,
5¾" h. (small flake on foot) 45.00

LEAF MOLD

*Though the maker of this attractive glass
pattern remains elusive, the Leaf Mold
pattern becomes more popular with
collectors each year. Thought to have been
made in the 1890s, there are several colors
and color combinations available and it was
made in both satin and shiny finish as well
as in a cased version.*

Creamer, pink, satin finish $85.00
Cruet, cased cranberry spatter 230.00
Pickle castor, vaseline w/cranberry &
white spatter insert, ornate footed
silverplate holder 185.00
Rose bowl, vaseline w/cranberry
spatter 175.00

Salt & pepper shakers w/original tops,
cased cranberry, pr.. . . . . .140.00
Sugar shaker w/original top, pink &
white spatter w/mica flecks 210.00
Sugar shaker w/original top, vaseline
w/cranberry spatter 165.00
Syrup jug w/original top, pink & white
spatter w/mica flecks 245.00
Toothpick holder, vaseline w/cran-
berry & white spatter 125.00
Tumbler, vaseline w/cranberry
spatter 85.00

LE GRAS

Le Gras Vases

*Cameo and enameled glass somewhat
similar to that made by Galle', Daum Nancy
and other factories of the period was made
at the Le Gras works in Saint Denis,
France, late last century and until the outbreak of World War I.*

Cameo vase, 5" h., bulbous, carved
green water lilies highlighted
w/gold, signed $280.00
Cameo vase, 5" h., carved & enamel-
ed lavender florals, signed 275.00
Cameo vase, 7½" h., carved &
enameled peach, beige & brown
boat scene w/two fishermen in the
largest boat, signed 750.00
Cameo vase, 9" h., carved dark brown
Art Deco birds in flight against
mottled red ground, signed 625.00
Cameo vase, 9" h., carved pink-
orange, light & dark blue
hydrangeas w/stems, signed 850.00
Cameo vase, 10¾" h., baluster-
shaped, carved & enameled sienna,
blue & green lakeside scene
w/stately fir trees in foreground
against lemon yellow & orange
ground, ca. 1900, signed (ILLUS.
left) 715.00

Cameo vase, 13¾" h., carved orange,
green & brown lake & forest scene,
signed 750.00
Cameo vase, 16" h., carved russet
grapevine against peach ground 500.00
Cameo vase, 20½" h., carved lavender & brown florals against blue
ground, signed 950.00
Vase, 8¼" h., swollen cylinder, clear
mottled w/lime green & white
splotches, w/cameo-carved medial
brown band of fans & leafage,
ca. 1925, signed (ILLUS. right). 412.00
Vases, 10" h., enameled tree scene,
signed, pr.. . . . . .375.00
Vase, 11" h., enameled orange &
yellow trees & snow-capped
mountains, signed 185.00
Vases, 15½" h., intaglio-cut Art
Nouveau designs, green, signed,
pr. 650.00

LE VERRE FRANCAISE

*This glass was made in France by Charles
Schneider and fairly large quantities of the
cameo ware were exported to the United
States in the early part of this century.
Much of it was sold by Ovingtons, New
York City. Also see SCHNEIDER.*

Cameo night light, carved pink &
lavender stylized florals on globe
fitted in metal Art Nouveau base
w/leaf-like feet, 5¼" d. globe,
overall 6" h.. . . . .$695.00
Cameo vase, 11" h., bottle-shaped,
carved green & shaded pink florals,
signed. 625.00
Cameo vase, 18½" h., carved light
red florals & dark red leaves,
signed Charder 585.00
Cameo vase, carved purple-brown to
rich orange Art Deco fruit trees &
carved orange beehive design at
rim against vivid yellow ground,
signed. 450.00

LIBBEY

*In 1878, William L. Libbey obtained a
lease on the New England Glass Company
of Cambridge, Mass., changing the name to
the New England Glass Works, W.L.
Libbey and Son, Proprietors. After his
death in 1883, his son, Edward D. Libbey,
continued to operate the company in
Cambridge until 1888 when the factory was*

closed. Edward Libbey moved to Toledo, Ohio, and set up the company subsequently known as Libbey Glass Co. During the 1880s, the firm's master technician, Joseph Locke, developed the now much desired colored art glass lines of Agata, Amberina, Peach Blow and Pomona. Renowned for its Cut Glass of the Brilliant Period, the company continues in operation today as Libbey Glassware, a division of Owens-Illinois, Inc. Also see AMBERINA and CUT GLASS.

Maize Syrup Jugs

Candlestick, clear bowl, opalescent
   silhouette of camel in stem, signed
   (single) $145.00
Champagne, clear bowl, opalescent
   silhouette of squirrel in stem 69.00
Cocktail, silhouette of crow in stem,
   clear 60.00
Cocktail, clear bowl, opalescent
   silhouette of kangaroo in stem 110.00
Cruet w/original steeple stopper,
   pedestal base, applied arched
   handle, paneled loop body,
   9½" h. 125.00
Dish, clear w/engraved wheat, 6" l. 40.00
Goblet, clear bowl, opalescent
   silhouette of cat in stem 160.00
Goblets, etched bowl, controlled bub-
   ble stem, signed, 5¼" h., set of 6 . . . 295.00
Maize bowl, 8¾" d., 4" h., white
   opaque w/green husks 165.00
Maize celery vase, white opaque
   w/green husks 135.00
Maize salt & pepper shakers w/orig-
   inal brass tops, creamy white
   w/gold-edged blue husks, pr. 185.00
Maize sugar shaker w/original top,
   pearlized cream lustre w/yellow
   husks, 5½" h. 160.00
Maize sugar shaker w/original top,
   custard color w/yellow
   husks . . . . 155.00 to 175.00
Maize syrup pitchers w/original pewter
   tops, clear w/iridescent gold & blue
   husks & creamy white w/green
   husks, 6" h., each (ILLUS.) 385.00

Maize tumbler, custard w/gold-edged
   yellow husks 170.00
Maize tumbler, clear w/iridescent gold
   & blue husks 180.00
Maize tumbler, creamy opaque
   w/green & brown husks 120.00
Milk jug, peridot green threading on
   clear, 1930s, signed 150.00
Toothpick holder, Little Lobe patt., pink
   to white w/enameled blue florals,
   green leaves & name in gold 112.50
Tumbler, custard color 50.00
Vase, 3" h., footed, clear w/applied
   dark green prunts, signed 110.00
Vase, 10¼" h., clear cylinder w/verti-
   cal panels of thumbprint & cable &
   w/horizontal wavy green lines encircling body from top rim to polished
   pontil on base 135.00
Wines, clear bowl, opalescent silhou-
   ette of polar bear in stem, signed,
   set of 4 . . . . 340.00

LOETZ

Loetz Iridescent Glass Vases

Iridescent glass, some of it somewhat resembling that of Tiffany and other contemporary glasshouses, was produced by the Bohemian firm of J. Loetz Witwe of Klostermule and is referred to as Loetz. Some cameo pieces were also made. Not all pieces are marked.

Basket, hat-shaped, iridescent
   green, applied clear handle,
   unsigned $225.00
Bowl, 6½" d., 4" h., 6 puffed-out
   melon ribs, iridescent green,
   unsigned 275.00
Bowl, 7" d., iridescent green to
   iridescent blue, signed 495.00
Bowl, 9½ x 5¼" oblong, 5¼" h.,
   textured ribs, pinched sides, folded
   rim, rainbow iridescence on green

w/red splashes, ground pontil,
signed...........................280.00

Bowl, 12" d., ruffled rim, deep cranberry to mottled green to clear
iridescent, signed..................400.00

Bowl, 4-cornered, Verre de Soie
coloring w/highly iridized amethyst
overlay, unsigned..................185.00

Pendant, iridescent turquoise on
yellow, solid gold fittings, 1½"
ovoid (no chain) 128.00

Salt dip, footed, iridescent green,
sterling silver rim, unsigned........95.00

Sweetmeat jar, cov., iridescent silver
spider web on green ground,
signed...........................400.00

Syrup pitcher, iridescent blue, original
silverplate top & handle, signed,
6½" h............................395.00

Vase, 4" h., gold spattered w/iridescent gold oil splashes, unsigned 135.00

Vase, 4" h., 3¼" d., ruffled rim,
green threading on clear w/gold
iridescence, ground pontil,
unsigned 235.00

Vase, 4" h., 3½" d., urn-shaped
w/vertical ribbing, lavender to iridescent clear w/applied iridescent
platinum on textured circular
handles, ground pontil, unsigned ...265.00

Vase, 5¼" h., 2¼" d., triple gourd
shape, iridescent blue waves on
salmon pink w/random platinum
raindrops, sterling silver overlay
marked "Alvin" 1,300.00

Vase, 6" h., tapering cylinder w/three
pinched sides, salmon pink w/iridescent blue striated lappets, ca. 1900,
signed (ILLUS. left) 485.00

Vase, 6" h., pale salmon pink w/deep
sapphire blue waves & iridescent
amber oil spots on lower portion,
sterling silver pierced overlay of iris
blossoms & undulating tendrils,
ca. 1900, unsigned (ILLUS. right) 325.00

Vase, 6½" h., Art Nouveau chalice
form, iridescent blue w/turquoise
green highlights w/shaded blue-
green horizontal feathering rising
from base tipped in platinum,
signed...........................765.00

Vase, 6½" h., iridescent purple,
unsigned 225.00

Vase, 7¼" h., tapered form w/triangular mouth, yellow w/silvery-
blue iridescent splashes, ca. 1900,
unsigned 550.00

Vase, 7 3/8" h., iridescent pink neck
& upper body, purple lower body
w/silvery-blue oil spots, ca. 1900,
unsigned 605.00

Vase, 7½" h., silvery-blue iridescent
concentric waves, red-washed
interior, ca. 1900, signed (ILLUS.) ...990.00

Loetz Vase

Vase, 8" h., glossy green & iridescent green combination, signed.....175.00

Vase, 8" h., twisted form, cobalt
blue textured surface w/gold &
raised gold foliage decor, unsigned .285.00

Vase, 9" h., iridescent purple w/blue
threading, signed.................295.00

Vase, 9" h., 6" d., iridescent silver
& green w/silver overlay berry &
leaf decor, signed.................450.00

Vase, 9½" h., floriform, iridescent
dark blue w/random criss-cross
threading, unsigned...............395.00

Vase, 9 7/8" h., baluster form
w/spreading foot, pale green
washed in golden-green iridescence & w/silvery-blue undulating
waves, ca. 1900, signed...........660.00

Vase, 10" h., crimped rim, iridescent gold-pink w/green pulled
design, unsigned 195.00

Vase, 10" h., ruffled top, iridescent
green & amethyst, signed 245.00

Vase, 11" h., 6" base, amethyst, red
& green w/overall threading,
unsigned 175.00

Vase, 13" h., slightly twisted form,
iridescent green to blue w/veined
gold design, signed 395.00

Vase, 13" h., variegated fan shape,
ribbed, iridescent green, amethyst
& gold, unsigned..................285.00

Vase, 13" h., 4-sided ruffled top, red to
blue w/pulled iridescent design,
unsigned 295.00

MARBLE

*Slag and Agate glass are other names
applied to this variegated glass ware made
from the middle until the close of the last*

century and now being reproduced. It is
characterized by variegated streaks of color.
Pink slag was made only in the Inverted
Fan & Feather Pattern and is rare.

Purple Marble Glasswares

Berry set: master bowl & 6 sauce
  dishes; Inverted Fan & Feather
  patt., footed, pink, 7 pcs.........$3,500.00
Bowl, 8" d., Dart Bar patt., purple 45.00
Compote, 4½", crimped, purple 65.00
Compote, jelly, threaded, purple 55.00
Creamer, Scroll with Acanthus patt.,
  purple, large 55.00
Cruet w/original stopper, Inverted Fan
  & Feather patt., pink............1,485.00
Novelty vase, Beads & Bark patt.,
  purple...........................35.00
Pitcher, water, Dart Bar patt., purple ...95.00
Pitcher, windmill & house scene,
  purple..........................200.00
Plate, 10½" d., lattice edge, purple ...100.00
Rose bowl, Beaded Cable patt.,
  purple...........................45.00
Salt shaker w/original top, Inverted
  Fan & Feather patt., pink
  (single) ....175.00 to 225.00
Sauce dish, footed, Inverted Fan &
  Feather patt., pink, 4 5/8" d.,
  2½" h. ....230.00 to 285.00
Sauce dish, purple 50.00
Spooner, Flower & Panel patt., purple ..80.00
Spooner, Flute patt., purple 80.00
Table set: cov. sugar bowl, creamer &
  spooner; Inverted Fan & Feather
  patt., footed, pink, 3 pcs.........2,250.00
Toothpick holder, British boat, purple ..30.00
Tumbler, Inverted Fan & Feather patt.,
  pink, 2¾" d., 4" h........375.00 to 410.00
Tumbler, dark purple, English Registry
  mark...........................30.00
Tumbler, rayed base, purple, signed on
  bottom w/dolphin 45.00
Vase, 5" h., 3-handled, purple, signed
  "Davidson" 95.00
Vase, molded country scene w/man,
  woman & child, purple, Sowerby &
  Co., England, miniature 75.00

MARY GREGORY

Mary Gregory Box

Glass enameled in white with silhouette-
type figures, primarily children, is now
termed Mary Gregory. Glass of this kind was
decorated at the Boston & Sandwich Glass
Works, reportedly by a decorator named
Mary Gregory, but also was made in numer-
ous other factories in this country and abroad.
Bohemian pieces are said to have tinted faces.
This type is now being widely reproduced.
Also see BARBER BOTTLES and PATCH
BOXES.

Box w/hinged lid, lime green, white
  enameled body, 2 3/8" d., 1¾" h. ...$140.00
Box w/hinged lid, sapphire blue, white
  enameled girl, white dot trim around
  sides, 3¼" d., 2 5/8" h. 150.00
Box w/hinged lid, ormolu feet,
  cobalt blue, white enameled girl on
  lid, white sprays around sides, brass
  rings on sides, 4" d., 4¼" h.
  (ILLUS.).........................235.00
Box w/hinged lid, cranberry, white
  enameled boy on lid, white garlands
  around sides, 5¼" d., 4¼" h.......375.00
Box w/hinged lid, ormolu feet, cobalt
  blue, white enameled girl holding
  bird on lid & sprays around sides,
  5 3/8" d., 5" h..................400.00
Box w/hinged lid, amethyst, white
  enameled girl & foliage, white dot
  trim around sides, 5½" l., 4½" h. ...205.00
Box w/hinged lid, oblong w/rounded
  ends, ormolu feet molded
  w/women's heads, periwinkle blue,
  white enameled boy feeding birds,
  white floral sprays & dot trim
  around sides, 5½ x 3½", 5" h.......445.00
Cologne bottle w/original stopper,
  ruby, white enameled boy feeding
  birds, 9¼" h.....................245.00
Dresser tray, cranberry, white enameled
  girl & boy, 9¼ x 6 3/8".............225.00
Mug, applied clear handle, cranberry,
  white enameled boy, 3" h. 98.00
Mug, applied blue handle, sapphire

blue, white enameled boy, 2 3/8" d.,
3¼" h. 88.00

Perfume bottle w/original blue ball
stopper, sapphire blue, white enameled boy, 1 3/8" d., 4" h. 165.00

Pin basket, ormolu handle & feet,
ruby, white enameled girl, 3½" d.,
3¼" h. 170.00

Pitcher, 6" h., sapphire blue, white
enameled boy w/sailboat 225.00

Pitcher, 12" h., paneled, applied amber
reeded handle, sapphire blue, white
enameled girl w/basket 375.00

Plate, 6 5/8" d., cobalt blue, white
enameled boy w/hat 118.00

Punch cup, applied reeded handle,
Baby Thumbprint patt., sapphire
blue, white enameled boy, gold
rim 85.00

Rose bowl, 8-crimp top, cranberry,
white enameled girl, 3¼" d., 3" h. ..225.00

Stein, applied handle, Inverted Thumbprint patt., sapphire blue, white
enameled boy w/butterfly, pewter
top w/clear glass insert, 5½" h. 175.00

Syrup pitcher w/original top, cobalt
blue, white enameled girl..........125.00

Toothpick holder, cranberry, white
enameled boy looking at bird.......65.00

Mary Gregory Tumbler

Tumbler, Baby Thumbprint patt.,
green, white enameled girl w/tinted
face, 3¾" h. (ILLUS.) 95.00

Tumbler, cobalt blue, white enameled
boy w/hoop, narrow gold band at
top...............................95.00

Tumble-up (water carafe & tumbler
top), sapphire blue, white enameled
girl, 8¼" h. 225.00

Vase, 1¾" h., 1½" d., cranberry, white
enameled girl 125.00

Vase, 2½" h., 2¾" d., cranberry, white
enameled boy 100.00

Vase, 5" h., 2¾" d., cranberry, white
enameled girl 135.00

Vase, 7¼" h., 4 1/8" d., applied amber
reeded snail handles w/gold trim,

scalloped top, amber, white
enameled boy 150.00

Vase, 8¼" h., amethyst, white
enameled boy w/butterfly net 295.00

Vase, 9" h., bottle-shaped, vaseline,
white enameled boy & girl 145.00

Vase, 10" h., long tapering neck
w/slightly flared rim, cranberry,
white enameled girl playing lyre
& singing, overall scrolling
& sprigs of flowers, leaves &
berries decor, reverse w/single
gold sprig of berries 215.00

Vase, 13" h., 5" d., applied clear
reeded snail handles, scalloped top,
cranberry, white enameled girl
w/flowers 425.00

Water set: pitcher & 2 tumblers; clear,
white enameled girls, 3 pcs........275.00

Wine bottle w/original clear
"bubble" stopper, cranberry,
white enameled girl holding sprays
of flowers, 3 1/8" d., 9" h..........150.00

MC KEE

McKee's Coach Bowl

*The McKee name has been associated
with glass production since 1834, first producing window glass and later bottles. In
the 1850s a new factory was established in
Pittsburgh, Pa., for production of flint and
pressed glass. The plant was relocated at
Jeannette, Pa. in 1888, and operated there
as an independent company, almost continuously until 1951 when it sold out to
Thatcher Glass Manufacturing Company.
Many types of collectible glass were produced by McKee through the years including Depression, Pattern, Milk White
and a variety of utility kitchen wares.*

Animal covered dish, Squirrel on split-
ribbed base, milk white, 5½".......$110.00

Batter bowl, Jade green opaque, 7" d. ...10.00

Bowl, 9 x 5¼", 4¼" h., model of a
coach, blue, 1886 (ILLUS.) 65.00

Bowl, 11" d., Laurel patt., French
ivory 15.00

McKee's Wiltec Pattern

Butter dish, cov., Wiltec patt., clear
(ILLUS.)............................42.50
Cake pan, white opal, 1947, 9" sq. 7.00
Candy jar, cov., Rock Crystal, ruby-
flashed, tall 90.00
Canister, cov., "Cereal," custard color,
6" h. 32.00
Casserole, cov., white opal, round,
w/metal holder, 1938 ....25.00
Centerpiece bowl, footed, Rock Crystal,
amber, 12" d. 40.00
Creamer, Jade green opaque ..15.00 to 20.00
Decanter set: decanter & 6 matching
whiskey shot glasses; "Life Saver"
decanter w/rings, pink, 7 pcs. 95.00
Goblet, Rock Crystal, clear 15.00
Measuring cup, Skokie green opaque,
2-cup..............................14.00
Measuring cup, milk white, 2-cup 12.00
Pie pan, white opal, 1916, 10" d. 10.00
Pitcher, water, Toltec patt., clear 45.00
Plate, 6" d., Laurel patt., Jade green
opaque 3.00
Plate, 7½" d., Laurel patt., Jade
green opaque 5.00
Plates, 8" d., Holly patt., Jade green
opaque, set of 6 ....48.00
Plate, 8½" d., Rock Crystal, clear 8.50
Punch set: bowl, base & 6 cups; Yutec
patt., Prescut, clear, 1901-15, 8 pcs. ..95.00
Refrigerator set: 1 large & 2 small
bowls w/covers; Jade green
opaque, 3 pcs.....................25.00
Relish, Prescut, milk white 18.00
Salt shaker w/original top, Skokie
green opaque 5.00
Syrup pitcher w/pewter top, Apollo
patt., pink 68.00
Tom & Jerry set: bowl & 8 mugs; milk
white, 9 pcs. 36.50
Tumblers, bell-shaped, Rock Crystal,
clear, pr. 22.00
Whiskey tumbler w/coaster base,
"Bottoms Up," caramel opaque 50.00
Whiskey tumbler w/coaster base,
"Bottoms Up," green
opaque ....35.00 to 45.00

MERCURY

Mercury Glass Candlesticks

*This glass has a silvery appearance due to
a coating of silver nitrate in double-walled
objects. A gold effect was obtained by
placing the silver nitrate in amber glass.
The hole through which the solution was
injected was subsequently sealed. It was
made in this country and England from the
middle of the 19th century.*

Bottle w/corked metal stopper, bulbous w/flashed amber panel-cut
neck, etched grapes & grape
leaves, 1840s, 4¼" d., 7½" h. $150.00
Bowl, 9 3/8" d., 4¾" h., 3 applied
clear feet (2 feet ground flat) 70.00
Candlestick, domed base, paneled
stem, candle cup w/tin liner, 4" h.
(single) 37.50
Candlestick, domed base, teardrop-
shaped stem, amber for gold-
washed effect, 6¼" h. (single).......40.00
Candlesticks, domed base, teardrop-
shaped stem, enameled white floral
decor, 5¼" h., pr.................50.00
Candlesticks, round base, baluster-
shaped stem, enameled decor,
12" h., pr. (ILLUS.)................165.00
Centerpice, spherical top mounted on
baluster-shaped stem & round base,
10" h. 57.50
Centerpiece, spherical top on
baluster-shaped stem & circular foot,
silver w/blue cast, transfer-printed
floral decor, 10 5/8" h.............130.00
Compote, 6 3/8" h., bowl w/enamel-
ed white floral decor, large cylindrical stem........................50.00
Compote, 8" d., 8¼" h., amber bowl
interior for gold-washed effect,
knobbed stem 85.00
Curtain tiebacks w/original pewter
shanks, etched grape clusters &
vines, 3½" d., pr. 22.00

Curtain tiebacks w/original pewter
shanks, embossed florals, 3 5/8" d.,
pr. 37.50
Doorknobs, pr. 30.00
Goblet, amber interior for gold-
washed effect, enameled white
floral band, 5 1/8" h. 20.00
Mug, applied clear handle, 2 7/8" h. 15.00
Perfume flacon w/original dauber,
amber glass for gold effect
w/striped design, 2¾" h. 20.00
Pitcher, water, 9¾" h., 5½" d.,
applied clear handle, bulbous
w/panel-cut neck, engraved lacy
florals & leaves, 1840s 200.00
Rose bowl, 3½" h. 10.00
Salt dip, master size, flat, 3" d.,
1½" h. 35.00
Salt dip, master size, pedestal base,
amber interior for gold-washed
effect, signed "W.H." on underside,
1840s, 2 5/8" h. 92.00

Mercury Glass Master Salt

Salt dip, master size, pedestal base,
etched florals, signed "N.E.G." (New
England Glass Co.), 3¼" d., 3" h.
(ILLUS.) 150.00
Sugar bowl & domed cover w/knob
finial, low foot, enameled white
foliage decor, 4¼" d., 6¼" h. 30.00
Vase, 6¾" h., spherical. 45.00
Vase, 7" h., amber interior for gold-
washed effect, enameled poly-
chrome floral decor 60.00
Vases, 7" h., baluster-shaped,
enameled light blue deer & foliage
decor, pr. 75.00
Wine, engraved Vintage patt., amber
interior for gold-washed effect 110.00
Wines, enameled decor, pr. 75.00

MILK WHITE

*This is opaque white glass that resembles
the color of and was used as a substitute for
white porcelain. Opacity was obtained by
adding oxide of tin to a batch of clear glass.*

*It has been made in numerous forms and
shapes in this country and abroad from
about the first quarter of last century. It is
still being produced, and there are many
reproductions of earlier pieces. Also see
COSMOS, HISTORICAL and PATTERN
GLASS and POLITICAL & CAMPAIGN
ITEMS.*

Animal covered dish, Boar's Head
w/glass eyes . . . .$775.00 to 950.00
Animal covered dish, Chick in Egg
on Sleigh 42.50
Animal covered dish, Chicks in Square
Basket, 2¾ x 4½" base, 3½" h. 150.00
Animal covered dish, Dog on ribbed
base 45.00
Animal covered dish, Duck w/glass
eyes, Atterbury. 115.00
Animal covered dish, Duck w/wavy base,
5¼" h. 100.00
Animal covered dish, Horse on split-
ribbed base, McKee 135.00
Animal covered dish, Lion on ribbed
base, Atterbury 130.00
Animal covered dish, Swan w/closed
neck on split-ribbed base 48.50
Animal covered dish, Swan w/raised
wings & glass eyes on lacy-edge
base 130.00
Animal covered dish, "square block"
Swan w/glass eyes, Atterbury,
8" l. 165.00
Animal covered dish, Turtle on 2-han-
dled oblong base 132.50
Animal covered dish, Woolly Lamb on
split rib base 52.50
Bowl, 9¼ x 8¾", Square Edge border. . .38.00
Bowl, 10" d., 4" h., Daisy patt.,
unpainted 75.00
Bowl, 10" d., 4½" h., Acanthus Leaf
patt. 50.00
Bread tray, basketweave, w/patent
date June 30, 1874, 12 x 9¾" 45.00
Butter dish, cov., Blackberry patt. 65.00

Trumpet Vine Cake Stand

Cake stand, Trumpet Vine patt.,
6½" d., 9" h. (ILLUS.). . . . . . .85.00 to 100.00
Candlesticks, Cruciform, 9½" to 10" h.,
each (ILLUS.) 35.00

Cruciform Candlesticks

mpote, 8¼" d., 7" h., openwork
edge, narrow-ribbed stem 58.00
mpote, 8¼" d., 8¼" h., Atlas stem,
scalloped rim, Atterbury ...80.00 to 100.00
mpote, 10" d., 8½" h., Open Hand
patt. 57.50
vered dish, Admiral Dewey on tile
base, 6½" l., 4" h. ....45.00 to 60.00
vered dish, Crawfish finial 150.00
vered dish, Cruiser, 7½" l. 48.50
vered dish, Entwined Fish on lacy
edge base 127.00
vered dish, Moses in Bullrushes,
6½" l. 110.00
vered dish, Royal Coach 65.00
vered dish, Strawberry, w/snail
on lid............................52.50
vered dish, Uncle Sam on Battleship, 4½" h., 6½" l. 55.50
eamer, Blackberry patt. 30.00
esser tray, Chrysanthemum patt.,
7½ x 10"..........................46.00
-, cov., figural Owl, Atterbury,
7" h. 105.00
kle dish, figural fish w/glass eyes,
waffle-type body, Challinor, Taylor
& Company, 9 x 4¼" 55.00
ate, 5½" d., Woof Woof............35.50
ate, 6¼" d., Easter Ducks 33.50
ate, 7" d., Eagles, Flags & Stars
border 24.50
ate, 7" d., Three Kittens 24.50
ate, 7" d., Three Owls 26.00
ate, 7" d., William Howard Taft
center, eagle, flag & star border 57.00
ate, 7¼" d., Chick & Eggs 36.50
ate, 7¼" d., "Easter" Rabbits 28.50
ate, 8" d., Angel & Harp 24.50
ate, 8" d., Half-Pinwheel border....30.00
ate, 8" d., Hearts & Anchor border....25.00
ate, 8" sq., Backward-C border.....35.00
ate, 8¼" d., Gothic & Chain border..25.00
ate, 8¼" d., 1-0-1 border...........35.00
ate, 8¼" d., Quarter-Circle border ...12.00

Plate, 8¼" d., Shell w/Grape Cluster
at handle 20.00
Plate, 8¼" d., Washington bust por-
trait in relief, 13-star border........65.00
Plate, 9½" d., Columbus bust center,
Club & Shell border................35.00
Plate, 11" d., Quarter-Circle border 35.00
Plate, Indian Head center, Beaded
Loop border 40.00
Plate, Indian Head center, Lacy Edge
border 55.00
Plate, Sunken Rabbit 28.00
Sugar shaker w/original top, Apple
Blossom patt. 125.00

Alba Syrup Pitcher

Syrup pitcher w/original top, Alba
patt., decorated, Didthridge, 1894
(ILLUS.)..........................65.00
Syrup pitcher w/original top, Creased
Scroll patt. 45.00
Syrup pitcher w/pewter top w/bird
finial, Stippled Dahlia patt..........50.00
Tumbler, Wild Rose patt.............30.00

MILLEFIORI

*Millefiori glass is decorated or patterned,
with tiny slices of thin multicolored glass
canes and is familiar in paperweights, often
filled with closely packed canes. These
flower pattern canes have also been used in
the production of other objects for many
years and the technique is ancient. This type
of glass is still being made in Murano, Italy,
and elsewhere. Also see PAPER-
WEIGHTS.*

Bowl, 4" d., applied handles, predominantly blue & white canes $85.00
Bowl, 8" w., 2½" h., tricornered
w/folded sides & scalloped edge,
multicolored canes in amethyst,
silver deposit trim 125.00

Cup & saucer, pink, yellow & red
  canes in base of saucer & cup,
  applied clear handle on cup 300.00
Sugar shaker w/original top, applied
  frosted handle, multicolored canes,
  4½" h. 475.00

Millefiori Tumbler

Tumbler, multicolored canes in blue,
  4" h. (ILLUS.) 150.00
Vase, 8" h., 2-handled, multicolored
  canes 195.00
Vase, 11" h., 4½" widest d., bulbous
  w/long neck, yellow, green & red
  canes 110.00

MONART

Monart Bowl

*This glass was produced by John
Moncrieff, Ltd., in Perth, Scotland, between
1924 and 1957. Much of it was signed on a
paper label.*

Bowl, flared, mottled reds & gold $95.00
Candle holder, 2-tone green w/gold-
  stone mica flecks, original label
  (single) 65.00
Vase, 6½" h., mottled shades of red
  & blue, white lining 95.00
Vase, 10" h., random bubbles through
  red & black web design 115.00
Vase, 11" h., 9" d. at shoulders,
  iridescent blue w/internal scrolls &
  bits of white mica at surface 79.00

MONOT & STUMPF

*A glassworks was established by E.S.
Monot at La Villette, near Paris, in 1850.
This operation was moved to Pantin in 1858
and became Monot & Stumpf as Mr. F.
Stumpf joined the firm in 1868. Monot's son
also entered the firm and, in 1873, it became
Monot, Pere et Fils, et Stumpf. According
to an article by Albert Christian Revi,
recognized authority on glasswares and
paperweights, their iridescent wares were
called "Chine Metallique," a patented
process they used beginning in 1878. The
firm continued business in Pantin into the
early 1890s but by the beginning of the 20th
century the company had become Cristallerie de Pantin and was operated by
Saint-Hilaire, Touvier, de Varreux &
Company.*

Monot & Stumpf Pitcher

Pitcher, 4" h., ruffled rim, applied
  handle & 6 applied crimped feet,
  striped lavender-pink, amber & rose
  iridescent (ILLUS.) $280.00
Salt dip, crimped edge, "Chine Metal-
  lique," soft opalescent pink-striped
  effect exterior w/gold lustred
  interior, 2 x 2¼" oval, 1¼" h. 67.50
Salt dip, fluted, "Chine Metallique,"
  soft opalescent pink-striped effect
  exterior w/gold lustred interior,
  3 1/8" d., 1 1/8" h. 60.00
Sauce dish, soft opalescent pink-
  striped effect, 4½" sq. 140.00
Shade, ruffled, softest pale pink opal-
  escent swirl w/lustred gold interior,
  3 7/8" d., 8½" h. 116.00
Vase, 4½" h., scalloped square rim,
  globular swirled body, opalescent
  pink to cranberry, iridescent
  interior 225.00
Vase, 7" h., 6 1/8" d., fan-shaped,
  rich pink opalescent to off-white
  opalescent . . . . 195.00 to 250.00

MONT JOYE

Mont Joye Vases

Cameo and enameled glass bearing this mark was made in Pantin, France, by the same works that produced pieces signed De Vez, which see.

Cameo vase, 4½" h., 5" d., carved roses against iridescent purple ground $310.00

Cameo vase, carved gold iris against light green ground 295.00

Pitcher, water, 10" h., enameled aqua, light blue, pink & gold florals on amethyst ground, signed 285.00

Vase, 8½" h., enameled butterflies, iris & foliage w/lacy gold trim on tomato red ground 132.00

Vase, 11½" h., bulbous body w/elongated neck, enameled burnt orange & gilt poppies on acid-etched green ground, ca. 1900, signed 247.50

Vases, 11¾" h., enameled florals & leaves on cranberry shaded to clear ground, geometric design border around top, signed, pr. (ILLUS.) 600.00

MOSER

Moser Punch Cup

High-quality Art Nouveau glass was produced from around the turn of the century by Moser, Ludwig & Sohne in

Carlsbad and Mierhofen. Much of the base glass was amethyst in color, but this expert craftsman turned out various types of glass, some with exquisite enameling.

Ash tray, triangular, cobalt blue w/frieze band of intaglio-cut classical ladies, signed $250.00

Bowl, 11" oval, emerald green shaded to clear w/intaglio-cut decor, signed 195.00

Cologne bottle w/original stopper, shaded green w/raised enamel nude Art Nouveau ladies & babies decor, signed, 8" h. 300.00

Compote, cov., 11½" h., black amethyst cut to clear, signed 265.00

Cup & saucer, demitasse, clear w/encrusted gold & enameled decor, signed..........................115.00

Cup & saucer, applied clear handle w/gold trim, clear w/heavy gold & dainty white enameled florals & cranberry windows w/gold foliage & white florals decor, signed..........................325.00

Decanter w/matching stopper, green cut to clear, signed, 8" h. 225.00

Goblet, cranberry w/enameled lady bug, dragonfly & floral decor, 4¼" h. 245.00

Punch cup, applied clear handle, enameled multicolored oak leaves w/lacy gold foliage & 8 applied lustred acorns, unsigned, 2 1/8" h. (ILLUS.) 225.00

Toothpick holder, fan-shaped, gold scroll feet, cranberry w/overall silver & gold foliage decor, 2¼ x 3¼"......................300.00

Moser Juice Tumblers

Tumbler, juice, cranberry or clear, enameled blue, white & gold decor, signed, each (ILLUS.) ....95.00 to 125.00

Tumbler, cranberry, gold panels w/enameled pink & blue florals alternating w/panels of enameled multicolored oak leaves, 2½" d., 4½" h. 100.00

Vase, 3½" h., 1¾" d., cylindrical,
ormolu foot, Inverted Thumbprint
patt., cranberry w/enameled
gold grape leaves & applied
clusters of green grapes, unsigned . . 185.00
Vase, 6¾" h., paneled, amethyst
w/intaglio-cut & gold-encrusted
band of Amazon women warriors,
signed 200.00
Vase, 7" h., translucent honey amber
crackle w/applied salamander
wrapped around body continuing
to form feet 385.00
Vase, 8½" h., pale lavender w/facet-
cut edges & acid-etched & tinted
scene of lovely girl beneath
flowering tree, signed 450.00
Vase, 12" h., 7" d., footed,
amethyst w/wide frieze band of
intaglio-cut & gold-encrusted
Etruscan warriors, signed 550.00
Vase, 23½" h., 7¼" d., cranberry,
raised enamel eagle in flight &
enameled multicolored oak leaves,
gold foliage & applied lustred
acorns, on matching stand w/smaller
bird sitting on a branch amidst
enameled oak leaaves & acorns,
signed 6,500.00

MT. WASHINGTON

Mt. Washington Cookie Jar

*A wide diversity of glass was made by the
Mt. Washington Glass Company, of New
Bedford, Mass., between 1869 and 1900. It
was succeeded in 1900 by the Pairpoint
Corporation. Miscellaneous types are listed
below, but also see AMBERINA, BUR-
MESE, CROWN MILANO, CUT, CUT
VELVET, PEACH BLOW, ROYAL
FLEMISH and SMITH BROTHERS
under Glass.*

Bowl, 8¾" d., 2 5/8" h., "Peppermint
Stick," clear acid finish w/"rosaria"
overlay at lip cut in picket fence
design, 24-point star-cut base $185.00

Bride's basket, cameo-carved pink to
white square bowl w/winged bird on
2 sides & florals opposite sides,
crimped rim, gold-washed silverplate frame signed "Reed & Barton,"
8" sq. 845.00
Cookie jar, bulbous, lustreless white,
acanthus leaf embossed corners,
h.p. chrysanthemum decor, silverplate rim & cover, late 19th c.,
unsigned, 6" w., 7" h. 330.00
Cookie jar, lustreless white, h.p.
chrysanthemum decor, silverplate
rim, cover & bail handle, signed 450.00
Cookie jar, melon-ribbed, lustreless
white, h.p. pansy decor, silverplate
rim, cover & bail handle, unsigned . . 400.00
Cookie jar, melon-ribbed, lustreless
white, h.p. thistles outlined in gold,
silverplate rim, cover & bail handle,
signed (ILLUS.) 600.00
Cookie jar, melon-ribbed, lustreless
white, h.p. bird on branch & floral
decor, silverplate cover 550.00
Flower holder, toad stool shape, lustreless white, enameled robin's egg
blue forget-me-nots decor 175.00
Hatpin holder, mushroom-shaped,
enameled ferns & red forget-me-
nots decor, satin finish 210.00
Rose bowl, lustreless white, pink &
blue enameled daisies decor, 6" w.,
5¼" h. 210.00
Salt shaker, model of a chick w/silver-
plate head, lustreless white, h.p.
floral decor, original paper label
(single) 365.00
Salt shaker w/original top, fig-shaped,
lustreless white, h.p. floral decor
(single) 145.00
Salt shaker w/original top, tomato-
shaped, lustreless white (single) 50.00
Salt & pepper shakers w/original
tops, egg-shaped, lustreless white,
h.p. green vines & red berries
decor, 1½" h., pr. 96.00
Salt & pepper shakers w/original tops,
egg-shaped, lavender, h.p. pansies
decor, pr. 75.00
Salt & pepper shakers w/original tops,
fig-shaped, lustreless white, one
w/h.p. yellow blossoms & green
leaves & other w/identical blossoms
in white & w/colored leaves, pr. 335.00
Salt & pepper shakers w/original tops,
flat-sided egg shape (lay-down type),
glossy white, black & red speckled
decor, pr. 150.00
Salt & pepper shakers w/original tops,
flat-sided egg shape (lay-down type),
blue, h.p. pink floral decor, pr. 125.00
Salt & pepper shakers w/original tops,
tomato-shaped, lustreless white,
h.p. dainty pink floral decor, pr. 65.00

Sugar shaker w/original top,
egg-shaped, lustreless white, h.p.
apple blossom decor 125.00

Sugar shaker w/original top, egg-
shaped, lustreless white, enameled
clusters of blue forget-met-nots,
green leaves & accented w/trailing
vines & orange florals 230.00

Sugar shaker w/original top, egg-
shaped, pale lemon yellow, h.p.
russet daisies decor 200.00

Sugar shaker w/original top, egg-
shaped, lustreless white, h.p.
decor 275.00

Sugar shaker w/original top, fig-
shaped, wavy-textured yellow-
green 500.00

Mt. Washington Sugar Shaker

Sugar shaker w/original silverplate
top, tomato-shaped, lustreless
white, h.p. autumn foliage decor
(ILLUS.) 325.00

MULLER FRERES

Muller Freres Vase

*The Muller Brothers made acid-etched
cameo and other fine glass at Luneville,*

*France, starting in 1910 and until the
outbreak of World War II in Europe. Also
see SHADES under Glass.*

Cameo bowl, 6" h., carved avocado
undulating blossoms & leafage
against avocade & dusty rose
ground, ca. 1920, signed $825.00

Cameo vase, 4" h., carved brown &
purple trees against yellow-flecked
to purple ground, signed 495.00

Cameo vase, 7¾" h., 4 3/8" d., carved
black storks (2) & green to blue to
gold chateau, mountains & trees
against frosted gold translucent
ground, signed 1,495.00

Cameo vase, 7¾" h., 5¾" d., carved
red to yellow roses & maroon leaves
against frosted salmon pink ground
w/soft blue mottling at base,
signed 1,212.00

Cameo vase, 8 5/8" h., 4 5/8" d.,
carved deep maroon to rose river
landscape against mottled off-white
frosted ground, signed 685.00

Cameo vase, 9" h., carved florals &
foliage against frosted translucent
ground, signed (ILLUS.) 950.00

Cameo vase, 9¾" h., 8½" w., flattened
bulbous form, carved dark blue
leaves w/rich blue florals against
frosted translucent gold ground
w/blue & coral mottling at base,
signed 2,265.00

Cameo vase, 10" h., carved stylized
parrots against lemon yellow ground,
encrusted w/gold mica flecks inter-
nally, signed .650.00

Cameo vase, 10 5/8" h., 6½" d.,
applied frosted handles, carved
black to green to peach trees along
a shore w/hills in background
against white opaque satin ground,
signed 1,910.00

Cameo vase, 11 3/8" h., compressed
bulbous form w/tapering neck,
carved deep plum trumpet blossoms
& leafage against pale dusty blue
ground, ca. 1900, signed 660.00

Cameo vase, 13¼" h., bulging ovoid,
carved brown river landscape
w/budding trees & doe & her young
in foreground against pumpkin
orange ground, ca. 1920, unsigned ..880.00

NAILSEA

*Glass was made at Nailsea, near Bristol,
England, from 1788 to 1873. Although the
bulk of the products were similar to Bristol
wares, collectors today visualize Nailsea
primarily as a glass characterized by swirls*

and loopings, usually white, on a colored ground. Much glass attributed to Nailsea was made in glasshouses elsewhere. Also see FAIRY LAMPS.

Nailsea Vases

Centerpiece, globe on trumpet-shaped
  vase, clear w/white loopings,
  8¼" h. vase, 7" d. ball $425.00
Cookie jar, cranberry w/white opaque
  loopings, silverplate lid chased
  w/bird & butterflies, 6¼" h. to top
  of finial 375.00
Flask, clear w/red, white & blue
  loopings, 7" l. 118.00
Flask, clear w/rust & white loopings,
  7½" l. 95.00
Flask, clear w/white loopings & ap-
  plied cobalt blue rim, cork closure,
  w/fitted leather 8" l. case 65.00
Perfume bottle w/stopper, opaque
  white w/deep blue loopings,
  6½" h. 125.00
Pitcher, 7¼" h., 5¼" d., bulbous
  w/round mouth, applied clear
  handle, cranberry w/white
  loopings 175.00
Rolling pin, clear w/red & white
  loopings, 15½" l. 118.00
Rolling pin, clear w/red loopings,
  16½" l. 118.00
Rolling pin, rose w/white loopings 200.00
Sugar shaker w/original top, footed
  pear shape, peacock blue w/white
  loopings, 5" h. 90.00
Sweetmeat jar, white w/pink & yel-
  low loopings, silverplate lid w/em-
  bossed designs, 4" d., 5" h. 485.00
Vase, 9" h., red w/white loopings,
  black amethyst base & earred
  handles 165.00
Vase, 9" h., bulbous bottom, ruffled
  rim, blue w/white loopings, ground
  pontil 175.00
Vases, 14" h., trumpet-shaped,
  opaque white w/blue loopings,
  19th c., pr. (ILLUS.) 660.00
Vase, 15 7/8" h., 5" d., trumpet-

shaped, opaque white w/deep rose
  loopings 157.00
Whimsey, model of a pipe w/curving
  stem, white w/pink loopings, 20" l. . . . 80.00

NAKARA

Nakara Tray

Nakara ware was made by the C.F. Monroe Company. For details see WAVE CREST.

Bon bon tray w/ormolu collar, diamond-
  shaped swirl mold, pink geometric
  & scrolling designs outlined in
  white enameled beading on blue
  bisque finish, signed (ILLUS.) $325.00
Box w/hinged lid, soft pink & white
  floral decor on blue ground, 3½" d.,
  3½" h. 375.00
Box w/hinged lid, crown mold, white
  reserve on lid w/portrait of woman
  & h.p. poppies on green ground,
  signed, 4¾" d. 295.00
Box w/hinged lid, pink & white
  florals & white enameled beading
  on soft moss green ground, signed,
  6" w., 3½" h. . . . . 400.00 to 550.00
Box w/hinged lid, octagonal mold,
  purple iris decor on butterscotch
  ground 225.00
Collars & cuffs box w/hinged lid,
  plain mold, white h.p. florals & white
  beading on blue ground, signed
  (clasp broken) 900.00
Dresser box w/hinged lid w/mirror
  inside, enameled daisies on yellow
  shaded to pink ground highlighted
  w/enameled white beading,
  6½" d. 575.00
Dresser dish w/ormolu rim & handles,
  pink, small, signed 85.00
Hair receiver, cov., diamond-shaped
  reserve w/scene of little girls at
  tea outlined in deep blue on pale
  blue ground w/white enameled
  beading decor, signed 385.00
Jewelry box w/hinged lid, enameled
  pink apple blossoms on avocado
  shaded to light rose ground,
  original lining, 4" d. 250.00

Jewelry box w/hinged lid, pink florals
& white enameled beading on moss
green ground, original lining,
6½" d., 3" h. 750.00

Jewelry tray, open, crown mold, h.p.
white florals on pink ground, signed,
6½" d. 275.00

Ring box w/hinged lid, enameled
blue florals on pink satin ground,
signed, 2¼" top d. 425.00

Tobacco jar w/metal lid, reserved
w/scene of frog reading newspaper on pale blue ground, lettered
"Tobacco," signed, 6¾" h. 700.00

Vase, 11½" h., 6" d., h.p. florals
& beaded rim, unsigned 500.00

Vase, 14" h., footed, enameled florals
& beading on matte green ground,
signed..........................875.00

Cordial, Chintz patt., blue & green,
4" h. 55.00

Goblet, Chintz patt., blue & silver,
signed, 5" h. (ILLUS.) 95.00

Goblet, flaring pink-threaded bowl,
twisted stem, wafer foot, signed
Libbey-Nash 99.00

Vase, 4¼" h., pedestal foot, ribbed
lower section, crimped top edge,
iridescent gold w/fiery blue interior, signed 225.00

Vase, 5" h., iridescent gold, signed....285.00

Vase, 5¾" h., Chintz patt., red &
silver, signed....................625.00

Vase, 10" h., trumpet-shaped, Chintz
patt., blue & green, signed 395.00

Vase, 12" h., iridescent gold, signed...175.00

Wine, Chintz patt., lavender & green,
signed, 6" h. 60.00

NASH

Nash Goblet

*This glass was made by A. Douglas Nash
Corp., which purchased the Corona Works
from L.C. Tiffany in December, 1928. Nash,
who formerly worked for Tiffany, produced
outstanding glass for a brief period of time
since the manufacture ceased prior to March
of 1931, when A. Douglas Nash became
associated with Libbey Glass in Toledo,
Ohio. This fine quality ware is scarce.*

Bowl, 10" d., 4" h., Chintz patt., red
w/silver, signed $425.00

Candlestick, Chintz patt., green &
blue stripes, signed (single) 85.00

Candlesticks, baluster-shaped stem,
flaring bobeche & base, Chintz patt.,
blood red w/blue & yellow, 4" h.,
pr..............................450.00

Cologne bottle w/clear stopper,
Chintz patt., pale green stripes separated by clear w/blue center
stripe, 5" h. 485.00

OPALESCENT

*Presently, this is one of the most popular
areas of glass collecting. The opalescent
effect was attained by adding bone ash
chemicals to areas of an item while still hot
and refiring this object at tremendous heat.
Both pressed and mold-blown patterns are
available to collectors and we distinguish
the types in our listing below. Opalescent
Glass From A to Z by William Heacock, is
the definitive reference book for collectors.
Also see PATTERN GLASS.*

MOLD-BLOWN OPALESCENT PATTERNS

ARABIAN NIGHTS
Pitcher, water, cranberry $325.00
Tumbler, blue 55.00

BUBBLE LATTICE
Pitcher, water, cranberry 175.00
Sugar bowl, cov., cranberry 105.00
Sugar shaker w/original top, blue.....135.00
Syrup pitcher w/original top, blue.....140.00
Syrup pitcher w/original top, canary
yellow..........................120.00

BUTTONS & BRAIDS
Pitcher, water, blue 155.00
Pitcher, water, green ....95.00 to 130.00
Tumbler, blue 25.00

CHRYSANTHEMUM BASE SWIRL
Pitcher, water, cranberry 500.00
Syrup pitcher w/original top, blue.....175.00
Toothpick holder, white 40.00

COIN SPOT
Creamer, blue, 4" h. 65.00

Creamer, cranberry, 4" h. 28.50
Pitcher, 5½" h., cranberry 32.00
Pitcher, water, 9¾" h., 5 5/8" d.,
    applied blue handle, ruffled top,
    blue. 125.00
Pitcher, water, applied handle, ruffled
    top, canary yellow 135.00
Pitcher, water, ruffled rim, cranberry. .145.00
Pitcher, water, green. 110.00
Pitcher, water, applied clear handle,
    white 95.00
Rose bowl, cranberry 55.00
Sugar shaker w/original top, green 85.00
Syrup pitcher w/original top, bulbous,
    blue. 125.00
Syrup pitcher w/original top, white . . .165.00
Tumbler, blue 35.00
Tumbler, cranberry 37.00
Vase, 6" h., 7½" d., scalloped rim,
    cranberry. 60.00
Vase, 7½" h., ruffled, cranberry 95.00
Water set: pitcher & 6 tumblers;
    white, 7 pcs. 250.00

Coin Spot Water Set

Water set: pitcher & 6 tumblers;
    cranberry, 7 pcs. (ILLUS.). 350.00

COIN SPOT & SWIRL
Syrup pitcher w/original top, blue. 120.00
Syrup pitcher w/original top, white 65.00

CONSOLIDATED'S CRISS-CROSS
Bowl, master berry, 8" d., cranberry. . .135.00
Celery vase, Rubina, satin finish 245.00
Salt shaker w/replaced top, cranberry. .58.00
Salt shaker w/original top, cran-
    berry, satin finish 110.00
Spooner, Rubina 125.00
Tumbler, cranberry 85.00
Tumbler, white .49.00

DAFFODILS
Celery vase, blue 72.00
Pitcher, water, blue 175.00
Pitcher, water, green. 180.00
Pitcher, water, white 145.00
Tumbler, blue 50.00
Tumbler, white .45.00

DAISY & FERN

Daisy & Fern Sugar Shaker

Barber bottle, cranberry 130.00
Creamer, cranberry 95.00
Cruet w/original stopper, blue 90.00
Cruet w/original stopper, white 55.00
Finger bowl, blue 30.00
Pitcher, 8½" h., 3-spout, blue 142.00
Pitcher, 9" h., applied clear handle,
    ruffled rim, white 75.00
Pitcher, milk, blue 60.00
Pitcher, water, bulbous, blue 165.00
Pitcher, water, cranberry 205.00
Pitcher, water, green. 145.00
Pitcher, water, white 125.00
Rose bowl, blue 35.00
Rose bowl, ruffled rim, cranberry 40.00
Sugar shaker w/original top, blue
    (ILLUS.). 110.00
Sugar shaker w/original top,
    cranberry 105.00
Syrup pitcher w/original top,
    bulbous base, blue 88.00
Syrup pitcher w/original top,
    cranberry 125.00
Syrup pitcher w/original top, white 65.00
Tumbler, blue 28.00
Tumbler, cranberry 40.00
Tumbler, green .35.00
Water set: pitcher & 4 tumblers; blue,
    5 pcs. 235.00
Water set: pitcher & 7 tumblers;
    cranberry, 8 pcs. 325.00

DAISY IN CRISS-CROSS
Pitcher, water, white 55.00
Syrup pitcher w/original top, blue. 250.00
Tumbler, blue 45.00
Tumbler, cranberry (edge flakes) 70.00

DIAMONDS
Tumbler, cranberry, 3 5/8" h. 55.00

FERN
Barber bottle, blue . . . . .90.00 to 95.00
Pitcher, water, tankard, applied
    handle, petal form rim, blue. 275.00

Pitcher, water, square top, cranberry . . 225.00
Spooner, cranberry 85.00
Sugar shaker w/original top, cran-
  berry 135.00
Syrup pitcher w/original top,
  blue . . . . 130.00 to 135.00
Syrup pitcher w/original top, white 85.00

HERRINGBONE
Cruet w/clear stopper, blue 85.00
Cruet w/original cut stopper, cran-
  berry 170.00
Tumbler, cranberry 75.00

HOBNAIL, HOBBS

Hobnail Pitcher

Barber bottle, blue 145.00
Bowl, 10" d., 4½" h., ruffled, blue 68.00
Butter dish, cov., blue 122.00
Butter dish, cov., vaseline 150.00
Celery vase, vaseline 52.50
Cruet w/original stopper, cran-
  berry 210.00
Cruet w/original stopper, vaseline 220.00
Finger bowl, cranberry 70.00
Ice cream set, vaseline, 7 pcs. 220.00
Pitcher, water, child's, vaseline 195.00
Pitcher, water, child's, white 125.00
Pitcher, water, square top, applied
  reeded handle, cranberry 230.00
Pitcher, water, bulbous w/square
  mouth, vaseline (ILLUS.) 165.00
Syrup pitcher w/original top, white . . . 125.00
Tumbler, blue 36.50
Tumbler, cranberry 58.00
Vase, 8" h., pineapple shape,
  ruffled rim, cranberry 125.00

NINE-PANEL COINSPOT
Sugar shaker w/original top, blue 85.00
Syrup pitcher w/original top, blue 90.00
Syrup pitcher w/original top,
  green . . . . 85.00 to 140.00
Syrup pitcher w/original top, white 47.50

POINSETTIA
Pitcher, water, tankard, 13" h., blue . . . 165.00
Pitcher, water, tankard, 13" h.,
  green 125.00
Tumbler, blue 43.00
Tumbler, green 33.00
Water set: bulbous pitcher w/crimped
  rim & 7 tumblers; blue, 8 pcs. 425.00

POLKA DOT
Barber bottle, blue 125.00
Barber bottle, cranberry 125.00
Cruet w/original stopper, cranberry . . . 120.00
Pitcher, 9" h., white 225.00
Pitcher, water, cranberry 185.00
Syrup pitcher w/original top,
  cranberry 220.00
Syrup pitcher w/original top, white 60.00

REVERSE SWIRL
Bowl, berry, 9" d., white 45.00
Carafe, blue 35.00
Celery vase, blue 68.00
Mustard jar, canary yellow 34.50
Pitcher, water, canary yellow 150.00
Pitcher, water, tankard, white 102.00
Salt shaker w/original top, blue 25.00
Salt shaker w/original top, canary
  yellow 25.00
Sauce dish, blue 20.00
Spooner, blue 55.00
Sugar bowl, cov., blue 115.00
Sugar shaker w/original top, blue 110.00
Sugar shaker w/original top, canary
  yellow 85.00
Sugar shaker w/original top,
  cranberry 125.00
Syrup pitcher w/original top, blue 135.00
Syrup pitcher w/original top, cran-
  berry, 7¼" h. 220.00
Toothpick holder, white 40.00
Tumbler, juice, white 25.00
Tumbler, canary yellow 38.00
Tumbler, cranberry 45.00
Tumbler, white 65.00
Vase, 8" h., blue 45.00
Water set: pitcher & 4 tumblers;
  white, 5 pcs. 165.00
Whiskey shot glass, white 22.00

RIBBED LATTICE
Celery vase, cranberry 87.00
Cruet w/original stopper, blue 150.00
Cruet w/original stopper, cranberry . . . 165.00
Cruet w/original stopper, white 55.00
Pitcher, water, white 130.00
Salt shaker w/original top, cranberry . . . 45.00
Sugar shaker w/original top, blue 85.00
Sugar shaker w/original top, cran-
  berry 110.00
Sugar shaker w/original top,
  white . . . . 50.00 to 75.00
Syrup pitcher w/original top,
  blue (ILLUS.) 160.00

Ribbed Lattice Sugar Shaker

Syrup pitcher w/original top, cran-
   berry..........................265.00
Toothpick holder, blue................65.00
Toothpick holder, cranberry..........72.50
Toothpick holder, white 30.00
Tumbler, cranberry 55.00
Tumbler, white 50.00

RING-NECK COINSPOT
Syrup pitcher w/original top, Rubina ..120.00
Syrup pitcher w/original top, white 75.00

SEAWEED
Barber bottle, blue..................110.00
Barber bottle, cranberry 115.00
Barber bottle, white.................85.00
Butter dish, cov., blue 200.00
Celery vase, blue 85.00
Cruet w/original stopper, blue 135.00
Cruet w/original stopper, white 85.00
Pitcher, water, blue.................250.00
Pitcher, water, cranberry 275.00
Pitcher, water, white 125.00
Salt shaker w/original top, cranberry...42.50
Spooner, cranberry, satin finish........90.00
Sugar bowl, cov., cranberry, satin
   finish.........................110.00
Sugar shaker w/original top, blue......95.00

SPANISH LACE
Bowl, 7" d., turned-up edge, white 40.00
Pitcher, water, 9" h., canary yellow ...145.00
Pitcher, water, tankard, 11½" h.,
   cranberry......................385.00
Pitcher, water, tankard, green 450.00
Rose bowl, blue 65.00
Rose bowl, canary yellow 50.00
Rose bowl, white 35.00
Spooner, blue ....60.00 to 75.00
Spooner, cranberry 75.00
Sugar shaker w/original top, blue......97.00
Sugar shaker w/original top, canary
   yellow.........................110.00
Sugar shaker w/original top, cran-
   berry..........................145.00
Syrup pitcher w/original top, blue.....115.00

Syrup pitcher w/original top,
   cranberry......................165.00
Tumbler, blue ....35.00 to 45.00
Tumbler, cranberry 45.00
Water set: pitcher & 4 tumblers;
   cranberry, 5 pcs.................375.00

STARS & STRIPES

Stars & Stripes Tumblers

Barber bottle, blue..................135.00
Barber bottle, white.................110.00
Finger bowl, white 15.00
Tumbler, blue 60.00
Tumbler, cranberry (ILLUS. of pair) 45.00
Tumbler, white 45.00

SWIRL
Barber bottle, cranberry, 10¼" h.......65.00
Bowl, master berry, white 50.00
Cruet w/original stopper, cranberry...160.00
Pitcher, water, bulbous w/square
   ruffled top, applied blue handle,
   blue...........................125.00
Pitcher, water, square ruffled top,
   cranberry ....185.00 to 235.00
Pitcher, water, green................130.00
Pitcher, water, white................90.00
Sugar shaker w/original top, blue......84.00
Syrup pitcher w/original top, blue.....105.00
Syrup pitcher w/tin top, canary
   yellow.........................125.00
Toothpick holder, blue...............42.50
Tumbler, blue 25.50
Tumbler, cranberry 35.50
Tumbler, white 20.00
Vase, 7" h., 10" d., scalloped
   rim w/ruffled edge, green 39.50
Water set: pitcher & 4 tumblers; blue,
   5 pcs..........................180.00
Water set: pitcher & 5 tumblers;
   cranberry, 6 pcs.................165.00
Water set: pitcher & 5 tumblers;
   green, 6 pcs....................235.00
Whimsey, hat, white 75.00
Whimsey, pipe, blue, 18" l............110.00

WINDOWS, PLAIN
Pitcher, water, cranberry 245.00
Pitcher, water, applied clear handle,
   white 150.00

Salt shaker w/original top, cranberry . . .40.00
Syrup pitcher w/original top, blue 135.00
Toothpick holder, white 40.00
Tumbler, blue 35.00
Vase, 9" h., ruffled top, blue 60.00
Water set: pitcher w/straight top &
   2 tumblers; cranberry, 3 pcs. 300.00

WINDOWS, SWIRLED
Finger bowl, blue, 4½" d. 35.00
Pitcher, water, white 135.00
Salt shaker w/original top, cranberry . . .32.00
Salt & pepper shakers w/original
   tops, blue, pr. 85.00
Sugar shaker w/original top, cran-
   berry, tall 195.00
Syrup pitcher w/original top, blue,
   tall 210.00
Syrup pitcher w/original top, cran-
   berry, tall 250.00
Syrup pitcher w/original top, white,
   tall 75.00
Tumbler, blue 85.00
Tumbler, cranberry . . . . .40.00 to 55.00
Tumbler, white .28.00

PRESSED OPALESCENT PATTERNS

ALASKA - See Pattern Glass

BARBELLS
Bowl, 6½" d., ruffled rim, blue 27.50
Candy dish, white 19.50

BEADED CABLE

Beaded Cable Bowl

Bowl, ruffled, green (ILLUS.) 45.00
Bowl, ruffled, white 28.00
Nut bowl, footed, blue 65.00

BEADS & BARK
Vase, blue . . . . .40.00 to 65.00
Vase, green 35.00
Vase, vaseline 35.00
Vase, white 75.00

BEATTY HONEYCOMB
Creamer, individual size, blue 45.00

Salt shaker w/original top, white 20.00
Toothpick holder, blue 45.00
Toothpick holder, white 25.00

BEATTY RIB

Beatty Rib Bowl

Bowl, master berry, 9" d., white
   (ILLUS.) 50.00
Celery vase, blue 50.00
Celery vase, white 50.00
Creamer, blue 22.00
Dish, blue, 4 7/8 x 3 5/8" oblong 25.00
Salt dip, individual size, white . . 16.00 to 22.00
Salt dip, master size, blue . . . . .40.00 to 65.00
Salt shaker w/original top, blue 35.00
Sauce dish, blue 14.50
Sauce dish, white 16.00
Sugar bowl, cov., white 42.50
Sugar shaker w/original top, blue 85.00
Toothpick holder, blue 35.00
Toothpick holder, white 24.00
Waste bowl, blue 35.00

BEATTY SWIRL

Beatty Swirl Pitcher

Banana boat, blue 40.00
Butter dish, cov., blue . . . . . . .125.00 to 140.00
Celery, white 25.00
Pitcher, water, blue (ILLUS.) 145.00
Sauce dish, blue 32.50
Spooner, white .65.00
Sugar bowl, cov., white 75.00
Water tray, blue . . . . .60.00 to 100.00
Water tray, canary yellow 85.00

BUTTON PANELS
Bowl, pedestal base, blue 25.00
Bowl, pedestal base, white 30.00
Rose bowl, blue 65.00
Rose bowl, white . . . . .35.00 to 45.00

CIRCLED SCROLL
Berry set: master bowl & 6 sauce
   dishes; blue, 7 pcs. 350.00
Bowl, master berry, green 65.00
Bowl, master berry, white 55.00
Butter dish, cov., green 150.00
Creamer, blue 65.00
Creamer, green 60.00
Pitcher, water, green 245.00
Sauce dish, footed, blue, 4¼" d. 25.00
Spooner, blue 57.00
Spooner, green 60.00
Table set: cov. butter dish, cov.
   sugar bowl, creamer & spooner;
   blue, 4 pcs. 750.00
Water set: pitcher & 6 tumblers; blue,
   7 pcs. .700.00

CORN VASE
Blue 80.00
Canary yellow . . . . .58.00 to 70.00
Green 82.00
White 60.00

DAISY & PLUME
Bowl, 3-footed, ribbon candy edge,
   blue 65.00
Bowl, 3-footed, white 35.00
Vase, blue 45.00

DIAMOND & OVAL THUMBPRINT
Vase, blue 20.00
Vase, white 11.00

DIAMOND SPEARHEAD
Bowl, master berry, blue 80.00
Bowl, master berry, vaseline 65.00
Butter dish, cov., vaseline 250.00
Celery vase, vaseline 95.00
Mug, blue 42.00
Plate, vaseline 70.00
Spooner, green . . . . .40.00 to 50.00
Spooner, vaseline 53.00
Sugar bowl, cov., blue 185.00
Sugar bowl, cov., vaseline 110.00
Toothpick holder, blue 90.00
Toothpick holder, green . . . . . . .45.00 to 55.00
Toothpick holder, vaseline 58.00
Tumbler, green 20.00

DOLLY MADISON
Bowl, berry, 9¼" d., green 50.00
Creamer, blue 70.00
Spooner, blue 70.00
Spooner, green 45.00
Sugar bowl, cov., green w/gold trim . . .85.00
Sugar bowl, cov., white 50.00

DOLPHIN COMPOTE
Blue 42.00
Canary yellow 35.00
White 20.00

DRAPERY
Berry set: master bowl & 6 sauce
   dishes; blue, 7 pcs. 225.00
Butter dish, cov., blue 200.00
Creamer, blue 45.00
Pitcher, water, blue . . . . .140.00 to 170.00
Pitcher, water, blue w/gold trim 225.00
Pitcher, water, white 125.00
Rose bowl, blue 49.50
Sauce dish, blue . . . . .20.00 to 30.00
Sauce dish, white 18.00
Spooner, blue w/gold trim 70.00
Spooner, white 25.00
Sugar bowl, cov., blue 100.00
Sugar bowl, cov., white 55.00
Table set: cov. butter dish, cov. sugar
   bowl, creamer & spooner; blue,
   4 pcs. .485.00
Table set, white, 4 pcs. 255.00
Tumbler, blue 28.00
Vase, 8" h., blue 75.00
Water set: pitcher & 6 tumblers; blue,
   7 pcs. .365.00

EVERGLADES

Everglades Spooner & Butter Dish

Berry set: master bowl & 6 sauce
   dishes; blue, 7 pcs. 295.00
Berry set: master bowl & 6 sauce
   dishes; canary yellow, 7 pcs. 485.00
Bowl, master berry, blue . . . .110.00 to 120.00
Butter dish, cov., blue w/gold trim
   (ILLUS. right) . . . . .250.00 to 300.00
Butter dish, cov., white 85.00
Candy compote, green 28.00
Compote, jelly, blue or green,
   each . . . . .40.00 to 60.00
Compote, jelly, canary yellow 90.00
Compote, jelly, white w/gold trim 35.00
Creamer, blue 60.00
Creamer, canary yellow 52.00
Creamer, white 40.00
Creamer & sugar bowl, white w/gold
   trim, pr. 90.00
Cruet w/original stopper, blue 370.00
Cruet w/original stopper, canary
   yellow .385.00

Pitcher, water, canary yellow 375.00
Sauce dish, blue 32.00
Sauce dish, canary yellow.............35.00
Spooner, blue w/gold trim (ILLUS. left)..90.00
Spooner, canary yellow ....55.00 to 78.00
Spooner, white 45.00
Sugar bowl, cov., blue w/gold
    trim ....120.00 to 150.00
Sugar bowl, cov., canary yellow 135.00
Sugar bowl, cov., canary yellow
    w/gold trim 150.00
Sugar bowl, cov., white...............75.00
Table set, blue, 4 pcs................450.00
Table set, canary yellow, 4 pcs.......515.00
Tumbler, blue ....58.00 to 65.00
Tumbler, canary yellow w/gold trim....65.00
Water set: pitcher & 4 tumblers;
    white w/gold trim, 5 pcs. 225.00

FAN

Fan Creamer

Bowl, footed, green 25.00
Creamer, blue (ILLUS.)................33.00
Dish, green 18.50
Gravy boat, blue......................35.00
Gravy boat, green 47.50
Sauce dish, blue 25.00

FINE-CUT & ROSES
Dish, green 25.00
Spooner, green 38.00
Spooner, white 19.00

FLORA
Berry set: master bowl & 6 sauce
    dishes; canary yellow, 7 pcs. 295.00
Bowl, master berry, blue..............63.00
Butter dish, cov., canary yellow 265.00
Butter dish, cov., white 95.00
Candy dish, tricornered, white, 7"....25.00
Celery vase, blue 125.00
Creamer, blue 65.00
Sauce dish, blue 34.00
Spooner, blue 75.00
Spooner, white 45.00
Sugar bowl, cov., blue 95.00

FLUTED BARS & BEADS
Rose bowl, green w/cranberry rim 38.00

Fluted Bars & Beads Vase

Vase, blue (ILLUS.) 35.00
Vase, vaseline w/cranberry rim 37.50

FLUTED SCROLLS

Fluted Scrolls Card Tray

Berry set: master bowl & 6 sauce
    dishes; vaseline, 7 pcs. 230.00
Bowl, 7½" d., turned down side, blue ..45.00
Bowl, master berry, blue..............60.00
Bowl, master berry, vaseline 85.00
Butter dish, cov., blue w/gold trim 200.00
Butter dish, cov., vaseline...........190.00
Butter dish, cov., white 125.00
Card tray, white, 7" (ILLUS.) 35.00
Creamer, blue.........................47.00
Creamer, vaseline ....45.00 to 60.00
Creamer, white 42.00
Cruet w/replaced stopper, blue.......125.00
Cruet w/original stopper, vaseline 150.00
Epergne, blue 120.00
Gravy bowl, vaseline..................65.00
Pitcher, water, blue 250.00
Pitcher, water, vaseline 200.00
Pitcher, water, white.................87.50
Puff jar, cov., blue ....50.00 to 75.00
Puff jar, cov., vaseline ....45.00 to 60.00
Puff jar, cov., white.................30.00
Rose bowl, white 45.00
Salt shaker w/original top, blue
    (single)............................37.50
Salt & pepper shakers w/original tops,
    blue, pr............................65.00

Sauce dish, blue w/enameled florals ...32.50
Sauce dish, vaseline..................25.00
Sauce dish, white w/enameled florals ..27.00
Spooner, blue 50.00
Spooner, white 42.00
Spooner, vaseline...................40.00
Sugar bowl, cov., blue..............85.00
Sugar bowl, cov., vaseline .....45.00 to 65.00
Sugar bowl, cov., vaseline w/enameled
   florals 150.00
Sugar bowl, open, vaseline 25.00
Table set, blue, 4 pcs. 485.00
Table set, vaseline, 4 pcs............455.00
Tumbler, blue w/enameled florals 65.00
Tumbler, vaseline w/enameled
   florals 65.00

FLUTED SCROLLS WITH VINE
Vase, 6" h., blue ....25.00 to 30.00

GONTERMAN SWIRL

Gonterman Swirl Spooner

Bowl, master berry, 10" d., blue top ...135.00
Celery vase, amber top 95.00
Creamer, applied amber handle,
   amber top 95.00
Pitcher, water, amber top...........245.00
Spooner, amber top (ILLUS.) ...80.00 to 95.00
Sugar bowl, cov., amber top ..85.00 to 105.00
Syrup pitcher w/original lid, amber
   top 250.00
Water set: pitcher & 5 tumblers; amber
   tops, 6 pcs.......................575.00

GRAPE & CHERRY
Bowl, master berry, 10" d.,
   blue ....35.00 to 45.00

GREEK KEY & RIBS
Bowl, 8½" w., 3" h., footed, ruffled
   rim, white 20.00
Bowl, 9" d., dome footed, green 35.00

GREEK KEY & SCALES
Bowl, blue 95.00

HOBNAIL, NORTHWOOD
Candle holders, blue, 4" base d.,
   2" h., pr...........................15.00
Cigarette box, cov., blue, 5 x 3½".....15.00
Creamer, white......................35.50
Creamer & sugar bowl, white, pr. 55.00
Nappy, ruffled, blue.................10.00
Pitcher, water, 8" h., 7" d.,
   bulbous, square mouth, applied
   clear handle, white 125.00
Powder jar, cov., white 15.00
Salt & pepper shakers w/original
   tops, blue, pr. 15.00
Tumbler, blue 20.00
Vase, 3½" h., fluted, cranberry........10.00
Vase, 4" h., crimped edge, vaseline 35.00
Vase, 5½" h., 5" d., ruffled top,
   canary yellow 25.00

HOBNAIL & PANELED THUMBPRINT

Hobnail & Paneled Thumbprint Table Set

Butter dish, cov. blue...............145.00
Creamer, blue.......................45.00
Pitcher, water, blue 135.00
Spooner, blue 60.00
Spooner, canary yellow ....50.00 to 65.00
Sugar bowl, cov., canary yellow 100.00
Table set, blue, 4 pcs...............425.00
Table set, canary yellow, 4 pcs.
   (ILLUS.)........................365.00
Tumbler, blue 25.00

HOBNAIL-IN-SQUARE
Bowl, master berry, 10" d., white 88.00
Pickle castor, white insert in silverplate
   holder w/apple decor 125.00

HONEYCOMB & CLOVER
Bowl, master berry, blue..............37.50
Bowl, master berry, green 35.00
Bowl, master berry, white 30.00
Pitcher, water, blue 265.00
Pitcher, water, green................175.00

IDYLL
Berry set: master bowl & 6 sauce
   dishes; green, 7 pcs. 45.00
Creamer, green 55.00
Creamer, white......................26.00
Pitcher, water, green...............245.00
Spooner, blue 80.00
Spooner, green 75.00
Sugar bowl, open, green 45.00
Toothpick holder, green 115.00

INTAGLIO

Berry set: master bowl & 6 sauce
  dishes; blue, 7 pcs. 400.00
Compote, jelly, blue. 27.50
Compote, jelly, canary yellow 45.00
Compote, jelly, white 22.50
Creamer, blue. 50.00
Creamer & sugar bowl, blue, pr. 125.00
Creamer & sugar bowl, white, pr. 62.00
Cruet w/original stopper, blue 125.00
Cruet w/original stopper, white 85.00
Pitcher, water, blue 215.00
Pitcher, water, white. 82.50
Sauce dish, blue 20.00
Sauce dish, white 16.50
Spooner, blue 60.00
Spooner, white 35.00
Table set, blue, 4 pcs. 850.00
Tumbler, white 30.00
Water set: pitcher & 6 tumblers; blue,
  7 pcs. 725.00

IRIS WITH MEANDER

Bowl, master berry, blue. 95.00
Butter dish, cov., blue 100.00
Compote, jelly, canary yellow 40.00
Pitcher, water, blue 150.00
Salt & pepper shakers w/original
  tops, blue, pr. 75.00
Sauce dish, canary yellow. 20.00
Toothpick holder, blue. 90.00
Toothpick holder, green 42.50
Water set: pitcher & 6 tumblers;
  blue, 7 pcs. 350.00

JACKSON

Cruet w/original stopper, canary
  yellow. 135.00
Pitcher, water, blue 195.00
Salt shaker w/original top, blue
  (single). 35.00
Salt & pepper shakers w/original
  tops, canary yellow, pr. 60.00
Sugar bowl, cov., blue 110.00
Sugar bowl, open, blue 55.00

JEFFERSON SPOOL

Vase, 6½" h., green 32.00
Vase, 6½" h., vaseline 39.00

JEWEL & FAN

Bowl, 7¾" d., ruffled edge, green. 26.50
Dish, blue, 7 x 5" oval . . . . 32.50 to 40.00
Dish, green, 7 x 5" oval 25.00
Dish, white, 9" oval 18.00
Rose bowl, blue 60.00
Sauce dish, green, oval 35.00

JEWELED HEART

Berry set: master bowl & 5 sauce
  dishes; green, 6 pcs. 165.00
Berry set: master bowl & 6 sauce
  dishes; white, 7 pcs. (ILLUS. of part) . . 95.00

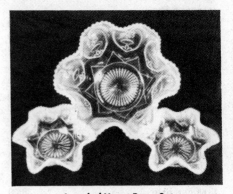

Jeweled Heart Berry Set

Bowl, master berry, ruffled, blue 35.00
Creamer, blue. 57.50
Creamer, white. 55.00
Dish, fluted rim, blue, 6". 22.50
Pitcher, water, white 135.00
Plate, 6½" d., footed, green 17.00
Sauce dish, green, 5½" d. 20.00
Spooner, green 45.00
Tumbler, green 37.50
Tumbler, white 27.50
Water set: pitcher & 4 tumblers;
  white, 5 pcs. 95.00

JOLLY BEAR

Bowl, 3 turned up sides, white
  w/"goofus" decor . . . . 85.00 to 125.00

LATTICE MEDALLIONS

Lattice Medallions Bowl

Bowl, scroll feet, blue 60.00
Bowl, fluted edge, scroll feet, green
  (ILLUS.). 25.00

LEAF CHALICE

Bowl-vase, blue 35.00
Bowl-vase, green. . . . . 45.00 to 55.00

LINED HEART

Vase, blue 27.50
Vase, green. 30.00

MANY LOOPS
Bowl, 8" d., blue .40.00
Bowl, 8" d., green. 35.00
Bowl, 8" d., white 15.50

MEANDER
Bowl, 9" d., crimped rim, 3-footed,
    blue. 42.50
Bowl, fluted edge, 3-footed, green 33.50

OPAL OPEN
Plate, 7" d., footed, ruffled, blue. 30.00
Rose bowl, pedestal base, blue 45.00

OVER-ALL-HOB
Creamer, blue. 38.00
Creamer, white. .41.50
Toothpick holder, blue. 42.50
Toothpick holder, canary yellow 45.00
Toothpick holder, white 22.50
Tumbler, blue 35.00

PALM BEACH
Berry set: master bowl & 6 sauce
    dishes; canary yellow, 7 pcs. 295.00
Bowl, master berry, blue. 70.00
Butter dish, cov., canary yellow. 225.00
Finger bowl, blue 115.00
Finger bowls, canary yellow, set of 8 . .275.00
Pitcher, water, blue 400.00
Pitcher, water, canary yellow 350.00
Plate, blue. . . . . .48.00 to 58.00
Sauce dish, canary yellow. 32.50
Spooner, canary yellow. 80.00
Sugar bowl, cov., blue 175.00
Sugar bowl, cov., canary yellow 145.00
Table set: cov. butter dish, cov. sugar
    bowl, creamer & spooner; blue or
    canary yellow, 4 pcs., each set. 690.00
Tumbler, canary yellow. 75.00
Water set: pitcher & 6 tumblers;
    canary yellow, 7 pcs. 695.00

PEARL FLOWERS

Pearl Flowers Bowl

Bowl, 6½" d., 4½" h., 3-footed,
    scalloped rim, blue. 35.00
Bowl, 6½" d., 4½" h., 3-footed,
    scalloped rim, white (ILLUS.) 25.00

PIASA BIRD
Cuspidor, lady's, white 32.50

Rose bowl, blue .55.00
Vase, 12" h., blue . . . . .48.50 to 60.00
Vase, 12" h., white . . . . .45.00 to 65.00

POPSICKLE STICKS
Bowl, green. 30.00
Compote, white .22.00

REGAL
Butter dish, cov., blue 195.00
Butter dish, cov., green. 150.00
Celery vase, blue 95.00
Compote, jelly, blue. 80.00
Creamer, blue. 60.00
Pitcher, water, blue 375.00
Sauce dish, blue 25.00
Spooner, blue 62.50
Spooner, green .50.00
Sugar bowl, cov., blue. 100.00
Sugar bowl, cov., green . . . . . .85.00 to 100.00
Sugar bowl, cov., white w/gold 75.00
Table set, blue, 4 pcs. 475.00
Tumbler, blue 75.00
Tumbler, green 42.50
Tumbler, white 32.50

RIBBED SPIRAL

Ribbed Spiral Pattern

Bowl, 9" d., white 27.50
Bowl, 9" d., canary yellow 37.50
Compote, jelly, blue (ILLUS.) 38.00
Compote, jelly, white 26.00
Creamer, blue. 52.50
Cup, blue (ILLUS.) 37.50
Cup & saucer, canary yellow. 60.00
Sauce dish, blue 25.00
Sauce dish, canary yellow. 18.00
Toothpick holder, blue. 82.50
Toothpick holder, canary yellow 65.00
Toothpick holder, white 55.00
Tumbler, blue 30.00
Tumbler, white 20.00
Vase, 10" h., canary yellow 24.50

RUFFLES & RINGS
Bowl, 8" to 9½" d., 3-footed,
    blue .35.00 to 58.00
Bowl, 8" to 9½" d., 3-footed,
    green . . . . .22.00 to 45.00
Bowl, 8" to 9½" d., 3-footed,
    white . . . . .22.00 to 38.00

S-REPEAT

S-Repeat Master Berry Bowl

Bowl, master berry, blue (ILLUS.) 60.00
Tumbler, blue ....35.00 to 45.00

SCROLL WITH ACANTHUS

Scroll with Acanthus Water Pitcher

Berry set: master bowl & 4 sauce
   dishes; white, 5 pcs................110.00
Bowl, master berry, 9½" d., blue 72.50
Bowl, master berry, 9½" d., white 45.00
Compote, jelly, blue ....28.00 to 40.00
Compote, jelly, white 22.50
Creamer, blue........................50.00
Creamer, canary yellow................52.50
Cruet w/original stopper, blue 135.00
Pitcher, water, blue (ILLUS.) 250.00
Sauce dish, white 12.50
Spooner, blue 57.50
Spooner, canary yellow................50.00
Spooner, white 30.00
Tumbler, blue 35.00

SEA SPRAY

Olive dish w/center ring handle, blue ..47.50
Olive dish w/center ring handle,
   green 25.00

SHELL

Compote, jelly, blue.................175.00
Creamer, blue........................60.00
Creamer, green 60.00

Creamer & open sugar bowl, blue,
   pr...............................110.00
Sauce dish, blue 25.00

SHELL & WILD ROSE

Shell & Wild Rose Bowl

Bowl, 8½" d., blue 33.00
Bowl, 8½" d., green (ILLUS.) 27.50
Bowl, 8½" d., white 32.50

SPOKES & WHEELS

Bowl, 8½" d., low, blue..............35.00
Bowl, 8½" d., low, green 32.50

SUNBURST ON SHIELD

Creamer, blue........................45.00
Sugar bowl, breakfast size,
   blue...........................35.00
Sugar bowl, breakfast size,
   white ....22.00 to 30.00

SWAG WITH BRACKET

Berry set: master bowl & 6 sauce
   dishes; green, 7 pcs. 210.00
Bowl, master berry, blue.............40.00
Butter dish, cov., canary yellow.......200.00
Butter dish, cov., green..............180.00
Compote, jelly, blue or canary yellow,
   each 35.00
Compote, jelly, green 25.00
Compote, jelly, white 20.00
Creamer, blue........................57.50
Creamer, green 52.50
Creamer, white.......................32.00
Cruet w/(replaced) stopper, canary
   yellow.........................150.00
Pitcher, water, blue 280.00
Pitcher, water, canary yellow 250.00
Sauce dish, blue or canary yellow,
   each 24.00
Spooner, blue 55.00
Spooner, canary yellow...............40.00
Spooner, green.......................45.00
Sugar bowl, cov., green 71.50
Sugar bowl, cov., white 50.00
Table set, canary yellow, 4 pcs........450.00
Table set, green, 4 pcs.......350.00 to 375.00
Toothpick holder, blue...............150.00
Tumbler, blue 65.00
Tumbler, canary yellow...............50.00
Tumbler, white.......................30.00

TREE TRUNK VASE

Novelty vase, blue 30.00
Novelty vase, green. 27.50
Novelty vase, white 35.00

WATERLILY WITH CATTAILS

Bowl, master berry, blue. 60.00
Bowl, master berry, white 55.00
Creamer, blue. .45.00
Creamer, white. 32.00
Pitcher, water, green. 185.00
Plate, 10" d., white. 25.00
Spooner, blue .50.00
Sugar bowl, cov., green 100.00
Tumbler, blue .34.00
Tumbler, white 20.00

WHEEL & BLOCK

Bowl, 9½" d., green. 35.00
Bowl, 9½" d., white 30.00

WILD BOUQUET

Wild Bouquet Spooner

Bowl, master berry, blue. 80.00
Butter dish, cov., blue 500.00
Compote, jelly, blue. 80.00
Compote, jelly, white 32.00
Creamer, blue. 77.50
Creamer, green 60.00
Cruet w/original stopper, blue 375.00
Pitcher, water, blue 250.00
Pitcher, water, white. 80.00
Sauce dish, blue 35.00
Sauce dish, green 27.50
Sauce dish, white 19.00
Spooner, blue (ILLUS.) 90.00
Spooner, green 75.00
Spooner, white 28.00
Sugar bowl, cov., blue. 175.00
Table set, blue, 4 pcs. 850.00
Toothpick holder, blue. 225.00
Tumbler, green 75.00

WREATH & SHELL

Berry set: master bowl & 6 sauce
    dishes; vaseline, 7 pcs. 185.00
Bowl, master berry, 10" d., blue 105.00
Bowl, master berry, 10" d., canary
    yellow. 85.00

Butter dish, cov., blue . . . . . . .185.00 to 240.00
Butter dish, cov., vaseline. 150.00
Celery vase, blue 150.00
Celery vase, white 85.00
Creamer, blue. 75.00
Cuspidor, lady's, vaseline 40.00
Pitcher, water, vaseline 325.00
Rose bowl, footed, blue . . . . . . .65.00 to 75.00
Rose bowl, footed, vaseline. 65.00
Rose bowl, footed, white 28.00
Salt dip, blue .75.00
Salt dip, canary yellow 60.00
Salt dip, vaseline 65.00
Salt dip, white .40.00
Sauce dish, blue 35.00
Sauce dish, canary yellow 27.50
Sauce dish, vaseline. 25.00
Sauce dish, white 20.00
Spooner, blue, enameled decor. 95.00

Wreath & Shell Spooner

Spooner, canary yellow (ILLUS.). 80.00
Spooner, canary yellow, enameled
    decor 125.00
Spooner, vaseline. 70.00
Spooner, white 40.00
Sugar bowl, cov., blue 150.00
Sugar bowl, cov., canary yellow 155.00
Sugar bowl, cov., vaseline 130.00
Sugar bowl, cov., white. 95.00
Toothpick holder, blue. 150.00
Toothpick holder, white 75.00
Tumbler, blue .50.00
Tumbler, vaseline. 65.00

OPALINE

*Also called opal glass (once a name applied
to milk-white glass), opaline is a fairly opaque
glass with a color resembling the opal; however, pieces in such colors as blue, pink, green
and others, also are referred to now as opaline glass. Many of the objects were decorated. Also see RING TREES.*

Opaline Vase

Bowl, pink, hinged brass handle & rim
   inscribed & dated "1882" $75.00
Cologne bottle w/bubble stopper, pink
   w/enameled cream scrolls & fan
   decor, gold trim, 3 1/8" d., 8" h. 165.00
Goblets, celestial blue, 6½" h., set
   of 6 . . . . .175.00
Perfume bottle w/stopper, pale blue,
   gold trim, 6¼" h. 68.00
Pitcher, 6½" h., applied handle, blue . . .50.00
Powder box w/hinged lid, footed, opal
   w/enameled ivy leaves & forget-me-
   nots decor, brass fittings 125.00
Tumbler, French blue, 2 1/8" h. 24.00
Vase, 12" h., pedestal foot, crenelated
   rim, enameled white carnations
   decor, gold trim (ILLUS.) 75.00
Vases, 15¼" h., pale turquoise
   w/crenelated rim w/gilt roundels
   enclosing Roman heads within
   jeweled, gilt & enameled foliate
   borders, silvered & gilt-bronze
   pierced foliate bases cast w/griffins
   by Elkington & Co., ca. 1860, pr. 330.00

PAIRPOINT

*Originally organized in New Bedford,
Massachusetts, in 1880, as the Pairpoint
Manufacturing Company, on land adjacent
to the famed Mount Washington Glass
Works, this company first manufactured
silver and plated wares. In 1894, the two
famous factories merged as the Pairpoint
Corporation and enjoyed renowned success
for more than forty years. The company was
sold in 1939, to a group of local business-
men and eventually bought out by one of
the group who turned the management over*

*to Robert M. Gunderson. Subsequently, it
operated as the Gunderson Glass Works
until 1952 when, after Gunderson's death,
the name was changed to Gunderson-
Pairpoint. This factory closed in 1956.
Subsequently, Robert Bryden took charge
of this glass works, at first producing glass
for Pairpoint abroad and eventually, in
1970, began glass production in Sagamore,
Massachusetts. Bryden's Pairpoint company continues in operation today
manufacturing fine quality blown and
pressed glass. Also see BURMESE, CUT
and PEACH BLOW under Glass.*

Bowl, clear swan handles, green,
   Gunderson-Pairpoint $100.00
Bride's bowl, "peppermint stick,"
   clear satin finish w/overlay rose
   rim cut to clear stripes, in footed
   silverplate frame w/embossed
   Greek warrior heads in medallions,
   9" d. 135.00
Candlesticks, mushroom-shaped top,
   green w/clear "controlled
   bubble" ball in stem, 4½" h., pr. 110.00
Centerpiece bowl, turned-down
   rim, amber w/ornate silver overlay
   decor 225.00
Compote, 6" d., 4" h., Auroria
   (reddish amber) 85.00
Compote, 6" d., 4¼" h., ruby w/clear
   "controlled bubble" ball in
   stem . . . . .70.00 to 95.00

Pairpoint Compote

Compote, 6" d., 7" h., cut &
   engraved design, ca. 1920 (ILLUS.) . . .95.00
Compote, 7½" d., amber w/clear
   "controlled bubble" ball in stem 110.00
Compote, 8" d., 8" h., green w/clear
   "controlled bubble" ball in stem,
   silver overlay floral garland
   decor, marked "Rockwell" 215.00
Compote, 12" d., 6½" h., amber
   w/clear "controlled bubble" paper-
   weight base 125.00

Console set: 12½" d. bowl & pr.
  3½" h. candlesticks; ruby w/clear
  "controlled bubble" base, 3 pcs. 195.00
Cordials, Amberina, Gunderson-
  Pairpoint, set of 10 . . . . .300.00
Cornucopia-vase, ruby w/clear
  "controlled bubble" base,
  8" h. . . . . .75.00 to 95.00
Paperweight, model of a fish,
  clear w/"controlled bubbles," 7" 30.00
Pitcher, water, clear w/"controlled
  bubble" paperweight base 110.00
Swan, Rosaria (cranberry) w/clear neck,
  large 450.00
Vase, 7½" h., gourd-shaped, green
  w/large random bubbles 50.00
Vase, 10" h., trumpet-shaped,
  Canaria (vaseline), engraved
  grape & leaf design, clear "controlled bubble" ball connector 110.00
Vase, 12" h., trumpet form, ruby
  w/clear "controlled bubble" ball
  stem .160.00 to 190.00
Vase, cov., 15" h., 5½" w., engraved
  grape design, amethyst 195.00

PATE DE VERRE

Pate de Verre Bowl-Vase

Pate de Verre, or "paste of glass," was molded by very few glass artisans. In the pate de verre technique, powdered glass is mixed with a liquid to make a paste which is then placed in a mold and baked at a high temperature. These articles have a finely-pitted or matte finish and are easily distinguished from blown glass. Duplicate pieces are possible with this technique.

Bookend, cast w/yellow fox leaping
  from a leaf-molded green ground
  to a trellis hung w/green & purple
  grapes & leafage, ca. 1925,
  signed A. Walter, Nancy, 5¾" h.
  (single) $770.00
Bowl, 3½" h., mottled pale grey sides
  cast w/deep purple, raspberry &
  Chinese red pendant fruit-laden
  grape vines, ca. 1925, signed G.
  Argy-Rousseau, France 2,750.00
Bowl-vase, 6" d., flared 6-sided form
  w/galleried rim, transparent navy

blue streaked w/cobalt blue,
  signed Decorchemont (ILLUS.) 1,100.00

Pate de Verre Table Lamp

Lamp, helmet-form shade & bulbous
  base, pale grey splashed w/laven-
  der & pumpkin orange, the shade
  cast w/deep purple & Chinese red
  stylized chrysanthemum blossoms
  w/graduated tiers of petals & cascading stamen, the base molded
  w/a gadrooned collar above base
  cast w/conforming chrysanthemum
  blossoms, ca. 1925, signed G. Argy-
  Rousseau, 7 1/8" d., 15¾" h.
  (ILLUS.) 13,200.00
Model of a fox sleeping, w/tail curled
  around him & ears erect, pale green,
  on mottled rust & blue square base,
  early 20th c., signed A. Walter,
  Nancy & M. Corrette, 4½" l. 770.00
Paperweight, molded in the form of
  a snail w/mustard yellow shell
  perched on a leaf green, ochre &
  olive green base cast w/grapes &
  foliage, ca. 1925, signed A. Walter,
  Nancy & F. Berge Sc., 5½" d. 5,170.00
Pendant, rounded triangle, cast
  w/deep blue & green chameleon
  perched on a leafy green olive
  branch w/purple olives on ground
  streaked w/azure, ca. 1920, signed
  AW N BS, 2¾" l., w/silk cord
  necklace 1,540.00
Plate, 12 1/8" d., grey boldly streaked
  w/blue-grey, lavender & deep turquoise, rim cast w/three square
  panels enclosing melons & leafage
  & conjoined by emerald green &
  lavender leaf-molded borders,
  ca. 1925, signed G. Argy-
  Rousseau .2,860.00
Vase, 7" h., sloping sides, cast w/two
  graduated bands of stylized chevron
  devices, pale grey splashed w/deep
  turquoise & lavender, ca. 1925,
  signed G. Argy-Rousseau,
  France 1,980.00

PATTERN GLASS

Though it has never been ascertained whether glass was first pressed in the United States or abroad, the development of the glass pressing machine revolutionized the glass industry in the United States and this country receives the credit for improving the method to make this process feasible. The first wares pressed were probably small flat plates of the type now referred to as "lacy" Sandwich, the intricacy of the design concealing flaws.

In 1827, both the New England Glass Co., Cambridge, Massachusetts and Bakewell & Co., Pittsburgh, took out patents for pressing glass furniture knobs and soon other pieces followed. This early pressed glass contained red lead which made it clear and resonant when tapped (flint). Made primarily in clear, it is rarer in blue, amethyst, olive green and yellow.

By the 1840s, early simple patterns such as Ashburton, Argus and Excelsior appeared. Ribbed Bellflower seems to have been one of the earliest patterns to have had complete sets. By the 1860s, a wide range of patterns were available.

In 1864, William Leighton of Hobbs, Brockunier & Co., Wheeling, West Virginia, developed a formula for "soda lime" glass which did not require the expensive red lead for clarity. Although "soda lime" glass did not have the brilliance of the earlier flint glass, the formula came into widespread use because glass could be produced cheaply.

By 1900, patterns had become ornate in imitation of the expensive brilliant cut glass.

ACTRESS

Pinafore Scene Celery Vase

Bowl, 6" d., footed $50.00
Bowl, 8" d., Adelaide Neilson,
  C.W. 1875 . . . . .75.00
Bread tray, Miss Neilson, 12½" l. 70.00
Butter dish, cov., all clear 85.00
Cake stand, 10" d., 7" h. 155.00
Celery vase, Pinafore scene, all clear
  (ILLUS.) 160.00
Celery vase, Pinafore scene, clear &
  frosted 120.00
Cheese dish, cov., "The Two
  Dromios," 8" d. 215.00
Cologne bottle w/original stopper,
  11" h. 48.50
Compote, cov., 6" d., 10" h. 130.00
Compote, cov., 8" d.,
  12" h. . . . . .140.00 to 235.00
Compote, open, 6" d., 11" h. 145.00
Compote, open, 7" d., 7" h.,
  Adelaide Neilson 45.00
Creamer, Miss Neilson & Fanny
  Davenport . . . . .62.50 to 75.00
Goblet, Lotta Crabtree & Kate Claxton . .80.00
Marmalade jar, cov., Maude Granger &
  Annie Pixley, frosted base . . .70.00 to 85.00
Pickle dish, Kate Claxton, "Love's
  Request is Pickles," 9¼ x 5¼" 36.50
Pitcher, water, 9" h. 250.00
Platter, 11½ x 7", Pinafore scene 60.00
Relish, Miss Neilson, 8 x 5" 30.00
Relish, Maude Granger, 9 x 5" 65.00
Salt & pepper shakers w/original
  tops, pr. 115.00
Sauce dish, footed, Maggie Mitchell &
  Fanny Davenport, all clear, 4½" d.,
  2½" h. 15.50
Sauce dish, footed, frosted base,
  4¾" d., 3" h. .17.50
Spooner, frosted base, Mary
  Anderson & Maude Granger 65.00
Sugar bowl, cov., Lotta Crabtree &
  Kate Claxton .90.00
Sugar bowl, open 60.00

ALABAMA (Beaded Bull's Eye with Drape)
Butter dish, cov., w/silver rim 57.50
Celery tray 25.00
Compote, cov., 5" d. 62.50
Creamer 32.50
Cruet w/original stopper 67.50
Honey dish, cov. 47.50
Pitcher, water 65.00
Relish 17.50
Spooner 35.00
Sugar bowl, cov. 42.50
Syrup pitcher w/original top 85.00
Toothpick holder 47.50
Tray, water, 10½" 20.00
Tumbler 22.00

ALASKA (Lion's Leg)
Banana boat, blue opalescent 255.00
Banana boat, emerald green 72.50
Banana boat, vaseline opalescent 225.00

Berry set: master bowl & 6 sauce
 dishes; blue opalescent, 7 pcs.......325.00
Berry set: master bowl & 6 sauce
 dishes; vaseline opalescent, 7 pcs. ..375.00
Bowl, 7" sq., blue opalescent
 w/enameled florals...............115.00
Bowl, master berry, blue opalescent ..125.00
Bowl, master berry, clear w/enameled
 florals.........................55.00
Bowl, master berry, green 55.00
Bowl, master berry, vaseline
 opalescent......................92.00
Butter dish, cov., blue opalescent 245.00
Butter dish, cov., green w/enameled
 florals..........................170.00

Alaska Butter Dish

Butter dish, cov., vaseline opalescent
 (ILLUS.).........................295.00
Celery tray, blue opalescent.........128.00
Celery tray, blue opalescent
 w/enameled florals 232.00
Compote, open, 7½" d., 3¼" h.,
 ruffled rim, blue opalescent 65.00
Creamer, blue opalescent............60.00
Creamer, green 35.00
Creamer, vaseline opalescent 70.00
Creamer & cov. sugar bowl, blue
 opalescent, pr. 225.00
Creamer & cov. sugar bowl,
 vaseline opalescent, pr. 200.00
Cruet w/original stopper, blue
 opalescent w/enameled florals 225.00
Cruet w/original stopper, green
 w/enameled florals.......175.00 to 225.00
Cruet w/original stopper, vaseline
 opalescent w/enameled florals 230.00
Pitcher, water, blue opalescent 420.00
Pitcher, water, clear w/enameled
 florals & gold trim................110.00
Pitcher, water, green...............55.00
Pitcher, water, vaseline opalescent ...375.00
Salt shaker w/original top, vaseline
 opalescent (single)................55.00
Salt & pepper shakers w/original
 tops, blue opalescent w/enameled
 florals, pr. 115.00
Sauce dish, blue opalescent 40.00
Sauce dish, clear to opalescent 22.50
Sauce dish, clear to opalescent
 w/enameled florals 25.00

Sauce dish, green w/enameled florals
 & leaves 45.00
Sauce dish, vaseline opalescent 32.50
Spooner, blue opalescent 56.50
Spooner, clear to opalescent 27.50
Spooner, green....................50.00
Spooner, vaseline opalescent 55.00
Spooner, vaseline opalescent
 w/enameled florals...............95.00
Sugar bowl, cov., blue opal-
 escent ....120.00 to 145.00
Sugar bowl, cov., green 65.00
Sugar bowl, open, clear to opalescent ..40.00
Sugar bowl, open, vaseline opalescent .85.00
Table set: creamer, open sugar bowl,
 spooner & cov. butter dish; blue
 opalescent, 4 pcs.................750.00
Table set: creamer, open sugar bowl,
 spooner & cov. butter dish; vaseline
 opalescent, 4 pcs.................600.00
Tumbler, blue opalescent 73.00
Tumbler, vaseline opalescent 65.00
Wine, blue opalescent...............90.00

ALEXIS - See Priscilla Pattern

ALMOND THUMBPRINT (Pointed Thumbprint)
Bowl, 4½" d., 4 7/8" h., footed 20.00
Butter dish, cov., ruby-stained........102.00
Champagne.......................25.00
Salt dip, master size, flint 12.00
Spooner, fluted....................20.00
Wine 30.00

AMAZON (Sawtooth Band)

Child's Sugar Bowl & Creamer

Banana stand 50.00
Bowl, 9" d........................22.00
Butter dish, cov....................38.50
Cake stand, 8" d....................36.00
Cake stand, 9¼" d. 38.00
Celery vase, etched 35.00
Champagne.......................35.00
Compote, cov., 7" d., 11½" h. 62.50
Compote, open, jelly 24.00
Compote, open, 6" d., high stand 21.00
Cordial, etched 27.50
Creamer..........................27.50
Creamer, child's miniature (ILLUS.).....27.50
Egg cup..........................14.00

Goblet, etched or plain 30.00
Nappy 25.00
Pitcher, water, etched 60.00
Salt dip, master size 14.00
Sauce dish, footed 10.00
Spooner, etched or plain . . . . . .25.00 to 30.00
Spooner, child's miniature 25.00
Sugar bowl, cov. .37.50
Sugar bowl, open 15.00
Sugar bowl, child's miniature (ILLUS.) . . .30.00
Syrup pitcher w/original top, etched . . .42.50
Table set: cov. butter dish, creamer,
  cov. sugar bowl & spooner; miniature,
  4 pcs. 150.00
Tumbler, etched or plain . . . . . .18.50 to 25.00
Wine, etched or plain . . . . .25.00 to 30.00

AMBERETTE (English Hobnail Cross or Klondike)

Amberette Salt Shaker

Berry set: 8" sq. master bowl & 6
  sauce dishes; clear w/amber cross,
  7 pcs. 165.00
Bowl, fruit, 7" sq., frosted w/amber
  cross 235.00
Bowl, fruit, 8½" sq., clear w/amber
  cross 55.00
Bowl, 11" sq., flared, clear w/amber
  cross 150.00
Bread plate, clear w/amber cross,
  11 x 8½" oval 135.00
Butter dish, cov., clear w/amber
  cross 115.00
Butter dish, cov., frosted w/amber
  cross 300.00
Celery tray, frosted w/amber cross,
  10 7/8 x 4½", 2 7/8" h. 175.00
Celery vase, frosted w/amber cross . . .195.00
Creamer, clear w/amber cross 60.00
Creamer, frosted w/amber cross 240.00
Goblet, clear w/amber cross 125.00
Pitcher, water, clear w/amber cross . . .125.00
Pitcher, water, frosted w/amber
  cross 545.00
Punch cup, frosted w/amber cross 135.00
Relish, clear w/amber cross, boat-
  shaped, 9 x 4" 118.00
Salt shaker w/original top, clear
  w/amber cross (single) 67.50

Salt & pepper shakers w/original tops,
  frosted w/amber cross, pr. (ILLUS. of
  one) 195.00
Sauce dish, flat or footed, clear
  w/amber cross . . . . .18.00 to 21.50
Sauce dish, flat or footed, frosted
  w/amber cross 78.50
Spooner, clear w/amber cross 50.00
Spooner, frosted w/amber cross 165.00
Sugar bowl, cov., frosted w/amber
  cross, 4" d., 6¾" h. 240.00
Sugar bowl, open, clear w/amber
  cross 75.00
Syrup pitcher w/original top, frosted
  w/amber cross 550.00
Toothpick holder, clear w/amber
  cross 145.00
Toothpick holder, frosted w/amber
  cross 375.00
Tumbler, clear w/amber cross 135.00
Tumbler, frosted w/amber cross 150.00
Vase, 10" h., trumpet-shaped, frosted
  w/amber cross 300.00

APOLLO

Bowl, 6" d. 12.00
Bowl, 8" d. 20.00
Butter dish, cov. .45.00
Celery dish, oblong 22.50
Celery vase, etched 37.50
Compote, open, 7" d., low stand 25.00
Compote, w/silverplate handle 85.00
Creamer, etched or
  plain . . . . .30.00 to 40.00
Goblet, etched or plain . . . . . . .27.50 to 42.50
Lamp, kerosene-type, amber or blue,
  9" h., ea. 190.00
Lamp, kerosene-type, frosted, 12" h. . . .65.00
Pitcher, water, bulbous 65.00
Plate, 9½" sq. 25.00
Salt dip, master size 25.00
Sauce dish, flat or footed . . . . . . .6.00 to 10.50
Spooner . . . . .30.00 to 35.00
Sugar bowl, cov., etched 40.00
Sugar shaker w/original top, etched . . .45.00
Syrup pitcher w/original top, etched . . .42.50
Tray, water 45.00
Tumbler, etched .21.50

ARGUS (Thumbprint by Bakewell, Pears & Co.)

Ale glass, footed, flint, 5½" h. 70.00
Ale glass, flint, 9" h. 65.00
Butter dish, footed, flint, 8" d. 85.00
Celery vase, flint 56.50
Champagne 42.50
Champagne (Hotel Argus) 18.50
Creamer w/applied handle, flint 70.00
Egg cup, flint 23.50
Goblet 32.50
Goblet (Barrel Argus) 42.50
Goblet (Hotel Argus) . . . . .16.00 to 20.00
Goblet, master size 45.00
Mug, applied handle 60.00

Pitcher, water, 8¼" h., applied handle, flint 200.00
Salt dip, master size 27.50

Argus Spillholder

Spillholder, flint (ILLUS.) 60.00
Spooner, flint 40.00
Sugar bowl, cov., flint 65.00
Sugar bowl, open, flint ....35.00 to 39.50
Tumbler (Barrel Argus) ....16.00 to 25.00
Tumbler, bar-type, flint 48.00
Tumbler, footed, 4" h. 46.50
Tumbler, footed, 5" h. 60.00
Tumbler, whiskey, handled 57.50
Wine, flint, 4" h. 47.50
Wine (Barrel Argus) 35.00
Wine (Hotel Argus)...................12.50

ART (Job's Tears)
Banana stand 97.50
Basket, fruit.......................165.00
Bowl, 7" d., flared rim, footed base 27.00
Bowl, 8½" d. 50.00
Butter dish, cov. 50.00
Butter dish, cov., ruby-stained 65.00
Cake stand, 9" d. 52.50
Cake stand, 10¼" d. 62.50
Celery vase 37.50
Compote, open, 7" d. 65.00
Compote, open, 9" d., 7¼" h. 48.00
Compote, open, 10" d., 9" h. ...50.00 to 68.00
Creamer ....40.00 to 50.00
Cruet w/original stopper 65.00
Goblet ....25.00 to 37.50
Pitcher, milk, ruby-stained....95.00 to 150.00
Pitcher, water 70.00
Relish, 7¾ x 4¼" 26.50
Relish, ruby-stained 65.00
Sauce dish, flat..............12.00 to 20.00
Sauce dish, footed 18.50
Spooner 28.50
Sugar bowl, cov. ....40.00 to 50.00
Sugar bowl, open 22.00
Tumbler 20.00

ASHBURTON
Ale glass, flint, 5" h. 87.50
Ale glass, flint, 6½" h. 65.00

Ale glass, non-flint..................25.00
Bitters bottle w/original pewter lid 55.00
Bowl, 6½" d., low, footed............72.50
Carafe 175.00
Celery vase, plain rim, flint 72.50
Celery vase, scalloped rim,
flint....................95.00 to 125.00
Champagne 48.50
Champagne, creased ovals...........55.00
Champagne, cut ovals 75.00
Champagne, double knob stem 68.00
Claret, flint, 5¼" h. 50.00
Compote, open, 7½" d., low stand 65.00
Cordial, flint, 4¼" h. 57.50
Cordial, vaseline, flint..............140.00
Creamer, applied handle, flint........175.00
Cup plate, 3" d.....................20.00
Decanter, no stopper, pt. 42.50
Decanter w/original stopper, flint,
qt. 48.00
Decanter, bar lip & facet-cut neck,
qt. 62.50
Decanter, bar lip & facet-cut neck,
canary yellow, qt. 600.00
Egg cup, clambroth, flint 125.00
Egg cup, flint 24.50
Egg cup, double 95.00
Flip glass, handled, flint 135.00
Goblet, flint, barrel-shaped 45.00
Goblet, flint, flared 45.00
Goblet, non-flint ....20.00 to 30.00
Goblet, disconnected ovals 26.50
Goblet, "giant," straight stem, flint 42.50
Honey dish, 3½" d. 13.00
Mug, applied handle, 3" h. 67.50
Mug, 4¾" h. 67.50
Pitcher, water, applied hollow handle .450.00
Plate, 6 5/8" d., flint................60.00
Sauce dish, flint 12.00
Spooner, flint 115.00

Ashburton Sugar bowl
Sugar bowl, cov., flint (ILLUS.) 140.00
Sugar bowl, open, non-flint 35.00
Toddy jar, cov. 110.00
Tumbler, bar, flint ....55.00 to 65.00
Tumbler, water, flint 80.00

Tumbler, water, footed........75.00 to 85.00
Tumbler, whiskey, applied handle,
  flint...........................75.00
Wine, barrel-shaped.............41.50
Wine, flint.....................32.00
Wine, cut ovals.................65.00
Wine, non-flint.................24.00

ATLANTA - See Lion Pattern

ATLAS (Crystal Ball or Cannon Ball)

Atlas Toothpick Holder

Bowl, cov., large, flat, clear...........35.00
Bowl, open, 9" d., clear...............20.00
Butter dish, cov., clear...............45.00
Cake stand, clear, 8" d...............22.50
Cake stand, clear, 9" d...............40.00
Cake stand, ruby-stained, 10" d.......95.00
Celery vase, clear...................26.50
Champagne, clear, 5½" h.............28.00
Compote, cov., 8" d., 8" h., clear......55.00
Compote, open, 8" d., 8" h., milk
  white.............................65.00
Compote, open, 9" d., milk white.....80.00
Cordial, clear......................27.50
Creamer, flat or pedestal base, clear...22.50
Creamer & sugar bowl, clear, pr........50.00
Goblet, clear.......................30.00
Pitcher, milk, tankard, applied
  handle, clear.....................30.00
Pitcher, water, tankard, applied
  handle, clear.....................38.00
Salt dip, individual size, clear...........8.00
Salt dip, master size, clear...........20.00
Salt & pepper shakers w/original tops,
  clear, pr.........................20.00
Sauce dish, flat or footed, clear..8.00 to 11.00
Sauce dish, footed, ruby-stained.......20.00
Spooner, flat, clear.................26.00
Spooner, ruby-stained, w/gold trim....35.00
Sugar bowl, cov., clear..............38.00
Sugar bowl, open, clear..............20.00
Toothpick holder, clear (ILLUS.)........18.00
Tumbler, clear......................27.50
Wine, clear.........................22.50

AURORA (Diamond Horseshoe)
Celery vase.........................35.00
Creamer, applied handle.............38.00

Decanter w/stopper, ruby-stained 135.00
Goblet, etched or plain..............30.00
Pitcher, water, tankard, 9½" h........40.00
Salt & pepper shakers w/original tops,
  pr...............................30.00
Tray, wine, 10" d.............25.00 to 30.00
Tray, wine, ruby-stained, 10" d........55.00
Wine........................17.50 to 25.00
Wine, ruby-stained..................35.00
Wine set: decanter w/original ruby
  stopper, 6 wines & tray; ruby-stained,
  8 pcs. 350.00

AZTEC

Aztec Creamer

Bon bon, footed, 7" d., 4½" h. 13.50
Bowl, 8½" d., sapphire blue..........45.00
Butter dish, cov. 40.00
Carafe, water.....................37.50
Creamer (ILLUS.)...................19.00
Creamer, individual size.............10.50
Cruet w/original stopper 35.00
Goblet 33.50
Punch cup.........................6.00
Relish 15.00
Salt & pepper shakers w/original tops,
  pr...............................35.00
Toothpick holder...................18.50
Tumbler 20.00
Tumbler, whiskey...................12.00
Wine..............................22.50

BABY FACE

Baby Face Compote

Compote, cov., 5¼" d.,
  6½" h. ....125.00 to 140.00

Compote, cov., 8" d., 13" h., scalloped
  rim 250.00
Compote, open, 8" d., 4¾" h. (ILLUS.) ..85.00
Compote, open, 8" d., 8" h. 58.00
Creamer.............................110.00
Goblet 85.00
Pitcher, water 175.00
Spooner 95.00

BABY THUMBPRINT - See Dakota Pattern

BALDER (Kamoni or Pennsylvania - Late)

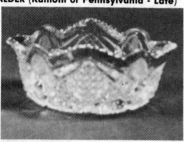

Balder Sauce Dish

Bowl, berry or fruit, 8½" d., clear
  w/gold trim 25.00
Bowl, 9" d., 2½" h., clear 29.50
Butter dish, cov., clear ....35.00 to 45.00
Carafe, clear 35.00
Celery tray, clear, 11 x 4½" ....25.00 to 30.00
Cheese dish, cov., clear 62.50
Cookie jar, cov., clear 42.00
Creamer, clear w/gold trim, small,
  3" h. 17.50
Creamer, green w/gold trim, small,
  3" h. 65.00
Creamer, clear, large, 4" h. 28.00
Creamer & open sugar bowl, individual
  size, clear, pr. 38.00
Cruet w/original stopper, clear 37.50
Decanter w/original stopper, clear,
  10¾" h. 87.50
Goblet, clear ....20.00 to 25.00
Mustard jar w/pewter lid, clear........40.00
Plate, 8" d., clear 29.50
Punch cup, clear 10.00
Relish, clear.........................11.50
Salt & pepper shakers w/original tops,
  clear, pr. 22.00
Sauce dish, boat-shaped, clear
  (ILLUS.)...........................22.00
Spooner, clear.......................26.50
Sugar bowl, cov., child's, clear
  w/gold trim 38.50
Sugar bowl, cov., clear 39.50
Sugar bowl, open, clear 14.00
Syrup pitcher w/original top, clear 37.50
Toothpick holder, clear 17.50
Toothpick holder, green 50.00
Tumbler, juice, clear 11.50
Tumbler, juice, green 21.00
Tumbler, water, clear 20.00
Tumbler, water, clear w/gold trim 23.50

Tumbler, water, ruby-stained 50.00
Tumbler, whiskey, clear 12.00
Tumbler, whiskey, green w/gold trim ..26.00
Whiskey shot glass, clear 61.50
Wine, clear 16.50
Wine, green w/gold trim..............42.50

BALTIMORE PEAR

Baltimore Pear Bowl

Bowl, 6" d. (ILLUS.) 29.00
Bowl, berry or fruit, 9" d. 40.00
Bread plate, 12½" l...................60.00
Butter dish, cov. 62.50
Cake plate, side handles, 10" octagon . 31.50
Celery vase 40.00
Compote, cov., 7" d...................80.00
Compote, cov., 8½" d., low stand......45.00
Compote, open, jelly 28.50
Compote, open, high stand...........30.00
Creamer..............................25.00
Goblet 26.00
Pitcher, milk 60.00
Pitcher, water.............75.00 to 90.00
Plate, 9" d...........................28.00
Sauce dish, flat or footed ......10.00 to 15.00
Spooner 28.00
Sugar bowl, cov. 48.00
Sugar bowl, open ....25.00 to 35.00

BAMBOO - See Broken Column Pattern

BANDED PORTLAND (Portland w/Diamond Point Band)
Bowl, berry, 9" d. 32.00
Butter dish, cov. 50.00
Butter pat............................18.00
Candlesticks, pr. 85.00
Carafe, water 82.50
Celery tray, gold-stained, 12 x 5" 25.00
Cologne bottle w/original stopper 55.00
Compote, cov., jelly 35.00
Compote, open, 8¼" d., 8" h., scalloped
  rim 40.00

Compote, open, 10" d., high stand 49.50
Creamer. 27.50
Creamer, small .13.50

Banded Portland Dresser Jar

Dresser jar, cov., 2 5/8" d.
  (ILLUS.) . . . . .30.00 to 38.00
Dresser set: large tray, pin tray, pr.
  cov. pomade jars, pr. perfume
  bottles w/original stoppers & ring
  tree; clear w/gold, 7 pcs. 195.00
Goblet 35.00
Pickle dish, 6 x 4" 16.00
Pin dish, cov., 2¼" 25.00
Pin tray, souvenir 15.00
Pitcher, water 50.00
Pitcher, child's. .33.50
Punch cup, gold rim 17.00
Relish, 8½ x 4" oval 10.00
Ring tree, gold-stained 40.00
Salt & pepper shakers w/original tops,
  pr. 55.00
Sauce dish 12.00
Spooner 28.00
Sugar bowl, cov., gold-stained. 37.50
Sugar shaker w/original top . . .40.00 to 45.00
Syrup jug w/original top 50.00
Toothpick holder. 20.00
Tumbler 30.00
Vase, 6" h., flared 15.50
Vase, 9" h. 24.00
Wine 30.00
Wine, gold-stained. 40.00

**BANDED PORTLAND W/COLOR - See Portland
Maiden Blush Pattern**

BAR & DIAMOND - See Kokomo Pattern

BARBERRY

Bowl, 8" oval 27.00
Bread plate 23.00
Butter dish, cov., shell finial 43.50
Cake stand, 9½" d. 27.50
Celery vase 30.00
Compote, cov., 8" d., low stand,
  shell finial 55.00
Compote, open, 8" d., high stand 36.00
Creamer. 28.00

Egg cup. 19.50
Goblet 24.00
Goblet, buttermilk 18.50

Barberry Water Pitcher

Pitcher, water, 9½" h., applied handle
  (ILLUS.) . . . . .85.00 to 110.00
Plate, 6" d., amber 38.00
Plate, 6" d., clear 15.00
Salt dip, master size 26.00
Sauce dish, flat 6.50
Sauce dish, footed 12.50
Spooner, footed .22.50
Sugar bowl, cov., shell finial 45.00
Sugar bowl, open 27.50
Syrup jug w/original top 120.00
Tumbler, footed .24.00
Wine 22.50

BARLEY

Barley Goblet

Bowl, 10" oval 20.00
Bread platter, plain rim, 11½ x 9½" 28.00
Bread platter, scalloped rim, 11½ x
  9½". 35.00
Butter dish, cov. .35.00
Cake stand, 8" d. 25.00
Cake stand, 9" d. 28.00

Celery vase 25.00
Compote, cov., 7" d., high stand 60.00
Compote, open, 6" d., high stand 30.00
Compote, open, 8½" d., 8" h. 35.00
Compote, open, 8¾" d., 6½" h.,
   scalloped rim. 35.00
Creamer 25.00
Goblet (ILLUS.) .26.00
Honey dish, footed, 3½" 5.00
Marmalade jar, cov. 28.50
Pickle castor w/frame & tongs 90.00
Pitcher, milk 30.00
Pitcher, water 45.00
Plate, 6" d. 35.00
Platter, 13 x 8" 25.00
Relish, 8 x 6" . . . . .16.00 to 20.00
Sauce dish, flat 9.00
Sauce dish, footed 12.00
Spooner 21.50
Sugar bowl, cov. 27.00
Wheelbarrow sugar cube dish w/metal
   wheels . . . . .60.00 to 75.00
Wine, 3¾" h. 25.00

BARRED HOBSTAR - See Checkerboard Pattern

BARRED STAR - See Spartan Pattern

BASKET WEAVE
Cup & saucer, amber 32.00
Goblet, amber 24.50
Goblet, clear 17.00
Goblet, vaseline .30.00
Mug, clear, 3" h. 12.00
Pitcher, vaseline. 60.00
Plate, 8¾" d., handled, clear 11.00
Tray, water, vaseline, w/scenic
   center, 12" 50.00

BEADED BULL'S EYE WITH DRAPE - See Alabama Pattern

BEADED DEWDROP - See Wisconsin Pattern

BEADED GRAPE (California)

Beaded Grape Compote

Bowl, 5½" sq., clear 16.50
Bowl, 5½" sq., green. 18.00
Bowl, 7¼ x 4" rectangle, green 25.00
Bowl, 7½" sq., clear 20.00
Bowl, 7½" sq., green. 28.00
Bowl, 8" sq., clear 26.00
Bowl, 8½ x 6½" rectangle, green 30.00
Bread tray, clear, 10 x 7". 20.00
Butter dish, cov., sq., clear 55.00
Butter dish, cov., sq., green. 95.00
Cake stand, clear, 9" sq. 67.50
Cake stand, green, 9" sq., 6" h. 85.00
Celery tray, clear 30.00
Celery tray, green 45.00
Compote, open, 5" sq., clear 55.00
Compote, open, 6" sq., green 75.00
Compote, open, 7" sq., high stand,
   clear (ILLUS.) 38.00
Compote, open, 8½" sq., high stand,
   clear 75.00
Creamer, clear .22.00
Creamer, green .37.50
Cruet w/original stopper, clear 47.50
Cruet w/original stopper, green 95.00
Egg cup, clear 16.00
Goblet, clear 23.00
Goblet, green 42.50
Pitcher, water, round, green 78.00
Pitcher, water, square, green 120.00
Plate, 8" sq., clear 28.00
Plate, 8" sq., green 40.00
Relish, clear, 7 x 4". 20.00
Sauce dish, clear. 12.00
Sauce dish, green 15.00
Spooner, clear. .30.00
Spooner, green .45.00
Sugar bowl, cov., clear 46.50
Sugar bowl, cov., green 55.00
Sugar bowl, open, clear 20.00
Sugar bowl, open, green. 28.00
Toothpick holder, clear 35.00
Toothpick holder, green 55.00
Tumbler, clear. .25.00
Tumbler, green .45.00
Vase, 7" h., green 48.00
Wine, clear 32.50
Wine, green. 65.00

BEADED GRAPE MEDALLION
Bowl, oval 24.50
Butter dish, cov. 45.00
Celery vase 55.00
Compote, open, 8¼" d., low stand 19.50
Compote, open, high stand. 31.00
Creamer, applied handle 33.00
Egg cup 25.00
Goblet 25.00
Goblet, buttermilk 34.00
Goblet, lady's 30.00
Honey dish. 10.00
Pitcher, water, applied handle. 80.00
Relish, oblong 15.00
Salt dip, flat. 15.00
Sauce dish 8.00

Spooner 30.00
Sugar bowl, cov. 46.50
Sugar bowl, open 23.00
Vegetable dish, cov., footed,
    dated 1869 .... 75.00
Wine 35.00

BEADED LOOP (Oregon)
Berry set, master bowl & 5 sauce
    dishes, 6 pcs. 50.00
Bowl, berry, 7" d. 17.00
Bowl, 8¼" d. 15.00
Bowl, 9¼ x 6¾" oval 22.00
Bread platter 30.00
Butter dish, cov. 60.00
Cake stand, 9" d. 30.00
Cake stand, 10½" d. 50.00
Celery vase, 7" h. 29.00
Compote, open, jelly 45.00
Compote, open, 7" d., 4½" h.,
    ruby-stained 55.00
Compote, open, 7½" d. 20.00
Creamer........................... 25.00
Cruet w/faceted stopper............ 60.00
Cruet, no stopper 45.00
Goblet 35.00
Honey dish......................... 8.00
Pickle dish, boat-shaped, 9" l. 15.00
Pitcher, milk, 8½" h. 46.00
Pitcher, water, tankard .... 45.00 to 55.00
Relish 12.00
Salt shaker w/original top (single) 20.00
Sauce dish, flat or footed .... 6.50 to 13.00
Spooner, clear..................... 28.00
Spooner, ruby-stained 40.00
Sugar bowl, cov., clear 30.00
Sugar bowl, cov., ruby-stained 47.50
Sugar bowl, open 15.00
Syrup pitcher w/original top.......... 60.00
Toothpick holder................... 32.50
Tumbler, clear..................... 42.50
Tumbler, ruby-stained 35.00
Whiskey carafe, individual size 35.00
Wine 32.50

BEADED MEDALLION - See Beaded Mirror Pattern

BEADED MIRROR (Beaded Medallion)
Butter dish, cov. 40.00
Castor bottle, mustard.............. 15.00
Castor bottle w/original stopper, oil.... 25.00
Castor set, 5 pcs. 75.00
Celery vase 48.00
Egg cup........................... 18.50
Goblet .... 15.00 to 21.50
Salt dip 18.00
Sauce dish, flat 6.00
Spooner 22.50
Sugar bowl, cov.................... 45.00
Sugar bowl, open 20.00

BEARDED HEAD - See Viking Pattern

BEARDED MAN (Old Man of the Woods or Neptune)

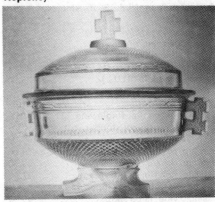

Bearded Man Compote

Butter dish, cov. 65.00
Celery vase 35.00
Compote, cov., 9" h. (ILLUS.) 55.00
Creamer........................... 40.00
Pitcher, water, 2 qt. 58.00
Spooner 40.00
Sugar bowl, open 50.00

BELLFLOWER

Bellflower Creamer

Bowl, 6" d., 1¾" h., single vine 75.00
Bowl, 8" d., 4½" h., scalloped
    rim .... 63.50 to 75.00
Bowl, 9 x 6" oval, rayed base 115.00
Butter dish, cov. 80.00
Castor bottle w/original stopper 28.00
Celery vase, fine rib, single vine 114.00
Celery vase, w/cut bellflowers 160.00
Champagne, barrel-shaped, fine rib,
    knob stem, plain base...... 95.00 to 115.00
Champagne, straight sides, plain stem,
    rayed base .... 70.00 to 90.00
Cologne w/stopper, clambroth 161.00
Compote, cov., 8" d., 8" h., fine rib,
    single vine 375.00
Compote, open, 4¾" d., low stand,
    scalloped rim.................... 88.00

Compote, open, 8" d., 5" h.,
  scalloped rim, single vine 72.50
Compote, open, 8" d., 8" h., single
  vine 225.00
Compote, open, 9½" d., 8½" h.,
  scalloped rim, single vine 150.00
Cordial, fine rib, single vine 115.00
Creamer, fine rib, double vine,
  applied handle (ILLUS.) 135.00
Decanter w/bar lip, fine rib, single
  vine, pt. 185.00
Decanter w/bar lip, single vine, qt. . . .140.00
Decanter w/original stopper, cut
  shoulder, qt. .160.00
Egg cup, cov., w/shield 450.00
Egg cup, coarse rib 22.50
Egg cup, fine rib, single vine 37.50
Goblet, barrel-shaped, fine rib,
  single vine, knob stem 45.00
Goblet, barrel-shaped, fine rib, single
  vine, plain stem 30.00
Goblet, coarse rib . . . . .30.00 to 35.00
Goblet, double vine 43.00
Goblet, fine rib, sun-colored
  amethyst 75.00
Goblet, single vine, rayed base 40.00
Honey dish, single vine 115.00
Lamp, kerosene-type, 8½" h. 135.00
Lamp, whale oil, brass stem, marble
  base 125.00
Pitcher, milk, double vine 350.00
Pitcher, water, 8¾" h., coarse rib,
  double vine 350.00
Plate, 6" d., fine rib, single vine 50.00
Salt dip, master size, footed, scal-
  loped rim, single vine 35.00
Sauce dish, double vine 20.00
Sauce dish, single vine . . . . .10.00 to 15.00
Spillholder 30.00
Spooner, low foot, double vine 48.50
Spooner, scalloped rim, single vine 35.00
Sugar bowl, cov., single vine 95.00
Sugar bowl, open, double vine .45.00 to 50.00
Sugar bowl, open, coarse rib, double
  vine 68.00
Syrup pitcher w/original top, applied
  handle, fine rib, single vine 410.00
Tumbler, bar 72.50
Tumbler, coarse rib, double vine 77.50
Tumbler, fine rib, single vine 82.50
Tumbler, whiskey 135.00
Wine, barrel-shaped, knob stem,
  fine rib, single vine, rayed base 90.00
Wine, straight sides, plain stem, rayed
  base 75.00

BIGLER

Bowl, 10" d. 75.00
Celery vase 105.00
Champagne 95.00
Cordial 60.00
Decanter w/bar lip, pt. 55.00
Decanter w/bar lip, qt. 80.00
Goblet, 6" h. (ILLUS.) 42.50

Bigler Goblet

Salt dip, master size 20.00
Tumbler .50.00 to 60.00
Whiskey, handled 100.00
Wine 45.00

BIRD & FERN - See Hummingbird Pattern

BIRD & STRAWBERRY (Bluebird)

Bird & Strawberry Tumbler

Berry set: master bowl & 6 sauce
  dishes; footed, clear, 7 pcs. 125.00
Bowl, 5½" d., clear 25.00
Bowl, 5½" d., w/color 35.00
Bowl, 7½" d., footed, clear 45.00
Bowl, 9" d., flat, clear 45.00
Bowl, 9½ x 6" oval, footed, clear 55.00
Bowl, 10" d., flat, clear 36.50
Bowl, 10" d., flat, w/color & gold trim . . .65.00
Butter dish, cov., clear 110.00
Butter dish, cov., w/color 255.00
Cake stand, clear, 9" to 9½" d. 48.00
Celery tray, clear, 10" l. 35.00
Celery vase, pedestal base, clear,
  7½" h. 65.00

Compote, cov., 5¼" d., 8" h., clear 55.00
Compote, cov., 6" d., low stand, clear . .50.00
Compote, cov., 6½" d., 9½" h., clear . . .95.00
Compote, open, 8" d., 6" h., scal-
  loped & ruffed rim, w/color 110.00
Creamer, clear 42.50
Creamer, w/color. 135.00
Dish, heart-shaped, clear . . . . . .35.00 to 42.00
Goblet, clear 40.00
Pitcher, water, clear 185.00
Pitcher, water, w/color 275.00
Plate, 12" d., clear 70.00
Punch cup, clear 20.00
Relish, clear, 8¼" oval 22.00
Sauce dish, flat or footed,
  clear. . . . . .17.50 to 25.00
Spooner, clear 47.50
Sugar bowl, cov., clear 60.00
Sugar bowl, open, clear 30.00
Table set, w/color, 4 pcs. 385.00
Tumbler, clear . . . . .35.00 to 45.00
Tumbler, w/color (ILLUS.) 58.00
Water set: pitcher & 5 tumblers; clear,
  6 pcs. 198.00
Water set: pitcher & 6 tumblers;
  w/color, 7 pcs. 395.00
Wine, clear 40.00

BLEEDING HEART

Bleeding Heart Spooner

Bowl, 8" 37.50
Brandy snifter 45.00
Butter dish, cov. 52.50
Cake stand, 9½" d. 58.50
Cake stand, 10" d. 85.00
Compote, cov., 9" d., 12" h., w/Bleeding
  Heart finial 78.00
Compote, open, 8½" d., low stand 24.00
Compote, open, 8½" d., high stand 30.00
Creamer. 35.00
Egg cup 40.00
Goblet, buttermilk 25.00
Goblet, knob stem 32.50
Honey dish . . . . .12.50 to 17.00
Mug, 3" h. 49.00

Pickle dish, pear-shaped w/scalloped
  rim, 5" w., 8¾" l. 37.00
Pitcher, water 115.00
Relish, 5 1/8 x 3 5/8" oval 33.00
Salt dip, master size, footed . . .32.50 to 45.00
Sauce dish, flat. . . . . .7.50 to 10.00
Spooner (ILLUS.) 31.50
Sugar bowl, cov. 52.50
Sugar bowl, open 23.00
Tumbler, flat 65.00
Wine 42.50

BLOCK (Also see Red Block Pattern)

Carafe, clear 25.00
Celery, clear 15.00
Creamer, large, clear 8.00
Cruet w/original stopper, clear 20.00
Pitcher, water, clear 65.00
Punch cup, applied handle, clear. 8.00
Sauce dish, flat, clear 5.00
Tumbler, clear. .40.00
Water set: pitcher & 6 tumblers; clear
  w/gold, 7 pcs. 110.00
Wine, clear 14.50

BLOCK & FAN

Block & Fan Rose Bowl

Bowl, berry, 8" d., footed 19.50
Bowl, 9¾" d. 32.50
Bowl, 10 x 6" rectangle 50.00
Butter dish, cov. 45.00
Cake stand, 9" d. 32.50
Cake stand, 10" d. 38.00
Carafe, water 50.00
Celery tray. 22.50
Celery vase 30.00
Compote, open, 8" d., high stand 40.00
Cookie jar, cov. .65.00
Creamer. 22.50
Cruet w/original stopper, small, 6" h. . .24.00
Cruet w/original stopper, medium 35.00
Cruet w/original stopper, large. 29.50
Finger bowl 29.50
Goblet 52.50
Ice bucket 40.00
Pitcher, milk 35.00
Pitcher, water 50.00
Plate, 6" d. 21.50
Plate, 10" d. 19.50
Relish, 9¾ x 6" oval 25.00

Rose bowl (ILLUS.) 25.00
Salt & pepper shakers w/original tops,
    pr. 40.00
Sauce dish, flat or footed . . . . . .8.00 to 12.00
Sauce dish, footed, ruby-stained 25.00
Spooner 25.00
Sugar bowl, cov. 40.00
Sugar bowl, open .18.00
Sugar shaker w/original top 35.00
Syrup pitcher w/original top, 7" h. 60.00
Tray, ice cream, 13½ x 8" 40.00
Tumbler 30.00
Wine 45.00

BLOCK & STAR - See Valencia Waffle Pattern

BLUEBIRD - See Bird & Strawberry Pattern

BOW TIE
Bowl, berry, 8" d. 32.50
Bowl, 10" d., 5" h. 75.00
Butter dish, cov. 68.00
Butter pat 25.00
Cake stand, 9" d. .60.00
Compote, open, 5½" d., 10½" h. 60.00
Compote, open, 6½" d., low stand 45.00
Compote, open, 8" d., low stand 47.50
Compote, open, 9¼" d., high stand 55.00
Creamer 45.00
Goblet 37.50
Marmalade jar w/cover 45.00
Pickle castor, amber insert, ornate
    footed silverplate frame & tongs 165.00
Pitcher, milk 65.00
Pitcher, water 75.00
Relish, rectangular 22.50
Salt dip, master size 32.50
Salt shaker w/original top (single) 18.00
Sauce dish, flat 18.00
Spooner 35.00
Sugar bowl, cov. 55.00
Sugar bowl, open .35.00
Tumbler 45.00

BROKEN COLUMN (Irish Column, Notched Rib or Bamboo)
Banana stand, clear 100.00
Basket, applied handle, clear, 15" l.,
    12" h. 150.00
Bowl, 7¼" d., clear 32.50
Bowl, 8" d., clear .35.00
Bowl, 9" d., clear . . . . .35.00 to 40.00
Bowl, cov., vegetable, clear 95.00
Butter dish, cov., clear. 65.00
Cake stand, clear, 9" d. 60.00
Cake stand, clear, 10" d. 72.50
Carafe, water, clear. 65.00
Celery vase, clear. .50.00
Celery vase, clear w/red notches 135.00
Claret, clear 45.00
Compote, cov., 4¾" d., clear 56.00
Compote, cov., 5¼" d., 10½" h., clear . .62.50
Compote, cov., 5¼" d., 10½" h.,
    clear w/red notches 200.00

Compote, cov., 7" d., 12" h.,
    clear .100.00 to 120.00
Compote, cov., 8" d., high stand,
    clear 150.00
Compote, open, jelly, clear w/red
    notches 110.00
Compote, open, 5" d., 6" h., clear 35.00
Compote, open, 6" d., flared rim,
    clear 55.00
Compote, open, 6" d., clear w/red
    notches 135.00
Compote, open, 8" d., clear . . . .42.00 to 55.00
Cookie jar, cov., clear 70.00
Creamer, clear 37.50
Creamer, clear w/red notches 92.50
Creamer & open sugar bowl, clear
    w/red notches, pr. 150.00
Cruet w/original stopper, clear 52.50
Cruet w/original stopper, clear w/red
    notches 110.00
Decanter w/original stopper, clear,
    10½" h. 95.00

Broken Column Goblet

Goblet, clear (ILLUS.) 46.00
Marmalade jar w/original cover, clear . .62.50
Pickle castor, clear, w/frame & tongs . . .95.00
Pickle castor, clear w/red notches,
    w/frame & tongs 425.00
Pitcher, water, clear 85.00
Pitcher, water, clear w/red notches . . .210.00
Plate, 5" d., clear .32.50
Plate, 7½" d., clear w/red notches 75.00
Plate, 8" d., clear .37.50
Powder jar, cov., clear 24.50
Punch cup, blue. 55.00
Relish, clear, 5 x 3¾". 15.00
Relish, clear, 6½" l. 20.00
Relish, clear, 8 x 5" 30.00
Salt shaker w/original top, clear
    (single) 30.00
Sauce dish, clear. .15.00
Sauce dish, clear w/red notches 37.50

Spooner, clear. 32.50
Spooner, clear w/red notches 110.00
Sugar bowl, cov., clear 67.50
Syrup pitcher w/metal top, clear 80.00
Syrup pitcher w/metal top, clear
    w/red notches . . . . .380.00 to 425.00
Tumbler, clear. 37.50
Tumbler, clear w/red notches 55.00
Waste bowl, clear. 30.00
Wine, clear 52.50

BRYCE - See Ribbon Candy Pattern

BUCKLE

Buckle Goblet

Bowl, 10" d., rolled edge. 60.00
Butter dish, cov. 68.00
Cake stand, 9¾" d., 5¼" h. 30.00
Champagne, flint 65.00
Compote, cov., 6" d., 8½" h. 95.00
Creamer, applied handle, flint. 110.00
Creamer, small size, non-flint 24.00
Egg cup, flint 30.00
Egg cup, non-flint 20.00
Goblet, flint 31.50
Goblet, non-flint (ILLUS.). 25.00
Goblet, buttermilk, non-flint 24.00
Lamp, kerosene-type, w/clambroth
    base 125.00
Pitcher, water, applied handle, flint . . .525.00
Salt dip, master size, footed, flint 24.00
Salt dip, master size, flat, oval. 30.00
Sauce dish, flint 10.00
Sauce dish, non-flint 7.00
Spooner, flint 35.00
Spooner, non-flint 25.00
Sugar bowl, cov., w/acorn finial, flint . .65.00
Sugar bowl, open, flint 45.00
Sugar bowl, open, non-flint 19.00
Tumbler, bar, flint 55.00
Tumbler, non-flint 30.00
Wine, non-flint .27.50

BUCKLE WITH STAR

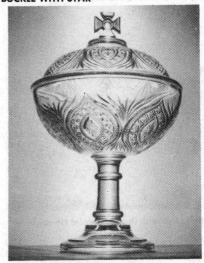

Buckle With Star Compote

Bowl, 8" oval 15.00
Butter dish, cov. 35.00
Cake stand, 9" d. 30.00
Celery vase 24.50
Compote, cov., 7" d. (ILLUS.) 60.00
Compote, open, 7" d., 5½" h. 19.50
Creamer. 24.00
Goblet 25.00
Pitcher, water, applied handle. 80.00
Relish, 7¼ x 5 1/8" oval 10.00
Salt dip 25.00
Sauce dish, flat or footed 6.50
Spillholder 60.00
Spooner 20.00
Sugar bowl, cov. 35.00
Sugar bowl, open 20.00
Tumbler, bar 55.00
Wine 36.00

BULL'S EYE

Carafe, flint, qt. .45.00
Celery vase, flint 72.50
Cordial, flint 45.00
Creamer, applied handle, flint. 110.00
Decanter w/bar lip, flint, qt. 120.00
Egg cup, flint 45.00
Goblet, flint . . . . .50.00 to 60.00
Goblet, giant bull's eye, flint 65.00
Lamp, kerosene-type, marble base,
    brass stem, 9" h. 110.00
Salt dip, rectangular 39.50
Spooner, flint 35.00
Spooner, non-flint 18.00
Sugar bowl, cov., flint 135.00
Tumbler, bar, flint 85.00
Tumbler, flat, flint 75.00
Wine, knob stem, flint 45.00

**BULL'S EYE VARIANT - See Texas Bull's Eye
Pattern**

BULL'S EYE WITH DIAMOND POINT

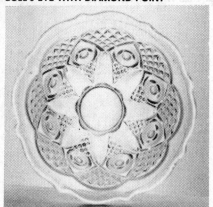

Bull's Eye with Diamond Point Honey Dish

Celery vase 180.00
Cologne bottle 85.00
Goblet ....95.00 to 125.00
Honey dish (ILLUS.)..................23.00
Lamp, kerosene-type, applied handle .150.00
Salt dip, basket-shaped.............100.00
Sauce dish 15.00
Spillholder 75.00
Spooner 80.00
Syrup pitcher w/tin top 45.00
Tumbler, bar 110.00
Tumbler, water 150.00
Wine 120.00

BULL'S EYE WITH FLEUR DE LIS

Bull's Eye With Fleur De Lis Pitcher

Celery vase, 11" h....................85.00
Creamer............................65.00
Goblet 80.00
Lamp, pear-shaped font on marble
  base 95.00
Lamp, pear-shaped font on brass
  standard..........................175.00
Pitcher, water (ILLUS.)..............485.00

Salt dip, master size.................52.50
Sugar bowl, open 55.00

BUTTON ARCHES

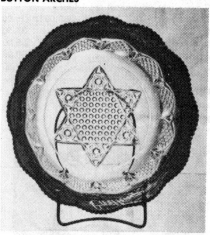

Button Arches Master Berry Bowl

Berry set: 8" d. master bowl & 6
  sauce dishes; ruby-stained, 7 pcs.
  (ILLUS. of bowl)..................135.00
Butter dish, cov., clear...............45.00
Butter dish, cov., ruby-stained 96.00
Compote, open, jelly, 4½" h.,
  ruby-stained 48.00
Creamer, clear 20.00
Creamer, ruby-stained 42.50
Creamer, ruby-stained, souvenir,
  3½" h. 47.50
Creamer, individual size, ruby-stained,
  souvenir...........................20.00
Goblet, clambroth 28.50
Goblet, clear.......................20.00
Goblet, ruby-stained 37.50
Goblet, ruby-stained, souvenir 32.00
Mug, child's, ruby-stained, souvenir 25.00
Mug, ruby-stained, souvenir, 3½" h. ...32.50
Pitcher, 7" h., ruby-stained, souvenir ...60.00
Pitcher, water, tankard, 12" h., clear ...85.00
Pitcher, water, tankard, 12" h.,
  ruby-stained 110.00
Punch cup, clear 9.00
Punch cup, ruby-stained 17.50
Salt shaker w/original top, clear
  (single)............................7.50
Salt shaker w/original top, ruby-
  stained (single)....................22.50
Spooner, clear......................24.50
Spooner, ruby-stained 32.50
Sugar bowl, cov., clear 30.00
Sugar bowl, cov., ruby-stained,
  etched ....65.00 to 80.00
Syrup pitcher w/original top, ruby-
  stained...........................125.00
Table set, clear, 4 pcs...............125.00
Toothpick holder, clambroth, souvenir ..30.00
Toothpick holder, clear 14.50

Toothpick holder, ruby-stained,
  souvenir 30.00
Tumbler, clambroth, souvenir 19.00
Tumbler, clear. 22.50
Tumbler, ruby-stained 25.00
Water set: tankard pitcher & 4 tum-
  blers; ruby-stained, souvenir,
  5 pcs. 210.00
Water set: pitcher & 5 tumblers; clear
  w/frosted band & gold, 6 pcs. 225.00
Water set: tankard pitcher & 5 tum-
  blers; ruby-stained, souvenir,
  6 pcs. 245.00
Whiskey shot glass, ruby-stained 14.50
Wine, clambroth 25.00
Wine, clear 12.00
Wine, ruby-stained 24.50

CABBAGE LEAF

Butter dish, cov., frosted 500.00
Celery vase, clear & frosted 65.00
Custard cup, frosted, marked Libbey
  Glass Co., "Columbian Expo" on
  base 80.00
Pitcher, water, frosted 135.00
Rose bowl, amber. 175.00
Sauce dish, frosted, w/rabbit center. . . .35.00

CABBAGE ROSE

Cabbage Rose Goblet

Bitters bottle, 6½" h. 85.00
Bowl, berry, 8½" oval 26.00
Butter dish, cov. 42.50
Cake stand, 11" d. 45.00
Celery vase 38.50
Champagne 50.00
Compote, cov., 7" d 85.00
Compote, cov., 8" d., high stand 100.00
Compote, open, 9¼" d., 7½" h. 34.00
Cordial 55.00
Creamer, applied handle 55.00
Egg cup. 30.00
Goblet (ILLUS.) 42.50
Pickle dish 28.00
Pitcher, water 100.00

Salt dip, master size. 23.00
Sauce dish 10.00
Spooner 32.00
Sugar bowl, cov. 55.00
Tumbler 38.00
Wine 35.50

CABLE

Cable Egg Cup

Bowl, 9" d. 70.00
Butter dish, cov. 100.00
Cake stand, 9" d. 37.00
Celery vase 65.00
Champagne 275.00
Compote, open, 5¼" d., high stand 62.50
Compote, open, 7" d., 5" h. 40.00
Compote, open, 8" d., 4¾" h. 38.00
Compote, open, 9" d., 4½" h. . .42.50 to 55.00
Creamer. 495.00
Decanter w/bar lip, qt. 125.00
Decanter w/stopper, qt. 195.00
Egg cup (ILLUS.) . . . . .35.00 to 40.00
Egg cup, clambroth, flint 550.00
Goblet 70.00
Honey dish, 3½" d., 1" h. 11.00
Lamp, whale oil, 8¾" h. 135.00
Pitcher, water, 9½" h., applied
  handle . . . . .350.00 to 500.00
Plate, 6" d. 65.00
Salt dip, individual size 20.00
Salt dip, master size. 45.00
Sauce dish 30.00
Spooner 39.00
Sugar bowl, cov. 95.00
Wine 77.50

CABLE WITH RING

Lamp, hand-type w/ring handle 175.00
Sugar bowl, cov., flint 78.00

CACTUS (See Chocolate & Greentown Glass)

CALIFORNIA - See Beaded Grape Pattern

CAMEO - See Classic Medallion Pattern

CANADIAN

Canadian Footed Sauce Dish

Bowl, berry, 7" d., 4½" h., footed 75.00
Bread plate, handled, 10" d. 35.00
Butter dish, cov. .80.00
Cake stand, 9¾" d., 5" h. 35.00
Celery vase 45.00
Compote, cov., 7" d., 11" h. 110.00
Compote, cov., 8" d., low stand 76.50
Compote, open, 7" d., 6" h. 35.00
Compote, open, 8" d., 5" h. 45.00
Cordial 36.50
Creamer 45.00
Goblet 57.50
Pitcher, milk, 8" h. 75.00
Pitcher, water 85.00
Plate, 6" d., handled 25.00
Plate, 7" d., handled 35.00
Sauce dish, flat or footed . . . . . .12.00 to 16.00
Spooner 45.00
Sugar bowl, cov. .80.00
Wine 38.50

CANE

Bowl, 9½" oval, amber 15.00
Bread platter, amber 24.00
Candlestick, clear (single) 15.00
Creamer, amber .27.50
Creamer, blue 35.00
Creamer, clear 22.50
Goblet, amber 30.00
Goblet, apple green 45.00
Goblet, blue 35.00
Goblet, clear 20.00
Honey dish, clear 15.00
Match holder, model of cauldron,
   amber 18.00
Match holder, model of cauldron,
   blue 16.00
Mustard jar, cov., amber 37.00
Pitcher, water, amber 57.50
Pitcher, water, blue 65.00
Pitcher, water, clear 35.00
Relish, amber, 7½ x 3½" 22.50
Sauce dish, flat, apple green 9.50
Sauce dish, footed, clear 15.00
Spooner, amber .42.00
Sugar bowl, cov., amber 55.00
Sugar bowl, cov., clear 40.00
Toddy plate, amber, 4½" d. 15.00
Toddy plate, apple green, 4½" d. 15.00

Toddy plate, blue, 4½" d. 17.50
Toddy plate, clear, 4½" d. 12.50
Tray, water, amber 29.50
Tumbler, apple green 28.50
Tumbler, blue 24.00
Tumbler, clear. 16.50
Waste bowl, amber 32.50
Waste bowl, apple green 30.00
Whimsey, slipper, amber 30.00

CANNON BALL - See Atlas Pattern

CAPE COD

Cape Cod Spooner

Bowl, 6" d., handled 20.00
Bread platter 45.00
Compote, cov., 8" d., 12" h. 145.00
Compote, open, 7" d., 6" h. 37.00
Compote, open, 8" d., 5½" h. 30.00
Cruet w/original stopper 25.00
Decanter w/original stopper 160.00
Goblet 35.00
Pitcher, water 65.00
Plate, 8" d., open handles 55.00
Sauce dish, flat or footed . . . . . .14.00 to 18.50
Spooner (ILLUS.) .35.00

CARDINAL BIRD

Cardinal Bird Footed Sauce Dish

Butter dish, cov. .65.00
Creamer. 30.00
Goblet 32.50
Honey dish, cov., 3½" h. 35.00
Honey dish, open 18.50
Sauce dish, flat 12.00
Sauce dish, footed (ILLUS.) 21.00
Spooner 32.50
Sugar bowl, cov. .60.00
Sugar bowl, open 30.00

CATHEDRAL

Cathedral Compote

Bowl, 6" d., crimped rim, vaseline. 35.00
Bowl, 8" d., amber 35.00
Bowl, 8" d., blue .40.00
Bowl, 8" d., vaseline 32.50
Butter dish, cov., clear. 38.50
Cake stand, blue, 10" d., 4½" h. 60.00
Cake stand, clear, 10" d. 38.00
Cake stand, vaseline 68.00
Compote, cov., 7¼" d., 10½" h.,
    clear 68.00
Compote, open, 5" d., clear 21.00
Compote, open, 7" d., high stand,
    fluted rim, amethyst 145.00
Compote, open, 7½" d., fluted rim,
    amber. 45.00
Compote, open, 9" d., 5½" h., amber. . .50.00
Compote, open, 9" d., 5½" h., blue 65.00
Compote, open, 9" d., 7" h., clear
    (ILLUS.) 48.00
Creamer, clear 18.50
Creamer, ruby-stained 50.00
Cruet w/original stopper, amber. 77.50
Dish, ruffled rim, ruby-stained, 5" d. . . .24.00
Goblet, amber 43.50
Goblet, amethyst 70.00
Goblet, clear. 30.00
Goblet, vaseline. 52.50
Lamp, kerosene-type, blue font,
    clear base, 12¾" h. 185.00
Pitcher, water, clear 125.00
Pitcher, water, ruby-stained. 105.00
Relish, fish-shaped, amber. 35.00
Relish, fish-shaped, blue. 35.00
Relish, fish-shaped, ruby-stained 55.00
Relish, fish-shaped, vaseline 35.00

Salt dip, canoe-shaped, vaseline 17.50
Sauce dish, flat, blue 20.00
Sauce dish, flat, clear 12.00
Sauce dish, flat, vaseline 24.00
Sauce dish, footed, amethyst 35.00
Sauce dish, footed, ruby-stained 22.00
Spooner, clear. 25.00
Spooner, ruby-stained 40.00
Sugar bowl, cov., clear 45.00
Sugar bowl, cov., ruby-stained 67.50
Sugar bowl, open, clear 22.50
Tumbler, amber .31.00
Tumbler, clear. 18.50
Tumbler, ruby-stained 34.00
Wine, amber 41.00
Wine, blue 55.00
Wine, clear 29.50
Wine, vaseline 45.00

CERES (Goddess of Liberty)

Butter dish, cov., lady's head finial,
    clear 75.00
Compote, open, 6" d., low stand,
    clear 25.00
Creamer, clear 22.50
Mug, amber. 25.00
Mug, blue. 22.00
Mug, clear 20.00
Mug, purple-black 60.00
Spooner, milk white 25.00
Sugar bowl, cov., clear 45.00

CHAIN

Chain Sauce Dish

Bread plate 23.50
Butter dish, cov. .35.00
Compote, cov., 7½" d., 8" h. 36.00
Compote, cov., 7½" d., 12" h. 45.00
Creamer. 18.50
Goblet 19.00
Plate, 7" d. 14.50
Relish, 8" oval 13.00
Sauce dish, footed (ILLUS.) 8.50
Spooner 24.00
Sugar bowl, cov. .32.00
Sugar bowl, open 20.00
Wine 18.00

CHAIN & SHIELD

Creamer. 30.00
Goblet 35.00
Pitcher, water 50.00
Platter, oval. 28.00

CHAIN WITH STAR

Chain with Star Goblet

Bread plate, handled	29.00
Butter dish, cov.	32.50
Cake stand, 8¾" d., 4¾" h.	27.00
Cake stand, 10" d.	32.50
Compote, open, 8" d., 6½" h.	22.50
Compote, open, 9½" d.	29.00
Creamer	21.50
Goblet (ILLUS.)	18.50
Pitcher, water	55.00
Plate, 7" d.	16.00
Plate, 7½" d.	18.00
Relish	11.00
Sauce dish	11.50
Spooner	18.00
Sugar bowl, cov.	37.50
Sugar bowl, open	27.00
Wine	20.00

CHANDELIER (Crown Jewel)

Chandelier Celery Vase

Bowl, 8" d., 3¼" h.	25.00
Butter dish, cov.	60.00
Cake stand, 10" d.	70.00

Celery vase (ILLUS.)	35.00
Compote, open, 6½" d.	38.00
Compote, open, 9¼" d., 7¾" h.	68.00
Creamer	35.00
Finger bowl	16.00
Goblet	55.00
Inkwell	85.00
Pitcher, water	68.00
Salt dip, footed	35.00
Sauce dish, flat	16.50
Spooner	30.00
Sugar bowl, cov.	40.00
Sugar shaker w/original top	60.00
Tumbler	35.00
Wine	32.00

CHECKERBOARD (Barred Hobstar)

Bowl, 9" d., flat	20.00
Butter dish, cov.	42.50
Celery vase, flat	30.00
Compote, jelly	25.00
Creamer	12.00
Goblet	17.00
Honey dish, cov., 5" w.	45.00
Pitcher, milk	35.00
Plate, 7" d.	21.50
Punch cup	5.00
Sauce dish, flat, ruby-stained w/gilt trim, 4½" d.	14.50
Spooner	22.50
Sugar bowl, cov.	25.00
Tumbler	14.50
Water set: pitcher & 4 tumblers; ruby-stained, 5 pcs.	210.00
Wine	12.00

CHERRY THUMBPRINT - See Paneled Cherry with Thumbprints Pattern

CLASSIC

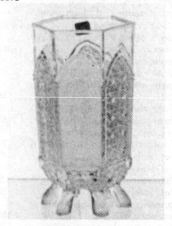

Classic Celery Vase

Berry set, master bowl & 4 sauce dishes, 5 pcs.	275.00
Bowl, cov., 7" hexagon, open log feet	125.00
Bowl, open, 8" hexagon, open log feet	47.50

Butter dish, cov., collared base 125.00
Butter dish, cov., open log feet 175.00
Celery vase, collared base 120.00
Celery vase, open log feet
  (ILLUS.) . . . . .180.00 to 225.00
Compote, cov., 6½" d., open log
  feet 240.00
Compote, cov., 6½" d., collared
  base 150.00
Compote, cov., 7½" d., 8" h., open
  log feet. 220.00
Compote, cov., 8½" d., collared
  base 175.00
Compote, cov., 12½" d., collared
  base 325.00
Compote, open, 7¾" d., open log
  feet 90.00
Creamer . . . . .118.00 to 145.00
Goblet 200.00
Pitcher, milk, open log feet 500.00
Pitcher, water. . . . . .265.00 to 285.00
Plate, 10" d., "Blaine," signed
  Jacobus 185.00
Plate, 10" d., "Cleveland" 179.00
Plate, 10" d., "Logan" 225.00
Plate, 10" d., "Warrior" 128.00
Plate, 10" d., "Warrior," signed
  Jacobus 160.00
Sauce dish . . . . .35.00 to 40.00
Spooner . . . . .90.00 to 125.00
Sugar bowl, cov., collared base 150.00
Sugar bowl, cov., open log feet 175.00
Sugar bowl, open, log feet 125.00

CLASSIC MEDALLION (Cameo)

Classic Medallion Spooner

Bowl, 6¾" d., 3½" h., footed 38.00
Bowl, 7½" d., footed 25.00
Celery vase 30.00
Compote, open, 7" d., 3¾" h. 30.00
Creamer. 25.00
Creamer & open sugar bowl, pr. 75.00
Pitcher, water 52.50
Sauce dish, footed 13.00
Spooner (ILLUS.) 23.50
Sugar bowl, open 20.00

COIN - See Columbian Coin & U.S. Coin Patterns

COLLINS - See Crystal Wedding Pattern

COLONIAL (Empire Colonial)

Colonial Claret

Celery vase, flint 75.00
Champagne, flint 55.00
Claret, 5½" h. (ILLUS.) 50.00
Creamer, applied handle, flint. 120.00
Goblet, flint 55.00
Salt dip, master size. 17.50
Spillholder 40.00
Spooner 40.00
Sugar bowl, cov. 95.00
Tumbler, footed, flint . . . . .25.00 to 45.00
Wine, flint 75.00

COLORADO

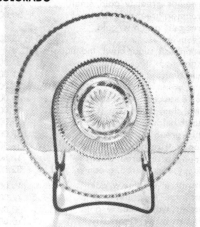

Colorado Plate

Berry set: master bowl & 4 sauce
  dishes; green, 5 pcs. 80.00

Berry set: master bowl & 6 sauce
dishes; green w/gold, 7 pcs. 165.00
Bowl, 5" d., flared edge, clear 12.00
Bowl, 5" d., green w/gold 45.00
Bowl, 6" d., clear 20.00
Bowl, 7" d., flat, green 23.00
Bowl, 7" d., footed, clear 15.00
Bowl, 7½" d., footed, turned-up sides,
green 30.00
Bowl, 8" d., turned-up sides, green
w/gold 60.00
Bowl, 8½" d., footed, crimped edge,
green 40.00
Bowl, 8½" triangle, clear 20.00
Bowl, 9" d., green w/gold 37.00
Bowl, 9¾" d., 4" h., footed, flared,
green 30.00
Bowl, 10" d., footed, fluted, green 42.50
Butter dish, cov., blue w/gold 200.00
Butter dish, cov., clear 52.50
Butter dish, cov., green 110.00
Candy dish, clear 9.50
Candy dish, green, souvenir 20.00
Card tray, clear 25.00
Card tray, green w/gold 32.50
Celery vase, clear 35.00
Celery vase, green w/gold 48.00
Compote, open, 6" d., 4" h., crimped
rim, clear 20.00
Compote, open, 8" d., 7" h.,
beaded rim, green 77.50
Compote, open, 9½" d., blue 95.00
Compote, open, 10½" d., 7" h.,
green w/gold 135.00
Creamer, blue w/gold 95.00
Creamer, clear 43.50
Creamer, clear w/ruby-staining 75.00
Creamer, clear w/gold, individual
size 22.50
Creamer, clear w/ruby-staining,
individual size 40.00
Creamer, green w/gold, small 30.00
Creamer, green w/gold, large 50.00
Creamer, green w/gold,
souvenir .... 40.00 to 55.00
Creamer & sugar bowl, individual size,
green, pr........................... 57.00
Cup, clear 11.00
Cup, green 26.00
Cup & saucer, green, souvenir 40.00
Dish, clear, 6" sq. 15.00
Match holder, green 35.00
Mug, green 25.00
Nappy, tricornered, blue w/gold 32.50
Nappy, tricornered, clear 17.50
Nappy, tricornered, green w/gold 32.50
Pitcher, 6" h., blue w/gold 115.00
Pitcher, 6" h., green w/gold 42.00
Pitcher, water, blue w/gold 400.00
Pitcher, water, clear w/gold 116.00
Pitcher, water, green
w/gold .... 175.00 to 200.00
Plate, 7" d., footed, clear (ILLUS.) 17.50
Plate, 8" d., blue 60.00

Punch cup, clear 20.00
Punch cup, green w/gold, souvenir 28.00
Salt shaker w/original top, blue
w/gold 58.00
Salt shaker w/original top, green
w/gold 95.00
Sauce dish, blue w/gold 38.50
Sauce dish, clear 14.50
Sauce dish, green w/gold 28.00
Spooner, clear 25.00
Spooner, green w/gold 50.00
Sugar bowl, cov., large, clear 32.00
Sugar bowl, cov., large, green 65.00
Sugar bowl, open, large, green 30.00
Sugar bowl, open, individual size, blue .26.50
Sugar bowl, open, individual size,
green 27.50
Table set, green w/gold, 4 pcs. 350.00
Toothpick holder, blue w/gold 48.00
Toothpick holder, clear w/gold 30.00
Toothpick holder, green w/gold 38.00
Tumbler, ruby-stained, souvenir 32.00
Vase, 12" h., blue w/gold ..... 95.00 to 145.00
Vase, 12" h., trumpet-shaped, green .. 52.50
Violet vase, blue 48.00
Wine, clear 24.50
Wine, green w/gold 37.50
Wine, ruby-stained w/gold 25.00

COLUMBIAN COIN

Columbian Coin Lamp

Berry set: master bowl & 6 sauce
dishes; gilded coins, 7 pcs. 295.00
Butter dish, cov., gilded coins 165.00
Celery vase, frosted coins 75.00
Champagne, frosted coins 65.00
Champagne, gilded coins 85.00
Claret, clear coins 90.00
Claret, frosted coins 140.00
Compote, cov., 8" d., frosted coins 187.50
Compote, open, 8" d., clear coins 80.00
Creamer, gilded coins 67.50
Cruet w/original stopper, frosted
coins 145.00
Goblet, frosted coins 80.00

Goblet, gilded coins 75.00
Lamp, kerosene-type, frosted coins,
   12" h. (ILLUS.) 160.00
Mug, beer, handled, gilded coins 75.00
Pickle dish 90.00
Pitcher, milk, gilded coins 155.00
Pitcher, water, 10" h., gilded coins 145.00
Salt shaker w/original top, clear
   (single) 95.00
Sauce dish, flat, gilded coins 32.50
Spooner, frosted coins 45.00
Spooner, gilded coins 55.00
Sugar bowl, cov., frosted coins 135.00
Syrup pitcher w/original top, frosted
   coins 135.00
Toothpick holder, gilded coins 72.50
Tray, 10" d. 112.00
Tumbler 46.50
Wine . . . . .55.00 to 85.00

COMET (Early)
Compote, low stand 135.00
Goblet . . . . .75.00 to 90.00
Pitcher, water, tankard 400.00
Spooner 85.00
Tumbler, bar 95.00
Tumbler, bar, canary yellow 750.00
Tumbler, water .110.00
Tumbler, whiskey, handled 110.00

COMPACT - See Snail Pattern

CORD & TASSEL

Cord & Tassel Goblet

Bowl, oval 20.00
Cake stand, 9½" d. 50.00
Castor bottle 32.00
Compote, cov., 8" d. 50.00
Compote, open, 8" d., low stand 26.50
Creamer 28.00
Goblet (ILLUS.) . . . . .25.00 to 32.00
Mug 25.00
Mustard jar 24.00
Pitcher, water 57.50
Salt & pepper shakers w/original
   tops, pr. 55.00
Sauce dish, flat .10.00
Spooner 32.50
Sugar bowl, open 28.00
Wine 28.50

CORD DRAPERY

Cord Drapery Relish

Bowl, 7½ x 4½" oval, clear 21.00
Bowl, 8½" oval, clear 30.50
Bowl, 10" d., 3½" h., clear 45.00
Butter dish, cov., clear 55.00
Butter dish, cov., green 150.00
Cake plate, clear, 10" d. 45.00
Compote, cov., jelly, blue 55.00
Compote, cov., jelly, clear 45.00
Compote, cov., 6½" d., clear 65.00
Compote, open, jelly, clear 18.00
Compote, open, 7½" d., 5½" h.,
   clear 40.00
Compote, open, 8½" d., 6¼" h.,
   clear 48.00
Creamer, clear 31.50
Cruet w/original stopper, amber 265.00
Cruet w/original stopper, clear 90.00
Goblet, clear 55.00
Mug, clear 27.00
Pitcher, water, amber 170.00
Pitcher, water, clear 59.00
Punch cup, clear 12.50
Relish, clear, 7 x 4" 21.50
Relish, clear, 9¼ x 5¾" (ILLUS.) 24.50
Salt shaker w/original top, clear
   (single) 43.00
Sauce dish, flat or footed, clear . .8.50 to 11.50
Spooner, clear 35.00
Sugar bowl, cov., amber 125.00
Sugar bowl, cov., clear 38.50
Sweetmeat dish, cov., amber, 6½" d.,
   5¼" h. 165.00
Syrup pitcher w/original top, amber . . .280.00
Toothpick holder, clear 65.00
Tumbler, clear 33.00

CORDOVA
Butter dish, cov. 35.00
Cake stand, square 67.50
Cologne bottle, 5" h. 20.00
Compote, open, 8" d. 35.00
Creamer 17.50
Inkwell 75.00
Mug 14.00
Pitcher, milk 32.50
Pitcher, water 40.00
Punch cup 8.00
Salt shaker w/original top (single) 15.00

Spooner 35.00
Sugar bowl, cov. ....35.00 to 40.00
Sugar bowl, cov., individual size 40.00
Syrup pitcher w/pewter top 125.00
Toothpick holder...................18.00
Tumbler 13.00
Vase, bud..........................15.00

COTTAGE (Dinner Bell or Fine Cut Band)

Cottage Bowl

Bowl, berry, 7" d., green (ILLUS.).......16.00
Bowl, berry, 9¼ x 6½" oval, clear 11.50
Butter dish, cov., clear...............45.00
Cake stand, blue....................55.00
Cake stand, clear 28.00
Celery vase, clear...................27.50
Champagne, clear 37.00
Compote, open, jelly, 4½" d., 4" h.,
   clear 20.00
Compote, open, jelly, 4½" d., 4" h.,
   green 40.00
Compote, open, 8¼" d., 7½" h., clear ..65.00
Creamer, amber....................37.50
Creamer, clear 22.00
Cruet w/original stopper, clear 37.00
Cup & saucer, clear 32.50
Goblet, amber 47.50
Goblet, clear 22.50
Pitcher, milk, clear..................28.00
Pitcher, water, clear, 2 qt. 40.00
Plate, 5" d., clear 5.00
Plate, 6" d., clear 12.50
Plate, 7" d., clear 16.00
Plate, 8" d., clear 22.00
Plate, 9" d., clear 32.50
Salt shaker w/original top, clear
   (single)..........................25.00
Sauce dish, clear....................8.00
Spooner, clear......................20.00
Sugar bowl, cov., clear 47.00
Syrup pitcher w/original top, clear 65.00
Tray, water, clear...................25.00
Tumbler, clear......................12.50
Wine, clear 18.00

CROESUS

Croesus Sauce Dish

Berry set: master bowl & 6 sauce
   dishes; green, 7 pcs. 300.00
Berry set: master bowl & 6 sauce
   dishes; purple, 7 pcs..............435.00
Bowl, 6¾" d., 4" h., footed, green 95.00
Bowl, 8" d., green..................125.00
Bowl, 8" d., purple 175.00
Bowl, berry or fruit, 9" d.,
   green ....100.00 to 125.00
Butter dish, cov., green .....120.00 to 165.00
Butter dish, cov., purple 215.00
Celery vase, green w/gold 135.00
Celery vase, purple 325.00
Compote, open, jelly, green.........215.00
Compote, open, jelly, purple 250.00
Condiment tray, clear 18.00
Condiment tray, green 40.00
Creamer, green 75.00
Creamer, purple...................150.00
Creamer & cov. sugar bowl, green,
   pr. 225.00
Cruet w/original stopper, clear 75.00
Cruet w/original stopper, green 200.00
Cruet w/original stopper, purple......350.00
Cruet w/original stopper, miniature,
   green, 4" h. 130.00
Pitcher, water, green...............250.00
Pitcher, water, purple 550.00
Plate, 8" d., scalloped rim,
   green w/gold 145.00
Relish, boat-shaped, purple 75.00
Salt & pepper shakers w/replaced
   tops, green, pr....................145.00
Sauce dish, green w/gold (ILLUS.)......32.50
Sauce dish, purple w/gold 52.50
Spooner, green 67.50
Spooner, purple 87.50
Sugar bowl, cov., clear 75.00
Sugar bowl, cov., green 105.00
Sugar bowl, cov., purple.....160.00 to 200.00
Sugar bowl, individual size, green 65.00
Table set: creamer, cov. sugar bowl
   & toothpick holder, clear, 3 pcs......275.00
Table set; green, 4 pcs. 525.00
   cov. butter dish & spooner; green,
   4 pcs. 525.00
Toothpick holder, green 72.50
Toothpick holder, purple 100.00
Tumbler, green 45.00
Tumbler, purple 72.50
Water set: pitcher & 5 tumblers;
   green, 6 pcs. 425.00

CROWN JEWEL - See Chandelier Pattern

CRYSTAL BALL - See Atlas Pattern

CRYSTAL WEDDING (Collins)

Crystal Wedding Celery Vase

Banana stand, 10" h. . . . . .75.00 to 110.00
Berry set, 8" sq. bowl & 6 sauce
   dishes, 7 pcs. 125.00
Bowl, cov., 7" sq. 75.00
Bowl, berry, 8" sq. 35.00
Butter dish, cov. .52.50
Butter dish, cov., amber-stained 100.00
Butter dish, cov., ruby-stained 75.00
Cake stand, 9" sq., 8" h. 42.50
Cake stand, 10" sq. . . . . .65.00 to 85.00
Celery vase (ILLUS.) 42.50
Compote, cov., 5" sq. 52.50
Compote, cov., 6" sq., 9½" h. 65.00
Compote, cov., 7" sq. 75.00
Compote, open, 4" sq., 6" h. 24.00
Compote, open, 5" sq. 42.50
Creamer . . . . .30.00 to 42.50
Creamer, ruby-stained 75.00
Creamer & cov. sugar bowl, amber-
   stained, pr. . . . . .180.00 to 195.00
Creamer & cov. sugar bowl, clear,
   pr. 75.00
Cruet w/original stopper, amber-
   stained 175.00
Goblet 50.00
Lamp base, kerosene, square font,
   10" h. 375.00
Pitcher, water 145.00
Relish 25.00
Salt dip 30.00
Sauce dish . . . . .10.00 to 15.00
Spooner, clear. 30.00
Spooner, ruby-stained 65.00
Sugar bowl, cov., clear 50.00
Sugar bowl, cov., ruby-stained 85.00
Sugar bowl, open, scalloped rim 30.00
Syrup pitcher w/original top, ruby-
   stained 210.00
Tumbler 37.50

CUPID & VENUS (Guardian Angel)

Cupid & Venus Footed Sauce Dish

Bowl, 8" d., scalloped rim, footed 28.00
Bowl, 9" oval, 2¼" h. 28.00
Bread plate, amber, 10½" d. 115.00
Bread plate, clear, 10½" d. 32.50
Butter dish, cov. . . . . .42.50 to 55.00
Cake plate 40.00
Celery vase 42.50
Champagne 100.00
Compote, cov., 7" d., low stand 55.00
Compote, cov., 10" d., high stand 63.00
Compote, open, 6" d., low stand 30.00
Compote, open, 7½" d., low stand 27.00
Compote, open, 8½" d., low stand,
   scalloped rim . . . . .25.00 to 35.00
Compote, open, 9½" d., low stand 36.00
Cordial 52.50
Creamer 36.50
Goblet 60.00
Mug, 2½" h. 25.00
Mug, 3½" h. 30.00
Pitcher, milk, amber 190.00
Pitcher, milk, clear 65.00
Sauce dish, footed, 3½" to 4½" d.
   (ILLUS.) . . . . .8.00 to 15.00
Spooner . . . . .30.00 to 38.00
Sugar bowl, cov. 65.00
Sugar bowl, open 35.00
Wine 80.00

CURRANT

Cake stand, 9¼" d., 4¼" h. 65.00
Cake stand, 11" d. 72.50
Celery vase 42.50
Creamer 36.50
Egg cup . . . . .20.00 to 25.00
Goblet 23.50
Goblet, buttermilk 40.00
Pitcher, water 70.00
Spooner 25.00
Wine 16.50

CURRIER & IVES

Bread plate, Balky Mule on Railroad
   Tracks, blue. 85.00
Bread plate, Balky Mule on Railroad
   Tracks, clear 62.50

Bread plate, children sawing felled
   log, frosted center 75.00
Compote, cov., 7½" d., high stand 95.00
Compote, open, 7½" d., 9" h.,
   scalloped rim, clear 45.00
Cordial, clear, 3¼" h. 25.00
Creamer, clear 30.00
Cup & saucer, clear 35.00
Decanter w/original stopper, clear 55.00
Goblet, clear . . . . .20.00 to 28.00
Lamp, kerosene-type, clear, 9½" h. 70.00
Pitcher, milk, clear. 45.00
Pitcher, water, blue 110.00
Pitcher, water, clear 52.50
Relish dish, clear, 10" oval . . . . .16.00 to 20.00
Salt shaker w/original top, amber
   (single). 45.00
Salt shaker w/original top, clear
   (single) 19.00
Salt shaker w/original top, vaseline
   (single) 50.00
Sauce dish, flat or footed, blue 28.50
Sauce dish, flat or footed,
   clear. . . . . .7.00 to 12.50
Spooner, blue .45.00
Spooner, clear. 30.00
Sugar bowl, cov., clear 35.00
Syrup jug w/original top, clear 55.00
Tray, wine, clear, 9½" d. . . . . . .40.00 to 48.00
Tray, water, Balky Mule on Railroad
   Tracks, blue, 12" d. 110.00

Currier & Ives Water Tray

Tray, water, Balky Mule on Railroad
   Tracks, clear, 12" d.
   (ILLUS.) . . . . .45.00 to 58.00
Tray, water, Balky Mule on Railroad
   Tracks, vaseline, 12" d. 125.00
Water set: pitcher & 6 goblets;
   clear, 7 pcs. 175.00
Wine, clear 17.50

CURTAIN
Bowl, 7½" d. 22.00
Bowl, 8" d. 60.00

Butter dish, cov. 50.00
Cake stand, 9½" d. 36.50
Celery boat 48.50
Celery vase 28.50
Compote, open, 10" d., 8" h. 38.00
Creamer. 25.00
Goblet 35.00

Curtain Pattern Salt Shaker

Salt shaker w/original top (ILLUS.) 15.00
Sauce dish, flat or footed, 4¾" d. 8.00
Spooner 25.00
Sugar bowl, cov. 32.00
Tumbler 20.00

CURTAIN TIE BACK

Curtain Tie Back Goblet

Bowl, 7½" sq., flat 18.00
Bread tray 35.00
Butter dish, cov. 38.00
Creamer. 25.00
Goblet (ILLUS.) 18.50
Pitcher, water .55.00
Relish 10.00
Sauce dish, flat or footed, 3¾" d. 10.00

Spooner 28.00
Sugar bowl, cov. 30.00
Sugar bowl, open 15.00

CUT LOG

Cut Log Creamer

Bowl, master berry, 8½" d.,
   scalloped rim .27.50
Butter dish, cov. . . . . .65.00 to 70.00
Cake stand, 9" d., 6" h. 58.00
Cake stand, 10" d. 65.00
Celery tray 14.50
Celery vase 35.00
Compote, cov., 5½" d., 7½" h. 55.00
Compote, cov., 8" d., 10" h. 85.00
Compote, cov., 8" d., 12½" h. 95.00
Compote, open, 5" d. 25.00
Compote, open, 6" d.,
   4¾" h. . . . . .35.00 to 40.00
Compote, open, 8" d., 6½" h. 22.50
Compote, open, 9" d., 6¼" h. 35.00
Compote, open, 9¾" d., 5¾" h. 55.00
Compote, open, 10" d., 8½" h.,
   scalloped rim . . . . .75.00 to 85.00
Creamer (ILLUS.) 37.50
Creamer, individual size . . . . . . .10.00 to 15.00
Cruet w/original stopper,
   small . . . . .35.00 to 45.00
Cruet w/original stopper, large 45.00
Goblet 45.00
Mug .14.00 to 20.00
Nappy, handled, 5" d. 18.50
Olive dish . . . . .15.00 to 22.50
Pitcher, water, tankard 75.00
Relish, boat-shaped, 7¼ x
   4½" .15.00 to 18.50
Salt shaker w/original tin top
   (single) . . . . .40.00 to 55.00
Sauce dish, flat or footed . . . . . .25.00 to 30.00
Spooner . . . . .25.00 to 35.00
Sugar bowl, cov. 48.00
Sugar bowl, open, individual size 19.50
Tumbler 45.00
Tumbler, juice .25.00
Wine 22.50

DAHLIA

Bowl, 9 x 6" oval, clear 16.50
Bread platter, clear, 12 x 8" 36.50

Butter dish, cov., clear 40.00
Cake stand, amber, 9" d. 65.00
Cake stand, clear, 9" d. 25.00
Cake stand, amber, 10½" d. 75.00
Champagne, clear 55.00
Creamer, clear .18.00
Egg cup, double, clear 55.00
Mug, amber 37.50
Mug, clear 30.00
Pitcher, milk, applied handle, clear 37.00
Pitcher, water, amber 67.50

Dahlia Water Pitcher

Pitcher, water, blue (ILLUS.) 100.00
Pitcher, water, clear 38.00
Pitcher, water, vaseline . . . . . . .75.00 to 95.00
Plate, 7" d., amber 42.50
Plate, 7" d., blue 36.00
Plate, 7" d., clear 20.00
Plate, 9" d., w/handles, amber 34.50
Plate, 9" d., w/handles, clear 15.00
Relish, clear, 9½ x 5" 13.00
Sauce dish, flat, amber 10.50
Sauce dish, flat, blue 12.00
Sauce dish, flat, clear 8.00
Spooner, blue .50.00
Spooner, clear .25.00
Wine, clear 37.50

DAISY & BUTTON

Bowl, 6" d., blue 45.00
Bowl, 8" d., flat, clear 20.00
Bowl, 8" d., 8¾" h., scalloped
   rim, clear 125.00
Bowl, 8" w., tricornered, vaseline 50.00
Bowl, berry or fruit, 8½" d., clear 42.50
Bowl, 10 x 7" rectangle, 2¼" h.,
   vaseline 45.00
Bowl, 11 x 8" oval, 3" h., amber 37.50
Bread tray, amber . . . . .22.00 to 34.00
Bread tray, clear 20.00
Bread tray, vaseline 25.00
Butter chip, fan-shaped, clear 9.50

Butter dish, cov., scalloped base,
  blue.................................60.00
Butter dish, cov., square, clear 40.00
Butter dish, cov., model of
  Victorian stove, blue 52.50
Butter tub, cov., 2-handled, vaseline ...28.00
Canoe, Amberina, 8" l.......650.00 to 850.00
Canoe, clear, 8" l....................25.00
Canoe, vaseline, 8" l.................90.00
Canoe, canary yellow, 12" l............50.00
Canoe, amber, 13" l. 60.00
Carafe, clear 37.50
Castor set, 3-bottle, clear, in glass
  frame w/toothpick holder at
  top...............................50.00
Castor set, 4-bottle, amber, in glass
  frame 80.00
Castor shaker bottle w/original
  top, amber........................18.00
Cheese dish, cov., clear 52.00

Daisy & Button Hat & Cologne

Cologne bottle w/original stopper,
  clear (ILLUS.)......................22.50
Creamer, amber.....................25.50
Creamer, clear 18.00
Creamer, pedestal base, vaseline,
  7" h..............................35.00
Cruet w/original stopper, amber......100.00
Dish, fan-shaped, clear, 10" w. 11.50
Dresser set: pr. cologne bottles,
  powder box, shoe form pin holder
  & tray; clear, 5 pcs................132.00
Gas shade, ruffled rim, vaseline 65.00
Goblet, amber 30.00
Goblet, blue 32.50
Goblet, clear 20.00
Hat shape, amber, 2½" h..............30.00
Hat shape, apple green, 2½" h.........35.00
Hat shape, blue, 2½" h. 28.00
Hat shape, clear, 2½" h. (ILLUS.).......20.00
Hat shape, vaseline, 2½" h............45.00
Hat shape, blue, from tumbler
  mold, 4¾" d.......................40.00
Ice cream dish, scalloped corners,
  Amberina, 5¾" d. 130.00
Ice cream dish, cut corners, clear,
  6" sq. 9.00

Mug, clear 10.00
Pickle castor, sapphire blue insert,
  w/silverplate frame & tongs........250.00
Pitcher, water, bulbous, applied
  handle, clear.....................55.00
Pitcher, water, bulbous, applied
  handle, clear w/ruby-stained
  buttons 200.00
Pitcher, water, square, clear 58.00
Plate, 7" sq., amber...........14.50 to 22.50
Plate, 7" sq., clear 13.50
Plate, 10" d., scalloped rim,
  amber.............................28.00
Platter, 13 x 9" oval, open
  handles, amber....................37.50
Platter, 13 x 9" oval, open handles,
  blue...............................39.50
Relish, "Sitz bathtub," amber 140.00
Relish, "Sitz bathtub," clear 72.50
Salt dip, master size, blue, 3½" d. 12.50
Salt dip, master size, vaseline, 3½" d. ...23.00
Salt & pepper shakers w/original
  tops, clear, pr.....................20.00
Sauce dish, amber, 4" to 5" sq. .12.50 to 30.00
Sauce dish, blue, 4" to 5" sq. ....13.50 to 32.00
Sauce dish, clear, 4" to 5" sq. 12.00
Sauce dish, clear w/ruby-stained
  buttons, 4" to 5" sq. 20.00
Sauce dish, vaseline, 4" to 5" sq. 16.00
Sauce dish, cloverleaf-shaped, amber ..14.50
Sauce dish, cloverleaf-shaped, clear ...24.00
Sauce dish, octagonal, vaseline........38.00
Sauce dish, tricornered, blue 13.00
Sauce dish, tricornered, vaseline 15.00
Slipper, "1886 patent," clear..........45.00
Slipper, clear w/ruby-stained buttons ..79.00
Smoke bell, amber 65.00
Spooner, amber ....30.00 to 35.00
Spooner, clear......................30.00
Sugar bowl, cov., amber 35.00
Sugar bowl, cov., barrel-shaped, blue ..45.00
Sugar bowl, open, purple 55.00
Toothpick holder (or salt dip),
  "Bandmaster's cap," vaseline........45.00
Toothpick holder, 3-footed, amber 34.50
Toothpick holder, 3-footed,
  Amberina.........................175.00
Toothpick holder, 3-footed, vaseline ...39.50
Toothpick holder, urn-shaped, clear 28.00
Toothpick holder, amber, w/brass rim
  & base............................22.00
Tray, heart-shaped, clear 32.00
Tray, ice cream, handled, clear,
  16½ x 9¼"........................45.00
Tray, water, amber, 11" d. 65.00
Tray, water, triangular, vaseline......62.00
Tumbler, juice, amber 17.00
Tumbler, water, amber 17.00
Tumbler, water, blue 35.00
Tumbler, water, clear 14.50
Tumbler, water, clear w/ruby-
  stained buttons 35.00
Tumbler, water, vaseline 25.00
Tumbler, whiskey, amber.............9.00

Vase, 6" h., hand holding cornu-
copia, blue.......................50.00
Vase, 6" h., hand holding cornu-
copia, clear w/ruby-stained buttons ..58.50
Waste bowl, clear....................30.00
Water set: bulbous pitcher & 2
tumblers; clear, 3 pcs.............185.00
Whimsey, sleigh, amber, 7¾ x 4½" ...115.00
Whimsey, "whisk broom" dish, amber ..37.50
Whimsey, "whisk broom" dish,
vaseline 22.50
Whiskey taster, blue 28.50

DAISY & BUTTON WITH CROSSBARS (Mikado)

Daisy & Button with Crossbars Goblet

Bread tray, clear.....................25.00
Butter dish, cov., clear...............42.00
Cake stand, clear 55.00
Celery vase, amber 36.00
Celery vase, blue 40.00
Celery vase, clear....................27.00
Celery vase, vaseline.................50.00
Compote, open, 6" h., canary yellow ...38.00
Compote, open, 7" d., 4" h., amber.....28.00
Compote, open, 8½" d., 7½" h., blue ..45.00
Creamer, amber ....37.00 to 45.00
Creamer, blue........................42.00
Creamer, clear..............24.00 to 35.00
Creamer, individual size, amber 23.50
Creamer, individual size, blue 30.00
Creamer, individual size, clear 16.00
Creamer & open sugar bowl, amber,
pr.................................70.00
Cruet w/original stopper, clear, 6" h....35.00
Cruet w/original stopper,
vaseline................110.00 to 135.00
Finger bowl, blue 25.00
Goblet, amber ....35.00 to 45.00
Goblet, blue 38.00
Goblet, clear (ILLUS.).................25.00
Goblet, vaseline ....35.00 to 50.00
Mug, amber, 3" h. 12.00
Mug, canary yellow, 3" h..............22.50
Mug, clear, 3" h......................12.50

Pitcher, milk, amber ....40.00 to 45.00
Pitcher, milk, clear...................50.00
Pitcher, water, amber.........70.00 to 85.00
Pitcher, water, clear 65.00
Relish, blue, 8 x 4½" 20.00
Salt shaker w/original top, blue
(single)...........................18.00
Sauce dish, flat or footed, amber.......12.50
Sauce dish, flat or footed, canary
yellow.............................14.50
Sauce dish, footed, vaseline...........22.00
Spooner, clear.......................25.00
Sugar bowl, cov., blue 40.00
Sugar bowl, cov., clear 25.00
Toothpick holder, clear 28.00
Tumbler, amber 20.00
Tumbler, blue 25.00
Tumbler, clear.......................17.50
Tumbler, vaseline....................25.00
Vase, vaseline 45.00
Waste bowl, canary yellow............22.50
Water set: pitcher & 8 tumblers;
amber, 9 pcs......................185.00
Wine, amber 20.00

DAISY & BUTTON WITH NARCISSUS

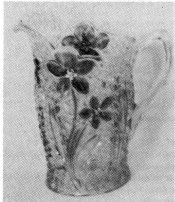

Daisy & Button with Narcissus Pitcher

Bowl, 9½ x 6" oval, footed 45.00
Butter dish, cov...............40.00 to 50.00
Decanter, no stopper 65.00
Goblet 22.50
Nappy, leaf-shaped 65.00
Pitcher, water (ILLUS.)................70.00
Punch cup...........................12.00
Sauce dish, flat or 3-footed ....10.00 to 15.00
Spooner 30.00
Sugar bowl, cov......................38.00
Tray, 10½" d..........................26.00
Tumbler 18.00
Wine 20.00

DAISY & BUTTON WITH THUMBPRINT PANELS
Bowl, berry, cov., 8" d., 8" h., clear
w/amber panels 130.00
Bowl, 8" sq., clear 25.00

Bowl, 9" oval, amber 50.00
Bowl, 11" d., collared base, clear
   w/amber panels 51.50
Butter dish, cov., clear 78.00
Cake basket, clear w/amber
   panels, 11 x 7", 5½" h. . . . .125.00 to 165.00
Celery vase, clear 30.00

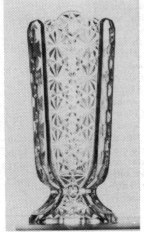

Daisy & Button with Thumbprint Panels

Celery vase, clear w/amber panels
   (ILLUS.) 78.00
Compote, cov., 6¾" d., 10½" h.,
   clear 62.50
Compote, open, 6" d., 6" h., clear 15.00
Creamer, footed, clear 20.50
Cruet w/original stopper, clear 28.00
Dish, triangular, clear, 5" w., 2" h. 10.00
Goblet, clear 27.50
Goblet, clear w/amber panels 65.00
Goblet, clear w/blue
   panels . . . . .45.00 to 50.00
Pitcher, water, applied handle,
   clear w/amber panels 160.00
Sauce dish, flat or footed, clear,
   5" sq. .5.00 to 12.50
Sauce dish, flat or footed, clear
   w/amber panels, 5" sq. . . . . .15.00 to 30.00
Sugar bowl, open, clear w/amber
   panels 36.00
Syrup jug w/original top, amber 125.00
Tumbler, amber .25.00
Tumbler, blue 18.00
Tumbler, clear 22.50
Wine, clear 18.50
Wine, clear w/amber panels 33.50
Wine, clear w/blue panels 40.00

DAISY & BUTTON WITH "V" ORNAMENT

Bowl, 9" d., clear 45.00
Butter dish, cov., blue 80.00
Butter dish, cov., clear 45.00
Celery vase, amber 45.00
Celery vase, canary yellow 65.00
Celery vase, clear 28.00
Creamer, clear 30.00

Dish, cut corners, clear, 9 x 6" 10.00
Finger bowl, blue 45.00
Mug, clear 17.50
Mug, miniature, vaseline 28.00
Pitcher, water, blue 90.00
Pitcher, water, clear 48.00
Pitcher, water, vaseline 59.00
Sauce dish, amber 16.50
Sauce dish, blue .15.00
Sauce dish, clear 10.00
Spooner, amber .37.50
Spooner, blue 36.00
Spooner, clear 20.00
Sugar bowl, cov., blue 49.00
Sugar bowl, open, vaseline 30.00
Toothpick holder, amber 25.00
Toothpick holder, blue 35.00
Toothpick holder, clear 29.00
Toothpick holder, vaseline 35.00
Tumbler, amber .22.00
Tumbler, clear 15.00
Waste bowl, amber 28.50
Waste bowl, clear 22.50

DAKOTA (Baby Thumbprint)

Hotel Size Shaker Bottle

Basket, etched, 10" l., 2" h. 165.00
Butter dish, cov., plain or
   etched . . . . .45.00 to 65.00
Cake stand, plain or etched,
   9¼" d. . . . . .38.00 to 50.00
Cake stand, plain or etched,
   10¼" d. . . . . .45.00 to 60.00
Celery vase, flat base, plain or
   etched . . . . .30.00 to 45.00
Celery vase, pedestal base, plain
   or etched . . . . .40.00 to 50.00
Compote, cov., jelly, 5" d., 5" h.,
   etched 55.00
Compote, cov., 6" d., high stand,
   etched 65.00
Compote, cov., 7" d., 11" h., etched 50.00
Compote, cov., 8" d., 8" h., plain
   or etched 31.50
Compote, cov., 8" d., 12" h., etched 72.50
Compote, open, jelly, 5" d., 5" h.,
   etched 35.00

Compote, open, 6" d., plain or
   etched . . . . .30.00 to 40.00
Compote, open, 7" d., plain or etched . .42.50
Compote, open, 8" d., low stand,
   etched . . . . .32.50 to 38.00
Compote, open, 8" d., 9" h.,
   etched . . . . .55.00 to 70.00
Compote, open, 10" d., etched. 75.00
Creamer, plain or etched . . . . . .35.00 to 50.00
Cruet w/original stopper,
   etched . . . . .50.00 to 75.00
Finger bowl, etched 45.00
Goblet, plain or
   etched . . . . .22.00 to 35.00
Goblet, ruby-stained, plain or etched. . .40.00
Lamp, kerosene-type, plain 140.00
Mug, ruby-stained, souvenir, 3½" h. . . .35.00
Pitcher, water, plain or
   etched . . . . .75.00 to 100.00
Pitcher, water, ruby-stained &
   etched . . . . .125.00 to 190.00
Plate, 10" d., plain or etched 85.00
Salt & pepper shakers w/original
   tops, plain, pr. 90.00
Sauce dish, flat or footed, plain or
   etched . . . . .15.00 to 20.00
Shaker bottle, hotel size, 6½" h.
   (ILLUS.). 45.00
Spooner, plain or etched . . . . . .25.00 to 37.50
Sugar bowl, cov., plain or
   etched . . . . .45.00 to 55.00
Sugar bowl, open, plain or
   etched . . . . .15.00 to 25.00
Sugar bowl, open, breakfast size,
   plain or etched 25.00
Tray, water, piecrust rim, plain
   or etched, 12½" to
   13½" d. . . . . .75.00 to 120.00
Tray, wine, plain or etched 77.50
Tumbler, plain or etched . . . . . .35.00 to 50.00
Tumbler, ruby-stained, plain or
   etched . . . . .35.00 to 40.00
Waste bowl, plain or etched 62.50
Wine, plain or etched . . . . .20.00 to 35.00
Wine, ruby-stained . . . . .35.00 to 45.00

DARBY - See Pleat & Panel Pattern

DART

Compote, cov., 8½" d., high stand 35.00
Compote, open, jelly 17.00
Creamer. 20.00
Goblet 24.00
Sauce dish, footed 8.50
Spooner 20.00
Sugar bowl, cov.. . . . . .32.50
Table set, creamer, spooner &
   cov. sugar bowl, 3 pcs. 85.00

DEER & DOG

Butter dish, cov., pedestal base &
   frosted dog finial, etched 125.00
Celery vase, scalloped rim, 8½" h. 70.00
Compote, open, 8" d.. . . . . .90.00

Creamer. 65.00
Goblet, straight sides . . . . .45.00 to 55.00
Goblet, U-shaped . . . . .65.00 to 95.00
Marmalade jar, no cover. 37.50
Pitcher, milk, 9" h. 165.00
Pitcher, water, applied reeded
   handle 145.00
Sauce dish, footed 22.00
Spooner 45.00
Sugar bowl, cov., frosted dog finial. 98.00

DEER & PINE TREE

Deer & Pine Tree Bread Tray

Bread tray, amber, 13 x 8" . . . . .65.00 to 85.00
Bread tray, apple green, 13 x 8" 78.00
Bread tray, blue, 13 x 8" . . . . . . .58.00 to 75.00
Bread tray, clear, 13 x 8" (ILLUS.). 45.00
Bread tray, vaseline, 13 x 8". 85.00
Butter dish, cov., clear. 90.00
Cake stand, clear . . . . .50.00 to 75.00
Celery vase, clear. 50.00
Compote, cov., 8" sq., 6" h., clear 68.00
Compote, cov., 8" sq., 12" h., clear 100.00
Compote, open, 8" sq., high stand,
   clear 48.00
Creamer, clear .65.00
Finger bowl, clear 55.00
Goblet, clear . . . . .45.00 to 55.00
Mug, child's, amber 45.00
Mug, child's, clear 37.00
Mug, child's, vaseline 55.00
Mug, large, apple green 90.00
Mug, large, clear 40.00
Pitcher, milk, clear. 70.00
Pitcher, water, clear . . . . .85.00 to 95.00
Relish, clear, 8 x 5". 38.00
Sauce dish, flat or footed,
   clear. . . . . .16.00 to 28.00
Spooner, clear. 35.00
Sugar bowl, cov., clear 50.00
Sugar bowl, open, clear 25.00
Tray, water, handled, amber,
   15 x 9". 68.00
Tray, water, handled, apple
   green, 15 x 9" 68.00
Tray, water, handled, clear, 15 x 9" 55.00

DELAWARE (Four Petal Flower)

Banana boat, amethyst w/gold,
   11¾" l.. . . . . .125.00

Delaware Pattern

Banana boat, clear w/gold, 11¾" l. 50.00
Banana boat, green w/gold, 11¾" l. . . .55.00
Banana boat, rose w/gold, 11¾" l. 65.00
Berry set: master bowl & 4 sauce
　　dishes; green w/gold, 5 pcs. 120.00
Bowl, 8" d., amethyst w/gold. 75.00
Bowl, 8" d., green w/gold . . . . .25.00 to 38.00
Bowl, 8" d., rose w/gold. . . . . . .45.00 to 55.00
Bowl, 9" d., clear w/gold 24.50
Bowl, 9" d., green w/gold. 45.00
Bowl, 9" d., rose w/gold 80.00
Bride's basket, boat-shaped open
　　bowl, green, w/silverplate frame,
　　11½" oval 115.00
Bride's basket, boat-shaped, open
　　bowl, rose w/gold, w/silverplate
　　frame, 11½" oval (ILLUS.) 135.00
Bride's basket, boat-shaped open
　　bowl, green w/gold, miniature 200.00
Butter dish, cov., clear. 60.00
Butter dish, cov., green
　　w/gold. . . . . .100.00 to 125.00
Butter dish, cov., rose w/gold
　　(ILLUS.) 125.00
Celery vase, clear w/gold. 37.00
Celery vase, green w/gold 65.00
Celery vase, rose w/gold 65.00
Claret jug, green w/gold. 175.00
Creamer, clear w/gold 35.00
Creamer, green w/gold . . . . . . .55.00 to 65.00
Creamer, rose w/gold (ILLUS.) 60.00
Creamer, individual size, clear
　　w/gold 17.50
Creamer & open sugar bowl, rose
　　w/gold, pr. 125.00
Cruet w/original stopper, clear
　　w/pink florals & gold trim 235.00
Dresser tray, rose w/gold. 65.00
Finger bowl, clear w/gold. 21.50
Marmalade dish w/silverplate holder,
　　amethyst w/gold 45.00
Marmalade dish w/silverplate holder,
　　green w/gold .47.00
Marmalade dish w/silverplate holder,
　　rose w/gold. 45.00

Pin tray, clear, 7 x 3½" 15.00
Pin tray, clear, 9 x 4¾" 17.50
Pin tray, rose w/gold 65.00
Pitcher, milk, green w/gold. . . .55.00 to 86.50
Pitcher, tankard, clear w/cran-
　　berry & green florals & gold trim 110.00
Pitcher, tankard, green w/gold 95.00
Pitcher, tankard, rose w/gold 165.00
Pitcher, water, bulbous, green
　　w/gold 158.00
Pitcher, water, bulbous, rose
　　w/gold (ILLUS.) 125.00
Pomade jar w/jeweled cover, green
　　w/gold 157.00
Pomade jar w/jeweled cover, rose
　　w/gold 215.00
Powder jar, cov., rose w/gold 100.00
Punch cup, clear 15.00
Punch cup, clear w/cranberry florals
　　& gold 28.00
Punch cup, green, souvenir 35.00
Punch cup, green w/gold 25.00
Punch cup, rose w/gold. 35.50
Salt shaker w/original top, rose
　　w/gold (single) 45.00
Sauce dish, boat-shaped, green
　　w/gold 25.00
Sauce dish, boat-shaped, rose
　　w/gold 32.50
Sauce dish, round, green w/gold. 20.00
Sauce dish, round, rose w/gold 25.00
Spooner, clear w/gold. 35.00
Spooner, green w/gold 45.00
Spooner, rose w/gold 55.00
Sugar bowl, cov., clear 65.00
Sugar bowl, cov., rose w/gold
　　(ILLUS.) 100.00
Sugar bowl, open, clear 37.00
Sugar bowl, open, green w/gold 60.00
Sugar bowl, open, rose w/gold 40.00
Sugar bowl, individual size, green 55.00
Table set, green w/gold, 4 pcs. 415.00
Toothpick holder, clear 25.00
Toothpick holder, green w/gold 75.00
Toothpick holder, rose w/gold .85.00 to 95.00
Tumbler, clear. 12.00
Tumbler, green w/gold 30.00
Tumbler, rose w/gold (ILLUS.) 40.00
Vase, 6" h., green w/gold. 39.50
Vase, 6" h., rose w/gold 70.00
Vase, 8" h., green w/gold. 55.00
Vase, 9½" h., green w/gold . . .80.00 to 95.00
Vase, 9½" h., rose w/gold 85.00
Water set: pitcher & 6 tumblers; clear
　　w/gold, 7 pcs. 165.00
Water set: pitcher & 6 tumblers;
　　green w/gold, 7 pcs. 260.00
Water set: pitcher & 6 tumblers;
　　rose w/gold, 7 pcs. 300.00

DEW & RAINDROP
Berry set, master bowl & 6 sauce
　　dishes, 7 pcs. 80.00
Bowl, berry, 8" d. 38.00

Cordial 14.50
Creamer. 30.00
Goblet 35.00
Pitcher, water 65.00
Punch cup. 5.00
Salt shaker w/replaced top (single) 27.50
Sauce dish, flat or footed . . . . . . .8.00 to 14.00
Spooner 26.00
Sugar bowl, cov. 50.00
Table set, cov. butter dish, creamer,
    open sugar bowl & spooner, 4 pcs. . .130.00
Tumbler .12.00 to 20.00
Vase, bud, 6" h. 20.00

Dew & Raindrop Wine

Wine (ILLUS.) 18.00

DEWDROP

Cheese dish, cov., clear 175.00
Cordial, clear 40.00
Creamer, clear .24.00
Creamer & cov. sugar bowl, clear, pr. . .76.00
Egg cup, double, clear 20.00
Goblet, amber .20.50
Goblet, blue 25.00
Goblet, clear 13.50
Mug, applied handle, clear. 19.50
Relish, clear. 15.00
Sauce dish, clear. 7.00
Spooner, clear. 25.00
Sugar bowl, open, clear 50.00
Tumbler, blue .25.00
Tumbler, clear. 14.50
Wine, clear 25.00

DEWDROP WITH STAR

Bowl, 6" d. 6.50
Bowl, 7" d. 14.00
Bowl, 9" d., footed 15.00
Butter dish, cov. 45.00
Cake stand, 9" d. 38.00
Celery vase 40.00
Cheese dish, cov. 80.00
Compote, cov., 5" d. 60.00

Creamer, applied handle 25.00
Plate, 5" d. 12.00
Plate, 8" d. 12.50
Relish, 10" l. 7.50
Salt dip, footed 16.00

Dewdrop with Star Sauce Dish

Sauce dish, flat (ILLUS.) 10.00
Sauce dish, footed 7.50
Sugar bowl, cov. 50.00

DEWEY (Flower Flange)

Dewey Spooner

Bowl, 8" d., amber 30.00
Bowl, 8" d., green. 45.00
Bowl, 8" d., yellow 45.00
Butter dish, cov., amber . . . . . . .65.00 to 75.00
Butter dish, cov., clear. 55.00
Butter dish, cov., green 65.00
Butter dish, cov., yellow 95.00
Butter dish, cov., amber,
    miniature . . . . .60.00 to 75.00
Creamer, amber 35.00
Creamer, clear .30.00
Creamer, green .45.00
Creamer, yellow 55.00
Creamer & cov. sugar bowl, breakfast
    size, vaseline, pr. 95.00
Cruet w/original stopper, amber. 110.00
Cruet w/original stopper, clear 72.50
Cruet w/original stopper, green 145.00

Cruet w/original stopper,
yellow ....95.00 to 125.00
Mug, amber.........................65.00
Mug, clear 25.00
Mug, green 42.50
Mug, yellow.......................55.00
Parfait, green 33.50
Parfait, yellow 50.00
Pitcher, water, clear 60.00
Plate, footed, amber 42.00
Plate, footed, clear 15.00
Plate, footed, green..............45.00
Plate, footed, yellow 55.00
Relish tray, serpentine shape,
amber, small.....................38.50
Relish tray, serpentine shape, clear,
small.............................19.00
Relish tray, serpentine shape, green,
small.............................36.50
Relish tray, serpentine shape, yellow,
small.............................42.50
Relish tray, serpentine shape, yellow,
large.............................55.00
Salt shaker w/original top, green
(single) 45.00
Salt shaker w/original top, yellow
(single) 45.00
Sauce dish, amber 22.00
Sauce dish, yellow 30.00
Spooner, amber (ILLUS.) 60.00
Sugar bowl, cov., clear 25.00
Sugar bowl, cov., green 45.00
Sugar bowl, cov., individual size,
yellow............................65.00
Sugar bowl, open, amber 32.50
Sugar bowl, open, green...........30.00
Table set, amber, 4 pcs. 210.00
Table set, yellow, 4 pcs. 225.00
Tumbler, clear.....................50.00
Tumbler, yellow ....55.00 to 65.00
Water set: pitcher & 6 tumblers;
yellow, 7 pcs. 225.00

DIAGONAL BAND

Diagonal Band Goblet

Berry set, master bowl & 5 sauce
dishes, 6 pcs......................48.00
Bread plate, "Eureka," 13 x 7½ " 40.00
Butter dish, cov. 35.00
Celery vase 22.50
Compote, cov., 7½" d., 9¼" h. 45.00
Compote, open, 7½" d., high stand 16.50
Creamer...........................22.50
Goblet (ILLUS.) ....15.00 to 25.00
Pitcher, milk 32.00
Pitcher, water 37.50
Plate, 8" d........................10.50
Relish, 6 7/8" oval 7.50
Salt & pepper shakers w/original tops,
pr................................30.00
Sauce dish, flat or footed ....5.50 to 9.00
Spooner 22.50
Sugar bowl, open 14.50
Wine 22.50

DIAGONAL BAND & FAN

Diagonal Band & Fan Relish

Butter dish, cov. 40.00
Goblet 17.50
Plate, 6" d.........................6.00
Plate, 8" d........................10.00
Relish, 8" oval (ILLUS.)...............15.00
Spooner 22.50
Wine 17.50

**DIAMOND AND BULL'S EYE BAND - See
Reverse Torpedo Pattern**

DIAMOND & SUNBURST

Diamond & Sunburst Goblet

Celery vase 35.00
Compote, cov., 7" d., high stand 45.00
Compote, open, jelly 15.00
Goblet (ILLUS.) 22.00
Salt dip, master size.................20.00
Spooner 21.50
Sugar bowl, open 25.00
Sugar shaker.......................22.00
Syrup jug w/original top, applied
    handle 45.00
Wine 20.00

DIAMOND BAR - See Lattice Pattern

DIAMOND HORSESHOE - See Aurora Pattern

DIAMOND MEDALLION (Finecut & Diamond or Grand)

Diamond Medallion Creamer

Bowl, 9 x 6¼" oval 10.50
Bread plate, 10" d. 21.50
Butter dish, cov. 35.00
Cake stand, 9" d. 25.00
Cake stand, 10" d. 35.00
Celery vase 22.50
Compote, cov., 7" d., high stand 36.00
Compote, open, 6" d., 6" h. 19.50
Compote, open, 8" d., 6" h. 19.50
Creamer, footed (ILLUS.)............24.50
Goblet 25.00
Pitcher, water 48.00
Relish, 7½" oval 8.00
Salt & pepper shakers w/original tops,
    pr..............................35.00
Sauce dish, flat or footed ....5.00 to 9.00
Spooner 20.00
Sugar bowl, cov. ....25.00 to 35.00
Sugar bowl, open 15.00
Wine 28.00

DIAMOND POINT
Bar bottle, flint 55.00

Bowl, 6" d..................20.00 to 25.00
Butter dish, cov., flint 95.00
Castor set, 6-bottle, w/silverplate
    frame 165.00
Celery vase, pedestal base w/knob
    stem, flint 70.00
Champagne, flint 65.00
Claret, flint 65.00
Compote, open, 7" d., 7" h., non-flint...37.50
Compote, open, 7½" d., low stand,
    non-flint.........................25.00
Creamer, applied handle, flint........130.00
Decanter w/original stopper, qt........87.50
Egg cup, clear, flint 40.00
Egg cup, clambroth, flint 115.00

Diamond Point Goblet

Goblet, flint (ILLUS.).................60.00
Goblet, non-flint.....................13.50
Honey dish, flint 18.00
Mug, non-flint 11.00
Pitcher, tankard, applied handle, qt. ..180.00
Plate, 6" d..........................16.00
Salt dip, cov., master size 27.50
Sauce dish, 3½" to 5½" d. ......6.00 to 12.50
Spillholder, flint 55.00
Spooner, flint ....40.00 to 55.00
Sugar bowl, cov., flint 65.00
Tumbler, flint 50.00
Tumbler, bar, flint 65.00
Tumbler, whiskey, handled, flint, 3" h. .65.00
Wine, flint 52.50
Wine, non-flint 16.50

DIAMOND POINT WITH PANELS - See Hinoto Pattern

DIAMOND QUILTED
Bowl, 6" d., amber 10.00
Bowl, 6" d., footed, amethyst.........20.00
Bowl, 7" d., amber 19.00
Bowl, 8" d., amber 50.00
Bowl, 8" d., vaseline 20.00
Bowl, 9" d., vaseline 22.50
Butter dish, cov., amber ....42.00 to 50.00
Celery vase, amber 37.50

Celery vase, blue 42.50
Celery vase, vaseline. 39.00
Champagne, amethyst 36.00
Champagne, clear 21.00
Compote, cov., 8" d., 13" h.,
    amber. 115.00

Diamond Quilted Compote

Compote, open, 6" d., 6" h., amber
    (ILLUS.) 35.00
Compote, open, 9" d., low stand,
    vaseline 32.00
Creamer, amethyst 40.00
Goblet, amber .26.50
Goblet, amethyst 37.50
Goblet, blue 38.00
Goblet, turquoise blue 40.00
Goblet, vaseline. 40.00
Mug, amethyst .30.00
Pitcher, water, blue 80.00
Sauce dish, flat or footed, amber,
    4" to 5" d. 10.00
Sauce dish, flat or footed, amethyst,
    4" to 5" d. . . . . .11.00 to 20.00
Sauce dish, flat or footed, turquoise
    blue, 4" to 5" d. . . . . .9.50 to 15.00
Sauce dish, flat or footed, vaseline,
    4" to 5" d. . . . . .11.00 to 20.00
Spooner, amber 30.00
Spooner, turquoise blue 40.00
Sugar bowl, cov., blue. 47.50
Sugar bowl, cov., vaseline 45.00
Sugar bowl, open, vaseline 28.00
Table set: cov. butter dish, cov.
    sugar bowl & spooner; vaseline,
    3 pcs. 175.00
Tumbler, amber 45.00
Tumbler, amethyst. 40.00
Tumbler, vaseline . . . . .25.00 to 35.00
Wine, amber 25.00
Wine, amethyst. 48.00
Wine, blue 38.00
Wine, clear 15.00
Wine, vaseline 21.00

DIAMOND THUMBPRINT
Bowl, 8" d., footed, scalloped rim 60.00
Butter dish, cov. 200.00
Cake stand, 12" d. 195.00

Carafe 115.00
Celery vase 168.00
Champagne. 295.00
Compote, open, 7" d., 4½" h.,
    extended scalloped rim 75.00
Compote, open, 8" d., 6" h. 82.50
Compote, open, 10½" d., 7½" h. 288.00
Creamer, applied handle 145.00
Cup plate 50.00
Goblet 325.00

Diamond Thumbprint Pitcher

Pitcher, water (ILLUS.) 425.00
Spillholder, clear 40.00
Spillholder, vaseline 875.00
Spooner 85.00
Sugar bowl, cov.. . . . . .125.00
Tumbler 95.00
Tumbler, bar, 3¾" h. 75.00
Tumbler, whiskey, handled 300.00
Wine 245.00

DINNER BELL - See Cottage Pattern

DORIC - See Indiana Pattern

DOUBLE LOOP - See Ribbon Candy Pattern

DOUBLE WEDDING RING

Double Wedding Ring Footed Tumbler

Champagne 52.50
Cruet, applied handle 110.00
Goblet 37.50
Lamp, kerosene, hand-type w/flat
　base, applied handle 80.00
Syrup pitcher w/original top, 6" h. 48.00
Tumbler, bar 90.00
Tumbler, footed (ILLUS.) 80.00
Wine 42.00

DRAPERY

Drapery Buttermilk Goblet

Butter dish, cov. 40.00
Cake plate, sq., footed . . . . . . .40.00 to 45.00
Creamer, applied handle 37.50
Egg cup 19.50
Goblet 26.50
Goblet, buttermilk (ILLUS.) 20.00
Plate, 6" d. 19.00
Sauce dish, flat .10.00
Spooner 28.50
Sugar bowl, cov. 42.00
Sugar bowl, open 18.00
Tumbler 27.00

EGG IN SAND

Egg in Sand Goblet

Bread tray, handled,
　clear . . . . .25.00 to 37.50

Butter dish, cov., clear. 48.00
Creamer, clear 25.00
Goblet, amber 45.00
Goblet, blue 40.00
Goblet, clear (ILLUS.) 30.00
Pitcher, milk, clear 45.00
Pitcher, water, clear 50.00
Relish, clear, 9 x 5½" 17.00
Sauce dish, clear 15.00
Spooner, amber .55.00
Spooner, clear. 25.00
Sugar bowl, cov., amber 65.00
Sugar bowl, cov., clear 40.00
Tray, water, clear, 12½" oblong 38.50
Tumbler, clear. 36.00

EGYPTIAN

Egyptian Sauce Dish

Berry set, master bowl & 5 sauce
　dishes, 6 pcs. 150.00
Bowl, 8½" d. 48.00
Bread platter, Cleopatra center,
　12 x 9". 50.00
Bread platter, Salt Lake Temple
　center 295.00
Butter dish, cov. 67.50
Celery vase 65.00
Compote, cov., 6" d., 6" h.,
　sphinx base .135.00
Compote, cov., 8" d., high stand,
　sphinx base .225.00
Compote, open, 6" d., low stand 45.00
Compote, open, 7½" d., sphinx base . . .70.00
Creamer 35.00
Goblet 50.00
Pickle dish, 8½ x 4½" oval 20.00
Pitcher, water 175.00
Plate, 10" d. 55.00
Relish, 8½ x 5½" 20.00
Sauce dish, flat 9.00
Sauce dish, footed (ILLUS.) 16.50
Spooner 35.00
Sugar bowl, cov. 67.50
Sugar bowl, open 30.00
Table set, 4 pcs. 235.00

**EMERALD GREEN HERRINGBONE - See
Paneled Herringbone Pattern**

EMPIRE COLONIAL - See Colonial Pattern

ENGLISH HOBNAIL CROSS - See Amberette Pattern

ESTHER

Esther Sauce Dish

Berry set: master bowl & 8 sauce
   dishes; green, 9 pcs. 245.00
Bowl, 9" d., footed, green. 24.50
Butter dish, cov., clear. 70.00
Butter dish, cov., clear w/amber stain
   & etching 110.00
Butter dish, cov., green 135.00
Celery vase, clear. 70.00
Celery vase, green. 135.00
Compote, cov., high stand, clear 80.00
Compote, open, jelly, green 55.00
Compote, open, 4" d., clear w/amber
   stain 60.00
Compote, open, 5" d., 6½" h., clear 65.00
Compote, open, 5" d., 6½" h., green . . .60.00
Creamer, clear .70.00
Creamer, green 135.00
Cruet w/ball-shaped stopper, green. . .190.00
Cruet w/original stopper, green,
   miniature. 90.00
Goblet, green 90.00
Pitcher, water, clear w/amber stain . . .250.00
Plate, 12" d., footed, scalloped rim,
   clear 65.00
Salt & pepper shakers w/original
   tops, green, pr.. . . . . .98.00
Sauce dish, clear (ILLUS.) 18.50
Sauce dish, green 35.00
Spooner, clear. .42.00
Spooner, green .52.50
Sugar bowl, cov., clear 40.00
Sugar bowl, cov., clear w/amber
   stain & etching 80.00
Sugar bowl, cov., green 68.50
Syrup jug w/original spring lid, clear
   w/amber stain & etching. 360.00
Toothpick holder, clear 40.00
Toothpick holder, clear w/amber
   stain & etching 72.50
Toothpick holder, green 90.00
Tray, ice cream, green. 150.00
Tumbler, clear. .30.00
Tumbler, green .55.00
Wine, clear 32.50
Wine, clear w/ruby stain & etching 43.00

EUREKA

Bowl, 9½" d.. . . . . .30.00
Bread tray 32.50
Compote, open, jelly 55.00
Creamer. 45.00
Egg cup 19.00
Goblet, plain or etched 26.50
Salt dip, master size. 24.50
Spooner 40.00
Sugar bowl, cov.. . . . . .55.00
Sugar bowl, open 29.50
Toothpick holder. 35.00
Tumbler, footed 25.00
Wine. 25.00

EXCELSIOR

Excelsior Goblet

Bar bottle, pt. .34.50
Butter dish, cov. 100.00
Candlestick, flint 96.00
Celery vase 65.00
Creamer. 60.00
Egg cup. 26.00
Egg cup, double 55.00
Egg cup, double, opalescent, flint 225.00
Flip glass, 8" h. 200.00
Goblet, "Barrel" 42.50
Goblet, flint (ILLUS.). 50.00
Lamp, hand-type, applied finger
   loop handle .95.00
Mug. 30.00
Pitcher, water, flint 325.00
Salt dip, master size. 18.50
Spillholder, flint 75.00
Spooner 35.00
Sugar bowl, cov.. . . . . .80.00
Syrup pitcher w/applied handle. 110.00
Syrup pitcher w/original top, green . . .750.00
Tumbler, bar, flint, 3½" h. 60.00
Tumbler, footed, flint. 47.50
Wine, flint . . . . .35.00 to 55.00

EYEWINKER

Banana boat, flat, 8½" l.. . . . . .85.00

Bowl, open, master berry or fruit,
  9" d., 4½" h. 42.50
Butter dish, cov. 65.00
Cake stand, 8½" to 9½" d. ....50.00 to 75.00
Compote, cov., 6½" d., 11" h. 52.50
Compote, open, 4" d., 5" h., scalloped
  rim 31.50
Compote, open, 6½" sq., 8½" h.......70.00
Compote, open, 7½" d., 4½" h. 45.00
Compote, open, 9½" d., 6½" h. 90.00
Creamer...............................42.50
Lamp, kerosene-type, w/original
  burner, 9½" h. 82.50
Pitcher, milk.........................85.00
Plate, 7" d., 1½" h., turned-up
  sides 27.50
Plate, 9" sq., 2" h., turned-up
  sides 37.50
Plate, 10" sq., 2" h., turned-up
  sides 65.00

Eyewinker Salt Shaker

Salt shaker w/original top (ILLUS.) 25.50
Sauce dish, square 13.50
Spooner 35.00
Sugar bowl, cov.......................60.00

FEATHER (Indiana Swirl or Finecut & Feather)

Feather Sugar Bowl

Banana boat, footed, clear 75.00
Bowl, 6½" d., clear 12.50
Bowl, 9¼" oval, flat, clear 16.00
Butter dish, cov., clear...............45.00
Butter dish, cov., green 125.00
Cake stand, clear, 8" d...............35.00
Cake stand, clear, 9½" d. 37.50
Cake stand, green, 9½" d. 125.00
Cake stand, clear, 11" d..............45.00
Celery vase, clear....................35.00
Compote, cov., 7" d., 10½" h., clear....85.00
Compote, cov., 8½" d., 12" h., clear...125.00
Compote, open, jelly, 5" d., clear 20.00
Compote, open, 8" d., clear 40.00
Cordial, clear, 3" h. 70.00
Creamer, clear 28.00
Creamer, green 65.00
Creamer & open sugar bowl, clear, pr...40.00
Cruet w/original stopper, clear 37.00
Cruet w/original stopper, green 185.00
Goblet, clear........................52.50
Honey dish, clear, 3½" d........9.00 to 15.00
Pitcher, milk, clear..................38.50
Pitcher, water, plain rim, clear 47.50
Pitcher, water, green...............190.00
Plate, 10" d., clear 35.00
Relish, clear, 8¼" oval 18.00
Relish, clear w/amber staining,
  8¼" oval 45.00
Salt & pepper shakers w/original tops,
  clear, pr. 45.00
Sauce dish, flat or footed, clear..9.50 to 14.00
Spooner, clear.......................22.50
Spooner, clear w/amber staining 40.00
Spooner, green 60.00
Sugar bowl, cov., clear (ILLUS.) 37.50
Sugar bowl, cov., child's, clear........15.00
Sugar bowl, open, clear, large........20.00
Syrup pitcher w/original top, clear 100.00
Table set, clear, 4 pcs...............125.00
Toothpick holder, clear 50.00
Tumbler, clear.......................50.00
Tumbler, green 75.00
Wine, clear 35.00
Wine, clear w/ruby staining 40.00

FESTOON

Festoon Cake Stand

Berry set, 9½" d. master bowl & 6
  sauce dishes, 7 pcs. 70.00
Bowl, berry, 7 x 4½" rectangle 25.00
Bowl, berry, 8" rectangle 27.00
Bowl, berry, 9 x 5½" rectangle 30.00
Butter dish, cov. 55.00
Cake stand, high stand, 9" d. (ILLUS.) . . .40.00
Creamer 22.50
Finger bowl, 4½" d., 2" h. 30.00
Marmalade jar, cov. 28.00
Pickle castor, silverplate frame & cover
  w/bird finial .87.50
Pitcher, water .47.50
Plate, 7½" d. 27.50
Plate, 9¼" d. 30.00
Relish, 7 x 4" 13.50
Relish, 9 x 5½" .40.00
Sauce dish 6.50
Spooner . . . . .22.50 to 35.00
Sugar bowl, cov. 45.00
Sugar bowl, open 15.00
Table set, 4 pcs. 185.00
Tray, water, 10" d. 32.50
Tumbler 20.00
Water set, pitcher, tray & 6 tumblers,
  8 pcs. 225.00

Pitcher, water, amber 95.00
Pitcher, water, blue 80.00
Pitcher, water, vaseline 55.00
Plate, 6" d., blue. 20.00
Plate, 6" d., clear 8.00
Plate, 7" d., amber 15.00
Plate, 7" d., clear 13.50
Plate, 7" d., vaseline 20.00
Relish, boat-shaped, clear, 10½" l. 18.00
Salt & pepper shakers w/original tops,
  clear, pr. (ILLUS.) 25.00
Spooner, clear. .17.00
Spooner, vaseline 38.00
Sugar bowl, cov., clear 35.00
Toothpick holder, hat shape on plate,
  vaseline 35.00
Tray, ice cream, lion's head handles,
  amber. 40.00
Tray, water, clear. 22.50
Tumbler, clear. .13.50
Tumbler, vaseline. 28.00
Waste bowl, vaseline. 32.50
Whimsey, shoe on skate, amber 30.00
Whimsey, slipper, amber, 4" l. 30.00
Whimsey, slipper, blue, 4" l. 30.00
Wine, clear 13.00

FINECUT

Finecut Salt & Pepper Shakers

Bowl, 8¼ x 5 1/8", flat, clear 12.00
Bowl, master berry, clear, w/silver-
  plate stand & spoon 95.00
Bread tray, amber 40.00
Butter dish, cov., clear. 45.00
Cake stand, clear 30.00
Celery vase, footed, 2-handled, clear . . .25.00
Celery vase, vaseline, ornate sq. base
  silverplate holder 115.00
Compote, cov., 9¼" d., 7" h., amber . .135.00
Compote, open, 9" d., lattice rim,
  clear 135.00
Creamer, blue. .40.00
Creamer, clear .16.00
Goblet, amber .45.00
Goblet, blue 55.00
Goblet, clear. 20.00
Goblet, vaseline 42.00
Pickle dish, clear, 9 x 6" 12.00

FINECUT & BLOCK

Finecut & Block Celery Tray

Bowl, fruit, 9" d., collared base, clear . .35.00
Butter dish, cov., 2-handled, clear. 75.00
Cake stand, clear 35.00
Celery tray, clear, 11" l. 27.50
Celery tray, clear w/blue blocks,
  11" l. 45.00
Celery tray, clear w/pink blocks, 11" l.
  (ILLUS.) 60.00
Compote, open, jelly, all blue 50.00
Compote, open, jelly, clear 18.00
Compote, open, jelly, clear w/amber
  blocks 75.00
Compote, open, 7¾" d., clear w/blue
  blocks 65.00
Compote, open, 8½" d., 6½" h., clear . .35.00
Cordial, clear 85.00
Creamer, clear .32.00
Creamer, clear w/amber blocks 67.00
Creamer, clear w/blue blocks . .48.00 to 65.00
Creamer, clear w/pink blocks 65.00
Creamer, clear w/yellow blocks 76.50
Egg cup, single, clear. 30.00
Goblet, clear. 35.00
Goblet, clear w/amber blocks 53.50
Goblet, clear w/blue blocks 65.00
Goblet, clear w/pink blocks 57.50
Goblet, buttermilk, clear . . . . . .25.00 to 35.00

Goblet, buttermilk, clear w/blue
   blocks 52.00
Goblet, buttermilk, clear w/pink
   blocks 85.00
Goblet, buttermilk, clear w/yellow
   blocks 60.00
Goblet, lady's, clear 42.50
Ice cream tray, clear w/amber blocks .. 85.00
Ice cream tray, clear w/yellow blocks .. 75.00
Pitcher, water, all amber 85.00
Pitcher, water, clear 42.50
Pitcher, water, clear w/amber blocks .. 85.00
Pitcher, water, clear w/blue blocks 90.00
Pitcher, water, clear w/pink blocks ... 125.00
Plate, 5¾" d., clear 23.50
Punch cup, clear 12.00
Relish, handled, clear w/amber blocks,
   7½" 55.00
Relish, handled, clear w/blue blocks,
   7½" 50.00
Sauce dish, all amber 18.50
Sauce dish, all blue 14.50
Sauce dish, clear 9.50
Sauce dish, clear w/amber blocks 16.00
Sauce dish, clear w/yellow blocks 17.50
Spooner, clear 30.00
Spooner, clear w/blue blocks 55.00
Sugar bowl, cov., clear w/yellow
   blocks 125.00
Sugar bowl, open, clear w/blue
   blocks 35.00
Table set, clear w/yellow blocks,
   4 pcs. 265.00
Tumbler, clear 17.50
Tumbler, clear w/pink blocks 40.00
Tumbler, clear w/yellow blocks 50.00
Waste bowl, all amber 45.00
Wine, clear 30.00
Wine, clear w/blue blocks 45.00

FINECUT & DIAMOND - See Diamond Medallion Pattern

FINECUT & FEATHER - See Feather Pattern

FINECUT & PANEL (Paneled Finecut)

Finecut & Panel Plate

Bowl, 8" oval, clear 18.00
Bread tray, amber, 13 x 9" 50.00
Bread tray, blue, 13 x 9" 45.00
Bread tray, clear, 13 x 9" 30.00
Butter dish, cov., amber 45.00
Celery vase, clear 17.50
Compote, open, high stand, amber 50.00
Compote, open, high stand, clear 32.00
Creamer, amber 35.00
Goblet, clear 21.50
Goblet, clear w/amber bars ... 35.00 to 50.00
Pitcher, milk, vaseline 50.00
Pitcher, water, amber 85.00
Plate, 6" d., amber (ILLUS.) 25.00
Plate, 6" d., blue 30.00
Plate, 6" d., vaseline 20.00
Plate, 7" d., clear 12.00
Salt shaker w/original top, clear
   (single) 10.00
Sauce dish, amber 7.50
Sauce dish, vaseline 13.50
Spooner, vaseline 30.00
Tray, water, blue 55.00
Tumbler, clear 18.00
Tumbler, vaseline 38.00
Wine, amber 30.00
Wine, blue 35.00
Wine, clear 17.50
Wine, vaseline 35.00
Wine set: decanter & 4 wines; vaseline,
   5 pcs. 185.00

FINECUT BAND - See Cottage Pattern

FINE RIB
Butter dish, cov. 75.00
Castor set, complete w/frame 190.00
Celery vase, flint 42.00
Champagne, flint 65.00
Compote, open, 7¾" d., 7" h., flint 50.00
Creamer, flint 125.00
Egg cup, flint 37.50
Goblet, flint 50.00
Goblet, non-flint 22.00
Honey dish, flint, 3½" d. 16.00
Pitcher, water, bulbous, applied
   handle, flint 350.00
Salt dip, individual size, flint 14.00
Salt dip, master size, footed, scal-
   loped rim, flint 22.50
Spoonholder, flint 52.50
Sugar bowl, cov. 75.00
Sugar bowl, open, non-flint 29.00
Tumbler, flint 65.00
Tumbler, whiskey, non-flint 18.00
Wine, flint 42.50
Wine, cut ovals, flint 98.00

FISHSCALE
Berry set, 8½" d. master bowl & 8
   sauce dishes, 9 pcs. (ILLUS.) 85.00
Bowl, cov., 9½" d. 42.50
Bowl, 7½" d. 16.00
Bowl, 8½" d. 22.00

Fishscale Pattern

Bread platter 26.00
Butter dish, cov. 35.00
Cake stand, 8" d. 36.00
Cake stand, 9" d. (ILLUS.) 30.00
Candy dish, 4½" d. 20.00
Celery vase 30.00
Compote, open, jelly 16.00
Compote, open, 8" d., high stand 26.00
Compote, open, 9" d., high stand 46.00
Condiment tray, rectangular 35.00
Creamer . . . . .25.00 to 35.00
Goblet 30.00
Lamp, hand-type w/finger grip 65.00
Mug. 30.00
Pickle dish 17.00
Pitcher, milk 30.00
Pitcher, water (ILLUS.) 42.50
Plate, 7" d. 15.00
Plate, 8" d. 26.00
Plate, 9" sq. 32.50
Salt shaker w/original top (single) 27.50
Sauce dish, flat or footed,
   4" sq. . . . . 6.50 to 15.00
Spooner 20.00
Sugar bowl, cov. 42.50
Tumbler 45.00

FLORIDA - See Paneled Herringbone Pattern

FLORIDA PALM

Florida Palm Creamer

Celery vase 18.00
Compote, cov., 7" d., high stand 35.00
Compote, open, 9" d. 35.00

Creamer (ILLUS.) 20.00
Goblet 17.50
Relish 12.00
Spooner 20.00
Sugar bowl, cov. 35.00
Tumbler, footed 18.00
Wine 21.50

FLOWER FLANGE - See Dewey Pattern

FLOWER POT (Potted Plant)

Flower Pot Sugar & Creamer

Bread tray 47.50
Butter dish, cov. 37.50
Cake stand, 10½" d. 45.00
Creamer (ILLUS.) 30.00
Goblet 40.00
Pitcher, milk 40.00
Pitcher, water 55.00
Salt shaker w/original top (single) 20.00
Sauce dish 9.00
Sugar bowl, cov. (ILLUS.) 40.00
Spooner 22.00

FLUTE

Flute Pattern Decanter

Ale glass 50.00
Celery vase 80.00
Claret 22.00
Compote, open, 9½" d., 3½" h. 35.00

Decanter w/bar lip & original pewter-
  rimmed glass stopper, amethyst, flint
  (ILLUS.) 600.00
Egg cup, double 28.00
Egg cup, handled 30.00
Goblet, Bessimer 24.00
Goblet, Brooklyn 35.00
Goblet, Connecticut or New England ...19.00
Goblet 29.00
Sugar bowl, open 35.00
Toothpick holder....................18.00
Tumbler, amethyst, 10 panels 100.00
Tumbler, clear, 3½" h...............16.00
Tumbler, whiskey, handled, clear.....28.00
Wine, New England 21.50
Wine, Pittsburgh, flint 45.00

FLYING ROBIN - See Hummingbird Pattern

FOUR PETAL

Four Petal Sugar Bowl

Creamer & cov. sugar bowl, pr. 135.00
Sugar bowl, cov. (ILLUS.).............57.50
Sugar bowl, open 35.00

FOUR PETAL FLOWER - See Delaware Pattern

FROSTED CIRCLE

Frosted Circle Compote

Bowl, 8" d., 3¼" h. 25.00
Butter dish, cov. 47.50
Cake stand, 9½" d. 40.00
Compote, cov., 5" d., 9" h. 43.50
Compote, open, 7" d., 6" h. 20.50
Compote, open, 9" d., 6" h. 40.00
Compote, open, 10" d., high stand,
  scalloped rim (ILLUS.) 55.00
Creamer...........................31.50
Goblet 35.00
Pitcher, water, tankard 65.00
Plate, 9" d........................22.00
Punch cup.........................15.00
Salt & pepper shakers w/original tops,
  pr...............................47.50
Sauce dish 8.50
Spooner 28.50
Sugar bowl, cov....................42.50
Sugar shaker w/original top..........40.00
Syrup pitcher w/original top..........85.00
Tumbler 30.00
Wine 35.00

FROSTED LEAF
Celery vase 145.00
Creamer...........................395.00
Egg cup...........................90.00
Goblet 82.50
Salt dip 50.00
Sauce dish 22.50

FROSTED LION (Rampant Lion)

Frosted Lion Celery Vase

Bowl, cov., 6 7/8 x 3 7/8" oblong,
  collared base......................110.00
Bowl, cov., 7 7/16 x 4 5/8" oblong,
  collared base......................110.00
Bowl, cov., 8 7/8 x 5½" oblong,
  collared base......................125.00
Bread plate, rope edge, close han-
  dles, 10½" d.......................62.50
Butter dish, cov., rampant lion finial....95.00
Celery vase, etched 110.00

Celery vase, plain (ILLUS.) 72.50
Cheese dish, cov., rampant lion finial. .298.00
Compote, cov., 6¾" oval, 7" h.,
  collared base, rampant lion finial . . .130.00
Compote, cov., 7" d., 11" h., lion
  head finial 95.00
Compote, cov., 7¾" oval, rampant
  lion finial 125.00
Compote, cov., 8" d., 13" h., rampant
  lion finial 137.50
Compote, cov., 8½ x 7¾" oval, col-
  lared base, rampant lion finial 80.00
Compote, open, 7¾" d., high stand 75.00
Compote, open, 8" oblong, low stand . . .96.50
Compote, open, 9" oblong, 9" h. 80.00
Creamer 62.50
Egg cup 72.50
Goblet 62.50
Marmalade jar, cov., rampant lion
  finial. .85.00 to 95.00
Paperweight, embossed "Gillinder &
  Sons, Centennial" 110.00
Pitcher, water. . . . . .195.00 to 225.00
Platter, 10½ x 9" oval, lion handles 80.00
Relish . . . . .35.00 to 45.00
Salt dip, master size, collared base,
  rectangular 250.00
Sauce dish, 4" to 5" d. . . . . .20.00 to 26.00
Spooner, plain or etched 60.00
Sugar bowl, cov., rampant lion finial . . .77.50
Sugar bowl, open 43.00
Table set, 4 pcs. 225.00
Wine, 4 1/8" h. . . . . .125.00 to 150.00

FROSTED RIBBON
Bowl, low 22.00
Bread platter 42.00
Butter dish, cov. .40.00
Celery vase 40.00
Cologne bottle w/stopper. 45.00
Compote, cov., 6½" d. 61.50
Compote, cov., 8" d., 11" h. 85.00
Compote, open, 8" d., low stand 60.00
Compote, open, 10" d., 9½" h.,
  etched 42.50
Creamer 35.00
Creamer & cov. sugar bowl, pr. 125.00
Goblet 27.50
Pitcher, water 62.50
Sauce dish 9.50
Spooner 29.50
Sugar bowl, cov. .50.00
Waste bowl, 4½" d., 3½" h. 45.00
Wine 65.00

FROSTED ROMAN KEY (With Flutes or Ribs)
Bowl, 9¾" d., 3½" h. 42.50
Butter dish, cov. .55.00
Celery vase 67.50
Champagne 55.00
Compote, cov., 7" d. 75.00
Compote, open, 9" d., 8" h. 60.00
Creamer, applied handle (ILLUS.) 56.00
Goblet (ILLUS.) . . . . .30.00 to 37.50

Frosted Roman Key Pattern

Goblet, buttermilk 42.50
Salt dip, master size 32.00
Sauce dish, 4" d. .14.00
Spooner . . . . .25.00 to 36.00
Sugar bowl, cov. .90.00
Sugar bowl, open 26.00
Tumbler, bar 85.00
Tumbler, footed .45.00
Wine 55.00

FROSTED STORK
Bowl, 9" oval, 101 border 50.00
Bread plate, round. . . . . .45.00 to 70.00
Butter dish, cov. .70.00
Creamer 60.00
Finger bowl 90.00
Goblet .55.00 to 60.00
Platter, 12 x 8" oval . . . . .40.00 to 48.00
Platter, deer & doe border 75.00
Relish, 101 border 58.00
Spooner 45.00
Sugar bowl, cov., stork finial 95.00
Sugar bowl, open 25.00
Tray, water, 15½ x 11" 125.00
Waste bowl 42.50

FROSTED WAFFLE - See Hidalgo Pattern

GALLOWAY (Virginia)
Berry set: master bowl & 6 sauce
  dishes; ruby-stained, 7 pcs. 135.00
Bowl, 6½" d. 11.50
Bowl, 9¾" d., flat 35.00
Bowl, ice cream, 11" d., 3½" h. 45.00
Butter dish, cov. .50.00
Butter dish, cov., ruby-stained 110.00
Cake stand, 9¼" d., 6" h. 60.00
Carafe 55.00
Celery vase 20.00
Celery vase, ruby-stained 75.00
Champagne 35.00
Compote, open, 4¼" d., 6" h. 30.00
Compote, open, 10" d., 8" h., scal-
  loped rim 55.00
Creamer 25.00
Creamer, individual size 12.50
Creamer & cov. sugar bowl, etched,
  pr. 95.00

Cruet w/stopper 35.00
Dish, 7" l. 17.00
Finger bowl, 4½" d., 3" h. 37.50
Goblet 70.00
Mug, 4½" d. 36.00
Nappy, handled, gold rim, 5" d. 16.00
Olive dish, ruby-stained, 6 x 4" 30.00
Pitcher, milk 40.00
Pitcher, lemonade, applied handle 75.00
Pitcher, water, 9" h. 62.50
Pitcher, water, ruby-stained. 125.00
Pitcher, child's. 19.00
Pitcher, child's, ruby-stained 85.00
Plate, 8" d. 20.00
Punch bowl 158.00
Punch cup. 9.50
Relish, 8¼" l. 18.00
Relish, ruby-stained 29.50
Salt dip, master size, scalloped rim,
    2" d. 24.00
Salt & pepper shakers w/original tops,
    gold trim, 3" h., pr. 30.00
Sauce dish, flat or footed . . . . . . .8.50 to 15.00
Spooner 30.00
Sugar bowl, cov. .52.50
Sugar shaker w/original top. 37.50
Syrup pitcher w/metal spring top 57.50
Toothpick holder. 28.50
Tumbler 22.50
Vase, 9½" h. 15.00
Vase, 12" h. 18.00
Vase, 14" h. 22.50
Waste bowl 25.00
Water set, child's, pitcher & 4 tumb-
    lers, 5 pcs. 50.00
Wine. 45.00

GARFIELD DRAPE

Garfield Drape Goblet

Bread plate, "We Mourn Our Nation's
    Loss," 11½" d. .52.50
Butter dish, cov. .59.00
Cake stand, 9½" d. 47.50
Celery vase, pedestal base. 35.00
Compote, cov., 6" d., low stand 60.00
Compote, cov., 8" d., 12½" h. 100.00

Compote, open, 8½" d., 6" h. 37.00
Creamer. 30.00
Goblet (ILLUS.) 35.00
Honey dish, 3½" .14.00
Lamp, kerosene-type, cobalt blue,
    9" h. 150.00
Pitcher, milk 55.00
Pitcher, water 75.00
Plate, 10" d. 60.00
Sauce dish, flat or footed 8.50
Spooner 22.50
Sugar bowl, cov. .60.00
Tumbler 30.00

GEORGIA - See Peacock Feather Pattern

GOBLETS WITH BIRDS & ANIMALS

Bear climber, etched 65.00
Deer & Doe, pressed 92.50
Giraffe, etched 75.00
Ibex, etched 75.00
Lion in the Jungle, etched 35.00
Ostrich Looking At Moon, pressed 76.50
Owl-Possum, pressed 68.50
Pigs in Corn, pressed 285.00
Squirrel, pressed 350.00
Stork & flowers, etched 62.50
Tiger, etched. 50.00

GODDESS OF LIBERTY - See Ceres Pattern

GOOD LUCK - See Horseshoe Pattern

GOOSEBERRY

Gooseberry Compote

Butter dish, cov. .50.00
Compote, cov., 6" d. 35.00
Compote, cov., 7" d. (ILLUS.) 65.00
Creamer. 32.50
Creamer & open sugar bowl, pr. 80.00
Goblet 25.00
Mug. 25.00
Mug, child's, blue opaque 25.50
Sauce dish 8.00

Spooner 19.00
Tumbler, bar 30.00
Tumbler, water 30.00

GOTHIC

Gothic Egg Cup

Bowl, master berry or fruit, flat 69.00
Celery vase 95.00
Champagne.........................125.00
Creamer, applied handle 75.00
Egg cup (ILLUS.)....................42.50
Goblet 56.50
Sauce dish 14.00
Spooner 42.50
Sugar bowl, cov.....................80.00
Sugar bowl, open 27.50
Tumbler 95.00
Wine, 3¾" h........................96.50

GRAND - See Diamond Medallion Pattern

GRAPE & FESTOON

Grape & Festoon Spooner

Butter dish, cov., stippled leaf 50.00
Celery vase, stippled leaf 35.00
Compote, cov., 8" d., high stand,
   acorn finial, stippled leaf 115.00

Compote, open, 8" d., low stand 75.00
Creamer, stippled leaf...............38.50
Egg cup, stippled leaf................18.00
Goblet, stippled leaf 31.50
Goblet, buttermilk, stippled leaf 33.00
Goblet, veined leaf 18.50
Pitcher, milk, 7" h., stippled leaf 65.00
Pitcher, water, stippled leaf 85.00
Plate, 6" d., stippled leaf.............17.50
Relish, stippled leaf 7.50
Salt dip, footed, stippled leaf 23.50
Sauce dish, flat, stippled leaf, 4" d.......7.50
Sauce dish, flat, veined leaf 12.50
Spooner, stippled leaf (ILLUS.) 28.00
Spooner, veined leaf 22.00
Sugar bowl, open, stippled leaf 22.00
Wine, stippled leaf 20.00

GRAPE & FESTOON WITH SHIELD

Compote, cov., 8" d., low stand 39.50
Creamer, applied handle 35.00
Goblet w/shield & grapes 26.00
Goblet w/American shield 65.00
Mug, clear, 1 7/8" h. 16.50
Mug, cobalt blue, 1 7/8" h. 26.00
Mug, clear, 3¼" h..................18.50
Pitcher, water, applied handle.........65.00
Sauce dish, flat or footed ....6.00 to 12.00
Spooner 26.50

GRASSHOPPER (Locust)

Berry set, footed, master bowl & 11
   sauce dishes, 12 pcs. 127.00
Bowl, cov., 7" d., etched 27.50
Bowl, open, 8" d. 20.00
Bowl, open, 11" d., shallow 15.00
Butter dish, cov....................58.00
Butter dish, cov., vaseline............95.00
Celery vase, w/insect 38.00
Compote, cov., 7" d., 7¾" h........49.00
Compote, cov., 8¼" d. 57.50
Creamer...........................32.50
Goblet, w/insect, amber.............85.00
Goblet, w/insect 32.50
Pitcher, water 60.00
Plate, 8½" d., footed 25.00
Salt dip 20.00
Sauce dish, footed 9.00
Spooner 49.50
Spooner, w/insect 55.00
Sugar bowl, cov., w/insect, etched.....65.00
Sugar bowl, open, w/insect 42.00
Table set, creamer without insect &
   spooner & cov. sugar bowl
   w/insect, 3 pcs....................125.00

GREEK KEY (Heisey's Greek Key)

Butter dish, cov. 125.00
Celery tray.........................40.00
Creamer & open sugar bowl, pr. 55.00
Goblet 45.00
Humidor, cov. 225.00
Ice tub, hotel size...........75.00 to 125.00

Lamp, kerosene-type, miniature 75.00
Nut dish, individual size 22.00
Pitcher, tankard, 1½ qt. . . . . . .95.00 to 110.00
Punch cup. 20.00
Sauce dish 20.00
Sherbet . . . . .15.00 to 20.00
Soda fountain (straw holder) jar 128.00
Tumbler 85.00

GUARDIAN ANGEL - See Cupid & Venus Pattern

HAIRPIN (Sandwich Loop)
Celery vase 38.00
Champagne 50.00
Compote, open, 9½" d., 9" h. 235.00
Decanter w/stopper, qt. 50.00
Egg cup. 18.50
Egg cup, fiery opalescent 74.50
Goblet 40.00
Salt dip, cov. 85.00
Salt dip, master size. 20.00
Sauce dish, 4" d. 10.50
Spooner. 36.50
Spooner, fiery opalescent 175.00
Sugar bowl, cov. 95.00
Tumbler 28.00
Tumbler, whiskey, handled 45.00
Wine 25.00

HALEY'S COMET

Haley's Comet Wine

Celery. 35.00
Goblet 37.50
Pitcher, water 85.00
Wine (ILLUS.) 22.00

HAMILTON
Butter dish, cov. .80.00
Cake stand. 175.00
Compote, open, 8" d., 5½" h. (ILLUS.) . .65.00

Hamilton Compote

Creamer. 75.00
Egg cup. 40.00
Goblet 46.50
Pitcher, water 175.00
Sauce dish 15.00
Spooner 38.00
Sugar bowl, cov. 80.00
Sugar bowl, open 30.00
Tumbler, bar 85.00
Tumbler, water 80.00
Tumbler, whiskey, applied handle 90.00
Wine 90.00

HAMILTON WITH LEAF
Butter dish, cov., frosted leaf 80.00
Compote, open, 6" d., 4½" h. 52.50
Compote, open, high stand, large 85.00
Creamer, frosted leaf 55.00
Egg cup, clear leaf 55.00
Goblet, clear leaf 50.00
Goblet, frosted leaf 55.00
Lamp, kerosene-type, brass stem,
   marble base, blue, 9" h. 320.00
Lamp base, kerosene-type, scalloped
   foot, clear leaf 80.00
Spooner, clear leaf 33.50
Sugar bowl, cov., clear leaf 75.00
Sweetmeat dish, cov., clear leaf 75.00
Tumbler, frosted leaf 125.00
Tumbler, bar, clear leaf. 70.00
Wine 65.00

HAND (Pennsylvania, Early)
Bowl, 9" d. 36.50
Bread plate, 10½ x 8" oval 20.00
Butter dish, cov. .70.00
Cake stand. 55.00
Celery vase 42.50
Compote, cov., 8" d., high stand 95.00
Compote, open, 9" d., low stand 20.00
Cordial 75.00
Creamer. 45.00
Creamer, child's 45.00
Goblet 41.50
Marmalade jar, cov. 40.00
Mug. 45.00
Pitcher, water 67.50
Sauce dish, 4½" d. 7.50
Spooner 25.00

Sugar bowl, cov. 75.00
Syrup pitcher w/original top, 4" h. 42.00
Toothpick holder. .20.00
Wine 30.00

HARP

Harp Spillholder

Goblet, flared sides 650.00
Goblet, straight sides 250.00
Spillholder (ILLUS.) 85.00

HEART WITH THUMBPRINT

Heart with Thumbprint Bowl

Banana boat, clear, 7½ x 6½" 50.00
Banana boat, clear, 11 x 6½" 50.00
Berry set: master bowl & 6 sauce
   dishes; clear, 7 pcs. 130.00
Bowl, 7" sq., 3½" h., clear 37.50
Bowl, 9" d., clear 27.50
Bowl, 9½" d., clear (ILLUS.) 31.50
Bowl, 10" d., scalloped rim, clear 35.00
Butter dish, cov., clear. 75.00
Cake stand, clear, 9" d., 5" h. 125.00
Card tray, folded edge, clear, 6" w. 35.00
Card tray, clear, 8 x 4¼" 20.00
Celery vase, clear. 49.00
Compote, open, 7½" d., 7½" h.,
   scalloped rim, clear 68.00
Cordial, clear, 3" h. 55.00
Creamer, clear 27.50
Creamer, individual size, clear 20.00
Creamer, individual size, green
   w/gold 36.50
Creamer, sugar bowl & tray, individual
   size, clear, 3 pcs. 47.50

Cruet w/original stopper, clear 60.00
Goblet, clear 49.50
Goblet, green w/gold 90.00
Ice bucket, clear 50.00
Lamp, kerosene-type, clear, 8" h. 51.50
Lamp, kerosene-type, green, 9" h. 117.00
Lamp, kerosene-type, green, 10" h. . . .160.00
Mustard jar w/silverplate cover, clear . .95.00
Nappy, heart-shaped, clear 32.50
Olive dish, handled, green 42.50
Plate, 6" d., clear 25.00
Plate, 6" d., green 65.00
Plate, 10" d., clear 35.00
Plate, 12" d., clear 40.00
Powder jar w/silverplate cover, clear . .65.00
Punch cup, clear 15.00
Relish, clear w/gold 17.50
Rose bowl, clear, 3¾" d. 26.50
Rose bowl, clear, 5" d. 30.00
Salt & pepper shakers w/original tops,
   clear, pr. 95.00
Sauce dish, clear, 4" to 5" d. . . .12.00 to 17.50
Sauce dish, green 32.00
Spooner, clear. .39.50
Sugar bowl, cov., large, clear 45.00
Sugar bowl, open, clear 24.50
Sugar bowl, open, individual size,
   clear w/pewter rim 15.00
Sugar bowl, open, individual size,
   green w/gold .31.50
Syrup jug w/pewter top, clear 68.50
Tray, clear, 8 1/8 x 4 1/8" 35.00
Tumbler, water, clear 38.50
Tumbler, water, ruby-stained 115.00
Vase, 6" h., trumpet-shaped, clear 35.00
Vase, 7" h., green 65.00
Vase, 10" h., trumpet-shaped, clear 58.00
Waste bowl, clear. 45.00
Wine, clear 42.50

HEARTS OF LOCH LAVEN - See Shuttle Pattern

HERCULES PILLAR (Pillar Variant)

Hercules Pillar Cordial

Ale glass, clear 30.00
Celery vase, clear .47.00
Champagne, clear 35.00
Cordial, clear, 3¾" h. (ILLUS.) 38.00
Syrup jug w/original top, blue 125.00
Toothpick holder, amber 100.00
Tumbler, clear 25.00
Whiskey taster, clear 13.50
Wine, clear 35.00

HERRINGBONE (Herringbone with Star & Shield Motif)

Celery vase 30.00
Creamer 27.00
Goblet 22.00
Goblet, buttermilk 23.00
Salt dip, master size 14.00
Sauce dish 10.50
Spooner 20.00
Sugar bowl, cov. .24.00
Wine 14.00

HERRINGBONE BAND

Egg cup 18.50
Goblet 13.50
Sauce dish, 4" sq. .9.50
Spooner, pedestal base, scalloped rim . .21.00
Sugar bowl, open 15.00
Wine 20.00

HICKMAN (Le Clede)

![Hickman Relish dish]

Hickman Relish

Banana stand, clear 65.00
Bowl, 5" d., green w/gold 8.00
Bowl, 7" sq., clear 15.00
Bowl, berry, 9" sq., clear 25.00
Butter dish, cov., clear 35.00
Cake stand, clear, 9¼" d. 35.00
Celery dish, boat-shaped, green 25.00
Champagne, clear 21.50
Compote, cov., 5" d., clear 37.00
Compote, cov., 7" d., clear 53.00
Compote, open, jelly, green 16.00
Compote, open, 7½" d., 5½" h., clear . .20.00
Compote, open, 8" d., 6½" h., clear 31.50
Condiment set: salt & pepper shakers
  & cruet w/original stopper, on
  cloverleaf-shaped tray; clear, mini-
  ature, 4 pcs. 48.00
Cookie jar, cov., clear 45.00

Cookie jar, cov., green, w/pewter
  bottom rim 75.00
Creamer, clear w/gold, 2½" h. 24.50
Creamer, green, 2½" h. 26.50
Creamer & open sugar bowl, indi-
  vidual size, green, oval, pr. 38.00
Cruet w/ball-shaped stopper, clear 42.50
Dish, pulled-out corners, clear,
  6½" sq. 11.00
Doughnut stand, scalloped rim,
  clear, 8" d. 45.00
Goblet, clear 30.00
Goblet, green w/gold 35.00
Ice tub, clear 42.50
Mustard jar w/cover & underplate,
  clear, 2 pcs. 45.00
Pickle dish, clear, 8 x 4" 14.50
Pickle dish, green 15.00
Pitcher, clear w/gold 55.00
Plate, 6" d., clear .7.00
Plate, 8½ x 7½" diamond shape,
  clear 13.00
Punch cup, clear .7.50
Punch cup, green 12.50
Relish, clear, 4" sq. (ILLUS.) 14.00
Relish, clear, 5½" l. 15.00
Relish, boat-shaped, cobalt blue
  w/gold 32.00
Rose bowl, clear .26.50
Salt shaker w/original top, clear
  (single) 9.50
Salt shaker w/original top, green
  (single) 18.00
Sauce dish, clear .8.00
Spooner, clear 22.50
Sugar bowl, cov., clear 38.00
Sugar bowl, cov., green 45.00
Sugar shaker w/original top, clear 45.00
Table set, clear w/gold, 4 pcs. 175.00
Toothpick holder, green 45.00
Tumbler, clear 27.50
Vase, 10" h., clear 38.50
Vase, 10½" h., purple 45.00
Wine, clear 25.00

HIDALGO (Frosted Waffle)

Hidalgo Compote

Bowl, 10" sq., frosted 22.00

Butter dish, cov., clear w/etching 45.00
Celery dish, boat-shaped, frosted,
    13" l. 50.00
Celery vase, clear. 25.00
Celery vase, clear w/etching 22.50
Celery vase, clear w/amber staining . . .32.50
Celery vase, frosted 25.00
Compote, open, 6½" d., clear (ILLUS.) . .20.00
Creamer, clear w/etching. 22.50
Creamer, frosted 41.50
Cruet w/original stopper, frosted 65.00
Egg cup, clear 30.00
Goblet, clear w/etching . . . . . . .15.00 to 20.00
Goblet, frosted 16.50
Pitcher, milk, frosted 39.50
Pitcher, water, clear 48.00
Pitcher, water, clear w/etching 50.00
Relish, shell-shaped, frosted 15.00
Sauce dish, handled, clear 9.00
Spooner, clear. 22.50
Sugar bowl, cov., clear 25.00
Sugar shaker w/original top, clear 30.00
Syrup pitcher w/original top, frosted . . .75.00

HINOTO (Diamond Point w/Panels)

Hinoto Creamer

Butter dish, cov. .90.00
Celery vase 42.50
Compote, open, 7½" d., 2½" h. 27.50
Creamer (ILLUS.). 75.00
Dresser set, 6 pcs. 95.00
Egg cup, handled 23.00
Goblet 55.00
Pitcher, tankard, 9" h., applied
    handle 110.00
Spooner 32.50
Sugar bowl, cov. .48.00
Tumbler, footed .45.00
Tumbler, whiskey, handled, footed 45.00
Wine 55.00

HOBNAIL

Barber bottle, blue, applied rigaree
    at neck 90.00
Bowl, 7½" d., ruffled rim, blue 35.00

Butter dish, cov., amber 35.00
Cake stand, pedestal base, square,
    clear 85.00
Creamer, fluted top, applied handle,
    amber, 3 x 2". .17.50

Hobnail Creamer

Creamer, scalloped & ornamented
    top, clear, 6" h. (ILLUS.) 45.00
Cruet w/original stopper, amber 100.00
Egg cup, double, amber 25.00
Goblet, clear 15.00
Hat shape, clear, 10" d., 6" h. 49.00
Lamp, hand-type, opaque white
    w/amber foot & handle, 4¼" d.,
    6" h. 110.00
Mayonnaise dish, cov., clear 12.00
Mug, child's, amber 35.00
Pitcher, 8" h., square top, clear 60.00
Pitcher, water, Rubina. 125.00
Punch cup, amber 21.00
Salt & pepper shakers w/original
    tops, sapphire blue, pr. 27.50
Spooner, ruffled rim, amber 32.00
Spooner, clear. 20.00
Syrup pitcher w/original top, clear 72.00
Toothpick holder, amber 21.00
Tray, water, clear, 11½" d. 18.50
Tumbler, amber .16.00
Tumbler, 10-row, blue 31.00
Tumbler, 10-row, clear 25.00
Tumbler, 10-row, Rubina Frosted. 92.00
Tumbler, ruby-stained 37.00
Tumbler, vaseline. 46.50
Wine, clear 19.50

HOBNAIL WITH FAN

Hobnail with Fan Bowl

Berry set: 9" d. master bowl & six
   4¾" d. sauce dishes; clear, 7 pcs. . . .138.00
Bowl, 6" d., clear .20.00
Bowl, 7" d., blue (ILLUS.) 50.00
Celery vase, clear. 38.00
Goblet, clear 30.00

HOBNAIL WITH THUMBPRINT BASE

Hobnail with Thumbprint Pitcher

Butter dish, cov., clear. 55.00
Creamer, amber .37.50
Creamer, blue 45.00
Creamer, miniature, amber 15.00
Creamer, miniature, blue 23.00
Finger bowl, scalloped rim, blue 45.00
Pitcher, 7" h., clear w/ruby-stained
   rim 45.00
Pitcher, 8" h., amber (ILLUS.) 90.00
Pitcher, 8" h., blue 85.00
Sugar bowl, cov., clear 35.00
Waste bowl, amber 40.00

HONEYCOMB

Vernon Honeycomb Vases

Ale glass 42.00
Barber bottle w/pewter top 45.00
Butter dish, cov., non-flint 45.00
Cake stand, 10½" d. 35.00
Celery vase, Laredo, flint 32.00

Celery vase, New York, non-flint. 18.00
Celery vase, Vernon, flint, 9" h. 65.00
Champagne, w/etching, flint 65.00
Claret 22.00
Compote, cov., 6½ x 8½", flint 80.00
Compote, cov., 9¼" d., 11½" h. 65.00
Compote, open, 7" d., 5" h., flint 32.00
Compote, open, 7" d., 7" h., flint 57.50
Compote, open, 8" d., 6¼" h., flint 55.00
Compote, open, 11" d., 8" h., flint 135.00
Cordial, flint, 3¼" h. 20.00
Creamer, applied handle, flint. 25.00
Decanter w/bar lip, flint 85.00
Decanter w/original stopper, qt. 56.00
Egg cup. 16.00
Finger bowl, flint 46.00
Goblet, flint 16.50
Goblet, non-flint .10.00
Goblet, Banded Vernon 22.00
Goblet, Barrel w/knob stem. 18.00
Goblet, buttermilk 24.00
Goblet, Laredo 25.50
Goblet, New York 20.00
Mug 22.50
Pitcher, water, 8½" h., molded han-
   dle, polished pontil, flint 100.00
Pitcher, water, 9" h., applied handle . . .56.50
Pomade jar, cov., flint 48.00
Relish 30.00
Salt dip, pedestal base, flint 35.00
Sauce dish, flint .11.00
Spillholder, flint .22.00
Spooner, flint 33.50
Spooner, non-flint 15.00
Sugar bowl, cov., flint 75.00
Sugar bowl, open, scalloped rim 35.00
Syrup pitcher w/pewter top 126.50
Tumbler, bar 25.00
Tumbler, footed .23.00
Tumbler, Vernon, flint 55.00
Tumbler, whiskey, footed, handled,
   flint 45.00
Tumbler, whiskey, Vernon 125.00
Vase, 7½" h., 4" d., Vernon, flint 45.00
Vases, 10¼" h., Vernon, flint, pr.
   (ILLUS.) 150.00
Wine, flint 24.00
Wine, non-flint 12.00

HORN OF PLENTY

Bar bottle w/original stopper, qt. 130.00
Bar bottle w/pewter pour spout, 8". . . .135.00
Bowl, 9 x 6¼" oval 145.00
Butter dish, cov. .150.00
Butter pat. 18.00
Celery vase . . . . .100.00 to 165.00
Champagne. 150.00
Compote, cov., 6¼" d., 7½" h. 175.00
Compote, open, 7" d., 3" h. 95.00
Compote, open, 7" d., high stand,
   waffle base 85.00
Compote, open, 8" d., low stand 55.00
Compote, open, 8" d., 8" h. 115.00
Compote, open, 9" d., low stand 82.50

Horn of Plenty Compote

Compote, open, 9" d., 8½" h.
(ILLUS.) 200.00
Compote, open, 10½" d., 8½" h. 140.00
Creamer, applied handle, 5½" h. 235.00
Creamer, applied handle, 7" h. 160.00
Decanter w/original stopper, pt. 185.00
Decanter w/original stopper, qt. 148.00
Dish, low foot, 7¼" d. 85.00
Dish, low foot, 8" d. 95.00
Egg cup, 3¾" h. 37.50
Goblet 65.00
Honey dish, cov. 19.50
Honey dish, open 10.50
Lamp, whale oil type, w/burner,
11" h. 195.00
Peppersauce bottle w/stopper. 142.50
Pitcher, water 575.00
Plate, 6" d. 65.00
Relish, 7 x 5" oval 30.00
Salt dip, master size, oval 69.50
Sauce dish . . . . .18.00 to 22.00
Spillholder 48.00
Spooner 38.00
Sugar bowl, cov. 96.50
Sugar bowl, open 62.50
Table set, 4 pcs. 450.00
Tumbler, bar 70.00
Tumbler, water, 3 5/8" h. 75.00
Tumbler, whiskey, 3" h. 85.00
Tumbler, whiskey, handled 235.00
Wine 120.00

HORSESHOE (Good Luck or Prayer Rug)

Horseshoe Cake Stand

Bowl, cov., 8 x 5" oval, flat, triple
horseshoe finial 195.00
Bowl, open, 6" d. 15.00
Bowl, open, 7" d., footed 20.00
Bowl, open, 8½" d., electric blue 150.00
Bowl, open, 9 x 6" oval 36.50
Bread tray, single horseshoe handles . . .33.50
Bread tray, double horseshoe handles . .42.50
Butter dish, cov. 55.50
Cake stand, 8" d., 6½" h. 49.50
Cake stand, 9" d. (ILLUS.) 55.00
Cake stand, 10" d. . . . . .60.00 to 75.00
Celery vase 41.50
Cheese dish, cov., w/woman churning
butter in base 230.00
Compote, cov., 6" d., 10½" h. 135.00
Compote, cov., 8" d., 9" h. 75.00
Compote, cov., 8" d., 11" h. 80.00
Compote, cov., 12" d. 95.00
Compote, open, 8" d., 7¾" h. 35.00
Creamer, hotel-type, 6½" h. 95.00
Creamer, regular 30.00
Creamer, individual size 38.50
Doughnut stand 57.50
Goblet 32.50
Marmalade jar, cov. 97.50
Pitcher, milk 72.50
Pitcher, water 80.00
Plate, 7" d. 30.00
Plate, 8" d. 41.50
Plate, 10" d. 45.00
Relish, 8 x 5" 11.50
Relish, 9 x 5½" .18.00
Salt dip, individual size 19.00
Salt dip, master size, horsehoe shape . .90.00
Sauce dish, flat or footed . . . . . .8.50 to 20.00
Spooner 30.00
Sugar bowl, cov. 55.00
Sugar bowl, open 16.00
Sugar shaker w/original top 29.00
Tray, double horseshoe handles,
15 x 10" 100.00
Waste bowl, 4" d., 2½" h. 55.00
Wine .145.00 to 180.00

HUBER

Huber Compote

Celery vase, non-flint	26.50
Celery vase, etched, small	45.00
Champagne, straight sides	23.50
Champagne, etched	40.00
Compote, open, 7" d.	55.00
Compote, open, 8" d., etched (ILLUS.)	75.00
Cordial	30.00
Creamer, flint	80.00
Egg cup, flint	15.00
Egg cup, non-flint	11.00
Egg cup, double, flint	30.00
Goblet, flint	23.50
Goblet, non-flint	12.00
Goblet, barrel, non-flint	20.00
Goblet, buttermilk	16.50
Goblet, lady's, non-flint	16.50
Mug, flint	22.50
Salt dip, master size, flint	17.50
Sugar bowl, cov.	41.50
Tumbler, bar	22.50
Tumbler, water	19.50
Vase, non-flint	18.50
Wine, flint	18.50
Wine, non-flint	12.50

HUMMINGBIRD (Flying Robin or Bird & Fern)

Butter dish, cov., clear	50.00
Celery vase, clear	37.50
Compote, open, 7" d., clear	48.00
Creamer, amber	52.50
Creamer, blue	50.00
Creamer, clear	28.50
Goblet, amber	55.00
Goblet, blue	60.00
Goblet, clear	32.50
Pitcher, milk, amber	65.00
Pitcher, milk, blue	92.00
Pitcher, milk, clear	50.00
Pitcher, water, amber	125.00
Pitcher, water, blue	125.00
Pitcher, water, clear	85.00
Sauce dish, clear	12.00
Sugar bowl, cov., clear	55.00
Sugar bowl, open, clear	20.00
Spooner, amber	40.00
Spooner, clear	29.50
Tray, water, amber	170.00
Tumbler, amber	45.00
Tumbler, clear	30.00
Waste bowl, clear	35.00
Water set: pitcher & 6 tumblers; amber, 7 pcs.	350.00
Wine, clear	46.50

HUNDRED EYE

Creamer, clear	18.50
Goblet, clear	15.50
Mug, blue	25.00
Wine, clear	9.00

ILLINOIS

Basket, applied reeded handle, 11½ x 7"	100.00

Bowl, 8" sq.	35.00
Butter dish, cov., 7" sq.	60.00
Candlestick (single)	70.00
Celery tray	40.00
Creamer, small	18.50
Creamer, large	35.00
Creamer & open sugar bowl, small, pr.	35.00
Marmalade jar in silverplate frame w/spoon, 3 pcs.	135.00
Pitcher, milk	31.00
Pitcher, water, tankard	60.00
Pitcher, water, silverplate rim, green	80.00
Plate, 7" sq.	15.00 to 22.00
Relish, 8½ x 3"	9.50
Salt dip, individual size	12.50
Sauce dish	15.00
Soda fountain (straw-holder) jar, cov., 12½" h.	180.00
Soda fountain (straw-holder) jar, cov., green, 12½" h.	300.00
Spooner	35.00
Sugar bowl, cov.	50.00
Sugar bowl, open	39.50
Sugar bowl, cov., individual size	30.00
Syrup pitcher w/original pewter top	95.00
Table set, creamer, open sugar bowl, cov. butter dish & spooner, 4 pcs.	197.50
Toothpick holder	25.00
Vase, 5¾" h.	26.00

INDIANA (Doric)

Butter dish, cov.	40.00
Creamer	23.00
Sugar bowl, open	23.00

INDIANA SWIRL - See Feather Pattern

INVERTED FERN

Inverted Fern Sugar Bowl

Butter dish, cov.	57.50
Cake stand	475.00
Champagne	114.00

Compote, open, 8" d. 55.00
Creamer, applied handle 122.00
Egg cup 27.50
Goblet 35.00
Honey dish, 4" d. 12.50
Salt dip, master size, footed 35.00
Sauce dish, 4" d. .7.50
Spooner 36.00
Sugar bowl, cov. (ILLUS.) 75.00
Sugar bowl, open 37.00
Tumbler 95.00
Wine 57.50

INVERTED LOOPS & FANS - See Maryland Pattern

IOWA (Paneled Zipper & Zippered Block)

Lamp, kerosene-type . . . . .95.00 to 125.00
Nappy, handled .10.00
Olive dish 18.00
Punch cup 15.00
Salt & pepper shakers w/original tops,
  pr. 35.00
Salt & pepper shakers w/original tops,
  ruby-stained, pr. 35.00
Sauce dish, flat, 4½" d. 6.50
Sugar bowl, cov., ruby-stained 45.00
Sugar bowl, cov., small 15.00
Table set, ruby-stained, 4 pcs. 235.00
Toothpick holder .22.00
Toothpick holder, ruby-stained 75.00
Tumbler 25.00
Tumbler, ruby-stained 35.00
Vases, gold trim, pr. 18.00
Wine 30.00

IRISH COLUMN - See Broken Column Pattern

IVY IN THE SNOW

Ivy in the Snow Compote

Bowl, 8 x 5½", flat 9.00
Butter dish, cov. .50.00
Cake stand, 8" d. 25.00
Cake stand, amber-stained ivy sprigs,
  10" sq. 125.00

Celery vase, 8" h. 27.50
Compote, cov., 8" d., 13" h. (ILLUS.) 60.00
Compote, open, jelly 20.00
Creamer 19.00
Egg cup 28.00
Goblet 25.00
Pitcher, 5½" h., ruby-stained ivy
  sprigs, souvenir 65.00
Pitcher, water 50.00
Plate, 7" d. 14.00
Plate, 10" d. 19.00
Relish 18.00
Sauce dish, flat or footed . . . . . . .7.00 to 10.00
Spooner 30.00
Sugar bowl, open .7.50
Syrup jug w/original top 69.50
Tumbler 20.00
Wine 22.00

JACOB'S LADDER (Maltese)

Jacob's Ladder Open Sugar Bowl

Bowl, 6¾" d., 4¾" h., footed 25.00
Bowl, 7¼" d., footed 30.00
Bowl, 7¾" oval, flat 15.00
Butter dish, cov., Maltese Cross finial . . .65.00
Cake stand, 8½" d. 30.00
Cake stand, 10½" d. 52.50
Candlesticks, pr. .38.00
Celery vase 41.50
Cologne bottle w/original Maltese
  Cross stopper, footed 125.00
Compote, cov., 7¼" d. 58.50
Compote, cov., 9½" d., high stand 175.00
Compote, open, 7" d., low stand 28.00
Compote, open, 7½" d., 7½" h. 35.00
Compote, open, 8½" d., scalloped rim . .28.50
Compote, open, 9½" d., 7½" h.,
  scalloped rim .38.00
Compote, open, 10" d., 7" h. 40.00
Creamer, footed .32.50
Cruet w/original stopper, footed 80.00
Goblet 62.50
Honey dish, open 10.00
Marmalade jar, cov. 85.00
Pickle dish 13.00
Pitcher, water, applied handle 150.00
Plate, 6" d. . . . . .22.00 to 28.00
Relish, Maltese Cross handles,
  10 x 5½" 16.50

Salt dip, master size, footed 26.00
Sauce dish, flat or footed . . . . . . .8.00 to 11.50
Spooner 30.00
Sugar bowl, cov. 43.50
Sugar bowl, open (ILLUS.) 28.00
Syrup jug w/pewter top 70.00
Tumbler 75.00
Wine 33.50

JEWEL & DEWDROP (Kansas)

Jewel & Dewdrop Pitcher

Berry set, master bowl & 6 sauce
   dishes, 7 pcs. 75.00
Bowl, 8½" d. 40.00
Bread tray, "Our Daily Bread," 10½"
   oval 45.00
Butter dish, cov. 55.00
Cake stand, 8" d. .60.00
Cake stand, 9" d. .46.50
Cake stand, 10" d. 60.00
Compote, cov., 9½" d. 55.00
Compote, open, jelly 23.50
Compote, open, 7½" d., 5" h. 45.00
Compote, open, 9½" d. 75.00
Creamer 38.00
Dish, cov., 4½" d. .40.00
Goblet 42.50
Mug 18.50
Pitcher, milk 50.00
Pitcher, water (ILLUS.) 55.00
Relish, 8½" oval 20.00
Sauce dish, 4" d. .11.50
Syrup jug w/original top 125.00
Toothpick holder 40.00
Tumbler, juice, handled 12.00
Tumbler, water, footed 35.00
Whiskey taster, 2-handled 12.50
Wine 50.00
Wine, ruby-stained, w/gilt trim 70.00

JEWEL & FESTOON (Loop & Jewel)

Champagne 42.00
Creamer 22.00
Creamer, individual size 32.00
Dish, 5½" sq. 7.50
Dresser bottle w/matching stopper,
   7½" h. 50.00

Goblet 16.50
Pickle dish 17.50
Punch cup 9.00
Sauce dish, flat, 4" d. 6.00
Spooner 29.00
Sugar bowl, cov. 29.00

Jewel & Festoon Small Open Sugar

Sugar bowl, open, individual size
   (ILLUS.) 25.00
Toothpick holder 30.00
Vase, 8¾" h. 40.00
Wine 30.00

JEWEL BAND (Scalloped Tape)

Jewel Band Creamer

Bowl, cov., 8" rectangle 32.00
Bread platter 22.50
Cake stand, 9½" d. 35.00
Celery vase, 8" h. .24.00
Compote, cov., 8¼" d., 12" h. 45.00
Creamer (ILLUS.) .27.50
Goblet 22.50
Pitcher, water, 9¼" h. 39.00
Sauce dish, flat or footed, 4" d. . .7.00 to 10.00
Sugar bowl, cov. 30.00
Wine 20.00

JEWELED MOON & STAR (Moon & Star with Waffle)

Bowl, 6¾" d., flat 13.50
Cake stand, 8½" d. 29.50
Carafe 39.00
Celery 30.00
Creamer w/amber & blue staining 50.00

Cruet. 19.50
Goblet, gilt trim 45.00
Sauce dish 3.50
Spooner w/amber & blue staining 50.00
Sugar bowl, cov. 120.00
Tumbler, gilt trim 24.50

JOB'S TEARS - See Art Pattern

JUMBO

Jumbo Spoon Rack

Butter dish w/frosted elephant finial,
    oblong 475.00
Castor holder (no bottles) 95.00
Castor set, w/four original bottles
    & metal tops .440.00
Compote, cov., 12" h., frosted
    elephant finial. 425.00
Compote, open, 12" h. 250.00
Creamer, w/Barnum head at handle . .185.00
Goblet 400.00
Marmalade jar, cov., Barnum head
    handles, frosted elephant finial. 237.50
Spooner 125.00
Spoon rack (ILLUS.). 550.00
Sugar bowl, cov., w/Barnum head
    handles, 9" h. 450.00

KAMONI - See Balder Pattern

KANSAS - See Jewel & Dewdrop Pattern

KENTUCKY
Cake stand, clear, 9½" d. 37.50
Cruet w/original stopper, clear 38.00
Pitcher, water, clear 55.00
Punch cup, green . . . . .12.00 to 18.00
Salt & pepper shakers w/original tops,
    clear, pr. 20.00
Sauce dish, footed, clear. 6.50
Sauce dish, footed, green 12.50
Sugar bowl, cov., clear 30.00

Toothpick holder, clear 26.50
Tumbler, green 21.50
Wine, clear 25.00
Wine, green. 35.00

KING'S CROWN (Also see Ruby Thumbprint)

King's Crown Mustard

Banana stand, clear 50.00
Bowl, 9¼" oval, scalloped rim, round
    base, clear. 50.00
Butter dish, cov., clear. 37.50
Cake stand, clear, 9" d., 7" h. 85.00
Celery vase, clear. 40.00
Champagne, clear 30.00
Compote, cov., 6" d., 6" h., clear 85.00
Compote, open, jelly, clear 35.00
Compote, open, 7½" d., high stand,
    clear 45.00
Compote, open, 8½" d., high stand,
    clear 67.50
Creamer, clear . . . . .35.00 to 45.00
Creamer, individual size, clear 18.50
Goblet, clear . . . . .18.50 to 30.00
Mustard jar, cov., clear (ILLUS.) 38.00
Pitcher, tankard, 8½" h., clear 75.00
Pitcher, tankard, 13" h., clear 95.00
Plate, 7" d., clear 20.00
Punch cup, clear 17.00
Punch set: bowl & 12 cups; clear,
    13 pcs. 90.00
Salt dip, individual size, clear. 10.00
Salt dip, master size, footed, clear 24.00
Sauce dish, clear, 4" d. 10.00
Sauce dish, boat-shaped, clear 22.50
Spooner, clear . . . . .40.00 to 50.00
Toothpick holder, clear 25.00
Tumbler, blue 75.00
Wine, clear . . . . .15.00 to 22.50

KOKOMO (Bar & Diamond)
Bowl, 8½" d., footed 15.00
Celery vase 14.50
Compote, cov., 7½" d., high stand 45.00
Compote, open, 7½" d., low stand 20.00
Creamer, applied handle 25.00
Cruet w/stopper .22.50

Decanter 65.00
Goblet 28.00
Pitcher, water, tankard 39.50
Salt & pepper shakers w/original tops,
    pr. 24.00
Sauce dish, footed 7.50
Spooner 22.50
Sugar bowl, cov. 45.00
Tray for condiment set 20.00
Tray, water 27.50
Wine 24.00

LATTICE (Diamond Bar)

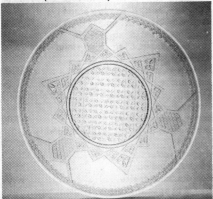

Lattice Plate

Bowl, 8" oval 18.00
Bread plate, "Waste Not - Want Not,"
    10" d. 40.00
Cake stand, 8¼" d., 5" h. 36.00
Creamer 27.00
Goblet 22.50
Pitcher, milk 35.00
Pitcher, water. . . . . .35.00 to 40.00
Plate, 6" d. 9.00
Plate, 7" d. (ILLUS.) 15.00
Sugar bowl, cov. 29.00
Syrup pitcher w/original tin top 70.00
Wine 20.00

LEAF & DART (Double Leaf & Dart)

Bowl, 8¼" d., low foot 25.00
Butter dish, cov., pedestal base 85.00
Celery vase, pedestal base 32.50
Creamer, applied handle 36.00
Egg cup. 20.00
Goblet 27.50
Honey dish, 3½" d. 5.00
Pitcher, water, applied handle 75.00
Relish 15.00
Salt dip, open, master size 24.50
Sauce dish 8.50
Spooner 22.50
Sugar bowl, cov. 40.00
Sugar bowl, open 20.00
Tumbler, footed (ILLUS.) 21.50
Water set, pitcher & 5 footed tumblers,
    6 pcs. 290.00
Wine. .30.00 to 38.00

Leaf & Dart Tumbler

LE CLEDE - See Hickman Pattern

LIBERTY BELL

"Signer's" Platter

Berry set, flat master bowl & 6 flat
    sauce dishes, 7 pcs. 195.00
Bread platter, "John Hancock," shell
    handles, clear, 11½ x 7 1/8" 100.00
Bread platter, shell handles, without
    John Hancock signature, clear,
    11½ x 7 1/8" 170.00
Bread platter, "Signer's," twig handles
    (ILLUS.) 85.00
Butter dish, cov. 125.00
Butter dish, cov., miniature 158.00
Creamer, applied handle . . . . .95.00 to 125.00
Goblet . . . . .48.00 to 70.00
Pickle dish, closed handles, 1776-1876,
    w/thirteen original states, 9¼ x
    5½" oval 42.50
Pitcher, water .535.00
Plate, 6" d., closed handles, scalloped
    rim, w/thirteen original states. 75.00
Plate, 6" d., no states, dated 57.50
Plate, 8" d., closed handles, scalloped
    rim, w/thirteen original states. 52.50
Plate, 10" d., closed handles, scalloped
    rim, w/thirteen original states. 80.00

Platter, 13 x 8¼", twig handles,
  w/thirteen original states ...55.00 to 75.00
Salt dip, individual size 32.50
Salt shaker w/original pewter top
  (single).........................85.00
Sauce dish, flat..............22.00 to 28.00
Sauce dish, footed...........25.00 to 35.00
Spooner...................65.00 to 80.00
Sugar bowl, cov....................100.00
Table set, 4 pcs. 495.00

LILY-OF-THE-VALLEY
Butter dish, cov. 75.00
Celery vase 40.00
Compote, cov., 8½" d., high stand 85.00
Creamer, 3-footed, molded handle....55.00
Creamer, plain base, applied handle ...65.00
Cruet w/original stopper 95.00
Egg cup............................35.00
Goblet 38.00
Pitcher, milk, applied handle 85.00
Pitcher, water, bulbous, applied
  handle............................110.00
Relish, 8 x 5½" 18.00
Salt dip, cov., master size, 3-footed ...125.00
Spooner 40.00
Sugar bowl, cov., 3-footed 75.00
Tumbler, flat 9.50
Tumbler, footed 55.00
Wine 130.00

LINCOLN DRAPE & LINCOLN DRAPE WITH TASSEL

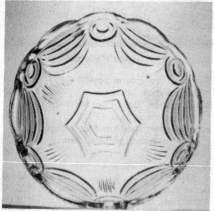

Lincoln Drape Sauce
Celery vase 90.00
Compote, open, 7½" d., 3½" h., flint ...55.00
Egg cup, flint 42.50
Goblet, flint.........................70.00
Goblet w/tassel, flint 120.00
Lamp, kerosene-type, miniature 125.00
Salt dip, master size..................25.00
Salt dip, master size, w/tassel 125.00
Sauce dish, 4" d. (ILLUS.).............20.00
Spillholder 45.00
Spooner 50.00

Sugar bowl, cov......................85.00
Sugar bowl, open 65.00
Syrup pitcher w/original pewter
  top ....95.00 to 125.00
Wine 57.50

LION (Square Lion's Head or Atlanta)
Bowl, 8½" sq. 25.00
Bread plate, "Give Us...," 12" sq. 125.00
Butter dish, cov. 65.00
Cake stand, large 82.50
Celery vase 82.50
Compote, cov., 5" sq., 6" h. 85.00
Compote, cov., 7" sq., low stand 95.00
Compote, cov., 7½" sq., 12½" h. ...175.00
Compote, open, 6" sq., 7½" h........40.00
Compote, open, 8" sq., high stand 75.00
Creamer............................40.00
Dish, cov., oblong...................75.00
Egg cup............................50.00
Goblet ....55.00 to 70.00
Honey dish.........................38.00
Lamp, kerosene-type................175.00
Marmalade jar, cov., w/lion's head
  finial 85.00
Pitcher, water 110.00
Platter, handled 75.00
Salt dip, master size.................40.00
Salt & pepper shakers w/original tops,
  pr................................45.00
Sauce dish 23.00
Spooner 50.00
Sugar bowl, cov.....................85.00
Sugar bowl, open 55.00
Syrup pitcher w/original top..........240.00
Toothpick holder ....35.00 to 42.00
Tumbler ....45.00 to 55.00

LION, FROSTED - See Frosted Lion Pattern

LION'S LEG - See Alaska Pattern

LOCUST - See Grasshopper Pattern

LOG CABIN

Log Cabin Pattern
Butter dish, cov. 285.00
Creamer, 4¼" h. (ILLUS.) 125.00
Pitcher, water 290.00
Sauce dish, flat oblong 85.00
Spooner (ILLUS.) 90.00
Sugar bowl, cov., 8" h. (ILLUS.) 250.00
Sugar bowl, cov., vaseline 675.00

LOOP (Seneca Loop)

Loop Goblet

Bowl, 9" d., flint .80.00
Cake stand, flint 150.00
Celery vase, flint . . . . .50.00 to 75.00
Celery vase, non-flint 20.00
Compote, open, 5¾" d., flint 45.00
Compote, open, 8" d., 6" h., non-flint . . .30.00
Compote, open, 9" d., 7" h., flint 125.00
Cordial, non-flint, 2¾" h. 18.00
Creamer, flint 60.00
Decanter, non-flint 35.00
Egg cup, flint 26.00
Egg cup, non-flint 18.00
Goblet, flint (ILLUS.) . . . . .25.00 to 35.00
Goblet, non-flint. 16.50
Pitcher, water, applied handle, flint . . .170.00
Pitcher, water, non-flint 60.00
Salt dip, individual size, flint 15.00
Salt dip, master size, flint 20.00
Spooner, non-flint 22.50
Sugar bowl, cov., flint 70.00
Sugar bowl, cov., non-flint 29.50
Syrup jug w/original pewter top,
    applied handle, flint. 95.00
Tumbler, flint 18.00
Tumbler, bar, non-flint 14.00
Wine, flint 25.00
Wine, non-flint .15.00

LOOP & DART

Bowl, 9 x 6" oval, round ornaments. 19.50
Butter dish, cov., diamond ornaments . .45.00
Butter dish, cov., round ornaments 80.00
Celery vase, round ornaments 35.00
Champagne, round ornaments 78.00
Compote, cov., 8" d., 10" h., round
    ornaments (ILLUS.) 85.00
Compote, cov., 8" d., low stand, round
    ornaments 65.00
Compote, open, 8" d., 4½" h., round
    ornaments 42.50
Creamer, applied handle, diamond
    ornaments 35.00

Compote with Round Ornaments

Creamer, applied handle, round
    ornaments 40.00
Egg cup, diamond ornaments 20.00
Egg cup, round ornaments 28.00
Goblet, diamond ornaments 22.50
Goblet, round ornaments 27.50
Goblet, buttermilk, diamond
    ornaments 20.00
Goblet, buttermilk, round ornaments. . .35.00
Lamp, kerosene-type, round orna-
    ments on font, milk white glass
    base 85.00
Pitcher, water, round
    ornaments. . . . . .85.00 to 90.00
Plate, 6" d., round ornaments 35.00
Relish, diamond ornaments 12.00
Relish, round ornaments 25.00
Salt dip, master size, diamond
    ornaments 15.00
Salt dip, master size, round
    ornaments 28.00
Sauce dish, diamond ornaments 4.50
Sauce dish, round ornaments 7.00
Spooner, diamond ornaments 21.50
Spooner, round ornaments 26.50
Sugar bowl, cov., diamond ornaments . .35.00
Sugar bowl, cov., round ornaments 57.50
Sugar bowl, open, diamond
    ornaments 19.00
Tumbler, flat or footed, diamond
    ornaments. . . . . .30.00 to 35.00
Tumbler, flat or footed, round
    ornaments. . . . . .25.00 to 30.00
Wine, diamond ornaments 32.50
Wine, round ornaments. 29.50

LOOP & JEWEL - See Jewel & Festoon Pattern

LOOP & PILLAR - See Michigan Pattern

LOOP WITH DEWDROPS

Butter dish, cov. 27.50

Creamer..............................22.50
Goblet 24.00
Pitcher, water.......................65.00
Sugar bowl, cov.....................25.00
Tumbler 17.00
Wine 25.00

LOOP WITH STIPPLED PANELS - See Texas Pattern

LOOPS & DROPS - See New Jersey Pattern

LOOPS & FANS - See Maryland Pattern

MAGNET & GRAPE
Butter dish, cov., frosted leaf, flint 185.00
Compote, open, 7½" d., high stand,
   stippled leaf, non-flint..............68.00
Creamer, frosted leaf, flint...........160.00
Egg cup, clear leaf, non-flint...........18.00
Egg cup, frosted leaf, flint............85.00
Goblet, clear leaf, non-flint 24.50
Goblet, frosted leaf, flint 65.00
Goblet, frosted leaf & American Shield,
   flint 220.00
Goblet, stippled leaf, non-flint........23.50
Salt dip, frosted leaf, flint...........50.00
Sauce dish, frosted leaf, flint 18.00
Sauce dish, stippled leaf, non-flint 4.50
Spooner, frosted leaf, flint 95.00
Spooner, stippled leaf, non-flint 28.00
Sugar bowl, cov., frosted leaf, flint 110.00
Sugar bowl, cov., frosted leaf &
   American Shield, flint...............285.00
Tumbler, frosted leaf, flint 75.00
Wine, stippled leaf, non-flint 40.00

MAINE (Stippled Flower Panels)
Bowl, master berry, 8½" d., green 35.00
Butter dish, cov., clear................42.50
Cake stand, green, 8½" d......27.00 to 45.00
Compote, cov., small, green...........65.00
Compote, open, 8" d., green 30.00
Pitcher, milk, green 85.00
Pitcher, water, clear 50.00
Pitcher, water, clear w/red & green
   stain 125.00
Relish, clear, 7¼" l...................15.00
Sauce dish, clear....................12.50
Spooner, clear.......................30.00
Sugar bowl, cov., green 60.00
Syrup pitcher w/original top, clear 55.00
Tumbler, clear w/red & green stain 45.00
Wine, clear 32.50

MALTESE - See Jacob's Ladder Pattern

MANHATTAN
Berry set, master bowl & 3 flat sauce
   dishes, 4 pcs.......................35.00
Bowl, 6" d...........................18.00
Bowl, 9" d...........................21.00
Butter dish, cov. 55.00
Cake stand, clear w/pink stain, 9" d. ...35.00

Cake stand, clear, 10" d..............30.00
Carafe, water 40.00
Cookie jar, cov......................60.00
Cookie jar, cov., clear w/pink stain 82.50
Creamer.............................12.50
Creamer, individual size 20.00
Creamer & open sugar bowl, pr. 32.00
Creamer & open sugar bowl, individual
   size, pr. 35.00
Cruet w/original stopper 30.00
Goblet 20.00
Pickle dish, w/advertising, 8 x 6" oval ..25.00
Plate, 5" d., clear w/pink stain 29.00
Plate, 6" d............................6.50
Plate, 10¾" d........................18.50
Punch bowl, 14" d., 8" h.............110.00
Punch cup............................8.50
Relish, 6" l..........................10.00
Sauce dish, flat, amber 12.00
Sauce dish, flat, clear 8.00
Sugar bowl, open 11.00
Toothpick holder.....................25.00
Vase, 7" h...........................15.00
Wine 21.50

MAPLE LEAF (Leaf)

Maple Leaf Bread Tray

Bowl, 7" oval, clear ....20.00 to 25.00
Bowl, 10 x 6" oval, footed, amber 40.00
Bowl, 10 x 6" oval, footed, clear 36.00
Bowl, 10 x 6" oval, footed, green.......60.00
Bowl, 10 x 6" oval, footed, vaseline 40.00
Bowl, 10" square, crimped rim, blue 85.00
Bowl, 12 x 7½" oval, amber 70.00
Bread plate, Grant, "Let Us Have
   Peace," amber, 9½" d..............65.00
Bread plate, Grant, "Let Us Have
   Peace," blue, 9½" d. 75.00
Bread plate, Grant, "Let Us Have
   Peace," clear, 9½" d...............40.00
Bread plate, Grant, "Let Us Have
   Peace," vaseline, 9½" d. 65.00
Bread tray, vaseline w/frosted maple
   leaves, 13¼ x 9¼" (ILLUS.)..........60.00
Butter dish, cov., clear................80.00
Celery vase, frosted stem, scalloped
   rim, clear 35.00
Compote, open, jelly, green...........45.00
Creamer, blue.......................65.00

Creamer, clear 25.00
Creamer, vaseline 55.00
Goblet, amber . . . . .95.00 to 140.00
Goblet, vaseline . . . . .90.00 to 110.00
Pitcher, water, clear 67.50
Plate, 9" d., blue 35.00
Platter, 10½" oval, blue 45.00
Platter, 10½" oval, clear 40.00
Platter, 10½" oval, vaseline 45.00
Sauce dish, leaf-shaped, clear, 5½" l. . .24.50
Spooner, blue 55.00
Spooner, clear .40.00
Spooner, green .45.00
Spooner, vaseline 65.00
Sugar bowl, cov., blue 95.00
Sugar bowl, open, clear 40.00

MARYLAND (Inverted Loops & Fans or Loops & Fans)

Maryland Tumbler

Banana bowl, flat, 11¼ x 5" 30.00
Bread platter 18.50
Butter dish, cov. 65.00
Cake stand, 8" d. 27.50
Celery vase 20.00
Compote, open, jelly 16.50
Compote, open, medium 32.50
Creamer 16.00
Goblet 25.00
Pickle dish 16.50
Pitcher, milk 30.00
Pitcher, water 50.00
Plate, 7" d. 10.00
Sauce dish 8.50
Spooner 30.00
Tumbler (ILLUS.) 26.00
Wine 40.00

MASCOTTE

Bowl, 9" d., 2¾" h. 35.00
Butter dish, cov. 48.00
Butter dish, cov., horseshoe-shaped,
  "Maude S." .100.00
Butter pat 10.00
Cake basket w/handle 70.00
Cake stand 35.00
Celery vase . . . . .30.00 to 38.00
Cheese dish, cov. . . . . .55.00 to 85.00
Compote, cov., 9" d., high stand 175.00
Creamer . . . . .30.00 to 38.00
Goblet 45.00

Pitcher, water 70.00
Salt shaker w/original top (single) 9.00
Sauce dish, flat .9.00
Sauce dish, footed 14.00
Spooner . . . . .25.00 to 32.00
Sugar bowl, cov. . . . . .35.00 to 45.00

Mascotte Open Sugar Bowl

Sugar bowl, open (ILLUS.) 25.00
Tray, wine 20.00
Tumbler 15.00
Wine 35.00

MASSACHUSETTS

Massachusetts Butter Dish

Banana boat, 8½ x 6½" 55.00
Bar bottle, 11" h. 62.50
Bowl, 6" sq. 16.00
Butter dish, cov. (ILLUS.) 52.50
Carafe 36.00
Cologne bottle w/stopper 37.50
Cordial 52.50
Creamer 24.00
Creamer, breakfast size 15.00
Cruet w/original stopper 40.00
Cruet w/original stopper, miniature 55.00
Decanter w/stopper 95.00
Goblet 45.00
Mug, 3½" h. 22.50
Olive dish, 5 x 3½" 8.50
Pitcher, water 75.00
Plate, 5" sq., serrated rim 19.00
Plate, 6" sq., w/advertising 16.50
Plate, 8" d. . . . . .25.00 to 32.00
Punch cup 13.50
Relish, 8½" l. 13.00

Rum jug, 5" h. 65.00
Sugar bowl, open, 2-handled 20.00
Toothpick holder . . . . .29.00 to 40.00
Tumbler, juice 20.00
Tumbler, water 30.00
Vase, 6½" h., trumpet-shaped, clear . . .13.00
Vase, 6½" h., trumpet-shaped, cobalt
   blue w/gold 28.00
Vase, 10" h., trumpet-shaped, green . . .45.00
Whiskey shot glass, clear 15.00
Wine 37.50

MELROSE

Butter dish, cov. 45.00
Cake stand, 8" d. 27.50
Celery vase 25.00
Compote, open, jelly, 5½" d 15.00
Compote, open, 7" d., 7" h. 25.00
Creamer 30.00
Goblet 17.50
Pitcher, water . . . . .35.00 to 40.00
Plate, 8" d. 9.00
Spooner 30.00
Tray, water, 11½" d. 38.00
Wine . . . . 15.00 to 25.00

MICHIGAN (Paneled Jewel or Loop & Pillar)

Michigan Goblet

Bowl, cov., master berry or fruit,
   clear 75.00
Bowl, 7½ x 5¼" oval, clear 12.50
Bowl, 8¾" d., scalloped & flared rim,
   clear 30.00
Bowl, 9" d., clear w/pink stain 55.00
Bowl, 10" d., clear 22.50
Butter dish, cov., clear 45.00
Butter dish, cov., clear w/pink stain . . .110.00
Butter dish, cov., clear w/yellow stain
   & enameled florals 190.00
Carafe, water, clear 150.00
Celery vase, clear . . . . .30.00 to 35.00
Celery vase, clear w/pink stain & gold . .75.00

Champagne, clear w/blue stain 50.00
Champagne, clear w/yellow stain 50.00
Compote, open, jelly, 4½" d., clear 23.00
Compote, open, 9¼" d., clear 57.50
Creamer, clear, 4" h. 30.00
Creamer, clear w/pink stain, 4" h. 65.00
Creamer, individual size, clear 15.00
Creamer & open sugar bowl, individual
   size, clear, pr. 45.00
Finger bowl, clear 14.50
Goblet, clear 26.50
Goblet, clear w/blue stain 35.00
Goblet, clear w/pink stain & gold
   (ILLUS.) 38.00
Honey dish, clear, 3½" d. 8.00
Mug, clear 17.50
Mug, clear w/pink stain & gold 35.00
Olive dish, clear w/pink stain 32.50
Parfait, clear 30.00
Pickle dish, clear 12.00
Pitcher, miniature, clear 22.00
Pitcher, water, 8" h., clear 50.00
Pitcher, water, 12" h., clear . . . .55.00 to 70.00
Pitcher, water, 12" h., clear w/pink
   stain 150.00
Punch cup, clear w/enameled decor 8.50
Relish, clear 18.50
Salt & pepper shakers w/original tops,
   clear, pr. 38.00
Sauce dish, clear 10.50
Sauce dish, clear w/pink stain 20.00
Sauce dish, clear w/yellow stain &
   enameled florals 21.00
Spooner, clear 25.00
Spooner, clear w/pink stain 50.00
Spooner, clear w/yellow stain &
   enameled florals 45.00
Sugar bowl, cov., clear 50.00
Sugar bowl, cov., clear w/pink stain &
   gold 65.00
Syrup jug w/pewter top, clear 75.00
Table set, clear w/pink stain, 4 pcs. . . .400.00
Toothpick holder, clear 25.00
Toothpick holder, clear w/yellow
   stain 40.00
Tumbler, clear 30.00
Tumbler, clear w/enameled decor 23.00
Tumbler, clear w/pink stain & gold 50.00
Vase, 6" h., clear 10.00
Vase, 6" h., clear w/pink stain & gold. . .17.50
Water set: pitcher & 6 tumblers; clear,
   7 pcs. 150.00
Water set: pitcher & 6 tumblers; clear
   w/pink stain, 7 pcs. 285.00
Wine, clear 20.00
Wine, clear w/yellow stain 35.00

**MIKADO - See Daisy & Button with Crossbars
Pattern**

MINERVA

Bread tray, 13" l. 77.50
Butter dish, cov. 52.50
Cake stand, 8" d. 95.00

Cake stand, 10½" d. . . . . .100.00 to 115.00
Compote, cov., 8" d., low stand 80.00
Compote, open, 10" d., 9" h. 55.00
Creamer 42.50
Creamer & open sugar bowl, pr. 75.00
Goblet 70.00
Marmalade jar, cov. 150.00
Pickle dish, "Love's Request is Pickles,"
    oval 25.00
Pitcher, milk, 7½" h. 72.50
Pitcher, water . . . . .150.00 to 175.00
Plate, 8" d., J.C. Bates portrait center,
    scalloped rim 50.00
Plate, 10" d., Mars center 60.00
Relish, 8 x 5" oblong 29.50
Sauce dish, flat .16.50
Sauce dish, footed 15.00
Spooner 36.50
Sugar bowl, cov. .60.00

Minerva Open Sugar Bowl

Sugar bowl, open (ILLUS.) 30.00

MINNESOTA

Minnesota Relish

Banana bowl, flat 50.00
Basket w/applied reeded handle 65.00
Berry set, 10" d. master bowl & 5 sauce
    dishes, 6 pcs. 55.00
Bowl, 8½" d. 30.00
Butter dish, cov. .52.50
Carafe 35.00
Celery tray, 13" l. 25.00

Compote, open, 9" sq. 47.50
Creamer, 3½" h. 23.50
Creamer, individual size 16.50
Cruet w/original stopper 32.50
Flower frog, green, 2 pcs. 45.00
Goblet 25.00
Mug. 18.00
Olive dish, oval .12.50
Pitcher, water, tankard 85.00
Plate, 7 3/8" d., turned-up rim 12.50
Relish, 8¾ x 6½" oblong (ILLUS.) 13.00
Sauce dish 15.00
Spooner 20.00
Sugar bowl, cov. .29.50
Syrup pitcher w/original top 55.00
Toothpick holder, 3-handled, clear 22.50
Tumbler 15.00
Wine 25.00

MIRROR

Mirror Pomade Jar

Ale glass . . . . .30.00 to 35.00
Celery vase 75.00
Champagne 31.00
Compote, open, 8" d., 7" h. 65.00
Compote, open, 10" d., 7½" h. 95.00
Goblet 28.00
Pomade jar w/ground stopper, 3½" h.
    (ILLUS.) 35.00
Salt dip, cov., master size 95.00
Spillholder 40.00
Spooner 22.00
Sugar bowl, cov. .60.00
Sugar bowl, open 18.50
Tumbler, bar 30.00
Tumbler, footed .45.00
Wine. . . . . .25.00 to 37.50

MISSOURI (Palm & Scroll)

Bowl, 8¾" d., green. 32.00
Butter dish, cov., clear 50.00
Butter dish, cov., green 65.00
Cake stand, clear, 9" d., 4¾" h. 30.00
Celery vase, clear 30.00
Creamer, clear 25.00
Creamer, green 40.00

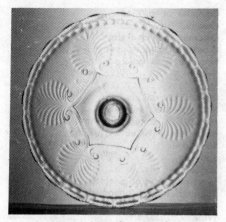

Missouri Doughnut Stand

Doughnut stand, clear, 6" d. (ILLUS.) . . . 35.00
Goblet, clear 50.00
Mug, green 40.00
Pitcher, milk, clear 49.00
Pitcher, water, clear 75.00
Pitcher, water, tankard, green 85.00
Relish, clear 10.00
Salt & pepper shakers, clear, no tops,
    pr. 25.00
Sauce dish, clear 10.50
Sauce dish, green . . . . .11.00 to 14.00
Spooner, clear 25.00
Sugar bowl, cov., clear 50.00
Sugar bowl, cov., green 55.00
Table set, clear, 4 pcs. 197.00
Wine, clear 40.00
Wine, green . . . . .42.50 to 50.00

MOON & STARS

Moon & Stars Compote

Berry set, master bowl & 6 sauce
    dishes, 7 pcs. 95.00
Bowl, nappy, 4" d. 25.00
Bowl, 6" d. 36.50
Bowl, 8" d. 30.00
Bowl, 10 x 7", teardrop-shaped 42.00
Bread tray, scalloped rim, 10¾ x 6½" . .26.00
Butter dish, cov. 57.50
Cake stand, 9" d. 35.00
Cake stand, 10" d. 55.00

Carafe, water 40.00
Celery vase 45.00
Champagne 32.00
Compote, cov., 6" d., 10" h. 55.00
Compote, cov., 6½" d., low stand 50.00
Compote, cov., 8" d., 12" h. 65.00
Compote, open, 7" d., 7½" h. 32.50
Compote, open, 8½" d., 7½" h. 47.50
Compote, open, 9" d., 6½" h. (ILLUS.) . .40.00
Compote, open, 10" d., high stand 125.00
Creamer 55.00
Goblet . . . . .35.00 to 45.00
Lamp, kerosene-type, table model,
    amber 190.00
Lamp, kerosene-type, table model,
    blue 190.00
Pickle dish, 8" l. . . . . .15.00 to 20.00
Relish, oblong 23.50
Salt & pepper shakers w/original tops,
    pr. 50.00
Sauce dish, flat 6.50
Sauce dish, footed 12.00
Spooner 45.00
Sugar bowl, open 40.00
Syrup pitcher w/original top 75.00
Tumbler, footed, flint 75.00
Wine 35.00

**MOON & STAR WITH WAFFLE - See Jeweled
Moon & Star Pattern**

NAILHEAD

Nailhead Goblet

Bowl, 6" d. 16.00
Butter dish, cov. . . . . .32.50 to 45.00
Cake stand, 9" d. 24.00
Cake stand, 10½" d. 28.00
Celery vase 50.00
Compote, cov., 6¼" d., 6¼" h. 40.00
Compote, cov., 7" d., low stand 45.00
Compote, open, 6½" d., 6¾" h. 25.00
Compote, open, 10" d., 7" h. . . .45.00 to 50.00
Creamer 22.50
Goblet (ILLUS.) .25.00

Pitcher, water 42.50
Plate, 7" sq. 16.50
Plate, 9" sq. 18.50
Relish, 8¾ x 5¼" .10.00
Spooner 22.50
Sugar bowl, cov. 30.00
Sugar bowl, open 13.50
Tumbler 36.50
Wine. . . . . .18.00 to 25.00

NEPTUNE - See Bearded Man Pattern

NEW ENGLAND PINEAPPLE

New England Pineapple Egg Cup

Bowl, 8" d., footed, scalloped rim 80.00
Cake stand. 115.00
Champagne 175.00
Compote, cov., 5" d., 8½" h. 150.00
Compote, open, 7" d., 4" h. 55.00
Compote, open, 8" d., 5" h. 75.00
Creamer, applied handle . . . .150.00 to 185.00
Decanter w/bar lip, qt. 120.00
Decanter w/original stopper 225.00
Egg cup (ILLUS.) .38.00
Goblet 55.00
Goblet, lady's 70.00
Plate, 6" d. 90.00
Salt dip, individual size 25.00
Salt dip, master size 42.50
Sauce dish 12.00
Spooner . . . . .38.00 to 45.00
Sugar bowl, cov. .95.00
Sugar bowl, open 35.00
Tumbler, water 80.00
Tumbler, bar 95.00
Whiskey tumbler, applied handle 145.00
Wine 135.00

NEW JERSEY (Loops & Drops)
Compote, open, jelly . . . . .20.00 to 30.00
Compote, open, 7" d., 3½" h. 12.50
Creamer 35.00
Cruet w/original stopper 45.00
Goblet 35.00
Olive dish. 18.00

Plate, 8" d. 12.00
Plate, 8¾" d. 13.00
Plate, 11" d. 18.50
Relish 15.00
Sauce dish, flat 11.50
Sugar bowl, cov. .40.00
Toothpick holder. 40.00
Tumbler 22.00
Water set, pitcher & 6 tumblers,
    7 pcs. 165.00
Wine 30.00

NORTHWOOD DRAPERY - See Opalescent Glass

NOTCHED RIB - See Broken Column Pattern

OAKEN BUCKET (Wooden Pail)

Oaken Bucket Pitcher

Butter dish, cov., blue . . . . . . .100.00 to 120.00
Creamer, amber .40.00
Creamer, amethyst 85.00
Creamer, clear 35.00
Match holder w/original wire handle,
    amber, 2 5/8" d., 2 5/8" h. 19.50
Pitcher, water, amber 75.00
Pitcher, water, amethyst. 150.00
Pitcher, water, blue (ILLUS.) . .75.00 to 110.00
Pitcher, water, clear 60.00
Spooner, amber .40.00
Spooner, blue 42.50
Spooner, vaseline. 55.00
Sugar bowl, cov., blue 48.00
Sugar bowl, cov., clear 35.00
Sugar bowl, cov., vaseline 55.00
Sugar bowl, open, amber 20.00
Sugar bowl, open, miniature,
    amethyst 22.50
Toothpick holder, blue. 22.50
Toothpick holder, vaseline 27.50
Tumbler, clear. 15.00

OAK LEAF BAND
Bowl, 8 x 5½" oval 9.50
Butter dish, cov. .45.00

Oak Leaf Band Goblet

Goblet (ILLUS.) 32.50
Mug, applied handle, 3½" h. 37.50
Pitcher, 6" h. 36.00
Relish 10.00
Sauce dish, 5" d. 16.00

OLD MAN OF THE MOUNTAIN - See Viking Pattern

OLD MAN OF THE WOODS - See Bearded Man Pattern

ONE HUNDRED ONE

One Hundred One Creamer

Creamer, 4¾" h. (ILLUS.) 24.50
Goblet 30.00

OPEN ROSE

Compote, open, 7½" d. 32.50
Creamer...............................40.00
Egg cup 21.50
Goblet (ILLUS.) 20.00
Goblet, lady's 28.00
Pitcher, water, applied handle........165.00
Relish, 8 x 5½" 12.50
Spooner 30.00

Open Rose Goblet

Sugar bowl, cov......................50.00
Sugar bowl, open 24.50
Tumbler 28.00
Tumbler, applied handle.............65.00
Water set, pitcher & 6 goblets,
    7 pcs. 325.00

OREGON NO. 1 - See Beaded Loop Pattern

OREGON NO. 2 (Skilton)

Oregon No. 2 Celery Vase

Bowl, 7¾" d., 2½" h., clear 12.50
Butter dish, cov., clear...............40.00
Cake stand, clear, 9" d................35.00
Celery vase, clear (ILLUS.) 25.00
Compote, open, 5½" d., 4½" h., clear ..22.50
Compote, open, 8½" d., low stand,
    clear 35.00
Compote, open, 8½" d., low stand,
    ruby-stained 55.00
Decanter, whiskey, clear 29.00
Pitcher, milk, clear...................25.00
Pitcher, water, tankard, clear 40.00
Pitcher, water, tankard, ruby-
    stained 125.00

Relish, clear	15.00
Sauce dish, clear	10.00
Spooner, ruby-stained	42.50
Syrup pitcher w/original top, clear	45.00
Tumbler, ruby-stained	35.00
Wine, clear	32.50

OWL IN FAN - See Parrot Pattern

PALM & SCROLL - See Missouri Pattern

PALMETTE

Palmette Goblet

Bowl, 9 x 6" oval, flat	15.00
Butter dish, cov.	52.50
Butter pat	45.00
Cake stand	45.00
Castor set, 5-bottle, complete	125.00
Celery vase	31.50
Champagne	68.00
Compote, cov., 8" d., high stand	58.00 to 75.00
Compote, open, 7" d., low stand	15.00
Creamer, applied handle	50.00
Cup plate	45.00
Egg cup	22.00
Goblet (ILLUS.)	30.00
Lamp, kerosene-type, table model w/stem, clear	72.50
Lamp, kerosene-type, table model w/stem, milk white	85.00
Pitcher, water, applied handle	95.00
Relish	17.50
Salt dip, master size, footed	22.00
Salt & pepper shakers, w/original tops, 5½" h., pr.	55.00
Sauce dish	6.50 to 10.00
Spooner	35.00
Sugar bowl, cov.	40.00
Sugar bowl, open	19.50
Tumbler, bar	58.00
Tumbler, water, footed	30.00

PANELED CANE

Creamer & cov. sugar bowl, clear, pr.	32.00
Goblet, amber	25.00
Goblet, clear	20.00

PANELED CHERRY WITH THUMBPRINTS

(All pieces in clear glass w/red-stained cherries & gilt cable trim)

Paneled Cherry with Thumbprints Bowl

Berry set, master bowl & 6 sauce dishes, 7 pcs. (ILLUS. of bowl)	135.00
Butter dish, cov.	85.00 to 110.00
Pitcher, water	110.00 to 125.00
Punch cup, footed	26.00
Sauce dish	12.00 to 15.00
Spooner	45.00
Sugar bowl, cov.	25.00
Table set, 4 pcs.	170.00
Toothpick holder	16.00
Tumbler	20.00
Water set, pitcher & 6 tumblers, 7 pcs.	250.00

PANELED DAISY

Paneled Daisy Pickle Dish

Berry set, master bowl & 6 sauce dishes, 7 pcs.	65.00
Bowl, 7 x 5" oval	9.00
Bowl, 8" sq.	12.00
Bowl, berry, 8¼ x 5¾" oval	20.00
Bowl, 10½" sq.	15.00
Butter dish, cov.	45.00
Cake stand, high stand, 8" d.	30.00
Cake stand, 11½" d.	45.00
Celery vase	32.50
Compote, cov., 5" d., high stand	35.00
Compote, cov., large	50.00
Creamer	35.00
Goblet	25.00
Mug	30.00
Pickle dish, handled (ILLUS.)	15.00
Pitcher, water	45.00
Plate, 7½" sq.	18.00
Plate, 9" sq.	22.50
Relish, 7 x 5" oval	12.50

Sauce dish, flat 5.50
Sauce dish, footed 12.00
Spooner 25.00
Sugar shaker w/original top..........35.00
Tray, water 32.00

PANELED DEWDROP

Bowl, 8½" oval 24.00
Butter dish, cov. 65.00
Celery vase 35.00
Cordial, 3¼" h.........................30.00
Creamer...............................30.00
Creamer, individual size 20.00
Goblet 28.00
Mug, applied handle 35.00
Pitcher, milk 42.50
Plate, 7" d............................15.00
Plate, 9" d............................30.00
Relish, 7 x 4½" ....12.50 to 16.00
Sauce dish, flat 6.00
Sauce dish, footed 9.50
Spooner 35.00
Sugar bowl, cov.......................37.50
Wine..................................21.50

PANELED FINECUT - See Finecut & Panel Pattern

PANELED FORGET-ME-NOT

Paneled Forget-Me-Not Compote

Bread platter, 11 x 7" oval............24.00
Butter dish, cov. 35.00
Cake stand, 10" d. 35.00
Cake stand, 11" d. 45.00
Celery vase 36.00
Compote, cov., 6" d., 9½" h. 47.50
Compote, cov., 7" d., 10" h. 65.00
Compote, cov., 8" d., high stand
  (ILLUS.).............................60.00
Compote, open, 10" d., 7½" h. 40.00
Creamer...............................32.50
Goblet 35.00
Pitcher, milk, clear...................36.50

Pitcher, water, clear 55.00
Relish, handled, 9 x 5"...............23.00
Salt & pepper shakers w/original tops,
  pr....................................65.00
Sauce dish, flat or footed 12.00
Spooner 22.00
Sugar bowl, cov.......................40.00
Sugar bowl, open 18.00
Water set, pitcher & 6 tumblers,
  7 pcs. 265.00
Wine..................................38.50

PANELED HEATHER

Paneled Heather Jelly Compote

Bowl, 8¼" d., 3¾" h..................24.00
Butter dish, cov., ruby-stained 40.00
Cake plate, 9½" d., 4" h. 32.00
Compote, cov..........................40.00
Compote, open, jelly (ILLUS.) 20.00
Compote, open, 8" d..................27.50
Creamer...............................22.50
Goblet 24.00
Pitcher, water 38.00
Plate, 12" d...........................15.00
Sauce dish, flat or footed ....7.00 to 10.00
Spooner 21.00
Sugar bowl, open 18.00
Table set, h.p. florals, gilt trim, 4 pcs. .175.00
Tumbler 16.00
Wine..................................18.50

PANELED HERRINGBONE (Emerald Green Herringbone or Florida)

Bowl, 7½" d., green..................35.00
Bowl, master berry, 9" sq.,
  green ....25.00 to 38.00
Bowl, oval vegetable, green, medium ..17.50
Bowl, oval vegetable, green, large.....45.00
Cake stand, green, 9½" d. 42.00
Cake stand, clear, 10½" d............25.00
Celery vase, green 55.00
Creamer, clear 22.00
Creamer, green 28.00
Cruet w/original stopper, green 95.00
Goblet, clear 14.50
Goblet, green (ILLUS.) 32.50
Mustard pot, cov., clear 22.50
Nappy, green 19.00
Pitcher, milk, green 58.00

Paneled Herringbone Goblet

Pitcher, water, clear 35.00
Pitcher, water, green................60.00
Plate, 7" sq., green 17.00
Plate, 9" sq., clear 15.00
Plate, 9" sq., green 21.50
Relish, green, 8 x 4½" oval..........14.50
Relish, green, 8½" sq................18.00
Salt shaker w/original top, green
  (single) 20.00
Sauce dish, green 11.50
Sugar bowl, open, green.............28.00
Table set, green, 4 pcs. 185.00
Tumbler, green......................21.50
Water set: pitcher & 6 goblets; green,
  7 pcs. 225.00
Water set: pitcher & 6 tumblers; green,
  7 pcs. 150.00
Wine, clear 20.00
Wine, green.........................49.00

PANELED JEWEL - See Michigan Pattern

PANELED STAR & BUTTON - See Sedan Pattern

PANELED THISTLE
Basket w/applied handle, 7 x 4¾",
  2½" h. plus handle................35.00
Bowl, cov., 5½" d., 4" h., w/bee 48.00
Bowl, 5½" d., 2½" h., footed 18.00
Bowl, 8" d., w/bee 18.00
Bowl, 9" d., deep, w/bee 30.00
Bowl, 10" d., flattened rim 19.50
Butter dish, cov., w/bee ....40.00 to 55.00
Cake stand, 9½" d., 5" h............35.00
Celery vase 30.00
Compote, open, 5" d., low stand 18.00
Compote, open, 6" d., high stand 55.00
Compote, open, 7½" d., 7" h. 35.00
Compote, open, 8" d., 7" h. 29.00

Compote, open, 9" d., 6½" h. 35.00
Creamer ....30.00 to 40.00
Cruet w/stopper 30.00
Goblet ....27.50 to 32.00
Honey dish, cov., square............48.00
Honey dish, open 12.00
Pitcher, milk 37.50

Paneled Thistle Pitcher

Pitcher, water, w/bee (ILLUS.) 68.00
Plate, 7" sq........................16.00
Plate, 7" sq., w/bee 20.00
Plate, 9½" d........................36.00
Rose bowl, extra large 50.00
Salt dip, master size................9.00
Salt dip, master size, w/bee..........15.00
Sauce dish, flat ....8.00 to 12.00
Sauce dish, footed ....12.00 to 20.00
Spooner, handled 22.50
Sugar bowl, cov....................29.50
Toothpick holder, w/bee.............27.50
Wine.......................20.00 to 25.00

PANELED ZIPPER - See Iowa Pattern

PARROT (Owl in Fan)
Goblet 26.50
Spooner 25.00
Wine..............................50.00

PAVONIA (Pineapple Stem)

(*Items can be plain or etched*)

Pavonia Finger Bowl

Butter dish, cov. 57.50
Butter dish, cov., ruby-stained 110.00

Cake stand, 10" d. . . . . .45.00 to 55.00
Celery vase .37.50
Creamer 45.00
Creamer, ruby-stained 65.00
Finger bowl, 7" d. (ILLUS.) 36.00
Goblet . . . . .20.00 to 35.00
Mug, applied handle 15.00
Pitcher, water, tall tankard . . . .55.00 to 75.00
Salt dip, master size 22.00
Sauce dish, flat or footed . . . . . . .7.00 to 12.00
Spooner . . . . .35.00 to 45.00
Sugar bowl, cov., ruby-stained 75.00
Table set, 4 pcs. 295.00
Tray, water . . . . .45.00 to 75.00
Tumbler . . . . .22.00 to 30.00
Tumbler, ruby-stained . . . . .28.00 to 45.00
Waste bowl 45.00
Waste bowl, ruby-stained 110.00
Water set: pitcher & 4 tumblers; ruby-
    stained, 5 pcs. 250.00
Wine . . . . .22.50 to 30.00

PEACOCK FEATHER (Georgia)

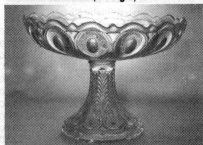

Peacock Feather Compote

Berry set, 8" d. bowl & 5 sauce
    dishes, 6 pcs. .35.00
Bon bon dish, footed 25.00
Bowl, 8" d. 22.00
Butter dish, cov. 42.50
Cake stand, 8½" d., 5" h. 35.00
Celery tray, 11¾" l. 35.00
Compote, open, jelly 28.00
Compote, open, 6½" d., high stand 25.00
Compote, open, 7½" d. (ILLUS.) 30.00
Compote, open, 10" d., low stand 27.00
Creamer 22.00
Creamer & cov. sugar bowl, pr. 100.00
Cruet w/original stopper 47.50
Cup plate 25.00
Decanter, no stopper 30.00
Lamp, kerosene-type, low hand-type
    w/handle, blue, 5¼" h. 135.00
Lamp, kerosene-type, table model
    w/handle, blue, 9" h. . . . . .225.00 to 255.00
Lamp, kerosene-type, table model
    w/handle, clear, 9" h. . . . . . .40.00 to 65.00
Lamp, kerosene-type, table model,
    blue, 12" h. 235.00
Mug 19.00
Pitcher, water .65.00
Relish, 8" oval .15.00

Salt & pepper shakers w/original
    tops, pr. 50.00
Sauce dish 8.00
Spooner 36.00
Sugar bowl, cov. 38.00
Tumbler 35.00

PENNSYLVANIA, EARLY - See Hand Pattern

PENNSYLVANIA, LATE - See Balder Pattern

PICKET

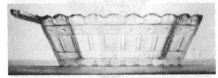

Picket Sauce Dish

Bread tray, 13 x 8" 67.50
Butter dish, cov. . . . . .45.00 to 55.00
Compote, cov., 8" d., low stand 125.00
Compote, open, 7" sq., 7" h. 35.00
Creamer 37.00
Goblet 35.00
Pitcher, water .90.00
Salt dip, master size 32.50
Sauce dish (ILLUS.) 7.50
Spooner 35.00
Sugar bowl, cov. 40.00
Toothpick holder 30.00
Wine 50.00

PILLAR

Ale glass, 6½" h. . . . . .42.50 to 55.00
Claret 55.00
Compote, open, 8" d. 55.00
Creamer 70.00
Decanter w/bar lip, ½ pt. 70.00
Decanter w/bar lip, qt. 45.00
Goblet .40.00 to 50.00
Wine 45.00

PILLAR VARIANT - See Hercules Pillar Pattern

PILLAR & BULL'S EYE

Decanter with Bar Lip

Decanter w/bar lip, 10" h. (ILLUS.) 95.00
Flip glass, 5" d., 7½" h. 150.00
Goblet . . . . .45.00 to 70.00
Pitcher, water, applied handle. 325.00
Tumbler 65.00
Wine. . . . . .50.00 to 65.00

PILLOW ENCIRCLED

(Called Ruby Rosette when ruby-stained)

Bowl, 8" d., clear 28.00
Bowl, 8" d., Ruby Rosette 52.50
Butter dish, cov., clear. 65.00
Butter dish, cov., Ruby Rosette. 75.00
Celery vase, clear. 25.00
Celery vase, Ruby Rosette. 50.00
Compote, clear .40.00
Creamer, clear .30.00
Creamer, Ruby Rosette 37.50
Creamer & cov. sugar bowl, clear, pr. . .55.00
Cruet w/original stopper, Ruby
    Rosette. 135.00
Pitcher, milk, Ruby Rosette. 85.00
Pitcher, water, tankard, clear 40.00
Pitcher, water, tankard, Ruby
    Rosette . . . . .95.00 to 105.00
Salt & pepper shakers w/original tops,
    clear, pr. 15.00
Sauce dish, footed, clear. 16.00
Sauce dish, footed, Ruby Rosette. 22.50
Spooner, clear . . . . .25.00 to 30.00
Spooner, Ruby Rosette . . . . .45.00 to 55.00
Sugar bowl, cov., clear 32.50
Sugar bowl, cov., Ruby Rosette 37.50
Table set: cov. butter dish, sugar bowl
    & spooner; Ruby Rosette, 3 pcs. 285.00
Tumbler, clear . . . . .15.00 to 20.00
Tumbler, Ruby Rosette. 30.00
Water set: tankard pitcher & 6
    tumblers; Ruby Rosette w/etching,
    7 pcs. 270.00

PINEAPPLE STEM - See Pavonia Pattern

PLEAT & PANEL (Darby)

Pleat & Panel Goblet

Bowl, cov., 8 x 5" 42.50
Bowl, 7" d., 4½" h., footed 22.50
Bread tray, closed handles,
    13 x 8½" . . . . .30.00 to 50.00
Butter dish, cov., footed 55.00
Cake stand, 9" sq. . . . . .40.00 to 50.00
Celery vase, footed 35.00
Compote, cov., 7" sq.,
    10½" h. . . . . .45.00 to 65.00
Creamer. 30.00
Goblet (ILLUS.) .23.50
Pickle dish 20.00
Pitcher, water. . . . . .45.00 to 55.00
Plate, 6" sq.. . . . . .19.50
Plate, 7" sq.. . . . . .22.00
Plate, 8" sq.. . . . . .35.00
Platter w/open handles . . . . . . .30.00 to 50.00
Relish, 7 x 4½" .15.00
Salt dip, master size. 18.00
Salt & pepper shakers w/original tops,
    pr.. . . . . .65.00
Sauce dish, flat, handled. 12.00
Sauce dish, footed . . . . .8.00 to 16.00
Spooner 25.00
Sugar bowl, cov.. . . . . .45.00
Sugar bowl, open 12.50
Waste bowl 25.00

PLUME

Plume Compote

Berry set: 8½" sq. master bowl & five
    4½" sq. sauce dishes; clear, 6 pcs. . . .80.00
Bowl, 6" d., clear 25.00
Butter dish, cov., clear. 50.00
Cake stand, clear, 9" d., 5¾" h.. . . . . . . .35.00
Cake stand, clear, 9" d., 7" h.. . . . . .45.00
Celery vase, clear. 30.00
Compote, cov., 6½" d., 12" h., clear. . . .95.00
Compote, open, 7" d., 6¾" h., clear
    (ILLUS.). 30.00
Compote, open, 8" d., 8" h., clear 42.50
Creamer, applied handle, clear 30.00
Creamer, ruby-stained 55.00
Creamer & cov. sugar bowl, clear, pr. . .65.00
Goblet, clear 28.00
Goblet, ruby-stained & etched 55.00
Pitcher, water, clear 70.00

Pitcher, water, ruby-stained 140.00
Relish, clear. 25.00
Sauce dish, flat, clear . . . . 8.50 to 10.00
Sauce dish, footed, clear. 12.50
Sauce dish, ruby-stained 20.00
Spooner, clear. .26.50
Spooner, ruby-stained 55.00
Sugar bowl, cov., clear 30.00
Sugar bowl, cov., ruby-stained 90.00
Sugar bowl, open, clear 20.00
Sugar bowl, open, ruby-stained. 37.50
Tumbler, clear. .35.00
Waste bowl, clear. 45.00

POLAR BEAR

Polar Bear Water Tray

Bread tray, frosted 175.00
Goblet, clear 100.00
Goblet, clear & frosted 115.00
Pitcher, water, frosted 240.00
Tray, water, clear, 16" l. 95.00
Tray, water, frosted, 16" l. (ILLUS.) 155.00
Waste bowl, clear. 90.00
Waste bowl, frosted. 110.00

POPCORN

Popcorn Cake Stand

Butter dish, cov. 52.50
Cake stand, 11" d. (ILLUS.) 78.00
Celery vase, 6½" h. 40.00
Creamer w/raised ears 40.00
Creamer & cov. sugar bowl, pr. 110.00

Goblet w/raised ears 42.50
Goblet 30.00
Pickle dish, oval 12.50
Pitcher, water 80.00
Spooner w/raised ears 40.00
Spooner 35.00
Sugar bowl, cov. 40.00
Wine w/raised ears 58.00
Wine 35.00

PORTLAND

Portland Goblet

Basket w/high handle 35.00
Butter dish, cov. 50.00
Cake stand, 10½". 45.00
Celery tray. 21.50
Celery vase 35.00
Compote, cov., 6½" d., high stand 110.00
Compote, open, 7½" d., 5½" h. 45.00
Creamer. 20.00
Creamer & open sugar bowl, oval, pr. . .28.00
Cruet w/original stopper 35.00
Dresser jar, cov., 5" d. 22.50
Goblet (ILLUS.) 26.50
Lamp, kerosene-type, 9" h. 65.00
Pitcher, water 75.00
Punch cup. 12.00
Relish, boat-shaped, 9" l. 12.50
Relish, boat-shaped, 12" l. 18.50
Salt & pepper shakers w/original tops,
   pr. 30.00
Sauce dish, 4½" d. 7.50
Spooner 27.50
Sugar bowl, cov. 38.00
Sugar bowl, open 17.50
Syrup pitcher w/original top. 125.00
Toothpick holder. 22.50
Tumbler 22.50
Vase, 6" h., scalloped rim 15.00
Wine 22.50

PORTLAND MAIDEN BLUSH (Banded Portland with Color)

Bowl, 9" d. 16.50

Butter dish, cov. . . . . .145.00 to 160.00
Celery tray, 10" oval 65.00
Celery vase 60.00
Creamer. 75.00
Creamer, breakfast size 35.00
Goblet 50.00
Marmalade jar w/silverplate cover,
   frame & spoon, 3 pcs. 95.00
Perfume bottle w/original stopper 85.00
Pin tray, souvenir 12.50
Pitcher, tankard, 11" h. 150.00
Powder jar, cov. 85.00
Punch cup . . . . .18.00 to 25.00
Relish, 6½ x 4" .22.50
Relish, boat-shaped, 8¾ x 4¼" 35.00
Salt & pepper shakers w/original
   tops, pr. 125.00
Sauce dish, boat-shaped, 4¾" l. 26.00

Portland Maiden Blush Sauce

Sauce dish, 4½" d. (ILLUS.) . . . .20.00 to 30.00
Sugar bowl, cov., large 115.00
Sugar shaker w/original top. 120.00
Table set, 4 pcs. 285.00
Toothpick holder. 47.50
Vase, 6" h. 30.00
Wine 55.00

PORTLAND WITH DIAMOND POINT BAND - See Banded Portland Pattern

POST (Square Panes)
Bowl, cov., 6¾" d., footed 45.00
Butter dish, cov. 42.50
Cake stand, 9½" d. 60.00
Celery vase 38.00
Compote, cov., 7½" d., high stand 70.00
Creamer. 40.00
Goblet . . . . .30.00 to 42.50
Pitcher, water 75.00
Relish, 7¼ x 4¾" 8.00
Salt dip, master size. 7.00
Spooner 28.00
Sugar bowl, cov. 47.50

POTTED PLANT - See Flower Pot Pattern

POWDER & SHOT
Butter dish, cov. 65.00
Creamer, applied handle, flint. 95.00
Egg cup, flint 45.00
Goblet, flint. 55.00

Goblet, buttermilk 37.50
Salt dip, master size. 48.00
Sauce dish 20.00
Spooner 45.00
Sugar bowl, cov. 90.00
Sugar bowl, open 31.50
Sugar shaker 35.00

PRAYER RUG - See Horseshoe Pattern

PRESSED LEAF

Pressed Leaf Spooner

Bowl, 7" oval 40.00
Butter dish, cov. 50.00
Champagne 21.50
Compote, cov., acorn finial, low stand . .37.50
Creamer, applied handle 35.00
Egg cup . . . . .20.00 to 25.00
Goblet 25.00
Goblet, buttermilk, non-flint 25.00
Pitcher, water, applied handle. 90.00
Relish, 7 x 5" 12.50
Salt dip, master size. 15.00
Sauce dish 9.00
Spooner (ILLUS.) 25.00
Sugar bowl, cov. 40.00
Sugar bowl, open 18.50
Wine 32.50

PRIMROSE
Bowl, 8" d., flat, clear 25.00
Butter dish, cov., clear. 40.00
Cake plate, 2-handled, clear, 9" d. 18.00
Cake stand, blue, 10" d. 47.00
Card tray, amber w/wire frame,
   4½" d. 32.00
Celery vase, clear. 18.50
Compote, cov., 5" d., milk white 28.00
Creamer, clear 30.00
Goblet, clear 40.00
Pitcher, milk, amber 48.00
Pitcher, milk, blue 65.00
Pitcher, milk, clear. 27.50
Pitcher, water, clear 37.50
Plate, 4½" d., amber 12.00

Plate, 4½" d., blue..................14.00
Plate, 4½" d., clear 9.00
Plate, 6" d., clear 15.00
Plate, 7" d., amber 16.00
Platter, 12 x 8", amber..............22.50
Relish, amber, 9¼ x 5" 18.00
Relish, clear........................15.00
Sauce dish, flat, blue 10.00
Sauce dish, flat, clear 8.00
Spooner, clear......................25.00
Sugar bowl, cov., clear 42.50
Tray, water, clear, 11" d............27.50
Wine, amber 37.50
Wine, clear ....17.50 to 25.00
Wine, opaque turquoise 60.00

PRINCESS FEATHER (Rochelle)

Princess Feather Compote

Bowl, cov., 7½" d....................35.00
Butter dish, cov. 51.50
Celery vase ....32.50 to 45.00
Compote, open, 8" d., low stand
   (ILLUS.).........................32.50
Creamer............................52.50
Egg cup.............................35.00
Goblet 30.00
Goblet, buttermilk 25.00
Honey dish..........................12.50
Lamp, kerosene-type, clear, 12" h. 50.00
Lamp, kerosene-type, cobalt blue,
   large 200.00
Pitcher, water, bulbous, applied
   handle, flint.....................85.00
Plate, 6" d..........................35.00
Plate, 9" d..........................27.50
Relish, 7 x 5" oval 17.50
Sauce dish 10.00
Sauce dish, blue, flint 145.00
Spooner 28.50
Sugar bowl, cov. ....45.00 to 55.00
Sugar bowl, open 29.50

PRISCILLA (Alexis)

Banana stand 75.00
Bowl, 8" d., 3½" h., straight sides,
   flat 50.00
Bowl, 8" d., 3½" h., w/pattern on
   base 75.00

Bowl, 8¾" d., 3 3/8" h., flared
   sides 55.00
Bowl, 9 7/8" d., 2" h. 35.00
Butter dish, cov. 145.00
Cake stand, 9" d. 35.00
Cake stand, 10" d., 7½" h. 90.00
Compote, cov., jelly 45.00
Compote, cov., 6" d., 10" h. ....55.00 to 65.00
Compote, open, 4¾" d., 4 7/8" h.,
   flared sides 35.00

Priscilla Compote

Compote, open, 8" d., 8" h. (ILLUS.) ...58.00
Compote, open, 8¾" d., 9¾" h.,
   flared rim........................55.00
Creamer.............................38.00
Creamer, individual size 32.50
Cruet w/original stopper 30.00
Doughnut stand, 5¾ x 4¼" 47.50
Doughnut stand, 10¾ x 6¼" 50.00
Mustard jar, open...................35.00
Pitcher, water..............85.00 to 115.00
Punch cup...........................18.00
Relish....................20.00 to 28.00
Rose bowl, 3¾" h....................30.00
Salt shaker w/original top (single) 35.00
Sauce dish, flat, 4½" d...............11.50
Spooner 31.50
Sugar bowl, cov.....................50.00
Sugar bowl, cov., individual size 35.00
Syrup pitcher w/original pewter top ...125.00
Table set, 4 pcs....................225.00
Toothpick holder....................35.00
Tumbler 30.00
Wine 25.00

PRISM

Bowl, 7" d., flat 8.00
Celery vase 30.00
Champagne 45.00
Claret, 6" h........................22.00
Compote, open, 7" d., 5" h. 65.00
Creamer............................55.00
Egg cup 25.00
Egg cup, double 26.50
Goblet (ILLUS.) 35.00

Prism Goblet

Pitcher, water 100.00
Plate, 7½" d. 25.00
Sauce dish 16.00
Spooner 36.50
Sugar bowl, open .18.00
Wine 38.00

PRISM WITH DIAMOND POINT
Goblet 25.00
Salt dip, master size 17.50
Tumbler, bar 65.00

PSYCHE & CUPID
Bread tray 40.00
Butter dish, cov. 65.00
Celery vase 42.50
Compote, open, 5" d., 6¾" h. 45.00
Creamer 45.00
Goblet 42.50
Pickle castor w/frame 195.00
Pitcher, water . . . . .65.00 to 75.00
Relish, 9½ x 6½" 32.50
Sauce dish, footed 11.50
Spooner 38.00
Sugar bowl, cov. .42.50
Sugar bowl, open, footed, 6½" h. 32.50

PYGMY - See Torpedo Pattern

RED BLOCK
Bowl, berry or fruit, 8" d. 65.00
Butter dish, cov. . . . . .65.00 to 80.00
Celery vase, 6½" h. 110.00
Creamer, large 55.00
Creamer & sugar bowl, individual
   size, pr. 135.00
Decanter, whiskey, w/original
   stopper, 12" h. 175.00
Goblet 32.50
Mug 22.50
Pitcher, tankard, 9 5/8" h. 145.00
Rose bowl 55.00

Salt & pepper shakers w/original
   tops, pr. 82.00
Sauce dish, 4½" .23.50

Red Block Spooner

Spooner (ILLUS.) 45.00
Sugar bowl, cov. .60.00
Sugar bowl, open 35.00
Table set, 4 pcs. . . . . .225.00 to 245.00
Tumbler 28.00
Tumbler, amber blocks 34.50
Water set, pitcher & 6 tumblers,
   7 pcs. 245.00
Wine 32.50

REVERSE TORPEDO (Diamond & Bull's Eye Band)

Reverse Torpedo Bowl

Banana stand 110.00
Bowl, cov., 9" d. .75.00
Bowl, 7½" d., piecrust rim (ILLUS.) 77.50
Bowl, 10¼" d., piecrust rim 95.00
Butter dish, cov. .80.00
Cake stand, 10" d. 72.00
Celery vase 70.00
Compote, cov., jelly 30.00
Compote, cov., 5½" d., high stand 95.00
Compote, open, 5" d., flared rim 45.00
Compote, open, 8" d., piecrust rim 65.00
Compote, open, 10" d., 6½" h. 70.00
Compote, open, 10 x 8½" oval,
   9¼" h., ruffled rim 145.00
Creamer 62.50
Goblet 70.00
Pitcher, water 165.00
Sauce dish 18.00
Spooner 55.00
Sugar bowl, cov. .70.00

Syrup pitcher w/original top.........165.00
Tumbler 85.00

RIBBED GRAPE

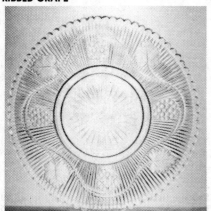

Ribbed Grape Plate

Compote, open, 8" d., 5" h. 90.00
Creamer, applied handle 130.00
Goblet 37.50
Plate, 6" d. (ILLUS.)..................25.00
Sauce dish, 4" d...................15.00
Spooner 38.50
Sugar bowl, cov......................95.00

RIBBED IVY

Berry set, master bowl & 4 sauce
   dishes, 5 pcs.......................105.00
Bitters bottle w/original tulip-shaped
   stopper.........................175.00
Bowl, 8" d., 2" h......................67.50
Butter dish, cov. 85.00
Compote, cov., 6" d., high stand 130.00
Compote, open, 7" d., low stand 55.00
Compote, open, 7½" d., high stand,
   rope edge rim 88.00
Compote, open, 8" d., 5" h. 60.00
Creamer, applied handle 110.00
Egg cup 27.50
Goblet 40.00
Salt dip, cov., master size 115.00
Salt dip, open, master size, beaded
   rim 40.00
Sauce dish 13.50
Spooner 40.00
Sugar bowl, cov......................87.50
Sweetmeat, cov......................165.00
Tumbler, bar 85.00
Tumbler, water.....................80.00
Tumbler, whiskey...................62.50
Tumbler, whiskey, handled 95.00
Wine..............................72.50

RIBBED PALM

Celery vase 65.00
Champagne..........................95.00
Creamer............................100.00

Ribbed Palm Egg Cup

Egg cup (ILLUS.)....................25.00
Goblet 37.50
Goblet, buttermilk 30.00
Pitcher, water, 9" h., applied handle ..170.00
Salt dip, master size.................27.50
Sauce dish 8.00
Spillholder 45.00
Spooner 45.00
Sugar bowl, cov......................75.00
Sugar bowl, open 27.50
Tumbler 85.00
Wine 47.50

RIBBON (Early Ribbon, Bakewell & Pears)

Early Ribbon Compote

Butter dish, cov..............50.00 to 65.00
Cake stand, 9¼" d. 35.00
Celery vase 55.00
Cheese dish, cov. 110.00
Compote, cov., 8" d. (ILLUS.) ...60.00 to 77.50

Compote, open, 7" d., low stand 30.00
Compote, open, 8 x 5¼" rectangular
  bowl, 7" h., frosted dolphin stem on
  dome base 225.00
Creamer. 32.00
Goblet .27.50 to 35.00
Pitcher, water. . . . . .60.00 to 70.00
Platter 32.50
Pomade jar, cov., squat. 28.00
Sauce dish, flat .11.50
Sauce dish, footed 14.00
Spooner 27.50
Sugar bowl, cov., 4¼" d., 7¾" h. 65.00
Sugar bowl, open 33.50
Tray, water 115.00
Waste bowl 38.00
Wine. 110.00

RIBBON CANDY (Bryce or Double Loop)

Ribbon Candy Plate

Bowl, cov., 6¼" d., footed 35.00
Bowl, 8" d., flat .19.00
Butter dish, cov. 45.00
Cake stand, child's, 6½" d., 3" h. 35.50
Cake stand, 8" to 10½" d. . . . . .32.00 to 40.00
Celery vase 28.00
Compote, open, jelly 24.50
Compote, open, 8" d. 30.00
Creamer. 26.50
Doughnut stand 35.00
Goblet 30.00
Pitcher, milk 55.00
Pitcher, water 75.00
Plate, 8½" d. 15.00
Plate, 10½" d. 32.00
Plate, 12" d. (ILLUS.). 45.00
Relish, 8½" l. 11.00
Salt & pepper shakers w/original tops,
  pr.. . . . . .55.00
Spooner . . . . .18.00 to 22.50
Sugar bowl, cov.. . . . . .35.00
Sugar bowl, open 17.00
Syrup pitcher w/original top. 95.00
Wine 27.50

RISING SUN

Berry set: master bowl & 4 sauce
  dishes; green suns, 5 pcs. 75.00
Celery vase, pink suns 30.00
Compote, open, jelly, purple suns. 17.50
Compote, open, 7" d., 6" h., clear 18.50
Creamer, clear .18.00
Goblet, clear 27.50
Goblet, gold suns 15.00
Goblet, green suns. 25.00
Goblet, pink suns 26.00
Goblet, purple suns 25.00
Pitcher, water, clear 75.00
Pitcher, water, gold suns 35.00
Punch cup, green suns 20.00
Spooner, gold suns. 18.00
Sugar bowl, open, scalloped rim,
  green suns 22.00
Toothpick holder, handled, clear. 18.00
Toothpick holder, handled, gold suns . . .23.00
Tumbler, clear. .15.00
Tumbler, gold suns 13.50
Tumbler, green suns 25.00
Tumbler, pink suns. 22.00
Water set: pitcher & 6 tumblers; gold
  suns, 7 pcs. 87.50
Wine, clear 20.00
Wine, green suns 30.00
Wine, pink suns 30.00
Wine, purple suns. 30.00

ROCHELLE - See Princess Feather Pattern

ROMAN KEY - See Frosted Roman Key Pattern

ROMAN ROSETTE

Roman Rosette Creamer

Bowl, 7" d.. . . . . .22.50
Bowl, 8½" d. 25.00
Bread platter, 11 x 9". 28.50
Butter dish, cov. 47.00
Cake stand, 9" to 10" d. . . . . . . .45.00 to 55.00
Celery vase 18.00
Compote, cov., 6½" d., 10" h. 62.50
Compote, open, jelly 20.00
Compote, open, 7½" d., 8" h. 23.50
Creamer (ILLUS.) 31.00

Goblet . . . . .30.00 to 37.00
Honey dish, cov. 65.00
Mug, 3" h. 15.00
Pitcher, milk 40.00
Pitcher, water 70.00
Plate, 5 3/8" d. .35.00
Plate, "A Good Mother Makes a Happy
    Home" 47.50
Relish, 8½ x 3½" 10.00
Salt & pepper shakers w/original tops,
    pr. 32.00
Sauce dish 10.00
Spooner 23.00
Sugar bowl, cov. 37.50
Wine 65.00

ROSE IN SNOW

Rose in Snow Compote

Berry set: 8¼" sq. footed bowl & 4
    footed sauce dishes; clear, 5 pcs. 75.00
Bowl, 7" d., footed, clear 22.50
Butter dish, cov., round, clear 40.00
Butter dish, cov., square, clear 55.00
Cake plate, handled, clear, 10" d. 35.00
Cake stand, clear, 9" d. 77.50
Cologne bottle w/original stopper,
    clear 90.00
Compote, cov., 6" d., 8" h., clear 70.00
Compote, cov., 7" d., 8" h., clear 57.50
Compote, cov., 8" d., 10" h., clear 80.00
Compote, open, jelly, clear 55.00
Compote, open, 5½" d., 4¾" h., clear . .22.50
Compote, open, 5¾" d., vaseline 55.00
Compote, open, 6¼" d., low stand,
    clear (ILLUS.) 20.00
Compote, open, 7" d., low stand,
    clear 24.00
Creamer, round, amber 45.00
Creamer, round, blue 55.00
Creamer, round, clear 40.00
Creamer, square, clear 45.00
Creamer, vaseline 60.00
Creamer & open sugar bowl, round,
    clear, pr. 90.00
Creamer & open sugar bowl, square,
    clear, pr. 95.00
Goblet, amber . . . . .30.00 to 40.00
Goblet, clear 30.00

Mug, clear, 3½" h. 35.00
Mug, applied handle, "In Fond
    Remembrance," clear 45.00
Pitcher, water, applied handle,
    amber 95.00
Pitcher, water, applied handle, clear . . .80.00
Pitcher, water, vaseline 165.00
Plate, 5" d., clear 30.00
Plate, 6" d., clear 22.50
Plate, 7" d., clear . . . . .19.50 to 25.00
Plate, 9½" d., clear 30.00
Powder jar, cov., clear 21.00
Relish, clear, 8 x 5½" oval 16.50
Relish, clear, 9¼ x 6¼" 18.50
Relish, double, clear 75.00
Sauce dish, flat, clear 12.00
Sauce dish, footed, clear 17.50
Spooner, round, clear 32.00
Spooner, square, clear 25.00
Sugar bowl, cov., round, clear 40.00
Sugar bowl, cov., square, clear 45.00
Sugar bowl, open, square, clear 20.00
Table set, square, clear, 4 pcs. 170.00
Tumbler, clear. 40.00

ROSE SPRIG

Rose Sprig Plate

Bowl, 9" d., footed, clear 25.00
Bowl, 9 x 8¼" oval, footed, clear 35.00
Bread tray, 2-handled, blue 35.00
Bread tray, 2-handled, yellow 40.00
Cake stand, amber, 9" octagon,
    6½" h. 60.00
Cake stand, blue, 9" octagon, 6½" h. . . .65.00
Cake stand, clear, 9" octagon, 6½" h. . . .58.00
Cake stand, yellow, 9" octagon,
    6½" h. 85.00
Celery vase, amber 45.00
Celery vase, clear. 35.00
Compote, cov., high stand, clear,
    large 75.00
Compote, open, 7" oval, amber 36.00
Compote, open, 9" d., high stand,
    amber. 37.50
Goblet, amber 32.50

Goblet, blue 48.00
Goblet, clear 27.50
Pitcher, milk, amber 55.00
Pitcher, water, clear 42.50
Pitcher, water, yellow 70.00
Plate, 6" sq., handled, amber........26.50
Plate, 6" sq., blue (ILLUS.)..........30.00
Plate, 6" sq., clear 20.00
Relish, boat-shaped, amber,
  8" l.....................25.00 to 32.00
Relish, boat-shaped, blue, 8" l. 37.50
Relish, boat-shaped, clear, 8" l.......19.50
Relish, boat-shaped, yellow, 8" l. 32.50
Sauce dish, footed, clear............12.50
Tumbler, clear......................45.00
Tumbler w/applied handle, clear 45.00
Wine, blue 49.50

ROSETTE

Rosette Jelly Compote

Bowl, cov., 7¼" d., flat 30.00
Bowl, open, 7½" d. 20.00
Bread plate, handled, 11" d...........26.50
Butter dish, cov. 40.00
Cake stand, 8½" to 11" d. .....25.00 to 35.00
Compote, cov., 6" d., 9" h. 70.00
Compote, open, jelly, 4½" d., 5" h.
  (ILLUS.) 18.50
Compote, open, 7¼" d., 6" h. 22.00
Creamer............................25.00
Goblet 30.00
Pitcher, milk 40.00
Pitcher, water, tankard...............55.00
Plate, 7" d.........................22.50
Plate, 9" d., 2-handled ....18.00 to 25.00
Relish, fish-shaped..................14.50
Salt shaker w/replaced top (single) 23.00
Sauce dish 8.00
Spooner 25.00
Sugar bowl, cov.....................30.00
Wine 27.50

ROYAL IVY

Berry set: master berry bowl & 4 sauce
  dishes; frosted rubina crystal,
  5 pcs. 175.00
Bowl, 8" d., rubina crystal............95.00

Bowl, fruit, 9" d., craquelle (cranberry
  & vaseline spatter) 125.00
Bowl, fruit, 9" d., frosted rubina
  crystal...........................100.00
Butter dish, cov., rubina crystal 210.00
Butter dish, cov., frosted rubina
  crystal...........................215.00
Creamer, clear & frosted 55.00
Creamer, rubina crystal 100.00
Creamer, frosted rubina crystal 175.00
Cruet w/original stopper, rubina
  crystal...........................275.00
Cruet w/original stopper, frosted
  rubina crystal 325.00
Cruet, no stopper, clear & frosted 95.00
Pickle castor, clear & frosted, com-
  plete w/frame...................140.00
Pickle castor, cased spatter (cranberry
  & vaseline w/white lining), complete
  w/silverplate frame & tongs 350.00
Pitcher, water, cased spatter 225.00
Pitcher, water, clear &
  frosted ....100.00 to 125.00
Pitcher, water, craquelle 450.00
Pitcher, water, rubina
  crystal ....165.00 to 225.00
Pitcher, water, frosted rubina
  crystal...........................275.00
Pitcher, water, frosted craquelle......400.00
Rose bowl, cased spatter 295.00
Rose bowl, clear & frosted 85.00
Rose bowl, frosted rubina crystal 85.00
Rose bowl, craquelle 110.00
Salt & pepper shakers w/original tops,
  clear & frosted, pr..................69.00
Salt & pepper shakers w/original tops,
  frosted rubina crystal, pr...........100.00
Sauce dish, rubina crystal 30.00
Sauce dish, frosted rubina crystal 35.00
Spooner, clear & frosted 40.00
Spooner, rubina crystal 79.00
Spooner, frosted rubina crystal 75.00
Sugar bowl, cov., rubina crystal.......130.00
Sugar bowl, frosted rubina crystal.....125.00
Sugar shaker w/original top, cased
  spatter...........................150.00
Sugar shaker w/original top, clear &
  frosted ....58.00 to 75.00
Sugar shaker w/original top, frosted
  craquelle 200.00
Sugar shaker w/original top, rubina
  crystal...........................110.00
Sugar shaker w/original top, frosted
  rubina crystal 165.00
Syrup pitcher w/original top, cased
  spatter 500.00
Syrup pitcher w/original top, rubina
  crystal ....225.00 to 295.00
Syrup pitcher w/original top, frosted
  rubina crystal 450.00
Table set, craquelle, 4 pcs. 850.00
Table set, clear & frosted, 4 pcs. 475.00
Table set, frosted rubina crystal,
  4 pcs. 495.00

Toothpick holder, rubina crystal 75.00
Toothpick holder, frosted rubina
   crystal. 95.00
Tumbler, clear & frosted 25.00
Tumbler, craquelle. 80.00
Tumbler, frosted craquelle 125.00
Tumbler, frosted rubina crystal 75.00
Water set: pitcher & 5 tumblers;
   cased spatter, 6 pcs. 850.00
Water set: pitcher & 5 tumblers;
   frosted rubina crystal, 6 pcs. 325.00
Water set: pitcher & 6 tumblers;
   rubina crystal, 7 pcs. . . . . . .425.00 to 500.00
Water set: pitcher & 6 tumblers; frosted
   rubina crystal, 7 pcs. 550.00

ROYAL OAK

Frosted Rubina Crystal Sugar Shaker

Butter dish, cov., frosted rubina
   crystal. 210.00
Butter dish, cov., rubina
   crystal . . . . .195.00 to 250.00
Creamer, frosted crystal 95.00
Creamer, frosted rubina crystal 245.00
Creamer, rubina crystal 100.00
Cruet w/original stopper, frosted
   rubina crystal 310.00
Cruet w/original stopper, rubina
   crystal. 425.00
Pickle castor, frosted rubina crystal
   insert, w/silverplate frame & cover . .240.00
Pitcher, 8½" h., frosted crystal . . .100.00
Pitcher, water, frosted rubina crystal . .325.00
Pitcher, water, rubina crystal 290.00
Salt & pepper shakers w/original tops,
   frosted crystal, pr. 135.00
Salt & pepper shakers w/original tops,
   frosted rubina crystal, pr. 150.00
Sauce dish, frosted crystal 12.50
Sauce dish, rubina crystal 35.00
Spooner, frosted crystal . . . . . .65.00 to 90.00
Spooner, frosted rubina crystal 100.00
Spooner, rubina crystal 70.00
Sugar bowl, cov., frosted rubina
   crystal. 130.00

Sugar bowl, cov., rubina crystal. 140.00
Sugar bowl, open, frosted rubina
   crystal. 60.00
Sugar shaker w/original top, frosted
   rubina crystal (ILLUS.) 165.00
Syrup pitcher w/original repaired top,
   rubina crystal 275.00
Table set, frosted rubina crystal,
   4 pcs. 600.00
Toothpick holder, frosted rubina
   crystal. 135.00
Toothpick holder, rubina crystal 82.00
Tumbler, frosted crystal 75.00
Tumbler, frosted rubina crystal 82.50

RUBY ROSETTE - See Pillow Encircled Pattern

RUBY THUMBPRINT

(Sometimes may have etched decorations)

Berry set, master bowl & 4 sauce
   dishes, 5 pcs. .135.00
Berry set: boat-shaped master bowl &
   6 boat-shaped sauce dishes; 7 pcs. . .235.00
Bowl, 8½" d. 45.00
Bowl, master berry or fruit, 10" l.,
   boat-shaped .125.00
Butter dish, cov. 125.00
Cake stand, 10" d. 125.00
Castor bottle 25.00
Castor set, 5-bottle, w/frame. 350.00
Celery vase 52.50
Champagne. 35.00
Cheese dish, cov., 7" d. 55.00
Claret 46.50
Compote, open, jelly, 5¼" h. 45.00
Compote, open, 7" d. 95.00
Cordial 28.00
Creamer. 60.00
Creamer, individual size 22.50
Creamer & sugar bowl, individual size,
   pr. 85.00
Cup & saucer 65.00
Goblet . . . . .35.00 to 42.50
Match holder. 20.00
Mustard jar, cov., souvenir 1893
   World's Fair .127.50
Pitcher, milk, 7½" h., bulbous. 100.00
Pitcher, milk, tankard, 8 3/8" h. 90.00
Pitcher, water, bulbous, large 250.00
Pitcher, water, tankard, 11" h.. . . . . . . .160.00
Punch cup. 24.00
Salt & pepper shakers w/original tops,
   individual size, pr. 95.00
Salt & pepper shakers w/original tops,
   pr. 70.00
Sauce dish, boat-shaped 27.50
Sauce dish, round 20.00
Spooner 40.00
Sugar bowl, cov.. . . . . .60.00
Sugar bowl, open 32.50
Table set, 4 pcs. . . . . .250.00 to 350.00
Toothpick holder . . . . .25.00 to 35.00

Tumbler 35.00
Water set, tankard pitcher & 6
    tumblers, 7 pcs. 385.00
Wine 32.50

SANDWICH LOOP - See Hairpin Pattern

SANDWICH STAR

Sandwich Star Spillholder

Bitters bottle 55.00
Compote, open, 8½" d...............60.00
Decanter w/bar lip, pt. 65.00
Decanter w/bar lip, qt. 77.50
Lamp, whale oil, 6-sided font,
    10½" h. 125.00
Spillholder (ILLUS.) 67.50
Spillholder, electric blue 425.00
Spooner 95.00

SAWTOOTH

Sawtooth Flint Celery Vase

Butter dish, cov., flint 87.50
Butter dish, cov., non-flint 38.00
Cake stand, non-flint, 9½" d., 4½" h. ..52.50

Celery vase, knob stem, flint (ILLUS.) ...75.00
Celery vase, knob stem,
    non-flint..................17.50 to 25.00
Champagne, knob stem, flint 55.00
Champagne, non-flint 32.00
Compote, cov., 9¼" d., 4" h., non-
    flint 48.00
Compote, cov., 9" d., 14" h., flint.....200.00
Compote, open, 8" d., 6" h., non-flint ...36.00
Compote, open, 8¼" d., 8¼" h., flint ...50.00
Creamer, applied handle, flint.........95.00
Creamer, applied handle, non-flint.....25.00
Decanter w/acorn stopper, flint,
    ½ pt.............................85.00
Egg cup, flint 42.50
Goblet, knob stem, flint 40.00
Goblet, knob stem, non-flint 20.00
Pitcher, water, applied handle, flint ...140.00
Salt dip, cov., individual size, footed,
    flint..............................35.00
Salt dip, individual size, footed, flint....18.00
Salt dip, cov., master size, footed,
    flint..............................80.00
Salt dip, master size, non-flint 15.00
Salt dip, master size, milk white 19.50
Salt shaker w/original top, milk white,
    non-flint (single)..................19.50
Spillholder, flint 45.00
Spooner, flint 45.00
Spooner, non-flint 19.50
Sugar bowl, cov., flint 75.00
Tumbler, bar, flint, 4½" h. 50.00
Tumbler, bar, non-flint 35.00
Tumbler, footed, flint................65.00
Wine, flint 35.00
Wine, non-flint 27.50

SAWTOOTH BAND - See Amazon Pattern

SCALLOPED TAPE - See Jewel Band Pattern

SEDAN (Paneled Star & Button)

Sedan Sauce Dish

Butter dish, cov. 38.00
Compote, open, high stand............20.00
Creamer.............................20.00
Goblet 22.00
Mug, miniature......................12.50
Pitcher, water.......................45.00
Sauce dish, flat, 4½" d. (ILLUS.).........8.00
Spooner 25.00
Sugar bowl, cov.....................45.00
Wine................................17.50

SENECA LOOP - See Loop Pattern

SHELL & JEWEL (Victor)

Shell & Jewel Tumbler

Bowl, 8" d., clear 20.00
Bowl, 10" d., clear 25.00
Butter dish, cov., clear...............60.00
Cake stand, clear, 10" d., 5" h..........45.00
Compote, cov., 8½" d., high stand,
  clear 75.00
Compote, open, 7" d., 7½" h., clear 40.00
Creamer, clear 40.00
Pitcher, water, amber 100.00
Pitcher, water, blue 98.00
Pitcher, water, clear 39.50
Pitcher, water, green.................70.00
Relish, oblong, clear 18.00
Sauce dish, amber 15.00
Sauce dish, clear ....7.00 to 10.00
Spooner, clear.......................26.50
Sugar bowl, cov., clear 35.00
Tumbler, amber 35.00
Tumbler, blue 30.00
Tumbler, clear (ILLUS.) 18.50
Tumbler, green.......................36.00
Water set: pitcher & 6 tumblers;
  amber, 7 pcs.....................260.00
Water set: pitcher & 6 tumblers; blue,
  7 pcs. 285.00
Water set: pitcher & 6 tumblers; clear,
  7 pcs. 87.50

SHELL & TASSEL
Berry set: 10" oval master berry bowl
  & 6 square footed sauce dishes;
  clear, 7 pcs......................150.00

Bowl, 9" oval, clear 33.00
Bowl, 10 x 5½" oval, amber 90.00
Bowl, 10 x 5½" oval, clear 36.50
Bowl, 12 x 6½" oval, clear 85.00
Bread tray, clear, 13 x 9"..............52.50
Butter dish, cov., round, dog finial,
  clear 115.00
Butter pat, shell-shaped, clear..........9.00
Cake stand, shell corners, clear, 9" to
  10" sq. ....50.00 to 65.00
Celery vase, round, handled, clear 67.50

Shell & Tassel Compote

Compote, open, 8½" sq., 8" h., clear
  (ILLUS.)...........................72.50
Creamer, round, clear 30.00
Creamer, square, clear 40.00
Creamer & sugar bowl, square, clear,
  pr...............................120.00
Goblet, round, knob stem, clear 40.00
Oyster plate, clear, 9½" d............210.00
Pitcher, water, round, clear 60.00
Pitcher, water, square, clear 67.50
Platter, 11 x 8" oblong, clear 65.00
Relish, clear, 8 x 5"..................22.00
Salt dip, clear 15.00
Salt & pepper shakers w/original tops,
  square, clear, pr. 40.00
Sauce dish, flat, clear, 4" to 5" d.........9.50
Sauce dish, footed, clear, 4" to 5" d. 12.50
Sauce dish, footed, w/shell handle,
  clear 13.50
Spooner, round, clear 37.00
Spooner, square, clear 38.00
Sugar bowl, cov., round, dog finial,
  clear 85.00
Sugar bowl, cov., square, shell finial,
  clear 75.00
Table set, clear, 4 pcs...............285.00
Tray, ice cream 45.00

SHERATON
Bowl, 6 5/8 x 4 7/8", amber 23.00
Bread platter, amber, 10 x 8".........42.50
Bread platter, blue, 10 x 8"...........32.50
Bread platter, clear, 10 x 8" 25.00

Butter dish, cov., blue 50.00
Butter dish, cov., clear. 25.00
Cake stand, clear, 10½" d. 32.00
Celery vase, clear. 22.50
Compote, open, 7" d., amber 25.00
Compote, open, 7 1/8" d., 5" h., clear . .20.00
Compote, open, 10" d., clear 45.00
Creamer, amber .27.00
Creamer, clear 22.50
Goblet, blue 42.50

Sheraton Goblet

Goblet, clear (ILLUS.) 18.00
Pitcher, milk, clear 27.50
Pitcher, water, amber 55.00
Pitcher, water, clear 32.50
Plate, 7" w., amber 20.00
Relish, handled, amber 16.50
Relish, handled, clear 12.50
Sauce dish, blue, 4" d. 12.00
Sauce dish, clear, 4" d. 9.50
Spooner, blue 35.00
Spooner, clear. .15.00
Tumbler, clear. .22.00
Wine, clear 20.00

SHOVEL

Shovel Goblet

Compote, open, jelly 18.00
Goblet (ILLUS.) . . . . .16.00 to 20.00
Tumbler 16.00
Wine 18.00

SHRINE

Butter dish, cov. 45.00
Compote, open, jelly 19.00
Creamer. 32.50
Goblet 42.50
Lamp, kerosene-type, w/finger grip,
   pedestal base, 10" h. 145.00
Mug. 38.50
Pickle dish 17.50
Pitcher, cider, ½ gal. . . . . . . .110.00 to 135.00
Pitcher, water 47.50
Salt & pepper shakers w/replaced
   tops, pr. 45.00
Sauce dish 13.00
Spooner 31.50
Sugar bowl, cov. 47.50
Toothpick holder. 85.00
Tumbler, 4" h. 37.50

SHUTTLE (Hearts of Loch Laven)

Shuttle Mug

Bowl, berry, large 30.00
Champagne 35.00
Cordial, small 20.00
Creamer, tall tankard 35.00
Goblet 40.00
Mug, amber 50.00
Mug (ILLUS.) 28.00
Pitcher, water 70.00
Punch cup . . . . 10.00 to 14.00
Salt shaker w/original top (single) 45.00
Wine. . . . . .12.00 to 20.00

SKILTON - See Oregon Pattern

SMOCKING

Bowl, 7" d., footed 38.50
Butter dish, cov. 90.00
Champagne, knob stem 85.00
Compote, 7¾" d., low stand. 52.00
Creamer, applied handle 105.00
Creamer, individual size 125.00
Creamer w/applied handle & cov.
   sugar bowl, pr. 275.00

Goblet 55.00
Spillholder 39.50
Spooner 37.50

Smocking Sugar Bowl

Sugar bowl, cov. (ILLUS.) 67.00
Sugar bowl, open 25.00

SNAIL (Compact)

Snail Banana Stand

Banana stand, 10" d., 7" h. (ILLUS.) 155.00
Bowl, berry, 8" d., 4" h. 37.50
Butter dish, cov. 110.00
Cake stand, 10" d. 100.00
Celery vase 60.00
Compote, cov., 7" d., 11½" h. 130.00
Compote, open, 8" d., 9" h. 65.00
Creamer. 58.00
Cruet w/original stopper 100.00
Goblet 75.00
Honey dish, cov. 95.00
Pitcher, cider, bulbous. 150.00
Pitcher, water, tankard . . . . . .95.00 to 125.00
Punch cup. 30.00
Relish, 7" oval 25.00
Rose bowl, large. 50.00
Salt dip, individual size 18.00

Salt shaker w/original top, ruby-
    stained (single) 50.00
Salt & pepper shakers w/original tops,
    clear, pr. 55.00
Salt & pepper shakers w/original tops,
    ruby-stained, pr. 95.00
Sauce dish 15.00
Spooner 32.50
Sugar bowl, cov. 60.00
Sugar shaker w/original top, ruby-
    stained 160.00
Syrup jug (no top) 65.00
Tumbler . . . . .40.00 to 47.50

SNAKESKIN & DOT
Celery vase, clear. 35.00
Creamer, clear 35.00
Goblet 30.00
Plate, 4½" d., amber 9.00
Plate, 7" d., milk white 15.00
Plate, 9" d., clear 25.00
Sugar bowl, cov., clear 45.00

SPARTAN (Barred Star)
Cordial 15.00
Goblet 25.00
Sauce dish, flat .10.00
Sugar bowl, cov. 60.00
Tumbler 17.50

SPIREA BAND
Butter dish, cov., amber 50.00
Butter dish, cov., blue 57.50
Butter dish, cov., clear. 40.00
Cake stand, blue, 10½" d. 56.00
Celery vase, blue 35.00
Compote, cov., 7" d., low stand, clear . .65.00
Compote, open, 7" d., low stand,
    amber. 27.00
Creamer, amber .36.50
Creamer, blue. 32.50
Creamer, clear 20.00
Goblet, amber 27.50
Goblet, blue 30.00
Goblet, clear. 22.50
Pitcher, water, amber 45.00
Pitcher, water, blue 90.00
Pitcher, water, clear. 45.00
Platter, 10½ x 8½", amber. 25.00
Platter, 10½ x 8½", clear. 20.00
Relish, amber, 7 x 4½" 10.00
Relish, amber, 9 x 5½" 18.50
Salt shaker w/original top, blue
    (single) 37.50
Salt & pepper shakers w/original tops,
    amber, pr. 30.00
Sauce dish, flat or footed,
    amber . . . . .6.00 to 12.00
Sauce dish, flat or footed, blue 14.00
Spooner, amber .26.50
Spooner, blue 33.00
Spooner, clear. 18.00
Spooner, vaseline 26.00
Sugar bowl, cov., blue 55.00

Sugar bowl, cov., clear 35.00
Tumbler, blue 35.00
Wine, amber 25.00
Wine, blue 35.00
Wine, clear 20.00

SPRIG

Sprig Relish

Berry set, 8½" d. master bowl & 6
   sauce dishes, 7 pcs. 80.00
Bowl, 8" oval, footed 42.00
Bread platter, 11" oval.............32.00
Butter dish, cov. 47.50
Cake stand.......................42.50
Celery vase 38.00
Compote, cov., 6" d., high stand 50.00
Compote, open, 6¾" d., 5½" h. 17.50
Compote, open, 7" d., low stand 28.50
Compote, open, 8" d., high stand 25.00
Compote, open, 10" d., high stand 42.50
Creamer.........................25.00
Goblet 27.50
Pickle castor, clear insert, resilvered
   frame & tongs 85.00
Pitcher, water 45.00
Relish, 6¾" oval 12.00
Relish, 7¾" oval 18.00
Relish, 8¾" oval (ILLUS.).............22.00
Salt dip, master size...............45.00
Sauce dish, flat or footed ....7.50 to 12.00
Spooner 23.50
Sugar bowl, cov. 48.00
Wine 35.00

SQUARE PANES - See Post Pattern

STAR ROSETTED

Star Rosetted Goblet

Bread plate 35.00
Butter dish, cov. 40.00
Creamer.........................30.00
Goblet (ILLUS.) 20.00
Plate, "A Good Mother Makes A Happy
   Home" 60.00
Sauce dish, flat or footed 4.50
Spooner 25.00
Sugar bowl, cov. 40.00

STATES (THE)

Bowl, 7" d., 3-handled 27.50
Bowl, 9" d. 25.00
Butter dish, cov. 67.50
Card tray, gold trim, 7 3/8 x 5".......15.00
Celery..........................32.50
Cocktail, flared 24.00
Compote, open, 9¼" d., 9" h...80.00
Creamer, gold trim 25.00
Creamer, individual size 29.00
Creamer & sugar bowl, individual size,
   pr..............................40.00
Goblet, clear....................35.00
Olive dish, gold trim 22.50
Pitcher, water 75.00
Punch cup.......................12.00
Relish, cov., w/silver holder & ladle,
   4" d. 125.00
Salt & pepper shakers w/original tops,
   pr..............................40.00
Sauce dish 12.00
Spooner 28.00
Sugar bowl, cov. 40.00
Sugar bowl, open, individual size ...17.50
Toothpick holder.................47.50
Tumbler 20.00
Water set, pitcher & 6 tumblers,
   7 pcs. 125.00
Wine 25.00

STEDMAN

Butter dish, cov. 45.00
Champagne......................35.00
Compote, open, 7½" d., 7" h. 45.00
Creamer.........................40.00
Egg cup.........................20.00
Goblet 32.50
Sauce dish, flat 10.00
Spooner 40.00
Sugar bowl, open 24.00
Syrup pitcher, applied handle, 4¼" d.,
   8¼" h. 100.00
Tumbler 38.00
Wine 45.00

STIPPLED CHAIN

Creamer.........................35.00
Goblet 22.50
Salt dip, master size...............19.50
Sauce dish 4.50
Spooner 22.50
Tumbler 20.00

STIPPLED CHERRY

Bowl, master berry, 8" d.	28.00
Bread platter	26.00
Butter dish, cov.	42.00
Creamer	22.50
Pitcher, water	55.00
Plate, 6" d.	20.00
Sauce dish, flat	6.50
Spooner	25.00
Tumbler	22.00

STIPPLED DOUBLE LOOP

Butter dish, cov.	40.00
Goblet	18.00
Spooner	22.00
Sugar bowl, cov.	35.00
Tumbler	15.00

STIPPLED FLOWER PANELS - See Maine Pattern

STIPPLED FORGET-ME-NOT

Stippled Forget-Me-Not Compote

Bread platter	35.00
Butter dish, cov.	48.00
Cake stand, 8" to 9" d.	42.50
Compote, open, 6" d., 6½" h. (ILLUS.)	30.00
Compote, open, 8" d.	45.00
Cup & saucer	28.00
Goblet	32.50
Mug	20.00
Pitcher, milk	36.00
Pitcher, water	55.00
Plate, 7" d.	22.50
Plate, 7" d., w/baby in tub reaching for ball on floor center	55.00
Plate, 7" d., w/kitten center	45.00
Plate, 9" d., closed handles	36.00
Salt dip, master size, oval	35.00
Sauce dish	17.00
Syrup pitcher w/original top	80.00
Tray, water	75.00
Tumbler	30.00
Wine	45.00

STIPPLED GRAPE & FESTOON

Celery vase	29.00

Creamer, w/clear leaf	38.50
Goblet	24.50
Spooner, w/clear leaf	28.50

STIPPLED IVY

Butter dish, cov.	45.00
Compote, cov., 6" d.	49.00
Compote, open, jelly, flint	35.00
Creamer, applied handle	35.00
Egg cup	28.00
Goblet	33.50
Pitcher, water	40.00
Salt dip, master size	30.00
Sauce dish, flat	8.00
Spooner	23.00
Sugar bowl, cov.	33.50
Sugar bowl, open	24.00
Tumbler, buttermilk	32.50
Tumbler, water	30.00
Water set: pitcher & 6 tumblers; gold trim, 7 pcs.	220.00

STIPPLED ROMAN KEY

Goblet	35.00
Tumbler	18.00

SUNK HONEYCOMB

Creamer, 4½" h., ruby-stained	24.00
Punch cup, clear	6.50
Salt shaker, w/original top, clear (single)	6.50
Salt shaker w/original top, ruby-stained (single)	19.50
Wine, clear, etched	15.00
Wine, ruby-stained	32.50
Wine, ruby-stained, etched	39.50

SWAN

Swan Spooner & Creamer

Butter dish, cov., swan finial, clear	90.00
Celery vase, clear	60.00
Compote, cov., 8" d., 12" h., clear	120.00
Compote, open, 8½" h., clear	45.00
Creamer, clear (ILLUS. right)	45.00
Dish, cov., clear	55.00
Goblet, canary yellow	65.00
Goblet, clear	50.00
Marmalade jar, cov., clear	57.50
Mug, footed, clear	27.50
Mug, footed, ring handle, opaque blue	68.00

Mug, footed, ring handle, opaque
   purple..............................68.00
Pitcher, water, clear 220.00
Sauce dish, footed, clear.............14.50
Spooner, clear (ILLUS. left) 37.00
Sugar bowl, cov., clear 195.00

TEARDROP & TASSEL

Teardrop & Tassel Butter Dish

Berry set: master bowl & 5 sauce
   dishes; cobalt blue, 6 pcs..........125.00
Bowl, 7½" d., clear 40.00
Bowl, 8½" d., emerald green.........150.00
Bowl, master berry or fruit, cobalt
   blue................................45.00
Butter dish, cov., clear (ILLUS.) 55.00
Butter dish, cov., emerald green 130.00
Butter dish, cov., teal blue 160.00
Compote, open, 5" d., clear 28.00
Compote, open, 6" d., clear 32.50
Compote, open, Nile green 250.00
Creamer, clear 30.00
Creamer, teal blue 100.00
Goblet, clear 95.00
Pitcher, water, clear 70.00
Pitcher, water, emerald green 195.00
Pitcher, water, teal blue 245.00
Relish, clear........................25.00
Relish, emerald green 45.00
Relish, Nile green 55.00
Salt shaker w/original top, clear
   (single).............................65.00
Sauce dish, clear....................11.50
Sauce dish, cobalt blue 20.00
Sauce dish, emerald green 15.00
Spooner, clear.......................30.00
Sugar bowl, cov., cobalt blue 135.00
Sugar bowl, cov., clear 47.50
Tumbler, clear.......................25.00
Tumbler, cobalt blue 45.00

TEASEL

Celery.............................20.00
Goblet 24.00
Plate, 7" to 9" d..............12.00 to 20.00
Sugar bowl, open 30.00
Wine 12.00

TEXAS (Loop with Stippled Panels)

Texas Individual Size Creamer

Bowl, 8" oval.................25.00 to 32.00
Butter dish, cov., ruby-stained 165.00
Cake stand, 9½" to 10¾" d...........75.00
Celery vase 55.00
Compote, cov., 6" d., 11" h. 90.00
Creamer............................17.50
Creamer, individual size (ILLUS.) 16.50
Creamer & sugar bowl, individual
   size, pr. 32.00
Cruet w/original stopper 50.00
Cruet w/original stopper, ruby-
   stained 165.00
Goblet, clear........................45.00
Goblet, ruby-stained 95.00
Pickle dish 24.00
Pitcher, water, 8½" h................120.00
Plate, 8¾" d........................62.00
Relish, handled, 8½" l................20.00
Salt dip, master size, footed, 3" d.,
   2¾" h.............................16.00
Sauce dish, flat or footed ......10.00 to 28.00
Spooner 54.00
Sugar bowl, cov......................60.00
Sugar bowl, open, individual size 15.00
Toothpick holder.....................26.50
Tumbler............................58.00
Vase, bud, 8" h......................20.00
Vase, 10" h.........................25.00
Wine 57.50
Wine, ruby-stained 95.00

TEXAS BULL'S EYE (Bull's Eye Variant)

Celery vase 32.00
Egg cup............................15.00
Goblet 25.00
Tumbler 24.00
Wine 18.50

THOUSAND EYE

Bowl, 8" d., 4½" h., footed, blue
   opaque.............................55.00
Bowl, 11½" sq., 1¾" h., folded
   corners, clear 45.00
Bread tray, blue 28.50
Bread tray, clear....................16.00
Butter dish, cov., blue 90.00

Butter dish, cov., clear 40.00
Butter dish, cov., vaseline 70.00
Cake stand, amber, 8½" to
    10" d. .47.50 to 60.00
Cake stand, apple green, 8½" to
    10" d. 75.00
Candle cup, amber 32.50
Candle cup, blue 35.00
Candle cup, vaseline 42.50
Celery vase, 3-knob stem, clear 40.00
Celery vase, plain stem, clear 31.00
Cologne bottle w/matching stopper,
    clear 26.00
Compote, cov., 12" h., clear 115.00
Compote, cov., 3-knob stem, apple
    green, large 120.00
Compote, open, 6" d., low stand,
    apple green .30.00
Compote, open, 6" d., low stand, blue . .37.50
Compote, open, 7½" d., 3-knob stem,
    amber 57.00
Compote, open, 7½" d., 3-knob stem,
    blue 55.00
Compote, open, 7½" d., 5" h., clear 25.00
Compote, open, 7½" d., 5" h., apple
    green 30.00
Compote, open, 7½" d., 5" h., blue 48.00
Compote, open, 8" d., 3¾" h., apple
    green 37.50
Compote, open, 8" d., 6" h., 3-knob
    stem, amber .34.50
Compote, open, 8" d., 6" h., 3-knob
    stem, apple green 37.50
Compote, open, 8" d., 6" h., 3-knob
    stem, blue 65.00
Compote, open, 10" d., 6½" h., apple
    green 45.00
Creamer, blue 50.00
Creamer, clear .30.00
Creamer, vaseline 47.50
Cruet w/original 3-knob stopper,
    amber 60.00
Cruet w/original 3-knob stopper,
    apple green .110.00
Cruet w/original 3-knob stopper,
    clear 45.00
Cruet w/original 3-knob stopper,
    vaseline 125.00
Dish, amber, 7 x 5" 21.00

Thousand Eye Dish

Dish, apple green, 7 x 5" (ILLUS.) 25.00
Egg cup, blue 75.00
Egg cup, clear .25.00
Egg cup, vaseline 65.00
Goblet, amber .30.00
Goblet, apple green 36.00
Goblet, blue 60.00
Goblet, clear 30.00
Hat shape, clear, small 12.00
Hat shape, vaseline, small 24.00
Inkwell, cov., amber 85.00
Inkwell, clear, 2" sq. 30.00
Lamp, kerosene-type, pedestal base,
    blue, 12" h. .165.00
Lamp, kerosene-type, flat base, ring
    handle, clear . . . . .105.00 to 120.00
Lemonade set: tankard pitcher, lemon
    dish, 12" tray & 3 goblets; apple
    green, 6 pcs. 165.00
Mug, amber, 3½" h. 25.00
Mug, clear, 3½" h. 15.00
Mug, vaseline, 3½" h. . . . . . . .25.00 to 35.00
Mug, miniature, amber 18.00
Mug, miniature, apple green 17.50
Mug, miniature, vaseline 25.00
Pitcher, milk, 3-knob stem, blue 85.00
Pitcher, milk, 3-knob stem, clear 35.00
Pitcher, water, 3-knob stem, amber . . .210.00
Pitcher, water, 3-knob stem, apple
    green 85.00
Pitcher, water, 3-knob stem, blue 100.00
Pitcher, water, blue w/clear handle 99.00
Pitcher, water, clear 57.50
Plate, 6" d., apple green 22.50
Plate, 6" d., clear 12.00
Plate, 8" d., amber 25.00
Plate, 8" d., clear 20.00
Plate, 10" sq., w/folded corners, clear . .27.50
Platter, 11 x 8", apple green 75.00
Platter, 11 x 8", clear 28.00
Salt shaker w/original top, clear
    (single) 22.50
Salt & pepper shakers w/brass tops,
    blue, pr. 80.00
Sauce dish, flat or footed,
    amber . . . . .9.00 to 12.00
Sauce dish, flat or footed, apple
    green .9.00 to 14.00
Sauce dish, flat or footed,
    blue . . . . .12.00 to 25.00
Sauce dish, flat or footed, clear . . .7.00 to 9.50
Sauce dish, flat or footed,
    vaseline . . . . .15.00 to 27.00
Spooner, 3-knob stem, amber 35.00
Spooner, 3-knob stem, apple green 35.00
Spooner, 3-knob stem, blue 32.00
Spooner, 3-knob stem, clear 18.00
Sugar bowl, cov., knob stem, blue 55.00
Sugar bowl, cov., clear 40.00
Syrup pitcher w/original pewter top,
    footed, apple green 85.00
Toothpick holder, amber 37.50
Toothpick holder, apple green 65.00
Toothpick holder, clear 21.50

Toothpick holder, vaseline 35.00
Tray, water, amber, 12½" d. 90.00
Tray, water, vaseline, 12½" d. 37.50
Tray, amber, 14" oval 60.00
Tray, apple green, 14" oval. 85.00
Tumbler, amber 22.50
Tumbler, blue 35.00
Tumbler, clear. .18.50
Vase, 5½" h., ruffled top, clear 15.00
Whimsey, model of a 4-wheeled cart,
    amber. 115.00
Wine, amber 125.00
Wine, apple green 42.50

THREE FACE

Three Face Compote

Bread plate 78.00
Butter dish, cov. 120.00
Cake stand, 8" to 10½" d. . . .100.00 to 175.00
Celery vase 110.00
Champagne 127.50
Claret 135.00
Compote, cov., 4½" d., 6½" h. 75.00
Compote, cov., 6" d. 125.00
Compote, cov., 8" d., 13" h. (ILLUS.) . . .160.00
Compote, cov., 10" d. 145.00
Compote, open, 6" d., 7½" h. 60.00
Compote, open, 8½" d., 8½" h. 95.00
Compote, open, 9½" d., 9½" h. 165.00
Creamer 85.00
Creamer w/mask spout. 125.00
Goblet 85.00
Lamp, kerosene-type, pedestal base,
    8" h. 145.00
Lamp, w/original whale oil burner 250.00
Pitcher, water .320.00
Salt dip 50.00
Salt & pepper shakers w/original tops,
    pr. 85.00
Sauce dish 22.50
Spooner 65.00
Sugar bowl, cov. 115.00
Sugar bowl, open 80.00

Toothpick holder. 55.00
Wine 98.00

THREE PANEL

Three Panel Creamer

Berry set: footed master bowl & 3
    footed sauce dishes; amber, 4 pcs. . . .55.00
Berry set: footed master bowl & 4
    footed sauce dishes; clear, 5 pcs. 60.00
Berry set: master bowl & 5 sauce
    dishes; clear, 6 pcs. 57.50
Berry set: master bowl & 6 sauce
    dishes; amber, 7 pcs. 110.00
Berry set: 9" d. master bowl & 6
    footed sauce dishes; clear, 7 pcs. 95.00
Berry set: master bowl & 6 sauce
    dishes; vaseline, 7 pcs. 67.50
Bowl, 7" d., footed, amber 25.00
Bowl, 7" d., footed, blue 38.00
Bowl, 7" d., footed, clear 19.00
Bowl, 7" d., footed, vaseline 33.00
Bowl, 9" d., footed, amber 35.00
Bowl, 9" d., footed, clear 20.00
Bowl, 9" d., footed, vaseline 45.00
Bowl, 10" d., amber 50.00
Bowl, 10" d., blue 55.00
Bowl, 10" d., clear 20.00
Bowl, 10" d., vaseline 46.00
Butter dish, cov., blue 60.00
Butter dish, cov., clear. 39.00
Celery vase, amber 40.00
Celery vase, blue 37.50
Celery vase, clear. 35.00
Celery vase, vaseline. 50.00
Compote, open, 7" d., low stand,
    amber. 25.00
Compote, open, 7" d., low stand, blue . .32.50
Compote, open, 7" d., low stand,
    clear 17.50
Compote, open, 7" d., low stand,
    vaseline 40.00
Compote, open, 8½" d., low stand,
    blue. 37.00
Compote, open, 8½" d., low stand,
    vaseline 38.50
Creamer, amber 35.00
Creamer, blue (ILLUS.). 55.00
Creamer, clear .22.00
Creamer, vaseline 36.00
Goblet, amber .35.00

Goblet, blue 40.00
Goblet, clear 30.00
Goblet, vaseline 40.00
Lamp, kerosene-type, amber 135.00
Mug, amber.........................30.00
Mug, blue..........................37.50
Mug, clear 22.00
Mug, vaseline 35.00
Pitcher, milk, 7" h., amber 65.00
Pitcher, milk, 7" h., clear 45.00
Pitcher, water, amber 85.00
Pitcher, water, blue 100.00
Sauce dish, footed, amber 17.50
Sauce dish, footed, blue 15.00
Sauce dish, footed, clear 10.00
Sauce dish, footed, vaseline 14.00
Spooner, amber 27.50
Spooner, blue 40.00
Spooner, clear.....................23.00
Spooner, vaseline..................30.00
Sugar bowl, cov., amber 40.00
Sugar bowl, cov., blue 65.00
Sugar bowl, cov., clear 28.00
Sugar bowl, cov., vaseline 65.00
Table set: creamer, open sugar bowl,
  spooner & cov. butter dish; amber,
  4 pcs. 135.00
Tumbler, amber 35.00

THUMBPRINT, EARLY

Early Thumbprint Tumbler

Ale glass, footed, 5" h. 32.50
Banana bowl, boat-shaped 145.00
Berry set: master bowl & 4 sauce
  dishes; boat-shaped, 5 pcs. 165.00
Berry set: master bowl & 6 sauce
  dishes; round, 7 pcs. 195.00
Bitters bottle 135.00
Bowl, 5" d., 5" h., footed 30.00
Bowl, 8" d., flat...................85.00
Bowl, 8" d., footed 20.00
Bowl, 9½" d. 40.00
Butter dish, cov. 135.00
Cake stand, 8" to 9½" d. 85.00
Celery vase, plain base 90.00
Compote, open, 5" d., 5½" h.,
  scalloped rim....................75.00
Compote, open, 6" d., low stand,
  scalloped rim....................40.00
Compote, open, 7½" d., 7¼" h.,
  scalloped rim....................90.00

Compote, open, 14" d., 12" h. 450.00
Creamer............................57.50
Egg cup............................40.00
Goblet, baluster stem 55.00
Honey dish.........................7.50
Mug, applied handle, footed 125.00
Paperweight, panel-cut top 350.00
Pitcher, water, 8¼" h..............275.00
Salt dip, master size, footed 30.00
Sauce dish 9.00
Spillholder 45.00
Spooner 48.00
Sugar bowl, cov....................55.00
Tumbler, bar (ILLUS.) 30.00
Tumbler, footed 48.50
Tumble-up (carafe w/tumbler lid) ...450.00
Wine, baluster stem................46.50

THUMBPRINT - See Argus Pattern

TORPEDO (Pygmy)

Torpedo Bowl

Bowl, cov., master berry, clear 85.00
Bowl, 7" d., flat, clear (ILLUS.) 17.50
Bowl, 7" d., flat, ruby-stained 35.00
Bowl, 8" d., clear 19.00
Bowl, 8" d., ruby-stained.............35.00
Bowl, 9" d., clear 32.50
Bowl, 9½" d., clear 55.00
Butter dish, cov., clear................75.00
Cake stand, clear, 9" to 11" d. ..70.00 to 95.00
Celery vase, clear ....35.00 to 41.50
Compote, cov., jelly, clear 44.50
Compote, cov., 6" d., clear 95.00
Compote, cov., 8" d., 14" h., clear ...125.00
Compote, open, jelly, 5" d., 5" h.,
  clear...................35.00 to 45.00
Compote, open, 7" d., 6" h., clear ...20.00
Compote, open, 8" d., high stand,
  flared rim, clear ....30.00 to 45.00
Compote, open, 9" d., low stand,
  clear 55.00
Creamer, clear 35.00
Cruet w/original faceted stopper,
  clear 60.00
Cup, clear 25.00
Cup & saucer, clear 60.00
Decanter, wine, clear 85.00
Goblet, clear 48.50
Lamp, kerosene-type, hand-type

w/finger-grip, clear, w/burner &
  chimney 67.50
Lamp, kerosene-type, pedestal base,
  clear, 8½" h. 75.00
Marmalade jar, cov., clear 55.00
Pickle castor insert, clear 28.00
Pitcher, milk, 7" h., clear 50.00
Pitcher, milk, 8½" h., clear 65.00
Pitcher, water, 10" h., clear 67.50
Pitcher, water, 10" h., ruby-stained 90.00
Pitcher, water, tankard, 12" h., clear . . .85.00
Salt dip, individual size, clear, 1½" d. . .32.50
Salt dip, master size, clear 40.00
Salt shaker w/original top, clear
  (single) 21.00
Sauce dish, clear. .16.00
Spooner, clear . . . . .35.00 to 45.00
Sugar bowl, cov., clear 80.00
Sugar bowl, open, clear 25.00
Syrup jug w/original top, clear 72.50
Syrup jug w/original top, ruby-
  stained 160.00
Tray, 9¾" d., clear. 75.00
Tumbler, clear. 37.00
Tumbler, ruby-stained 45.00
Waste bowl, clear. 45.00
Wine, clear 30.00

TREE OF LIFE - PITTSBURGH (Tree of Life With Hand)

Pittsburgh Tree of Life Creamer

Butter dish, cov. 55.00
Cake stand, 8¾" d. 72.50
Celery vase 32.50
Compote, cov., 5½" d., 10" h., frosted
  hand & ball stem 70.00
Compote, open, 5½" d., 5½" h.,
  frosted hand & ball stem 56.00
Compote, open, 8" d., 8½" h., frosted
  hand & ball stem 57.50
Compote, open, 9" d., frosted hand &
  ball stem 75.00
Compote, open, 10" d., 10" h., frosted
  hand & ball stem 90.00

Creamer, w/hand & ball handle
  (ILLUS.) 47.50
Creamer & sugar bowl, pr. 95.00
Pitcher, water, 9" h. 65.00
Relish, oval 29.00
Sauce dish, flat or footed . . . . . .12.00 to 20.00
Spooner 37.00
Sugar bowl, cov. .45.00
Tumbler 23.00
Wine 28.00

TREE OF LIFE - PORTLAND

Portland Tree of Life Ice Cream Tray

Bowl, 5½" d., flat, clear 12.00
Bowl, 8½ x 7½", shell-shaped, footed,
  clear 68.00
Bread tray, clear. .40.00
Butter dish, cov., clear. 55.00
Butter pat, blue. 25.00
Butter pat, clear 13.00
Butter pat, vaseline 25.00
Cake stand, signed "Davis," clear, 9"
  to 11½" d. . . . . .45.00 to 60.00
Celery vase, clear, in metal holder 75.00
Champagne, clear 60.00
Cologne bottle w/faceted stopper,
  clear 48.00
Compote, cov., 5" d., clear 50.00
Compote, open, 6" d., 6" h., clear 35.00
Compote, open, 7¾" d., signed "PG
  Co.," clear 85.00
Compote, open, 7¾" d., 11" h., Infant
  Samuel stand, signed "Davis,"
  clear 175.00
Compote, open, 8½" d., 6½" h.,
  signed "Davis," clear 120.00
Compote, open, 9½" d., Infant Samuel
  stand, clear 200.00
Compote, open, 10" d., 6" h., signed
  "Davis," clear .90.00
Creamer, signed "Davis," clear 65.00
Creamer, clear, in silverplate holder . . .56.00
Creamer, cranberry, in silverplate
  holder 85.00
Cruet w/original stopper, blue 90.00
Epergne, Infant Samuel stand, signed
  "Davis," clear, 2 pcs. 125.00
Finger bowl, clear 16.00
Goblet, clear . . . . .32.50 to 42.00
Goblet, signed "Davis," clear . .50.00 to 65.00
Mug, applied handle, clear, 3½" h. 25.00
Pitcher, water, applied handle, clear . .140.00

Pitcher, water, applied handle, signed
"Davis," amber . . . . .225.00 to 250.00
Plate, 6½" d., amber 35.00
Plate, 6½" d., clear 18.00
Plate, 12" l., 3-footed, shell-shaped,
clear 85.00
Salt dip, flat, clear, 3" d. 12.00
Salt dip, footed, clear 60.00
Salt shaker w/original top, clear
(single) 25.00
Sauce dish, melon-ribbed, clear, 4½"
to 5½" d. 18.00
Sauce dish, leaf-shaped, amber 10.50
Spooner, clear, in handled silverplate
holder w/two Griffin heads 57.50
Sugar bowl, cov., clear 55.00
Sugar bowl, open, clear 15.00
Sugar bowl, clear, in silverplate
holder 70.00
Toothpick holder, vaseline 55.00
Tray, ice cream, clear, 14" rectangle
(ILLUS.) 35.00
Tray, ice cream, vaseline, 14"
rectangle 85.00
Tumbler, clear, 4½" h. 22.50
Tumbler, footed, clear, 6" h. 35.00
Wine, clear 45.00

TULIP WITH SAWTOOTH

Tulip with Sawtooth Celery Vase

Butter dish, cov., non-flint 80.00
Celery vase, flint (ILLUS.) 70.00
Celery vase, non-flint 30.00
Champagne, non-flint 40.00
Compote, cov., 6" d., high stand,
flint 120.00
Compote, open, 7" d., low stand, non-
flint 22.50
Compote, open, 8" d., low stand, flint . .80.00
Creamer, applied handle, flint 85.00
Decanter w/tulip-form stopper, flint,
12" h., pt. 95.00
Decanter w/pewter stopper, flint,
12½" h., qt. .130.00
Decanter w/bar lip, flint, pt. 68.00

Goblet, flint 42.00
Goblet, non-flint 26.00
Marmalade jar, cov., non-flint 30.00
Pitcher, water, flint 175.00
Salt dip, master size, footed, flint,
w/metal lid 35.00
Salt dip, master size, scalloped rim,
flint 25.00
Sauce dish, flat, non-flint, 3 7/8" d. 8.00
Spooner, flint 35.00
Spooner, non-flint 28.00
Sugar bowl, open, non-flint 40.00
Tumbler, bar, flint 85.00
Tumbler, bar, non-flint 27.50
Tumbler, flint 30.00
Tumbler, footed, flint. 45.00
Wine, flint 45.00
Wine, non-flint .16.50

TWO PANEL (Daisy in Panel)

Two Panel Fruit Bowl

Berry set: 9" oval master bowl & 6
sauce dishes; blue, 7 pcs. 125.00
Bowl, cov., 7" oval, vaseline 55.00
Bowl, 7 x 5½" oval, amber 25.00
Bowl, 8 x 6" oval, amber 30.00
Bowl, 8 x 6" oval, blue 30.00
Bowl, 9 x 7½" oval, amber 35.00
Bowl, 9 x 7½" oval, clear 15.00
Bowl, 10 x 8" oval, blue (ILLUS.) 65.00
Bowl, 10 x 8" oval, vaseline 50.00
Bread tray, apple green 35.00
Bread tray, blue 45.00
Butter dish, cov., amber 50.00
Butter dish, cov., blue 90.00
Butter dish, cov., vaseline 55.00
Celery vase, amber 30.00
Celery vase, apple green 38.00
Celery vase, blue 50.00
Compote, cov., 8 x 6½", 11" h.,
vaseline 85.00
Compote, open, 9" oval, amber 37.00
Compote, open, 9" oval, blue 40.00
Compote, open, 9" oval, clear 32.00
Compote, open, 9" oval, 4" h.,
vaseline 45.00
Creamer, apple green 40.00
Creamer, blue. 35.00
Creamer, clear 16.00
Creamer, vaseline 35.00
Dish, amber, 11 x 9" 34.00
Flower pot, apple green 22.50

Goblet, amber 32.50
Goblet, apple green. 35.00
Goblet, blue 32.50
Goblet, clear. .30.00
Goblet, vaseline 35.00
Lamp, kerosene-type, pedestal base,
    blue, 8½" h. 125.00
Lamp, kerosene-type, pedestal base,
    vaseline, 7¾" h. 130.00
Marmalade jar, cov., clear 36.50
Marmalade jar, cov., vaseline 65.00
Pitcher, water, amber 50.00
Pitcher, water, apple green 55.00
Pitcher, water, blue 95.00
Pitcher, water, clear 35.00
Pitcher, water, vaseline 75.00
Relish, amber .16.00
Relish, blue 22.50
Relish, vaseline 22.50
Salt dip, master size, amber 20.00
Salt dip, master size, apple green 18.50
Salt dip, master size, blue. 17.50
Salt dip, master size, vaseline 22.00
Salt dip, individual size, apple green . . .15.00
Sauce dish, flat or footed,
    amber . . . . .9.00 to 12.00
Sauce dish, flat or footed, apple
    green . . . . .13.50 to 22.00
Sauce dish, flat or footed, blue . .9.00 to 18.00
Sauce dish, flat or footed,
    clear. . . . . .7.50 to 15.00
Sauce dish, flat or footed,
    vaseline . . . . .15.00 to 19.00
Spooner, amber 35.00
Spooner, blue 37.50
Spooner, clear. 25.00
Spooner, vaseline. 32.50
Sugar bowl, cov., clear 30.00
Sugar bowl, open, vaseline 35.00
Tray, water, cloverleaf shape, vase-
    line, 12 x 12", 1½" h. 45.00
Tray, water, amber, 15 x 10" 47.50
Tumbler, amber 25.00
Tumbler, blue .32.00
Tumbler, vaseline. 35.00
Waste bowl, amber 30.00
Waste bowl, blue 30.00
Water set: pitcher & 6 tumblers; blue,
    7 pcs. 300.00
Wine, amber .23.50
Wine, apple green 32.50
Wine, blue 33.50
Wine, clear 17.50
Wine, vaseline 30.00

U.S. COIN

Bowl, 8" oval, frosted coins 250.00
Bread tray, dollars & half dollars 325.00
Butter dish, dollars & half dollars. 500.00
Cake stand, clear dollars, 10" d. 235.00
Cake stand, frosted dollars,
    10" d. . . . . .300.00 to 400.00
Celery vase, clear dimes 135.00
Champagne, frosted dimes. 325.00

Compote, cov., 6 x 9½", w/dollar
    finial 375.00
Compote, cov., 6 7/8" d., high stand,
    frosted coins 475.00
Compote, open, 6½" d., 8" h., frosted
    dimes & quarters 215.00
Compote, open, 7" d., 5¾" h., frosted
    dimes & quarters 395.00
Compote, open, 8½" d., 6½" h.,
    frosted quarters on bowl, dimes on
    stem 245.00
Goblet, frosted dimes 265.00
Lamp, kerosene-type, round font,
    handled, clear quarters in base 350.00
Mug, frosted coins 360.00
Pickle dish, clear coins, 7½ x 3¾" 205.00
Pitcher, water, frosted dollars 485.00
Relish, frosted coins 195.00
Salt shaker w/original top (single) 125.00

U.S. Coin Sauce Dish

Sauce dish, frosted quarters, 4" d.
    (ILLUS.) . . . . .110.00 to 195.00
Spooner, frosted quarters 310.00
Sugar bowl, cov., frosted
    coins. . . . . .325.00 to 450.00
Toothpick holder, clear coins 180.00
Tumbler, frosted dollar in base 175.00
Wine, frosted half dimes 450.00

VALENCIA WAFFLE (Block & Star)

Valencia Waffle Salt Dip

Bread platter, amber 45.00
Bread platter, clear 27.00
Butter dish, cov., amber 70.00
Butter dish, cov., apple green 75.00
Butter dish, cov., clear. 42.50
Cake stand, amber . . . . .60.00 to 75.00
Cake stand, clear, 10" d. 70.00
Celery vase, blue 42.50
Celery vase, clear. 35.00
Celery vase, yellow 35.00

Compote, cov., 6" sq., 8½" h., apple
   green 67.50
Compote, cov., 6" d., 10" h., clear 75.00
Compote, cov., 7" sq., low stand,
   amber 65.00
Compote, cov., 7" sq., apple green 75.00
Compote, cov., 7" sq., flat, clear 55.00
Compote, cov., 8" sq., 9" h., amber 90.00
Compote, open, 8" d., blue 29.50
Creamer, clear 35.00
Creamer, vaseline 32.50
Goblet, amber 37.50
Goblet, blue 40.00
Goblet, canary yellow 35.00
Goblet, clear 25.00
Pitcher, water, 7½" h., amber 65.00
Pitcher, water, apple green 65.00
Pitcher, water, clear 40.00
Relish, amber, 10¾ x 7½" 30.00
Relish, clear, 10¾ x 7½" 10.00
Salt dip, master size, amber 22.50
Salt dip, master size, yellow (ILLUS.) 26.00
Salt shaker w/original top, clear
   (single) 20.00
Salt shaker w/original top, yellow
   (single) 20.00
Salt & pepper shakers w/original tops,
   apple green, pr. 50.00
Sauce dish, footed, amber 13.50
Sauce dish, footed, blue 12.50
Sauce dish, footed, clear 12.50
Spooner, amber .40.00
Spooner, blue 37.50
Spooner, clear 18.00
Syrup jug w/original top, amber 125.00
Syrup jug w/original top, blue 90.00
Tray, amber, 13¼ x 9½", amber 45.00

VICTOR - See Shell & Jewel Pattern

VICTORIA

Victoria Compote

Bowl, 8½" d., footed 100.00
Compote, cov., 10½" h. (ILLUS.) 150.00
Creamer, applied handle 100.00

VIKING (Bearded Head or Old Man of the Mountain)

Viking Butter Dish

Apothecary jar w/original stopper 95.00
Bowl, cov., 8" oval 45.00
Bowl, cov., 9" oval 55.00
Bread tray, Cupid hunt scene center 50.00
Butter dish, cov. (ILLUS.) . . . . . . .55.00 to 70.00
Cake stand, 10" d. 67.50
Celery vase 38.50
Compote, cov., 7" d., low stand 44.50
Compote, cov., 8" d., low stand 67.50
Compote, cov., 9" d., low stand 75.00
Compote, cov., 12" h. 150.00
Compote, open, 8" d., high stand 62.50
Compote, open, 9½" d., 10½" h. 125.00
Creamer 42.50
Dish, cov., 8" oval 85.00
Egg cup 35.00
Goblet 80.00
Honey dish, cov., footed 65.00
Mug, applied handle 65.00
Pickle dish, 7" l. .45.00
Pitcher, water, 8¾" h. 92.50
Salt dip, master size 45.00
Sauce dish, footed 12.50
Spooner 30.00
Sugar bowl, cov., clear . . . . .50.00 to 75.00

VIRGINIA - See Galloway Pattern

WAFFLE

Celery vase, flint .42.50
Compote, open, 7" d., 5¼" h. 32.50
Compote, open, 9½" d., 8" h. 75.00
Creamer, applied handle 75.00
Cruet 27.50
Egg cup 25.00
Goblet 69.50
Salt dip, master size 27.50
Sugar bowl, cov. .60.00
Syrup pitcher, applied handle 85.00
Tumbler, bar 75.00
Waste bowl, ruffled top 75.00

WAFFLE & THUMBPRINT

Waffle & Thumbprint Spillholder

Bowl, 7¼" d., flint .30.00
Bowl, 9 x 7" rectangle, non-flint. 26.00
Celery vase, flint 110.00
Compote, open, 7" d., high stand, non-
    flint 33.00
Cordial, flint 85.00
Creamer, applied handle, flint. 250.00
Decanter, no stopper, flint, pt. 70.00
Egg cup, flint 32.50
Flip glass, flint. .145.00
Goblet, flint 57.50
Lamp, w/original whale oil burner,
    flint, 11" h. . . . . .135.00 to 170.00
Pitcher, water, flint 300.00
Salt dip, master size, flint 25.00
Spillholder, flint (ILLUS.) 115.00
Tumbler, bar, flint 62.50
Tumbler, whiskey, flint 92.00
Wine, flint 50.00

WASHINGTON, EARLY

Claret, flint 135.00
Egg cup, flint 65.00
Goblet, flint . . . . .60.00 to 80.00
Lamp, kerosene-type, cast iron base . .125.00
Pitcher, water, flint 225.00
Salt dip, individual size 12.50
Salt dip, master size, flat, round 27.50

WASHINGTON CENTENNIAL

Bowl, 8½" oval 22.50
Bread platter, Carpenter's Hall, clear . . .82.50
Bread platter, Carpenter's Hall,
    frosted 125.00
Bread platter, George Washington
    center, clear . . . . .85.00 to 100.00
Bread platter, George Washington
    center, frosted . . . . .95.00 to 110.00
Bread platter, Independence Hall
    center, clear .80.00
Butter dish, cov., footed 87.50
Cake stand, 8½" to 11½" d. 45.00
Celery vase 45.00

Champagne 42.50
Compote, cov., 7" d., 11" h. 65.00
Compote, open, 6" d., 7¾" h. 38.00
Compote, open, 7½" d., 8" h. 42.00
Compote, open, 8" d., 6½" h. 37.50
Compote, open, 8" d., high stand 36.50
Creamer 80.00
Dish, 8" oval, 2" h. 25.00
Egg cup 42.50
Goblet 50.00
Honey dish 12.00
Pickle dish 20.00
Pitcher, milk 80.00
Pitcher, water 82.50
Relish, bear paw handles, dated 1876. . .30.00
Salt dip, master size 25.00
Sauce dish, flat or footed . . . . . . .9.00 to 11.50
Spooner 35.00
Sugar bowl, cov. .75.00
Sugar bowl, open 20.00
Syrup pitcher w/metal top, applied
    handle, milk white 140.00
Toothpick holder 60.00
Tumbler 72.50
Tumbler, bar 68.00
Wine .38.00 to 45.00

WEDDING BELLS

Bowl, master berry, clear, w/gold
    trim 28.00
Butter dish, cov., clear. 30.00
Celery tray, pink-stained 27.50
Celery vase, clear 27.50
Creamer, 4-footed, clear. 48.00
Goblet, clear 50.00
Pitcher, water, clear 60.00
Pitcher, water, alternate ruby-stained
    panels. 85.00
Punch cup, clear .15.00
Spooner, clear. 32.50
Toothpick holder, clear, w/gold trim . . .33.00
Toothpick holder, pink-stained 80.00
Tumbler, clear. 17.50
Wine, clear w/gold trim 18.00
Wine, pink-stained. 40.00

WEDDING RING

Decanter w/stopper, qt. 55.00
Goblet 50.00
Sauce dish, 4" d. .8.50
Tumbler 45.00
Wine. . . . . .20.00 to 35.00

WESTWARD HO

Bread platter 95.00
Butter dish, cov. . . . . .180.00 to 210.00
Celery vase 120.00
Compote, cov., 6" d., low stand 145.00
Compote, cov., 6" d., 12" h. 195.00
Compote, cov., 6¾ x 4½" oval 150.00
Compote, cov., 7¾ x 5" oval, 10" h. . . .160.00
Compote, cov., 8" d., low stand 275.00
Compote, cov., 8 x 5½" oval, 12" h. . . .290.00
Compote, cov., 8" d., 14" h. 290.00

Compote, cov., 10 x 6½" oval, low
  stand............................235.00
Compote, open, 8 1/16" d., 8" h.......65.00

Westward Ho Creamer

Creamer (ILLUS.) ....95.00 to 125.00
Creamer & open sugar bowl, pr. 175.00
Goblet....................65.00 to 100.00
Pickle dish, oval 45.00
Pitcher, milk, 8" h....................250.00
Pitcher, water............185.00 to 225.00
Sauce dish, footed 30.00
Spooner ....65.00 to 95.00
Sugar bowl, cov. ....125.00 to 160.00

WHEAT & BARLEY

Wheat & Barley Tumbler

Bowl, cov., 8" d., flat, clear 40.00
Bread plate, amber 25.00
Bread plate, blue 35.00
Bread plate, clear.....................25.00
Butter dish, cov., blue 75.00
Butter dish, cov., clear................35.00
Cake stand, amber, 8" to 10" d........35.00
Compote, cov., 8½" h., clear 56.00

Compote, open, jelly, blue 32.50
Compote, open, jelly, clear 19.50
Compote, open, 8¾" d., 6¾" h.,
  clear 35.00
Creamer, amber 26.00
Creamer, blue 45.00
Creamer, clear 22.50
Goblet, amber 36.50
Goblet, blue 40.00
Goblet, clear.......................25.00
Mug, amber.........................32.50
Mug, blue..........................40.00
Pitcher, milk, blue 65.00
Pitcher, water, amber 85.00
Pitcher, water, blue 72.50
Pitcher, water, clear 40.00
Pitcher, water, vaseline 98.00
Plate, 7" d., blue....................30.00
Plate, 7" d., clear 18.00
Plate, 9" d., closed handles, clear 20.00
Salt shaker w/original top, blue
  (single) 33.50
Salt & pepper shakers w/original tops,
  clear, pr. 30.00
Sauce dish, flat, handled, amber 10.00
Sauce dish, flat, handled, clear 10.00
Sauce dish, footed, amber 14.50
Sauce dish, footed, clear............15.00
Spooner, amber 32.50
Spooner, clear......................18.00
Sugar bowl, cov., clear 32.00
Tumbler, amber 32.50
Tumbler, blue 32.50
Tumbler, clear (ILLUS.) 25.00
Wine, amber 20.00

WILDFLOWER

Wildflower Goblet

Bowl, 5¾" sq., clear 10.00
Bowl, 6½" sq., blue 22.50
Bowl, 7" sq., footed, apple green 18.50
Bowl, 8" sq., apple green 22.50
Butter dish, cov., flat, blue 46.50
Butter dish, cov., flat, clear 34.00
Cake stand, amber, 9½" to
  11" ....48.50 to 65.00
Cake stand, apple green, 9½" to
  11" ....60.00 to 95.00

Cake stand, blue, 9½" to
  11" . . . . .50.00 to 85.00
Cake stand, clear, 9½" to
  11" .40.00 to 55.00
Cake stand, vaseline, 9½" to
  11" 75.00
Celery vase, amber 57.50
Celery vase, blue 62.50
Celery vase, clear 27.50
Celery vase, vaseline 55.00
Champagne, amber 57.50
Compote, cov., 6" d., amber 40.00
Compote, cov., 6" d., blue 70.00
Compote, cov., 7" d., amber 49.00
Compote, open, 7" d., low stand,
  apple green 26.50
Compote, open, 7" d., low stand, blue . .38.00
Creamer, amber .30.00
Creamer, apple green 40.00
Creamer, blue 35.00
Creamer, clear 25.00
Creamer, vaseline 40.00
Goblet, amber 30.00
Goblet, apple green 37.50
Goblet, blue 27.00
Goblet, clear (ILLUS.) 23.50
Pitcher, water, amber 52.50
Pitcher, water, apple green 75.00
Pitcher, water, blue 75.00
Pitcher, water, clear 43.50
Pitcher, water, vaseline 58.50
Plate, 7" sq., apple green 24.50
Plate, 10" sq., amber 35.00
Plate, 10" sq., apple green . . . . .30.00 to 45.00
Plate, 10" sq., blue 35.00
Plate, 10" sq., clear 17.50
Platter, 11 x 8", apple green . . .45.00 to 69.00
Platter, 11 x 8", clear 35.00
Relish, amber 17.50
Relish, apple green 19.50
Relish, clear 22.50
Salt & pepper shakers w/original tops,
  amber, pr. 50.00
Salt & pepper shakers w/original
  tops, blue, pr. 70.00
Sauce dish, flat or footed,
  amber .9.00 to 12.00
Sauce dish, flat or footed, apple
  green .11.00 to 16.00
Sauce dish, flat or footed,
  blue .10.00 to 30.00
Sauce dish, flat or footed,
  clear . . . . .6.00 to 9.00
Sauce dish, flat or footed, vaseline 15.00
Spooner, amber .30.00
Spooner, apple green 35.00
Spooner, blue 27.00
Spooner, clear 22.50
Spooner, vaseline 35.00
Sugar bowl, cov., blue 48.00
Sugar bowl, cov., clear 35.00
Sugar bowl, open, amber 19.00
Sugar bowl, open, apple green 35.00
Sugar bowl, open, clear 22.00

Tray, dresser, amber, 9 x 4" 25.00
Tray, water, amber, 13 x 11" 60.00
Tray, water, apple green, 13 x 11" 55.00
Tray, water, blue, 13 x 11" 35.00
Tray, water, clear, 13 x 11" 35.00
Tray, water, vaseline, 13 x 11" 45.00

WILLOW OAK

Willow Oak Water Pitcher

Bowl, cov., 7" d., flat, clear 35.00
Bowl, 7" d., amber 20.00
Bowl, 7" d., blue .30.00
Bowl, 7" d., clear 16.00
Bowl, 8" d., 2½" h., clear 19.50
Bread plate, amber, 11" d. 25.00
Bread plate, blue, 11" d. 22.00
Bread plate, clear, 11" d. 21.50
Butter dish, cov., amber 57.50
Butter dish, cov., blue 65.00
Cake stand, amber, 8" to
  10" d. . . . . .40.00 to 60.00
Cake stand, blue, 8" to
  10" d. . . . . .58.00 to 85.00
Cake stand, clear, 8" to 10" d. 35.00
Celery vase, clear 42.50
Compote, cov., 6½" d., 9" h., clear 45.00
Compote, cov., 7½" d., 10" h., clear 40.00
Compote, open, 6" d., scalloped top,
  clear 25.00
Compote, open, 7" d., high stand,
  blue 60.00
Creamer, amber .37.50
Creamer, blue 42.50
Creamer, clear 27.50
Goblet, amber 42.50
Goblet, blue 47.50
Goblet, clear 33.50
Mug, blue 42.50
Pitcher, milk, amber 65.00
Pitcher, milk, clear 38.50
Pitcher, water, amber (ILLUS.) 75.00
Pitcher, water, blue 65.00
Pitcher, water, clear 50.00
Plate, 7" d., amber 30.00
Plate, 7" d., clear 25.00

Plate, 9" d., handled, amber 30.00
Plate, 9" d., handled, blue 45.00
Plate, 9" d., handled, clear 22.50
Sauce dish, flat or footed,
  clear......................10.00 to 18.00
Spooner, amber 40.00
Spooner, blue 38.00
Spooner, clear....................25.00
Sugar bowl, cov., amber 62.50
Sugar bowl, cov., clear 35.00
Sugar bowl, open, clear 20.00
Tray, water, clear, 10½" d. 25.00
Tumbler, amber 35.00
Tumbler, blue 39.50
Tumbler, clear....................32.00

WINDFLOWER
Bowl, 7 x 5" oval 27.50
Butter dish, cov. 55.00
Celery vase 40.00
Compote, cov., 8½" d., low stand 60.00
Creamer..........................28.00
Egg cup 20.00
Goblet 32.50
Pitcher, water 67.50
Sauce dish 10.00
Spooner 26.00
Tumbler, bar 35.00
Tumbler, water 40.00

WISCONSIN (Beaded Dewdrop)

Wisconsin Water Pitcher

Banana stand, turned-up sides, 7½" w.,
  4" h. 75.00
Bowl, 6½" d. 28.00
Bowl, 8½" oblong..................35.00
Bread tray 42.00
Butter dish, cov. 62.50
Cake stand, 9¾" d. ....45.00 to 50.00
Celery tray, flat, 10 x 5"............35.00
Celery vase 36.50
Compote, cov., 10½" d. 65.00
Compote, open, 6½" d., 6½" h. 22.50
Compote, open, 7½" d., 5½" h. 39.00
Creamer, individual size 47.00

Cup & saucer 45.00
Goblet 35.00
Nappy, handled, 4" d. 20.00
Olive dish, 2-handled...............35.00
Pickle dish 18.50
Pitcher, water, 8" h. 65.00
Plate, 6½" sq.....................21.00
Punch cup........................15.00
Relish, 8½ x 4" 25.00
Salt & pepper shakers w/original tops,
  pr................................45.00
Sauce dish 10.00
Spooner 29.50
Sugar bowl, cov., 5" h..............37.50
Sugar shaker w/original top..........65.00
Syrup pitcher w/original top, 6½" h. ...56.00
Tumbler 38.00
Wine 48.50

WOODEN PAIL - See Oaken Bucket Pattern

ZIPPER
Bowl, 8" oval 18.00
Bowl, 10" d. 17.50
Butter dish, cov. 40.00
Celery vase 18.00
Cheese dish, cov. 60.00
Compote, cov., low stand 40.00
Compote, open 25.00
Creamer..........................20.00
Cruet w/original stopper, clear 38.00
Cruet w/original stopper, ruby-
  stained 145.00
Goblet 17.50
Marmalade jar, cov.................35.00
Pitcher, water 35.00
Relish 15.00
Sauce dish, flat or footed ....6.00 to 8.00
Spooner 19.00
Sugar bowl, cov...................25.00
Sugar shaker w/silverplate top 28.00
Toothpick holder...................15.00
Toothpick holder, ruby-stained 25.00
Wine 16.00

ZIPPERED BLOCK - See Iowa Pattern

(End of Pattern Glass Section)

PEACH BLOW

*Several types of glass lumped together by
collectors as Peach Blow were produced by
half a dozen glass houses. Hobbs, Brockunier & Co., Wheeling, West Va., made
Peach Blow as a plated ware that shaded
from red at the top to yellow at the bottom
and is referred to as Wheeling Peach Blow.
Mt. Washington Glass Works produced an
homogeneous Peach Blow shading from a*

rose color at the top to pale blue in the lower portion. The New England Glass Works' Peach Blow, called Wild Rose, shaded from rose at the top to white. Gunderson—Pairpoint Co. also reproduced some of the Mt. Washington Peach Blow in the early 1950s, and some glass of a somewhat similar type was made by Steuben Glass Works, the Boston & Sandwich Factory and by Thomas Webb & Sons and Stevens & Williams of England. Sandwich Peach Blow is a one-layered glass and the English is two-layered. A relative newcomer to the fold is called New Martinsville "Peach Blow." It is a single-layered glass.

GUNDERSON - PAIRPOINT

Cup & saucer, applied white reeded
    handle $200.00
Goblet, enameled blue & white
    forget-me-nots decor, 6¾" h. 100.00
Rose bowl, pinched & ruffled top,
    4¼" d., 3½" h. 50.00
Tumbler 125.00
Vase, 3" h., glossy, enameled decor . . .365.00

MOUNT WASHINGTON

Perfume bottle w/original stopper,
    ribbed, h.p. apple blossom
    decor 1,850.00
Vase, 3¼" h., 3" d., flower-form top,
    acid finish 905.00
Vase, 6¼" h., 2½" d., trumpet-
    shaped, acid finish 1,110.00

NEW ENGLAND

New England Peach Blow

Bowl, 4½" d., 2¾" h., glossy finish. . . .435.00
Bowl, 5½" w., 2¾" h., flared &
    scalloped rim. 745.00
Celery vase, crimped top 795.00
Darning egg, acid finish, 6" l. 105.00

Darning egg, glossy finish,
    6" l. . . . . .140.00 to 150.00
Pear, acid finish, together w/clear
    glass dome cover, 2 pcs. 225.00
Pitcher, water, applied frosted ribbed
    handle, Hobnail patt. 700.00
Punch cup, 2½" h. 325.00
Salt & pepper shakers w/original tops,
    in metal holder 850.00
Shade, glossy finish, 6¼" top d.,
    4½" h. 385.00
Sugar bowl, 2-handled, lettered
    "World's Fair 1893". 450.00
Toothpick holder. 375.00
Tumbler, acid finish (ILLUS. left) 195.00
Tumbler, glossy finish, 3¾" h. (ILLUS.
    right) . . . . .385.00 to 450.00
Vase, 7" h., double gourd shape, acid
    finish. 575.00
Vase, 8¼" h., lily form, acid finish,
    w/most of original paper label
    (ILLUS.). 845.00
Vase, 9¾" h., lily form, glossy finish . .785.00

NEW MARTINSVILLE

Bowl, 8" d., fluted rim 98.00
Bowl, ruffled rim, large 115.00
Bride's bowl, crimped & ruffled rim,
    10¾" d. . . . . .125.00 to 175.00

SANDWICH

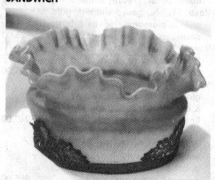

Sandwich Peach Blow Bowl

Bowl, 5" d., 2¾" h., ruffled & crimped
    rim, faint Diamond Quilted patt.
    (ILLUS.) 600.00
Vase, 5¾" h., applied camphor thorn
    handles & ruffled edge 265.00
Vase, applied camphor base (few
    flakes on base) 145.00

WEBB

Bowl, 4" d., acid finish, glossy creamy
    white lining 265.00
Cookie jar, enameled floral decor,
    silverplate rim, cover & bail
    handle 325.00
Rose bowl, acid finish, glossy creamy
    white lining, 4" 190.00

Webb Peach Blow Vase

Vase, 3¼" h., ovoid, raised gold
enameled dots overall, creamy
white lining (ILLUS.) 700.00
Vase, 4¼" h., 4 3/8" d., squat bulbous
shape, glossy finish, gold & silver
florals & gold & silver butterfly
w/blue enameled trim decor,
creamy white lining 280.00
Vase, 5" h., 4½" d., applied clear
feet w/gold enameling, gold & silver
dragonfly & bee decor 320.00
Vase, 6" h., gold leaves, florals &
insect decor, creamy white lining . . .270.00
Vase, 6½" h., gourd-shaped, gold
prunus blossoms, leaves & butterfly
decor, creamy white lining 325.00
Vase, 7" h., 3 1/8" d., stick-type,
Diamond Quilted patt., acid finish,
creamy white lining 395.00
Vase, 7" h., 3 3/8" d., stick-type,
glossy finish, gold branches, florals
& butterfly decor, creamy white
lining 240.00
Vase, 7½" h., 4 3/8" d., swelling
cylinder, glossy finish, gold-
encrusted florals, leaves & butterfly
decor & gold-ornamented bands
around bottom half 895.00
Vase, 8" h., 3" d., acid finish, gold
florals & butterfly decor, creamy
white lining 495.00
Vases, 8" h., glossy finish, gold florals
& butterfly decor, creamy white
lining, pr. 995.00
Vase, 8½" h., 3¾" d., glossy finish,
gold branches of florals & leaves
pendant from top edge, creamy
white lining 425.00
Vase, 9" h., ribbon candy crimped rim,
enameled gold butterfly decor,
creamy white lining 695.00
Vase, 10¼" h., 4" d., knobbed neck,
glossy finish, gold foliage, silver
florals & silver & gold-encrusted
hummingbird decor w/gold band at
neck, creamy white lining 495.00

PEKING

Peking Cameo Vases

*This is Chinese glass, some of it cameo-
carved, that has attracted collector interest.*

Bowls, 3¼" h., spherical w/everted
rim, cameo-carved cloud dragon &
O noga doni bird motifs, yellow,
19th c., pr. $550.00
Bowl, 9½" d., deep rounded sides
resting on a ring foot, mazerine blue,
18th c. (rim slightly ground) 605.00
Cup, deep sides flaring to lipped rim,
mazerine blue, within silver sepal
form holder engraved w/dragon &
cloud motifs, 19th c., 3" d. 220.00
Goblet, thick stem, amethyst, marked
"China," 6¼" h. 85.00
Vase, 5 x 10", cameo-carved red ducks
& water lilies against white
ground 210.00
Vases, 8¾" h., ovoid, cameo-carved
w/quatrefoil panels of birds & florals
reserved on an incised trellis ground
between pendant leaves & petals,
yellow, pr. (ILLUS.) 1,320.00
Vases, 9" h., bottle-shaped, cameo-
carved yellow birds against white
ground, pr. 500.00
Vases, 9¼" h., double gourd form,
cameo-carved Chinese red bird &
florals against opaque white ground,
late 19th c., pr. 302.50
Vase, 9 3/8" h., spherical w/tall
cylindrical neck tapering towards the
rim, burgundy, 18th c. 357.00
Vases, 10" h., baluster-shaped, cameo-
carved red goldfish & water lily
against white ground, pr. 650.00

PELOTON

*Made in Bohemia, Germany and England
in the late 19th century, this glassware is
characterized by threads or filaments of*

glass rolled into the glass body of the object in random patterns. Some of these wares were decorated.

Cookie jar, ribbed body, pale blue w/pastel "coconut" threading, silverplate rim, cover & bail handle $585.00

Cruet w/clear stopper, 3-petal top, applied clear handle, amber w/blue, pink, yellow & white "coconut" threading, 3½" d., 6¼" h. 325.00

Pitcher, applied clear reeded handle, pale pink w/blue, pink, yellow & white "coconut" threading, small . . .225.00

Rose bowl, 6-crimp top, opaque white w/pink, blue, yellow & white "coconut" threading, 2 3/8" d., 2¼" h. 265.00

Vase, 4" h., applied clear curling rigaree foot, ribbed body, opaque white w/blue, rose & yellow "coconut" threading 130.00

Peloton Vase

Vase, 4" h., clear w/white "coconut" threading (ILLUS.) 165.00

Vase, 4 1/8" h., 4 5/8" d., squat form w/bulbous ribs & folded-over tricornered top, opaque white w/pink, blue & off-white "coconut" threading, cased in clear 295.00

Vase, 4½" h., fan-shaped w/ruffled rim & clear foot, rich pink w/pink, blue, yellow & white "coconut" threading, cased in clear 225.00

Vase, 5" h., 4 3/8" d., ruffled fan-shaped top, shaded lavender to pink w/pink, blue, yellow & white "coconut" threading, cased in clear 295.00

Vase, 6" h., 4" d., clear wafer foot, mauve w/multicolored "coconut" threading 275.00

PHOENIX

Phoenix Vase

This ware was made by the Phoenix Glass Co. of Beaver County, Pa., which produced various types of glass from the 1880s. One special type that attracts collectors now is a molded ware with a vague resemblance to cameo in its "sculptured" decoration.

Bowl, 14" oval, sculptured green diving nudes on white ground $100.00

Bowl, 14" d., sculptured water lilies on milk white ground 135.00

Centerpiece, boat-shaped, sculptured cocoa brown lovebirds on custard ground, 15 x 8" 279.00

Dish, cov., sculptured lotus blossoms & dragonflies on amber ground, 8½" oval 65.00

Rose bowl, sculptured white star-flowers & bands on rose pink ground 125.00

Vase, 5½" h., sculptured amethyst owls 70.00

Vase, 6" h., sculptured turquoise boughs & tan owls on white ground. . .75.00

Vase, 7" h., 8" widest d., ovoid, sculptured light green leaves & tan grass-hopppers on cream ground. 85.00

Vase, 7" h., sculptured amethyst praying mantis 110.00

Vase, 9" h., pillow-shaped, sculptured flying geese, frosted & clear. 120.00

Vase, 9 x 8", sculptured blue goldfish on pink ground 95.00

Vase, 9½" h., sculptured blue florals on cream ground 95.00

Vase, 9½" h., sculptured blue fish on yellow ground 250.00

Vase, 10" h., sculptured yellow love-birds on white ground 210.00

Vase, 10¼" h., sculptured white bust of the Madonna on cream ground . . . . .225.00 to 275.00

Vase, 10½" h., 9" d., sculptured white daisies on light brown ground (ILLUS.) 125.00

Vase, 10½" h., 9¼" d., sculptured

salmon pink blossoming branches &
turquoise lovebirds on white
ground 150.00
Vase, 11" h., sculptured blue foxgloves
on white ground 100.00
Vase, 11" h., sculptured white fern
fronds on slate blue ground 135.00
Vase, 12" h., "Dance of the Veils,"
sculptured iridescent white nudes on
salmon pink ground 150.00
Vase, 12" h., sculptured frosted
emerald green cosmos 140.00
Vase, 14½" h., sculptured nude
fitgures, blue & white, original
label 475.00

PIGEON BLOOD

Bulging Loops Pattern Shakers

*This name refers to the color of the glass,
which was blood-red, and many wares have
been lumped into this category.*

Butter dish, cov., Venecia patt.
w/enameled decor..............$350.00
Cookie jar, Florette patt., silverplate
rim, cover & bail handle 165.00
Creamer, Venecia patt. w/enameled
decor 125.00
Pitcher, milk, applied strap handle,
8-sided, w/heavy gold leaves
decor 125.00
Pitcher, tankard, Diamond Quilted
patt. 185.00
Pitcher, water, Torquay patt., glossy ..245.00
Salt & pepper shakers w/original
tops, Ada patt., pr...............125.00
Salt & pepper shakers w/original
tops, Bulging Loops patt., pr.
(ILLUS.) 125.00
Salt & pepper shakers w/original
tops, Flower Band patt., pr. 125.00
Salt & pepper shakers w/original
tops, Periwinkle patt., pr............85.00
Sugar shaker w/original top,
Torquay patt....................250.00
Vase, 8" h., gilt & white enamel decor ..68.00
Vase, 11½" h., applied clear foot &
rigaree 145.00

POMONA

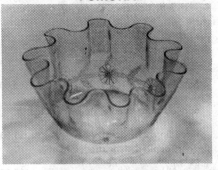

2nd Grind Pomona Bowl

*First produced by the New England
Glass Works in the 1880s, Pomona has a
frosted ground on clear glass decorated with
mineral stains, most frequently amber-
yellow, sometimes pale blue. It may be
recognized by its background of finely-
etched lines crossing one another. Some
pieces bore floral decorations. Two types
were made. One called "first grind" was
etched by acid that cut into the numerous
etched lines made with a needle on glass
that had been given an acid resistant
coating. A cheaper method, "second grind,"
consisted of rolling the glass article in
particles of acid-resisting material which
were picked up by it. The glass was then
etched by acid which attacked areas not
protected by the resistant particles. A
favorite design on Pomona was the
cornflower.*

Bowl, 5½" d., 2½" h., amber-stained
ruffled rim, blue cornflower decor,
1st grind $175.00
Bowl, 6" d., amber-stained ruffled rim,
blue cornflower decor, 2nd grind
(ILLUS.) 100.00
Bowl, 6" d., 3½" h., collared base,
amber-stained ruffled & crimped rim,
1st grind 110.00
Creamer, amber-stained top, blueberry
decor, 2nd grind 250.00
Cruet w/clear stopper & handle,
footed, crimped lip, Thumbprint
patt., 2nd grind 85.00
Finger bowl & underplate, amber-
stained ruffled rim on bowl, 2nd
grind, pr. 75.00
Pitcher, 4½" h., amber-stained square
top, 1st grind ....145.00 to 165.00
Pitcher, 5" h., square top, cornflower
decor, 2nd grind 225.00
Pitcher, 5½" h., amber-stained top,
enameled blue cornflower decor,
1st grind 325.00
Pitcher, square top, 1st grind, miniature size 110.00

Punch cup, amber-stained rim, blue
cornflower decor, 1st grind 65.00
Punch cup, ornate border separating
amber rim from clear, 1st grind 130.00
Toothpick holder, blue cornflower
decor, 1st grind 235.00
Toothpick holder, amber scalloped rim
& applied clear rigaree, 2nd grind . . .210.00
Tumbler, juice, tapered, Hobnail
interior, 1st grind, 3¾" h. 67.50
Tumbler, juice, amber rim & acanthus
leaves, 2nd grind 114.00
Tumbler, cornflower decor, 2nd
grind .75.00 to 110.00
Tumbler, Inverted Thumbprint patt.,
honey amber stain, enameled pink &
white florals & green, blue & pink
fern-like branches decor, 2nd
grind 125.00
Vase, 4½" h., blue cornflower decor,
1st grind 195.00
Water carafe, blue cornflower decor,
2nd grind 190.00
Water set: tankard pitcher & 6
tumblers; honey amber stain, 1st
grind, 7 pcs. .750.00

QUEZAL

Quezal Vase

*These wares resembled those of Tiffany
and other lustred "Art" glass houses of the
late 19th and early 20th centuries and were
made by the Quezal Art Glass and Decorating Co. of Brooklyn, N.Y., early in the
century and until its closing in the mid-20s.
Also see SHADES under Glass.*

Candle holder, iridescent gold lustre,
signed, 5" base d., 10" h. $350.00
Cuspidor, lady's, gold & green
feathering at base rising to white
& green w/lavender highlights,
gold interior, signed, 6¾" w.,
3 3/8" h. 1,150.00
Rose bowl, opal w/imbedded gold
leaves & vines, 4¾" h. 1,250.00
Salt dip, ruffled rim, iridescent gold,
signed, 1" h. .135.00

Salt dips, ruffled rims, iridescent
gold, signed, 1" h., set of 6 in
original box .725.00
Sweet pea vase, opal w/pulled green
lustre threads, gold lustre lining 990.00
Vase, 3" h., dimpled, iridescent blue,
signed. 325.00
Vase, 4" h., 2½" w., squat bottom,
narrow top, gold hooked feathering
rising from bottom to opal top,
iridescent gold interior, signed 877.50
Vase, 4¼" h., wide bottom w/gold
hooked feathering, white & green
swirls, signed 775.00
Vase, 5" h., bulbous w/everted
neck, deep iridescent green
w/pulled ivory & silver feathering,
1905-25, signed (ILLUS.) 1,650.00

Quezal Vase with Label

Vase, 5" h., shaped flaring lip, slender stem, flaring rounded foot,
iridescent amber w/green & silver-
blue striated feathering devices,
1905-20, original paper label
(ILLUS.) 550.00
Vase, 5½" h., green & gold feather-
ing on opal, gold interior, signed. . . .895.00
Vase, 5½" h., iridescent gold lustre
w/pink highlights & pulled green
feathering, signed 895.00
Vase, 6½" h., gold feathering on opal
w/pronounced darker shades out-
lined in brown, signed 1,305.00
Vase, 7¼" h., floriform, gold ribbed
pedestal base w/knobbed stem
spreading in a trumpet shape
w/gold & green feathered leaves
on opal, flaring opal & gold "onion
skin" top, signed 1,440.00
Vase, 8" h., white & gold dama-
scene, signed. 2,250.00
Vase, 8" h., iridescent gold w/pink
& maroon highlights, signed. 400.00
Vase, 8" h., 4" d., urn-shaped,
iridescent gold lustre, signed 450.00

Quezal Jack-in-Pulpit Vase

Vase, 10" h., jack-in-pulpit, iridescent
gold lustre w/stretched edges
(ILLUS.) 975.00
Vase, 10" h., trumpet-shaped
w/bulbous base, orange-gold lustre
w/pink highlights, signed 495.00

QUILTED PHLOX

*This attractive pattern was first made,
about 1889, by Hobbs Glass Company of
Wheeling, West Virginia in opaque blue,
white, pink, green and mauve and was
sometimes cased. Later, a company that
acquired the old Hobbs' glass molds
produced items in amethyst, light blue and
emerald and apple green. A limited variety
of items is available to collectors.*

Rose bowl, blue opaque $45.00
Rose bowl, cased, green opaque 55.00
Rose bowl, cased, pink opaque 50.00
Rose bowl, green opaque 29.50
Salt dip, blue opaque 25.00
Salt shaker w/original top, cased,
pink opaque 35.00
Salt shaker w/original top, blue
opaque 37.50
Salt shaker w/original top, green
opaque 35.00
Spooner, emerald green 30.00
Sugar shaker w/original top,
blue opaque 125.00
Sugar shaker w/original top, cased,
pink opaque 95.00
Sugar shaker w/original top,
translucent sapphire blue 81.50
Toothpick holder, cased, blue opaque .. 22.00
Water set: pitcher & 6 tumblers;
pink opaque, satin finish, 7 pcs...... 350.00

RICHARD

Cameo Vase by Richard

This is cameo glass made in France.

Cameo atomizer, carved shaded purple
florals, signed, 7" h. $525.00
Cameo vase, 3¼" h., 2 1/8" d.,
carved burnt orange tree landscape
along a river bank against frosted
ground, signed 265.00
Cameo vase, 5" h., carved &
enameled scene w/pine trees,
signed 350.00
Cameo vase, 8" h., 5" d., applied
frosted cobalt blue vine-like feet,
carved navy blue mountainous scene
w/house, bridge & water against
orange opaque satin ground,
signed 650.00
Cameo vase, 8" h., footed carved
dark blue river, castle & mountain
scene against yellow, signed 350.00
Cameo vase, 10¼" h., 7" d., carved
deep blue trees, mountains, river
& castle scene against golden
orange ground, signed 915.00
Cameo vase, 10½" h., carved brown
pine cones & needles against
orange opaque frosted ground, signed
(ILLUS.) 650.00
Cameo vase, 16" h., carved deep
red oasis w/palm trees shading a
river village against pale avocado
to grey & cherry red ground,
ca. 1920, signed 385.00

ROYAL FLEMISH

*This ware, made by Mt. Washington
Glass Co., is characterized by very heavy
gold enameled lines dividing the surface*

into separate areas or sections. *The body, with a matte finish, is variously decorated.*

Cookie jar, square form, gold line segments separating shades of pink to maroon, veined leaves & thistles outlined in gold decor, silverplate rim, cover & bail handle, 5" sq., 7½" h. $2,195.00
Cookie jar, gold line segments separating colors of pink, mauve & maroon & gold coin discs on front & reverse, silverplate rim, cover & bail handle 2,250.00

Royal Flemish Ewer

Ewer, rope handle, 9¼" h. (ILLUS.) . .3,950.00
Pitcher, 7¼" h., 7¼" widest d., characteristic geometric segments in gold & silver florals w/raised enamel dots center 1,950.00
Vase, 5¾" h., 7¼" widest d., squat bulbous shape, bulbous collar w/enameled gold pansies, body w/colorful pansies outlined in gold & maiden hair fern in gold tracery within segmented sections 1,750.00
Vase, 10½" h., tan & red serpent w/gold highlights front & gold falcon reverse, red top w/gold encrusted decor & gold beading at neck & base. 3,500.00

RUBINA CRYSTAL

This glass, sometimes spelled "Rubena," is a flashed ware, shading from ruby to clear. Some pieces are decorated, others are plain. Also see BRIDES' BASKETS and JACK-IN-PULPIT VASES under Glass.

Basket, applied clear braided handle, ribbon candy rim, ca. 1880, small . . .$85.00

Bowl, 6" d., Honeycomb patt. 75.00
Box w/sterling silver lid, paneled body, 2 x 1½" 95.00
Butter dish, cov. 125.00
Condiment set: 2 square bottles & rectangular salt dip; cut & polished panels, in silverplate holder, 5¾" h. 175.00
Cookie jar, melon-ribbed, silverplate rim, cover & bail handle marked "EPNS" . . . . .195.00 to 235.00
Cruet w/original stopper, Medallion Sprig patt. 200.00
Decanter w/stopper, threaded, signed Northwood, 8" h. 175.00
Decanter w/hollow stopper, 10½" h. . . .195.00

Rubina Crystal Finger Bowl

Finger bowl, Inverted Thumbprint patt., 4½" d. (ILLUS.) 55.00
Jelly dish, triangular w/crimped rim, threaded body w/applied vaseline rigaree, in silverplate holder 165.00
Perfume bottle w/clear facet-cut stopper, cut panels on body, 1¾" d., 5 3/8" h. 79.00
Pitcher, 7½" h., bulbous w/square mouth, applied clear rope twist handle & neck collar, Inverted Thumbprint patt. 165.00
Pitcher, water, applied clear handle, bulbous, interior panels 125.00
Rose bowl, jack-in-pulpit type, enameled floral decor 95.00
Salt dip, floriform top, applied clear rigaree around center, in silverplate stand, 2¾" d., 2" h. 99.00
Salt dip, applied clear shell trim around center, in silverplate stand, 2 7/8" d., 2" h. 100.00
Sugar shaker w/Georgian-style silverplate top, square w/diagonal-cut stripes, 6½" h. 135.00
Sugar shaker w/original top, bulbous, melon-ribbed .95.00
Syrup pitcher w/original top, tapered, Inverted Thumbprint patt. 150.00
Syrup pitcher w/original top, threaded 295.00
Tumbler, Diamond Quilted patt., enameled floral & leaves decor 45.00

Tumbler, Inverted Thumbprint patt.,
  enameled decor 65.00
Tumbler, "overshot" . . . . .95.00 to 125.00
Vase, 11" h., 5¼" d., jack-in-pulpit
  type, applied vaseline edging 125.00
Vase, 13" h., 4½" d., trumpet-
  shaped, clear pedestal foot, applied
  clear threads & applied branch
  w/three pink spatter leaves 145.00

RUBINA VERDE

Rubina Verde Vase

*This glass shades from ruby or deep
cranberry to green. Also see JACK-IN-
PULPIT VASES under Glass.*

Creamer, bulbous, reeded handle,
  Inverted Thumbprint patt., 5" h. . . .$265.00
Cruet w/matching stopper, Inverted
  Thumbprint patt., 6¾" h. 325.00
Finger bowl, threaded 80.00
Pitcher, water, bulbous w/square top,
  applied handle, Inverted Thumbprint
  patt., ground pontil . . . . . . .175.00 to 290.00
Salt & pepper shakers w/original tops,
  pr. 195.00
Sweetmeat dish, 8-sided top w/notch-
  cut edge, applied vaseline shell trim
  around center, in silverplate basket
  frame, 5¾" d., 5¾" h. 118.00
Syrup pitcher w/original hinged pewter
  lid marked "Mar. 20, '83," Inverted
  Thumbprint patt., 6¾" h. 450.00
Tumbler, 10-row Hobnail patt., 4" h. . . .225.00
Vase, 4½" h., 3½" d., bulbous,
  w/ruffled rim, interior panels,
  enameled pink & white florals & green
  green leaves decor (ILLUS.) 135.00
Vase, 7" h., 9½" widest d., scalloped
  rim, enameled decor 225.00
Vase, 8¼" h., 4" d., jack-in-pulpit
  type, applied vaseline feet 98.00
Vase, 13" h., opalescent, narrow stem
  w/ruffled rim, English, in silverplate base marked "E.P.N.S." 175.00

RUBY

Souvenir Mugs

*This name derives from the color of the
glass — a deep red. Much ruby glass was
flashed or stained and was produced as
souvenir items late last century and in the
present one. Most items listed below are
flashed glass. Also see PATTERN GLASS.*

Berry set: master bowl & 4 sauce
  dishes; Star in Square patt., 5 pcs. $95.00
Berry set: master bowl & 6 sauce
  dishes; New Jersey patt., 7 pcs. 175.00
Butter dish, cov., Button Arches patt.,
  souvenir, dated "1907" 70.00
Butter dish, cov., Loop & Block patt. 75.00
Celery vase, Loop & Block patt. 75.00
Celery vase, Thumbprint patt., 6" h. 58.00
Creamer, Pioneer's Victoria patt. 55.00
Creamer, Roanoke patt. 35.00
Goblet, Nail patt. 40.00
Goblet, Roanoke patt. 30.00
Goblet, Yoked Spearpoint patt. 35.00
Mug, Arched Oval patt., souvenir 35.00
Mug, Bordered Ellipse patt. 30.00
Mug, Heart Band patt., souvenir
  (ILLUS. right) 30.00
Mug, Lacy Medallion patt., souvenir
  (ILLUS. left) .22.50
Mug, New Hampshire patt. 60.00
Pitcher, tankard, 12" h., York Herring-
  bone patt. 95.00
Pitcher, water, Block & Sunburst patt. . .70.00
Pitcher, water, Greek Key patt. 115.00
Pitcher, water, Late Block patt. 100.00
Punch cup, Late Block patt. 15.00
Punch cup, Tacoma patt. 16.00
Sauce dish, flat, Nail patt. 11.00
Sauce dish, handled, Riverside's
  Victoria patt. 20.00
Spooner, Adam's Saxon patt. 50.00
Spooner, Box-in-Box patt. 35.00
Spooner, Roanoke patt. 35.00
Spooner, Thumbprint patt., etched 40.00
Syrup pitcher w/original top, Royal
  Crystal patt. .265.00
Syrup pitcher w/metal top, Torpedo
  patt. . . . . .135.00 to 150.00
Table set: cov. butter dish, open sugar
  bowl, creamer & spooner; River-
  side's Victoria patt., 4 pcs. 375.00
Table set, Spearpoint Band patt.,
  4 pcs. 185.00
Toothpick holder, Box-in-Box patt. 45.00
Toothpick holder, Cordova patt. 40.00

Toothpick holder, Heart Band patt.,
  souvenir.........................15.00
Toothpick holder, Prince of Wales -
  Plumes patt. 210.00
Toothpick holder, Truncated Cube
  patt. 45.00
Tumbler, Arched Oval patt., souvenir ..27.50
Tumbler, Beaded Swirl patt...........45.00
Tumbler, Broken Column patt.........50.00
Tumbler, Cathedral patt..............32.00
Tumbler, Tacoma patt. 25.00
Tumbler, Triple Triangle patt. 30.00
Water set: pitcher & 5 tumblers;
  Beaded Swag patt., gold trim,
  6 pcs. 285.00
Water set: pitcher & 6 tumblers;
  Roanoke patt., 7 pcs.......255.00 to 285.00
Water set: bulbous pitcher & 6
  tumblers; Royal Crystal patt.,
  7 pcs. 265.00

Souvenir Wine

Wine, Button Arches patt., souvenir,
  4" h. (ILLUS.) 25.00
Wine, King's Crown patt., souvenir 20.00
Wine, Truncated Cube patt. 35.00
Wine set: decanter & 6 wines; Tiny
  Fine Cut patt., 7 pcs. 225.00

SANDWICH

Numerous types of glass were produced at the Boston & Sandwich Glass Works, Cape Cod, Mass., from 1826 to 1888. Those listed here represent a sampling. Also see PATTERN and PEACH BLOW under Glass.

Bowl, 7" d., Rayed Peacock Eye patt.,
  clear $65.00
Bowls, 8" oval, lacy, Double Horn
  of Plenty & Princess Feather
  patterns, clear, pr................425.00
Bowl, 6-sided, lacy, Star Medallion
  patt. 155.00

Candlesticks, stepped base, columnar
  stem, petal socket, clear, pr. 250.00

Dolphin Candlesticks

Candlesticks, square base, dolphin
  stem, vaseline, pr. (ILLUS.) 625.00
Celery vase, Loop patt., canary
  yellow...........................295.00
Creamer, Ivy patt., flint, clear 165.00
Curtain tieback w/original pewter
  shank, fiery blue opalescent flower
  form (single) 35.00
Curtain tiebacks w/original pewter
  shanks, clear flower forms,
  3½" d., pr........................75.00
Curtain tiebacks, amber flower
  forms, pr. (no shanks) 35.00
Dish, lacy, Hairpin patt., clear,
  oblong 385.00
Perfume bottle w/stopper, vaseline ...175.00

Pitcher with Ice Bladder

Pitcher w/ice bladder, 13" h.,
  clear "overshot" (ILLUS.) 200.00
Plate, 5" d., lacy, Heart & Sheaves
  of Wheat patt., clear 45.00
Pomade jar, figural muzzled bear,
  blue opaque 175.00
Salt basket, Bull's Eye & Diamond
  Point patt., clear..................100.00
Salt dip, lacy, clear..................75.00

Salt dip, "Lafayette Boat," purple-blue .550.00
Salt shaker, "Christmas" salt w/agitator
   & dated top, amber or amethyst,
   2½" h., each 110.00
Salt shaker, "Christmas" salt
   w/agitator & dated top, clear 50.00
Salt shaker, "Christmas" salt
   w/agitator & dated top, cobalt blue ..95.00
Salt & pepper shakers w/pewter tops,
   blue opaque, flint, 6" h., pr. 110.00
Sauce dish, lacy, Crossed Swords
   patt., clear.......................23.00
Sauce dish, lacy, Peacock Feather
   patt., clear, flint 28.00
Sauce dish, lacy, Princess Feather
   patt. 145.00
Spillholder, Sawtooth & Thumbprint
   patt., clear.......................60.00
Spillholder, Star patt., canary yellow ..395.00
Sugar bowl, cov., lacy, Gothic Arch
   patt., clear......................600.00
Sugar bowl, cov., lacy, Gothic Arch
   patt., violet, 5½" h. 850.00
Sugar bowl, cov., lacy, Roman
   Rosette patt., clear, flint, 6" h.......125.00
Vase, 7" h., Midnight Lace patt.,
   black amethyst, ca. 1880 ....65.00
Vase, 9 3/8" h., 6¾" d., bulbous,
   smoke-colored w/applied
   sapphire blue icicles & blue trim
   around top edge 650.00
Whiskey taster, fiery opalescent 225.00
Whiskey taster, vaseline............150.00

SATIN

Mother-of-Pearl Satin Pitcher

*Satin and Mother-of-Pearl wares were
made by numerous glasshouses over a large
part of the world. They continue in
production today.*

Bowl, 4 x 5", 4" h., applied frosted
   feet & top ruffle, shaded blue
   mother-of-pearl Ribbon patt. $365.00

Bowl, 8 x 7" oblong, 5" h., 4
   applied feet, blue mother-of-pearl
   Diamond Quilted patt..............285.00
Box w/hinged lid, applied frosted
   feet, lavender-pink w/overall
   green, blue, white & gold
   enameled leaves & scrolls decor,
   white lining, ornate brass bail
   handle, 3½" d., 4¾" h..............180.00
Celery vase, ruffled top w/frosted
   edging, shaded lemon yellow
   w/blue & white enameled floral
   decor, white lining, silverplate
   holder w/bow ribbon handles,
   5½" d., 8 7/8" h..................232.00
Cookie jar, pale green w/enameled
   chrysanthemums decor, silverplate
   rim, cover & bail handle 125.00
Creamer, applied blue frosted reeded
   handle, bulbous w/round top,
   heavenly blue mother-of-pearl
   Raindrop patt., white lining,
   3 1/8" d., 4½" h..................230.00
Ewer, applied frosted handle, rainbow
   mother-of-pearl Herringbone patt.,
   9¾" h. 945.00
Pitcher, 6" h., 4½" d., bulbous w/oval
   top, applied frosted handle, shaded
   heavenly blue w/enameled pink &
   yellow florals & green foliage 232.00
Pitcher, 7" h., blue mother-of-pearl
   Diamond Quilted patt. (ILLUS.)......225.00
Pitcher, 8¼" h., applied frosted
   handle, brilliant lemon yellow
   mother-of-pearl Diamond Quilted
   patt. 145.00
Rose bowl, 8-crimp top, shaded brown
   to tan mother-of-pearl Diamond
   Quilted patt., cream lining,
   2 3/8" d., 2 1/8" h. 275.00
Rose bowl, white mother-of-pearl
   Ribbon patt. w/gold floral decor,
   gold top & base trim, 3" d.,
   2½" h. 495.00
Rose bowl, 9-crimp top, Amberina
   mother-of-pearl Diamond
   Quilted patt., cream lining, Webb,
   7" d., 7" h. 1,360.00

Mother-of-Pearl Satin Salt & Pepper Shakers

Salt & pepper shakers w/original tops,
    deep rose shaded to white mother-
    of pearl Diamond Quilted patt.,
    enameled floral decor, pr. (ILLUS.) . .250.00
Syrup pitcher w/original top, Beaded
    Drape patt., red 350.00
Tumbler, shaded deep pink mother-
    of-pearl Diamond Quilted patt.
    w/blue daisies & yellow & green
    leaves decor, 2 7/8" d., 3 7/8" h. 200.00
Tumbler, shaded pink w/blue & white
    florals & green leaves decor, gold
    trim, white lining, 3" d., 4 1/8" h. . . .130.00
Tumbler, yellow shaded to white
    mother-of-pearl Diamond Quilted
    patt. 100.00
Tumbler, Rubina mother-of-pearl
    Herringbone patt., white lining 95.00
Vase, 5¾" h., 4¼" d., American
    Beauty Rose mother-of-pearl Flower
    & Acorn patt., white lining 405.00
Vase, 6" h., 4½" widest d., square
    folded-over top, golden yellow
    shaded to white mother-of-pearl
    Hobnail patt. 600.00
Vase, 6 3/8" h., 3¾" d., bridal white
    mother-of-pearl Ribbon patt. w/gold
    garlands & bows decor 907.00
Vase, 8" h., crimped top, pinched
    sides, apple green mother-of-pearl
    Raindrop patt. 295.00

Mother-of-Pearl Satin Vase

Vase, 8½" h., 4 3/8" d., bulbous
    w/narrow neck, soft peach mother-
    of-pearl Diamond Quilted patt.,
    white lining (ILLUS.) 150.00
Vase, 10" h., ruffled top, chartreuse
    green mother-of-pearl Diamond
    Quilted patt., white lining, ormolu
    foot w/applied flowers 450.00
Vase, 10¾" h., 8" d., bulbous base,
    butterscotch mother-of-pearl
    "Federzeichnung" patt., gold
    tracery, marked "Patent" 1,750.00

SCHNEIDER

Schneider Vases

    *This ware is made in France at
Cristallerie Schneider, established in 1913
near Paris by Ernest and Charles Schneider.
Some pieces of cameo were marked "Le
Verre Francais" and others were signed
"Charder." Also see LE VERRE
FRANCAIS.*

Bowl, 9" d., flared, mottled orange,
    signed $75.00
Centerpiece bowl, red bowl shading
    to mottled yellow at foot, in
    handled wrought iron frame cast
    w/roses & leaves, signed, 10" w.,
    4" h. 225.00
Compote, 6" d., 8" h., Art Deco style
    flattened bowl w/upright rim, tubu-
    lar stem & rounded foot, shaded
    from purple to orange to deep
    purple, signed 550.00
Ewer, shaded mottled amethyst to red,
    applied amethyst handle, signed,
    6½" h. 175.00
Jardiniere, shaded speckled light to
    dark purple, in wrought iron ribbed
    oblong frame cast w/foliate han-
    dles & 4 feet, early 20th c., 8¼" h. 550.00
Rose bowl, shaded mottled yellow to
    mottled brown at rim, 4" d. top
    opening 125.00
Urn, 2-handled, deep maroon to
    tomato red, internally decorated
    in undulating waves in body & con-
    trolled bubbles in upper portion,
    signed, 9" d., 11" h. 1,250.00
Vase, 5½" h., blue, black & clear
    w/orange lining, blown into
    wrought iron footed base, ca. 1925,
    signed 250.00
Vase, 7½" h., globular w/waisted
    neck, marbleized pink & yellow
    shaded to amethyst at base,
    signed 375.00
Vase, 8½" h., bulbous, grey-amber

w/applied lavender opalescent
band near top, signed 375.00

Vase, 14½" h., translucent amber
footed cylinder w/waisted neck,
band of intaglio-carved leafage at
shoulder applied w/cast mustard
yellow opaque cabochons cut as
stylized pinecones, "Guirlande"
series, 1924-25, signed (ILLUS.
right) 1,760.00

Vase, 14¾" h., clear mottled w/dusty
rose shading to white, purple &
blue-grey elongated ovoid raised
on domed purple foot, 1924-25,
signed (ILLUS. left) 770.00

SHADES

Fostoria Festoon Pattern Shade

*The popularity of collecting fine early Art
Glass gas and electric shades has recently
soared and values have escalated accordingly. Listed below, by manufacturer or
type of glass, is a random sampling of
shades offered for sale within the past six
months.*

Durand, white w/blue & gold hearts &
gold threading, gold lining,
5½" h. $120.00

Fostoria, Festoon patt., gold pulled
design on white, gold lining
(ILLUS.) 125.00

Fostoria, green w/platinum King Tut
patt. 350.00

Lustre Art, Calcite w/green leaves
& gold threading, corset-shaped 65.00

Lustre Art, iridescent gold w/opal
leaves edged in green w/overall
gold threading 245.00

Lustre Art, iridescent gold w/pulled
brownish feathering edged in iridescent green, pr. 285.00

Lustre Art, opal w/gold feathering
edged in green, gold lining, scalloped edge......................125.00

Muller Freres, creamy white w/cobalt
blue mottling & touches of yellow,
6" h., set of 3 ....245.00

NuArt, iridescent marigold Carnival
glass, paneled....................35.00

NuArt, iridescent marigold Carnival
glass, fishscale decor, pr. 65.00

Quezal, Calcite w/gold feathering,
gold lining, set of 3..............300.00

Quezal, Calcite w/pulled green
feathering outlined in gold, gold
lining, 6½" h. 225.00

Quezal Shade

Quezal, iridescent gold w/blue &
purple highlights, 6" h. (ILLUS.) 150.00

Quezal, iridescent gold w/opal snakeskin, flaring green border..........125.00

Quezal, iridescent platinum w/opal
feathering outlined in green &
applied platinum spider webbing
overall, notched rim, set of 3 ....450.00

Quezal, opal w/green & gold leaves
& overall gold threading, gold lining,
pr. 220.00

Quezal, opal w/iridescent gold
feathering, gold lining, 5½" h., set
of 4 ....475.00

Quezal, opal w/iridescent gold trellis,
gold lining, 7" d. 715.00

Quezal, opal w/platinum feathering
on dark green, gold lining..........275.00

Steuben, Calcite w/blue feathering
outlined in gold, gold lining,
6¼" h. 275.00

Steuben, iridescent brown Aurene
w/blue drape, Calcite lining........350.00

Steuben, iridescent gold Aurene,
Calcite lining 110.00

Steuben, iridescent green Aurene
w/platinum leaf & vine, Calcite
lining, 4½" h. 950.00

Steuben, iridescent tan Aurene w/gold
leaves & threading, gold lining 175.00

Steuben, opal w/bright yellow
feathering outlined in green, gold
lining, set of 4 ....525.00

Steuben, Verre de Soie, bell-shaped....75.00

Tiffany, damascened in silvery-blue,
green & iridescent amber, waisted
domical form, 1900-20, 10" d........990.00

Tiffany, floriform w/ruffled rim,

varying feather devices in opalescent cream, green, yellow & amber on a light ground, 1899-1920, 5¼" to 5¾" h., set of 4 .... 935.00
Tiffany, iridescent orange w/green King Tut patt., opal lining, pr. 500.00
Tiffany, quilted spherical deep iridescent amber upper body above pale amber iridescent deep ruffled lip, 1900-20, 4½" h. (minor upper rim chips).......................... 1,430.00

SILVER OVERLAY & SILVER DEPOSIT

Vase with Silver Overlay

Silver Deposit and Silver Overlay have been made commercially since the last quarter of the 19th century. Silver is deposited on the glass by various means, the most widely adopted utilizing an electric current. The glass was very popular during the first three decades of this century, and some pieces are still being produced. During the late 1970's, silver commanded exceptionally high prices and this was reflected in a surge of interest in silver overlay glass, especially in pieces marked "sterling" or "925" on the heavy silver overlay.

Bottle w/original stopper, cobalt blue w/sterling silver overlay leaf design, 9¼" h. $110.00
Bowl, 12½" d., scalloped rim, clear w/frosted florals & silver deposit 60.00
Candy jar, cov., black-amethyst w/silver deposit florals & trim, 7" d. .. 45.00
Cologne bottle w/original stopper, corset-shaped, clear w/silver overlay scrolls & florals, 7¾" h. 135.00
Compote & underplate, clear w/etched florals & silver deposit trim, pr. 55.00
Console set: footed bowl & pr. low

candlesticks; black w/sterling silver overlay, 3 pcs. 290.00
Loving cup, 3-handled, cranberry w/sterling silver overlay, 3½" 595.00
Perfume bottle w/ball-shaped stopper, clear w/silver deposit florals & vines, 4¼" h. 55.00
Perfume bottle w/sterling silver stopper, clear w/sterling silver overlay designs, 6" h. 85.00
Pitcher, water, 8¼" h., clear w/sterling silver overlay floral & leaf decor 245.00
Vase, bud, 6½" h., clear w/silver deposit florals 55.00
Vase, 7½" h., mottled iridescent gold w/green & purple highlights & sterling silver overlay decor, unsigned .. 395.00
Vase, 8" h., clear w/silver deposit iris & butterflies decor 37.00
Vase, 8" h., 3-footed, clear w/three panels of silver deposit floral wreaths joining horizontal band at shoulder, fluted & flared lip w/sterling rim band 67.50
Vase, 9½" h., amethyst w/silver deposit geometric design 59.00
Vase, 10¾" h., green satin finish w/sterling silver overlay rim & pendant blossoming branch (ILLUS.) 225.00
Vase, 12" h., emerald green w/silver overlay long-stemmed tulips, marked "Alvin Sterling" in design ... 935.00
Vase, 12" h., green w/sterling silver overlay latticework & scrolls 475.00
Vase, 14" h., clear w/sterling silver overlay Art Nouveau florals, marked "Gorham" on silver 295.00
Water set: pitcher & 6 tumblers; cobalt blue w/sterling silver overlay, 7 pcs. 285.00
Whiskey decanter, clear w/sterling silver overlay Art Nouveau vines & thistles, 12" h. 125.00

SINCLAIRE

H.P. Sinclaire & Co., Corning, New York, operated from 1904 until 1928, turning out fine quality cut and engraved glasswares on blanks supplied by Dorflinger, Pairpoint, Baccarat, Steuben and other glassworks. Its founder, H.P. Sinclaire, Jr., had been associated with T.G. Hawkes & Co., from 1883, and had risen to a high position with that firm. Sinclaire showed a preference for engraved glass over deeply cut glass and this was to be the specialty of the firm that carried his name. From 1920 on, most of the crystal and colored blanks were of the company's own manufacture and, after 1926, engraving gave way to acid-etched designs. Their trademark of an acid-stamped "S" within a laurel wreath interrupted by two shields was used on all perfect pieces but seconds were sold without the trademark from a special salesroom on the premises. Also see CUT GLASS.

Candlestick, swirl-ribbed stem, light green, signed, 10¼" h. (single) $70.00

Candlesticks, round foot, trapped "air bubble" baluster-shaped standard w/engraved scroll motif, faceted knop, paneled candle cup, clear, early 20th c., 14 1/8" h., pr. 605.00

Console set: 13" d. bowl w/rolled rim & pr. low candlesticks; yellow-topaz, engraved floral medallions, signed, 3 pcs. 275.00

Console set: bowl & pr. candlesticks; amethyst, signed, 3 pcs. 250.00

Cordials, Greek Key patt., star-cut base, clear, signed, pr. 60.00

Vase, 5" h., 8" d., rose bowl shape, clear w/engraved florals, signed . . . 100.00

Vase, 7" h., sapphire blue, signed. 75.00

Water set: pitcher & 5 tumblers; apple green pitcher w/applied amber handle & apple green tumblers w/amber bases, etched Vintage patt., 6 pcs. 400.00

SMITH BROTHERS

Smith Brothers Syrup Pitcher

This company first operated as a decorating department of the Mt. Washington Glass Works in the 1870s and later on as an independent business in New Bedford, Mass. The firm was noted for its outstanding decorating work on glass and also carried on a glass cutting trade.

Bowl, 5½" d., 3" h., melon-ribbed, beaded rim, h.p. pale blue & violet pansies on biscuit-colored ground, signed. $275.00

Bowl, 5½" w., melon-ribbed, enameled prunus blossoms & leaves on beige-cream ground, signed 225.00

Creamer & cov. sugar bowl, enameled gold florals on cream ground, "repousse" silverplate lid & bail handle, pr. 500.00

Hatpin holder, h.p. florals on glossy ground, unsigned, 3¾" h. 165.00

Humidor, enameled pastel pansies on cream ground, silverplate cover w/"repousse" florals & molded pipe, signed, 5" d., 7" h. 485.00

Planter, melon-ribbed, h.p. tan & brown florals on cream satin finish ground, silverplate insert, 8" d., 4" h. 260.00

Plate, 7" d., "Santa Maria," shades of brown, signed . . . . 375.00 to 395.00

Salt dip, master size, gold-beaded rim, h.p. green & lavender florals & beading on satin finish ground, unsigned, 3" d., 1½" h. 65.00

Sugar shaker w/embossed silverplate top, melon-ribbed, h.p. purple columbines on stark white ground, signed, 4" d., 3" h. 485.00

Syrup pitcher w/original silverplate domed lid & embossed handle, h.p. scene of stork amidst rushes on yellow ground, dark green band at base, 7" h. (ILLUS.) 300.00

Vase attributed to Smith Brothers

Vase, 6" h., h.p. scene of heron in rushes & pink bands decor, unsigned (ILLUS.) 65.00

Vase, 6¾" h., swirl-molded, h.p. blue florals & gold decor, signed 450.00

Vase, 9¾" h., 6¼" d., enameled gold dots around top edge, h.p. pink & yellow chrysanthemums on brown shaded to tan semi-glossy ground, unsigned 175.00

SPANGLED

Spangled Glass Basket

Spangled glass incorporated particles of mica or metallic flakes and variegated colored glass particles imbedded in the transparent glass. Usually made of two layers, it might have either an opaque or transparent casing. The Vasa Murrhina Glass Company of Sandwich, Mass., first patented the process for producing Spangled glass in 1884 and this factory is known to have produced great quantities of this ware. It was, however, also produced by numerous other American and English glasshouses. This type, along with Spatter, which see below, is often erroneously called "End of Day." Also see JACK-IN-PULPIT VASES under Glass.

Basket, crimped & ruffled rim, applied clear twisted loop handle, multi-colored spatter & silver mica flecks in clear, white lining (ILLUS.) $165.00
Bride's basket, cranberry w/silver mica flecks, ornate silverplate footed frame 185.00
Candlesticks, shaded pink w/white spatter & green aventurine mica flecks, white lining, 8¾" h., pr. 110.00

Spangled Glass Pitcher

Pitcher, 8¾" h., applied clear reeded handle, crimped rim w/applied clear edge, deep rose w/burgundy spatter & silver mica flecks (ILLUS.) 300.00
Pitcher, water, bulbous w/tricornered top, applied clear reeded handle, green w/white spatter & gold mica flecks 80.00
Rose bowl, 8-crimp top, sapphire blue & white spatter w/mica flecks, 3 5/8" d., 3¼" h. 85.00
Rose bowl, 8-crimp top, soft beige w/pink & brown spatter & mica flecks in a swirl patt., white lining, 4" d., 3¼" h. 100.00
Rose bowl, 8-crimp top, applied clear wishbone feet, heavenly blue w/silver mica flecks, white lining, 2 5/8" d., 3½" h. 84.00
Rose bowl, 8-crimp top, rose w/silver mica flecks in coral-like patt., white lining, 3¾" d., 3¾" h. 90.00
Rose bowl, blue to white w/silver mica flecks, 5¼" d., 5" h. 95.00
Rose bowl, egg-shaped, yellow w/gold mica flecks. 70.00
Vase, 7¾" h., 4 5/8" d., jack-in-pulpit type, green w/brown & white spatter & mica flecks 100.00
Vase, 7¾" h., ruffled top w/applied clear rigaree, rainbow spatter w/silver mica flecks. 75.00
Vase, 7 7/8" h., 4" d., ewer form w/ruffled rim & applied clear thorn handle, blue w/silver mica flecks in coral-like patt., white lining 115.00
Vases, 8" h., 4 1/8" d., tan, beige, ox blood & pink spatter w/mica flecks, white lining, pr. 132.00
Vase, 8½" h., yellow w/multicolor mica flecks, white lining 125.00
Vase, 9" h., 4 5/8" d., ruffled rim w/applied clear edge, pink & soft blue w/maroon spatter & metallic mica flecks, white lining 100.00
Vase, 9¾" h., 4¼" d., applied vase-line handles & shell trim, pink w/silver mica flecks, white lining . . . 100.00

SPATTER

This variegated-color ware is similar to Spangled glass but does not contain metallic flakes. The various colors are applied on an opaque white or colored body. Much of it was made in Europe and England. It is sometimes called "End of Day." Also see JACK-IN-PULPIT VASES under Glass.

Basket, applied blue thorn handle, blue spatter in clear, white lining, 8½" h. (ILLUS.) $175.00

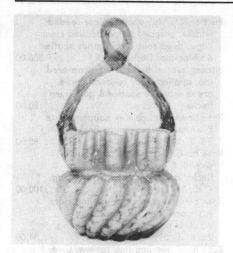

Spatter Glass Basket

Box w/hinged lid, egg-shaped, 3
   applied clear gold decorated feet,
   yellow spatter w/blue bell-shaped
   florals & gold & white leaves
   & branches decor, 4½" d., 7½" h. . . . 245.00
Candlestick, ruffled base, clear w/pink
   spatter, 4" base d., 9 3/8" h.
   (single) 70.00
Celery vase, cranberry w/white
   spatter 85.00
Dresser set w/ormolu mounts &
   attached mirror, heavenly blue &
   white spatter ruffled center bowl
   w/ornate ormolu mounts flanked
   w/floriform sides supporting pr.
   matching perfume bottles w/original
   stoppers & w/ornate mirror at rear
   cast w/ormolu leaves & vines,
   French, 13¾" w., 18" h. 405.00
Jar & cover w/applied clear finial,
   yellow spatter w/blue forget-me-nots
   decor, 3½" d., 6¼" h. 65.00
Pitcher, 5¼" h., 4 1/8" d., applied
   clear reeded handle, bulbous
   w/three-petal top & embossed
   patterning on body, maroon & white
   spatter in clear, yellow lining 85.00
Pitcher, 7 7/8" h., 5¼" d., applied
   clear reeded handle, bulbous w/three-
   way top, pink & white spatter
   w/clear "overshot" outer casing 165.00
Pitcher, water, 8" h., 5¾" d., applied
   clear handle, bulbous w/round
   mouth, Inverted Thumbprint patt.,
   maroon & white spatter in clear 110.00
Pitcher, water, 9¼" h., 5½" d.,
   applied clear reeded handle,
   6-sided top, royal blue & white
   spatter in clear 110.00
Rose bowl, pink & blue spatter in
   clear, 4½" 35.00
Tumbler, royal blue & white spatter
   in clear, 2 5/8" d., 3¾" h. 35.00

Tumbler, Swirl patt., green & white
   spatter in clear, 2¾" d., 3¾" h 45.00
Tumbler, yellow spatter in clear,
   enameled orange & blue florals
   w/gold decor 20.00
Vase, 3¼" h., 3¼" d., applied clear
   rigaree at top, cranberry w/white
   spatter 75.00

Spatter Glass Vase

Vase, 5" h., 4" widest d., blue & white
   spatter & single red spot in clear
   (ILLUS.) 50.00
Vases, 8" h., maroon, turquoise,
   yellow & green spatter in clear,
   white lining, pr. 120.00
Vase, 9" h., applied clear thorn
   handles, pastel rainbow spatter
   in clear 95.00
Vase, 9" h., ruffled top w/black
   edge, yellow & red spatter in clear . . . 65.00
Vase, 9¼" h., 5½" d., jack-in-pulpit
   type, Diamond Quilted patt. base,
   green, white & peach spatter in
   clear 100.00
Vases, 10" h., ruffled rim, green &
   white spatter in clear satin finish,
   enameled purple florals & blue
   leaves decor, pr. 500.00

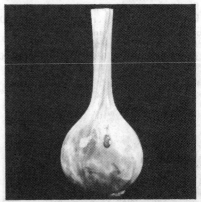

Spatter Glass Stick Vase

Vase, 10½" h., stick-type w/long
   narrow neck, white & rose spatter
   in pink (ILLUS.) 110.00

STEUBEN

The Steuben glass listed below was made at the Steuben Glass Works, now a division of Corning Glass, between 1903, when the factory was organized by T.G. Hawkes, Sr., the late Frederick Carder, and others, until about 1933. Mr. Carder devised many types of glass and revived many old techniques. Also see ANIMALS and SHADES under Glass.

ACID CUT BACK

Acid Cut Back Bowl

Ginger jar, cov., Jade green cut to
  Alabaster Art Deco flower, rough-
  textured double etching, solid
  green Jade cover w/white Alabaster
  knob, 5½" h. $950.00
Bowl, 8" d., green Jade cut in
  Canton patt., signed (ILLUS.) 800.00
Lamp, Jade green cut to Alabaster
  oriental motif, 12" h. base
  (complete) 850.00
Rose bowl, green Jade cut to
  Alabaster Matzu patt., signed
  Carder, 7½" d., 4" h. 725.00
Vase, 7½" h., 8" w., green Jade cut
  to Alabaster florals 1,450.00
Vase, 9" h., Rosaline cut to
  Alabaster stylized bouquets of
  blossoms & leafage, ca. 1920,
  unsigned 715.00
Vase, 12" h., green Jade cut to
  Alabaster butterflies & florals 1,800.00

AURENE

Aurene Bowl & Candlesticks

Atomizer, blue "mirror-finish" Aurene,
  6¼" h. 275.00
Bowl, 8" d., pedestal foot, blue
  Aurene, signed 495.00
Bowl, 8" d., 3½" h., gold Aurene
  (ILLUS.) 425.00
Candlesticks, domed foot, 4 prunts
  each side, rolled-over top, gold
  Aurene, signed, 3 7/8" base,
  3½" h., pr. 650.00
Candlesticks, twisted stems, gold
  Aurene, signed, 8" h., pr. (ILLUS.) . . .850.00
Candlesticks, twisted stems, blue
  Aurene, signed, 10" h., pr. 1,500.00
Candy dish, gold Aurene, signed,
  5" w., 1½" h. 225.00
Compote, 8" d., 5¼" h., gold Aurene
  & Calcite, unsigned 345.00
Creamer, gold Aurene, signed,
  3¼" h. 700.00
Cup & saucer, gold Aurene, signed 325.00
Finger bowl & underplate, floriform,
  gold Aurene interior, Calcite
  exterior 400.00
Perfume bottle w/flame stopper,
  melon-ribbed, gold Aurene w/purple
  highlights 375.00
Rose bowl, ruffled rim, decorated
  gold Aurene w/green hooked pulls .825.00
Salt dip, ruffled stretch edge,
  gold Aurene, signed & "Haviland"
  mark 275.00
Sherbet & underplate, blue Aurene
  & Calcite, pr. 400.00
Tumbler, blue Aurene, signed 285.00
Tumbler, gold Aurene, signed 220.00
Vase, 2¾" h., turned out rim, gold
  Aurene w/pink highlights, signed
  & numbered .195.00
Vase, 5¼" h., blue Aurene, signed
  & numbered .425.00
Vase, 8½" h., stick-type, blue
  Aurene, signed & numbered 295.00
Vase, 9" h., trumpet-shaped w/ruffled
  rim, blue Aurene, signed 395.00
Vase, green Aurene, signed 7,200.00

BRISTOL YELLOW

Bristol Yellow Goblets with Amethyst Stems

Chalice, signed, 8" h. 75.00
Finger bowl & underplate, 9" d. plate
   w/lotus rim, signed, pr. 125.00
Goblet, Bristol yellow bowls, amethyst
   twisted stems, signed, 8½" h., each
   (ILLUS. of pair). 120.00
Salt dip, pedestal base, w/bubbles
   & self-threading, signed, 2¼" d.,
   1½" h. 95.00

BUBBLY

Candlesticks, green w/controlled
   bubbles throughout & self-reeding
   on flattened tops, 5" d., 4½" h.,
   pr. 165.00
Compote, 7" d., 7" h., clear
   w/controlled bubbles throughout &
   applied green reeding under rim,
   signed. 80.00
Vase, 5½" h., 4½" d., French blue
   w/controlled bubbles throughout,
   signed. 85.00
Vase, 6½" h., ovoid, amethyst w/con-
   trolled bubbles & pulled up lily
   pads 120.00
Vase, 8" h., 6¼" top d., clear w/con-
   trolled bubbles & amber reeding at
   top, signed. .95.00
Vase, 8¼" h., 3-tier Art Deco shape,
   clear w/bubbles throughout & blue
   reeding around upper portion,
   signed. 110.00

CALCITE

Bowl, fruit, 12" d., bulbous base,
   Calcite w/gold Aurene lining 345.00
Compote, 8" w., 5¼" h., Calcite
   w/pink highlights in center, original
   factory sticker. 405.00
Finger bowl & underplate, Calcite
   w/gold Aurene, pr. 185.00
Salt dip, master size, Calcite w/blue
   Aurene. 400.00
Salt dip, master size, Calcite w/gold
   Aurene. 310.00
Vase, 7" h., ruffled, Calcite w/gold
   Aurene interior, signed Carder 285.00

CELESTE BLUE

Cordial 50.00
Goblet 99.00
Candlesticks, Celeste blue & Topaz,
   8" h., pr. 145.00

CLUTHRA

Bowl-vase, 7¾" oval, 4¼" h.,
   lavender w/random trapped air
   bubbles, signed & numbered 550.00
Cologne bottle w/stopper, pink shaded
   to white w/random trapped air
   bubbles, 7" h. 400.00
Vase, 4½" h., lavender w/random
   trapped air bubbles, signed 550.00

Vase, 6¼" h., blue w/random trapped
   air bubbles. .700.00
Vase, 8½" h., classical shape, straw-
   berry pink w/random trapped air
   bubbles 550.00

Cluthra Vase

Vase, 11" h., tapering triangle, lime
   green w/random trapped air
   bubbles, signed (ILLUS.) 412.00

FLEMISH BLUE

Bowl, 4½" d., 2" h., flared rim,
   applied threading. 40.00
Candelabra lamp, 2-arm, w/swirl-
   ribbed flame finial center, signed . . .250.00
Wine, applied random threading on
   lower half of bowl, 7½" h. 75.00

FRENCH BLUE

Candlestick, 4½" h. (single). 40.00
Champagne, self-reeding on bowl,
   graceful stem w/wafer, signed,
   7¼" h. 55.00
Console bowl, rolled rim, signed,
   14" d., 5½" h. 250.00
Vase, 7¾" h., diagonal ribbing,
   signed. 95.00
Vase, 8½" h., ribbed fan shape, ball
   stem, signed .75.00
Wine, self-reeding on bowl, graceful
   stem w/wafer, signed, 6½" h. 45.00

GROTESQUE

Steuben Grotesque Bowl

Bowl, 8" d., 4¾" h., shaded purple to
   clear, signed .225.00
Bowl, 7¾" w., 6" h., shaded emerald
   green to clear, signed (ILLUS.) 195.00
Bowl, 12" w., 6½" h., cranberry 275.00
Bowl, 12" oval, 6½" h., folded, Ivory,
   signed. 225.00
Bowl, 13" d., 6" h., clear, signed 110.00
Vase, 5¾" h., 8" d., green Jade. 125.00
Vase, 6½" h., 11½" w., shaded green
   to clear, signed 250.00
Vase, 9" h., shaded blue to clear,
   signed. 185.00
Vase, 19" h., floriform, shaded clear to
   deep green, signed 675.00

IVRENE

Ivrene Vase

Centerpiece bowl, lotus leaf form
   on pedestal base, white w/irides-
   cent pink highlights, signed,
   14" w., 6" h. 350.00
Cornucopia vase on pedestal foot,
   ribbed w/ruffled top, signed,
   6½" h. 250.00
Vase, 6" h., fan-shaped,
   signed . . . . .200.00 to 225.00
Vase, 6½" h., signed (ILLUS.) 325.00
Vase, 8" h. 285.00
Vase, 10" h., signed 350.00

JADE

Bowl, 7" w., 4" h., pulled 6-sided
   shape, diagonally ribbed, green
   Jade w/Alabaster foot, signed 165.00
Bowl, 12½" d., 2" h., green Jade,
   signed Carder 350.00
Centerpiece bowl, light blue Jade,
   signed, 16" d., 4¾" h. 425.00
Champagne, green Jade w/twisted
   Alabaster stem, signed, 5½" h. 110.00
Cologne bottle w/original stopper,
   yellow Jade, 7¾" h. 450.00
Cup & saucer, yellow Jade w/Ala-
   baster handle 105.00
Perfume bottle, melon-ribbed, green

Jade, w/original Alabaster long
   dauber, 4¾" h. 175.00
Sherbet & underplate, light blue Jade
   w/Alabaster stem on sherbet, pr. . . .400.00
Vase, 5" h., black Jade w/platinum
   Aurene highlights. 250.00
Vase, 5" h., light blue Jade
   w/Alabaster pedestal base,
   signed. 375.00

Steuben Three-Prong Vase

Vase, 6" h., 3-pronged tree stump,
   green Jade, signed (ILLUS.) 425.00
Vase, 9½" h., swirl-ribbed body
   w/ball stem, green Jade
   w/Alabaster foot, signed 235.00
Vase, 10" h., green Jade w/Alabaster
   handles 575.00
Wine, light blue Jade w/Alabaster
   stem & foot . . . . .100.00 to 200.00

MARINA BLUE
Candlesticks, ribbed stem w/double
   ball, domed foot, 12" h., pr. 250.00
Vase, 16" h., fold-over rim, optic ribs . .295.00

MILLEFIORI

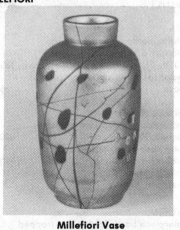

Millefiori Vase

Finger bowl & underplate, ruffled,
iridescent gold Aurene w/imbedded
white millefiori florettes, green
heart-shaped leaves & vines,
5" d. bowl, 6" d. underplate,
pr. 1,575.00
Rose bowl, gold Aurene w/imbedded
white millefiori florettes & deep
green vines 1,275.00
Vase, 4" h., baluster-shaped, iridescent
amber w/imbedded white millefiori
blossoms, green leaves & tendrils,
1905-25, signed 1,210.00
Vase, 5½" h., iridescent gold Aurene
w/imbedded white millefiori
florettes, green leaves & vines
(ILLUS.) 1,750.00

MOSS AGATE

Moss Agate Vase by Steuben

Bowl, 9½" d., fold-over rim 150.00
Vase, 10¾" h., footed cylinder
w/rounded shoulders & short wide
neck, variegated blues & greens
within amber, ca. 1920, signed
(ILLUS.) 800.00

ROSA

Perfume bottle w/flame-shaped
stopper & long dauber, signed,
10" h. 135.00
Powder jar, cov., signed on cover &
base 65.00

SILENIUM RUBY

Candlesticks, ribbed foot & nozzle,
signed, 12½" h., pr...............400.00
Centerpiece bowl, ribbed body,
scalloped rim, signed, 12" d. 150.00
Goblet, signed, 8" h. 110.00
Vase, 5" h., signed 125.00

SILVERINA

Centerpiece bowl, footed, air-trapped

& mica-flecked decoration, signed,
11" w., 4¾" h. 700.00
Vase, 8" h., amethyst w/diamond-form
air-trapped & silver mica fleck
decoration, signed 375.00
Vase, 12¼" h., flaring rim, green
w/air-trapped & mica-flecked
decoration 395.00

THREADED

Dresser set: cov. powder box, perfume
bottle & pin dish; clear w/applied
green threading & green faceted
stopper, signed, 3 pcs.............200.00
Jar, cov., clear ribbed body w/Pomona
green threading & green floral
stopper, signed, 6" h. 160.00
Wine, deep blue crystal, applied
threads on bowl, thin stem, signed,
7½" h. 55.00

TOPAZ

Ash tray, blue leaf handle, signed.....125.00
Candlesticks, swirl-ribbed, signed,
10" h., pr.......................190.00
Centerpiece bowl, turned-over rim,
swirl-ribbed, signed, 12" d., 4½" h. ..85.00
Compote, 6 7/8" d., 7" h., spiral
twist stem, unsigned 70.00
Sugar bowl & cover w/leaf finial,
signed, 3½" d. 95.00
Vase, 6" h., footed, ribbed, signed 85.00
Vase, 8" h., 6-sided top, ribbed,
on green pedestal foot, signed 115.00
Vase, 8½" h., Topaz fan-shaped
ribbed top & double-knobbed stem
on green pedestal, signed 95.00

STEVENS & WILLIAMS

Stevens & Williams "Threaded" Pitcher

*This long-established English glass house
has turned out scores of types of glass
through the years. The following represents
a cross-section of its wares. Also see
APPLIQUE GLASS.*

Bowl, 5½" d., 4" h., footed,
ruffled rim pulled to diamond
points, salmon pink w/threading,
clear berry pontil $85.00
Creamer, applied amber handle,
ornate scissors-cut top edge,
white w/applied blue florals &
green leaves, pink lining, 2 5/8" d.,
2 7/8" h. 195.00
Ewer, applied amber branch handle,
oyster white w/rose lining, applied
amber edging at ruffled rim &
applied amber acorns & oak
leaves on body, 11½" h. 250.00
Jar, cov., jade blue, signed. 150.00
Perfume bottle w/silver-gilt ball-
shaped screw-on cap, yellow satin
w/enameled overall red stars & gold
prunus branches & sparrow in flight,
ca. 1885, 5" h. 385.00
Pitcher, 7" h., 6" widest d., amber,
threaded & w/applied clear prunts &
rigaree, ca. 1887 (ILLUS.). 150.00
Rose bowl, blue mother-of-pearl Swirl
patt., attached to light blue opalescent tray-like base, 3½" d. rose
bowl, 5¾" d. base, overall 4" h. 485.00
Sweetmeat jar, embossed ribs, blue &
white opaque swirl stripes,
silverplate rim, cover & handle,
4 1/8" d., 4¼" h. 135.00
Tumbler, cased butterscotch to white
opal, applied florals 240.00
Vase, 5½" h., 5" d., pink-lined tri-
cornered top w/green edging, light
cream exterior w/applied cranberry
branch w/ruffled green & amber
leaf 150.00
Vase, 5¾" h., 5" d., alternating deep
purple & lavender Swirl patt., satin
finish, white lining 995.00
Vase, 7½" h., 3½" w., white
w/applied amber ruffled edge &
amber florettes, leaves & stem
on body 165.00
Vase, 8½" h., pedestal base, tapering
body w/waisted neck & flaring rim,
clear w/applied overall green
trailing lily pads 100.00

STIEGEL & STIEGEL-TYPE

*This glass was made at the American
Flint Glass Works of "Baron" Henry W.
Stiegel at Manheim, Pennsylvania, from
1765 until the 1770s. It is difficult to
attribute pieces positively to Stiegel.*

Flask, rectangular w/chamfered
corners, enameled red, yellow,
white & blue man holding a walking

stick within red & yellow dash
borders w/white stylized vines,
reverse w/inscription in German,
early 19th c., 5½" h. $275.00
Flip glass, clear w/simple copper
wheel-engraved tulip, 5 5/8" h. 65.00
Flip glass, 12-panel base, clear
w/simple copper wheel-engraved
rim, 6" h. 75.00
Flip glass, 24-panel, clear w/wheel-
engraved vesica & dot, 6¼" h. 230.00
Salt dip, blown, expanded 20-diamond
mold, applied foot, deep violet-blue
w/opalescent rim, 3 1/8" h. 225.00

Tumblers attributed to "Baron" Stiegel

Tumblers, blown, clear w/enameled
polychrome bands above inscription
"My love you Like me do" above
2 doves on basket & floral sprays
on one & 2 doves centering floral
sprays on second, attributed to
Henry William Stiegel's Manheim,
Pennsylvania Glass Works, 1772-74,
4 5/8" & 4¾" h., pr. (ILLUS.) 3,300.00
Wine, blown, conical bowl, folded
foot rim, 18th c. 85.00

STRETCH

Stretch Glass Bowl

*Collectors have given this name to a
Carnival-type glass that is iridescent and
with a surface somewhat resembling the skin
of an onion. It was made in various glass factories and some is now being reproduced.*

Basket, vaseline, 3" h. plus handle $25.00
Bowl, 7½" d., celeste blue, Fenton 27.50

Bowl, 8" d., turned-in rim, collared
  base, vaseline (ILLUS.)............25.00
Bowl, 10" d., blue, Imperial..........55.00
Bowl, 10¾" d., rolled edge, vaseline,
  Fenton..........................32.00
Candlesticks, hexagonal, vaseline,
  h.p. florals on alternating side
  panels, 7" h., pr..................75.00
Candlesticks, blue, Imperial, 8" h., pr...67.50
Candlesticks, scalloped base, fluted
  cup & rim, blue, 9" h...........68.00
Candy jar, cov., pink, 9½" h..........30.00
Compote, 6" d., 7" h., purple..........45.00
Compote, 10" d., 4" h., lime green
  w/rainbow highlights.............30.00
Console bowl, rolled edge, blue,
  Fenton, 12" d....................35.00
Console bowl, red, 14"............175.00
Console set: 9¾" d. bowl & pr. 9½" h.
  candlesticks; Ritz blue, 3 pcs........85.00
Powder jar, cov., ice blue.............35.00
Vase, 7" h., fan-shaped, vaseline......25.00

TIFFANY

Tiffany Favrile Perfume Bottle

This glassware, covering a wide diversity of types, was produced in glasshouses operated by Louis Comfort Tiffany, America's outstanding glass designer of the Art Nouveau period, from the last quarter of the 19th century until the early 1930s. Tiffany revived early techniques and devised many new ones. Also see SHADES under Glass, LIGHTING DEVICES and METALS.

Bowl, 5" d., inverted pyriform,
  uncarved agate, polished sides
  w/overall lozenge devices in
  shaded milky blue, lavender &

olive green between milky green &
  white trellises, interior shading
  from olive green to sunset red,
  1892-1928, signed & w/original
  paper label..................$4,400.00
Bowl, 7" d., 2½" h., ribbed flaring
  form w/scalloped rim, engraved
  leaves interior, signed............385.00
Bowl, 9 7/8" d., ruffled rim, iridescent
  gold w/purple highlights, signed....650.00
Compote, 6" d., 4" h., iridescent gold
  w/stretched edge, signed L.C.
  Tiffany Favrile................500.00
Compote, 7½" h., clear yellow-
  feathered bowl w/opaque yellow
  rolled rim, twisted stem & feathered
  foot, signed & w/paper label......675.00
Creamer & sugar bowl, iridescent gold,
  signed, pr......................425.00
Decanter, pale iridescent gold, signed
  L.C.T., 10½"...................560.00
Finger bowl & underplate, ruffled,
  iridescent gold w/pink & blue highlights, signed, 5½" d., 2" h. bowl &
  7" d. plate, pr...........250.00 to 375.00
Goblet, Wisteria patt., ribbed turquoise opalescent bowl, clear ribbed
  stem, opalescent ribbed mushroom
  foot, signed L.C.T. Favrile, 8¾" h....375.00
Perfume bottle w/original lobed
  stopper, mirror black w/striated
  ochre & olive green lappets on body,
  signed L.C.T. & numbered, 9" h.
  (ILLUS.)......................2,200.00
Pitcher, 4¼" h., corset-shaped,
  iridescent blue, signed L.C.T.
  Favrile........................750.00
Plate, 8" d., turquoise, signed &
  w/paper label..................275.00
Plate, 11" d., scalloped rim,
  turquoise w/white opalescent
  radiants from center, signed.......250.00
Punch cup, footed, iridescent gold,
  signed, 3½" h...........140.00 to 200.00
Salt dip, 2-handled bean pot shape,
  iridescent gold, signed...........190.00
Salt dip, 4 pulled feet, iridescent blue,
  signed & numbered..............275.00
Salt dip, ruffled rim, iridescent gold,
  signed L.C.T............135.00 to 195.00
Toothpick holder, light green to iridescent blue w/red artistic stripe,
  signed, 2½ x 2".................300.00
Toothpick holder, iridescent gold,
  signed L.C.T. & w/original paper
  label, 2½" h....................292.50
Toothpick holder, iridescent gold
  w/pigtail prunts, signed L.C.T. &
  numbered......................285.00
Vase, 3¼" h., spherical w/short neck,
  pulled iridescent blue design over
  iridescent red, signed L.C. Tiffany
  Favrile & numbered............2,310.00

Vase, 3¾" h., iridescent gold & green pulled feathering on ivory, signed L.C.T. 375.00

Vase, 4" h., bulbous w/flaring cylindrical neck, opaque to clear lime green, neck & shoulder w/intaglio-carved lozenge devices enclosing stylized leafage, 1892-1928, signed L.C.T. Favrile 1,540.00

Vase, 4¼" h., "millefiori," imbedded green leaves, vines & florettes on golden rainbow ground, signed ... 1,980.00

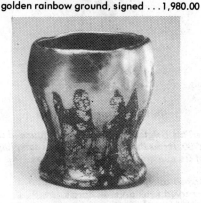

Tiffany "Cypriote" Vase

Vase, 4½" h., "lava," waisted ovoid, midnight blue pitted sides w/thick patches of amber iridescence, wide mouth w/amber-pink iridescent drippings, ca. 1918, signed L.C. Tiffany Inc. Favrile (ILLUS.) 7,700.00

Vase, 6" h., 8" d., oyster white iridescent striped exterior w/clear opalescent-edged iridescent foot, iridescent pastel green inside flaring trumpet rim, signed L.C.T. Favrile ... 373.00

Vase, 6" h., footed, pastel pink, signed & numbered 385.00

Vase, 7" h., classical shape, deep iridescent blue, signed 425.00

Tiffany "Lava" Glass Vase

Vase, 7¾" h., "cypriote," double conical form w/lobed neck, pitted

iridescent amber w/iridescent golden amber trailings, ca. 1899, signed L.C.T. (ILLUS.) 935.00

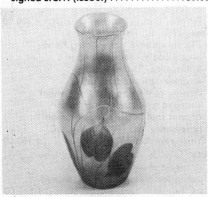

Vase with Intaglio-carved Decoration

Vase, 9" h., ovoid, iridescent amber w/imbedded trailing green vines & intaglio-carved green leaves, ca. 1917, signed L.C. Tiffany-Favrile (ILLUS.) 1,760.00

Vase, 15 3/8" h., paperweight-type, slender baluster form, clear w/creamy white narcissus blossoms on elongated stalks alternating w/shaded green & blue-green leafage, whole washed in iridescence, 1899-1920, signed L.C. Tiffany Inc. Favrile 2,860.00

Vase, 16" h., floriform, iridescent gold, in thin-stemmed bronze pedestal, both signed 1,250.00

Tiffany Vases

Vase, 16" h., trumpet-shaped, gold w/green pulled feathering, signed (ILLUS. left) 1,200.00

Vase, 17¾" h., baluster-shaped, iridescent w/intaglio-carved white 5-petal blossoms at the

slightly bulging shoulder, whole
further decorated w/undulating
pendant green leafage & vines,
ca. 1915, signed L.C. Tiffany
Favrile 4,400.00
Vase, 17¾" h., floriform, ovoid
slightly waisted cup shading from
pearly opalescence to amber
iridescence, lower section
w/green striated feathering
devices continuing into the slender
knopped rod standard, domed
circular foot in deep & pale amber
iridescence, ca. 1905, signed L.C.
Tiffany Favrile (ILLUS. right) 4,950.00
Vase, 18½" h., baluster-shaped, ivory
w/sprays of iridescent amber
pulled feathering, ca. 1907, signed
L.C.T. 1,540.00
Whiskey shot glass, iridescent, gold,
signed & numbered 150.00
Wine, curved stem, iridescent gold,
signed, 4" h. 158.00
Wine, pastel green, signed 225.00

TORTOISE SHELL

*Tortoise Shell glass is primarily amber
with splotches of darker amber or brown
and resembles the actual tortoise shell,
hence the name. Some of this ware is attributed to Sandwich, but it was also made
in numerous European glasshouses. Readily
identified by its peculiar coloring, it is*
Bottle, square form w/sloping
shoulders $75.00
Bowl, 4¾" d., attributed to
Boston & Sandwich 89.50
Bowl, 6" sq., pulled-out corners &
folded-in sides, gilt decor 85.00
Cruet w/amber stopper, applied
handle .... 125.00 to 150.00
Pitcher, 8" h., applied amber
handle .... 65.00 to 95.00
Pitcher, 8½" h., cylindrical, applied
amber handle, attributed to
Boston & Sandwich .... 110.00 to 125.00
Pitcher, 9" h., applied reeded amber
handle, bulbous body, square
mouth, swirl-ribbed body w/cream
panels alternating w/deep brown
tortoise shell spattered panels 300.00
Pitcher, 9½" h., applied amber
handle 135.00
Plate, 10" d. 28.00
Vase, 8" h., paneled body, English,
ca. 1910 .... 135.00
Vase, 8" h., quatrefoil top, ribbed
bulbous base, raised gold enamel
berries & leaves decor, attributed to
to Stevens & Williams 165.00

VAL ST. LAMBERT

Val St. Lambert Cameo Vase

*This Belgian glass works was founded in
1790. Items listed here represent a sampling
of its numerous types of production.*

Cameo cologne bottle w/stopper,
carved Rubina Verde florals,
8½" h. $475.00
Cameo dish, boat-shaped, purple overlay w/cameo-carved & wheel-cut
designs, signed, 11¼" l. 375.00
Cameo vase, 11¼" h., lobed form
w/tapering neck & ruffled lip, carved
deep olive brown upright thorny
flowering thistle branches against
grey ground splashed w/opalescent
cream, ca. 1910, signed (ILLUS.) 550.00
Candlesticks, 4 molded birds at base,
satin finish, 11" h., pr. 110.00
Finger bowls, blue cut to clear, notched
sides, ca. 1920, unsigned, 4¾" d.,
set of 6 .... 65.00
Tray, Art Deco decor, green, signed,
16¼" d. 175.00

VASELINE

*This glass takes its name from its color,
which is akin to that of petroleum jelly used
for medicinal purposes. Pieces below are miscellaneous. Also see JACK-IN-PULPIT
VASES, OPALESCENT and PATTERN
GLASS.*

Bowl, footed, ruffled edges w/pink
trim $45.00
Butter dish, cov., sad iron shape, Daisy
& Button patt. 125.00
Candlesticks, etched florals, ground
pontil, 3¼" h., pr. 35.00
Candlesticks, hexagonal base & stem,

petal form candle cup, mid-19th c.,
9 7/8" h., pr. 350.00
Candy dish, cov., footed, h.p. floral
decor, 7" h. 85.00
Celery vase, scalloped top, overall
pattern, 3 3/8" d., 7 7/8" h.........73.00
Cheese keeper, large 95.00
Compote, 4¾", Inverted Fan & Feather
patt., Northwood 150.00
Compote, 6¾" d., 4" h., rolled edge,
Twirl patt., U.S. Glass Co...........29.00
Compote, 8½" w., 6" h., Fine Cut &
Button patt. 45.00
Decanter w/clear stopper, applied
ribbon foot & handle, etched florals
& butterfly decor, 11½" h. 65.00
Dish, cover w/bubble finial & matching
underplate, scallop-cut rims & other
cutting on dish & lid, overall 6½" d.,
6" h. 140.00
Finger bowl, Optic Rib patt. 45.00
Gum stand, "Clark's Tea-
berry" ....35.00 to 55.00
Loving cup, mold-blown, 8½" h. 60.00
Mug, paneled, polished pontil, 3½" d.,
5¼" h. 65.00
Plate, luncheon, 8½" d. 10.00
Platter, 13 x 9½", notched corners 37.50
Salt dip, double, ribbed, w/original
metal bail handle 30.00
Spooner, Diamond Quilted patt. 30.00

Vaseline Spooner

Spooner, pressed pattern, 5" h.
(ILLUS.) 24.00
Table set: cov. butter dish, cov. sugar
bowl, creamer & spooner; Queen
patt., McKee Glass Co., 4 pcs. 210.00
Vase, 9" h., cylindrical, enameled
daisies decor 35.00
Water set: pitcher & 4 goblets on tray;
Basketweave patt., 6 pcs. 100.00
Wine server, acid-etched Vintage
patt., silver base, spigot, handles &
top, 15½" h. 750.00

VENETIAN & VENETIAN-TYPE

Venetian Glass Swans

Venetian glass has been made for six centuries on the island of Murano, where it continues to be produced. The skilled glass artisans developed numerous techniques, subsequently imitated elsewhere.

Candlesticks, dragon form stem,
yellow, 10" h., pr................$250.00
Jar, cov., pedestal base, rosy pink
w/applied gold-flecked bubble stem
& finial, 7" h. 80.00
Models of swans, translucent purple
bodies overlaid in clear & w/applied
clear gold-flecked feathering wings,
12½" h., pr. (ILLUS.)..............300.00
Vase, bud, 12" h., 3-sided, clear
w/wide heavy gold top & bottom
border bands & raised cloverleaf &
florals at sides w/applied sawtooth
rigaree 95.00
Whiskey set: decanter & 3 shot glasses;
clear w/raised gold scrollwork over
much of body & enameled white
violets & pale green leaves decor,
4 pcs. 145.00

VERLYS

This glass is a relative newcomer for collectors and is not old enough to be antique, having been made for less than half a century in France and the United States, but fine pieces are collected. Blown and molded pieces have been produced.

Ash tray, model of bird at rear, clear,
signed..........................$30.00
Ash tray, "Swallow," blue, signed......85.00
Bowl, 5½" d., sculptured roses, clear...60.00
Bowl, 6¾" d., Pinecone patt., clear 60.00
Bowl, 8½" d., 3-footed, Alpine Thistle
patt., frosted, signed 77.50
Bowl, 8 5/8" d., Thistle patt., amber 95.00

Bowl, 11½" d., 3½" h., sculptured
flying seagulls & fish amidst swirling
waves, frosted & clear, signed 225.00
Bowl, 12" d., sculptured birds & bees,
frosted & clear, signed 125.00
Bowl, 13½" w., Poppy patt., frosted &
clear, signed 110.00
Bowl, 13½" d., 2½" h., Waterlily patt.,
frosted, signed 140.00
Bowl, Tassel patt., Directoire blue 185.00
Charger, Waterlily patt., frosted,
signed, 13¾" d. 195.00
Charger, sculptured flying seagulls &
fish amidst waves, blue, signed,
14" d. 225.00
Model of a pigeon, frosted, signed,
4¼" h. 285.00
Planter, Chrysanthemum patt., clear,
10 1/8" l. 80.00
Vase, 5" h., fan-shaped, Lovebirds
patt., clear 115.00
Vase, 8½" h., 5" top d., clear
w/frosted maidens either side, 1
dancing w/veil & other kneeling
w/sheaf of wheat 95.00

Verlys Alpine Thistle Vase

Vase, 9" h., Alpine Thistle patt.,
amber, signed (ILLUS.) 255.00
Vase, 9½" h., Wheat patt., blue,
signed 295.00
Vase, 10½" h., 8½" d., Laurel patt.,
clear, signed 125.00
Vase, 11" h., 7" d., sculptured mer-
maids & seahorses, amber, signed . . 400.00

WAVE CREST

*Now much sought after, Wave Crest was
produced by the C.F. Monroe Co., Meriden,
Conn., in the late 19th and early 20th centuries from opaque white glass blown into
molds. It was then hand-decorated in enamels
and metal trims were often added. Boudoir*

*accessories such as jewel boxes, hair
receivers, etc., were predominant. Also see
KELVA and NAKARA.*

"Collars and Cuffs" Box

Box w/hinged lid, Helmschmied Swirl
mold, enameled blue & white
florals on creamy white ground,
3" d. $140.00
Box w/hinged lid, Baroque Shell mold,
h.p. florals on pale blue to white,
signed, 4" d., 3" h. 250.00
Box w/hinged lid, Helmschmied Swirl
mold, h.p. florals on creamy white,
signed, 4" d., 3¾" h. 325.00
Box w/hinged lid, Blownout Pansy
mold on lid w/realistic colors,
bronze shaded to yellow ground,
4½" d. 425.00
Box w/hinged lid, puffy Egg Crate
mold, h.p. pink & blue florals on
yellow ground, signed, 5" d. 450.00
Box w/hinged lid, Baroque Shell mold,
h.p. floral reserves on creamy
white, signed, 7" d. 565.00
Box w/hinged lid, plain mold, white
reserve on lid w/full-length portrait of two women & white
enameled beading on moss green,
sides w/pink roses, 7" d. 850.00
Collars & cuffs box w/hinged lid,
puffy Egg Crate mold, blue florals
& enameled highlights on creamy
white, 7" d. 750.00
Collars & cuffs box w/hinged lid,
Embossed Scroll mold, floral decor
on creamy white, "Collars and Cuffs"
in gold, ormolu collar & ormolu
base w/lion masks above feet,
signed (ILLUS.) 950.00
Cookie jar, puffy Egg Crate mold, apple
blossoms decor on creamy white,
silverplate rim, cover & bail handle,
signed in lid 295.00
Cookie jar, square, Embossed Scroll
mold, colorful pansies decor on
creamy white, silverplated-brass
rim, cover & bail handle 265.00
Cookie jar, Helmschmied Swirl mold,

creamy white, silverplate rim, cover
& bail handle, unsigned 285.00
Creamer, Helmschmied Swirl patt.,
floral decor on creamy white, silverplate collar, rim & handle, unsigned,
3½" h. 85.00
Dresser dish, ormolu collar, Helm-
schmied Swirl patt., enameled florals
on creamy white, unsigned, 5" d.,
2¼" h. 105.00
Fernery, puffy Egg Crate mold, violets
decor w/raised gold tracery on
creamy white, ormolu rim, unsigned,
7" w. . . . . 265.00 to 340.00
Glove box w/hinged lid, Embossed
Scroll mold, pink florals on sky blue
ground, signed, 8½" l., 4½" w. 650.00
Humidor, cov., Embossed Scroll mold,
forget-me-nots decor on creamy
ivory ground, signed, 4" d., 5" h. 450.00
Humidor, cov., plain mold, floral decor
on green ground, unsigned 425.00

Wave Crest Jardiniere

Jardiniere, wild flowers picked out
w/enameled white beading on
creamy white, signed, 10" d., 7¾" h.
(ILLUS.) 850.00
Jewelry box w/hinged lid, Embossed
Scroll mold, enameled florals on
creamy ivory ground, original lining,
signed, 3½" d., 3" h. 195.00
Jewelry box w/hinged lid, Helm-
schmied Swirl mold, blue forget-me-
nots decor on creamy ivory, original
lining, unsigned, 7" d., 4" h. 500.00
Jewelry box w/hinged lid, Baroque
Shell mold, enameled floral decor on
pale blue ground, original lining,
signed, 7½" d. 695.00
Jewelry casket w/hinged lid, Embossed
Scroll mold, white cartouches w/blue
florals on dark brown ground,
original lining, ormolu rims & feet,
signed, 8½ x 4". 995.00
Letter holder, puffy Egg Crate mold,
blue florals & white beading on
creamy white, ormolu rim, 6 x 3 x
4½" . . . . 225.00 to 265.00
Letter holder, Embossed Scroll mold,
h.p. florals on creamy white, ormolu
footed base & collar 285.00

Pin dish w/brass rim & handle, Helmschmied Swirl mold, enameled
decor on white, unsigned, 4" d.,
1¼" h. 75.00
Pin dish w/pewter beaded rim & side
handles, puffy Egg Crate mold, pink
florals & green leaves on creamy
white, 4½" across handles 150.00
Vase, 8" h., expanding cylinder
w/ormolu collar & ornate handles,
h.p. florals on creamy white,
signed. 375.00
Vase, 12" h., 9" widest d., ormolu
collar, handles & feet, iris decor
on royal blue ground, signed 575.00
Watch box w/hinged lid, Baroque
Shell mold, h.p. florals on creamy
white, signed, 3½" d. 185.00
Whisk broom holder, Embossed Scroll
mold, pastel floral decor on creamy
white, ormolu rim, base & ornate
wallplate, signed, 8½" across
backplate. 625.00

WEBB

Webb Cameo Vase

*This glass is made by Thomas Webb &
Sons, of Stourbridge, one of England's most
prolific glasshouses. Numerous types of
glass, including cameo, have been produced
by this firm through the years. The
company also devised various types of
novelty and "art" glass during the late
Victorian period. Also see AMBERINA,
BURMESE, CORALENE, PEACH BLOW
and SATIN GLASS.*

Bowl, fruit, 8" d., 6" h., 3 applied
textured feet, enameled 2-tone gold

bird w/outstretched wings standing
upon flowering branch on white
opalescent ground, melon pink
lining, signed $485.00
Cameo bowl, 7½" widest d., melon-
ribbed, carved shaded pink to white
fishscale design & enameled gold
morning glory vine & butterfly decor,
signed 1,000.00
Cameo creamer, carved white florals &
butterfly against yellow satin ground,
ornately carved handle, signed,
3½" h. 975.00
Cameo rose bowl, 3 applied blue feet,
carved white morning glory blossoms & foliage & butterfly against
blue ground, 6" d., 4" h. 750.00
Cameo scent bottle w/hallmarked
silver hinged top, carved white to
pink florals on heavenly blue satin
ground, 2¾" d., 2" h..............895.00
Cameo scent bottle w/hallmarked
silver screw-on top, carved opaque
white leaves against rich yellow
satin ground, 1 3/8" d., 2¼" h. 375.00
Cameo scent bottle w/hallmarked
silver screw-on top, flattened
bulbous shape, carved white
nasturtiums & leaves against deep
rose satin ground, opaque white
lining, 2½" d., 3½" h. 795.00
Cameo vase, 6¼" h., elongated teardrop form, carved white & pink
chrysanthemum blossoms, leafage
& butterfly against lemon yellow
ground, ca. 1900, signed (ILLUS.) ..1,870.00
Cameo vase, 6½" h., 3¼" d., carved
opaque white florals & leaves
against deep red satin ground,
white band at top & base 1,395.00
Cameo vase, 9" h., carved white
florals, branches & leaves against
deep raspberry ground, w/carved
white band at top 2,850.00
Cameo vase, 10½" h., carved fruits,
gnarled branches & leaves against
golden tan satin, carved border at
top & above base, signed.........5,500.00
Cologne bottle w/hallmarked silver
top, Amberina over green satin,
white lining, 5 7/8" h. 335.00
Compote, blue satin, on silverplate
pedestal 175.00
Finger bowl & underplate, cranberry
w/overall encrusted gold vine,
leaves & butterfly & enameled pink
florals, 4¼" d. bowl & 9 1/8" d.
plate, pr. 375.00
Potpourri (rose petal) jar, panels of
pink, blue & yellow florals & green
leaves outlined in gold & gold-
trimmed green bands on ivory satin,
pierced top rim & lid w/hinged
inside cover, 4¾" d., 6½" h. 607.00

Rose bowl, 8-crimp top, shaded rose
satin, white lining, 2¾" d.,
2 3/8" h..........................175.00
Scent bottle w/hallmarked silver top,
gold prunus & branches w/gold
butterfly on ivory satin finish
ground, 2 3/8" d., 3¼" h. 235.00
Scent bottle w/silver top, square shape
w/dimpled sides, light mauve &
yellow florals & foliage on shaded
sapphire blue satin ground, 3" w.,
4½" h. 235.00
Vase, 5¼" h., ovoid, blue satin,
signed...........................275.00
Vase, 7" h., gold florals & blue
dragonflies on Peach Blow pink
satin ground 360.00
Vase, 7" h., cased rainbow satin swirl
w/coin gold decor at top 675.00
Vase, 7" h., enameled bird in flight
& gold florals on white shaded to
dark pink ground, signed 395.00
Vase, 9" h., melon-ribbed, ivory to
rust-red marbleized swirls, white
enameled blossoms & dragonfly 415.00
Vase, 9" h., 5" d., paneled body,
lavender-blue, signed 195.00
Vases, 11" h., 4½" d., enameled gold
florals, leaves & branches on
shaded rose satin finish ground, pr. .595.00
Vase, 11¾" h., footed, cased, cream
w/applied amber pinched & ruffled
rigaree around top & pink & amber
rosette & leaves, rose lining 198.00

Webb Vase with enameled Decoration

Vase, 12½" h., enameled colorful
florals outlined in gold on ivory satin
finish ground (ILLUS.) 900.00

(End of Glass Section)

GRANITEWARE

Graniteware Cake Pan

This is a name given to metal (customarily iron) kitchenwares covered with an enamel coating. Featured at the 1876 Philadelphia Centennial Exposition, it became quite popular for it was lightweight, attractive, and easy to clean. Although it was made in huge quantities and is still produced, it has caught the attention of a younger generation of collectors. Though prices remain fairly stable, there is a consistent demand for the wide variety of these utilitarian articles turned out earlier in this century. Also see ADVERTISING ITEMS, AUTOMOBILE ACCESSORIES and SIGNS & SIGNBOARDS.

ABC plate, brown alphabet on white . . $40.00
Angel food cake pan, tube-type, blue
   & grey mottled .22.00
Basting spoon, grey mottled. 10.00
Beer growler w/bail handle (carry-out
   pail), grey mottled 24.00
Berry bucket, bail handle, turquoise
   blue & white mottled, 10 x 8" 25.00
Bowl, blue & white marbleized, 7" d. . . .22.00
Bowl, grey mottled, 10 x 8" oval 25.00
Bowl, child's, bunny center decor on
   pink ground w/cobalt blue trim 11.00
Bowl, fruit, solid blue w/pierced
   design. 41.00
Bread box, blue mottled, large 69.00
Bread pan, blue & white marbleized,
   15" l. 30.00
Bread pan, grey mottled 13.00
Bread riser w/tin lid, turquoise
   mottled. 85.00
Butter bucket w/lid & bail handle,
   cobalt & light blue marbleized,
   small. 31.00
Butter bucket, lid & bail handle, grey
   mottled, 3-lb. size. 35.00
Cake pan, grey mottled (ILLUS.). 12.00
Canister, cov., blue mottled, lettered
   "Sugar". 35.00
Canning kettle, blue speckled, marked
   "Lisk," large 32.00

Coffee boiler, cov., blue & white
   marbleized, large . . . . .58.00 to 72.00
Coffee pot, cov., child's, grey
   mottled, 6" h. .75.00

Graniteware Coffee Pot

Coffee pot, cov., gooseneck spout,
   blue & white marbleized (ILLUS.) 45.00
Colander, circular pierced design,
   solid blue, 11" d. 23.00
Cream can, tin cover & side handle,
   grey mottled 65.00
Creamer, solid medium blue 40.00
Cup, blue & white marbleized 25.00
Cuspidor, lady's, blue & white
   marbleized 95.00
Dipper w/long handle, brown mottled . .22.00
Dipper w/tubular handle, robin's egg
   blue w/black trim, 14" l. 18.00
Dishpan, cobalt blue & white marble-
   ized. 45.00
Dishpan, turquoise blue & white
   marbleized 30.00
Double boiler, blue & white speckles . . .60.00
Double boiler, green & white marble-
   ized exterior, white interior 45.00
Flask w/screw-on cap, oval, grey
   mottled. 75.00
Food mold, child's, ruffled rim, grey
   mottled. 48.00
Food mold, grey mottled, 8" w., 2" h. . . .28.00
Funnel, canning-type, light blue &
   white marbleized 48.00
Funnel w/handle, grey mottled, 4½" d.,
   5" h. 20.00
Funnel, turquoise blue & white
   marbleized . . . . .45.00 to 50.00
Grater, turquoise blue & white marble-
   ized 48.00
Kettle w/bail handle, deep brown &
   white marbleized, marked "Majestic,"
   large 85.00
Kettle w/side handles, blue & white
   mottled, 8½" d. 42.00
Kettle, preserving, grey mottled,
   marked "L. & G.," 22" d. 40.00

Kettle w/swing-away lid & bail handle,
   blue & white marbleized 85.00
Ladle, brown & white marbleized 26.00
Ladle, grey mottled 10.00
Liquid measure, grey mottled, 1-cup 25.00
Liquid measure, cobalt blue w/white
   lining, pt. 45.00
Liquid measure, grey mottled, pt. 24.00
Liquid measure, grey mottled, 2-qt. 40.00
Loaf pan, cobalt blue & white
   marbleized, large 18.00
Lunch bucket, miner's type, brown
   & white marbleized 45.00

Graniteware Milk Can

Milk can w/wire bail handle, cov.,
   grey mottled, 1-qt. (ILLUS.) 55.00
Milk cooling basin, brown & white
   marbleized, 12½ " d. 20.00
Mixing bowl, medium blue & white
   marbleized, small 20.00
Molasses pitcher, hinged lid w/thumb-
   lift, grey mottled 52.00
Muffin pan, fluted, 6-cup, grey
   mottled 65.00
Pie pan, brown & white marbleized 28.00
Pie pan, green & white marbleized 26.00

Graniteware Pitcher

Pitcher, cream, squatty, grey mottled
   (ILLUS.) 45.00
Pitcher, water, hinged lid, green &
   white marbleized 37.50
Pitcher, child's, pink 17.00
Plate, cobalt blue & white or turquoise
   blue & white marbleized, 10" d.,
   each 25.00
Plate & bowl, child's, branding iron
   decor, yellow & brown, 2 pcs. 15.00
Platter, light blue & white mottled,
   18 x 14" oval 60.00
Pudding mold, grey mottled 65.00
Pudding pan, cobalt blue & white
   marbleized 36.00
Roaster, turquoise blue & white
   marbleized, marked "Lisk, pat. May
   2, 1911" 65.00
Salt box w/hinged wooden lid,
   hanging-type, white 60.00
Sauce pan, handled, grey mottled,
   4½" d. 33.00
Sauce pan w/bail handle, pouring lip,
   emerald green & white marbleized,
   9¼" d., 4" h. 55.00
Skimmer, brown & white marbleized . . . 38.00
Soap dish, shell-shaped, grey mottled . . 55.00
Spooner, white w/floral decor &
   pewter rim 100.00
Syrup pitcher, original pewter top
   w/lady's head finial, grey mottled . . 195.00
Teapot, cov., child's, green mottled 15.00

Teapot with Pewter Trim

Teapot, cov., grey mottled w/pewter
   gooseneck spout, handle & cover
   w/ornate finial, 11" h. (ILLUS.) 300.00
Tea steeper, cov., Chrysolite 85.00
Tea strainer, grey mottled . . . . . 30.00 to 45.00
Tray, blue & white marbleized,
   26 x 18" 65.00
Trivet, yellow, marked "Portland Stove
   Foundry," oval 35.00
Tumbler, blue & white speckled 15.00
Utensil rack, hanging-type, blue &

green scenic decor on white w/blue
trim .125.00 to 185.00
Utility rack w/three containers marked
"Zeep," "Zand" & "Soda," grey
mottled, 4 pcs. . . . . .95.00 to 125.00
Vegetable rack, hanging-type, blue
windmill decor on white, lettered
"Zwiebeln" (onions) 55.00
Wash basin & pitcher, grey mottled 55.00
Water pail, turquoise blue & white
marbleized 85.00

GREENAWAY (Kate) ITEMS

Kate Greenaway

Numerous objects in pottery, porcelain, glass and other materials were made in or with the likenesses of the appealing children created by the famous 19th century English artist, Kate Greenaway. These are now eagerly sought along with the original Greenaway books. Also see NAPKIN RINGS.

Almanack for 1883, published by
George Routledge $80.00
Almanack for 1887, published by
George Routledge & Sons 57.50

Almanack for 1888

Almanack for 1888, published by
George Routledge & Sons (ILLUS.) 90.00

Almanack for 1892, published by
George Routledge & Sons 77.50
Book, "A - Apple Pie," muslin,
published by Saalfield, 1907 . . . . .55.00
Book, "Chatterbox Hall," illustrated by
Kate Greenaway, 1884 . . . . .40.00
Book, "The Language of Flowers," by
Kate Greenaway, w/illustrations,
leather cover, 1880s 65.00
Book, "Marigold Gardens," engraved &
printed by Edmond Evans, London
(some writing & slight tear on one
page) 35.00
Book, "Mother Goose," illustrated by
Kate Greenaway 40.00
Book, "Pied Piper of Hamelin," by
Robert Browning, illustrated by
Greenaway 80.00
Book, "Under the Window," by Kate
Greenaway, published by Frederick
Warne, London 45.00
Christmas card, chromolithograph, 8
children w/song, 4 x 6½" 35.00
Figure of a girl w/basket, glossy off
white finish w/flesh tones & gold
trim, Royal Worcester, 1882, 2¾ x
3½" base, 6¾" h. 400.00
Figure of a Greenaway girl
w/tambourine beside a tree trunk,
Royal Worcester, 9" h. 420.00
Figures, bisque, girl seated & holding
tin umbrella & boy standing holding
tin umbrella, 2" & 2½" h. respec-
tively, pr. 90.00
Match holder w/striker, bisque, figural
Greenaway boy holding rabbit
beside container 65.00
Match safe, pocket-type, silverplate,
embossed Greenaway children 50.00
Nodding figures, porcelain, Greenaway boy w/book & girl knitting,
white & gold clothing, each seated
on pale blue chair, 5" h., pr. 175.00
Salt shaker, china, figural Greenaway
girl wearing beige coat w/fur trim,
blue bonnet & brown muff (single) . . .50.00
Salt & pepper shakers, china, figural
Greenaway girl & boy, wearing tan
coats, black & green hats, 4¼" h.,
pr. 125.00
Tea set: cov. teapot, cov. sugar bowl &
6 c/s; china, decal of Greenaway
children decor, 14 pcs. 110.00
Toothpick holder, silverplate, figural
Greenaway girl standing on footed
acorn shape container, marked "J.
Tufts" 155.00
Toothpick holder, silverplate, figural
Greenaway girl, wearing coat & hat,
seated beside container, large 175.00
Vase, china, decal of 2 Greenaway-
type girls on white, 6" h. 35.00

HATPIN HOLDERS

R.S. Germany Hatpin Holder

Also see SCHLEGELMILCH.

Austrian china, multicolored floral
   decor $95.00
German china, pink roses & green
   foliage on tan shaded to cream
   ground, 3¼" d., 5" h. 35.00
Nippon china, h.p. violets & green
   leaves decor on blue shaded to
   green ground between gold panels
   w/enameled dot trim, 3½" d.,
   4½" h. 75.00
Nippon china, hexagonal w/bulbous
   base, h.p. pink floral decor, heavy
   gold trim, w/attached pin tray 65.00
Nippon china, h.p. ships decor, bisque
   finish. 60.00
Nippon china, cylindrical, h.p. yellow
   roses decor, w/attached pin tray 45.00
R.S. Germany china, floral decor on
   shaded ground, 4½" h. (ILLUS.) 60.00
R.S. Germany china, peach florals &
   green & brown leaves on shaded
   yellow ground .45.00
R.S. Germany china, h.p. bands of
   roses on shaded pink ground, gold
   trim 50.00
R.S. Prussia china, scalloped petticoat
   base, h.p. portrait of a young girl . . .165.00
R.S. Prussia china, footed, hexagonal,
   Swans on Lake decor, pearlized
   finish. 135.00
Silver lustre china, figural portly man
   wearing tri-cornered hat 96.00
Silverplate, sphinx decor 28.00
Sterling silver, hockey stick in center . . .75.00

HATPINS

Brass w/faceted purple glass inset $18.00
Carnival glass, butterfly, purple 27.50
Carnival glass, cattails, purple. 32.50
Carnival glass, rooster, marigold 35.00
Celluloid, plain, 1920s 3.00
Rhinestone-studded, 1½" d. top 24.50
Sterling silver, Art Nouveau lady's
   head 35.00

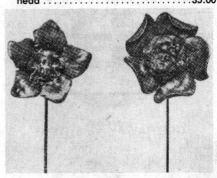

Sterling Silver Hatpins

Sterling silver, Art Nouveau style,
   by Unger Bros., ca. 1904, each
   (ILLUS.) 100.00
Sterling silver, golf clubs (2 drivers & 2
   putters) in leather golf bag hatpin
   holder, marked "Milwaukee,"
   7¼" l., 5 pcs. .165.00
Sterling silver, love knot 22.00
Sterling silver, set w/amethyst stone . . .32.00

HOOKED RUGS

A true form of American folk art, hooked rugs have caught the attention of numerous collectors. It is believed this rug-making technique (pulling yarn or fabric strips through a woven fabric background) originated in America. Jute burlap (gunny-sacking) provides the ideal background material and after this fabric was brought out around the 1850s, rug hooking became quite a vogue. It provided the opportunity to thriftily use up leftover burlap sacks and the remnants of discarded clothing to produce attractive floor coverings. Geometric and floral design rugs are the most common while animals, houses, figures, landscapes and ships are scarcer. Bold colorful, original designs are most appealing to collectors, but those hooked on stamped burlap patterns, even during the 20th century, are also avidly sought. Also see CAT COLLECTIBLES.

Abstract floral design w/circles
   of red & gold on a striped &
   swirled brown ground within

multicolored striped border,
37 x 32".........................$195.00
Basket of kittens in shades of grey,
red, brown, green & blue, 39½ x
25"...............................250.00
Cat & 3 kittens w/ball of yarn in
beige, black, brown & white on
grey ground w/diamond border,
35½ x 24" (minor edge wear).......725.00
Checkerboard design in beige &
cream w/houses, anchors,
flowers, etc., in the light
squares, 9 x 6' (minor wear).......700.00

Dog Rug

Dog w/beige striped coat & button
eyes on black, brown & olive
green abstract background
w/rainbow stripes in corners,
minor fading, 44 x 28" (ILLUS.) 1,000.00
Floral design in grey, yellow &
red on black ground, wide multicolored zig-zag border, 40 x 31".....375.00
Geometric & floral designs, brown
grid filled w/stylized pastel
flowers & foliage on cream ground,
9 x 6'............................450.00
Horse running, black horse outlined
in red on beige ground w/vining
floral border in shades of red,
yellow, blue & brown, shaggy
yarn edge, 46 x 42"..............1,700.00

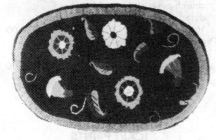

Morning Glory Rug

Morning glory blossoms, buds &
trailing vines in maroon, magenta,
lavender, green, grey & beige,
52 x 33" oval (ILLUS.) 192.00
Mother cat & 2 kittens, 1 playing
w/ball of yarn, corners w/elaborate

scrolling, red, beige, blue & brown,
19th c., 51½ x 26½" 1,100.00
Nautical design w/fish, lobster,
whales, etc., in shades of blue,
white, grey & maroon on 2-tone
green ground, 43 x 31" (some
wear) 100.00
Owl on a branch, white & brown
polka dot bird on yellow ground
w/red, black & white border
design, 4'8" x 2'6"................600.00
Pig standing, spotted pink animal on
dark ground within half-circle
border 235.00
Rabbit, white animal on beige ground
within multicolored diamond
border 225.00
Rooster in faded yellow & blue
w/red comb on black ground
w/large white corner flowers,
44 x 25½"........................800.00
Snowflake & flowers, blue & red on
white ground, 36 x 26"..............225.00
Stylized palm trees in black, brown,
purple, green & beige within
black border w/white circles each
w/a colored dot, 38½ x 28½" 165.00
White geese (2) on grey ground,
scalloped border design in soft pink,
green & orange, 50 x 27½" (minor
damage & repair) 325.00

HORSE & BUGGY COLLECTIBLES

Horse Brass

Buggy brush, crescent-shape, 18" l. ...$35.00
Buggy seat, pine, original brown paint
w/green & salmon striping & salmon
pink seat top, 38¾ x 8", 21½" h......65.00
Buggy whip socket, nickel & wood.......8.00
Carriage robe, horse hide, Chestnut
sorrel color w/black & gold double
border, fully lined................140.00
Carriage robe, horse hide w/woven
mohair lining, colorful felt binding ...90.00

Conestoga wagon jack, dated
  "1785" ....80.00 to 100.00
Conestoga wagon jack, wrought iron &
  wood, simple tooling w/"No. 592" &
  date "1802," 21" h. 165.00
Fly nets for horses (or mules), orange
  cord, pr. 60.00
Horse blanket pins, brass, on holder,
  set of 10 ....33.00
Horse brass, owl within pierced border
  (ILLUS.) 35.00
Horse brass, 11-tooth comb form
  w/high scalloped pierced crest 170.00
Horse hames w/brass tips, pr. 60.00
Horse hitching pot, cast iron, model of
  a circus horse's head, 13¾" h.
  (column post missing) 325.00
Horse hoof scraper, iron 20.00
Horseshoe & harness repair kit, "The
  Summers Automatic," original tools
  in dovetailed box w/sliding lid,
  14 x 4 x 4". 50.00
Horse sweat scraper, wooden, curved ..28.00
Saddle, leather w/woven horse hair
  cinch, McLellan Army-type, 1904 ....175.00
Saddle bags, leather pouches w/rein-
  forced flaps, on wide leather strap
  w/buckle, 19th c. (minor breaks in
  leather) 72.00
Side saddle, lady's, off-white leather
  w/red stitching, double horn 295.00
Spurs, silver w/engraved scrolling
  decor, Mexican, pr. 275.00
Wagon lantern, red lens, Dietz 35.00
Wagon seat, maple & pine, 3 acorn
  finials above a double slat-back &
  strapwork seat, turned legs joined by
  box stretchers (1 slat replaced),
  19th c., 34 x 18", 24½" h. 352.00

HUMPHREY (MAUD) ILLUSTRATIONS

Maud Humphrey was an accomplished artist whose illustrations appeared in more than twenty children's books and numerous women's magazines during the 1890s and in the early years of the 20th century. Although many of her illustrations are unsigned, most of her book illustrations carry at least her initials if not the full signature. The mother of actor Humphrey Bogart, she died in Hollywood, in 1940, at the age of 72.

Book, "Babes of the Year," 12 color
  illustrations $285.00
Book, "Cosy Corner Stories," 6 color
  illustrations 65.00
Book, "Favorite Fairy Tales" 95.00

Book, "Little Grownups," 12 color
  illustrations 400.00
Book, "Little Rosebuds," 6 color
  illustrations 400.00
Book, "Mother Goose" 365.00
Book, "Old Youngsters," 6 color
  illustrations, decorative borders,
  1897 ....95.00
Calendar, 1895, advertising, "Hood's
  Sarsaparilla," 6 color-illustrated
  pp., 13½ x 11".....................200.00
Calendar, 1901, advertising, "Cold
  Spring Tea," 2 little girls w/many
  roses, 16 x 12", framed 47.50
Calendar, 1904, advertising, "Equitable
  Insurance," beautiful children, 6
  color-illustrated pp., 12½ x 10" 100.00
Calendar, 1905, advertising, "Elgin
  Watch Co.," 4 color-illustrated pp.
  w/Father Time & beautiful
  woman on each ....95.00 to 135.00
Christmas card for subscription to
  "Farm Journal of Philadelphia,"
  scene of bringing in the Yule log,
  signed..............................19.00
Poster, advertising, "Fairy Soap,"
  entitled "Kitty's Bath," 2 pretty
  well-dressed little girls wearing
  bonnets about to bathe a white
  angora cat, 21 x 15", framed 275.00
Print, entitled "April Shower," little
  girl dressed in pink, 1888, 9 x 7" 20.00
Print, entitled "Bride," dated 1900,
  matted & framed, 14 x 11¾".........45.00
Print, entitled "Little Boy Blue,"
  matted & framed, 14 x 11".........190.00
Print, untitled, depicting baby playing
  w/roses, signed, 10 x 8" 45.00
Print, untitled, bust of little girl
  wearing large-brimmed white
  hat & surrounded by flowers,
  dated 1890, 13 x 10, framed,
  overall 21 x 17" 67.50
Print, untitled, child seated in
  church pew, elaborately dressed,
  dated 1898, original frame, overall
  16 x 12¾"..........................150.00
Print, untitled, child wearing poke
  bonnet & holding a lily, dated
  1888, 14 x 12" 125.00

ICART PRINTS

The works of Louis Icart, the successful French artist whose working years spanned the Art Nouveau and Art Deco movements, first became popular in the United States shortly after World War I. His limited edition etchings were much in vogue during

those years that the fashion trends were
established in Paris. These prints were later
relegated to closet shelves and basements
but they have now re-entered the art market
and are avidly sought by collectors. Listed
by their American titles, those appearing
below have been sold within the past eighteen months.

Autumn, 1928, 6½ x 9"	$300.00
Black Shawl (The), 1925, 12½ x 16½"	302.00
Casanova, 1928, 14 x 21"	535.00
Cinderella, 1927, 14½ x 18¼" oval	385.00 to 420.00
Dalilah, 1929, 13½ x 20½"	600.00 to 660.00
Eve, 1928, 19½ x 14" oval	900.00

Golden Veil

Golden Veil, 1930, 20 x 15" (ILLUS.)	1,700.00
In the Open, 1925, 16 x 10½"	522.00
Joy of Life, 1929, 15 x 23½"	1,710.00
Orchids, 1937, 19½ x 28"	990.00
Paris Flowers, 1930, 19 x 15"	935.00
Sleeping Beauty, 1927, 19½ x 15½" oval	995.00
Springtime, 1932	250.00
Venus, 1928, 19½ x 14" oval	1,125.00
White Underwear, 1925, 19 x 15"	640.00
Wounded Dove, 1929, 16 x 21"	550.00
Youth, 1930, 15½ x 24"	500.00
Zest, 1928, 14 x 19"	1,010.00

INDIAN RELICS

Bag, Nez Perce, entwined corn husks
decorated w/diamond, triangle &
terrace designs in burgundy, red,
grey, vegetal green, pastel orange &
black commercial yarn, red trade
cloth edging, ca. 1900, 9½" w.,
13½" l. $200.00
Belt, Nez Perce, buffalo hide, wide
band decorated in large & small
brass & silver tacks forming a quatrefoil flanked by 2 crosses & various
other devices, 40¼" l. 357.00
Belt, lady's, Plains, plain German
silver conchos on commercial leather
belt, 29" l. 115.00
Blanket, Navajo, woven in German-
town wool, concentric serrated
lozenges & hooked crosses in auber-
gine, navy blue, bright green &
white outlined in black on bright red
ground, linear bands on short side
borders, 67¾ x 51¾" 4,125.00
Cap, maiden's, Hupa, woven
basketry 300.00
Cradleboard, Sioux, beaded hide,
stitched in dark blue, pale green &
translucent red detail against white
ground w/rows of crosses alternating w/stylized butterflies along
each side, green panel containing a
diamond & triangle pattern at top
of the head, fringed hide panel
attached below, strands of translucent blue cylindrical glass beads
attached behind the crest, remains of
indigo pigment, 27¼" l. 2,750.00
Game bag, Sioux, leather, large 90.00
Leggins, child's, Sioux, buckskin
w/multicolored beading & fringe,
15" l., pr. 550.00

Sioux Plains Leggins

Leggins, Sioux Plains, fringed buckskin, painted design & quillwork,
24" w. at top, 30" l., pr. (ILLUS.) 600.00
Moccasins, Sioux, beaded hide, yellow
& white crosses on dark blue, green
& red, ca. 1900, pr. 150.00
Necklace, Plains, 7 rows of bone segments divided by leather spacers,
center ornament of white beading,
metal button & ermine tail bound in
red wool, 12" l. plus string ends 225.00
Pipe bag, Sioux, beaded & fringed
hide, attached each side in white,
dark blue & translucent red over a
bright blue beaded ground w/a
column of crosses, fringe wrapped in

red & yellow rectangular patterned quillwork, 30¾" l 1,100.00

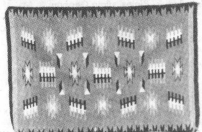

Navajo Rug

Rug, Navajo, Ganado area, black, white & grey on analine red ground, ca. 1930, 48 x 30½" (ILLUS.) 325.00

Rug, Navajo, woven black, white, red & shaded brown pr. of concentric terraced zig-zags flanking a row of terraced full & halved concentric diamonds, against finely striped ground, 81 x 64" 770.00

Saddle blanket, Sioux, woven red & blue wool w/multicolor beaded floral border, 43½ x 28" 1,200.00

Shirt, Assiniboin, beaded buckskin, ca. 1900, large 500.00

Strike-a-light bag, Sioux, front panel w/blue, green & white beading, w/fringe of copper cone dangles, blue horsehair & long twisted ochre leather tails, ca. 1880, 5" l. plus fringe 175.00

Tomahawk, Sioux, iron head w/spiked blade, wooden handle, 20" l 675.00

Vest, boy's, Sioux, beaded hide, stitched in yellow, bright blue & translucent red on a white beaded ground w/column of graduated fringed rectangles on front, similar devices flanking a concentric diamond & arrow device on reverse, edged w/dark blue beaded strips containing tiny rectangles, 14½" l. . . 660.00

IVORY

Also see FANS and NETSUKES.

Card case, carved w/figures, pagodas & trees, Chinese, 19th c. $175.00

Cup, footed, carved scenes depicting deer, bear, stag & boar hunts & 4 huntsmen w/attributes, metal-lined, German, late 19th c., 10¼" h. 3,300.00

Figure of a boy, wearing patterned robes & examining a nest of small

birds held in his hand, artist-signed, Japanese, ca. 1900, 7½" h. 1,100.00

Figure of a nude woman, standing demurely w/her hands clasped together to one side of her head, onyx socle, Continental, ca. 1900, 9 7/8" h. 660.00

Figure group, The Three Graces, Continental, 19th c., 7½" h. 1,320.00

Glove stretcher, hinged, small 45.00

Mirror surround, carved w/heraldic emblems, putti & eagles & centering a banner inscribed "Montjoye St Deny," whole on a background of carved lappet motifs, centering an oval mirror, French, probably Dieppe, late 19th c., 34" h. 2,310.00

Pastry wheel, handle open carved w/chamfered column between beaded & scrolled borders, joined w/steel pin to an exceptionally large fluted wheel, mounted on black Anton base, San Francisco, ca. 1875, 7" l. 1,760.00

Carved Ivory Table Screen

Table screen, rectangular, carved in medium relief depicting nymph being showered w/flowers by cupids, on twisted standard & 3 C-scroll foliate-carved feet, Continental, late 19th c., 19¾" h. (ILLUS.) 880.00

Tankard, carved in medium relief w/Alexander the Great in battle, finial carved in the form of the warrior on horseback, C-scroll foliate handle carved w/captured slave, Continental, late 19th c., 16¼" h. 5,500.00

Triptych, carved depicting the coronation of St. Stephen flanked by priests & holy men within a Gothic surround, Continental, late 19th c., wood frame, 23¾" l. 3,740.00

JADE

Carved Jade Incense Burner

Also see SNUFF BOTTLES.

Bowl, overlapping petals of an open
chrysanthemum blossom carved in
crisp high relief on interior &
exterior, pale sage green w/dusty
grey clouds, w/wooden stand,
7½" d. $1,540.00

Bowls, deep flaring sides carved
w/concentric rows of petal flutes,
mossy green, w/wooden stand,
7¾" d., pr. .2,200.00

Box, pierced cover w/carved figural
lady finial, pierced sides, ornate
brass trim, soft creamy white,
China, 4 x 4" 345.00

Incense burner (koro) w/domed cover
w/pierced coiled dragon finial,
carved in low relief w/archaistic
dragons amongst scrolling foliage,
shallow body on 3 masked pad feet,
horned dragon-headed loops suspending loose rings, pale spinach
green w/dark flecks, 18th c.,
6¼" d. (ILLUS.). 3,520.00

Ink box, cov., top carved in low relief
w/a shou medallion, cover & base
rims crisply ridged, separate short
flaring foot ring, eggshell mottled
apple green, 3¼" d. 5,500.00

Model of a toad holding a pomegranate, its body slightly turned &
carved w/bumpy skin, bulging eyes
& long webbed feet, pale greyish
white w/brown streaks, Ming
Dynasty, 2 1/8" l. 1,540.00

Vases, carved in high relief & openwork w/exotic long-tailed bird
standing beside deeply carved
magnolia blossom growing from
stylized pierced rockwork, long-
tailed parrot perched on the rim of
one, shaded celadon to apple green
w/russet suffusions, wooden
stands, 14½" h., pr. 4,400.00

JEWELRY (Victorian)

Gold Chain Bracelet

*Also see STICKPINS, WATCH FOBS
and WATCHES.*

Bar pin, 14k gold, black enamel trim
& 9 seed pearls across center, 1" l. . .$45.00

Bar pin, 14k green gold set w/fresh
water pearls (6) alternating
w/amethysts (5), 2¼" l. 145.00

Bracelet, child's, bangle-type w/hinge,
14k gold, engraved & enameled,
¼" w. 150.00

Bracelet, bangle-type w/hinged snap-in
lock & safety chain, 9k gold, ½" w. . .259.00

Bracelet, bangle-type, gold-filled
tubular style w/two turquoise sets,
raised beading & rope trim 50.00

Bracelet, 14k gold chain w/heart-
shaped catch mechanism & guard
chain, 1880's (ILLUS.) 175.00

Brooch, coin silver, coiled snake set
w/seed pearl eyes & 32 small
coral stones .48.00

Brooch, cameo carved w/bust of young
girl in 10k gold frame 225.00

Brooch, large veined turquoise
cabochon in wide 14k gold inter-
twined mesh frame 135.00

Brooch, 14k green gold crab form set
w/mine-cut white diamond, 1 x 1" . .150.00

Chatelaine, sterling silver, filigree
work & Art Nouveau mask w/four
drops (perfume flask, ivory tablet,
coin holder & pencil holder) 265.00

Earrings, 10k gold, 2" l. drops, pr. 45.00

Amber Hair Comb

Hair comb, amber w/colored sets, 6" h.
(ILLUS.). 65.00

Hairpin, 14k gold, 3 small seed pearls
at crest, marked "Tiffany"...........95.00

Mourning locket, gutta percha, floral
decorated w/bow-shaped clasp, on
38" l. chain......................195.00

Mourning pin, 14k gold crescent shape,
black enamel trim, 1" l..............30.00

Mourning pin, 14k gold crescent shape,
black enamel trim & 12 graduated
seed pearls, 1 1/8" l. 45.00

Mourning ring, 14k gold, entwined
hearts set w/diamond within filigree, hinged top opening to reveal
braided lock of hair 275.00

Ring, friendship-type, 9k gold, in the
form of a belt & buckle.............99.00

Ring, poison-type, 14k gold, bezel-set
oval sardonyx, engraved & w/hinged
secret compartment...............175.00

Ring, lady's, 14k gold, bezel-set cameo-
carved black & white onyx oval
within rope-twist border 110.00

Ring, lady's, 14k gold, large center opal
& 6 small rubies...................175.00

Ring, lady's, 14k white gold, emerald
green citrine quartz, chased floral
sides 135.00

Ring, lady's, 14k gold, Tiffany-type
prong-set peridot 99.00

Ring, lady's, 15k gold band set
w/rubies (3) alternating w/rose-cut
diamonds (2), scroll-carved, English
hallmarks.......................140.00

Ring, lady's, 18k white gold, green
peridot within filigree engraving,
butterfly & leaf at sides 140.00

Ring, man's, 14k green gold, bezel-set
carnelian, scroll-carved sides,
English hallmarks 150.00

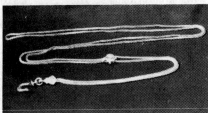

Lady's Slide Chain

Watch chain, lady's, 14k gold,
w/bright-cut slide & hinged swivel
ring, 50" l. (ILLUS.) 700.00

Watch chain, man's, braided human
hair w/gold-filled fittings, 1890s 55.00

Watch pin, 9k gold, self-beaded
border, 1" l......................55.00

Watch pin, 14k rose gold 4-leaf clover,
black enamel top & fresh water
pearl center......................70.00

KELLOGG PRINTS

Kellogg lithograph prints are not as well known as those of their rival firm, Currier and Ives, who issued far more titles and distributed them more widely. However, many collectors feel that Kellogg's work is superior in many respects. The four Hartford, Connecticut brothers involved in printmaking from about 1883 until 1875 were Jarvis G., Daniel W., Edmond B. and Elijah C. Kellogg. Their lithograph prints will be found variously signed: J.G. Kellogg, D.W. Kellogg, Kellogg & Hanmer, Kellogg & Thayer, E.B. & E.C. Kellogg and Kellogg & Buckley. Values of these prints are rising.

"Falls of Niagara," Kellogg & Com-
stock, trimmed margins, old beveled
mahogany veneer frame,
16 1/4 x 12 1/4"....................$40.00

"Household Pets," woman & child
w/dog & cat......................35.00

"John Tyler," matted, 1844 ....75.00

"Lady of the Lake," lady seated in
boat & man & dog watching from
shore, w/four lines of verse from
Sir Walter Scott's poem 38.00

"Little Drummer Boy".................35.00

"Married," man, woman & three
children 40.00

"Martin Van Buren," matted, 1844......75.00

"The May Queen," Kellogg & Thayer,
framed, 16 7/8 x 12 7/8"............45.00

"William Penn's Treaty with the
Indians," Kellogg & Thayer, framed,
16 1/2 x 12 3/4".......................85.00

KEWPIE COLLECTIBLES

Kewpie Easter Card

Rose O'Neill's Kewpies were so popular in their heyday that numerous objects de- picting them were produced and are now collectible. The following represents a sampling.

Bank, bisque, Kewpie kneeling on
rock, original paint, 8½" h. $85.00

Booklet, "The Kewpies & the Little Mermaid," signed Rose O'Neill, 1917,
3 pp. 30.00

Candle holder, metal, 2-light, Kewpie
seated on bar 65.00

Christmas postcard, Kewpie in
stocking, signed Rose O'Neill 22.00

Clock, jasper ware case, white relief
action Kewpies on blue, signed Rose
O'Neill 250.00

Coloring book, "Kewpies to Color,"
Artcraft 19.00

Creamer, china, Kewpie farmer &
Kewpie carpenter cavorting, signed
Rose O'Neill Wilson 125.00

Creamer, jasper ware, white relief
action Kewpies on blue, signed Rose
O'Neill 180.00

Easter greeting card, signed Rose
O'Neill (ILLUS.) 30.00

Feeding spoon, sterling silver, Kewpie
handle 95.00

Figure, Kewpie w/guitar, bisque,
2" h. 115.00

Figure, Kewpie Confederate soldier,
bisque, 3½" h. 275.00

Figure, Kewpie sitting & gazing at bug
on foot, bisque, 3½" h. 400.00

Figures, Kewpie wedding party:
minister wearing glasses, bride,
groom, 3 bridesmaids & 3 ushers;
bisque, wearing original cloth &
crepe paper clothing, 4½" h.,
9 pcs. 1,200.00

Bisque Kewpie "Traveler" & "Sweeper"

Figure, Kewpie "Sweeper," bisque,
signed Rose O'Neill, 5" h. (ILLUS.
right) 300.00

Figure, Kewpie "Traveler," bisque,
signed Rose O'Neill, 5½" h. (ILLUS.
left) 300.00

Figures, Kewpie bride & groom,
composition, 10" h., pr. 235.00

Figure, Kewpie wearing sunsuit,
composition, signed Rose O'Neill,
12" h. 110.00

Flannel square, Kewpie at the sea-
shore, signed & dated 1914, 5 x 7" 15.00

Lapel pin, bisque, Kewpie, 2" h. 100.00

Letter opener, pewter, Kewpie in relief
on handle, heart touch mark 55.00

Magazine sheet, "Woman's Home
Companion," 1912, "Kewpie
Kutouts," uncut 12.50

Mug, sterling silver, 4 action Kewpies
& bird decor, Matthews Silver Co. . . . 390.00

Night light, bisque, Kewpie seated, on
metal base, 4½" h. 125.00

Perfume bottle, figural Kewpie, clear
glass w/painted features, 3" h. 35.00

Plate, china, action Kewpies (3) decor,
floral border, signed Mrs. Rose
O'Neill Wilson, Bavaria, 6" d. 95.00

Postcard, Kewpie wearing Santa mask,
signed Rose O'Neill 25.00

Salt dip, china, Kewpie & turkey
decor 250.00

Sand pail, tin, Kewpie & Scooties,
signed Rose O'Neill 150.00

Tea set: cov. teapot, creamer, sugar
bowl & 5 c/s; china, action Kewpies
on blue lustre ground, signed Rose
O'Neill, 13 pcs. 600.00

KITCHENWARES

Utilitarian Bowl

*Also see ADVERTISING ITEMS, BAS-
KETS, BOTTLE OPENERS, CANS &
CONTAINERS, CERAMICS, COFFEE
GRINDERS, COOKBOOKS, COOKIE
CUTTERS, FIREPLACE & HEARTH
ACCESSORIES, FOOD, CANDY & MIS-
CELLANEOUS MOLDS, GLASS, ICE
BOXES under Furniture, METALS,
SHAKER ITEMS and WOODENWARES.*

Apple butter stirrer, wooden, pierced
paddle at right angle to handle,
43" l. $55.00

Apple corer, heavy tin, T-shaped
tubular form, 1880-1900, 6" l. 5.00

Apple parer, cast iron, "Harbster
Bros.," 1867 patent 50.00

Apple parer, cast iron, "C.L. Hudson
Parer Co., Leominster, Mass.,
Rocking Table," 1882 patent . . 48.00 to 55.00

Apple parer, cast iron, "Sargeant & Fosters," 3-gear table clamp-on model, 1856 patent, w/partial paper label 80.00

Apple parer, cast iron, "Sinclair, Scott Co., Made in U.S.A.," 3-gear, w/heart motif on one wheel 40.00

Apple parer, cast iron, "White Mountain, Goodell Co., Antrim, New Hampshire," 5-gear, 1898 patent 35.00

Apple parer, cherrywood base w/wrought iron fork & hand crank, dovetailed pivoting blade holder, old dark patina, 14½ x 10¼" base (no blade) . .65.00

Baking pan, copper, dovetailed corners, wrought iron end handles, worn tin lining, marked "Willibald Meckel - Wien (Vienna)," 22 x 14½" 65.00

Beater jar, grey stoneware w/blue band decor 50.00

Bowl, utilitarian crockery, Wedding Ring patt., yellow & green, 5½" d. . . .40.00

Bowl, utilitarian crockery, Greek Key patt., blue & white, 8" d. 60.00

Bowl, yellowware pottery w/brown & green mottled glaze, ridged sides, attributed to Morton Pottery Co., 8" d., 3¾" h. (ILLUS.) 40.00

Bowl, utilitarian crockery, Basketweave patt., blue & white, 9½" d., 6½" h. . . .60.00

Bowl, utilitarian crockery, Greek Key patt., blue & white, 10" d. 70.00

Bread cutting board, wooden, machine-carved border w/"Bread" 45.00

Bread mixer, tin pail w/hand crank in lid, table clamp-on model, "White House," 1902 patent 45.00

Bread pan, tin, embossed "Deckers" in bottom 6.50

Bread pan, tin, "Majestic" 10.00

Bread slicing knife, iron loop handle stamped "Nov. 12, 1890, Fremont, Ohio," scalloped-edge blade, 12" l. . .15.00

Bread slicing knife, wooden handle, scalloped-edge blade, "Simmon's, 12¼" l. 10.00

Bundt pan, copper, dovetailed con-struction, tin lining & brass ring handle, ca. 1820, 10" d., 4½" h. 140.00

Butter churn, "The Dazey Churn," embossed glass jar w/original gears, 2-qt. 45.00

Butter churn, "The Dazey Churn," model B, embossed glass jar, original gears & red egg-shaped iron finial on lid, 4-qt. 35.00

Butter churn, "The Dazey Churn," blue galvanized tin, wooden lid & 2-wheel paddle, 1917 patent, 3-gal., 25" h. 60.00

Butter churn, wooden cylinder floor model, tin lid, iron crank, wooden blades, original yellow paint w/gold stenciled decoration & label

"Manufactured by Cornish & Curtis, Fort Atkinson, Wis. for Wm. E. Linnchlin, Warren, Mass.," 35" h. . . .100.00

Butter churn, wooden cylinder floor model, dovetailed construction, wrought iron clamp-on lid spins when wooden crank is turned, mortised frame w/shoe feet, old worn dark finish, 37" h. 160.00

Butter churn, dasher-type, oak, stave construction, original stenciling, "Star," & "No. 0," red-painted top . . .175.00

Butter crock w/lid, utilitarian crockery, Apricot patt., blue & white 150.00

Butter crock w/lid, utilitarian crockery, Butterfly patt., blue & white 95.00

Butter crock w/lid, utilitarian crockery, Cow patt., blue & white . . . .85.00 to 110.00

Butter crock w/lid, utilitarian crockery, Daisy & Waffle patt., blue & white 95.00

Butter crock w/lid, utilitarian crockery, Eagle patt. on stippled ground, blue & white 170.00

Cabbage cutting board, maple, plain, 6 x 18" 15.00

Cabbage cutting board, poplar w/single steel blade & pierced heart design in crest, 7" w., 20" l. 165.00

Cabbage cutting board, walnut w/single blade & pierced heart in crest, 8" w., 20¾" l. (crack in top of heart) 125.00

Cabbage cutting board, oak, plain, 9 x 25" 20.00

Cabbage cutting board, pine w/single steel blade & pierced heart design in fishtail crest, original worn red paint, 9" w., 26½" l. 175.00

Cabbage cutting board, "Keen Kutter," wooden w/single blade, original square cabbage head box & kraut stomper, large . . . . .45.00 to 65.00

Cake pans, tin, heart-shaped, hand-seamed, 7 x 7", pr. 60.00

Early Tin Cake Pan

Cake pan w/center tube, tin, 10-sided, hand-seamed, 12½" top d., 3¾" h. (ILLUS.) 40.00

Canister, transparent green glass jar w/metal screw-on lid, 64-oz., 1930s 22.00

Canister, cov., utilitarian crockery,

"Sugar," Basketweave patt., blue &
white 125.00
Canisters, cov., porcelain w/white
iridescent glaze, lettered
"Oatmeal," "Rice," "Flour,"
"Tea," "Coffee" & "Sugar," marked
"Made in Germany," 8" h., set of 6 . .115.00
Can opener, cast iron, figural bull's
head & tail, 6¼" l. 68.00
Can opener, cast iron, "Delmonico,"
1890s. 12.00
Can opener, cast iron, "Keen Kutter,"
1895 . . . . .32.50
Carpet beater, bent wire Art Nouveau
tulip shape in wooden
handle . . . . .20.00 to 24.00
Carpet beater, bent wire double loop
in wooden handle . . . . .10.00 to 19.00
Carpet beater, wire heart-shaped
loop in wooden handle, miniature
size. .16.00 to 35.00
Charcoal iron w/brass rooster
finial 125.00
Charcoal iron, w/Vulcan head finial 58.00
Cherry pitter, cast iron, "Enterprise
1883" .22.00 to 29.00
Cherry pitter, cast iron, double,
"Goodell Co., Antrim, New
Hampshire," clamp-type. . . . .28.00 to 45.00
Cherry pitter, cast iron, "Holman,"
clamp-type. .25.00
Cherry pitter, cast iron, "New
Standard, Mt. Joy, Pa.". . . . . .20.00 to 30.00
Cherry pitter, cast iron, "Rollman Mfg.
Co.," clamp-type . . . . .22.50 to 30.00
Clothesline reel, wooden "niddy-
noddy" form, 12¾" l. 10.00
Coffee boiler, cov., copper, large 75.00

Tin Coffee Boiler

Coffee boiler, cov., tin w/copper
bottom, strap-handled grip at base,
wire bail handle at top, 3-qt.,
9½" base d., 9½" h. (ILLUS.) 40.00
Coffee pot, cov., tin, Shaker-style 37.50
Coffee pot, cov., utilitarian crockery,
Swirl patt., blue & white 595.00
Cookie board, carved granite, bird

on branch one side, initials & flowers
reverse, 6½ x 4" oblong 200.00
Cookie board, carved pine, florals &
leaves in circles, 10 x 6½" oblong . . .130.00
Cornstick pan, cast iron, 7-ear,
"Griswold Crispy Cornsticks,"
No. 273 . . . . .18.00 to 35.00
Cottage cheese drainer, tin, strap handle,
small. 25.00
Cream skimmer, pierced brass bowl
w/wrought iron handle, 18¾" l. 75.00
Cream skimmer, wooden, hand-hewn,
5½" d. 75.00
Cream whip, cov., tin, "Hodge's,"
footed, 1890-1910 . . . . .45.00
Cream whip, cov., tin, cast iron &
wood, "Fries," crank handle at side,
footed, 1890s, 6 x 4", 8" h. 85.00
Cucumber slicer, cast iron, clamp-on
type w/crank handle, ca. 1877 . . . . . .75.00

Pot Scrubber

Pot scrubber, wire chain links on
handle, 7½" l. (ILLUS.). 15.00
Scrub board, wooden frame
w/corrugated glass insert, "Good
Housekeeper," 18 x 8½" . . . .12.00 to 22.00
Scrub board, wooden frame w/brass
insert, "Sunset," 24 x 12½" . .10.00 to 20.00

"Griswold" Waffle Iron

Waffle iron, cast iron, grid design
w/heart & star, "Griswold" (ILLUS.) . .75.00
Waffle iron w/bail handle, cast iron,
"Wagner," ca. 1910, 2-pc. . . . .15.00 to 20.00
Waffle iron, cast iron grid w/wrought
iron handle, overall 25" l. 60.00

KNIFE RESTS

China, flow blue $85.00
Cut glass, dumbbell shape, faceted
ends, large 35.00

Cut glass, dumbbell shape, notched
   prism cutting on bar, star-cut ends,
   5¼" l. 35.00
Glass, signed "Lalique" 60.00
Pottery, peasant decor, marked "H. B.
   Quimper".........................65.00
Pressed glass, dumbbell shape, large ..32.50
Silverplate, figural boy sitting on fence
   at each end, 1½ x 4", 1 7/8" h........40.00
Silverplate, figural butterfly at each
   end 38.00
Silverplate, figural child w/bowed
   head at each end 35.00
Silverplate, figural Cocker Spaniel dog
   at each end 30.00

Silverplate Knife Rest

Silverplate, figural Greyhound dog at
   each end (ILLUS.) 35.00
Silverplate, figural squirrel at each
   end 30.00
Silverplate, figural steer's head at each
   end 30.00
Silverplate, figural swan at each end ...35.00

KNIVES

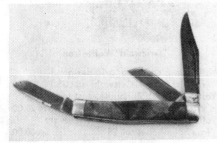

Remington Pocket Knife

Advertising, "American Boy
   Magazine," pocket knife $12.00
Advertising, "Franklin Fire Ins.,"
   Remington pocket knife 35.00
Bertram (Hen & Rooster trademark),
   Solingen, Germany, pocket knife,
   mother-of-pearl handle............100.00
Bowie knife, antler handle, 9" l. blade ..50.00

Camillus Cutlery Co., Camillus, N.Y.,
   Boy Scout knife 9.00
Case XX 1-blade Bulldog (clasp knife),
   stag handle, 1950s, No. 5172, 5½" l.
   closed 150.00
Case XX 1-blade pocket knife, red bone
   handle, No. 6143..................45.00
Case XX 3-blade pocket knife, green
   bone handle, No. 6347 ....75.00
Cattaraugus Cutlery Co., Little Valley,
   N.Y., 2-blade pocket knife, serpen-
   tine handle, 3 1/8" l. closed 30.00
Cattaraugus Cutlery Co., sheath knife,
   No. 2250 ....115.00
Fleam (lancet) knife, 2-blade, in horn
   case ....65.00 to 85.00
Ka-Bar pocket knife, stag handle
   w/dog's head 150.00
Ka-Bar, Union Cut. Co., Olean, N.Y.,
   3-blade fish knife, black handle.....150.00
Keen Kutter pocket knife, mother-of-
   pearl handle, No. 0153 ....62.00
Pal Cutlery Co., Plattsburg, N.Y.,
   4-blade pocket knife, bone handle,
   marked "U.S.M.C." 100.00
Remington Arms Co., Boy Scout pocket
   knife, bone handle, No. R3843 .....300.00
Remington Arms Co., "Bullet" knife,
   bone handle, No. R4353...........500.00
Remington Arms Co., 3-blade pocket
   knife, green marbleized Pyremite
   handle w/emblem shield, No. R3555,
   4" l. closed (ILLUS.)...............55.00
Schrade Cutlery Co., Bridgeport, Conn.,
   pocket knife w/switchblade, dated
   1916 ....65.00
Souvenir, pocket knife, "Brooklyn
   Bridge"..........................85.00
Sterling silver pocket knife, 1-blade
   w/nut pick, Gorham Silver Co.......175.00
Valley Forge Cutlery Co., Newark,
   N.J., 2-blade pocket knife, nickel
   silver handle, 3¼" l. closed 175.00

LACQUER

*Most desirable of the lacquer articles
available for collectors are those of Japanese
and Chinese origin, and the finest of these
were produced during the Ming & Ching
dynasties, although the Chinese knew the
art of fashioning articles of lacquer
centuries before. Cinnabar is carved red
lacquer.*

Box w/hinged lid, spade-shaped, top
   w/gold butterflies in flight decor
   on black ground, black interior,
   8 x 7¾ x 3¼"...................$350.00

Leaf-shaped Japanese Lacquer Box

Box, cov., leaf-shaped, "takamakie"
& "hiramakie" (raised gold) chrysanthemums adorned w/a ladybug &
mother-of-pearl inlaid butterfly,
sides inlaid w/bone & mother-of-
pearl designs, corresponding
interior tray painted w/a vine on
green ground, rosewood lining,
Japan, 19th c., 9½" l. (ILLUS.) 1,600.00
Breakfast tray on legs, painted w/bird
in flight over chrysanthemum blossoms in salmon-red & grey-green
on black ground, China, early
20th c., 16" l. 220.00
Cinnabar stools, overall carved red
lacquer, pr. 3,300.00
Cinnabar tray, carved w/various birds
in & around flowering tree, magnolia blossoms & birds border,
China, late 19th c., 14 7/8" sq. 275.00
Glove box w/hinged lid, painted
w/Geisha girls, child, birds &
dragons in tones of red & gold on
black ground, 11½" l., 3½" w. 55.00
Picnic box, 5-tier, floral decor in red,
yellow & green on stippled black
ground, red interior, 11" h. 412.00

LAW ENFORCEMENT ITEMS

*All types of objects relating to law
enforcement activities of earlier days are
now being collected, just as are fire-fighting
mementoes. The range extends from badges
and insignia to leg irons and weapons. The
following compilation represents a cross-
section.*

Badge, "Captain, Winfield, Kansas,"
w/sunburst & eagle top, hall-
marked. $70.00
Badge, "Deputy Investigator, Jackson
County, Missouri," w/Jackson
County seal 65.00
Badge, "Police, Miami, Florida". 70.00
Badge, "Police, Selma, Alabama,"
shield-shaped w/eagle top. 95.00

Badge, "Sheriff's Patrol, Jackson
County Missouri," sunburst
w/Jackson County seal 60.00
Badge, "Special Police, New York
State," w/New York State seal & cut-
out numbers, 1930s 100.00
Handcuffs, "Hiatt," w/keys, pr. 65.00
Handcuffs, "Matlock," w/key, pr. 90.00
Handcuffs, "Mattatuck," pr. 45.00
Handcuffs, "Peerless, Pat. 1912-25,"
w/key, pr. 27.50
Handcuffs, "Smith & Wesson," w/key,
pr. 38.00

Solid Iron Handcuffs

Handcuffs, iron, "Towers, Pat. May 26,
1874," w/key, 9" across, pr. (ILLUS.) . .80.00
Leg irons, "U.S.M.C., 1887," pr. 145.00
Wrist iron w/keys 105.00

LIGHTING DEVICES

*Also see CANDLESTICKS & CANDLE
HOLDERS, CARNIVAL and PATTERN
GLASS.*

CHANDELIERS

18th Century Brass Chandelier

Candle chandelier, brass, 3-light,
baluster-shaped stem w/three
scrolling candle arms ending in

shaped candle nozzles w/drip pans, 18th c., overall 11" h., w/wrought iron chain (ILLUS.) $1,100.00

Candle chandelier, gilt bronze & cut glass, 6-light, cast w/stylized acanthus leafage, 3 candle arms set w/two lights each, hung overall w/faceted or rounded teardrop prisms, France, late 19th c., overall 27" h.........................1,760.00

Louis XV Style Chandelier

Candle chandelier, gilt bronze & cut glass, 8-light, cage frame w/eight scrolling candle arms hung overall w/facet-cut glass drops & w/facet-cut sphere at base, Louis XV style, early 20th c., overall 38" h. (ILLUS.) 1,870.00

Candle chandelier, gilt metal & cut glass, 8-light, 5 graduated gilt metal tiers hung w/facet-cut glass pendants & lower tier fitted w/curved candle arms interspersed by cut glass spires, Louis XVI period, late 18th c., overall 41" h. 11,000.00

Candle chandelier, ormolu & cut glass, 12-light, the crown fitted w/cut glass pendants forming palmettes & hung w/facet-cut glass beading attached to lower pierced ormolu ring fitted w/a red glass plate & curved candle arms w/pierced drip pans, hung overall w/facet-cut glass teardrop pendants, Russia, 19th c., 31" d. at lower ring, overall 38" h.......................17,600.00

Candle chandelier, gilt bronze & cut glass, 12-light, upper tier formed as 8 upright acanthus palmettes & lower tier supporting 12 candle arms, all joined by facet-cut glass beading & hung w/similar swags, France, late 19th c., overall 44" h.............2,310.00

Chandelier shade, Custard glass, Paneled Poppies patt., 16" d. 500.00

Tiffany Type Chandelier Shade

Chandelier shade, Tiffany-type leaded glass, mottled green & white glass panels w/red, yellow & green floral border, 26½" d. (ILLUS.) 275.00

LAMPS, MISCELLANEOUS

Astral lamp, marble stepped base, brass fluted stem, original font, acid-etched glass pyriform shade, w/prisms, mid-19th c., 22½" h. 522.50

Baker's lamp, tin, oval font w/cylindrical handle, brass whale oil burner, 9¼" l. 75.00

Banquet lamp, brass base & stem, aqua Bristol glass globe-shaped shade w/pink roses decor (electrified) 275.00

Banquet lamp, onyx base, brass & onyx stem, cased yellow-gold over white glass globe-shaped shade, 29½" h. 325.00

Betty lamp, wrought iron, w/pick & twisted hanger, 18th c. ....105.00 to 230.00

Bouillotte lamp, ormolu, 3-light, circular stop-fluted stem w/three candle arms & molded nozzles cast w/foliate scrolls supporting drip pans on pierced slightly dished circular base, Charles X period, France, 1st quarter 19th c., 28" h..................4,170.00

Bradley & Hubbard signed banquet lamp, polished brass & onyx base & stem, etched glass globe-shaped shade (electrified) 350.00

Bradley & Hubbard signed hanging central room fixture, cast iron frame, clear glass font, 14" d. opaline glass conical shade 275.00

Bradley & Hubbard signed hanging country-store fixture, brass font & frame, original green-painted tin shade 300.00

Bradley & Hubbard signed table lamp, kerosene-type, brass bulbous base, 12" d. floral-etched frosted clear glass domical shade, original clear glass chimney 250.00

Desk lamp, "Emeralite," brass base & adjustable stem, cased green over white glass oblong shade, 15" h. ....275.00 to 400.00

Desk lamp, bronze base w/adjustable
stem, oblong etched glass shade
w/reverse-painted florals, late
19th c., 13¾" h. 247.50
Fluid lamp, stepped marble base
w/applied brass mounts, baluster-
shaped white overlay cut to clear
glass stem w/brass knop, clear
pyriform glass font w/cut foliate
design, Sandwich, mid-19th c.,
16" h. 176.00
Gone-with-the-Wind lamp, green-
washed opaline glass ball-shaped
shade & matching base w/enameled
pink & red dogwood blossoms decor,
slip-in brass font signed "Royal" &
dated "1895," 23" h. 595.00
Gone-with-the-Wind lamp, red Satin
glass puffy ball-shaped shade &
matching base, slip-in brass font,
"Pittsburgh Lamp & Glass Co.,"
ca. 1890, 24½" h. 695.00

Red Satin Gone-With-The-Wind Lamp

Gone-with-the-Wind lamp, red Satin
glass Baby Face patt. ball-shaped
shade & inverted pear-shaped base
(ILLUS.) 950.00
Gone-with-the-Wind lamp, white Satin
glass Regal Iris patt. ball-shaped
shade & matching base, slip-in brass
font, 27" h. 695.00
Grease lamp, wrought iron triangular
pan w/wick support, on sawtooth
trammel hanger adjusting from
24" 175.00
Kerosene lamp, "Angle Lamp Co.,
N.Y." signed, single, nickel-plated
brass reservoir, frosted glass shade &
milk white glass chimney 325.00
Kerosene lamp, "Angle Lamp Co.,
N.Y." signed, double, embossed
brass reservoir, frosted glass shades
& milk white glass
chimneys ....375.00 to 495.00

Kerosene lamp, hanging central room
(or library) fixture, milk white glass
domical 14" d. shade w/bluebird
decor, clear glass font, original brass
frame & chains, w/prisms 795.00
Kerosene lamp, hanging hall fixture,
8" d. shaded pink mother-of-pearl
Satin glass Diamond Quilted patt.
shade w/white lining, brass frame
& chains, 16½" h. 850.00

Cranberry Glass Hall Lamp

Kerosene lamp, hanging hall fixture,
pull-down type, cranberry glass Swirl
patt. shade, brass frame & chains
(ILLUS.) 295.00
Kerosene hand lamp w/finger grip,
blown-mold cranberry glass
w/panels, applied clear handle,
brass burner, 4 3/8" d., 5½" h. 125.00
Kerosene hand lamp w/finger grip,
blown-mold sky blue overlay
glass w/embossed designs, applied
clear glass reeded handle, 4¼" d.,
6" h. 125.00
Kerosene hand lamp w/finger grip,
pressed glass, Double Bar Band
patt., amber ....75.00 to 95.00
Kerosene hand lamp w/finger grip,
pressed glass, Gothic Arches patt.,
sapphire blue w/applied clear
crimped handle..................195.00
Kerosene hand lamp w/finger grip,
pressed glass, Greek Key patt.,
clear 45.00
Kerosene hand lamp w/finger grip,
footed, pressed glass, King Comet
patt., clear ....55.00 to 75.00
Kerosene hand lamp w/finger grip,
pressed glass, King Melon patt.,
clear 40.00
Kerosene hand lamp w/finger grip,

pressed glass, Little Buttercup patt.,
amethyst 145.00
Kerosene table lamp, "Rayo," brass
base, milk white glass shade, clear
glass chimney ....95.00 to 125.00

"Aladdin" Table Lamp

Kerosene table lamp, "Aladdin," brass
base "Model No. 9," (replaced) milk
white glass shade, clear glass
chimney (ILLUS.) 90.00
Kerosene table lamp w/stem, blown-
mold cranberry opalescent Coin Dot
patt. font, clear glass ribbed stem &
expanding base, original burner &
clear glass chimney 500.00
Kerosene table lamp w/stem,
"Aladdin," pressed glass, Corinthian
patt., clear font, black base 85.00
Kerosene table lamp w/stem,
"Aladdin," pressed glass, Hobnail
patt., clear.......................80.00
Kerosene table lamp w/stem,
"Aladdin," pressed glass, Lincoln
Drape patt., ruby, short............325.00
Kerosene table lamp w/stem,
"Aladdin," pressed glass, Lincoln
Drape patt., ruby, tall 325.00
Kerosene table lamp w/stem,
"Aladdin," pressed glass, Venetian
patt., clear, "B" burner 110.00
Kerosene table lamp w/stem,
"Aladdin," pressed glass, Vertique
patt., green moonstone............155.00
Kerosene table lamp w/stem, pressed
glass, Aquarius patt., amber
w/amber chimney 160.00
Kerosene table lamp w/stem, pressed
glass, Beaded Diamond Band patt.,
amber............................100.00
Kerosene table lamp w/stem, pressed
glass, Bolton patt., clear 37.50

Coolidge Drape Pattern Lamp

Kerosene table lamp w/stem, pressed
glass, Coolidge Drape patt., clear,
overall 22" h. (ILLUS.)..............125.00
Kerosene table lamp w/two burners,
"Ripley Marriage (or Wedding) Lamp,"
blue opaline glass double fonts &
center match holder, milk white
glass base, w/brass connectors,
collars & burners, clear glass chimneys, "Ripley & Co., Pat. Feb. 1st,
1870" on base........1,000.00 to 1,500.00
Kerosene wall bracket lamps, lacy cast
iron bracket, clear pressed glass
lamp w/burner, original mercury
glass reflector, pr. 120.00
Lacemaker's lamp, brass base
w/handle, cranberry "overshot" glass
shade, clear glass chimney, 10"
widest d. shade, overall 16" h.......375.00

Kinnear's Patent Lard Lamp

Lard oil lamp, tin, saucer base,
tubular stem & cylindrical font joined
by applied strap handle, "Kinnear's
Patent Feb. 4, 1851" (ILLUS.) 495.00

Loom lamp, wrought iron, rush light w/candle socket counter balance on hanging arm, overall 18" l. (some rust damage)....................215.00

Miller Lamp Co. signed table lamp, reverse-painted 18" d. shade w/woodland scene, 3-socket metal base........................1,195.00

Moe Bridges signed table lamp, 16" d. reverse-painted shade w/green, lavender & brown mountain & desert scene w/large tree in foreground, bronze base............1,695.00

Moe Bridges signed table lamp, shade w/winter sunset scene, original base........................2,200.00

Nursing lamp, tin & copper double boiler w/brass hinges & hasp at top, "Badger" brass burner inside, overall 9" h. 150.00

Pairpoint signed boudoir lamp, 5" d. "puffy" Rose Bouquet shade, tree trunk base 1,750.00

Pairpoint signed floor lamp, reverse-painted "Garden of Allah" shade, metal base 3,500.00

Pairpoint signed table lamp, 8" d. "puffy" Papillon patt. shade w/rose on top & 4 groups of flowers & 4 butterflies, brass base.........2,500.00

Pairpoint signed table lamp, 8" d. "puffy" Dogwood Blossom Border shade, brass base 1,800.00

Pairpoint Lamp with Papillon Shade

Pairpoint signed table lamp, 14" d. "puffy" Papillon patt. shade w/four groups & flowers & 4 butterflies, brass finish base, 21" h. (ILLUS.)...3,500.00

Peg lamp, shaded rose to pink Satin overlay glass font & shade w/white lining, brass candlestick base, original burner, shade holder & clear glass chimney, 6" d., 17¼" h.......607.00

Peg lamps, yellow overlay Swirl patt. Satin glass font & shade, oriental

style brass candlestick base, original shade holder, burner & clear glass chimney, 6" d. shade, overall 17" h., pr. 1,250.00

Peg lamp, tin, petticoat-type, original worn dark japanned finish, whale oil burner, 5¼" h................65.00

Rush light holder, wrought iron shaft w/candle socket counter balance set in wooden base, 7¾" h. 155.00

Rush light holder, wrought iron shaft w/broad bill w/faceted acorn finial as counter balance set in wooden block, 18th c., 9½" h..............295.00

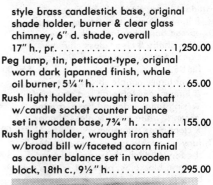

Solar Lamp

Solar lamp, bronze "dore" stem, square marble base, acid finish glass shade w/cut florals & leaves, signed "Cornelius & Co.," 1840s, 26" h. (ILLUS.) 895.00

Sparking lamp, pewter, matching burner w/brass single tube spout, 4" h. 120.00

Student Lamp

Student lamp, single, brass reservoir
& lamp adjustable on rod standard &
domed base, original milk white
glass shade & clear glass chimney,
signed Bradley & Hubbard, 20" h.
(ILLUS.) 550.00

Student lamp, double, brass reservoir
& lamps adjustable on rod standard
w/ring finial & domed base, original
green & white overlay glass shades
& clear glass chimneys 1,250.00

Tiffany-type table lamp w/leaded glass
shade, 24" d. shade w/pale blue
wisteria blossoms, brown & mauve
branches & green leaves on green
ground, patinated metal tree trunk
form standard w/pierced roots at
circular base, American, early
20th c., 30½" h.................3,025.00

Time Indicating lamp, "Pride of
America," clear glass base-font
embossed w/various hours from
"8 p.m. to 6 a.m.," milk white glass
ridged shade, 7½" h...............48.00

Whale oil lamps, brass, saucer base
w/handle, baluster-shaped stem,
swiveling acorn-shaped font in
holder, 5¾" h., pr...............110.00

Whale oil lamp, blown clear glass
pear-shaped font on stepped serpen-
tine-sided square base, original
whale oil burner & brass collar,
11 1/8" h.......................105.00

Whale oil lamp, pewter, disc-shaped
base, baluster-turned stem, original
burner, American, 4½" h. 220.00

Whale oil lamp, pressed glass, Moon
& Star patt., clear, original burner...150.00

Whale oil lamp, tin, petticoat-type,
egg-shaped oil font w/filling spout,
petticoat base w/handle, original
burner, remnants of original
asphaltum, 4" h..................55.00

HANDEL LAMPS (All Signed)

Handel Table Lamp

Boudoir lamp, leaded glass conical
shade w/tapering white panels inter-
cepted by band of purple, patinated
metal base.....................425.00

Piano lamp, leaded glass shade
w/poppy blossoms on rose ground,
bronze base, 14" h. 750.00

Table lamp, 18" d. domical shade
w/caramel glass panels overlaid
w/metal filigree, patinated metal
base, early 20th c.,
26" h.................1,200.00 to 1,800.00

Table lamp, 18" d. reverse-painted
shade w/scene of lake & trees in
shades of sage & deep green, grey
& black, patinated metal base, early
20th c., 22" h....................4,510.00

Table lamp, 18" d. reverse-painted
domical shade w/autumn forest land-
landscape w/birds perched in the
colorful leafy branches against pale
grey & green ground, patinated
metal base w/standard raised on 3
scrolling acanthus-molded supports
& circular 2-tier foot, w/finial, early
20th c., 23¼" h.................3,630.00

Table lamp, 18" d. reverse-painted
domical "chipped ice" shade w/red
roses, white dogwood, small blue
florals & black border on yellow
ground, oriental-style bronze base
w/three applied handles, early
20th c., 24" h...................1,900.00

Table lamp, 18" d. reverse-painted
domical "chipped ice" shade
w/exotic red-orange & blue parrots
perched on lush tropical trees
against shaded blue, green & yellow
ground, patinated metal urn form
Chinese-style base, w/finial, early
20th c., 24½" h. (ILLUS.)..........7,425.00

Table lamp, 20" d. leaded glass
domical shade w/yellow-centered
pink apple blossoms & green leaves,
bronze base cast w/band of floral
panels, early 20th c., 29½" h......3,080.00

TIFFANY LAMPS (All Signed)

Bridge lamp, counter-balance type,
10" d. damascene iridescent amber
shade, bronze S-scroll bifurcated
arm w/sphere counter-balance
terminal, cylindrical standard
molded w/leafage, circular base on
leaf-molded scrolling feet, early
20th c., 54" h........4,950.00 to 6,600.00

Candle lamp, iridescent blue glass
ruffled umbrella-type shade & swirl-
ribbed base, 14" h. 1,850.00

Candle lamp, iridescent green glass
ruffled umbrella-type shade & swirl-
ribbed base, 14" h. 2,250.00

Candlestick lamp, alabaster glass

pyriform shade w/green striated
feathering devices edged in iridescent amber, fitting into a bronze urn-
form socket supported by 3 prongs &
cylindrical standard splitting at base
to form 3 root-form feet, early
20th c., 18¾" h. 1,870.00
Desk lamp, flattened ovoid bronze
shade, set w/two deep blue glass
"turtle-back" tiles, pivoting on
bronze harp-form support, pierced
standard, footed hexagonal base
cast w/Zodiac motifs, 1899-1920,
14¾" h. 3,080.00
Desk lamp, counter-balance type, 7" d.
domical lime green glass shade
w/intaglio-carved band of leafage,
bronze scrolling arm w/sphere
counter-balance terminal, raised on
2 scrolling legs continuing to dished
circular base, early 20th c.,
14¾" h. 2,860.00
Desk lamp, 7" d. domical iridescent
gold glass shade pivoting on bronze
harp-form support, American Indian
patt. base . . . . .1,250.00 to 1,500.00
Desk lamp, 7" d. domical yellow-green
damascene glass shade pivoting on
bronze harp-form support, baluster
standard, domed circular base cast
w/gadroon edge, 5 ball feet, early
20th c., 17½" h. 2,310.00
Floor lamp, "Bamboo," 22" d. leaded
glass domical shade w/overall pale
lime green to emerald green bamboo leafage, pale yellow & green
bamboo stalks on variegated blue
ground, bronze cylindrical standard,
circular slightly dished base, 4
spatulate feet, bamboo finial, early
20th c., 63½" h. 39,600.00
Floor lamp, "Curtain Border," 24½" d.
leaded glass domical shade w/band
of rippled lime green panels at rim
beneath band of green lozenge-
shaped panels on mottled green
ground, bronze standard & base, 5
ball feet, w/pigtail finial,
76½" h. .13,200.00
Floor lamp, "Tulip," 22" d. leaded glass
domical shade w/deeply mottled
orange & yellow blossoms amidst
green leafage on bright blue
ground, bronze base, pigtail finial,
67½" h. . . . . .23,100.00 to 38,500.00
Lily lamp, 3-light, opalescent white
glass lily-form shades w/green
pulled feathering, bronze base
w/dark patina 2,750.00
Lily lamp, 6-light, iridescent opaque
white glass lily-form shades
w/striated green feathering, bronze
base w/adjustable holder on central
column, 20½" h. 4,840.00

Tiffany Lily Lamp

Lily lamp, 12-light, iridescent gold
glass lily-form shades, bronze stems
& lily pad base, 21¾" h.
(ILLUS.) . . . . .12,100.00 to 15,400.00

Tiffany Student Lamp

Student lamp, double, bronze base
w/upright rods supporting cylindrical oil reservoir & adjustable
arms w/fitted ring supports for iridescent glass shades w/silver-blue &
amber waves, 29¼" h. (ILLUS.). . . .4,070.00
Table lamp, "Acorn," 16" d. leaded
glass domical shade w/radiating
bands of mottled green above lower
border of mottled amber acorns &
leafage, bronze urn-form base, 4
scrolling legs w/shaped square
feet, early 20th c.,
21" h. . . . . .2,750.00 to 5,225.00

Table lamp, "Clematis," 18½" d.
leaded glass conical shade w/opal-
escent white to mottled yellow-white
blossoms w/pale yellow centers on
mottled green to mottled blue-green
ground, bronze base, early 20th c.,
22" h. (upper rim of shade
releaded) 7,700.00

Table lamp, "Dragonfly," 20" d. leaded
glass conical shade w/band of
inverted dragonflies w/filigreed
green & red wings & red eyes on
emerald green jeweled & multi-hued
purple-blue ground, bronze base,
25¾" h.......................19,800.00

Table lamp, "Laburnum," 22" d. leaded
glass bulging domical shade
w/clusters of golden laburnum blossoms & green leafage pendant from
mauve branches on mottled blue-
grey ground, bronze cylindrical
standard & 4 branching legs cast to
resemble organic roots, w/finial,
early 20th c., 30½" h..........44,000.00

Table lamp, "Peacock," 18" d. leaded
glass domical shade w/two radiating
bands of purple & turquoise peacock
eyes amidst brown-green plumage
shading to deep purple at top &
w/lower band of green feathers,
bronze base, 25½" h...........14,300.00

Tiffany Table Lamp

Table lamp, "Peony," 18" d. leaded
glass domical shade w/overall white
to crimson, maroon & lavender blossoming peonies & green leafage,
bronze paneled standard & base
w/applied stringing, 5 ball feet,
w/finial, early 20th c., 24¾" h.
(ILLUS.) 15,400.00

Table lamp, "Pond Lily," 20" d. leaded
glass conical shade w/orange-
centered pink & textured white

blossoms amidst variegated green
lily pads on bright mottled blue
ground, bronze band cast w/band of
cattails above overlapping lily pads,
25 1/8" h. 67,100.00

MINIATURE LAMPS

Eagle and Block & Dot Pattern Lamps

*Numbers following our listing of lamps
are those assigned to the various miniature
lamps pictured in Frank R. & Ruth E.
Smith's book, "Miniature Lamps," now
often referred to as Smith's Book I.*

Amber glass Bull's Eye patt. variant
stem lamp, Nutmeg burner, clear
glass chimney, No. 111 ....125.00

Amber (or blue) glass Bull's Eye patt.
stem lamp, Nutmeg burner, clear
glass chimney, advertised as "Daisy"
in Butler Brothers "Our Drummer"
1912 catalogue, 5" h., No. 112,
each 100.00

Blue glass Block patt. stem lamp,
Nutmeg burner, clear glass
chimney, 5¼" h. base, No. 106 ......80.00

Blue glass Buckle patt. stem lamp,
Nutmeg burner, clear glass chimney,
5½" h., No. 118.................118.00

Blue opaque glass multi-ribbed base &
matching globe-chimney, Acorn
burner, 6½" h., No. 176 ....150.00

Blue opaque glass w/swirl-ribbed band
on base & globe-chimney, Hornet
burner, 7¾" h., No. 215 ....425.00

Brass "Beauty Night Lamp" embossed
wall lamp, w/filling spout on wall
reservoir & lion's mouth supporting
tubing to burner, milk glass beehive
chimney-shade, No. 77 ....70.00

Brass ball-shaped base w/three large
ball-shaped feet, foreign burner,
green opaque glass umbrella-type
shade w/brass crown ring, 10½" h.,
No. 101 ....95.00

Cased butterscotch over custard glass base & globe-chimney w/embossed florals, Hornet burner, 8" h., No. 372 ....375.00

Cased pink glass melon-ribbed base & melon-ribbed umbrella-type shade, Nutmeg burner, clear glass chimney, by Consolidated Lamp & Glass Co., Pittsburgh, 7" h., No. 390 ....550.00

Clear & frosted glass Octagon-type patt. globular base & overlapping leaf patt. umbrella-type shade, Nutmeg burner, clear glass chimney, No. 148 ....90.00 to 135.00

Clear glass base embossed w/elephant, 2 moons & 2 stars, applied handle, Acorn burner, clear glass chimney, 2¾" h., No. 37 ....98.00

Cranberry glass Inverted Thumbprint patt. base & umbrella-type shade, Nutmeg burner, clear glass chimney, 8" h., No. 434....................225.00

Cranberry glass base & globe-shaped shade w/fired-on gold decor, Nutmeg burner, 8¾" h., No. 441 ....360.00

"Evening Star" embossed on clear glass font, Olmsted burner, white Bristol glass chimney-shade, 2½" h., No. 12...........................145.00

Goofus glass w/fired on red paint & relief-molded grape clusters, Acorn burner, clear glass chimney, 3¼" h., No. 123 ....28.00 to 40.00

Green glass Bull's Eye patt. stem lamp, Nutmeg burner, clear glass chimney, advertised as "Daisy" in Butler Brothers "Our Drummer" 1912 catalogue, 5" h., No. 112 ....75.00 to 95.00

Green glass stem lamp w/frosted & floral-embossed font, Acorn burner, clear glass chimney, 5½" h., No. 114 ....95.00 to 135.00

Green Satin glass Beaded Drape patt. base & ball-shaped shade, Nutmeg burner, clear glass chimney, 9" h., No. 400..........................395.00

"Improved Banner" & 3 stars embossed on clear glass pedestal base, Olmsted burner, white Bristol glass shade, No. 20 ....85.00

"Little Buttercup" embossed on cobalt blue glass base w/handle, Nutmeg burner, clear glass chimney, 2¾" h., No. 36............................90.00

"Little Duchess" & 3 stars embossed on milk white glass font in brass saucer base w/brass spring-type clamp, Acorn burner, clear glass chimney, 3" h., No. 32.....80.00 to 110.00

"Little Jewel" embossed on clear glass footed base, applied handle, Acorn burner, clear glass chimney, 4" h., No. 44..........................70.00

"Little Twilight" embossed on clear

glass ribbed pedestal base, Olmsted burner, white Bristol glass chimney-shade, 7" h., No. 19 ....145.00

Milk white glass Block & Dot patt. footed base & ball-shaped shade, Acorn burner, clear glass chimney, 7½" h., No. 190 (ILLUS. right)........98.00

Milk white glass Cosmos patt. base & umbrella-type shade w/painted flowers & yellow band decor, Nutmeg burner, 7½" h., No. 286 ....285.00

Milk white glass Eagle patt. base & ball-shaped shade w/American Eagle in relief in diamond form w/beaded & leaf-molded framework, Nutmeg burner, clear glass chimney, 7½" h., No. 275 (ILLUS. left) 345.00

Milk white glass Greek Key patt. base & matching globe-chimney w/h.p. floral decor, Acorn burner, 6" h., No. 169......................145.00

Milk white glass Pineapple on Basket patt. base & ball-shaped shade, Nutmeg burner, clear glass chimney, 7¼" h., No. 276 ....290.00

Milk white glass w/pink-washed paint Rib patt. font on brass pedestal, Acorn burner, matching Rib patt. umbrella shade, clear glass chimney, 7¾" h., No. 128................140.00

Milk white glass Rib & Panel patt. footed base, Acorn burner, milk white glass Rib & Panel patt. chimney-shade, No. 126 ....120.00

"Nellie Bly" Miniature Lamp

Milk white glass footed base w/painted blue & white florals & frosted glass globe-chimney w/conforming decoration, Hornet burner, often called "Nellie Bly," No. 219 (ILLUS.).........................250.00

"Nutmeg" embossed on cobalt blue glass font w/narrow brass band forming removable handle, Nutmeg

burner, clear glass chimney, 2¾" h.,
No. 29 . . . . .80.00
Pink-painted clear glass Hobnail patt.
globular base & umbrella-type
shade, Nutmeg burner, clear glass
chimney, No. 142 . . . . .95.00
Pink Satin glass base & rounded
petal-molded ball-shaped shade,
Nutmeg burner, clear glass chimney,
7" h., No. 385 . . . . .375.00 to 450.00
Spangled glass flattened globular
base & globe-chimney in clear
w/cranberry, vaseline & white mica
flecks, Nutmeg burner, 6½" h.,
No. 555 . . . . .175.00
White mother-of-pearl Satin glass
Raindrop patt. ball-shaped base on
applied frosted feet & upturned &
fluted shade, Nutmeg burner, clear
glass chimney, 8" h., No. 601 . . . . . . .600.00

LANTERNS

Barn Lantern

Barn lantern, kerosene-type, "Dietz D-
Lite," brass & tin w/clear glass
globe, wire bracing & wire bail
handle, cleaned & polished, 12" h.
plus handle (ILLUS.) 75.00
Bicycle lantern, kerosene-type, "Silver
King of the Road - Jos. Lucas &
Son" 42.50
Candle lantern, pierced tin cylinder
w/conical top & ring handle (so-
called Paul Revere lantern), old
black repaint, 13½" h. 135.00
Candle lantern, pierced tin half-round
w/flat-glazed door at front, 18th c.,
18" h. 395.00
Candle lantern, tin, square w/three
glass sides, conical pierced top
w/crimped wafer, strap handle,
14" h. 140.00
Carriage lantern, kerosene-type,
painted tin, 2 glazed sides & hinged
opening to silvered-copper interior

fitted w/burner & wick, 14½" h.,
pr. 300.00
Folding lantern, tin w/isinglass sides,
"Stonebridge," dated 1908 . . .30.00 to 50.00
Kerosene lantern, tin, half-round
w/sliding front glass panel, shallow
font in base w/burner, bail & strap
handles, painted black, 17½" h. 105.00
Miner's lantern, brass, carbide-type,
complete . . . . .22.50 to 35.00
Miner's lantern, brass, carbide-type,
"DeWar" 47.50
Miner's lantern, brass, carbide-type,
"Justrite" 28.00
Miner's lantern, tin, teakettle-type
w/straight spout at side, marked
"C. George, Hazelton, Pa.,"
3 5/8" h. 35.00
Motorcycle lantern, brass, carbide-type,
"Old Sol Hawthorne" 85.00
Police (so-called burglar's) lantern,
kerosene-type, tin, w/hand-oper-
ated shutter cover for clear glass
lens, 7½" h. 50.00
Ship's masthead lantern, brass,
embossed "Dressel, Arlington, N.J.
U.S.A.," 10½" base d., 23" h. 185.00

Skater's Lantern

Skater's lantern, brass w/clear glass
pear-shaped globe & bail handle,
overall 11½" h. (ILLUS.) 60.00
Skater's lantern, tin w/clear glass
pear-shaped globe & bail handle,
6¾" h. plus bail handle . . . . . .22.50 to 35.00
Street lantern, tin w/amethyst glass
pear-shaped globe marked "C. T.
Ham Mfg. Co's No. 9 Globe Street,"
w/iron bracket marked "Dietz No.
3," overall 36" h. 300.00

(End of Lighting Devices Section)

LIGHTNING ROD BALLS

Lightning Rod Ball

These small colored glass balls from early lightning rods have attracted a number of collectors.

Amber glass, "Electra" $12.00
Amber glass, "Hawkeye" 35.00
Blue milk glass, "D. & S.,"
    10-sided.................22.00 to 30.00
Blue milk glass, Moon & Star patt.......40.00
Blue milk glass, plain, round ....8.00 to 15.00
Blue milk glass, plain, together
    w/bronze spear w/ornate arrow
    point & roof stand 50.00
Cobalt blue glass, "National" 18.00
Lemon yellow glass 25.00
Milk white glass, plain, round,
    "Electra".........................10.00
Milk white glass, "National"...........12.50
Milk white glass, ribbed, belted
    middle, "W.C. Shinn Mfg. Co.," 4" d.,
    5½" h. (ILLUS.) ....16.00 to 22.00
Red glass 24.00

LITHOPHANES

Lithophane Panel

*Lithophanes are pictorial panes of porce-
lain cast in molds, the layer of clay varying
in thickness so that when light is trans-*

*mitted through the panels, the picture is
seen in highlights and shadows. Said to
have been invented in France in the 1830s
they were also made elsewhere. The panes
are utilized in lamps, steins and also as
scenic plaques.*

Night lamp (or tea warmer), 3 panels
    w/scenes of ladies & gentlemen,
    4¾" h. $495.00
Night lamp (or tea warmer), 1-piece
    cylindrical panel depicting 4 seasonal
    landscapes w/children, in copper
    frame w/finger grip & molded base,
    late 19th c., 5 7/8" h. 220.00
Night lamp (or tea warmer), 5 panels
    w/scenes of children, w/original base
    base & burner, marked K.P.M.......815.00
Panel, scene entitled "Rheinstein,"
    castle on a hill above a meandering
    river, in cobalt blue leaded glass
    frame w/cut to clear spandrels,
    German, late 19th c., 7½ x 5¾" 110.00
Panel, entitled "Paul & Virginia,"
    scene w/young man holding a bird's
    nest & lemon w/his arm around a
    young woman in a tropical setting,
    19th c., 7¾ x 6"....................88.00
Panel, scene entitled "William Penn's
    Treaty with the Indians," 19th c.,
    8¼ x 6½" (ILLUS.) 265.00
Panel, scene entitled "Le Seaux du Parc
    de Versailles," self-framed,
    numbered, 8¼ x 6¾" 140.00
Panel, view of Paterson Falls, marked
    P.P.M...........................165.00
Panel, young boy in Scottish attire
    w/dog............................150.00
Panels, one depicting a man & woman
    w/dog overlooking a water scene, the
    the other a scene of a young man
    & woman in 18th century dress in a
    garden, he playing the flute & she
    seated holding his music, pr. 200.00
Table lamp w/lithophane shade
    consisting of 3 colored & 2 plain
    panels w/landscape scenes, gilded
    metal figural cherub base, German,
    ca. 1900, 10" h. 550.00

LOCKS & KEYS

Box lock, iron w/brass knobs, keeper,
    escutcheons & key, old white paint,
    5 x 7 5/8" $115.00
Box lock, wrought iron "bear trap" type
    from early blanket chest, w/key &
    lid pin, 7" l. 25.00
Door lock, bronze, early 19th c........145.00
Key, brass, 7" l.......................9.00

Key, folding-type, brass, 3½" l. 5.00
Keys, folding-type, cast steel, 1880s,
   pr. 9.00

Iron Keys

Key, gate-type, iron, 5" to 7" l.,
   each (ILLUS.). . . . . .5.00 to 10.00
Key, skeleton-type, "Keen Kutter"
   (E.C. Simmons) .6.00
Padlock, brass, "Eureka," 1884 patent,
   w/key. 25.00
Padlock, brass, "Good Luck,"
   horseshoe-shaped, Barnes,
   1870s .40.00 to 60.00
Padlock, brass, "Harvard" 25.00
Padlock, brass, "Keen Kutter,"
   w/key . . . . .65.00 to 85.00
Padlock, brass, "Pioneer," w/em-
   bossed Indian head 40.00
Padlock, brass, "Van Camps Hard-
   ware," w/(replaced) key. 75.00
Padlock, brass, embossed bulldog,
   small. 7.50
Padlock, cast iron, "Bruno," embossed
   dog's face, w/key. 12.00
Padlock, cast iron, "Winchester,"
   6-lever, w/key 95.00
Padlock, cast steel, "Eagle," 6-lever,
   w/key. 10.00
Padlock, cast steel, "Victory," w/key . . .10.00
Padlock, railroad, brass, heart-shaped,
   "MR & BT," lead belt short line 235.00
Padlock, railroad, cast iron, potato-
   type, w/"P.R.R." monogram. 75.00

LORGNETTES, OPERA GLASSES
& SPECTACLES

Tortoise Shell Lorgnette

Lorgnette, gilt silver, Art Nouveau
   style folding-type w/handle,
   w/case $75.00
Lorgnette, gilt silver, reticulated over-
   all, 4¼" l. 135.00
Lorgnette, 18k gold, Art Nouveau
   style w/initial "M" monogram,
   heavy 895.00
Lorgnette, gold, enamel & diamond,
   edges applied w/scrolling foliage &
   shellwork, 1 side w/profile of a
   maiden wearing a diamond-set head
   ornament & her face w/enameled
   details, ca. 1900, 4½" l. 935.00
Lorgnette, white gold w/sterling silver
   chain, folding-type, original case 50.00
Lorgnette, sterling silver, hanging-
   type. 95.00
Lorgnette, sterling silver & marcasite,
   w/folding handle 130.00
Lorgnette, tortoise shell, pierce-
   carved floral scroll at handle
   terminal, 6½" l. handle (ILLUS.). 30.00
Opera glasses, brass & nickel, birds in
   relief, marked "Paris" 35.00
Opera glasses, gold, engine-turned
   dotted pattern, each lens surmounted by a diamond-set monogram within an oval reserve,
   w/diamond-set borders, w/case,
   Continental, ca. 1900, 3½" l. 3,300.00
Opera glasses, gold-plated, marked
   "Zeiss," w/lady's alligator skin
   compact & case combination 98.50
Opera glasses, mother-of-pearl &
   brass, marked "France" . . . . .50.00 to 65.00
Opera glasses, mother-of-pearl &
   brass, marked "Lefils Paris," w/tele-
   scopic handle . . . . .65.00 to 85.00
Opera glasses, mother-of-pearl &
   brass, marked "LeMaire, Paris,"
   w/original leather case. 70.00
Opera glasses, mother-of-pearl &
   brass, marked "Mermod Jaccard,"
   w/leather case. . . . . .40.00 to 60.00
Opera glasses, mother-of-pearl &
   brass, w/lorgnette-type handle. 75.00
Opera glasses, mother-of-pearl &
   gold-plated brass, w/velvet case
   marked "Tiffany & Co." 125.00
Pince nez, 14k white gold frame,
   w/retractable chain & clip, w/case . . .32.50
Pince nez, 12k gold-filled, w/chain &
   case 15.00
Pince nez, 14k white gold w/sterling
   silver chain, folding-type, w/leather
   case marked "The Huttem, Oxford,"
   ca. 1910 . . . . .95.00
Pince nez, sterling silver, w/sterling
   silver chain 32.50
Spectacles, 14k gold, Ben Franklin
   style 30.00
Spectacles, gold-plated wire rims,
   1½" d. lens 8.00

Spectacles, granny-type, gold-filled
    wire frames 10.00

Early Spectacles with Papier Mache Case

Spectacles, granny-type, gold-filled
    wire frames, original papier mache
    case w/gilt stenciling on black
    ground, 6½ x 1½" case (ILLUS) 45.00
Spectacles, sterling silver frames
    w/sliding side pieces, ca. 1860 . . . . 30.00

LUSTRES

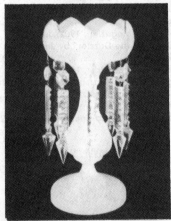

Bristol Glass Lustre

*Lustres are glass vase-like decorative
vessels with prisms designed to hold
candles and intended as mantel and table-
top decorative adjuncts.*

Bohemian glass, ruby w/frosted &
    clear Deer & Castle patt., single
    row of clear prisms, pr. $320.00
Bristol glass, pale blue w/gold decor,
    frosted finish, single row of clear
    spear-point prisms, 10¾" h., pr.
    (ILLUS. of one) 295.00
Green cut to clear, single row of clear
    cut prisms, 5" d., 10½" h., pr. 285.00
White opaline, single row of clear
    spear-point prisms, 10 ¼" h., pr. 250.00
White opaque overlay cut to emerald

green, w/portrait of beautiful girl &
    ornate gold trim, pedestal base,
    w/single row of notch-cut prisms,
    6" d., 14½" h., pr. 350.00

MAGAZINES

Harper's Bazar Magazine

Aero Digest, 1935, April $20.00
Allure, 1937, July, Vol. 1, No. 1, Carole
    Lombard pin-ups 35.00
American Architect Weekly, 1915,
    January through June, 6 months
    bound 50.00
Ballou's Pictorial Weekly, 1855, full
    year . . . . 135.00 to 150.00
Burr-McIntosh Monthly, 1903, April,
    Vol. 1, No. 1 . . . . 25.00
Century, 1890-91, November through
    April, illustrations by Remington
    & Gibson & Joel Chandler Harris
    stories, 6 months bound 65.00
Child Life, 1929, January, doll pages 6.50
Collier's, 1900, October 6, Galveston
    Disaster, Violet Oakley color cover . . . 15.00
Collier's, 1957, January 4, last issue,
    Princess Grace cover 15.00
Cosmopolitan, 1901, September,
    Buffalo Exposition 10.00
Cosmopolitan, 1926, June 7.00
Country Gentleman, 1921, July 2,
    Norman Rockwell cover 15.00
Decorator & Furnisher, 1897,
    November 4.00
Delineator, 1907, April, color fashion
    plates 10.00
Delineator, 1917, April, Maud
    Humphrey cover 30.00
Farmer's Wife, 1929, April 4.00

Fortune, 1939, July, New York City
featured, w/fold-out map 15.00
Frank Leslie's Weekly, 1909, June 17,
Alaska-Yukon Pacific Exposition 10.00
Gleason's Pictorial Weekly, 1853, July
through December, 26 issues 70.00
Godey's Lady's Book, 1858, December,
color fashion plates 12.50
Good Housekeeping, 1932, September,
Mother Goose Series 10.00
Graham's Magazine, 1850, full year
bound 50.00
Harper's Bazar, 1907, October, Rose
O'Neill illustrations 10.00
Harper's Monthly, 1864, Civil War
articles & pictures, full year bound . . .95.00
Harper's Weekly, 1858, full year
bound 350.00
Hearst's International, 1922, March,
Alphonse Mucha cover, Maxfield
Parrish Jell-O ad 65.00
Ladies' Home Journal, 1892-93, Palmer
Cox Brownies series, "Brownies
'Round the World," 12 issues 60.00
Ladies' Home Journal, 1895, April,
Kate Greenaway cover 10.00
Ladies' Home Journal, 1910, July,
Harrison Fisher cover, Lettie Lane
Japanese girl & boy paper dolls . . .16.00
Ladies' Repository, 1872, full year
bound 60.00
Life, 1938, August 22, Fred Astaire &
Ginger Rogers cover & article 10.00

1950 Life Magazine

Life, 1950, June 26, Cecile Aubry cover
(ILLUS.) 2.00
Literary Digest, 1922, February 22,
Norman Rockwell cover 5.75
Look, 1962, March 27, John Wayne
cover 4.00

McClure's, 1909, October 15.00
Modern Priscilla, 1924, January, full
page Maxfield Parrish Jell-O ad 15.00
Modern Screen, 1934, December,
Dolores Del Rio cover 35.00
Motion Picture Classic, 1926, January,
John Gilbert cover 25.00
Motor Age, 1904, May 12, St. Louis
Car Family Tree 13.50
Munsey's, 1894, full year bound 30.00
National Geographic, 1928, July
through December, 6 months bound . .35.00
New Movie, 1932, October, Kay Francis
cover 25.00
Our Young Folks, 1865, February 3.00
Penthouse, 1969, September, Vol. 1,
No. 1 . . . . .95.00
Peterson's, 1848, January through
June, fashion plates & steel
engravings, 6 months bound 40.00
Photoplay, 1938, July, Clark Gable
cover 25.00
Pictorial Review, 1912, July, Howard
Chandler Christy "Revolutionary
Girl" cover 15.00
Playboy, 1953, December, Vol. 1,
No. 1 . . . . .750.00
Popular Aviation & Aeronautics, 1909,
March 20.00
St. Nicholas Magazine, 1902, July,
"Cruise of the Dazzler" by Jack
London 12.50
Saturday Evening Post, 1909,
November 16, Harrison Fisher cover . .10.00
Saturday Evening Post, 1922, October
14, Leyendecker cover, full page
Haynes car & Coca-Cola ads 25.00

December 1937 Woman's Day

Woman's Day, 1937, December 2
(ILLUS.) 2.50
Youth's Companion, 1888, full year
bound 190.00

MARBLES

Assorted Slag Marbles

Bennington-type, mottled brown,
1" d. $7.00
Bennington-type, mottled brown,
2" d. 55.00
China, unglazed, 1" d. 35.00
Clay, 1" d., set of 5 ....5.00
Clay, 2" d. 15.00
Glass, Akro Agate, brown & white,
15/16" d. 10.00
Glass, clear w/white mica flecks,
1" d. 30.00
Glass, comic strip type, "Betty Boop"
or "Orphan Annie," each 45.00
Glass, comic strip type, "Skeezix" 42.50
Glass, comic strip type, "Moon
Mullins"...................75.00 to 85.00
Glass, Lutz-type, yellow & aventurine
swirls, 1" d. 150.00
Glass, "onionskin," pink, white &
green, 1½" d. 85.00
Glass, slag, w/single pontil, blue,
brown, green & yellow, ½" to 1" d.,
each (ILLUS.) ....5.00 to 10.00
Glass, sulphide, w/ape 225.00
Glass, sulphide, w/baby in cradle 225.00
Glass, sulphide, w/boar 68.00
Glass, sulphide, w/dog seated,
1¼" d. 40.00
Glass, sulphide, w/dog standing,
1 3/8" d. 45.00
Glass, sulphide, w/fox, 1¾" d. 80.00
Glass, sulphide, w/horse standing,
1¼" d. 50.00
Glass, sulphide, w/lamb standing,
1¾" d. 75.00
Glass, sulphide, w/lion reclining,
1¾" d. 95.00
Glass, sulphide, w/papoose, 2" d. 200.00
Glass, sulphide, w/rabbit,
2" d. ....60.00 to 85.00
Glass, sulphide, w/ram, 1 7/8" d. 125.00
Glass, sulphide, w/robin 55.00
Glass, sulphide, w/squirrel,
1 7/8" d. 100.00
Glass, sulphide, w/squirrel,
2 1/8" d. 125.00
Glass, swirl w/white latticino center
& red & yellow outer swirls,
1 9/16" d. 50.00
Glass, swirl, yellow & white, 1¾" d. 68.00
Glass, swirl, w/divided core, red,
blue, yellow, green & white, 1¾" d. ...45.00
Glass, swirl, w/divided core, red,
yellow, blue, green & white,
2 1/8" d. 60.00

Glass, swirl, w/latticino core, red,
blue, green, yellow & white, 2¼" d. ...65.00
Glass, swirl, w/solid core, red, blue,
white, green & yellow, 1 7/8" d. 60.00

MATCH SAFES & CONTAINERS

Brass Skull Match Safe

*Also see ADVERTISING ITEMS, ART
NOUVEAU, GREENAWAY COL-
LECTIBLES and MAJOLICA under
Ceramics.*

Advertising container, wall-type, tin,
"DeLaval Cream Separators" $65.00
Advertising container, wall-type, tin,
"Dockash Stoves," factory
pictured 25.00
Advertising safe, pocket-type, cell-
uloid, "Charles Granes Jewelers
Chicago," pocket watch decor 24.00
Advertising safe, pocket-type, cell-
uloid & tin, "Neverslips Horseshoes,"
horse's head pictured, dated 1905 ....18.00
Advertising safe, pocket-type, cell-
uloid & metal, "Sharples Cream
Separators," woman & cows
pictured 85.00
Bisque container, table model, figural
girl w/beading on dress beside
container, 4" h. 45.00
Bisque container, table model, figural
Victorian girl w/basket on back,
w/striker, 6" h. 60.00
Brass container, table model, model of
lady's high button shoe, w/striker....50.00
Brass container, wall-type, double
pocket, hanging game in relief,
7½" w. 55.00
Brass safe, pocket-type, model of a
skull w/hinged jaws as opening,
striker on chin, 1½" h. (ILLUS.) 225.00
Cast iron container, table model,
model of lady's high button shoe, old
worn black & red repaint...........50.00

Cast iron container, wall-type, figural
  devil's head, red painted finish 75.00
Cast iron container, wall-type,
  openwork backplate cast w/rabbit,
  powder horn, game bird & pouch,
  single pocket, residual red & green
  paint 85.00

Three-Dolphin Match Holder

Glass container, table model, pressed
  cylindrical jar on 3-dolphin base,
  sapphire blue (ILLUS.) 55.00
Glass container, table model, model
  of a top hat, cobalt blue, w/striker
  at base 34.00
Glass container, table model, bust of
  black boy wearing high collar, milk
  white, 1886 ....135.00
Gold safe, pocket-type, chased
  w/flowering foliage on a matted
  ground, cover engraved "Annette"
  within a shield, interior w/inner
  striking cover, France, mid-19th c.,
  2 1/8" l. 550.00
Gutta percha safe, pocket-type 25.00
Ivory safe, pocket-type, cylindrical
  w/screw-on lid 130.00
Majolica container, table model,
  acorns & leaves exterior decor,
  orchid-pink interior, cover signed
  George Jones, striker on base,
  4 1/8" oval 65.00
Silverplate safe, pocket-type, model of
  a pig, 2 1/2 x 3/4", 1 1/2" h. 75.00
Silverplate safe, pocket-type,
  engraved "I'm Your Match" on front ..22.00
Staffordshire pottery container, table
  model, figural boy holding boot 65.00
Sterling silver safe, pocket-type,
  engraved boar's head one side,
  hooked fish reverse, English hallmarks 52.50
Sterling silver safe, pocket-type,
  chased ornate sea monsters & florals
  in relief.........................125.00
Sterling silver safe, pocket-type,
  chased Art Nouveau flower & leaves
  in low relief (ILLUS.) 65.00

Sterling Silver Pocket Safe

Tin container, wall-type, double
  pocket, stamped Maltese Cross
  decor, 3 1/2" w., 5" h................20.00
Tin container, wall-type, backplate
  w/crimped crest, original worn
  brown japanned finish, 4 3/8" w.,
  7 1/2" h. 55.00
Tortoise shell safe, pocket-type, low
  relief designs each side............65.00
Wooden container, hanging-type,
  double pocket, fleur-de-lis & heart on
  scalloped backplate, leaves on
  pockets, 4 x 6".....................35.00
Wooden container, hanging-type,
  walnut, carved w/game pouch, birds
  & powder horn, 6 1/4" l..............95.00

MEDICAL QUACKERY ITEMS

*Numerous devices and contrivances
offered last century and early in the present
one as "cures" or palliatives for a host of
ailments and subsequently found to be
worthless, dangerous or at least unequal to
their claims are now sought by some
collectors. The following represents a
sampling of items being collected.*

Apollo medical apparatus, w/attach-
  ments $65.00
Bunnel Medical Battery, w/wooden
  case 38.00
Calbro Magnowave Radionic machine,
  large black switchboard w/two
  meters, 52 rheostats & 34 toggle
  switches, ornate gold numerals &
  lettering, in oak secretary desk
  w/roll top, 4' 8" x 2', 4' 4" h. 875.00
Cambridge Electrocardiograph machine,
  portable, 1930s 165.00
Davis & Kidder's Magneto Electric

machine, for treatment of nervous
diseases, patent date of 1854 . . . . . . .100.00
Electreat Arthritis Remedy apparatus,
w/roller 15.00
Electro Medical machine, w/original
oak case & instructions, Sears
Roebuck 145.00
Master Violet Ray machine, w/original
leather-bound suitcase & illustrated
booklet, 12 x 9" 45.00
Overbeck's Rejuvenator device 85.00
Thermo-Faradic machine by D'Arson-
aul, paneled quarter-sawn oak on 4
sides w/brass ball electrodes on top,
operates on alternating current,
dated 1909, 30 x 23", 41" h. 2,375.00
Tucker's Violet Ray medical device 40.00

METALS

*Also see ABC PLATES, ADVERTIS-
ING ITEMS, ART DECO, ART NOU-
VEAU, AVIATION COLLECTIBLES,
BABY MEMENTOES, BANKS, BELLS,
BILLIKEN COLLECTIBLES, BOOK-
ENDS, BOOTJACKS, BOTTLE OPEN-
ERS, BRONZES, BROWNIE COLLECT-
IBLES, BUCKLES, BUSTER BROWN
COLLECTIBLES, BUTTON HOOKS,
BUTTONS, CAMPBELL KID COLLECT-
IBLES, CANDLESTICKS & CANDLE
HOLDERS, CANS & CONTAINERS,
CARD CASES, CASH REGISTERS,
CHARACTER COLLECTIBLES, CIGAR
& CIGARETTE CASES, HOLDERS &
LIGHTERS, CIGAR & TOBACCO
CUTTERS, COCA-COLA ITEMS, COF-
FEE GRINDERS, COOKIE CUTTERS,
CORKSCREWS, COW CREAMERS, DIS-
NEY COLLECTIBLES, DOLL FUR-
NITURE & ACCESSORIES, DOOR
KNOCKERS, DOOR STOPS, FABERGE,
FARM COLLECTIBLES, FIRE FIGHT-
ING COLLECTIBLES, FOOD, CANDY &
MISC. MOLDS, FOOT & BED WARM-
ERS, FOOT & BOOT SCRAPERS,
GREENAWAY ITEMS, HATPIN HOLD-
ERS, HORSE & BUGGY COLLECT-
IBLES, JEWELRY, KEWPIE COL-
LECTIBLES, KITCHENWARES, KNIFE
RESTS, LAW ENFORCEMENT ITEMS,
LIGHTING DEVICES, LOCKS & KEYS,
LORGNETTES & OPERA GLASSES,
MATCH SAFES & CONTAINERS,
MORTARS & PESTLES, MUSTACHE
CUPS & SAUCERS, NAPKIN RINGS,
NAUTICAL GEAR, NUTCRACKERS,
POWDER HORNS & FLASKS, RAIL-
ROADIANA, ROYCROFT ITEMS,
SCALES, SEWING ADJUNCTS,
SHAKER ITEMS, SIGNS & SIGN-
BOARDS, SPICE CABINETS, SPOOL,
DYE & ALLIED CABINETS, SUGAR
BOWLS, TOOLS, TOYS, TRAPS, TRAYS,
VANITY CASES & COMPACTS,
VIENNA ART TIN PLATES, VIN-
AIGRETTES, WATCH FOBS, WEATH-
ERVANES, WORLD FAIR COLLECT-
IBLES and ZEPPELIN COLLECTIBLES.*

BRASS

Chinese Incense Pot

Bill clip, hanging-type, spring-form
figural duck's head w/glass eyes $40.00
Bill clip, embossed woodland scene,
signed Bradley & Hubbard 30.00
Bootblack's shoe stands, 15" h., pr. 55.00
Box, cov., engraved geometric &
foliage designs, lion's head drop
ring handles, cast claw-and-ball feet,
7½" l. 115.00
Bread tray, almond-shaped w/reticulated
sides, 13 x 7", 3" h. 95.00
Bullet mold, 6" l. .25.00
Calipers, lady's legs form, 3" l. 70.00
Candle sconce, oblong backplate
w/rolled edge & frontispiece con-
cealing candle nozzle, hand-wrought,
early 20th c., 8" h. 42.50
Candlewick trimmer & snuffer, scissors-
type, 7 1/8" l. 40.00
Chestnut roaster, brass & copper,
English, 19th c., 16½" l. handle 75.00
Coal hod, helmet-style w/bail handle,
burnished 220.00
Cow tag, polished . . . . .3.00 to 5.00
Cream skimmer, pierced blade w/simple
tooled edge, polished, overall
21¼" l. 65.00
Cuspidor w/removable top & cover,
concave 60.00
Cyclist's cup, folding-type, dated 1897 . .20.00
Desk set, Art Nouveau style, signed
Bradley & Hubbard, 3 pcs. 75.00
Easel, cast w/foliate & bulbous details,
Victorian, 61" h. 265.00
Incense pot, 3-footed, w/seal mark
& "China," 1890-1915, 4" across
handles (ILLUS.) 20.00
Kettle, spun brass w/iron bail
handle, stamped "H.W. Hayden's
Patent, Dec. 16, 1851, by the
Ansonia Brass Co.," 8½" d. 75.00

Brass Kettle

Kettle, spun brass w/iron bail handle,
  12" d., 6½" h. (ILLUS.) 65.00
Kettle, spun brass w/iron bail handle,
  stamped "H.W. Hayden's Patent,"
  20½" d. 130.00
Pepper mill, cylindrical w/jointed
  crank handle, 18th c., 9" h. 85.00
Pipe tampers, Dicken's type man &
  woman, pr. 75.00
Plate warmer, Georgian, shaped plate
  supports above hinged & pierce-
  molded olbong lid opening to a
  coal receptacle, shaped bail handle
  attached, molded base, flattened
  ball feet, England, 1750-70, 11½" w.
  (1 plate support missing) 247.00
Posnet, circular w/molded rim & short
  channel-molded handle, 3 round
  splayed legs, England, mid-18th c. . .176.00
Scale pan (for candy scale), 12 x 7" 45.00
Siren, hand-crank model, "Tyfon -
  Made in Sweden," 24" h. 65.00
Stencils for apple crate, months &
  numbers, set of 35, in oblong tin
  hanging pocket 65.00
Stencil for barrel, numbers, letters &
  rotating placer, signed & dated 1868,
  13" d. 90.00
"Taster" spoon, ornate tooled handle,
  6" l. 45.00
Tea kettle, cov., straight sides &
  straight spout, 8" h. 85.00
Teapot, cov., globular w/overhead
  handle w/amber glass grip, marked
  "J.C.B.," Dutch, 8¼" h. 65.00
Tinder box w/candle socket on lid &
  handle on side, Lititz, Pennsylvania,
  4 3/8" d., plus 3" l. handle 180.00
Tobacco box, cov., reeded moldings,
  engraved figures & inscriptions on
  cover & bottom, Dutch, 18th c.,
  5¾" oval 220.00
Umbrella stand, cylindrical w/lion's
  mask drop ring handles at sides 75.00

BRONZE

Tiffany Gilt-Bronze Bowl

Ash tray, ribbed & scalloped rim,
  "dore" finish, signed Tiffany Studios,
  5½" oval 95.00
Ash tray, Venetian patt., signed Tiffany
  Studios & numbered, 5½ x 3¾" 125.00
Ash tray, w/figural parrot, Vienna 50.00
Ash tray, floor standing model,
  adjustable baluster-shaped standard,
  concave round base, signed Tiffany
  Studios, New York, ca. 1910, 28" h. . .550.00
Blotter, rocker-type, Chinese patt.,
  "dore" finish, signed Tiffany Studios .150.00
Blotter, rocker-type, Venetian patt.,
  signed Tiffany Studios 175.00
Blotter ends, Venetian patt., signed
  Tiffany Studios, pr. 175.00
Blotter ends, Zodiac patt., signed Tiffany
  Studios, 19½" l., pr. . . . . . .140.00 to 175.00
Bowl, shallow w/flaring lip, loop handle,
  gilt-bronze w/enameled red, pink &
  dusty rose circle & rectangle
  design, signed L.C. Tiffany Inc.,
  Favrile, ca. 1920, 9½" d. (ILLUS.) 715.00
Box w/hinged lid, Adams patt., "dore"
  finish w/pastel enameled highlights,
  signed Tiffany Studios & numbered,
  4½ x 3½" oval, 1½" h. 165.00

Bronze Smoking Set

Cigarette set, full figure Chinese
"nodder" holding a long-stemmed
pipe & standing beside an open tobacco
bale cigarette holder & baluster-shaped
jardiniere match container on tassel-
molded base, hinged door in man's
back for incense, France, 19th c.,
9 3/16" w. base, 8 3/8" h. (ILLUS.) ...440.00
Desk set: inkwell, letter rack & rocker-
type blotter; Abalone patt., signed
Tiffany Studios, 3 pcs. 550.00

Tiffany Desk Set

Desk set: inkwell w/hinged lid, letter
rack, rocker-type blotter &
tray; Nautical patt., "dore" finish,
signed Tiffany Studios, 4 pcs.
(ILLUS.)..........................880.00
Desk set: inkwell w/glass insert, pr.
blotter ends, rocker-type blotter,
pen tray & pen brush; Graduate
patt., signed Tiffany Studios, 6 pcs...625.00
Desk set: desk lamp, pr. blotter ends,
rocker-type blotter, ash tray, letter
opener, match box cover, memorandum
pad, perpetual calendar, letter rack
& pen stand; Zodiac patt., signed
Tiffany Studios, 11 pcs............1,760.00
Dish, wide openwork border, "dore"
finish w/enameled blue & red decor,
signed "Louis C. Tiffany Furnaces,
Inc.," 8" d., 1" h..................185.00
Dish, Abalone patt., "dore" finish,
signed Tiffany Studios, 9" d. 125.00
Ewer, bulbous base w/long narrow
neck enveloped in leafage,
figural youthful nude maiden forming
handle & peering inside, green
patina, signed Jeanne Jozon, ca.
1900, 13½" h. 715.00
Frame, Grapevine patt., signed
Tiffany Studios & numbered,
8 x 10" picture opening, overall
12 x 14"..........................425.00
Frame, Zodiac patt., "dore" finish,
signed Tiffany Studios .....285.00 to 350.00
Humidor, cov., Pine Needle patt.,
gilt liner, signed Tiffany Studios......475.00
Incense burner, phoenix bird &
elephant decor, Japanese,
19th c., 15" h. 375.00

Ink stand, Abalone patt., signed Tiffany
Studios 275.00
Ink stand, American Indian patt.,
original glass insert, signed
Tiffany Studios 295.00
Ink well, Bookmark patt., signed
Tiffany Studios 295.00
Ink well, Chinese patt., signed Tiffany
Studios, 6" w., 4¾" h. 395.00
Inkwell, Spider Web patt. w/glass
insert & pen tray, gold "dore"
finish, signed Tiffany Studios, pr. ...250.00
Letter rack, American Indian patt.,
signed Tiffany Studios 225.00
Letter rack, Zodiac patt., "dore"
finish, signed Tiffany Studios,
9½ x 6 1/8" 235.00
Note pad holder, Chinese patt.,
"dore" finish, signed Tiffany Studios .225.00
Paperweight, Zodiac patt., signed
Tiffany Studios ....165.00 to 225.00
Paperweight, model of a squirrel
in seated position eating corn,
original paint, 2" h. 65.00
Paperweight, model of a tiger, signed
Tiffany Studios ....275.00 to 350.00
Pen tray, Byzantine patt. w/blue &
green enameled highlights, signed
Tiffany Studios & numbered 110.00
Pen tray, Venetian patt., signed Tiffany
Studios 150.00
Pen tray, Zodiac patt., "dore" finish,
signed Tiffany Studios .....100.00 to 150.00
Planter, Grapevine patt. w/glass grapes,
signed Tiffany Studios, 10 x 8½"
oblong...........................1,250.00
Plate, red enameled floral & leaf
border, signed Tiffany
Studios...............100.00 to 175.00
Postage scale, Zodiac patt., signed
Tiffany Studios 250.00
Stamp box, cov., Pine Needle patt.
w/glass inserts, signed Tiffany
Studios 195.00
Stamp box, cov., Venetian patt., signed
Tiffany Studios & numbered 195.00
Stamp box, cov., Zodiac patt., "dore"
finish, signed Tiffany Studios &
numbered ....125.00 to 195.00
Urns, elaborate rosette-topped handles,
mounted on rouge marble bases
w/applied bronze floral swags &
elaborate cast feet, France, 19th c.,
8 1/8" h. urns, overall 13¼" h.,
pr...............................975.00
Vase, bronze w/silver overlay reeds &
geese in flight, marked Silvercrest,
14" h. 135.00
Vase, conch shell rising from a wave
cast w/a fish, surmounted by nude
female struggling w/baby triton,
parcel-gilt, green patina, signed
Francois Mage, ca. 1900, 15¼" h. 550.00

COPPER

Copper Pan

Ale warmer w/hinged lid & finial,
turned wood handle at side, oval,
6" h. 175.00
Apple butter kettle, 35-gal. 285.00
Basin, hand-hammered, tapering sides,
flat rim, free swinging loop
handle, 19th c., 10" d. 145.00
Bowl, scalloped rim, Russian, w/Cyrillic
inscription & dated 1832 on reverse,
9¼" d. 65.00
Coffee boiler & cover w/ring handle,
applied handle at base, wire bail
handle at top, 10-cup 65.00
Coffee pot & tin lid w/copper ring
handle, expanding cylinder,
ca. 1850 ....75.00
Coffee pot, cov., stripped & burnished
nickel-plated copper w/silverplate
spout, handle & finial...............65.00
Cream skimmer, hand-tooled, overall
20" l. 95.00
Fish brazier w/wrought iron handles,
New York, ca. 1870, 13½ x 8" oval ..145.00
Funnel, 9" l. 30.00
Kettle, cov., w/brass handles riveted
to sides, 13" d., 13½" h. 115.00
Measure, cylindrical w/wide strap
handle, brass base & name plate
embossed "Chas G. Schenck, Mfr.,
Columbus, O., Patented Nov. 8,
1898," 8" h. 35.00
Measure, haystack-type, dovetailed
seams, wrought copper handle,
stamped "½ gallon" on rim, 8½" h. ..115.00
Pan, rolled rim, applied wrought copper
handles at rim, French, 15" d.
(ILLUS.).........................125.00
Pan, hand-hammered, dovetail
construction, earred handles, flaring
sides, 7¼" d., 40" h. 40.00
Sauce pan, dovetail construction,
w/wrought copper handle, 7" d.,
8" l. handle 70.00
Sauce pan, dovetail construction,
straight sides, wrought iron handle,
7¼" d., 8" l. handle 85.00
Sauce pan, dovetail construction,
wrought copper handle, 8" d.,
9" l. handle 95.00

Revere Ware Tea Kettle

Tea kettle, cov., straight sides &
straight spout, bail handle w/wooden
grip, marked "Solid Copper Revere
Ware Rome, N.Y.," early 20th c.,
7¼" d., 7½" h. (ILLUS.) 50.00
Tea kettle, domed cov., ovoid body
w/base made to fit into stove-top
opening, dovetail construction, struck
w/initials "C.E.E." in three places,
tin lining, 19th c., 11" h.............192.50
Tea kettle, cov., gooseneck spout, bail
handle w/movable handgrip,
13½" h. 95.00
Tea kettle, domed cover w/turned
finial, globular body, dovetail construction, gooseneck spout, bail
handle w/heart-shaped terminals,
late 18th-early 19th c., 11" d.,
13½" h. 275.00

Teapot by Rochester Stamping Co.

Teapot, cov., globular, stripped &
burnished nickel-plated copper
body, silverplate handle & spout,
brass finial on lid, marked Rochester
Stamping Co. (ILLUS.)...............70.00
Tray, hand-hammered, Russian hallmark,
16" oval 125.00
Wash boiler w/tin lid & wooden
handles at sides ....48.00 to 75.00

IRON

Baker's rack, hand-wrought, oblong wall
piece w/horizontal iron bars
supporting 3 graduated shelves,
each w/brass rails & baluster-turned
gallery, scrolled side supports &
lower shelf, columnar front legs,

late 19th - early 20th c., 20½" w.,
21 5/8" deep, 72¾" h. 2,420.00

Bill hook, wall-type, cast, "Starr,
1883". 21.00

Bowl, cast, collared base, straight
sides, 18th c., 8¾" d., 3¼" h. 45.00

Brazier, vertical rods forming cage-like
basket, 3-legged w/feet, 9" d.,
15½" h. 135.00

Candlewick trimmer & snuffer, scissors-
type, 3-footed . . . . 40.00 to 45.00

Cauldron, cast, 3 short feet, hand-
wrought bail handle, 12" d., 6¼" h. . .25.00

Ceiling hook, hand-wrought, half ram's
horn type, 7" l. 18.00

Christmas tree stand, cast, ornate,
Germany, 19th c. 100.00

Cigar press, cast, well-detailed leafy
base & dog on handle, 9½" l. 30.00

Coffee roaster, sheet iron, 10½ x 8½"
pan, 20" l. handle 21.00

Cookie board, cast, lyre design,
5¼ x 3 7/8" oval 65.00

Cookie board, cast, cornucopia of
fruit design, 5¾ x 4¼" oval 105.00

Cuspidor, cast, mechanical-type,
figural turtle, step-on head to lift
cover, 14 x 10". 125.00

Cuspidor, cast, w/porcelain interior,
ca. 1850 . . . . .30.00 to 50.00

Dipper, cast, side pouring spout,
ornate handle, 5½" d., 5" l. handle. . .35.00

Ember tongs, hand-wrought . . .30.00 to 55.00

Fork, hand-wrought, 2-tine, scrolling
heart & curliques on handle
w/hanging ring at end, 11" l. 20.00

Fork, hand-wrought, 3-tine, slender
handle w/elongated diamond-
shaped end w/hanging ring, 16¼" l. . .90.00

Fork, hand-wrought, 2-tine, well-shaped
handle w/simple tooling, 17¾" l. 95.00

Garden urns, cast, flared rim, round
reeded standard on square base
w/reeded sides, 23" h., pr. (layers
of old paint) 190.00

Garden urns, cast, elaborate scrolling
foliage & scroll handles, 27" d.,
38" h., pr. 450.00

Gate section, cast, silhouette of willow
tree w/sheep lying beneath within
scrollwork, American, ca. 1875,
28" w., 31½" h. 302.50

Rotary Hearth Grill

Hearth grill, hand-wrought, rotary-type,
4 sections of scrollwork revolving

on tripod base, strap handle
w/pierced end, probably American,
early 19th c., 22 3/8" l. (ILLUS.) 286.00

Hinges, strap-type, hand-wrought,
decorative curving bird's beak ends,
38½" l., pr. 90.00

Hinges, strap-type, hand-wrought,
primitive tulip-like ends, 44½" l.,
pr. 80.00

Kettle stand, cast, round reticulated
shelf w/thistle design, 3 legs,
old painted finish, 10" d., 11½" h. 55.00

Ladle, hand-wrought, small hearts
stamped on handle, 17½" l. 45.00

Ladle, hand-wrought, 4½" d. bowl
w/crude pouring spout, long
handle w/hanging hole at end &
attached footrest near top, 19½" l. 80.00

Lantern hooks, hand-wrought w/spike
ends to hang, 11" & 14" l., pr. 95.00

Meat hanging hook, hand-wrought,
4-prong w/each hook 7" l.,
overall 23" l. 55.00

Model of a top hat, cast, 7" h. (flaking
paint on interior) 85.00

Muffin pan w/skillet handle, 6 heart
cups & single star cup center, 8½" d. .30.00

Oven peel, hand-wrought, ram's horn
handle ends, signed "Londonderry,"
34½" l. 95.00

Oven peel, hand-wrought, ram's horn
handle ends, 49" l. 115.00

Pan, cast, oblong w/invected corners
& cast design in bottom, 7½ x 5½" . . .14.00

Porringer, cast, marked Kendrick,
18th c., 4 1/8" d. . . . . .60.00 to 75.00

Posnet pan, cast, 3 tapering legs,
straight handle, 18th c., 7 1/8" d.,
3" h. bowl, 6" l. handle 45.00

Pot, cast, 3-footed, iron bail handle
fastened to tabs at sides, 5½" d. 30.00

Shelf brackets, cast, lacy, ornate, pr. . . .15.00

Shooting Gallery Target

Shooting gallery target, cast, model of
an owl (ILLUS.) 35.00

Shooting gallery target, cast, model of
a running rabbit, traces of white
paint, 11" l. 80.00

Skillet, hand-wrought, handle stamped

"Whitfield 2," 9½" d. pan,
11" handle 55.00
Skillet, hand-wrought, deep pan, long
handle w/side supports, 11½" d.
pan, 20½" l. handle 210.00
Snow birds, cast, model of eagle,
6½" h., pr. 55.00
Spatula, hand-wrought, broom-
shaped blade, 10½" l. 45.00
Spatula, hand-wrought, blade
w/rounded front, well-shaped
handle w/doughnut terminal,
13¾" l. 105.00
Spatula, hand-wrought, tapering handle
w/decorative end, 19¾" l. 75.00
Stake, hand-wrought, w/heart-shaped
top, 40½" h. .65.00
Store counter feet, cast, ornate,
set of 4 . . . . .20.00
Stove feet, cast, scrolling foliate
design, 8½" h., pr. 10.00
Stove plate, cast, 2 stylized tulips
in arched panels, German inscription
& date "1756," 23" w., 21" h.
(surface pitting & small crack) 275.00
Tea kettle, cov., cast, bulbous, footed,
gooseneck spout, w/wrought iron
handle, 18th c. 190.00
Utensil rack, hand-wrought, flat bar
w/five hooks, detailed scrolling
crest, 13½" l. 250.00
Utensil rack, hand-wrought, flat bar
w/seven hooks, scrolling & twisted
crest, 32¾" l., overall 13½" h. 105.00
Wafer iron, cast grid w/musical
instruments, wrought iron handle,
29" l. 125.00

Cast Iron Rabbit Garden Ornament

Yard or garden ornament, cast, model
of a rabbit, weathered white paint,
11½" h. 105.00

PEWTER
Basin, rim engraved "R.B.L.K. 1785,"
angel touchmarks for Johann Georg
Klingling, 11¾" d., 2½" h. (some
wear & minor dents) 165.00

18th & 19th Century Pewter

Bowl, lovebird mark, Philadelphia,
last half 18th c., 6½" d. (ILLUS.
left front) 495.00
Bowl, shallow, plain wide rim, Town-
send & Compton, London, 12" d.,
1¾" h. (minor dents) 185.00
Candlesticks, domed base, baluster-
shaped stem, cylindrical candle
nozzle, 1820-30, 9¼" h., pr. 185.00
Charger, Joseph Danforth, Middletown,
Connecticut, 1780-88, 12 1/8" d.
(some wear & dents) 325.00
Charger, Graham & Wardrop, London,
14¾" d. (wear & minor rim dent) 165.00
Coffee pot, cov., paneled body, S-scroll
handle, gooseneck spout, Sellew &
Co., Cincinnati, 1832-60, 9½" h. 175.00
Coffee pot w/hinged domed lid,
stepped cylinder w/pedestal base,
double S-scroll handle, gooseneck
spout, Josiah Danforth, Middletown,
Connecticut, 1825-37, 10¼" h. (repair
to lid hinge) 375.00
Coffee pot, cov., gooseneck spout,
American, ca. 1867 . . . . .85.00
Cream pitcher w/hinged conical lid,
straight sides w/slightly flared base,
C-scroll handle, American,
6 1/8" h. 200.00
Dish, deep, Thomas Danforth, Phila-
delphia, ca. 1800, 11½" d. (ILLUS.
back). 330.00
Egg cup, 2 5/8" h. 30.00
Measure, James Yates, England, ½
gill. 30.00
Measure, tulip-shaped, handled, Yates
crown mark, England, ½ pt. 57.00
Measure, tankard form, engraved name,
½ pt., 3 3/8" h. 55.00
Measure, tankard form, pear-shaped
body, scroll handle, James Yates,
England, pt., 5 1/8" h. 80.00
Measure, tankard form, labeled
"Barclay, Perkins & Co., Entire 7
Broad Street," qt., 6" h. 85.00
Mug, N. Harding, last half 19th c.,
3" h. (ILLUS.) .50.00
Pen box w/hinged lid & recessed ring
handle, 7" l. 35.00
Pitcher & porringer, 7" h. pitcher by
Boardman & Hart, New York, 1830-50
& scroll-handled porringer by Robert

Bush, Bristol, England, late 18th c.,
2 pcs. (ILLUS. right) 275.00
Plate, 18th c., w/remnant of English
touchmark, 7 3/4" d. 75.00
Plate, George Lightner, Baltimore,
Maryland, ca. 1815, 8¾" d. (slightly
dented)........................225.00
Salt & pepper shakers w/screw-in
bottom plugs, attributed to Thomas
Danforth II, 5¾" h., pr. 145.00
Teapot, cov., footed, melon-ribbed,
James Dixon & Sons, 4½" d.,
7¼" h. 115.00
Teapot, cov., bulbous body, conical
lid, gooseneck spout, scroll
handle, pedestal base, unmarked
American, 8¼" h. 245.00
Tray, deep scalloped rim, Reed &
Barton, Taunton, Massachusetts,
after 1840, 15½ x 11"..............150.00
Tray, Samuel Duncomb, England,
1740-80, 16 x 11¼"...............150.00
Whale oil lamps, acorn-shaped fonts
on baluster-turned standard, domed
base, Taunton Britannia Manufacturing
Co., Taunton, Massachusetts, 1830-35,
9¾" h., pr......................467.50

PLATED SILVER (Hollowware)

Silverplate Cake Basket

Bowl, footed, ruffled rim, 2-handled,
chased floral decor, Pairpoint,
New Bedford, Massachusetts,
7½" d., 3" h. 125.00
Box & cover w/full figure rat on lid,
chased basketweave body w/sheaf
of wheat tied at each end 55.00
Bread tray, ornate reticulated rim,
Forbes Silver Co., Meriden,
Connecticut, 15 x 7" 45.00
Butter dish, cover & liner, 2-handled,
engraved & bright-cut floral decor,
James W. Tufts, Boston, Massa-
chusetts 55.00
Cake basket, footed, embossed fruit,

ornate bail handle, Pairpoint, New
Bedford, Massachusetts, small 55.00
Cake basket, shaped oblong, 4-footed,
"repousse" reeds, grasses & fruit on
sides & owls in relief below ornate
handle, Reed & Barton, Taunton,
Massachusetts (ILLUS.) 195.00

Candle Snuffer

Candle snuffer, bulldog's head (ILLUS.) .65.00
Card holder, figural cherub pushing
holder on small oblong base,
Pairpoint, New Bedford, Massa-
chusetts 55.00
Coffee urn, cover & burner, applied
Egyptian masks decor, spigot
w/ivory handle, Meriden Britannia
Company, Meriden, Connecticut,
ca. 1868, 16" h. 250.00
Gravy boat & undertray, gadroon
borders, Gorham Corporation,
Providence, Rhode Island 40.00
Ice water pitcher & underplate,
porcelain-lined, Rogers Smith & Co.,
7¾" d., 14½" h. 190.00
Jewelry box, cov., "repousse" roses
decor, Pairpoint, New Bedford,
Massachusetts, 4" sq. 40.00
Nosegay holder, in original velvet-lined
box 185.00
Nut bowl, footed, figural squirrel
seated at one end, Pairpoint,
11" l..................95.00 to 115.00
Pitcher, bulbous, "repousse" pears &
leaves w/bright-cut florals, Barbour
Bros. Co., Hartford, Connecticut,
7¾" h. 45.00
Plateau mirror, beveled mirror plate
within chased floral & scroll framework, openwork feet, ornate,
Pairpoint, 8" d. 100.00
Plateau mirror, beveled mirror plate
within chased florals, scrolls
& open lattice framework
w/gargoyle heads at feet, 10" d. 65.00
Punch set: banquet size 21" d. tray,
16" d., 12½" h. footed punch bowl,
12 footed punch cups w/scroll
handles & 16½" l. ladle w/twisted
handle; fans & scrolls in high relief,
English hallmarks w/crown, 15 pcs. .395.00

Silverplate Sardine Box

Sardine box & cover w/fish finial,
5½" l. (ILLUS.) .80.00
Sugar bowl-spoonholder combination,
12 spoon slots, domed lid, ornate
footed frame, amber glass Inverted
Thumbprint patt. insert, Rogers
Brothers 120.00
Syrup pitcher & cover w/lion finial,
footed, Reed & Barton, 7½" h. 45.00
Tea & coffee service: cov. hot water urn
w/spigot, cov. coffee & tea pots,
creamer, cov. sugar bowl, waste
bowl & 2-handled tray; overall
"repousse" florals, 1890s, 7 pcs. 1,800.00
Teapot, cov., ornate spout & handle,
engraved floral decor, Pairpoint,
1 qt. 75.00
Tray, footed, engraved scrolls & relief-
molded fans at rim, crown & star
hallmark, on copper, 25 x 15½" 125.00
Vase, applied textured diamonds
w/engraved floral sprays, gold-
washed accents, James W. Tufts 70.00
Water tipling stand w/original stand,
drip tray & goblet, ornate, 19th c.,
overall 20" h. . . . . .255.00 to 295.00

SILVER, AMERICAN, ENGLISH & OTHERS

American Silver Coffee Pot

Bowl, hand-hammered, Georg Jensen,
5" d. 298.00

Bowl, hexagonally lobed form, flat
"repousse" rim w/six clusters of
pierced chrysanthemums &
sunflowers, Dominick & Haff,
New York, late 19th c., 8½" d. 200.00
Bowl, embossed & chased to
resemble overlapping leaves
w/curling stems forming handles,
applied grape vines & clusters &
2 insects of copper alloy, George
W. Shiebler & Co., New York, for
J.E. Caldwell, Philadelphia,
Pennsylvania, ca. 1890, 10¾"
across handles 1,045.00
Butter pat, Bailey Banks & Biddle,
late 19th c., 3" sq. 72.00
Cake basket, George III, boat-shaped
w/undulating reeded rim & swing
handle, bright-cut & pierced swags of
trefoils in arches & paterae, pierced
foot rim, center w/monogram of
later date, Peter & Jonathan Bateman,
London, 1790, 15" l. (restored
base) 1,100.00
Cann, cov., pyriform w/circular slightly
domed lid w/thumbpiece, double
scroll handle, circular molded foot,
"repousse" & chased w/florals,
leaves & grapevine, engraved crest,
Samuel Kirk, Baltimore, 1828,
6 5/8" h. 1,760.00
Coffee pot, cov., George II, plain
tapering cylinder, engraved crest &
decorated spout, urn finial,
Benjamin Cartwright, London, 1750,
9¾" h. 2,640.00
Coffee pot, cov., baluster form
on pedestal base, chased stylized
leaf sprays & flowerheads, swan's neck
spout, bud finial, borders of running
thistles, J. Ewan, Charleston, South
Carolina, ca. 1828, 11½" h.
(ILLUS.) 1,430.00
Creamer, ovoid w/shaped rim & pouring
spout, pedestal base, applied
handle, chased w/scene of swan
on river & cow in dooryard, England,
ca. 1816, 4¼" h. 99.00
Creamer, ewer form w/punch-beaded
rim, "repousse" ribboned swag body,
flat scrolling handle, convex foot
w/conforming engraved decor,
Hester Bateman, London, ca. 1790,
4½" h. 154.00
Creamer, George III, compressed
vase form, partly lobed pedestal
foot, guilloche border, double serpent
handle, gilt interior, Paul Storr,
London, 1813, 4½" h. 1,100.00
Creamer, helmet form, pedestal base,
C-scroll strap handle, beaded
borders, engraved w/foliate monogram
one side, Christian Wiltberger,
Philadelphia, ca. 1795, 7¼" h. 880.00

Dish, molded high relief foliate
strawberry clusters alternating
w/vine-like scrolls forming
border, Tiffany & Co., 5¾" d. 115.00

Entree dish, cov., George IV, oblong
w/gadroon borders, cover engraved
w/armorials one side, detachable
leaf-capped double scroll handle
centered w/shell, Jospeh Angell,
London, 1820, 11½" l. 1,210.00

Fruit basket, boat-shaped, vertically
ribbed base, wide reticulated border,
engraved rim, handle divided by
3 balls, German Reich mark, dated
1906, 11¾ x 8¼" 385.00

Meat dish, cov., George III, shaped oval,
molded gadroon rim alternating
w/beads & anthemia at intervals,
engraved each side w/armorials,
domed cover w/wide band of lobes
w/acanthus at intervals & conforming
armorials, acanthus-capped reeded
handles rising from lion's masks above
patera, Paul Storr, London, 1818,
24" l. 10,450.00

Mug, George III, plain baluster form,
leaf-capped double scroll handle,
pedestal foot, Peter & Jonathan
Bateman, London, 1790, 4½" h. 467.00

Pitcher, water, vase-shaped body
w/foliate ribs, domed base w/foliate
& scroll border, scrolling foliate
handle & molded border, engraved
w/initials, Tiffany & Co., New
York, 20th c., 9¾" h. 825.00

Pitcher, water, pear-shaped body on
molded base, shaped rim, chased
w/brace of duck on side & brace of
pheasant reverse, engraved crest,
foliate scroll handle, Robert
Hennell, London, 1856, 11" h. 1,650.00

Porringer, bombe sides, keyhole
handle engraved w/monogram,
John W. Forbes, New York,
ca, 1830, 5 3/8" d. 605.00

Porringer, George III, slightly bombe
sides, molded reeded rim, pierced
keyhole handle engraved
w/crest, James Mince, London,
1802, 6½" rim d. 2,750.00

Sauceboats, slightly bulbous oval
form, molded gadroon rim w/foliate
shells each side, leaf-capped scroll
handle, acanthus-capped scroll feet,
Robert Hennell, London, 1840,
9" l., pr. 3,410.00

Sugar boat, George III, boat-shaped
w/undulating reeded rim & swing
handle, bright-cut florals & pierced
swags of arches enclosing trefoils,
pierced foot rim, w/blue glass liner,
Peter & Jonathan Bateman, London,
1790, 5½" l. 1,320.00

American Silver Sugar Bowl

Sugar bowl, cov., inverted pear
form on pedestal base, engraved
contemporary monogram below
molded rim, domed cover w/pineapple
finial, punch-beaded borders,
Joseph & Nathaniel Richardson,
Philadelphia, ca. 1780, 6½" h.
(ILLUS.) 6,600.00

Teapot, cov., George III, oval straight-
sided form w/reeded rims,
bright-cut & engraved borders
w/formal foliage & vacant
octagonal shield each side, domed
cover w/pineapple finial, Hester
Bateman, London, 1790, 6 5/8" h. . .1,320.00

Tray, circular w/lobed & hammer-
faceted rim, Gorham Manufacturing
Co., Providence, Rhode Island,
1928, 19 1/8" d. 1,100.00

Tray, shaped oblong, 2-handled,
engraved reserve w/trailing
foliage, florals & monogram,
border embossed & chased w/scrolls,
foliage & florals, The Gorham
Co., Providence, Rhode Island,
ca. 1905, 31½" l. 1,540.00

TIN & TOLE

Tin Beer Growler

Apple roasting oven, tin, reflector-type,
hinged at top rear & w/two rear
feet, original insert pan, original
darkened finish, 11 x 10 x 9½" 110.00

Basket, tin, crimped sides, rigid
overhead double-curve handle,
9" d., overall 8½" h. 165.00

Beer growler w/cover, tin, bail
handle, 6¼" d. (ILLUS.)......12.50 to 18.00

Berry pail, tin 12.00

Berry picker, tin, blue 37.50

Box w/domed lid, tole, yellow striping
& white band w/red & green
decor, original bail handle, 4¼" l. ...150.00

Bun tray, tole, boat-shaped w/open
handles at ends, free-hand brushed
central flower, leaves & buds in
red, yellow & green on brown
asphaltum, probably New York,
ca. 1830, 12" l...................325.00

Candle box, hanging-type, tin,
cylindrical w/hinged lid, strap
hangers at back, original hasp,
oxidized slightly greenish cast,
11½" l.........................135.00

Candle box, hanging-type, tin,
cylindrical w/hinged lid, hanging
tabs at back, old black finish,
19th c., 15" l....................165.00

Candle mold, tin, single tube, square
tapered form, 3" h.................60.00

Candle mold, tin, single tube, crimped
circular top & base, w/handle,
10½" h. 135.00

Candle mold, tin, 2-tube, oblong tray
top w/ring handles, 10" h. 45.00

Candle mold, tin, 3-tube, w/vertical
wire strut brace, signed "Manson,"
7½" h. 395.00

Candle mold, tin, 3-tube, oblong tray
top w/strap handles, 11" h. 45.00

Candle mold, tin, 4-tube, 10 5/8" h. 85.00

Candle mold, tin, 8-tube, brace rods at
base, strap handles at top sides,
7½ x 3¾" base, 11¼" h. ...75.00 to 145.00

Candle mold, tin, 9-tube, widely spaced
tubes, 12" h. 130.00

Candle mold, tin, 12-tube, single
handle, 10½" h.............75.00 to 95.00

Candle mold, tin, 18-tube, 2 rows of
9 each, 10½" h...................110.00

Candle mold, tin, 18-tube, 2 rows of 9
in wooden frame, 10½ x 9¼",
16" h. 150.00

Candle mold, tin, 24-tube 125.00

Candle mold, tin, 36-tube 195.00

Candle sconce, wall-type, tin, Gothic
arch backplate reflector, drum-
shaped base, 8" h. 60.00

Candle sconce, wall-type, tin,
sunburst-ribbed reflector plate,
crimped saucer pan w/cylindrical
candle nozzle, 9¾" w., 9" h........215.00

Candle snuffer, tin, cone-shaped,
japanned finish ....30.00 to 38.00

Cheese drainer, pierced tin, heart-
shaped, handled, Pennyslvania
Deutsch 150.00

Cheese drainer, pierced tin, built-up
foot, strap handle, attributed to the
Shakers 95.00

Coffee pot w/slightly domed lid, tin,
tapering cylinder, short spout, braced
strap handle at side & iron wire
bail handle w/wooden grip at top 50.00

Comb case, wall-type, tin, arched
scalloped top w/two doves in relief,
blue finish, 7 x 7" 39.00

Comb case, wall-type, tin, embossed
design, worn red japanned finish,
8 x 8" ....12.50 to 20.00

Cup, tole, straight sides, strap handle,
stenciled design & inscription "My
Girl" on faded pink ground,
2 7/8" d., 1¾" h...................35.00

Document Box

Document box w/domed lid, tole,
original free-hand yellow, orange &
green florals & scrolls on dark brown
japanned ground, original brass
bail handle, 9¾" l. (ILLUS.) 300.00

Document box w/flat lid, free-hand
orange & yellow design on worn
black ground, 9¾" l. 90.00

Knitting needle case, tole, free-hand
red & yellow decor on worn original
black ground, 9 3/8" l. 75.00

Lamp Filler

Lamp filler, tin, funnel-shaped top,
strap handle, straight spout w/angled
end, bail handle w/wooden grip,
original cork stopper, early 1900s,
overall 13" h. (ILLUS.)...............45.00
Lunch pail, cov., tin, 4-part w/soup
tray, late 19th-early 20th c. ..28.00 to 40.00
Mitten drying rack, tin, stove pipe
clamp-on type, rolled edge bracing,
flat surface pierced w/holes,
1870 patent, 20 x 13" 55.00
Quilt pattern, tin, 6-petal flower, 5" d...15.00
Scoop, tin, original red paint, 17" l......85.00
Snuff box, tole, lid w/landscape
scene depicting boy fishing on black
ground, 2 3/8" d., 1¾" h. 60.00
Sugar shaker, tole, strap handle, free-
hand green & yellow decor on
brown japanned ground, 3¼" h.
(old resoldering at base of handle) ...80.00
Syrup pitcher w/slightly domed lid, tole,
tapering cylinder, strap handle,
red, green, yellow & white
florals on worn black ground,
4¼" h. 120.00
Tea bin, w/hinged slant-front lid, tole,
gilt-stenciled house, leaves &
fruit decor on red, 8 x 9½ x 10" 190.00
Teapot w/slightly domed lid, tole,
tapering cylinder, straight
spout, strap handle, red, yellow &
green florals on worn brown
japanned ground, 8¾" h. 300.00

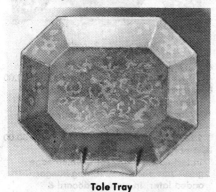

Tole Tray

Tray, tole, octagonal, gilt-stenciled
florals on red, 12 x 9" (ILLUS.).......95.00
Tray, tole, oblong w/pierced sides &
carrying handles, free-hand
polychrome pastoral scene within
gilt borders, Regency period,
ca. 1810, now on stand of later
date w/square tapering legs, 27" w.,
18" h.........................1,430.00
Tray, tole, oblong, stenciled foliate
scrolls & flowerheads on black
ground, mid-19th c., now on stand
of later date, 34" w..............198.00
Urns & covers w/pinecone finials,

tole, shaped & squared body
flanked by scrolling handles, socle
foot above conformingly lobed foot,
"chinoiserie" overall decor in
gilt on black ground, 19th c.,
11½" h., pr...................528.00
Wall box, tin, box w/canted sides, high
arched backplate, faded out
stenciling on original blue
ground, mid-19th c., 6½" w.,
5¾" h. backplate 55.00
Wash boiler w/lid, tin w/copper bottom,
17¼ x 10½" oval 40.00
Watch holder, tin, round w/hinged lid,
hook inside 17.00

(End of Metals Section)

MILITARY COLLECTIBLES

Civil War Bullet Mold

*Also see FIREARMS and PAPER COL-
LECTIBLES.*

Civil War artillery shell, empty shell
w/lead rifling plugs & unused
wooden nose, 3¼" d., 6½" l......$240.00
Civil War belt buckle, Union Naval
officer's, w/belt & "frog"...........125.00
Civil War book, "Society of the Army
of the Cumberland 23rd Reunion -
1892," Chicamauga, Georgia,
w/photographs...................25.00
Civil War bullet mold, 4¾" l. (ILLUS.) ...28.00
Civil War canteen, Confederate States,
wooden model made from two
hollowed pieces of turned wood 350.00
Civil War cap, Union soldier's visored
Kepi-style........................55.00
Civil War dagger, Sheffield silver
handle, 5¾" blade, w/sheath,
marked "Slater Bros."..............150.00
Civil War discharge papers, Union
Infantry Corporal, dated July 8,
1865 ....40.00
Civil War saddle, Confederate
officer's, leather 250.00
Civil War stirrups, "U.S. Cavalry,"
wooden w/leather tapaderos, pr.....45.00
Civil War sword, Confederate States

artillery model w/star, original
wooden scabbard 575.00
Nazi ammunition pouch, black leather ..12.00
Nazi arm band......................35.00
Nazi badge, "Tank Assault" division ...195.00
Nazi cane, officer's model w/pewter
bust of soldier wearing helmet
w/swastica insignia on handle......125.00
Nazi dagger & scabbard, Luftwaffe 1st
model..........................225.00
Nazi flag, black swastica on white
circle on red ground, muslin,
52 x 31".........................55.00
Nazi helmet, metal w/winged emblem
on front & "Luftschutz".............75.00
Nazi mess kit, steel, combination large
spoon, fork, knife & can opener,
w/steel case, dated 1942 ....55.00
Nazi parade banner, long & narrow 65.00
Nazi parade dagger w/"S.S." marks
& inscription on blade, maker's mark
"E. & A. Helbig, Steinback" in oval
cartouche, w/black scabbard......247.50
War of 1812 sword, U.S. Navy officer's,
fluted ivory grip, brass scabbard,
engraved blade, sea serpent back-
strap 600.00
World War I gas mask, in canvas
carrying bag, w/instructions 25.00
World War I helmet, French 28.00
World War I helmet, German, metal,
spike-top 65.00
World War I helmet, U.S. Army,
doughboy-style, metal,
w/liner ....18.00 to 25.00
World War I mess kit, German
officer's model, w/leather case 110.00
World War I pilot's helmet, U.S.
Air Force, leather 70.00
World War I postcard, scene of
destruction at Verdun, France 3.00
World War I sword w/scabbard,
German cavalry 95.00
World War I trench periscope,
w/wooden tripod 135.00
World War I uniform, U.S. Army
"doughboy" jacket, shirt, jodhpurs,
cap & helmet, 5 pcs...............125.00
World War I uniform, U.S. Navy, blue
wool 75.00
World War II banner, "U.S.O. Overseas
Shows," red, white & blue satin,
52 x 41".........................75.00
World War II bayonet, Japanese 25.00
World War II field telephone,
German 135.00
World War II helmet, Dutch, steel 35.00
World War II helmet, Japanese,
complete 65.00
World War II "pith" helmet, British
officer's desert model w/insignia 39.00
World War II "ID" bracelet, U.S. Navy
Air Force insignia, sterling silver
w/gold inlay insignia (ILLUS.)........75.00

World War II Insignia Bracelet

World War II life jacket, "Mae
West".................20.00 to 30.00
World War II parachute, Japanese,
silk, complete, w/chair 37.00
World War II uniform, U.S. Air Force
jacket 110.00
World War II uniform, U.S. Navy
Commander, khaki, complete
w/hat 55.00

MINIATURES (Paintings)

Madonna on Porcelain

Andrew Jackson on ivory, framed,
3½ x 4"......................$400.00
Bust portrait of gentleman wearing
glasses on ivory, gilt-metal case
w/sample of black cloth visible
through clear glass back lens,
2 1/8" oval 150.00
Bust portrait of gentleman on ivory,
in locked case w/clear beveled edge
glass lens each side, w/ring hanger
added later, in worn cardboard &
wooden case, 2 3/8" h. 200.00
Bust portrait of gentleman in blue
frock coat on ivory, original paper
backing w/label, ornate gilt frame,
6¾ x 7½" oval 150.00
Bust portrait of lady in early 19th century attire on ivory, in oval gold
bezel & wooden frame, Continental,
early 19th c., overall 5" h. 110.00
Bust portrait of young woman on ivory,
wearing draped headdress w/large
blue jewels & pearls, w/matching
necklace, under glass, brass & fruitwood frame, ca. 1830, 2½" d. 175.00
Bust portrait of young woman w/long

hair on porcelain, embossed ormolu
frame w/ring, 3½ x 3".............200.00
Empress Elizabeth of Austria on ivory,
tortoise shell frame, 4¾ x 5½"
oval..........................290.00
Fanny Eisler (actress) on ivory, tortoise
shell frame, 4¾ x 5½" oval........290.00
Hot air balloon ascension on ivory,
scene w/spectators watching
balloon rising, French, ca. 1795.....450.00
Madonna w/Child & St. John the
Baptist on porcelain, folding book-
type frame, overall 5¾ x 4¾"
(ILLUS.).......................225.00
Napoleon & Josephine on porcelain,
framed, 4 x 5", pr...............400.00
Theodore Roosevelt on ivory, framed,
3½ x 4".........................400.00

MINIATURES (Replicas)

Miniature Decorated Chest of Drawers

Blanket chest, maple, hinged lid
w/applied edge lifting to deep well
w/large till & secret drawer in case
w/drawer below main storage compartment, cut-out bracket feet, old
worn original brown finish,
26½" w., 13½" deep, 22¾" h.....$5,250.00
Blanket chest, poplar, oblong top on
original wrought iron hinges lifting
to well w/till in case w/inlaid
whalebone diamond-shaped keyhole escutcheon, scalloped bracket
feet, "alligatored" original red &
black graining, original spring lock,
14¾ x 8½", 8¼" h...............475.00
Bucket, stave construction w/tin
banding, wire bail handle w/wooden
grip, worn yellow paint, 5½" d.,
4½" h..........................35.00

Cake stand, cut glass, teardrop stem,
sterling silver rim, 3" d., 2" h......150.00
Candlesticks, brass, circular base,
turned baluster form column,
4" h., pr......................50.00
Chamber pot, yellowware w/white
band, applied handle, 2 1/8".......30.00
Cheese dish, porcelain, autumn-
colored florals & leaves on cream
ground, Vienna mark, 3" l.........52.00
Chest of drawers, Federal, mahogany,
bowed rectangular top above conforming case of 2 short & 3 long
graduated drawers w/turned pulls
over a scalloped skirt on French
feet, 1790-1810, 14½ x 7½", 16" h...935.00
Chest of drawers, Victorian cottage-
style, painted & decorated, oblong
top w/shaped backboard above case
w/pr. set back short drawers over
deep drawer faced to simulate 2
molded long drawers above one
molded long drawer, painted fruit &
flowers on yellow ground, signed
"A. Snow" on reverse, mid-19th c.,
13½ x 12", 20" h. (ILLUS.).........1,100.00
Chest of drawers, walnut, oblong top
w/high scalloped backboard above
case w/pr. handkerchief boxes over
3 long drawers, original porcelain
drawer pulls, ca. 1880, 15½ x 7½",
15" h..........................245.00
Coffee grinder, wood & iron..........85.00
Compote, cut glass, diamond, fan &
bull's eyes, 3½" d. bowl, 2" d. foot,
2" h...........................60.00
Fireplace andirons, cast iron, ornate
scrolling, black, 4¼ x 2½", 4¾" h.,
pr.............................110.00
Frying pan, cast iron, footed, 3" d.,
3" l. handle....................25.00
Herb drying rack, wood, 7" w., 6" h.....75.00
Ink stand, silver, rectangular w/bun
feet, fitted w/removable sander &
inkwell (later cover) & fixed pen
holder/taperstick, Dutch, maker's
mark a tree, probably for Jan
Bogaert, Amsterdam, 1785, 2¾" l...522.00
Mirror, giltwood frame w/ornate
corner posts, "eglomise" panel of
cottage & tree in a hilly landscape,
4¼" w., 9" h...................195.00
Mortar & pestle, brass, flaring cylinder,
2" h...........................45.00
Mug, handled, cut glass, strawberry
diamond & fan..................85.00
Pitcher, lime green glass w/applied
green handle, bulbous w/round
mouth, dainty pink flowers & green
leaves decor w/gold trim, 1 3/8" d.,
2¼" h..........................45.00
Pitcher, tankard, cranberry glass,
applied clear handle, overall lacy
gold scrollwork, 1¼" d., 3½" h......85.00

Plates, pewter, scalloped rims, angel
   touch mark, 3¾" d., set of 3 . . . . 25.50
Settee, painted & carved, shaped back
   comprising 3 arched crests above
   vase-form splats, scrolled arms,
   plank seat, ring-turned legs joined by
   by stretchers, painted w/floral
   motifs in polychrome on a brown
   ground w/yellow & brown highlights, Pennsylvania, ca. 1845,
   23" l. 1,980.00
Table, tilt-top, walnut, 6½" h. 125.00
Tea set: 1¼" h. cov. teapot, creamer
   & sugar bowl; silver, hallmarks for
   Birmingham, 1906, 3 pcs. 135.00
Vase, green opaline pressed glass,
   Hobnail patt., ca. 1900, 3" h. 95.00

Cast iron 6¾" d., 6¾" h. mortar
   w/flaring lip, w/pestle . . . . . 34.00 to 55.00
Ironstone mortar, w/9" l. pestle 29.00
Maple 6½" h. mortar, w/double-
   headed pestle 49.00
Tiger maple mortar, w/pestle 220.00
Turned curly maple 8¼" h. mortar,
   w/plain maple pestle. 180.00
Turned walnut 7¼" h. mortar,
   w/pestle (ILLUS.) 125.00
Turned wood 5 5/8" h. mortar,
   w/pestle 55.00
Walnut 6¾ x 6" mortar, w/pestle 75.00
Walnut 7" h. octagonal mortar
   w/pedestal base, w/chestnut pestle . 30.00

MORTARS & PESTLES

Turned Wood Mortar & Pestle

Also see MINIATURES (Replicas).

Brass 4" d., 4" h. mortar,
   w/pestle $55.00
Brass 4½" h. mortar w/knob
   handles, w/pestle 75.00
Brass 5½" d., 4½" h. mortar w/turned
   detail, w/pestle 99.00
Burl 4¼" d., 5¾" h. mortar w/tapering
   sides, w/lignum vitae pestle 145.00
Burl (ash) 6" h. mortar w/pedestal base,
   w/beechwood pestle 115.00
Burl 6¼" h. mortar, w/curly maple
   pestle 155.00
Burl 8" h. mortar w/footed base &
   tooled rings, w/stone pestle 200.00
Cast iron 5" h. mortar, w/pestle 30.00
Cast iron 5¾" h. mortar, w/pestle 45.00
Cast iron 6" d. mortar w/flaring lip,
   w/8" l. pestle 39.00

MUSIC BOXES

Baker-Troll "Sublime Harmony" Music Box

Baker-Troll "Sublime Harmony" (Swiss)
   cylinder music box, 6-tune w/zither
   attachment & 10 bells, fast-slow &
   stop-start adjustment, tune indicator
   & original tune card, burl walnut
   case w/fruitwood banding &
   matching base w/single drawer,
   late 19th c., w/three 16" cylinders
   (ILLUS.) $4,400.00
Conchon (F.) cylinder music box, 6-tune
   w/zither attachment, fast-slow adjustment & tune indicator, lever-
   wound at side, rosewood case
   w/inlaid boxwood stringing, on
   matching stand w/cylinder storage
   drawer, ca. 1880, 11" cylinder,
   39" l. case, w/six cylinders 1,980.00
Criterion (F.G. Otto & Sons) disc music
   box, double comb, mahogany case,
   11½" disc 2,100.00

Criterion disc music box, double
  comb, mahogany case, 15¾" disc . 2,500.00
Criterion disc music box, double comb,
  oak console cabinet, w/twenty
  15½" discs 3,400.00
Ducommun-Girod cylinder music box,
  w/forte piano comb, lever-wound
  at side (restored) 2,250.00
Heller (J.H.) cylinder music box,
  double comb, 8-tune w/piccolo &
  harp attachment, original tune card,
  lever-wound at side, rosewood
  case w/fruitwood banding, ca. 1880,
  19½" cylinder, 32½" l. case 2,750.00
Mermod Freres (Swiss) cylinder music
  box, 11" cylinder, 22" l. case 795.00
Mira (Mermod Freres) disc music box,
  oak console model, w/fifty 15¾"
  discs 3,800.00

"Mira" Console Music Box

Mira disc music box, console model,
  ca. 1905, w/thirty 18½" discs
  (ILLUS.) 4,500.00
Mojon Manger (London) cylinder music
  box, 12-tune w/zither attachment &
  6 bells (soprano bells in view), tune
  indicator & original tune card, lever-
  wound at side, walnut veneer case
  w/inlaid cartouche, ca. 1900, 13"
  cylinder, 26" l. case 990.00
Orphenion (Bruno Ruckert, Leipzig,
  Germany) upright disc music box,
  walnut case 4,000.00
Paillard (Swiss) cylinder music box,
  6-tune w/flute attachment,
  (fragmented) original tune card,
  lever-wound at side, kingwood case
  w/tulipwood banding, late 19th c.,
  13" cylinder, 23" l. case 1,540.00
Paillard (Swiss) cylinder music box, 12-
  tune w/piccolo & harp attachment,
  double comb, original tune card,
  lever-wound at side, rosewood

veneer case inlaid w/musical
  cartouche, ca. 1890, 28" l. 1,870.00
Perfection (Perfection Music Box Co.,
  Jersey City, New Jersey) disc music
  box, oak case 1,500.00
Regina disc music box, single comb,
  oak case, w/nine 15½" discs 1,600.00
Regina disc music box, double comb,
  Style 9 upright model, ornately
  carved walnut case w/gilt trim,
  15½" disc . . . . 2,500.00 to 4,000.00
Regina disc music box, double comb,
  Style 11, lever-wound at side,
  stained oak case w/drawer, ca.
  1895, w/six 15½" discs, 22½" l.
  case . . . . 1,450.00 to 2,650.00
Regina disc music box, double comb,
  Style 19, carved walnut Art Nouveau
  style case, 15½" disc . . 2,000.00 to 2,700.00
Regina disc music box, double comb,
  Style 26, 20½" disc 4,200.00
Regina disc music box, Style 40 console
  model, Rookwood finish case
  w/Victorian oil painting decor,
  1902-15 . . . . 5,000.00
Regina disc music box, double comb,
  Style 50, mahogany serpentine case,
  15½" disc 2,800.00
Stella (Mermod Freres) disc music box,
  mahogany case, 1885-97, w/eleven
  15½" discs 2,600.00
Stella disc music box, double comb,
  mahogany console model w/disc
  storage cabinet below, w/eighteen
  15½" discs 3,600.00
Stella disc music box, double comb,
  mahogany console model w/disc
  storage cabinet below, w/thirty
  17½" discs 2,950.00
Swiss cylinder music box, 6-tune,
  (refinished) case, 11" cylinder 1,650.00

Swiss Music Box with Bells & Drums

Swiss cylinder music box, 8-tune
  w/zither attachment & bells & drums
  "in view," w/stop-start adjustment,
  tune indicator & original tune card,

kingwood case w/fruitwood floral
inlay on lid, late 19th c., 10¾"
cylinder, 21" l. case (ILLUS.) 2,200.00
Swiss cylinder music box, 10-tune,
inlaid rosewood case, 24 x 8" 1,000.00
Swiss cylinder music box, 12-tune
w/zither attachment, rosewood
case w/inlaid musical trophy on
lid, ca. 1900, 24" l. 850.00
Symphonion disc music box, w/original
tune card, lever-wound at side,
mahogany case w/inlaid musical
trophy on lid, w/thirty 15½" discs,
22 x 18" case 1,100.00

MUSICAL INSTRUMENTS

Rosewood and Ebony Zither

Autoharp, "Zimmerman" $85.00
Banjo, 4-string, "Steward," mother-
of-pearl inlay....................550.00
Banjo, 5-string, "S.S. Steward"
Universal Favourite, 5000s serial
number.........................300.00
Banjo-mandolin, 8-string, bird's eye
maple w/mother-of-pearl inlay,
ivory keys 110.00
Banjo-mandolin, "Orpheum No. 1" 300.00
Cello, tiger maple sides, spruce front
& back w/line inlay, brass keys,
paper label "Abraham Prescott
Manufacturer & Dealer in Musical
Instruments of every description --
Concord, N.H.," early 19th c., 50" l.
(minor damage, fret missing).......635.00
Clarinet, "Selmer" Contrabass E-flat,
rosewood w/silverplate trim,
original case 750.00
Dulcimer, painted poplar, 5 scroll-

carved heads w/pins for 25
strings, compass star design on
face, worn original red & black
paint, w/inscription "Szaba Pall,
1876," 36" l......................450.00
Guitar, "Gibson," Model L-5, 1932 ...1,150.00
Harmonica, "Hohner - Model No.
34B," Germany, original box 25.00
Harp, "Lyon & Healy," single action,
ca. 1910.......................2,800.00
Mandolin, "Orville Gibson - Model
A"....................450.00 to 500.00
Melodeon, portable, "MacNutt, Philadelphia," folding carved legs
(refinished & restored) 700.00
Ocarina (Sweet Potato), pottery, gold
seal, Austria 85.00
Organ, "Estey," church model, 16
stops, 1 manual, oak, dovetail
construction 3,000.00
Piano, baby grand, "Chickering,"
rosewood, 1857 (restored).......10,000.00
Piano, square grand, "Weber," rosewood, carved legs, w/matching
stool, 2 pcs. 2,000.00
Piano, upright, "Steinway & Sons,
New York," ebonized wood,
Renaissance Revival style w/pierce-
carved music rack & flat pilasters
w/ornate capitals & scrolled base
panels, ca. 1920, w/adjustable
piano stool labeled "Cook &
Company," 2 pcs. 650.00
Pianoforte, "H. & W. Geib, New
York," inlaid mahogany w/brass
mounts, oblong cross-banded top
opening to 5-octave keyboard
w/maker's name within geometric
stencil, brass-mounted frieze
w/drawers, acanthus- and spiral-
carved legs on casters, w/Empire-
style piano stool, ca. 1830, 2 pcs. ..3,025.00
Piccolo, ebony, nickel-plated brass
fittings, 12¼" l....................50.00
Violin, lady's, "Amati," 1817, w/bow
& case 1,950.00
Violin, "Stainer," scrimshaw inlay,
handmade wooden case, ca. 1860 ...975.00
Zither, rosewood & carved ebony,
"Kerschensteiner, Regensburg, Bayern,"
in original case, w/pitch pipe,
ca. 1880, 28½" l. (ILLUS.)...........550.00

MUSICAL INSTRUMENTS,
MECHANICAL

Band organ, "Artizan Style X-A-2
Military Band," 46 keys, w/eight
rolls $12,500.00

Band organ, "Herschell-Spillman,"
  w/brass trumpets & piccolos 6,500.00
Band organ, "North Tonawanda
  Musical Instrument Works," plays
  Wurlitzer Type 125 rolls 15,000.00

German Barrel Organ

Barrel organ, "Wilhelm Bruder Sohne,
  Orgelbauer in Waldkirch, Baden,"
  10-tune w/twenty keys & 2 ranks of
  39 pipes, walnut case w/fruitwood
  banding & floral inlay, 21" h.
  (ILLUS.) 2,860.00
Barrel organ, 2 barrels, each capable
  of playing 10 tunes, 46 metal pipes,
  16 stopped wooden pipes, triangle
  & drum (restored) 10,500.00
Calliope, "Cozatt," 44-note, keyboard
  or roll play 9,500.00
Calliope, "Tangley," 43-note, keyboard
  or roll play 7,500.00
Coin-operated piano, "Nelson-
  Wiggen Casino X Model," case
  w/original art glass panels,
  mid-1920s 6,000.00
Coin-operated piano, "Seeburg Style
  A," w/mandolin attachment, oak
  case w/art glass panel 6,800.00
Coin-operated piano, "Seeburg Style
  E," w/wood xylophone attachment
  (restored) 12,000.00
Coin-operated piano, "Western
  Electric Mascot Model," oak case
  w/stained glass panel
  (restored) . . . . 7,200.00 to 8,500.00
Music box, "Polyphon" upright disc
  model, walnut case w/glazed
  door flanked by carved columns,
  w/drawer in base, ca. 1900,
  w/forty-three 24½" discs 7,425.00
Music box, "Regina" automatic disc
  changer, mahogany floor model
  case w/carved dragons, 20¾"
  disc 9,500.00
Music box, "Regina Orchestral Corona
  Style 8" automatic disc changer,
  mahogany floor model, 27" disc
  (ILLUS.) 15,000.00

Regina Orchestral Corona Music Box

Orchestrion (self-contained musical
  instrument equipped w/several
  different instruments in imitation of
  an orchestra), "Paul Losche Leipzig
  Orchestrion Works, Leipzig,
  Germany" 5,500.00
Orchestrion, "Seeburg Style L," hard-
  wood case w/art glass front 39,750.00
Organ, "Orchestrelle Aeolian Style A,"
  w/twenty-five rolls 3,400.00
Organ, "Orchestrelle Aeolian Style F,"
  mahogany case, restored (uses
  116-note or 58-note rolls) 19,500.00
Pianino (small upright piano),
  Wurlitzer, 44-note 4,500.00
Reproducing piano, "Fisher Ampico
  Model B Grand," mahogany case,
  ca. 1930 (player mechanism
  restored) 5,500.00
Reproducing piano, "Knabe Ampico
  Model A Grand," Louis XVI style
  walnut case 7,500.00
Reproducing piano, "Marshall &
  Wendall Ampico Model A Grand,"
  mahogany case w/carved floral
  accents & gilt highlights, w/bench &
  90 rolls 5,500.00
Reproducing piano, "Mason & Hamlin
  Ampico Grand," 1925, w/adjustable
  bench & 205 Ampico rolls 14,500.00
Reproducing piano, "Seeburg Style
  X" 5,200.00
Violano (violin player), "Mills," single
  violin, mahogany case 8,600.00
Violano, "Mills," double violins,
  restored & refinished case 25,000.00

MUSTACHE CUPS & SAUCERS

China Mustache Cup

China, Austrian, overall tiny pink
  roses decor $65.00
China, Coalport, dark blue birds &
  bamboo decor on white ground,
  wide geometric border, 1881-91 . . . . .85.00
China, E.S. Germany, orange flowers
  & green leaves decor 85.00
China, Limoges, gold decor on white
  ground 45.00
China, R.S. Prussia, shaded cream
  ground w/gold, yellow & green
  floral decor 98.00
China, cobalt blue & white decor, gold
  trim, marked Germany 65.00
China, h.p. gold, red, yellow & green
  florals, ca. 1910 (ILLUS. of
  cup) .45.00 to 65.00
China, lettered "Brother" in relief
  w/ornate gold outlining on hunter
  green ground 45.00
China, lettered "Christmas 1884,"
  Germany 48.00
China, lettered "Remember Me" &
  floral decor, Germany 40.00
Silverplate, bright-cut butterfly
  design, engraved w/date "Dec. 25,
  1902," James Tufts 90.00
Silverplate, bright-cut floral design,
  Barbour Bros. Co. 60.00
Silverplate, crimped rim, engraved
  florals, Derby Silver Co. 45.00
Silverplate, engraved & embossed
  florals, James Tufts 85.00
Silverplate, engraved decor, James
  Tufts .65.00 to 95.00
Silverplate, gold washed interior,
  Rogers (cup only) 65.00

NAPKIN RINGS

Baby in cradle beside ring $225.00
Bird standing on large leaf beside
  ring 145.00

Bird w/long tail perched beside ring
  on leaf-shaped base, Meriden 90.00
Birds sitting on branch atop flattened
  oval ring, 1¾" h., 2¼ x 2½" 40.00
Boy w/raised drumsticks beside ring,
  Pairpoint 182.00
Boy carrying ring on his shoulder
  on round base, Rogers Bros. 165.00
Bumble bee atop leaf-engraved ring,
  George W. Shiebler & Co. 325.00
Butterflies (2) supporting ring,
  handled fan base, Meriden 140.00

Cherry Cluster Napkin Ring

Cherry cluster attached to ring on
  ball-footed platform base, marked
  "Meriden," 3½" l. (ILLUS.) 50.00
Cherub & bird beside ring, Wilcox 95.00
Cherub pulling ring cart w/movable
  wheels 179.00
Cherubs (2) each side of floral
  engraved ring, Victor Silver Co. 59.00
Chick on wishbone base beside egg-
  shaped ring engraved "Best
  Wishes," Derby Silver Co. 70.00
Cow standing beside bucket-shaped
  ring on floral embossed circular
  base, Meriden 180.00
Cupids (2) carrying barrel-shaped
  ring on flat base 100.00
Cupid w/arrow reclining beside ring
  w/four bulbous sections on heart-
  shaped base, Wilcox 125.00
Dog barking at bird on ring, footed
  base, 1901 . . . . .85.00
Dog w/front paws on ring, barking
  at cat w/arched back atop ring,
  oval base 220.00
Dog pulling ornate ring cart
  w/movable wheels 229.00
Eagle holding ring between raised
  wings, Rogers, Smith & Co., 4" h. 125.00
Fox beside ring w/applied grapes &
  vines 85.00
Greenaway boy beside hexagonal
  ring 155.00
Greenaway girl w/goat beside ring
  on oval base .225.00
Kewpie standing beside ring 92.00

NAUTICAL GEAR

Diving Helmet

The romantic lure of the sea, and of ships in general, has opened up a new area of collector interest. Nautical gear, especially items made of brass or with brass trim, is sought out for its decorative appeal. Virtually all items that can be associated with ships, along with items used or made by sailors, is now considered collectible for technological advances have rendered it obsolete. Listed below are but a few of the numerous nautical items sold in recent months.

Binnacle (non-magnetic compass
   stand) & Oriental compass,
   copper, ca. 1835 . . . . $295.00
Boson's whistle, sterling silver,
   marked "Tiffany," 1¾" l. 100.00
Cane, shark vertebrae & baleen,
   handle w/six baleen spacers &
   end w/baleen tip, ca. 1850,
   34½" l. 220.00
Corset busk, baleen, scrimshawed on
   front w/armorous verse within
   geometric borders centering
   initials & scrimshawed w/flowers,
   hearts, trees & American flags
   reverse, ca. 1835, 13¾" l. 330.00
Diving helmet, copper & brass,
   w/three circular glazed face
   plates, "Schrader's & Son Inc."
   (ILLUS.) 467.00
Fid, carved gnarled sapling, 7¼" l. 20.00
Float ball, aqua glass, egg-shaped,
   indented ridge for net rope,
   "S.H. Davis & Co. Gill Net Float -
   patented 1877," 5 x 3½ x 3¼" 65.00
Life preserver, "Winston" on one side,
   17" d. 65.00
Octant, ebony, marked "Gilbert,
   London," w/box 650.00
Porthole, brass, 17" d. 100.00
Rolling pin, blown cobalt blue glass,
   enameled "I Love a Sailor," &
   flags, ca. 1850 . . . . 125.00
Sailor's knot board, 30 knots mounted
   on oblong mahogany board, each
   labeled, by Clifford W. Ashley,
   ca. 1925, 23½ x 16¾" 440.00

Seaman's chest, pine, hinged lid on
   wrought iron strap hinges opening
   to fitted interior w/sliding tray &
   3 dovetailed drawers in dovetailed case w/"becket" handles,
   old worn finish, 43 x 18", 18¼" h. . . .125.00
Sextant, brass, "Plath," in wooden
   case, German, w/sales & manifest
   papers 500.00
Ship's starboard lantern, copper &
   brass, kerosene burner, "Seahorse
   Trade Mark - Made in England,"
   polished, 20th c., 8¾" h. 70.00
Ship's telegraph, polished brass,
   1940s, 42" h. 650.00
Telescope, 4-draw, 9½" l. 75.00
Telescope, w/braided leather grip,
   3-draw, 29" l. 185.00
Telescope, brass, 5-draw, 36" l. 175.00

Telescope

Telescope, brass, "Edinburgh Lennie,"
   39" l. unextended (ILLUS.) 425.00
Telescope, walnut & brass, engraved,
   ca. 1850 . . . . 375.00

NEEDLEWORK PICTURES

Berlin Wool Work Picture

Berlin wool work is embroidery with wool on a canvas pattern, sometimes erroneously referred to as tapestry, which was a popular pastime of ladies of the 19th century. Wool embroidery with glass beads worked in the design became fashionable about 1850 and this type is known as "German Embroidery." Stool and book covers, panels for fire screens and pictures are among the items available to collectors today.

Berlin wool work, depicting the fully rigged vessel "Ethel" within central circular reserve flanked by large draped English, American, Norwegian & Swedish flags, w/roses & thistles, red, green, beige & blue, English, 19th c., 23 x 25" (ILLUS.)...........$770.00

Needlework embroidered on homespun fabric, colorful lilies, roses & daisies, framed, 10½ x 3"...........90.00

Needlework embroidered on homespun fabric, petit point & satin stitch verse & pheasant perched on a branch surrounded by twining floral border, in shades of green, gold, red, brown & white, signed & dated 1830, bird's eye maple ogee frame, 15¼" w., 19" h...........160.00

Needlework embroidered on linen, floral wreath w/strawberries worked in raised stitches on black ground centering inscription "Julia Anderson Gregory Hopewell 1856 Ont. Co. N.Y.," in recessed giltwood frame, 17½" sq. 220.00

Needlework embroidered on linen, depicting woman, birds, animals, floral sprays in urns & bleeding heart above garland w/initials, early 19th c., framed, 28¾ x 21½" ..550.00

Needlework embroidered on silk, single large tulip in pot w/spray of roses above, in shades of soft yellow, green, blue & white, signed & dated 1811 in lower section, framed, 9½ x 8"..................570.00

Needlework embroidered on silk, depicting 2 women in classical dress personifying the sciences within a landscape scene, signed, in giltwood frame, early 19th c., 10¾" sq. 242.00

Needlework embroidered on silk, depicting a spray of colorful flowers, silk thread, early 19th c., framed, 16 x 11½".......................154.00

Needlework embroidered on silk, basket of flowers in shades of faded blue, gold, brown, green & salmon pink, mahogany frame w/corner buttons, 18" sq. 225.00

Needlework embroidered & painted on silk, mourning picture, depicting young maiden seated beneath a weeping willow tree w/a white lamb at her feet, cottage in back-

ground & monument inscribed "In memory of Emma Corbet," in shades of pink, green, blue & white, in original black glass mat, early 19th c., 13 x 10".............385.00

Needlework embroidered & painted on silk, depicting classical figures under a portico rendered in various stitchery including chenille, "Miss Rowson's Academy, Hollis Street, Boston, Mass.," ca. 1811, 13¼ x 10¼"......................220.00

NETSUKES

Ivory Cat Netsuke

These are decorative toggles, or fasteners, used by the Japanese to secure a purse or other small personal articles by means of a cord slipped behind the Kimono sash. They are carved of ivory, jade and other materials. There are many reproductions.

Figure of a dancer, inlaid lacquered wood, wearing a Kitsune mask & elaborate robes w/red hair streaming over the back, in gold, red & colored fundame w/ivory inlays, ca. 1900, signed Issai.............$660.00

Figure of Hotei, carved ivory, immortal wearing bordered & stippled robes & carrying a karako within the treasure sack suspended from his neck, ca. 1800, signed Masatomo ...990.00

Figure of a Mongolian archer, carved ivory, wearing typical outfit w/conical hat & holding bow & arrow, early 18th c., unsigned 1,980.00

Figure of Tobosaku, carved ivory, smiling immortal holding a large peach as he balances on one foot, inlaid dark horn eyes, himotoshi deeply carved, 18th c., signed Yohsimasa......................412.00

Group of a dog & puppy, carved ivory, adult seated w/head turned, wearing a cloth collar & protecting the puppy beneath a raised paw, inlaid dark horn eyes, himotoshi naturally formed, 18th c., attributed to Takanobu....................1,430.00

803　OCCUPIED JAPAN

Group of monkey & young, carved
ivory, adult simian seated on its
haunches while subduing a smaller
monkey beneath its paws, each
w/incised hairwork stained to
enhance the details, ca. 1800,
signed Garaku 412.00

Group of Oni disguised as Yama Uba
carrying a child, carved ivory, wearing
a long sleeved coat belted at the
waist & falling open to reveal
his bony chest, holding a long staff
& supporting the child on his
shoulder, unsigned 715.00

Model of a basket, lacquered wood,
ovoid form narrowing toward the foot,
carved overall to simulate wickerwork & lacquered w/a flower sprig
in layers of red & black, 19th c.,
unsigned 275.00

Model of a cat, carved ivory,
climbing over an awabi shell to watch
a venus clam opening up, 18th c.,
unsigned (ILLUS.). 1,045.00

Model of a goat, carved ivory,
resting on folded legs w/its head
turned to the right, face carved
w/an alert expression, horns
turned inward for compactness,
coat formed from thick pleats, large
eyes inlaid in dark horn, ca. 1800,
unsigned. 3,300.00

Model of a mushroom cluster, carved
wood, smooth caps & stems, underside engraved w/numerous gills, 19th c.,
unsigned 495.00

Model of a squirrel, carved & stained
ivory, standing on its hind legs
while resting its forepaws on a
bunch of grapes, large tail raised
above the back, w/inlaid dark
horn eyes, 19th c., signed Ranichi . . .605.00

Boxwood "Tiger" Netsuke

Model of a tiger, carved & stained
boxwood, seated on its haunches
w/head raised & turned slightly
w/tail trailing up the back, well-
etched stripes, ca. 1800, signed
Kokei (ILLUS.). 1,540.00

NUTCRACKERS

Cast Iron Nutcracker

Brass, figural Bill Sykes & Fagin $45.00
Brass, lady's legs, 4½" l. . . . . . .25.00 to 35.00
Brass, model of an alligator, 8½" l. 35.00
Brass, model of a dog on base, 10" l.,
5¼" h., 7" base. 75.00
Bronze, lady's legs, 18th c. 55.00
Bronze, model of a dog on base,
marked "L. A. Althoff & Co." 135.00
Bronze w/"dore" finish, model of a
pheasant, France 93.50
Bronze, model of a squirrel on
branch . . . . .40.00 to 55.00
Cast iron, model of an alligator,
16" l. 100.00
Cast iron, model of a dog, worn
black & yellow repaint over blue,
4 5/8" h. 75.00
Cast iron, model of dog's head. 60.00
Cast iron, model of an elephant,
original paint, ca. 1920, 10 x 5" 69.00
Cast iron, model of a parrot, worn
original polychrome paint, marked
"Novelty Mfg. Co.," 5¾" h. (ILLUS.) . .85.00
Cast iron, model of a St. Bernard
dog 65.00
Cast iron, model of a squirrel
sitting on a leaf. 35.00
Cast iron, vise-type, "Perfection Nut
Cracker Co., Waco, Texas,
patented 1914" 17.50
Nickel-plated steel, model of a dog
on rectangular low footed base,
marked "The L. A. Althoff Mfg. Co.,
Inc., Chicago, Ill.," 5¼" h. 45.00
Wooden, carved model of a sitting
squirrel eating a nut, handle
screws up to crack nut, 7" h. 52.00
Wooden, hand-carved bust of gentle-
man, 9" h. 65.00
Wooden, hand-carved model of a hand
holding a cup, intricate detailing,
7 5/8" l. 105.00

OCCUPIED JAPAN

*American troops occupied the country of
Japan from September 2, 1945 until April*

28, 1952, following World War II. All wares made for export during this period were required to be marked "Made in Occupied Japan." Now these items, mostly small ceramic and metal trifles of varying quality, are sought out by a growing number of collectors.

Occupied Japan Cup & Saucer

Binoculars, metal, embossed Egyptian
   figures $32.00
Character mug, china, Indian Chief
   bust, 2½" h. 35.00
Character mug, china, bust of man
   w/large hat & bow tie, 5" h. 16.00
Cigarette set: 9 x 3½" tray w/pierced
   handles, 4 ash trays, cigarette
   lighter w/pedestal base & scroll
   handles, 2½" h. handled cigarette
   holder; metal, ornate decor, 7 pcs. 45.00
Clock, model of an owl, rolling
   eyes, original box, 11" h. 350.00
Creamer & sugar bowl, china, diamond-
   shaped, floral decor, large, pr. 35.00
Cup & saucer, china, Blue Willow patt. ...35.00
Cup & saucer, china, lustre & coralene
   floral decor (ILLUS.) 22.50
Doll house chair w/seated man,
   porcelain, 2½" h. 8.50
Tea set: cov. teapot, creamer & cov.
   sugar bowl; china, cottage scene
   decor, 3 pcs. 75.00
Tea set, child's, china, floral decor
   on white ground, 24 pcs. 105.00
Toy, windup celluloid boy w/tin
   suitcase 45.00
Toy, windup celluloid dog, tail spins
   & head shakes old shoe 27.50
Toy, windup celluloid lion 32.00
Toy, windup "Crawling Baby," tin,
   body w/celluloid head, arms & legs,
   Kewpie-type, original box 150.00
Toy, windup "Easter on Parade,"
   celluloid rabbit pulling metal sled
   w/basket of chicks, original box 125.00
Whimsey, china, lady's Victorian slippers,
   ornate, pr. 20.00
Wine set: tray & 4 wines; lacquer-
   ware, 5 pcs. 35.00

PAPER COLLECTIBLES

G.A.R. Annual Encampment Broadside

Also see ADVERTISING ITEMS, ALMANACS, AUDUBON PRINTS, AUTOGRAPHS, AUTOMOBILE LITER-ATURE, BASEBALL MEMORABILIA, BIG LITTLE BOOKS, BOOKMARKS, BOY SCOUT COLLECTIBLES, CHILDREN'S BOOKS, COCA-COLA ITEMS, COOKBOOKS, CURRIER & IVES PRINTS, FISHER GIRLS, GREENAWAY COLLECTIBLES, HUM-PHREY ILLUSTRATIONS, ICART PRINTS, KEWPIE COLLECTIBLES, PAPER DOLLS, PARRISH ARTWORK, POSTCARDS, POSTERS, SHAKER COL-LECTIBLES, SHEET MUSIC, SIGNS & SIGNBOARDS, SILHOUETTES, SUN-BONNET BABY COLLECTIBLES, TEDDY BEAR COLLECTIBLES, THEOREMS, TRADE CATALOGUES, VALENTINES, WALLACE NUTTING PRINTS, WORLD FAIR COLLECT-IBLES, YARD LONG PICTURES and ZEPPELIN COLLECTIBLES.

Autograph album, maroon cover
   w/h.p. gold ferns, flowers, birds &
   people in colonial-style dress,
   Illinois, ca. 1885 ....$35.00
Bond, Eclipse Oil Co., 1870s 35.00
Booklet, souvenir, "Coney Island,"
   1904, illustrated, 30 pp., 6½ x 9".....12.50
Broadside, "G.A.R. Annual Encamp-
   ment, Cleveland, Ohio, September
   10-14, 1901," w/Union Pacific
   Railroad excursion information,
   10½ x 28" (ILLUS.) 75.00
Broadside, Indian medicine show,
   "Rolling Thunder Chief Medicine Man
   of the Kiowa Nation is Here Tonight
   with His Medicine & Vaudeville
   Company," small picture of Rolling

Thunder & Mrs. L. B. Newell, the
business manager of the company,
early 20th c., 12 x 4½" 10.00

Brochure, "Palmer House, Chicago,"
1876, w/full page engravings of
hotel exterior & interior, 67 pp. 40.00

Brochure, "San Francisco Hotel
Gazette," 1905, w/timetables, etc.,
96 pp. 20.00

Calendar for 1913, Indian maiden in
feathered headdress, signed E.H.
Clapsaddle 35.00

Calendar for 1924, Navy recruiting
theme, Norman Rockwell 75.00

Calendar for 1943, Betty Grable type
"Petty Girl," 12 x 19" 43.00

Calendar for 1955, each month
w/sketch of "Petty Girl" 75.00

Calligraphic specimen, pen & ink
drawing of a bird in red & black
ink, framed, 9½ x 7½" 55.00

Circus magazine & daily review,
"Barnum & Bailey," 1909, 30 pp.,
7¼ x 9¼". 45.00

City directory, Harrisburg, Pennsylvania, 1887, w/fold-out map of city . . . 35.00

Civil War letters, written by New
Hampshire volunteer to his brother
between 1861 & 1864, stories of
combat, marches, etc., in South
Carolina, set of 40 (most in
envelopes). 440.00

Map of the western territories of
Montana, Idaho & Wyoming, by
Gray, 1873 . . . . 36.00

Menu, "Nantasket Hotel," Boston,
Massachusetts, 1880 . . . . 22.50

Movie program, "Birth of a Nation,"
produced by D. W. Griffith, 1915 . . . . . 50.00

Newspaper, "Daily Mirror," May 8,
1945, w/headline "Nazis Quit War" . . . 5.00

Opera program from Covent Garden,
"Norma," w/Rosa Ponselle, 1929. . . . . . 6.00

Program, "Billy Rose's Aquacade,"
1940 . . . . 13.50

Buffalo Bill's Wild West Show Program

Program, "Buffalo Bill's Wild West"
show, "Historical Sketches &
Programme," chromolithograph
covers, 64 pp., 7¼ x 9¼" (ILLUS.) 75.00

Program, "Chicago Art Institute,
Napoleon Exhibit," 1901 . . . . 10.00

Program, Dedication of Grauman's
Chinese Theater, combined
w/premiere of Cecil B. DeMille's
"King of Kings," 90 pp., 8 x 11". 75.00

Program, "Follies Bergere," 1926 . . . . . . 10.00

Program, football, Army vs. Notre
Dame, 1940, cover by Howard
Chandler Christy. 15.00

Program, "Horse Show, Madison
Square Garden," 1891, 176 pp. 28.00

Program, ice show, "Sonja Henie
Hollywood Ice Review," 1940 . . . . 15.00

Program, "Kentucky Derby," 1936,
history, photographs, past
performances of horses, etc.,
76 pp. 25.00

Program, "National Air Races," Cleve-
land, 1932 . . . . 12.00

Program, "Radio City Music Hall,"
opening night, 1933 . . . . 35.00

Ration book, World War II, w/leather
folder for book & tokens 10.00

Sale bill, "Public Sale of Vermont
Sheep," Salem, Ohio, 1865, old
carved walnut frame, 16¾ x 14¾" . . . 95.00

Social Register, Boston, 1944 . . . . 18.00

Theater program, "This is the Army,"
by Irving Berlin, Special Armed
Forces show, photographs of Irving
Berlin w/soldiers, 1942 . . . . 20.00

U.S. Income Tax Guide Books, 1943 &
1944, 2 pcs. 20.00

PAPER DOLLS

Advertising, "Clark's O.N.T.," Dolls of
All Nations series - Spanish Boy $7.50

Advertising, "Clark's O.N.T.," Wedding
series - Bridesmaid. 8.50

Advertising, "Cream of Wheat,"
Rastus, uncut, in original envelope . . . 75.00

Advertising, "Fidelity Hams," pig
w/one costume, 1901. . . . . 8.00

Advertising, "Hood's Sarsaparilla,"
family, uncut, in original folder 95.00

Advertising, "Lion Coffee," The Miller,
No. 1 . . . . 35.00

Advertising, "McLaughlin's Coffee,"
monkey w/two jackets 15.00

Advertising, "Minard's Liniment," 21"
doll w/two outfits. 150.00

"Alice in Wonderland," uncut book,
Saalfield No. 964, 1934 . . . . 25.00

Betty Grable, uncut book, Whitman
No. 989, 1941 . . . . .75.00
Bobby Butterick, uncut "Delineator"
magazine sheet, 1913 . . . . .20.00
"Children 'Round the World," uncut
book, Merrill, 1955 . . . . .22.00
"Coronation Paper Doll & Coloring
Book," uncut book, Saalfield, 1953 . . .30.00
Deanna Durbin, uncut book, Merrill
No. 4804, 1941 . . . . .175.00
Dennis the Menace, uncut book, Whit-
man No. 1991, 1960 . . . . .12.00 to 16.00
Dinah Shore, uncut book, Whitman
No. 1963, 1958 . . . . .40.00
Dolly Dingle, bridesmaid, uncut
"Pictorial Review" magazine sheet,
1929 . . . . .15.00
Doris Day, uncut book, Whitman No.
2103, 1952 . . . . .40.00
Douglas Fairbanks, uncut "Movy Dols"
sheet, 1920, 8 x 11" 30.00
Faye Emerson, uncut book, Saalfield
No. 2722 . . . . .35.00
"First Ladies of the White House,"
uncut book, Saalfield, 1937 . . . . .45.00
Gale Storm, uncut book, Whitman No.
2089, 1959 . . . . .40.00
Gloria Jean, uncut book, Saalfield No.
1666, 1941 . . . . .50.00
Greer Garson, uncut book, Merrill
No. 4858, 1944 . . . . .62.00
Jane Russell, uncut book, Saalfield
No. 2651, 1955 . . . . .65.00
Janet Leigh, uncut book, Lowe No.
2405, 1957 . . . . .25.00
Jeanette MacDonald, uncut book,
Merrill No. 3460, 1941 . . . . .62.00
Marilyn Monroe, uncut book, Saalfield
No. 1586, 1954 . . . . .75.00
"Mouseketeers," Karen & Cubby,
uncut book, Whitman No. 1974,
1957 . . . . .30.00
Nancy & Her Dolls, uncut book, Saal-
field No. 2478, 1944 . . . . .22.00
Patti Page, uncut book, Lowe No. 1804,
1957 . . . . .25.00
Queen Holden, "All Size Dolls," uncut
book, Whitman No. 982, 1945 . . . . .35.00
Queen Holden, "Baby Sandy of the
Movies," uncut book, Whitman
No. 996, 1940 .25.00
"Quiz Kids," uncut book, Saalfield
No. 2430, 1942 . . . . .70.00
Raggedy Ann & Andy, uncut book,
Saalfield No. 2497, 1944 . . . . .12.00
Shirley Temple, uncut book, Saalfield
No. 1761, 1937 . . . . .68.00
Sonja Henie, uncut book, Merrill No.
3492, 1940 . . . . .45.00
"Style Shop," uncut book, Saalfield,
ca. 1943 . . . . .14.00
Teddy Bear, "Ted E. Bear Goes A
Hunting," uncut magazine sheet,
1909 . . . . .15.00

"Three Little Nixons," uncut "Life"
magazine sheets, 1970, 4 pp. 12.00
Tricia Nixon, uncut book, Saalfield
No. 1248, 1970 . . . . .15.00

Raphael Tuck Paper Doll

Tuck (Raphael), Artistic Series No. 1,
1894 (ILLUS.) .35.00
Tuck (Raphael), "Belle of the South,"
in original folder 80.00
Tuck (Raphael), "Darling Hilda," in
original box 125.00
"Uncle Tom's Cabin," uncut "Boston
Sunday Globe" newspaper sheet,
January 26, 1896 . . . . .24.00
"Wild West," uncut book, McLoughlin
No. 123, ca. 1890, 4 x 5" 6.00

Women's Suffrage Paper Dolls

"Women's Suffrage," Set No. 2, uncut
sheet, Decalco Litho Co. (ILLUS.) 12.00
"Ziegfeld Girl," uncut book, Merrill
No. 3466, 1941 . . . . .125.00

PAPERWEIGHTS

Baccarat "Strawberry" Paperweight

Baccarat, miniature "Pompon" weight, clear w/white flower composed of numerous rows of recessed petals w/yellow stamen center growing from a curved green stalk w/two green leaves & 3 further leaves about the flower, star-cut base, 2" d. $660.00

Baccarat, "Strawberry" weight, clear w/two ripe red fruits growing from green stalks w/numerous shaded green leaves, star-cut base, 2¾" d. (ILLUS.) 3,575.00

Baccarat, sulphide of Winston Churchill, blue ground 300.00

Baccarat, sulphide of Dwight Eisenhower, blue ground 300.00

Baccarat, sulphide of LaFayette, blue ground 75.00

Baccarat, sulphide of Thomas Paine, turquoise ground 250.00

Baccarat, sulphide of Adlai Stevenson, purple overlay....................125.00

Baccarat, sulphide of Woodrow Wilson, yellow overlay, 1972 ....150.00

Bacchus (George), Birmingham, England, "Sodden Snow" millefiori weight, brightly colored assorted canes set deeply into a white "sodden snow" ground within a basket of green staves lined in white & w/green center, 1845-55, 3 1/8" d. 1,430.00

Banford (Bob), faceted "Dragonfly" weight, lacy-winged dragonfly hovering above blue & white flower w/two buds & green foliage, 2½" d. 600.00

Banford (Ray), double overlay weight, 3 shaded pink roses in full bloom growing from entwined green stalks w/numerous green leaves about the flowers, bright red & white overlay cut w/large circular window at the top & 3 rows of circular side printies, star-cut base, 2½" d. 660.00

Clichy, miniature swirl weight, alternating opaque white & cobalt blue threads radiating from a large claret, green, yellow & pink florette, 1 7/8" d. 880.00

Clichy, "Flower" weight, 9 white overlapping petals w/green spots near the pale turquoise & white honeycomb center growing from a straight green stalk w/two green leaves & 3 further leaves about the flower, lush moss green ground, 2 7/8" d. 11,000.00

Cristal d'Albret, sulphide of Christopher Columbus.......................90.00

Cristal d'Albret, sulphide of Paul Revere, grey overlay, 1969 ....150.00

Kaziun (Charles), miniature "Spider Lily" weight on pedestal base, brilliant red lily w/yellow center & 4 slender green leaves set on opaque green ground flecked w/gold, 2" h. 302.50

Mt. Washington "Rose" Paperweight

Mt. Washington Glass Co., "Rose" weight, shaded blue & white mottled petals w/yellow, white & aventurine center, growing from a long green leafy stem w/one yellow & one white bud, the flower set amidst 5 serrated green leaves, 4 1/8" d. (ILLUS.) 19,800.00

New England Glass Co., faceted upright "Bouquet" weight, clear w/central red flower w/white & red cane center & 3 buds in white, cobalt blue & red, w/three millefiori canes in shades of blue, white & red, set amongst numerous green leaf tips on a swirling white latticino basket-type ground, 2 5/8" d................2,420.00

New England Glass Co., "Poinsettia" weight, 10 overlapping deep salmon pink petals about a white cane center growing from a short green stalk w/two serrated green leaves at the base w/three further leaves about the flower, set in a concave white latticino basket, 2¾" d. 605.00

St. Louis, "Clematis" weight, large pink
double clematis blossom w/yellow
cane center growing from a curved
leafy green stalk, within a white
latticino torsade, set on a green
aventurine ground, 3" d. 6,050.00
Stankard (Paul), faceted "Forget-Me-
Not" weight, clear w/five 4-petaled
opaque blue flowers w/clusters of
buds & green leaves growing from
a long green stalk, set on an opaque
white ground, top & sides faceted,
2 3/8" d. .1,320.00
Stankard, "Blackberry Blossom & Bud"
weight, plant in 3 stages of growth
w/small buds at base, 3 fully opened
& 1 half-opened w/stamen at center
& 3 ripe blackberries at the top,
w/variegated green foliage growing
from entwined vines, 1979, 3" d. . .1,045.00
Tarsitano (Delmo), "Cherry" weight,
clear w/three ripe red cherries hanging from yellow stems growing from
brown branches w/numerous shaded
green leaves, 2¾" d. 467.00
Whittemore (Francis), "Bouquet"
weight, clear w/five-petaled blue
clematis w/yellow center, white lily
& yellow spray of blossoms growing
from conjoined stalks w/four green
leaves, set on a translucent pink
ground, 2½" d. 247.00
Ysart (Paul), "Heart" weight, clear
w/blue, green, purple & white
millefiori heart enclosing a tiny
circlet of shaded purple & white
millefiori canes w/a central cane,
row of purple, yellow & white spaced
canes at periphery, set on a translucent cobalt blue ground,
2 7/8" d. .1,100.00

PAPIER MACHE

Papier Mache Candy Containers

*Various objects including decorative
adjuncts were made of papier mache, which
is a substance made of pulped paper mixed
with glue and other materials or layers of
paper glued and pressed and then molded.
Also see CHRISTMAS TREE ORNA-
MENTS.*

Bracelet box, lacquered black
w/mother-of-pearl inlay in the form
of a spray of wild roses, gilt
trim, 4¾ x 3½", 1" h. $195.00
Candy container, figure of a devil,
painted, 3¾" h. 85.00
Candy container, model of a black cat
on a pumpkin, painted, 2½" h. 60.00
Candy container, model of a fish,
painted, 5" l. 80.00
Candy container, model of a seated
Poodle dog, applied fluffy "fur"
covering, glass eyes, Germany,
6" h. 225.00
Candy container, model of a skull,
painted, Germany, 2¼" h. 70.00
Candy containers, models of rabbits
w/removable heads, 8" h. standing
rabbit & 7" l. walking rabbit, pr.
(ILLUS.). 65.00
Figure of a clown Hobo, sack over
his shoulder, big feet, 15" h. 65.00
Figure of Father Christmas, 9" h. 75.00
Match holder, black w/gold figures
& scenes, w/striker, China, 7" l. 30.00
Model of a horse on wooden stand,
Germany, 8½" h. 85.00
Nodding figure, "Happy Hooligan,"
4½" h. 48.00
Nodding figure candy container,
gentleman in top hat & tails,
painted, Germany, 8" h. 90.00
Nodding figure candy container,
musical-type, rabbit playing a
banjo, marked Germany, 13½" h. . .255.00
Nodding figure w/growler, model
of a Bulldog. 350.00
Patch box, inlaid pewter border &
center decor, 1¼ x ¾" rectangle 30.00
Sewing box w/hinged lid, fitted box
w/inlaid mother-of-pearl grapes &
leaves decor & painted flowers &
vines w/ornate gilt edging, signed
Tiffany, Young & Ellis (1848-52),
12½ x 10", 7" h. (minor damage
to 2 feet). .375.00
Snuff box, cov., lid w/colorful transfer
scene of girl w/basket of flowers,
2¾" d. 65.00
Snuff box, cov., crescent-shaped,
inlaid pewter border & center decor,
3" l. 38.00
Snuff box, cov., black lacquer
w/inlaid mother-of-pearl decor
on lid, small. 36.00
Spectacle case, inlaid pewter border
& center decor, 4½ x 1½". 30.00

Papier Mache Tea Caddy

Tea caddy, lacquered black w/mother-of-pearl floral inlay on hinged lid, h.p. design on front, 5 x 5½ x 9" (ILLUS.) 100.00
Toy, "hidden surprise," mouse in loaf of bread, painted, 3½" l. 100.00
Toy, "hidden surprise," frog in shoe, painted, 5" l. 105.00
Tray, h.p. gilt florals on black ground, Regency, early 19th c., 25" l. (on 19" h. bamboo stand of later date) 935.00
Tray, gilt chinoiserie decor on black ground, early 19th c., 32" l. 522.00

PARRISH (Maxfield) ARTWORK

Maxfield Parrish Poster

During the 1920s and 1930s, Maxfield Parrish (1870-1966) was considered the most popular artist-illustrator in the United States. His illustrations graced the covers of the most noted magazines of the day--Scribner's, Century, Life, Harper's, Ladies Home Journal and others. High quality art

prints, copies of his original paintings usually in a range of sizes, graced the walls of homes and offices across the country. Today all Maxfield Parrish artwork, including magazine covers, advertisements and calendar art, is considered collectible but it is the fine art prints that command the most attention.

Book, "Dream Days," by Kenneth Grahame, illustrated by Maxfield Parrish, 1898 .... $60.00
Book, "The Golden Age," by Kenneth Grahame, illustrated by Maxfield Parrish, 1899 .... 65.00
Book, "Italian Villas & Their Gardens," by Edith Wharton, illustrated by Maxfield Parrish, 1904 .... 105.00
Book, "Knickerbocker's History of New York," by Washington Irving, illustrated by Maxfield Parrish, 1900 .... 175.00
Book, "Poems of Childhood," by Eugene Field, illustrated by Maxfield Parrish, 1904 .... 65.00 to 80.00
Book, "A Wonderbook of Tanglewood Tales," by Nathaniel Hawthorne, illustrated by Maxfield Parrish, 1910 .... 75.00 to 90.00
Calendar, 1928, for Edison-Mazda, entitled "Contentment" 600.00
Calendar, 1931, for Edison-Mazda, entitled "The Waterfall," 18½ x 38½" 535.00
Calendar, 1932, for Edison-Mazda, entitled "Solitude" .... 175.00 to 350.00
Calendar, 1936, for Brown & Bigelow Publishing Co., entitled "Peaceful Valley," 18½ x 13½" 125.00
Calendar, 1940, for Brown & Bigelow Publishing Co., winter landscape scene entitled "Silent Night" 145.00
Calendar, 1949, for Brown & Bigelow Publishing Co., entitled "The Village Church," overall 22 x 16" 195.00
Candy box, "Crane's Chocolates," illustration entitled "Garden of Allah" on cover 225.00
Christmas cards, for Clark-Wells Metals Co., St. Louis, Missouri, entitled "Sunup" & "At Close of Day," 4¾ x 6¼", each .... 15.00 to 20.00
Magazine cover, "Collier's," November 30, 1907 .... 45.00
Magazine cover, "Collier's," March 20, 1909 .... 20.00
Magazine cover, "Ladies Home Journal," January, 1931, skier 25.00
Magazine cover, San Francisco Call, June 29, 1913, "Independence Day" 200.00
Playing cards, for Edison-Mazda, entitled "Reveries," w/original box .. 95.00
Poster, "Pennsylvania Academy of the Fine Arts, Philadelphia, Poster

Show," lithograph on paper, w/two
young ladies carrying programs,
in shades of brown, ochre, ivory &
black, framed, 24" w.,
34" h. (ILLUS.).................4,950.00
Print, "Air Castles," 17 x 13"..........75.00
Print, "The Black Prince," framed,
14 x 17".........................40.00
Print, "Cassim in the Cave of the
Forty Thieves," 1905, Collier's
Publishing Co., 13 x 18"............65.00
Print, "Cleopatra," large, original
frame..................750.00 to 800.00
Print, "Dawn," 32 x 20".............150.00
Print, "Daybreak," original frame,
10 x 18"..........................85.00
Print, "Dinkey Bird," original frame,
16 x 12".........................90.00
Print, "Garden of Allah," 1918, framed,
9 x 17"..........................80.00
Print, "Hilltop," medium 235.00
Print, "Interlude," original frame,
18 x 30".........................170.00
Print, "The Knave," 10 x 12" 85.00
Print, "Lute Players," 12 x 18".........95.00
Print, "Night Has Fled," small........150.00
Print, "Peace at Twilight," 8 x 11".....70.00
Print, "Prince Codadad," 9 x 11" 70.00
Print, "Reveries," large 290.00
Print, "Romance," 16½ x 26" 195.00
Print, "Rubaiyat," original frame,
8 x 30"..........................265.00
Print, "Stars," framed, 7 x 11" 105.00
Print, "Sunrise," framed, 12 x 16" 40.00
Print, "Twilight," 1937, small 70.00
Print, "Under Summer Skies,"
18 x 15½"........................70.00

PATCH BOXES

Staffordshire Enamel Patch Boxes

Enamel on copper, 2 boxes w/bust
portraits of Lord Nelson, one inscribed
"Nelson and Victory" & the other

"May all British Admirals Prove a
Nelson," the third box w/a bust
portrait of Wellington & inscribed
"The Most Noble Marquis Wellington,
Salamanca," Staffordshire, early
19th c., 1 5/8" to 2 1/8" l., 3 pcs.
(ILLUS.) $1,100.00
Glass, clear w/enameled green 4-leaf
clover on hinged lid, mirror inside,
1 3/8" d.......................125.00
Glass, clear w/enameled bluebirds on
hinged lid, 1 7/8" d............120.00
Glass, cobalt blue w/overall yellow
scrollwork decor, 2" d., 1¼" h. 85.00
Glass, cranberry w/enameled decor
on hinged lid, 2" d..............110.00
Glass, cranberry w/overall enameled
floral decor 175.00
Glass, lime green w/overall gold
leaves & foliage decor, 2¼" d.,
1¼" h. 85.00
Glass, Mary Gregory type, cobalt blue
w/white enameled boy on hinged
lid, white dots around sides, 2" d.,
1 1/8" h. 170.00
Glass, Mary Gregory type, cranberry
w/white enameled boy, 1¾" d......175.00
Glass, Mary Gregory type, golden
amber w/white enameled girl, 2" d.,
1 1/8" h. 150.00
Glass, Mary Gregory type, lime green
w/white enameled boy on hinged
lid, 2¼" d., 1" h...............165.00
Glass, sapphire blue w/enameled
white daisy & leaves decor, 2" d.,
1" h. 95.00
Glass, sapphire blue w/overall gold
stars centering a brown & white
owl, 2" d., 1¼" h................95.00
Ivory & gold, braid of hair under glass
in center of cover, rose gold inlay
& fittings, 3½" oval 275.00

PHONOGRAPHS

Berliner Trade-Mark Gramophone. .$2,100.00
Busy Bee, disc model 450.00
Columbia Model A Graphophone,
w/original horn 350.00
Columbia Model AT Graphophone,
w/original horn & crane 285.00
Columbia Model BI Disc Graphophone,
w/large oak horn 1,600.00
Edison Amberola Model 30, table
model 300.00
Edison Amberola Model 50, table
model 355.00
Edison Fireside Model B, w/cygnet
horn & crane 535.00

Edison Gem Model, w/original horn,
  oak case 445.00
Edison Home Model F, w/No. 10
  cygnet horn 750.00

Edison Standard Model

Edison Standard Model A, oak
  suitcase model w/decal banners
  (ILLUS.) 510.00
Edison Standard Model H, w/brass bell
  horn & cast iron crane, oak case 425.00
Edison Triumph Model, w/brass bell
  horn & chromed crane 625.00
Edison Triumph Model, w/oak
  horn 1,600.00
Mikiphone, folds to fit into 4½" d.
  nickel-plated case, Switzerland,
  1920s 150.00
Perophone (Vernon Lockwood Mfg.
  Co., London), w/black horn 350.00
Thorens, portable, brown leather case
  resembling folding camera, Switzer-
  land 115.00
Victor Model I, oak case & small oak
  horn 1,500.00
Victor Model II, w/brass bell horn 750.00
Victor Model II, w/oak horn 1,225.00
Victor Model III, w/oak horn 1,500.00
Victor Model IV, w/mahogany case &
  morning glory horn 1,000.00
Victor Model V, w/wooden horn 1,175.00
Victor Monarch Senior, ornate oak
  case, brass bell horn 850.00

PHOTOGRAPHIC ITEMS

Also see SCRAPBOOKS & ALBUMS.

Albumen print, railroad station (Winchester, Massachusetts), w/people,
  Western Union Telegraph office,
  buildings & trade signs, 1870s,
  11 x 16¼" $75.00
Albumen prints, "Beauvoir," home of

Jefferson Davis, matted & framed,
  8 x 6", set of 3 . . . . 55.00
Ambrotype, ninth plate, young lady
  wearing off-the-shoulder dress &
  ornate jewelry, w/case 25.00
Ambrotype, sixth plate, "The Blind
  Beggar," in thermoplastic case 125.00
Ambrotype, sixth plate, Civil War
  soldier w/saber, wearing long jacket
  & visored cap 145.00
Ambrotype, sixth plate, Civil War
  Union soldier, in thermoplastic case
  w/chain & buckle design 125.00
Ambrotype, half plate, young girl, in
  thermoplastic frame 110.00
Book, "Photographic Optics," by R.S.
  Cole, 1899, 330 pp. 20.00
Cabinet photograph, "Capt. Bogardus &
  Sons, World Champion Shooters" 50.00
Cabinet photograph, Ferris Wheel at
  Columbian Exposition, 1893 . . . . 25.00
Camera, Ansco Jr. No. 1, folding-type,
  original box & instructions, 1912 . . . . . 35.00
Camera, Century, folding-type,
  4 x 5" 150.00
Camera, Eastman Kodak Panoram No.
  4, 1899 . . . . 85.00
Camera, Eastman Kodak Quick Focus
  Model 3-B, 1906 . . . . 115.00
Camera, Korona II, 4 x 5" 95.00
Camera, Mentor Reflex, 1920s 95.00
Camera, Steineck ABC wristwatch,
  original case, 1948 . . . . 500.00
Camera, Voightlander w/Compur
  shutter, folding-type, w/case 100.00
Camera set, Wollensak Optical Co.,
  Jr. Model camera, black throw cloth,
  film holders & original case 125.00
Carte de visite, Golden Spike
  Ceremony, Promontory Point,
  1869 . . . . 300.00
Carte de visite, Jefferson Davis,
  1860s 65.00
Carte de visite, Robert E. Lee, by
  Vannerson, published by Fredericks,
  1864 . . . . 135.00
Carte de visite, Sudley Ford & Church,
  Battle of Bull Run, by Brady, 1860s 50.00
Carte de visite, Wild Bill Hickok,
  1870s 125.00
Daguerreotype, ninth plate, image of
  post-mortem baby 65.00
Daguerreotype, sixth plate, image of
  naval officer in dress uniform,
  w/case 375.00
Daguerreotype, sixth plate, image of
  post-mortem young girl holding
  china doll 225.00
Daguerreotype, sixth plate, image of
  Sir Henry Havelock, in thermoplastic
  case, ca. 1850 . . . . 120.00
Daguerreotype, sixth plate, image of
  well-dressed young lady, w/case
  (ILLUS.) 47.00

Daguerreotype in Case

Daguerreotypes, sixth plate, image of
 young girl standing in front of table
 w/china doll in cradle & image of
 pert young girl seated in chair
 holding china doll, pr. 375.00
Daguerreotype, whole plate, Niagara
 Falls scene, in leather case 1,100.00
Daguerreotype case, thermoplastic,
 faithful hound design, 4-part,
 37/8 x 6¼" 210.00
Daguerreotype case, thermoplastic,
 Fruits of Harvest patt., 1 7/8 x
 2 1/8" oval 50.00
Daguerreotype case, thermoplastic,
 intricate floral design, embossed
 gilded brass liner, 2¼ x 3" 25.00
Daguerreotype lens, brass 300.00

Kodak Darkroom Lantern

Darkroom lantern, tin, Kodak (ILLUS.) . .30.00
Darkroom photograph enlarger
 w/bellows, wooden frame, Elwood . .30.00
Graphoscope (viewing device that
 provides a magnified image of a
 transparent photograph), mother-of-
 pearl inlaid scene of fish & water
 lilies 450.00
Photograph, Admiral Richard Byrd's
 expedition ship, signed by radio
 engineer, 8 x 10" 100.00

Photograph, cigar factory, Galena,
 Illinois, 1890s. 15.00
Photograph, Civil War soldier & lady,
 16 x 18". 59.00
Photograph, "Sutter's Fort,
 Sacramento," Sept. 9, 1895, 8 x 5" 20.00
Photograph, U.S. Army Officers'
 Missouri Rifle Team, 1889, oak
 frame, 16 x 20" 100.00
Post-mortem photograph, child in
 casket in family home parlor, ornate
 brass frame w/convex glass,
 14 x 24". 130.00
Tintype, sixth plate, butchers (2)
 w/implements 14.00
Tintype, sixth plate, card players,
 w/case 30.00
Tintype, half plate, Civil War Union
 soldier wearing infantryman's frock
 coat, bummer's cap, leather
 accoutrements & holding a Model
 1861 rifle musket, New York,
 unmounted 132.50
Tintype, half plate, horse & buggy 18.00
Tintype, Connecticut Volunteer w/rifle,
 back pack, bedroll, etc. 185.00
Tintype, hunter w/Kentucky rifle,
 powder horn around his neck 50.00

PIN CUSHION DOLLS

Assorted Pin Cushion Dolls

*These china half figures were never
intended to use as dolls, but rather to serve
as ornamental tops to their functional pin
cushion bases which were discreetly covered
with silk and lace skirts. They were produced in a wide variety of forms and
quality, all of which are now deemed collectible, and were especially popular during
the first quarter of this century.*

Bisque half figure of a nude lady w/out-
 stretched arms, mohair wig,
 3½" h. $135.00

Bisque half figure of a nude lady
w/arms extended, grey hair
w/applied pink & yellow roses &
green leaves, 3" d., 4¾" h.........200.00

China half figure of a Colonial lady
w/one hand extended & other hand
on bosom, pompadour-styled grey
hair held in place w/blue ribbon,
pink cushion base, 4" h. 75.00

China half figure of a "flapper"
w/arms extended, black hair, tan
palette-shaped hat & green blouse
w/tan wrist bands, 2½" d., 4¼" h. . .300.00

China half figure of a "flapper" w/red
ribbon in her black hair, red cushion
trimmed w/lace, impressed
"Germany," 7" h. 85.00

China half figure of a girl w/green
bonnet & tie, impressed "Germany
8038," 3¾" h. 50.00

China half figure of Jenny Lind,
marked "Munzer, 1926, Patented,"
Germany (mold attributed to
Goebel), 3½" h. 95.00

China half figure of lady in 18th c.
costume w/arms extended, white
hair, Schneider mark, impressed
"Germany, 13944," 4" h. 98.00

China half figure of a lady wearing
a plumed hat, arms extended from
body & holding a fan in one hand,
Goebel Crown mark, 4½" h. 235.00

China half figure of a lady w/arms
extended from body & holding a rose
in one hand, 4½" h. 165.00

China half figure of a lady w/grey
hair, arms extended from body &
holding a bouquet of flowers in one
hand, 4¾" h. 195.00

China, half figure of lady w/hands
away from body, wearing a
crocheted dress, blonde hair, 5" h. . . .75.00

China half figure of a lady w/arms
away from body, curling plumes in
her hair, red eye liner, 5" h. 125.00

China half figure of a lady seated
w/arms extended from body &
holding a rose in one hand, dusty
rose colored satin dress, china legs,
4½" d., 5¼" h. 125.00

China half figure of a lady w/yellow
ribbon in her hair, one hand on
bosom & other hand at waist,
Germany, 6" h. 65.00

China half figure of a little girl holding
a red ball in one hand, light brown
hair partially covered by a blue
bonnet trimmed w/red bows,
impressed "57.08," 3½" h. 48.00

China half figure of Pierrette seated on
a powder puff, original box, France . .95.00

PIPES

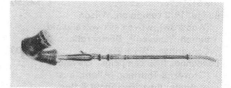

Briar Root Pipe

Briar root, carved w/bust of George
Washington, amber stem $475.00
Briar root, w/silverplate bowl cover,
30" l. (ILLUS.) 125.00
Meerschaum, carved w/horse on bowl,
amber stem, original case, 3¾" l.....75.00
Meerschaum, carved bareheaded black
man's head as bowl, amber stem,
9k gold fittings, late 19th c., 6" l. 198.00
Meerschaum, carved lion's head as
bowl, amber stem, 6½" l...........95.00
Meerschaum, carved w/nude lady on
bowl, amber stem, 8½" l..........150.00
Meerschaum, carved as a ball held in
the outstretched hands of a lepre-
chaun, amber stem, fitted case 110.00
Meerschaum, carved Elizabethan lady
w/ornate hat as bowl, amber stem . .150.00
Meerschaum, carved Turk's head as
bowl, amber stem ....95.00 to 130.00
Rosewood, hand-carved w/stag on
bowl 100.00
Wooden w/sterling silver overlay,
scene of dogs & trees on bowl 40.00
Wooden w/sterling silver overlay,
scene of jockeys racing horses on
bowl 85.00

POLITICAL & CAMPAIGN ITEMS

Theodore Roosevelt Pocket Knife

Arm band, 1932 campaign, Roosevelt
(Franklin D.), "Repeal & Roosevelt,"
blue machine-stitched lettering on

red felt, framed, overall 18¼
x 5¼" $47.50

Badge, 1912 campaign, Wilson
(Woodrow), woven silk w/celluloid
button, "Souvenir, Democratic
Convention," 9½ x 2¼" 35.00

Bandanna, 1888 campaign, Cleveland
(Grover) & Thurman (Allan), bust
portraits, American Eagle & flag,
crossed pennants each corner, red,
black & white, framed, 29½ x 26" ...160.00

Button, jugate, 1884 campaign,
Cleveland (Grover) & Hendricks
(Thomas), brass 32.00

Button, jugate, 1896 campaign,
McKinley (William B.) & Hobart
(Garret A.).......................55.00

Button, jugate, 1900 campaign,
McKinley (William B.) & Roosevelt
(Theodore).......................45.00

Button, jugate, 1904 campaign, Debs
(Eugene V.) & Hanford (Ben-
jamin) ....125.00 to 150.00

Flag banner, 1884 campaign, Cleveland
(Grover), oval bust portrait center
within starred border, red, blue,
brown & white, framed, 29¾ x 27" ..300.00

Flag banner, 1892 campaign, Harrison
(Benjamin), silk, bust portrait &
"1892" superimposed on flag, red,
white & blue, framed, 13¾ x 10¼" ..235.00

Knife, pocket-type, 1920 campaign,
Harding (Warren G.), embossed bust
portrait & "Warren Harding President
of U.S.A." on handle 65.00

Knife, pocket-type, Roosevelt (Theodore), bust portrait center w/eagle
above & flag below, gold finish metal
w/magnetic steel blades, Germany,
3" l. (ILLUS.) 75.00

Lapel pin, 1920 campaign, Cox (James
M), rooster-shaped 90.00

Lapel pin, 1928 campaign, Hoover
(Herbert), figural elephant, green
enamel w/gold outline 55.00

Lapel pin, 1940 campaign, Willkie
(Wendell), figural elephant, brass....10.00

Franklin D. Roosevelt Mug

Mug, Roosevelt (Franklin D.), mustard
yellow glazed pottery, embossed
bust portrait in shield & "The New
Deal," 4" h. (ILLUS.) 20.00

Necktie, 1948 campaign, Dewey
(Thomas E.), bust portrait & White
House scene 22.00

Plate, 1896 campaign, McKinley
(William), china, bust portrait on
white ground w/gold trim, 8" d. 20.00

McKinley Portrait Plate

Plate, 1900 campaign, McKinley
(William B.), milk white glass
w/black & white laminated photograph on purple ground w/gold
border, 8½" d. (ILLUS.) 45.00

Poster, 1916 campaign, Wilson
(Woodrow), "Wilson Fights for
America & Humanity," w/portraits
of Wilson, Washington & Lincoln,
framed, 20 x 18" 90.00

Puzzle, "Playing Possum with Taft,"
lithographed paper on wood,
original box......................79.50

Ribbon, 1836 campaign, Harrison
(William H.), "Tippicanoe Club" 100.00

Stickpin, 1868 campaign, Grant
(Ulysses S.), ferrotype in brass
frame 32.00

Toby jug, 1928 campaign, Hoover
(Herbert), Gold Medal China Co.,
7" h. 55.00

Token, 1840 campaign, Harrison
(William H.), "The People's Choice" ..52.00

Umbrella, 1896 campaign, McKinley
(William) & Hobart (Garret A.), red,
white & blue panels 525.00

Watch fob, 1916 campaign, Wilson
(Woodrow), celluloid, disc-type,
Wilson pictured & "Woodrow Wilson
for President," red, white & blue,
1½" d., 5½" l.....................45.00

ADVERTISING POSTCARDS

by Sally S. Carver

The use of advertising on old postcards presents a telling view into American life during the first two decades of this century. No other category of postcards so accurately allows us to examine the fascination which the postcard held, and still holds today for collectors. Before the advent of television and radio commercials, the postcard presented a major advertising force through which thousands of products were paraded and sold. This topical chronicled the spectrum of everyday living and was unparalleled in its influence in many diverse areas of life. It would not be wrong to state that the advertising postcard of the early 1900s was a form of *media.*

The advertising postcard first appeared in the late decades of the nineteenth century printed on government postals and replaced the non-mailable trade card. A line drawing, a vignette, a full size picture or a small logo was enough to qualify as an advertising card as long as the product was prominently pictured or mentioned on the *front* of the card. (In postcards, we refer to the address side as the back). Unfortunately these early cards are often overlooked by the postcard collector while prized by the postal historian.

Collectors will find cards advertising almost every conceivable consumer product or service. One could choose to be a general collector or a specialist in one specific area. One might also wish to use the advertising postcard as a *cross-over* item with another type of collectible. For example, the collector of Sleepy Eye Flour material will be pleased that there is a set of nine postcards devoted to this food product. Along this same line, many popular artists were known for their contributions to the advertising postcard. The Campbell Kids, well-known as the purveyors of their famous products, need not have the name of their creator *Grace Weiderseim Drayton* signed on the card. The pictures of the dimpled children were signature enough!

Artist *Richard Felton Outcault* used the characters of Buster Brown, Mary Jane and Tige not only to advertise shoes but to illustrate so-called calendar postcards, which showed a scene and a monthly calendar with the name of the store, imprinted independently by the owner, thus creating a popular means of private advertising. Many of the early Expositions produced a goodly amount of postcards that advertised a large variety of products ranging from shoes to cigarettes. Because so many people attended these splendid fairs, they became an obvious means of advertising one's wares and, since most people enjoyed sending a "Wish You Were Here...." postcard home, the advertisements became widespread.

Food and drinks that are still popular today can be found on postcards from the early years of this century. Schlitz Beer, Coca-Cola, Hires Root Beer, Domino Sugar, many Heinz products, and even Cracker Jacks are good examples of foods that have endured the passing of time.

Clothing, like food, was a perfect product to illustrate on the postcard. Many of the names are still familiar today. Fabrics, furs, shoes, hosiery, galoshes, and corsets were popular advertising items. The *Walkover Shoe Company* produced an interesting group of twelve different series, depicting everything from famous people and literary scenes to nursery rhymes. Their most common set features illustrations of the Puritan traditions and is the one which most collectors equate with Walkover.

The telephone and its many uses had to be "sold" to the public in the early years of this century. It was often pictured as a convenient method of calling the butcher, contacting the doctor, finding a plumber or hurriedly reaching the fire department in an emergency. The use of the picture postcard proved more convincing than the written word. The Bell Telephone Company produced an important series showing the uses and needs of the telephone. This series is an important indication that advertising served a useful purpose.

The automobile which was both a source of laughter and questioning interest when it was first marketed, proved to be the subject of many, different cards. Not only was the early auto advertised, but also tires, gasoline, motor oil, brakes and even trade journals are found on postcards. The bicycle was also an important means of transportation and several series of cards were issued illustrating this method of mobility.

If one still wanted "safety," the horse was always available, and advertisers ranged from blacksmiths to those selling blankets to keep the animals warm. One of the most popular series was known as the "*5-A Horse Blanket*," which consisted of thirteen cards showing how to keep the horse and/or rider warm. Unfortunately the printing process used in this series was vastly inferior to the product, and although it was and still is one of the most popular sets, the pictures often tend to be fuzzy, while the name of the product is always clear and did not leave anyone with doubt!

Railroad lines and steamship companies used the postcard to great advantage, producing cards showing both the exteriors of trains and ships and the luxuries and comforts of their interiors, as well as the practicality of using such means of transportation. Sometimes the final destination of the journey (rather than the means) provided the subject of the advertisement. Popular artist *Rose O'Neill* with whom we associate the Kewpie doll, was the person responsible for a series of cards put out for the Rock Island Railroad showing beach and mountain scenes. These cards are found as line drawings on sepia cards and are sometimes in color. There are no *Kewpies* on the cards, but the cherubic faces of the children (sometimes with a well-hidden signature) are unmistakably the work of O'Neill.

The important area of farming and agricultural equipment provided another area which reflects the time period of the advertisement. From plows to seed catalogues, this is certainly a major category. It is interesting to note that people yesterday were no less conscious of their appearances and health than we are today. Beauty aids and medicines can be broken down into several sections. Cards advertising men's toupees, as well as lotions and creams, are to be found along with toothpastes, soaps and the ever-popular Lydia Pinkham compounds.

Home furnishings is a category with many subdivisions. At a time when new appliances such as electric and gas stoves and washing machines appeared on advertising postcards, they were becoming more than simply "fashionable" items; they were necessities. Carpeting, wallpaper, fences, paints, and sewing machines represented some of the household products which were popular advertising items. In this section, we might also include the postcards featuring store interiors with rooms of furniture. These store cards served a dual purpose as they not only advertised the seller (the store) but also the product -- in this case, furniture.

One intriguing group of postcards dealt with theatrical productions, the new and very popular motion pictures, books, magazines, and even song sheets. This entire area which might be classified under "Entertainment" would, in itself, be enough to make up a large collection. Of particular interest in this category are those cards which are brightly colored and have a poster-like appearance along with the "song" cards which showed a replica of an actual song sheet cover. Collectors of sheet music might wish to enhance their collections by adding these postcards again proving that the cards can be used as *cross-overs*.

It is important to mention that beer and breweriana, as well as the hard liquor companies, issued enough cards to fill a large album. This is an especially popular topical and many of the cards are highly collectible. Again, we often find these cards to be of the poster-style. In a related category are advertisements for tobacco products that ranged from cigars and cigarettes to the tobacco itself.

If one wished to publicize a product or a service, it was pictured on a postcard. Prices tend to fluctuate greatly with both poster-style and scarcity creating the higher prices. However, one should realize that many cards can be found in the below $10.00 range. It is also important to stress that although several sets and series were issued, the major portion of advertising postcards were published as individual cards. So far no checklist has been published and, judging from the vast amount of cards that were published privately, it can be assumed that no checklist can ever be considered complete. The field is extensive enough so that there is enough material to please even the most eclectic tastes.

The promotion of these cards does not end in 1925. It continues even today with the chrome cards of restaurants, hotels, and especially automobiles. These cards can be picked up at very reasonable prices, often less than $1.00.

Finally, it is recommended that new collectors stay with the American material since one is usually not that familiar with the European market where the prices seem to fluctuate rapidly. The American advertising postcard provides a rich and virtually inexhaustible field to be explored. It posesses great variety while lacking the vastness of the European market, so begin with the U.S. cards before collecting other countries. There is enough material to be found here to please almost all collectors.

(Editor's Note: *Sally S. Carver, one of the country's foremost authorities on postcards, is a collector, dealer, columnist, and author who specializes in postcards. Her book,* The American Postcard Guide To Tuck, *now in its fifth printing, is the largest selling book devoted to postcards of all time. For details you may write Sally Carver at 179 South St., Chestnut Hill, Massachusetts 02167.*)

*   *   *   *   *

All evaluations for postcards listed below are for cards in perfect condition whether used or unused. All creases, tears, bends, scuffs or cancel marks will reduce the price accordingly. Any number in parenthesis such as (12) indicates the number of cards known to be in a set. Those cards without parenthesis can be considered to be one of a kind whether issued by a known publisher or a private printing. All prices are for individual cards whether in a set or not.

PRODUCTS

BEVERAGES

BEER:

Conrad-Seipp Brewing Company

Anheuser-Busch - series of 5 western
  scenes $15.00
Anheuser-Busch - black & white views
  of brewery interiors 8.00
Conrad-Seipp Brewing Company
  (ILLUS.)..........................30.00
Falstaff Beer - photo card showing bar-
  maid rising from beer stein..........17.50
Feigenspan Bock Beer - children in
  goat-drawn carriage 15.00
Schlitz - young girl carrying beer bottle
  on tray 25.00

SOFT DRINKS:

Cherry Smash - Mt. Vernon lawn
  scene 15.00
Cherry Smash - bust of George Washington. Very scarce 125.00
Coca-Cola - signed by illustrator

Hamilton King. Considered rare
  when found in perfect condition 350.00
Dr. Swett's Root Beer - Nursery Rhyme
  series (6) 10.00
Hires Root Beer - picture of lovely
  woman, "Alice." Copyr. 1912 ....6.00
Moxie - series of at least 4 cards with
  blank backs 45.00

COFFEE AND TEA:

White House Teas

Chase and Sanborn Salesman's Calling
  Card - 1899........................17.50
Formosa Oolong Tea - Japanese scenes
  and/or costumes 4.00
Lipton Teas and Coffees - scenes
  showing production 7.50
Turkey Coffee - Uncle Sam sipping
  from cup..........................18.00
White House Teas - young girls at tea
  party (ILLUS.).....................12.00

FOOD

FOOD, CANDY, CEREALS ETC.

Best Flour

Allentown Adpostals - showing several
  products on Government postal
  (7)........................25.00 to 40.00
Beech-Nut - little boys seated at table.
  Embossed card 15.00
Beech-Nut - interior of plant, Canajo-
  harie, N.Y. (6) 4.00
Best Flour - woman baking (ILLUS.) 7.50
Bulte's Best Flour - children baking (6) ..15.00
Campbell Soup - horizontal series
  (ILLUS.)..........................20.00

Campbell's Soup

Campbell Soup - vertical series, shows
   Campbell Kids as above 25.00
Cracker Jack Bears - given as
   premiums in Cracker Jack boxes
   (16) 18.00
Daniel Webster Bread - baby & loaf of
   bread 7.00
Egg-O-See Cereal - child at table. Very
   common 3.50
Fralinger Salt Water Taffy - signed by
   artist F. Burd (24) 10.00
Gold Medal Flour - woman feeding pie
   to tramp 10.00
Heinz Products - early Atlantic City
   series 7.50

H.J. Heinz Pittsburg Company

Heinz Products - Pittsburg plant
   interiors (ILLUS.)...................7.50
Heinz Products - female factory
   workers 10.00
Hershey Chocolate Company - numer-
   ous black & white scenes on narrow
   cards. Common....................3.00
Horn and Hardart Baking Company -
   shows interiors of Automat in New
   York 6.00
Kellogg's Corn Flakes - smaller cards
   approx. 3 x 5" (8) 7.50
Korn Kinks - black girl on stilts. Orange
   & brown colors. Common 3.50
Nabisco Biscuits - boy in yellow slicker..12.00
Nestles Food (for babies) - stork in
   nest of infants. Copyr. 1910 ....12.00
Postum Cereal - Battle Creek, Mich.
   interior/exterior of factory scenes 5.00
Quaker Puffed Rice 10.00
Red Cross Brand - woman & cow in
   field 12.50

Shredded Wheat - bowl of cereal &
   strawberries 15.00

Shuyler's Candy

Shuyler's Candy - Santa Claus scene
   (ILLUS.).........................12.00
Shuyler's Candy - other scenes.........7.50
Sleepy Eye Flour - Indian series (9) 40.00
Swift's Premium - 4 series of 6 cards
   each showing children..............6.00
Velvet Candy Kisses................10.00

TOBACCO:

Happy Thought Chewing Tobacco

Bull Durham Smoking Tobacco - series
   of different countries (33) 30.00
Daniel Webster Cigars - series (6) 6.00
Happy Thought Chewing Tobacco -
   cartoon scenes (ILLUS.) 15.00
Mecca Cigarettes 10.00
Mogul Cigarettes - black & white
   scenes from 1904 St. Louis World's
   Fair (25) 3.50

CLOTHING & SHOES

WEARING APPAREL:

Bear Brand Hosiery

Bear Brand Hosiery (ILLUS.) 7.50
Buster Brown Shoes 9.00
College Brand Clothes - drawings of
   college men (4) .12.00
Hart Schaffner & Marx (Copyr.) -
   historical scenes by artist Edward
   Penfield (10) 8.00
Humpty-Dumpty Stockings - nursery
   rhyme characters 10.00
Kuppenheimer & Company - men's &
   women's fashions 7.50
Minneapolis Knitting Works - nursery
   rhyme characters (6) 10.00
Patrick-Duluth Woolen Mills - scenes by
   artist Peter Newell (4) 10.00
Walkover Shoes - 12 different series
   of 8-24 cards. The most common
   scenes depict Puritans. All cards
   carry only Walkover logo 3.50
Walkover Shoes - other than Puritan
   scenes mentioned above . . . . .7.00 to 10.00

Woonsocket Rubber Company

Woonsocket Rubber Company - man
   rowing in rubber-shaped boat
   (ILLUS.) 9.00
Woonsocket Rubber Company - "Foot-
   wear of Nations" colorful series of 10..7.00

PERSONAL ACCESSORIES & HEALTH AIDS

CLEANSERS:

Buchanan Soap

Buchanan Soap - little girl & bear (6)
   (ILLUS.) 20.00
Gold Dust Twins Washing Powder (4).
   Polishing globe 25.00
La France Soap - 6 historical scenes
   of Revolutionary times 5.00
Swifts Pride Soap - various
   series .6.00 to 10.00

Wyandotte Cleanser - Indian motifs 15.00

PATENT MEDICINE AND HEALTH AIDS:

Burrill's Tooth Powder

Bromo-Seltzer - black & white view of
   horse-drawn wagon 15.00
Burrill's Tooth Powder (ILLUS.) 6.00

Frog In Your Throat Lozenges

Frog In Your Throat Lozenges (10).
   Scarce (ILLUS.) 25.00
Frog In Your Throat Lozenges (12) 25.00
Lydia Pinkham Compounds - college
   series. Fairly common (12) 5.00
Mentholatum Salve 8.00
Patent Toupee and Wigs - for men 12.00
Sanitol Tooth Powder - lovely smiling
   woman 5.00

MISCELLANEOUS ACCESSORIES:
American Thermos Bottle Company -
   pictures utilizing product (10) 20.00
Elgin Watches - scenes with children 7.50

Ives Toys

Ives Toys - boy playing with toy trains
   (ILLUS.) 10.00
"Red Pig" Household Knives - large pig
   & cutlery. Scarce (10) 15.00
Rockford Watches - calendar cards by

artist Richard Outcault (12). Different
card for each month 12.00
Teddy Go-Cars - large bear & baby
carriage 12.00

FARM & HOME-RELATED ITEMS

HOME FURNISHINGS:

Furniture Store Calendar by Outcault

Free Sewing Machine (The) - scene
with mother & baby 7.00
Fuller Floor Wax - people dancing on
waxed floor 5.00
Furniture Store - private advertising
imprinted on calendar card by
Outcault (ILLUS.) 12.00
Grand Rapids Furniture - 18 different
showing refrigerator, stove, etc. 7.50
Hartford Carpet Company - shows
Indian against vivid carpet. Also
advertises 1909 Alaska-Yukon Expo-
sition 4.00

Herrick Refrigerator Company

Herrick Refrigerator Company
(ILLUS.) 10.00
Jones Sewing Machine 8.00
Lindsay Gas Lights - woman & gas
fixtures 7.00
Maxwell Wallpaper - differently
decorated rooms. Series of 8 . . . . 4.00
Round Oak Stoves - Indian scenes
showing months of year 8.00
Singer Sewing Machine - several
different issues . . . . 6.00 to 9.00
Westinghouse Electric Iron (ILLUS.) 10.00

Westinghouse Electric Iron

FARM & HOME NECESSITIES:

Berry Brothers Varnishes

Berry Brothers Varnishes (12). Children
in advertising wagons (ILLUS.) 7.50
Bird & Poultry Breeding (U.S. Pheas-
antry Company) - early issues (25) 7.50
Buckbees Seeds - colorful. Several
different scenes . . . . 8.00 to 10.00
Case Threshing Machines & Steam
Rollers 5.00
Dutch Boy Paints - superb poster-style . . 20.00
Fertilizer Spreaders - only those show-
ing large equipment. Several issues . . 10.00
International Harvester 10.00

International Harvester Nations Series Card

International Harvester - large series
showing use in other nations
(ILLUS.) . . . . 7.00 to 10.00
Luther Burbank - large grouping
showing enlarged fruits/vegetables.
Artist drawn 5.00
Philadelphia Lawn Mower 7.00
Pratt Food Company - animal feed (10) . . . 6.00

Sharples Cream Separators

Sharples Cream Separators - several
cards showing children or woman
with product (ILLUS.) 9.00

SERVICES

BUSINESS:

Bell Telephone Company

Bell Telephone Company (10). Scene
w/round insert picture (ILLUS.) 10.00
Eberhard Faber Company - pencils &
erasers 6.00
National Cash Register Company -
scenes of buildings & interiors 4.00

Underwood Typewriter

Underwood Typewriter - giant typewriter exhibit at Atlantic City
(ILLUS.) 7.50

INSURANCE:

Glens Falls Insurance Company -
historical series published by Detroit
Publishing Company (10) 7.50
Metropolitan Life Insurance - series
showing home office building &
interiors (12) 3.50

Mutual Fire Insurance Company

Mutual Fire Insurance Company -
poster-style (ILLUS.) 12.00
Prudential Insurance Company - histor-
ical series. 4.00
Prudential Insurance Company - ships . . .3.00
Prudential Insurance Company - views . . .3.00

ENTERTAINMENT

LITERARY & THEATRICAL:

*(Prices in this grouping vary according to
actual artist, author, or song writer. These
are almost never found in series with some
listed exceptions below.)*

"The Auction Block" - card of book
illustrated by Charles Dana Gibson . . .12.00
"Baltimore and Ohio" magazine -
poster-style covers (12) 7.00
"Bambi" - card is book illustration.
Artist-signed 7.50

"Ben Hur"

"Ben-Hur" - shows chariot race. Sears
Roebuck edition (ILLUS.) 5.00
"The Blue Bird" - play by Maeterlinck.
Poster-style 8.00
"Boston Herald" - boys & girls of New
England (6) 10.00
"Ladies Home Journal" - various issues
ranging from common to poster-
style . . . . .7.00 to 10.00
"Somebody's Coming To My House" -
by Irving Berlin. Illustrated song-
sheet showing stork 8.00
"There's A Little Spark Of Love....
Burning" - songsheet simulation
(ILLUS.) 8.00

"There's A Little Spark of Love. . .Burning"

"Tip Top Weekly" - youth magazine
  showing sports (6) 12.00
"Tip Top Weekly" - cover showing
  poster-style drawing of Frank
  Merriwell 15.00

AMUSEMENTS:

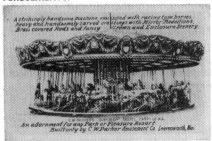

C.W. Parker Amusement Company

Columbia Phonograph Co. - man in
  canoe w/phonograph 7.50
Edison Phonograph (The) - older man &
  woman listening to phonograph 5.00
Farrand Company (The) - angel playing
  piano 5.00
Parker (C.W.) Amusement Company -
  black & white photos of carousels.
  Different scenes (ILLUS.) 17.00

TRANSPORTATION & ACCESSORIES

MISCELLANEOUS:

Automobile Trade Journal

Autocar - 1907 Model 18.00
Auto Factories - exteriors of named
  companies 4.00

Auto Factories - interiors of named
  companies 6.00
Automobile Trade Journal - different
  issues of cards (ILLUS.) 6.00
Babcock Electric Carriage Company -
  artist drawing 12.00
Blacksmith Shops - black & white
  photos w/close-up views 12.00

Pennsylvania Railroad "Broadway Limited"

Broadway Limited--Pennsylvania R.R.
  (ILLUS.) 6.00
Buick - 1910 open roadster model.
  Photo issued by manufacturer 25.00
Corbin Coaster Brakes - excellent
  drawings of bikes in cartoon style
  (10) 18.00
Durkee (C.D.) & Co. - marine goods 7.00
Evinrude Motor - photo-style w/girl in
  boat 8.00
Firestone Tire - putting tire under
  Christmas tree 10.00
Fisk Tire - various poster-style issues
  showing little boy in pajamas........12.00
Fisk Tire - one issue by Norman Rock-
  well 25.00

5-A Horse Blanket

5-A Horse Blanket (ILLUS.) 12.00
Glidden Tours - advertising U.S. tour
  in Glidden auto (24) 8.00
Goodrich Tire 18.00
Havoline Oil - poster-style 15.00
Holland-American Lines - artist
  drawings of ships & Dutch costumes
  (6) 12.00
Hupmobile 4-Passenger Touring Car....18.00
Indian Motorcycle - various artist
  drawings (ILLUS.) 22.00

Indian Motorcycle

New Departure Coaster Brakes For
  Bikes - 3 series of 6 & 8 cards 15.00

Oilzum

Oilzum - oils & lubrications (ILLUS.) 12.00
Rock Island Railroad Line - vacation
  spots by artist Rose O'Neill 25.00

(End of Special Focus)

POSTERS

Poster by Toulouse-Lautrec

Ammunition, "Remington Arms - Union
  Metallic Cartridge Co.," 2 men in

canoe surprising a drinking bear,
  ca. 1920, 25¾ x 17¼" $302.50
Ammunition, "Winchester," cowboy
  w/rifle in hand & foot on ram, 1904 ..675.00
Baking soda, "Arm & Hammer Soda,"
  2 young hunters w/dog attacked by
  bees, 1910, 25 x 17" 185.00
Cigarettes, "Oasis," seated young
  woman wearing a hat, w/pack of
  cigarettes, "Always Refreshing,"
  30 x 19" 121.00
Cigars, "Big Major 5c Cigar," girl & dog
  pictured 95.00
Country fair, "Trotting & Pacing
  Races," blue ribbon cows & bull
  pictured, 42 x 27" 150.00
Farm equipment, "John Deere,"
  harvest scene w/man operating corn
  sheller, 1929, 37 x 25" 215.00
French artist, Henri de Toulouse-
  Lautrec, "Prochainement au Theatre
  A. Bruant," lithograph, 31 x 22½"
  (ILLUS.) 2,860.00
Gasoline, "Tydol," lady driving, 1920s,
  55 x 36" 250.00
Gun powder, "DuPont," various game
  birds, 1920 ....165.00
Gun powder, "Hercules Powder,"
  "Right in the Blind," 1922 ....150.00
Movie, "A Close Call For Ellery
  Queen," William Gargan & cast,
  Columbia Pictures, 1941 ....35.00
Movie, "The Great Dictator," Charlie
  Chaplin, United Artists, 38 x 30" 75.00

Army Recruiting Poster

Recruiting, "Men Wanted for the
  Army," gun crew manning coast
  defense gun, American Lithograph
  Co., New York, 1909, 35½ x 24¾"
  (ILLUS.) 88.00
Seeds, "Burpee," nasturtiums, 1934 ...135.00

Snuff, "Red Seal," girl & checkerboard,
"Two Comforts in Life" 75.00
Soap, "Pears'," "Bubbles," 1890,
36 x 24" 245.00
Stove polish, "Dixon," little girl
wearing feathered hat 275.00
Travel, "Imperial Airways," comical
scene, "Fly Through Europe," by
Schurich, 1935, 38 x 24" 85.00
Vaudeville, "8 Bells," 8 dancing young
women clad in sailor suits,
Strobridge Lithograph Co., Cincin-
nati, Ohio, ca. 1910, 40 x 30" 121.00
World War I, "Boys and Girls! You can
Help your Uncle Sam Win the War,
Save your Quarters, Buy War Savings
Stamps," Uncle Sam w/girl & War
Savings Certificate while boy looks
on, James Montgomery Flagg,
30 x 20" 75.00
World War I, "Carrying the World to
Victory," Uncle Sam, President
Wilson & General Pershing, by
Johnson, 1918, 20 x 15" 65.00
World War I, "Have You Answered the
Red Cross Christmas Roll Call?"
nurse w/outstretched arms, soldiers
in background, Harrison Fisher,
30 x 20" 45.00
World War I, "It Takes a Man to Fill
It," Navy recruiting, uniform draped
over empty chair, Charles Stafford
Duncan, 1918, 42 x 28" 88.00
World War I, "You Buy a Liberty Bond,
Lest I Perish," Statue of Liberty,
McCauley, 30 x 20" 175.00
World War II, "Buy War Bonds! Save
Freedom of Speech!," Norman
Rockwell, 1943 . . . . .55.00
World War II, "Don't Let the Shadow
Touch Them," 20 x 14" 55.00
World War II, "This is the Enemy,"
28 x 22" 75.00
World War II, "You Buy 'Em, We'll Fly
'Em," 28 x 20" 60.00

POWDER HORNS & FLASKS

Brass Powder Flask

Brass flask, embossed ribs, 8¼" l. $55.00
Brass flask, embossed hound & dead
game in relief (ILLUS.) . . . . . . .50.00 to 75.00

Copper flask w/brass trim, embossed
rifles, cannon & crossed flags,
Civil War era, 8" l. 105.00
Copper flask, embossed shell pattern,
8 3/8" l. 65.00
Horn, engraved clipper ship, eagle,
shield & fish, w/initials & dated
"1870," 6½" l. 105.00
Horn, engraved scene of Indian
sighting a rifle, animals & snake,
dated "1845," wooden plug
w/brass nailheads, 8" l. 192.50
Horn, engraved w/eagle, fish, stars &
initials, w/relief carved hearts &
crescents, 8½" l. 1,025.00
Horn, engraved w/simple design,
brass tip & wooden plug, 9" l. 60.00
Horn, engraved village scene w/trees,
houses & church, brass end ring,
9½" l. 125.00
Horn, engraved w/inscription "Henry
Muller, His Horn. 12th Penna. Regt.
Dauphin County, Jan. Ye 19. 1781,"
& scene of town identified as
"Frederickstown," sides engraved
w/large tulips & bird, wooden
base w/metal ring, turned throat
w/wooden plug, 10½" l. 385.00
Horn, engraved self-portrait w/wife &
5 children & various animals including
a cow, spotted dog, roosters &
eagle in flight, signed "S. Merrill,
Peacham, Vermont" & dated "1847,"
crimped neck, 13¾" l. (plug
missing) 4,400.00

RADIOS & ACCESSORIES

*Early model radios, transmitting equip-
ment and components are now being sought
by a special group of collectors. Also see
ADVERTISING ITEMS and SIGNS &
SIGNBOARDS.*

Book, "1001 Radio Questions &
Answers," Vol, I, No. 1, 1926 . . . . . .$19.50
Book, "How To Locate Troubles In
Your Radio Set," by Benson, 1924 . . . .14.50
Book, "Practical Radio," by Moyer,
hardbound, 1926, 273 pp. 12.50
Instruction book for Atwater Kent
Model 55 & 60 radios 20.00
Poster, "Sparton Radio," early foot-
ball game, parlor scene, etc., 78" l. . .225.00
Radio, Andrews Type II, battery-
operated, Art Deco front panel 325.00
Radio, Atwater Kent Model 20,
w/speaker horn 125.00
Radio, Atwater Kent Model 33, 1927,
w/separate speaker 75.00

Radio, Atwater Kent Model 42, 1928,
w/type E-3 speaker 165.00
Radio, Bendix Aviation Co. table
model, Art Deco style white plastic
case . . . . .35.00 to 50.00
Radio, Crosley Model 4-29, 1926,
battery-operated . . . . .100.00 to 135.00
Radio, Crosley Model 53, cabinet
w/Victorian-style carving & 5"
Queen Anne-style legs, 1930, 26" h. .300.00
Radio, Crosley "Cathedral" Model 148 . .85.00
Radio, Doron Bros. (Hamilton, Ohio)
crystal set 85.00
Radio, FADA shelf-model, Art Deco
bullet-shaped bakelite butterscotch
yellow case w/red trim, 10½ x 5½",
6" h. . . . . .220.00 to 250.00
Radio, Freed-Eisemann NR 6, w/manuals
& extras 110.00
Radio, Grimes 4DL Inverse Duplex
Reflex model, 1925, w/tubes 200.00
Radio, Hallicrafter S-38 AM/Shortwave
to 30 megacycle 50.00
Radio, Metrodyne Super 7, 1925. . . . . . .250.00

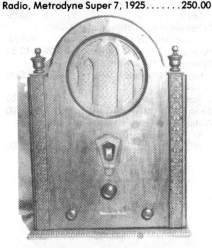

Northland "Cathedral" Radio

Radio, Northland "Cathedral"
(ILLUS.) 145.00
Radio, Philco "Cathedral" Model 20,
1930 . . . . .165.00
Radio, Philco "Cathedral" Model 37-61,
1937 . . . . .75.00
Radio, Philco Model 624, 6-volt 95.00
Radio, Philco Transitone, maroon
plastic case 20.00
Radio, RCA Model 20, 1925 . . . . .125.00
Radio, Scott Philharmonic, Gothic-
style cabinet .795.00
Radio, Silvertone portable, Art Deco
green marbleized bakelite case,
8 x 7". 25.00
Radio, Sparton "Blue Mirror" table
model 650.00
Radio, Sparton Nocturne Model 1186
console, Art Deco "Blue Mirror"

cabinet designed by Walter Dorwin
Teague, 43" d., on bracket feet,
46" h. 25,000.00
Radio, Steinite Model A.C. 1 . . . . .165.00
Radio, Zenith Model 6G-601M, battery-
operated "Wavemagnet" 52.00
Radio, Zenith Model 5S-338, table
model 135.00
Radio speaker, Atwater Kent 65.00
Radio speaker, Kolster Mod. KG, claw-
footed. 50.00
Radio speaker, cast iron & wood,
sailing ship decor, 17" d. 95.00
Radio speaker, celluloid gooseneck-
type. 100.00
Tube, Deforest D-01A, w/original box . .15.00
Tube tester, General Electric Supreme
No. 40, 1933 . . . . .55.00

RAILROADIANA

"Frisco System" Pocket Mirror

Ash tray, "Pullman," bronze $65.00
Book, "Railroads of the U.S.," by Henry
M. Flint, 1868 . . . . .25.00
Booklet, "Western Pacific Railway,"
"From Salt Lake City to San Fran-
cisco by Feather River Canyon
Route," illustrated, ca. 1900 . . . . .45.00
Bowl, cereal, "Wabash R.R.," china,
Banner patt. .72.50
Brakeman's cap, badge & button,
"N.Y.C." (New York Central) 40.00
Butter pat, "Chicago, Milwaukee, St.
Paul & Pacific R.R.," china, Traveler
patt. 15.00
Calendar, 1938, wall-type, "Chesa-
peake & Ohio R.R.," w/Chessie cat,
3 pp., 19 x 14" 22.00
Celery tray, "Baltimore & Ohio," china,
Capital patt. .135.00

Coffee pot, cov., "Great Northern,"
silverplate, 54 oz. 85.00
Compote, "Atlantic Coast Line," china,
Flora of the South patt., Buffalo
Pottery 200.00
Conductor's hat w/badge, "M.K.T."
(Missouri-Kansas-Texas) 70.00
Conductor's lantern, brass, M.M. Buck
& Co. 265.00
Conductor's step stool, "Mo. Pac. Ry."
(Missouri Pacific) 110.00
Creamer & cov. sugar bowl, "Union
Pacific," silverplate, pr. 125.00
Cup & saucer, "Chicago, Milwaukee,
St. Paul & Pacific R.R.," china,
Olympian patt. .85.00
Cuspidor, "M.K.T." (Missouri-Kansas-
Texas), china. 65.00
Depot bench, 2-sided, oak w/bentwood
seat, 8' l. 450.00
Dispatcher's telephone, "Santa Fe,"
oak box 195.00
Egg cup, "Chicago & North Western,"
black & red logo 18.00
Finger bowl, "Northern Pacific," silver-
plate 16.00
Fire extinguisher, "C. & N.W. Ry."
(Chicago & North Western), glass,
rolling pin shape 85.00
Kerosene can, "Santa Fe Route," cone-
top, 2-gal. 65.00
Lantern, "B. & A. R.R." (Boston &
Albany), brass bell bottom, clear
globe, last patent date Dec. 12,
1882 . . . . .295.00
Mirror, pocket-type, "Frisco System,"
celluloid, 2 1/8" d. (ILLUS.) 95.00
Oil can w/long spout, "Atchison,
Topeka & Santa Fe R.R." 50.00
Oyster plate, "Chicago, Rock Island &
Pacific," china, Golden State patt. 47.00
Padlock, "Illinois Central R.R.,"
6-lever, "pancake" 80.00

"Rock Island Route" Paperweight

Paperweight, "Rock Island Route,"
glass, ca. 1880, 3" octagon, 1" h.
(ILLUS.) 85.00

Paperweight, "Soo Line," clear glass,
magnifying-type, "1883-1958 - 75th
Anniversary". 35.00
Plate, "Western Pacific," china,
Feather River patt., 5½" d. 27.50
Plate, "Illinois Central," china, French
Quarter patt., 10½" d. 275.00
Platter, "Illinois Central R.R.,"
Louisiane patt., 9 x 6" 125.00
Playing cards, "Union Pacific - Over-
land Route," 35 views 40.00
Print, "Chesapeake & Ohio," Negro
porter peeking at sleeping Chessie
cat, framed, 15 x 13" 70.00
Stock certificate, Lawrenceburgh &
Indianapolis R.R. Co., 1830s 150.00
Sugar tongs, "Wabash Railroad," silver-
plate 45.00
Switch key, "C. & N.W." (Chicago &
North Western), brass 14.00
Switch lantern, 2 red & 2 green lens,
Dressel, 17". 95.00
Teapot, cov., "Pennsylvania R.R.,"
Keystone logo, International Silver
Co. 150.00
Ticket validator, "Hills Model A Cen-
tennial Machine" 225.00
Timetable, "Atlantic Coast Line," 1928 . .12.50
Timetable, "New York, New Haven &
Hartford Railroad," 1895 . . . . .8.00
Tumbler, "Union Pacific R.R.," blue
glass 20.00
Wash basin, "Missouri Pacific," tin 25.00
Water can w/bail handle, "A.T. & S.F.
RY." (Atchison, Topeka & Santa Fe),
10" h. 22.00

RAZORS - STRAIGHT EDGE

Celluloid Razor

Aluminum handle w/overall chased
design, stamped "J.R. Torrey, Wor-
cester, Mass." on tang. $62.00
Celluloid (black) handle, etched
"Henckles Razor" (Germany) on
blade 45.00
Celluloid (green transparent) handle,
stamped "Otto Deutsch" (Germany),
w/case 48.00
Celluloid (ivory) handle w/embossed
Art Nouveau woman w/flowing hair,
etched "Suredge" on blade 25.00
Celluloid (ivory) handle w/embossed
cowboy on horse, scrolls & inset

moonstones, stamped "Hibbard
Spencer Bartlett & Co." on tang, 6" l.
(ILLUS.) 40.00
Celluloid (ivory) handle w/embossed
florals, etched "Wyeth Our Best
Brand" on blade 18.00
Celluloid (ivory) handle w/embossed
green peacock, Germany 30.00
Celluloid (ivory) handle w/embossed
stork eating fish 30.00
Celluloid (ivory) handle w/embossed
windmill & boat scene stained red,
Germany 23.00
Celluloid (ivory) handle w/raised gold
scrolling, stamped "Wostenholm" on
tang 30.00
Celluloid (ivory) handle w/nude in
relief on front, etched "The Farmer's
Beauty" on blade, w/original box 50.00
Celluloid (ivory) handle w/inlaid silver
lyre & leaves 20.00
Celluloid (ivory) handle, stamped "Win-
chester No. 8625" on tang 57.50
Celluloid (red) handle w/embossed
Art Nouveau lady's head...........25.00
Celluloid (white) handle, stamped
"Wester Bros." (New York &
Germany) on tang 25.00
Corn razor (small size razor designed
for removing corns), celluloid (ivory)
handle, 4" l......................35.00
Horn handle, early 1820s............88.00
Horn handle, stamped "Boker & Co."
on tang, etched "American Lines S.S.
St. Louis" on blade, original box 55.00
Horn handle, etched angel & cornu-
copia on blade....................50.00
Horn handle, etched Statue of Liberty
on blade.........................50.00
Mother-of-pearl handle, etched "Hess
Hair Milk" on blade 25.00

style leaf-carved rectangular frame,
Chinese Export, 18th c., 33 x
26½" 3,300.00
Hongs at Canton, showing French,
American, British & Dutch flags,
Chinese Export, ca. 1840, framed,
17¾ x 14¼" 2,310.00
Man playing harpsichord w/lady
looking on, silver leaf mirror on the
wall, gilt ground, signed Koehler,
giltwood frame, 19th c., 10¼
x 7¼" 605.00

The Sailor's Farewell

"Sailor's Farewell," w/seaman carrying
a black & gold teapot & pointing to
a lady wearing a red, white & blue
dress standing at the foot of a path
leading to a large white building
w/another building on distant hill,
Chinese Export, ca. 1860, framed,
15¾ x 11¾" (ILLUS.)............2,750.00
Statue of Liberty, framed, 22 x 16"
oval...........................65.00

REVERSE PAINTINGS ON GLASS

Also see SIGNS & SIGNBOARDS.

Battle scene w/warriors brandishing
swords, shields & daggers, pitched
tents in back & foreground, banners
flying, Chinese Export, 19th c.,
framed, 16 x 22½" $1,100.00
Battleship, "S.S. Maine," 1896, 8 x 13" .125.00
Bust portrait of Abraham Lincoln,
ca. 1870, framed, overall 17½
x 23¾" 72.50
Courtyard scene w/temple background,
Chinese Export, 19th c., 8 x 12" 450.00
European gentleman in court dress,
silver mirror backing, within rococo

"Washington"

"Washington," three-quarter length
  portrait posed against green ground,
  Continental, mid-19th c., framed,
  10 x 7" (ILLUS.) 990.00
Young woman w/large red bow in her
  dark hair, wearing yellow low-cut
  dress, entitled "Joseffina," original
  frame, 9½ x 12" 475.00

RING TREES

Bavarian China Ring Tree

China, Austrian, pink & green floral
  decor, gold trim, marked "M.Z." $35.00
China, Bavarian, model of a hand,
  h.p. florals on saucer base (ILLUS.) ...38.00
China, German, figural lady seated
  beside tree stump, marked "Erphila,
  Germany," 2¾" h. 45.00
China, Minton, h.p. pastel florals at
  top, gilt edge & knob, 3½" d., 3" h....38.00
China, Nippon, model of a hand, h.p.
  ship scene & gold edge on base 60.00
China, Nippon, h.p. roses, green stem
  & ribbons & gold trim, blue Maple
  Leaf mark................45.00
Glass, blue opaline, footed, h.p. gold,
  blue & white floral decor, 3¾" d.,
  4¼" h. 68.00
Glass, ruby, w/gold, blue, pink & white
  floral decor, 3½" d., 3 1/8" h. 58.00
Glass, yellow spatter, w/gold band
  enameled w/blue, white, pink &
  yellow florals, 3½" d., 3¼" h. 58.00
Parian, model of a child's hand
  w/ornate cuff molded w/ribbon &
  pearls, white, English Registry
  mark (1842-83), 2 7/8" d., 4" h. 33.50

ROYCROFT ITEMS

*Elbert Hubbard, eccentric entrepreneur
of the late 19th century, founded Roycroft*

*Shops and established a craft community in
East Aurora, New York in 1895. Individuals
were trained in the trades of bookbinding,
leather tooling and printing. Craft-style
furniture in the manner of Gustav Stickley
and known as "Aurora Colonial" furniture
was produced. A copper workshop, begun in
1908, turned out numerous items. All of
these, along with the Buffalo Pottery china
which was produced exclusively for use at
the Roycroft Inn and carries the Roycroft
symbol, constitute a special category
associated with the Arts and Crafts movement. Also see FURNITURE.*

Roycroft Bookends & Desk Accessories

Book, "Elbert Hubbard's Scrapbook,"
  by Elbert Hubbard II, 1923, cloth
  bound $15.00
Books, "Little Journeys to the Homes of
  the Great," by Elbert Hubbard, 14-
  volume set, 1925.................175.00
Book, "No Enemy But Himself," by
  Elbert Hubbard, 1934 ....14.00
Book, "The Notebook of Elbert
  Hubbard," by Elbert Hubbard II,
  1926 ....28.00 to 35.00
Book, "The Rubiat of Omar Khayam,"
  by Fitzgerald, 1908, leather cover
  (stained).........................10.00
Bookends, hand-hammered copper
  w/Art Nouveau style florals in
  relief, pr. 55.00
Bookends, hand-hammered copper,
  clipper ship design, pr. 50.00
Candle holders, hand-hammered
  copper, w/mottled green patina,
  7½" h., pr........................80.00
Catalogue, "Roycroft Books," 1902,
  suede cover, 16 photos 36.00
Cigarette box, cov., hand-hammered
  copper 65.00
Desk set: letter holder, rocker blotter,
  calendar & cov. inkwell w/glass
  insert; hammered copper, Sunburst
  patt., 4 pcs. 100.00
Frame, hammered copper, incised Art
  Nouveau florals & tracery, 5 x 6" 125.00
Inkwell w/hinged lid, hammered
  copper, riveted decor, dark
  patina ....65.00 to 100.00
Lamp, hammered copper, domical-type
  shade, straight standard w/flaring
  base 625.00
Letter opener, hammered brass 15.00

Letter opener, hammered copper,
  advertising "Buffalo Envelope Co.,"
  8" l. 25.00
Magazine, "The Fra," 1914-16, set of 50 .87.50
Maple syrup jug, original tags, 13½ oz. ..25.00
Pen tray, hammered copper, 11" l. 28.00
Plate, china, Roycroft logo center, 8" d. .85.00
Prints, portrait of Elbert Hubbard,
  different poses, signed by Elbert
  Hubbard, pr. 125.00
Purse, hand-tooled leather, Arts &
  Crafts line 60.00
Vase, hand-hammered copper, 4" h. ...25.00
Vase, hand-hammered copper,
  5½" h. 125.00
Vase, bud, hand-hammered copper
  w/glass insert, 6" h................45.00
Vase, hand-hammered copper, incised
  stylized pendant bellflowers,
  10¾" h. 175.00
Wall sconce, hand-hammered copper,
  arrowhead-shaped backplate, 8" h. ...95.00

SCALES

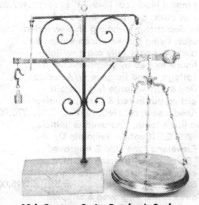

18th Century Swiss Butcher's Scale

Apothecary scale, balance-type,
  brass pan & gram weights to 500,
  "Toledo"........................$55.00
Baby weighing scale, w/wicker basket .25.00
Butcher's scale, iron & brass on stone
  base, iron standard w/brass ball
  finial supporting iron & brass scale,
  Switzerland, 18th c., overall 45½" h.
  (ILLUS.) 990.00
Butcher's steelyard scale, hanging-type,
  "Koch Butchers Supply Co., Kansas
  City, Mo.," ornate..................69.00
Butter scale, balance-type, wooden,
  turned post balancing scrolled arm
  w/string supports to flat wooden
  pans, 19th c., 7" d. pans, 23" across
  balance beam 825.00

Candy scale, cast iron w/brass scoop,
  "Toledo Model No. 415-T," 3-lb.......85.00
Candy scale, cast iron w/brass pan,
  "Buffalo," red w/gold lettering 50.00
Candy scale, fan-type w/indicating
  chart in glass-faced housing, brass
  platform & side mounts, "Exact
  Weight" 210.00
Coin-operated sidewalk scale,
  "National," claw-footed base, dial
  on column, 1-cent play...975.00 to 1,200.00
Cotton scale, Texas 42.50
Countertop scale, cast iron, "Fairbanks,
  No. 8," w/tin scoop 65.00
Countertop scale, cast iron base
  w/brass oval dish supported on arm,
  w/six iron weights, 23" l. 75.00
Countertop scale, computing-type,
  brass w/marble platform, "Hobard
  Scales, Pat. Mar. 31, 1895, Dayton,
  Ohio" on brass plate 365.00
Countertop scale, platform-type, cast
  iron, "Howe Scale Co., Rutland, Vt.,
  No. 12," old worn yellow repaint
  w/black trim, 28½" h..............137.50
Egg grading scale, tin, various makers,
  1920s ....15.00 to 25.00
Fur trader's hide scale, brass insert
  for 0-40 & 20-350 lbs. 90.00
Gold scale, brass, w/three brass
  weights (troy ounces), original
  velvet-lined box 75.00
Grain scale, brass, "Fairbanks,"
  w/bucket................150.00 to 170.00
Grain scale, brass, "Winchester,"
  1887 patent 250.00
Jockey's weight scale, chair-type,
  leather upholstery 950.00
Kitchen scale, tin, "Pelouze," ivory
  paint 16.00
Postage scale, brass, "Property of P.O.
  Dept., 1931, Chicago, Ill.," 10" 65.00
Postage scale, cast iron w/brass weight
  & beam, "Fairbanks" 55.00
Postage scale, tin, various makers,
  early 20th c. ....15.00 to 22.00
Spring scale, hanging-type, brass,
  "Chatillon," 24-lb., 8½" l. 18.00
Spring scale, iron w/polished brass
  face plate, "Chatillon's Improved
  Spring Balance, N.Y.," 200-lb.,
  19" l.......................25.00 to 45.00
Steelyard scale, wrought iron, good
  detail, 15" l.......................35.00

SCRAPBOOKS & ALBUMS

Album, photograph, celluloid cover
  w/portrait of Admiral Dewey.......$90.00

Celluloid Album on Stand

Album, photograph, celluloid, bluebirds & wedding bells on ivory
ground, on base & stand w/drawer
(ILLUS.) 85.00
Album, photograph, celluloid cover
w/scene of beautiful girl seated at a
table within a floral border,
w/photographs 85.00
Album, photograph, celluloid cover
w/scene of peasant girl in field of
flowers, w/photographs 60.00
Album, photograph, lacquer cover,
"Typhoon at Hong Kong, September
18, 1906," w/twenty-nine
photographs 225.00
Album, photograph, leather cover
w/tooled floral design, w/fifty
photographs, 16 x 7" 55.00
Album, photograph, gold plush cover
w/mirrored insert etched "Our
Friends," w/pedestal stand 55.00
Album, photograph, 65 assorted World
War I photographs, including
General Pershing & airplanes 45.00
Album, musical-type, celluloid,
w/portrait of lady on silk cover,
1890s ....175.00 to 200.00
Album, w/65 postcards, including
Clapsaddle, Tuck, Osgood &
Twelvetrees......................245.00
Album, w/144 postcards, including
Thanksgiving & children 200.00
Scrapbook, w/70 pages of trade
cards 200.00
Scrapbook, w/Cunard Lines menus,
postcards & other memorabilia 24.00
Scrapbook, w/trade cards & die-cuts
of children & animals, 1890s 75.00

SCRIMSHAW

The Susan's Tooth

*In recent years a flood of fine grade hard
plastic scrimshaw reproductions have
appeared on the market and the novice
collector is urged to learn to distinguish
these new items from the 19th century
pieces.*

Corset busk, whale baleen, engraved
whalers (2) & Neptune's boaters
harpooning, dated 1882, 7½" l. $300.00
Corset busk, pan bone, engraved
American eagle, flowers & initials
within floral surround one side &
engraved w/sentimental verse on
reverse, details picked out in red,
green & black, ca. 1845, 11" l. 467.00
Corset busk, pan bone, engraved
w/depiction of whaling ship w/furled
sails, flying the American ensign &
anchored near hilly coast w/light-
house topped by weathervane, a
cottage, large flagpole w/American
flag & fort w/large flag, details
picked out in red & black, in velvet-
lined frame, ca. 1860, 13¼" l. 770.00
Sea lion's tooth, engraved w/initials
"B.D.C." (Captain Benjamin D.
Cleveland) one side & engraved
"Daisy 1907" reverse, mounted on
chrome & mirrored lucite stand,
5¼" l. 495.00
Walrus tusks, engraved & stippled
both sides: 1st engraved w/pin-
wheels, stars, facade of a pillared
house, 2-masted sailing ship above
compass-drawn flowerheads &
inscribed "Walrus Tusk" one side
& w/freely drawn flowers, sprigs &
leaves reverse; 2nd engraved
w/large gabled house, man in foreground w/horse, palm trees, pinwheels & flowers one side &
w/compass-drawn stars, flowers &
a heart reverse; each w/details
picked out in red, green & yellow &
w/crowns pierced for hanging,
19th c., 21¾" l., pr...............2,750.00
Whale's tooth, "Susan's Tooth,"
engraved by Frederick Myrick w/the
ship "Susan" cutting-in, her boats
down, harpooning & lancing sperm

whales & inscribed above the boat
"The Susan on the coast of Japan,"
w/American eagle, shield & "E
Pluribus Unum" banner above crossed
American flags one side & w/depiction
of the "Susan" beneath banner inscribed "The Susan on her homeward
bound passage" & further engraved
w/legend "The Susan of Nantucket,
March 24, 1829" one side & "Death
to the living, long life to the killers,
Success to sailors, wives & greasy
luck to whalers," 5 5/8" l.
(ILLUS.) 11,000.00
Whale's tooth, engraved w/figure of
man in top hat holding a riding crop,
Nantucket, ca. 1850, 7¼" l., mounted
on stand 1,650.00
Whale's tooth, engraved American
naval vessel, the "Hornet," lying at
anchor in foreign harbor, another
ship w/sails furled in distance &
w/inscription one side & w/squadron
of naval vessels in formation & inscription reverse, details picked out
in red, green & black, ca. 1830,
7½" l. 3,190.00

Scrimshawed Whale's Tooth

Whale's tooth, engraved w/large
footed compote planted w/large
leafy tree w/star-like flowers &
w/American eagle perched on shield
above on one side & w/full-length
figure of Victorian lady wearing
checkered dress & carrying a small
parasol reverse, mid-19th c., 8" l.
(ILLUS.)........................660.00
Whale's tooth, engraved w/scene of
battle between the American &
English naval ships, "Constitution"
& "Guerriere," during the War of
1812 one side & w/the American
vessels the "Wasp" & "Frolic," large
American flag & floral sprays
reverse, details picked out in black
& red, 19th c., 8" l..............3,410.00

Whale's teeth, engraved square-rigged
ships under full sail beneath moon
& stars, signed "J.F.C.," Nantucket,
ca. 1835, 4¼" l., pr. 2,750.00

SEWING ADJUNCTS

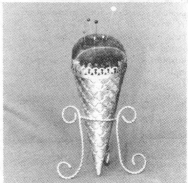

"Ice Cream Cone" Pin Cushion

*Also see ADVERTISING ITEMS and
BREWERIANA.*
Buttonhole scissors, marked "Wol-
cott's Boston, 1852" $25.00
Darner, blown cobalt blue glass 48.00
Darner blown Pigeon Blood red glass,
ground end 105.00
Darner, blown white opaline glass,
egg-shaped 45.00
Darner, celluloid.................6.00
Darner, pressed clear glass 10.00
Darner, turned wood 5.00
Embroidery scissors, sterling silver
"repousse" handles, "Gorham,"
3¾" l...................28.00 to 35.00
Eyelet punch, sterling silver, ornate,
w/adjustable gauge...............22.00
Glove darner, sterling silver, Art
Nouveau style...................40.00
Needle case, beaded cloth, book-
shaped worked w/beaded glass
roses & lyre, dated 1839, original
silk lining......................95.00
Needle case, boxwood, barrel-shaped,
"Accept My Best Wishes,"
Germany 25.00
Needle case, brass, w/hinged lid,
model of sheaf of wheat, "W. Avery
& Son, Redditch, England," 3½ x
2¼".............................135.00
Needle case, brass, 4-compartment,
hinged lid, dial on base for
numbered compartments, engraved
butterfly & leaf both sides, "Thomas
Savage, London," dated 1868, 2¾ x
1½"............................95.00
Needle case, brass, 6-compartment,

hinged lid, front & reverse w/hinged
covers for closing each compartment,
florals in relief on cover ends, "The
Gem-Perry & Co., London," 7¾" l. . .135.00
Needle case, celluloid, model of
umbrella, 3½" h. 20.00
Needle case, ivory, carved model of
a parasol, 4¼" l. 135.00
Needle case, sterling silver, Art
Nouveau style 65.00
Pin cushion, beaded cloth, model of a
bird on olive branch, 7 x 9 x 4" 40.00
Pin cushion, beaded cloth, shoe-
shaped, Victorian, 7" l. 14.50
Pin cushion, beaded cloth, star-shaped,
maple leaf & "Montereal" worked in
design, 6" l. 28.00
Pin cushion, brass, model of a footed
basket w/kitten w/amethyst glass
eyes perched on edge, red velvet
cushion, 2¼" d. 22.00
Pin cushion, brass, model of an ice
cream cone, velvet cushion top,
6" h. (ILLUS.) .20.00

Celluloid Slipper Pin Cushion

Pin cushion, celluloid, slipper form,
painted forget-me-nots decor
(ILLUS.) 15.00
Pin cushion, painted silk, apple form,
3" d. 17.00
Pin cushion, silverplate, heart-shaped,
ornate. 15.00
Pin cushion, silverplate, model of
a lady's high heel boot, Meriden,
1890s. 35.00
Pin cushion, turned wood, model of a
bucket w/velvet cushion on top &
mirror on inside, original white
paint w/blue floral decor, 2" h.
(minor age cracks) 45.00
Ruler, sterling silver, w/inches &
centimeters demarcated, "Tiffany,"
6" l. 225.00
Seam ripper, celluloid, green mottled . . .8.50
Sewing bird, brass, single cushion,
w/patent date of Feb. 15,
1853 . . . . .85.00 to 125.00
Sewing bird, brass, single cushion,
w/heart-shaped thumbscrew 130.00

Sewing bird, brass, double cushion,
dated Sept. 15, 1853 . . . . . .105.00 to 145.00
Sewing bird, silverplate, "Norton's
Improved Patent 1853" . . . .100.00 to 125.00
Sewing clamp, brass, table screw cast
as hand holding a bar, dated 1859 . . .65.00
Sewing clamp, cast iron, openwork
lyre form 65.00

Early Sewing Kit

Sewing kit: pin cushion, thread holder,
thimble case & scissors case; woven
reed, 4 pcs. (ILLUS.) 25.00
Sewing kit: tooled leather purse
w/original brass thimble, bee's wax
& ivory tool; Victorian, 4 pcs. 55.00
Tailor's shears, iron, "Wm. Braithwait
Shear Steel". 35.00
Tape measure, advertising, "Edison
Mazda Lights," Maxfield Parrish
artwork w/two medieval boys &
light bulb one side, early electric
stove reverse 65.00
Tape measure, advertising, "Frigi-
dare," celluloid, man carrying
frigidare. 30.00

Tape Measure with Advertising

Tape measure, advertising, "General
Electric Refrigerators," celluloid,
white refrigerator on dark blue with
light blue outer band, 1½" d.
(ILLUS.). 22.50
Tape measure, advertising, "Hoover
Sweeper" 12.50

Tape measure, brass, model of German spike helmet w/enameled black Maltese Cross, dated 1914 . . . . . 65.00

Tape measure, brass & silverplate, model of a straw hat 47.00

Tape measure, celluloid, beehive w/two bees at top & bee pull 40.00

Tape measure, celluloid, bust of an Oriental man 37.00

Tape measure, celluloid, model of an apple w/lady bug pull 20.00

Tape measure, celluloid, model of a tulip 40.00

Tape measure, gilt metal, model of a book, marked "Austria," 1¾" l 25.00

Tape measure, silverplate, model of a clam shell 35.00

Tape measure, silverplate, model of a shoe, embossed "Three Feet in One Shoe" 39.00

Tape measure, sterling silver, chased holly decor 65.00

Tatting shuttle, mother-of-pearl shell . . . 18.00

Tatting shuttle, sterling silver 65.00

Thimble, advertising, "Silk Hosiery, Indianapolis," aluminum 4.00

Thimble, 10k gold, double bands of bright cut at rim 82.50

Thimble, 14k gold, narrow bright-cut band . . . . 85.00 to 95.00

Thimble, 14k gold, chased cherub band 125.00

Thimble, 18k pink & yellow gold, chased leaves in band 95.00

Thimble, sterling silver, "Charles Horner," dated 1900 . . . . 45.00

Thimble, sterling silver, "Pat. May 28, 1889" & anchor mark 25.00

Thimble, sterling silver, cat in relief on body 42.00

Thimble case, brass, model of an egg, w/hanging loop 47.00

Thimble case w/hinged lid, sterling silver, "repousse" strawberry form . . 155.00

Thimble case, turned wood, model of an acorn 35.00

Thimble case, glass, cobalt blue model of a slipper, w/original sterling silver thimble, 2" l., 2 pcs 95.00

Thread caddy, brass, domed base, rod standard supporting thread spools & w/needlepoint pin cushion top, original glass dome cover, 1880s, 11" h. 245.00

Thread caddy, cast iron, w/pin cushion top 65.00

Thread caddy, cherrywood, box form w/lift-up pin cushion top, 6 spool holders & drawers, 5 x 7 x 6" 55.00

Thread caddy, ivory, barrel-shaped w/spool insert, 2" l 80.00

SHAKER ITEMS

Shaker Clothespin

The Shakers, a religious sect founded by Ann Lee, first settled in this country at Watervliet, N.Y., near Albany, in 1774 and by 1880 there were nine settlements in America. Workmanship in Shaker crafts is an extension of their religious beliefs and features plain and simple designs reflecting a chaste elegance that is now much in demand though relatively few early items are available. Also see BASKETS and FURNITURE.

Apple box, pine, canted sides, attributed to Canterbury Shakers, 7½" sq., 2 5/8" h. $75.00

Bed rug, wool, deep red, gold, green & grey 325.00

Berry basket, splint ribs w/bentwood rim & base bands, 4" d., 2½" h. 105.00

Berry box, wooden, square w/holes pierced in sides 95.00

Bonnet, tightly woven split poplar, w/blue or black silk trim, 1880s . . . . 175.00 to 220.00

Book binding press, walnut, dovetail construction, wooden-threaded screw, 3 x 8 x 9" 110.00

Bottle, aqua glass w/yellow label printed "Extract of Butternut - Prepared in the United Society, New Lebanon, N.Y." in black, 8" h. 39.00

Broadside, printed paper, entitled "The American Shakers," listing history & goals of the Shakers in America, ca. 1900, matted & framed, 19" w., 27" h. (minor discoloration & stains) 165.00

Broom, round style, original paper label "Shaker Broom, Geo. Salmon," 37" l. 115.00

Bucket, stave construction w/brass bandings & wire bail handle w/wooden grip, marked "N.E. Shakers, Enfield, N.H.," 9½" d., 7½" h. 155.00

Cape (sister's garment), red wool, w/lined hood 225.00

Carrier, bentwood oval, 4-finger lappet construction, bentwood handle, w/satin lining & bows 385.00

Cheese box, cov., bentwood round w/finger lappet bands secured by copper tacks, attributed to Sabbathday Lake Community, 17" d., 7" h. 185.00

Clothespin, 8" l. (ILLUS.) 10.00

Coffee pot, cov., tin, classic style

w/side spout, old black finish,
9½" h. 75.00
Doll's bonnet, woven straw, silk
lining ....155.00 to 225.00
Drying rack, painted pine, 2 uprights
joined by 2 horizontal bars, shoe
feet, painted grey, ca. 1830, 42" w.,
26" h. ....190.00 to 295.00
Dry measure, wooden, 4-qt...........40.00
Dusting brush, natural bristles in round
w/shaped wooden handle, 11½" l....22.00
Dust pan, tin, old black finish,
w/hanging ring at handle, 13 x 8¼"
pan, 5" l. handle 40.00
Flour scoop, maple, 1-piece w/ribbed
finger grip 85.00
Fly swatter, woven splint oval
w/handle 85.00
Funnel w/removable strainer, tin,
4¾" d., 4" handle 45.00
Grain shovel, hand-hewn, open "D"
handle, early 1800s, 1-pc. 150.00
Hat form for wide-brimmed straw hats,
wooden, worn old black paint,
12¾ x 14¾"......................400.00
Kitchen utensils: pr. forks & strainer
ladle; iron w/cherrywood handles,
Hancock, Massachusetts, ca. 1840,
3 pcs. 247.00
Lamp filler, tin, tapering cylinder
w/side handle & gooseneck spout,
old darkened finish 42.00
Mitten dryer, wooden, double-ended
w/cut-out mitten form each end 235.00
Pantry box, cov., bentwood oval,
2-finger lappet construction, copper
tacks, old worn yellow paint, 6 1/8 x
4 3/8" 400.00
Pantry box, cov., bentwood oval, single
finger lappet construction, copper
tacks, natural finish, 6½ x 5" 200.00
Pantry box, bentwood oval, 3-finger
lappet construction, copper tacks,
traces of old brown stain, 8¾ x 6"...425.00
Pantry box, cov., bentwood oval,
3-finger lappet construction, copper
tacks, original dark greyish green
paint, 11¼ x 8 3/8" 735.00
Pantry box, cov., bentwood round,
Harvard single finger lappet
w/copper tacks, nice honey brown
finish, 6¼" d. 85.00

Pantry Box with Straight Seam

Pantry box, cov., bentwood round,
straight-lapped sides w/copper
tacks, 7" d., 3½" h. (ILLUS.) 75.00
Pie lifter, iron tongs in wooden
handle, 17½" l....................32.50
Pill box, cov., bentwood round
w/copper fasteners, faded stamped
label, 3¼" l. 65.00

Shaker Rolling Pin

Rolling pin w/"stick" handles, maple
(ILLUS.)..........................60.00
Seed box, cov., wooden, paper label
"Shaker's Genuine Garden Seeds,
Mount Lebanon, N.Y.," original
reddish brown paint, 23½ x 11½"...550.00
Sieve, bentwood sides, woven horse
hair sieve, 5 7/8" d. 125.00
Soap scoop, hand-hewn hickory, long
handle w/hole for hanging, oval-
shaped bowl, 35" l................75.00
Thread caddy, pine & butternut, square
corner posts w/conical finials, one
drawer & top compartment w/eight
ivory eyelets for thread, worn blue
cloth pincushion on turned wood
base, worn original natural & red
stain finish, 7¼ x 7 x 5½" 325.00
Warming shelf, tin, 3 round shelves
clamp to stove pipe, each is
9½" d. 205.00

SHAVING MUGS

FRATERNAL

Masonic Shaving Mug

F.O.E. (Fraternal Order of Eagles).....$95.00
G.A.R. (Grand Army of the Republic),
w/emblem, owl & moon scene &
name 90.00

Knights of Columbus 95.00
Masonic, gold Masonic emblem, name
&trim on white, 3½" h. (ILLUS.)......95.00
Royal Order of Moose 95.00

GENERAL

Silverplate Shaving Mug

China, Limoges, Lady Liberty w/Eagle
shield, holding banner w/name......95.00
China, R.S. Prussia, w/mirror inset,
shaded green floral decor on white
ground, gold trim, 3½" h. 325.00
China, R.S. Prussia, roses decor on
shaded blue ground 150.00
China, h.p. American Flag & inscription
"The Union Forever," Civil War era ..135.00
China, color transfer of horse's head
within horseshoe & floral wreath,
w/name 65.00
China, color transfer of pink florals
on white ground, pink lustre trim 28.00
China, copper lustre w/blue bands,
large 85.00
China, scuttle-type, color transfer of
flowers, marked Germany 22.00
China, scuttle-type, color transfer of
hand holding 4 playing cards,
"Lucky Spots" 70.00
China, scuttle-type, h.p. blue &
peach blossoms w/rust leaves on
white ground, Smith Bros., 1876-77
patent, Boston, Mass. 65.00
Glass, clambroth, scuttle-type, Robin
& Wheat patt. 100.00
Silverplate, engraved scrolling
foliage, Derby Silver (ILLUS.) 35.00
Silverplate, ornate figural handle,
James W. Tufts 65.00
Sterling silver, bulbous, w/monogram
& dated 1891 ....150.00

OCCUPATIONAL

Accountant, roll-top desk 200.00
Butcher, large steer center surrounded
by knife, saw & hatchet, w/name in
gold............................225.00

Farmer, man plowing field w/two
horses, w/name in gold 280.00
Fisherman, oval medallions of fisherman smoking pipe one side &
wearing whaler's hat & coat reverse,
on black ground, 3¾" h. 100.00
Motorist, early car & driver w/trees
& house in background 200.00
Physician, skull & crossbones,
w/name 135.00

Occupational Shaving Mug

Railroadman, baggage car, w/name
(ILLUS.) 250.00
Sulky driver, man driving sulky,
driving time of race & name in
gold...........................395.00
Telegrapher, w/name 125.00
Trolleyman, w/early trolley car &
name 340.00
Wallpaper hanger, man working at
table w/paper, ladder & partially
papered room in background,
w/name in gold 395.00

SHAVING STANDS

Cherrywood, Federal, Hepplewhite-
style, w/mirror plate in frame
swiveling on tapering squared uprights w/ball finials above bow-
fronted case w/single drawer, ball
feet, 15¾" w., 21½" h. $150.00
Mahogany veneer, Federal, Hepplewhite-style, rectangular mirror
plate within frame w/scrolling crest
& cross-banded inlay swiveling on
square supports w/turned finials
above serpentine-fronted base
w/three short drawers on small
ogee-cut feet, 18¼" w., 24½" h.
(ILLUS.) 550.00

Mahogany Shaving Stand

Mahogany w/inlay, Federal, Sheraton-
style, rectangular mirror within
inlaid frame swiveling on turned
posts above bow-fronted case
w/three small drawers inlaid
w/stringing, short bulbous-turned
feet, early 19th c., 23" w., 25" h.
(replaced brasses) 495.00
Mahogany veneer, Victorian, rectan-
gular mirror plate pivoting between
turned columnar supports above
base w/pr. short line-inlaid drawers,
ball feet, 18½" w., 24" h. (minor
veneer damage) 105.00
Walnut, mirror plate in canted frame
swiveling on spool-turned uprights
on plane base, 21¼" w., 18 3/8" h. . . . 55.00

SHEET MUSIC

*Also see BROWNIE and DISNEY COL-
LECTIBLES.*

"Ain't She Sweet," 1927, "Flapper" on
cover $4.00
"America Today," 1917, President
Wilson on cover 8.00
"Bell Bottom Trousers," dancing sailors
on cover 5.00
"The Bible Tells Me So," Roy Rogers
& Dale Evans on cover 12.50
"Check & Doublecheck," 1930, Amos 'n
Andy on cover 10.00
"Everybody's Teddy" (march), 1901,
Theodore Roosevelt on cover 14.00
"Everything I Have Is Yours," 1933,
Joan Crawford & Clark Gable on
cover 15.00

"Girl of Mine," Rolf Armstrong girl on
cover 10.00
"Give a Little Whistle," Pinocchio on
cover 8.00
"High Noon," Grace Kelly & Gary
Cooper on cover 10.00
"How Can I Thank You," Shirley Temple
on cover 20.00
"I'm an Old Cowhand," 1936, Bing
Crosby on cover 6.00
"In the Baggage Coach Ahead," steam
locomotive on cover 6.00
"Lily of the Prairie," 1909, Indian
maiden on cover 8.00
"Little Old Log Cabin in the Lane,"
Fibber McGee & Molly on cover 4.00
"Lovely Lady," Alice Faye on cover 8.00
"Make Hay While the Sun Shines," Bing
Crosby & Marion Davies on cover 7.00
"The Minstrels March Two-Step," by Al
J. White, 1913, black minstrels on
cover 15.00
"My Doughnut Girl," 1919, Salvation
Army girl w/pan of doughnuts on
cover 15.00
"My Sweetheart Went Down with the
Ship," Titanic on cover 12.00
"Oh By Jingo," Charlotte Greenwood
on cover 4.00
"One in a Million," Sonja Henie on
cover 10.00
"Our Darling Comodore," Admiral
Dewey on cover 7.00
"Polly-Wolly-Doodle," Shirley Temple
on cover 14.00
"The Pussy Cat Song," 1948, Bob
Crosby & Patty Andrews on cover 10.00
"Shortnin' Bread," 1939, black woman
baking bread on cover 8.00
"Smilin' Through," Norma Shearer on
cover 4.00

"The One Rose That's Left in My Heart"

"The One Rose That's Left in My Heart,"
Bing Crosby on cover (ILLUS.) 7.00

"There Will Never Be Another You"

"There Will Never Be Another You,"
Sonja Henie, John Payne, Jack Oakie
& Sammy Kaye on cover (ILLUS.) 9.50

"Under the Train," train wreck on
cover 20.00

"When Dixie Stars are Playing Peek-a-
Boo," 1924, black women picking
cotton on cover .7.50

SIGNS & SIGNBOARDS

Ale, "Carlings Red Cap Ale," tin over
cardboard, w/"Nine Pints of the
Law" policeman scene $85.00

Ammunition, "Western," embossed tin,
hunting scene w/rifle & dogs,
19 x 13" 225.00

Barber pole, turned wood w/acorn
ends, old worn red & white paint,
original iron mounting bracket,
34½" h. 225.00

Barber pole, revolving red & white
graniteware cylinder, "Kochs,"
76" h. 1,750.00

Bus depot, "Continental Trailways,"
graniteware, 36 x 18" 150.00

Butcher, wooden plank w/relief-
carved "Pork" gold leaf lettering on
red ground, 31 x 20" oval 400.00

Chocolates, "Blue Banner Chocolates,"
tin, w/wooden frame, 17 x 8" 95.00

Chocolates, "Pangburn's Chocolates,"
reverse painting on glass 95.00

"Egyptienne Straights"

Cigarettes, "Egyptienne Straights,"
cardboard, young woman in bonnet
against red background, original
frame, 31 x 20½" (ILLUS.) 121.00

Cigarettes, "Fatima," tin, veiled lady,
35 x 24" oval .395.00

Cigars, "Cubanola Cigar," lithographed paper on wood, beautiful
girl wearing yellow dress playing
mandolin, 1890s, 32 x 20" 195.00

Cigars, "Frances Wilson Cigars,"
printed tin, ornately carved table
w/cigar box, matches, ash trays &
lighted cigar & 3 well-dressed young
men, ca. 1895 . . . . .275.00 to 325.00

Clothing, "Kuppenheimer Clothes,"
reverse painting on glass w/ornate
gold leaf, electric clock as part of
background, 23" sq. 325.00

Coffee, "Arbuckles," embossed tin,
small girl taking steaming cup of
coffee to her beaming father 350.00

Farm Machinery, "Buy the McCormick,"
chromolithographed paper, farm
machinery & beautiful woman,
framed 14 x 16" 295.00

Flour, "Duluth Imperial," printed tin,
black man holding baked bread,
1910, 25 x 18" 675.00

Flour, "Kismet," printed tin, curved
corners, beautiful woman in
window, 1913 .325.00

Flour, "Sleepy Eye Millling Co.," cardboard, lithograph of Chief Sleepy
Eye, 1905, 15" d. 500.00

Food product, "Knox Gelatin," lithographed paper, black woman
preparing strawberry gelatin dish
for small white girl, 1901 . . . . .375.00

Furniture, "Globe Wernicke Book-
cases," self-framed tin, man &
woman filling bookcase, "Heart of
the Home," 29 x 40" 275.00
Gasoline, "Mobilgas," graniteware,
flying red horse, 10 x 12"...........22.50
Gum, "Oh Boy," printed tin, young boy
w/sticks of gum in hand, 1930s,
16 x 8"..........................50.00
Gum, "Wrigley's Chewing Gum,"
printed tin, 3 packs of gum & packs
of mints 120.00
Gun powder, "DuPont Powders," self-
framed tin, 2 hunting dogs, 1908,
28 x 22"...............750.00 to 1,200.00

Hatter's Trade Sign

Hatter, tin, model of a top hat, painted
red w/blue & pink bow-knotted
band, 19th c., 8" h. (ILLUS.).........990.00
Ice cream, "Metropolitan Velvet Ice
Cream," printed tin, bowl of ice
cream, sodas & vase of flowers,
ca. 1900 ....295.00
Insurance, "Connecticut Fire," reverse
painting on glass, silver lettering on
green, 29½ x 14½" ....130.00 to 165.00
Jeweler, cast iron & tin, pocket watch
shape, late 19th c. 350.00

Optometrist's Trade Sign

Optometrist, cast iron & glass, oval
eyeglass frames w/colored glass
lenses (one cracked) on metal
support, early 20th c., overall
35" h. (ILLUS.) 990.00
Paint, "Wetherill's Paint," printed tin,
Atlas holding the world & cherubs
flying overhead...................165.00

Patent medicine, "Doctor Drake's
Cough & Croup Remedy," self-framed
tin, man & woman standing over
baby in wicker crib 475.00

"Dr. Fitler's Rheumatic Syrup" Sign

Patent medicine, "Dr. Fitler's Rheu-
matic Syrup," printed tin, portrait of
Dr. center w/gold lettering on blue
ribbons, by F. Tuchfarber & Co., Cin-
cinnati, Ohio, ca. 1880, 19½ x 13½"
(ILLUS.) 2,310.00
Radios, "Majestic," reverse painting
on glass, 5 colors w/lightning bolt
through center, framed 175.00
Railway express, "Railway Express
Agency," graniteware, 36 x 36".....100.00
Shipping lines, "Hamburg American
Lines," self-framed tin, brass plaque
w/"Around the World Annual
Cruises $650 & up," ca. 1905,
36 x 48"......................1,650.00
Shoe polish, "Whittemore's Shoe
Polish," self-framed tin, mother
polishes shoes w/daughter seated
at her knee 145.00

Shoe Repair Trade Sign

Shoe repair, carved wooden low boot, painted red w/black heel & lettered "Shines - Repairs," on wrought iron support, 34" h. (ILLUS.) 660.00

Shoes, "Red Goose Shoes," embossed tin, Emmet Kelly clown face w/Red Goose shoes on forehead, double-sided, happy clown one side & sad reverse, large 450.00

Soft drink, "Moxie," printed tin, horse & rider in Rolls Royce rolling down highway in front of billboard 400.00

Soft drink, "Pepsi Cola," cardboard, Art Nouveau portrait of girl holding flowers, 1914, framed, 31 x 36" . .850.00

Stove polish, "Vulcanol," printed tin, bulldog, wooden frame, 41 x 15" 145.00

Stoves, "Doe-Wah-Jack (Dowagiac, Michigan) Round Oak Stoves," pressed paperboard, 8" d. 125.00

Stoves, "Favorite Stoves & Ranges," graniteware, rising sun 275.00

Tires, "Firestone," cardboard, tire-shaped 125.00

Tobacco, "Bull Durham," paperboard, bull fighting scene, original wooden frame, 1909, 35 x 23" 450.00

Tobacco, "Duke's Mixture," paper-board, "Duke's Twins" carrying suit-case, wooden frame, 1910, 24 x 30" 295.00

"Red Indian Cut Plug" Sign

Tobacco, "Red Indian Cut Plug," chromolithographed paper, Indian in feathered headdress shooting arrow at package of Cut Plug, ca. 1900, framed, 28 x 22" (ILLUS.) 302.50

Veterinary medicine, "Wilbur's Stock Tonic," lithographed paper, delivery wagon scene, 1904, framed 135.00

Watches, "Hamilton Watch Co.," printed tin, small girl w/blonde curls & wearing pink dress, "America's

Standard R.R. Timekeeper," 19 x 13" 310.00

Whiskey, "Belle of Milton Whiskey-Levy Schier & Co., Kansas City, USA," printed tin, camping scene w/hunters, dogs, tent, campfire, guns & equipment & 2 cases whiskey, 27 x 39" 350.00

Whiskey, "Edgewood Kentucky Sour Mash Whiskey," printed tin, bottle, full glass & lighted cigar, ca. 1895, oak frame 325.00

Whiskey, "Four Roses Whiskey," printed tin, slain fox & game birds hanging on wall next to rifle, 1900, 48 x 32" 450.00

Whiskey, "Old Boone Distilling Co., Louisville, Ky.," self-framed tin, log cabin scene w/Daniel Boone holding rifle & other figures, dated 1904 . . . . .450.00

Whiskey, "Volunteer Whiskey," reverse painting on glass, Civil War soldiers w/flag & saber, & "It's Pure - That's Sure - John Barth Co., Milwaukee, Wis." 165.00

SILHOUETTES

Hollow-Cut Silhouettes

These cut-out paper portraits in profile were named after Etienne de Silhouette, Louis XV's unpopular minister of finance and an amateur profile cutter. As originally applied, the term was synonymous with cheapness, or anything reduced to its simplist state. These substitutes for the more expensive oil paintings or miniatures were popular from about 1770 until 1860 when daguerreotype images replaced the vogue. Silhouettes may be either hollow-cut, with the head cut away leaving the white paper frame for mounting against a dark background, or the profile itself may be cut from black paper and pasted to a light background.

Bust portrait of boy, cut & pasted & brushed w/artwork highlights,

beveled rosewood frame, 5" w.,
6¾" h. $150.00

Bust portrait of a gentleman wearing
high wing collar, hollow-cut &
mounted on black fabric, w/black
ink detail, black reeded frame,
4 5/8 x 3 5/8"......................115.00

Bust portrait of a lady with elaborate
coiffure, hollow-cut & mounted on
black fabric, molded pine frame,
4 5/8 x 3 5/8".....................115.00

Bust portraits of a lady & gentleman,
lady wearing black dress & carrying
tiny green umbrella & blue reticule,
man wearing black coat & magenta
vest, carrying red book, each
w/hollow-cut heads, details in
watercolor, anonymous, New England, ca. 1840, 3¾ x 3", pr.........715.00

Bust portraits of a lady & gentleman,
hollow-cut & mounted on black
paper, original yellow varnished
maple frames, 5 1/8 x 4 1/8", pr.....240.00

Bust portraits of a lady & gentleman,
hollow-cut & mounted on black,
embossed "Peale's" on one &
"Museum" on second, mounted
w/"eglomise" glass mat in gilt
frame, 9½" w., 6 5/8" h...........450.00

Bust portraits of a young lady &
Joshua Bailey, hollow-cut, young
lady wearing yellow dress, enclosed
w/black & gold oval glass mat,
Joshua Bailey, age 37, dated
November 20, 1835, in painted
frames, New England, 4" & 4½" h.,
pr. (ILLUS.).......................880.00

Bust portraits of a young man &
young woman, hollow-cut & mounted
on black fabric, ink inscriptions
"Rachel Morris done by Baches
Patent, 1820 Phila." & "--Morris,"
black reeded frames, 4¾ x 3¾",
pr. 400.00

Gentleman wearing top hat & carrying an umbrella in an Italianate
setting, full-length, cut & pasted,
signed "Aug. Edouart fecit 1833,"
framed, 10¼ x 7½"..............462.00

Three-quarter profile portrait of
woman in frilly & beribboned attire,
hollow-cut & mounted on black
w/"eglomise" mat in gilt-edge
frame, 6 7/8" w., 7 7/8" h.........125.00

SNUFF BOTTLES & BOXES

*The habit of taking snuff (powdered
tobacco meant for inhaling) began in 17th*
century France and reached its peak during
the 18th century, spreading to England,
elsewhere on the Continent, and even to
China, probably introduced there by
Spanish or Portuguese traders. In Europe,
tightly hinged porcelain or metal boxes were
considered desirable containers to house the
aromatic snuff. Orientals favored bottles of
porcelain or glass, or carved of agate, ivory
or jade, often modeled in the form of a
human figure or fruit. By mid-19th century
the popularity of snuff declined and
consequently production of these exquisite
containers diminished.

BOTTLES

Carved Coral Snuff Bottle

Coral, carved as a basket of flowers,
wickerwork basket w/large lotus
flowers sprouting from it & a small
boy standing on its edge, w/match-
ing stopper, wooden stand, 19th c.
(ILLUS.) $1,320.00

Hornbill ivory, pyramidal form, carved
in relief w/a Phoenix bird & writhing
dragon, 3¾" h....................265.00

Interior painted crystal, painted w/a
continuous lush garden scene, coral
stopper, 3¼" h.....................130.00

Ivory, carved in relief w/little boy &
girl on either side of a gourd-shaped
vase filled w/flowers, 2" w., 3" h....150.00

Jade, flattened rounded oblong, front
carved in low relief w/a gnarled tree
& mushroom, creamy white,
carnelian stopper, 19th c., 2¾" h....165.00

BOXES

Gold Snuff Box

Agate, boat-shaped w/stepped base,
molded silver mounts, Continental,
3rd quarter 18th c., 2¾" l. 440.00

Gold, 18k, oblong, hinged cover
"repousse" & chased in the center
w/bouquet of flowers within
cartouche-form reserve, borders
w/shellwork & scrolling foliage,
sides & central cartouche-form
reserve engine-turned, Swiss,
ca. 1820, 3½" l. (ILLUS.) 1,870.00

Horn, engraved floral design on lid &
a bird at either end, brass fittings,
3 7/8" l. 125.00

Lacquer, oval, sprays of flowers on red
ground w/gilded borders, gilt-metal
mounts w/neo-rococo thumbpiece,
Continental, mid-19th c., 3 5/8" l. . . .715.00

Pewter, hinged lid w/engraved floral
decor, American, 1810. . . . . .85.00

Tortoise shell, molded in the form of a
recumbent lion, hinged cover
w/molded gilt-metal mounts, shell-
form thumbpiece, German, ca. 1770,
3" l. 1,045.00

Wooden, hand-carved model of a
lady's shoe, inlaid w/brass & con-
trasting wood, 4½" l. 100.00

Bookends, carved figure group of
Oriental man on water buffalo,
7½" h., pr. $50.00

Candle holder, carved w/three lion's
heads, marked "China" 185.00

Figure of Kuan Yin, her eyes down-
cast & w/serene expression, standing w/her hands clasped & wearing
long robes open at the chest to
reveal a lotus necklace, pale green-
yellow w/grey mottling, on wooden
stand, 14½" h. 715.00

Figure group, European youth, wearing
cloak over pleated tunic, standing
before his recumbent dog, on scalloped base, celadon green, China,
18th c., 6 3/8" h. (ILLUS.) 1,430.00

Mantel garniture, carved fruit com-
pote, ca. 1900 . . . . .275.00

Model of a Foo dog on tomb, 7½" h. 92.00

Toothpick holder, carved w/three
monkeys 48.00

Vase, carved ornate florals, leaves &
w/two squirrels, 6 x 7" 75.00

Vase, double, carved w/two monkeys,
birds & tree, shaded brown, 7 x 5". . . .95.00

SOAPSTONE

Soapstone Figure Group

Soapstone Vases

Vases & covers w/"o noga doni" bird
finials, pierce-carved intertwining
chrysanthemum blossoms & lava
formations w/conforming birds
perched amidst flowers, variegated
beige, tan, carnelian & dark brown,
China, ca. 1900, 13¼" h., pr.
(ILLUS.) 231.00

*This mineral used in producing all sorts of
soapstone wares has a greasy feel and has
been utilized, among other things, for
carved figure groups by the Chinese and
others. It also has been fashioned into
utilitarian pieces.*

SOUVENIR SPOONS

Alligator & grapefruit handle, Palm
Beach, Florida in bowl $47.50

Art Nouveau lady holding Texas State
   Seal handle, Laredo, Texas in bowl . . .25.00
Chief Seattle bust atop Alaska totem
   pole, reverse stamped Totem Pole,
   Pioneer Square, Seattle 30.00
Christ, angels (2) & nude cherub
   handle, Tulsa in bowl, 1906 . . . . .45.00
Columbine floral handle, Auditorium,
   Denver, Colorado in bowl
   (demitasse) 12.50
Commodore Perry bust handle, plain
   bowl 35.00
Easter, cherubs (3) figural handle,
   cross & lilies in bowl 45.00
Fish figural handle, Patchogue, Long
   Island in bowl (demitasse) 40.00
Gold miner's pan, pick axe & shovel
   figural handle, Idaho in bowl 45.00
Indian full figure handle, salmon in
   bowl, Portland, Oregon, 4" l. 75.00
Indian maiden on handle, Monroe
   Street Bridge, Spokane, Washington
   in bowl 65.00
Miner holding gold nugget full figure
   handle, Results at Last, Denver,
   Colorado in bowl (demitasse) 45.00
Mission bell handle, Pasadena,
   California in bowl 45.00

Columbian Exposition Souvenir Spoon

Mrs. Potter Palmer bust atop handle,
   Woman's Pavillion - World's
   Columbian Exposition in bowl
   (ILLUS.) . . . . .85.00 to 125.00
New York City skyline, Statue of
   Liberty in bowl 65.00
Pilgrim full figure handle, Philadelphia
   buildings in bowl 35.00
Pope Leo XIII bust portrait handle,
   St. Peter's Square in bowl 50.00
San Francisco Post Office handle,
   plain shell-shaped bowl 38.00
Santa Claus on handle, Nativity scene
   in bowl 195.00

SPICE CABINETS & BOXES

Cherrywood cabinet, hanging-type,
   8-drawer, original white porcelain
   pulls $225.00
Oak cabinet, hanging-type, 4-drawer,

w/two compartments in each
   drawer 100.00
Oak cabinet, hanging-type, 8-drawer,
   arched top pierced w/hole to
   hang . . . . .85.00 to 100.00
Pine cabinet, hanging-type, 8-drawer,
   stenciled spice names on each,
   rounded top . . . . .125.00 to 145.00
Tin box, cov., w/six inner containers
   & nutmeg grater, round, 8 pcs 60.00
Tin box, cov., w/six square containers
   & nutmeg grater, original japanned
   finish & pin stripes, 10 x 7" box,
   8 pcs. 85.00
Tin box, cov., w/seven cylindrical
   containers w/original lids,
   "Chautauqua Spices," 8 pcs. 55.00
Tin cabinet, hanging-type, 8-drawer,
   blue stenciling on white, marked
   "Germany" 150.00

Queen Anne Period Spice Cabinet

Walnut cabinet, Queen Anne period,
   molded projecting top over arched
   paneled door opening to arrangement of 10 short drawers over single
   long drawer, paneled sides, molded
   base bracket feet, Pennsylvania,
   ca. 1750, 17" w., 24" h. (ILLUS.) . . .22,000.00
Wooden box, cov., bentwood round
   w/five 3½" d. inner boxes
   w/stenciled label on each, "Spices"
   stenciled on lid of large 8" d. box,
   6 pcs. 85.00
Wooden box, cov., bentwood round
   w/eight inner containers, 9 pcs. 195.00

SPOOL, DYE & ALLIED CABINETS

Dye, "Diamond," oak case w/litho-
   graphed tin front w/scene of five

children around hot air
balloon ....$300.00 to 500.00
Dye, "Diamond," oak case w/litho-
graphed tin front depicting the
"Evolution of Woman" 575.00

Diamond Dye Cabinet

Dye, "Diamond," oak case w/litho-
graphed tin front w/children playing
at steps of mansion, early 20th c.
(ILLUS.) ....450.00 to 695.00
Dye, "Peerless Dyes for Home Use,
N. Spencer Thomas, Elmira, N.
York," wooden, roll-top, lithographed tin insert (poor condition) front
depicts young eastern woman, late
19th c., 18 x 10", 31¾" h. 192.50
Dye, "Putnam," tin, w/lithographed
scene of General Putnam 125.00
Spool, "Brainerd & Armstrong," oak,
2-drawer 250.00
Spool, "Clark's," oak, 3-drawer,
original porcelain pulls,
9 x 14 x 22" ....98.00 to 150.00
Spool, "Clark's O.N.T. Spool Cotton,"
walnut, 3-drawer, w/ruby glass
drawer fronts ....260.00 to 325.00
Veterinary medicines, "Pratt's Veterinary Remedies," wooden, shaped
crest, lithographed tin front panel
w/horse portrait in round reserve
over list of "specifics" & opening to
numerous small numbered
drawers 275.00

STEINS

Character, "Bismarck," porcelain,
w/pewter thumblift, marked
"Musterschutz" (patented or protected by law) on base, ½ liter $425.00

Character, "Bismarck Radish," porcelain, w/porcelain-inset pewter lid
w/green leaf finial, marked
"Musterschutz" on base ...395.00 to 450.00
Character, "Bowling Pin," porcelain,
marked "Musterschutz" on
base ....350.00 to 375.00

Kaiser Wilhelm II Character Stein

Character, "Kaiser Wilhelm II,"
porcelain, w/spread-winged eagle
finial on helmet, ornate pewter
handle, marked "Musterschutz" on
base (ILLUS.) 500.00
Character, "Sad Radish," porcelain,
pewter lid inset w/porcelain leaf
finial, ½ liter....................300.00
Character, "Skull," bisque,
"Gaudeamus Igitur," pewter lid
w/porcelain inset, ½ liter.........255.00
Character, "Smoking Pig," porcelain,
marked "Musterschutz" on base,
7" h. 350.00
Glass, amber, w/h.p. deer in forest
scene decor, 1890's, 1½ liter 225.00
Glass, clear w/cut geometric designs,
pewter lid w/porcelain inset painted
w/scene of city along river & family
walking in foreground, artist-
signed, ½ liter 175.00
Lithophane base w/tavern scene, body
w/h.p. florals & "Gruss Aus
Sonneberg," pewter lid,
¼ liter ....145.00 to 175.00
Mettlach, No. 171, relief-molded
figures around body representing
activities during months of the year,
pewter lid w/porcelain inset,
½ liter 225.00
Mettlach, No. 675, relief-molded barrel
form, pewter lid, ½ liter 125.00
Mettlach, No. 1028, oval cameo relief
panel of man carrying hay & walking
w/woman on bark ground, inlaid
pewter lid, ½ liter ....165.00 to 225.00
Mettlach, No. 1161, etched German

eagle, city shields & 2 ladies, inlaid
pewter lid, 7 liter 2,500.00
Mettlach, No. 1394, etched German
card symbols, inlaid pewter lid,
½ liter 435.00

Mettlach No. 1467 & No. 1675

Mettlach, No. 1467, cameo relief-
molded panels of farming, weaving,
hunting & picking fruit, inlaid pewter
lid, ½ liter (ILLUS. left) . . . .200.00 to 260.00
Mettlach, No. 1527, etched scene of
four men drinking, signed "Warth,"
inlaid pewter lid, 1 liter 700.00
Mettlach, No. 1577, etched scene of
12 people at dinner, inlaid pewter
lid, 4½ liter 1,800.00
Mettlach, No. 1650, tapestry,
Mountaineer, pewter lid, 1 liter 350.00
Mettlach, No. 1675, etched scene of
Heidelberg, "1386-1886" on reverse
medallion, inlaid pewter lid, ½ liter
(ILLUS. right) 500.00
Mettlach, No. 1725, etched scene of
lovers w/man holding stein, signed
"Warth," inlaid pewter lid, ½ liter . .460.00
Mettlach, No. 1786, etched St. Florian,
pewter tile roof lid, dragon's head
thumblift, ½ liter 750.00
Mettlach, No. 1794, etched figure of
Bismarck in uniform, signed
"Warth," inlaid pewter lid, ½ liter . .450.00
Mettlach, No. 1795, etched scene of
Freiburg, signed "Warth," inlaid
pewter lid, ½ liter 345.00
Mettlach, No. 1932, etched cavaliers
drinking scene, signed "Warth,"
inlaid pewter lid, ½ liter 650.00
Mettlach, No. 2009, etched scene from
"Trumpeter from Sackingen"
w/Werner & Margarete dancing,
signed "Stuck," inlaid pewter lid,
½ liter 575.00
Mettlach, No. 2093, "card" stein,
etched w/four playing cards around

bulbous body, inlaid pewter lid,
½ liter 725.00
Mettlach, No. 2107, etched King
Gambrinius, signed "Schlitt,"
jeweled base, inlaid pewter lid,
2½ liter 1,200.00
Mettlach, No. 2184, printed under
glaze dancing bearded gnomes
w/mugs one side & man playing
bagpipes for dancing turnips
reverse, inlaid pewter lid, ½ liter . . .250.00
Mettlach, No. 2190, etched bicycling
scene w/seven riders, inlaid pewter
lid, ½ liter 650.00
Mettlach, No. 2780, etched scene of
man playing guitar for lady seated
at table, inlaid pewter lid, ½ liter . . .685.00
Mettlach, No. 2800, etched Art
Nouveau blackberries, inlaid pewter
lid, ½ liter 495.00
Regimental, German Battalion, w/lith-
ophane of nude lady in base, soldiers w/cannon, drinking scene &
list of names on body, pewter lid
w/cannon finial & floral thumblift,
1890-1910, 10" h. 260.00

STEREOSCOPES

Cadwell's Revolving Stereoscope

*Hand stereoscope viewers with an
adjustable slide may be found at $20.00 to
$35.00 each in good condition. Elaborate
table models are priced much higher. Prices
of view cards depend on the subject material
and range from less than $1.00 to $10.00, or
more.*

Stereoscope viewer, hand-type, brushed
aluminum & wood, ca. 1900 . . . .**$25.00**

Stereoscope viewer, hand-type, oak ...29.00
Stereoscope viewer, hand-type, wooden
  w/sliding adjustment ....35.00 to 40.00
Stereoscope viewer, hand-type, tin,
  miniature, w/twenty-five assorted
  view cards 75.00
Stereoscope viewer, hand-type, silver
  finish metal w/sixty-three assorted
  view cards 100.00
Stereoscope viewer, hand-type, wooden,
  w/four-hundred Alaska Klondike
  & early Colorado town view cards ...275.00
Stereoscope viewer, table model,
  rotary-type, holds 100 cards,
  "J.W. Cadwell," 1874 (ILLUS.) 375.00
View card, Minnesota Indian, 1870s 15.00
View card, Niagara Falls tightrope
  walker 5.00
View card, nude woman, early 1900s 8.00
View cards, 1893 Columbian Exposition
  & 1904 St. Louis World's Fair, set
  of 10 ....50.00
View cards, "The New Cook," set of 12..25.00
View cards, Mammoth Cave, published
  by E. & H.T. Anthony, dated
  1866, set of 14 ....21.00
View cards, whaling voyage, set of 14 ..50.00
View cards, "Life of Christ," published
  by Keystone, set of 20 ....9.50
View cards, World War I scenes,
  published by Keystone, set of 25 .....48.00
View cards, 1933 Chicago World's Fair -
  A Century of Progress, published by
  Keystone, set of 50.................65.00
View cards, Sportsmans Series, colored,
  by T.W. Ingersoll, dated 1898, set of
  50 in original box 150.00
View cards, "Views of the World," by
  T.W. Ingersoll, set of 89 in original
  box 75.00

STICKPINS

Assorted Stickpins

Also see ADVERTISING ITEMS.

Advertising, "Case Threshing
  Machine" $10.00
Advertising, "Gold Medal Flour" 15.00
Advertising, "Studebaker" 25.00
Brass, bear w/wide hat, "Big Stick" 8.00
Cameo, chalcedony cameo head
  depicting the god Mercury surmounted by curling locks & a winged
  helmet carved in 14k gold,
  accented w/a small round diamond,
  ca. 1900 (ILLUS. center) 770.00
Enamel & diamond, oval-shaped panel
  enameled w/a miniature portrait
  of a warrior in armor against a
  black ground, set w/two rose-cut
  diamonds, gold mounting, 19th c.
  (ILLUS. left center) 550.00
Enamel & diamond birds, swimming duck
  w/head enameled in bright green
  & plumage accented w/rose-cut
  diamonds; bird w/yellow enameled
  feet & plumage dotted w/white
  enamel & wings set w/rose-cut
  diamonds, 19th c., pr. (ILLUS. right) .880.00
Gold, 14k, w/oval moonstone 45.00
Gold, 14k, bezel-set pearl, filigree
  scroll trim, ca. 1900 ....65.00
Gold, 14k, octagonal filigree frame
  set w/faceted amethyst, ca. 1900 ....68.00
Gold & silver, fox, set w/rose-cut
  diamonds, 19th c.................385.00
Labradorite & green garnet,
  carved labradorite owl's head set
  w/two round green garnet eyes,
  gold pin, 19th c. (ILLUS. left) 275.00

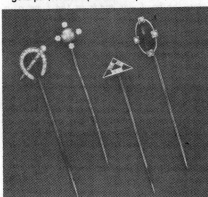

Collection of Stickpins

Moonstone & diamond, carved "man in
  the moon" moonstone quartered by
  4 diamonds, mounted in gold (ILLUS.
  left center).......................275.00
Platinum, diamond horseshoe & nail
  motif, gold shaft, ca. 1910 (ILLUS.
  left)............................247.00
Platinum, oval-shaped cabochon sapphire
  set within frame of conforming
  design, quartered by 4 single-cut

diamonds, 14k gold shaft, early
20th c. (ILLUS. right) 440.00
Platinum & gold, triangle motif set
w/three cabochon rubies & 7 square-
cut diamonds, ca. 1910 (ILLUS. right
center) 330.00

STIRRUP CUPS

Derby Porcelain Stirrup Cup

*The stirrup cup was a small variety of
tumbler, used in England in the late 18th
and 19th centuries, which held a single
drink to be consumed by the hunter while
mounted on his horse. In the most familiar
form, the bowl was made in the form of a
fox's mask or more rarely a hound's mask.
While these were made primarily of silver,
fox or hound mask stirrup cups were also
made of earthenware at a number of English
potteries.*

Creamware pottery, modeled as a dog
mask, black, brown, amber & white,
4 7/8" l. $260.00
Derby porcelain, modeled as a fox
mask, iron-red head w/fur delineated in black & w/black features
& yellow eyes, neck w/gilt collar
inscribed "Tallyho," ca. 1820, 4¾" l.
(ILLUS.) 1,650.00
English porcelain, modeled as a hound
mask, white w/brown marking
about eyes & continuing to top of
head & ears, pale peach muzzle,
details picked out in iron-red enamel
& w/random darker brown spots,
wearing black collar outlined in
gilding, 1820-30, 6" l. 605.00
Silver, modeled as a fox mask, realistically cast & chased, collar engraved "Mr. Reynard with the
morning air, scents his foe, and
leaves his lair," maker's mark
H.A.S., London, 1903, 8" l. 2,640.00

Silver, modeled as a hare mask,
realistically chased head w/collar
chased w/ribbon-tied oak leaves,
the border below collar flat-chased
w/formal foliage & scrollwork on a
matted ground, applied w/pendant
ring, Continental, late 19th c.,
5¾" l. 1,870.00
Staffordshire earthenware pottery,
modeled as a dog mask, brown &
white, 4¼" l. 255.00
Staffordshire earthenware pottery,
modeled as hound masks, black &
white w/gilt collar, late 19th c.,
4½" h., pr. 495.00

SUGAR SHAKERS

Reverse Swirl Pattern Sugar Shaker

*Called "muffineers" by the English who
favored sifting a small amount of sugar on
their muffins, sugar shakers are a popular
collectible. All listed have their original tops
unless otherwise noted.*

China, floral decor, marked Ger-
many. $40.00
Copper, tapering cylinder, pierced
brass screw-on top, 1860, 9" h. 44.00
Glass, Acorn patt., clear w/enameled
decor 95.00
Glass, Challinor's Forget-Me-Not patt.,
blue, green or pink, each . . .95.00 to 125.00
Glass, Cone patt., green or pink
opaque, each .75.00
Glass, Inverted Thumbprint patt.,
cranberry, bulbous, 3½" d., 5" h. 65.00
Glass, Reverse Swirl patt., cranberry
opalescent, 6" h. (ILLUS.) 125.00
Glass, Ribbed Scroll patt., green
opaque 65.00
Glass, Zipper patt., clear 26.00

SUGAR BOWLS

by Kyle Husfloen

Since the days of the Ancients, sugar, the product of the treasured "honey-bearing reed," as sugar cane was called by early Greeks, has been a highly prized seasoning and sweetener. Until the Middle Ages sugar was seldom available in Western Europe and what little was seen was imported from the Middle East and North Africa. Venice was the center of this trade and it was there, sometime in the 15th century, that sugar was first pressed into loaves or cones, the form in which it was most commonly sold for the next 400 years.

It was not until well into the 18th century that sugar became more widely available, largely due to the tremendous growth of the sugar cane industry in the New World colonies. Throughout America's colonial period sugar was a scarce and costly commodity for the average man, although in some areas raw honey and sugar from the sugar maples might substitute. Molasses, another product of the sugar cane, was also widely used as a sweetener in those early times.

Since sugar was such a rare and costly item in the past, it was mainly available to the wealthy who, as with other treasures, kept it under lock and key in a small chest or box. By the 18th century other forms of storage developed and as sugar became more widely available, such containers became more common and their forms multiplied. The earliest sugar chests, boxes or bowls are very rare and would be quite costly if they came on the market. However, examples of sugar containers from the 18th century are more common and these may be found by collectors, although they would still be on the expensive side.

By the 18th century all sorts of materials were used for making sugar bowls and boxes. Examples in *treen* (turned wooden-ware), various types of pottery and earthenware and pewter were probably most usual at that time and would have been found in less affluent homes in America and Europe. For the wealthy, fine examples in silver, porcelain and glass became stylish.

Up until the 18th century, sugar was kept in its own distinctive storage container but as it became more available the sorts of containers for storing and serving it also became more common and their forms proliferated. By the late 1700s we find that sugar was stored and served in such diverse items as castors, caddies, boxes, basins, bowls, baskets and even "urns," though the most usual form remained the covered bowl. With the introduction of tea and its spreading use in the 18th century, it soon evolved that a sugar container was appropriate to have along with the teapot and cream basin, since most tea drinkers required a nip of sugar for their cup of tea. Other tea equipage developed in the 18th century included the sugar "nipper," a little scissor-like implement for cutting off bits of sugar from the unwieldly sugar loaf or cone. In the late 18th century the sugar bowl or basin had become a standard part of the specialized "tea set," and so it remains to this day. It was not until into the 19th century, however, when whole dinner services of china or earthenware became common, that the sugar bowl was included in those sets also.

From the late 17th century onward, the sugar bowl's shape evolved gradually and began to follow the prevailing styles of expensive chinawares and silver. In its most mundane form, made of treen, pottery or pewter, it remained basically a simple rounded bowl, usually with a lid. However, examples in silver, porcelain and, to a certain extent, glass, became fancier and more highly decorated, showing off the refined rococo or neoclassical designs of their times. In whatever material, sugar bowls needed to be fairly large. Although sugar was expensive, it was also bulky and the chunks broken or "nipped" off the sugar loaf and ground up, needed fairly roomy containers. Until well into the 19th century, when purer, refined white sugar became widely available, sugar bowls in all materials remained quite large, at least by modern standards.

As mentioned earlier, for collectors, the earliest sugar bowls and related containers will be hard to find and expensive. Earthenwares became more common in America in the late 18th century and sugar bowls became proportionately more available too. Quite a variety from this period are still found on the market, although perfect examples are scarce.

A fairly good selection of late 18th century and early 19th century pewter, silver and porcelain examples may be found with diligent searching, but these will be more expensive than the commoner earthenware pieces. Most of the better earthenwares (in early times usually referred to as "pearlware" or "queensware"), were imported from England in great quantities by 1800. Pewter and silver bowls made in America before this date are very rare and expensive with pewter examples more scarce than silver pieces due to the attrition rate of that soft, often "recycled" alloy.

Glass sugar bowls from the period 1750-1850, are also quite scarce and since little glass was made in America before the 19th century, early documented American examples are extremely rare and most are in museums. There are a few pieces attributed tentatively to the 18th century glasshouses of Casper Wistar, "Baron" Stiegel and John Frederick Amelung, but since their forms and decorations are so close to English and European prototypes these early rarities are difficult to attribute with certainty. It is only with Amelung glass that we find a few engraved presentation pieces which we know for certain came from his factory and thus we can tentatively attribute other closely related pieces. All such examples, however, are beyond the purse of the average collector.

It is in the realm of pottery and, later, porcelain, that a collector can put together a well-rounded collection of sugar bowls from the late 18th and throughout the 19th century. With the growing abundance of dinnerwares, again, mainly from England, sugar bowls became a routine adjunct to the dining table. Transfer-printed Staffordshire examples from the 1820s onward are quite common and, later, ironstone china and related wares made the sugar bowl even more commonplace. The styles and decorations of 19th century sugar bowls matched the dinner or tea sets to which they belonged and, though finding a complete dinner or tea set may be difficult, the very substantial sugar bowls have survived in quite a variety and can make an interesting specialized collection.

During the 19th century the other most commonly found medium for sugar bowls became pressed glass. This industry was widely developed in the United States by 1850 and during the rest of the 19th century American pressed glass was found on tables all over the world. Whereas early free-blown sugar bowls from the late 18th and early 19th century are rare, pressed glass examples do still exist in great numbers. Before about 1850, a smaller selection of pressed glass items in flint glass was made, chiefly such forms as pitchers, decanters, bowls, lamps, and candlesticks, but also sugar bowls. After the introduction of the cheaper soda-lime glass formula in 1865, the American pressed glass industry mushroomed and hundreds of varied glass patterns, with dozens of different pieces available in each pattern, made glassware affordable to all. Sugar bowls then became an integral part of the four-piece glass "table set" (sugar, creamer, spoon holder and butter dish), found in nearly every Victorian kitchen or dining room.

Sugar and the sugar bowl are today an accepted part of our mealtimes, but a collection of early sugar bowls helps to bring to mind an ancient age when sugar, this "sort of hard honey," as Dioscorides wrote Roman emperor Nero, was a rare treasure brought from afar and available to only the privileged few.

(Editor's Note: *Kyle Husfloen, Editor of* THE ANTIQUE TRADER WEEKLY *newspaper for the past 13 years, is a dedicated collector of early Americana, especially early American glass before 1860. Sugar bowls are one facet of his varied collection.*)

*   *   *   *   *

EARLY FREE-BLOWN GLASS

Clear sugar bowl w/galleried rim & domed cover. Applied chain decoration to both base & cover. Thomas Cains' South Boston or the Phoenix Glass Works, ca. 1820. 5 1/8" d., 5 7/8" h...............$2,000.00

Clear sugar bowl & cover tooled in the Beehive design. Footed base & bowl w/seven heavy rings & cover w/six rings plus applied finial. Probably Boston & Sandwich Glass Co. 5¼" d., 7" h. 1,900.00

Cobalt blue sugar bowl w/galleried rim & domed cover. Pear-shaped body w/applied foot. Domed cover w/folded rim & flat knob finial. Pittsburgh, ca. 1830, 4" d. at mouth, 6¾" h. (ILLUS. on cover) ....1,200.00 to 1,800.00

Greenish aqua sugar bowl w/galleried rim & very high domed cover. Applied circular foot & applied Type I Lilypad decoration. Domed cover w/folded rim & solid "button" finial. 4 1/8" d. at mouth, 7½" h.........3,600.00

EARLY BLOWN EXPANDED-MOLD GLASS

Stiegel-type Sugar Bowl

Amethyst sugar bowl & domed cover pattern-molded in the 12-vertical panel design. Pear-shaped footed bowl w/galleried rim. Bakewell, Page and Bakewell, Pittsburgh, ca. 1830. 4 1/8" d., 7" h. 5,300.00

Clear sugar bowl & domed cover pattern-molded in the 12-panel design. Panels at base of bowl w/galleried rim, applied pedestal foot & knop-wafered stem. Engraved w/fine designs of leaves & daisies. 4 7/8" d., 7 3/8" h. . . . . . .2,800.00 to 4,000.00

Cobalt blue Stiegel-type sugar bowl & cover. Pattern-molded in the 16-Diamond patt. Applied foot & applied double-tiered swirled finial on cover. 4¾" d., 6 1/8" h. (ILLUS.) 5,800.00

Purple-blue sugar bowl & domed cover. Pattern-molded in the 12-vertical rib design. Footed pear-shaped bowl w/galleried rim. Attributed to Bakewell, Page and Bakewell, Pittsburgh, ca. 1830. 4 1/8" d. at mouth, 6¾" h. 2,000.00

Clear w/greyish tint sugar bowl & cover. Pillar-molded in 8-rib design. Applied solid circular foot w/pontil. Cover w/design drawn into high peak & applied w/solid finial. Pittsburgh, Pennsylvania, 1840-50. 4¾" d. at mouth, 8 1/8" h. 2,300.00

EARLY LACY PRESSED GLASS (1830s and 1840s)

Canary yellow Gothic Arch patt. sugar bowl & cover. 5 1/8" h. (shallow non-disfiguring spall on underside of lid & mold roughness) 450.00

Canary-vaseline California design sugar bowl & cover. 5¾" h. (shallow 1" chip under lip of cover which does not detract) 400.00

Deep blue Gothic Arch patt. sugar bowl & cover. 5½" h. (rim of base w/overall roughness & cover w/non-disfiguring chip under lip & short 1½" crack) 350.00

Midwestern Gothic Arch Pattern

Electric blue Gothic Arch patt. sugar bowl w/petal foot & cover (unseen chips on underside edge of cover). Midwestern version. 5 3/8" h. (ILLUS.) 360.00

Fiery opal Gothic Arch patt. sugar bowl & cover. 5¼" h. 500.00

PATTERN GLASS (1840s and on)

All sugar bowls listed are clear glass and with a lid unless otherwise noted.

CLEAR FLINT GLASS PATTERNS (1840-60)

Four Petal Sugar Bowl

Argus	.65.00
Bellflower, single vine	.95.00
Bull's Eye	135.00
Cable	.95.00
Colonial	.95.00
Diamond Point	.95.00
Diamond Thumbprint	125.00

Excelsior 80.00
Four Petal (ILLUS.) 70.00
Honeycomb 75.00
Horn of Plenty 95.00

1870's Frosted & Clear Patterns
Frosted Circle 45.00
Frosted Lion.........................75.00
Frosted Ribbon 45.00
Three Face 120.00
Westward Ho ....125.00 to 160.00

1870's & 80's Geometric & Beaded Motif Patterns

Inverted Fern Sugar Bowl

Inverted Fern (ILLUS.) 75.00
Loop 70.00
Mirror..............................60.00
New England Pineapple 95.00
Ribbed Grape 95.00
Ribbed Ivy 90.00
Ribbon 65.00

Feather Sugar Bowl

Art ....40.00 to 50.00
Atlas...............................38.00
Beaded Loop 47.50
Beaded Mirror......................45.00
Buckle (open) 19.00
Cane, amber 55.00
Cane, clear 40.00
Chain 32.50
Chain with Star 37.50
Chandelier.........................40.00
Cordova..................35.00 to 40.00
Dewdrop with Star 50.00
Feather (ILLUS.) 37.50
Finecut 35.00
Hand 75.00
Herringbone 24.00
Jacob's Ladder 43.50

Sawtooth Sugar Bowl

Sawtooth (ILLUS.) 75.00
Waffle & Thumbprint 135.00

NON-FLINT GLASS PATTERNS

1870's Floral & Fruit Motifs
Barley..............................27.00
Beaded Grape or Beaded Grape
  Medallion........................46.50
Cabbage Rose 55.00
Grape & Festoon....................45.00
Lily-of-the-Valley 75.00
Paneled Forget-me-not 40.00
Rose in Snow, round or
  square ....40.00 to 45.00
Wheat & Barley 32.50

Jacob's Ladder Open Sugar

Jacob's Ladder, open (ILLUS.) 28.00
Kokomo 45.00
Lattice 29.00
Nailhead 30.00
One-Hundred-One 45.00
Picket 40.00
Pleat & Panel (open) 13.50

Priscilla Pattern

Priscilla (ILLUS.) .50.00

Snail Sugar Bowl

Snail (ILLUS.) 60.00
Spirea Band, blue 52.50
Spirea Band, clear 35.00
Three Panel, amber 40.00
Three Panel, blue .55.00
Three Panel, clear 28.00
Three Panel, vaseline 60.00
Two Panel 30.00
Zipper 25.00

Late Imitation Cut Glass Patterns

Aztec 25.00
Brazilian (ILLUS.) .25.00
Pineapple & Fan .40.00
Wiltec 40.00

Brazilian Pattern

States Patterns

Colorado, green, large . . . . .65.00 to 95.00
Dakota . . . . .55.00 to 65.00
Delaware, rose w/gold 100.00
Florida Palm 35.00
Illinois 50.00
Iowa 20.00
Maryland 55.00
Massachusetts (open) 20.00
Michigan 50.00
Minnesota 30.00
Missouri 50.00
Texas 60.00
Wisconsin 37.50
(The) States 40.00

ART GLASS

While sugar bowls are sometimes found in various late 19th century art glass forms, one encounters the sugar shaker (muffineer) more frequently in this type of glass.

CARNIVAL GLASS (early 20th c.)

Most sugar bowls sell within the $50 to $150 price range but there are exceptions. Check the various patterns of Carnival Glass.

DEPRESSION GLASS (1930 and on)

In some patterns of Depression Glass sugar bowls sell for under $10 and almost all Depression Glass sugar bowls are priced under $30, but a few scarce colors in certain patterns are more costly. Check the various patterns of Depression Glass.

GRANITEWARE (late 19th - early 20th c.)

Graniteware Sugar Bowl

Mottled blue & white, bulbous body
w/loop handles at sides, double-
domed lid w/self-finial (ILLUS.) 25.00
Robin's egg blue w/black trim, cov.,
4" d., 4½" h. 28.50
White, w/decal on body, pewter rim,
handles & lid .100.00

METALS

PLATED SILVER (Victorian)

Forbes Silver Co. sugar bowl, domed
cover, pedestal base, ca. 1895 . . . . . . .40.00
Wilcox Silverplate Co. sugar bowl,
domed cover, hoof feet, ca. 1870 . . . . .45.00
Sugar bowl-spoonholder combination,
footed, bird-inset handles, 12 spoon
slots at rim, cover w/ornate finial,
w/sapphire blue glass sugar bowl
insert 175.00
Sugar bowl-spoonholder combination,
pedestal base, engraved bowl
w/rabbit handles & 12 spoon slots
at rim, cover w/pointed finial,
w/cranberry glass sugar bowl
insert 185.00

SILVER, AMERICAN & OTHERS

American sugar urn & cover, pedestal
base, beaded rims & pierced gallery
rim, engraved w/monogram within
oval shield suspended from bow-tied
ribbon flanked by husk pendants &
ribbon-tied floral spray below at
front, reel-shaped cover w/pine-
apple finial w/leaves at base & top,
Joseph & Nathaniel Richardson,
Philadelphia, ca. 1785, 8½" h. 6,050.00
American sugar urn & cover, flaring
cylindrical foot on square base, body
& foot w/beaded moldings & rim
w/bright-cut border, body w/shield-
shaped bright-cut reserve, cover
w/urn finial, Ephraim Brasher, New
York, 1786-1807, 9½" h. 1,650.00
American sugar urn & cover, flaring
cylindrical stem w/beaded edge on
square foot, body w/beaded &
molded rim w/engraved initials,
cover w/stepped & beaded edge
w/urn-shaped finial, Joseph
Richardson, Jr., Philadelphia, 1785-
1800, 9¾" h. .2,420.00

American Silver Sugar Urn

American sugar urn & cover, beaded
borders on pedestal raised on square
base, body w/engraved ribbon-tied
shield enclosing contemporary
monogram & pierced gallery, reel-
form cover w/pineapple finial,
Richards & Williamson, Philadelphia,
ca. 1800, 10 1/8" h. (ILLUS.) 3,520.00
American sugar urn & cover, pedestal
foot on square base, beaded
borders, reel-form cover w/urn
finial, Christian Wiltberger, Philadelphia, ca. 1800, 10 1/8" h. 1,760.00
Dutch sugar urn & cover, fluted
pedestal foot, beaded borders, body
w/engraved crest & English presentation inscription, cover w/engraved
ribbonwork rim & bud finial, maker's
mark "J.H.V." in monogram struck
4 times on base, 8 5/8" h. 1,210.00
German sugar box w/hinged lid,
octagonal form on paw feet,
grapevine at rim & oval plaque
w/playful tritons on body, Gottlob
Ludwig Howaldt, Berlin, ca. 1825,
5¾" w. 522.00

TIN & TOLE

Tole, cov., white band w/free-hand red
& green fruit & leaves & yellow
striping on old black repaint,
3½" h. 245.00

Tole, domed cover, free-hand red fruit
  & yellow leaves on black ground,
  Pennsylvania, 19th c. 550.00

CERAMIC

ENGLISH

Early Flow Blue Sugar Bowl

Flow blue, octagonal, brush stroke
  Aster & Grapeshot patt., ca. 1850,
  7" h. (ILLUS.) 300.00

St. Louis Pattern Flow Blue

Flow blue, St. Louis patt., Johnson
  Bros., ca. 1900, 5¾" d., 4¾" h.
  (ILLUS.) 60.00
Ironstone, Boote's 1851 Octagon patt.,
  all white 35.00
Ironstone, Ceres shape, all white,
  Ellsmore & Forster, 1853-71 . . . . 125.00
Ironstone, Cone with Leaves patt., all
  white, James Edwards, 1842-51 . . . . . . 45.00
Ironstone, Corn & Oats patt., all white,
  John Wedge Wood, 1841-60 . . . . 50.00
Ironstone, Gothic patt., all white,
  Ridgway 60.00
Ironstone, Hyacinth patt., all white,
  Alcock 35.00
Ironstone, Moss Rose patt., Alfred
  Meakin, 7" h. (ILLUS.) 40.00

Moss Rose Pattern Ironstone

Ironstone, Tea Leaf Lustre patt., Lily-
  of-the-Valley mold, Anthony Shaw . . . 75.00
Ironstone, Tea Leaf Lustre patt., small . . 55.00

Walley's Lustreberry Pattern

Ironstone, octagonal, Walley's Lustre-
  berry patt., copper lustre sprigs,
  Edward Walley, ca. 1842, 8 1/8" h.
  (ILLUS.) 125.00

Leeds Pottery Sugar Bowl

Leeds earthenware, brush stroke dark
  blue leaves on pale blue-washed
  ground, 1790-1800, 4" h. (ILLUS.) 200.00
Silver Lustre ware, Staffordshire
  district, 1800-15, 5¼" w., 5¼" h.
  (ILLUS.) 125.00

Silver Lustre Ware Sugar Bowl

Spatter ware, Peafowl patt., free-hand
blue, ochre, red & black peafowl on
blue spatter ground, 4 3/8" h. 400.00

Spatter Ware Sugar Bowl

Spatter ware, purple spatter at
shoulders, rim & cover, ca. 1830,
4½" h. (ILLUS.) 300.00
Spatter ware, Rainbow patt., red,
green, yellow & black spattered
diagonal stripes, 5 3/8" h. (edge
chip on flat lid) 285.00

Staffordshire Bowl with Oriental Scene

Staffordshire earthenware, blue transfer of Oriental landscape w/temples
& boat in foreground, ca. 1810,
7" w., 5" h. (ILLUS.)...............120.00

Staffordshire Sugar Bowl

Staffordshire earthenware, pink transfer florals, scrolls & Oriental figures,
unmarked, 5½" w., 6¾" h. (ILLUS.) ..85.00

Chelsea Sprig Pattern

Staffordshire earthenware, Chelsea
Blue Sprig patt. by J. Wedge Wood,
ca. 1845, 6¼" d., 8¾" h. (ILLUS.).....55.00
Staffordshire earthenware with Historical American scene, dark blue
transfer of Lafayette at Franklin's
Tomb, w/floral border, Wood,
4¾" h. (chip on rim & bowl w/pin-
point edge flake) 375.00

Historical Staffordshire Sugar Bowl

Staffordshire earthenware with Historical American scene, dark blue
transfer of Lafayette at Franklin's
Tomb, w/floral border, 6" h.,
Thomas Mayer (ILLUS.) 358.00
Staffordshire earthenware, Athens patt.
by Adams, mulberry transfer,
ca. 1849 . . . . .179.00
Staffordshire earthenware, Beehive
patt. by Adams, purple transfer. 79.00

Porcelain Sugar Bowl

Unattributed English porcelain, h.p.
pink roses, green leaves, blue floral
sprigs & gold bands decor, 1810-20,
6¼" w., 4¾" h. (ILLUS.). 200.00

FRENCH PORCELAIN

Chantilly Sugar Bowl

Chantilly, h.p. colorful scattered floral
sprays, cover w/lemon branch finial
& chocolate brown rim, iron-red
hunting horn mark & painter's mark,
ca. 1745 (ILLUS.) 550.00
Haviland & Co., Autumn Leaf patt.,
early 20th c.. .45.00
Haviland & Co., tiny blue floral decor,
early 20th c.. .40.00
Limoges (T. & V.), model of a basket
w/scalloped rim & overhead handle,
h.p. purple floral decor, 4" w., 5" to
top of handle (open). 75.00
Sevres, h.p. portrait of court lady
reserved within turquoise jeweling at
at front & w/interlaced floral initials

reverse on blue ground w/gilt
diamond pattern enclosing white
enameled fleur-de-lis, cover
w/flowerhead finial, 18th c.,
3½" d. 660.00

Unmarked French Porcelain Sugar Bowl

Unattributed French porcelain, h.p.
moss rose decor, ca. 1870, 5¼" d.,
7" h. (ILLUS.) .60.00

GERMAN & AUSTRIAN PORCELAIN

Bluebird Pattern Austrian Sugar Bowl

Austrian, Carlsbad, Victoria, Bluebird
patt., decal of bluebird & h.p. blue
trim, small size (ILLUS.) 25.00
Austrian, h.p. pink florals & green
leaves, blue trim. 20.00

Carlsbad-Austria Sugar Bowl

Austrian, Carlsbad, embossed scrollwork, transfer print & h.p. pink,
white & green blossoms w/brown
leaves & branches, 6½" h. (ILLUS.) ...40.00

German, Meissen, Blue Onion patt.,
late 19th c........................125.00

German, Royal Bayreuth, peasants &
house scene w/blue sky & clouds
decor 50.00

German, Royal Bayreuth, figural
lobster (open) 80.00

German, Royal Bayreuth, figural
poppy, purple 125.00

German, Royal Bayreuth, figural
poppy, red......................160.00

Royal Bayreuth Rose Sugar Bowl

German, Royal Bayreuth, figural rose,
open (ILLUS.) 175.00

German (or Germanic Provinces),
Schlegelmilch, E.S. Prov. Saxe, pink
primroses decor on yellow ground,
light blue rim band & heavy gold
tracery 45.00

German (or Germanic Provinces),
Schlegelmilch, R.S. Poland, wavy
mold, pink roses decor on shaded
lavender ground.................125.00

German, Schlegelmilch, R.S. Prussia,
10-scallop base, Castle Scene
decor 275.00

R.S. Prussia Cottage Scene Sugar Bowl

German, Schlegelmilch, R.S. Prussia,
Cottage Scene (ILLUS.)............300.00

German, Schlegelmilch, R.S. Prussia,
Hanging Flower Basket patt. on
shaded lavender, yellow, blue &
green ground, gold trim 140.00

R.S. Prussia with Madame Lebrun

German, Schlegelmilch, R.S. Prussia,
Madame Lebrun self portrait
(ILLUS.) 175.00

German, Schlegelmilch, R.S. Prussia,
icicle mold, Pond Lilies reflecting
in Water, light blue ground.........150.00

German, Schlegelmilch, R.S. Prussia,
feather plume mold, poppy cluster
decor, gilt trim 110.00

German, Schlegelmilch, R.S. Prussia,
Summer Season portrait 750.00

German, Schlegelmilch, R.S. Prussia,
icicle mold, Swans (3) on Lake Scene,
dark & light blue & tan 375.00

Winter Season Portrait

German, Schlegelmilch, R.S. Prussia,
poppy mold, Winter Season portrait
(ILLUS.) 650.00

German, Schlegelmilch, R.S. Prussia,
4-footed mold, scalloped rim, pink
florals on light shaded to dark cobalt
blue ground, gilt trim.............110.00

German, Schlegelmilch, R.S. Prussia,
plain mold, pink & white bellflowers
on shaded green ground 75.00

German, Schlegelmilch, R.S. Tillowitz,
white peonies on shaded light russet

R.S. Tillowitz Sugar Bowl

to green ground, gold trim, 5" h.
(ILLUS.) 65.00

IRISH & AMERICAN BELLEEK

Irish Belleek, Limpet patt., gold trim,
3rd black mark 100.00
Irish Belleek, Neptune patt., pink trim,
2nd black mark, small 65.00
Irish Belleek, Shamrock-Basketweave
patt., 3rd black mark 55.00
Irish Belleek, Tridacna patt., pink trim,
2nd black mark 100.00
American Belleek, dragon handles,
mask spout, small h.p. multicolored
florals, Willets pink mark 100.00
American Belleek, pedestal base,
factory-decorated gold paste swags
& baskets w/pink roses, Willets..... 125.00

JAPANESE & CHINESE

Chinese Export, reserved on front &
reverse w/brown & gilt-edged oval
panel w/scene of pr. of coopers
working on barrel with other figures
looking on, buildings & small boat in
distance & mother seated w/child on
her knee before turreted castle in
shades of brown, green, yellow,
blue, turquoise "grisaille" & touches
of rose & iron-red, ca. 1740,
4 5/8" d. 880.00

Chinese Export Armorial Sugar Bowl

Chinese Export, Armorial decor,
painted on front & reverse "en
grisaille" w/arms of John Boyle, 3rd
Earl of Glasgow above motto
beneath a gold floral & foliate
border & w/gilt peach-form knop on
cover, ca. 1755, 5¼" h. (ILLUS.) ... 1,760.00
Chinese Rose Medallion patt., marked
"Made in China," early 20th c. 85.00
Japanese, Nippon "M" in Wreath mark,
pedestal base, open handles at
sides, h.p. roses on white, Wedgwood blue borders w/slip-trailed
moriage scrolls 65.00
Japanese, Nippon "M" in Wreath mark,
h.p. woodland scene in shades of
brown & green, 3½" h. 45.00
Japanese, Noritake, Azalea patt.,
20th c. 45.00
Japanese, marked "Made in Japan,"
Geisha Girl patt., red trim 12.00

AMERICAN PORCELAIN
(Early 20th Century)

Lenox, cobalt blue w/sterling silver
overlay (open) 55.00
Pickard, h.p. long-stemmed flowers,
gold handles, borders & finial 55.00
Pickard, currants decor, artist-signed... 65.00
Pickard, roses decor, heavy gold trim... 50.00

AMERICAN UTILITARIAN POTTERY

Frankoma Pottery, Wagon Wheel patt.,
brown & green, 4" h. 5.00
Hall China Co. Jewel Tea Company's
Autumn Leaf patt., pre-1940......... 25.00
Homer Laughlin China Co., Fiesta
ware, chartreuse or grey, each 17.00
Homer Laughlin China Co., Fiesta
ware, light or forest green or tur-
quoise, each .... 10.00 to 14.00
Homer Laughlin China Co., Fiesta
ware, red .... 17.00 to 25.00
Hull Pottery, Little Red Riding Hood
(figural) patt..................... 60.00
Shawnee Pottery, Corn King line 17.50
Shawnee Pottery, Corn Queen line 20.00
Western Stoneware Co., Old Sleepy
Eye patt., cobalt blue on white,
1906-37, 4" h..................... 390.00

AMERICAN ART POTTERY

Rookwood Pottery, underglaze slip-
painted florals, standard glaze,
dated 1893 .... 285.00
Rookwood Pottery, floral decor on pink
ground, artist-signed & dated 1928 .. 120.00
Rookwood Pottery, pink glaze, dated
1949 .... 25.00
Roseville Pottery, Bushberry line,
berries & leaves on russet bark-
textured ground 15.00

Roseville Pottery, Dutch line 55.00
Roseville Pottery, Landscape line 55.00
Roseville Pottery, Peony line, rose
   ground 20.00
Roseville Pottery, Zephyr Lily line,
   green ground 20.00
Weller Pottery, Wild Rose line 18.00

(End of Special Focus)

SUNBONNET BABY COLLECTIBLES

"Sunbonnet Babies Coloring Book"

Bertha L. Corbett, creator of these faceless children, proved a figure did not need a face to express character. Her pastel drawings appeared in "Sunbonnet Primer" by Eulalie Osgood Grover, published in 1900. Later Miss Corbett did a series showing the babies at work, one for each day of the week, and they became so popular advertisers began using them. Numerous objects including cards and prints with illustrations of, or in the shape of the Sunbonnet Babies are now being collected.

Book, "Sunbonnet Babies Coloring
   Book," published by Rand McNally,
   1937, 12½ x 10¾" (ILLUS.) $30.00
Book, "Sunbonnet Babies Primer,"
   by Eulalie Osgood Grover, illus-
   trated by Bertha Corbett,
   1900 . . . . 85.00 to 110.00
Book, "Sunbonnet Twins," color illus-
   trations by Bertha Corbett, 1907 . . . . . 65.00
Box, cov., china, spade-shaped,
   Sunbonnet Babies washing & iron-
   ing decor, 3¼ x 3" 150.00
Cup, demitasse, china, Sunbonnet
   Babies fishing decor, gold trim 85.00
Cup, china, "Days of the Week"
   series, 1¾" 30.00
Feeding dish, china, "Mending Day,"
   Cleveland China, 8" d. 95.00

Feeding dish, china, Sunbonnet Girl
   serving tea to Overall Boy, B.E.
   McNichol Pottery Co. 250.00
Plate, china, Sunbonnet Babies decor
   around rim, 5" d. 20.00
Plate, china, "Scrubbing Day," 6¼" d. . . 85.00
Postcard, "Last Day of Summer,"
   signed Dorothy Dixon (pseud. for
   Bertha Corbett), 1905 . . . . 15.00
Postcard, "Paying Toll," signed
   Dorothy Dixon, 1905 . . . . 15.00
Postcard, "Saying Grace," signed
   Dorothy Dixon, 1905 . . . . 12.50
Postcards, "Month of the Year" series,
   1906 copyright by the Ullman Mfg. Co.,
   New York, framed, set of 12 . . . . 120.00
Print, "Family Cares," original frame,
   1905, 7½ x 9½" 38.00
Print, "Fishing," by B. L. Corbett,
   framed 20.00
Print, "The Good Old Summertime,"
   by B. L. Corbett, framed 20.00
Quilt, appliqued Sunbonnet Babies
   decor, ca. 1930, single bed size 135.00
School set: calendar, crayons, pen,
   ruler & tablet in leather case; Sunbonnet Babies decor, 1936, 6 pcs. 20.00

TEDDY BEAR COLLECTIBLES

"The Roosevelt Bears" Book

Theodore (Teddy) Roosevelt had become a national hero during the Spanish-American War by leading his "Rough Riders" to victory at San Juan Hill in 1898. He became the 26th President of the United States in 1901 when President McKinley was assassinated. The gregarious Roosevelt was fond of the outdoors and hunting. Legend has it that while on a hunting trip, soon after becoming President, he refused to shoot a bear cub because it was so small and helpless. The story was picked up by a political cartoonist who depicted President Roosevelt, attired in hunting garb, turning away and refusing to shoot a small bear cub. Shortly thereafter, toy plush bears began appearing in department stores labeled "Teddy Bear" and they became an immediate success. Books on the adventures of "The Roosevelt Bears" were written and illustrated by Paul Piper under the pseudonym of Seymour Eaton and this version of the Teddy Bear became a popular decoration on children's dishes.

Baby rattle w/teething ring, silver-
plate, w/figural Teddy Bear $70.00
Book, "Mother Goose's Teddy Bears,"
Frederick L. Cavally, Jr., 1907 . . . . . . 85.00
Book, "The Roosevelt Bears, Their
Travels & Adventures," Seymour
Eaton (Paul Piper), illustrations by
Floyd V. Campbell, published by
Edward Stern & Co., Philadelphia,
hard cover, 1906 (ILLUS.) . . . . 85.00 to 95.00
Book, "The Teddy Bear That Prowled
at Night," Edna G. Deihl, illus-
trations by Mary Russell, 1924 . . . . . . 24.00
Book, "The Traveling Bears in
England," Seymour Eaton, hard
cover, 1907 . . . . 62.50
Book, "The Traveling Bears in
Fairyland," Seymour Eaton, hard
cover, 1907 . . . . 60.00
Fork, silverplate, figural Teddy Bear
atop handle 30.00
Match holder, ceramic, Teddy Bear
standing by hat 50.00
Paper doll, Teddy Bear w/five outfits,
Selchow & Righter, 1904, original
envelope (1 hat missing) 250.00
Plate, china, Roosevelt Bears digging
Panama Canal, w/verse on foreign
aid, pink lustre border, 6¼" d. 47.50
Postcard, bear standing w/a walking
stick in one paw & "Rough Rider" hat
in the other, "Teddy B," ca. 1913 . . . . . 10.00
Prints, "The Roosevelt Bears Abroad,"
colorful scenes, set of 16 . . . . 100.00
Tea set: cov. teapot, creamer, sugar
bowl & 4 c/s; child's, china, Roosevelt Bears decor w/pink lustre trim,
11 pcs. 325.00
Teddy bear, white mohair straw-
stuffed body w/hump back, swivel
head & articulated limbs, shoe buton
eyes, Steiff, early 1900s, 3½" h. 235.00
Teddy bear, brown plush body, glass
eyes, dressed in green felt jacket,
6¼" h. 52.50
Teddy bear, shaggy reddish brown
mohair straw & excelsior stuffed
body, articulated limbs, glass eyes,
narrow nose, w/blanket, 9" h. 220.00

Teddy bear, dark brown mohair body
w/hump back, articulated limbs,
shoe button eyes, original felt
padded feet & paws, 12" h. 185.00
Teddy bear, maize-colored plush body
w/hump back, swivel head & articulated limbs, embroidered nose &
mouth, muslin feet & paws
w/embroidered nails, w/working
growler, ca. 1910, 16" h. 400.00
Toothpick holder, porcelain, "Teddy &
His Bear," souvenir 125.00
Whistle, tin, lithographed Teddy Bears
decor, Germany 24.00

TELEPHONES

Candlestick-type, "AT & T," 1920 . . . . . . $95.00
Candlestick-type, "Automatic Electric
Co.," brass 90.00
Candlestick-type, "Kellogg," oak bell
box, 1901 . . . . 135.00 to 150.00
Candlestick-type, "Stromberg Carlson,"
brass, oil can shape, ca. 1900 . . . . 90.00
Desk-type, "Stromberg Carlson," hand
crank on side 45.00
Wall-type, "Green Telephone & Electric
Mfg., Milwaukee," oak case
w/cathedral top, picture frame front,
8" w., 25" h. (refinished) 215.00
Wall-type, "Kellogg," oak
case . . . . 150.00 to 195.00
Wall-type, "Sumpter Telephone Co.,"
oak case 950.00
Wall-type, oak case, 1914,
21" h. . . . . 135.00 to 165.00

TEXTILE COLLECTIBLES

BATTENBURG LACE
Doily, thread-drawnwork center
w/initial "H," 17" sq. $45.00
Dresser scarf, grape & leaf border on
3 sides, 24 x 80" 145.00
Table centerpiece, 6" Battenburg
border, 26" sq. 98.00
Table centerpiece, white satin stitched
florals on linen center, Battenburg
border, 26" d. 90.00
Table centerpiece, thread-drawnwork
center, 29" sq. 115.00
Tablecloth, linen center, Battenburg
border, 45" d. 58.00
Tablecloth, 50" d. 110.00

Tablecloth, 60" d. 45.00
Tablecloth, linen center, Battenburg
 border, 64" d. .95.00
Tablecloth, 68" d. 150.00
Tablecloth & 8 napkins, 68 x 88"
 tablecloth, 9 pcs. . . . . .200.00 to 250.00
Table runner, solid squares w/Batten-
 burg medallions, 18 x 50" 115.00
Table runner, wide Battenburg border,
 18 x 52". 95.00
Table runner, 3 squares center w/thread-
 drawnwork, 19 x 52" 78.00
Table runner, 15 x 54" 63.50

BEDSPREADS, COVERLETS & QUILTS

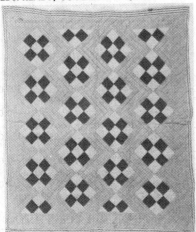

Crib Size Quilt

Bedspread, Battenburg lace, 90 x 90" . .350.00
Bedspread, hand-crocheted cotton,
 Candlewick patt., ecru, 100 x 100"
 (very minor wear). 200.00
Bedspread, hand-crocheted cotton,
 Pinwheel patt., white, full size. 175.00
Bedspread, hand-crocheted cotton,
 Star & Popcorn patt., scalloped
 edges, queen size. 250.00
Bedspread, white trapunto work,
 Marseilles patt., full size. 60.00
Coverlet, jacquard single weave,
 1-piece, blue, white, red & gold
 floral medallions alternating w/stars
 center, urn of flowers border, signed
 "D. Cosley, Xenia, Greene Co.,
 Ohio, 1849" in corner, 92 x 78
 (some wear) 300.00
Coverlet, jacquard single weave,
 1-piece, floral & foliage medallion
 center, stylized floral & geometric
 medallions border, red, blue, green
 & white, signed "Made by J. Haag
 Inemaus for J.O. 1850," original
 fringe, 96 x 76" 455.00
Coverlet, jacquard single weave,
 2-piece w/center seam, floral medallions

center, vintage border, blue & white,
 signed "Loudonville, Ohio 1868, wove
 by Peter Grimm," 82 x 72" (minor
 wear) 400.00
Coverlet, jacquard weave, double
 woven, 2-piece w/center seam, blue,
 white & red rose medallions,
 86 x 74". 350.00
Coverlet, jacquard weave, double woven,
 2-piece w/center seam, snowflakes
 center, pine tree border, blue & white,
 97 x 74". 325.00
Coverlet, overshot weave, 2-piece,
 red, navy blue, white & teal blue,
 82 x 68". 235.00
Coverlet, overshot weave, 2-piece,
 red & white, 88 x 76" 275.00
Quilt, crib size, pieced Flower Garden
 patt., purple & black silk, 33 x 24" 85.00
Quilt, crib size, pieced Flying Geese
 patt., multicolor calico patches,
 ca. 1860, 32 x 32" 295.00
Quilt, crib size, pieced Nine Patch
 patt., navy blue, white & pink calico
 patches, w/line quilting, late 19th c.,
 25 x 22" (ILLUS.) 220.00
Quilt, crib size, pieced & embroidered
 Mother Goose patt., each block
 w/scene from a nursery rhyme &
 alternating w/solid pale blue
 blocks. 352.00
Quilt, appliqued Album patt., white
 squares appliqued w/plain & printed
 cotton, several signed in ink, backed
 w/white cotton, late 19th-early 20th c.,
 80 x 80". 990.00
Quilt, appliqued floral medallions
 (6) w/meandering vine border, red,
 yellow & yellow-green, 90 x 88"
 (minor wear & fading) 250.00
Quilt, appliqued & pieced Bud & Blos-
 som patt., red & green calico
 patches on white cotton field w/leaf
 sprig quilting, 19th c., 104 x 92" 880.00

Feathered Star Pattern Quilt

Quilt, pieced Feathered Star patt.,
moss green stars feathered in pale
beige triangular patches, field
w/flowerhead & cable quilting,
bordered on 2 sides w/moss green
& beige, dated "1890," 84 x 80"
(ILLUS.) 412.00

Quilt, pieced House patt., yellow
& lavender, 82 x 70" 150.00

Quilt, pieced Maltese Cross patt.,
salmon, light green & white cotton
patches, w/decorative stitching,
ca. 1920, 86½ x 76" 286.00

Quilt, pieced Nine Patch patt., dark
colors & blue & white plaid print on
brown, reverse w/cotton print w/dogs
& cats, 84 x 70" 250.00

Quilt, pieced Old Maid's Puzzle patt.,
black, blue, red & white, 76 x 76" ...185.00

Quilt, pieced Pinwheel Block patt., blue
& white polka dot calico patches,
white cotton field w/diagonal line
& diamond quilting, 19th c.,
76 x 76" 825.00

Quilt, pieced Robbing Peter to Pay Paul
patt., beige & blue cotton patches,
field w/conforming line quilting,
19th c., 84 x 84" 660.00

Rose Blossom & Bud Pattern Quilt

Quilt, pieced Rose Blossom & Bud patt.,
red, green, yellow-printed & solid
calico patches, white cotton field
w/diamond quilting divided into
square reserves, each bordered by
brilliantly colored chintz fabric,
wide borders w/green, rose & blue
floral chintz, signed "C.A. Harris" &
dated "October 1855," 100 x 88"
(ILLUS.) 1,430.00

Quilt, pieced Seven Sisters patt.,
yellow, pink, green & blue printed
& solid calico patches, field

w/flowerhead quilting, ca. 1930,
100 x 80".........................880.00

Quilt, pieced Star of Bethlehem patt.,
lavender, green & white cotton patches,
scalloped border, field w/feather &
interlacing circle quilting, ca. 1930,
84 x 80".........................495.00

Quilt, pieced Wild Goose Chase patt.,
red & olive green "linsey woolsey"
patches, field w/diagonal line
quilting, notched for a tester
bedstead, probably Pennsylvania,
late 18th c., 90 x 90" 935.00

Quilt, pieced & embroidered Log Cabin
patt., pink, grey, maroon, green & gold
silk & satin patches embroidered
w/floral or tree motif, made for
Dr. C. Cole Bradley, Connecticut,
dated 1899, 80 x 64" 880.00

Quilt, pieced Sunshine & Shadow patt.,
all cotton, blue, green, brown, grey &
black, w/blue & grey borders, Amish,
ca. 1940, 77 x 64" 775.00

SAMPLERS

Alphabet Sampler

Alphabets, numbers, house, trees &
young ladies, green, gold, blue & white
stitched on homespun fabric, signed
& dated 1810, 9½ x 8"............1,225.00

Alphabets above house w/trees,
birds & man & woman in garden
within flowering border blue,
olive green, brown, gold, black &
white stitched on homespun linen
fabric, signed & dated 1784,
framed, 12¾ x 12¼" 525.00

Alphabets, birds & stylized flowering
trees in multicolors stitched on
homespun linen fabric, mahogany
veneer frame, 16¾ x 12¾" 275.00

Alphabets, numbers & deer within
vining border, brown, blue, green &
white stitched on homespun fabric,
signed & dated 1820s, framed,
17¾ x 14¾".......................260.00

Alphabets, numerals, row of vining
flowers, house, fence, trees w/birds,

"Martha Walker, Aged thirteen years AD 1813" & verse, green, blue, brown, pink & white stitched on homespun linen fabric, flame mahogany veneer frame, 18¼ x 14¾" (ILLUS) 1,325.00

Meadow scene w/large stylized tree, sheep, shepherd & maiden in foreground, large brick house on a hill w/farm buildings & picket fence, birds & floral baskets, stitched on linen fabric, signed & dated 1812, gilt frame, 24 x 20"................625.00

Pious verse above register w/figures of Adam & Eve, serpent, tree & flowers within floral border, stitched on linen, signed & dated 1843, framed, 24¼ x 20" 280.00

Pious verse above flowering tree, recumbent deer & oversized bird in smaller tree, w/birds, pots of flowers & central floral wreath w/name & date below within vining floral border, gold, brown, red, blue & green stitched on homespun fabric, signed & dated 1829 within wreath, oak frame, 26¼ x 23½".........1,325.00

Shepherd & flock beside cottage below large colorful floral medallion surrounded by birds & floral baskets within floral spray border, signed & dated 1839, cherrywood frame, 25¾ x 21¾"....................400.00

Tree flanked by birds & basket of fruit above a verse over stylized birds & animals centering a flowering tree over inscription "Esther Jesse Paris Aged 12 Years 1837" within a floral border, cross & Irish stitched, polychrome wool yarns, framed, 16½ x 11¾"....................220.00

STEVENGRAPHS

Grover Cleveland Bookmark

Bookmark, "A Birthday Gift" 65.00
Bookmark, "A Blessing" 32.00
Bookmark, "Greetings of the Season," Christmas colors 65.00
Bookmark, "Grover Cleveland," w/shield, red, white & blue (ILLUS.) 130.00
Bookmark, "Happy May Thy Birthday Be" ....50.00 to 58.00
Bookmark, "Home Sweet Home".......75.00
Bookmark, "Honor Thy Father & Mother" 75.00
Bookmark, "Last Rose of Summer," Columbian Exposition, 1893 ....110.00
Bookmark, "Little Busy Bee"..........50.00
Bookmark, "Merry Christmas & Happy New Year" 35.00
Bookmark, "Norwich Anniversary"....150.00
Bookmark, "Old Arm Chair"..........50.00
Bookmark, "To My Father" 45.00
Bookmark, "To My Dear Mother"..................50.00 to 55.00
Bookmark, "Unchanging Love" 55.00
Picture, "The Good Old Days," framed 150.00
Picture, hunting series, "The Death," matted & framed..................175.00
Picture, hunting series, "The Finish," framed 185.00
Picture, hunting series, "Full Cry," matted & framed ....150.00 to 175.00
Picture, hunting series, "The Meet," framed.................165.00 to 185.00
Picture, hunting series, "The Start," framed 185.00
Picture, "The Present Time," matted & framed 425.00
Picture, "The Water Jump," framed ...185.00

TAPESTRIES

Flemish, Baptism of an Emperor, Pope before the throne center foreground, flower & acanthus border, mid-17th c., 9'7" x 9'7" 4,675.00

Flemish, Biblical, Old Testament scene, probably from the story of Jacob & Laban, late 16th c., 16'6" x 9'6" 2,750.00

Flemish, Diana the huntress & her attendants, each wearing richly embroidered vestments in late gothic style, pursuing stags, armed w/bows & arrows, border woven w/Ulysses & Circe, Pyramus & Thisbe in either bottom border, centered by Cupid riding the Quadriga armed w/bow & arrow, mid-16th c., 12'10" x 11'..6,600.00

Flemish, mythological, Ulysses taking leave from Nausicaa & King Alcinous, border boldly woven w/garlands of fruit, centered by grotesque masks & inhabited by monkeys, parrots & eagles, Brussels, 1620-30, 14'8" x 10'8" 11,000.00

Brussels Tapestry

Flemish, "verdure," densely forested landscape by a river, framework border, Brussels, early 18th c., 9' 9" x 9' 1" (ILLUS.) 3,300.00

THEOREMS

During the 19th century, a popular pastime for some ladies was theorem painting, or stencil painting. Paint was allowed to penetrate through hollow-cut patterns of paper placed on cotton velvet. Still-life compositions, such as bowls of fruit or vases of flowers, were the favorite themes, but landscapes and religious scenes found some favor among amateur artists who were limited in their ability and unable to do freehand painting. Today these colorful pictures, with their charming arrangements, are highly regarded by collectors. The following theorems are by unknown American artists.

Basket of fruit on silk, framed, early 19th c., 8½ x 11½" $528.00
Basket of fruit on velvet, green, yellow, red & blue fruit in yellow basket, painted yellow frame, ca. 1830, 9½ x 10½" 3,850.00
Basket of fruit, berries & leafy vines on velvet, framed, ca. 1840, 12½ x 16" 770.00
Basket of fruit w/parrot on velvet, giltwood frame, mid-19th c., 16 x 18½" 770.00
Basket of lilacs on velvet, 14 x 19½" ...148.00
Basket w/long curled earred handles overflowing w/variety of fruits & leafy vines on velvet,

rose, blue, green & yellow, borders w/basting stitches, probably New England, ca. 1830, 21½ x 18½" ...3,080.00
Basket w/melons, peaches, grapes, cherries & other fruit & leafy vines on velvet, green, yellow, blue, red & brown, basket on green-painted slab, inscribed in the upper right hand corner "Painted in 1825," framed, 17¾ x 22½" 4,125.00

Bird & Butterfly Theorem

Bird & butterfly amongst basket of fruit on velvet, framed, early 19th c., 18 x 15" (ILLUS.) 1,760.00
Bowl of fruit on paper, applied printed paper border, framed, 11 5/8 x 9 5/8" (some damage) 325.00
Fruits & vines in woven basket on velvet, bright blue, red, yellow, pink & green, probably New England, 19th c., 13 x 14½" 1,100.00
Vase of flowers on velvet, faded shades of blue, gold & brown, graphite wash, gilded frame, 18¼ x 21¼" 250.00
Watermelon, peaches, pears, grapes & berries in straw basket resting on patch of grass on velvet, 19th c., 16 x 17½" 1,815.00

TOOLS

Also see ADVERTISING ITEMS, AUTOMOBILE ACCESSORIES and FARM COLLECTIBLES.

Blacksmith's carriage jack, lever-type w/wooden handle, No. 00 ....$25.00
Blacksmith's rule, "Starrett" 53.00
Butcher's gambrel, wooden, hand-hewn w/notched hook ends, 30" 6.00
Cabinet maker's clamp, curly maple & hickory, 15" l. 65.00

Cabinet maker's gauge, wooden, dove-
  tail construction, adjustable 65.00
Cabinet maker's scraping plane, "Keen
  Kutter No. K-312" 150.00
Carpenter's adjustable dado plane,
  "Ohio Tool Co.," 11½" l. 65.00
Carpenter's bit brace, maple w/brass
  fittings, 1830 . . . . .95.00
Carpenter's bit brace, wooden w/brass
  trim, "Bower, Chesterworks, Shef-
  field," 13" l. plus spoon bit 105.00
Carpenter's block plane, "Stanley No.
  140" 80.00
Carpenter's circular plane, "Keen
  Kutter No. 115" 150.00
Carpenter's corner brace, "Miller's
  Falls" 20.00
Carpenter's corner plane w/added
  wooden wings, "Stanley No. 57,"
  11 x 10" 130.00
Carpenter's doweling jig, "Stanley No.
  59" 25.00
Carpenter's folding rule, wooden
  w/brass trim, "Stanley No. 54" 50.00
Carpenter's frame saw, curly maple,
  mortised construction w/wrought
  iron fittings, 31 x 30" 105.00
Carpenter's joiner gauge, "Stanley No.
  386," original box 15.00
Carpenter's level, cherrywood w/brass
  trim, "Disston & Sons, patd. 1912,"
  18" l. 12.00
Carpenter's level, mahogany w/brass
  template, "Allen," 19th c., 24" l. 42.50
Carpenter's level, cherrywood, "Stan-
  ley No. 0," 26" 45.00
Carpenter's maul, maple burl block
  w/turned hickory handle, 10½" l. 30.00
Carpenter's mitre box, laminated oak
  & maple, letter-marked quadrant
  setting, w/original paper label
  instructions, "Stanley No. 115," 16" . . .75.00
Carpenter's nail rake, "Tower & Lyons
  Cyclops," ca. 1890 . . . . .25.00
Carpenter's plane, "Bailey No. 6" 15.00
Carpenter's plane, "Keen Kutter No.
  5" . . . . .25.00 to 35.00

Stanley Universal Combination Plane

Carpenter's plane, "Stanley Universal
  Combination No. 55," w/set of 52
  cutters in 4 boxes & all attachments,
  original wooden box, ca. 1908
  (ILLUS. of part) 350.00
Carpenter's plumb bob, pulley-type,
  brass, "Stanley" 45.00
Carpenter's rabbet plane, wooden,
  adjustable, "Philada Warranted,
  D.H.," 11" l. .30.00
Carpenter's smoothing plane,
  "Norris" 200.00
Carpenter's square, wooden w/brass
  trim, "B.N.," 7" l. 12.00
Carpenter's tenon saw, brass trim,
  "Sheffield" 65.00
Cobbler's box, oak, w/seven iron lasts
  & hammer 40.00
Cooper's adze, "D.R. Bart," 7¼" l. 27.50
Cooper's measure, brass, wooden
  handle (replaced), 13" l. 65.00
Cooper's sun plane, curved, "French &
  Co." 90.00
Farrier's carry-all, pine 70.00
Harness maker's vise, wooden, on
  4-footed base, 34" h. 40.00
Ice man's chisel, cast iron, "Yankee
  No. 27" 65.00
Ice man's tongs, iron, "Straatsburg" 26.00
Leather worker's awl, ornate cast
  brass handle w/iron punch, 7¼" l. . . .25.00
Lineman's pliers, "Winchester No.
  2117," 7" l. 45.00
Lumberman's broad axe, "Keen
  Kutter," embossed logo 115.00
Lumberman's brush axe, "Keen
  Kutter" 18.00
Lumberman's safety axe, w/folding
  blade guard, "Marbles No. 2" 125.00
Machinist's level, "Stanley No. 34,"
  10" l. 37.00
Painter's comb graining tools, steel, in
  japanned tin case w/paper label
  "Henry H. Taylor's Graining Combs,"
  5½ x 3¾" 80.00
Plumber's crescent wrench, "Keen
  Kutter No. K-8" 20.00
Plumber's monkey wrench, "B.J. pat'd.
  '96," 10" l. 24.00
Plumber's "S" wrench, "Winchester
  No. 1537" 30.00
Plumbers slip joint pliers, "Keen
  Kutter" 12.00
Shipwright's slick, steel blade w/turned
  wood handle, "Ohio Tool Co.,"
  24½" l. 75.00
Surveyor's compass, brass, silver-
  colored metal face engraved "A.
  Platt, Columbus, O.," w/brass cover,
  7" d. 400.00
Surveyor's transit level w/tripod base
  & leather case, "Warner & Swasey,"
  1898 . . . . .200.00
Tailor's buttonhole cutter, wrought

iron, flat faceted head, 2 blades at
right angle, 18th cent., 5" l. 85.00
Violin maker's compass plane, curved
sole, ¾ x 5/8 x 2½" long 140.00
Violin maker's finger plane, 2" l. 50.00
Wheelwright's spoke shave, "Stanley
No. 67" 35.00
Wheelwright's spoke shave, brass,
"Syracuse," 7" 45.00
Wheelwright's spoke shave, "Win-
chester No. 3250," original blade 95.00
Wheelwright's traveler, wrought iron
w/curved spokes & open handle,
"Wiley & Russell Mfg. Co., Green-
field, Mass.," 12" 35.00
Wheelwright's traveler, cast iron
w/brass band 85.00

TORTOISE SHELL

*The horny, translucent mottled substance,
obtained from the backs of certain species of
turtles, was widely used, from the mid-18th
century onward, to fashion small objects such
as snuff boxes and combs. It is noted for its
warm mottled colors which were often further
enhanced by silver ornamentation. Collectors
should beware of modern imitations in celluloid.*

Box, cover mounted w/gold cartouche,
inlaid mother-of-pearl border
w/gold "pique" edging, 5¾ x 2½",
1½" h. $335.00
Card case, inlaid mother-of-pearl
checkerboard design, Victorian 150.00
Hair comb, curved, inlaid gold design
w/rhinestone highlights, 4¼ x 3" 70.00
Hair comb, Art Nouveau style, large 35.00
Hair pin, Art Nouveau style, 4" l. 20.00
Mirror, hand-type, beveled mirror,
4" d. 68.00
Mustache brush, inlaid mother-of-pearl
decor 25.00
Tea caddy, cask form w/hinged lid
opening to 2 compartments, 19th c.,
7" l., 5½" h. 385.00

TOYS

*Also see ADVERTISING ITEMS,
BABY MEMENTOES, BANKS, BASE-
BALL MEMORABILIA, BROWNIE
COLLECTIBLES, BUSTER BROWN
COLLECTIBLES, CAMPBELL KID*

*COLLECTIBLES, CHARACTER COL-
LECTIBLES, CHILDREN'S DISHES,
DISNEY (Walt) COLLECTIBLES, DOLL
FURNITURE & ACCESSORIES, DOLLS,
GAMES, KEWPIE ITEMS, MAGIC
LANTERNS, MARBLES, PAPER
DOLLS, SUNBONNET BABY ITEMS,
TEDDY BEAR and ZEPPELIN COL-
LECTIBLES.*

African Safari Rhinoceros

African Safari animal, Rhinoceros,
wooden, glass eyes, Schoenhut
(ILLUS.) $350.00
African Safari figure, Teddy Roosevelt,
wooden, Schoenhut, ca. 1909 . . . . . 1,250.00
Army tractor, tin, Marx (New York
City), 1950 . . . . 55.00
Airplane, "Spirit of St. Louis," cast
iron, 8½" l., 11½" wing span 75.00
Airplane, wooden, Cass Toys 25.00
Automobile, Cadillac station wagon,
tin, ca. 1940 . . . . 30.00
Automobile, 1953 Corvette, cast iron,
Hubley 350.00
Automobile, Ford Model A w/rumble
seat, sheet metal, old worn black
paint shows red below, 8¼" l. 30.00
Automobile, LaSalle, Tootsietoy 15.00
Automobile, Nash, painted die cast,
white rubber tires, Banthrico,
6½" l. 25.00
Automobile, limousine, lithographed
tin, Chein, 5½" l. 40.00
Automobile, racer, cast iron,
streamlined design, red, Hubley,
4" l. 80.00
Automobile, sedan, cast iron,
Kenton, 6½" l. 210.00
Automobile, sedan, cast iron, Arcade,
7" l. (repainted) 95.00
Battery-operated, "Bubble Blowing
Monkey" 75.00
Battery operated, "Charlie Weaver
Bartender" 44.00
Battery-operated, "Fred Flintstone
on Dino" 140.00

Battery-operated, "Miss Friday
Typist" 100.00
Battery-operated, "Mr. Fox - Bubble
Blower" 100.00
Battery-operated, "Piggy Cook" 85.00
Battery-operated, "Telephone Bear" ...75.00
Battery-operated, "V.I.P. Boss Bear" ...75.00
Bell ringer toy, boy riding dog,
painted cast iron & tin, 6" l..........600.00
Bell ringer toy, cast iron clown
holding hoop w/original cloth tatters
through which a dog jumps,
pivoting to ring a bell at each end,
green-painted base cast w/scrolls
& "No. 44 Bell Toy," Gong Bell
Mfg. Co., 12½" l................3,025.00
Bell ringer toy, Negro entering hollow
cast iron log from one end & raccoon
from other end, Gong Bell Mfg.
Co., 1880s, 9" l. 3,300.00
Bell ringer toy, Negro on log, cast
iron 395.00
Bicycle horn, "Ooga," Seiss Products
Mfg. (Toledo, Ohio) 30.00
Blackboard-desk, oak easel-type frame
w/fold-down front, w/paper roller
alphabet & numbers & counting
beads 45.00
Blocks, alphabet, wooden, painted,
19th c., set of 26 ....50.00
Blocks, alphabet, w/chromolithographed
paper on wood, ABCs & children's
scenes, McLoughlin, dated 1907,
original box.....................180.00
Blocks, building-type, chromolithographed paper on wood, animals
& birds corresponding to letter of
alphabet, 1880s, 2½ x 1¾ x 3/8",
complete set 85.00
Blocks, building-type, stone (3 colors),
in original box w/sliding lid, marked
"Richters Comet Blocks" 95.50
Blocks, nesting-type, color-printed
heavy cardboard, ABCs, animals,
etc., ca. 1920, nested set of 7 ....50.00
Blocks, nesting-type, chromolitho-
graphed paper on wood, ABCs,
Victorian children, animals, Santas
& fairy tale characters, stacks to
58" h. 395.00
Boat, sidewheeler, cast iron, 4" l. 135.00
"Britains" (soldiers), Royal Scots
Marching, Set No. 212, 8 pcs. 175.00
"Britains" (soldiers), Attendants to the
State Coach, Set No. 1475, 28 pcs. 250.00
Bus, "Greyhound," cast iron, Century
of Progress, 1934 ....75.00
Bus, cast iron, white rubber tires,
Kenton, 9" l.....................325.00
Cannon, firecracker-type, cast iron,
"Dewey," partially rotating on frame
w/bust of Admiral George Dewey
in relief, marked "Dewey" & "Kenton
Brand," ca. 1899, 11½ x 5¼ x 6" 175.00

Cap pistol, "Big Bill," cast iron 25.00
Cap pistol, "Big Scout," cast iron,
Hubley 50.00
Cap pistol, "Buffalo Bill," cast iron.....80.00
Cap pistol, "Long Boy," cast iron 60.00
Cap pistol, "Pony," cast iron 15.00
Cap pistol, "Preston," cast iron 18.00
Cap pistol, "Wizard," cast iron 25.00
Carpet sweeper, "Burlington,"
wooden 10.00
Cash register, "American Flyer,"
metal, w/cash drawer & key, 9 x
9 x 10"...........................32.00
Cash register, "Tom Thumb," red 21.50
Cement mixer, "Jaeger," cast iron,
50% original green & red paint,
white rubber tires, Kenton Hardware
Co., ca. 1935, 7" l................175.00
Cement roller, cast iron w/wooden
rollers ....65.00 to 95.00
Carpet sweeper, "Universal," tin.......22.00
Circus animal, Camel (Dromedary),
wooden, painted eyes, Schoenhut,
regular size 160.00
Circus animal, Giraffe, wooden,
Schoenhut, reduced size 140.00
Circus animal, Goat, wooden, painted
eyes, Schoenhut, regular size 105.00
Circus animal, Mule, wooden, painted
eyes, Schoenhut, regular size 75.00
Circus animal, Poodle, wooden, painted
eyes, Schoenhut, regular size 120.00

Schoenhut Circus Animal

Circus animal, Tiger, wooden,
Schoenhut, regular size (ILLUS.).....120.00
Circus performer, "Girl Bare-back
Rider," wooden w/bisque head,
Schoenhut, 8½" h. 225.00
Circus performer," Hobo," wooden,
Schoenhut, reduced size 150.00
Circus performer, "Humpty Dumpty"
Clown, wooden, Schoenhut, 8½" h. ..80.00
Circus performer, "Lady Acrobat,"
wooden, Schoenhut, reduced size ...130.00
Circus performer, "Lion Tamer,"
wooden, Schoenhut, regular size ...145.00
Circus performer, "Ringmaster,"
wooden, Schoenhut 125.00
Circus prop, barrel, wooden,
Schoenhut 20.00
Circus prop, chair, wooden,
Schoenhut 8.00

Circus set: ringmaster, elephant,
donkey, chair, ladder, barrel & stool;
wooden, Schoenhut, reduced size,
7 pcs. 255.00
Circus wagon w/two horses & 9 figures,
"Overland," cast iron, Kenton,
16" l........................375.00
Clockwork mechanism "General Grant
Smoking Cigar" automaton, cast
iron head & hands, stuffed body in
blue uniform, holding brass cigar, on
wooden base w/bank coin slot
w/brass clockwork movement, Ives,
Blakeslee & Co. (Bridgeport,
Connecticut), 1875-85 (repainted &
redressed) 1,870.00
Coaster wagon, wooden, "Dan Patch -
1:55," spoke wheels.............600.00
Drum, "Playtime Circus," tin
w/wooden sticks, Chein, 1930s 12.00
"Duck" rocking chair, wooden cut-out
duck sides w/seat between, painted
bold duck colors 58.00

Buddy "L" Dump Truck

Dump truck, pressed steel, spoke
wheels, Buddy "L," 12" l. (ILLUS.)....100.00

Farm Animal

Farm animal, sheep w/bell around
neck, blue eyes, wooden legs, 3½" l.
(ILLUS.)..........................22.00
Farm animal, steer, wood &
composition w/"flocked" brown coat
& glass inset eyes, 6¼" l. 25.00
Farm wagon, cast iron, Kenton,
14½" l............................100.00

Fire ladder truck, red, Tootsietoy 10.00
Fire pumper truck, cast iron, (new)
white rubber tires, Kenton, 10" l. ...120.00
Fire pumper truck, metal, 2 yellow
ladders each side, "Pumper" written
on it, metal tires, "Structo" on
radiator, 21" l.....................225.00
Friction-type toy, horse pulling man
in chariot, painted sheet metal,
ca. 1910 ....295.00
Friction-type toy, Yellow Taxi, painted
pressed steel, Ohio Friction Toy
Co., 10" l..........................150.00
Goat & cart, cast iron & tin 130.00

"Dandy" Gryoscope

Gyroscope, "Dandy," metal, made in
U.S.A., Pat. 1919 & 1923, original
box (ILLUS.) 15.00
Hobby horse on rockers, wooden,
painted light grey horse w/black
splotches, red rockers w/ochre
stripes, 19th c., 40" l., 21" h........275.00
Horn, tin, old worn red paint, 13¾" l....10.00
Ice skates, steel, clamp-on type, pr. 9.00
"Ice" wagon w/horse, lithographed tin
& wood, Converse, 18" l...........370.00
Ice wagon w/horse, cast iron, yellow
wagon w/red wheels, silver horse,
8½" l., 3¾" h.....................110.00
Ironing board, wooden, folding-type,
24 x 17".............................12.50
Jack-in-the-box, clown, red ostrich
feather hair, red grosgrain body,
h.p. face, silk fringe trim on red
wooden box........................45.00
Jigsaw puzzle, "Fighters for Victory,"
paperboard, Louis Marx & Co. 20.00
Jigsaw puzzle, "St. Bernard & Child,"
paperboard, 1895, 12 x 8" 15.00
Kaleidoscope, tube-like container
w/brass end, wheel-turn rotates
colored glass fragments, marked
"G.G. Bush & Co., Prov., R.I.," on
turned wooden stand, 19th c.,
10¼" l. kaleidoscope, overall
11½" h. 467.50
Kaleidoscope, tin, Germany, early
20th c..............................20.00
Marble "solitaire" game, 9½" d.
mahogany board & bag of glass
swirl marbles 95.00
Milk wagon w/horse & driver, cast
iron, white & red wheels, 1920s,
6 x 12"..........................275.00

Motorcycle w/driver, cast iron, Barclay
(New Jersey), 1923-71, 3½" l. 25.00
Motorcycle w/policeman driver, "Harley
Davidson," cast iron, original red
paint, white rubber wheels, Hubley .125.00
Motorcycle w/policeman driver &
sidecar, cast iron, Hubley, 9" l. 130.00
Motorcycle w/sidecar, cast iron,
"Champion," 7" l. 160.00
Noah's ark, lithographed paper on
wood on wooden wheels w/lift-
off roof, complete w/seven lithographed paperboard figures of Noah
& animals, Bliss, overall 11" l. 160.00
Noah's ark, lithographed paper on
wood, house & platform w/spruce
branches trim & blue paper cathedral-
shaped windows, complete w/forty
figures & animals, overall 12" l. 325.00
Ox cart w/Negro driver, cast iron,
1880s, 12½" l. 425.00
Pail w/lid & bail handle, tin, embossed
alphabet letters on sides, 1880s,
2 5/8" d., 1 7/8" h. 97.50
Pail w/bail handle, printed & embossed
tin w/flower & leaf in relief & "A
Good Child" in base, printed ship
picture 27.50

"Schoenhut" Piano

Player piano, "Pianolodeon," w/five
rolls, Chein, 20 x 20¼" 250.00
"Police Patrol" wagon w/horse, driver
& 3 policemen seated in wagon, cast
iron, yellow wagon w/red wheels &
black horse, Hubley, ca. 1910, 11" l. .165.00
Pull toy, Alphonse & Gaston "teeter-
totter," cast iron, 7½" l. 270.00
Pull toy, elephant on platform base
w/wheels, papier mache animal,
wooden base, iron wheels, ca. 1900 . .80.00

"Panama" Pile Driver

"Panama" pile driver, tin, green & red
paint w/gold lettering, complete
w/marbles (ILLUS.). 95.00
Pedal car, "Ace," 1915 . . . . .475.00
Pedal car, "Austin," trunk & hood
raise, balloon tires, 1952 . . . . .750.00
Phonograph, "Spear," tin, plays 78 rpm
records 40.00
Piano, upright model, 8-key, wooden,
w/dancing maidens & cherubs
decor, 9¼" l., 7" h. (ILLUS.) 85.00

Goat on Wheels

Pull toy, goat w/real fur coat on
wooden platform w/iron wheels,
large (ILLUS.) 1,210.00
Puzzle blocks, "Aunt Louisa," chromolithographed paper on wood, original
wooden box w/colorful pictures
front & reverse, McLoughlin 395.00
Sand toy w/cart & hopper, tin, "Sandy
Cindy, Wolverine Supply & Mfg.
Co.," 14¾" h. .30.00
School slate, oak frame, 10 x 7"
oblong .10.00 to 16.00
Sled, wooden w/iron-covered runners,

painted green, yellow & black &
w/faded Santa Claus image center
top, signed "Paris Mfg. Co. - St.
Nicholas Sled" 295.00
Sled, wooden w/iron runners, painted
dark brown, red, green, yellow &
silver & lettered "Champion" 225.00
Sprinkling can, printed tin, gooseneck
spout, picture of child in window
on yellow & red ground, Chein,
early 1920s. 22.00

"Huber" Steam Roller

Steam roller, "Huber," cast iron, traces
of original painted finish, Hubley
Mfg. Co., ca. 1928, 8" l. (ILLUS.) 350.00
Straw-stuffed animal, beaver,
Steiff .30.00 to 45.00
Straw-stuffed animal, cat, "Diva,"
Steiff, 12" h. .160.00
Straw-stuffed animal, dog, Schnauzer,
"Tessie," Steiff 35.00
Straw-stuffed animal, dog, Wire-haired
Terrier, Steiff, 9½" l., 9" h. 50.00
Straw-stuffed animal, elephant, Steiff,
4" 50.00
Straw-stuffed animal, kangaroo,
"Linda," Steiff, 11" h. 95.00
Straw-stuffed animal, lamb, "Floppy
Lamby," Steiff, 10" l. 80.00
Straw-stuffed animal, llama, Steiff,
11 x 7½". 135.00
Straw-stuffed animal, raccoon, Steiff,
10" l. .40.00 to 65.00
Straw-stuffed animal, squirrel,
"Perri," Steiff. .35.00
Taxicab, cast iron, yellow, Arcade,
8" l. 550.00
Telegraph set: pr. transmitters,
"Western Union" sheets, wire &
instruction folder & original box;
Gilbert, 1935, 9 x 12" 60.00
Tractor, "Fordson," cast iron, blue,
Arcade, 3½" 45.00
Train, "Zephyr," red-painted white
metal, Tootsietoy 10.00
Train set, "American Flyer": steam
engine No. 1218, passenger car No.
1205 & pr. No. 1206 passenger cars;
ca. 1925, set. .180.00

Typewriter, "American Flyer," Pat.
No. 1-907-379 . . . . .45.00
Typewriter, "Marx Jr. Dial," tin 19.00
Wagon, "Burnam Coaster, Charles City,
Iowa," iron wheels, early 1900s 137.50
Wagon, "Flexible Flyer," 22" l. 41.00
Wagon, "Speed Boy," wooden 125.00
Wash boiler w/lid, tin, early 19th c.,
5" l. 30.00
Wash day set, corrugated tin tub
w/wooden wringer & wooden
agitator, wooden ironing board
& metal sad iron trivet, set 65.00
Washing machine, "Little Queen" 160.00

"Toy Columbia Washer"

Washing machine, "Toy Columbia
Washer," wood & cast iron,
10½" d., 19" h. (ILLUS.) 250.00
Windup tin "Alabama Coon Jigger,"
Ferdinand Strauss, 1923, 10" h. 240.00
Windup tin "Alabama Coon Jigger,"
Lehmann, patented 1912. . . . . .330.00
Windup tin alligator w/man on back,
Chein 65.00
Windup tin "Amos & Andy Fresh Air
Taxi," Louis Marx & Co., 1929 . . . . . . .545.00
Windup tin Amos & Andy walking
figures, Louis Marx & Co., 1930s,
pr. 935.00
Windup tin "Am Pol," 3-wheeled
vehicle w/driver & figure seated
behind twirling a parasol, Lehmann,
ca. 1911, 5¼" l. 1,200.00
Windup tin "The Anxious Bride," chauf-
feur erratically driving a tricycle
pulling a 2-wheeled car w/woman,
Lehmann, ca. 1915, 8½" l. 1,290.00
Windup tin "Balky Mule," Lehmann,
ca. 1930 . . . . .180.00
Windup tin "Balky Mule," Louis Marx &
Co., 1930s . . . . .50.00 to 85.00
Windup tin "Barnacle Bill in Barrel,"
Chein, 1930s, 7" h. . . . . .100.00 to 150.00

"Barnacle Bill"

Windup tin "Barnacle Bill the Sailor,"
  walking, 1930s (ILLUS.) 190.00
Windup tin beetle, Lehmann, 4" l. 125.00
Windup tin "Betty," walking, Lind-
  strom, 1930, 8" h. 130.00
Windup tin "Big Parade," Louis Marx
  & Co., 1929 ....195.00 to 225.00
Windup tin "Blonde Jalopy" 250.00
Windup tin "B.O. Plenty w/Sparkle,"
  Louis Marx & Co., ca. 1938 ....125.00
Windup tin boy on skis, Chein 35.00
Windup tin boy on tricycle, Louis
  Marx & Co., 1920.................195.00
Windup tin "Bucking Broncho,"
  Lehmann, 1930s, 6½" l.............355.00
Windup tin bus "788," white rubber
  tires, Kingsbury, 16" l.............385.00
Windup tin "Butter & Egg Man," Louis
  Marx & Co., 1930s, 7½" h. 295.00
Windup tin "Charlie Chaplin," shuffles
  along spinning his cane, 1920s 575.00
Windup tin "Charlie McCarthy in His
  Benzine Buggy," Louis Marx & Co. 230.00
Windup tin "Charlie McCarthy"
  walker 175.00
Windup tin "City Meat Market" car,
  Louis Marx & Co..................45.00
Windup tin clown driving a donkey
  cart, clown w/cloth shirt, flocked
  donkey w/string tail, Lehmann, early
  20th c., 7¼" l. 105.00
Windup tin "Coo Coo" car, Louis Marx
  & Co......................160.00
Windup tin "Dagwood the Driver,"
  Louis Marx & Co..................435.00
Windup tin "EHE" truck, Lehmann 685.00
Windup tin ferris wheel, Chein.......110.00
Windup tin "Galop Cowboy," zebra
  cart, Lehmann, original box 120.00
Windup tin "G.I. Joe & His Jouncing
  Jeep," Unique Art, ca. 1940 ....85.00
Windup tin "G.I. Joe & the K-9
  Pups," Unique Art.................110.00

Windup tin "Ham & Sam," Ferdinand
  Strauss, 1921.............325.00 to 450.00
Windup tin "Happy Hooligan," Chein,
  1932 ....195.00
Windup tin Harold Lloyd "Funny
  Face" walker, Louis Marx & Co.,
  1929 ....360.00
Windup tin "Haul A Way" truck,
  Ferdinand Strauss................145.00
Windup tin "Honeymoon Express,"
  Louis Marx & Co., 1929............120.00

"Honeymoon Express"

Windup tin "Honeymoon Express,"
  Louis Marx & Co., 1947 (ILLUS.) 60.00
Windup tin "Howdy Doody Band,"
  w/Bob Smith seated at piano &
  Howdy Doody dancing alongside....415.00
Windup tin "Inter State" double decker
  bus, Ferdinand Strauss 365.00
Windup tin "Jazzbo Jim on Roof,"
  Ferdinand Strauss, 1921 ....220.00
Windup tin "Jazzbo Jim" dancer,
  Unique Art, 1921.................245.00
Windup tin "Jenny the Balky Mule,"
  Ferdinand Strauss................155.00
Windup tin "Joe Penner & His Duck,"
  Louis Marx & Co..................300.00
Windup tin "Joe Penner & His Duck,"
  Ferdinand Strauss, 1930s...........300.00
Windup tin "Rapid Transit Co." trolley
  car, 8½" l. 80.00
Windup tin "Sandy" carrying Orphan
  Annie's valise in mouth, Louis Marx
  & Co., 1930s, 5" l. 150.00
Windup tin seal, Lehmann...........150.00
Windup tin "Skyrangers," Unique Art,
  U.S.A., 1933....................140.00
Windup tin "Speed Boy Delivery,"
  motorcycle w/attached delivery
  wagon, Louis Marx & Co., 1930s,
  10" l..........................100.00
Windup tin "Speed King," kid riding
  soap box scooter, Wyandotte,
  1920s ....225.00 to 250.00
Windup tin "Spic & Span," Louis Marx
  & Co., 1924.....................650.00

"Tidy Tim"

Windup tin "Tidy Tim," old man pushing
  trash barrel, Louis Marx & Co.,
  ca. 1938 (ILLUS.) ....225.00 to 250.00
Windup tin "Tombo" Coon Jigger,
  Negro dances on box, Ferdinand
  Strauss 280.00
Windup tin "Toonerville Trolley,"
  Fontaine Fox, copyright 1922,
  7¾" h. 470.00
Windup tin "Trixo," climbing monkey,
  Ferdinand Strauss, ca. 1924, 10" 45.00
Windup tin "Uncle Wiggily Car," Louis
  Marx & Co., 1935.................385.00
Windup tin "Whoopie Car," w/cowboy
  driver, Louis Marx & Co., 9" l.......180.00
Windup tin World War I German soldier
  w/spike helmet & rifle, crawls on
  ground 656.00
Windup tin Zeppelin "SR-47," Ferdinand
  Strauss, 9½" l. 325.00
Windup tin "Zig-Zag," Lehmann,
  1903..........................1,055.00
Windup tin "Zilotone," musical toy,
  clown standing on platform before
  xylophone & holding wood-tipped
  mallet, w/three records, Wolverine,
  ca. 1920, 7" h. 220.00

TRADE CATALOGUES

Alaska Refrigerator, 1922, ice boxes . . $40.00
American Booksellers, 1883,
  Christmas........................12.00
Bausch & Lomb, 1915, projection
  apparatus, "Edison Kinetoscopes"....39.00
Belknap Hardware, 1932, 3024 pp. 150.00
Blair & Letts, 1889, horse clothing,
  harnesses & saddlery, illustrated,
  9¼ x 5¾", 25 pp. (ILLUS.) 35.00

Blair & Letts Catalogue

Burpee Seed Catalog, 1935, 144 pp. 12.00
Butler Bros., 1892, general merchandise, 95 pp. 19.00
Carson Pirie Scott & Co., 1932,
  jewelry, silverware, pewter, leather
  & radios, hard cover, 300 pp. 32.50
Cattaraugus Cutlery Co., 1910, color
  illustrations 30.00
Crane Co., 1924, bathtubs............15.00
Davisson Co., 1904, laces & linens 24.00
DeLaval Cream Separator, 1928, farm &
  dairy equipment, Golden Anniver-
  sary issue, "First in 1878, best in
  1928," 11 x 8", 36 pp. 42.50
Diebold Office Safes, 1928 ....10.00
Dunlop Tires, 1895, 16 pp. 12.50
Eagle Lock Co., 1930, hard cover,
  11 x 8½", 750 pp. 25.00
F.A.O. Schwartz, 1939, Christmas,
  Disney items, toys, dolls & doll
  houses, 12½ x 9½", 64 pp..........55.00
Fischer, 1923, musical instruments,
  hard cover, 239 pp.................45.00
Grange Blue Book, 1913, costumes,
  badges, jewels, pins, misc. supplies, color centerfold, 5½ x 9",
  52 pp. 17.50
Harley-Davidson, 1917, motorcycles 40.00
Harris (B.J.) Co., 1914, celluloid &
  metal souvenirs, trays, watch fobs,
  match safes, mirrors, etc., 9¼ x 6",
  36 pp. 23.00
Houghton, Mifflin & Company, 1885,
  books, portraits of authors &
  reviews, 96 pp. 12.50
Howe Sewing Machine, 1876, 32 pp. 22.00
Indian Motorcycles, 1912, colorful
  embossed Indian head cover, 24 pp. ...60.00
Kendall & Whitney, 1893, farm &
  garden supplies 25.00
Kodak Cameras, 1918, 5½ x 3½",
  32 pp. 20.00

Lane Bryant, 1929, Spring & Summer
fashions, 111 pp. 45.00
Lyon & Healy, 1892, band instruments,
uniforms & supplies 25.00
Marshall Field & Co., 1930, Christmas,
cover by Howard Chandler Christy,
50 pp. 10.00
Meir Co., Chicago, Illinois, 1920, police
& fireman's uniforms, accessories,
nightsticks, badges, etc., 9 x 6",
47 pp. 35.00
Millers Falls Tools, 1934, 240 pp. 13.00
National Cloak & Suit Co., 1908,
Christmas, cover by Howard
Chandler Christy, 47 pp. 17.00
Osborne Farm Machinery, 1887 . . . . . . .21.50
Pick (Albert) & Co., 1907, "Hotel, Res-
taurant & Saloon World," cut &
pattern glass, Majolica, Mettlach &
German steins, cigar lighters, Mills
vending machines, slot machines,
roulette wheels, Faro tables, etc.,
color illustrations, 11½ x 8½",
730 pp. 75.00
Plymouth Clothing House, 1899-1900,
31 pp. 15.00
Remington Arms Cartridge Co.,
1918-19, 208 pp. 37.50
Sears & Roebuck, 1913, furniture,
108 pp. 42.00
Spiegel Co., 1899, Victorian furniture,
illustrated, 14 x 11½", 103 pp. 65.00
Stickley (L. & J.G.) Co., 1930, furniture,
90 pp. 40.00
Tiebout, W. & J., 1912, marine
hardware 40.00
Underwood Typewriters, 1911 . . . . .20.00
Vantine's Oriental Store, 1918 . . . . .40.00
Vitanola Phonographs, models pic-
tured & priced, 1911 . . . . .10.00
White (S.S.), 1905, porcelain teeth,
10 x 7", 194 pp. 35.00
Winchester Firearms & Ammunition,
1916, 224 pp. .45.00
Yale & Towne Co., 1905, locks & hard-
ware, hard cover, 9 x 6", 206 pp. 45.00

TRAPS

Also see ADVERTISING ITEMS.

Bear, hand-forged iron, 34" l. $225.00
Bear, "Newhouse No. 15," cast iron,
jaws open to 14", ovearll 34½" 450.00
Beaver, "Triumph No. 3," cast iron 30.00
Fly, blown glass . . . . .65.00 to 75.00
Fly, "Columbia," wire screen sphere on
tin removable base, w/original
instructions 45.00

Fly, pressed glass .50.00
Fly, "Shur Katch," wire screen dome on
removable base 39.00
Fly, wire screen cone shape on wooden
removable base 10.00
Mink, "Newhouse Oneida Community
No. 2," cast iron, double spring 30.00
Mouse, "Catchem Alive," tin & wood,
w/original instructions 40.00
Mouse, "McGill Metal Products" 10.00
Mouse, "Star," wooden 12.00
Mouse, "Victor No. 3," double spring 8.00
Mouse, wire cage w/wire bail handle
& tin door, 8½" 18.00

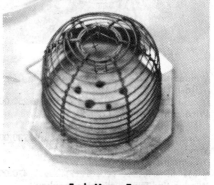

Early Mouse Trap

Mouse, wire cage on wooden base
(ILLUS.) 32.00
Muskrat, "Newhouse Oneida Com-
munity No. 1," cast iron, single
spring 25.00
Rat, "Erie," wooden w/iron hinge 30.00
Wolf, "Newhouse No. 4½" 115.00

TRAYS, SERVING & CHANGE

Anheuser-Busch Oval Tray

*Both serving & change trays once used in
taverns, cafes and the like and usually*

bearing advertising for a beverage maker are now being widely collected. All trays listed are heavy tin serving trays, unless otherwise noted. Also see BREWERIANA.

American Brewing Company, "Liberty Beer," Rochester, New York, wood-grained background, 12" d. $65.00

American Brewing Company, "Liberty Beer," Rochester, New York, bust of Indian maiden center (change) 90.00

American Line Steamship Company, ship, 4" d. (change) 85.00

Anheuser-Busch, St. Louis, Missouri, maiden holding Eagle & "A" logo symbol aloft surrounded by winged cherubs, ca. 1900, 16½ x 13½" oval (ILLUS.) 550.00

Anheuser-Busch "Bevo" (non-alcoholic beverage of prohibition era), Anheuser-Busch delivery wagon & team of horses (change) 67.50

Atlas Brewery, Chicago, Illinois, American eagle astride Western hemisphere, pre-prohibition 125.00

Ballentine Beer, Newark, New Jersey, 3 rings (change) 40.00

Bartels Brewing Co., Syracuse, New York, "Night Watchman," pre-1920 (change) 125.00

Bartholomay Brewing Co., Rochester, New York, lady seated on winged wheel (change) . . . . .110.00 to 125.00

Beverwyck Brewing Co., Albany, New York, golfer 85.00

Beverwyck Brewing Co., "Beverwyck Beer," Albany, New York, wood-grained background, after 1935, round 65.00

Bissantz Ice Cream, beautiful lady 75.00

Boedecker Ice Cream, Dallas, Texas, pretty lady eating ice cream 175.00

Bolton's (Samuel) Sons, "Home Brewed Ale," Troy, New York, group of monks w/keg, pre-prohibition, 18½" oval . . . . .110.00 to 175.00

Buffalo Cooperative Brewing Co., Buffalo, New York, bottles, pre-prohibition 250.00

Calumet Brewing Co., Chilton, Wisconsin, cavalier, 17 x 12" 250.00

Casey & Kelly Brewing Co., Scranton, Pennsylvania, king holding mug, pre-prohibition 225.00

Chean Tea (change) 65.00

Chero-Cola, bottle pictured, "There's None So Good - 5 cents," 1905 . . . . .125.00 to 165.00

Cottolene Shortening, black woman & child picking cotton (change) 42.50

Cutter (J.H.) Whiskey, ship pictured, 17" d. 250.00

Darne's Carnation Gum (change) 65.00

Davenport Malt & Brewing Co., Daven-

port, Iowa, "The Invitation," roses & lady holding up glass of beer (change) 95.00

Dixie Queen Tobacco (change) 60.00

Dobler Brewing Co., Albany, New York, 3 beer wagons, 1906, oval 175.00

Don Fino Cigars (change) 25.00

Eagle Brewing Co., Newark, New Jersey, pretty girl holding rose, 1911, 13 x 10" 225.00

Ehret's Hell Gate Brewery, New York, entwined "G.E." within star, pre-prohibition, large oval 155.00

El Verso Cigars, man in chair w/girl in smoke dreams (change) 45.00

Enterprise Brewing Co., San Francisco, California, Victorian lady in large oval, pre-prohibition 200.00

Everess Sparkling Water, red parrot & "Thank You" (change) 20.00

Eye Fix Remedy, beautiful woman & cherub (change) 77.50

Fairy Soap Change Tray

Fairy Soap, little girl w/violets sitting on large bar of soap, change (ILLUS.) 45.00

International Brewing, Buffalo, New York, blacksmith at lunch, 12" wedge shape 300.00

Jersey Creme, profile of pretty girl wearing bonnet, 12" d. 125.00

Jones (Frank), "Homestead Ale," Portsmouth, New Hampshire (change) 42.50

Kenny (C.D.) Coffee, "America's Pride," flag raising at Valley Forge (change) 65.00

Kentucky Best Whiskey, woman & horse 110.00

Koppitz-Melchers, "Pale Select Beer," Detroit, Michigan, 4 seasons depicted w/drinking figures, early 1900s 295.00

Lewis 66 Whiskey, man eating lobster & drinking (change) 55.00

Miller "High Life Beer," Milwaukee, Wisconsin, girl on crescent moon, 13" d. 52.50

Miller "High Life Beer," Milwaukee,

Wisconsin, scene of men in top hats
on stagecoach w/innkeeper serving
glasses of beer, red border, oblong
(change).........................35.00

Monrow Brewing Co., Rochester, New
York, king holding goblet, pre-prohibition..........................180.00

Monticello Whiskey, fox hunt scene
(change)..........................80.00

Narrangasett Brewing Co., "Lager &
Ale," Arlington, Rhode Island, Chief
Pansett, round....................47.50

Neuweiller (Louis F.) Beer, Allentown,
Pennsylvania, German gentleman in
old world costume holding beer
stein, 13¼" d.....................42.50

New York Brewery, Spokane,
Washington, pretty lady...........175.00

Occident Flour (change)...........25.00

Oertel's Brewing, Louisville, Kentucky,
lady & dove, early 1900s (change)....70.00

Oneida Brewing Co., Utica, New York,
spaniel dog, "Roderick," 1904......350.00

Oshkosh Brewing Co., "Chief Oshkosh
Beer," Oshkosh, Wisconsin, Chief in
top hat...........................175.00

Owatonna Flour (change)...........12.00

Passaic Metal Ware Co., lady & factory
scene, 1914 (change)..............30.00

Pepsi-Cola, Coney Island scene, 1950s..20.00

Peter's (William), "Palisades Beer,"
Union City, New Jersey, factory on
Hudson River "Palisades,"
oval.................150.00 to 200.00

Plymouth Gin, monk drinking
(change)..........................75.00

Polar Maid Ice Cream, 1916........45.00

President Suspenders, 4½" d.
(change)..........................40.00

Red Raven Splits, bird pouring drink
from bottle, 1910, 12" d..........150.00

Red Raven Splits, bird pouring drink
from bottle, 1905 Pittsburgh Exposition (change)...................65.00

Red Raven Splits, lobster, rabbit & red
raven, 13¾ x 10½".................90.00

Red Raven Whiskey, girl hugging
raven, "Ask the Man" (change)......60.00

Roessle Brewery, "Lager," Boston,
Massachusetts, 2 old gentleman
seated at table drinking, pre-prohibition.........................150.00

Rubsan & Hormann Brewing Co.,
Staten Island, New York, 1930s......41.50

Ruhstaller's Beer, Sacramento,
California, factory scene, 1910,
large oval........................450.00

Ruhstaller's Beer, Sacramento,
California, "California Invites the
World," 1915......................125.00

Ruhstaller's Beer, Sacramento, California, lady & dove...............225.00

Ruhstaller's Beer, Sacramento, California, lady & dove (change)........85.00

Ruhstaller's "Gilt Edge Lager," Sacramento, California, man pouring
beer for ladies in touring car, pre-
prohibition.............275.00 to 365.00

Ruppert's (Jacob) Beer, New York,
New York, cartoon-type (change)....47.50

Ryan's (Thomas) Consumer's Brewing
Company, Syracuse, New York,
Indian head center, red, white &
blue, 16" oval....................75.00

Ryan's (Thomas) Beer, Syracuse, New
York, gypsy girl (change)..........75.00

San Antonio Brewing Association, San
Antonio, Texas, malt, hops & beer
glass.............................300.00

Savannah Brewing Co., Savannah,
Georgia, lady on lion rug, 13" d....145.00

Savannah Brewing Co., Savannah,
Georgia (change)..................70.00

Sears, Roebuck & Co., scales of Justice
& Chicago home office, 6 x 4½" oval
(change)..........................60.00

Seitz Beer, Easton, Pennsylvania, eagle
(change)..........................90.00

"Simon Pure" Beer Tray

Simon (William) Brewing, "Simon
Pure," Buffalo, New York, winged
hops, change (ILLUS.)..............15.00

Spokane Brewery, Spokane,
Washington, elk standing by water,
pre-prohibition...................155.00

Star Union Brewing Co., Peru, Illinois,
"Janice" in white fur hat, dated
1913..............................65.00

Stegmaier Beer, Wilkes Barre, Pennsylvania, factory scene, "The Home of
Stegmaier Beer," 6" oval (change)..125.00

Tam O'Shanter Ale, Scotsman holding
glass (change)....................125.00

Tivoli Brewing Co., "Altes Lager,"
Detroit, Michigan, Bavarian waiter,
1910.................95.00 to 135.00

Tivoli Brewing Co., Detroit, Michigan
(change)..........................50.00

Wagener (Henry) Brewing Co., Salt
Lake City, Utah, bottle of beer, 1894
(change)..........................100.00

Weatherly Ice Cream Tray

Weatherly Ice Cream, "Janice" in
white fur hat & stole w/holly, 1920s
(ILLUS.) 155.00
Weinhard (Henry) Beer, Portland,
Oregon, factory scene, oval 550.00
Weinhard (Henry) Brewing Co., Port-
land, Oregon, eagle, pre-pro-
hibition 150.00
Welsbach Lighting, child playing
w/toys, mother reading (change) 55.00
West End Brewing Co., "Utica Beer,"
Utica, New York, 2 dogs seated at
table drinking beer & smoking
cigars, "The Famous Utica Beer," ca.
1910, 13¼ x 10¼" 82.50
West End Brewing Co., Utica, New
York, Miss Liberty draped in
American flag & eagle on barrel,
pre-prohibition 300.00

TRIVETS

"Best On Earth" Trivet

*When numbers are noted following trivets
listed below they refer to numbers in Dick*

Hankenson's "Trivets," Book I or "Trivets,
Old and Re-Pro," Book II. All are cast iron
except where otherwise noted.

Best on Earth, Book 1, No. 107
(ILLUS.) $19.00
Colebrookdale Crown & Maltese Cross
No. 1, Book I, No. 119 .... 16.50
Enterprise "E," Book 1, No. 114 .... 12.00
Ferrosteel Urn, Book 1, No. 121 .... 16.00
"God Bless Our House," sailor's house
blessing w/anchor center & star at
edge, Book II, No. 4 .... 40.00
Heart on 3 double scrolled feet, hand-
wrought, 18th c., 7½" l. 55.00
Heart on chamfered legs w/drake
feet, small heart handle, hand-
wrought, 18th c., overall 9" l. 265.00
Heart shape (brass) 40.00
Hearts & diamonds openwork motif,
9" l. (brass) 85.00
Horseshoe, embossed "Take Simmons
Liver Regulator in Time" (brass) 35.00
"Howell H," "The W.H. Howell Co.,
Geneva, Ill." embossed in recessed
panels, wavy railing, Book 1,
No. 125 .... 16.00
Iwantu Spade, "Iwantu Comfort Iron,
Strause Gas Iron Co., Phila., Pa.,
U.S.A.," Book 1, No. 148 .... 26.00
Jenny Lind, Book 1, No. 16 .... 22.50
Lyre form on turned feet, 6" l. (brass) ... 65.00
Lyre form w/turned wooden handle,
stamped "Gray, Bradford St.,
Birmh.," 12" l. (one leg replaced) 45.00
N.R. Streeter, Crown & Maltese Cross,
Book 1, No. 118 .... 15.00
Odd Fellows, 3-footed, Book 1, No. 6 ... 37.50
Odd Fellows, w/heart in hand, Book 1,
No. 12 .... 22.00
Scrolling openwork w/twisted open
handle, 9½" l. (brass) 40.00
Serpentine form w/three drawn legs &
flat feet, hand-wrought, 18th c., 7" l.,
2½" h. 150.00
Spider Web, Book 1, No. 90 .... 12.00
Thistles, leaves & rose, signed & dated
on back, 1907 (brass) 65.00
Triangular frame w/handle through to
point of triangle & pierced to hang,
hand-wrought, 10" l. 75.00
Waffle, Book 1, No. 95 .... 10.00

TRUNKS

*These box-like portable containers are used
for transporting or storing personal pos-
sessions. There are many styles to choose
from since they have been made from the 16th
century onward. Thousands arrived in this*

country with the immigrants and more were turned out to accommodate the westward movement of the population. The popular dome-top trunk was designed to prevent water from accumulating on the top. Hinges, locks and construction, along with condition and age, greatly determine the values of older trunks.

Painted Dome-Top Trunk

Dome-top, wooden, top painted w/large green, red & yellow open fan, the front painted w/a stylized flower & leaf motif in red & yellow, all on a black ground w/outlining in green & red, probably New England, 19th c., 22½ x 10", 9" h. (ILLUS.) $440.00

Dome-top, pine w/hand-carved wooden eagle on lid, refinished, 29½ x 15", 16" h. (open knot hole in lid, replaced lock & hinges) 325.00

Dome-top, leather covered wood w/decorative brass studding, wrought iron hasp & lock, 39½ x 21", 26" h. 110.00

Dome-top, pine, dovetail construction, wrought iron hinges, hasp & lock, 19th c. 500.00

Flat-top, painted pine, dovetail construction, wrought iron hinges, hasp & side handles, painted simulated graining in brown, original shipping labels w/New Hampshire & later Ohio destinations, 20½ x 18", 15¾" h. 195.00

Immigrant-type, leather-covered wood w/brass nailhead decor, wrought iron side handles & lock, lined w/early floral print fabric, 22 x 13 x 11½" (incomplete hasp) 95.00

Immigrant-type, wooden w/camel top, interior till, sheet iron banding, refinished, 1880, 28 x 17" 100.00

Immigrant-type, wooden w/dome top, interior till w/secret compartment, wrought iron strap hinges, bear trap lock & banding, free-hand red, blue, yellow & black flowers, foliage & birds decor & German inscription, front panel w/date "1790" & lid interior w/date "1767," 38 x 19", 19" h. 650.00

Immigrant-type, pine, dome-top w/canted sides, dovetail construc-

tion, wrought iron hinges, lock & side handles, refinished, 39" l.......300.00

Immigrant-type, painted & decorated pine, dovetail construction, front panels painted w/full-length figures of a man & woman, side panels w/original rose maaled decor in shades of red, blue, green & white, all on brown grain-painted ground, turned feet, wrought iron strap hinges, bear trap lock & side handles, 47 x 23", 20" h. 550.00

Immigrant-type, wooden, dome-top, blue over original mustard yellow paint, "Bitville Co., Iowa, Nord Amerika" & name, small 225.00

TYPEWRITERS

Hammond Typewriter

Franklin, semi-circular keyboard.....$175.00

Hammond, patent date of Feb. 3, 1880, w/original oak cover for case (ILLUS.) 300.00

Oliver No. 9, 1915-22 ....40.00

Remington No. 7, late 1920s 30.00

Royal No. 10, beveled glass sides, ca. 1920 ....40.00

Smith Premier, double keyboard 325.00

World, indicator-type, original box 435.00

UNGER BROTHERS

Unger Brothers Hair Brush

Herman and Eugene Unger worked as jewelers and silversmiths in Newark, New Jersey, from 1881. Their early productions were designed with elaborate rococo scrolls but after a visit to Paris, in 1901, their work began to reflect the Art Nouveau movement. They became masters of this style, characterized by limply swaying, curving lines enhanced with flowers and tendrils and by the appearance of figures, predominantly female, that seemed to melt away within the lines of the objects they adorned. Dresser and desk sets, along with ash trays, cigarette and match cases, sewing accessories and pocket flasks reflect an exquisite development of the Art Nouveau taste, so popular in the first decade of this century and collectors vie to acquire items bearing the interlaced U and B trademark of the Unger Brothers. The company's Art Nouveau productions ceased about 1910, but they continued to produce a simpler line of silver until 1914 when the firm switched their production to airplane parts.

Almond scoop, sterling silver, Springfield patt. $125.00
Berry spoon, sterling silver, Passaic patt. 95.00
Butter pick, sterling silver, Duvaine patt. 65.00
Cigarette case, sterling silver, Love's Dream patt. 188.00
Claret ladle, sterling silver, Passaic patt. 115.00
Cream ladle, sterling silver, Duvaine patt. 65.00
Demitasse spoon, sterling silver, Passaic patt. 25.00
Dresser set, sterling silver, Le Secrete de Fleurs patt., 8 pcs. 950.00
Gravy ladle, sterling silver, Passaic patt. 65.00
Hair brush, sterling silver, Love's Dream patt. (ILLUS.) 115.00
Handbag, black velvet, leather interior, sterling silver frame w/embossed cupids & scrolls, tortured chain handle, w/monogram applied one side, 6½" w., 7¾" l. 195.00
Hat brush, sterling silver, He Loves Me patt. 88.00
Hatpin, sterling silver, English bulldog head w/ruby set eyes, overall 7¾" l. 125.00
Luncheon fork, sterling silver, Dawn patt. 125.00
Luncheon fork, sterling silver, He Loves Me patt. 95.00
Luncheon fork, sterling silver, Jonquil patt. 35.00
Luncheon fork, sterling silver, Le Secrete de Fleurs patt. 95.00
Luncheon knife, sterling silver, Jonquil patt. 30.00
Match safe, sterling silver, overall "repousse" vintage decor 115.00
Military brushes, sterling silver back, Tulip patt., 4¼ x 3" oval, pr. 185.00

Mirror, hand-type w/ring handle, sterling silver, Love's Dream patt. 348.00
Mustard ladle, sterling silver, Narcissus patt. .45.00
Napkin ring, sterling silver, Art Nouveau ladies in relief 65.00
Olive spoon, sterling silver, Narcissus patt. 42.00
Pen rack, sterling silver, Love's Dream patt. 115.00
Pin, sterling silver, owl head w/ruby set eyes, 1 5/8" w. 300.00
Powder jar, cut glass base, sterling silver lid in Love's Dream patt. 175.00
Sardine fork, sterling silver, Passaic patt. 55.00
Shaving mug, sterling silver, bust of an Indian chief w/full headdress in relief 300.00
Shoe horn, sterling silver, Love's Dream patt. .65.00
Sugar shell, sterling silver, Peep O'Day patt. 38.00
Sugar spoon, sterling silver, Duvaine patt. 65.00
Sugar tongs, sterling silver, Narcissus patt. 45.00
Tea caddy, sterling silver, Narcissus patt. 60.00
Teaspoon, sterling silver, Narcissus patt. 26.00
Teaspoon, sterling silver, Passaic patt. 40.00
Tomato server, sterling silver, Duvaine patt. 144.00

UNIFORMS, COSTUMES & PERIOD CLOTHING

Christening Gown

Recent interest in period clothing, uniforms and accessories from the 18th and 19th centuries and from specific periods in the 20th century, compelled us to add this category to our compilation. While style and fabric play an important role in the values of older garments of previous centuries, designer dresses of the 1920s and 30s, especially evening gowns, are enhanced by the original label of *a noted couturier such as Worth, or Adrian. Prices vary widely for these garments which we list by type, with infant's and children's apparel so designated. Also see BABY MEMENTOES, MILITARY COLLECT-IBLES and SHAKER ITEMS.*

Apron, red & white calico $25.00
Baby bunting, hand-quilted blue silk,
 together w/matching blanket embroidered w/tiny flowers, 2 pcs. 45.00
Bathing suit, lady's, wool, 1930s 15.00
Bathing tunic, lady's, black sateen,
 1910 . . . . .22.00
Bloomers, child's, white cotton w/lace
 edging, 1890 . . . . .5.00 to 8.00
Blouse, lady's, silk, middy-type 12.00
Blouse, white lawn w/embroidered
 bodice, collar & sleeves, w/hand-
 made lace trim & insert in bodice,
 celluloid collar stays 90.00
Boa, peach ostrich feathers 60.00
Bonnet, lady's, wool, Amish, 1930s 55.00
Bonnet, lady's, pioneer-style, quilted
 black silk 30.00
Camisole, girl's, white cotton w/lace
 inserts 18.00
Cape, lady's, black wool, waist length
 w/black buttons & fringe, Amish 45.00
Cape, lady's, black wool w/satin lining,
 ankle-length Victorian style 85.00
Cape, lady's, black velvet, long, 1930s . .50.00

1920s-style Cape & Dresses

Cape, blue panne velvet, embroidered
 w/white & crystal beads in Art Deco
 style floral & abstract designs,
 w/grey fox collar, together w/black
 georgette bias-cut evening gown
 embroidered w/rhinestones &
 crystal beads, 1920s-30s, 2 pcs.
 (ILLUS. of cape center) 242.00
Cape, brown wool w/monkey fur trim,
 silk lining, 1880s 85.00
Chemise, nasturtium chiffon w/inset &

edged w/bands of ivory lace sewn
 to the waist w/narrow pintucks &
 narrowly pleated from the waist to
 the hem, w/"Callot Soeurs Paris
 Nouvelle Marque Depose Made in
 France" label .495.00
Chemise, white cotton w/tucks & lace
 panels, 28" l. 25.00
Christening gown, white batiste
 w/tucked yoke (ILLUS.) 15.00
Coat, girl's, black crushed velvet
 w/fur-trimmed buttons, Victorian 38.00
Coat, lady's, apricot velveteen w/white
 fox collar & cuffs 65.00
Coat, lady's, beige wool w/metallic
 braid trim, ankle length, 1920s,
 size 10 . . . . .80.00
Coat, lady's, sleeveless caftan-style,
 black velvet w/gold stenciled border
 of stylized trees & undulating vines,
 w/"Mariano Fortuny, Venise"
 label 1,210.00
Coat, man's, black bear skin, full
 length 125.00
Dress, child's, long-waisted, white
 lawn w/lace inserts, tucks & ruffles,
 ca. 1900, size 4 . . . . .65.00
Dress, child's, white flower-sprigged
 calico, w/matching sunbonnet,
 ca. 1880, size 4, 2 pcs. 85.00

Dress, chemise-style, black georgette,
 heavily embroidered w/white & jet
 beads & rhinestones in a starburst
 motif at center, bodice & skirt hung
 w/crystal beaded fringe, 1920s
 (ILLUS. left) .208.00
Dress, chemise-style, cream georgette,
 embroidered w/black, white &
 crystal beaded geometric designs,
 skirt hung w/beaded fringe, 1920s
 (ILLUS. right) .176.00
Dress, Edwardian, oyster white lawn,
 high waist w/ruffled detail, satin
 ribbon bands & sash, elbow-length
 net sleeves, 1900 . . . . .60.00
Dress, Edwardian, white cotton
 w/drawnwork yoke & sleeves &
 tucked skirt, 1905-10, size 8 . . . . .95.00
Dress, Victorian, 2-piece, brown
 polished cotton w/cream print:
 bodice w/high puffed sleeves, lace
 collar & row of tiny buttons; tightly
 gathered skirt w/embroidered band,
 ca. 1880, size 10 . . . . .210.00
Evening coat, lady's, black satin
 w/wide glossy fur collar to waist,
 cream silk lining, 1920s 85.00
Evening dress, crepe & lace, black,
 sleeveless bodice falling from
 V-back in a triangle of lace-edged
 crepe continuing across the bosom
 in an arch, shirred waist, skirt inset
 w/panels of lace-edged crepe
 ending in a handkerchief hem,

w/matching satin slip, w/"Jean
Patou, Paris" label, late 1920s 220.00
Evening dress, silk velvet, royal blue,
bias-cut w/V neck, flowing bat-wing
sleeves trimmed w/rhinestones,
1930s, size 10......................50.00
Evening gloves, lady's, white kid,
23" l., pr. 27.50
Gloves, child's, white kid, 5" l., pr. 18.00
Gym suit, black serge bloomers
w/middy blouse 35.00
Handkerchief, 2" ecru chantilly-type
lace border, pale lime green chiffon,
18" sq. 20.00
Hat, child's, blue straw w/red streamer
ribbon...........................22.00
Hat, gentleman's, Derby-type,
w/"Stetson" label.................27.00
Hat, gentleman's, brown Homburg-
type.............................25.00
Hat, lady's, green velvet turban
w/plume, 1920s 30.00
Kimono, silk, pale lavender w/hand-
printed & embroidered florals,
lined 45.00
Knickers, boy's, wool, checkerboard
pattern, 1920s 8.00
Knickers, man's, linen 36.00
Maid's uniform, grey chambray, 1915 ...30.00

Militiaman's Great Coat

Militiaman's great coat w/attached
cape. coarse blue wool w/brown
wool inner lining & linen-lined
sleeves, Massachusetts, ca. 1855
(ILLUS.)........................770.00
Muff, child's, ermine 30.00
Muff, black seal, gathered pocket in
bottom, pleated satin around
openings, braid trim w/tassel,
18 x 16"........................35.00
Muff, raccoon, round, large 75.00
Nightgown, lady's, white cotton
w/crochet yoke & short sleeves,
small...........................26.00

Nightgown, lady's, white cotton w/em-
broidered & tucked yoke & cuffs,
tucked back, late 19th c............88.00
Nightgown, lady's, peach satin w/eye-
let embroidery trim on puffed
sleeves & pockets, 1930s...........24.00
Parasol, child's, black lace lined
w/ivory silk, ivory handle inlaid
w/coral & gold monogram, ivory &
coral floral finial.................110.00

Black Silk Parasol

Parasol, folding-type, black pleated
silk (ILLUS.) ....35.00 to 50.00
Parasol, linen, wide ribbon edge.......35.00
Petticoat, child's, white cotton
w/embroidery & cutwork, Victorian ..18.00
Petticoat, grey flannel w/red crochet
edging 36.00
Petticoat, purple wool w/blue & white
homespun waistband..............60.00
Petticoat, white cotton w/rows of
drawnwork, tucks & crochet inserts,
1880 ....50.00
Petticoat, reversible, quilted cotton,
brown reversing to gold
calico ....95.00 to 110.00
Shawl, silk, black on black florals &
foliage, 68" sq. plus 6" fringe 48.00
Shawl, silk, light pink w/dark pink
embroidered florals, 50" sq. plus 15"
fringe 80.00
Shoes, boy's, black leather w/brass
pegs, ca. 1850, pr. 36.00
Shoes, child's high button style, black
suede, pr. 30.00
Shoes, child's high button style, light
blue, scalloped edge, white buttons,
pr. 28.00
Shoes, lady's, high top white canvas,
leather soles, Victorian, pr. 25.00
Shoes, man's lace-up high style,
kangaroo leather, pr. 35.00
Skirt, Edwardian, black cotton w/two
rows of satin flounces at hemline,
35" waist 18.00
Skirt, Edwardian, green ribbed velvet
w/appliqued peacock eyes, ca. 1910 .95.00
Skirt, Victorian, black taffeta, high-
waisted, ca. 1890 ....20.00
Smoking jacket, black velvet, silk
lining, 1904 ....50.00

Spats, cream poplin w/pearl buttons ...25.00
Stockings, lady's, pink cotton, pr. 3.50
Suit, boy's, sailor-type, white linen
   w/red piping 18.00
Suit, boy's, wool tweed, brownish
   olive coat & knee pants w/"Trump
   Clothes, Age 4" label 35.00
Suit, girl's, middy blouse & pleated
   skirt of raw silk, pocket of blouse
   embroidered in navy blue w/an
   abstract motif, navy blue blazer
   trimmed w/white braid, w/"Modele
   Molyneux 5 rue Royale Made in
   France" label, 3 pcs. 467.00
Suit, lady's, beige cashmere, jacket
   w/velvet, embroidery, applique &
   braid trim, 1890s, size 10, 3 pcs. 125.00
Suit, lady's, jacket & skirt of black
   charmeuse, jacket sewn w/top-
   stitched curved lines & curved
   pockets, faceted "jet" buttons,
   rounded collar faced w/ivory charmeuse, 1 lapel sewn w/black & white
   chiffon chrysanthemum, skirt sewn
   w/further rounded line seams, ivory
   charmeuse blouse w/French cuffs &
   rounded neckline w/row of buttons
   & working buttonholes down one
   side & w/band of black charmeuse
   around hem, w/"Chanel, Model No.
   36751" label 7,150.00
Suit, man's, black wool, early 1900s,
   3 pcs. 75.00
Top hat, gentleman's, beaver,
   w/"Lamson & Hubbard, Boston"
   label 50.00
Top hat, gentleman's, collapsible,
   silk ....55.00 to 65.00
Tuxedo, black wool w/white silk vest,
   ca. 1910 ....85.00
Wedding gown, ivory silk, tiered skirt,
   high neck, Victorian ......200.00 to 225.00
Wedding gown, white satin, beaded
   neckline, knee-length hemline front
   tapering down to mid-calf back,
   1920s............................85.00
Wedding veil, gathered cap w/ribbon
   rosettes on sides, waist length,
   1910-20 ....45.00

VALENTINES

Assorted, pre-1900, lot of 15 ....$140.00
Assorted, fold-out & mechanical-type,
   lot of 18 ....40.00
Assorted, Whitney, Germany, set of
   60 ....40.00
Assorted, children's, 1930s & early
   1940s, lot of 150 ....32.00

Fold-out type, lacy, w/tissue paper
   honeycomb 16.00

Fold-out Type Valentine

Fold-out type, die-cut, Cupid emerging
   from water lily, w/tissue paper
   honeycomb (ILLUS.) 45.00

Gibson-type Girl Valentine

Gibson-type girl & Cupid, sepia
   tones (ILLUS.) 20.00
Mechanical, small girl w/bellows
   camera, 1920s, large 18.00
"Punch & Judy," 1900, 6 x 8" 30.00
Raphael Tuck publisher, farmer boy 12.00
Silk, heart-shaped, pre-1920 ....2.00
Walt Disney, Snow White, 1938 ....5.00

VANITY CASES & COMPACTS

Brass compact, lid w/embossed stork
   & "Stork Club," ca. 1935, 2½" d. $30.00
Enameled compact, Art Deco style,
   black w/four rhinestone fleur-de-lis,
   Volupte 25.00

Enameled compact, Art Deco style,
geometric design in blue enamel on
silver finish metal. 35.00
Gold-washed metal compact, enameled
maroon & white Art Deco decor 10.00

Gold and Enamel Compact

Gold & enamel compact, opaque black
enameled geometric design in the
Art Deco taste, w/push thumbpiece,
Continental, ca. 1930, 3½" l.
(ILLUS.) 1,650.00
Gold & enamel compact, rectangular,
Art Deco style, enameled Chinese
red & w/gilded scroll borders in the
Oriental style, hinged cover
w/diamond-set monogram & concealed push-button opening, interior
fitted w/powder compartment,
lipstick holder & mirror, chain
handle, Cartier, Paris, ca. 1925,
2 5/8" l. 3,300.00
Gold & enamel compact, rectangular,
hinged cover & base enameled
w/trails of butterflies between
diamonds, sides w/geometric
pattern, w/diamond-set thumbpiece,
interior fitted w/mirror, powder
compartment & lipstick holder,
Cartier, Paris, 2¾" l. 2,970.00
Gold, enamel & diamond compact, rectangular, Art Deco style, enameled
black on both sides w/plain gold
borders, hinged cover applied
w/diamond-set monogram, thumbpiece set w/three diamonds, interior
fitted w/mirror & 2 compartments,
diamond-set pendant loop & rope
handle, ca. 1925, 3" l. 1,870.00
Gold finish metal compact, embossed
petit point decor center . . . . .10.00 to 15.00
Leather & brass compact, Art Deco
style, compartments for powder,
rouge & mascara. 50.00
Lucite compact w/blue mirrored lid 30.00
Mother-of-pearl compact, iniaid red
mariner's wheel w/black border,
interior inscription, 2½" d. 25.00
Mother-of-pearl compact, rhinestone-
studded, Evans, w/felt case 15.00

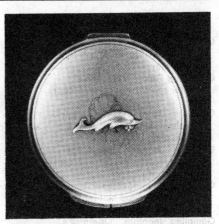

Silver Compact by Georg Jensen

Silver compact, lid w/dolphin in relief
& a chased oyster shell, Georg
Jensen, w/suede case, 3½" d.
(ILLUS.) 330.00
Sterling silver compact, engraved floral
decor, 4" d. 70.00
Sterling silver compact, shell-shaped,
engraved butterflies & florals. 60.00
Sterling silver compact, hand-chased
Art Deco floral motif 85.00
Sterling silver & enamel compact,
geometric design in blue enamel,
Tiffany, 2 1/8" d. 65.00
Sterling silver & enamel compact,
octagonal, lid w/scene of Siamese
dancing girl in black enamel, artist-
signed. 110.00
Sterling silver & 14k gold vanity case,
w/coin slots for nickels & dimes &
compartments for powder & rouge . .150.00

VENDING & GAMBLING MACHINES

Arcade, "Play Golf," Chester
Pollard Amusement Co., 1928 . . . .$1,650.00
Arcade, "Tiger Pull," catch the tiger
by the tail & tug, the harder the
pull, the louder the roar, cast iron
figure realistically painted, mounted
on oak, Exhibit Supply, ca. 1928 . . .2,200.00
Gambling, Bally's "Double Bell"
counter-top slot machine, 5-cent
& 25-cent play 3,375.00
Gambling, Bally's "Reliance" dice
counter-top slot machine, 25-cent
play 3,100.00
Gambling, Berger's "Chicago Ridge"
floor model slot machine, oak
cabinet w/central semi-circular

glass revealing gambling color wheel, late 1890s, 56" h. 4,400.00

Gambling, Caille's "Superior Jack-pot" counter-top slot machine, 25-cent play 1,735.00

Gambling, Field's "Five Jacks" counter-top slot machine, 5-cent play 750.00

Gambling, Jennings' "Challenger" console slot machine 5-cent & 25-cent play, 1947 . . . . 1,100.00

Gambling, Jennings' "Dutch Boy" counter-top slot machine, 5-cent play 1,250.00

Gambling, Jennings' "Four Star Chief" counter-top slot machine, 5-cent play, 1936 . . . . 1,275.00

Gambling, Jennings' "Operator's Bell" counter-top slot machine, 5-cent play, 1920 . . . . 1,565.00

Gambling, Jennings' "Witch" counter-top slot machine, 5-cent play 4,500.00

Gambling, Mills' "Blue Front" counter-top slot machine, 10-cent play 1,270.00

Gambling, Mills' "Cherry Front" counter-top slot machine, 10-cent play, 1937 . . . . 1,075.00

Gambling, Mills' "Dewey" double upright slot machine, 5-cent & 25-cent play 25,330.00

Gambling, Mills' "Diamond" counter-top slot machine, 5-cent play, 1937 . . . . 1,310.00

Gambling, Mills' "Golden Falls" counter-top slot machine, 5-cent play 1,240.00

Gambling, Mills' "Hi-Top" counter-top slot machine, 5-cent play 1,140.00

Mills' "Poinsettia"

Gambling, Mills' "Poinsettia" counter-top slot machine, 25-cent play (ILLUS.) 1,285.00

Gum vendor, "Columbus," Columbus Vending Co., 1-cent, ca. 1927 . . . . 145.00

Gum vendor, "Cop," Pulver Mfg. Co., 1-cent, ca. 1930 . . . . 260.00

Gum vendor, "Masters," 1-cent, ca. 1913, 16" h. 150.00

Match book vendor, "Diamond Matches," Beaton & Calkwell, 1-cent, ca. 1915, 14" h. 215.00

Peanut vendor, "Advance," 1-cent, football-shaped globe, red metal case, polished brass front, 1923 . . . . . . 87.50

Peanut vendor, "Red Star," 1-cent, original paint & pin striping, ca. 1905 . . . . 850.00

Peanut vendor, "Sel-Mor," cast iron, 1-cent 130.00

Peanut vendor, "Smilin' Sam - from Alabam," cast aluminum, embossed "The Salted Peanut Man" on base, painted red, General Mds. Co., 1931 . . . . 1,100.00 to 1,275.00

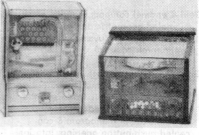

Trade Stimulators

Trade stimulator, "Official Sweep-stakes," racing horses revolve on a track, 1-cent play, w/gumball prize, Rock-Ola Mfg. Co., 1935 (ILLUS. right) 495.00

Trade stimulator, "Kicker & Catcher," player kicks the ball & mechanical football player moves to catch it, Baker Novelty Co., ca. 1935 (ILLUS. left) 220.00

VIENNA ART TIN PLATES

Beautiful woman wearing flowing gown, advertising "Y-B Havana Cigars," 10" d. $65.00

Boy w/dog center, holly berries & foliage border, Christmas adver-tising promotion for C.D. Kenney Co. 55.00

Bust portrait of beautiful brunette woman, ornate border, Royal Art, 10" d. 47.00

Bust portrait of beautiful woman holding urn of flowers, ornate vining border, 10" d. 48.00

Bust portrait of beautiful woman,
advertising "Dr. Pepper" 225.00
Bust portrait of beautiful woman
w/flowing dark hair, advertising
"Anheuser-Busch Malt
Nutrine" . . . . .95.00 to 110.00

Knights of Columbus Plate

Columbus bust portrait center, Knights
of Columbus souvenir w/K.C.
emblems, T. C. Gleason & Co.,
Chicago, Illinois, w/1905 patent
date, 10" d. (ILLUS.) 65.00
Francis Scott Key & flag center, history
of "The Star Spangled Banner"
w/flags & shields around sides &
"1814-1914," 9½" d. 85.00
Girl w/doll center, holly berries &
foliage border, Christmas advertising promotion for C. D. Kenney
Co. 62.50
Jamestown Exposition souvenir, scene
of Indian attack center w/John Smith
& Pocahontas on border & dates 1607
& 1907 on pages of open book,
1905 patent, 9" d. 85.00
Roses center, advertising "Dr.
Pepper" 175.00

VINAIGRETTES

*These were originally tiny boxes, usually
silver, with an inner perforated lid enclosing
a sponge soaked in aromatic vinegar to
lessen offensive odors. Later versions made
of glass in this country contained perfumes.*

Gold-washed sterling silver, "repousse" Vintage grape design on
lid $260.00
Silver, bright-cut florals, reticulated
inner lid & gold-washed interior,

rabbit head mark, France, ca. 1830,
1¼ x ¾" 95.00
Sterling silver, book-shaped w/hinged
lid, lacy filigree of twisted wires,
1¾ x 1¼" 125.00
Sterling silver, heart-shaped,
embossed cherubs & florals, hinged
opening to insert cotton pad,
ca. 1880 . . . . .195.00
Sterling silver, walnut-shaped,
1840-60 . . . . .250.00

WALLACE NUTTING PRINTS

"A Cape Mill"

*In 1898, Wallace Nutting published his first
hand-tinted pictures and these were popular
for more than 20 years. An "assembly line"
subsequently colored and placed a signature
and (sometimes) a title on the mat of these
copyrighted photographs. Interior scenes
featuring Early American furniture are considered the most desirable of these photographs.*

"A Bit of Gossip," interior scene,
framed, 16" w. $85.00
"A Bit of Sewing," interior scene,
11 x 13½" 90.00
"A Cape Mill," outdoor scene, framed
(ILLUS.) 40.00
"A Favorite Corner," outdoor scene
w/sheep grazing, rock walls & road,
framed, 16" .72.00
"A Garden of Larkspur," 9½ x 12" 37.50
"A Joyous Anniversary," 11 x 13" 35.00
"A Little River," outdoor scene,
framed, overall 12½ x 18½" 32.00
"A Peep at the Hills," outdoor scene,
framed, overall 11 x 17" 35.00
"A Sheffield Heirloom," interior scene,
framed, overall 18½ x 15¾" 95.00
"A Sip of Tea," interior scene, framed,
18 x 15" 95.00

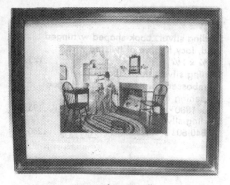

"A Stitch in Time"

"A Stitch in Time," interior scene,
 framed, 11½" (ILLUS.) 70.00
"A Tunnel of Bloom," framed,
 14½ x 17½" 38.00
"A Warm Spring Day," outdoor scene
 w/sheep grazing near water & trees
 against blue sky, framed 18¼" w. 65.00
"An Absorbing Tale," interior scene,
 lady reading book in home, framed,
 10½" 65.00
"An Old Drawing Room," interior
 scene, framed, 15" 77.00
"An Overflowing Cup," outdoor scene,
 framed, overall 10½ x 12½" 32.00
"Bonny Dale," outdoor scene, framed,
 overall 15½ x 18½" 35.00
"By A Berkshire Pool," outdoor scene,
 14½ x 18" 55.00
"Comfort & A Cat," lady sewing near
 fireplace w/cat in basket on a chair,
 framed, 13¼ x 11½" 85.00
"Hollyhock Cottage," outdoor scene,
 framed, overall 11 x 13" 30.00
"Honeymoon Stroll," 5 x 7" 30.00
"Litchfield Minster," outdoor scene of
 cathedral w/spires, houses & leafy
 trees from across shimmering blue
 water, framed, 16½" w. 67.00
"Locust Cottage," framed, 12¾ x
 10¾". 30.00
"Nearing the Crest," outdoor scene,
 framed, overall 11½ x 17½" 30.00
"New Hampshire Birches," outdoor
 scene, framed, overall 12 x 15" 35.00
"On the Heights," outdoor scene, gilt
 frame, 16" h. .55.00
"Orta in Blossom Time," outdoor
 scene of houses, wharf & tree-
 covered hilltop, framed, 11½" 55.00
"Path of Joy," 9½ x 12" 37.50
"Posing," outdoor scene of mother &
 child under bower of roses before
 doorway, framed, overall 7½ x
 9½" 65.00
"Spring in the Berkshires," outdoor
 scene, framed, overall 15 x 18" 35.00
"The Swimming Pool," outdoor scene,
 framed, overall 12 x 18" 32.00

"The Way Through the Orchard,"
 outdoor scene, framed, overall
 14 x 16". 35.00
"Westmore Drive," framed, 7¼ x 9¼" . .45.00

WASH BASINS & PITCHERS

Graniteware Wash Basin & Pitcher

Graniteware, grey mottled, 11" h.
 pitcher & 13" d. bowl, pr. (ILLUS.) . . .$70.00
Ironstone china, Cyprus patt., mulberry transfer, Davenport, 13" h.
 pitcher, pr. 175.00
Ironstone china, Panama patt., mul-
 berry transfer, pr. 175.00
Ironstone china, Tea Leaf Lustre patt.,
 Bamboo shape, Alfred Meakin, pr. . .350.00
Ironstone china, Tea Leaf Lustre patt.,
 melon-ribbed, Burgess, 1864-92,
 pr. 350.00
Ironstone china, Wheat & Blackberry
 patt., all white, J. & G. Meakin,
 Staffordshire, ca. 1865, pr. 175.00
Ironstone china, embossed ivy, all
 white, Bridgwood & Clarke, Stafford-
 shire, 1857-64, pr. 185.00
Royal Doulton pottery, octagonal, blue
 & lavender lilacs w/green foliage &
 black trim, navy blue & gold
 borders, 10½" h. pitcher & 16¼" d.
 bowl, pr. 250.00
Utilitarian crockery, Bow Tie w/Bird
 patt., blue & white, pr. 275.00

WATCH FOBS

Also see COCA-COLA ITEMS.

Advertising, "Adams' Road Machinery," horse-drawn grader pictured . .$45.00
Advertising, "Atkins' Saws," saws
 intertwined 50.00

Advertising, "Barker-Wheeler Co.,
 Peoria," Art Nouveau lady decor.....40.00

"Hamlight" Watch Fob

Advertising, "Hamlight, Ham's No. 2
 Cold Blast" farm lantern, nickel-
 plated brass, 2¼ x 1 1/8" (ILLUS.) 75.00

"Henry Bosch Company" Watch Fob

Advertising, "Henry Bosch Company,"
 white metal, embossed name, wall
 paper roll & tools, 1½ x 1 1/8" oval
 (ILLUS.)..........................35.00
Advertising, "Hohner Little Lady
 Harmonica," 1 3/8" 14.00
Advertising, "International Harvester,"
 twin globes w/corn stalks & wheat ...80.00
Advertising, "Leisey Brewery,"
 porcelain 175.00
Advertising, "Maxwell Motor Co.,"
 enameled.........................25.00
Advertising, "NCR, National Cash
 Registers Benefit Everybody,"
 register pictured ....65.00 to 85.00

Advertising, "Old Reliable Coffee,"
 brass.............................32.00
Advertising, "Reo Motor Car"........60.00
Advertising, "Rockford Watch Co.,
 Rockford, Ill.," bell-shaped.........25.00
Advertising, "Savage Rifles," Indian
 w/rifle pictured 85.00
Advertising, "Star Brand Shoes," red
 porcelain.........................50.00
Advertising, "Turkey Coffee".........60.00
Advertising, "Wear-Ever Aluminum" ...15.00
Braided human hair, gold-filled
 attachments set w/ruby & pearl......75.00
Brass, embossed hunter shooting lion ..12.00
Brass, Massachusetts motorcycle
 registration, 1912 ....75.00
Bronze, American Eagle w/spread
 wings 30.00
Bronze, figural Statue of Liberty 35.00
Gold-plated, Great Seal of the United
 States 18.00
Silverplate, shield-shaped w/ornate
 monogram, w/ornate hook & mesh
 strap, marked "Patd. '03" 45.00
Souvenir, "1909 Alaska Yukon Pacific
 Expo."...........................75.00
Souvenir, "1916 Milwaukee Automobile
 Dealers Show," w/strap 65.00
Souvenir, "1921 New York State Fair"...20.00
Sterling silver, Art Nouveau decor 24.00

WATCHES

Man's Hunting Case Watch

Hunting case, lady's, American
 Waltham Watch Co., Waltham, Massachusetts, 7-jewel movement, 6 size
 (1 11/30"), ornate yellow gold-filled
 case, 1899 ....$195.00
Hunting case, lady's, Columbia Watch
 Co., Waltham, Massachusetts,

7-jewel movement, 6 size, lever set,
ornate gold-filled case, 1896 ......165.00
Hunting case, lady's, Elgin Watch Co.,
Elgin, Illinois, 7-jewel movement,
6 size, ornate yellow gold-filled
case, 1901 ....165.00
Hunting case, lady's, Elgin Watch Co.,
17-jewel movement, 0 size (1 5/30"),
gold case 225.00
Hunting case, lady's, Hampden Watch
Co., Springfield, Massachusetts,
Molly Stark, 7-jewel movement,
3/0 size (1 3/30"), gold-filled case ...135.00
Hunting case, lady's, New York
Standard Watch Co., Jersey City,
New Jersey, 7-jewel movement,
0 size..........................225.00
Hunting case, man's, American Watch
Co., Waltham, Massachusetts, 14
size (1 19/30"), half plate nickel
lever movement, bi-metallic compen-
sation balance, white enamel dial
w/Roman numerals, 18k gold box
hinged case, 1876, in original fitted
wooden box.....................880.00
Hunting case, man's, Appleton, Tracy
& Co., Waltham, Massachusetts, 18
size (1 23/30"), gilt damascened full
plate lever movement, white enamel
double sunk dial w/Roman numerals,
14k yellow gold case chased w/ever-
green branches & stars, 1889 ......935.00
Hunting case, man's, Elgin Watch Co.,
lever-set 7-jewel movement, 18 size,
yellow gold case 105.00
Hunting case, man's, Hampden Watch
Co., full plate nickel lever movement, adjusted, double sunk white
enamel dial w/Roman numerals,
14k gold case w/box hinge, chased
w/a stag within vari-colored gold
foliate lozenge set w/four single-cut
diamonds, reverse w/similar
lozenge design centered by a blank
cartouche surrounded w/vari-
colored foliage, ca. 1884, 2 1/8" d.
(ILLUS.) 2,090.00
Hunting case, man's, E. Howard & Co.,
Roxbury, Massachusetts, 23-jewel
movement, 14k gold case, 1896 ...1,400.00
Open face chronograph, man's,
American Waltham Watch Co., gilt
lever movement, bimetallic compen-
sation balance, white enamel dial
w/Arabic numerals, subsidiary dials,
bezels & band chased w/scrolls,
14k gold case, 1886, 2" d.........1,210.00
Open face, man's, American Waltham
Watch Co., 11-jewel movement,
18 size, silver case, 1893 ....125.00
Open face, man's, Ball Watch Co.,
19-jewel movement, 12 size
(1 17/30"), 14k white gold-filled
case, 1906 ....325.00

Open face, man's, Elgin Watch Co.,
G. M. Wheeler model, 17-jewel
movement, 18 size, lever set, yellow
gold-filled case, 1888 ....135.00
Open face, man's, Hamilton Watch Co.,
Lancaster, Pennsylvania, Model 914,
17-jewel movement, 12 size, 14k
white gold-filled case 135.00
Open face, man's, Hampden Watch
Co., Gladiator model, 11-jewel
movement, 18 size, lever set, silver-
oid case, 1885 ....95.00
Open face, man's, Illinois Watch Co.,
Sangamo Special, 23-jewel movement, 16 size 600.00
Open face, man's, South Bend Watch
Co., South Bend, Indiana, Model
No. 429, 19-jewel movement, 12
size, adjusted to temperature,
4-position, yellow gold-filled case...135.00
Railroad, Hamilton Watch Co., Grade
992, 21-jewel movement, 16 size,
yellow gold-filled case, 1909 ....175.00
Railroad, Hamilton Watch Co., Grade
992-B, 21-jewel movement, 16 size,
ornate 10k yellow gold-filled case...235.00

WEATHERVANES

Copper Cow Weathervane

Banner, sheet copper, pierced
w/scrollwork & geometric devices
enclosing the letter "W," on rod
standard w/ball finial sprouting 4
flowers set in black metal stand,
J.W. Fiske & Co., New York, late
19th c., 48" l., overall 8' 7" h. $770.00
Boar, copper, full-bodied animal
w/sheet copper incisors, ears &
corkscrew tail, on rod standard,
J.W. Fiske & Co., New York, late
19th c., 31½" l., overall 17" h. 2,090.00
Centaur, copper, flattened full-bodied
figure of a Centaur drawing his bow,
w/molded & ridged sheet copper

tail, original gilding, mounted on black metal stand, American, 3rd quarter 19th c., 41½" l., overall 33" h. (2 bullet holes) 11,000.00

Cow, copper, full-bodied animal w/zinc horns & ears, remnants of old yellow & polychrome paint & w/weathered verdigris, New England, 19th c., 31½" l., 20¼" h. (ILLUS.) 2,750.00

Fish, zinc, full-bodied, painted in variegated green, yellow & white, on black metal stand, American, late 19th c., 24" l., overall 15" h. 825.00

Goddess of Liberty, copper & cast zinc, flattened full-bodied figure w/right arm grasping the standard of an American flag w/pierced 5-point stars, left hand grasping fasces w/traditional axe, short cloak at her shoulders & w/Phrygian cap, on large arrow directional, w/original gilding, on black metal stand, New England, late 19th c., 37" l., overall 43" h. 23,100.00

Horse prancing, sheet iron silhouette, w/flowing tail, mounted on rod standard w/directional arrow in later black metal stand, American, late 19th c., 48" l., overall 36" h. 1,650.00

Horse running, copper, flattened full-bodied animal w/cast zinc head & molded sheet copper tail, on rod standard in black metal stand, Cushing & White, Waltham, Massachusetts, ca. 1880, 28" l., overall 17¼" h. 1,320.00

Copper Horse Weathervane

Horse running, copper, full-bodied animal w/tail flying, on black metal stand, 19th c., 40" l., 19" h. (ILLUS.) 2,200.00

Horse trotting, carved wood, flattened silhouette w/indented eye, painted terra cotta red body w/black mane & tail, mounted on rod standard in wooden base, American, 19th c., 29" l., overall 23¼" h. 935.00

Horse & rider, copper, flattened full-bodied animal w/applied sheet copper tail & rider, traces of original gilding, on rod standard in

contemporary metal stand, American, 3rd quarter 19th c., 18¾" l., overall 20½" h. 5,500.00

Hound pursuing a fox, copper, flattened full-bodied animals, mounted on rod standard & black metal stand, Cushing & White, Waltham, Massachusetts, ca. 1880, 48" l., overall 24½" h. 7,975.00

Mercury shooting an arrow, sheet iron silhouette, on molded brass sphere above cast iron directionals, in cast iron base, traces of original gilding, 47" h. 440.00

Pig, copper, flattened full-bodied animal w/cast zinc head & tail & applied sheet copper ears, green patina, on rod standard, L. W. Cushing & Sons, Waltham, Massachusetts, 3rd quarter 19th c., 21" l., overall 13" h. 6,875.00

Pig, hammered copper, flattened full-bodied animal w/large sheet copper ears & molded curly tail, on rod standard, E.G. Washburne & Co., New York City, New York, late 19th c., 46" l., overall 26" h. 11,000.00

Pigeon, copper, full-bodied figure perched on a large directional arrow, w/original gilding, on rod standard & black metal base, J. W. Fiske & Co., New York, late 19th c., 24¼" l., overall 30¼" h. 1,980.00

Plow, sheet copper & zinc, fashioned in the full round, w/turning wheels & blades, mounted on a black metal stand, American, 19th c., 41½" l., overall 22½" h. 3,300.00

Ram, copper & zinc, flattened full-bodied animal w/cast zinc head applied w/molded sheet copper horns, green patina, on rod standard, American, mid-19th c., 28½" l., overall 22" h. 7,700.00

Wooden Rooster Weathervane

Rooster, carved & painted wood,
flattened form w/rounded edges,
incised feathering, head w/traces of
old yellow paint, red wattles &
comb, tail w/overlapping feather
detail, on wooden rod standard &
black wooden base, American, early
19th c., 10¾" l., overall 18¼" h.
(ILLUS.) 2,310.00

Rooster, zinc & copper, full-bodied
cast zinc figure w/deeply molded
feather detail, applied & "repousse"
sheet copper tail & legs, w/green
patina & majority of original gilding,
on contemporary black metal stand,
J. Howard & Co., West Bridgewater,
Massachusetts, 3rd quarter 19th c.,
12½" l., overall 13¾" h. 5,500.00

Stag leaping, copper, full-bodied
animal w/cast zinc antlers, on black
metal stand, L.W. Cushing & Sons,
Waltham, Massachusetts, 19th c.,
19¾" l., overall 18" h. 4,125.00

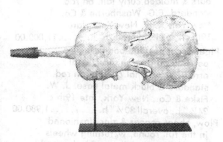

19th Century Violin Weathervane

Violin, carved & gilded wood, flattened
stylized form w/pierced "sound"
holes, fingerboard w/sheet-iron
sheathing, bottom w/wrought-iron
peg, on rod standard & black
metal base, American, 19th c.,
23¼" l., overall 11¾" h. (ILLUS.) 880.00

WITCH BALLS

*Several versions exist as to the origin of
these hollow balls of glass. Some believe they
were originally designed to hold the then precious commodity of salt in the chimney where
it would be kept dry. Eventually these blown
glass spheres became associated with ward-
ing off the "evil eye" and it is known they
were hung in the windows of numerous 18th
century English glass blowers. The tradition
was carried to America where the balls were
made from the 19th century on. They are
scarce.*

Aqua w/white loopings, 3¼" d. $30.00
Clear w/green & opalescent loopings ...95.00
Clear w/white loopings, w/shaded pink
Satin glass holder w/ruffled rim, pr.
6" d. balls & pr. 6 3/8" h. holders,
4 pcs. 275.00

Cobalt Blue Witch Ball with Vase

Cobalt blue ball & matching vase
w/crimped foot, South Jersey, mid-
19th c., 3¼" d. ball, 5½" h. vase
(ILLUS.) 175.00
Deep olive green (black), New England
area, 3½" d. 50.00
Fiery opalescent w/bright red & pink
loopings, 3½" d. 90.00
Green w/opalescent loopings, 5" d. 75.00
Olive green w/large white speckles on
one side, Saratoga, New York,
2¾" d. 160.00
Red-amber, closed pontil, 5¼" d. 80.00

WOODENWARES

Burl Bowl

*The patina and mellow coloring, along
with the lightness and smoothness that
come only with age and wear, attract
collectors to old woodenwares. The earliest
forms were the simplest and the shapes of
items whittled out in the late 19th century
varied little in form from those turned out in*

the American colonies two centuries earlier. Burl is a growth, or wart, on some trees in which the grain of the wood is twisted and turned in a manner which strengthens the fibers and causes a beautiful pattern to be formed. Treenware is simply a term for utilitarian items made from "treen," another word for wood. While maple was the primary wood used for these items, they are also abundant in pine, ash, oak, walnut, and other woods. "Lignum Vitae" is a West Indies species of wood that can always be identified by the contrasting colors of the dark heartwood and light sapwood and by its heavy weight, which causes it to sink in water. Also see BUTTER MOLDS & STAMPS, COFFEE GRINDERS, DE-COYS, KITCHENWARES, MORTARS & PESTLES, NAUTICAL ANTIQUES, SHAKER ITEMS, TOYS, WEATHER-VANES, WOOD SCULPTURES, WRITING ACCESSORIES and YARN WINDERS.

Alms box, hanging-type, w/carved & painted angel at front, 14½" h. $170.00
Alms box, hanging-type, oak, plain 45.00
Apple butter scoop, hand-hewn from single piece of wood w/D-shaped opening in handle, 6" w. bowl, overall 15" l. 220.00
Apple tray, curly poplar, canted sides, w/traces of old red, 9½ x 10½" squared form 85.00
Baker's cooling rack, poplar, 6 removable slatted shelves, mortised base w/chamfered shoe feet, original red paint, 22¾" w., 63¼" h. 250.00
Bed steps, inlaid mahogany & cherry-wood, 2-step model, top step w/hinged lid enclosing deep compartment, step faces w/line-inlay borders & inlaid fish form in each corner, on short square tapering legs, Rhode Island, 1790-1820, 20" w., 21" h. 990.00
Bed wrench (for rope bed), 15" l. 60.00
Bowl, turned, 8" d., 4" h. 40.00
Bowl, burl, good figuring, traces of green paint on exterior, 8¼" d., 3 7/8" h. 400.00
Bowl, burl, well figured, 11" d., 3¼" h. 225.00
Bowl, factory-turned, maple, 11" d. 15.00
Bowl, burl, oval w/rim handles, well figured, 12½ x 10¼" 805.00
Bowl, burl, 18th c., 14" d., 5" h. (ILLUS.) 725.00
Bowl, burl, oval w/protruding rim handles, 18 x 11½", 5" h. 1,400.00
Bowl, hand-hewn oblong w/simple rim handles, worn blue exterior paint, 20 x 10¾" 125.00

Bowl, turned wood, flared rim, 24 x 23" warped d., 8¼" h. 110.00

Hand-Hewn Bowl

Bowl, hand-hewn w/prominent chisel marks, deep oblong w/outward flaring lip handles, 19th c., 26½" l., 7" h. (ILLUS.) 385.00
Box w/sliding lid, painted pine, dove-tail construction, old worn brown-painted graining w/black edge stripe, 10¼ x 7 3/8" 65.00
Box w/hinged slant-lid, painted pine, old brown paint w/white edge stripe, 12 x 8¼", 5¾" h. 35.00
Bread (or pastry) board, poplar, fish-tail crest, 18¾ x 14¾" 75.00
Breadboard, poplar, tombstone crest pierced w/hole to hang, 22 x 15" 45.00
Bucket w/"piggin" handle, stave construction w/brass & iron bandings, 10½" d., 8¼" h. 105.00
Butter churn, painted poplar, pump-type w/squared body on molded base w/cut-out feet, original red & black-painted flame graining on brown ground, overall 34" h. (skillfully matched handle replacement) 160.00
Butter paddle, maple w/some curl, well-shaped handle w/carved bird looking over back, dark worn finish & some age cracks, 6" l. 175.00
Butter paddle, maple, shaped blade, good finish, 9" l. . . . . 15.00 to 20.00
Butter paddle, curly maple, scoop-carved blade, overall 11¾" l. 120.00
Cutlery tray, maple, 2-compartment w/scalloped divider pierced w/heart-shaped handle grip, canted sides w/scalloped tops, wire nail construction, dark patinated finish, 13½ x 8¾" (minor base damage at 1 corner) 135.00
Dipper, burl ash bowl w/straight grain in handle, open knot hole in side, never had finish, 9½" d., 11½" l. handle 90.00
Dipper w/pouring lip, hand-shaped bowl & flattened handle, nice form, 12¼" l. 175.00
Door stop, turned lignum vitae, pedestal base, bulbous solid body w/tall turned finial, 12" h. 110.00

Pine Dough Trough

Dough trough, pine, canted sides,
old refinishing, 28" l. (ILLUS.) 65.00

Dough trough, painted pine, dovetailed
box w/canted sides & lid on base
w/turned legs joined by box
stretcher, turned feet, worn original
red paint 300.00

Dough trough, pine box on hardwood
stand, canted box w/applied molding
on bottom edge, base w/turned &
splayed legs joined by H-stretchers,
old worn reddish brown finish,
28½ x 48" top, overall 29¼" h.
(2-board pine top is old
replacement). 215.00

Dry measure, 2-part, stave construction w/wire bands, top holds 1
peck, bottom holds half peck,
stamped label w/anchor & "R.C.W.
Richmond, Va.," 12½" h. 75.00

"Star" Egg Carrier

Egg carrier w/interior trays & lid,
marked "Star, Mfg. by John G. Elbs,
Rochester, N.Y., Pat. 1903-1906,"
8¼ x 6½", 2¾" h. (ILLUS.) 35.00

Egg crate, slat-type, 2-layer, 13" sq.,
7" h. 25.00

Egg crate, solid sides, locking cover,
"Farmer's Friend" 48.00

Flour sifter, pine, sides continuing to
form cut-out feet, crank handle at
side to turn roller above sieve,
w/label "Blood's Patent" 240.00

"Hasty pudding" stirrer, flattened blade,
turned handle, 20" l. . . . . 20.00 to 26.00

Lap board, pine, 14 x 29" 25.00

Lemon squeezer, all wood . . . . . 36.50 to 45.00

Mangling or Smoothing Board

Mangling (or smoothing) board, carved
stylized horse handle, relief & chip-
carved board w/crown monogram &
dated 1817, medium brown finish,
26½" l. (ILLUS.) 775.00

Mangling (or smoothing) board, oak,
shaped cut-out handle, chip-carved
geometric starburst medallion &
large heart on flat surface, Scandinavian origins, 4½" w., 28½" l. 220.00

Noggin (pitcher hewn from single
block of wood), maple, 7" h. 220.00

Noodle cutting board, 15" d. board
w/handle pierced w/hanging hole,
overall 24½" l. to end of handle 68.00

Ox yoke, 35" l. 60.00

Ox yoke, 49" l. 165.00

Pantry box, cov., bentwood round,
straight-lapped seams, original dark
brown finish w/minor edge wear,
8¼" d., 3¾" h. 35.00

Pantry box, cov., bentwood round,
straight-lapped seams, original
black paint, 9½" d., 6" h. 55.00

Pantry box, cov., bentwood round,
V-lapped lid & straight-lapped base,
natural finish w/darkened patina,
9½" d. 85.00

Pantry box w/cover & wire bail
handle w/wooden grip, bentwood
round, straight-lapped seams,
painted pewter grey finish, 11" d.,
7" h. 55.00

Pantry box, cov., bentwood round
w/laced seams, original colorful
Norwegian-type rosemaaling w/black,
blue & yellow scrolling foliage on
red ground, 12½" d., 4" h. 355.00

Pantry Box with Rosemaaling Decor

Pantry box, cov., finger-lapped seams,
original colorful Norwegian-style
rosemaaling decor, 14" d. (ILLUS.)...325.00
Pantry boxes, cov., straight-lapped
seams, natural finish, graduated
sizes from 6" to 9", set of 3 ....115.00
Pickle barrel, cov., die-stamped
"Heinz"...........................95.00
Pie peel, pine, short handle, 1-pc.,
15½" l..............................65.00
Piggin (stave-constructed bucket
w/single stave extending beyond
rim as handle), bentwood bandings
w/locked laps, 18th c., 7½" d.,
6½" h. 275.00
Pill box, cov., bentwood round,
straight seams, good patina, 2" d.....28.00
Pipe box, hanging-type, walnut,
elaborately chip-carved hearts,
pinwheels & stellate devices, 2
dolphins one side & other w/whaling
scene w/a whaleboat, sperm whale
& harpooner ready w/iron dart,
probably Pennsylvania, ca. 1830,
10¼" h. 990.00
Plate, turned curly maple, branded
"Wallace Nutting," 9" d. 65.00
Rolling pin, curly maple, w/movable
black-painted handles, 19½" l. 50.00
Rolling pin, walnut, 1-piece 22.00
Salt dip, turned treenware, pedestal
base, original grey-blue paint,
2½" d., 2 3/8" h.................200.00
Scoop, burl cup shape w/cone
handle, New England, 18th c.,
5" d. 275.00
Scrubbing stick, corrugated, 1-piece,
29" l.............................150.00
"Secret" ballot box, cov., dovetail
construction, w/marbles...........70.00
Shoes, child's Dutch-style, pr. 20.00

Wooden Shoulder Yoke

Shoulder yoke, replaced sapling hooks
& rope, 37" l. (ILLUS.) 27.50
Shovel, maple, carved from single
piece of wood, natural finish,
attributed to the Shakers, overall
56" l..............................82.50
Skimmer, shell-shaped, honey-colored
patina, 6¾" l. 120.00
Soap stirring paddle (for making lye
soap), hand-hewn, pierced blade,
19th c., 28" l. 85.00
Soft soap dish, turned, 5½" d. 50.00
Spoon, burl, small tapered handle,
18th c., 3½" l. 330.00

Spoon, long-handled, early 19th c.,
20" l..............................55.00
Stocking stretcher, maple, die-bossed
size "11".........................20.00
Storage bin, pine, hinged lid lifting to
deep dovetailed bin on turned feet,
worn original dark paint, 36½" w.,
24" deep, 28" h. 175.00
Storage box w/domed lid, painted &
decorated poplar, dovetail construction, original red & black painted
graining w/green & yellow striping &
free-hand pomegranate & foliage
decor, original brass bail handle,
11¾" w...........................395.00
Strawberry picking box, pine, w/four
berry boxes, 5 pcs.................37.50
Sugar bowl, cov., ovoid body on
molded base, slightly domed fitted
cover, sponge daubed brown, yellow
& green decor, New England, early
19th c., 4½" h. (small crack).......302.50

Sugar Firkin

Sugar firkin (bucket of stave construction) w/lid, bentwood bandings
& swing handle, 9¾" d., 10" h.
(ILLUS.)..........................65.00
Sugar firkin w/lid, wooden bandings
& bentwood swing handle, old blue
repaint, 14¼" d., 13½" h............85.00
Tankard, cov., stave construc-
tion w/locked hoops, 18th c., 9" h. ..660.00
Tape loom, early 19th c., small size,
6½" w., 17" l. 125.00
"Taster" spoon, hand-hewn maple,
18th c., 12" l. 30.00
"Tina" box, bentwood oval w/laced
seams, w/initials & dated 1877,
Norwegian.......................195.00
Toddy stick, maple, mushroom end,
tapered handle, overall 11" l........30.00
Tool tote box, walnut, square nail
construction, 23 x 13" oblong 55.00
Towel rack, hanging-type, double, oak,
wide top ball & spindle panel,
19 x 22"..........................90.00
Towel rack, floor standing type, 4-bar,

turned posts & feet, refinished,
27¼" w., 32" h. 36.00
Towel rack, floor-standing type,
Victorian cottage-style, maple,
T-shaped ends w/two mortised bars,
spool-turned legs, w/stretchers, ball
feet, late 19th c. 125.00
Trencher plate, turned treenware,
9 x 9½" warped d. 145.00
Trencher plate, birch, hand-hewn, ca.
1800, 23½ x 13½" oval 140.00
Violin case w/hinged lid, pine 85.00
Wall box, painted pine, arched crest
pierced w/hole to hang, hinged
slant-lid opening to small well above
single drawer w/turned wood pull,
applied molding at base, original
yellow paint, 12" w., 6" deep, overall
12" h. to crest .750.00
Wall pocket w/shelf, pine, cut-out
sides, old red paint, 9" w.,
22½" h. 195.00

Norwegian "Wedding" Spoon

"Wedding" spoon, hand-hewn,
traditional Norwegian form,
probably made in Minnesota
(ILLUS.) 25.00
Wood storage bin, pine, oblong
top-shelf over narrower shelf within
bin w/arched sides continuing to
scalloped front, wide board construction throughout, old mellow
refinishing, 35" w., 17" deep,
33¼" h. to top shelf at rear 275.00
Writing box w/hinged lid, walnut, dovetailed case w/small dovetailed drawer
at side, lid w/replaced brass bail
handle, old dark finish, 22 x 14",
8½" h. 75.00

WOOD SCULPTURES

*American folk sculpture is an important
part of the American art scene today. Skilled
wood carvers turned out ship's figureheads,
cigar store figures, plaques and carousel
animals of stylized beauty and great appeal.
The wooden shipbuilding industry, which had
originally nourished this folk art, declined*

*after the Civil War and the talented carvers
then turned to producing figures for tobac-
conist's shops, carousel animals and show
figures for the circuses. These figures and
other early ornamental carvings that have
survived the elements and years are eagerly
sought. Also see DECOYS and
WEATHERVANES.*

Carousel figure of a camel, hand-
carved, painted tan coat w/dark
green saddle & colorful saddle
blanket w/"jewels" & incised tassels,
Looff, 78" l., 66" h. $6,900.00
Carousel figure of a donkey, hand-
carved, w/saddle & bridle, worn
original polychrome paint, American, 3rd quarter 19th c., 45" l.,
47" h. 2,750.00
Carousel figure of a horse jumping,
hand-carved, original polychrome
paint, mounted on rocking
mechanism, Spillman, ca. 1930 . . . .3,200.00

Carved & Painted Carousel Horse

Carousel figure of a horse prancing,
hand-carved, painted black coat &
red, ochre & pale blue saddle,
20th c., 60" l. (ILLUS.) 1,320.00
Carousel figure of a horse prancing,
hand-carved, Dentzel, ca. 1890,
restored 5,500.00
Carousel figure of a rooster running,
hand-carved, w/glass eyes, mounted
on spiral brass & wrought iron
standard, probably European, ca.
1900, 48" l., 48" h. 1,980.00
Cigar store figure of an Indian chief,
hand-carved, wearing feathered
headdress, red cloak w/yellow
fringe over a blue-green costume,
holding tobacco leaves in one hand
& box of cigars in other, on base
w/number "413," attributed to
Samuel Robb, New York, ca. 1880,
45" h. 6,600.00
Cigar store figure of an Indian princess,
hand-carved, w/plumed headdress
centering a star & wearing a fringed
shawl & dress, right hand pressing 2
cigar boxes to her chest, on
chamfered rectangular base, late
19th c., 59½" h. 4,400.00

19th Century Cigar Store Figure

Cigar store figure of a Scotsman, hand-carved, wearing feathered hat & colorful costume, arm outstretched holding a snuff horn, probably New York, late 19th c., 81" h. (ILLUS.) . . 4,400.00

Figure of a mermaid, hand-carved pine, w/scroll pressed to her breast, her hair in braids & tied w/ribbons, scrolled tail, probably American, early 19th c., 22½" l., 18" h. 1,045.00

Figures, Abraham Lincoln, George Washington & Uncle Sam holding an eagle & American flag, hand-carved, w/painted clothing, each on titled base, M. Rothloff, ca. 1920, 12" to 14½" h., set of 3 . . . . 1,430.00

Model of a Sandpiper

Model of a sandpiper, hand-carved, body painted white w/black streaks & spots & w/yellow beak, rotating

on single iron bar (without base), East Coast States, 20th c., 14" w., 15" h. (ILLUS.) 770.00

Model of the American clipper ship "Flying Cloud," hand-carved, detailed figurehead & deck w/two deckhouses & lifeboats, mounted on stand, A. Jansen, Roxbury, 1894, 36 x 26¼" 605.00

Plaque, hand-carved, spread-winged American eagle w/head turned to the right, grasping a banner in its beak & poised above a shield flanked by draped American flags ending in cross-hatched tassels, gilt & polychrome, attributed to John Haley Bellamy, Kittery Point, Maine, ca. 1900, 25" l., 8" h. 2,640.00

Plaque, relief-carved figure of a rooster wearing a top hat, original red paint, 15¾" h. (mounting board removed from back) 4,500.00

Ship's figurehead, hand-carved pine, bust length figure of a young woman, white repaint, 18th c., 19" h. 990.00

Whirligig, hand-carved figure of an Indian w/tin feather headdress, old dark red repaint w/features in white & black, dark yellow breech cloth & high moccasins trimmed in black, mounted on black wooden base, 13¾" h. plus base 3,025.00

Whirligig, hand-carved Negro minstrel dancer, ca. 1900, 12 x 6" 250.00

Hand-carved Whirligig

Whirligig, hand-carved stylized figures of 2 Indians seated in a canoe, one w/long leather headdress & the other w/leather feathers, w/metal paddle arm baffles, mounted on a rod standard w/large ball finial, in black metal stand, American, late 19th c., overall 16¼" h. (ILLUS.) . . . 1,210.00

Whirligig, hand-carved stylized figure of
a man, wearing a blue jacket, yellow
trousers w/bright blue stripe, arm
baffles set in at right angles, paddles
painted w/red, green & white stripes,
on black metal stand, Pennsylvania,
19th c., 17" h. 3,850.00
Whirligig, hand-carved stylized figure
of a sailor, wearing white bell-
bottom trousers, blue middy blouse
w/white collar, black tie & hat
w/painted tin brim, w/paddle arm
baffles, mounted on metal stand,
ca. 1890, 20½" h. 715.00

WORLD FAIR COLLECTIBLES

*There has been great interest in collecting
items produced for the great fairs and expositions held through the years. During the
1970s, there was particular interest in items
produced for the 1876 Centennial Exhibition
and now interest is focusing on those items
associated with the 1893 Columbian Exposition. Listed below is a random sampling of
prices asked for items produced for the various fairs.*

1876 PHILADELPHIA EXHIBITION
Book, "Centennial Exhibition Guide,"
22 fold-out steel engravings $85.00
Calendar, "Home Insurance Company,"
7½ x 5½", 12 pp. 50.00
Handkerchief, printed cotton, 3 Exhi-
bition buildings pictured center, bust
portraits of George Washington &
Ulysses S. Grant in upper corners,
framed, 29¾ x 25½" 100.00
Pail, tin, "Naphey's Leaf Lard, Phila-
delphia, 1776-1876," 2½" h. 26.00
Paperweight, frosted & clear glass,
Women's Pavillion pictured,
Gillinder & Sons, 5¼ x 4" oval 95.00
Picture, woven silk, scene depicting
Betsy Ross sewing the first American
flag, marked "Anderson Bros.,
Paterson, N.J.," original frame,
13 x 10". 150.00
Plate, ironstone china, color transfer,
view of buildings "Philadelphia Exhi-
bition 1876," bright blue border,
8½" d. 25.00
Press ticket 12.00
Scarf, printed cotton, Memorial Hall
center w/other buildings, black &
white w/orange border,
26½ x 24½". 55.00
Whimsey, lady's shoe, clear glass,
marked "Gillinder & Sons," 5" l 35.00

1893 COLUMBIAN EXPOSITION

Columbian Exposition Glass Bell

Advertising cards, "Singer Sewing
Machines," Costumes of All Nations
series, set of 36 . . . . .110.00
Bell, clear glass, "World's Fair
Columbian Exposition - 1893," 3" d.,
4½" h. (ILLUS.) 95.00
Bone dish, ironstone china, brown
transfer "The Lagoon Looking
South". 18.00
Book, "The City of Palaces," illustrated,
embossed hard cover, 160 pp.,
11 x 14". 25.00
Book, "Glimpses of the World's Fair &
the Midway Plaisance," soft cover,
190 pp., 5 x 7" 12.00
Book, "Shepp's World's Fair Photo-
graphed," w/descriptions of
exhibits, 538 pp. 45.00
Creamer & open sugar bowl, china,
gold handles, shell decor w/gold
trim on cream ground, marked
"Coalport, England," small, pr. 150.00
Cup & saucer, china, Fisheries & Transportation Building scene 38.00
Demitasse spoon, sterling silver,
Queen Isabella on handle, Women's
Building in bowl 33.00
Doll house living room furniture:
settee, rocking chair & 2 arm chairs;
metal w/velvet seats, painted scene
depicting landing of Columbus on
backs, 4 pcs. .275.00
Knife, pocket-type, sterling silver,
embossed bust of Columbus, small . . .20.00
Mustard jar w/original lid, ruby-
flashed glass, Thumbprint patt.,
etched souvenir 125.00
Paperweight, clear glass, melon-
ribbed, rim embossed "World's
Columbian Exposition 1492-1892,"
3½" d. 45.00
Paperweight, glass, U.S. Government
Building pictured on thin film of
milk white glass on underside

enclosed in clear, signed "Libbey,"
4 x 2½" oblong 32.00
Pen, bone handle w/Fair scene in
Stanhope viewer. 85.00
Pencil sharpener, model of a world
globe, razor-type sharpener in cast
iron base, "World's Fair Columbian
Exposition Chicago, Illinois, 1893,"
9" d., 5½" h. 125.00
Pin tray, tin, Electrical Building
pictured, 5 x 3¼" 23.00
Plate, china, "Horticultural Building,"
pink & white floral border, marked
"Wedgwood, Etruria," 8¼" d. 33.00
Plate, lustreless white glass, color
transfer view of buildings, Mt.
Washington Glass Co., 7¾" d. 55.00
Postcards, "Official Souvenir U.S.
Postals," by Charles W. Goldsmith,
set of 10 . . . . .100.00
Print, chromolithograph view of the
Ferris Wheel, framed, 24 x 20". 65.00
Razor, straight edge, etched scene on
blade 35.00
Stickpin, sterling silver, bust of
Columbus. 35.00
Ticket, admission to "Manhattan Day" . .12.00
Toothpick holder, ruby-flashed glass,
Thumbprint patt., etched souvenir . . .30.00
Vase, pink shaded to lavender satin
glass, pear-shaped w/narrow double-
ringed neck, Illinois State Building
scene, 7¾" h. 150.00

1901 PAN AMERICAN EXPOSITION

Pan American Exposition Paperweight

Cup, ruby-flashed glass, etched
souvenir, Heisey Glass Co. 35.00
Match safe, pewter & brass, embossed
Art Nouveau lady decor, w/cigar
cutter end 35.00
Model of a hatchet, clear glass
w/embossed Indian head, 7" l. 75.00
Mug, stoneware, blue & grey
w/embossed buffalo decor. 150.00
Paperweight, bronze-finish pot metal,
model of a buffalo, w/Feb. 5, 1901
patent (ILLUS.). 48.00
Plaque, bronze, buffalo in high relief
& "Buffalo, New York," 7 x 5¼" 75.00

Teaspoon, silverplate, Indian head
handle, Electrical Building in bowl. . . .15.00
Teaspoon, sterling silver, full figure
Indian & buffalo handle w/Niagara
Falls reverse, Art Nouveau decor
bowl 65.00
Tumbler, pewter, embossed scene of
buildings, Niagara Falls & buffalo
head, 3½" h. .35.00
Viewbook 9.00

1904 ST. LOUIS WORLD FAIR

1904 World's Fair Letter Opener

Billfold, leather, embossed scenes 25.00
Card tray, metal, Palace of Industry
pictured 12.00
Change tray, metal, Cascade Gardens
pictured, 5" 20.00
Dresser box, glass, Cascade Gardens
decor 35.00
Letter opener, bronze, eagle perched
atop handle, 7¼" l. (ILLUS.) 75.00
Match holder, pocket-type, tin,
Jefferson & Napoleon pictured. 25.00
Model of a hatchet, clear glass 65.00
Mug, china, Administration Building,
pictured, 4" h. 45.00
Mug, ruby-stained glass, etched
souvenir. 20.00
Napkin ring, white metal, Cascade
Gardens & other views 12.00
Necktie, spun glass, in original box 18.00
Padlock, "1904 St. Louis World's Fair"
one side & Missouri State seal
reverse. 150.00
Picture, reverse painting on glass,
"Palace of Varied Industries,"
framed 55.00
Plate, china, U.S. Government Building
pictured, 5" d. 35.00
Postcard, bust portraits of Lewis &
Clark. 12.00
Postcard, hold-to-light type, Transpor-
tation Building pictured 22.00
Teaspoon, silverplate, Jefferson
handle, Palace of Electricity in
bowl. . . . . 12.00 to 15.00
Tumbler, milk white glass, scenes of
Cascade Gardens & Palace of
Machinery, 5" h. 30.00
Vase, white metal, Palace of Liberal
Arts pictured, 3½" h. 45.00

1909 ALASKA-YUKON-PACIFIC EXPOSITION

Alaska-Yukon-Pacific Exposition Plate

Ash tray, metal, embossed scenes 14.50
Booklet, illustrated, 24 pp. 9.00
Card tray, white metal, Alaska
    Building pictured 12.00
Handkerchief, silk 12.00
Plate, china, blue transfer of Alaska
    Building, Mt. Ranier, Princess
    Angeline & Snoqualmie Falls,
    marked "Rowland & Marsellus Co.,"
    10¼" d. (ILLUS.) 55.00
Scarf, silk, eagle center surrounded by
    Exposition scenes 32.00

1915 PANAMA-PACIFIC INTERNATIONAL EXPOSITION

Book, "Panama-Pacific International
    Exposition," 70 views, miniature 18.00
Compact, celluloid 20.00
Medal, bronze, 2¾" d. 60.00
Paperweight w/pen holder, glass,
    4 x 7" 26.00
Pennant, "Panama-Pacific International
    Exposition, San Francisco, 1915,"
    29" l. 25.00
Pin tray, metal, Tower of Jewels
    pictured, 3½ x 2½" oval 15.00
Plate, metal, embossed panorama
    of Exposition, 12" d. 30.00
Ribbon threader, metal, advertising
    "Singer Sewing Machines" 4.00
Teaspoon, sterling silver, advertising
    "California Perfume Co." 65.00
View book 10.00
Watch fob, ship passing through
    Panama Canal pictured, die-cut
    bear at top, w/strap.............. 28.00

1933-34 CHICAGO WORLD FAIR

Ash tray, copper, Sky Ride, 1934 .... 7.00
Ash tray, milk white glass, advertising
    "Stewart's Coffee, 40th Anniversary" ..5.00

Baby spoon, brass 38.50
Bank, advertising "American Can Co.,"
    model of a tin can w/multicolored
    lithographed label, 3½" h. 11.00
Book, "A Century of Progress, Official
    View Book," color photographs,
    w/dust jacket 25.00

Chicago World's Fair Guide Book

Book, "Official Guide Book of the
    Fair," illustrated, hard cover,
    175 pp., 6 x 9½" (ILLUS.) 10.00
Candlestick, silverplate, 6" h. 28.00
Cigarette case, metal, black & gold
    Art Deco geometric design 35.00
Cocktail shaker, metal, "Happy Days at
    the Century of Progress, Chicago,
    1934," 15 drink recipes engraved on
    sides, 11" h...................... 40.00
Creamer & cov. sugar bowl, china,
    transfer scene of Chicago Court
    House & Art Institute, made for
    Marshall Field & Co., 4½" h., pr. 150.00
Letter opener, brass, Lincoln Exhibit....12.00
Medal, bronze, "Century of Progress,"
    2¾" d. 30.00
Napkin ring, sterling silver, Hall of
    Science pictured 30.00
Paperweight, paper view of Hall of
    Science under glass 9.00
Parasol, paper, "A Century of
    Progress" and "Galaxy" logo, 30" l. ..50.00
Plate, china, Hall of Science pictured,
    marked "Pickard"................. 20.00
Plate, pottery, nursery rhyme decor,
    marked "Shenango," 9" d. 47.50
Program, "Wings of a Century," trans-
    portation exhibit, illustrated, 18 pp. ...10.00
Tapestry, aerial view of fair, Zeppelin,
    airplane & skyride, 41 x 25" 125.00
Tea strainer, teapot shape w/Century
    of Progress logo on attached disc 12.50
Teaspoon, silverplate, Administration
    Building in bowl, Rogers 15.00
Token, Indian Head penny center, Fort
    Dearborn reverse, 2¼" d............ 15.00

Toy, cast iron, touring bus, "A Century
of Progress, Chicago, 1933, Greyhound Lines," replica of vehicle used
to transport visitors around Fair,
marked "Arcade," 10¼ x 2",
1¾" h. 100.00
Tray, metal, Buckingham Fountain
bordered by 12 Fair buildings, 4¾"....6.00
Watch fob, brass.....................32.00

1939 NEW YORK WORLD FAIR

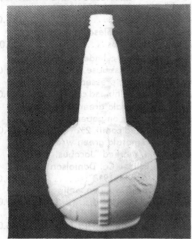

1939 New York World's Fair Bottle

Ash tray, brass, embossed Trylon &
Perisphere.......................17.00
Bank, metal, model of a typewriter,
advertising "Remington"...........47.00
Book, "1939 World's Fair in Pictures,"
8½ x 11".........................18.00
Book, "Your World of Tomorrow,"
interior photos of Trylon &
Perisphere, 12 x 9"...............17.50
Bottle, milk white glass, embossed map
map of the world, "World's Fair
1939," 9" h. (ILLUS.) ....20.00 to 25.00
Bracelet, gold, embossed bust of
George Washington & Trylon &
Perisphere.......................85.00
Candle holders, double, pink glass,
replicas of Trylon & Perisphere, pr....30.00
Coasters, glass, acid etched Trylon &
Perisphere decor, made in Holland,
set of 12 ....85.00
Model of a key, advertising "The Yale
& Towne Mfg. Co.," in original
cellophane packet w/Trylon &
Perisphere logo, 3" l...............5.00
Mug, 2-handled, ceramic, bust of
George Washington wearing tri-
cornered hat, "The American Potter
-- Joint Exhibit of Capital & Labor,
New York World's Fair, 1939".......23.00
Pencil sharpener, Trylon & Perisphere ..30.00
Pin, gold-tone metal, Trylon &

Perisphere hinged for use as a
locket, 2 x 1½" 18.00
Postcards, advertising "Borden's," Elsie,
the Cow, pictured, original envelope,
set of 5 ....25.00
Program, Billy Rose's Aquacade 15.00
Salt & pepper shakers, celluloid,
replicas of Trylon & Perisphere, pr....16.00
Sewing box, lithographed cardboard,
advertising "J. & P. Coats,"
w/needle & thread 35.00
Stereoscope viewer, hand-type,
w/seventy-five Fair view cards,
original box 38.50
Teaspoons, silverplate, Trylon & Peri-
sphere on handle, various buildings
in bowl, set of 9..................75.00
Teaspoon, sterling silver, Empire State
Building on handle w/eagle atop,
Trylon & Perisphere in bowl 26.00
Thermometer, wooden, Trylon &
Perisphere........................5.00
Vase, china, white "pate sur pate"
Trylon & Perisphere decor on green
ground, marked "Lenox," dated,
7" h. 125.00

WRITING ACCESSORIES

*Early writing accessories are popular
collectibles and offer a wide variety to select
from. A collection may be formed around
any one segment--pens, letter openers, lap
desks or ink wells--or the collection may
revolve around choice specimens of all
types. Material, design and age usually
determine the value. Pen collectors like the
large fountain pens developed in the 1920s
but also look for pens and mechanical
pencils that are solid gold or gold-plated.
Also see ART NOUVEAU, METALS and
ROYCROFT ITEMS.*

FOUNTAIN & DIP PENS
Dip pen, mother-of-pearl handle,
gold nib ....$12.00 to 15.00
Dip pen, mother-of-pearl handle, gold
nib, original case, ca. 1900 ....30.00
Dip pen, mother-of-pearl & gold
handle, original plush case.........65.00
Arnold fountain pen..................9.00
Conklin fountain pen, 14k rolled
gold............................275.00
Conklin "Endura Senior" fountain
pen, black 110.00
Grieshaber fountain pen, 10k gold
barrel & 14k gold cap 750.00
Mable, Todd & Dard fountain pen &
pencil, gold-filled metal, ornate,
England, set......................60.00

Parker "51" Pen

Parker, "51," dove grey (ILLUS.)........12.50
Parker "Black Giant Lucky Curve,"
  black, ca. 1915 ....260.00
Parker "Duofold Jr." fountain pen
  & pencil, red, 1922, set 95.00
Parker, "Lucky Curve with Jack Knife
  Safety," black w/nickel-platinum,
  1920 ....150.00
Parker "Vacuumatic" fountain pen,
  man's, gold stripes, 1934...........28.00
Sheaffer "Lifetime" fountain pen, pat.
  Aug. 25, 1908, Ft. Madison, black
  w/gold band, clip & tip 25.00
Sheaffer "White Dot Imperial
  Triumph" fountain pen, gold-filled,
  1972 ....125.00
Sheaffer "White Dot 777" fountain pen,
  1970 ....50.00
Wahl-Eversharp "Gold Seal" fountain
  pen, black & pearl 75.00
Wahl-Eversharp "Skyline" fountain pen,
  maroon barrel, gold-filled cap, 1942..20.00
Wahl-Eversharp fountain pen, Art
  Deco design, jade green 185.00
Wahl-Eversharp fountain pen, gold-
  filled, 1925......................75.00
Wahl-Eversharp fountain pen, green
  marbled 20.00
Wahl-Eversharp "Tempoint" fountain
  pen, lady's, 14k gold 250.00
Waterman "Commando" fountain pen ..20.00
Waterman "Gothic" fountain pen,
  gold-filled barrel & cap, 1925 ....75.00
Waterman "Ideal" fountain pen, ornate
  14k gold Art Nouveau overlay 225.00
Waterman "Ideal" fountain pen,
  ornate sterling silver Art Nouveau
  overlay barrel & cap...............150.00
Waterman "Patrician" fountain pen,
  onyx, 1929-36 ....300.00
Waterman "Red Dot No. 7," black 55.00
Waterman "Ripple" fountain pen,
  orange, large 90.00

INK WELLS & STANDS

Bronze Crab Ink Well

Brass well w/hinged lid, malachite
  stone on cover, 5" d. 200.00
Bronze stand, lion's head & paw
  feet, griffin pen rests, dated
  1887 ....300.00
Bronze well, model of a crab
  w/hinged back opening to small
  stamp compartment & holding bucket
  w/hinged shell-mounted lid opening to
  well fitted w/glass liner,
  impressed "Tiffany Studios, New
  York" & numbered, 1892-1902,
  8½" l. (ILLUS.) 2,090.00
Glass well, blue opalescent, kettle
  shape w/deep ribs 435.00
Glass well, clear, cylinder w/brass
  hinged lid & brass base, 3" d. 20.00
Glass well, clear, pressed model of
  a Scotty dog w/hinged cover, 3" h. ...47.00
Glass well, emerald green, blown hat
  shape w/cover on paperweight
  base, polished pontil, 2¾" d........135.00
Glass well, emerald green w/clear
  domed lid, marked "Jacobus,
  General Eclipse Co. Danielson
  Ct., Pat. May 14, 1918".............45.00
Leather-covered wooden well,
  traveling-type, 1½" d..............49.00
Nickel-plated well, model of an
  antique car w/hinged lid, 5" l. 65.00
Pot metal well, model of an antique
  car w/hinged hood for well &
  hinged back for stamps, 9" l. 135.00
Pot metal well, model of a frog
  seated & holding a water lily,
  w/hinged lid, 3" h. 65.00
Redware pottery well, house-shaped
  w/slanting lid, original glass
  insert, 1¾" h. 135.00
Silverplate stand, boat-shaped w/pr.
  cobalt blue glass wells w/silver-
  plate collars......................98.00
Silverplate stand, bun feet, 2 clear
  glass wells, w/silverplate collars &
  serpentine lids 185.00
Silverplate well, model of a fish
  w/hinged lid, 5" l. 85.00
Staffordshire pottery stand, scroll-
  molded base, center figure of a
  classical Greek woman seated on a
  cushioned stool, wearing a flowing
  gown & holding a caduceus,
  flanked by 3" d. wells w/dome
  covers w/pineapple finials, impressed
  "H" mark, ca. 1800, 12 x 7" 350.00
Stoneware pottery well, cylindrical,
  center well & 2 quill holes,
  olive green shaded to rust glaze,
  3½" d., 1½" h. 55.00
Wooden well, carved model of an old
  shoe w/sock forming hinged lid,
  4½" l. 120.00
Wooden well, cherrywood, carved head
  of Boxer dog w/glass eyes, hinged

lid, glass insert w/original lid,
ca. 1840, 4½ x 4½" 260.00
Wooden well, traveling-type, lathe-
turned cylinder w/two glass inserts,
original brown sponging & gilt hearts
& arrows on body, black-painted
lid, original paper label "Manufactured
by S. Silliman & Co., Chester,
Conn.," 3 5/8" d., 2¼" h. 115.00

LAP DESKS

Oak Roll-Top Lap Desk

Mahogany w/brass strapwork, oblong
top lifting to a felt-covered writing
surface flanked by fitted compartments, English Regency period,
early 19th c., 12 x 10½", 7¼" h. 418.00
Oak, cylinder roll opening to stationery
& letter slots & perpetual calendar at
top, w/removable small lap desk in
lower drawer, late 19th c., 14 x 14",
10½" h. (ILLUS.) 385.00
Oak, lady's .185.00
Pine, original red paint 195.00
Rosewood, brass hinges, inlaid decor,
19th c. (minor interior damage) 121.00
Rosewood w/mother-of-pearl inlay
border, original purple velvet lining,
ca. 1850, 15½ x 10½ x 6" 135.00

LETTER OPENERS

Brass Figural Letter Opener

Brass, embossed lion head on handle,
"Lion Bonding & Surety Co., Omaha,
Nebraska" 24.00
Brass, figural handle, 7" l. (ILLUS.) 15.00
Bronze, handle cast w/Noh masks,
Japan 125.00
Bronze, Abalone patt., Tiffany
Studios 150.00

Bronze, Zodiac patt., signed Tiffany
Studios & numbered . . . . . .135.00 to 150.00
Cast iron, handle cast in the form of
a rifle 7.00
Celluloid, figural elephant handle 3.50
Celluloid, bust of George Washington
on handle, White House on blade 18.00
Chrome, Art Deco model of rapier
w/sheath 70.00
Copper, w/strap handle, hammered,
Arts & Crafts, large 20.00
Pewter, Caduceus handle, chrome
blade, 20th c. 11.00
Pipestone . . . . .12.00 to 15.00
Silver-gilt & rhodonite, faceted rho-
donite handle applied w/silver-gilt
foliage, w/cabochon sapphire finial,
Faberge, Moscow, ca. 1910, in
original fitted holly wood case,
9" l. 2,310.00
Sterling silver, Calvert patt. handle
w/monogram, S. Kirk & Son,
5 5/8" l. 45.00
Sterling silver, Repousse patt. handle,
S. Kirk & Son . . . . .40.00 to 50.00
Sterling silver, 3-dimensional jockey
figure on handle, Tiffany & Co.,
7" l. 150.00
Wooden, carved figure of young man
in Alpine costume on handle,
11¼" l. 12.50

PAPER CLIPS

Brass, American Eagle w/two crossed
flags, 5½" 45.00
Brass, figural owl 25.00
Brass, model of hanging fowl, glass
eyes 40.00
Bronze, embossed facade of Sperry &
Hutchinson Building, Union Square,
N.Y., 1896-1925, 2¼ x 3½" 32.00
Celluloid, advertising "Kansas Saddlery
Co." 8.50

POUNCE SANDERS

Maple, flared top, incised bands 50.00
Tin, asphaltum finish, 19th c. 58.00
Tin, cylindrical w/large base & top,
old worn finish, 2½" h. 18.00
Turned treenware, cylindrical
w/banded center & flaring top, brass
shaker insert, old dark finish,
2 7/8" h. 55.00

WAX LETTER SEALS

Brass seal w/foreign script engraving,
well-turned handle, 1¼" d.,
3 5/8" l. 10.00
Brass seal, Wells Fargo, Renfrew,
Pa. 195.00
Bronze seal w/Chinese foo dog
handle 60.00
Bronze seal w/figural dog's head
handle, signed Fremiet 230.00

Glass seal, green w/dark patinated
vintage overlay, signed Tiffany
Studios, 3" h. 325.00

Silver Mounted Rock Crystal Letter Seal

Silver mounted rock crystal seal
w/Napoleon bust finial, fluted knob
shape capped w/tiers of swags &
wreaths, 19th c., 5 3/8" h. (ILLUS.). . .715.00
Sterling silver seal, amethyst mounted
on handle. 48.00

YARD LONG PICTURES

*These out of proportion colorful prints
were fashionable wall decorations in the
waning years of the 19th century and early
in the 20th century. They are all 36" wide
and between 8" and 10" h. A wide variety of
subjects, ranging from florals and fruits to
chicks and puppies, is available to collectors. Prices for these yard-long prints
have shown a dramatic increase within the
past two years. All included in this list are
framed unless otherwise noted.*

A Carnation Symphony (unframed) $25.00
Asters, signed (unframed) 21.00
Bridal Favors, ca. 1890 . . . . .135.00
Chickens, signed Ben Austrian. 140.00
Fruit arrangement, multicolored 95.00
Pink roses, signed Paul de Longpre 77.50
Polar Animals .137.50
Poppies, signed Beaugart 60.00
Poppies & asters, signed S. Clarkson . . .45.00
Puppies, signed Van
   Vredenburgh . . . . .95.00 to 130.00
Red puffy roses, signed Califano 85.00
Roses, signed LeRoy. 55.00
Roses, signed Paul de Longpre
   (unframed) .35.00
Roses & hydrangeas 45.00
Show Dogs 135.00
Shower of Lilacs, signed Muller, 1897 . .100.00

Study of Roses, signed Paul de
   Longpre, 1895 . . . . .55.00
Violets, signed Mary E. Hart, 1900. . . . . .60.00
Yellow, pink & red roses, Klein 75.00

YARN WINDERS

Floor Model Yarn Winder

Floor model yarn winder, maple &
other hardwood, whittled legs,
chamfered block & well detailed
frame w/molded & chamfered
edges, worn red paint, 26" reel,
36" h. $175.00
Floor model yarn winder, walnut,
4-arm reel w/turned arms, original
geared clicker mechanism w/clock
face dial to side, on chip-carved
platform base w/four splayed
tapering legs, 26½" reel, 38½" h. . . .115.00
Floor model yarn winder, wooden,
4-arm reel & original clicker-counter
mechanism on turned post, one arm
hinged for yarn removal, chip-carved
base on 4 raking turned legs,
old dark red paint, 24" d. reel,
26½" h. overall. 175.00
Floor model yarn winder, wooden,
19th c., 24" w., 24" h. (ILLUS.). 100.00
Niddy noddy hand reel, butternut,
18" l. . . . . .35.00 to 50.00
Niddy noddy hand reel, maple &
chestnut, 18" l. 45.00
Niddy noddy hand reel, pine,
punched decor 75.00
Niddy noddy hand reel, wooden,
mortised construction, early 19th c.,
10" l. 155.00

Table model yarn "swift," maple, Shaker, expandable reel on turned standard, original mustard yellow paint 165.00

Table model yarn "swift," rosewood & brass, clamp-on type 125.00

Table model yarn "swift," carved whalebone & ivory, shaft & slats of whalebone, retaining most of the original pink & green ribbons, finial & shaft collars of whale ivory elaborately turned & scribed in red & green to match the ribbons, turned & scribed swift clamp from large pieces of whale ivory, clamp screw of whale ivory w/heart-carved thumbpiece, mounted on black metal Anton base, ca. 1840, 15¼" h. 1,760.00

Table model yarn, "swift," carved whalebone & ivory, cup finial, cage collars & shaft clamp of whale ivory, shaft & cage of whalebone, swift clamp turned in the shape of a barrel scribed in red & green, whalebone clamp screw is old replacement, mounted on black Anton base, ca. 1850, 21½" h. 1,210.00

ZEPPELIN COLLECTIBLES

Santa Claus in Zeppelin Calendar Plate

Not all airships are zeppelins. Only those lighter-than-aircraft ships that resemble the huge cigar-shaped type designed by Count Ferdinand von Zeppelin of Germany are referred to as zeppelins. The famed "Graf Zeppelin" was the only airship to fly around the world, making this trip in twenty-one days, eight hours, in 1929. Used for commercial flights from 1933 until 1937, its success led to the building of the "Hindenburg," the largest airship ever built. The tragic crash of the "Hindenburg" on May 6, 1937, ended regular airship service. Also see STILL BANKS.

Airmail cover, "The Hindenburg," envelope w/two commemorative stamps, canceled May 5, 1936 . . . . . $100.00

Ash tray, aluminum, Zeppelin replica . . . 30.00

Badge, metal, marked "Hindenburg Landing Crew -- Lakehurst," w/embossed Iron Cross & Zeppelin, 1¾" d. 400.00

Book, "Zeppelin, Fahrt Um Die Welt," 161 illustrations, German text, ca. 1929 . . . . .35.00

Brochure, "Graf Zeppelin" 25.00

Calendar plate, 1909, Santa Claus in Zeppelin center dropping presents to children, w/advertising, 7½" d. (ILLUS.) 50.00

Cigarette cards, photographs of Zeppelins, 5 x 7", set of 6 . . . . .15.00

Fish bowl, clear glass, Zeppelin replica, w/patent number on observation deck, 1930s, 14" l 100.00

Game, "Hang the Zeppelin" 65.00

Medal, sterling silver, bust of Count von Zeppelin front, reverse commemorating first flight of the "Graf Zeppelin," July 8, 1929 . . . . .95.00

Needle book, Zeppelin pictured on cover, Germany, 7" l 10.00

Newspaper, St. Louis, "Hindenburg" disaster, 1937 . . . . .25.00

Photograph, Count Ferdinand von Zeppelin, 9 x 13" 35.00

Pilot's wings 200.00

Pin tray, "Hindenburg" pictured 25.00

Plate, children looking at Zeppelin in sky, small 50.00

Pocket knife, brass, "Graf Zeppelin" pictured 25.00

Postcard, Zeppelin at mooring, 1908 . . . .25.00

Postcard, photograph of Zeppelin lounge, 1936 .10.00

Soft drink bottle, Graf Zeppelins in relief, advertising John Graf Co., Milwaukee 50.00

Stereoscope view card, Zeppelin pictured 8.00

Stickpin, "Graf Zeppelin," enameled . .100.00

Toy, pull-type, tin replica of a Zeppelin, marked "Lil' Giant," ca. 1930, 26" l 125.00

Toy, cast iron replica of "Graf Zeppelin" 75.00

Toy, cast iron replica of "Hindenburg," original paint, 27" l 145.00

Watch, pocket-type, Zeppelin on face, engraved back, dated 1929 . . . . .95.00

INDEX

*Denotes "Special Focus" section